Negotiating Difference

CULTURAL CASE STUDIES FOR COMPOSITION

Negotiating Difference

CULTURAL CASE STUDIES FOR COMPOSITION

Edited by

PATRICIA BIZZELL
College of the Holy Cross

BRUCE HERZBERG
Bentley College

BEDFORD/ST. MARTIN'S
BOSTON ◆ **NEW YORK**

FOR BEDFORD/ST. MARTIN'S

President and Publisher: Charles H. Christensen
General Manager and Associate Publisher: Joan E. Feinberg
Managing Editor: Elizabeth M. Schaaf
Developmental Editor: Pam Ozaroff
Editorial Assistants: Mark Reimold, Joanne Diaz
Production Editor: Ann Sweeney
Production Assistants: Karen Baart, Maureen Murray
Copyeditor: Barbara G. Flanagan
Text Design: Claire Seng-Niemoeller
Cover Design: Diane Levy
Cover Art: Confrontation by Ben Shahn, 1964. Reprinted by courtesy of The Lane
     Collection, Museum of Fine Arts, Boston. Copyright © 1995, Estate of
     Ben Shahn. Licensed by VAGA, New York, NY.

Library of Congress Catalog Card Number 95–80789

5   4   3   2   1

i   h   g   f

For information, write: Bedford/St. Martin's, 75 Arlington Street, Boston, MA 02116
(617-399-4000)

ISBN: 0–312–06846–8

ACKNOWLEDGMENTS

William Bradford. From *History of Plymouth Plantation 1620–1647* by William Bradford, edited
     by Samuel Eliot Morison. Copyright © 1952 by Samuel Eliot Morison and renewed 1980 by
     Emily M. Beck. Reprinted by permission of Alfred A. Knopf, Inc.
Harold "Light Bulb" Bryant. Oral history from *Bloods* by Wallace Terry. Copyright © 1984 by
     Wallace Terry. Reprinted by permission of Random House, Inc.
William Z. Foster. Excerpt from *Pages from a Worker's Life* by William Z. Foster. Copyright ©
     1939 by International Publishers Co., Inc. Reprinted by permission of the publisher.
Jeanne Wakatsuki Houston. Excerpts from *Farewell to Manzanar* by James D. and Jeanne
     Wakatsuki Houston. Copyright © 1973 by James D. Houston. Reprinted by permission of
     Houghton Mifflin Co. All rights reserved. Lyrics from "Girl of My Dreams." Words and

Preface for Instructors

WHAT DOES "NEGOTIATING DIFFERENCE" MEAN?

Since the moment the first native inhabitants met the first immigrants from Europe, since the first African slaves were brought here in chains, America has been a multicultural land. People from virtually every nation in the world have worked and struggled here. Part of their struggle has been to communicate across cultural boundaries, and not only to communicate but to argue for rights, to capture cultural territory, to change the way America was imagined so that it would include those who were newer or less powerful or spoken about but not listened to — in short, to negotiate the differences of culture, race, gender, class, and ideology. Multiculturalism and its difficulties are not phenomena only of our own day: They are embedded deeply in the nation's history.

To learn to communicate in the overlapping discourse communities of such a society, students must understand the historical contexts in which cultural conflicts have taken place. They must master the rhetorical strategies that constitute what comparative literature scholar Mary Louise Pratt calls "the arts of the contact zone." Pratt defines a contact zone as a particular cultural conflict in which the contending groups have unequal power. The typical contact zone is bounded both historically and geographically. Within the zone, the contending groups must negotiate not only their political and social differences but also the very concepts of difference or otherness that each applies to the other. Each group must develop effective rhetorical strategies for communicating both within and across cultural boundaries, taking into consideration its position of relative power in the conflict.

Negotiating Difference is organized around this concept of contact zones. Each of its six case studies focuses on a historical moment when groups with unequal power have struggled to define some significant part of their common experience. The selections are the actual primary sources through which the negotiations took place.

This contextualized analysis of firsthand materials also characterizes the cultural studies perspective. *Negotiating Difference* facilitates such a perspec-

v

tive through the presentation of public discourse in a variety of genres —
memoirs, speeches, sermons, oral history, Senate testimony, government
documents, and so on — to show how individual and group identities are
shaped by negotiated interpretations of experience.

Although *Negotiating Difference* contains much new material, it also
meets the traditional needs of the composition course. It is writing intensive in its approach to text study, it calls for personal reflection as well as
analysis and argument, and it suggests projects for further research. The
book's focus on rhetorical strategies encourages the development of critical thinking. At the same time, its historical approach to multiculturalism
deflects the tensions that often arise in the composition classroom, allowing students to deal with sensitive issues by focusing on the analysis of texts
rather than on students' personal lives and reactions. As the United States
becomes ever more diverse, educating students to communicate across the
boundaries of culture, race, class, and gender grows increasingly crucial.
Negotiating Difference seeks to further that end and, ultimately, to promote
education for citizenship in a multicultural democracy.

CASE STUDIES, CONTACT ZONES, AND THE WRITING COURSE

The six units of *Negotiating Difference* are case studies that explore past conflicts in American culture. The units progress chronologically from the
English colonization of New England to the Vietnam War. Each unit focuses on a struggle for the power to define some significant part of American culture, to say what America is or means. These struggles are represented in texts that constitute the actual rhetorical sites of conflict. In
them we hear the voices of the participants in those struggles and gain a
sense of the variety of perspectives and arguments about the issues at
hand.

This last point is particularly important: The texts represent moments
in the struggles themselves, the negotiations and arguments through
which people strove to keep or win a place — physical, political, economic,
social, or spiritual — in the United States. The struggles were not confined
to debates, to be sure. Guns and knives, military force, police lines, laws,
and court decisions were weapons in the conflicts between English settlers
and Native Americans, between whites and blacks, men and women, bosses
and workers. But though decisive battles may have been won in the fields
or the streets, the meaning of each conflict is found in its participants' attempts to articulate the positions they were fighting over. This part of the
struggle is unending, for two reasons. First, we are engaged in a retrospec-
tive search for greater understanding. We want to know what really happened, what the participants felt and thought, and how we should now
evaluate the events of our history. But second — and this is in some ways
more important for us — the struggles themselves are by no means over.

Every case study in *Negotiating Difference* concerns a cultural problem with relevance today. In Unit One, the English colonizers of New England negotiate among themselves as well as with the "Indians" to position the two groups in their respective visions of the "new world." The native peoples — underdogs by the time they could participate in the European linguistic forms that have come to constitute the rhetorical arena — respond to the European vision not only in retrospect but in prospect: How can native Americans get their voices into American history and by doing so mark out a more satisfactory ideological and cultural place in the American landscape? This is not a simple history lesson; their problems have not been solved. The native peoples' struggle for official recognition in the legal system and cultural institutions of the United States continues, challenging other Americans to enter the struggle, to take positions (if not sides), to learn to hear the various arguments and understand their import. At least this challenge goes out to Americans who wish to recognize the fundamental multiculturalism of the United States and to participate in civic life.

The same is true for the issues raised in the other case studies. The debate over the Declaration of Independence in Unit Two raises questions about the American ideal of equality and the treatment of African Americans that have not receded into history or passed beyond the realm of debate with the abolition of slavery. The place of women in American society, discussed in Unit Three, has hardly been definitively settled. And so with the other issues — economic class differences in a capitalist economy, the treatment of Japanese immigrants as unassimilable aliens, and the political rifts revealed by the war in Vietnam — all continue to exercise ideological force and demand engagement.

The need to negotiate the differences among cultures is perhaps the most pressing rhetorical challenge in American civic life today. If, as we maintain, the development of American culture is in great part a rhetorical activity, then its study in a writing course is not only appropriate but also an important means of addressing current concerns about multiculturalism. If we hope to see America as multicultural or wish to debate the issues of global multiculturalism, we must do what we can to teach the arts of the contact zone.

Negotiating Difference invites readers to study contact zones — places where cultures clash, where power between groups is unequal, where positions of power are unstable. The book asks its readers — both students and teachers — to analyze original materials so that they can understand historical circumstances, positions taken and refuted, audiences addressed, and rhetorical strategies employed. In the apparatus, we ask readers to locate themselves in the systems and institutions that are the sites of debate. We invite them to explore issues in greater depth or to follow them to different times and places, to find them in their own regions or their own families.

We have designed this book for a course in serious writing and strong reading, a course in *rhetoric* strongly defined. Rhetoric in its strong definition is a form of action, personal and civic and as well as academic. The writing course that adopts this definition asks students to read texts that make public statements about important issues using powerful arguments. It asks students to talk and write their way into these issues, to understand them and to take possession of them, to transform them and engage them in their own lives.

HOW THE APPARATUS WORKS

The apparatus of *Negotiating Difference* attempts to reinforce the idea that important issues are joined through negotiation, not through the simple assertion of a position; that negotiation requires an understanding of other arguments and positions; that positions (including — especially — one's own) are grounded in material circumstances and ideological premises.

The case study method allows students to read a variety of statements from the same time period on the same issue. Often, the texts directly respond to each other or stake out positions in clear recognition of other arguments used and other ground occupied. The unit introductions and selection headnotes provide historical information that will help students understand the issues. The "Reading Critically" questions following each selection asks students to identify key arguments and rhetorical strategies and may be used as stimuli for class journals or class discussions. The "Writing Analytically" questions after each selection call for analysis, evaluation, comparison, and even imitation of the texts.

Each unit ends with three or four assignment sequences that suggest various ways to cluster the readings around a central theme raised in the unit. Each combination of readings is followed by a sequence of writing assignments that asks students to place the texts in dialogue with one another by synthesizing and comparing arguments, engaging in debate with the issues, or assessing an exchange or conflict. The assignments in each sequence build on each other, increasing in complexity as the sequence progresses.

Unavoidably, *Negotiating Difference* is an incomplete book. We have not been able to represent every nuance of the issues addressed in the six units. We have had to omit significant writers because of limitations. Moreover, we know that in six units we have not been able to explore every significant rhetorical moment in American history or to represent every group that has played a significant role in the development of American rhetoric. Many readers may find that the social group to which they feel the closest allegiance is not represented here.

An important feature of *Negotiating Difference* addresses these difficulties. We have concluded every unit with a Research Kit that provides a large number of suggestions for research projects. These are divided into two sets. The first set, "Ideas from the Unit Readings," contain suggestions for projects that will expand students' knowledge of the issues raised by the readings — for example, by investigating the way the conflict represented in the unit was played out in another region or at a later period. The second set, "Branching Out," contains suggestions for topics on issues analogous to those in the unit but pertaining to other social groups as well as topics that fill in the historical context of the period.

The Research Kits invite students to go beyond the resources offered within the covers of this book. Students need to be empowered as independent inquirers who can define and pursue research agendas on their own. Each Research Kit provides the tools students can use for their own investigative purposes. The Research Kits give students leads to a variety of information sources. In addition to providing bibliographies that cite the works included in the unit and related primary and secondary texts, the kits also point to resources in the community, such as historical societies, churches, civic groups, and so on. In using this key feature of the book, students will learn that research includes, but is not limited to, library searching.

Research is a social act. Most successful research is collaborative in some way — at the very least, in the sense that it builds on the recorded work of others and is often conducted in teams, especially in the social and natural sciences and in the world beyond school. For this reason, many of the research projects suggested in the Research Kits lend themselves to group work.

THE CHALLENGE OF NEGOTIATING DIFFERENCE

Many of the texts we have selected are challenging, but we have found this challenge salutary in our own classes. Students at a wide variety of ability levels have found these materials so stimulating that we regard the effort to engage them as well worthwhile.

An issue related to difficulty is the question of whether the units are too long to be managed in the usual span of a writing course. We admit that the units are long, but the assignment sequences provide you with a variety of ways to engage a unit without having to use all of its selections. We wanted the units to be ample, both to give the best possible picture, within our space constraints, of the complexity of the historical and rhetorical situation and to provide room for teachers and students to roam around, make unexpected discoveries, and design their own pathways through the material.

Teachers have also asked us whether they need to become experts in the historical periods that form the basis of the units in order to teach them. We don't think so. *Negotiating Difference* is not a history book and does not claim to be representing the history of any period in a complete way. For example, we make no claim that Unit Five fully represents the history of Japanese American internment during World War II. We focus, more narrowly, on the ways that writers represent the internment experience in texts directed to a diverse audience. Some minimal historical knowledge is needed to appreciate the writers' struggles and strategies, and we've provided this context in the unit introductions and selection headnotes. But the main focus on *Negotiating Difference* is on how the texts work.

It is our hope that instead of creating problems, *Negotiating Difference* will successfully address some concerns that have been plaguing teachers in composition and English studies. We believe that the book's organizational principle provides the best approach for teachers who want to represent the multicultural richness of American rhetoric in their classes. We believe that this principle allows for the teaching of writing in a serious, contextualized way. And we believe that the book's rhetorical approach points the way to methodological reunion of composition and literature in a newly strengthened and socially relevant English studies.

ACKNOWLEDGMENTS

Assembling *Negotiating Difference* has been a collaborative process, not only between the two editors but among us and all the people who have read parts of the manuscript, discussed it with us, helped us find readings, and polished and revised the text until it was a genuine Bedford Book. Fittingly, this collaboration could be called a process of negotiating difference. It would not be correct to say that the people we are thanking here have "helped" us with the book. It would be more correct to say that the book could not exist in its present form without them. We have learned much from our differences and negotiations with them.

We would like to thank, first, our text reviewers: David Bartholomae, University of Pittsburgh; Tom Fox, California State University at Chico; William Hochman, University of Southern Colorado; Thomas Recchio, University of Connecticut; Louise Z. Smith, University of Massachusetts, Boston; Irwin Weiser, Purdue University; and Stephen Wilhoit, University of Dayton. We are especially grateful to our principal reviewer, Kay Halasek, Ohio State University, who not only gave detailed attention to the readings and apparatus but also helped up keep focused on the book's purpose and concept. In addition, we are grateful for the assistance of experts in a variety of fields other than composition and rhetoric who helped refine the selection of texts and polish the historical introductions and headnotes: Dale Bauer, University of Wisconsin, Madison; Daniel H. Borus, University of Rochester; Catherine Clinton, W.E.B. Du Bois Institute, Harvard University; Colin G. Calloway, Dartmouth College; Roger Daniels, University of Cincinnati; H. Bruce Franklin, Rutgers University; Judith Fetterly, State University of New York at Albany; Donald Teruo Hata Jr., California State University, Dominguez Hills; Nadine Ishitani Hata, El Camino College; Carolyn L. Karcher, Temple University; Barry O'Connell, Amherst College; and Bruce J. Shulman, Boston University.

We would also like to thank Phil Rule at Holy Cross and Marc Stern at Bentley, colleagues whose generosity in discussing the project with us over the four years of its development has been so helpful and encouraging. In addition, Alexa Mayo and the other research librarians at Holy Cross have provided invaluable assistance. We would also like to thank the librarians at the American Antiquarian Society in Worcester.

One colleague has to be thanked posthumously. Americanist Cynthia Jordan, who generously advised us about the readings for Unit Three, died unexpectedly shortly after her return from Holy Cross to Indiana University. Her wit and warm good wishes toward the project were sustaining and are sorely missed.

The team at Bedford Books, as so often before, showed faith in an experimental idea through all the difficult stages of its coming to birth. Pam Ozaroff edited the book with an astonishing degree of care and personal investment. Decisions and revisions major and minor were made at her urging and with her acute judgment. Ann Sweeney managed the production process and kept us on a pitiless schedule with unfailing good cheer. Barbara Flanagan brought good sense as well as inerrant grammar to the copyediting. Mark Reimold, Joanne Diaz, Karen Baart, and Maureen Murray attended to many of the quite innumerable details of editing and production. We thank them all, without whom there would be silence.

Bedford Books is Chuck and Joan. To the paeans of much-deserved praise for Chuck Christensen and Joan Feinberg that can be found in the preface of every Bedford Book, we add our moiety. Their excellent judgment and perceptive suggestions for shaping and improving the book have been inspiring to us. Joan in particular always provides light in the darker passages and keeps us from leaving the profession to become lumberjacks.

Finally we would like to thank our daughters, Anna and Rachel, for being so patient when Mommy or Daddy disappeared into the cave (the basement room where the computer lives) one more time. We dedicate this book to our students, but we like to imagine our daughters' beautiful faces in the front row.

Contents

By following these ordinances, Native American converts to Christianity attempt to adopt the English way of life.

UNIT THREE

Defining "Woman's Sphere" in Nineteenth-Century American Society **285**

scendentalist movement argues that women need civil rights — but only to give greater scope to their innate "oracular," or spiritual powers, which must still be nourished by a primary focus on the home.

With this speech, a major women's rights activist persuades the all-male New York legislature to liberalize married women's property laws, arguing that the condition of married white women compares unfavorably with that of black men, both free and slave.

Criticizing the racism of white suffragists, this African American educator stresses the world's need for the influence of college-educated women to resist the prevailing "might makes right" philosophy and to spread mercy and peace.

Laws, Contracts, and Proclamations on Women's Rights 387

This proclamation, coauthored by Elizabeth Cady Stanton and other activists for the first American women's rights convention, begins with language that closely parallels that of the Declaration of Independence, amended to include women.

These laws guarantee married women's control over various kinds of property, as well as guardianship over their children. The 1848 reforms were extended in 1860 in part because of agitation by Elizabeth Cady Stanton.

These documents, typical of agreements signed by women's rights activists and their marriage partners, denounce the advantages given to husbands by nineteenth-century law.

Intended to extend the vote to male former slaves, and thereby institute universal male suffrage, this amendment does not include women.

This amendment, aimed to bolster the provisions of the Fourteenth Amendment, bars any form of racial discrimination in voting. It does not mention discrimination on the basis of gender.

The United States Supreme Court states that while women are citizens, they are not thereby guaranteed the right to vote.

Arguing for gradual state and local suffrage for literate, American-born white women, these resolutions show a breakdown in the solidarity be-

should spend less time preaching about temperance and more time reforming the bad working conditions that lead to drinking.

Testimony of the Interned   676

drafted — and the long-lasting ambivalence about his ultimate decision to serve in Vietnam.

An African American veteran who specialized in disarming bombs describes atrocities committed by fellow soldiers in Vietnam and his own attempts to find an "explanation" for the war upon returning home.

A nurse who elected to serve in Vietnam tells of her hatred of the Vietnamese, her disorientation after the war, and her need to be with other veterans.

Paralyzed by a war wound, a former marine describes his motives for fighting, his eventual disillusionment, and his return to antiwar activity, including a dramatic protest at the 1972 Republican National Convention in Miami.

Negotiating Difference

CULTURAL CASE STUDIES FOR COMPOSITION

Introduction for Students

NEGOTIATING DIFFERENCE IN AMERICA

The United States is one of the most diverse countries in the world, consisting of many groups of Americans who are different from one another in ethnic background, race, religion, sexual orientation, social class, and many other dimensions. The United States is sometimes called a "multicultural" democracy. But even that term is not inclusive enough because it can obscure the significance sometimes carried by differences other than racial or ethnic, such as in sexual orientation or social class.

In a country that is so diverse, a great deal of negotiation is necessary. People with different backgrounds and competing goals will fight for their own prerogatives, the right to live as they wish, to have a share of political freedom, to participate in civic life, to make a living, and to have their beliefs and cultural practices accepted. All too often, conflicts between different racial, ethnic, and religious groups, between men and women, bosses and workers, and adherents of different political positions have broken out — and continue to break out — in violent confrontations. But even when conflicts do not come to open violence, constant negotiation of contending needs must go on. The ability to engage in such negotiations is an important prerequisite for being a good citizen in a multicultural democracy.

The United States is a country, in short, where we are constantly negotiating difference. To do so intelligently and well, we need to know something about the history of previous negotiations: What have the conflicts been? What arguments have been employed? What forms have the arguments taken? What effects have they had? We also need to know how to talk and write about cultural differences: What are our own positions and why have we taken them? What forms are available to us for making a case? How can we use our knowledge to advance the democratic principles of the country?

Our goal in this book is to introduce some of the American conflicts that have been negotiated but that, even so, have not been entirely settled. The selections in each unit are statements by the participants in a particu-

1

lar conflict and, taken together, they show what we mean by "negotiation." We ask students to think about the conflicts and the arguments, to discuss them in groups, to write about them informally and formally, like historians or political scientists or literary critics, or like advocates of a position.

All of this thinking, discussing, and writing is the essence of *rhetoric*. Rhetoric has a bad name these days — "mere rhetoric" means talk and no action, campaign promises, spin control, lies, and slick talk. But rhetoric has a more positive sense. In Greece, twenty-five hundred years ago, rhetoric appeared as part of a new political order called democracy. Debate and persuasive public speaking on public issues were essential if the citizens were to take part in the government of the country. The negotiations we present in this book and ask students to write about are examples of this form of rhetoric.

We've organized this book into six case studies of moments in American history that illustrate the negotiations of difference. To have a say in a situation of contention, a writer has to negotiate — has to think about how to persuade or to create change in readers who may be very different, even hostile. It isn't enough just to take a stand, which will often only alienate, not persuade, those who don't already agree.

Furthermore, in many contentious situations, the issues involved do not split easily into two sides, pro or con. Usually more than two groups are engaged in the struggle. Also, people who might consider themselves to be within the same group can still disagree about how to approach a particular issue. And many people feel connected to more than one group, so when they present their ideas, they have to negotiate among their own multiple allegiances as well as their various readers' needs and expectations. Taking a stand may fail not only because it isn't persuasive, but also because it isn't accurate — it doesn't represent the complexity of the situation. The writers in our selections are dealing with these rhetorical complexities. We want to help you learn how to recognize and deal with them, too.

THE STRUCTURE OF THIS BOOK

A brief look at the six units in this book will give you a better idea of what we mean by "negotiating difference." These case studies focus on moments in American history when different groups were contending for the power to make their views of a conflict or contentious situation prevail.

Unit One is entitled, "First Contacts between Puritans and Native Americans." In one sense, we all know what happened in New England: The English came in increasing numbers and eventually killed or displaced most of the Native American population. But how are we to understand this historical process? Who was generous, treacherous, compassionate, or excessively violent? These questions can receive only partial answers, as we try to piece together the story of that time from the narratives left by various participants. In Unit One, we see how the narrative form itself is partial, both in the sense that it necessarily selects some, but not all, details to include in the story and in the sense that the writer's partialities, or prejudices, are reflected in the selection process. We will study how these narrative choices affect readers dealing with similar issues today.

Unit Two is entitled "The Debate over Slavery and the Declaration of Independence." Most Americans would now interpret the famous phrase from the Declaration of Independence "all men are created equal" to include all people. But this interpretation was not widely accepted before the Civil War, when many wished to restrict its application as a way to defend the institution of slavery. African American intellectuals were largely responsible for mounting the arguments that broadened the meaning of this phrase to its present-day understanding, in the process providing powerful, effective arguments against slavery. Here we see how arguments over the interpretation of a text affect real-world issues of vital importance.

Unit Three is entitled "Defining 'Woman's Sphere' in Nineteenth-Century American Society." This unit focuses on a time in American history, similar to our own day, when gender roles were hotly debated. Nineteenth-century women violated norms for female behavior when they tried to become political activists against slavery, and they were roundly criticized and told to stay at home. In this unit, male and female, African American and European American writers are represented. All were dealing with the tricky business of mounting arguments concerning the ideal behavior for women, while at the same time attending to the way they presented themselves in their texts — not wanting either to violate the gender norms they themselves were advocating or to alienate readers who might disagree with them. Strategies for dealing with hostile audiences have many applications in present-day debates, not only over gender roles but also over other controversial, emotionally charged issues.

Unit Four is entitled "Wealth, Work, and Class Conflict in the Industrial Age." The industrial revolution following the Civil War created enormous wealth in the United States, but not for everyone. Was the United States truly a land of unlimited wealth and equal opportunity? Those who thought so subscribed to the "Gospel of Wealth," which considered the successful better than the unsuccessful — more diligent, clever, and virtuous. What did the Gospel of Wealth mean, though, to the huge group of industrial workers, many of whom were chronically underemployed and underpaid? In this unit, we find stories, essays, and even congressional testimony about individualism and the "self-made man," about unions and workers, about the acceptance of African Americans as regular working citizens of the United States, and about the American ideals of liberty and fairness. The arguments in this unit are directed both toward shaping beliefs about the United States and toward the public policies that reflect those beliefs.

Unit Five is entitled "Japanese American Internment and the Problem of Cultural Identity." Beginning in 1942, about 120,000 Japanese and Japanese American men, women, and children were removed from their homes on the West Coast and interned in ramshackle "camps" farther inland because they were considered to be aiding imperial Japan, with which the United States was at war. This internment has since been recognized as a grave injustice, and reparations have been paid to the survivors. But the interned people did not react just with indignation or bitterness; their responses were much more complex. In their personal accounts they addressed such questions as these: How is a member of a racially and culturally distinctive group to understand the experience of such injustice? What does that experience say about whether such a group can, or should, assimilate into mainstream American culture? This unit invites you to consider how personal experiences can illuminate the complexities of such issues — both your own experiences and those of the writers you will study.

Unit Six is entitled "Policy and Protest over the Vietnam War." The Vietnam War, which lasted from 1954 to 1975, caused extensive damage to the people and the land of a small Southeast Asian country and many thousands of casualties to the American soldiers who fought there. But the war in Southeast Asia also caused conflict in the United States itself, as many Americans protested the government's policies and questioned the truth of its claims, both about the need to fight and about the progress of the war effort. Even today, the issue remains unresolved, with Americans continuing to argue over why we fought.

READINGS AND APPARATUS

Clearly, the focus of this book is historical; texts have been selected from as far back as the seventeenth century, when Europeans first began to settle on the North American continent. We believe that a historical perspective allows us to appreciate the full richness of the rhetorical traditions that have developed in the United States, in various periods of contention. Each unit includes a historical introduction and headnotes for each reading selection to help orient you to the time period.

The readings in these case studies are the real texts in which the negotiation of difference was conducted. Though sometimes excerpted for use in a writing class, they are the texts written by the actual players in each contested situation. Often we have chosen texts that address, support, or refute one another. The writers employ a wide range of strategies to persuade their readers, and the book provides questions to help reveal these strategies.

First, reading questions focus on the text itself, asking you to locate definitions of key terms, supporting reasons for arguments, uses of personal testimony, invocations of tradition, humor, and more. Our approach in *Negotiating Difference* treats all of these features of a text as legitimate choices made by the writer in an attempt to make his or her text persuasive. Our assumption is that persuasion always relies on a mixture of techniques, just as human beings are "mixed" creatures who are usually moved to action by a combination of rational and emotional motives. *Negotiating Difference* does not separate these diverse rhetorical strategies into logical and emotional elements. To do so would tend to privilege the logical and downgrade the emotional, and that distinction would not give you an accurate picture of how persuasion is accomplished. The reading questions in *Negotiating Difference* ask for a genuine understanding of what a writer is saying and how the writer tries to make his or her view persuasive. Using these questions to take notes, as starters for a reading journal, or for class discussion should help prepare you for the writing questions that follow.

The writing questions ask you to write about issues such as whether the text is persuasive, in your now-informed opinion; how the writer presents his or her views to readers who may know little about the writer's cultural heritage and may be indifferent or even hostile to the writer's views; how the text responds or would respond to opposing positions articulated in another text in the unit; and how you can relate issues raised in the text to social issues of contention that concern you today.

While it is good practice to write about issues such as these after reading any one selection in a unit, we strongly suggest studying and writing about a number of texts together. This is the rationale for the case study approach, which groups a number of texts around a common issue. It is also the rationale for the use of assignment sequences. At the end of each unit, we suggest various ways to cluster readings around central themes raised in the unit. Each cluster of readings is followed by three or four sequences of writing assignments that draw on various combinations of readings within the cluster. As each sequence progresses, the assignments increase in complexity.

There have been many other occasions for the negotiation of difference in American history besides the ones represented in the case studies in this book. In that sense, the book is necessarily incomplete. To partly address this limitation, we have included a "Research Kit" at the end of each unit with both writing assignments for further research into the historical moment that is the unit's focus and assignments that point outward to research on similar issues in other times and places. For example, some of the Research Kit assignments at the end of Unit I suggest ways to find out more about the relations between European Americans and Native Americans in colonial New England, while other assignments point to topics on the relations between Native Americans and immigrant groups elsewhere in the United States. For use in these assignments, the Research Kit provides a basic bibliography and ideas on where to look for further information, including community sources.

WRITING AS NEGOTIATION

In the broadest perspective, *Negotiating Difference* suggests the model of negotiating difference as a way of understanding all reading and writing. The effort of "negotiating difference" can be generalized to describe any occasion in which readers encounter texts. Difficulties in reading or writing can arise from differences between writer and readers. But if there were no differences between writer and readers, then no one would stand to learn very much from the exchange.

Writing is a form of negotiation. The effective writer's task is not simply to dump the meaning out of her head onto the paper as quickly as possible. Writers have to think about how to present what they want to say. They have to imagine the readers who are going to be negotiating the text, and offer them some inducement to do the work.

Writers must, for example, consider what order of ideas will be clearest for readers, even if it's not the order that immediately presents itself. Writers ought also to think about what kinds of cultural allusions will be most persuasive, even if they are not ones that are already familiar to readers. What kind of person does the writer wish to appear to be: Cool and analytical? Warm and caring? Which self-presentation will be most credible with readers?

Effective writers attempt to anticipate readers' needs and expectations in these ways in order to inform readers, to influence them, to change their minds. Communication is rarely, probably never, neutral: Writers want their readers to know or believe something they did not know or believe before, to adopt a new point of view. For readers, this will take work — as all of us who read know from our own negotiations with the texts of others. Writers who hope to be taken seriously must offer readers some accommodations to make the work worth their effort.

When a writer stops working on a piece of writing, she may feel that it does not accomplish all that she had hoped it would. In the effort to accommodate readers, the writer may not state her own views in exactly the way that she originally wished to do. And to express her own point of view, the writer may not do all she could to accommodate her readers. But what gets written, finally, is a negotiated settlement among these contending forces.

Writing rarely begins with a predetermined meaning for which the writer simply finds words. Much more often, ideas actually develop as a result of these rhetorical negotiations with readers. Texts emerge that would not have been written if there had been no negotiation, or if the negotiation had occurred with a different group of readers.

Negotiation among significant differences requires knowledge of both the issues in dispute and the assumptions made by the disputants. Negotiation also requires some ability to analyze, compare, and evaluate arguments. By including in this book a substantial number of selections that reveal the various perspectives represented in the conflicts, we aim to provide a knowledge base for negotiation. Through the questions and assignments, we mean to suggest entries for analysis, points of comparison, and frameworks for interpretation. With this guidance, you should feel empowered to begin grappling in your writing with these important civic issues and intellectual strategies.

We hope this book will improve your abilities to engage in the rhetorical activities we call "negotiating difference." But even more important, we hope this book will help you to appreciate the advantages of negotiating difference. We hope you will see that difference itself is an advantage, not a "problem" to be overcome, for it is the multicultural richness of the United States that gives our country its strength, creative force, and idealistic commitment to social justice, however tarnished. The celebration of difference is the ever-receding utopian goal to which we dedicate this book.

UNIT ONE

First Contacts
between Puritans
and Native Americans

NEGOTIATIONS

How do we know what happened in the past? How do we know, for example, what happened in New England in the 1600s, when English people were first beginning to settle there? One way is through narratives of the events written by participants, such as the *History of Plymouth Plantation* by early colonist William Bradford. But narratives are inevitably partial accounts of events: partial in the sense that the narrator selects, from among all the available things he or she could tell us, just those things that he or she considers significant; and partial in the sense that the narrator makes these selections on the basis of his or her own assumptions, loyalties, and prejudices.

Even to speak of "New England" and the "1600s" is already to take a partial perspective. "New England" is the name given to the region not by its original inhabitants, the Native Americans, but by settlers who came there from England. And the date refers to the calendar in use by these settlers, not to Native American ways of recording time.

The way William Bradford selects events to narrate, based on his own assumptions, is evident in the following passage describing the colonists' arrival in 1620:

> And for the season it was winter, and they that know the winters of that country know them to be sharp and violent, and subject to cruel and fierce storms, dangerous to travel to known places, much more to search an unknown coast. Besides, what could they see but a hideous and desolate wilderness, full of wild beasts and wild men — and what multitudes there might be of them they knew not. (p. 22)

Bradford emphasizes the hazards of the colonizing journey that he and his comrades undertook, as well he might, considering that more than half of them died that first winter. He omits to tell us, however, that they eventually settled at the site they called Plymouth precisely because it had been one of the area's Wampanoag villages, Patuxet, surrounded by cleared fields. The Wampanoag people farmed as well as hunted — they were hardly "wild men" — and after a few initial, minor skirmishes, they welcomed the colonists warmly. Bradford also omits to tell us that Patuxet was empty because its inhabitants had recently died from diseases brought by European sailors, who had been visiting the region since around 1500 and whose maps the Plymouth expedition followed — the coast was not totally "unknown."

This brief example from Bradford is meant to suggest that when we read any narrative that claims to tell what happened in the past, we must be cautious, not only about what the text says, but also about what it doesn't say. Caution is needed even more when we are investigating a period in history that is controversial, such as the 1600s in New England. The controversy here revolves around the interactions between the English immigrants and the Native Americans. We all know the ultimate outcome of these interactions: The English took over, and the population and landholdings of the Native Americans were greatly reduced. But how did this come about? Who was generous, treacherous, conciliatory, or excessively violent?

Given our understanding of the partiality of historical narratives, we know that the answers to these questions are going to depend on whose narratives we read. Even by piecing together different accounts, we probably will not be able to arrive at a complete story — especially in the case of New England in the 1600s, where one major group of participants, the Native Americans, were mostly not literate in English. The record of their version of what happened must come largely from words of theirs that were taken down by English storytellers or from retellings of their history by later Native American writers.

With these cautions in mind, we focus in Unit One on the negotiation of difference that takes place when two groups attempt to tell conflicting versions of history — in this case, the history of relations between the English and the Native Americans in seventeenth-century New England. How, in their written representations of the situation, did the English "negotiate," or deal with, the "difference" they perceived between themselves and the Native Americans? How, in their spoken and written texts, did the Native Americans negotiate the difference between interpretations the English imposed on Native American culture and the Native Americans' own perceptions of themselves? How were these textual negotiations affected by the unequal and changing political power relations among the groups involved? These are some of the questions we will consider.

OVERVIEW OF THE SELECTIONS

The texts we present are grouped into four categories: dominant and alternative English accounts, Native American accounts, and documents such as treaties, laws, and deeds. All focus on English–Native American relations in the seventeenth century, especially on the two wars that marked these relations, the so-called Pequot War (1637) and King Philip's War (1675–76).

Dominant English accounts were written by religious and social leaders of the English colonies in New England. In part because of their authors' social power, these texts have for a long time been virtually the only ones studied in literature courses on the period. In addition to Bradford's narrative of the founding of Plymouth, included here are an account of the Pequot War by John Underhill, one of the two leaders of the attacking colonists, and accounts of King Philip's War by the Puritan minister Increase Mather and by Mary Rowlandson, a minister's wife who was a captive of the Native Americans during the war.

We use the term "alternative English accounts" for the writings of English people who were not part of the social elite in New England. These accounts have been very little studied in literature courses. Lion Gardener's narrative of the Pequot War presents the perspective of a professional soldier who was highly critical of Puritan dealings with the Native Americans. Quaker John Easton's account of the origins of King Philip's War emphasizes the justice of the Native Americans' complaints against the Puritan settlers.

Native American accounts have also been largely overlooked until very recently. Moreover, Native American voices have been muted because few Native Americans in the 1600s could produce written texts in English. We present English transcriptions of Native American reactions at the time of King Philip's War: a defiant note left on the bridge post of an English settlement destroyed by Native American fighters and a speech of both conciliation and grievance addressed to the English by Waban, a leader of the few Christian Native Americans to survive harsh treatment during the war. We also present lengthy excerpts from *Eulogy on King Philip*, a revisionist history covering the whole period and critiquing many of the dominant sources, by a Pequot writer of the early nineteenth century, William Apess.

Finally, we present a selection of legal documents, such as treaties and deeds, illustrating the ways in which the English tried to regulate their relations with Native Americans according to English law.

HISTORICAL BACKGROUND

"Puritans" and "Indians": Who Were They?

Most of the English people who came to New England in the early 1600s left England because they did not want to practice Christianity according to the state-established rite in England, the Anglican Church. They were Protestant Christians of other denominations. Some of them were known as Puritans because their religious practices, they claimed, "purified" the Anglican Church. Although "Puritan" was intended to be an insulting name, it became commonly used even by members of the group themselves.

Puritans who remained in England during this period continued to struggle against the royal government, finally coming to open warfare, overthrowing King Charles I and executing him in 1649. A Puritan commonwealth governed England until 1660 when the son of the executed monarch was restored to the throne as Charles II. The Anglican Church, disestablished under the Puritans, was restored as the state religion.

The term "Puritan" is commonly applied to all Protestant Christians in seventeenth-century New England; some, however, were orthodox Anglicans, and some, such as the Society of Friends, or Quakers, had separated from the Anglican Church completely. Bradford's group at Plymouth, also known as Separatists because they had separated from the Anglican Church, called themselves Pilgrims to recognize the pious aspirations motivating their journey to America. Because the Puritans quickly became the most numerous group in New England in the seventeenth century, we use this term to refer to the religious majority in the colonies and their leadership. We use other, more specific terms such as "Pilgrim" when they apply.

The name "Indians," used by Europeans to refer to the Native Americans, was not intended to be insulting. It resulted from the mistaken idea of early European explorers that they had reached not a continent unknown to them, but the coast of India in Asia. Although this name occurs frequently in the English texts included here, in our own accounts we use the term "Native Americans" except when we can refer to members of a specific tribe by their tribal name.

Native American Culture

It is extremely difficult to estimate the Native American population of the New England region. Only the roughest estimates can be given. It is important to realize, however, that the region was well populated and far from empty before the Europeans arrived. Around the year 1500, before much European contact had taken place, the population may have been around 150,000, with 45,000 concentrated in eastern New England. As a result of contacts between Native Americans and early European sailors and traders, however, epidemic disease took a steady toll of Native American lives from the sixteenth through the eighteenth century. A particularly devastating plague swept eastern Massachusetts from 1617 to 1619, killing more than half of the native Massachusett and Wampanoag tribes (and emptying Patuxet).

Tribes in eastern New England had a common culture and spoke closely related Algonkian languages. Tribal subgroups, kin-related, might total as many as five hundred to seven hundred people. They might gather their easily portable houses, called *wetus*, into larger settlements near their fields of maize (corn), kidney beans, squash, and tobacco. Or families or small groups could move with the seasons, in search of wild berries, fish, and game.

Each tribal subgroup had both a political leader, called a *sachem* or *sagamore*, and a religious leader, called a *powwow*. Both leaders were usually, but not always, men. The sachem provided day-to-day guidance and managed relations with other groups, whether for trade or for war. Trade among tribes, and later with the English settlers, was sometimes conducted by exchanging wampum, beads made from shells, for desirable goods. War might provide additional territory, such as the use of choice hunting grounds, and additional people for the tribe, captives who would be adopted into families. A sachem particularly noted for wisdom and power might be acknowledged as the supreme sachem over several tribal bands.

Sachems traditionally came from certain families, but inheritance was not guaranteed. People acknowledged the authority of a sachem only if he or she was considered fit to lead, and the sachem stayed in power only so long as he or she consulted other respected persons and made wise decisions. Unlike a European ruler, the sachem did not have the power to impose an unpopular decision on his or her people or to permanently dispose of tribal land by sale or treaty.

The religious leader, or powwow, performed several functions, such as leading ceremonies to mark the seasons of the year or give thanks for successful hunts. The powwow also helped the sick, using a combination of curative rituals and herbal remedies. The person who became a powwow was perceived as having special sensitivity to the spirit world. But all people felt they had some capacity to communicate with local spirits and with Manitou, the chief spirit or source of all spiritual power. Hence the powwow was helpful, but not essential, to a person's religious life, and allegiance to a powwow who seemed more powerful could be transferred rather easily. This religious structure would later facilitate the conversion of Native Americans to Christianity during times when Christians appeared to have more power over disease or human enemies, but it would also make church discipline distasteful to the Native Americans.

The Founding of the English Colonies

This complex and thriving Native American culture was hardly acknowledged by the region's first English visitors, sailors and traders who began arriving about 1500. They were looking mainly to find whatever they could carry away for profit — including a few unfortunate, unsuspecting Native Americans who were kidnapped when they came to trade. The English took them to Europe to sell as slaves or exhibit as curiosities.

Ironically, this practice of kidnapping turned out to benefit English people, such as Bradford's group, who came to settle permanently in New England. It accidentally provided them with resident Native Americans who already spoke some English and who, remarkably under the circumstances, were willing to help. One of the most famous of these was Squanto, a Wampanoag man who had been kidnapped by an English sea captain in 1614 and taken to Spain to be sold as a slave. Squanto escaped to England and eventually returned to Massachusetts in 1619, only to find that his home village of Patuxet had been emptied by the plague.

Bradford's band of Pilgrims arrived in November 1620, built Plymouth on the site of Patuxet, and suffered an agonizing first winter. In the spring of 1621, a sachem named Samoset came into Plymouth and surprised the colonists by addressing them in English, which he had learned from sailors. He introduced them to Squanto, whose English was better than his, and to Osamequin, who was the massasoit, or supreme sachem, of the Wampanoag people (and who was usually known by his title). John Carver, then governor of Plymouth, concluded a treaty of peaceful coexistence with Massasoit, and the Wampanoags proceeded to give the Pilgrims vital advice on farming, hunting, and fishing.

Other English settlements followed. One group attempted to establish a town at Wessagusset, on Massachusetts Bay north of Plymouth, in 1622. Hardship drove the men to steal maize from the nearby Massachusett people, who angrily decided to attack both Wessagusset and Plymouth. Enlisted for aid by the Massachusetts, the Wampanoag leader Massasoit instead informed the Pilgrims, and Plymouth sent Captain Myles Standish with armed men to Wessagusset, where they first invited the Massachusetts to parley and then killed their sachem and several others when they came to talk. In spite of this intervention, the Wessagusset settlement fell apart.

In 1630 a group of about one thousand Puritans, led by John Winthrop, established a settlement on Massachusetts Bay. Miantonomo, a supreme sachem of the Narragansetts, who lived to the east and south of Plymouth and the Wampanoags in what is now Rhode Island, soon signed a treaty of peaceful coexistence with the Massachusetts Bay colony. The Massachusetts Bay Puritans sought this treaty in part because it seemed to confirm their control in the region. Increasingly in seventeenth-century New England, the English interpreted a treaty of alliance with a sachem as establishing not partnership, as the sachem may have thought, but Native American submission and English control over lands the tribe occupied.

The Pequot War: 1637

By 1637 the English were extending their colonizing efforts to what are now Long Island and Connecticut. But they continued to be fearful of attacks by Native Americans and particularly wary of what they called "conspiracies," or combinations of tribes, against them. They were therefore extremely disturbed by trouble between the Pequots of eastern Connecticut and English traders; several traders had been killed. Some contemporary witnesses, such as Lion Gardener, as well as some twentieth-century historians place much blame on the English for stirring up these troubles by their insensitive behavior and unwillingness to negotiate in good faith with the Native Americans. Finally, though, the Pequots attacked the settlement of Wethersfield, and the Puritans decided to retaliate with all-out war.

In May 1637, armed settlers under Captains John Underhill and John Mason launched a dawn surprise attack against a major Pequot village at what is now Mystic, Connecticut. Uncas, sachem of the Mohegans, who lived near the Pequots in Connecticut, joined in this attack, seeking to increase his own power. Some of his own warriors and some neighboring Narragansetts participated. In the space of about an hour, five hundred to seven hundred men, women, and children were killed.

So many Pequots were killed or captured that they were not even signers of the Treaty of Hartford, which ended the Pequot War by distributing Pequot survivors between Uncas and the Mohegans and Miantonomo and the Narragansetts. Other Pequot captives were sold into slavery in Bermuda. The English claimed most of the Pequot territory for themselves. Not long after the war, several English colonies banded together to form the New England Confederation, in part to protect themselves against future trouble with the Native Americans. Members of this confederation were Plymouth, Massachusetts Bay, New Haven, and Connecticut. The Rhode Island colony, a haven for Quakers and other religious dissenters, was pointedly excluded.

"Civilizing" and Christianizing the Native Americans

After the Pequot War, the English began to make more attempts to peacefully conform Native American society to English customs. For example, they began to try to apply English law more consistently to the Native Americans. The Puritans also began efforts to convert the Native Americans to Christianity. Unlike other missionaries (such as the Roman Catholics in Canada), the Puritans were convinced that the Native Americans had to be "reduced to civility," that is, converted to a "civilized" English way of life, before they could be Christianized.

Perhaps for this reason, Puritan attempts to convert the Native Americans were not very successful. The best-known Puritan preacher to the Native Americans was the Reverend John Eliot, who learned their language from a Pequot War captive. Eliot established his Christian Native Americans, or "Praying Indians," as they were called, in their own towns west of Boston, where they were to follow the English way of life. The first of these towns, Natick, was established in 1650. By 1674, although Eliot had set up fourteen such "praying towns," their total population was only about eleven hundred.

Moreover, what turned out to be the longest-lived praying town was not one of Eliot's. It grew up on Cape Cod, founded at Mashpee in 1665 by Wampanoags converted by local settler Richard Bourne. Within ten years, the town's Congregational church had more members than the English church in nearby Sandwich, and by 1682 Mashpee had its own Wampanoag minister, Simon Popmonet, son of the sachem Paupmunnuck, who had sanctioned the original settlement. Protected by its location on Cape Cod, Mashpee survived the war that raged between the English and the Native Americans in 1675–76. Most of Eliot's towns did not.

King Philip's War: 1675–76

Tensions leading to war were increased by the 1660 overthrow of the Puritan regime in England and the restoration of the monarchy. English colonies in New England became increasingly anxious about what these changes would mean for their charters, and they were eager to enlarge and confirm their landholdings by treaties with the Native Americans. Plymouth colony, in particular, feared being absorbed by the much larger Massachusetts Bay colony (as it finally was in 1691) and consequently began putting more pressure on the Wampanoags to sign treaties that would seem to give Plymouth control over a larger area.

Just at this time, the Wampanoag supreme sachem Massasoit, who had always been friendly to Plymouth, died. He was succeeded first by his son Wamsutta, known to the colonists as Alexander. Wamsutta resisted Plymouth's efforts to change their treaty relations. In 1664 the colonists forced him to come to Plymouth for another pressured negotiating session, in spite of the fact that he was ill; he died on the way home. He was succeeded as supreme sachem by his brother Metacomet, known to the colonists as Philip, now King Philip. By 1674 Metacomet had attempted to accommodate Pilgrim demands by signing a treaty that Plymouth interpreted as placing the Wampanoags under Plymouth's control. But Metacomet resented this interpretation. He was also angry because, in individual court cases, the English seemed to apply English law in their own favor at Native American expense; and he was annoyed by visits from preachers attempting to Christianize his people.

Early in 1675, John Sassamon, a Christian Native American and Harvard student who had been sent by John Eliot to preach to Metacomet and his people, came to Plymouth with the news that Metacomet was planning war against the colonists. Soon after, Sassamon was killed, and three of Metacomet's men were convicted of his murder in a Plymouth court. Contemporary commentators such as Increase Mather and John Easton disagree about who killed Sassamon and whether Metacomet was planning war. Nevertheless, Plymouth sent out soldiers to launch a preemptive strike against Metacomet's Wampanoags.

Metacomet dodged the first attack. He sent the women and children in his band to harbor with the Narragansetts (who loudly announced their neutrality) and began guerrilla warfare against all the English, starting with the settlements near Plymouth. Thus, what would be known as King Philip's War began. Attacks were soon launched against the English by other Wampanoags under the sachem Weetamoo (Wamsutta's widow); by Abenakis to the north; and by Nipmucks, Mahicans, and other western New England tribes. All the English settlements rallied to aid Plymouth and one another.

The English were convinced that Metacomet had organized these attacks, that the so-called conspiracy of tribes they had long dreaded was finally upon them. Historians disagree about the extent to which Metacomet did organize the attacks. But it seems clear that most of the Native

Americans in the region had finally become disgusted with English land taking and efforts to impose their culture and were determined to retaliate. They achieved a considerable degree of unity in their war efforts and considerable success, inflicting heavy losses on the English.

Unable to catch Metacomet, frustrated and fearful because of their losses, the English troops invaded Narragansett territory in the winter of 1675, in spite of protestations by the English in Rhode Island that the Narragansetts were indeed neutral. English troops surrounded the main Narragansett village and repeated the tactics they had used against the Pequot village at Mystic. With gunshot and fire they killed about seven hundred men, women, and children, including Wampanoag noncombatants who had sheltered there. The attacking English also suffered heavy casualties during the battle and during their withdrawal afterward in severe winter weather.

Meanwhile, Metacomet and his warriors, who had also taken substantial losses, circled out to western Massachusetts, to their allies the Mahicans. The Massachusetts Bay leadership then asked the English colonists at New York to send their allies the Mohawks against them. The Mohawks were the traditional, dreaded enemies — known as Maquas, or cannibals — of all the Native American tribes to the east of them. They attacked, reducing Metacomet's forces still further. In the spring of 1676, Metacomet and his few remaining warriors returned to his home village of Pokanoket, where they were killed. According to the eyewitness account of Benjamin Church, who commanded the troops that cornered Metacomet, the Native American leader was actually killed by a Native American fighting for the English.

King Philip's War was one of the bloodiest in American history. The English, unaccustomed to dealing with Native American methods of guerrilla warfare, lost the highest percentage of soldiers killed or wounded that has ever been suffered in an American war, and they took significant civilian casualties as well. They came very close to losing the war. Native American casualties were also high: About three thousand were killed in the fighting, a few on the English side. Christian Native Americans also died as a result of wartime persecution; for example, a number were interned over the winter on bleak Deer Island in Boston Harbor with very little food or shelter.

While English numbers rebounded after the war, the Native American population of the region dwindled. Although Christian Native Americans were allowed to return to their towns after the war, their numbers were so reduced, and the pressure of encroachments on their lands by surrounding colonists was so great, that most of these towns were gone completely within seventy-five years. Many Native Americans, whether Christian or not, left New England to resettle farther west. King Philip's War turned the tide decisively in favor of English dominance in New England.

The 1700s and Later

After King Philip's War greatly reduced the Native American population in New England, the colonists still feared the attacks of Native Americans from the north, who were French allies. Sporadic warfare culminated in what the English called the French and Indian War (1756–63). It finally ended in 1763 with a treaty that ceded all French rights in North America to Great Britain.

In the eighteenth century, the Native Americans remaining in New England were pushed to the margins of society, and efforts to "civilize" and convert them slowed. Small reservations were created for Massachusett, Wampanoag, and Nipmuck groups in Massachusetts; for the Narragansetts in Rhode Island; and for the Mohegans and Pequots in Connecticut. Like the Christian Native American towns, these reservations were under constant pressure during the eighteenth and early nineteenth centuries from Europeans seeking new lands. They were gradually whittled away but never disappeared completely. Native Americans also continued to live together in small groups all over New England.

Puritan accounts of what had happened between the Native Americans and the English immigrants in New England in the seventeenth century became dominant. Puritan writers such as Increase Mather were highly learned and prolific, seeming hardly to leave room in the historical record for rebuttal by Native Americans, who could rarely become literate in English. Yet some Native American historians such as the nineteenth-century William Apess spoke for them, and Native Americans continued to struggle for their rights — as they have done up to the present day.

DOMINANT ENGLISH ACCOUNTS

WILLIAM BRADFORD

From *History of Plymouth Plantation* (1630–1645)

William Bradford (1590–1657) traveled with fellow Separatists to the Netherlands in 1609 and then on to North America on the *Mayflower* in 1620, to found a settlement that they called Plymouth. Bradford's wife fell overboard and drowned just before the group moved ashore; many historians believe she took her own life rather than face the impending hardships. Bradford, although not a robust man, survived the first harsh winter and became governor of the "plantation," or settlement, the following spring. For the rest of his life, the Plymouth colony was his main concern. He served as governor almost continuously until 1656, the year before he died. His *History of Plymouth Plantation* was not published in his lifetime. Some eighteenth-century historians had access to it in manuscript, but during the Revolutionary War the manuscript disappeared and was not found again until 1855, in London. It was returned to Massachusetts and published for the first time in 1856.

In the first eight chapters of his history, Bradford details the reasons his group decided to move to North America: to make a living, to practice their religion, and to bring up their children free from the distractions of "corrupt" European society. In chapters 9–12 (the first section we have excerpted), Bradford describes the voyage to North America, settlement at Plymouth, and initial relations with Native Americans. The rest of our selection excerpts brief passages (from chapters 14 and 28) in which Bradford reports on the Wessagusset incident and the war with the Pequots.

CHAPTER IX

Of their Voyage, and how they Passed the Sea; and of their Safe Arrival at Cape Cod

September 6. These troubles being blown over, and now all being compact together in one ship,[1] they put to sea again with a prosperous wind, which continued divers days together, which was some encouragement

William Bradford, *History of Plymouth Plantation, 1620–1647*, edited with an introduction and notes by Samuel Eliot Morison (New York: Knopf, 1952), 58–90, 116–19, 294–97.

In the notes, WB = William Bradford, SEM = Samuel Eliot Morison, EDS. = Patricia Bizzell and Bruce Herzberg.

[1]The Pilgrims first left England in two ships but had to turn back because one proved unseaworthy. Some of the people from the leaky ship remained in England, while others joined the group in the *Mayflower*. — EDS.

unto them; yet, according to the usual manner, many were afflicted with sea-sickness. And I may not omit here a special work of God's providence. There was a proud and very profane young man, one of the seamen, of a lusty,[2] able body, which made him the more haughty; he would alway be contemning the poor people in their sickness and cursing them daily with grievous execrations; and did not let to tell them that he hoped to help to cast half of them overboard before they came to their journey's end, and to make merry with what they had; and if he were by any gently reproved, he would curse and swear most bitterly. But it pleased God before they came half seas over, to smite this young man with a grievous disease, of which he died in a desperate manner, and so was himself the first that was thrown overboard. Thus his curses light on his own head, and it was an astonishment to all his fellows for they noted it to be the just hand of God upon him.

After they had enjoyed fair winds and weather for a season, they were encountered many times with cross winds and met with many fierce storms with which the ship was shroudly[3] shaken, and her upper works made very leaky; and one of the main beams in the midships was bowed and cracked, which put them in some fear that the ship could not be able to perform the voyage. So some of the chief of the company, perceiving the mariners to fear the sufficiency of the ship as appeared by their mutterings, they entered into serious consultation with the master and other officers of the ship, to consider in time of the danger, and rather to return than to cast themselves into a desperate and inevitable peril. And truly there was great distraction and difference of opinion amongst the mariners themselves; fain would they do what could be done for their wages' sake (being now near half the seas over) and on the other hand they were loath to hazard their lives too desperately. But in examining of all opinions, the master and others affirmed they knew the ship to be strong and firm under water; and for the buckling of the main beam, there was a great iron screw the passengers brought out of Holland, which would raise the beam into his place; the which being done, the carpenter and master affirmed that with a post put under it, set firm in the lower deck and otherways bound, he would make it sufficient. And as for the decks and upper works, they would caulk them as well as they could, and though with the working of the ship they would not long keep staunch, yet there would otherwise be no great danger, if they did not overpress her with sails. So they committed themselves to the will of God and resolved to proceed.

In sundry of these storms the winds were so fierce and the seas so high, as they could not bear a knot of sail, but were forced to hull[4] for divers days together. And in one of them, as they thus lay at hull in a mighty storm, a lusty young man called John Howland, coming upon some occasion above the gratings was, with a seele[5] of the ship, thrown into sea; but

---

[2]"Lusty" here means "lively" or "robust"; it has no sexual connotation. — EDS.
[3]Shrewdly, that is, severely. — EDS.
[4]To "hull" means to take down most of the sails and to let the boat drift. — EDS.
[5]Roll or pitch. — SEM

it pleased God that he caught hold of the topsail halyards which hung overboard and ran out at length. Yet he held his hold (though he was sundry fathoms under water) till he was hauled up by the same rope to the brim of the water, and then with a boat hook and other means got into the ship again and his life saved. And though he was something ill with it, yet he lived many years after and became a profitable member both in church and commonwealth. In all this voyage there died but one of the passengers, which was William Butten, a youth, servant to Samuel Fuller, when they drew near the coast.

But to omit other things (that I may be brief) after long beating at sea they fell with that land which is called Cape Cod; the which being made and certainly known to be it, they were not a little joyful. After some deliberation had amongst themselves and with the master of the ship, they tacked about and resolved to stand for the southward (the wind and weather being fair) to find some place about Hudson's River for their habitation. But after they had sailed that course about half the day, they fell amongst dangerous shoals and roaring breakers, and they were so far entangled therewith as they conceived themselves in great danger; and the wind shrinking upon them withal, they resolved to bear up again for the Cape and thought themselves happy to get out of those dangers before night overtook them, as by God's good providence they did. And the next day they got into the Cape Harbor where they rid in safety.

A word or two by the way of this cape. It was thus first named by Captain Gosnold and his company,[6] Anno 1602, and after by Captain Smith was called Cape James; but it retains the former name amongst seamen. Also, that point which first showed those dangerous shoals unto them they called Point Care, and Tucker's Terrour; but the French and Dutch to this day call it Malabar by reason of those perilous shoals and the losses they have suffered there.

Being thus arrived in a good harbor, and brought safe to land, they fell upon their knees and blessed the God of Heaven who had brought them over the vast and furious ocean, and delivered them from all the perils and miseries thereof, again to set their feet on the firm and stable earth, their proper element. And no marvel if they were thus joyful, seeing wise Seneca was so affected with sailing a few miles on the coast of his own Italy, as he affirmed, that he had rather remain twenty years on his way by land than pass by sea to any place in a short time, so tedious and dreadful was the same unto him.

But here I cannot but stay and make a pause, and stand half amazed at this poor people's present condition; and so I think will the reader, too, when he well considers the same. Being thus passed the vast ocean, and a sea of troubles before in their preparation (as may be remembered by that which went before), they had now no friends to welcome them nor inns to entertain or refresh their weatherbeaten bodies; no houses or much less

[6]Because they took much of that fish [cod] there. — WB

towns to repair to, to seek for succour. It is recorded in Scripture as a mercy to the Apostle and his shipwrecked company, that the barbarians showed them no small kindness in refreshing them, but these savage barbarians, when they met with them (as after will appear) were readier to fill their sides full of arrows than otherwise. And for the season it was winter, and they that know the winters of that country know them to be sharp and violent, and subject to cruel and fierce storms, dangerous to travel to known places, much more to search an unknown coast. Besides, what could they see but a hideous and desolate wilderness, full of wild beasts and wild men — and what multitudes there might be of them they knew not. Neither could they, as it were, go up to the top of Pisgah[7] to view from this wilderness a more goodly country to feed their hopes; for which way soever they turned their eyes (save upward to the heavens) they could have little solace or content in respect of any outward objects. For summer being done, all things stand upon them with a weatherbeaten face, and the whole country, full of woods and thickets, represented a wild and savage hue. If they looked behind them, there was the mighty ocean which they had passed and was now as a main bar and gulf to separate them from all the civil parts of the world. If it be said they had a ship to succour them, it is true; but what heard they daily from the master and company? But that with speed they should look out a place (with their shallop)[8] where they would be, at some near distance; for the season was such as he would not stir from thence till a safe harbor was discovered by them, where they would be, and he might go without danger; and that victuals consumed apace but he must and would keep sufficient for themselves and their return. Yea, it was muttered by some that if they got not a place in time, they would turn them and their goods ashore and leave them. Let it also be considered what weak hopes of supply and succour they left behind them, that might bear up their minds in this sad condition and trials they were under; and they could not but be very small. It is true, indeed, the affections and love of their brethren at Leyden was cordial and entire towards them, but they had little power to help them or themselves; and how the case stood between them and the merchants at their coming away hath already been declared.

What could now sustain them but the Spirit of God and His grace? May not and ought not the children of these fathers rightly say: "Our fathers were Englishmen which came over this great ocean, and were ready to perish in this wilderness; but they cried unto the Lord, and He heard their voice and looked on their adversity,"[9] etc. "Let them therefore praise the Lord, because He is good: and His mercies endure forever." "Yea, let them which have been redeemed of the Lord, shew how He hath delivered them from the hand of the oppressor. When they wandered in the desert wilder-

---

[7]"Pisgah" is the mountain from which Moses viewed Palestine, the Promised Land to which he led the Jewish people but which he was not allowed to enter. — EDS.

[8]A "shallop" is a small boat that could be used for coastal exploration. — EDS.

[9]Deuteronomy 26:5, 7. — WB

ness out of the way, and found no city to dwell in, both hungry and thirsty, their soul was overwhelmed in them. Let them confess before the Lord His loving kindness and His wonderful works before the sons of men."[10]

CHAPTER X

Showing How they Sought out a place of Habitation; and What Befell them Thereabout

Being thus arrived at Cape Cod the 11th of November, and necessity calling them to look out a place for habitation (as well as the master's and mariners' importunity); they having brought a large shallop with them out of England, stowed in quarters in the ship, they now got her out and set their carpenters to work to trim her up; but being much bruised and shattered in the ship with foul weather, they saw she would be long in mending. Whereupon a few of them tendered themselves to go by land and discover those nearest places, whilst the shallop was in mending; and the rather because as they went into that harbor there seemed to be an opening some two or three leagues off, which the master judged to be a river. It was conceived there might be some danger in the attempt, yet seeing them resolute, they were permitted to go, being sixteen of them well armed under the conduct of Captain Standish,[11] having such instructions given them as was thought meet.

They set forth the 15th of November; and when they had marched about the space of a mile by the seaside, they espied five or six persons with a dog coming towards them, who were savages; but they fled from them and ran up into the woods, and the English followed them, partly to see if they could speak with them, and partly to discover if there might not be more of them lying in ambush. But the Indians seeing themselves thus followed, they again forsook the woods and ran away on the sands as hard as they could, so as they could not come near them but followed them by the track of their feet sundry miles and saw that they had come the same way. So, night coming on, they made their rendezvous and set out their sentinels, and rested in quiet that night; and the next morning followed their track till they had headed a great creek and so left the sands, and turned another way into the woods. But they still followed them by guess, hoping to find their dwellings; but they soon lost both them and themselves, falling into such thickets as were ready to tear their clothes and armor in pieces; but were most distressed for want of drink. But at length they found water and refreshed themselves, being the first New England water they drunk of, and was now in great thirst as pleasant unto them as wine or beer had been in foretimes.

[10]Psalm 107:1–5, 8. — WB

[11]Myles Standish was a mercenary soldier hired to give the Pilgrims military advice. He did not originally share the Pilgrims' religious beliefs but later converted out of admiration for his employers. — EDS.

Afterwards they directed their course to come to the other shore, for they knew it was a neck of land they were to cross over, and so at length got to the seaside and marched to this supposed river, and by the way found a pond of clear, fresh water, and shortly after a good quantity of clear ground where the Indians had formerly set corn, and some of their graves. And proceeding further they saw new stubble where corn had been set the same year; also they found where lately a house had been, where some planks and a great kettle was remaining, and heaps of sand newly paddled with their hands. Which, they digging up, found in them divers fair Indian baskets filled with corn, and some in ears, fair and good, of divers colours, which seemed to them a very goodly sight (having never seen any such before).[12] This was near the place of that supposed river they came to seek, unto which they went and found it to open itself into two arms with a high cliff of sand in the entrance but more like to be creeks of salt water than any fresh, for aught they saw; and that there was good harborage for their shallop, leaving it further to be discovered by their shallop, when she was ready. So, their time limited them being expired, they returned to the ship lest they should be in fear of their safety; and took with them part of the corn and buried up the rest. And so, like the men from Eshcol, carried with them of the fruits of the land and showed their brethren;[13] of which, and their return, they were marvelously glad and their hearts encouraged.

After this, the shallop being got ready, they set out again for the better discovery of this place, and the master of the ship desired to go himself. So there went some thirty men but found it to be no harbor for ships but only for boats. There was also found two of their houses covered with mats, and sundry of their implements in them, but the people were run away and could not be seen. Also there was found more of their corn and of their beans of various colours; the corn and beans they brought away, purposing to give them full satisfaction when they should meet with any of them as, about some six months afterward they did, to their good content.

And here is to be noted a special providence of God, and a great mercy to this poor people, that here they got seed to plant them corn the next year, or else they might have starved, for they had none nor any likelihood to get any till the season had been past, as the sequel did manifest. Neither is it likely they had had this, if the first voyage had not been made, for the ground was now all covered with snow and hard frozen; but the Lord is

---

[12]The English had never seen corn before because the plant is native to the Americas. Indian corn, as it is now called, has kernels of many colors — red, purple, and blue as well as yellow and white. — EDS.

[13]The "men from Eshcol" are the spies whom Moses sent into the Promised Land before the Jewish people entered. They found grapes growing in the valley of Eshcol that were so big the men needed to hang one bunch over a pole and carry it between them to bring back a sample of the land's produce (Numbers 13:23–26). — EDS.

never wanting unto His in their greatest needs; let His holy name have all the praise.

The month of November being spent in these affairs, and much foul weather falling in, the 6th of December they sent out their shallop again with ten of their principal men and some seamen, upon further discovery, intending to circulate that deep bay of Cape Cod. The weather was very cold and it froze so hard as the spray of the sea lighting on their coats, they were as if they had been glazed. Yet that night betimes they got down into the bottom of the bay, and as they drew near the shore they saw some ten or twelve Indians very busy about something. They landed about a league or two from them, and had much ado to put ashore anywhere — it lay so full of flats. Being landed, it grew late and they made themselves a barricado with logs and boughs as well as they could in the time, and set out their sentinel and betook them to rest, and saw the smoke of the fire the savages made that night. When morning was come they divided their company, some to coast along the shore in the boat, and the rest marched through the woods to see the land, if any fit place might be for their dwelling. They came also to the place where they saw the Indians the night before, and found they had been cutting up a great fish like a grampus,[14] being some two inches thick of fat like a hog, some pieces whereof they had left by the way. And the shallop found two more of these fishes dead on the sands, a thing usual after storms in that place, by reason of the great flats of sand that lie off.

So they ranged up and down all that day, but found no people, nor any place they liked. When the sun grew low, they hasted out of the woods to meet with their shallop, to whom they made signs to come to them into a creek hard by, the which they did at high water; of which they were very glad, for they had not seen each other all that day since the morning. So they made them a barricado as usually they did every night, with logs, stakes and thick pine boughs, the height of a man, leaving it open to leeward, partly to shelter them from the cold and wind (making their fire in the middle and lying round about it) and partly to defend them from any sudden assaults of the savages, if they should surround them; so being very weary, they betook them to rest. But about midnight they heard a hideous and great cry, and their sentinel called "Arm! arm!" So they bestirred them and stood to their arms and shot off a couple of muskets, and then the noise ceased. They concluded it was a company of wolves or such like wild beasts, for one of the seamen told them he had often heard such a noise in Newfoundland.

So they rested till about five of the clock in the morning; for the tide, and their purpose to go from thence, made them be stirring betimes. So after prayer they prepared for breakfast, and it being day dawning it was

---

[14]A kind of dolphin. — EDS.

thought best to be carrying things down to the boat. But some said it was not best to carry the arms down, others said they would be the readier, for they had lapped them up in their coats from the dew; but some three or four would not carry theirs till they went themselves. Yet as it fell out, the water being not high enough, they laid them down on the bank side and came up to breakfast.

But presently, all on the sudden, they heard a great and strange cry, which they knew to be the same voices they heard in the night, though they varied their notes; and one of their company being abroad came running in and cried, "Men, Indians! Indians!" And withal, their arrows came flying amongst them. Their men ran with all speed to recover their arms, as by the good providence of God they did. In the meantime, of those that were there ready, two muskets were discharged at them, and two more stood ready in the entrance of their rendezvous but were commanded not to shoot till they could take full aim at them. And the other two charged again with all speed, for there were only four had arms there, and defended the barricado, which was first assaulted. The cry of the Indians was dreadful, especially when they saw their men run out of the rendezvous toward the shallop to recover their arms, the Indians wheeling about upon them. But some running out with coats of mail on, and cutlasses in their hands, they soon got their arms and let fly amongst them and quickly stopped their violence. Yet there was a lusty man, and no less valiant, stood behind a tree within half a musket shot, and let his arrows fly at them; he was seen [to] shoot three arrows, which were all avoided. He stood three shots of a musket, till one taking full aim at him and made the bark or splinters of the tree fly about his ears, after which he gave an extraordinary shriek and away they went, all of them. They left some to keep the shallop and followed them about a quarter of a mile and shouted once or twice, and shot off two or three pieces, and so returned. This they did that they might conceive that they were not afraid of them or any way discouraged.

Thus it pleased God to vanquish their enemies and give them deliverance; and by His special providence so to dispose that not any one of them were either hurt or hit, though their arrows came close by them and on every side [of] them; and sundry of their coats, which hung up in the barricado, were shot through and through. Afterwards they gave God solemn thanks and praise for their deliverance, and gathered up a bundle of their arrows and sent them into England afterward by the master of the ship, and called that place the First Encounter.

From hence they departed and coasted all along but discerned no place likely for harbor; and therefore hasted to a place that their pilot (one Mr. Coppin who had been in the country before) did assure them was a good harbor, which he had been in, and they might fetch it before night; of which they were glad for it began to be foul weather.

After some hours' sailing it began to snow and rain, and about the middle of the afternoon the wind increased and the sea became very rough, and they broke their rudder, and it was as much as two men could do to steer her with a couple of oars. But their pilot bade them be of good cheer for he saw the harbor; but the storm increasing, and night drawing on, they bore what sail they could to get in, while they could see. But herewith they broke their mast in three pieces and their sail fell overboard in a very grown sea, so as they had like to have been cast away. Yet by God's mercy they recovered themselves, and having the flood[15] with them, struck into the harbor. But when it came to, the pilot was deceived in the place, and said the Lord be merciful unto them for his eyes never saw that place before; and he and the master's mate would have run her ashore in a cove full of breakers before the wind. But a lusty seaman which steered bade those which rowed, if they were men, about with her or else they were all cast away; the which they did with speed. So he bid them be of good cheer and row lustily, for there was a fair sound before them, and he doubted not but they should find one place or other where they might ride in safety. And though it was very dark and rained sore, yet in the end they got under the lee of a small island and remained there all that night in safety. But they knew not this to be an island till morning, but were divided in their minds; some would keep the boat for fear they might be amongst the Indians, others were so wet and cold they could not endure but got ashore, and with much ado got fire (all things being so wet); and the rest were glad to come to them, for after midnight the wind shifted to the northwest and it froze hard.

But though this had been a day and night of much trouble and danger unto them, yet God gave them a morning of comfort and refreshing (as usually He doth to His children) for the next day was a fair, sunshining day, and they found themselves to be on an island secure from the Indians, where they might dry their stuff, fix their pieces and rest themselves; and gave God thanks for His mercies in their manifold deliverances. And this being the last day of the week, they prepared there to keep the Sabbath.

On Monday they sounded the harbor and found it fit for shipping, and marched into the land and found divers cornfields and little running brooks, a place (as they supposed) fit for situation.[16] At least it was the best they could find, and the season and their present necessity made them glad to accept of it. So they returned to their ship again with this news to the rest of their people, which did much comfort their hearts.

On the 15th of December they weighed anchor to go to the place they had discovered, and came within two leagues of it, but were fain to bear up again; but the 16th day, the wind came fair, and they arrived safe in this harbor. And afterwards took better view of the place, and resolved where to pitch their dwelling; and the 25th day began to erect the first house for common use to receive them and their goods.

[15]The tide. — EDS.

[16]This is the famous landing of the Pilgrims on Plymouth Rock. The rock is not mentioned here, however, and may have been used as a landing stage only by later travelers. Note that the land had already been cleared for "cornfields" — because it was the site of Squanto's home village of Patuxet, which had been emptied by the plague. — EDS.

CHAPTER XI

The Remainder of Anno 1620
[The Mayflower Compact][17]

I shall a little return back, and begin with a combination made by them before they came ashore; being the first foundation of their government in this place. Occasioned partly by the discontented and mutinous speeches that some of the strangers amongst them had let fall from them in the ship: That when they came ashore they would use their own liberty, for none had power to command them, the patent they had being for Virginia and not for New England, which belonged to another government, with which the Virginia Company had nothing to do.[18] And partly that such an act by them done, this their condition considered, might be as firm as any patent, and in some respects more sure.

The form was as followeth:

IN THE NAME OF GOD, AMEN.

We whose names are underwritten, the loyal subjects of our dread Sovereign Lord King James, by the Grace of God of Great Britain, France, and Ireland King, Defender of the Faith, etc.

Having undertaken, for the Glory of God and advancement of the Christian Faith and Honour of our King and Country, a Voyage to plant the First Colony in the Northern Parts of Virginia, do by these presents solemnly and mutually in the presence of God and one of another, Covenant and Combine ourselves together into a Civil Body Politic, for our better ordering and preservation and furtherance of the ends aforesaid; and by virtue hereof to enact, constitute and frame such just and equal Laws, Ordinances, Acts, Constitutions and Offices, from time to time, as shall be thought most meet and convenient for the general good of the Colony, unto which we promise all due submission and obedience. In witness whereof we have hereunder subscribed our names at Cape Cod, the 11th of November, in the year of the reign of our Sovereign Lord King James, of England, France and Ireland the eighteenth, and of Scotland the fifty-fourth. Anno Domini 1620.

After this they chose, or rather confirmed, Mr. John Carver (a man godly and well approved amongst them) their Governor for that year. And after they had provided a place for their goods, or common store (which were long in unlading for want of boats, foulness of the winter weather and sickness of divers) and begun some small cottages for their habitation;

[17]Bracketed subtitles are SEM's.

[18]The Virginia Company was the group of investors who helped to finance the Pilgrims' voyage. The company had rights granted by the English king to establish settlements in a large tract of land running from present-day Virginia up to the Hudson River. Settlers financed by the company received a patent, a document confirming their right to settle in the area, according to English law. But the Pilgrims landed too far north and were unable to sail south because of the weather and navigational difficulties. They had to stay in the land called New England ("the Northern Parts of Virginia"), to which their patent did not apply. Feeling the need for some form of legal document to organize their settlement, the Pilgrims drew up a "combination" or "compact," modeled on the agreements whereby their church congregations were organized. — EDS.

as time would admit, they met and consulted of laws and orders, both for their civil and military government as the necessity of their condition did require, still adding thereunto as urgent occasion in several times, and as cases did require.

In these hard and difficult beginnings they found some discontents and murmurings arise amongst some, and mutinous speeches and carriages in others; but they were soon quelled and overcome by the wisdom, patience, and just and equal carriage of things, by the Governor and better part, which clave faithfully together in the main.

[The Starving Time]

But that which was most sad and lamentable was, that in two or three months' time half of their company died, especially in January and February, being the depth of winter, and wanting houses and other comforts; being infected with the scurvy and other diseases which this long voyage and their inaccommodate condition had brought upon them. So as there died some times two or three of a day in the foresaid time, that of one hundred and odd persons, scarce fifty remained.[19] And of these, in the time of most distress, there was but six or seven sound persons who to their great commendations, be it spoken, spared no pains night nor day, but with abundance of toil and hazard of their own health, fetched them wood, made them fires, dressed them meat, made their beds, washed their loathsome clothes, clothed and unclothed them. In a word, did all the homely and necessary offices for them which dainty and queasy stomachs cannot endure to hear named; and all this willingly and cheerfully, without any grudging in the least, showing herein their true love unto their friends and brethren; a rare example and worthy to be remembered. Two of these seven were Mr. William Brewster, their reverend Elder, and Myles Standish, their Captain and military commander, unto whom myself and many others were much beholden in our low and sick condition. And yet the Lord so upheld these persons as in this general calamity they were not at all infected either with sickness or lameness. And what I have said of these I may say of many others who died in this general visitation, and others yet living; that whilst they had health, yea, or any strength continuing, they were not wanting to any that had need of them. And I doubt not but their recompense is with the Lord.

But I may not here pass by another remarkable passage not to be forgotten. As this calamity fell among the passengers that were to be left here to plant, and were hasted ashore and made to drink water that the seamen might have the more beer, and one[20] in his sickness desiring but a small

[19]Of the 102 *Mayflower* passengers who reached Cape Cod, 4 died before she made Plymouth; and by the summer of 1621 the total deaths numbered 50. Only 12 of the original 26 heads of families and 4 of the original 12 unattached men or boys were left; and of the women who reached Plymouth, all but a few died. Doubtless many of the deaths took place on board the *Mayflower* at anchor, since there was not enough shelter ashore for all; and Plymouth Harbor is so shallow that she was moored about $1\frac{1}{2}$ nautical miles from the Rock. — SEM

[20]Which was this author himself. — WB

can of beer, it was answered that if he were their own father he should have none. The disease began to fall amongst them also, so as almost half of their company died before they went away, and many of their officers and lustiest men, as the boatswain, gunner, three quartermasters, the cook and others. At which the Master was something strucken and sent to the sick ashore and told the Governor he should send for beer for them that had need of it, though he drunk water homeward bound.

But now amongst his company there was far another kind of carriage in this misery than amongst the passengers. For they that before had been boon companions in drinking and jollity in the time of their health and welfare, began now to desert one another in this calamity, saying they would not hazard their lives for them, they should be infected by coming to help them in their cabins; and so, after they came to lie by it, would do little or nothing for them but, "if they died, let them die." But such of the passengers as were yet aboard showed them what mercy they could, which made some of their hearts relent, as the boatswain (and some others) who was a proud young man and would often curse and scoff at the passengers. But when he grew weak, they had compassion on him and helped him; then he confessed he did not deserve it at their hands, he had abused them in word and deed. "Oh!" (saith he) "you, I now see, show your love like Christians indeed one to another, but we let one another lie and die like dogs." Another lay cursing his wife, saying if it had not been for her he had never come this unlucky voyage, and anon cursing his fellows, saying he had done this and that for some of them; he had spent so much and so much amongst them, and they were now weary of him and did not help him, having need. Another gave his companion all he had, if he died, to help him in his weakness; he went and got a little spice and made him a mess of meat once or twice. And because he died not so soon as he expected, he went amongst his fellows and swore the rogue would cozen him, he would see him choked before he made him any more meat; and yet the poor fellow died before morning.

[Indian Relations]

All this while the Indians came skulking about them, and would sometimes show themselves aloof off, but when any approached near them, they would run away; and once they stole away their tools where they had been at work and were gone to dinner. But about the 16th of March, a certain Indian came boldly amongst them and spoke to them in broken English, which they could well understand but marveled at it. At length they understood by discourse with him, that he was not of these parts, but belonged to the eastern parts where some English ships came to fish, with whom he was acquainted and could name sundry of them by their names, amongst whom he had got his language. He became profitable to them in acquainting them with many things concerning the state of the country in the east parts where he lived, which was afterwards profitable unto them; as also of the people here, of their names, number and strength, of their situation and distance from this place, and who was chief amongst them. His name was Samoset.[21] He told them also of another Indian whose name was Squanto, a native of this place, who had been in England and could speak better English than himself.

Being, after some time of entertainment and gifts dismissed, a while after he came again, and five more with him, and they brought again all the tools that were stolen away before, and made way for the coming of their great Sachem, called Massasoit. Who, about four or five days after, came with the chief of his friends and other attendance, with the aforesaid Squanto. With whom, after friendly entertainment and some gifts given him, they made a peace with him (which hath now continued this 24 years) in these terms:[22]

1. That neither he nor any of his should injure or do hurt to any of their people.
2. That if any of his did hurt to any of theirs, he should send the offender, that they might punish him.
3. That if anything were taken away from any of theirs, he should cause it to be restored; and they should do the like to his.
4. If any did unjustly war against him, they would aid him; if any did war against them, he should aid them.
5. He should send to his neighbours confederates to certify them of this, that they might not wrong them, but might be likewise comprised in the conditions of peace.
6. That when their men came to them, they should leave their bows and arrows behind them.

After these things he returned to his place called Sowams, some 40 miles from this place, but Squanto continued with them and was their interpreter and was a special instrument sent of God for their good beyond their expectation. He directed them how to set their corn, where to take fish, and to procure other commodities, and was also their pilot to bring them to unknown places for their profit, and never left them till he died. He was a native of this place, and scarce any left alive besides himself. He was carried away with divers others by one Hunt, a master of a ship, who thought to sell them for slaves in Spain. But he got away for England and was entertained by a merchant in London, and employed to Newfoundland and other parts, and lastly brought hither into these parts by one Mr. Dermer, a gentleman employed by Sir Ferdinando Gorges and others for discovery and other designs in these parts. Of whom I shall say something,

[21]Samoset was an Algonkian sagamore of Pemaquid Point, Maine, a region much frequented by English fishermen. He probably shipped with Capt. Dermer from Monhegan to Cape Cod shortly before the Pilgrims landed and worked his way overland to Plymouth. . . . — SEM

[22]For a slightly different version of this treaty, see p. 136. — EDS.

because it is mentioned in a book set forth Anno 1622 by the President and Council for New England, that he made the peace between the savages of these parts and the English, of which this plantation, as it is intimated, had the benefit; but what a peace it was may appear by what befell him and his men.

This Mr. Dermer was here the same year that these people came, as appears by a relation[23] written by him and given me by a friend, bearing date June 30, Anno 1620. And they came in November following, so there was but four months difference. In which relation to his honoured friend, he hath these passages of this very place:

> I will first begin (saith he) with that place from whence Squanto or Tisquantum, was taken away; which in Captain Smith's map is called Plymouth; and I would that Plymouth had the like commodities. I would that the first plantation might here be seated, if there come to the number of fifty persons, or upward. Otherwise, Charlton, because there the savages are less to be feared. The Pocanockets,[24] which live to the west of Plymouth, bear an inveterate malice to the English, and are of more strength than all the savages from thence to Penobscot. Their desire of revenge was occasioned by an Englishman, who having many of them on board, made a greater slaughter with their murderers[25] and small shot when as (they say) they offered no injury on their parts. Whether they were English or no it may be doubted; yet they believe they were, for the French have so possessed them. For which cause Squanto cannot deny but they would have killed me when I was at Namasket, had he not entreated hard for me.
>
> The soil of the borders of this great bay may be compared to most of the plantations which I have seen in Virginia. The land is of divers sorts, for Patuxet is a hardy but strong soil; Nauset and Satucket are for the most part a blackish and deep mould much like that where groweth the best tobacco in Virginia. In the bottom of that great bay is store of cod and bass or mullet, etc. But above all he commends Pocanocket for the richest soil, and much open ground fit for English grain, etc.
>
> Massachusetts is about nine leagues from Plymouth, and situated in the midst between both, is full of islands and peninsulas, very fertile for the most part.

With sundry such relations which I forbear to transcribe, being now better known than they were to him.

He [Dermer] was taken prisoner by the Indians at Manamoyick, a place not far from hence, now well known. He gave them what they demanded for his liberty, but when they had got what they desired, they kept him still, and endeavoured to kill his men. But he was freed by seizing on some of them and kept them bound till they gave him a canoe's load of corn. . . . But this was Anno 1619.

---

[23]"Relation" here means a narrative or account, perhaps in a letter. — EDS.

[24]The Pocanockets were the same as the Wampanoags, Massasoit's tribe. Their country lay around Mount Hope and the Taunton and Dighton Rivers, which flow into Narragansett Bay. — SEM

[25]A ship's gun that used small bullets and slugs. — SEM

After the writing of the former relation, he came to the Isle of Capawack[26] (which lies south of this place in the way to Virginia) and the aforesaid Squanto with him, where he going ashore amongst the Indians to trade, as he used to do, was betrayed and assaulted by them, and all his men slain, but one that kept the boat. But himself got aboard very sore wounded, and they had cut off his head upon the cuddy of the boat, had not the man rescued him with a sword. And so they got away and made shift to get into Virginia where he died, whether of his wounds or the diseases of the country, or both together, is uncertain. By all which it may appear how far these people were from peace, and with what danger this plantation was begun, save as the powerful hand of the Lord did protect them.

These things were partly the reason why they kept aloof and were so long before they came to the English. Another reason as after themselves made known was how about three years before, a French ship was cast away at Cape Cod, but the men got ashore and saved their lives, and much of their victuals and other goods. But after the Indians heard of it, they gathered together from these parts and never left watching and dogging them till they got advantage and killed them all but three or four which they kept, and sent from one sachem to another to make sport with, and used them worse than slaves. Of which the aforesaid Mr. Dermer redeemed two of them; and they conceived this ship was now come to revenge it.

Also, as after was made known, before they came to the English to make friendship, they got all the Powachs[27] of the country, for three days together in a horrid and devilish manner, to curse and execrate them with their conjurations, which assembly and service they held in a dark and dismal swamp.

But to return. The spring now approaching, it pleased God the mortality began to cease amongst them, and the sick and lame recovered apace, which put as [it] were new life into them, though they had borne their sad affliction with much patience and contentedness as I think any people could do. But it was the Lord which upheld them, and had beforehand prepared them; many having long borne the yoke, yea from their youth. . . .

CHAPTER XII

Anno 1621
[Mayflower *Departs and Corn Planted*]

They now began to dispatch the ship away which brought them over, which lay till about this time, or the beginning of April. The reason on their part why she stayed so long, was the necessity and danger that lay

---

[26]Now called Martha's Vineyard. — EDS.
[27]Powwows, or religious leaders and healers. — EDS.

upon them; for it was well towards the end of December before she could land anything here, or they able to receive anything ashore. Afterwards, the 14th of January, the house which they had made for a general rendezvous by casualty fell afire, and some were fain to retire aboard for shelter; then the sickness began to fall sore amongst them, and the weather so bad as they could not make much sooner any dispatch. Again, the Governor and chief of them, seeing so many die and fall down sick daily, thought it no wisdom to send away the ship, their condition considered and the danger they stood in from the Indians, till they could procure some shelter; and therefore thought it better to draw some more charge upon themselves and friends than hazard all. The master and seamen likewise, though before they hasted the passengers ashore to be gone, now many of their men being dead, and of the ablest of them (as is before noted), and of the rest many lay sick and weak; the master durst not put to sea till he saw his men begin to recover, and the heart of winter over.

Afterwards they (as many as were able) began to plant their corn, in which service Squanto stood them in great stead, showing them both the manner how to set it, and after how to dress and tend it. Also he told them, except they got fish and set with it in these old grounds it would come to nothing. And he showed them that in the middle of April they should have store enough come up the brook by which they began to build, and taught them how to take it, and where to get other provisions necessary for them. All which they found true by trial and experience. Some English seed they sowed, as wheat and pease, but it came not to good, either by the badness of the seed or lateness of the season or both, or some other defect.

[Bradford Succeeds Carver; Civil Marriage]

In this month of April, whilst they were busy about their seed, their Governor (Mr. John Carver) came out of the field very sick, it being a hot day. He complained greatly of his head and lay down, and within a few hours his senses failed, so as he never spake more till he died, which was within a few days after. Whose death was much lamented and caused great heaviness amongst them, as there was cause. He was buried in the best manner they could, with some volleys of shot by all that bore arms. And his wife, being a weak woman, died within five or six weeks after him.

Shortly after, William Bradford was chosen Governor in his stead, and being not recovered of his illness, in which he had been near the point of death, Isaac Allerton was chosen to be an assistant unto him who, by renewed election every year, continued sundry years together. Which I here note once for all.

May 12 was the first marriage in this place which, according to the laudable custom of the Low Countries,[28] in which they had lived, was thought

---

[28]What is now Holland. — EDS.

most requisite to be performed by the magistrate, as being a civil thing, upon which many questions about inheritances do depend, with other things most proper to their cognizance and most consonant to the Scriptures (Ruth 4) and nowhere found in the Gospel to be laid on the ministers as a part of their office. "This decree or law about marriage was published by the States of the Low Countries Anno 1590. That those of any religion (after lawful and open publication) coming before the magistrates in the Town, or State house, were to be orderly (by them) married one to another.". . . And this practice hath continued amongst not only them, but hath been followed by all the famous churches of Christ in these parts to this time — Anno 1646.

[Indian Diplomacy]

Having in some sort ordered their business at home, it was thought meet to send some abroad to see their new friend Massasoit, and to bestow upon him some gratuity to bind him the faster unto them; as also that hereby they might view the country and see in what manner he lived, what strength he had about him, and how the ways were to his place, if at any time they should have occasion. So the second of July they sent Mr. Edward Winslow and Mr. Hopkins, with the foresaid Squanto for their guide; who gave him a suit of clothes and a horseman's coat, with some other small things, which were kindly accepted; but they found but short commons and came both weary and hungry home. For the Indians used then to have nothing so much corn as they have since the English have stored them with their hoes, and seen their industry in breaking up new grounds therewith.

They found his place to be forty miles from hence, the soil good and the people not many, being dead and abundantly wasted in the late great mortality, which fell in all these parts about three years before the coming of the English, wherein thousands of them died. They not being able to bury one another, their skulls and bones were found in many places lying still above the ground where their houses and dwellings had been, a very sad spectacle to behold. But they brought word that the Narragansetts lived but on the other side of that great bay, and were a strong people and many in number, living compact together, and had not been at all touched with this wasting plague.

About the latter end of this month, one John Billington lost himself in the woods, and wandered up and down some five days, living on berries and what he could find. At length he light on an Indian plantation twenty miles south of this place, called Manomet; they conveyed him further off, to Nauset among those people that had before set upon the English when they were coasting whilst the ship lay at the Cape, as is before noted. But the Governor caused him to be inquired for among the Indians, and at length Massasoit sent word where he was, and the Governor sent a shallop for him and had him delivered. Those people also came and made their peace; and they gave full satisfaction to those whose corn they had found and taken when they were at Cape Cod.

Thus their peace and acquaintance was pretty well established with the natives about them. And there was another Indian called Hobomok come to live amongst them, a proper lusty man, and a man of account for his valour and parts amongst the Indians, and continued very faithful and constant to the English till he died. He and Squanto being gone upon business among the Indians, at their return (whether it was out of envy to them or malice to the English) there was a sachem called Corbitant, allied to Massasoit but never any good friend to the English to this day, met with them at an Indian town called Namasket, fourteen miles to the west of this place, and began to quarrel with them and offered to stab Hobomok. But being a lusty man, he cleared himself of him and came running away all sweating, and told the Governor what had befallen him. And he feared they had killed Squanto, for they threatened them both; and for no other cause but because they were friends to the English and serviceable unto them. Upon this the Governor taking counsel, it was conceived not fit to be borne; for if they should suffer their friends and messengers thus to be wronged, they should have none would cleave to them, or give them any intelligence, or do them service afterwards, but next they would fall upon themselves. Whereupon it was resolved to send the Captain and fourteen men well armed, and to go and fall upon them in the night. And if they found that Squanto was killed, to cut off Corbitant's head, but not to hurt any but those that had a hand in it.

Hobomok was asked if he would go and be their guide and bring them there before day. He said he would, and bring them to the house where the man lay, and show them which was he. So they set forth the 14th of August, and beset the house round. The Captain, giving charge to let none pass out, entered the house to search for him. But he was gone away that day, so they missed him, but understood that Squanto was alive, and that he had only threatened to kill him and made an offer to stab him but did not. So they withheld and did no more hurt, and the people came trembling and brought them the best provisions they had, after they were acquainted by Hobomok what was only intended. There was three sore wounded which broke out of the house and assayed to pass through the guard. These they brought home with them, and they had their wounds dressed and cured, and sent home. After this they had many gratulations from divers sachems, and much firmer peace; yea, those of the Isles of Capawack sent to make friendship; and this Corbitant himself used the mediation of Massasoit to make his peace, but was shy to come near them a long while after.

After this, the 18th of September they sent out their shallop to the Massachusetts, with ten men and Squanto for their guide and interpreter, to discover and view that Bay and trade with the natives. The which they performed, and found kind entertainment. The people were much afraid of the Tarentines, a people to the eastward which used to come in harvest time and take away their corn, and many times kill their persons.[29] They returned in safety and brought home a good quantity of beaver, and made report of the place, wishing they had been there seated. But it seems the Lord, who assigns to all men the bounds of their habitations, had appointed it for another use. And thus they found the Lord to be with them in all their ways, and to bless their outgoings and incomings, for which let His holy name have the praise forever, to all posterity.

[First Thanksgiving]

They began now to gather in the small harvest they had, and to fit up their houses and dwellings against winter, being all well recovered in health and strength and had all things in good plenty. For as some were thus employed in affairs abroad, others were exercised in fishing, about cod and bass and other fish, of which they took good store, of which every family had their portion. All the summer there was no want; and now began to come in store of fowl, as winter approached, of which this place did abound when they came first (but afterward decreased by degrees). And besides waterfowl there was great store of wild turkeys, of which they took many, besides venison, etc. Besides they had about a peck a meal a week to a person, or now since harvest, Indian corn to that proportion. Which made many afterwards write so largely of their plenty here to their friends in England, which were not feigned but true reports.[30] . . .

[29]The Tarentines were also called the Abenakis; they lived in what is now Maine. — EDS.

[30]Edward Winslow's letter of December 11, 1621 to a friend in England describing this "First Thanksgiving" is printed in *Mourt's Relation* pp. 60–65:

"Our harvest being gotten in, our Governor sent four men on fowling, that so we might after a more special manner rejoice together, after we had gathered the fruit of our labours. They four in one day killed as much fowl as, with a little help beside, served the Company almost a week. At which time, amongst other recreations, we exercised our arms, many of the Indians coming amongst us, and amongst the rest their greatest king, Massasoit with some ninety men, whom for three days we entertained and feasted. And they went out and killed five deer which they brought to the plantation and bestowed on our Governor and upon the Captain and others."

The actual date of this festival is nowhere related. . . . — SEM. *Mourt's Relation* is a collection of English letters and journals published anonymously in 1622 by a printer named Morton, abbreviated "Mourt." Some of the selections in *Mourt's* were written by Edward Winslow, William Bradford, and other Plymouth settlers. A modern edition is *A Journal of the Pilgrims at Plymouth: Mourt's Relation* (1622; reprint, edited with notes by Dwight B. Heath, New York: Corinth Books, 1963). — EDS.

CHAPTER XIV

Anno Dom: 1623
[Sad Straits of Weston's Men, and
the Great Indian Conspiracy]

It may be thought strange that these people[31] should fall to these extremities in so short a time; being left competently provided when the ship left them, and had an ambition by that moiety of corn that was got by trade, besides much they got of the Indians where they lived, by one means and other. It must needs be their great disorder, for they spent excessively whilst they had or could get it; and, it may be, wasted part away among the Indians; for he that was their chief was taxed by some amongst them for keeping Indian women, how truly I know not. And after they began to come into wants, many sold away their clothes and bed coverings; others (so base were they) became servants to the Indians, and would cut them wood and fetch them water for a capful of corn; others fell to plain stealing, both night and day, from the Indians, of which they grievously complained. In the end, they came to that misery that some starved and died with cold and hunger. One in gathering shellfish was so weak as he stuck fast in the mud and was found dead in the place. At last most of them left their dwellings and scattered up and down in the woods and by the watersides, where they could find ground nuts[32] and clams, here six and there ten.

By which their carriages[33] they became contemned and scorned of the Indians, and they began greatly to insult over them in a most insolent manner. Insomuch that many times as they lay thus scattered abroad and had set on a pot with ground nuts or shellfish, when it was ready the Indians would come and eat it up; and when night came, whereas some of them had a sorry blanket or such like to lap themselves in, the Indians would take it and let the other lie all night in the cold, so as their condition was very lamentable. Yea, in the end they were fain to hang one of their men whom they could not reclaim from stealing, to give the Indians content.

Whilst things went in this manner with them, the Governor and people here had notice that Massasoit their friend was sick and near unto death. They sent to visit him, and withal sent him such comfortable things as gave him great content and was a means of his recovery. Upon which occasion he discovers the conspiracy of these Indians, how they were resolved to cut off Mr. Weston's people for the continual injuries they did them, and would now take opportunity of their weakness to do it, and for that end

[31]"These people" are a small group of Englishmen — not particularly religious — who were settled by the London investor Weston at a site near the present-day Boston. They did not prosper, according to Bradford, because they were poorly organized and wasted their provisions. Then hunger drove them to steal from the nearby Massachusetts and otherwise to stir up trouble that the Pilgrims feared would provoke the Native Americans to attack all the English. — EDS.

[32]A low plant with edible tubers on its roots, once very common in New England. — SEM
[33]I.e., conduct. — SEM

had conspired with other Indians their neighbours thereabout; and, thinking the people here would revenge their death, they therefore thought to do the like by them, and had solicited him to join with them. He advised them therefore to prevent it, and that speedily, by taking of some of the chief of them before it was too late, for he assured them of the truth hereof.[34]

This did much trouble them, and they took it into serious deliberation, and found upon examination other evidence to give light hereunto, too long here to relate. In the meantime, came one of them from the Massachusetts with a small pack at his back, and though he knew not a foot of the way, yet he got safe hither but lost his way; which was well for him for he was pursued, and so was missed. He told them here, how all things stood amongst them, and that he durst stay no longer; he apprehended they (by what he observed) would be all knocked in the head shortly.

This made them make the more haste, and dispatched a boat away with Captain Standish and some men, who found them in a miserable condition, out of which he rescued them and helped them to some relief, cut off some few of the chief conspirators,[35] and according to his order, offered to bring them all hither if they thought good, and they should fare no worse than themselves, till Mr. Weston or some supply came to them. Or, if any other course liked them better, he was to do them any helpfulness he could. They thanked him and the rest, but most of them desired he would help them with some corn, and they would go with their small ship to the eastward, where haply they might hear of Mr. Weston or some supply from him, seeing the time of the year was for fishing ships to be in the land; if not, they would work among the fishermen for their living and get their passage into England, if they heard nothing from Mr. Weston in time. So they shipped what they had of any worth, and he got them all the corn he could (scarce leaving to bring him home), and saw them well out of the bay, under sail at sea, and so came home, not taking the worth of a penny of anything that was theirs. I have but touched these things briefly, because they have already been published in print more at large.

This was the end of these, that some time boasted of their strength (being all able, lusty men) and what they would do and bring to pass in comparison of the people here, who had many women and children and weak ones amongst them. And said at their first arrival, when they saw the wants here, that they would take another course and not to fall into such a condition as this simple people were come to. But a man's way is not in his own power, God can make the weak to stand. Let him also that standeth take heed lest he fall. . . .

[34]That is, according to Bradford, Massasoit advised the English to capture the leaders of the Massachusetts before they could act on their plan to attack Weston's men and the Plymouth settlement. — EDS.

[35]Standish invited the Massachusett leaders to a parley and then killed them when they came to talk. — EDS.

CHAPTER XXVIII

Anno Dom: 1637
[The Pequot War]

In the fore part of this year, the Pequots fell openly upon the English at Connecticut, in the lower parts of the river, and slew sundry of them as they were at work in the fields, both men and women, to the great terrour of the rest, and went away in great pride and triumph, with many high threats. They also assaulted a fort at the river's mouth,[36] though strong and well defended; and though they did not there prevail, yet it struck them with much fear and astonishment to see their bold attempts in the face of danger. Which made them in all places to stand upon their guard and to prepare for resistance, and earnestly to solicit their friends and confederates in the Bay of Massachusetts to send them speedy aid, for they looked for more forcible assaults. Mr. Vane, being then Governor, writ from their General Court to them here to join with them in this war. To which they were cordially willing, but took opportunity to write to them about some former things, as well as present, considerable hereabout. . . .

In the meantime, the Pequots, especially in the winter before, sought to make peace with the Narragansetts, and used very pernicious arguments to move them thereunto: as that the English were strangers and began to overspread their country, and would deprive them thereof in time, if they were suffered to grow and increase. And if the Narragansetts did assist the English to subdue them, they did but make way for their own overthrow, for if they were rooted out, the English would soon take occasion to subjugate them. And if they would hearken to them they should not need to fear the strength of the English, for they would not come to open battle with them but fire their houses, kill their cattle, and lie in ambush for them as they went abroad upon their occasions; and all this they might easily do without any or little danger to themselves. The which course being held, they well saw the English could not long subsist but they would either be starved with hunger or be forced to forsake the country. With many the like things; insomuch that the Narragansetts were once wavering and were half minded to have made peace with them, and joined against the English. But again, when they considered how much wrong they had received from the Pequots, and what an opportunity they now had by the help of the English to right themselves; revenge was so sweet unto them as it prevailed above all the rest, so as they resolved to join with the English against them, and did.

The Court here agreed forthwith to send fifty men at their own charge; and with as much speed as possibly they could, got them armed and had made them ready under sufficient leaders, and provided a bark to carry them provisions and tend upon them for all occasions. But when they were ready to march, with a supply from the Bay, they had word to stay; for the enemy was as good as vanquished and there would be no need.

---

[36] This is the fort commanded by Lion Gardener (see p. 85). — EDS.

I shall not take upon me exactly to describe their proceedings in these things, because I expect it will be fully done by themselves who best know the carriage and circumstances of things. I shall therefore but touch them in general. From Connecticut, who were most sensible of the hurt sustained and the present danger, they set out a party of men, and another party met them from the Bay, at Narragansetts', who were to join with them.[37] The Narragansetts were earnest to be gone before the English were well rested and refreshed, especially some of them which came last. It should seem their desire was to come upon the enemy suddenly and undiscovered. There was a bark of this place, newly put in there, which was come from Connecticut, who did encourage them to lay hold of the Indians' forwardness, and to show as great forwardness as they, for it would encourage them, and expedition might prove to their great advantage. So they went on, and so ordered their march as the Indians brought them to a fort of the enemy's (in which most of their chief men were) before day. They approached the same with great silence and surrounded it both with English and Indians, that they might not break out; and so assaulted them with great courage, shooting amongst them, and entered the fort with all speed. And those that first entered found sharp resistance from the enemy who both shot at and grappled with them; others ran into their houses and brought out fire and set them on fire, which soon took in their mat; and standing close together, with the wind all was quickly on a flame, and thereby more were burnt to death than was otherwise slain; it burnt their bowstrings and made them unserviceable; those that scaped the fire were slain with the sword, some hewed to pieces, others run through with their rapiers, so as they were quickly dispatched and very few escaped. It was conceived they thus destroyed about four hundred at this time. It was a fearful sight to see them thus frying in the fire and the streams of blood quenching the same, and horrible was the stink and scent thereof; but the victory seemed a sweet sacrifice,[38] and they gave the praise thereof to God, who had wrought so wonderfully for them, thus to enclose their enemies in their hands and give them so speedy a victory over so proud and insulting an enemy.

The Narragansett Indians all this while stood round about, but aloof from all danger and left the whole execution to the English, except it were the stopping of any that broke away. Insulting over their enemies in this their ruin and misery, when they saw them dancing in the flames, calling them by a word in their own language, signifying "O brave Pequots!" which

---

[37]As Bradford explains in the previous paragraph, no fighters from Plymouth were involved in the Pequot War because it was over before they could set out. The two main English forces were from the colonies of Connecticut, commanded by John Mason, and Massachusetts Bay, commanded by John Underhill. They were joined by Narragansett and Mohegan fighters and the Mohegan sachem Uncas. — EDS.

[38]Bradford alludes to the ancient Jewish practice, described in the Bible, of slaughtering animals in ritual fashion and burning them on an altar as an offering or "sacrifice" to God. He compares the Pequots burning in their town to the sacrificial animals. — EDS.

they used familiarly among themselves in their own praise in songs of triumph after their victories. After this service was thus happily accomplished, they marched to the waterside where they met with some of their vessels, by which they had refreshing with victuals and other necessaries. But in their march the rest of the Pequots drew into a body and accosted them, thinking to have some advantage against them by reason of a neck of land. But when they saw the English prepare for them they kept aloof, so as they neither did hurt nor could receive any.

After their refreshing, and repair together for further counsel and directions, they resolved to pursue their victory and follow the war against the rest. But the Narragansett Indians, most of them, forsook them, and such of them as they had with them for guides or otherwise, they found them very cold and backward in the business, either out of envy, or that they saw the English would make more profit of the victory than they were willing they should; or else deprive them of such advantage as themselves desired, by having them become tributaries unto them, or the like. . . .

That I may make an end of this matter, this Sassacus (the Pequots' chief sachem) being fled to the Mohawks, they cut off his head, with some other of the chief of them, whether to satisfy the English or rather the Narragansetts (who, as I have since heard, hired them to do it)or for their own advantage, I well know not; but thus this war took end.[39] The rest of the Pequots were wholly driven from their place, and some of them submitted themselves to the Narragansetts and lived under them. Others of them betook themselves to the Mohegans under Uncas, their sachem, with the approbation of the English of Connecticut, under whose protection Uncas lived; and he and his men had been faithful to them in this war and done them very good service. But this did so vex the Narragansetts, that they had not the whole sway over them, as they have never ceased plotting and contriving how to bring them under; and because they cannot attain their ends, because of the English who have protected them, they have sought to raise a general conspiracy against the English, as will appear in another place.

READING CRITICALLY

1. What aspects of the Plymouth settlers' experience does Bradford emphasize in the last two paragraphs in chapter 9?

2. What did the treaty with Massasoit require the Native Americans to do? What did it require the English to do?

---

[39]Sassacus, said to have been seventy-seven years old at the time of this war, was the most powerful sachem in southern New England. At the height of his power he ruled from Narragansett Bay to the Hudson, and a great part of Long Island too. It is believed that the Mohawks slew him in order to get possession of a treasure of wampum which he carried in his escape. — SEM

3. Why, in Bradford's view, were the Native Americans hesitant to approach Plymouth at first?

4. According to Bradford, why did the colonists raid the house where Corbitant might be found? What did they do there?

5. Why, according to Bradford, did the English at Wessagusset get into trouble with the Native Americans there? What did the Plymouth colonists do to help them? What lesson does Bradford draw from the story?

6. According to Bradford, what arguments did the Pequots use to persuade the Narragansetts to ally with them against the English? Their arguments were unsuccessful. The Narragansetts allied with the English but then, according to Bradford, were dissatisfied with the outcome of the war. Why?

WRITING ANALYTICALLY

1. Consider the passage at the end of chapter 9 that you analyzed in reading question 1. Bradford seems to be working for a certain effect here, to depict the Plymouth settlers in particular ways. How would you describe his characterization? Do you respond to it as you think Bradford wanted readers to respond? Why or why not? Write a paper in which you analyze what Bradford is trying to do in this passage and evaluate whether he succeeds. Option: You may extend this work into a longer paper in which you compare this passage with the ways Bradford depicts Native Americans and the New England landscape in chapter 10. How does the picture change in chapter 10 from the one at the end of chapter 9? What is the effect on you of having these two rather different pictures next to each other? Analyze and evaluate chapter 10, as well as the passage from chapter 9, and then compare the effects of the two sections and discuss the effects of their juxtaposition.

2. The Native American tribes in New England had their own political relations before the English came and provided a new factor — their own allegiance or hostility — in the regional balance of power. What sort of picture does Bradford paint of the relations among the different groups in the region in connection with the Pequot War (your response to reading question 6 can help you here)? Compare his picture with the relations implied by the Treaty of Hartford that ended the Pequot War (p. 137). Write a paper in which you analyze the political situation in New England at the end of the Pequot War, using the evidence from Bradford and from the treaty. Option: You may write as if you were a seventeenth-century English colonist reporting to friends in England who want to know if it's safe for them to join you in New England.

3. How does Bradford deal with the violence of the English attack on the Pequot town (chapter 28)? Compare and contrast his treatment with that of John Underhill (p. 44), who specifically answers charges that the English were excessively violent. Does either of these writers persuade you that the violence was justified? How do you react to their strategies? Write a paper in which you argue that Bradford and Underhill do or do not successfully deal with charges that the English were excessively violent in their assault on the Pequot town.

JOHN UNDERHILL

From *Newes from America* (1638)

John Underhill (c. 1597–1672), a Massachusetts Bay colonist, was one of two English commanders of the forces that attacked the Pequot town at what is now Mystic, Connecticut, in 1637. The other commander was John Mason, whose account of the battle *(An Epitome or brief History of the Pequot War, 1677)* differs significantly from Underhill's. The English fighters were accompanied by the Mohegan sachem Uncas, several hundred of his warriors, and also some of the neighboring Narragansetts. While Mason led the group that breached the main entrance in the palisade protecting the Pequot town, Underhill led the group that surrounded the town and attacked any who fled. Underhill promptly published his own account of the Pequot War, *Newes from America*, in 1638. He was later banished from the Massachusetts Bay colony for religious views taken to be unorthodox, but still later he was allowed to return, and he served as a military leader of the colonists in later conflicts.

In our excerpts, first Underhill gives an explanation of why the Pequots dared to begin hostilities against the English settlers in spite of the establishment of a fort at Saybrook, Connecticut, which Lion Gardener commanded (see p. 85). Then he describes the battle at the town and its immediate aftermath, the point at which his narrative ends.

I TOLD YOU BEFORE, that when the Pequeats heard and saw Seabrooke fort was supplied, they forbore to visit us.[1] But the old serpent, according to his first malice, stirred them up against the church of Christ, and in such a furious manner, as our people were so far disturbed and affrighted with their boldness that they scarce durst rest in their beds; threatening persons and cattle to take them, as indeed they did. So insolent were these wicked imps grown, that like the devil, their commander, they run up and down as roaring lions, compassing all corners of the country for a prey, seeking whom they might devour. It being death to them for to rest without some wicked employment or other, they still plotted how they might wickedly attempt some bloody enterprise upon our poor native countrymen. . . .

[*Underhill tells some stories about Native American violence against English settlers in Connecticut, including the capture and brutal treatment of two young girls (who were eventually rescued).* — EDS.]

John Underhill, *Newes from America*, reprinted in *History of the Pequot War*, edited with notes by Charles Orr (1897; reprint, New York: AMS, 1980), 66, 77–86.

In the notes, EDS. = Patricia Bizzell and Bruce Herzberg.

[1]"Pequeats" is an alternative spelling of Pequots. "Seabrooke" is Saybrook, Connecticut. — EDS.

Having embarked our soldiers, we weighed anchor at Seabrooke fort, and set sail for the Narraganset Bay, deluding the Pequeats thereby, for they expected us to fall into the Pequeat river; but crossing their expectation, bred in them a security.[2] We landed our men in the Narraganset Bay, and marched over land above two days' journey before we came to Pequeat. Quartering the last night's march within two miles of the place, we set forth about one of the clock in the morning, having sufficient intelligence that they knew nothing of our coming. Drawing near to the fort, yielded up ourselves to God, and entreated his assistance in so weighty an enterprise. We set on our march to surround the fort;[3] Captain John Mason, approaching to the west end, where it had an entrance to pass into it; myself marching to the south side, surrounding the fort; placing the Indians, for we had about three hundred of them, without side of our soldiers in a ring battalia, giving a volley of shot upon the fort. So remarkable it appeared to us, as we could not but admire at the providence of God in it, that soldiers so unexpert in the use of their arms, should give so complete a volley, as though the finger of God had touched both match and flint. Which volley being given at break of day, and themselves fast asleep for the most part, bred in them such a terror, that they brake forth into a most doleful cry; so as if God had not fitted the hearts of men for the service, it would have bred in them a commiseration towards them. But every man being bereaved of pity, fell upon the work without compassion, considering the blood they had shed of our native countrymen, and how barbarously they had dealt with them, and slain, first and last, about thirty persons.

Having given fire, we approached near to the entrance, which they had stopped full with arms of trees, or brakes. Myself approaching to the entrance, found the work too heavy for me, to draw out all those which were strongly forced in. We gave order to one Master Hedge, and some other soldiers, to pull out those brakes. Having this done, and laid them between me and the entrance, and without order themselves, proceeded first on the south end of the fort. But remarkable it was to many of us. Men that run before they are sent, most commonly have an ill reward. Worthy reader, let me entreat you to have a more charitable opinion of me (though unworthy to be better thought of) than is reported in the other book.[4] You may remember there is a passage unjustly laid upon me, that when we should come to the entrance I should put forth this question, Shall we enter? Others should answer again, What came we hither for else? It is well known to many, it was never my practice, in time of my command,

---

[2] The Pequots expected the English to come from the west, as Saybrook fort was located west of the main Pequot village at what is now Mystic, Connecticut. Instead, the English sailed around Mystic, landing near what is now Rhode Island and approaching the Pequot village from the east. — EDS.

[3] The Pequot "fort" was a town surrounded by a palisade made of tree trunks driven into the ground next to one another. — EDS.

[4] Another published account of the Pequot War, by Philip Vincent, suggests that Underhill hesitated to enter the Pequot village out of fear. — EDS.

when we are in garrison, much to consult with a private soldier, or to ask his advice in point of war; much less in a matter of so great a moment as that was, which experience had often taught me was not a time to put forth such a question; and therefore pardon him that hath given the wrong information.

Having our swords in our right hand, our carbines or muskets in our left hand, we approached the fort, Master Hedge being shot through both arms, and more wounded. Though it be not commendable for a man to make mention of anything that might tend to his own honor, yet because I would have the providence of God observed, and his name magnified, as well for myself as others, I dare not omit, but let the world know, that deliverance was given to us that command, as well as to private soldiers. Captain Mason and myself entering into the wigwams, he was shot, and received many arrows against his head-piece. God preserved him from many wounds. Myself received a shot in the left hip, through a sufficient buff coat, that if I had not been supplied with such a garment, the arrow would have pierced through me. Another I received between neck and shoulders, hanging in the linen of my head-piece. Others of our soldiers were shot, some through the shoulders, some in the face, some in the head, some in the legs, Captain Mason and myself losing each of us a man, and had near twenty wounded. Most courageously these Pequeats behaved themselves. But seeing the fort was too hot for us, we devised a way how we might save ourselves and prejudice them. Captain Mason entering into a wigwam, brought out a firebrand, after he had wounded many in the house. Then he set fire on the west side, where he entered; myself set fire on the south end with a train of powder. The fires of both meeting in the centre of the fort, blazed most terribly, and burnt all in the space of half an hour. Many courageous fellows were unwilling to come out, and fought most desperately through the palisadoes, so as they were scorched and burnt with the very flame, and were deprived of their arms — in regard the fire burnt their very bowstrings — and so perished valiantly. Mercy did they deserve for their valor, could we have had opportunity to have bestowed it. Many were burnt in the fort, both men, women, and children. Others forced out, and came in troops to the Indians, twenty and thirty at a time, which our soldiers received and entertained with the point of the sword. Down fell men, women, and children; those that scaped us, fell into the hands of the Indians that were in the rear of us. It is reported by themselves, that there were about four hundred souls in this fort, and not above five of them escaped out of our hands. Great and doleful was the bloody sight to the view of young soldiers that never had been in war, to see so many souls lie gasping on the ground, so thick, in some places, that you could hardly pass along. It may be demanded, Why should you be so furious? (as some have said). Should not Christians have more mercy and compassion? But I would refer you to David's war.[5] When a people is

---

[5]David is depicted in the Bible as making war and totally exterminating the enemy people — men, women, and children — supposedly at God's command. — EDS.

grown to such a height of blood, and sin against God and man, and all confederates in the action, there he hath no respect to persons, but harrows them, and saws them, and puts them to the sword, and the most terriblest death that may be. Sometimes the Scripture declareth women and children must perish with their parents. Sometimes the case alters; but we will not dispute it now. We had sufficient light from the word of God for our proceedings.

Having ended this service, we drew our forces together to battalia. Being ordered, the Pequeats came upon us with their prime men, and let fly at us; myself fell on scarce with twelve or fourteen men to encounter with them; but they finding our bullets to outreach their arrows, forced themselves often to retreat. When we saw we could have no advantage against them in the open field, we requested our Indians for to entertain fight with them. Our end was that we might see the nature of the Indian war; which they granted us, and fell out, the Pequeats, Narragansets, and Mohigeners changing a few arrows together after such a manner, as I dare boldly affirm, they might fight seven years and not kill seven men. They came not near one another, but shot remote, and not point-blank, as we often do with our bullets, but at rovers, and then they gaze up in the sky to see where the arrow falls, and not until it is fallen do they shoot again. This fight is more for pastime, than to conquer and subdue enemies.

But spending a little time this way, we were forced to cast our eyes upon our poor maimed soldiers, many of them lying upon the ground, wanting food and such nourishable things as might refresh them in this faint state. But we were not supplied with any such things whereby we might relieve them, but only were constrained to look up to God, and to entreat him for mercy towards them. Most were thirsty, but could find no water. The provision we had for food was very little. Many distractions seized upon us at the present. A chirurgeon[6] we wanted; our chirurgeon, not accustomed to war, durst not hazard himself where we ventured our lives, but, like a fresh water soldier, kept aboard, and by this means our poor maimed soldiers were brought to a great strait and faintness, some of them swounding away for want of speedy help; but yet God was pleased to preserve the lives of them, though not without great misery and pain to themselves for the present.

Distractions multiplying, strength and courage began to fail with many. Our Indians, that had stood close to us hitherto, were fallen into consultation, and were resolved for to leave us in a land we knew not which way to get out. Suddenly after their resolution, fifty of the Narraganset Indians fell off from the rest, returning home. The Pequeats spying them, pursued after them. Then came the Narragansets to Captain Mason and myself, crying, Oh help us now, or our men will be all slain. We answered, How dare you crave aid of us, when you are leaving of us in this distressed condition, not knowing which way to march out of the country? But yet you shall see it is not the nature of Englishmen to deal like heathens, to requite evil for

[6]A surgeon, a physician. — EDS.

evil, but we will succor you. Myself falling on with thirty men, in the space of an hour rescued their men, and in our retreat to the body, slew and wounded above a hundred Pequeats, all fighting men, that charged us both in rear and flanks.

Having overtaken the body we were resolved to march to a certain neck of land that lay by the sea-side, where we intended to quarter that night, because we knew not how to get our maimed men to Pequeat river. As yet we saw not our pinnaces[7] sail along, but feared the Lord had crossed them, which also the master of the barque much feared. We gave them order to set sail on the Narraganset Bay, about midnight, as we were to fall upon the fort in the morning, so that they might meet us in Pequeat river in the afternoon; but the wind being cross, bred in them a great perplexity what would become of us, knowing that we were but slenderly provided, both with munition and provision. But they being in a distracted condition, lifted up their hearts to God for help. About twelve of the clock the wind turned about and became fair; it brought them along in sight of us, and about ten o'clock in the morning carried them into Pequeat river. Coming to an anchor at the place appointed, the wind turned as full against them as ever it could blow. How remarkable this providence of God was, I leave to a Christian eye to judge. Our Indians came to us, and much rejoiced at our victories, and greatly admired the manner of Englishmen's fight, but cried Mach it, mach it; that is, It is naught, it is naught, because it is too furious, and slays too many men. Having received their desires, they freely promised, and gave up themselves to march along with us, wherever we would go. God having eased us from that oppression that lay upon us, thinking we should have been left in great misery for want of our vessels, we diverted our thoughts from going to that neck of land, and faced about, marching to the river where our vessels lay at anchor. One remarkable passage. The Pequeats playing upon our flanks, one Sergeant Davis, a pretty courageous soldier, spying something black upon the top of a rock, stepped forth from the body with a carbine of three feet long, and, at a venture, gave fire, supposing it to be an Indian's head, turning him over with his heels upward. The Indians observed this, and greatly admired that a man should shoot so directly. The Pequeats were much daunted at the shot, and forbore approaching so near upon us. Being come to the Pequeat river we met with Captain Patrick, who under his command had forty able soldiers, who was ready to begin a second attempt. But many of our men being maimed and much wearied, we forbore that night, and embarked ourselves, myself setting sail for Seabrooke fort. Captain Mason and Captain Patrick marching over land, burned and spoiled the country between the Pequeat and Conetticot river, where we received them.

The Pequeats having received so terrible a blow, and being much affrighted with the destruction of so many, the next day fell into consultation. Assembling their most ablest men together, propounded these three

---

[7]Light, sailing ships. — EDS.

things. First, whether they would set upon a sudden revenge upon the Narragansets, or attempt an enterprise upon the English, or fly. They were in great dispute one amongst another. Sasachus, their chief commander, was all for blood; the rest for flight, Alleging these arguments: We are a people bereaved of courage, our hearts are sadded with the death of so many of our dear friends; we see upon what advantage the English lie; what sudden and deadly blows they strike; what advantage they have of their pieces to us, which are not able to reach them with our arrows at distance. They are supplied with everything necessary; they are flote[8] and heartened in their victory. To what end shall we stand it out with them? We are not able; therefore let us rather save some than lose all. This prevailed. Suddenly after, they spoiled all those goods they could not carry with them, broke up their tents and wigwams, and betook themselves to flight. Sasachus, flying towards Conetticot plantation, quartered by the river side; there he met with a shallop[9] sent down to Seabrooke fort, which had in it three men; they let fly upon them, shot many arrows into them. Courageous were the English, and died in their hands, but with a great deal of valor. The forces which were prepared in the Bay were ready for to set forth. Myself being taken on but for three months, and the soldiers willing to return to the Bay, we embarked ourselves, and set to sail. In our journey we met with certain pinnaces, in them a hundred able and well appointed soldiers, under the the conduct of one Captain Stoughton, and other inferior officers; and in company with them one Mr. John Wilson, who was sent to instruct the company. These falling into Pequeat river, met with many of the distressed Indians. Some they slew, others they took prisoners.[10]

READING CRITICALLY

1. According to Underhill, in what ways did God intervene in the battle with the Pequots?

2. Underhill says that another account of the battle "unjustly" criticized his conduct. What was he accused of doing, and how does he refute the charge?

3. How does Underhill answer charges that the English were too "furious" in their killing of men, women, and children trying to surrender?

4. Underhill has little respect for the Native American way of fighting. Why?

---

[8]Numerous. — EDS.   [9]A small sailing vessel. — EDS.

[10]Underhill and his men returned home to the Massachusetts Bay colony before the Pequot War's final battle, in which most of the remaining Pequot fighters were trapped in a swamp and killed. The Pequot sachem Sassacus (Underhill calls him ("Sasachus") fled west to the Mohawks, who killed him. Some Pequot survivors were sold into slavery in Bermuda, it being thought too risky to keep them in New England (see p. 107). Other survivors were adopted into the Narragansett and Mohegan tribes (see the Treaty of Hartford, which ended the war, p. 137). — EDS.

WRITING ANALYTICALLY

1. Underhill seems quite concerned about presenting himself as a valiant soldier. How does he do this? (Your responses to reading questions 2 and 4 may help you here.) Do you find his presentation convincing? Write a paper in which you argue that it is or is not convincing, supporting your position with evidence from the text.

2. Compare and contrast Underhill's account of the Pequot War with Bradford's. Underhill was an eyewitness to the attack on the Pequot town, whereas Bradford remained behind the lines and heard about it from witnesses; these differences certainly influence what each man tells us. But what differences, if any, do you see in their accounts that cannot be attributed simply to the fact that Underhill was there and Bradford wasn't? Write a paper in which you argue either that the two men's histories of the war have different agendas because they are trying to create different images of the Native Americans and the colonists, or that they basically agree on how to interpret the war and depict it for posterity. Support your position with evidence from the texts.

3. Compare and contrast Underhill's account of the war with that of Lion Gardener (p. 85), who was not an eyewitness but who was a soldier much closer to the field of battle than Bradford was. What similarities and differences do you see? Write a paper in which you argue either that the two men's histories of the war have different agendas because they are trying to create different images of the Native Americans and the English, or that they basically agree on how to interpret the war and depict it for posterity. Support your position with evidence from the texts.

INCREASE MATHER

From *A Brief History of the War with the Indians in New-England* (1676)

Increase Mather (1639–1723) was born in the Massachusetts Bay colony and educated at Harvard College and in England. He was a scholar of many interests who published 130 books. An ordained minister, Mather was pastor of Second Church, Boston, from 1664 until his death. He was also head of Harvard College from 1685 to 1701, where he encouraged the study of science. Moreover, he was an important colonial political leader. (Mather's son Cotton Mather, also a minister, succeeded his father at Second Church and was an even more notable scholar, scientist, and colonial leader.)

Increase Mather, *A Brief History of the War with the Indians in New-England,* reprinted in *So Dreadfull a Judgment: Puritan Responses to King Philip's War, 1676—1677,* ed. Richard Slotkin and James Folsom (Middletown, Conn.: Wesleyan University Press, 1978), 86–92, 106–9, 136–44.

In the notes, RS/JF = Richard Slotkin and James Folsom, EDS. = Patricia Bizzell and Bruce Herzberg.

Excerpted here is Increase Mather's *A Brief History of the War with the Indi-ans in New-England,* a chronicle first published in 1676. We have selected pas-sages dealing with the death of John Sassamon, the assault on the Narra-gansett town, and the death of Metacomet (Philip), the final excerpt taking us to the end of Mather's narrative. In his preface (not included here), Mather acknowledges a need to rebut accounts of the war by Quaker Rhode Islanders such as John Easton (p. 93), who were highly critical of the Massa-chusetts colonists' conduct.

THAT THE HEATHEN PEOPLE AMONGST WHOM WE LIVE, and whose Land the Lord God of our Fathers hath given to us for a rightfull Possession, have at sundry times been plotting mischievous devices against that part of the English Israel which is seated in these goings down of the Sun,[1] no man that is an Inhabitant of any considerable standing, can be ignorant. Espe-cially that there have been (*nec injuria*)[2] jealousies concerning the Narra-gansets and Wompanoags, is notoriously known to all men. And whereas they have been quiet untill the last year, that must be ascribed to the won-derfull Providence of God, who did (as with Jacob of old, and after that with the Children of Israel) lay the fear of the English, and the dread of them upon all the Indians. The terror of God was upon them round about. Nor indeed had they such advantages in former years as now they have, in respect of Arms and Ammunition, their bows and arrows not being comparably such weapons of death and destruction, as our guns and swords are, with which they have been unhappily furnished. Nor were our sins ripe for so dreadfull a judgment, untill the Body of the first Genera-tion was removed, and another Generation risen up which hath not so pursued, as ought to have been, the blessed design of their Fathers, in fol-lowing the Lord into this Wilderness, whilst it was a land not sown.

As for the Grounds, justness, and necessity of the present War with these barbarous Creatures which have set upon us, my design is not to in-large upon that Argument, but to leave that to others whom it mostly con-cerns, only in brief this. The irruption of this flame at this time was occa-sioned as followeth.

In the latter end of the year 1674, an Indian called John Sausaman, who had submitted himself unto, and was taken under the protection of the English, perceiving that the profane Indians were hatching mischief against the English, he faithfully acquainted the Governour of Plimouth with what he knew, and also what his fears were together with the grounds thereof, withall declaring, that he doubted such and such Indians belong-ing to Philip the Sachem of Pokanoket or Mount-hope, would murder

---

[1]The "English Israel" is the band of English Puritan settlers. The Puritans often referred to themselves in terms of the biblical story of Israel's (that is, the Jewish people's) flight from Egypt, wandering in the wilderness, and arduous conquest of their "Promised Land" in Pales-tine. "Goings down of the Sun" refers to the west (relative to England). — EDS.

[2]"Not because of injury (by the English to the Indians)." — RS/JF

him; which quickly hapned accordingly: for soon after this, John Sausaman was barbarously murthered by an Indian called Tobias (one of Phillip's chief Captains and Counsellors) and by his son, and another Indian, who knocked him on the head and then left him on the Ice on a great Pond. Divine providence which useth to bring murther to light, so ordered as that an Indian unseen by those three that killed Sausaman, beheld all that they did to him, and spake of it, so as that a Praying (and as there is cause to hope) a godly Indian, William Nahauton by name, heard of it, and he forthwith revealed what he knew to the English. Whereupon the three Indians who had committed the murther were apprehended, and the other Indian testified to their faces that he saw them killing Sausaman. They had a fair tryall for their lives, and that no appearance of wrong might be, Indians as well as English sate upon the Jury, and all agreed to the condemnation of those Murtherers, who were accordingly executed in the beginning of the 6th Month called June Anno 1675. They stoutly denied the fact, only at last Tobias's son confessed that his father and the other Indian killed Sausaman, but that himself had no hand in it, only stood by and saw them doe it.[3]

No doubt but one reason why the Indians murthered John Sausaman, was out of hatred against him for his Religion, for he was Christianized and baptiz'd, and was a Preacher amongst the Indians, being of very excellent parts, he translated some part of the bible into the Indian language, and was wont to curb those Indians that knew not God on the account of their debaucheryes; but the main ground why they murthered him seems to be, because he discovered their subtle and malicious designs, which they were complotting against the English. Philip perceiving that the Court of Plimouth had condemned and executed one of his Counsellors, being (as is upon strong grounds supposed) conscious to the murther committed upon John Sausaman, must needs think that ere long they would do to him (who had no less deserved it) as they had done to his Counsellour: wherefore he contrary to his Covenant and Faith engaged to Plimouth Colony, yea and contrary to his promise unto some in this Colony (for about five years agoe Philip made a disturbance in Plimouth Colony, but was quieted by the prudent interposition of some in our Colony, when he ingaged, that if at any time hereafter he should think the English among whome he lived did him wronge he would not cause any disquietments before such time as he had acquainted the English of Mattachusets, but contrary to these solemn ingagements he) doth call his men together and Arme them, and refused to come when sent for by the authority of Plimouth, unto whose government he had subjected himself.

Hereupon the English in Plimouth Jurisdiction sent a small Army to those towns next Mount-Hope in order to reducing Philip to his obedi-

---

[3]Native Americans often did sit on colonial juries trying cases involving Native Americans, at least in the seventeenth century, but it is not clear that they were voting members of the jury. They may have served only as translators. — Eds.

ence, and for the security of those places which were in great danger and in no less fear by reason of the insolency of the Heathen.

June 24 (Midsummer-day) was appointed and attended as a day of solemn Humiliation throughout that Colony, by fasting and prayer, to intreat the Lord to give success to the present expedition respecting the Enemy. At the conclusion of that day of Humiliation, as soon as ever the people in Swanzy were come from the place where they had been praying together, the Indians discharged a volly of shot whereby they killed one man & wounded others. Two men were sent to call a Surgeon for the relief of the wounded, but the Indians killed them by the way: and in another part of the town six men were killed, so that there were nine english men murthered this day.

Thus did the War begin, this being the first english blood which was spilt by the Indians in an hostile way.[4] The Providence of God is deeply to be observed, that the sword should be first drawn upon a day of Humiliation, the Lord thereby declaring from heaven that he expects something else from his People besides fasting and prayer.

Plimouth being thus suddenly involved in trouble, send to the other united Colonyes for aid, and their desires were with all readiness complyed with.

Souldiers marched out of Boston toward Mount-Hope, June 26th and continued marching that night, when there hapned a great Eclipse of the Moon, which was totally darkned above an hour. Only it must be remembred that some dayes before any Souldiers went out of Boston Commissioners were sent to treat with Philip, that so if possible ingaging in a War might be prevented. But when the Commissioners came near to Mount-Hope, they found diverse english men on the ground weltring in their own blood having been newly murthered by the Indians, so that they could not proceed further. Yea the Indians killed a man of this Colony as he was travelling in the roade before such time as we took up arms: in which respect no man can doubt of the justness of our cause, since the enemy did shed the blood of some of ours who never did them (our enemyes themselves being judges) the least wrong before we did at all offend them, or attempt any act of hostility towards them.

June 29th was a day of publick Humiliation in this Colony appointed by the Council in respect of the war which is now begun.

This morning our army would have ingaged with the enemy, the Indians shot the Pilot who was directing our Souldiers in their way to Philips Countrey, and wounded several of our men, and ran into Swamps, rainy weather hindred a further pursuit of the Enemy. An awfull Providence happened at this time: for a souldier (a stout man) who was sent from Watertown, seing the English Guide slain, and hearing many profane oathes among some of our Souldiers (namely those Privateers, who were also Vol-

---

[4]Compare Easton's account (p. 93), in which the first person killed in the war was a Native American shot by an English boy. — EDS.

unteers) and considering the unseasonableness of the weather was such, as that nothing could be done against the Enemy; this man was possessed with a strong conceit that God was against the english, whereupon he immediately ran distracted, and so was returned home a lamentable Spectacle.

In the beginning of July there was another Skirmish with the Enemy, wherein several of the Indians were killed, amongst whome were Philips chief Captain, and one of his Counsellors.

Now it appears that Squaw-Sachem of Pocasset her men were conjoyned with the Womponoags (that is Philips men) in this Rebellion.[5]

About this time they killed several English at Taunton, and burnt diverse houses there. Also at Swanzy they caused about half the Town to be consumed with merciless Flames. Likewise Middlebury and Dartmouth in Plimouth Colony did they burn with Fire, and barbarously murthered both men and women in those places, stripping the slain whether men or women, and leaving them in the open field as naked as in the day wherein they were born. Such also is their inhumanity as that they flay of[f] the skin from their faces and heads of those they get into their hands, and go away with the hairy Scalp of their enemyes.

July 19. Our Army pursued Philip who fled unto a dismal Swamp for refuge: the English Souldiers followed him, and killed many of his Men, also about fifteen of the English were then slain. The Swamp was so Boggy and thick of Bushes, as that it was judged to proceed further therein would be but to throw away Mens lives. It could not there be descerned who were English and who the Indians. Our Men when in that hideous place if they did but see a Bush stir would fire presently, whereby 'tis verily feared, that they did sometimes unhappily shoot English men instead of Indians. Wherefore a Retreat was Sounded, and night coming on, the Army withdrew from that place. This was because the desperate Distress which the Enemy was in was unknown to us: for the Indians have since said, that if the English had continued at the Swamp all night, nay, if they had but followed them but one half hour longer, Philip had come and yielded up himself. But God saw that we were not yet fit for Deliverance, nor could Health be restored unto us except a great deal more Blood be first taken from us: and other places as well as Plimouth stood in need of such a course to be taken with them.[6] It might rationally be conjectured that the unsuccessfulness of this Expedition against Philip would embolden the Heathen in other parts to do as he had done, and so it came to pass. For July 14, the Nipnep (or Nipmuck) Indians began their mischief at a Town called Mendam (had we amended our ways as we should have done, this Misery might have been prevented) where they committed Barbarous Murders. This Day deserves to have a Remark set upon it, considering that

[5]The "Squaw-Sachem of Pocasset" is Weetamoo, whom Mary Rowlandson served in her captivity (see p. 67). — EDS.

[6]The reference here is to the medical practice of bleeding the sick, a "course" of treatment God prescribes for curing the body politic of New England. — RS/JF

Blood was never shed in Massachusets Colony in a way of Hostility before this day. Moreover the Providence of God herein is the more awful and tremendous, in that this very day the Church in Dorchester was before the Lord, humbling themselves by Fasting and Prayer, on account of the Day of trouble now begun amongst us.

The news of this Blood-shed came to us at Boston the next day in Lecture time, in the midst of the Sermon, the Scripture then improved being that, Isai. 42.24. Who gave Jacob to the spoil, and Israel to the robbers? did not the Lord, He against whom we have sinned?

As yet Philip kept in the Swamp at Pocasset, but August 1 (being the Lords day) he fled. The English hearing that Philip was upon flight, pursued him, with a party of Monhegins, i.e., Unkas (who approved himself faithful to the English almost forty years ago in the time of the Pequod Wars, and now also in this present War) his Indians. They overtook Philips Party and killed about thirty of his men, none of ours being at that time cut off. Had the English pursued the Enemy they might easily have overtaken the Women and Children that were with Philip, yea and himself also, and so have put an end to these tumults: but though Deliverance was according to all Humane probability near, God saw it no good for us as yet. Wherefore Philip escaped and went to the Nipmuck Indians who had newly (as hath been intimated) done Acts of Hostility against the English. But mean while endeavours were used to keep those Indians from engaging in this War, and that those persons who had committed the Murder at Mendam might be delivered up to Justice. Captain Hutchinson with a small party was sent to Quahaog where there was a great Rendezvouze of Nipnep Indians. They appointed time and place of Treaty to be attended, August 2. Accordingly Captain Hutchinson rode to the Place fixed on to Treat in. But the Indians came not thither according to their Agreement, whereupon Captain Hutchinson resolved to go further to seek after them elsewhere, and as he was riding along, the Perfidious Indians lying in ambuscado in a Swamp, shot at him and wounded him, of which Wounds he after dyed, and eight men that were with him were struck down dead upon the place. Captain Wheeler who was in that Company was shot through the Arm, his dutiful Son alighting to relieve his Father, was himself shot and sorely wounded, willingly hazarding his own life to save the life of his Father. The English were not in a capacity to look after their dead, but those dead bodies were left as meat for the Fowls of Heaven, and their Flesh unto the Beasts of the Earth, and there was none to bury them.

Captain Hutchinson and the rest that escaped with their lives, hastened to Quahaog, and the Indians speedily followed, violently set upon the Town, killed divers, burning all the Houses therein down to the ground, except only one unto which the Inhabitants fled for succour, and now also (as since we have understood) did Philip with his broken Party come to Quahaog. Hundreds of Indians beset the House, and took possession of a Barn belonging thereunto, from whence they often shot into the House, and also attempted to fire it six times, but could not prevail, at last they took a Cart full of Flax and other combustible matter, and brought it near the House, intending to set it on fire; and then there was no appearing possibility, but all the English there, Men and Women and Children must have perished, either by unmerciful flames, or more unmerciful hands of wicked Men whose tender Mercies are cruelties, so that all hope that they should be saved was then taken away: but behold in this Mount of Difficulty and Extremity (יהוה יראה) the Lord is seen.[7]

For in the very nick of opportunity God sent that worthy Major Willard, who with forty and eight men set upon the Indians and caused them to turn their backs, so that poor People who were given up for dead, had their lives given them for a prey.[8] Surely this was a token for good, that however we may be diminished and brought low through Oppression, Affliction, and Sorrow, yet our God will have compassion on us, and this his People shall not utterly perish. And this Salvation is the more remarkable, for that albeit the Indians had ordered Scouts to lye in the way, and to give notice by firing three Guns, if any English came to the relief of the Distressed; yet although the Scouts fired when Major Willard and his Souldiers were past them, the Indians were so busie and made such a noise about the House, that they heard not the report of those Guns; which if they had heard, in all probability not only the People then living at Quahaog, but those also that came to succour them had been cut off.

Things being brought to this state, the Tumult of those that are risen up increaseth continually. . . .

. . . The Sword having marched Eastward, & Westward, and Northward, now beginneth to face toward the South again. The Narragansets, who were the greatest body of Indians in New-England; there being no less then six Sachims amongst them, having not as yet appeared in open Hostility. Nevertheless Philips and Squaw-Sachims men, when routed by the English Forces, were harboured amongst the Narragansets. When the Commissioners of the united Colonies sat at Boston, in the latter end of September, one of the Narraganset Sachims, and Messengers from other Sachims there, made their appearance in Boston; they pretended nothing but good-will to the English, and promised that those Enemies of ours, who had burnt so many houses, and committed so many Murders, and had fled to them for refuge, should be delivered up by the latter end of October. But when the time prefixed for the surrendry of the Wompanoags and Squaw-Sachems Indians was lapsed, they pretended they could not do as they had ingaged at present, but after winter they would do it. In the meanwhile, when the English had any ingagement with the Indians, wounded Indians came home to the Narragansets, especially after the fight at Hatfield, Octob. 19th, about fourty wounded men were seen crossing the woods towards the Narragansets; also some (at least two Indians) from amongst themselves, came to the English, and told them that the Narragansets were resolved (if they could) to destroy the English; but they

---

[7]Hebrew. Actually, "The Lord will see." — RS/JF

[8]That is, their lives were all that they were able to take away from this scene of destruction. — EDS.

were loth to begin to fall upon them before winter, but in the Spring when they should have the leaves of trees and Swamps to befriend them, they would doe it: wherefore it was judged necessary to send out Forces against them, and preparations were made accordingly.[9]

There was some agitation amongst those whom it did concern, where a person suitable for so great a trust might be found as General; and that worthy Gentleman Josiah Winslow Esq, who succeeds his Father (of blessed memory) as Governour of Plimouth, was pitched upon for this Service.

Under his conduct therefore, an Army consisting of at first a thousand, and at last about fifteen hundred men, were sent forth to execute the vengeance of the Lord upon the perfidious and bloudy Heathen. But before they set out, the Churches were all upon their knees before the Lord, the God of Armyes, entreating his favour and gracious success in that undertaking, wherein the welfare of his people was so greatly concerned. This day of Prayer and Humiliation was observed Decemb. 2d when also something hapned intimating as if the Lord were still angry with our Prayers, for this day all the houses in Quonsickamuck were burnt by the Indians.

Decemb. 8th. The Army set out from Boston. Whilst they were upon this march, an Indian whose name was Peter, having received some disgust among his Country-men, came to the English, and discovered the plotts of the Indians, told where they were, and promised to conduct the Army to them. They were no sooner arrived in the Narraganset Country, but they killed and took captive above fourty Indians. Being come to Mr. Smith's house, they waited some dayes for Connecticut Forces. In the mean while a party of the enemy did treacherously get into the house of Jerem. Bull (where was a Garison) burned the house, and slew about fourteen persons.

Decemb. 18. Connecticut Forces being come, a March toward the enemy was resolved upon: Peter Indian having informed that the Body of Indians (only Ninnigret being one of their old crafty Sachems, had with some of his men withdrawn himself from the rest, professing that he would not ingage in a War with the English, therefore did he goe into a place more remote) was in a Fort about eighteen miles distant from the place where our Army now was.[10] The next day, although it were the Sabbath, yet, provisions being a[l]most spent by our Souldiers, waiting so long for Connecticut Forces, the Councill of War resolved to give Battle to the enemy. The English Souldiers played the men wonderfully; the Indians also fought stoutly, but were at last beat out of their Fort, which was taken

---

[9]On the English reasons for attacking the Narragansetts, compare Easton (p. 93) and Apess (p. 107). — EDS.

[10]This "fort" was a large Native American village surrounded by a palisade, much like the Pequot town at what is now Mystic, Connecticut; this Narragansett town received the same treatment at the hands of the English as the Pequot town did (see Bradford, p. 19, and Underhill, p. 44). — EDS.

by the English, There were hundreds of Wigwams (or Indian houses) within the Fort, which our Souldiers set on fire, in the which men, women and Children (no man knoweth how many hundreds of them) were burnt to death. Night coming on, a Retreat was sounded.

Concerning the number of Indians slain in this Battle, we are uncertain: only some Indians which afterwards were taken prisoners (as also a wretched English man that apostatized to the Heathen, and fought with them against his own Country-men, but was at last taken and executed) confessed that the next day they found three hundred of their fighting men dead in their Fort, and that many men, women and children were burned in their Wigwams, but they neither knew, nor could conjecture how many: it is supposed that not less than a thousand Indian Souls perished at that time. Ninnigret whose men buried the slain, affirmeth that they found twenty & two Indian Captains among the dead bodyes. Of the English there were killed and wounded about two hundred and thirty, whereof only eighty and five persons are dead. But there was a solemn rebuke of Providence at this time, in that six of our Captains were slain, viz. Captain Johnson of Roxbury, Captain Gardner of Salem, Captain Davenport of Boston (son to that Captain Davenport who did great Service in the expedition against the Indians in the Pequod war, Anno 1637) Captain Gallop of New-London, Captain Marshal of Windsor, Captain Siely of Stratford, who dyed of his wounds some dayes after the fight was over. The three Captains first mentioned, belonged to Mattachusets Colony, the three last to Connecticut, of Plimouth Colony Captain Bradford (one of their faithfull Magistrates, and son of him that was many years Governour there) was sorely wounded, but God had mercy on him, and on his people in him, so as to spare his life, and to restore him to some measure of health, albeit the bullet shot into him is still in his body. Also Captain Goram of Barnstable in Plimouth Colony fel sick of a feaver whereof he dyed.

Thus did the Lord take away seven Captains out of that Army. Also four Leiutenants were wounded in that Fort fight, so that although the English had the better of it, yet not without solemn and humbling Rebukes of Providence. At night as the army returned to their Quarters, a great Snow fell, also part of the army missed their way, among whom was the General himself with his Life-guard. Had the enemy known their advantage, and pursued our Souldiers (and we have since heard that some of the Indians did earnestly move, that it might be so, but others of them through the overruling hand of Providence would not consent) when upon their retreat, they might easily have cut off the whole Army: But God would be more gracious to us. Here then was not only a Victory, but also a signal Preservation, for which let the Father of mercyes have eternal Glory.

After this God seemed to withdraw from the English, and take part with the enemy. The next day the Indians finding but few English men dead in the Fort amongst their three hundred Indians that were slain, were much troubled and amazed, supposing that no more of ours had been killed; this blow did greatly astonish them, and had the English immediately pursued the Victory begun, in all likelyhood there had been an end of our troubles: but God saw that neither yet were we fit for deliverance[.] Wherefore Connecticut Forces withdrew to Stonington, and there being so many killed and wounded amongst those that remained in the Narraganset Country, also bread for the Souldiers being wanting, by reason the extremity of the weather was such, as that the Vessels loaden with provision could not reach them, therefore the army lay still some weeks. . . .

August 1. Captain Church[11] with thirty English-men, and twenty Indians following Philip and those with him, by their track, took twenty and three Indians. The next morning they came upon Philips head quarters, killed and took about an hundred and thirty Indians, with the loss of but one English-man. In probability many of the English-Souldiers had been cut off at this time, but that an Indian called Matthias, who fought for the English, when they were come very near the Enemy, called to them in their own Language with much vehemency, telling them they were all dead men if they did but fire a Gun, which did so amuse and amaze the Indians that they lost a great advantage against the English. Philip hardly escaped with his life this day also. He fled and left his Peag[12] behind him, also his Squaw and his Son were taken Captives, and are now Prisoners in Plimouth. Thus hath God brought that grand Enemy into great misery before he quite destroy him. It must needs be bitter as death to him, to loose his Wife and only Son (for the Indians are marvellous fond and affectionate towards their Children) besides other Relations, and almost all his Subjects and Country too.

August 3. This day the Lord smiled upon this Land by signal favour, in another respect which concerns not the present War. For whereas in the month of July, there had been a sore Drought, which did greatly threaten the Indian Harvest, God opened the bottles of Heaven and caused it to rain all this night, and the day after, so as that the Indian corn is recovered to admiration, the English Harvest being already gathered in, and more plentifull then in some former years, insomuch that this which was expected to be a year of Famine, is turned to be a year of plenty as to provision.[13]

Whilst I am writing this, good information is brought to me, that in some parts of Connecticut Colony, the Drought was sorer then in this Colony, inasmuch as the Trees began to languish, and the Indians to despair of an harvest, wherefore Unkas (for although he be a friend to the English, yet he and all his men continue Pagans still) set his Powaws[14] on

[11]Benjamin Church, a nominal Puritan who homesteaded in the heart of Wampanoag country, was the most successful English fighter against the Native Americans, in part because he won many Native American fighters over to his side and imitated their tactics in battle. Church later published his own narrative of King Philip's War (see p. 132). — EDS.

[12]"Peag" refers to wompompeag, or wampum, the Native American shell money. — EDS.

[13]"Indian harvest" refers to the harvest of "Indian corn" or maize planted by the English; "English harvest" is of "English corn" or wheat. — RS/JF

[14]Powwows, or religious leaders and healers. — EDS.

work to see if they could by powawing (i.e., conjuring) procure rain, but all in vain, He therefore sent Westward to a noted Powaw, to try his skill, but neither could that Wizzard by all his hideous and diabolical howlings, obtain Showers. Whereupon he (i.e., Uncas) applyed himself to Mr. Fitch (the faithfull and able Teacher of the Church in Norwich) desiring that he would pray to God for rain. Mr. Fitch replyed to him that if he should do so, and God should hear him, as long as their Powaws were at work, they would ascribe the rain to them, and think that the Devill whome the Indians worship, and not God had sent that rain, and therefore he would not set himself to pray for it, untill they had done with their vanities and witcheries. Uncas and his son Oweneco declared that they had left off Powawing, despairing to obtain what they desired. Mr. Fitch therefore called his Church together, and they set themselves by Fasting and Prayer, to ask of the Lord Rain in the time of the latter Rain, and behold! that very night, and the next day, He that saith to the small rain, and to the great rain of his Strength be thou upon the earth, gave most Plentifull Showers, inasmuch as the Heathen were affected therewith, acknowledging that the God whom we serve is a great God, and there is none like unto him.

August 6. An Indian that deserted his Fellows, informed the inhabitants of Taunton that a party of Indians who might be easily surprised, were not very far off, and promised to conduct any that had a mind to apprehend those Indians, in the right way towards them, whereupon about twenty Souldiers marched out of Taunton, and they took all those Indians, being in number thirty and six, only the Squaw-Sachem of Pocasset, who was next unto Philip in respect of the mischief that hath been done, and the blood that hath been shed in this Warr, escaped alone; but not long after some of Taunton finding an Indian Squaw in Metapoiset newly dead, cut off her head, and it hapned to be Weetamoo, i.e., Squaw-Sachem her head. When it was set upon a pole in Taunton, the Indians who were prisoners there, knew it presently, and made a most horrid and diabolical Lamentation, crying out it was their Queens head. Now here it is to be observed, that God himself by his own hand, brought this enemy to destruction. For in that place, where the last year, she furnished Philip with Canooes for his men, she her self could not meet with a Canoo, but venturing over the River upon a Raft, that brake under her, so that she was drowned, just before the English found her. Surely Philips turn will be next.

August 10. Whereas Potock a chief Counsellor to the old Squaw-Sachem of Narraganset, was by some of Road-Island brought into Boston, and found guilty of promoting the War against the English, he was this day shot to death in the Common at Boston. As he was going to his execution, some told him that now he must dy, he had as good speak the truth, and say how many Indians were killed at the Fort-Fight last winter. He replyed, that the English did that day kill above seven hundred fighti[n]g men, and that three hundred who were wounded, dyed quickly after, and that as to old men, women and Children, they had lost no body could tell how many, and that there were above three thousand Indians in the Fort, when our Forces assaulted them, and made that notable slaughter amongst them.

August 12. This is the memorable day wherein Philip, the perfidious and bloudy Author of the War and wofull miseryes that have thence ensued, was taken and slain. And God brought it to pass, chiefly by Indians themselves. For one of Philips men (being disgusted at him, for killing an Indian who had propounded an expedient for peace with the English) ran away from him and coming to Road-Island, informed that Philip was now returned again to Mount-Hope, and undertook to bring them to the Swamp where he hid himself. Divine Providence so disposed, as that Capt. Church of Plymouth was then in Road-Island, in order to recruiting his Souldiers, who had been wearied with a tedious march that week, But immediately upon this Intelligence, he set forth again, with a small company of English and Indians. It seemeth that night Philip (like the man in the Host of Midian) dreamed that he was fallen into the hands of the English, and just as he was saying to those that were with him, that they must fly for their lives that day, lest the Indian that was gone from him should discover where he was, Our Souldiers came upon him, and surrounded the Swamp (where he with seven of his men absconded)[.] Thereupon he betook himself to flight, but as he was coming out of the Swamp, an English-man and an Indian endeavoured to fire at him, the English-man missed of his aime, but the Indian shot him through the heart, so as that he fell down dead. The Indian who thus killed Philip, did formerly belong to Squaw-Sachim of Pocasset, being known by the name of Alderman. In the beginning of the war, he came to the Governour of Plymouth, manifesting his desire to be at peace with the English, and immediately withdrew to an Island not having ingaged against the English nor for them, before this time. Thus when Philip had made an end to deal treacherously, his own subjects dealt treacherously with him. This Wo was brought upon him that spoyled when he was not spoyled.[15] And in that very place where he first contrived and began his mischief, was he taken and destroyed, and there was he (Like as Agag was hewed in pieces before the Lord)[16] cut into four quarters, and is now hanged up as a monument of revenging Justice, his head being cut off and carried away to Plymouth, his Hands were brought to Boston. So let all thine Enemies perish, O Lord! When Philip was thus slain, five of his men were killed with him, one of which was his chief Captain's son, being (as the Indians testified) that very Indian, who shot the first gun at the English, when the War began. So that we may hope that the War in those parts will dye with Philip.[17]

---

[15]"Spoyled" here means "despoiled" or "plundered"; Mather means that Philip attacked and plundered the colonists even though (according to Mather) he had not suffered any such assaults at English hands. — EDS.

[16]See 1 Samuel 15:33. — EDS.

[17]On the death of Philip (Metacomet), compare Apess (p. 107) and Church (p. 132). — EDS.

A little before this, the Authority in that Colony had appointed the seventeenth of this instant to be observed as a day of publick Thanksgiving throughout that Jurisdiction, on the account of wonderful success against the Enemy, which the Lord hath blessed them with, ever since they renewed their Covenant with him, and that so they might have hearts raised and enlarged in ascribing praises to God, he delivered Philip into their hands a few dayes before their intended Thanksgiving. Thus did God break the head of that Leviathan, and gave it to be meat to the people inhabiting the wilderness, and brought it to the Town of Plimouth the very day of their solemn Festival: yet this also is to be added and considered, that the Lord (so great is the divine faithfulness) to prevent us from being lifted up with our successes, and that we might not become secure, so ordered as that not an English-man but an Indian (though under Churches influence) must have the honour of killing Philip. And the day before this, was attended with a doleful Tragedy in the Eastern parts of this Country, viz. at Falmouth in Casco-bay, where some of those treacherous and bloody Indians who had lately submitted themselves, and promised Fidelity to the English, killed and took Captive above thirty Souls. The chief author of this mischief, was an Indian called Simon, who was once in the hands of the English, and then known to have been active in former Murders, having bragged and boasted of the mischief and murders done by him: we may fear that God, who so awfully threatned Ahab,[18] when he had let go out of his hand a Blasphemous, Murderous Heathen, whom the Lord had devoted to destruction, was not well pleased with the English for concluding this, and other bloody Murders, in the late Eastern peace. What the issue of this new flame thus breaking forth, shall be, or how far it shall proceed is with him whose wisdome is infinite; and who doth all things well: inasmuch as it is too evident that a French Coal hath kindled this unhappy fire (blood and fire being the Elements which they delight to swim in) it is not like to be extinguished in one day.[19] But we must leave it to God and time, fully to discover what hath been, and what shall be.

Thus have we a brief, plain, and true Story of the War with the Indians in New-England, how it began, and how it hath made its progress, and what present hopes there are of a comfortable closure and conclusion of this trouble; which hath been continued for a whole year and more. Designing only a Breviary of the History of this war; I have not enlarged upon the circumstances of things, but shall leave that to others, who have advantages and leasure to go on with such an undertaking.

Magna dabit, qui magna potest, mihi parva potenti,
Parvaq[ue], poscenti, parva dedisse sat est.[20]

[18]See 1 Kings 20:42. — EDS.

[19]With his reference to "a French Coal," Mather accuses the French settlers in Canada of stirring up Native Americans in northern New England against the English. Wars between the French and their Native American allies and the English and their allies would continue well into the eighteenth century. — EDS.

[20]"He will give much who can do so; for me, little able and demanding little, it is sufficient to have given little." — RS/JF

There is one thing admirable to consider; I mean the providence of God in keeping one of these three United Colonies, in a manner untouched all this while: For Connecticut Colony hath not been assaulted by this Enemy, only a few houses in one deserted Plantation were burnt: and it is possible that one Indian alone might do that. Whether God intends another tryal for them, or for what reason he hath hitherto spared them, no one may as yet determine. Christ said unto Peter, What I do thou Knowest not now, but thou shalt know hereafter: even so, although we do not at present fully perceive the meaning of this providence, yet hereafter it will be manifest. And albeit the same sins and provocations have been found with them that are to be charged upon others, nevertheless, it must needs be acknowledged (for why should not that which is praise-worthy in Brethren be owned, that so God may have the glory of his grace towards and in his Servants?) they have in the management of this affair, acquitted themselves like men and like Christians. It was prudently done of them, not to make the Indians who lived amongst them their Enemies, and the Lord hath made them to be as a Wall to them, and also made use of them to do great service against the common Enemies of the English. The Churches there have also given proof of their charity and Christianity, by a liberal Contribution towards the necessity of the Saints impoverished by this War in the other two Colonies,[21] having collected and transported above a thousand Bushels of Corn, for the relief and comfort of those that have lost all through the Calamity of War; God will remember and reward that pleasant fruit. Nor have some of the Churches in this Colony (especially in Boston, which the Grace of Christ hath alwayes made exemplary, in works of that nature) been unwilling to consider their poor Brethren according to their Ability.

To Conclude this History, it is evident by the things which have been expressed, that our deliverance is not as yet perfected;[22] for the Nipmuck Indians are not yet wholly subdued: Moreover, it will be a difficult thing, either to subdue or to come at the River Indians, who have many of them withdrawn themselves, and are gone far westward, and whilst they and others that have been in hostility against us, remain unconquered, we cannot enjoy such perfect peace as in the years which are past. And there seems to be a dark Cloud rising from the East in respect of Indians in those parts, yea a Cloud which streameth forth blood. But that which is the saddest thought of all, is that of late some unhappy scandals have been, which are enough to stop the current of mercy, which hath been flowing in upon us, and to provoke the Lord to let loose more Enemies upon us, so as that the second error shall be worse then the first. Only God doth deliver for his own Names sake: the Lord will not forsake his people for his great Names

---

[21]That is, Massachusetts Bay and Plymouth; Mather takes no account of Rhode Island. — EDS.

[22]Mather drafted this history before the war was completely over, and he anticipated future hostilities, such as with "Indians" from the "East" (Maine), which would indeed trouble the colonists for some time to come (see note 19). — EDS.

sake; because it hath pleased the Lord to make us his people. And we have reason to conclude that Salvation is begun, and in a gracious measure carried on towards us. For since last March there are two or three thousand Indians who have been either killed, or taken, or submitted themselves to the English. And those Indians which have been taken Captive, (& others also[)], inform that the Narragansets are in a manner ruined, there being (as they say) not above an hundred men left of them who the last year were the greatest body of Indians in New-England, and the most formidable Enemy which hath appeared against us. But God hath consumed them by the Sword & by Famine and by Sickness, it being no unusual thing for those that traverse the woods to find dead Indians up and down, whom either Famine, or sickness hath caused to dy, and there hath been none to bury them. And Philip who was the Sheba, that began & headed the Rebellion, his head is thrown over the wall, therefore have we good reason to hope that this Day of Trouble is near to an end, if our sins doe not undoe all that hath been wrought for us.[23] And indeed there is one sad consideration which may cause humble tremblings to think of it, namely in that the Reformation which God expects from us is not so hearty and so perfect as ought, to be. Divines observe, that whereas upon Samuels Exhortations, the people did make but imperfect work of it, as to the Reformation of provoking evils, therefore God did only begin their deliverance by Samuel, but left scattered Philistines unsubdued, who afterwards made head and proved a sore scourge to the Children of Israel, untill David's time, in whose Reign there was a full Reformation, and then did the Lord give unto his people full deliverance. Nevertheless a sad Catastrophe will attend those that shall magnifie themselves against the people of the Lord of Hosts. It hath been observed by many, that never any (whether Indians or Others) did set themselves to do hurt to New-England, but they have come to lamentable ends at last. New-England hath been a burthensome stone, all that have burthened themselves with it, have been cut in pieces. The experience of the present day, doth greatly confirm that observation, and give us ground to hope, that as for remaining enemies, they shall fare as others that have gone before them, have done. Yet this further must needs be acknowledged, that as to Victoryes obtained, we have no cause to glory in anything that we have done, but rather to be ashamed and confounded for our own wayes. The Lord hath thus far been our Saviour for his Names sake, that it might not be profaned among the Heathen whither he hath brought us. And God hath let us see that he could easily have destroyed us, by such a contemptible enemy as the Indians have been in our eyes, yea he hath convinced us that we our selves could not subdue them. They have advantages that we have not, knowing where to find us, but we know not where to find them, who nevertheless are alwayes at home, and have in a manner nothing but their lives and souls (which they think not of) to loose; every Swamp is a Castle to them, and they can live comfortably

---

[23]Sheba the son of Bichri, a rebel against King David, is meant. 2 Samuel 20. — RS/JF

on that which would starve English-men.[24] So that we have no cause to glory, for it is God which hath thus saved us, and not we our selves. If we consider the time when the enemy hath fallen, we must needs own that the Lord hath done it. For we expected (and could in reason expect no other) that when the Summer was come on, and the bushes and leaves of trees come forth, the enemy would do ten times more mischief then in the winter season, whenas since that the Lord hath appeared against them that they have done but little hurt comparatively. Had there not been, Θεὸω ἀπὸ μηχανῆς a divine hand beyond all expectation manifested, we had been in a state most miserable this day.[25] Also if we keep in mind the means and way whereby our deliverance hath thus been accomplished, we must needs own the Lord in all. For it hath not been brought to pass by our numbers, or skill, or valour, we have not got the Land in possession by our own Sword, neither did our own arm save us.[26] But God hath wasted the Heathen, by sending the destroying Angell amongst them, since this War began, and (which should alwayes be an humbling consideration unto us) much hath been done towards the subduing of the enemy, by the Indians who have fought for us, sometimes more than by the English. And no doubt but that a great reason why many of them have, of late been desirous to submit themselves to the English, hath been, because they were afraid of the Mohawgs who have a long time been a Terror to the other Indians. I have received it from one who was returned out of Captivity this Summer, that the Indians where he was would not suffer any fires to be made in the night, for fear lest the Mohawgs should thereby discern where they were, and cut them off.

Now, as the Lord, who doth redeem Israel out of all his troubles, hath graciously and gloriously begun our Salvation, so let him perfect it, in such a way as that no honour at all may come unto us, but that great glory may be to his own blessed Name for ever. Let him bring health and cure unto this Jerusalem, and reveal the abundance of peace and truth: And it shall be unto him a Name of joy, a Praise and an honour before all the Nations of the earth, which shall hear all the good that he will doe unto us, and they shall fear and tremble for all the goodness, and for all the prosperity that he will procure. If wee hearken to his voice in these his solemn Dispensations, it surely shall be so. Not unto us O Lord, not unto us, but unto thy Name give Glory for thy mercy and for thy Truths sake.[27] Amen!

Δόξα ἐν ὑχίστοις θεῷ. [28]

---

[24]On this contrast of English and Native American lifestyles, compare the paper left by a Native American fighter on the bridge post at Medfield (p. 102). — EDS.

[25]The Greek phrase is usually rendered in English "Deus ex machina," the god who intervenes in classical Greek tragedy to shape the outcome. — EDS.

[26]Psalms 44:3. — EDS.

[27]Psalms 96:7. — RS/JF

[28]"Glory to God in the highest" (*Gloria in excelsis deo*). — RS/JF

READING CRITICALLY

1. Mather says that King Philip's War is a punishment sent by God to the colonists. Why does he feel they are being punished?

2. According to Mather, why was John "Sausaman" (Sassamon) killed?

3. Why does Mather insist that the Native Americans struck first?

4. What reasons does Mather give for the colonists' decision to attack the Narragansett town even though the Narragansetts had "not as yet appeared in open Hostility" (p. 56)?

5. Why does Mather say that the English "have no cause to glory" in their victory (p. 65)?

WRITING ANALYTICALLY

1. Why do you think Mather includes so many biblical references and Latin, Greek, and Hebrew quotations in his history? Write a paper in which you analyze the effect of the religious allusions and classical languages, using evidence from the text and your own reactions to support your position.

2. Mather says he writes to rebut alternative voices such as John Easton's (p. 93). Two episodes on which Mather and Easton disagree are the death of John Sassamon and the assault on the Narragansett town. Choose one of these events, and compare and contrast what the two men tell us about it. Clearly they have different agendas because they are trying to create different images of the Native Americans and the colonists. Which one — if either — do you find convincing? Write a paper in which you evaluate the persuasiveness of the two accounts, supporting your position with evidence from the texts.

3. Puritans writing about their wars with the Native Americans drew moral lessons from the stories they told. History, for them, was important mainly because it enabled people to see these moral lessons. Write a paper in which you describe both the moral lesson Mather draws from King Philip's War and the moral lesson drawn from the Pequot War by either Bradford (p. 19) or Underhill (p. 44). You may build up your description by comparing and contrasting the two texts, noting similarities and differences. If you wish, you may turn the paper into an argumentative essay, using your comparison of the two Puritan historians to illustrate your own position about whether historians ought to try to draw moral lessons from the stories they tell.

MARY ROWLANDSON

From *A Narrative of the Captivity and Restoration of Mrs. Mary Rowlandson* (1682)

Mary Rowlandson (c. 1635–c. 1678) was the daughter of a wealthy Puritan settler in Lancaster, Massachusetts, and the wife of the town's minister. In February 1675, during King Philip's War, while Rowlandson's husband was in Boston, Lancaster was attacked and Rowlandson and three of her children were carried away captive. One child soon died, and she was separated from the other two. Rowlandson remained captive for eleven weeks, but eventually she and the two surviving children were ransomed. Rowlandson wrote an account of her experiences, entitled *The Sovereignty and Goodness of God, Together with the Faithfulness of His Promises Displayed; Being a Narrative of the Captivity and Restoration of Mrs. Mary Rowlandson,* published in 1682 with a preface by Increase Mather. The exact date of Rowlandson's death is unknown, but scholars believe that her narrative was published posthumously.

Our excerpts describe the attack on Lancaster; Rowlandson's encounters with Metacomet (King Philip); episodes in her captivity leading up to the negotiations for her release; and the final four paragraphs of her narrative. Her "master" and protector, Quinapin, was the husband of Weetamoo, who became an important sachem and war leader upon the death of her first husband, Wamsutta. Rowlandson complains bitterly about her treatment among the Native Americans, and she suffered terrible personal losses as a result of the attack. But it is clear from her narrative that she was no worse fed or clothed than the Native Americans and worked no harder than any of them. As was typical of captives among Native Americans of the Northeast, Rowlandson was not sexually molested. Rowlandson's narrative immediately became tremendously popular, going through many editions from the seventeenth century to the present day and inaugurating what would become a very popular American genre, the captivity narrative.

ON THE TENTH OF FEBRUARY 1675 came the Indians with great numbers upon Lancaster. Their first coming was about sunrising. Hearing the noise of some guns, we looked out; several houses were burning and the smoke ascending to heaven. There were five persons taken in one house; the fa-

Mary Rowlandson, *The Sovereignty and Goodness of God, Together with the Faithfulness of His Promises Displayed; Being a Narrative of the Captivity and Restoration of Mrs. Mary Rowlandson* (1682), reprinted in *Puritans among the Indians: Accounts of Captivity and Redemption, 1676–1724,* ed. Alden Vaughan and Edward W. Clark (Cambridge: Harvard University Press, Belknap Press, 1981), 33–75.

In the notes, AV/EWC = Alden Vaughan and Edward W. Clark, EDS. = Patricia Bizzell and Bruce Herzberg.

ther and the mother and a sucking child they knocked on the head; the other two they took and carried away alive. There were two others, who being out of their garrison upon some occasion were set upon; one was knocked on the head, the other escaped. Another there was who running along was shot and wounded and fell down; he begged of them his life, promising them money (as they told me), but they would not hearken to him but knocked him in [the] head, stripped him naked, and split open his bowels. Another, seeing many of the Indians about his barn, ventured and went out but was quickly shot down. There were three others belonging to the same garrison who were killed; the Indians, getting up upon the roof of the barn, had advantage to shoot down upon them over their fortification. Thus these murderous wretches went on, burning and destroying before them.

At length they came and beset our own house,[1] and quickly it was the dolefullest day that ever mine eyes saw. The house stood upon the edge of a hill. Some of the Indians got behind the hill, others into the barn, and others behind anything that could shelter them; from all which places they shot against the house so that the bullets seemed to fly like hail; and quickly they wounded one man among us, then another, and then a third. About two hours (according to my observation in that amazing time) they had been about the house before they prevailed to fire it (which they did with flax and hemp which they brought out of the barn, and there being no defense about the house, only two flankers at two opposite corners and one of them not finished). They fired it once, and one ventured out and quenched it, but they quickly fired it again and that took.

Now is that dreadful hour come that I have often heard of (in time of war as it was the case of others), but now mine eyes see it. Some in our house were fighting for their lives, others wallowing in their blood, the house on fire over our heads, and the bloody heathen ready to knock us on the head if we stirred out. Now might we hear mothers and children crying out for themselves and one another, "Lord, what shall we do?" Then I took my children (and one of my sisters, hers) to go forth and leave the house, but as soon as we came to the door and appeared, the Indians shot so thick that the bullets rattled against the house as if one had taken an handful of stones and threw them so that we were fain to give back. We had six stout dogs belonging to our garrison, but none of them would stir although another time, if any Indian had come to the door, they were ready to fly upon him and tear him down. The Lord hereby would make us the more to acknowledge His hand and to see that our help is always in Him. But out we must go, the fire increasing and coming along behind us roaring, and the Indians gaping before us with their guns, spears, and hatchets to devour us. No sooner were we out of the house, but my

---

[1]The Rowlandson house contained thirty-seven persons, including Mrs. Rowlandson, her three children, her two sisters (Hannah White Divoll and Elizabeth White Kerley) with their families, and several neighboring families. — AV/EWC

brother-in-law [John Divoll] (being before wounded, in defending the house, in or near the throat) fell down dead; whereat the Indians scornfully shouted, hallooed, and were presently upon him, stripping off his clothes. The bullets flying thick, one went through my side, and the same (as would seem) through the bowels and hand of my dear child in my arms. One of my elder sister's children, named William [Kerley], had then his leg broken, which the Indians perceiving, they knocked him on the head. Thus were we butchered by those merciless heathen, standing amazed, with the blood running down to our heels.

My eldest sister [Elizabeth] being yet in the house and seeing those woeful sights, the infidels hailing mothers one way and children another and some wallowing in their blood, and her elder son telling her that her son William was dead and myself was wounded, she said, "And, Lord, let me die with them." Which was no sooner said, but she was struck with a bullet and fell down dead over the threshold. I hope she is reaping the fruit of her good labors, being faithful to the service of God in her place. In her younger years she lay under much trouble upon spiritual accounts till it pleased God to make that precious scripture take hold of her heart, 2 Cor. 12:9, "And he said unto me, my grace is sufficient for thee." More than twenty years after I have heard her tell how sweet and comfortable that place was to her. But to return: the Indians laid hold of us, pulling me one way and the children another, and said, "Come go along with us." I told them they would kill me. They answered, if I were willing to go along with them they would not hurt me.

Oh, the doleful sight that now was to behold at this house! "Come, behold the works of the Lord, what desolation He has made in the earth." Of thirty-seven persons who were in this one house none escaped either present death or a bitter captivity save only one, who might say as he, Job 1:15, "And I only am escaped alone to tell the news." There were twelve killed, some shot, some stabbed with their spears, some knocked down with their hatchets. When we are in prosperity, oh, the little that we think of such dreadful sights, and to see our dear friends and relations lie bleeding out their heart-blood upon the ground! There was one who was chopped into the head with a hatchet and stripped naked, and yet was crawling up and down. It is a solemn sight to see so many Christians lying in their blood, some here and some there, like a company of sheep torn by wolves, all of them stripped naked by a company of hell-hounds, roaring, singing, ranting and insulting, as if they would have torn our very hearts out. Yet the Lord by his almighty power preserved a number of us from death, for there were twenty-four of us taken alive and carried captive.

I had often before this said that if the Indians should come I should choose rather to be killed by them than taken alive, but when it came to the trial, my mind changed; their glittering weapons so daunted my spirit that I chose rather to go along with those (as I may say) ravenous beasts than that moment to end my days. And that I may the better declare what happened to me during that grievous captivity, I shall particularly speak of the several removes[2] we had up and down the wilderness. . . .

THE EIGHTH REMOVE

On the morrow morning we must go over the river, i.e., Connecticot, to meet with King Philip. Two canoesful they had carried over; the next turn I myself was to go, but as my foot was upon the canoe to step in, there was a sudden outcry among them, and I must step back. And instead of going over the river, I must go four or five miles up the river farther northward. Some of the Indians ran one way and some another. The cause of this rout was, as I thought, their espying some English scouts who were thereabout. In this travel up the river about noon the company made a stop and sat down, some to eat and others to rest them. As I sat amongst them musing of things past, my son Joseph unexpectedly came to me. We asked of each other's welfare, bemoaning our doleful condition and the change that had come upon us. We had husbands and father, and children, and sisters, and friends, and relations, and house, and home, and many comforts of this life, but now we may say as Job, "Naked came I out of my mother's womb, and naked shall I return. The Lord gave, and the Lord hath taken away, blessed be the name of the Lord." I asked him whether he would read; he told me he earnestly desired it, [so] I gave him my Bible, and he lighted upon that comfortable scripture, Psal. 118:17, 18, "I shall not die but live and declare the works of the Lord: the Lord hath chastened me sore, yet he hath not given me over to death." "Look here, Mother," says he, "did you read this?" And here I may take occasion to mention one principal ground of my setting forth these lines, even as the psalmist says to declare the works of the Lord and His wonderful power in carrying us along, preserving us in the wilderness while under the enemy's hand and returning of us in safety again and His goodness in bringing to my hand so many comfortable and suitable scriptures in my distress.

But to return, we traveled on till night, and in the morning we must go over the river to Philip's crew. When I was in the canoe, I could not but be amazed at the numerous crew of pagans that were on the bank on the other side. When I came ashore, they gathered all about me, I sitting alone in the midst. I observed they asked one another questions and laughed and rejoiced over their gains and victories. Then my heart began to fail and I fell a-weeping, which was the first time to my remembrance that I wept before them. Although I had met with so much affliction and my heart was many times ready to break, yet could I not shed one tear in their sight but rather had been all this while in a maze and like one astonished. But now I may say as Psal. 137:1, "By the rivers of Babylon there we sat

---

[2]A "remove" is a journey to a new camping place. Rowlandson divides her narrative by removes, describing twenty in all. — EDS.

down; yea, we wept when we remembered Zion." There one of them asked me why I wept; I could hardly tell what to say, yet I answered they would kill me. "No," said he, "none will hurt you." Then came one of them and gave me two spoonfuls of meal to comfort me, and another gave me half a pint of peas which was more worth than many bushels at another time. Then I went to see King Philip. He bade me come in and sit down and asked me whether I would smoke it (a usual compliment nowadays among saints and sinners), but this no way suited me. For though I had formerly used tobacco, yet I had left it ever since I was first taken. It seems to be a bait the devil lays to make men lose their precious time.[3] I remember with shame how formerly when I had taken two or three pipes I was presently ready for another, such a bewitching thing it is. But I thank God He has now given me power over it; surely there are many who may be better employed than to lie sucking a stinking tobacco pipe.

Now the Indians gather their forces to go against Northampton. Overnight one went about yelling and hooting to give notice of the design, whereupon they fell to boiling of groundnuts and parching of corn (as many as had it) for their provision, and in the morning away they went. During my abode in this place Philip spoke to me to make a shirt for his boy, which I did, for which he gave me a shilling.[4] I offered the money to my master, but he bade me keep it, and with it I bought a piece of horse-flesh. Afterwards he asked me to make a cap for his boy, for which he invited me to dinner. I went, and he gave me a pancake about as big as two fingers; it was made of parched wheat, beaten and fried in bear's grease, but I thought I never tasted pleasanter meat in my life. There was a squaw who spoke to me to make a shirt for her *sannup* [husband], for which she gave me a piece of bear. Another asked me to knit a pair of stockings, for which she gave me a quart of peas. I boiled my peas and bear together and invited my master and mistress to dinner, but the proud gossip [i.e., companion], because I served them both in one dish, would eat nothing except one bit that he gave her upon the point of his knife.

Hearing that my son was come to this place, I went to see him and found him lying flat upon the ground. I asked him how he could sleep so. He answered me that he was not asleep but at prayer and lay so that they might not observe what he was doing. I pray God he may remember these things now he is returned in safety. At this place (the sun now getting higher) what with the beams and heat of the sun and the smoke of the wigwams, I thought I should have been blind. I could scarce discern one wig-

[3]In the seventeenth century, as in the second half of the twentieth, the medical and moral reasons for smoking tobacco were hotly debated. Most Puritans frowned on the habit, partly because it wasted time, partly because it presented a serious fire hazard in an age of wooden buildings and thick forests. — AV/EWC

[4]The Indians had no woven cloth before the arrival of European traders and settlers, from whom they rapidly began to acquire it in considerable quantities. It took time, however, for the Indians to learn sewing skills, and they consequently took advantage of the talents of their captives. Cloth clothes supplemented, rather than replaced, the Indians' traditional animal-skin garments. — AV/EWC

wam from another. There was here one Mary Thurston of Medfield who, seeing how it was with me, lent me a hat to wear, but as soon as I was gone, the squaw who owned that Mary Thurston came running after me and got it away again. Here was the squaw that gave one spoonful of meal. I put it in my pocket to keep it safe, yet notwithstanding somebody stole it but put five Indian corns in the room of it, which corns were the greatest provision I had in my travel for one day.

The Indians, returning from Northampton, brought with them some horses, and sheep, and other things which they had taken. I desired them that they would carry me to Albany upon one of those horses and sell me for powder, for so they had sometimes discoursed. I was utterly hopeless of getting home on foot the way that I came. I could hardly bear to think of the many weary steps I had taken to come to this place. . . .

THE THIRTEENTH REMOVE

Instead of going toward the Bay, which was that I desired, I must go with them five or six miles down the river into a mighty thicket of brush where we abode almost a fortnight. Here one asked me to make a shirt for her papoose, for which she gave me a mess of broth which was thickened with meal made of the bark of a tree, and to make it the better she had put into it about a handful of peas and a few roasted groundnuts. I had not seen my son a pretty while, and here was an Indian of whom I made inquiry after him and asked him when he saw him. He answered me that such a time his master roasted him and that himself did eat a piece of him as big as his two fingers and that he was very good meat. But the Lord upheld my spirit under this discouragement, and I considered their horrible addictedness to lying and that there is not one of them that makes the least conscience of speaking of truth. In this place on a cold night as I lay by the fire, I removed a stick that kept the heat from me; a squaw moved it down again at which I looked up, and she threw a handful of ashes in mine eyes. I thought I should have been quite blinded and have never seen more, but lying down, the water run out of my eyes and carried the dirt with it that by the morning I recovered my sight again. Yet upon this and the like occasions I hope it is not too much to say with Job, "Have pity upon me, have pity upon me, oh, ye my friends, for the hand of the Lord has touched me."

And here I cannot but remember how many times sitting in their wigwams and musing on things past I should suddenly leap up and run out as if I had been at home, forgetting where I was and what my condition was. But when I was without and saw nothing but wilderness and woods and a company of barbarous heathens, my mind quickly returned to me, which made me think of that spoken concerning Sampson, who said, "I will go out and shake myself as at other times, but he wished not that the Lord was departed from him."

About this time I began to think that all my hopes of restoration would come to nothing. I thought of the English army and hoped for their coming and being taken by them, but that failed. I hoped to be carried to Albany as the Indians had discoursed before, but that failed also. I thought of being sold to my husband, as my master spake, but instead of that my master himself was gone and I left behind so that my spirit was now quite ready to sink. I asked them to let me go out and pick up some sticks that I might get alone and pour out my heart unto the Lord. Then also I took my Bible to read, but I found no comfort here neither, which many times I was wont to find. So easy a thing it is with God to dry up the streams of scripture-comfort from us. Yet I can say that in all my sorrows and afflictions God did not leave me to have my impatience work towards Himself, as if His ways were unrighteous. But I knew that He laid upon me less than I deserved. Afterward, before this doleful time ended with me, I was turning the leaves of my Bible and the Lord brought to me some scriptures, which did a little revive me, as that Isai. 55:8, "'For my thoughts are not your thoughts, neither are your ways my ways,' saith the Lord." And also that Psal. 37:5, "Commit thy way unto the Lord, trust also in Him, and He shall bring it to pass."

About this time they came yelping from Hadley where they had killed three Englishmen and brought one captive with them, *viz.* Thomas Read. They all gathered about the poor man, asking him many questions. I desired also to go and see him, and when I came he was crying bitterly, supposing they would quickly kill him. Whereupon I asked one of them whether they intended to kill him; he answered me they would not. He being a little cheered with that, I asked him about the welfare of my husband; he told me he saw him such a time in the Bay, and he was well but very melancholy. By which I certainly understood (though I suspected it before) that whatsoever the Indians told me respecting him was vanity and lies. Some of them told me he was dead, and they had killed him. Some said he was married again, and that the governor wished him to marry and told him he should have his choice, and that all persuaded [him] I was dead. So like were these barbarous creatures to him who was a liar from the beginning.

As I was sitting once in the wigwam here, Philip's maid came in with the child in her arms and asked me to give her a piece of my apron to make a flap for it. I told her I would not. Then my mistress bade me give it, but still I said no. The maid told me if I would not give her a piece she would tear a piece off it. I told her I would tear her coat then; with that my mistress rises up and takes up a stick big enough to have killed me and struck at me with it, but I stepped out, and she struck the stick into the mat of the wigwam. But while she was pulling of it out, I ran to the maid and gave her all my apron, and so that storm went over.

Hearing that my son was come to this place, I went to see him and told him his father was well but very melancholy. He told me he was as much grieved for his father as for himself; I wondered at his speech, for I thought I had enough upon my spirit in reference to myself to make me mindless of my husband and everyone else, they being safe among their friends. He told me also that a while before his master, together with other Indians, were going to the French for powder, but by the way the Mohawks met with them and killed four of their company which made the rest turn back again, for which I desire that myself and he may bless the Lord. For it might have been worse with him had he been sold to the French than it proved to be in remaining with the Indians.[5]

I went to see an English youth in this place, one John Gilberd of Springfield. I found him lying without doors upon the ground; I asked him how he did. He told me he was very sick of a flux with eating so much blood. They had turned him out of the wigwam and with him an Indian papoose almost dead (whose parents had been killed) in a bitter cold day without fire or clothes. The young man himself had nothing on but his shirt and waistcoat. This sight was enough to melt a heart of flint. There they lay quivering in the cold, the youth [curled] round like a dog, the papoose stretched out with his eyes, nose, and mouth full of dirt and yet alive and groaning. I advised John to go and get to some fire; he told me he could not stand, but I persuaded him still, lest he should lie there and die. And with much ado I got him to a fire and went myself home. As soon as I was got home, his master's daughter came after me to know what I had done with the Englishman; I told her I had got him to a fire in such a place. Now had I need to pray Paul's prayer, 2 Thess. 3:2, "That we may be delivered from unreasonable and wicked men." For her satisfaction I went along with her and brought her to him, but before I got home again, it was noised about that I was running away and getting the English youth along with me, that as soon as I came in they began to rant and domineer, asking me where I had been, and what I had been doing, and saying they would knock him on the head. I told them I had been seeing the English youth and that I would not run away. They told me I lied, and taking up a hatchet, they came to me and said they would knock me down if I stirred out again and so confined me to the wigwam. Now may I say with David, 2 Sam. 24:14, "I am in a great strait." If I keep in, I must die with hunger, and if I go out, I must be knocked in [the] head. This distressed condition held that day and half the next. And then the Lord remembered me, whose mercies are great.

Then came an Indian to me with a pair of stockings that were too big for him, and he would have me ravel them out and knit them fit for him. I showed myself willing and bid him ask my mistress if I might go along with him a little way; she said yes, I might, but I was not a little refreshed with that news that I had my liberty again. Then I went along with him, and he gave me some roasted groundnuts which did again revive my feeble stomach.

---

[5]Rowlandson feels that her son would be "worse" among the French because she knows that English captives redeemed by the French were often persuaded or compelled to convert to Roman Catholicism, which she abhors. — EDS.

Being got out of her sight, I had time and liberty again to look into my Bible, which was my guide by day and my pillow by night. Now that comfortable scripture presented itself to me, Isa. 54:7, "For a small moment have I forsaken thee, but with great mercies will I gather thee." Thus the Lord carried me along from one time to another and made good to me this precious promise and many others. Then my son came to see me, and I asked his master to let him stay awhile with me that I might comb his head and look over him, for he was almost overcome with lice. He told me when I had done that he was very hungry, but I had nothing to relieve him but bid him go into the wigwams as he went along and see if he could get anything among them, which he did. And it seems [he] tarried a little too long, for his master was angry with him and beat him, and then sold him. Then he came running to tell me he had a new master, and that he had given him some groundnuts already. Then I went along with him to his new master who told me he loved him and he should not want. So his master carried him away, and I never saw him afterward till I saw him at Pascataqua in Portsmouth.

That night they bade me go out of the wigwam again. My mistress's papoose was sick, and it died that night, and there was one benefit in it that there was more room. I went to a wigwam and they bade me come in and gave me a skin to lie upon, and a mess of venison and groundnuts, which was a choice dish among them. On the morrow they buried the papoose and afterward, both morning and evening, there came a company to mourn and howl with her though I confess I could not much condole with them. Many sorrowful days I had in this place, often getting alone "like a crane, or a swallow, so did I chatter; I did mourn as a dove, mine eyes fail with looking upward. Oh, Lord, I am oppressed; undertake for me," Isa. 38:14. I could tell the Lord as Hezekiah, ver. 3, "Remember now, O Lord, I beseech Thee, how I have walked before Thee in truth."

Now had I time to examine all my ways. My conscience did not accuse me of unrighteousness toward one or other, yet I saw how in my walk with God I had been a careless creature. As David said, "Against Thee, Thee only, have I sinned," and I might say with the poor publican, "God be merciful unto me a sinner." On the Sabbath days I could look upon the sun and think how people were going to the house of God to have their souls refreshed and then home and their bodies also, but I was destitute of both and might say as the poor prodigal, "He would fain have filled his belly with the husks that the swine did eat, and no man gave unto him," Luke 15:16. For I must say with him, "Father I have sinned against heaven and in thy sight," ver. 21. I remembered how on the night before and after the Sabbath when my family was about me and relations and neighbors with us, we could pray and sing, and then refresh our bodies with the good creatures of God, and then have a comfortable bed to lie down on. But instead of all this I had only a little swill for the body and then like a swine must lie down on the ground. I cannot express to man the sorrow that lay upon my spirit; the Lord knows it. Yet that comfortable scripture would often come to my mind, "For a small moment have I forsaken thee, but with great mercies will I gather thee." . . .

THE NINETEENTH REMOVE

They said when we went out that we must travel to Wachuset this day. But a bitter weary day I had of it, traveling now three days together without resting any day between. At last, after many weary steps, I saw Wachuset Hills but many miles off. Then we came to a great swamp through which we traveled up to the knees in mud and water, which was heavy going to one tired before. Being almost spent, I thought I should have sunk down at last and never got out, but I may say, as in Psal. 94:18, "When my foot slipped, Thy mercy, O Lord, held me up." Going along, having indeed my life but little spirit, Philip, who was in the company, came up and took me by the hand and said, "Two weeks more and you shall be mistress again." I asked him if he spake true. He answered, "Yes, and quickly you shall come to your master again who has been gone from us three weeks." After many weary steps we came to Wachuset where he was, and glad I was to see him. He asked me when I washed me. I told him not this month. Then he fetched me some water himself and bid me wash and gave me the glass to see how I looked and bid his squaw give me something to eat. So she gave me a mess of beans and meat and a little groundnut cake. I was wonderfully revived with this favor showed me, Psal. 106:46, "He made them also to be pitied, of all those that carried them captives."

My master had three squaws, living sometimes with one and sometimes with another one. This old squaw at whose wigwam [now] I was, my master had been [with] those three weeks. Another was Wettimore [Weetamoo], with whom I had lived and served all this while. A severe and proud dame she was, bestowing every day in dressing herself neat as much time as any of the gentry of the land, powdering her hair and painting her face, going with necklaces, with jewels in her ears, and bracelets upon her hands. When she had dressed herself, her work was to make girdles of wampum and beads. The third squaw was a younger one by whom he had two papooses. By that time I was refreshed by the old squaw with whom my master was. Wettimore's maid came to call me home, at which I fell a-weeping. Then the old squaw told me, to encourage me, that if I wanted victuals I should come to her, and that I should lie there in her wigwam. Then I went with the maid and quickly came again and lodged there. The squaw laid a mat under me and a good rug over me; the first time I had any such kindness showed me. I understood that Wettimore thought that if she should let me go and serve with the old squaw, she would be in danger to lose not only my service but the redemption pay also. And I was not a little glad to hear this, being by it raised in my hopes that in God's due time there would be an end of this sorrowful hour. Then came an Indian and asked me to knit him three pair of stockings, for which I had a hat and a silk handkerchief. Then another asked me to make her a shift, for which she gave me an apron.

Then came Tom and Peter[6] with the second letter from the council about the captives. Though they were Indians, I got them by the hand and burst out into tears; my heart was so full that I could not speak to them, but recovering myself, I asked them how my husband did and all my friends and acquaintances. They said they [were] all very well but melancholy. They brought me two biscuits and a pound of tobacco. The tobacco I quickly gave away; when it was all gone, one asked me to give him a pipe of tobacco. I told him it was all gone. Then began he to rant and threaten. I told him when my husband came I would give some. "Hang [the] rogue," says he, "I will knock out his brains if he comes here." And then again in the same breath they would say that if there should come a hundred without guns they would do them no hurt, so unstable and like madmen they were, so that fearing the worst, I durst not send to my husband though there were some thoughts of his coming to redeem and fetch me, not knowing what might follow. For there was little more trust to them than to the master they served.

When the letter was come, the sagamores met to consult about the captives and called me to them to inquire how much my husband would give to redeem me. When I came, I sat down among them as I was wont to do as their manner is. Then they bade me stand up and said they were the General Court. They bid me speak what I thought he would give. Now knowing that all we had was destroyed by the Indians, I was in a great strait. I thought if I should speak of but a little, it would be slighted and hinder the matter; if of a great sum, I knew not where it would be procured. Yet at a venture, I said twenty pounds yet desired them to take less, but they would not hear of that but sent that message to Boston that for twenty pounds I should be redeemed. It was a praying Indian that wrote their letter for them. There was another praying Indian who told me that he had a brother that would not eat horse; his conscience was so tender and scrupulous (though as large as hell for the destruction of poor Christians). Then he said he read that scripture to him, 2 Kings, 6:25, "There was a famine in Samaria, and behold they besieged it, until an ass's head was sold for fourscore pieces of silver, and the fourth part of a kab of doves' dung for five pieces of silver." He expounded this place to his brother and showed him that it was lawful to eat that in a famine which is not at another time. And now, says he, he will eat horse with any Indian of them all.

[6]Christian Indians Tom Dublet (Nepanet) and Peter Conway (Tatatiquinea) from the praying town of Nashobah. — AV/EWC. In the sixteenth remove, Rowlandson explains that a letter came from the Massachusetts Bay colony governing council to the Native American leaders at Wachuset opening negotiations on the redemption of captives. This letter announced that a second letter would arrive within two weeks, and Rowlandson is brought to Wachuset to be handy if her master, Quinapin, decides that the terms of this second letter are attractive enough to allow her friends to ransom her. — EDS.

There was another praying Indian who, when he had done all the mischief that he could, betrayed his own father into the English hands thereby to purchase his own life. Another praying Indian was at Sudbury fight, though, as he deserved, he was afterward hanged for it. There was another praying Indian so wicked and cruel as to wear a string about his neck strung with Christians' fingers. Another praying Indian, when they went to Sudbury fight, went with them and his squaw also with him with her papoose at her back.

Before they went to that fight, they got a company together to powwow; the manner was as followeth. There was one that kneeled upon a deerskin with the company round him in a ring, who kneeled, and striking upon the ground with their hands and with sticks, and muttering or humming with their mouths; besides him who kneeled in the ring, there also stood one with a gun in his hand. Then he on the deerskin made a speech, and all manifested assent to it, and so they did many times together. Then they bade him with the gun go out of the ring, which he did, but when he was out, they called him in again. But he seemed to make a stand; then they called the more earnestly till he returned again. Then they all sang. Then they gave him two guns, in either hand one. And so he on the deerskin began again, and at the end of every sentence in his speaking, they all assented, humming or muttering with their mouths and striking upon the ground with their hands. Then they bade him with the two guns go out of the ring again, which he did a little way. Then they called him in again, but he made a stand; so they called him with greater earnestness, but he stood reeling and wavering as if he knew not whether he should stand or fall or which way to go. Then they called him with exceeding great vehemency, all of them, one and another. After a little while he turned in, staggering as he went, with his arms stretched out, in either hand a gun. As soon as he came in, they all sang and rejoiced exceedingly awhile. And then he upon the deerskin made another speech unto which they all assented in a rejoicing manner, and so they ended their business and forthwith went to Sudbury fight.

To my thinking they went without any scruple but that they should prosper and gain the victory. And they went out not so rejoicing, but they came home with as great a victory, for they said they had killed two captains and almost an hundred men. One Englishman they brought along with them; and he said it was too true for they had made sad work at Sudbury, as indeed it proved. Yet they came home without that rejoicing and triumphing over their victory which they were wont to show at other times but rather like dogs (as they say) which have lost their ears. Yet I could not perceive that it was for their own loss of men. They said they had not lost but above five or six, and I missed none except in one wigwam. When they went, they acted as if the devil had told them that they should gain the victory, and now they acted as if the devil had told them they should have a fall. Whither it were so or no, I cannot tell, but so it proved for quickly they began to fall and so held on that summer till they came to utter ruin.

They came home on a Sabbath day, and the powwow that kneeled upon the deerskin came home (I may say without abuse) as black as the devil. When my master came home, he came to me and bid me make a shirt for his papoose of a Holland lace pillowbeer.7 About that time there came an Indian to me and bid me come to his wigwam at night, and he would give me some pork and groundnuts, which I did. And as I was eating, another Indian said to me, "He seems to be your good friend, but he killed two Englishmen at Subury, and there lie their clothes behind you." I looked behind me, and there I saw bloody clothes with bullet holes in them, yet the Lord suffered not this wretch to do me any hurt. Yea, instead of that, he many times refreshed me; five or six times did he and his squaw refresh my feeble carcass. If I went to their wigwam at any time, they would always give me something, and yet they were strangers that I never saw before. Another squaw gave me a piece of fresh pork and a little salt with it and lent me her pan to fry it in, and I cannot but remember what a sweet, pleasant and delightful relish that bit had to me to this day. So little do we prize common mercies when we have them to the full.

THE TWENTIETH REMOVE

It was their usual manner to remove when they had done any mischief, lest they should be found out, and so they did at this time. We went about three or four miles, and there they built a great wigwam big enough to hold a hundred Indians, which they did in preparation to a great day of dancing. They would say now amongst themselves that the governor would be so angry for his loss at Sudbury that he would send no more about the captives, which made me grieve and tremble. My sister [Hannah] being not far from the place where we now were, and hearing that I was here, desired her master to let her come and see me, and he was willing to it and would go with her. But she, being ready before him, told him she would go before and was come within a mile or two of the place. Then he overtook her and began to rant as if he had been mad and made her go back again in the rain so that I never saw her till I saw her in Charlestown. But the Lord requited many of their ill doings, for this Indian, her master, was hanged afterward at Boston.

The Indians now began to come from all quarters, against their merry dancing day. Among some of them came one Goodwife Kettle. I told her my heart was so heavy that it was ready to break. "So is mine, too," said she. But yet [she] said, "I hope we shall hear some good news shortly." I could hear how earnestly my sister desired to see me, and I as earnestly desired to see her and yet neither of us could get an opportunity. My daughter was also now about a mile off, and I had not seen her in nine or ten weeks as I had not seen my sister since our first taking. I earnestly desired them to let me go and see them; yea, I entreated, begged, and persuaded them but to

7That is, pillowcases made of Dutch lace. — AV/EWC

let me see my daughter, and yet so hardhearted were they that they would not suffer it. They made use of their tyrannical power whilst they had it, but through the Lord's wonderful mercy their time was now but short.

On a Sabbath day, the sun being about an hour high in the afternoon, came Mr. John Hoar (the council permitting him and his own forward spirit inclining him) together with the two forementioned Indians, Tom and Peter, with their third letter from the council. When they came near, I was abroad; though I saw them not, they presently called me in and bade me sit down and not stir. Then they catched up their guns and away they ran as if an enemy had been at hand, and the guns went off apace. I manifested some great trouble, and they asked me what was the matter. I told them I thought they had killed the Englishman (for they had in the meantime informed me that an Englishman was come). They said, "No." They shot over his horse and under, and before his horse, and they pushed him this way and that way at their pleasure, showing what they could do. Then they let them come to their wigwams. I begged of them to let me see the Englishman, but they would not; but there was I fain to sit their pleasure. When they had talked their fill with him, they suffered me to go to him. We asked each other of our welfare, and how my husband did and all my friends. He told me they were all well and would be glad to see me. Amongst other things which my husband sent me, there came a pound of tobacco which I sold for nine shillings in money, for many of the Indians for want of tobacco smoked hemlock and ground ivy. It was a great mistake in any who thought I sent for tobacco, for through the favor of God that desire was overcome.

I now asked them whether I should go home with Mr. Hoar. They answered, "No," one and another of them. And it being night, we lay down with that answer. In the morning Mr. Hoar invited the sagamores to dinner, but when we went to get it ready, we found that they had stolen the greatest part of the provision Mr. Hoar had brought out of his bags in the night. And we may see the wonderful power of God in that one passage in that when there was such a great number of the Indians together and so greedy of a little good food and no English there but Mr. Hoar and myself that there they did not knock us in the head and take what he had, there being not only some provision but also trading cloth, a part of the twenty pounds agreed upon. But instead of doing us any mischief, they seemed to be ashamed of the fact and said it were some *matchit* [bad] Indian that did it. Oh, that we could believe that there is nothing too hard for God! God showed His power over the heathen in this as He did over the hungry lions when Daniel was cast into the den. Mr. Hoar called them betime to dinner, but they ate very little, they being so busy in dressing themselves and getting ready for their dance, which was carried on by eight of them — four men and four squaws, my master and mistress being two. He was dressed in his Holland shirt with great laces sewed at the tail of it; he had his silver buttons, his white stockings, his garters were hung round with shillings, and he had girdles of wampum upon his head and shoulders. She had a kersey coat and [was] covered with girdles of wampum from the loins upward; her arms from her elbows to her hands were covered with bracelets; there were handfuls of necklaces about her neck and several sorts of jewels in her ears. She had fine red stockings and white shoes, her hair powdered and face painted red that was always before black. And all the dancers were after the same manner. There were two other singing and knocking on a kettle for their music. They kept hopping up and down one after another with a kettle of water in the midst, standing warm upon some embers, to drink of when they were dry. They held on till it was almost night, throwing out wampum to the standersby.

At night I asked them again if I should go home. They all as one said no except my husband would come for me. When we were lain down, my master went out of the wigwam, and by and by sent in an Indian called James the Printer who told Mr. Hoar that my master would let me go home tomorrow if he would let him have one pint of liquors. Then Mr. Hoar called his own Indians, Tom and Peter, and bid them go and see whether he would promise it before them three, and if he would, he should have it, which he did, and he had it. Then Philip, smelling the business, called me to him and asked me what I would give him to tell me some good news and speak a good word for me. I told him I could not tell what to give him. I would anything I had and asked him what he would have. He said two coats and twenty shillings in money and half a bushel of seed corn and some tobacco. I thanked him for his love, but I knew the good news as well as the crafty fox.[8]

My master, after he had had his drink, quickly came ranting into the wigwam again and called for Mr. Hoar, drinking to him and saying he was a good man. And then again he would say, "Hang [the] rogue." Being almost drunk, he would drink to him, and yet presently say he should be hanged. Then he called for me. I trembled to hear him, yet I was fain to go to him, and he drank to me, showing no incivility. He was the first Indian I saw drunk all the while that I was amongst them. At last his squaw ran out, and he after her round the wigwam with his money jingling at his knees, but she escaped him. But having an old squaw, he ran to her, and so through the Lord's mercy, we were no more troubled that night.

Yet I had not a comfortable night's rest, for I think I can say I did not sleep for three nights together. The night before the letter came from the council I could not rest, I was so full of fears and troubles, God many times leaving us most in the dark when deliverance is nearest. Yea, at this time I could not rest night nor day. The next night I was overjoyed, Mr. Hoar being come and that with such good tidings. The third night I was even swallowed up with the thoughts of things, *viz.* that ever I should go home again and that I must go, leaving my children behind me in the wilderness so that sleep was now almost departed from mine eyes.

On Tuesday morning they called their General Court (as they call it) to

---

[8]Rowlandson declines to pay Philip for his assistance because she believes her master will allow her to be redeemed no matter what Philip says. She's right. She goes home with Mr. Hoar, Tom, and Peter. — EDS.

consult and determine whether I should go home or no. And they all as one man did seemingly consent to it that I should go home except Philip who would not come among them. . . .

I can remember the time when I used to sleep quietly without workings in my thoughts whole nights together, but now it is other ways with me. When all are fast about me and no eye open but His who ever waketh, my thoughts are upon things past, upon the awful dispensation of the Lord towards us, upon His wonderful power and might in carrying of us through so many difficulties in returning us in safety and suffering none to hurt us. I remember in the night season how the other day I was in the midst of thousands of enemies and nothing but death before me. It [was] then hard work to persuade myself that ever I should be satisfied with bread again. But now we are fed with the finest of the wheat, and, as I may say, with honey out of the rock. Instead of the husk, we have the fatted calf. The thoughts of these things in the particulars of them, and of the love and goodness of God towards us, make it true of me what David said of himself, Psal. 6:5 [actually 6:6]. "I watered my couch with my tears." Oh, the wonderful power of God that mine eyes have seen, affording matter enough for my thoughts to run in that when others are sleeping mine eyes are weeping!

I have seen the extreme vanity of this world. One hour I have been in health and wealth, wanting nothing, but the next hour in sickness and wounds and death, having nothing but sorrow and affliction. Before I knew what affliction meant, I was ready sometimes to wish for it. When I lived in prosperity, having the comforts of the world about me, my relations by me, my heart cheerful, and taking little care for anything, and yet seeing many whom I preferred before myself under many trials and afflictions, in sickness, weakness, poverty, losses, crosses, and cares of the world, I should be sometimes jealous lest I should have my portion in this life, and that scripture would come to mind, Heb. 12:6, "For whom the Lord loveth he chasteneth and scourgeth every son whom He receiveth." But now I see the Lord had His time to scourge and chasten me. The portion of some is to have their afflictions by drops, now one drop and then another, but the dregs of the cup, the wine of astonishment, like a sweeping rain that leaveth no food, did the Lord prepare to be my portion. Affliction I wanted and affliction I had, full measure (I thought) pressed down and running over. Yet I see when God calls a person to anything and through never so many difficulties, yet He is fully able to carry them through and make them see and say they have been gainers thereby. And I hope I can say in some measure, as David did, "It is good for me that I have been afflicted."

The Lord hath showed me the vanity of these outward things. That they are the vanity of vanities and vexation of spirit, that they are but a shadow, a blast, a bubble, and things of no continuance. That we must rely on God himself and our whole dependence must be upon Him. If trouble from smaller matters begin to arise in me, I have something at hand to check myself with and say, why am I troubled? It was but the other day that if I had had the world I would have given it for my freedom or to have been a servant to a Christian. I have learned to look beyond present and smaller troubles and to be quieted under them, as Moses said, Exod. 14:13, "Stand still and see the salvation of the Lord."

READING CRITICALLY

1. During the Eighth Remove, Rowlandson meets Metacomet (Philip). What does she notice about him? What does she seem to think of him? What impression of him do you get from her description?

2. How does Rowlandson fit into Native American society? What kinds of work does she do? How much freedom of movement does she seem to have? What bad treatment does she suffer, and what kindnesses? Collect evidence from the reading to build a composite answer.

3. On page 76, Rowlandson describes Weetamoo, the Native American woman whom she served while in captivity. Looking at this description and at other references to her "mistress" throughout the narrative, describe Rowlandson's attitude toward her female captor.

4. Rowlandson seems very negative about "Praying Indians" (Native Americans who have converted to Christianity). What are her main problems with them?

5. In concluding her narrative, Rowlandson says that she has trouble sleeping, now that she has returned to her family after her captivity. What does she think about while she is lying awake? What lesson does she draw from her experience?

WRITING ANALYTICALLY

1. Rowlandson clearly intends to present a particular image of the Native Americans in this narrative. What is that image, and how does she go about creating it? Collect evidence from the text and use it to support your own argument about whether Rowlandson is successful in creating this image or whether you find yourself resisting her portrayal of the Native Americans.

2. Puritan women were generally expected to attend to household duties and not appear in the public sphere. It was daring, then, for Rowlandson to call attention to herself by writing a narrative about her captivity, especially with such intimate details about her experiences. What does Rowlandson do to "excuse" this boldness and to make her narrative acceptable to Puritan readers? Collect evidence from the text and use it to support your own argument about whether Rowlandson succeeds in presenting herself as humble and submissive to God's actions and whether at the same time she manages to enlarge the acceptable sphere of activity for women.

3. Although Rowlandson and Increase Mather (p. 50) have written very different kinds of texts about King Philip's War — a captivity narrative and a history — they are very similar in their outlook on life, both being upper-class members of

the late-seventeenth-century American Puritan community. Write a paper in which you compare and contrast both the ways in which they infuse moral meaning into their stories and the kinds of moral lessons they draw. Option: You may turn this paper into an argumentative essay on the trustworthiness of Rowlandson and Mather as reporters on King Philip's War. To support your argument use your analysis of both their lessons and their techniques for enforcing these lessons.

LION GARDENER

From *"Relation of the Pequot Wars"* (c. 1660)

Lion Gardener was an English mercenary hired in the Netherlands to help
the Puritan colonists. He chose the site at Saybrook, Connecticut, for a fort
(actually a palisaded settlement defended with guns), directed its construction, and commanded this outpost during the Pequot War in 1637. Gardener was not a Puritan and was highly critical of the way the Puritans handled their relations with the Native Americans. It is clear from his narrative
that he thought the English did much to provoke the Pequot violence that
was the immediate cause of the war. He suspected the Puritan leaders of fostering their own interests at the expense of people like himself who were trying to work out practical and peaceful ways of living in the new country. He
clearly felt that some Native Americans could be made into firm allies, and
he berated the Puritan leaders for ignoring both their and his advice. Gardener's narrative was written around 1660 at the request of John Mason
(one of the two commanders of the 1637 Puritan attack on the Pequot town
at Mystic) and other colonists. Its complete title was "Leift. [Lieutenant]
Lion Gardener His Relation of the Pequot Warres."

We have excerpted the beginning of the narrative, which shows Gardener's doubts about the Puritan leadership and his own practical priorities;
Gardener's account of the assault on the Pequot town, during which he remained behind at Fort Saybrook; and the conclusion of his narrative, in
which he calls for proper recognition of the English and Native American
fighters who protected the colonists during this war.

IN THE YEAR 1635, I, Lion Gardener, Engineer and Master of works of Fortification in the legers of the Prince of Orange, in the Low Countries,
through the persuasion of Mr. John Davenport, Mr. Hugh Peters with
some other well-affected Englishmen of Rotterdam, I made an agreement
with the forenamed Mr. Peters for £100 per annum, for four years, to
serve the company of patentees, namely, the Lord Say, the Lord Brooks,
Sir Arthur Hazilrig, Sir Mathew Bonnington, Sir Richard Saltingstone, Esquire Fenwick, and the rest of their company, I was to serve them only in

Lion Gardener, "Leift. Lion Gardener His Relation of the Pequot Warres" (c. 1660),
reprinted in *History of the Pequot War*, edited with notes by Charles Orr (1897; reprint, New
York: AMS, 1980), 122–48.
    In the notes, EDS. = Patricia Bizzell and Bruce Herzberg.

the drawing, ordering and making of a city, towns or forts of defence.[1] And so I came from Holland to London, and from thence to New-England, where I was appointed to attend such orders as Mr. John Winthrop, Esquire, the present Governor of Conectecott, was to appoint, whether at Pequit [Pequot] river, or Conectecott, and that we should choose a place both for the convenience of a good harbour, and also for capableness and fitness for fortification. But I landing at Boston the latter end of November, the aforesaid Mr. Winthrop had sent before one Lieut. Gibbons, Sergeant Willard, with some carpenters, to take possession of the River's mouth, where they began to build houses against the Spring; we expecting, according to promise, that there would have come from England to us three hundred able men, whereof two hundred should attend fortification, fifty to till the ground, and fifty to build houses. But our great expectation at the River's mouth, came only to two men, viz. Mr. Fenwick, and his man, who came with Mr. Hugh Peters, and Mr. Oldham and Thomas Stanton, bringing with them some Otter-skin coats, and Beaver, and skeins of wampum, which the Pequits had sent for a present, because the English had required those Pequits that had killed a Virginean, one Capt. Stone, with his Bark's crew, in Conectecott River, for they said they would have their lives and not their presents; then I answered, Seeing you will take Mr. Winthrop to the Bay to see his wife, newly brought to bed of her first child, and though you say he shall return, yet I know if you make war with these Pequits, he will not come hither again, for I know you will keep yourselves safe, as you think, in the Bay, but myself, with these few, you will leave at the stake to be roasted, or for hunger to be starved, for Indian corn is now 12s. per bushel, and we have but three acres planted, and if they will now make war for a Virginian and expose us to the Indians, whose mercies are cruelties, they, I say, they love the Virginians better than us: for, have they stayed these four or five years, and will they begin now, we being so few in the River, and have scarce holes to put our heads in? I pray ask the Magistrates in the Bay if they have forgot what I said to them when I returned from Salem? For Mr. Winthrop, Mr. Haines, Mr. Dudley, Mr. Ludlow, Mr. Humfry, Mr. Belingam, Mr. Coddington, and Mr. Nowell; — these entreated me to go with Mr. Humfry and Mr. Peters to view the country, to see how fit it was for fortification. And I told them that Nature had done more than half the work already, and I thought no foreign potent enemy would do them any hurt, but one that was near. They asked me who that was, and I said it was Capt. Hunger that threatened them most, for, (said I,) War is like a three-footed Stool, want one foot and down comes all; and these three feet are men, victuals, and munition, therefore, seeing in peace you are like to be famished, what will or can be done if war? Therefore I think, said I, it will be best only to fight against Capt. Hunger, and let fortification alone awhile; and if need hereafter require it,

---

[1]Gardener describes himself as a professional soldier, what we would call a mercenary. He is hired in Holland (the "Low Countries") by the wealthy English investors ("Lord Say" and the others) who hold the patent, or license, to settle and develop Connecticut. — Eds.

I can come to do you any service: and they all liked my saying well. Entreat them to rest awhile, till we get more strength here about us, and that we hear where the seat of the war will be, may approve of it, and provide for it, for I had but twenty-four in all, men, women, and boys and girls, and not food for them for two months, unless we saved our corn-field, which could not possibly be if they came to war, for it is two miles from our home. Mr. Winthrop, Mr. Fenwick, and Mr. Peters promised me that they would do their utmost endeavour to persuade the Bay-men to desist from war a year or two, till we could be better provided for it; and then the Pequit Sachem was sent for, and the present returned, but full sore against my will. So they three returned to Boston, and two or three days after came an Indian from Pequit, whose name was Cocommithus, who had lived at Plimoth, and could speak good English; he desired that Mr. Steven Winthrop would go to Pequit with an £100 worth of trucking cloth and all other trading ware, for they knew that we had a great cargo of goods of Mr. Pincheon's, and Mr. Steven Winthrop had the disposing of it. And he said that if he would come he might put off all his goods, and the Pequit Sachem would give him two horses that had been there a great while. So I sent the Shallop,[2] with Mr. Steven Winthrop, Sergeant Tille, (whom we called afterward Sergeant Kettle, because he put the kettle on his head,) and Thomas Hurlbut and three men more, charging them that they should ride in the middle of the river, and not go ashore until they had done all their trade, and that Mr. Steven Winthrop should stand in the hold of the boat, having their guns by them, and swords by their sides, the other four to be, two in the fore cuddie, and two in aft, being armed in like manner, that so they out of the loop-holes might clear the boat, if they were by the Pequits assaulted; and that they should let but one canoe come aboard at once, with no more but four Indians in her, and when she had traded then another, and that they should lie no longer there than one day, and at night to go out of the river; and if they brought the two horses, to take them in at a clear piece of land at the mouth of the River, two of them go ashore to help the horses in, and the rest stand ready with their guns in their hands, if need were, to defend them from the Pequits, for I durst not trust them. So they went and found but little trade, and they having forgotten what I charged them, Thomas Hurlbut and one more went ashore to boil the kettle, and Thomas Hurlbut stepping into the Sachem's wigwam, not far from the shore, enquiring for the horses, the Indians went out of the wigwam, and Wincumbone, his mother's sister, was then the great Pequit Sachem's wife, who made signs to him that he should be gone, for they would cut off his head; which, when he perceived, he drew his sword and ran to the others, and got aboard, and immediately came abundance of Indians to the water-side and called them to come ashore, but they immediately set sail and came home, and this caused me to keep watch and ward, for I saw they plotted our destruction. And

---

[2]A small boat. — EDS.

suddenly after came Capt. Endecott, Capt. Turner, and Capt. Undrill, with a company of soldiers, well fitted, to Seabrook,[3] and made that place their rendezvous or seat of war, and that to my great grief, for, said I, you come hither to raise these wasps about my ears, and then you will take wing and flee away; but when I had seen their commission I wondered, and made many allegations against the manner of it, but go they did to Pequit, and as they came without acquainting any of us in the River with it, so they went against our will, for I knew that I should lose our corn-field; then I entreated them to hear what I would say to them, which was this: Sirs, Seeing you will go, I pray you, if you don't load your Barks with Pequits, load them with corn, for that is now gathered with them, and dry, ready to put into their barns, and both you and we have need of it, and I will send my shallop and hire this Dutchman's boat, there present, to go with you, and if you cannot attain your end of the Pequits, yet you may load your barks with corn, which will be welcome to Boston and to me: But they said they had no bags to load them with, then said I, here is three dozen of new bags, you shall have thirty of them, and my shallop to carry them, and six of them my men shall use themselves, for I will with the Dutchmen send twelve men well provided; and I desired them to divide the men into three parts, viz. two parts to stand without the corn, and to defend the other one third part, that carried the corn to the water-side, till they have loaded what they can. And the men there in arms, when the rest are aboard, shall in order go aboard, the rest that are aboard shall with their arms clear the shore, if the Pequits do assault them in the rear, and then, when the General shall display his colours, all to set sail together. To this motion they all agreed, and I put the three dozen of bags aboard my shallop, and away they went, and demanded the Pequit Sachem to come into parley. But it was returned for answer, that he was from home, but within three hours he would come; and so from three to six, and thence to nine, there came none. But the Indians came without arms to our men, in great numbers, and they talked with my men, whom they knew; but in the end, at a word given, they all on a sudden ran away from our men, as they stood in rank and file, and not an Indian more was to be seen: and all this while before, they carried all their stuff away, and thus was that great parley ended. Then they displayed their colours, and beat their drums, burnt some wigwams and some heaps of corn, and my men carried as much aboard as they could, but the army went aboard, leaving my men ashore, which ought to have marched aboard first. But they all set sail, and my men were pursued by the Indians, and they hurt some of the Indians, and two of them came home wounded. The Bay-men killed not a man, save that one Kichomiquim, an Indian Sachem of the Bay, killed a Pequit; and thus began the war between the Indians and us in these parts. . . .

---

[3]"Capt. Undrill" is John Underhill (see p. 44). At this time the fort at Saybrook ("Seabrook"), essentially a small group of buildings within a palisade, was unfinished, understaffed, and undersupplied. — EDS.

. . . Two days after came to me, as I had written to Sir Henerie Vane, then Governor of the Bay, I say came to me Capt. Undrill, with twenty lusty men, well armed, to stay with me two months, or 'till something should be done about the Pequits. He came at the charge of my masters. Soon after came down from Harford Maj. Mason, Lieut. Seely, accompanied with Mr. Stone and eighty Englishmen, and eighty Indians, with a commission from Mr. Ludlow and Mr. Steel, and some others; these came to go fight with the Pequits. But when Capt. Undrill and I had seen their commission, we both said they were not fitted for such a design, and we said to Maj. Mason we wondered he would venture himself, being no better fitted; and he said the Magistrates could not or would not send better; then we said that none of our men should go with them, neither should they go unless we, that were bred soldiers from our youth, could see some likelihood to do better than the Bay-men with their strong commission last year. Then I asked them how they durst trust the Mohegin Indians, who had but that year come from the Pequits. They said they would trust them, for they could not well go without them for want of guides. Yea, said I, but I will try them before a man of ours shall go with you or them; and I called for Uncas and said unto him, You say you will help Maj. Mason, but I will first see it, therefore send you now twenty men to the Bass river, for there went yesternight six Indians in a canoe thither; fetch them now dead or alive, and then you shall go with Maj. Mason, else not. So he sent his men who killed four, brought one a traitor to us alive, whose name was Kiswas, and one ran away. And I gave him fifteen yards of trading cloth on my own charge, to give unto his men according to their desert. And having staid there five or six days before we could agree, at last we old soldiers agreed about the way and act, and took twenty insufficient men from the eighty that came from Harford and sent them up again in a shallop, and Capt. Undrill with twenty of the lustiest of our men went in their room, and I furnished them with such things as they wanted, and sent Mr. Pell, the sergeon, with them; and the Lord God blessed their design and way, so that they returned with victory to the glory of God, and honour of our nation, having slain three hundred, burnt their fort, and taken many prisoners.[4] Then came to me an Indian called Wequash, and I by Mr. Higgisson inquired of him, how many of the Pequits were yet alive that had helped to kill Englishmen; and he declared them to Mr. Higgisson, and he writ them down, as may appear by his own hand here enclosed, and I did as therein is written. Then three days after the fight came Waiandance, next brother to the old Sachem of Long Island, and having been recommended to me by Maj. Gibbons, he came to know if we were angry with all Indians. I answered No, but only with such as had killed Englishmen. He asked me whether they that lived upon Long-Island might come to trade with us. I said No, nor we with them, for if I should send my boat to trade for corn, and you have Pequits

---

[4]"Harford" is Hartford. Gardener describes his part in the attack on the Pequot town as, first, consulting on the best military strategy for what he regarded as an ill-considered attack and, second, providing supplies for the attacking forces. — EDS.

with you, and if my boat should come into some creek by reason of bad weather, they might kill my men, and I shall think that you of Long Island have done it, and so we may kill all you for the Pequits; but if you will kill all the Pequits that come to you, and send me their heads, then I will give to you as to Weakwash, and you shall have trade with us. Then, said he, I will go to my brother, for he is the great Sachem of all Long Island, and if we may have peace and trade with you, we will give you tribute, as we did the Pequits. Then I said, If you have any Indians that have killed English, you must bring their heads also. He answered, not any one, and said that Gibbons, my brother, would have told you if it had been so; so he went away and did as I had said, and sent me five heads, three and four heads for which I paid them that brought them as I had promised.

Then came Capt. Stoten with an army of three hundred men, from the Bay, to kill the Pequits; but they were fled beyond New Haven to a swamp. I sent Wequash after them, who went by night to spy them out, and the army followed him, and found them at the great swamp, who killed some and took others, and the rest fled to the Mowhakues [Mohawks], with their Sachem. Then the Mohawks cut off his head and sent it to Hartford, for then they all feared us,[5] but now it is otherwise, for they say to our faces that our Commissioners meeting once a year, and speak a great deal, or write a letter, and there's all, for they dare not fight. But before they went to the Great Swamp they sent Thomas Stanton over to Long Island and Shelter Island to find Pequits there, but there was none, for the Sachem Waiandance, that was at Plimoth when the Commissioners were there, and set there last, I say, he had killed so many of the Pequits, and sent their heads to me, that they durst not come there; and he and his men went with the English to the Swamp, and thus the Pequits were quelled at that time. But there was like to be a great broil between Miantenomie and Unchus [Uncas] who should have the rest of the Pequits, but we mediated between them and pacified them; also Unchus challenged the Narraganset Sachem out to a single combat, but he would not fight without all his men; but they were pacified, though the old grudge remained still, as it doth appear. Thus far I had written in a book, that all men and posterity might know how and why so many honest men had their blood shed, yea, and some flayed alive, others cut in pieces, and some roasted alive, only because Kichamokin, a Bay Indian, killed one Pequit; and thus far of the Pequit war, which was but a comedy in comparison of the tragedies which hath been here threatened since, and may yet come, if God do not open the eyes, ears, and hearts of some that I think are wilfully deaf and blind, and think because there is no change that the vision fails, and put the evil-threatened day far off, for say they, We are now twenty to one to what we were then, and none dare meddle with us. Oh! wo be to the pride and se-

---

[5]The Mohawks were allied with the English, as much for mutual advantage as out of "fear" on the Mohawks' part. But the Mohawks were also traditionally enemies of the tribes to the east of them, and they typically refused to help them in their struggles against the New England colonists, as Metacomet would later discover during King Philip's War. — EDS.

curity which hath been the ruin of many nations, as woful experience has proved. . . .

. . . But now I am at a stand, for all we English would be thought and called Christians; yet, though I have seen this before spoken, having been these twenty-four years in the mouth of the premises, yet I know not where to find, or whose name to insert, to parallel Ahasuerus lying on his bed and could not sleep, and called for the Chronicles to be read; and when he heard Mordecai named, said, What hath been done for him? But who will say as he said, or do answerable to what he did? But our New-England twelve-penny Chronicle is stuffed with a catalogue of the names of some, as if they had deserved immortal fame; but the right New-England military worthies are left out for want of room, as Maj. Mason, Capt. Undrill, Lieut. Sielly, &c., who undertook the desperate way and design to Mistick Fort, and killed three hundred, burnt the fort and took many prisoners, though they are not once named. But honest Abraham thought it no shame to name the confederates that helped him to war when he redeemed his brother Lot; but Uncas of Mistick, and Waiandance, at the Great Swamp and ever since your trusty friend, is forgotten, and for our sakes persecuted to this day with fire and sword, and Ahasuerus of New-England is still asleep, and if there be any like to Ahasuerus, let him remember what glory to God and honor to our nation hath followed their wisdom and valor. Awake! awake Ahasuerus, if there be any of thy seed or spirit here, and let not Haman destroy us as he hath done our Mordecai! And although there hath been much blood shed here in these parts among us, God and we know it came not by us. But if all must drink of this cup that is threatened, then shortly the king of Sheshack shall drink last, and tremble and fall when our pain will be past.[6] O that I were in the countries[7] again, that in their but twelve years truce, repaired cities and towns, made strong forts, and prepared all things needful against a time of war like Solomon. I think the soil hath almost infected me, but what they or our enemies will do hereafter I know not. I hope I shall not live so long to hear or see it, for I am old and out of date, else I might be in fear to see and hear that I think ere long will come upon us. . . .

---

[6]Ahasuerus, king of Shushan ("Sheshack"), remembered the good deed of his Jewish subject Mordecai when the chronicles that recorded it were read to him. Ahasuerus subsequently resisted the scheme of his councilor Haman to kill all the Jews in the kingdom, including Mordecai's cousin Esther who was Ahasuerus's queen. Gardener implies that the colonists should be wise like Ahasuerus and listen to their "Chronicles"—such as Gardener's own narrative. They will then realize they should reward their "Mordecais," the "military worthies" Gardener praises, and ignore their dangerously misleading "Hamans" who would neglect these men. Gardener insists that the colonists recognize not only their own best war leaders but also their faithful Native American allies. — Eds.

[7]The Low Countries, or Holland. The Dutch used their time wisely during a truce to rebuild and prepare for the resumption of war — unlike the New England colonists, according to Gardener. — Eds.

READING CRITICALLY

1. What actions by the colonists does Gardener condemn for provoking hostilities with the Pequots?

2. According to Gardener, how did the war with the Pequots begin?

3. How does Gardener deal with Native Americans who want to be allies of the English, such as Uncas and Waiandance?

4. Gardener says that if his version of the Pequot War is ignored, certain "tragedies" threaten (p. 90). What does he seem to be afraid of?

5. What is Gardener's complaint about the treatment of "military worthies" such as Mason and Underhill and their "confederates" Uncas and Waiandance (see p. 91)?

WRITING ANALYTICALLY

1. Gardener clearly intends his story of the Pequot War to change English behavior. What does he want done? Write a paper in which you describe his recommendations, illustrating with evidence from the text. If you wish, you may write as a seventeenth-century English colonist reporting on Gardener's views to the investors in England who support the colonies, with the intent of helping the investors to judge whether the colonial leaders are doing a good job.

2. Compare and contrast Gardener's account of the Pequot War with that of either William Bradford (p. 19) or John Underhill (p. 44). Bradford is the kind of colonial leader, distant from the actual battlefield, of whom Gardener is most critical in his account (although he does not mention Bradford by name here). Underhill is the kind of military leader championed by Gardener (he is included in Gardener's concluding list of "worthies"). Choosing one of these other writers, discuss the similarities and differences you find between the two accounts. Then use these details to write a paper in which you argue that these writers basically agree or disagree about the events they are describing. Option: You can turn this argument into an essay assessing the accuracy of our placement of Gardener in the "Alternative English Accounts" section of this unit. His has not been a dominant account, since it is seldom studied; but you might argue that his perspective is more like that of the dominant historians than it is truly "alternative."

JOHN EASTON

"A Relation of the Indian War" (1675)

John Easton (1617–?) was born in England but came with his father to the Massachusetts Bay colony in 1634. The family was soon forced to relocate to Rhode Island because of their membership in the Society of Friends (Quakers), which was considered unorthodox by the Puritans. Easton's father was governor of Rhode Island for many years, and John Easton served as the colony's attorney general from 1652 to 1674, when he became deputy governor. Easton's "A Relation of the Indian War," written in 1675, describes only the beginning stages of King Philip's War, including the death of Sassamon ("Sausimun"). Apparently Easton intended to provide an account that was more favorable to the Native Americans than versions put out by Increase Mather (p. 50) and other leading Puritans. He may also have wanted to discredit the Massachusetts Bay writers: Rhode Island needed to challenge its credibility with readers in England to counteract the larger colony's maneuvers to reduce Rhode Island's territory or dissolve the colony altogether. Easton's *Relation* circulated in manuscript but was not published until 1858.

Our version is taken from Charles Lincoln's 1913 collection *Narratives of the Indian Wars, 1675–1699*, but we have changed spelling and punctuation to approximate the conventions of modern English. (We have kept Easton's spellings of proper names.)

IN THE WINTER IN THE YEAR 1674 an Indian was found dead, and by a Coroner's inquest of Plymouth Colony judged murdered. He was found dead in a hole through ice broken in a pond, with his gun and some fowl by him. Some English supposed him thrown in; some Indians that I judged intelligible and impartial in that case did think he fell in and was so drowned, and that the ice did hurt his throat. The English said it was cut, but acknowledged that sometimes naughty Indians would kill others but, not as ever they heard, to obscure the deed as if the dead Indian was not murdered. The dead Indian was called Sausimun, a Christian that could read and write. Report was he was a bad man. King Philip got him to write his will, and he made the writing for a great part of the land to be his but read as if it had been as Philip would, but it came to be known and then he ran away from him.

Now one Indian informed that three Indians had murdered him, and showed a coat that he said they gave him to conceal them. The Indians reported that the informer had played away his coat, and these men sent

John Easton, "A Relacion of the Indyan Warre, by Mr. Easton, of Roade Isld., 1675," reprinted in *Narratives of the Indian Wars, 1675–1699*, ed. Charles H. Lincoln (1913; reprint, New York: Barnes and Noble, 1966), 7–17.

In the notes, EDS. = Patricia Bizzell and Bruce Herzberg.

him that coat, and afterward demanded pay, and he not wanting to pay so accused them, and knowing it would please the English so to think him a better Christian. And the report came, that the three Indians had confessed and accused Philip so to employ them, and that the English would hang Philip. So the Indians were afraid, and reported that the English had flattered them (or by threats) to belie Philip that they might kill him to have his land. If Philip had done it, it was their law so to execute whom their kings judged deserved it, so that he had no cause to hide it.

So Philip kept his men in arms. The Plymouth Governor required him to disband his men, and informed him his jealousy[1] was false. Philip answered he would do no harm, and thanked the Governor for his information. The three Indians were hung, and to the last denied the fact. But one broke the halter, as it was reported, then desired to be saved, and so was a little while, then confessed they three had done the fact and then he was hanged.[2] It was reported Sausimun before his death had informed of the Indian plot, and that if the Indians knew it, they would kill him. People feared that the heathen might destroy the English for their wickedness as God had permitted the heathen to destroy the Israelites of old.

So the English were afraid and Philip was afraid and both increased in arms. But for forty years' time reports and jealousies of war had been very frequent, so that we did not think that now a war was breaking forth. But about a week before it did, we had cause to think it would. Then to endeavor to prevent it, we sent a man to Philip to say that if he would come to the ferry, we would come over to speak with him. About four miles we had to come thither. When our messenger came to them, they, not aware of it, behaved themselves as furious, but suddenly appeased when they understood who he was and what he came for. He [Philip] called his council and agreed to come to us; he came himself unarmed and about forty of his men armed. Then five of us went over. Three were magistrates.

We sat very friendly together. We told him our business was to endeavor that they might not receive or do wrong. They said that was well, they had done no wrong, the English wronged them. The Indians said the English wronged them, but our desire was the quarrel might rightly be decided in the best way, and not as dogs decided their quarrels. The Indians owned that fighting was the worst way. Then they propounded how right might take place. We said by arbitration. They said all English agreed against them, and so by arbitration they had had much wrong, many miles square of land so taken from them, for English would have English arbitrators. Once, they were persuaded to give in their arms, that thereby jealousy might be removed, and the English having their arms would not deliver them as they had promised, until they consented to pay one hundred pounds. Now they had not so much land or money, that they were as good

---

[1]His fear that the English meant to punish him for Sassamon's death. — EDS.

[2]Easton refers here to an old hangman's trick, causing the noose, or "halter," to break so that the terrified victim could be manipulated into further disclosures. Compare accounts of Sassamon's death and the trial of his accused murderers in Mather (p. 50) and Apess (p. 107). — EDS.

be killed as leave all their livlihood. We said they might choose an Indian king, and the English might choose the Governor of New York, so that neither had cause to say either were parties in the difference. They said they had not heard of that way and said we honestly spoke; so we were persuaded if that way had been tendered, they would have accepted.

We did endeavor not to hear their complaints, said it was not convenient for us now to consider of, but to endeavor to prevent war. We said to them when in war against English, [English] blood was spilled, that engaged all Englishmen, for we were to be all under one king. We knew what their complaints would be, and in our colony had removed some of them in sending for Indian rulers in so far as the crime concerned Indians' lives, which they very lovingly accepted and agreed with us to their execution and said so they were able to satisfy their subjects when they knew an Indian suffered duly. But they said in what was only between their Indians and not in townships that we had purchased, they would not have us prosecute. They had a great fear lest any of their Indians should be called or forced to be Christian Indians. They said that such were in everything more mischievous, only dissemblers, and then the English made them not subject to their kings, and by their lying to wrong their kings. We knew it to be true. We promised them, however, that in government to Indians, all should be alike, and that we knew it was our king's will it should be so. Although we were weaker than other colonies, they having submitted to our king to protect them, others dared not otherwise to molest them. So they expressed they took that to be well. We had little cause to doubt but that to us under the king, they would have yielded to our determinations in what any should have complained to us against them. But Philip charged it to be dishonesty in us to put off the hearing the complaints; therefore, we consented to hear them.

They said they had been the first in doing good to the English, and the English the first in doing wrong. When the English first came, their king's father[3] was as a great man and the English as a little child. He constrained other Indians from wronging the English and gave them corn and showed them how to plant and was free to do them any good and had let them have a hundred times more land, than now the king had for his own people. But their king's brother, when he was king, came miserably to die by being forced to court, as they judged poisoned.[4] Another grievance was, if twenty of their honest Indians testified that an Englishman had done them wrong, it was as nothing, and if but one of their worst Indians testified against any Indian or their king, when it pleased the English, that was sufficient. Another grievance was, when their kings sold land, the English would say it was more than they agreed to and a writing must be proof against all them, and some of their kings had done wrong

---

[3]That is, Philip's father, Massasoit, who helped the colonists at Plymouth, as described in Bradford (p. 19). — EDS.

[4]Philip's brother was Wamsutta, or Alexander, as the colonists called him; he died after being forced to march to Plymouth for a negotiating session when he was ill. — EDS.

to sell so much.[5] He left his people none. And some being given to drunkeness, the English made them drunk and then cheated them in bargains. But now their kings were forewarned not for to part with land for nothing in comparison to the value thereof. Now whom the English had owned for[6] king or queen they would disinherit, and make another king that would give or sell them their land, that now they had no hopes left to keep any land. Another grievance was that the English cattle and horses still increased. When they removed thirty miles from where English had anything to do, they could not keep their corn from being spoiled, they never being used to fence. They thought when the English bought land of them that they would have kept their cattle upon their own land. Another grievance was that the English were so eager to sell the Indians liquors that most of the Indians spent all in drunkeness and then ravened upon the sober Indians and, they did believe, often did hurt the English cattle, and their kings could not prevent it. We knew before these were their grand complaints, but then we only endeavored to persuade that all complaints might be righted without war. But we could have no other answer but that they had not heard of that way for the Governor of [New] York and an Indian king to have the hearing of it. We had cause to think if that had been tendered, it would have been accepted. We endeavored, however, that they should lay down their arms, for the English were too strong for them. They said, then the English should do to them as they did when they were too strong for the English. So we departed without any discourteousness, and suddenly had a letter from the Plymouth Governor saying they intended in arms to conform Philip, but no information what that was that they required or what terms he refused to have their quarrel decided, and in a week's time after we had been with the Indians the war thus begun.

Plymouth soldiers were come to have their headquarters within ten miles of Philip. Then most of the English thereabout left their houses. We had a letter from the Plymouth Governor to desire our help with some boats, if they had such occasion, and for us to look to ourselves. From the General at the headquarters, we had a letter telling the day they intended to come upon the Indians and desiring for some of our boats to attend. So we took it to be of necessity for one half of our Islanders one day and night to attend, and the other half the next, so by turns for our own safety. In this time some Indians fell a-pilfering some houses that the English had left, and an old man and a lad going to one of those houses did see three Indians run out thereof. The old man bid the young man shoot, so he did and an Indian fell down but got away again. It is reported that then some Indians came to the garrison and asked why they shot the Indian. They asked whether he was dead. The Indians said yea. An English lad said it was no matter. The men endeavored to inform them it was but an idle lad's words, but the Indians in haste went away and did not harken to

[5]According to traditional Native American practice, the king, or sachem, had no right to sell any tribal land, although he or she could negotiate arrangements whereby other people would be permitted to use the land. — EDS.

[6]Acknowledged as. — EDS.

them. The next day, the lad that shot the Indian and his father and five English more were killed. So the war begun with Philip.[7]

But there was a queen[8] that I knew was not a party with Philip, and the Plymouth Governor recommended to her that if she would come to our Island, it would be well. She desired she might, if it were but with six of her men. I can sufficiently prove, but it is too large here to relate, that she had practiced much that the quarrel might be decided without war. But some of our English also, in fury against all Indians, would not consent she should be received to our Island, although I preferred to be at all the charge to secure her and those she desired to come with her. So at length I prevailed we might send for her, but one day accidently we were prevented. Then our men had seized some canoes on her side, supposing they were Philip's, and the next day an English house was there burned. Then mischief of either side endeavored to the other and much done, and her houses burned, so we were prevented of any means to attain her.

The English army came not down as we were informed they would, so Philip got over and they could not find him. Three days after, they came down and we had a very stormy night. In the morning the foot soldiers were disabled to return before they had refreshment. They were free to accept, as we were willing to relieve them, but the troopers said, by their captain they despised it, and so left the foot [soldiers]. After the foot had refreshed themselves, they also returned to their headquarters. After hunting Philip from all sea shores, they could not tell what was become of him. The Narragansett kings informed us that the queen aforesaid must be in a thicket a-starving or conformed to Philip, but they knew she would be glad to be from them, so from us had encouragement to get her and as many as they could from Philip.

After the English army, without our consent or informing us, came into our colony and brought the Narragansett Indians to articles of agreement to them, Philip being fled, about 150 Indians came in to a Plymouth garrison voluntarily. The Plymouth authorities sold all for slaves (but about six of them) to be carried out of the country. It is true the Indians generally are very barbarous people, but in this war I have not heard of their tormenting any. But I have heard that the English army caught an old Indian and tormented him. He was well known to have been a long time a very decrepit and harmless Indian of the queen's.

As Philip fled, the aforesaid queen got to the Narragansetts and as many of her men as she could get. But one part of the Narragansetts' agreement with Boston was to kill or deliver as many as they could of Philip's people. Therefore Boston men demanded the aforesaid queen and others that they had so received, for which the Indians were unfree and made many

[7]Compare Mather's account (p. 50) of who drew first blood in King Philip's War. — EDS.

[8]The sachem Weetamoo, widow of Wamsutta, Philip's brother. Note how Easton explains Weetamoo's eventual participation with Philip against the English. Compare Rowlandson's description of Weetamoo (p. 67). — EDS.

excuses, as that the queen was none of them, and some others were but so-journers with Philip because removed by the English having got their land, and were of their kindred, which we know is true. Not but we think they did shelter many they should not, and that they did know some of their men did assist Philip, but according to their barbarous rules they accounted so was no wrong or they could not help it. Some enemies' heads they did send in and told us they were informed that, however, when winter came, they might be sure the English would be their enemies. And so the Narragansetts stood doubtful for about five months.

The English were jealous that there was a general plot of all Indians against English and the Indians were in like manner jealous of the English. I think it was general that they were unwilling to be wronged; that the Indians do judge the English partial against them; and that among all there was a filthy crew that did desire and endeavor for war and others, those of any solidity were against it and endeavored to prevent the war. Concerning Philip, we have good intelligence that he advised some English to be gone from their outplaces where they lived or they were in danger to be killed. But whether it were to prevent a war, or because by their priests they were informed that if they began they should be beaten and otherwise not so, I know not. We have good intelligence that most of them had a desire the English would begin, and if the English be not careful to manifest, the Indians may expect equity from them, they may have more enemies than they would and more cause of jealousy.

The report is that to the eastward the war thus began, by supposing that some of those Indians were at a fight in these parts and that there, they say, a man was wounded. So authority sent some forth to discover, having before disarmed those Indians and confined them to a place, which the Indians were not offended at. But those men coming upon them in a warlike posture, they fled, so that the men caught but three of them. Those in authority sent out again to excuse themselves, but they could only come to the speech with one man, as he kept out of their reach. They excused themselves and said his father was not hurt, one of the Indians they had taken. He said he could not believe them, for if it were so, they would have brought his father. They had been deceitful to disarm them and so would have killed them all, and so he ran away. And then English were killed, and the report is that up in the country here away, they had demanded the Indians' arms and went again to parley with them and the Indians by ambuscade treacherously killed eight that were going to treat with them.

When winter was come, we had a letter from Boston from the United Commissioners,[9] that they were resolved to reduce the Narragansetts to

---

[9]The "United Commissioners" were the leaders of Plymouth, Massachusetts Bay, Connecticut, and New Haven, the four colonies joined in the United Colonies of New England. This protective confederation pointedly excluded Easton's Rhode Island colony on the grounds of unorthodoxy both in matters of religion and in dealings with the Native Americans (the Rhode Islanders were perceived as too friendly with the Native Americans). It can be seen from Easton's account that Rhode Island nevertheless felt obliged to aid the other English colonies in wartime. — EDS.

conformity, not to be troubled with them any more, and they desired some help of boats and otherwise, if we saw cause, and that we should keep secret concerning it. Our governor sent them word we were satisfied the Narragansetts were treacherous, and had aided Philip, and as we had assisted to relieve their army before, so we should be ready to assist them still. We advised that terms might be tendered that such might expect compassion that would accept not to engage in war, and that there might be a separation between the guilty and the innocent, which in war could not be expected, we not in the least expecting they would have begun the war and not before proclaimed it or not given them defiance, I having often informed the Indians that Englishmen would not begin a war otherwise, it was brutish so to do. I am sorry so the Indians have cause to think me deceitful, for the English thus began the war with the Narragansetts, we having sent off our Island many Indians and informed them if they kept by the watersides and did not meddle, the English would do them no harm although it was not safe for us to let them live here.

The army first took all those prisoners, then fell upon Indian houses, burned them, and killed some men. The war began without proclamation, and some of our people did not know the English had begun mischief to the Indians, and being confident and had cause therefore, that the Indians would not hurt them before the English began, so did not keep their garrison exactly. But the Indians, having received that mischief, came unexpected upon them, and destroyed fourteen of them besides other great loss. The English army say they supposed Connecticutt forces had been there. They sold the Indians that they had taken as aforesaid, for slaves, but one old man that was carried off our Island upon his son's back. He was so decrepit he could not go, and when the army took them, the son upon his back carried him to the garrison. Some would have had him devoured by dogs, but the tenderness of some of them prevailed to cut off his head. After, they came suddenly upon the Indians where the Indians had prepared to defend themselves and so received and did much mischief. About six weeks since hath been spent as for both parties to recruit, and now the English army is out to seek after the Indians, but it is most likely that such most able to do mischief will escape and women and children and impotent may be destroyed, and so the most able will have the less incumbrance to do mischief.

But I am confident it would be best for English and Indians that a peace were made upon honest terms, for each to have a due property and to enjoy it without oppression or usurpation by one to the other. But the English dare not trust the Indians' promises, neither the Indians to the Englishes' promises, and each have great cause therefore. I see no way likely but if a cessation from arms might be procured until it might be known what terms King Charles would propound, for we great cause to think the Narragansett kings would trust our king and that they would have accepted him to be umpire if it had been tendered about any difference. We do know the English have had much contention against those Indians to invalidate the King's determination for Narragansett to be in our colony, and we have cause to think it was the greatest cause of the war against them.[10] I see no means likely to procure a cessation from arms except the Governor of New York can find a way to intercede, and so it will be likely a peace may be made without troubling our king. Not but it always hath been a principle in our colony that there should be but one supreme to English men, and in our native country wherever English have jurisdiction. So we know no English should begin a war and not first tender for the King to be umpire, and not persecute such that will not conform to their worship, and their worship be what is not owned by the King. The King not to mind to have such things redressed, some may take it that he hath not power, and that there may be a way for them to take power in opposition to him. I am so persuaded of New England priests, they are so blinded by the spirit of persecution and to maintain to have hire, and to have room to be mere hirelings, that they have been the cause that the law of nations and the law of arms have been violated in this war.[11] The war had not been if there had not been a hireling that for his managing what he calleth the gospel, by violence to have it chargeable for his gain from his quarters, and if any in magistracy be not so as their pack horses, they will be trumpeting for innovation or war.

READING CRITICALLY

1. In the first two paragraphs of his account, what evidence does Easton present to cast doubt on the idea that "Sausimun" (John Sassamon) was murdered? What evidence does he present against the idea that Sassamon was a good man? Against the charge that three followers of Philip killed him?

2. Easton describes at length a conference he and some fellow leaders of the Rhode Island colony attended with Philip and his advisers just before the war broke out. Easton says that he and his friends recommended that the Native Americans submit their grievances against the English to arbitration. What plans for arbitration does Easton put forth, and how does he claim Philip reacts?

3. What grievances against the English do the Native Americans express during their conference with Easton? To what extent does Easton admit that these grievances are justified?

4. How does Easton explain the Narragansetts' harboring of enemy Native Americans? What was the Rhode Island colony's position concerning the preemptive strike against the Narragansett town?

---

[10]Easton implies that the United Colonies attacked the Narragansetts so that they could claim Narragansett territory for themselves, rather than allow it to remain within the boundaries of the Rhode Island colony as determined by the English king. — EDS.

[11]Easton implies that the other colonies' ministers, here called "priests" (an insult as applied to these anti-Catholics), fomented hostilities in hopes of benefiting through their stipends from the profits that would presumably come in from increased English territory in New England, gained through war. — EDS.

5. How does Easton deal with the prevailing English view that "there was a general plot [or conspiracy] of all Indians against English" in King Philip's War (p. 98)?

WRITING ANALYTICALLY

1. Easton is determined in this account to create a particular image of Native Americans. What is that image, and how does he promote it? Collect evidence from the text to support your own argument that Easton does or does not successfully depict a particular image of Native Americans.

2. Increase Mather (p. 50) says that the colonists decided on a preemptive strike against the Narragansetts because, although the Narragansetts were neutral, they were harboring enemy Native Americans and refusing to help the English. How does Easton deal with these charges? Write a paper in which you analyze the Narragansett position in this war and recommend what you think the colonists should have done about the Narragansetts, based on the arguments in Mather and Easton. You will have to explain how you are dealing with two sources that disagree, why you are favoring one over the other or how you are reconciling them, and so forth. Option: You may write as if you were a seventeenth-century English colonist reporting to the English government on the conduct of the colonial leaders — what they did and should have done.

3. What happened to John Sassamon? Mather (p. 50) and Easton give very different accounts of his death. Piecing together the evidence from these two sources, write a paper in which you explain what we can know about answers to the following questions: Was Sassamon murdered? If so, did the three men who were executed for murdering him actually do the deed? If they did, were they acting on the orders of Philip? If they were, was Philip justified in ordering Sassamon's death? Option: You may write as if you were a seventeenth-century English colonist reporting to the English government on the conduct of the colonial leaders — what they did and should have done.

NATIVE AMERICAN ACCOUNTS

Paper Left on a Bridge Post
at Medfield, Massachusetts (February 1675)

The following text is taken from the Historical Account of the Doings and Sufferings of the Christian Indians in New England in the Years 1675, 1676, 1677 *by Daniel Gookin (c. 1612–87; for more information on Gookin, see p. 103). According to Gookin, an English soldier found this paper on a bridge post at Medfield after the town was burned by Native American fighters during King Philip's War. Gookin asserts that this paper was written "by the enemy Indians," and he reprints it to show "the pride and insolence of these barbarians at this time." We cannot be sure that a Native American wrote this text; it might have been created by some English person precisely to "prove" the evils about Native Americans that Gookin attributes to them. But some Native Americans were literate in English by the time of King Philip's War, most likely through instruction in Christianity; and some of them joined other Native Americans attacking the English.*

KNOW BY THIS PAPER, that the Indians that thou hast provoked to wrath and anger, will war this twenty-one years if you will; there are many Indians yet, we come three hundred at this time. You must consider the Indians lost nothing but their life; you must lose your fair houses and cattle.

READING CRITICALLY

If this paper was written by a Native American, it can be construed as showing a Native American perspective on cultural differences between Native Americans and English immigrants. What values does the paper appear to elevate and denigrate?

WRITING ANALYTICALLY

It must have been particularly upsetting to the English to find a paper written in English left by an attacking Native American: This meant that someone whom they had instructed in Christianity — the usual context for literacy instruction — had gone over to the enemy. We can say that the Native American who wrote this paper took the literacy he had acquired from the English and used it for decidedly differ-

Paper Left on a Bridge Post at Medfield, Massachusetts (1675), in Daniel Gookin, *An Historical Account of the Doings and Sufferings of the Christian Indians in New England, in the Years 1675, 1676, 1677* (1677; reprint, New York: Arno Press, 1972), 424.

ent purposes than those for which it was intended: to put forward his own Native American values and goals rather than English and Christian ones. Can you think of another example in recent history of someone who used schooling for such alternative purposes, turning literacy to his or her own ends rather than the ends intended by the dominant society? Malcolm X might be one example. If an example comes to mind, write an essay in which you use that example and the bridge post paper to illustrate an argument about what happens when people use literacy for purposes that resist the dominant order in society.

WABAN

Speech at the End of King Philip's War, Recorded and with a Reply by Daniel Gookin (1677)

Daniel Gookin (c. 1612–87) came to Boston from the southern English colony of Virginia in 1644. He held the post of superintendent of Indians for the Massachusetts Bay colony from 1656 until his death, working closely with the Reverend John Eliot in converting Native Americans to Christianity and promoting their interests. During King Philip's War, Christian Native Americans were subjected to violent persecution within the colonies, despite the fact that many of the adult men were fighting for the English. A large group of women, children, and old men were interned on Deer Island in Boston Harbor, where many died of hunger, exposure, and disease. Gookin remained an outspoken advocate for the Christian Native Americans even though he was attacked for it during King Philip's War. Immediately after the war, he wrote a sympathetic and indignant account of their persecution, intended as a report for the English missionary society funding his work. This report, *Historical Account of the Doings and Sufferings of the Christian Indians in New England, in the Years 1675, 1676, 1677*, was first published by the American Antiquarian Society in 1836.

Waban, a Nipmuck, was a leader of the Christian Native Americans at Natick. At the time of King Philip's War, he was an old man. According to Gookin, Waban encouraged Native American participation in the war effort against Metacomet (Philip). He provided early information on the warring tribes' plans, urged younger men to fight for the colonists, and accompanied the group that submitted (on his counsel) to internment on Deer Island. Waban himself almost died from the hardships there. Excerpted here is the final passage from Gookin's *Historical Account*, in which Gookin reports a speech given by Waban at a meeting held after the war by Gookin and Eliot with the Deer Island internees and other Christian Native American survivors.

Waban, Speech at the End of King Philip's War, in Daniel Gookin, *An Historical Account of the Doings and Sufferings of the Christian Indians in New England, in the Years 1675, 1676, 1677* (1677; reprint, New York: Arno Press, 1972), 522–23.
   In the notes, EDS. = Patricia Bizzell and Bruce Herzberg.

We cannot know for sure whether Waban actually said the words reported by Gookin. Gookin evidently regards his speech as a model of Christian humility and patience, and we may suspect that some English person might have contrived it to provide just such evidence of the success of the Christian missionaries. But oratory was an indigenous Native American art form; and Waban, from his long association with the English, would certainly have been capable of making this speech in English.

AT A COURT HELD AMONG THE PRAYING INDIANS, where was a full meeting of them, it being also Mr. Elliot's lecture, who was present with Major Gookin and some other English,[1] Waban, the chief ruler among the Indians, in the name of all the rest, made an affectionate speech to this effect: "We do, with all thankfulness, acknowledge God's great goodness to us, in preserving us alive to this day. Formerly, in our beginning to pray unto God, we received much encouragement from many godly English, both here and in England. Since the war begun between the English and wicked Indians, we expected to be all cut off, not only by the enemy Indians, whom we know hated us, but also by many English, who were much exasperated and very angry with us. In this case, we cried to God, in prayer, for help. Then God stirred up the governor and magistrates to send us to the Island, which was grievous to us; for we were forced to leave all our substance behind us, and we expected nothing else at the Island, but famine and nakedness. But behold God's goodness to us and our poor families, in stirring up the hearts of many godly persons in England, who never saw us, yet showed us kindness and much love, and gave us some corn and clothing, together with other provision of clams, that God provided for us. Also, in due time, God stirred up the hearts of the governor and magistrates, to call forth some of our brethren to go forth to fight against the enemy both to us and the English, and was pleased to give them courage and success in that service, unto the acceptance of the English; for it was always in our hearts to endeavour to do all we could, to demonstrate our fidelity to God and to the English, and against their and our enemy; and for all these things, we desire God only may be glorified." Piambow, the other ruler next to Waban, spake to the same, giving all glory to the Lord. After this, upon occasion of an inquiry concerning the messengers sent, in winter last, to Mohegan, to stir the Mohegans up to pray to God, some English reported, that those messengers enticed some of the Indian servants, at Norwich, to run away with those messengers, from their masters; but the messengers utterly denied any such thing.[2] Waban took this occasion, further to speak to this effect: "That God knew,

---

[1]The "Court" is a meeting of Christian Native Americans to hear a "lecture," or sermon, by the Reverend John Eliot. — EDS.

[2]The "messengers" are Christian Native Americans from Waban's eastern Massachusetts group, sent to proselytize the Mohegans in Connecticut. — EDS.

that they had done their utmost endeavours to carry themselves so that they might approve their fidelity and love to the English. But yet, some English were still ready to speak the contrary of them, as in this matter instanced; and in that business at Cocheco, lately, when the Indians were carried away by the Maquas; yet the English say, they ran away to the Maquas[3] and were not carried away; yet," said he, "I know the governor and magistrates and many good men had other thoughts of them and more charity toward them." To this speech of his, Major Gookin made this answer: "That Christ in the Gospel teacheth all his disciples to take up the cross daily. And he himself, though most innocent, and always did good, yet some said of him, he had a devil; others, that he was an enemy to Cesar; others, that he was a friend to publicans and sinners, and raised many other reproaches against him; yet he bore all patiently, and referred the case to God; and herein we should follow his example. Waban, you know all Indians are not good; some carry it rudely, some are drunkards, others steal, others lie and break their promises, and otherwise wicked. So 't is with Englishmen; all are not good, but some are bad, and will carry it rudely; and this we must expect, while we are in this world; therefore, let us be patient and quiet, and leave this case to God, and wait upon him in a way of well-doing, patience, meekness, and humility; and God will bring a good issue in the end, as you have seen and experienced."

There are many other things, that I might have recorded, concerning these poor, despised sheep of Christ. But I fear that which I have already written will be thought (by some) impertinent and tedious. But when I call to mind, that great and worthy men have taken much pains to record, and others to read, the seeming small and little concerns of the children of God; as well in the historical books of Scripture, as other histories of the primitive times of Christianity, and of the doings and sufferings of the poor saints of God; I do encourage my heart in God, that He will accept, in Christ, this mean labor of mine, touching these poor despised men; yet such as are, through the grace of Christ, the first professors, confessors, if I may not say martyrs, of the Christian religion among the poor Indians in America.

READING CRITICALLY

1. In the first part of Waban's speech, what actions does he attribute to the intervention of God?

2. In the first part of his speech, Waban reminds the English of how the Christian Native Americans helped the English against their enemies in King Philip's War. What did they do?

---

[3]"Maquas" means "Mohawks" in Waban's language. They were the traditional enemies of the tribes to the east of their upper Hudson River domain, and it would be extremely unlikely for any New England Native American to run to them voluntarily. — EDS.

3. According to Waban, why were the English so ready to believe the lie that some of his people ran away with the Mohawks?

4. Gookin interprets Waban's speech as complaining about English treatment of the Christian Native Americans. What responses does Gookin give?

5. In his concluding paragraph, Gookin compares the history of the Christian Native Americans ("these poor, despised sheep of Christ") with what two other kinds of history?

WRITING ANALYTICALLY

1. Although Waban's speech is full of expressions of humility and loyalty to the English and to God, it can also be interpreted as a complaint about English treatment of the Christian Native Americans (this is apparently how Gookin interpreted it, given his reply). Waban is obviously in a very difficult rhetorical position here. His people are destitute and entirely dependent on uncertain English protection, so he cannot risk offending the English; yet, precisely because his people's situation is desperate, he feels that he must make the attempt to improve English treatment of them. What evidence can you find in Waban's speech that he is attempting to placate the English? (Your response to reading question 1 may help you here.) What evidence can you find that Waban is making charges against the English, either directly or indirectly? (Your responses to reading questions 1, 2, and 3 may help you here.) Use this evidence to write a paper in which you argue that Waban is or is not an effective speaker for his people.

Option: Compare and contrast Waban's effectiveness with that of Andrew Pittimee and his fellow Native American petitioners on behalf of Native American captives taken in King Philip's War (p. 149). Both Waban and the petitioners are in the tricky situation of pro-English Native Americans who must nevertheless criticize English behavior and ask for better treatment for Native Americans.

2. Gookin is in a difficult rhetorical position in his account of the "doings and sufferings" of the Christian Native Americans. He is a devout Puritan and firm enemy of non-Christian Native Americans. At the same time, he sympathizes deeply with the Christian Native Americans and champions their cause, at great personal risk. He has to persuade other Puritans to see the Christian Native Americans as he does without discrediting himself in Puritan eyes. How do you see Gookin grappling with this rhetorical problem? (Your response to reading questions 4 and 5 may help you here.) Use this evidence to argue that Gookin is or is not an effective defender of Christian Native Americans.

Alternative: Compare and contrast how Gookin and John Easton (p. 93) attempt to represent Native American perspectives to indifferent or hostile English audiences. Both cast themselves in the role of mediator between their own people and Native American groups. Use the evidence you gather from this comparison to support an argument about how — or whether — a member of a dominant social group can be an effective speaker for the interests of a disadvantaged group.

WILLIAM APESS

From *Eulogy on King Philip* (1836)

William Apess (1798–?) was born in Massachusetts. In his autobiography, he identifies himself as a member of the Pequot tribe but also claims descent from the Wampanoag sachem Metacomet (Philip) on his mother's side. He is thus connected with the two tribes most involved in the two wars treated in this unit.

His poverty-stricken family unable to take care of him, Apess was placed with a European American family as an indentured servant and attended school intermittently. He converted to Methodist Christianity in his teens and was ordained a minister by the Protestant Methodists in 1829. Apess then began a career as what we would now call an activist for Native American rights. He traveled around New England preaching to Native American groups who would otherwise have had no minister. He published five books critiquing white society from a Native American perspective, including a spiritual autobiography; *Indian Nullification of the Unconstitutional Laws of Massachusetts*, an account of the civil disobedience action that he led at the Cape Cod praying town of Mashpee in 1833; and his *Eulogy on King Philip*, which went through two editions. The *Eulogy*, excerpted here, was originally delivered as a public lecture in Boston in January 1836.

Apess suddenly disappears from the historical record after 1838, when his name is listed in legal accounts as a debtor, and his work was neglected until very recently. One of his twentieth-century editors speculates that he may have been murdered for his activism, as was his Boston contemporary, African American abolitionist David Walker (see Unit Two, p. 193).

Clearly Apess was not afraid of confrontation, either in political action or in print. It must have been very provocative in Boston to eulogize publicly the biggest villain in the dominant accounts of Puritan–Native American relations. Moreover, Apess names and argues against many of the canonical historians, such as Bradford (see p. 19), Mather (see p. 50), Rowlandson (see p. 67), and others. He also insists that the seventeenth-century conflict echoes in the unjust treatment of Native Americans and other people of color in his own day. At the same time, Apess employs a number of strategies (such as using his subject's English name, Philip) to make his argument accessible to a European American audience. Yet it is remarkable how bold in fact he was, considering his own vulnerable position, representing marginalized people and suffering economic hardship himself.

We have excerpted almost the entire text of the *Eulogy*, cutting only a few sections that deal with historical incidents not treated in the other readings in Unit One.

William Apess, *Eulogy on King Philip as Pronounced at the Odeon, in Federal Street, Boston* (1836), reprinted in *On Our Own Ground: The Complete Writings of William Apess, a Pequot*, edited with an introduction and notes by Barry O'Connell (Amherst: University of Massachusetts Press, 1992), 277–310.

In the notes, WA = William Apess, BOC = Barry O'Connell, EDS. = Patricia Bizzell and Bruce Herzberg.

I DO NOT ARISE TO SPREAD BEFORE YOU the fame of a noted warrior, whose natural abilities shone like those of the great and mighty Philip of Greece, or of Alexander the Great, or like those of Washington — whose virtues and patriotism are engraven on the hearts of my audience. Neither do I approve of war as being the best method of bowing to the haughty tyrant, Man, and civilizing the world. No, far from me be such a thought. But it is to bring before you beings made by the God of Nature, and in whose hearts and heads he has planted sympathies that shall live forever in the memory of the world, whose brilliant talents shone in the display of natural things, so that the most cultivated, whose powers shown with equal luster, were not able to prepare mantles to cover the burning elements of an uncivilized world. What, then? Shall we cease to mention the mighty of the earth, the noble work of God?

Yet those purer virtues remain untold. Those noble traits that marked the wild man's course lie buried in the shades of night; and who shall stand? I appeal to the lovers of liberty. But those few remaining descendants who now remain as the monument of the cruelty of those who came to improve our race and correct our errors — and as the immortal Washington lives endeared and engraven on the hearts of every white in America, never to be forgotten in time — even such is the immortal Philip honored, as held in memory by the degraded but yet grateful descendants who appreciate his character; so will every patriot, especially in this enlightened age, respect the rude yet all-accomplished son of the forest, that died a martyr to his cause, though unsuccessful, yet as glorious as the *American* Revolution. Where, then, shall we place the hero of the wilderness?

Justice and humanity for the remaining few prompt me to vindicate the character of him who yet lives in their hearts and, if possible, melt the prejudice that exists in the hearts of those who are in the possession of his soil, and only by the right of conquest — is the aim of him who proudly tells you, the blood of a denominated savage runs in his veins. It is, however, true that there are many who are said to be honorable warriors, who, in the wisdom of their civilized legislation, think it no crime to wreak their vengeance upon whole nations and communities, until the fields are covered with blood and the rivers turned into purple fountains, while groans, like distant thunder, are heard from the wounded and the tens of thousands of the dying, leaving helpless families depending on their cares and sympathies for life; while a loud response is heard floating through the air from the ten thousand Indian children and orphans, who are left to mourn the honorable acts of a few — civilized men.

Now, if we have common sense and ability to allow the difference between the civilized and the uncivilized, we cannot but see that one mode of warfare is as just as the other; for while one is sanctioned by authority of the enlightened and cultivated men, the other is an agreement according to the pure laws of nature, growing out of natural consequences; for nature always has her defense for every beast of the field; even the reptiles of the earth and the fishes of the sea have their weapons of war. But though frail man was made for a nobler purpose — to live, to love, and adore his

God, and do good to his brother — for this reason, and this alone, the God of heaven prepared ways and means to blast anger, man's destroyer, and cause the Prince of Peace[1] to rule, that man might swell those blessed notes. My image is of God; I am not a beast.

But as all men are governed by animal passions who are void of the true principles of God, whether cultivated or uncultivated, we shall now lay before you the true character of Philip, in relation to those hostilities between himself and the whites; and in so doing, permit me to be plain and candid.

The first inquiry is: Who is Philip? He was the descendant of one of the most celebrated chiefs in the known world, for peace and universal benevolence toward all men;[2] for injuries upon injuries, and the most daring robberies and barbarous deeds of death that were ever committed by the American Pilgrims, were with patience and resignation borne, in a manner that would do justice to any Christian nation or being in the world — especially when we realize that it was voluntary suffering on the part of the good old chief. His country extensive, his men numerous, so as the wilderness was enlivened by them, say, a thousand to one of the white men, and they also sick and feeble — where, then, shall we find one nation submitting so tamely to another, with such a host at their command? For injuries of much less magnitude have the people called Christians slain their brethren, till they could sing, like Samson: With a jawbone of an ass have we slain our thousands and laid them in heaps. It will be well for us to lay those deeds and depredations committed by whites upon Indians before the civilized world, and then they can judge for themselves.

It appears from history that, in 1614, "There came one Henry Harly unto me, bringing with him a native of the Island of Capawick [Chappaquiddick], a place at the south of Cape Cod, whose name was Epenuel. This man was taken upon the main by force, with some twenty-nine others," very probably good old Massasoit's men,[3] "by a ship, and carried to London, and from thence to be sold for slaves among the Spaniards; but the Indians being too shrewd, or, as they say, unapt for their use, they refused to traffic in Indians' blood and bones." This inhuman act of the whites caused the Indians to be jealous[4] forever afterward, which the white man acknowledges upon the first pages of the history of his country.[5]

How inhuman it was in those wretches, to come into a country where nature shone in beauty, spreading her wings over the vast continent, sheltering beneath her shades those natural sons of an Almighty Being, that shone in grandeur and luster like the stars of the first magnitude in the heavenly world; whose virtues far surpassed their more enlightened foes,

---

[1]Jesus Christ. — EDS.

[2]Philip's father was the Pokanoket [Wampanoag] sachem Massasoit who, as the rest of the *Eulogy* makes clear, became the Pilgrims' crucial ally. — BOC

[3]See Harlow's Voyage, 1611. — WA

[4]"Jealous" here means suspicious, fearful of violence. — EDS.

[5]See Drake's *History of the Indians*, 7. — WA

notwithstanding their pretended zeal for religion and virtue. How they could go to work to enslave a free people and call it religion is beyond the power of my imagination and outstrips the revelation of God's word. O thou pretended hypocritical Christian, whoever thou art, to say it was the design of God that we should murder and slay one another because we have the power. Power was not given us to abuse each other, but a mere power delegated to us by the King of heaven, a weapon of defense against error and evil; and when abused, it will turn to our destruction. Mark, then, the history of nations throughout the world.

But notwithstanding the transgression of this power to destroy the Indians at their first discovery, yet it does appear that the Indians had a wish to be friendly. When the Pilgrims came among them (Iyanough's men),[6] there appeared an old woman, breaking out in solemn lamentations, declaring one Captain Hunt had carried off three of her children, and they would never return here. The Pilgrims replied that they were bad and wicked men, but they were going to do better and would never injure them at all. And, to pay the poor mother, gave her a few brass trinkets, to atone for her three sons and appease her present feelings, a woman nearly one hundred years of age. O white woman! What would you think if some foreign nation, unknown to you, should come and carry away from you three lovely children, whom you had dandled on the knee, and at some future time you should behold them and break forth in sorrow, with your heart broken, and merely ask, "Sirs, where are my little ones?" and some one should reply: "It was passion, great passion." What would you think of them? Should you not think they were beings made more like rocks than men? Yet these same men came to these Indians for support and acknowledge themselves that no people could be used better than they were; that their treatment would do honor to any nation; that their provisions were in abundance; that they gave them venison and sold them many hogsheads of corn to fill their stores, besides beans. This was in the year 1622. Had it not been for this humane act of the Indians, every white man would have been swept from the New England colonies. In their sickness, too, the Indians were as tender to them as to their own children; and for all this, they were denounced as savages by those who had received all the acts of kindness they possibly could show them. After these social acts of the Indians toward those who were suffering, and those of their countrymen, who well knew the care their brethren had received by them — how were the Indians treated before that? Oh, hear! In the following manner, and their own words, we presume, they will not deny.

December (O.S.)[7] 1620, the Pilgrims landed at Plymouth, and without asking liberty from anyone they possessed themselves of a portion of the

---

[6]Iyanough was a Cape Cod sachem, among the first encountered by the Plymouth settlers. The incident Apess notes here concerning the old woman is also told in *Mourt's Relation,* a collection of journals kept by Plymouth settlers (see note 30, p. 37). The facts of the case agree substantially in both accounts. — EDS.

[7]Old Style. Dates were ten days earlier than they would be currently. — BOC

country, and built themselves houses, and then made a treaty, and commanded them to accede to it.[8] This, if now done, it would be called an insult, and every white man would be called to go out and act the part of a patriot, to defend their country's rights; and if every intruder were butchered, it would be sung upon every hilltop in the Union that victory and patriotism was the order of the day. And yet the Indians (though many were dissatisfied), without the shedding of blood or imprisoning anyone, bore it. And yet for their kindness and resignation toward the whites, they were called savages and made by God on purpose for them to destroy. We might say, God understood his work better than this. But to proceed: It appears that a treaty was made by the Pilgrims and the Indians, which treaty was kept during forty years; the young chiefs during this time was showing the Pilgrims how to live in their country and find support for their wives and little ones; and for all this, they were receiving the applause of being savages. The two gentleman chiefs were Squanto and Samoset, that were so good to the Pilgrims.

The next we present before you are things very appalling. We turn our attention to the dates 1623, January and March, when Mr. Weston's colony came very near starving to death; some of them were obliged to hire themselves to the Indians, to become their servants, in order that they might live.[9] Their principal work was to bring wood and water; but, not being contented with this, many of the whites sought to steal the Indians' corn; and because the Indians complained of it, and through their complaint, some one of their number being punished, as they say, to appease the savages. Now let us see who the greatest savages were; the person that stole the corn was a stout athletic man, and because of this they [colonists] wished to spare him and take an old man who was lame and sickly and that used to get his living by weaving, and because they thought he would not be of so much use to them, he was, although innocent of any crime, hung in his stead. O savage, where art thou, to weep over the Christian's crimes? Another act of humanity for Christians, as they call themselves, that one Captain Standish, gathering some fruit and provisions, goes forward with a black and hypocritical heart and pretends to prepare a feast for the Indians; and when they sit down to eat, they seize the Indians' knives hanging about their necks, and stab them to the heart. The white people call this stabbing, feasting the savages. We suppose it might well mean themselves, their conduct being more like savages than Christians. They took one Wittumumet, the chief's head, and put it upon a pole in their fort and, for aught we know, gave praise to their God for success in murdering a poor Indian; for we know it was their usual course to give praise to God for this kind of victory, believing it was God's will and command for them to do so. We wonder if these same Christians do not think it the command of God

---

[8]One version of this treaty appears in our Bradford excerpt (p. 31); another version, from *Mourt's Relation*, appears in the "Treaties, Laws, and Deeds" section (p. 136). — EDS.

[9]This is the colony of Wessagusset; compare Bradford's account (p. 19) of what happened there. — EDS.

that they should lie, steal, and get drunk, commit fornication and adultery. The one is as consistent as the other. What say you, judges, is it not so, and was it not according as they did? Indians think it is. . . .

It does not appear that Massasoit or his sons were respected because they were human beings but because they feared him; and we are led to believe that, if it had been in the power of the Pilgrims, they would have butchered them out and out, notwithstanding all the piety they professed.

Only look for a few moments at the abuses the son of Massasoit received. Alexander being sent for with armed men, and while he and his men were breaking their fast in the morning, they were taken immediately away, by order of the governor, without the least provocation but merely through suspicion. Alexander and his men saw them and might have prevented it but did not, saying the governor had no occasion to treat him in this manner; and the heartless wretch informed him that he would murder him upon the spot if he did not go with him, presenting a sword at his breast; and had it not been for one of his men he would have yielded himself up upon the spot. Alexander was a man of strong passion and of a firm mind; and this insulting treatment of him caused him to fall sick of a fever, so that he never recovered. Some of the Indians were suspicious that he was poisoned to death.[10] He died in the year 1662. "After him," says that eminent divine, Dr. Mather,[11] "there rose up one Philip, of cursed memory." Perhaps if the Doctor was present, he would find that the memory of Philip was as far before his, in the view of sound, judicious men, as the sun is before the stars at noonday. But we might suppose that men like Dr. Mather, so well versed in Scripture, would have known his work better than to have spoken evil of anyone, or have cursed any of God's works. He ought to have known that God did not make his red children for him to curse; but if he wanted them cursed, he could have done it himself. But, on the contrary, his suffering Master commanded him to love his enemies and to pray for his persecutors, and to do unto others as he would that men should do unto him. Now, we wonder if the sons of the Pilgrims would like to have us, poor Indians, come out and curse the Doctor, and all their sons, as we have been by many of them. And suppose that, in some future day, our children should repay all these wrongs, would it not be doing as we, poor Indians, have been done to? But we sincerely hope there is more humanity in us than that.

In the history of Massasoit we find that his own head men were not satisfied with the Pilgrims, that they looked upon them to be intruders and had a wish to expel those intruders out of their coast; and no wonder that from the least reports the Pilgrims were ready to take it up. A false report was made respecting one Tisquantum, that he was murdered by an Indian, one of Coubantant's men.[12] Upon this news, one Standish, a vile and mali-

---

[10]Compare the version of Alexander's death given in Easton (p. 93) — EDS.

[11]"Dr. Mather" is Increase Mather, whose account of King Philip's War (p. 50) can be compared with Apess's at many points. — EDS.

[12]"Tisquantum" is another name for Squanto, and "Coubantant" for Corbitant; compare Bradford's description of the incident (p. 19). — EDS.

cious fellow, took fourteen of his lewd Pilgrims with him, and at midnight, when a deathless silence reigned throughout the wilderness; not even a bird is heard to send forth her sweet songs to charm and comfort those children of the woods; but all had taken their rest, to commence anew on the rising of the glorious sun. But to their sad surprise there was no rest for them, but they were surrounded by ruffians and assassins; yes, assassins, what better name can be given them? At that late hour of the night, meeting a house in the wilderness, whose inmates were nothing but a few helpless females and children; soon a voice is heard — "Move not, upon the peril of your life." I appeal to this audience if there was any righteousness in their proceedings. Justice would say no. At the same time some of the females were so frightened that some of them undertook to make their escape, upon which they were fired upon. Now, it is doubtless the case that these females never saw a white man before, or ever heard a gun fired. It must have sounded to them like the rumbling of thunder, and terror must certainly have filled all their hearts. And can it be supposed that these innocent Indians could have looked upon them as good and trusty men? Do you look upon the midnight robber and assassin as being a Christian and trusty man? These Indians had not done one single wrong act to the whites but were as innocent of any crime as any beings in the world. And do you believe that Indians cannot feel and see, as well as white people? If you think so, you are mistaken. Their power of feeling and knowing is as quick as yours. Now this is to be borne, as the Pilgrims did as their Master told them to; but what color he was I leave it. But if the real sufferers say one word, they are denounced as being wild and savage beasts.

But let us look a little further. It appears that in 1630 a benevolent chief bid the Pilgrims welcome to his shores and, in June 28, 1630, ceded his land to them for the small sum of eighty dollars, now Ipswich, Rowley, and a part of Essex.[13] The following year, at the July term, 1631, these Pilgrims of the New World passed an act in court, that the friendly chief should not come into their houses short of paying fifty dollars or an equivalent, that is, ten beaver skins. Who could have supposed that the meek and lowly followers of virtue would have taken such methods to rob honest men of the woods? But, for this insult, the Pilgrims had well-nigh lost the lives and their all, had it not been prevented by Robbin, an Indian, who apprised them of their danger. And now let it be understood, notwithstanding all the bitter feelings the whites have generally shown toward Indians, yet they have been the only instrument in preserving their lives.

The history of New England writers say that our tribes were large and respectable. How, then, could it be otherwise, but their safety rested in the hands of friendly Indians? In 1647, the Pilgrims speak of large and respectable tribes. But let us trace them for a few moments. How have they been destroyed? Is it by fair means? No. How then? By hypocritical proceedings, by being duped and flattered; flattered by informing the Indians

[13]This is Masconomo, and the "Pilgrims" he is welcoming were actually the Puritans of the Massachusetts Bay colony, whose governor was John Winthrop. — BOC

that their God was a going to speak to them, and then place them before the cannon's mouth in a line, and then putting the match to it and kill thousands of them. We might suppose that meek Christians had better gods and weapons than cannon; weapons that were not carnal, but mighty through God, to the pulling down of strongholds. These are the weapons that modern Christians profess to have; and if the Pilgrims did not have them, they ought not to be honored as such. But let us again review their weapons to civilize the nations of this soil. What were they? Rum and powder and ball, together with all the diseases, such as the smallpox and every other disease imaginable, and in this way sweep off thousands and tens of thousands. And then it has been said that these men who were free from these things, that they could not live among civilized people. We wonder how a virtuous people could live in a sink of diseases, a people who had never been used to them.

And who is to account for those destructions upon innocent families and helpless children? It was said by some of the New England writers that living babes were found at the breast of their dead mothers. What an awful sight! And to think, too, that these diseases were carried among them on purpose to destroy them. Let the children of the Pilgrims blush, while the son of the forest drops a tear and groans over the fate of his murdered and departed fathers. He would say to the sons of the Pilgrims (as Job said about his birthday), let the day be dark, the 22nd day of December 1622;[14] let it be forgotten in your celebration, in your speeches, and by the burying of the rock that your fathers first put their foot upon. For be it remembered, although the Gospel is said to be glad tidings to all people, yet we poor Indians never have found those who brought it as messengers of mercy, but contrawise. We say, therefore, let every man of color wrap himself in mourning, for the 22nd of December and the 4th of July are days of mourning and not of joy. (I would here say, there is an error in my book; it speaks of the 25th of December, but it should be the 22nd. See *Indian Nullification*.) Let them rather fast and pray to the great Spirit, the Indian's God, who deals out mercy to his red children, and not destruction.

O Christians, can you answer for those beings that have been destroyed by your hostilities, and beings too that lie endeared to God as yourselves, his Son being their Savior as well as yours, and alike to all men? And will you presume to say that you are executing the judgments of God by so doing, or as many really are approving the works of their fathers to be genuine, as it is certain that every time they celebrate the day of the Pilgrims they do? Although in words they deny it, yet in the works they approve of the iniquities of their fathers. And as the seed of iniquity and prejudice was sown in that day, so it still remains; and there is a deep-rooted popular

---

[14]Apess takes December 22 as the date of the Pilgrims' landing at Plymouth. The year 1622 given here must be an accidental error, for Apess earlier gives the year correctly as 1620. He alludes to the tradition that a particular rock on the Plymouth shore was the spot where the Pilgrims first set foot (this tradition is now disputed). — EDS.

opinion in the hearts of many that Indians were made, etc., on purpose for destruction, to be driven out by white Christians, and they to take their places; and that God had decreed it from all eternity. If such theologians would only study the works of nature more, they would understand the purposes of good better than they do: that the favor of the Almighty was good and holy, and all his nobler works were made to adorn his image, by being his grateful servants and admiring each other as angels, and not, as they say, to drive and devour each other. And that you may know the spirit of the Pilgrims yet remains, we will present before you the words of a humble divine of the Far West. He says, "The desert becomes an Eden." Rev. Nahum Gold, of Union Grove, Putnam, writes under the date June 12, 1835, says he, "Let any man look at this settlement, and reflect what it was three years ago, and his heart can but kindle up while he exclaims, 'what God has wrought!' the savage has left the ground for civilized man; the rich prairie, from bringing forth all its strengths to be burned, is now receiving numerous enclosures, and brings a harvest of corn and wheat to feed the church. Yes, sir, this is now God's vineyard; he has gathered the vine, the choice vine, and brought it from a far country, and has planted it on a goodly soil. He expects fruit now. He gathered out the stones thereof, and drove the red Canaanites from trampling it down, or in any way hindering its increase."[15]

But what next should we hear from this very pious man? Why, my brethren, the poor missionaries want money to go and convert the poor heathen, as if God could not convert them where they were but must first drive them out. If God wants the red men converted, we should think that he could do it as well in one place as in another. But must I say, and shall I say it, that missionaries have injured us more than they have done us good, by degrading us as a people, in breaking up our governments and leaving us without any suffrages whatever, or a legal right among men? Oh, what cursed doctrine is this! It most certainly is not fit to civilize men with, much more to save their souls; and we poor Indians want no such missionaries around us. But I would suggest one thing, and that is, let the ministers and people use the colored people they have already around them like human beings, before they go to convert any more; and let them show it in their churches; and let them proclaim it upon the housetops; and I would say to the benevolent, withhold your hard earnings from them, unless they do do it, until they can stop laying their own wickedness to God, which is blasphemy. . . .

But having laid a mass of history and exposition before you, the purpose of which is to show that Philip and all the Indians generally felt indignantly toward whites, whereby they were more easily allied together by Philip, their king and emperor, we come to notice more particularly his history. As to His Majesty, King Philip, it was certain that his honor was put to the test, and it was certainly to be tried, even at the loss of his

[15]*New York Evangelist*, August 1. — WA

life and country. It is a matter of uncertainty about his age; but his birth-place was at Mount Hope, Rhode Island, where Massasoit, his father, lived till 1656, and died, as also his brother, Alexander, by the governor's ill-treating him (that is, Winthrop), which caused his death, as before mentioned, in 1662; after which, the kingdom fell into the hands of Philip, the greatest man that ever lived upon the American shores. Soon after his coming to the throne, it appears he began to be noticed, though, prior to this, it appears that he was not forward in the councils of war or peace. When he came into office it appears that he knew there was great responsibility resting upon himself and country, that it was likely to be ruined by those rude intruders around him, though he appears friendly and is willing to sell them lands for almost nothing, as we shall learn from dates of the Plymouth colony, which commence June 23, 1664. William Benton of Rhode Island, a merchant, buys Mattapoisett of Philip and wife, but no sum is set which he gave for it. To this deed, his counselors, and wife, and two of the Pilgrims were witnesses. In 1665 he sold New Bedford and Compton for forty dollars. In 1667 he sells to Constant Southworth and others all the meadowlands from Dartmouth to Mattapoisett, for which he received sixty dollars. The same year he sells to Thomas Willet a tract of land two miles in length and perhaps the same in width, for which he received forty dollars. In 1668 he sold a tract of some square miles, now called Swansea. The next year he sells five hundred acres in Swansea, for which he received eighty dollars. His counselors and interpreters, with the Pilgrims, were witnesses to these deeds.

Osamequan,[16] for valuable considerations, in the year 1641 sold to John Brown and Edward Winslow a tract of land eight miles square, situated on both sides of Palmer's River. Philip, in 1668, was required to sign a quit claim of the same, which we understand he did in the presence of his counselors. In the same year Philip laid claim to a portion of land called New Meadows, alleging that it was not intended to be conveyed in a former deed, for which Mr. Brown paid him forty-four dollars, in goods; so it was settled without difficulty. Also, in 1669, for forty dollars, he sold to one John Cook a whole island called Nokatay, near Dartmouth. The same year Philip sells a tract of land in Middleborough for fifty-two dollars. In 1671 he sold to Hugh Cole a large tract of land lying near Swansea, for sixteen dollars. In 1672 he sold sixteen square miles to William Breton and others, of Taunton, for which he and his chief received five hundred and seventy-two dollars. This contract, signed by himself and chiefs, ends the sales of lands with Philip, for all which he received nine hundred and seventy-four dollars, as far as we can learn by the records.

Here Philip meets with a most bitter insult, in 1673, from one Peter Talmon of Rhode Island, who complained to the Plymouth court against Philip, of Mount Hope, predecessor, heir, and administrator of his brother

---

[16]"Osamequan," or Osamequin, was the name of Philip's father, who is usually identified instead by his title of Massasoit, meaning "supreme sachem." — EDS.

Alexander, deceased, in an action on the case, to the damage of three thousand and two hundred dollars, for which the court gave verdict in favor of Talmon, the young Pilgrim; for which Philip had to make good to the said Talmon a large tract of land at Sapamet and other places adjacent. And for the want thereof, that is, more land that was not taken up, the complainant is greatly damnified. This is the language in the Pilgrims' court. Now let us review this a little. The man who bought this land made the contract, as he says, with Alexander, ten or twelve years before; then why did he not bring forward his contract before the court? It is easy to understand why he did not. Their object was to cheat, or get the whole back again in this way. Only look at the sum demanded, and it is enough to satisfy the critical observer. This course of proceedings caused the chief and his people to entertain strong jealousies of the whites.

In the year 1668 Philip made a complaint against one Weston, who had wronged one of his men of a gun and some swine; and we have no account that he got any justice for his injured brethren. And, indeed, it would be a strange thing for poor unfortunate Indians to find justice in those courts of the pretended pious in those days, or even since; and for a proof of my assertion I will refer the reader or hearer to the records of legislatures and courts throughout New England, and also to my book, *Indian Nullification*.

We would remark still further: Who stood up in those days, and since, to plead Indian rights? Was it the friend of the Indian? No, it was his enemies who rose — his enemies, to judge and pass sentence. And we know that such kind of characters as the Pilgrims were, in regard to the Indians' rights, who, as they say, had none, must certainly always give verdict against them, as, generally speaking, they always have. Prior to this insult, it appears that Philip had met with great difficulty with the Pilgrims, that they appeared to be suspicious of him in 1671; and the Pilgrims sent for him, but he did not appear to move as though he cared much for their messenger, which caused them to be still more suspicious. What grounds the Pilgrims had is not ascertained, unless it is attributed to a guilty conscience for wrongs done to Indians. It appears that Philip, when he got ready, goes near to them and sends messengers to Taunton, to invite the Pilgrims to come and treat with him; but the governor, being either too proud or afraid, sends messengers to him to come to their residence at Taunton, to which he complied. Among these messengers was the Honorable Roger Williams, a Christian and a patriot and a friend to the Indians, for which we rejoice.[17] Philip, not liking to trust the Pilgrims, left some of the whites in his stead to warrant his safe return. When Philip and his men had come near the place, some of the Plymouth people were ready to attack him; this rashness was, however, prevented by the commissioner of Massachusetts, who met there with the governor to treat with Philip; and it was agreed

---

[17]Roger Williams was the founder of the colony of Rhode Island. Later, just before the war started, Rhode Islanders met with Philip to recommend arbitration, as recorded in Easton (p. 93). One Native American grievance that Easton reports is the colonists' holding of Native American weapons for ransom, which Apess mentions here. — EDS.

upon to meet in the meetinghouse. Philip's complaint was that the Pilgrims had injured the planting grounds of his people. The Pilgrims, acting as umpires, say the charges against them were not sustained; and because it was not, to their satisfaction, the whites wanted that Philip should order all his men to bring in his arms and ammunition; and the court was to dispose of them as they pleased. The next thing was that Philip must pay the cost of the treaty, which was four hundred dollars. The pious Dr. Mather says that Philip was appointed to pay a sum of money to defray the charges that his insolent clamors had put the colony to. We wonder if the Pilgrims were as ready to pay the Indians for the trouble they put them to. If they were, it was with the instruments of death. It appears that Philip did not wish to make war with them but compromised with them; and in order to appease the Pilgrims he actually did order his men, whom he could not trust, to deliver them up; but his own men withheld, with the exception of a very few.[18] . . .

But it appears that the Pilgrims could not be contented with what they had done, but they must send an Indian, and a traitor, to preach to Philip and his men, in order to convert him and his people to Christianity. The preacher's name was Sassamon.[19] I would appeal to this audience: Is it not certain that the Plymouth people strove to pick a quarrel with Philip and his men? What could have been more insulting than to send a man to them who was false, and looked upon as such? For it is most certain that a traitor was, above all others, the more to be detested than any other. And not only so; it was the laws of the Indians that such a man must die, that he had forfeited his life; and when he made his appearance among them, Philip would have killed him upon the spot if his council had not persuaded him not to. But it appears that in March 1674 one of Philip's men killed him and placed him beneath the ice in a certain pond near Plymouth, doubtless by the order of Philip. After this, search was made for him, and they found there a certain Indian, by the name of Patuckson; Tobias, also, his son, were apprehended and tried. Tobias was one of Philip's counselors, as it appears from the records that the trial did not end here, that it was put over, and that two of the Indians entered into bonds for $400, for the appearance of Tobias at the June term, for which a mortgage of land was taken to that amount for his safe return. June having arrived, three instead of one are arraigned. There was no one but Tobias suspected at the previous court. Now two others are arraigned, tried, condemned, and executed (making three in all) in June the 8th, 1675, by hanging and shooting. It does not appear that any more than one was guilty, and it was said that he was known to acknowledge it; but the other two persisted in their innocence to the last.

This murder of the preacher brought on the war a year sooner than it was anticipated by Philip. But this so exasperated King Philip that from that day he studied to be revenged of the Pilgrims, judging that his white

[18]Compare Easton's account (p. 93). — Eds.
[19]Compare accounts of Sassamon in Mather (p. 50) and Easton (p. 93). — Eds.

intruders had nothing to do in punishing his people for any crime and that it was in violation of treaties of ancient date. But when we look at this, how bold and how daring it was to Philip, as though they would bid defiance to him, and all his authority; we do not wonder at his exasperation. When the governor finds that His Majesty was displeased, he then sends messengers to him and wishes to know why he would make war upon him (as if he had done all right), and wished to enter into a new treaty with him. The king answered them thus: "Your governor is but a subject of King Charles of England; I shall not treat with a subject; I shall treat of peace only with a king, my brother; when he comes, I am ready."

This answer of Philip's to the messengers is worthy of note throughout the world. And never could a prince answer with more dignity in regard to his official authority than he did — disdaining the idea of placing himself upon a par of the minor subjects of a king; letting them know, at the same time, that he felt his independence more than they thought he did. And indeed it was time for him to wake up, for now the subjects of King Charles had taken one of his counselors and killed him, and he could no longer trust them. Until the execution of these three Indians, supposed to be the murderers of Sassamon, no hostility was committed by Philip or his warriors. About the time of their trial, he was said to be marching his men up and down the country in arms; but when it was known, he could no longer restrain his young men, who, upon the 24th of June [1675], provoked the people of Swansea by killing their cattle and other injuries, which was a signal to commence the war, and what they had desired, as a superstitious notion prevailed among the Indians that whoever fired the first gun of either party would be conquered, doubtless a notion they had received from the Pilgrims. It was upon a fast day, too, when the first gun was fired; and as the people were returning from church, they were fired upon by the Indians, when several of them were killed. It is not supposed that Philip directed this attack but was opposed to it.[20] Though it is not doubted that he meant to be revenged upon his enemies; for during some time he had been cementing his countrymen together, as it appears that he had sent to all the disaffected tribes, who also had watched the movements of the comers from the New World[21] and were as dissatisfied as Philip himself was with their proceedings.

> Now around the council fires they met,
>   The young nobles for to greet;
> Their tales of woe and sorrows to relate,
>   About the Pilgrims, their wretched foes.

[20]Compare accounts of the war's beginning in Mather (p. 50) and Easton (p. 93) — EDS.

[21]His "comers from the New World" may only be a slip of the pen, referring as he is to the Europeans, who are conventionally, of course, from the "Old" World, having "discovered" the "New." This is, however, so like Apess's wit and his delight in inverting the conventions of language through which Europeans validated their presence and their dominance in the Americas that it may be entirely deliberate — for the Europeans were of course from a new world from the perspective of Native Americans. — BOC

And while their fires were blazing high,
    Their king and Emperor to greet;
His voice like lightning fires their hearts,
    To stand the test or die.

See those Pilgrims from the world unknown,
    No love for Indians do know:
Although our fathers fed them well
    With venison rich, of precious kinds.

No gratitude to Indians now is shown,
    From people saved by them alone;
All gratitude that poor Indian do know,
    Is, we are robbed of all our rights.

At this council it appears that Philip made the following speech to his chiefs, counselors, and warriors:

Brothers, you see this vast country before us, which the Great Spirit gave to our fathers and us; you see the buffalo and deer that now are our support. Brothers, you see these little ones, our wives and children, who are looking to us for food and raiment; and you now see the foe before you, that they have grown insolent and bold; that all our ancient customs are disregarded; the treaties made by our fathers and us are broken, and all of us insulted; our council fires disregarded, and all the ancient customs of our fathers; our brothers murdered before our eyes, and their spirits cry to us for revenge. Brothers, these people from the unknown world will cut down our groves, spoil our hunting and planting grounds, and drive us and our children from the graves of our fathers, and our council fires, and enslave our women and children.

This famous speech of Philip was calculated to arouse them to arms, to do the best they could in protecting and defending their rights. The blow had now been struck, the die was cast, and nothing but blood and carnage was before them. And we find Philip as active as the wind, as dexterous as a giant, firm as the pillows of heaven, and fierce as a lion, a powerful foe to contend with indeed, and as swift as an eagle, gathering together his forces to prepare them for the battle. And as it would swell our address too full to mention all the tribes in Philip's train of warriors, suffice it to say that from six to seven were with him at different times. When he begins the war, he goes forward and musters about five hundred of his men and arms them complete, and about nine hundred of the other, making in all about fourteen hundred warriors when he commenced. It must be recollected that this war was legally declared by Philip, so that the colonies had a fair warning. It was no savage war of surprise, as some suppose, but one sorely provoked by the Pilgrims themselves. But when Philip and his men fought as they were accustomed to do and according to their mode of war, it was more than what could be expected. But we hear no particular acts of cruelty committed by Philip during the siege. But we find more manly nobility in him than we do in all the head Pilgrims put together, as we shall see during this quarrel between them. Philip's young men were eager to do exploits and to lead captive their haughty lords. It does appear that every Indian heart had been lighted up at the council fires, at Philip's speech, and that the forest was literally alive with this injured race. And now town after town fell before them. The Pilgrims with their forces were marching ever in one direction, while Philip and his forces were marching in another, burning all before them, until Middleborough, Taunton, and Dartmouth were laid in ruins and forsaken by its inhabitants.

At the great fight at Pocasset, Philip commanded in person, where he also was discovered with his host in a dismal swamp. He had retired here with his army to secure a safe retreat from the Pilgrims, who were in close pursuit of him, and their numbers were so powerful they thought the fate of Philip was sealed. They surrounded the swamp, in hopes to destroy him and his army. At the edge of the swamp Philip had secreted a few of his men to draw them into ambush, upon which the Pilgrims showed fight, Philip's men retreating and the whites pursuing them till they were surrounded by Philip and nearly all cut off. This was a sorry time to them; the Pilgrims, however, reinforced but ordered a retreat, supposing it impossible for Philip to escape; and knowing his forces to be great, it was conjectured by some to build a fort to starve him out, as he had lost but few men in the fight. The situation of Philip was rather peculiar, as there was but one outlet to the swamp and a river before him nearly seven miles to descend. The Pilgrims placed a guard around the swamp for thirteen days, which gave Philip and his men time to prepare canoes to make good his retreat, in which he did, to the Connecticut River, and in his retreat lost but fourteen men. We may look upon this move of Philip's to be equal, if not superior, to that of Washington crossing the Delaware. For while Washington was assisted by all the knowledge that art and science could give, together with all the instruments of defense and edged tools to prepare rafts and the like helps for safety across the river, Philip was naked as to any of these things, possessing only what nature, his mother, had bestowed upon him; and yet makes his escape with equal praise. But he would not even [have] lost a man had it not been for Indians who were hired to fight against Indians, with promise of their enjoying equal rights with their white brethren; but not one of those promises have as yet been fulfilled by the Pilgrims or their children, though they must acknowledge that without the aid of Indians and their guides they must inevitably been swept off. It was only, then, by deception that the Pilgrims gained the country, as their word has never been fulfilled in regard to Indian rights.

Philip having now taken possession of the back settlements of Massachusetts, one town after another was swept off. . . .

The Pilgrims determined to break down Philip's power, if possible, with the Narragansetts: Thus they raised an army of fifteen hundred strong, to go against them and destroy them if possible.[22] In this, Massachusetts, Plymouth, and Connecticut all join in severally, to crush Philip. Accordingly,

---

[22]Compare Mather (p. 50) and Easton (p. 93) on the assault on the Narragansett town. — EDS.

in December, in 1675, the Pilgrims set forward to destroy them. Preceding their march, Philip had made all arrangements for the winter and had fortified himself beyond what was common for his countrymen to do, upon a small island near South Kingston, R.I. Here he intended to pass the winter with his warriors and their wives and children. About five hundred Indian houses was erected of a superior kind, in which was deposited all their stores, tubs of corn, and other things, piled up to a great height, which rendered it bulletproof. It was supposed that three thousand persons had taken up their residence in it. (I would remark that Indians took better care of themselves in those days than they have been able to since.) Accordingly, on the 19th day of December, after the Pilgrims had been out in the extreme cold for nearly one month, lodging in tents, and their provision being short, and the air full of snow, they had no other alternative than to attack Philip in the fort. Treachery, however, hastened his ruin; one of his men, by hope of reward from the deceptive Pilgrims, betrayed his country into their hands. The traitor's name was Peter. No white man was acquainted with the way, and it would have been almost impossible for them to have found it, much less to have captured it. There was but one point where it could have been entered or assailed with any success, and this was fortified much like a blockhouse, directly in front of the entrance, and also flankers to cover a crossfire — besides high palisades, an immense hedge of fallen trees of nearly a rod in thickness. Thus surrounded by trees and water, there was but one place that the Pilgrims could pass. Nevertheless, they made the attempt. Philip now had directed his men to fire, and every platoon of the Indians swept every white man from the path one after another, until six captains, with a great many of the men, had fallen. In the meantime, one Captain Moseley with some of his men had somehow or other gotten into the fort in another way and surprised them, by which the Pilgrims were enabled to capture the fort, at the same time setting fire to it and hewing down men, women, and children indiscriminately. Philip, however, was enabled to escape with many of his warriors. It is said at this battle eighty whites were killed and one hundred and fifty wounded, many of whom died of their wounds afterward, not being able to dress them till they had marched eighteen miles, also leaving many of their dead in the fort. It is said that seven hundred of the Narragansetts perished, the greater part of them being women and children.

It appears that God did not prosper them much, after all. It is believed that the sufferings of the Pilgrims were without a parallel in history; and it is supposed that the horrors and burning elements of Moscow will bear but a faint resemblance of that scene.[23] The thousands and ten thousands assembled there with their well-disciplined forces bear but little comparison to that of modern Europe, when the inhabitants, science, manners,

---

[23]Apess is probably referring to Napoleon Bonaparte's (1769–1821) destruction of Moscow by fire and his subsequent retreat through the deadly Russian winter of 1812. Like the French troops under Napoleon, the English, on withdrawing from this Narragansett fight, suffered terribly from the winter weather. Apess finds it barbaric that the English would be willing to risk their men this way just for the sake of killing Indians. — EDS.

and customs are taken into consideration. We might as well admit the above fact and say the like was never known among any heathen nation in the world; for none but those worse than heathens would have suffered so much, for the sake of being revenged upon those of their enemies. Philip had repaired to his quarters to take care of his people and not to have them exposed. We should not have wondered quite so much if Philip had gone forward and acted thus. But when a people calling themselves Christians conduct in this manner, we think they are censurable, and no pity at all ought to be had for them.

It appears that one of the whites had married one of Philip's countrymen; and they, the Pilgrims, said he was a traitor, and therefore they said he must die. So they quartered him; and as history informs us, they said, he being a heathen, but a few tears were shed at his funeral. Here, then, because a man would not turn and fight against his own wife and family, or leave them, he was condemned as a heathen. We presume that no honest men will commend those ancient fathers for such absurd conduct. Soon after this, Philip and his men left that part of the country and retired farther back, near the Mohawks, where, in July 1676, some of his men were slain by the Mohawks. Notwithstanding this, he strove to get them to join him; and here it is said that Philip did not do that which was right, that he killed some of the Mohawks and laid it to the whites in order that he might get them to join him. If so, we cannot consistently believe he did right. But he was so exasperated that nothing but revenge would satisfy him. All this act was no worse than our political men do in our days, of their strife to wrong each other, who profess to be enlightened; and all for the sake of carrying their points. Heathenlike, either by the sword, calumny, or deception of every kind; and the late duels among the [so-] called high men of honor is sufficient to warrant my statements. But while we pursue our history in regard to Philip, we find that he made many successful attempts against the Pilgrims, in surprising and driving them from their posts, during the year 1676, in February and through till August, in which time many of the Christian Indians joined him. It is thought by many that all would have joined him, if they had been left to their choice, as it appears they did not like their white brethren very well. It appears that Philip treated his prisoners with a great deal more Christian-like spirit than the Pilgrims did; even Mrs. Rowlandson, although speaking with bitterness sometimes of the Indians, yet in her journal she speaks not a word against him. Philip even hires her to work for him, and pays her for her work, and then invites her to dine with him and to smoke with him. And we have many testimonies that he was kind to his prisoners; and when the English wanted to redeem Philip's prisoners, they had the privilege.[24]

Now, did Governor Winthrop or any of those ancient divines use any of his men so? No. Was it known that they received any of their female captives into their houses and fed them? No, it cannot be found upon history.

---

[24]We have excerpted passages from Mary Rowlandson's narrative in which these incidents are described (p. 67). — EDS.

Were not the females completely safe, and none of them were violated, as they acknowledge themselves? But was it so when the Indian women fell into the hands of the Pilgrims? No. Did the Indians get a chance to redeem their prisoners? No. But when they were taken they were either compelled to turn traitors and join their enemies or be butchered upon the spot. And this is the dishonest method that the famous Captain Church used in doing his great exploits; and in no other way could he ever gained one battle.[25] So, after all, Church only owes his exploits to the honesty of the Indians, who told the truth, and to his own deceptive heart in duping them. Here it is to be understood that the whites have always imposed upon the credulity of the Indians. It is with shame, I acknowledge, that I have to notice so much corruption of a people calling themselves Christians. If they were like my people, professing no purity at all, then their crimes would not appear to have such magnitude. But while they appear to be by profession more virtuous, their crimes still blacken. It makes them truly to appear to be like mountains filled with smoke, and thick darkness covering them all around.

But we have another dark and corrupt deed for the sons of Pilgrims to look at, and that is the fight and capture of Philip's son and wife and many of his warriors, in which Philip lost about 130 men killed and wounded; this was in August 1676. But the most horrid act was in taking Philip's son, about ten years of age, and selling him to be a slave away from his father and mother. While I am writing, I can hardly restrain my feelings, to think a people calling themselves Christians should conduct so scandalous, so outrageous, making themselves appear so despicable in the eyes of the Indians; and even now, in this audience, I doubt but there is men honorable enough to despise the conduct of those pretended Christians. And surely none but such as believe they did right will ever go and undertake to celebrate that day of their landing, the 22nd of December. Only look at it; then stop and pause: My fathers came here for liberty themselves, and then they must go and chain that mind, that image they professed to serve, not content to rob and cheat the poor ignorant Indians but must take one of the king's sons and make a slave of him. Gentlemen and ladies, I blush at these tales, if you do not, especially when they professed to be a free and humane people. Yes, they did; they took a part of my tribe and sold them to the Spaniards in Bermuda, and many others,[26] and then on the Sab-

[25]Benjamin Church was the most successful of the leaders of the forces of the United Colonies [Massachusetts Bay, Connecticut, Plymouth, New Haven — EDS.] against Philip. His sympathy with the Indians, his close knowledge of them, and his careful wooing of groups who were either unfriendly to Philip or otherwise uncertain about the war enabled him, as Apess rightly argues, to succeed where most of the other English commanders failed — in part because of their disdain for the Indians and a refusal to consider their ways. — BOC

[26]At the end of the Pequot War of 1637 the English sold a number of Pequots, men, women, and children, into slavery in Bermuda as part of their determination to wipe out the culture so they would never again be at risk of being challenged by it. The Pequots on Bermuda, though long out of touch with their New England brethren, have maintained a somewhat distinctive cultural identity to the present. — BOC This is the only mention in the *Eulogy* of the history of Apess's own tribe, the Pequots. — EDS.

bath day, these people would gather themselves together and say that God is no respecter of persons; while the divines would pour forth, "He says that he loves God and hates his brother is a liar, and the truth is not in him" — and at the same time they [are] hating and selling their fellow men in bondage. And there is no manner of doubt but that all my country-men would have been enslaved if they had tamely submitted. But no sooner would they butcher every white man that come in their way, and even put an end to their own wives and children, and that was all that pre-vented them from being slaves; yes, *all.* It was not the good will of those holy Pilgrims that prevented. No. But I would speak, and I could wish it might be like the voice of thunder, that it might be heard afar off, even to the ends of the earth. He that will advocate slavery is worse than a beast, is a being devoid of shame, and has gathered around him the most corrupt and debasing principles in the world; and I care not whether he be a min-ister or member of any church in the world — no, not excepting the head men of the nation. And he that will not set his face against its corrupt prin-ciples is a coward and not worthy of being numbered among men and Christians — and conduct, too, that libels the laws of the country, and the word of God, that men profess to believe in.

After Philip had his wife and son taken, sorrow filled his heart, but notwithstanding, as determined as ever to be revenged, though [he] was pursued by the duped Indians and Church into a swamp, one of the men proposing to Philip that he had better make peace with the enemy, upon which he slew him upon the spot. And the Pilgrims, being also repulsed by Philip, were forced to retreat with the loss of one man in particular, whose name was Thomas Lucas, of Plymouth. We rather suspect that he was some related to Lucas and Hedge, who made their famous speeches against the poor Marshpees, in 1834, in the Legislature, in Boston, against freeing them from slavery that their fathers, the Pilgrims, had made of them for years.[27]

Philip's forces had now become very small, so many having been duped away by the whites and killed that it was now easy surrounding him. There-fore, upon the 12th of August, Captain Church surrounded the swamp where Philip and his men had encamped, early in the morning, before they had risen, doubtless led on by an Indian who was either compelled or hired to turn traitor. Church had now placed his guard so that it was im-possible for Philip to escape without being shot. It is doubtful, however,

[27]Apess alludes here to the plight of the "Marshpee," or Mashpee, band of Christian Na-tive Americans, whose civil disobedience action he led. Part of the terms of their survival as a community required the Mashpees to accept and support a European American minister who was appointed for them. The man in this office in the 1830s neglected their spiritual needs and exploited them. Apess, a visiting preacher in Mashpee, led the group in a lock-out of the offending minister, inspiring them to action by reading aloud portions of the *Eulogy.* Although Apess spent some time in jail for his actions, the ultimate result was to force the Mashpee Overseers to remove the minister and to grant the Mashpees much more control over their own affairs. Apess's book *Indian Nullification of the Unconstitutional Laws of Massachu-setts* (1835), documents this event. — EDS.

whether they would have taken him if he had not been surprised. Suffice it to say, however, this was the case. A sorrowful morning to the poor Indians, to lose such a valuable man. When coming out of the swamp, he was fired upon by an Indian and killed dead upon the spot.

I rejoice that it was even so, that the Pilgrims did not have the pleasure of tormenting him. The white man's gun, missing fire, lost the honor of killing the truly great man, Philip. The place where Philip fell was very muddy. Upon this news, the Pilgrims gave three cheers; then Church ordering his body to be pulled out of the mud, while one of those tender-hearted Christians exclaims, "What a dirty creature he looks like." And we have also Church's speech upon that subject, as follows: "For as much as he has caused many a Pilgrim to lie above ground unburied, to rot, not one of his bones shall be buried." With him fell five of his best and most trusty men, one the son of a chief, who fired the first gun in the war.

Captain Church now orders him to be cut up. Accordingly, he was quartered and hung up upon four trees, his head and one hand given to the Indian who shot him, to carry about to show, at which sight it so overjoyed the Pilgrims that they would give him money for it, and in this way obtained a considerable sum. After which his head was sent to Plymouth and exposed upon a gibbet for twenty years; and his hand to Boston, where it was exhibited in savage triumph; and his mangled body denied a resting place in the tomb,[28] and thus adds the poet,

> Cold with the beast he slew, he sleeps,
> O'er him no filial spirit weeps.

I think that, as a matter of honor, that I can rejoice that no such evil conduct is recorded of the Indians, that they never hung up any of the white warriors who were head men. And we add the famous speech of Dr. Increase Mather; he says, during the bloody contest the pious fathers wrestled hard and long with their God, in prayer, that he would prosper their arms and deliver their enemies into their hands. And when upon stated days of prayer the Indians got the advantage, it was considered as a rebuke of divine providence (we suppose the Indian prayed best then), which stimulated them to more ardor. And on the contrary, when they prevailed they considered it as an immediate interposition in their favor. The Doctor closes thus: "Nor could they, the Pilgrims, cease crying to the Lord against Philip, until they had prayed the bullet through his heart." And in speaking of the slaughter of Philip's people at Narragansett, he says, "We have heard of two and twenty Indian captains slain, all of them, and brought down to hell in one day." Again, in speaking of a chief who had sneered at the Pilgrims' religion, and who had withal added a most hideous blasphemy, "Immediately upon which a bullet took him in the head, and dashed out his brains, sending his cursed soul in a moment among the devils and blasphemers in hell forever." It is true that this lan-

---

[28]Compare Apess's account of Philip's death with Benjamin Church's (p. 132). — EDS.

guage is sickening and is as true as the sun is in the heavens that such language was made use of, and it was a common thing for all the Pilgrims to curse the Indians, according to the order of their priests. It is also wonderful how they prayed, that they should pray the bullet through the Indians' heart and their souls down into hell. If I had any faith in such prayers, I should begin to think that soon we should all be gone. However, if this is the way they pray, that is, bullets through people's hearts, I hope they will not pray for me; I should rather be excused. But to say the least, there is no excuse for their ignorance how to treat their enemies and pray for them. If the Doctor and his people had only turned to the 23rd of Luke, and the 34th verse,[29] and heard the words of their Master, whom they pretended to follow, they would see that their course did utterly condemn them; or the 7th of Acts, and the 60th verse, and heard the language of the pious Stephen, we think it vastly different from the Pilgrims; he prayed: "Lord, lay not this sin to their charge." No curses were heard from these pious martyrs.

I do not hesitate to say that through the prayers, preaching, and examples of those pretended pious has been the foundation of all the slavery and degradation in the American colonies toward colored people. Experience has taught me that this has been a most sorry and wretched doctrine to us poor ignorant Indians. I will mention two or three things to amuse you a little; that is, as I was passing through Connecticut, about fifteen years ago, where they are so pious that they kill the cats for killing rats, and whip the beer barrels for working upon the Sabbath, that in a severe cold night, when the face of the earth was one glare of ice, dark and stormy, I called at a man's house to know if I could not stay with him, it being about nine miles to the house where I then lived, and knowing him to be a rich man, and withal very pious, knowing if he had a mind he could do it comfortably, and withal we were both members of one church. My reception, however, was almost as cold as the weather, only he did not turn me out-of-doors; if he had, I know not but I should have frozen to death. My situation was a little better than being out, for he allowed a little wood but no bed, because I was an Indian. Another Christian asked me to dine with him and put my dinner behind the door; I thought this a queer compliment indeed.

About two years ago, I called at an inn in Lexington; and a gentleman present, not spying me to be an Indian, began to say they ought to be exterminated. I took it up in our defense, though not boisterous but coolly; and when we came to retire, finding that I was an Indian, he was unwilling to sleep opposite my room for fear of being murdered before morning. We presume his conscience pled guilty. These things I mention to show that the doctrines of the Pilgrims has grown up with the people.

But not to forget Philip and his lady, and his prophecy: It is (that is, 1671), when Philip went to Boston, his clothing was worth nearly one

---

[29]"Then Jesus said, 'Father, forgive them; for they know not what they do.'" — BOC

hundred dollars. It is said by some of the writers in those days that their money[30] being so curiously wrought, that neither Jew nor devil could counterfeit it — a high encomium upon Indian arts; and with it they used to adorn their sagamores in a curious manner. It was said that Philip's wife was neatly attired in the Indian style; some of the white females used to call her a proud woman because she would not bow down to them and was so particular in adorning herself. Perhaps, while these ladies were so careful to review the queen, they had forgot that she was truly one of the greatest women there was among them, although not quite so white. But while we censure others for their faults in spending so much time to view their fair and handsome features, whether colored or white, we would remind all the fair sex it is what they all love, that is, jewels and feathers. It was what the Indian women used to love, and still love — and customs, we presume, that the whites brought from their original savage fathers, one thousand years ago. Every white that knows their own history knows there was not a whit of difference between them and the Indians of their days.

But who was Philip, that made all this display in the world, that put an enlightened nation to flight and won so many battles? It was a son of nature, with nature's talents alone. And who did he have to contend with? With all the combined arts of cultivated talents of the Old and New World. It was like putting one talent against a thousand. And yet Philip, with that, accomplished more than all of them. Yea, he outdid the well-disciplined forces of Greece, under the command of Philip, the Grecian emperor; for he never was enabled to lay such plans of allying the tribes of the earth together, as Philip of Mount Hope did. And even Napoleon patterned after him, in collecting his forces and surprising the enemy. Washington, too, pursued many of his plans in attacking the enemy and thereby enabled him to defeat his antagonists and conquer them. What, then, shall we say? Shall we not do right to say that Philip, with his one talent, outstrips them all with their ten thousand? No warrior, of any age, was ever known to pursue such plans as Philip did. And it is well known that Church and nobody else could have conquered, if his people had not used treachery, which was owing to their ignorance; and after all, it is a fact that it was not the Pilgrims that conquered him; it was Indians. And as to his benevolence, it was very great; no one in history can accuse Philip of being cruel to his conquered foes; that he used them with more hospitality than they, the Pilgrims, did cannot be denied; and that he had knowledge and forethought cannot be denied. As Mr. Gookin,[31] in speaking of Philip, says, that he was a man of good understanding and knowledge in the best things. Mr. Gookin, it appears, was a benevolent man and a friend to Indians.

How deep, then, was the thought of Philip, when he could look from Maine to Georgia, and from the ocean to the lakes, and view with one look all his brethren withering before the more enlightened to come; and how true his prophecy, that the white people would not only cut down their

---

[30]Their "money" is wampum, also used for personal adornment. — EDS.
[31]Daniel Gookin, Waban's interlocutor (p. 103). — EDS.

groves but would enslave them. Had the inspiration of Isaiah been there, he could not have been more correct. Our groves and hunting grounds are gone, our dead are dug up, our council fires are put out, and a foundation was laid in the first Legislature to enslave our people, by taking from them all rights, which has been strictly adhered to ever since. Look at the disgraceful laws, disfranchising us as citizens. Look at the treaties made by Congress, all broken. Look at the deep-rooted plans laid, when a territory becomes a state, that after so many years the laws shall be extended over the Indians that live within their boundaries. Yea, every charter that has been given was given with the view of driving the Indians out of the states, or dooming them to become chained under desperate laws, that would make them drag out a miserable life as one chained to the galley; and this is the course that has been pursued for nearly two hundred years. A fire, a canker, created by the Pilgrims from across the Atlantic, to burn and destroy my poor unfortunate brethren, and it cannot be denied. What, then, shall we do? Shall we cease crying and say it is all wrong, or shall we bury the hatchet and those unjust laws and Plymouth Rock together and become friends? And will the sons of the Pilgrims aid in putting out the fire and destroying the canker that will ruin all that their fathers left behind them to destroy? (By this we see how true Philip spoke.) If so, we hope we shall not hear it said from ministers and church members that we are so good no other people can live with us, as you know it is a common thing for them to say Indians cannot live among Christian people; no, even the president of the United States tells the Indians they cannot live among civilized people, and we want your lands and must have them and will have them. As if he had said to them, "We want your land for our use to speculate upon; it aids us in paying off our national debt and supporting us in Congress to drive you off.

"You see, my red children, that our fathers carried on this scheme of getting your lands for our use, and we have now become rich and powerful; and we have a right to do with you just as we please; we claim to be your fathers. And we think we shall do you a great favor, my dear sons and daughters, to drive you out, to get you away out of the reach of our civilized people, who are cheating you, for we have no law to reach them, we cannot protect you although you be our children. So it is no use, you need not cry, you must go, even if the lions devour you, for we promised the land you have to somebody else long ago, perhaps twenty or thirty years; and we did it without your consent, it is true. But this has been the way our fathers first brought us up, and it is hard to depart from it; therefore, you shall have no protection from us." Now, while we sum up this subject, does it not appear that the cause of all wars from beginning to end was and is for the want of good usage? That the whites have always been the aggressors, and the wars, cruelties, and bloodshed is a job of their own seeking, and not the Indians? Did you ever know of Indians hurting those who was kind to them? No. We have a thousand witnesses to the contrary. Yea, every male and female declare it to be the fact. We often hear of the wars breaking out upon the frontiers, and it is because the same spirit reigns there that reigned here in New England; and wherever there are any Indians, that spirit still reigns; and at present, there is no law to stop it. What, then, is to be done? Let every friend of the Indians now seize the mantle of Liberty and throw it over those burning elements that has spread with such fearful rapidity, and at once extinguish them forever. It is true that now and then a feeble voice has been raised in our favor. Yes, we might speak of distinguished men, but they fall so far short in the minority that it is heard but at a small distance. We want trumpets that sound like thunder, and men to act as though they were going at war with those corrupt and degrading principles that robs one of all rights, merely because he is ignorant and of a little different color. Let us have principles that will give everyone his due; and then shall wars cease, and the weary find rest. Give the Indian his rights, and you may be assured war will cease.

But by this time you have been enabled to see that Philip's prophecy has come to pass; therefore, as a man of natural abilities, I shall pronounce him the greatest man that was ever in America; and so it will stand, until he is proved to the contrary, to the everlasting disgrace of the Pilgrims' fathers.

We will now give you his language in the Lord's Prayer.

Noo-chun kes-uk-qut-tiam-at-am unch koo-we-su-onk, kuk-ket-as-soo-tam-oonk pey-au-moo-utch, keet-te-nan-tam-oo-onk ne nai; ne-ya-ne ke-suk-qutkah oh-ke-it; aos-sa-ma-i-in-ne-an ko-ko-ke-stik-o-da-e nut-as-e-suk-ok-ke fu-tuk-qun-neg; kah ah-quo-an-tam-a-i-in-ne-an num-match-e-se-ong-an-on-ash, ne-match-ene-na-mun wonk neet-ah-quo-antam-au-o-un-non-og nish-noh pasuk noo-na-mortuk-quoh-who-nan, kah chaque sag-kom-pa-ginne-an en qutch-e-het-tu-ong-a-nit, qut poh-qud-wus-sin-ne-an watch match-i-tut.

Having now given historical facts, and an exposition in relation to ancient times, by which we have been enabled to discover the foundation which destroyed our common fathers in their struggle together; it was indeed nothing more than the spirit of avarice and usurpation of power that has brought people in all ages to hate and devour each other. And I cannot, for one moment, look back upon what is past and call it religion. No, it has not the least appearance like it. Do not then wonder, my dear friends, at my bold and unpolished statements, though I do not believe that truth wants any polishing whatever. And I can assure you that I have no design to tell an untruth, but facts alone. Oft have I been surprised at the conduct of those who pretend to be Christians, to see how they were affected toward those who were of a different cast, professing one faith. Yes, the spirit of degradation has always been exercised toward us poor and untaught people. If we cannot read, we can see and feel; and we find no excuse in the Bible for Christians conducting toward us as they do.

It is said that in the Christian's guide, God is merciful, and they that are his followers are like him. How much mercy do you think has been shown toward Indians, their wives, and their children? Not much, we think. No. And ye fathers, I will appeal to you that are white. Have you any regard for your wives and children, for those delicate sons and daughters? Would you like to see them slain and lain in heaps, and their bodies devoured by the vultures and wild beasts of prey, and their bones bleaching in the sun and air, till they molder away or were covered by the falling leaves of the forest, and not resist? No. Your hearts would break with grief, and with all the religion and knowledge you have, it would not impede your force to take vengeance upon your foe that had so cruelly conducted thus, although God has forbid you in so doing. For he has said, "Vengeance is mine, and I will repay." What, then, my dear affectionate friends, can you think of those who have been so often betrayed, routed, and stripped of all they possess, of all their kindred in the flesh? Can or do you think we have no feeling? The speech of Logan, the white man's friend, is no doubt fresh in your memory, that he intended to live and die the friend of the white man; that he always fed them and gave them the best his cabin afforded; and he appealed to them if they had not been well used, to which they never denied. After which they murdered all of his family in cool blood, which roused his passions to be revenged upon the whites. This circumstance is but one in a thousand.

Upon the banks of Ohio, a party of two hundred white warriors, in 1757 or about that time, came across a settlement of Christian Indians and falsely accused them of being warriors, to which they denied, but all to no purpose; they were determined to massacre them all. They, the Indians, then asked liberty to prepare for the fatal hour. The white savages then gave them one hour, as the historian said. They then prayed together; and in tears and cries, upon their knees, begged pardon of each other, of all they had done, after which they informed the white savages that they were now ready. One white man then begun with a mallet and knocked them down and continued his work until he had killed fifteen, with his own hand; then, saying it ached, he gave his commission to another. And thus they continued till they had massacred nearly ninety men, women, and children, all these innocent of any crime. What sad tales are these for us to look upon the massacre of our dear fathers, mothers, brothers, and sisters; and if we speak, we are then called savages for complaining. Our affections for each other are the same as yours; we think as much of ourselves as you do of yourselves. When our children are sick, we do all we can for them; they lie buried deep in our affections; if they die, we remember it long and mourn in after years. Children also cleave to their parents; they look to them for aid; they do the best they know how to do for each other; and when strangers come among us, we use them as well as we know how; we feel honest in whatever we do; we have no desire to offend anyone. But when we are so deceived, it spoils all our confidence in our visitors. And although I can say that I have some dear, good friends among white people, yet I eye them with a jealous eye, for fear they will betray me. Having been deceived so much by them, how can I help it? Being brought up to look upon white people as being enemies and not friends, and by the whites treated as such, who can wonder? Yes, in vain have I looked for the Christian to take me by the hand and bid me welcome to his cabin, as my fathers did them, before we were born; and if they did, it was only to satisfy curiosity and not to look upon me as a man and a Christian. And so all of my people have been treated, whether Christians or not. I say, then, a different course must be pursued, and different laws must be enacted, and all men must operate under one general law. And while you ask yourselves, "What do they, the Indians, want?" you have only to look at the unjust laws made for them and say, "They want what I want," in order to make men of them, good and wholesome citizens. And this plan ought to be pursued by all missionaries or not pursued at all. That is not only to make Christians of us, but men, which plan as yet has never been pursued. And when it is, I will then throw my might upon the side of missions and do what I can to favor it. But this work must begin here first, in New England.

Having now closed, I would say that many thanks is due from me to you, though an unworthy speaker, for your kind attention; and I wish you to understand that we are thankful for every favor; and you and I have to rejoice that we have not to answer for our fathers' crimes; neither shall we do right to charge them one to another. We can only regret it, and flee from it; and from henceforth, let peace and righteousness be written upon our hearts and hands forever, is the wish of a poor Indian.

[*The following excerpt presents an eyewitness account of the death of Metacomet (Philip). Benjamin Church (1639—1718) was born at Plymouth and followed his father's trade as a carpenter. When King Philip's War broke out in 1675, Church's suggestions for ending the conflict through a combination of diplomacy and imitation of Native American military tactics initially brought him nothing but rebuffs from the Puritan leaders and accusations that he was an "Indian lover." Church persevered, however, and became the most successful English military commander of the war (see note 25, p. 124). Church's son Thomas worked from his father's diaries, letters, and personal testimony to prepare* Entertaining Passages Relating to Philip's War, *an account that is highly critical of the Puritan leadership and unembarrassed about depicting Benjamin Church as the prototypical American frontier hero.*]

BENJAMIN CHURCH, AS TOLD
TO HIS SON THOMAS CHURCH

From *Entertaining Passages Relating to Philip's War* (1716)

ONE OF PHILIPS GANG GOING FORTH to ease himself, when he had done, look'd round him, & Capt. Golding thought the Indian looked right at him (tho' probably 'twas but his conceit) so fired at him, and upon his firing, the whole company that were with him fired upon the Enemies shel-

Benjamin Church with Thomas Church, *Entertaining Passages Relating to Philip's War* (1716), reprinted in *So Dreadfull a Judgment: Puritan Responses to King Philip's War, 1676—1677,* ed. Richard Slotkin and James Folsom (Middletown, Conn.: Wesleyan University Press, 1978), 450–52.

ter, before the Indians had time to rise from their sleep, and so over-shot them. But their shelter was open on that side next the Swamp, built so on purpose for the convenience of flight on occasion. They were soon in the Swamp and Philip the foremost, who starting at the first Gun threw his Petunk [sling pouch] and Powder horn over his head, catch'd up his Gun and ran as fast as he could scamper, without any more clothes than his small breeches and stockings, and ran directly upon two of Capt. Churches Ambush; they let him come fair within shot, and the English mans Gun missing fire, he bid the Indian fire away, and he did so to purpose, sent one Musket Bullet thro' his heart, and another not above two inches from it; he fell upon his face in the Mud & Water with his Gun under him. By this time the Enemy perceived they were way laid on the east side of the Swamp, tack'd short about. One of the Enemy who seem'd to be a great surly old fellow, hollow'd with a loud voice, & often called out, *iootash, iootash,* Capt. Church called to his Indian Peter and ask'd him, Who that was that called so? He answered, it was old Annowon Philips great Captain, calling on his Souldiers to stand to it and fight stoutly. Now the Enemy finding that place of the Swamp which was not Ambush'd, many of them made their escape in the English Tracks. The Man that had shot down Philip, ran with all speed to Capt. Church, and informed him of his exploit, who commanded him to be Silent about it, & let no man more know it, until they had drove the Swamp clean; but when they had drove the Swamp thro' & found the Enemy had escaped, or at least the most of them; and the Sun now up, and so the dew gone, that they could not so easily Track them, the whole Company met together at the place where the Enemies Night shelter was; and then Capt. Church gave them the news of Philips death; upon which the whole Army gave Three loud Huzza's. Capt. Church ordered his body to be pull'd out of the mire on to the Upland, so some of Capt. Churches Indians took hold of him by his Stockings, and some by his small Breeches, (being otherwise naked) and drew him thro' the Mud unto the Upland, and a doleful, great, naked, dirty beast, he look'd like. Capt. Church then said, That for asmuch as he had caused many an English mans body to lye unburied and rot above ground, that not one of his bones should be buried. And calling his old Indian Executioner, bid him behead and quarter him. Accordingly, he came with his Hatchet and stood over him, but before he struck he made a small Speech directing it to Philip; and said, He had been a very great Man, and had made many a man afraid of him, but so big as he was he would now chop his Ass for him; and so went to work, and did as he was ordered. Philip having one very remarkable hand being much scarr'd, occasioned by the splitting of a Pistol in it formerly. Capt. Church gave the head and that hand to Alderman, the Indian who shot him, to show to such Gentlemen as would bestow gratuities upon him; and accordingly he got many a Peny by it. This being on the last day of the Week, the Captain with his Company returned to the Island, tarryed there until Tuesday; and then went off and ranged thro' all the Woods to Plymouth, and received their Premium, which was Thirty Shillings per head, for the Enemies which they had killed or taken, instead of all Wages; and Philips head went at the same price. Methinks it's scanty reward and poor incouragement; tho' it was better than what had been some time before. For this March they received Four Shillings and Six Pence a Man, which was all the Reward they had, except the honour of killing Philip. This was in the latter end of August, 1676.

READING CRITICALLY

1. How does Apess deal with Increase Mather's claims that God is on the side of the English and will help them kill Native Americans?

2. What reasons does Apess give for saying that Christian missionaries have done more harm than good to the Native Americans?

3. According to Apess, why did the English attack the Narragansett town, and what happened when they did?

4. What point does Apess make about Mary Rowlandson's description of Philip?

5. According to Apess, how did Benjamin Church persuade Native Americans to fight for him? What does Apess's attitude toward Church seem to be?

6. What details in the text show that Apess is trying to treat the death of Philip with dignity, so that Philip can still appear as a hero?

7. How does Apess answer the charge that Philip's wife was excessively proud of her appearance?

WRITING ANALYTICALLY

1. On page 114, why does Apess say that "every man of color" should "wrap himself in mourning" on the days commemorating the Pilgrims' landing (December 22) and the signing of the Declaration of Independence (July 4)? What point is he trying to make in calling for all people of color, not just Native Americans, to mourn? Consider your responses to these questions in light of the fact that the *Eulogy*'s audience was primarily European Americans, who did regard those two days as holidays. Write a paper in which you analyze Apess's rhetorical strategy and evaluate how effective you think it would have been.

2. Apess provides details from court records (pp. 116–17) to suggest that Philip initially tried to deal peacefully with the English through legal land sales and appeals to English law but that he was not treated fairly. Why do you think Apess is concerned about presenting this evidence before going on to discuss the war? Write a paper in which you analyze his rhetorical strategy and evaluate how effective you think it would have been.

3. Throughout the *Eulogy*, Apess confronts the dominant accounts of seventeenth-century New England history written by English historians and counters with his own version of events. Here are several examples: Apess (pp. 109–11) and Bradford (pp. 30–37) on early relations between the Plymouth settlers and Massasoit and the Wampanoags; Apess (p. 111) and Bradford (pp. 38–39) on the Wessagusset incident; Apess (pp. 112–13) and Bradford (p. 36) on the Puritan raid against Corbitant; Apess (p. 118), Mather (pp. 51–52), and Easton (pp. 93–94) on the death of John Sassamon; Apess (pp. 121–22) and Mather (pp. 57–59) on the

battle at the Narragansett town; Apess (pp. 125–26), Church (p. 133), and Mather (pp. 61–62) on the death of Philip.

Choose one of these examples and compare and contrast how the different writers present the incident. Drawing on this comparison, write a paper in which you analyze how Apess copes with the difficult rhetorical situation of knowing that these earlier writers have great authority while he has little. Does Apess convince you of his credibility as a historian? Why or why not?

TREATIES, LAWS, AND DEEDS

Treaty of Peace and Alliance between Massasoit and the Plymouth Colonists (March 22, 1621)

This treaty was signed by the Wampanoag sachem Massasoit and John Carver, governor of Plymouth. The "he" in the treaty refers to Massasoit, and the "we" refers to the colonists. The treaty is included in William Bradford's *History of Plymouth Plantation* (p. 19), but we are also including this version, originally printed in *Mourt's Relation,* because it differs slightly from Bradford's. *Mourt's Relation* is the common name given to *A Relation or Journal of the Beginning and Proceedings of the English Plantation Settled at Plymouth in New England,* published in England in 1622 over the signature "G. Mourt.," or George Morton, a printer. Morton compiled narratives written by Bradford, Edward Winslow, and perhaps other colonists.

1. That neither he nor any of his should injure or do hurt to any of our people.
2. And if any of his did hurt to any of ours, he should send the offender, that we might punish him.
3. That if any of our tools were taken away when our people were at work, he should cause them to be restored, and if ours did any harm to any of his, we would do the like to them.
4. If any did unjustly war against him, we would aid him; if any did war against us, he should aid us.
5. He should send to his neighbor confederates, to certify them of this, that they might not wrong us; but might be likewise comprised in the conditions of peace.
6. That when their men came to us, they should leave their bows and arrows behind them, as we should do our pieces when we came to them.

Lastly, that doing thus, King James would esteem of him as his friend and ally.

Treaty of Peace and Alliance between Chief Massasoit of the Wampanoags and Governor Carver of Plymouth, in Alden Vaughan, *New England Frontier: 1620–1675* (1965; 2nd ed., New York: Norton, 1979), 339–40.

READING CRITICALLY

1. What does this treaty require the Native Americans to do? What does it require the English to do? Make two lists.

2. Turn to Bradford's version of this treaty on page 31. What is the significance of the differences you note?

WRITING ANALYTICALLY

This treaty maintained peace for more than fifty years, until King Philip's War broke out after Massasoit's death. Considering the terms of the treaty as you have outlined them, why do you think it might have lasted so long? Who seems to get the better deal? Write a paper in which you argue that this was, or was not, a good treaty from the standpoint of the Wampanoags, the English, or both.

Treaty of Hartford (September 21, 1638)

This is the treaty that ended the Pequot War. The Pequots themselves did not sign it because so many of them had been killed their chief sachem Sassacus was actually in flight at the time the treaty was signed and was killed a few weeks later. This treaty tries not so much to make peace with the Pequots but rather to divide the spoils of war, including Pequot lands and captives, among the three uneasy victorious allies. The Narragansett sachem Miantonomo was concerned that the Mohegan Uncas would gain too much power from the victory. In the treaty, the English appear to be mediating between these two powerful sachems, but it might be just as accurate to say that they are playing one against the other, ultimately to bolster their own power. Later, when the English began to fear Miantonomo, they stirred up the animosity between him and Uncas and eventually delivered him captive to Uncas, who killed him.

ARTICLES BETWEEN THE INGLISH IN CONNECTICUT AND THE INDIAN SACHEMS

A COVENANT AND AGREEMENT BETWEEN THE ENGLISH Inhabiting the Jurisdiction of the River of Connecticut of the one part and Miantinomy the chief Sachem of the Narragansetts in the behalf of himself and the other Sachems there; and Poquim or Uncas the chief Sachim of the Indians

Treaty of Hartford, in Alden Vaughan, *New England Frontier: 1620 –1675* (1965; 2nd ed., New York: Norton, 1979), 340–41.
    In the notes, EDS. = Patricia Bizzell and Bruce Herzberg.

called the Mohegans in the behalf of himself and the Sachims under him, as Followeth, at Hartford the 21st of September, 1638.

1. Imp'r. There is a peace and a Familiarity made between the sd Miantinome and Narragansett Indians and the sd Poquim and Mohegan Indians, and all former Injuryes and wrongs offered each to other Remitted and Burryed and never to be renued any more from henceforth.

2. It is agreed if there fall out Injuryes and wrongs for fuetur to be done or committed Each to other or their men, they shall not presently Revenge it But they are to appeal to the English and they are to decide the same, and the determination of the English to stand And they are each to do as is by the English sett down and if the one or the other shall Refuse to do, it shall be lawfull for the English to Compel him and to side and take part if they see cause, against the obstinate or Refusing party.

3. It is agreed and a conclusion of peace and friendship made between the sd Miantinome and sd Narragansetts and the sd Poquim and the sd Mohegans as long as they carry themselves orderly and give no just cause of offence and that they nor either of them do shelter any that may be Enemyes to the English that shall or formerly have had hand in murdering or killing any English man or woman or consented thereunto, They or either of them shall as soon as they can either bring the chief Sachem of our late enemies the Peaquots that had the chief hand in killing the English, to the sd English, or take of their heads, As also for those murderers that are now agreed upon amongst us that are living they shall as soon as they can possibly take off their heads, if they may be in their custody or Else whensoever they or any of them shall come Amongst them or to their wigwams or any where if they can by any means come by them.

4. And whereas there be or is reported for to be by the sd Narragansetts and Mohegans two hundred Peaquots living that are men besides squawes and paposes. The English do give unto Miantinome and the Narragansetts to make up the number of Eighty with the Eleven they have already, and to Poquime his number, and that after they the Peaquots shall be divided as abovesd, shall no more be called Peaquots but Narragansetts and Mohegans and as their men and either of them are to pay for every Sanop one fathom of wampome peage[1] and for every youth half so much — and for every Sanop papoose one hand to be paid at Killing time of Corn at Connecticut yearly and shall not suffer them for to live in the country that was formerly theirs but is now the Englishes by conquest neither shall the Narragansets nor Mohegans possess any part of the Peaquot country without leave from the English And it is always expected that the English Captives are forthwith to be delivered to the English, such as belong to the Connecticut to the Sachems there, And such as belong to the Massachusetts; the sd agreements

---

[1]A "sanop" is an adult male Native American; the word is also sometimes used to mean "husband." The Native American money, wampum, is here called "wampome peage." The treaty does not mention that in addition to dispersing some Pequot captives among the Narragansett and Mohegan tribes, others were sold into slavery in Bermuda; see Apess (p. 107). Nevertheless, the Pequots have survived as a tribe to this day. They now run a successful gambling casino on their small reservation in Connecticut. — EDS.

are to be kept invoylably by the parties abovesd and if any make breach of them the other two may joyn and make warr upon such as shall break the same, unless satisfaction be made being Reasonably Required.

The Mark of MIANTINOMMY,

The Marks of POQUIAM alias UNKAS.

JOHN HAINES,

ROG'R LUDLOW,

EDW'RD HOPKINS.

READING CRITICALLY

1. What are the Narragansetts and the Mohegans given, and what are they required to do by this treaty? What are the English given and what are they required to do? Make lists.

2. If the provisions of this treaty were carried out in full, what would happen to the Pequot tribe?

WRITING ANALYTICALLY

Usually a treaty ending a war is signed by the parties that have been fighting each other, but here the three groups that signed were all allies during the war. What can you infer about English–Native American relations from this treaty? How are the three signers positioned with respect to one another? Does this look to you like a treaty arrangement that will last? Why or why not? Write a paper in which you analyze English–Native American relations in New England in 1638, based on the evidence of this treaty. If you wish, you may write as if you were a seventeenth-century English colonist reporting on the situation to people in England who are wondering if it's safe to join you in Massachusetts. Option: Add to your response evidence drawn from one or two of the following sources: Bradford (p. 19), Underhill (p. 44), and Gardener (p. 85).

Unrestricted Deed (January 12, 1642)

This deed was signed by a representative of the English settlers at Shawomet, now known as Warwick, Rhode Island, and by Miantonomo, the powerful Narragansett sachem, and his subordinate sachems. In signing an unrestricted deed, Native Americans retained no rights to the land under English law. The English regarded such transfers as the equivalent of a sale and assumed that the Native Americans would now vacate the territory. According to Native

Unrestricted Deed, in Alden Vaughan, *New England Frontier: 1620—1675* (1965; 2nd ed., New York: Norton, 1979), 348–49.

American practice, however, sachems did not have the right to permanently convey tribal lands to other parties, and they probably were not aware of the English interpretation. They most likely thought that they were merely agreeing to let the English use portions of the land for their houses and fields and perhaps hunting while the Native Americans would also go on hunting and farming on the land in other areas of the same territory.

These misunderstandings led to later problems such as the destruction of unfenced Native American crops by free-ranging English cattle and hogs (a problem addressed in the Massachusetts colony laws pertaining to Indians, p. 143). To combat such problems, the English and the Native Americans sometimes signed restricted land deeds (see p. 148), which attempted to spell out co-use protocols more in keeping with Native American ideas of land sharing. Unfortunately, the English often did not comply with such compromise arrangements.

KNOW ALL MEN: that I, Myantonomy, Cheefe Sachem of the Nanhey-gansett, have sould unto the persons heare named, one parsell of lands with all the right and privileges thereoff whatsoever, lyinge uppon the west syde of that part of the sea called Sowhomes Bay, from Copassanatuxett, over against a little Iland in the sayd Bay, being the North bounds, and the outmost point of that neck of land called Shawhomett; beinge the South bounds ffrom the sea shoare of each boundary uppon a straight lyne westward twentie miles. I say I have truly sould this parsell of lande above sayde, the proportion whereof is according to the mapp under written or drawne, being the forme of it unto Randall Houlden, John Greene, John Wickes, ffrancis Weston, Samuell Gorton, Richard Waterman, John Warner, Richard Carder, Sampson Shotten, Robert Potter, William Wuddall, ffor one hundreth and fortie foure ffathom of wampumpeage. I say I have sould it, and possession of it given unto the men above sayed, with the ffree and joynt consent of the present inhabitants, being natives, as it appeares by their hands hereunto annexed.

Dated the twelfth day of January, 1642. Beinge enacted uppon the above sayed parsell of land in the presence off

> PUMHOMM [his mark, a pipe]
> JANO [his mark, a bird]
> JOHN GREENE, Jun'r
> MYANTONOMY, Sachem of Shawhomett,
>   [his mark, a vertical bow and arrow]
> TOTANOMANS, his marke, [a musket].

READING CRITICALLY

According to what is said in the Unit One introduction about the rights and powers of Native American sachems, in what ways does this transaction conform to or violate Native American custom?

WRITING ANALYTICALLY

Compare this document with the restricted deed of land included on page 148. If the restricted deed assumes that Native American and English people will try to share the same parcel of land, this unrestricted deed assumes the opposite: that the land can have only one group occupying it. The Native Americans, having transferred it, will have to move out. What are the implications of this kind of separation for the ways of life of both the Native Americans and the English? Write a paper in which you explain what you think the consequences of this land transfer will be. If you wish, you may write as if you were an adviser either to Miantonomo or to the English signers.

Treaty of Submission (March 8, 1644)

By this treaty, several sachems of the Massachusett people "submitted" to the Massachusetts Bay colony and to English law. The Native Americans might have understood such a treaty as placing them in the position of a dependent, but still nominally autonomous, ally. Their territory already was overtaken with so much English settlement (and many minor but galling daily disputes between them and the settlers) that accepting the authority of English law may well have seemed the safest course. And if the Native Americans were going to accept the rule of English law, then they would be obligated to protect the government that administered the law, such as by giving "speedy notice of any conspiracy" of other Native Americans against the colonists. The sachems may also have calculated that the treaty would entitle them to English protection should they be attacked by other Native American groups.

In spite of such agreements, English law did not always protect Native Americans who submitted to it, as suggested in some of the grievances presented by Metcomet (Philip) to John Easton (p. 93). Moreover, the English sometimes regarded such treaties not merely as registering a dependent ally but actually as conveying the Native Americans' lands to the colony. In other words, these treaties were sometimes used by the colonies to enlarge their own holdings.

WEE HAVE AND BY these presents do voluntarily, and without any constraint or perswasion, but of our owne free motion. put ourselves, our subjects, lands, and estates under the government and jurisdiction of the Massachusets, to bee governed and protected by them, according to their just lawes and orders, so farr as wee shalbee made capable of understanding them;

Treaty of Submission, in Alden Vaughan, *New England Frontier: 1620 —1675* (1965; 2nd ed., New York: Norton, 1979), 342.

and wee do promise for ourselves, and all our subjects, and all our posterity, to bee true and faithfull to the said government. and ayding to the maintenance thereof, to our best ability, and from time to time to give speedy notice of any conspiracy, attempt, or evill intension of any which wee shall know or heareof against the same; and wee do promise to bee willing from time to time to bee instructed in the knowledge and worship of God. In witnes whereof wee have hereunto put our hands the 8th of the first month, anno 1643–1644

CUTSHAMACHE,
NASHOWANON,
WOSSAMEGON,
MASKANOMETT,
SQUA SACHIM.

READING CRITICALLY

What does this treaty require the Native Americans to do? What does it require the English to do? Make two lists.

WRITING ANALYTICALLY

1. Why do you think the colonists wanted to require the Native Americans to listen to instruction "in the knowledge and worship of God"? Write a paper analyzing the colonists' motives. Option: You may write as if you were one of the English colonists who negotiated the treaty, defending the religious instruction requirement either to the Native American sachems or to the Massachusetts Bay colony governor.

2. Compare and contrast this treaty with the 1621 Treaty of Peace and Alliance (p. 136) and the 1638 Treaty of Hartford (p. 137). What kind of relationship between Native Americans and English is assumed in each document? Who gets the better deal in each, in your opinion? Write a paper in which you describe English–Native American relations in seventeenth-century New England based on the evidence of these treaties. Option: You may argue that these relations changed over time, again based on the treaty evidence.

Rules for the Praying Indian Town of Concord, Massachusetts (January 1647)

Reverend John Eliot, a principal preacher to the Native Americans, encouraged his converts, called "Praying Indians," to form themselves into their own towns. Here they could live apart from both the English Christians and the non-Christian Native Americans, while attempting to model the lifestyle of the English by conforming to rules like the following.

CONCLUSIONS AND ORDERS MADE AND AGREED UPON BY DIVERS SACHIMS AND OTHER PRINCIPALL MEN AMONGST THE INDIANS AT CONCORD, IN THE END OF THE ELEVENTH MONETH, AN. 1646

1. THAT EVERYONE THAT SHALL abuse themselves with wine or strong liquors, shall pay for every time so abusing themselves, 20 s.
2. That there shall be no more Pawwowing[1] amongst the Indians. And if any shall hereafter Pawwow, both he that shall Powwow, & he that shall procure him to Powwow shall pay 20 s apeece.
3. They doe desire that they may be stirred up to seek after God.
4. They desire they may understand the wiles of Satan, and grow out of love with his suggestions, and temptations.
5. That they may fall upon some better course to improve their time, then formerly.
6. That they may be brought to the sight of the sinne of lying, and whosoever shall be found faulty herein shall pay for the first offence 5 s. the second 10 s. the third 20 s.
7. Whosoever shall steale any thing from another, shall restore fourfold.
8. They desire that no Indian hereafter shall have any more but one wife.
9. They desire to prevent falling out of Indians one with another, and that they may live quietly one by another.
10. That they may labour after humility, and not be proud.

Rules for the Praying Indian Town of Concord Massachusetts, in Alden Vaughan, *New England Frontier: 1620–1675* (1965; 2nd ed., New York: Norton, 1979), 346–47.

In the notes, EDS. = Patricia Bizzell and Bruce Herzberg.

[1]"Pawwowing" is the Native American ritual led by the powwows, or religious leaders. The Puritans consider these rites to be nothing more than devil worship. — EDS.

11. That when Indians doe wrong one to another, they may be lyable to censure by fine or the like, as the English are.
12. That they pay their debts to the English.
13. That they doe observe the Lords-Day, and whosoever shall prophane it shall pay 20 s.
14. That there shall not be allowance to pick lice, as formerly, and eate them, and whosoever shall offend in this case shall pay for every louse a penny.
15. They weill weare their haire comely, as the English do, and whosoever shall offend herein shall pay 5 s.
16. They intend to reforme themselves, in their former greasing themselves, under the Penalty of 5 s. for every default.
17. They doe all resolve to set up prayer in their wigwams, and to seek to God both before and after meats.
18. If any commit the sinne of fornication, being single persons, the man shall pay 20 s and the woman 10 s.
19. If any man lie with a beast he shall die.
20. Whosoever shall play at their former games shall pay 10 s.
21. Whosoever shall commit adultery shall be put to death.
22. Wilfull murder shall be punished with death.
23. They shall not disguise themselves in their mournings, as formerly, nor shall they keep a great noyse by howling.
24. The old Ceremony of the Maide walking alone and living apart so many dayes 20 s.[2]
25. No Indian shall take an English mans Canooe without leave under the penaltie of 5 s.
26. No Indian shall come into any English mans house except he first knock: and this they expect from the English.
27. Whosoever beats his wife shall pay 20 s.
28. If any Indian shall fall out with, and beats another Indian, he shall pay 20 s.
29. They desire they may bee a towne, and either to dwell on this side the Beare Swamp, or at the east side of Mr. Flints Pond.

READING CRITICALLY

1. What are the Native Americans forbidden to do by these rules? What are they required to do? Make two lists.

2. Which rules seem specifically aimed at eliminating traces of Native American customs among the Praying Indians? Which rules seem designed to promote English customs among them?

---

[2]The "Maide walking alone" is a woman practicing ritual seclusion during her menstrual period. — EDS.

WRITING ANALYTICALLY

1. If you assume that these rules were written by the English to be imposed on the Christian Native Americans, what would you say these rules are trying to do to or for them? Write a paper in which you answer this question, drawing on your responses to the reading questions.

2. Let us suppose that these rules were not imposed on the Christian Native Americans, but rather that the Native Americans had a hand in their framing and that they wanted them published. Consider that the Christian Native Americans were a small and vulnerable minority, separated from their non-Christian tribes and settled near the English, who distrusted and occasionally persecuted them. Suppose the Christian Native Americans wanted this document, the Praying Indian town rules, to be available to any English people who might inquire about what the Native Americans were doing in their separate town. How might this document be construed as a sort of "public relations" effort for the Christian Native Americans? What image of themselves would they be trying to create by publishing these rules? Write a paper in which you analyze the effectiveness of this document as an effort at public relations. If you have the knowledge, you can also discuss the situation of the Praying Indians in light of that of another group with which you are familiar, whose members may be concerned about how they appear to a possibly hostile outside world.

Laws Pertaining to Indians, Massachusetts Bay Colony (1648)

These laws were framed to deal with Native American and English people living in close proximity to one another.

IT IS ORDERED BY AUTHORITIES of this Court; that no person whatsoever shall henceforth buy land of any Indian, without licence first had & obtained of the General Court: and if any shall offend heerin, such land so bought shall be forfeited to the Countrie.

Nor shall any man within this Jurisdiction directly or indirectly amend, repair, or cause to be ammended or repaired any gun, small or great, belonging to any Indian, nor shall indeavour the same. Nor shall sell or give to any Indian, directly or indirectly anysuch gun, or any gun-powder, shot or lead, or shot-mould, or any militarie weapons or armour: upon payn of ten pounds fine, at the least for everie such offence: and that the court of

Laws Pertaining to Indians, Massachusetts Bay Colony, in Alden Vaughan, *New England Frontier: 1620 —1675* (1965; 2nd ed., New York: Norton, 1979), 343–45.

Assistants shall have power to increase the Fine; or to impose corporall punishment (where a Fine cannot be had) at their discretion.

1. It is also ordered by the Authoritie aforesaid that everie town shall have power to restrein all Indians from profaning the Lords day.

2. Whereas it appeareth to this Court that notwithstanding the former laws, made against selling of guns, powder and Amunition to the Indians, they are yet supplyed by indirect means, it is therefore ordered by this Court and Authoritie thereof;

That if any person after publication heerof, shall sell, give or barter any gun or guns, powder, bullets, shot or lead to any Indian whatsoever, or unto any person inhabiting out of this Jurisdiction without licence of this Court, or the court of Assistants, or some two Magistrates, he shall forfeit for everie gun so sold, given or bartered ten pounds: and for everie pound of powder five pounds: and for everie pound of bullets, shot or lead fourty shillings: and so proportionably for any greater or lesser quantitie.

3. It is ordered by this Court and Authoritie therof, that in all places, the English and such others as co-inhabit within our Jurisdiction shall keep their cattle from destroying the Indians corn, in any ground where they have right to plant, and if any of their corn be destroyed for want of fencing, or hearding; the town shall make satisfaction, and shall have power among themselves to lay the charge where the occasion of the damage did arise. Provided that the Indians shall make proof that the cattle of such a town, farm, or person did the damage. And for encouragement of the Indians toward the fencing in of their corn fields, such towns, farms or persons whose cattle may annoy them that way, shall direct, assist and help them in felling of trees, ryving, and sharpening of rayks & holing of posts: allowing one Englishman to three or more Indians. And shall also draw the fencing into place for them and allow one man a day or two toward the setting up the same and either lend or sell them tools to finish it. Provided that such Indians, to whom the Countrie, or any town hath given, or shall give ground to plant upon, or that shall purchase ground of the English shall fence such their corn fields or ground at their own charge as the English doe or should doe; and if any Indians refuse to fence their corn ground (being tendred help as aforesaid) in the presence and hearing of any Magistrate or selected Townsmen being met together they shall keep off all cattle or lose one half of their damages.

And it is also ordered that if any harm be done at any time by the Indians unto the English in their cattle; the Governour or Deputie Governour with two of the Assistants or any three Magistrates or any County Court may order satisfaction according to law and justice.

4. Considering that one end in planting these parts was to propagate the true Religion unto the Indians: and that divers of them are become subjects to the English and have ingaged themselves to be willing and ready to understand the law of God, it is therfore ordered and decreed,

That such necessary and wholsom Laws, which are in force, and may be made from time to time, to reduce them to civilitie of life shall be once in the year (if the times be safe) made known to them, by such fit persons as the General Court shall nominate, having the help of some able Interpreter with them.

Considering also that interpretation of tongues is appointed of God for propagating the Truth: and may therfore have a blessed successe in the hearts of others in due season, it is therfore farther ordered and decreed,

That two Ministers shall be chosen by the Elders of the Churches everie year at the Court of Election, and so be sent with the consent of their Churches (with whomsoever will freely offer themselves to accompany them in that service) to make known the heavenly counsell of God among the Indians in most familiar manner, by the help of some able Interpreter; as may be most available to bring them unto the knowledge of the truth, and their conversation to the Rules of Jesus Christ. And for that end that somthing be allowed them by the General Court, to give away freely unto those Indians whom they shall perceive most willing & ready to be instructed by them.

And it is farther ordered and decreed by this Court that no Indian shall at any time *powaw*, or performe outward worship to their false gods: or to the devil in any part of our Jurisdiction; whether they be such as shall dwell heer, or shall come hither: and if any transgresse this Law, the Powawer shall pay five pounds; the Procurer five pounds; and every other countenancing by his presence or otherwise being of age of discretion twenty shillings.

READING CRITICALLY

1. What specific actions are the English directed to perform here? What are they forbidden to do? What are the Native Americans required to do and forbidden to do? Make lists.

2. Look more closely at item number 3 in the laws, concerning Native American crops and English cattle. What problem is being addressed here, and how — that is, what are the Native Americans and the English required to do about it?

3. What kinds of laws do you think the English have in mind to "reduce them [the Native Americans] to civilitie of life" (p. 146)? What is "civilitie of life," as far as you can tell?

WRITING ANALYTICALLY

What assumptions do these laws make about the relative merits of the English and Native American ways of life? How can you tell? Do you think these laws will enable English and Native American people to live together peacefully? Why or why not? Write a paper in which you argue that these are or are not good laws. If you have the knowledge, you can discuss this issue in comparison with a contemporary situation. For example, how do American communities today respond to residents who do not follow the prevailing lifestyle, such as recent immigrants whose customs are very different from American norms? Are such newcomers able to integrate peacefully into the community? Why or why not? You can turn this paper into an argumentative essay about how such situations should be handled, using evidence from both the Massachusetts Bay colony laws and the contemporary example.

Restricted Deed (May 1648)

This deed was issued by Paupmunnuck, a Wampanoag sachem, to Myles Standish and other English settlers at what is now known as Barnstable, Massachusetts. Paupmunnuck is the same man who also ceded land for the establishment of the Praying Indian town of Mashpee. The deed is "restricted" in the sense that it prohibits the English from taking total control over the ceded property and retains some rights for the Native Americans. For more information on the complexities of these transactions, see pages 139–40.

AN AGREEMENT MADE THE 17TH of May, 1648, betweene Paupmunnuck, with the consent of his brother, and all the rest of his associats on the one part, and Captaine Myles Standish in the behalfe of the inhabitants of Barnestable on the other part, as followeth, viz: —

That the said Paupmunnucke hath, with the free and full consent of his said brother and associats, freely, fully, and absolutely bargained and sould unto the said Captaine Myles Standish in the behalfe and for the use of the inhabytants of Barnstable aforesaid, all his and thayer right, title, and intereste in all his and thayer lands lying and beeing within the precincts of Barnstable afforesaid, faring upon the sea, commonly called the South Sea, buting home to Janno his land eastward,[1] and a little beyond a brooke, called the First Hearing Brooke, weastward, and to Nepoyetums and Seqqunneks lands northward, exsepting thirty acars which hee the said Paupmunnuck hath retained to the proper use and behoofe of himselfe, his brother, and associates, for and in consideration of 2 brasse kittells and one bushell of Indian corn, to bee dewly and trewly payed unto him, the said Paupmunnuck by the said inhabytants of Barnstable, between the date heerof and November next inseuing; allso, one halfe part of so mutch fence as will fence in the thirty acars of land afforesaid for the said Paupmunnuck, to bee dewly and trewly made by the laste of Aprill next insewing the date heerof; allso, the said Paupmunnuck and his associates shall have free leave and liberty to hunt in the said lands, provided thay give notice to the said inhabitants before thay sett any trappes, as allso fully and diligenttly to see all thair trappes evry day, that soe in case any are taken or intrapped therin, thaye shall speedyli lett them out, and acquainte the said inhaby-

Restricted Deed, in Alden Vaughan, *New England Frontier: 1620—1675* (1965; 2nd ed., New York: Norton, 1979), 349–50.

In the notes, EDS. = Patricia Bizzell and Bruce Herzberg.
[1]That is, abutting, or lying next to, Janno's land on the east. — EDS.

tants forthwith therof; as allso to acquainte them if thay shall perceive any cattell to have broken out of thayer trapps before they come unto them.

In wittnes of all and singuler the preemises heerof, thay have heerunto sett thayer hands the day and yeare above written.

All which conditions, in case thay doe not dilligently observe, thay shall pay whatsoever damage comes to any mans cattell through thayer default heerin.

READING CRITICALLY

What rights do the Native Americans retain here?

WRITING ANALYTICALLY

This restricted deed might be considered a legal instrument that attempts to make it possible for two groups of people with very different lifestyles to use the same land. Just considering what is said in this document, write an argumentative essay in which you assess how successful you think this attempt is likely to be. Consider: What problems might arise to make it difficult for either group to exercise the rights this document aims to give them? Can you recommend changes in the document that would prevent the difficulties you anticipate? Or do you believe that people with such different ways of life cannot live so close together?

ANDREW PITTIMEE AND OTHER NATIVE AMERICAN FIGHTERS FOR THE ENGLISH IN KING PHILIP'S WAR

Petition (June 1676)

During King Philip's War, a number of Native Americans, many of them Christians, fought for the English, although this sometimes put them in the agonizing position of fighting against people from their own tribes. In this petition a group of such fighters are writing to the governor and council of the Massachusetts Bay colony, attempting to rescue Native American captives who fought, or who were related to those who fought, against them. The reply by the clerk of the council suggests they were partially successful in their plea.

Andrew Pittimee and Other Native American Fighters for the English in King Philip's War, Petition, in Daniel Gookin, *An Historical Account of the Doings and Sufferings of the Christian Indians in New England, in the Years 1675, 1676, 1677* (1677; reprint, New York: Arno Press, 1972), 527–29.

In the notes, EDS. = Patricia Bizzell and Bruce Herzberg.

To the Honourable the Govournour
and Councill of the Massachusetts Colony,
Assembled at Boston this ___ of June 1676

THE HUMBLE PETITION of Andrew Pittimee, Quanahpohkit, *alias* James Rumney Marsh, John Magus, and James Speen, officers unto the Indian souldiers, now in your service, with the consent of the rest of the Indian souldiers being about eighty men;

Humbly imploreth your favour and mercies to be extended to some of the prisoners taken by us, (most of them) near Lanchaster, Marlborough, &c: In whose behalf we are bold to supplicate your Honoures. And wee have three reasons for this our humble supplication; first, because the persons we beg pardon for, as we are informed, are innocent; and have not done any wrong or injury unto the English, all this war time, only were against their wills, taken and kept among the enemy. Secondly, because it pleased your Honours to say to some of us, to encourage us to fidelity and activity in your service, that you would be ready to do any thing for us, that was fitt for us to ask and you to grant. Thirdly, that others that are out, and love the English, may be encouraged to come in.[1] More that we humbly intercede for, is the lives and libertyes of those few of our poor friends and kindred, that, in this time of temptation and affliction, have been in the enemy's quarters; we hope it will be no griefe of heart to you to shew mercy, and especially to such who have (as we conceive) done no wrong to the English. If wee did think, or had any ground to conceive that they were naught, and were enemies to the English, we would not intercede for them, but rather bear our testimony against them, as we have done. We have (especially some of us) been sundry times in your service to the hazzard of our lives, both as spyes, messengers, scouts, and souldiers, and have through God's favour acquitted ourselves faithfully, and shall do as long as we live endeavour will all fidelitie to fight in the English cause, which we judge is our own cause, and also God's cause, to oppose the wicked Indians, enemies to God and all goodness. In granting this our humble request, you will much oblige us who desire to to remain

Your Honoures Humble and Faithful Servants,

> ANDREW PITTIMEE,
> JAMES QUANAPOHKIT,
> JOB,
> JOHN MAGUS,
> JAMES SPEEN.

The persons we supplicate for, are Capt. Tom, his son Nehemiah, his wife and two children, John Uktuek, his wife and children, Maanum and her child.

---

[1]"Others that are out" are Native Americans who are avoiding the English and possibly hiding among hostile Native Americans; if they "come in," they will come out of hiding, submit to English law, and put aside any idea of hostility. — EDS.

And if the Councill please not to answer our desires in granting the lives and liberties of all these, yett if you shall please to grant us the women and children, it will be a favour unto us.

In Answer to the Petition of James Quanhpohkit, James Speen, Job, Andrew Pittimee, and Jno. Magus

Capt. Tom being a lawful prisoner at warr, there needs no further evidence for his conviction; yet hee having had liberty to present his plea before the Councill why he should not be proceeded against accordingly, instead of presenting any thing that might alleviate his withdrawing from the government of the English and joyning with the enemy, it doth appear by sufficient evidence that hee was not only (as is credibly related by some Indians present with him) an instigator to others over whom he was by this government made a Captain, but also was actually present and an actor in the devastation of some of our plantations; and therefore it cannot consist with the honour and justice of authority to grant him a pardon.[2]

Whereas the Council do, with reference to the faithful service of the Petitioners, grant them the lives of the women and children by them mentioned. And, further, the Councill do hereby declair, that, as they shall be ready to show favour in sparing the lives and liberty of those that have been our enemys, on their comeing in and submission of themselves to the English Government and your disposal, the reality and complacency of the government towards the Indians sufficiently appearing in the provisions they have made, and tranquility that the Pequots have injoyed under them for over forty years; so also it will not be availeable for any to plead in favour for them that they have been our friends while found and taken among our enemyes.

Further the Councill do hereby declare that none may expect priviledge bye his declaration, that come not in and submit themselves in fourteen days next coming.

By the Council,

EDW. RAWSON, *Clerke*

READING CRITICALLY

1. What reasons do the Native American petitioners give for the release of the Native American captives they have delivered to the English?

2. Why do the colonists refuse to release Capt. Tom? Apparently they do release the other captives named in the petition; what other requests in the petition do they grant?

[2]Note that, according to the council, Capt. Tom is a Native American who originally commanded Native American troops fighting for the English, but then turned against the English. — EDS.

3. What is the point of the clerk's reference to English treatment of the Pequots?

WRITING ANALYTICALLY

Native American fighters for the English during King Philip's War were often suspected of disloyalty. In fact, one of the captives for whom the petitioners plead here, Capt. Tom, is charged with changing sides and assisting the enemy. It might be risky, then, for the Native American petitioners to raise doubts about their own loyalty by pleading for "enemy" people. How do the petitioners grapple with this risk? That is, what do they do to reassure the English that they are indeed loyal and at the same time to press the English to grant their request? Write a paper in which you evaluate the success of this petition, in terms of its effect on those to whom it was addressed and its effect on you.

ASSIGNMENT SEQUENCES

SEQUENCE 1

How did Native Americans negotiate with the English colonists in power?

- Increase Mather, From *A Brief History of the War with the Indians*
- William Bradford, From *History of Plymouth Plantation*
- Paper Left on a Bridge Post
- Waban, Speech at the End of King Philip's War
- William Apess, From *Eulogy on King Philip*
- Rules for the Praying Indian Town of Concord
- Andrew Pittimee and Other Native American Fighters, Petition

1. Consider this situation: You need to request something from a person in authority (coach, teacher, employer, and so on). You believe that there may be barriers to getting your request granted. They may be personal, for example if this person does not particularly like you; or they may be related to your or the person's group memberships — gender, race, religion, and so on. (For example, you may be a person of color addressing a white person whom you feel is prejudiced against people of color.) Still, you have to try to persuade this person to grant your request. What do you do? Write a personal narrative in which you tell the story of how you handled this situation, paying particular attention to how you attempted to overcome any barriers.

2. The Praying Indian town rules seem intended to conform the Christian Native Americans to an English way of life. Write a parody of these rules as you might imagine they would have been written if the Wampanoags had attempted to provide the Plymouth settlers with rules for living in their vicinity without offending the Native American way of life.

3. The Praying Indian town rules and the speech by Waban can both be read as presenting the English with the image of Christian Native Americans that they want to see. But should these two texts, then, be regarded as doing nothing more than appealing for English approval? Write a paper in which you explain how these two texts attempt to placate the English, and then argue whether or not you think that is all they do (you may compare and contrast them in the process).

4. The petition by Andrew Pittimee and other Native American fighters takes a great risk. The petitioners know that they might be accused of disloyalty for pleading for the lives of "enemy" Native Americans; yet it is important to them to press their request. So they have to reassure the English of their commitment while at the same time insisting that their petition be granted. Write a paper in which you explain how they try to negotiate this complicated rhetorical situation, and then argue whether or not you think they have done a good job, based on both your own response to their rhetoric and the response of the Massachusetts Council. If you wish, you may write this paper as if you were a seventeenth-century colonist making recommendations to council members on how they should respond to the petitioners. Alternative: Compare the petitioners and Waban,

and write an argumentative essay on how a marginalized group can best approach a dangerous authority, using the petitioners and Waban as good, or bad, examples.

5. William Apess aggressively contests the version of history presented in dominant Puritan texts such as William Bradford's. While Bradford tells the story of the early days of Plymouth as a story of courage, struggle, and gradual success, Apess says that the day Bradford's people landed should be a "day of mourning" for all people of color, and he tells the story as one of Native American generosity betrayed by brutal invaders. What differences in facts do you find in these two accounts? How does Bradford promote his version of the story? How does Apess promote his? Use the evidence in the texts to support an argumentative essay on whether Apess does or does not persuade you to question Bradford's account.

6. In contesting the version of history presented in texts written by the English, Apess questions not only the colonists' accounts of the facts but also the interpretation they place on these facts. For example, Apess discusses the attack on the Narragansett town during King Philip's War, as does Increase Mather. What approach to this incident does each writer promote, and how does he promote it? What seem to be the main points that each attempts to make with his account of this incident? How are the points made about this incident related to the overall purpose of each work? Use the evidence in the texts to support an argumentative essay on whether Apess does or does not persuade you to question the very different account by Mather. Option: You may write this paper in the form of an argument about why either or both of these writers should be included in a course on colonial American literature or history.

7. Apess, the Native American petitioners, and the Native American writer of the paper left at Medfield all can be said to be using literacy in English for oppositional purposes — not to conform to the English way of life, but to challenge it. They all want to speak aggressively for Native American values and rights. At the same time, they all need to address a primarily white audience and to persuade that audience not only to listen carefully but also to change their behavior accordingly. What strategies are effective for a rhetorician in this position? Compare and contrast the evidence in these three texts regarding this question; also consider your own response to question 1. Write an argumentative essay on what strategies oppositional or marginalized rhetoricians should employ if their goal is both to preserve the perspective of their own people and at the same time to persuade those in power to improve their treatment of those people. Texts included in this sequence may be used as positive or negative examples.

SEQUENCE 2

How did English writers create favorable images
of themselves for the historical record?

- William Bradford, From *History of Plymouth Plantation*
- John Underhill, From *Newes from America*
- Increase Mather, From *A Brief History of the War with the Indians*
- Mary Rowlandson, From *A Narrative of the Captivity and Restoration*
- Lion Gardener, From "Relation of the Pequot Wars"

- John Easton, "A Relation of the Indian War"
- Waban, Speech at the End of King Philip's War, Recorded and with a Reply by Daniel Gookin

1. You have faced a rhetorical problem similar to that confronting the writers included in this sequence if you have ever written an autobiography (perhaps as part of a college application or a job application). Think about how you did it: What did you tell? What did you leave out? Was there anything in your background that you felt might be damaging but that you had to tell while trying to put it in the best light possible? In your writing, did you talk about the autobiographical process at all ("It's hard for me to write about myself, but . . ."); if so, why? Answer these questions with a personal narrative in which you tell about a time you had to prepare an autobiography, a "history" of yourself. If possible, attach a copy of the autobiography you wrote.

2. All histories, of course, are selective. The historian chooses to tell certain things and to omit others. William Bradford, for example, does not mention his wife's death in his history. Choose from Bradford either the last two paragraphs of chapter 9 (pp. 21—23) or the references to Native Americans throughout chapters 9–12. Consider what is included and also, based on your reading in other sources, what might be omitted. Using this information, write an argumentative essay explaining what image of the English settlers you think Bradford is trying to create, and whether you think he succeeds.

3. Sometimes historians shape our perceptions of their stories not only by selecting what to tell us, but also by telling us what to think about what they have selected. Increase Mather and John Underhill, for example, frequently interpret the meaning of what they are telling us. Collect evidence of such editorial comments from these two writers, and use it to support an argumentative essay on the interpretation that you think Mather and Underhill are trying to promote and whether you think they succeed (you may compare and contrast them in the process). Option: You may evaluate the degree to which Mather and Underhill can be taken as trustworthy reporters of colonial history.

4. Interpreting as well as selecting, Mary Rowlandson comments frequently on the meaning of events recounted in her captivity narrative. Most scholars agree that her perspective is generally that of an orthodox Puritan. But Rowlandson has an additional rhetorical problem. She not only has to convince her readers of the correctness of her interpretation, but she also has to gain her readers' permission even to advance this interpretation. She needs permission because Puritan women were usually expected to attend to household duties and not to appear in the public sphere. They were not expected to discuss their experiences publicly as Rowlandson does. What does Rowlandson do to excuse her "boldness" and make her narrative acceptable to Puritan readers? What does she do to show that in spite of her orthodoxy, she isn't completely weak, meek, and submissive and that she is willing to enlarge the sphere of activity available to women? Use evidence from the text to support your own argument about whether Rowlandson succeeds in justifying an enlarged sphere of activity for women, thus gaining permission to advance her interpretation, both to Puritan readers and to you.

5. Sometimes historians acknowledge that other historians present views of the facts different from their own — in effect, acknowledging that the writing of history is an interpretive enterprise and that histories compete with one another to

persuade readers to accept their points of view. For example, in depicting his own behavior during the Pequot War, John Underhill attempts to contradict another history that presented him as less than heroic. Also, John Easton, writing about King Philip's War from the Quaker colony of Rhode Island, attempts to contradict negative interpretations of Native American behavior put forward by the English in the Plymouth and Massachusetts Bay colonies. For example, Easton contradicts Increase Mather both on the death of John Sassamon and on the reasons for attacking the Narragansett town — a challenge Mather acknowledges in the preface of his own history, written, he says, to correct mistakes spread around by Rhode Islanders like Easton. How do Underhill and Easton attempt to call other accounts into question and persuade readers that their version is more reasonable? (In answering this question for Easton, you might also want to look at the corresponding passages in Mather.) Use evidence from the texts to support an argumentative essay on how these writers rebut their opponents. Then evaluate the persuasiveness of their rebuttals (you may compare and contrast them in the process).

6. Sometimes historians comment on the power of history-writing itself to shape perceptions. For example, Lion Gardener uses the Bible story of King Ahasuerus and Mordecai (in which the record of Mordecai's good deeds in the kingdom's history book moved Ahasuerus to reward him) to try to persuade New Englanders to awaken to the debt they owe their defenders, both English and Native American. Daniel Gookin attempts to establish the importance of his account of Christian Native Americans by comparing it to the "doings and sufferings" of other religious martyrs. In general, as you can see from the readings for this sequence, seventeenth-century English colonists in New England had a strong sense that it was important to carefully record what they were doing. Looking at evidence in Gardener and Gookin (in the Waban selection), and all the other work you've done for this sequence, write a paper in which you discuss the power of history to shape perception. Does history actually shape its readers' perceptions both of what happened in the past and of how readers should understand themselves as inheritors of this past? If we know that historians aim to affect us in these ways, does this mean that we should not trust the historical record? Write an argumentative essay answering one or both of these questions.

SEQUENCE 3

How did the English colonists attempt to conform the Native Americans to an English way of life?

- Mary Rowlandson, From *A Narrative of the Captivity and Restoration*
- Waban, Speech at the End of King Philip's War, Recorded and with a Reply by Daniel Gookin
- William Apess, From *Eulogy on King Philip*
- Treaty of Peace and Alliance between Massasoit and the Plymouth Colonists
- Treaty of Hartford
- Unrestricted Deed
- Treaty of Submission
- Laws Pertaining to Indians
- Restricted Deed

1. Unlike some other documents in this sequence, the peace treaty between Massasoit and the Plymouth settlers does not call for large-scale changes in the Native Americans' way of life to conform to English customs. This treaty held for more than fifty years. Considering the terms of the treaty, do you see reasons why it might have lasted so long? Exactly what is the treaty trying to accomplish? Write a paper in which you argue that this was, or was not, a good treaty. You may argue from the point of view of either a seventeenth-century English colonist advising Governor Carver about the treaty or a Wampanoag advising Massasoit.

2. Compare and contrast the peace treaty with Massasoit (1621), The treaty of Hartford (1638), and the treaty of submission (1644). What kind of relationship between Native Americans and English is assumed in each document? Who gets the better deal in each, in your opinion? Using the evidence in these treaties, write a paper in which you describe English–Native American relations in seventeenth-century New England. You may argue that these relations changed over time. Option: You may write as if you were a seventeenth-century English colonist telling the colonies' financial backers in England about the progress of your relations with the Native Americans or as if you were a Native American speaking at a tribal meeting about relations with the English and what the tribe should do.

3. The restricted deed granted by Paupmunnuck to the Barnstable settlers might be considered a legal instrument that makes it possible for two groups of people with very different lifestyles to use the same land. Using only what is said in the document, write an argumentative essay in which you assess how successful you think this attempt is likely to be. Consider: What problems, if any, might arise to make it difficult for either group to exercise the rights this document aims to give them? If you anticipate difficulties, can you recommend changes in the document that would prevent them? Or do you think that the document attempts the impossible and that people with such different ways of life cannot live together? Option: You may write this paper as if you were an English adviser to Myles Standish or a Wampanoag adviser to Paupmunnuck.

4. In many of their dealings with the Native Americans, the English attempted to "reduce them to civilitie of life," as the Massachusetts laws put it. That is, the English assumed that it would be better if the Native Americans learned to live more like English people. Look at the unrestricted deed of land, the laws pertaining to Indians, and the way Gookin talks about, and to, the Christian Native Americans (in Waban). Where in these examples do you see evidence of assumptions about "civilitie"? Use this evidence to support an argument that the English did try to change the Native Americans in particular ways. Option: If you yourself have immigrant experience, you may also compare the ways the English attempted to change the Native Americans with the ways mainstream American culture attempts to change immigrants from very different ways of life today. If you add this dimension to your paper, then your argument will be about how American society in general has treated and still treats members who do not conform to the dominant lifestyle.

5. William Apess contests the pressure of European Americans to make Native Americans move away from their traditional way of life. For example, he calls the treaty with Massasoit an "insult," and he criticizes missionary efforts such as Gookin's (even though he himself is a Christian minister). Collect evidence from the text to help you explain exactly what Apess's grievances are and how he goes about presenting them to make them persuasive to his largely European American audience. Use this evidence to support an argument about what you think a minor-

ity group can do when it is pressured into conforming to the dominant culture. Apess will be your example of a minority group spokesperson, and you will have to say whether you think he is effective in this role. If you wish, you can add another example of a minority group spokesperson you know about, from any time period, and compare and contrast this person's effectiveness with Apess's. Bear in mind that you are looking for examples of a situation in which the minority group is trying to preserve a distinctive way of life. One possible avenue to explore might be current controversies over the extent to which children should be encouraged to preserve a native language other than English in the public schools.

6. In captivity narratives such as Rowlandson's, a relatively isolated member of one culture is immersed in a different, hostile culture to which the person must adjust in order to survive. This is an extreme example of pressure to assimilate such as we have been discussing in this sequence. What does a person do under such circumstances? In response to this question, describe a general model of behavior, using evidence from Rowlandson's text as your prime example. Also use evidence from at least two other texts included in this sequence. Option: If you have the knowledge, you may also use as evidence the experience of someone who has come to the United States from a different culture and adjusted to life here; compare and contrast this immigrant's experience with the captive's and the Native American's. Use this evidence to support an argument about how you think cultural differences should be dealt with in the United States today. How much difference can be tolerated? How much pressure to conform can the dominant culture fairly — or productively — exert?

SEQUENCE 4

How can readers today piece together a biography of Metacomet or Weetamoo?

- Increase Mather, From *A Brief History of the War with the Indians*
- Mary Rowlandson, From *A Narrative of the Captivity and Restoration*
- John Easton, "A Relation of the Indian War"
- William Apess, From *Eulogy on King Philip*

1. As is evident from the portraits of Metacomet (Philip) and Weetamoo in the texts in this sequence, different people often see the same person in different ways. To test this proposition, choose six people who know you; try to choose people from different aspects of your life, such as family, friends, work, school, and so on. Now write a one-paragraph description of yourself as you think each of these six people would write it. If you wish, trade your six paragraphs anonymously with another member of your class and see if the person can identify who is being described.

2. Mary Rowlandson and John Easton met Metacomet face to face; he is the principal speaker in the conference with Native American leaders that Easton attends. Increase Mather and William Apess also write about him. Go through each of these sources and collect all references to Metacomet (Philip). You might simply make a list of page references for each source. Then for each source, write a one-paragraph summary of how you think that source treats Metacomet. In general, what kind of picture is being conveyed?

3. Mary Rowlandson and John Easton met Weetamoo face to face; Increase Mather also writes about her. Go through each of these sources and collect all references to Weetamoo. Rowlandson often calls her simply "my mistress," Easton refers to her as a "queen" (p. 97), and Mather calls her the "squaw-sachem." You might simply make a list of page references for each source. Then write a one-paragraph summary of how you think that source treats Weetamoo. In general, what kind of picture does the writer convey? Option: You may also include Apess in your summary. He does not talk about Weetamoo directly, but his discussion of the charge that Native American women were excessively concerned about their appearance (see p. 128) can be applied to Rowlandson's discussion of Weetamoo's use of adornments and cosmetics.

4. Write a biography of Metacomet, using the information you collected in response to question 2. You will have to decide whether to call him Metacomet or Philip and explain your decision. You will also have to explain how you have handled sources that appear to conflict or to be incomplete or biased.

5. Write a biography of Weetamoo, using the information you collected in response to question 3. You will have to explain how you have handled sources that appear to conflict or to be incomplete or biased.

6. Write a paper in which you argue for particular guidelines that anyone writing a biography ought to follow. Draw on all your work for this sequence to illustrate why each guideline is necessary. Be sure to consider the special problems posed by a biographical subject who left no written record of his or her own and who may be represented in the written record only by strongly biased reporters (whether positive or negative) or by reporters from a different culture who cannot fully understand the subject's way of life. Your response to this assignment might be added as a final section to the biography you write for question 4 or 5.

RESEARCH KIT

Negotiating Difference is an unfinished book: There are many other stories to tell in the history of "negotiating difference" in the United States. This Research Kit is intended to help you expand on the readings provided in this unit. In "Ideas from the Unit Readings," we suggest ways to find out more about relations between English people and Native Americans in colonial New England. In "Branching Out," we suggest ways to transfer some of the issues of negotiating difference raised in this unit to other times and places — specifically, to relations between Native Americans and immigrant groups in your home region. You can pursue these research ideas individually or as group or class projects.

To compile materials, you can start with the short bibliography included in this unit and with standard library search techniques that your teacher or a librarian can explain. Here are some other places where you can inquire for resources (not all regions will have all materials):

- The Smithsonian Institution's *Handbook of North American Indians.* This work is an excellent place to start researching Native American tribes in your region, although not all volumes have been published yet and not all tribes are discussed; see particularly volume 4 of this set, *Indian-White Relations.* Here you can find out what tribes have lived in your region and what some of the significant moments in their relations with European and other immigrant groups have been.
- Town and state historical societies, antiquarian societies, and local historical museums.
- Native American tribal councils, reservation governing bodies, and the state Council or Bureau of Indian Affairs.
- Historical preservation societies, historic sites that are relevant to interactions between Native Americans and other groups and that have been preserved for tourist visits, and the gift shops of these sites.
- Natural history or anthropological museums.
- State university presses, which often have a list of titles on local history that may include works on relations between Native Americans and other groups.

Remember that whenever possible, you want to look at primary source material, that is, texts written by actual participants — Native Americans or others — in the history you are studying. You may have to rely on non–Native Americans' reporting on Native Americans. This is a particularly difficult issue in this unit, as few Native Americans were literate in English before the nineteenth century. Note the caution with which we have treated material taken from Gookin, for example, and emulate that caution.

You are not responsible for representing an authentic or complete Native American point of view in your research. Such authenticity might not be possible, anyway, given the limitations of the written record, even if you yourself are Native American. The focus should not be only on Native American life; nor should it be on the history of non–Native American pioneer efforts in your region. The focus should be on *relations* between Native Americans and the various immigrant groups, and on the texts created out of these contacts.

IDEAS FROM THE UNIT READINGS

1. Find out about the life and writings (if any) of one of these European Americans: John Mason, Benjamin Church, Roger Williams, John Eliot, Thomas Morton; or one of these Native Americans: Squanto, Massasoit, Uncas, Miantonomo, Metacomet, William Apess, Samson Occom. Your focus should be on what each of these people experienced in Native American–European American relations and what each contributed to the record of these relations (through texts they authored, transcribed accounts of their words, or whatever).

2. How did Native Americans use the land in New England, and how did the region's ecology change under English practices (see Cronon, Russell in the bibliography)? Write a paper in which you evaluate the validity of the common idea that Native Americans left the land untouched while European immigrants despoiled it.

3. Trace the history of the town of Natick, Massachusetts — originally a praying town and later depicted in Harriet Beecher Stowe's *Old Town Folks* — from the seventeenth to the nineteenth century. Focus on Native American–European American relations.

4. Trace the history of Mashpee, the Cape Cod praying town, from 1700 to the present. Pay special attention to the civil disobedience action led at Mashpee by William Apess in the early nineteenth century and the Mashpee Native Americans' battle in the twentieth century for federal recognition as a tribe (see Apess, *Indian Nullification,* in the O'Connell edition of Apess's work; Hutchins; and Peters in the bibliography). Or trace the history of some other Native American group in New England from 1700 to the present. Pay particular attention to land-taking controversies such as the Passamaquoddies' in Maine in the twentieth century and recent efforts by New England tribes to open gambling casinos on their property, such as the Pequots' successful enterprise, Foxwood, on their Connecticut reservation.

5. Read several more captivity narratives and develop a picture of the genre. You might concentrate on narratives written in New England in the 1600s and 1700s, perhaps comparing men's and women's versions (see the Vaughan and Clark collection); or you might compare some of the New England narratives with later versions from other parts of the country (such as Seaver and Jemison), including fictionalized accounts. Focus on how the captives experienced resistance to and integration with Native American culture.

6. Find out about Native American religious beliefs and practices in New England before the English settlers came, how these interacted with the religions the settlers brought, and how Native American religious practices developed up to 1800 (see Axtell, *Invasion;* Bowden; Salisbury, *Manitou;* and Simmons in the bibliography).

7. Read a historical novel set in seventeenth-century New England, such as Lydia Maria Child's *Hobomok* or Catherine Sedgwick's *Hope Leslie,* and compare their depictions with the historical sources you have read for this unit, some of which are mentioned in these works.

BRANCHING OUT

1. Research the lives of people or the history of places that you discover have been significant in the relations between Native Americans and other groups in your region.

2. Find out about the religions of Native Americans in your region.

3. Read Frances FitzGerald's book on the writing of history, *America Revised.* She contends that textbook accounts of the past are often manipulated for commercial or ideological reasons. Test her thesis by examining histories of Native American relations with other groups in your region.

4. Trace the history of Native American reservations in your region from the time of their establishment to the present.

5. Find out about different approaches to educating Native Americans in your region, both by Native Americans and by the dominant society, from the times before the first settlement by non–Native Americans to the present.

6. Create an annotated bibliography of visual materials on relations between Native Americans and other groups in your region. Keep in mind that your focus here is not to represent authentic Native American culture but rather to document various media of communication between Native Americans and non–Native Americans (including non–Native Americans' representations of Native Americans). Consider artwork, photography, video, films, handicrafts, "souvenir" items, and so on. Your annotations should describe each entry in light of your awareness of the need to negotiate difference in crossing cultural boundaries — a need the items may address with varying degrees of success.

BIBLIOGRAPHY

Works Included or Excerpted

Apess, William. *Eulogy on King Philip as Pronounced at the Odeon, in Federal Street, Boston.* 1836. Reprinted in *On Our Own Ground: The Complete Writings of William Apess, a Pequot,* edited with an introduction and notes by Barry O'Connell. Amherst: University of Massachusetts Press, 1992.

Bradford, William. *History of Plymouth Plantation, 1620–1647.* Edited with an introduction and notes by Samuel Eliot Morison. New York: Knopf, 1952.

Church, Benjamin, As Told to His Son Thomas Church. *Entertaining Passages Relating to Philip's War.* 1716. Reprinted in *So Dreadfull a Judgment: Puritan Responses to King Philip's War, 1676–1677,* edited by Richard Slotkin and James Folsom. Middletown, Conn.: Wesleyan University Press, 1978.

Easton, John. "A Relation of the Indian War." 1675. Reprinted in *Narratives of the Indian Wars, 1675–1699,* edited by Charles H. Lincoln. 1913. Reprint, New York: Barnes and Noble, 1966.

Gardener, Lion. "Leift. Lion Gardener His Relation of the Pequot Warres." c. 1660. Reprinted in Orr, *History of the Pequot War.*

Gookin, Daniel. *An Historical Account of the Doings and Sufferings of the Christian Indians in New England, in the Years 1675, 1676, 1677.* 1677. Reprint, New York: Arno Press, 1972.

Laws pertaining to the Indians. Reprinted in Vaughan, *New England Frontier.*

Mather, Increase. *A Brief History of the War with the Indians in New-England.* 1676. Reprinted in *So Dreadfull a Judgment: Puritan Responses to King Philip's War, 1676–1677,* edited by Richard Slotkin and James Folsom. Middletown, Conn.: Wesleyan University Press, 1978.

Orr, Charles, ed. *History of the Pequot War.* 1897. Reprint, New York: AMS, 1980.

Paper Left on a Bridge Post at Medfield, Massachusetts. Reprinted in Gookin, *An Historical Account.*

Pittimee, Andrew. Petition. Reprinted in Gookin, *An Historical Account.*

Restricted Deed. Reprinted in Vaughan, *New England Frontier.*

Rowlandson, Mary. *The Sovereignty and Goodness of God, Together with the Faithfulness of His Promises Displayed; Being a Narrative of the Captivity and Restoration of Mrs. Mary Rowlandson.* 1682. Reprinted in *Puritans among the Indians: Accounts of Captivity and Redemption, 1676–1724,* edited by Alden Vaughan and Edward W. Clark. Cambridge: Harvard University Press, Belknap Press, 1981.

Rules for the Praying Indian Town of Concord, Massachusetts. Reprinted in Vaughan, *New England Frontier.*

Treaty of Hartford. Reprinted in Vaughan, *New England Frontier.*

Treaty of Peace and Alliance between Chief Massasoit of the Wampanoags and Governor Carver of Plymouth. Reprinted in Vaughan, *New England Frontier.*

Treaty of Submission. Reprinted in Vaughan, *New England Frontier.*

Unrestricted Deed. Reprinted in Vaughan, *New England Frontier.*

Underhill, John. *Newes from America.* 1638. Reprinted in Orr, *History of the Pequot War.*

Vaughan, Alden. *New England Frontier: 1620—1675.* 1965. 2nd ed., New York: Norton, 1979.

Waban. Speech at the End of King Philip's War. Reprinted in Gookin, *An Historical Account.*

Other Sources

Axtell, James. *The European and the Indian.* New York: Oxford University Press, 1981.

———. *The Invasion Within: The Contest of Cultures in Colonial North America.* New York: Oxford University Press, 1985.

———, ed. *The Indian Peoples of Eastern American: A Documentary History of the Sexes.* New York: Oxford University Press, 1981.

Blodgett, Harold. *Samson Occom.* Hanover, N.H.: Dartmouth College Press, 1935.

Bourne, Russell. *The Red King's Rebellion: Racial Politics in New England, 1675—1678.* New York: Atheneum, 1990.

Bowden, Henry Warner. *American Indians and Christian Missions: Studies in Cultural Conflict.* Chicago: University of Chicago Press, 1981.

Cronon, William. *Changes in the Land: Indians, Colonists, and the Ecology of New England.* New York: Hill and Wang, 1983.

Demos, John. *The Unredeemed Captive: A Family Story from Early America.* New York: Knopf, 1994.

Eliot, John. *John Eliot's Indian Dialogues.* 1671. Reprint, edited by Henry Bowden and James Ronda. Westport, Conn.: Greenwood Press, 1980.

FitzGerald, Frances. *American Revised: History Schoolbooks in the Twentieth Century.* New York: Random House, 1979.

Hauptman, Laurence M., and James D. Wherry, eds. *The Pequots in Southern New England: The Fall and Rise of an American Indian Nation.* Norman: University of Oklahoma Press, 1990.

Hutchins, Francis. *Mashpee: The Story of Cape Cod's Indian Town.* West Franklin, N.H.: Amarta Press, 1979.

Jennings, Francis. *The Invasion of America: Indians, Colonialism, and the Cant of Conquest.* Chapel Hill: University of North Carolina Press, 1975.

A Journal of the Pilgrims at Plymouth: Mourt's Relation. 1622. Reprint, edited with notes by Dwight B. Heath. New York: Corinth Books, 1963.

Kolodny, Annette. *The Land before Her.* Chapel Hill: University of North Carolina Press, 1984.

Kupperman, Karen. *Settling with the Indians.* New York: Rowman and Littlefield, 1980.

Love, W. Deloss. *Samson Occom and the Christian Indians of New England.* Boston: Pilgrim Press, 1899.

Mason, John. *An Epitome or Brief History of the Pequot War.* 1677. Reprinted in *History of the Pequot War,* edited with notes by Charles Orr. 1897. Reprint, New York: AMS, 1980.

Morton, Thomas. *New English Canaan.* 1637. Reprint, Amsterdam, N.Y.: Da Capo Press, 1969.

Mourt's Relation. See *A Journal of the Pilgrims at Plymouth.*

Nabokov, Peter, ed. *Native American Testimony.* New York: Harper, 1978.

Peters, Russell. *The Wampanoags of Mashpee.* Somerville, Mass.: Nimrod Press, 1987.

Ruoff, A. LaVonne Brown, and Jerry W. Ward, Jr., eds. *Redefining American Literary History.* New York: Modern Language Association, 1990.

Russell, Howard S. *Indian New England before the Mayflower.* Hanover, N.H.: University Press of New England, 1980.

Salisbury, Neal. *The Indians of New England: A Critical Bibliography.* Bloomington: Indiana University Press, 1982.

——. *Manitou and Providence: Indians, Europeans, and the Making of New England, 1500—1643.* New York: Oxford University Press, 1982.

Seaver, James E., and Mary Jemison. *A Narrative of the Life of Mrs. Mary Jemison.* 1824. Reprint, Syracuse: Syracuse University Press, 1990.

Simmons, William S. *Spirit of the New England Tribes: Indian History and Folklore, 1620—1984.* Hanover, N.H.: University Press of New England, 1986.

Sturtevant, William C., ed. *Handbook of North American Indians.* 20 vols. Vol. 4, *Indian-White Relations,* ed. William Washburn. Washington: Smithsonian Institution, 1988.

Vanderwerth, W. C., ed. *Indian Oratory.* Norman: University of Oklahoma Press, 1971.

Vaughan, Alden, and Edward W. Clark, eds. *Puritans among the Indians: Accounts of Captivity and Redemption, 1676—1724.* Cambridge: Harvard University Press, Belknap Press, 1981.

Williams, Roger. *A Key into the Language of America.* 1643. Reprint, edited by John J. Teunissen and Evelyn J. Hinz. Detroit: Wayne State University Press, 1973.

Wood, William. *New England's Prospect.* 1634. Reprint, edited by Alden Vaughan. Amherst: University of Massachusetts Press, 1977.

The Debate over Slavery and the Declaration of Independence

NEGOTIATIONS

The Declaration of Independence helped to create the United States of America. It announced the separation of the United States from Great Britain on July 4, 1776, shortly after the start of the Revolutionary War. Because of the importance of this document in shaping our nation, it has often been taken as a summary of the high ideals that the nation was intended to embody. Its words are often cited as the philosophical guidelines that should inform legislation in the United States. Given this power imputed to the Declaration's words, it is crucial for us to be able to say exactly what they mean. But can we do that?

Consider what is perhaps the best-known phrase from the Declaration: "All men are created equal." Can we say exactly what this phrase means? Today, most people would agree that it means that all people, regardless of race, sex, or other variables, deserve equal civil rights and equal opportunities to better themselves and attain the good things of life for themselves and their loved ones. We like to think that we are working to achieve this equality through legislation and through the way we interact with one another as citizens.

But even the most casual glance at American history reveals times when, apparently, "all men are created equal" was not given the broad interpretation to which most people subscribe today. For example, the men who signed the Declaration of Independence went on to create a new government in which women and other classes of citizens were disenfranchised — denied the right to vote — and in which the enslavement of African Americans was legal. These legal inequalities, seemingly so at odds with our current understanding of the Declaration, persisted well past the Revolutionary era, and their consequences are still with us today.

What we learn from these apparent inconsistencies between Declaration ideals and social practice is that the meaning of words is hard to determine. Different interpretations of the words of the Declaration have been negotiated many times in American history, and there is no reason to think that the process will stop.

The debate over slavery became the focus of one of the first and most intense periods of contention over the meaning of the Declaration. Beginning in Revolutionary times, some people argued that the ideals of the Declaration precluded slavery and that, therefore, the nation that revered the Declaration ought to abolish slavery. But these antislavery crusaders were opposed by defenders who either denied that the Declaration could be interpreted as opposing slavery or, admitting that it could be so interpreted, attempted to demote the Declaration from its position of respect.

In addition to contending over the legal status of slavery, the debaters also addressed the larger issue of race relations in this country. Slavery's defenders often argued that both African Americans and the rest of American society were better off with African Americans in slavery. Slavery's attackers sometimes argued that African Americans, whether born free or freed from slavery, must be admitted to full American civil rights; others argued that African Americans could never live on terms of equality with whites and should be resettled elsewhere (such as in Africa) once slavery was abolished. Although slavery was finally abolished in 1865, after the Civil War, the larger issues surrounding equitable race relations are still unresolved to this day.

In Unit Two we will focus on the negotiation of difference that took place in the dispute over whether the ideals of the Declaration of Independence required the abolition of slavery. We are not trying to represent the full history of pre-Civil War race relations. Nor are we representing the full complexity of the battle over slavery. Rather, we are focusing on only one aspect of that battle, namely how the Declaration of Independence figured in the debate.

Furthermore, we are narrowing our focus more sharply to highlight the contributions of African American thinkers to the debate. These contributions are important because many historians now agree that African Americans were among the first to argue that there was a contradiction between the ideals of the Declaration of Independence and the practice of slavery. In opposition to their views were the interpretations of the Declaration put forward by defenders of slavery. We have included two selections that attempt to discredit the Declaration's doctrine of equality and a third that argues that the Declaration supports slavery. We have also provided a historical context for these debates by including two relevant texts by Thomas Jefferson as well as speeches and documents relating to the slavery controversy.

OVERVIEW OF THE SELECTIONS

In the first section of the unit, "Jefferson's Views on Slavery," we present Jefferson's original draft of the Declaration of Independence, including a clause condemning slavery, and an account from his *Autobiography* of why the clause was dropped from the final draft. Next is a selection from Jefferson's *Notes on Virginia*, which gives further evidence of his views on slavery and race.

The second section, "The Antislavery Battle," presents the work of five of the many African Americans who contested the meaning of the Declaration as it applied to slavery and black civil rights. Benjamin Banneker, Jefferson's contemporary, accosts Jefferson directly about what Banneker feels is a contradiction between the values expressed in the Declaration and Jefferson's failure to push for an end to slavery. David Walker and Maria Stewart, Boston abolitionists active around 1830, exhort African Americans to act against slavery and discrimination. Walker also vigorously condemns Jefferson's views as expressed in his *Notes on Virginia* and underscores a contradiction between Americans' professed ideals in the Declaration and their support of slavery. Speaking in the 1850s, Frederick Douglass taxes a largely white audience with the tragic irony of the July Fourth holiday for both slaves and free African Americans, playing masterfully on a theme common in African American July Fourth sermons of the period. Charles Langston, arrested for disobeying the Fugitive Slave Law, defends himself on Revolutionary principles. In one way or another, all of these African American intellectuals enlist Declaration ideals on the side of abolition and black civil rights.

In the third section, "The Proslavery Defense," we see what three European American defenders of slavery made of the Declaration. Southern political thinkers George Fitzhugh and Albert Bledsoe interpret the Declaration as opposing slavery — but they then condemn the Declaration. Fitzhugh's method of discrediting the Declaration emphasizes the impiety and malleability of its principal framers, especially Jefferson, whom Fitzhugh portrays as a wild-eyed radical. Bledsoe stresses the damage to a well-ordered society that could be caused by literal application of Declaration ideals. Northern journalist David Christy takes a different tack entirely, denying that the Declaration was ever intended to oppose slavery and adducing historical arguments to support his position.

In the last section of the unit, we present proclamations and public statements relating to the debate over slavery and the Declaration. Most of this section consists of a sampling of documents and speeches showing Revolutionary-era feeling about African Americans and slavery, ranging from a paper manumitting, or freeing, a slave in the spirit of 1776 to a proslavery petition that also draws on Declaration values. The last piece is an antislavery declaration, clearly modeled on the Declaration of Independence, by well-known European American abolitionist William Lloyd Garrison.

HISTORICAL BACKGROUND

The Institution of Slavery in the United States

Although Africans had visited the North American continent with earlier exploring parties, the first African slaves were brought to Virginia in 1619. American slavery was "chattel" slavery, a type of slavery that was much harsher than other forms (which often granted slaves at least some rights). As this system evolved, the owner gained complete power over the slave's body, including the right to control the slave's labor and to sell the slave or the slave's children. A slave was a slave for life unless manumitted, or freed, by the owner; and the children of slave mothers were automatically slaves (even if their fathers were free white men). Slave owners usually had the power to sexually exploit, physically punish, and even kill their slaves, although slave laws at times tried to mitigate this power and to compel at least subsistence support for slaves.

As the institution of slavery evolved in North America, people gradually came to feel that it was a status appropriate only for African Americans. Earlier, Native Americans had also been enslaved, and so had some Europeans, although increasingly in the eighteenth century the institution of indentured servitude was used for white workers. Its restrictions may be contrasted with the harsher terms of chattel slavery. The indentured servant was usually a young teenager compelled to labor for a limited number of years, often until he or she reached the age of twenty-one. Indentured servants could not leave their masters and could be physically punished by them. The indentured servant's master was supposed to provide subsistence support and sometimes to teach the servant a trade. The contracts of indentured servants (and, consequently, the servants' labor) could be bought and sold. Upon the expiration of the contract, however, the servant was free. The condition of indentured servitude was not hereditary.

By 1770, slavery was legal in all the colonies, and there were also free black people in all the colonies. At that time, the percentage of African Americans in the population was the highest it has ever been, ranging from 3 percent in New England to 30–50 percent in the South. By the Revolutionary era, a strong American antislavery movement had developed, led by members of the Society of Friends, or Quakers. Quaker John Woolman's 1754 tract *Some Considerations on the Keeping of Negroes* was one of the most influential colonial antislavery tracts; Anthony Benezet, another important Quaker antislavery leader, helped pioneer racially integrated Quaker schools. Several Quaker meetings banned their members from holding slaves. Antislavery organizations enlisted some prominent Americans, such as Benjamin Franklin. Free African Americans, such as Prince Hall, whose antislavery petition is included here, were also active against slavery.

American Attitudes toward Slavery, 1776–1820

The complexities of Revolutionary-era attitudes concerning slavery and race are well represented in the work of Thomas Jefferson. On the one hand, Jefferson (in *Notes on Virginia*) denounces slavery as a corrupting institution and (in the draft of the Declaration of Independence) attempts to throw it off as another imposition of the tyrannical English king. On the other hand, Jefferson did not fight for the antislavery clause in the Declaration when other delegates wanted to remove it; and in the *Notes,* while advocating gradual emancipation, he also voices suspicions about black inferiority and recommends that, when free, blacks be settled somewhere far away from white society.

African American thinkers challenged Revolutionary leaders to live up to their highest ideals of equality by eliminating slavery. Benjamin Banneker sent a letter to Jefferson responding to Jefferson's comments about African Americans' inferiority in *Notes on Virginia* and urging him to recognize the inconsistency between his sentiments in the Declaration of Independence and his refusal to push for emancipation. Later, in *The Colored Patriots of the American Revolution* (1855), African American historian and abolitionist William C. Nell compiled much testimony by black veterans of the Revolutionary War. Some slaves won their freedom by fighting in the Revolution, and some masters were moved to free their slaves by egalitarian Revolutionary rhetoric. Citing the ideals of the Declaration of Independence, African Americans frequently petitioned the white government for relief from slavery and from laws that discriminated against free blacks.

Antislavery sentiments spread, as antislavery organizations were formed and antislavery ideas were reflected in legislation. Vermont banned slavery in the state in its constitution (1777). Other northern states passed laws for immediate or gradual emancipation. Gradual emancipation usually meant that while adult slaves would remain slaves, their children born after a certain date — often the Fourth of July in a given year — would become free upon reaching adulthood. Immediate emancipation, also called abolition, required the immediate liberation of all slaves. In 1787 Congress passed the Northwest Ordinance banning slavery in the territory north of the Ohio River and east of the Mississippi River, which had not yet been organized into states.

Yet there was still much popular support for slavery. The United States Constitution, ratified in 1789, specified that an African American slave in the southern states counted as three-fifths of a white person in determining the population of these states. Since a state's representation in Congress depended on its population, this provision protected slavery by increasing the representation of the slaveholding states, which refused to ratify the Constitution without it.

Support for slavery grew in the South with the invention of the cotton gin in 1793, which made possible the profitable cultivation of short-staple cotton and created a new economic demand for slaves. After 1800, the year in which Jefferson won the presidency, debates in Congress on the subject of slavery and agitation by antislavery societies dwindled. Increasing legal restrictions were placed not only on slaves but also on free blacks, even in states that had abolished slavery. Intermarriage was banned, and free blacks were limited in where they could live, work, and go to school. Free blacks began to lose the right to vote, either by legal action or by brutality that discouraged their appearance at the polls. By 1820 virtually the only enfranchised African Americans in the country were the few men who voted in northern states.

Colonization schemes could also be seen as detrimental to African

American rights within the United States. The American Colonization Society, founded in 1816, advocated emancipation, but only if joined by "colonization," that is, by forced emigration of all African Americans to some place outside the United States, often Africa. Jefferson supported colonization schemes, including the founding of Liberia in Africa in 1822. Some well-known African Americans, such as Paul Cuffe, also supported colonization plans, but most opposed them. Maria Stewart led protests against colonization, among her other activities on behalf of African American civil rights.

Statehood and Slavery: The Missouri Compromise of 1820

Meanwhile, the question of whether slavery should be allowed to spread within the United States became an explosive political issue. The South was eager to protect slavery within the original slave states by encouraging its spread into territories that would become new states. In spite of the three-fifths rule for counting slaves in legislative representation, population growth in the North was reducing southern representation in Congress to about 40 percent by the early 1800s. New proslavery votes had to come from new slave states.

The North, however, was reluctant to let slavery spread not only because new slave states would presumably vote with the South on many issues besides slavery, but also because considerable distaste for slavery existed. Furthermore, free labor in the North feared competition from increasing numbers of slave workers. Thus, as new states were carved out of the territory west of the Allegheny Mountains, both the North and the South watched carefully to see that the number of slave and free states remained the same.

In 1800 Vermont, New Hampshire, Massachusetts, Connecticut, Rhode Island, New York, New Jersey, and Pennsylvania were the eight free states; Delaware, Maryland, Virginia, Kentucky, North Carolina, Tennessee, South Carolina, and Georgia were the eight slave states. Between 1800 and 1819, Ohio, Indiana, and Illinois joined the Union as free states and Mississippi, Alabama, and Louisiana as slave states. The Northwest Ordinance of 1787 had effectively determined in which of these new states slavery could be permitted. But the Northwest Ordinance did not apply to land west of the Mississippi River.

A crisis arose in 1819 when Missouri applied for statehood. If Missouri was admitted as a slave state, not only would the even balance between slave and free states be disrupted, but the spread of slavery west of the Mississippi would be allowed in principle. In 1820 Congress passed the so-called Missouri Compromise to resolve this crisis. Missouri was admitted as a slave state, and the new state of Maine was carved off of Massachusetts and admitted as a free state. The Compromise also provided that slavery would be banned in any new states formed in the territory north of the southern border of Missouri (a line across the continent at 36° 30' north latitude). The proslavery states assumed that, as with the Northwest Ordinance, slavery would be permitted in the territory where it was not explicitly banned by the Missouri Compromise.

Slavery, Public Agitation, and Politics, 1830–1870

It was during the debate over the Missouri Compromise, according to some historians, that the Declaration of Independence began to be cited frequently in antislavery arguments. Public agitation on the issue of slavery grew, and antislavery movements became more active than they had been since the 1790s. Many women, white and black, who had previously been reluctant to get involved in politics felt compelled to act on the slavery issue, and their activism gave rise to controversies about their place in public life (see Unit Three).

In 1830, the first national convention of free African Americans was held in Philadelphia to work for abolition and greater rights for free blacks. This convention resolved to transform the July Fourth holiday into a day of fasting and prayer over the evils of slavery and racism. Connected to this observance was the development of a rhetorical genre, the Fourth of July sermon denouncing slavery in terms of Declaration ideals. Escaped slave Frederick Douglass, whose Fourth of July address is included here, became one of the most important national leaders of the abolition movement.

In 1831 William Lloyd Garrison, a European American, began to publish the influential abolitionist newspaper *The Liberator* in Boston and to wage a vigorous and highly visible campaign for abolition, supported, at first, by a largely African American readership. Garrison opposed not only colonization but also violent resistance to slavery. Frequently persecuted for his views, Garrison was jailed in 1835, ostensibly to protect him from a mob (abolitionist publisher Elijah Lovejoy had, indeed, been killed by a mob in Illinois). In his cell, Garrison left graffiti stating that the mob had attacked him "for preaching the abominable and dangerous doctrine, that 'all men are created equal,' and that all oppression is odious in the sight of God."[1] Other signs of antislavery and antidiscrimination activity in the 1830s included the founding of the largely white American Anti-Slavery Society in 1833, whose founding document, composed by Garrison, is included here, and the activism on behalf of Native Americans and other people of color by the Pequot minister and writer William Apess (see Unit One).

By 1840 antislavery forces became strong enough to run a candidate for president on their own Liberty Party ticket, and presidential politics throughout the 1840s and 1850s revolved around the issue of slavery, its protection and its spread. While those advocating abolition remained in the minority, some people advocated banning slavery everywhere except in the states where it already existed. Others called for "popular sovereignty," that is, a provision that voters in a territory could determine

---

[1]Quoted in Truman Nelson, ed., *Documents of Upheaval* (New York: Hill and Wang, 1966), 93.

whether that territory would join the Union as a slave or free state. The admission of Texas as a slave state was delayed from 1837 to 1845, while the admission of a corresponding free state, Oregon, was pending. California's proposal to join as a free state, without a balancing slave state and immediately after the election of President Zachary Taylor, who was seen as lukewarm in defending slavery, provoked a crisis in which talk of secession was heard from some southern states.

Congress passed the Compromise of 1850 to address this crisis. This agreement admitted California as a free state but allowed the newly created territories of New Mexico and Utah to decide the slavery question through popular sovereignty. It also included a new Fugitive Slave Law that compelled the residents of free states to help capture escaped slaves. Although the Compromise temporarily quieted southern talk of secession, the Fugitive Slave Law incensed many northerners. Free African Americans such as Charles Langston openly violated the law and defended themselves on grounds of service to the ideals of the Declaration of Independence. Harriet Beecher Stowe, a European American writer, was moved by outrage at the Fugitive Slave Law to write *Uncle Tom's Cabin* (1852), a powerful antislavery novel that both her contemporaries and later historians credited with significantly increasing northern abolitionist sentiments.

Meanwhile, anxiety about slavery in the new western states was exacerbated again by the need to organize Nebraska and Kansas into formal territories. After bitter debate, another "compromise" bill passed Congress in 1854, allowing both regions to follow the popular sovereignty doctrine but with the understanding that Nebraska would be a free territory (and presumably, later, a free state) and Kansas a slave territory (and state). People on both sides of the slavery issue refused to accept this compromise, however, and fighting began in Kansas over whether the territory could become free soil. Bloody battles occurred between proslavery and antislavery settlers, and the fighting continued until Kansas entered as a free state in 1861, just before the start of the Civil War.

While this fighting was raging, the United States Supreme Court's 1857 decision in the *Dred Scott* case dealt a stunning blow both to abolition and to African American civil rights. Dred Scott was a slave who sued for his freedom on the grounds that his master had taken him from Missouri, a slave state, into Illinois, a free state, and then into free Wisconsin Territory. The Court ruled that Scott had no right to sue because African Americans could not become citizens of the United States. A principal basis for this ruling was the justices' interpretation of the Declaration of Independence. The justices ruled that this document and the government it founded were never intended to include blacks because the white political leaders of the time believed that blacks "had no rights which the white man was bound to respect."[2] These words were widely quoted with outrage

[2]United States Supreme Court, "The Dred Scott Decision" (1856), in *Cotton Is King and Pro-Slavery Arguments*, ed. E. N. Elliott (1860; reprint, New York: Negro University Press, 1969), 753.

in the North. Furthermore, the Court ruled that the laws forbidding slavery in the territories — specifically the Missouri Compromise — were unconstitutional, and therefore Scott was still a slave. This ruling on the Missouri Compromise suggested that any congressional attempt to limit slavery in new states would be unconstitutional.

As much as the North felt outraged by the Fugitive Slave Law and the *Dred Scott* decision, the South also felt threatened by the prospect of violent opposition to slavery, already seen in the battles in Kansas. Slave revolts, although quickly suppressed, had occurred periodically since the late 1700s and were the terror of southern whites. Then in 1859, northern white abolitionist John Brown, who had previously been involved in the fighting in Kansas, attempted to start a slave rebellion at Harpers Ferry, Virginia (now West Virginia). He and a small band of African American and white fighters occupied the federal arsenal at Harpers Ferry and offered arms to the local slaves, many of whom joined them. Their revolt was unsuccessful, however, and Brown and others were executed for the raid. But Brown, whose incursion had been funded by well-known abolitionists, was treated as a martyred hero in the North.

In this highly charged situation, the Democratic Party split in the presidential election of 1860. Northern Democrats supported a popular sovereignty platform, while southern Democrats pushed for explicit protection for slavery in the territories. The new Republican Party ran an antislavery candidate, Abraham Lincoln, and Lincoln won.

One month after Lincoln's victory, in December 1860, South Carolina seceded from the United States, precipitating a chain of secessions by other southern states. They formed a separate nation, the Confederate States of America, and inaugurated their president, Jefferson Davis, even before Lincoln was installed in office. Davis cited the Declaration of Independence in his inaugural address as support for the southern states' decision to break away. When Lincoln attempted to provision the federal garrison at Fort Sumter in the harbor of Charleston, South Carolina, in the spring of 1861, South Carolina attacked and the Civil War began.

In his 1863 Gettysburg Address, Lincoln defended this war on the grounds that he was protecting the principle that "all men were created equal." Also in 1863, Lincoln announced the Emancipation Proclamation, freeing slaves in the rebel states and allowing blacks to enlist as Union soldiers. Slavery was not abolished everywhere, however, until the Thirteenth Amendment to the U.S. Constitution was ratified at the war's end, in 1865. The Fifteenth Amendment (1870) guaranteed the right to vote to all American men regardless of race (African American women, along with other American women, did not receive the vote until the Nineteenth Amendment was passed in 1920). African American civil rights, however, were not yet secure; the promises of the Declaration of Independence were not yet realized for them. Even today, much remains to be done.

THOMAS JEFFERSON

Draft of the Declaration of Independence (1776)

Thomas Jefferson (1743–1826) was born in Virginia, son of a wealthy, slave-holding plantation owner. Trained as a lawyer, he became active in colonial politics and was a leading writer on resistance to British authority. At the Continental Congress in 1776, which he attended as a representative from Virginia, Jefferson was asked to head a committee preparing a declaration of the meeting's resolve for independence from Great Britain. Jefferson wrote the draft himself, later incorporating suggestions from other members of the congress. The changes are indicated in the text reprinted here, accompanied by Jefferson's commentary. (Both are taken from his *Autobiography*, first published in 1829.) Jefferson's Declaration of Independence, signed by the congress on July 4, 1776, has become a foundational document of American belief, and the date of its signing a national holiday. Jefferson was an important leader in the new United States government. In 1800 he was elected the third president of the United States and served for two terms. In later life, Jefferson founded and nurtured the University of Virginia. He died on July 4, 1826.

Then and now, many observers have questioned Jefferson's inactivity in opposing slavery (see, for example, the challenge of his African American contemporary Benjamin Banneker, p. 189). Jefferson continued to hold slaves throughout his life, declining to participate in a friend's scheme to free both families' slaves and settle them on their plantations as tenant farmers. Jefferson was also suspected of having several children with his slave Sally Hemmings. Although modern biographers have generally discounted this charge, it kept a powerful hold on the nineteenth-century American imagination, and one of the first novels by an African American writer, an escaped slave, depicted the tragic fate of Jefferson's supposed mulatto daughter (*Clotel, or the President's Daughter*, by William Wells Brown, 1853).

CONGRESS PROCEEDED THE SAME DAY[1] to consider the Declaration of Independence, which had been reported and lain on the table the Friday pre-

Thomas Jefferson, Draft of the Declaration of Independence, reprinted in vol. 1 of *The Writings of Thomas Jefferson*, ed. Andrew A. Lipscomb and Albert Ellery Bergh (Washington, D.C.: Thomas Jefferson Memorial Society, 1903), 27–38.

In the notes, EDS. = Patricia Bizzell and Bruce Herzberg.

[1]The "same day" is July 4, 1776, when the Continental Congress voted for the resolution to declare the colonies' independence from Great Britain. In the following paragraph, Jefferson describes how the congress completed its deliberations on the wording of the document and then signed it. — EDS.

ceding, and on Monday referred to a committee of the whole. The pusil-
lanimous idea that we had friends in England worth keeping terms with,
still haunted the minds of many. For this reason, those passages which conveyed censures on the people of England were struck out, lest they should
give them offence. The clause too, reprobating the enslaving the inhabitants of Africa, was struck out in complaisance to South Carolina and
Georgia, who had never attempted to restrain the importation of slaves,
and who, on the contrary, still wished to continue it. Our northern
brethren also, I believe, felt a little tender under those censures; for
though their people had very few slaves themselves, yet they had been
pretty considerable carriers of them to others. The debates, having taken
up the greater parts of the 2d, 3d, and 4th days of July, were, on the
evening of the last, closed; the Declaration was reported by the committee,
agreed to by the House, and signed by every member present, except Mr.
Dickinson. As the sentiments of men are known not only by what they receive, but what they reject also, I will state the form of the Declaration as
originally reported. The parts struck out by Congress shall be distinguished by a black line drawn under them;[2] and those inserted by them
shall be placed in the margin, or in a concurrent column.

A DECLARATION BY THE REPRESENTATIVES OF THE UNITED STATES OF AMERICA, IN GENERAL CONGRESS ASSEMBLED

DRAFT DOCUMENT	TEXT ADDED
When, in the course of human events, it becomes necessary for one people to dissolve the political bands which have con- nected them with another, and to assume among the powers of the earth the separate and equal station to which the laws of nature and of nature's God entitle them, a decent respect to the opinions of mankind requires that they should declare the causes which impel them to the separation.	
We hold these truths to be self evident: that all men are created equal; that they are endowed by their Creator with [*inherent and*] inalienable rights; that among these are life, liberty, and the pursuit of happiness; that to secure these rights, governments are instituted among men, deriving their just powers from the consent of the governed; that whenever any form of government becomes destructive of these ends, it is the right of the people to alter or to abolish it, and to insti- tute new government, laying its foundation on such prin- ciples, and organizing its powers in such form, as to them shall seem most likely to effect their safety and happiness.	*certain*

[2]In this book the parts struck out are printed in italics and enclosed in brackets. — EDS.

TEXT ADDED   DRAFT DOCUMENT

Prudence, indeed, will dictate that governments long established should not be changed for light and transient causes;
and accordingly all experience hath shown that mankind are
more disposed to suffer while evils are sufferable, than to
right themselves by abolishing the forms to which they are accustomed. But when a long train of abuses and usurpations,
[*begun at a distinguished period and*] pursuing invariably the
same object, evinces a design to reduce them under absolute
despotism, it is their right, it is their duty to throw off such
government, and to provide new guards for their future security. Such has been the patient sufferance of these colonies;
alter   and such is now the necessity which constrains them to [*ex-
punge*] their former systems of government. The history of
repeated   the present king of Great Britain is a history of [*unremitting*]
all having   injuries and usurpations, [*among which appears no solitary fact
to contradict the uniform tenor of the rest, but all have*] in direct
object the establishment of an absolute tyranny over these
states. To prove this, let facts be submitted to a candid world
[*for the truth of which we pledge a faith yet unsullied by falsehood.*]

He has refused his assent to laws the most wholesome and
necessary for the public good.

He has forbidden his governors to pass laws of immediate
and pressing importance, unless suspended in their operation till his assent should be obtained; and, when so suspended, he has utterly neglected to attend to them.

He has refused to pass other laws for the accommodation
of large districts of people, unless those people would relinquish the right of representation in the legislature, a right inestimable to them, and formidable to tyrants only.

He has called together legislative bodies at places unusual,
uncomfortable, and distant from the depository of their public records, for the sole purpose of fatiguing them into compliance with his measures.

He has dissolved representative houses repeatedly [*and
continually*] for opposing with manly firmness his invasions on
the rights of the people.

He has refused for a long time after such dissolutions to
cause others to be elected, whereby the legislative powers, incapable of annihilation, have returned to the people at large
for their exercise, the state remaining, in the meantime, exposed to all the dangers of invasion from without and convulsions within.

He has endeavored to prevent the population of these
states;[3] for that purpose obstructing the laws for naturaliza-
tion of foreigners, refusing to pass others to encourage their
migrations hither, and raising the conditions of new appropriations of lands.

[3] That is, British law has discouraged the growth of the English immigrant population in
the colonies. — EDS.

DRAFT DOCUMENT   **TEXT ADDED**

He has [*suffered*] the administration of justice [*totally to*   *obstructed*
cease in some of these states] refusing his assent to laws for estab-   *by*
lishing judiciary powers.

He has made [*our*] judges dependent on his will alone for
the tenure of their offices, and the amount and payment of
their salaries.

He has erected a multitude of new offices, [*by a self-*
assumed power] and sent hither swarms of new officers to harass our people and eat out their substance.

He has kept among us in times of peace standing armies
[*and ships of war*] without the consent of our legislatures.

He has affected to render the military independent of,
and superior to, the civil power.

He has combined with others[4] to subject us to a jurisdiction foreign to our constitutions and unacknowledged by our
laws, giving his assent to their acts of pretended legislation for
quartering large bodies of armed troops among us; for protecting them by a mock trial from punishment for any murders which they should commit on the inhabitants of these
states; for cutting off our trade with all parts of the world; for
imposing taxes on us without our consent; for depriving us
[ ] of the benefits of trial by jury; for transporting us beyond   *in many cases*
seas to be tried for pretended offences; for abolishing the free
system of English laws in a neighboring province,[5] establishing therein an arbitrary government, and enlarging its boundaries, so as to render it at once an example and fit instrument
for introducing the same absolute rule into these [*states*]; for   *colonies*
taking away our charters, abolishing our most valuable laws,
and altering fundamentally the forms of our governments; for
suspending our own legislatures, and declaring themselves invested with power to legislate for us in all cases whatsoever.

He has abdicated government here [*withdrawing his gover-*   *by declaring us out*
nors, and declaring us out of his allegiance and protection.]   *of his protection,*
                                                                      and waging war
He has plundered our seas, ravaged our coasts, burnt our   *against us.*
towns, and destroyed the lives of our people.

He is at this time transporting large armies of foreign mercenaries to complete the works of death, desolation and
tyranny already begun with circumstances of cruelty and per-
fidy [ ] unworthy the head of a civilized nation.   *scarcely paralleled*
                                                                      in the most
He has constrained our fellow citizens taken captive on   *barbarous ages, and*
the high seas, to bear arms against their country, to become   *totally*
the executioners of their friends and brethren, or to fall   *excited domestic*
themselves by their hands.   *insurrection among*
                                                                      us, and has
He has [ ] endeavored to bring on the inhabitants of our
frontiers, the merciless Indian savages, whose known rule of
warfare is an undistinguished destruction of all ages, sexes
and conditions [*of existence*].

[4]These "others" are the British Parliament. — EDS.
[5]Canada. — EDS.

TEXT ADDED   **DRAFT DOCUMENT**

[*He has incited treasonable insurrections of our fellow citizens, with the allurements of forfeiture and confiscation of our property.*

He has waged cruel war against human nature itself, violating its most sacred rights of life and liberty in the persons of a distant people who never offended him, captivating and carrying them into slavery in another hemisphere, or to incur miserable death in their transportation thither. This piratical warfare, the opprobium of INFIDEL *powers, is the warfare of the* CHRISTIAN *king of Great Britain. Determined to keep open a market where* MEN *should be bought and sold, he has prostituted his negative*[6] *for suppressing every legislative attempt to prohibit or to restrain this execrable commerce. And that this assemblage of horrors might want no fact of distinguished die, he is now exciting those very people to rise in arms among us, and to purchase that liberty of which he has deprived them, by murdering the people on whom he also obtruded them: thus paying off former crimes committed against the* LIBERTIES *of one people, with crimes which he urges them to commit against the* LIVES *of another.*]

In every stage of these oppressions we have petitioned for redress in the most humble terms: our repeated petitions have been answered only by repeated injuries.

A prince whose character is thus marked by every act which *free* may define a tyrant is unfit to be the ruler of a [ ] people [*who mean to be free. Future ages will scarcely believe that the hardiness of one man adventured, within the short compass of twelve years only, to lay a foundation so broad and so undisguised for tyranny over a people fostered and fixed in principles of freedom*].

Nor have we been wanting in attentions to our British brethren. We have warned them from time to time of at-
an unwarrantable tempts by their legislature to extend [*a*] jurisdiction over
us [*these our states*]. We have reminded them of the circumstances of our emigration and settlement here, [*no one of which could warrant so strange a pretension: that these were effected at the expense of our own blood and treasure, unassisted by the wealth or the strength of Great Britain: that in constituting indeed our several forms of government, we had adopted one common king, thereby laying a foundation for perpetual league and amity with them: but that submission to their parliament was no part of our con-*
have *stitution, nor ever in idea, if history may be credited: and,*] we [ ]
and we have appealed to their native justice and magnanimity [*as well as*
conjured them by *to*] the ties of our common kindred to disavow these usurpa-
would inevitably tions which [*were likely to*] interrupt our connection and correspondence. They too have been deaf to the voice of justice and of consanguinity, [*and when occasions have been given them, by the regular course of their laws, of removing from their councils the disturbers of our harmony, they have, by their free election, reestablished them in power. At this very time too, they are permitting their chief magistrate to send over not only soldiers of our common blood, but Scotch and foreign mercenaries to invade and destroy us. These*

[6]Veto power; that is, the king has misused this power. — EDS.

DRAFT DOCUMENT   **TEXT ADDED**

*facts have given the last stab to agonizing affection, and manly spirit
bids us to renounce forever these unfeeling brethren. We must endeavor to forget our former love for them, and hold them as we hold
the rest of mankind, enemies in war, in peace friends. We might have
been a free and a great people together; but a communication of
grandeur and of freedom, it seems, is below their dignity. Be it so,
since they will have it. The road to happiness and to glory is open to
us, too. We will tread it apart from them, and]* acquiesce in the
necessity which denounces our [*eternal*] separation [   ]!

*We must therefore
and hold them as we
hold the rest of
mankind, enemies
in war, in peace
friends.*

We therefore the representatives of
the United States of America in General
Congress assembled, do in the name,
and by the authority of the good people
of these [*states reject and renounce all allegiance and subjection to the kings of Great
Britain and all others who may hereafter
claim by, through or under them; we utterly
dissolve all political connection which may
heretofore have subsisted between us and the
people or parliament of Great Britain: and finally we do assert and declare these colonies to
be free and independent states,*] and that as
free and independent states, they have
full power to levy war, conclude peace,
contract alliances, establish commerce,
and to do all other acts and things which
independent states may of right do.

And for the support of this declaration, we mutually pledge to each other
our lives, our fortunes, and our sacred
honor.

*We, therefore, the representatives of the
United States of America in General Congress
assembled, appealing to the supreme judge of
the world for the rectitude of our intentions, do
in the name, and by the authority of the good
people of these colonies, solemnly publish and
declare, that these united colonies are, and of
right ought to be free and independent states;
that they are absolved from all allegiance to
the British crown, and that all political connection between them and the state of Great
Britain is, and ought to be, totally dissolved;
and that as free and independent states, they
have full power to levy war, conclude peace,
contract alliances, establish commerce, and to
do all other acts and things which independent states may of right do.*

*And for the support of this declaration,
with a firm reliance on the protection of divine providence, we mutually pledge to each
other our lives, our fortunes, and our sacred
honor.*

The Declaration thus signed on the 4th, on paper, was engrossed on
parchment, and signed again on the 2d of August.

READING CRITICALLY

1. In the deleted Declaration clause condemning slavery, what does Jefferson
say is wrong with slavery?

2. According to Jefferson, why was the passage condemning slavery taken out of
the Declaration?

3. Go through the Declaration and try to explain why the Continental Congress
made each of the changes Jefferson notes.

WRITING ANALYTICALLY

1. Imagine that you are a member of the Continental Congress who either supports or rejects the Declaration passage condemning slavery. Compose a brief speech to the other members of the congress, trying to persuade them to agree with you. Option: Only free middle- and upper-class white men were members of the Continental Congress. Imagine that you are a member of some other social group (such as a free black woman or a white male indentured servant) addressing the congress, pro or con, on the slavery passage.

2. In arguing that both African Americans and the rest of society are better off if African Americans are kept in slavery, Albert Bledsoe (p. 250) writes:

> No greater want is known to man, indeed, than the restraints of law and government. Hence, all men have an equal right to these, but not to the same restraints, to the same laws and governments. All have an equal right to that government which is the best for them. But the same government is not the best for all. A despotism is best for some; a limited monarchy is best for others; while, for a third people, a representative republic is the best form of government. (255)

Write a paper in which you imagine what Jefferson would say to the general principles that Bledsoe expresses here, basing your argument on what you know about Jefferson from the Declaration of Independence. Option: Add a section to your paper in which you speculate about how Jefferson would react to Bledsoe's specific application of this general argument to the defense of slavery.

THOMAS JEFFERSON

From *Notes on Virginia* (1788)

While Thomas Jefferson (1743–1826) was serving as governor of Virginia during the Revolutionary War (1779–81), he received a request from the French legation in Philadelphia to provide more information on the state. In response, and using as an organizational scheme the specific questions in the French request, Jefferson wrote his *Notes on Virginia* (first American edition, 1788). The *Notes* survey the geography, plants, animals, and human inhabitants of Virginia from the perspective of a naturalist who wishes to prove that America is in no way inferior to Europe. We have excerpted two passages from the *Notes*. One, like the antislavery clause that other Continental Congress members removed from Jefferson's first draft of the Declaration, expresses a strong condemnation of slavery. In the other, Jefferson makes

Thomas Jefferson, *Notes on Virginia*, reprinted in vol. 2 of *The Writings of Thomas Jefferson*, ed. Andrew A. Lipscomb and Albert Ellery Bergh (Washington, D.C.: Thomas Jefferson Memorial Society, 1903), 179–228.

In the notes, TJ = Thomas Jefferson, EDS. = Patricia Bizzell and Bruce Herzberg.

many negative generalizations about African Americans and voices his suspicion that they are mentally inferior to whites. For further information on Jefferson, see page 174.

For further information on Jefferson, see page 174.

QUERY XIV

The Administration of Justice and the Description of the Laws?

. . . IT WILL PROBABLY BE ASKED, Why not retain and incorporate the blacks into the State, and thus save the expense of supplying by importation of white settlers, the vacancies they will leave?[1] Deep-rooted prejudices entertained by the whites; ten thousand recollections, by the blacks, of the injuries they have sustained; new provocations; the real distinctions which nature has made; and many other circumstances, will divide us into parties, and produce convulsions, which will probably never end but in the extermination of the one or the other race. To these objections, which are political, may be added others, which are physical and moral. The first difference which strikes us is that of color. Whether the black of the negro resides in the reticular membrane between the skin and scarf-skin, or in the scarf-skin itself; whether it proceeds from the color of the blood, the color of the bile, or from that of some other secretion, the difference is fixed in nature, and is as real as if its seat and cause were better known to us. And is this difference of no importance? Is it not the foundation of a greater or less share of beauty in the two races? Are not the fine mixtures of red and white, the expressions of every passion by greater or less suffusions of color in the one, preferable to that eternal monotony, which reigns in the countenances, that immovable veil of black which covers the emotions of the other race? Add to these, flowing hair, a more elegant symmetry of form, their own judgment in favor of the whites, declared by their preference of them, as uniformly as is the preference of the Oran-ûtan for the black woman over those of his own species. The circumstance of superior beauty, is thought worthy attention in the propagation of our horses, dogs, and other domestic animals; why not in that of man? Besides those of color, figure, and hair, there are other physical distinctions proving a difference of race. They have less hair on the face and body. They secrete less by the kidneys, and more by the glands of the skin, which gives them a very strong and disagreeable odor. This greater degree of transpiration, renders them more tolerant of heat, and less so of cold than the whites. Per-

---

[1]In the passage immediately preceding this excerpt, Jefferson recommends emancipating all slaves born after a certain date and using public money to educate them in useful trades and, when they reach adulthood, to equip them as homesteaders and send them away from the United States to start their own colony. — EDS.

haps, too, a difference of structure in the pulmonary apparatus, which a late ingenious experimentalist has discovered to be the principal regulator of animal heat, may have disabled them from extricating, in the act of inspiration, so much of that fluid from the outer air, or obliged them in expiration, to part with more of it. They seem to require less sleep. A black after hard labor through the day, will be induced by the slightest amusements to sit up till midnight, or later, though knowing he must be out with the first dawn of the morning. They are at least as brave, and more adventuresome. But this may perhaps proceed from a want of forethought, which prevents their seeing a danger till it be present. When present, they do not go through it with more coolness or steadiness than the whites. They are more ardent after their female; but love seems with them to be more an eager desire, than a tender delicate mixture of sentiment and sensation. Their griefs are transient. Those numberless afflictions, which render it doubtful whether heaven has given life to us in mercy or in wrath, are less felt, and sooner forgotten with them. In general, their existence appears to participate more of sensation than reflection. To this must be ascribed their disposition to sleep when abstracted from their diversions, and unemployed in labor. An animal whose body is at rest, and who does not reflect must be disposed to sleep of course. Comparing them by their faculties of memory, reason, and imagination, it appears to me that in memory they are equal to the whites; in reason much inferior, as I think one could scarcely be found capable of tracing and comprehending the investigations of Euclid;[2] and that in imagination they are dull, tasteless, and anomalous. It would be unfair to follow them to Africa for this investigation. We will consider them here, on the same stage with the whites, and where the facts are not apocryphal on which a judgment is to be formed. It will be right to make great allowances for the difference of condition, of education, of conversation, of the sphere in which they move. Many millions of them have been brought to, and born in America. Most of them, indeed, have been confined to tillage, to their own homes, and their own society; yet many have been so situated, that they might have availed themselves of the conversation of their masters; many have been brought up to the handicraft arts, and from that circumstance have always been associated with the whites. Some have been liberally educated, and all have lived in countries where the arts and sciences are cultivated to a considerable degree, and all have had before their eyes samples of the best works from abroad. The Indians, with no advantages of this kind, will often carve figures on their pipes not destitute of design and merit. They will crayon out an animal, a plant, or a country, so as to prove the existence of a germ[3] in their minds which only wants cultivation. They astonish you with strokes of the most sublime oratory; such as prove their reason and sentiment strong, their imagination glowing and elevated. But never yet

[2]Euclid was an ancient Greek mathematician who developed geometry — by no means the most difficult form of mathematics with which Jefferson was acquainted. — EDS.

[3]"Germ" here means a beginning spark of life, or more precisely in Jefferson's metaphor, a spark of the "higher" intelligence he claims is shown by whites. — EDS.

could I find that a black had uttered a thought above the level of plain narration; never saw even an elementary trait of painting or sculpture. In music they are more generally gifted than the whites with accurate ears for tune and time, and they have been found capable of imagining a small catch.[4] Whether they will be equal to the composition of a more extensive run of melody, or of complicated harmony, is yet to be proved. Misery is often the parent of the most affecting touches in poetry. Among the blacks is misery enough, God knows, but no poetry. Love is the peculiar oestrum of the poet. Their love is ardent, but it kindles the senses only, not the imagination. Religion, indeed, has produced a Phyllis Whately;[5] but it could not produce a poet. The compositions published under her name are below the dignity of criticism. The heroes of the Dunciad are to her, as Hercules to the author of that poem.[6] Ignatius Sancho has approached nearer to merit in composition; yet his letters do more honor to the heart than the head.[7] They breathe the purest effusions of friendship and general philanthropy, and show how great a degree of the latter may be compounded with strong religious zeal. He is often happy in the turn of his compliments, and his style is easy and familiar, except when he affects a Shandean fabrication of words.[8] But his imagination is wild and extravagant, escapes incessantly from every restraint of reason and taste, and, in the course of its vagaries, leaves a tract of thought as incoherent and eccentric, as is the course of a meteor through the sky. His subjects should often have led him to a process of sober reasoning; yet we find him always substituting sentiment for demonstration. Upon the whole, though we admit him to the first place among those of his own color who have presented themselves to the public judgment, yet when we compare him with the writers of the race among whom he lived and particularly with the epistolary class in which he has taken his own stand, we are compelled to enrol him at the bottom of the column. This criticism supposes the letters published under his name to be genuine, and to have received amendment

[4]The instrument proper to them is the Banjar, which they brought hither from Africa, and which is the original of the guitar, its chords being precisely the four lower chords of the guitar. — TJ

[5]Phillis Wheatley (1753–84) was brought from Africa as a child in the mid-eighteenth century and sold to the Wheatley family in Boston, who educated her and encouraged her writing. Her *Poems on Various Subjects, Religious and Moral* (1773) received wide acclaim. Twentieth-century literary scholarship recognizes her as an important early voice in the African American literary tradition. — EDS.

[6]The *Dunciad* (1729) was a long mock epic poem by English poet Alexander Pope, in which he satirized people he considered to be bad poets. Pope was small and frail. Hercules was the Greek mythic hero of enormous strength. — EDS.

[7]Ignatio Sancho was born on a slave ship bound for the West Indies and then sent to England. The aristocratic Montagu family rescued him from cruel owners and gave him a prestigious and lucrative position as butler in their home. Here he met and struck up a correspondence with a number of English literary figures, including Laurence Sterne (see note 8). He wrote poetry and plays as well as letters published after his death (*Letters of the Late Ignatius Sancho, an African*, 1782). — EDS.

[8]A "Shandean fabrication of words" refers to the elaborate verbal habits of the protagonist of the novel *Tristram Shandy* (1760–67) by English writer Laurence Sterne. — EDS.

from no other hand; points which would not be of easy investigation. The improvement of the blacks in body and mind, in the first instance of their mixture with the whites, has been observed by every one, and proves that their inferiority is not the effect merely of their condition of life. We know that among the Romans, about the Augustan age especially, the condition of their slaves was much more deplorable than that of the blacks on the continent of America. The two sexes were confined in separate apartments, because to raise a child cost the master more than to buy one. Cato,[9] for a very restricted indulgence to his slaves in this particular, took from them a certain price. But in this country the slaves multiply as fast as the free inhabitants. Their situation and manners place the commerce between the two sexes almost without restraint. The same Cato, on a principle of economy, always sold his sick and superannuated slaves. He gives it as a standing precept to a master visiting his farm, to sell his old oxen, old wagons, old tools, old and diseased servants, and everything else become useless. "Vendat boves vetulos, plaustrum vetus, feramenta vetera, servum senem, servum morbosum, et si quid aliud supersit vendat." Cato de re rustica, c. 2.[10] The American slaves cannot enumerate this among the injuries and insults they receive. It was the common practice to expose in the island Aesculapius, in the Tyber, diseased slaves whose cure was like to become tedious. The emperor Claudius, by an edict, gave freedom to such of them as should recover, and first declared that if any person chose to kill rather than to expose them, it should not be deemed homicide. The exposing them is a crime of which no instance has existed with us; and were it to be followed by death, it would be punished capitally. We are told of a certain Vedius Pollio, who, in the presence of Augustus, would have given a slave as food to his fish, for having broken a glass. With the Romans, the regular method of taking the evidence of their slaves was under torture. Here it has been thought better never to resort to their evidence.[11] When a master was murdered, all his slaves, in the same house, or within hearing, were condemned to death. Here punishment falls on the guilty only, and as precise proof is required against him as against a freeman. Yet notwithstanding these and other discouraging circumstances among the Romans, their slaves were often their rarest artists. They excelled too in science, insomuch as to be usually employed as tutors to their master's children. Epictetus, Terence, and Phaedrus, were slaves.[12] But they were of the race of whites. It is not their condition then, but nature, which has produced the distinction. Whether further observation will or will not verify the conjecture, that nature has been less bountiful to them in the endowments of

[9]Cato the Younger, or Cato of Utica (95 B.C.E.–46 B.C.E.), Roman statesman, renowned for his honesty and incorruptibility. — EDS.

[10]"Sell old oxen, old wagons, old tools, old servants, mortally ill servants, sell everything that is useless." — EDS.

[11]Slaves could not give evidence in American courts. — EDS.

[12]These men were all well-known ancient Roman writers: Epictetus was a philosopher, Terence was a comedic playwright, and Phaedrus was a writer of fables in the style of Aesop. — EDS.

the head, I believe that in those of the heart she will be found to have done them justice. That disposition to theft with which they have been branded, must be ascribed to their situation, and not to any depravity of the moral sense. The man in whose favor no laws of property exist, probably feels himself less bound to respect those made in favor of others. When arguing for ourselves, we lay it down as a fundamental, that laws, to be just, must give a reciprocation of right; that, without this, they are mere arbitrary rules of conduct, founded in force, and not in conscience; and it is a problem which I give to the master to solve, whether the religious precepts against the violation of property were not framed for him as well as his slave? And whether the slave may not as justifiably take a little from one who has taken all from him, as he may slay one who would slay him? That a change in the relations in which a man is placed should change his ideas of moral right or wrong, is neither new, nor peculiar to the color of the blacks. Homer tells us it was so two thousand six hundred years ago.[13]

> 'Emisu, ger t' aretes apoainutai euruopa Zeus
> Haneros, eut' an min kata doulion ema elesin.
> — *Odd. 17, 323.*
>
> Jove fix'd it certain, that whatever day
> Makes man a slave, takes half his worth away.

But the slaves of which Homer speaks were whites. Notwithstanding these considerations which must weaken their respect for the laws of property, we find among them numerous instances of the most rigid integrity, and as many as among their better instructed masters, of benevolence, gratitude, and unshaken fidelity. The opinion that they are inferior in the faculties of reason and imagination, must be hazarded with great diffidence. To justify a general conclusion, requires many observations, even where the subject may be submitted to the anatomical knife, to optical glasses, to analysis by fire or by solvents. How much more then where it is a faculty, not a substance, we are examining; where it eludes the research of all the senses; where the conditions of its existence are various and variously combined; where the effects of those which are present or absent bid defiance to calculation; let me add too, as a circumstance of great tenderness, where our conclusion would degrade a whole race of men from the rank in the scale of beings which their Creator may perhaps have given them. To our reproach it must be said, that though for a century and a half we have had under our eyes the races of black and of red men, they have never yet been viewed by us as subjects of natural history. I advance it, therefore, as a suspicion only, that the blacks, whether originally a distinct race, or made distinct by time and circumstances, are inferior to the whites in the endowments both of body and mind. It is not against experience to

---

[13]Homer was the ancient Greek poet who composed both the *Iliad*, an epic poem about the Trojan War, and the epic from which Jefferson quotes here, the *Odyssey*, about the wanderings of the warrior Odysseus on his way home from the Trojan War. — EDS.

suppose that different species of the same genus, or varieties of the same species, may possess different qualifications. Will not a lover of natural history then, one who views the gradations in all the races of animals with the eye of philosophy, excuse an effort to keep those in the department of man as distinct as nature has formed them? This unfortunate difference of color, and perhaps of faculty, is a powerful obstacle to the emancipation of these people. Many of their advocates, while they wish to vindicate the liberty of human nature, are anxious also to preserve its dignity and beauty. Some of these, embarrassed by the question, "What further is to be done with them?" join themselves in opposition with those who are actuated by sordid avarice only. Among the Romans emancipation required but one effort. The slave, when made free, might mix with, without staining the blood of his master. But with us a second is necessary, unknown to history. When freed, he is to be removed beyond the reach of mixture. . . .

QUERY XVIII

The Particular Customs and Manners That May Happen to Be Received in That State?

It is difficult to determine on the standard by which the manners of a nation may be tried, whether *catholic*[14] or *particular*. It is more difficult for a native to bring to that standard the manners of his own nation, familiarized to him by habit. There must doubtless be an unhappy influence on the manners of our people produced by the existence of slavery among us. The whole commerce between master and slave is a perpetual exercise of the most boisterous passions, the most unremitting despotism on the one part, and degrading submissions on the other. Our children see this, and learn to imitate it; for man is an imitative animal. This quality is the germ of all education in him. From his cradle to his grave he is learning to do what he sees others do. If a parent could find no motive either in his philanthropy or his self-love, for restraining the intemperance of passion towards his slave, it should always be a sufficient one that his child is present. But generally it is not sufficient. The parent storms, the child looks on, catches the lineaments of wrath, puts on the same airs in the circle of smaller slaves, gives a loose to the worst of passions, and thus nursed, educated, and daily exercised in tyranny, cannot but be stamped by it with odious peculiarities. The man must be a prodigy who can retain his manners and morals undepraved by such circumstances. And with what execration should the statesman be loaded, who, permitting one half the citizens thus to trample on the rights of the other, transforms those into despots, and these into enemies, destroys the morals of the one part, and the *amor pa-*

[14]That is, universal; no reference to Roman Catholicism is meant. — EDS.

triae[15] of the other. For if a slave can have a country in this world, it must be any other in preference to that in which he is born to live and labor for another; in which he must lock up the faculties of his nature, contribute as far as depends on his individual endeavors to the evanishment of the human race,[16] or entail his own miserable condition on the endless generations proceeding from him. With the morals of the people, their industry also is destroyed. For in a warm climate, no man will labor for himself who can make another labor for him. This is so true, that of the proprietors of slaves a very small proportion indeed are ever seen to labor. And can the liberties of a nation be thought secure when we have removed their only firm basis, a conviction in the minds of the people that these liberties are of the gift of God? That they are not to be violated but with His wrath? Indeed I tremble for my country when I reflect that God is just; that his justice cannot sleep forever; that considering numbers, nature and natural means only, a revolution of the wheel of fortune, an exchange of situation is among possible events; that it may become probable by supernatural interference! The Almighty has no attribute which can take side with us in such a contest. But it is impossible to be temperate and to pursue this subject through the various considerations of policy, of morals, of history natural and civil. We must be contented to hope they will force their way into every one's mind. I think a change already perceptible, since the origin of the present revolution.[17] The spirit of the master is abating, that of the slave rising from the dust, his condition mollifying, the way I hope preparing, under the auspices of heaven, for a total emancipation, and that this is disposed, in the order of events, to be with the consent of the masters, rather than by their extirpation.

READING CRITICALLY

1. What are the "political" objections (p. 181) that Jefferson says make it impossible for African Americans and whites to live together?

2. What judgment does Jefferson pass on the physical differences between African Americans and whites? What does he mean by his assertion that, "in general, their existence appears to participate more of sensation than reflection" (p. 182)? What evidence does Jefferson provide to support this view?

3. What is the point of Jefferson's comparison between African Americans and Native Americans?

4. What is the point of Jefferson's comparison between African slaves in the United States and white slaves in ancient Rome?

[15]Love of country, patriotism. Jefferson argues that slavery destroys African Americans' feelings of patriotism toward the United States. — EDS.

[16]"Contribute . . . to the evanishment of the human race": refrain from having children. — EDS.

[17]That is, the American Revolution, which was in progress when Jefferson began writing the *Notes*. — EDS.

5. Jefferson contends that African Americans are just as moral as whites; how does he defend them from the charge of being prone to theft?

6. Jefferson says that "an unhappy influence on the manners of our people" is "produced by the existence of slavery among us" (p. 186). What is this negative influence? That is, what bad behavior does slavery create in both masters and slaves, according to Jefferson?

7. What changes in masters and slaves does Jefferson see coming about since the start of the American Revolution?

WRITING ANALYTICALLY

1. In general, Jefferson takes the tone of the naturalist or scientific investigator in the *Notes*, as shown in the excerpt from query 14. How do you as a reader react to his discussing race and race relations in such terms? Write a paper in which you quote specific passages from the text to illustrate this scientific tone and, further, evaluate the appropriateness of this tone to the subject matter. Option: Also analyze the tone of query 18, in which Jefferson departs somewhat from his naturalist persona to denounce slavery. Set up your paper as a comparison of queries 14 and 18, arguing for the style you prefer.

2. Catalog and compare the points in Jefferson's attacks on slavery in the draft of the Declaration of Independence and in the *Notes*. Exactly what seem to be Jefferson's primary concerns about slavery, according to this textual evidence? Write a paper in which you argue for an answer to this question.

3. Jefferson argues that slavery among the Romans was more severe than in America and that even under these harsher conditions, Roman slaves achieved more. Jefferson implies by this argument that African Americans owe their lack of achievement more to mental inferiority than to the rigors of slavery. How does antislavery writer David Walker (p. 193) deal with this argument? Whom do you find more persuasive, Jefferson or Walker? Write a paper responding to these questions.

4. Slavery defender George Fitzhugh (p. 239) argues that inequality, such as that institutionalized in slavery, is natural and right. He writes:

> Men are not "born entitled to equal rights!" It would be far nearer the truth to say, "that some were born with saddles on their backs, and others booted and spurred to ride them," — and the riding does them good. They need the reins, the bit and the spur. (p. 241)

Write a paper in which you imagine what Jefferson would say about Fitzhugh's opinion, basing Jefferson's reaction on the excerpts from his work included in this unit.

THE ANTISLAVERY BATTLE

BENJAMIN BANNEKER

Letter to Thomas Jefferson (1791)

Benjamin Banneker (1731–1806) was born to free African American parents who owned a tobacco farm in Maryland. He was educated in an integrated Quaker elementary school and from an early age showed great aptitude in mathematics and mechanical design. Banneker was part of the surveying team that laid out the nation's new capital in Washington, D.C. In 1791, in response to Thomas Jefferson's comments about African Americans' inferiority in *Notes on Virginia,* Banneker sent an almanac he had calculated to Jefferson, then secretary of state, along with the letter reprinted here criticizing Jefferson's lack of support for the abolition of slavery. Jefferson sent him a reply a few weeks later, in which he acknowledged that Banneker's letter and almanac gave evidence that African American mental powers were equal to those of whites. Jefferson was very interested in this evidence and sent copies of Banneker's work to a French scientific correspondent, Condorcet. Fifteen years later, however, Jefferson wrote to the American poet Joel Barlow that Banneker's intelligence was not distinguished and proved nothing. Banneker published the almanac he sent Jefferson, along with their correspondence, and five other almanacs from 1792 to 1797. They went through many editions.

SIR I AM FULLY SENSIBLE of the greatness of that freedom which I take with you on the present occasion; a liberty which Seemed to me scarcely allowable, when I reflected on that distinguished, and dignified station in which you Stand; and the almost general prejudice and prepossession which is so prevalent in the world against those of my complexion.

I suppose it is a truth too well attested to you, to need of proof here, that we are a race of Beings who have long labored under the abuse and censure of the world, that we have long been looked upon with an eye of contempt, and that we have long been considered rather as brutish than human, and Scarcely capable of mental endowments.

Sir, I hope I may Safely admit, in consequence of that report which hath reached me, that you are a man far less inflexible in Sentiments of this nature, than many others, that you are measurably friendly and well disposed

Benjamin Banneker, Letter to Thomas Jefferson, reprinted in *The Black Presence in the Era of the American Revolution, 1770—1800,* ed. Sidney Kaplan and Emma Nogrady Kaplan (Amherst: University of Massachusetts Press, 1989), 138–44.

In the notes, BB = Benjamin Banneker, EDS. = Patricia Bizzell and Bruce Herzberg.

towards us, and that you are willing and ready to Lend your aid and assistance to our relief from those many distresses and numerous calamities to which we are reduced.

Now Sir if this is founded in truth, I apprehend you will readily embrace every opportunity to eradicate that train of absurd and false ideas and opinions which so generally prevail with respect to us, and that your Sentiments are concurrent with mine, which are that one universal Father hath given being to us all, and that he hath not only made us all of one flesh, but that he hath also without partiality afforded us all the Same Sensations, and endued us all with the same faculties, and that however variable we may be in Society or religion, however diversified in Situation or color, we are all of the Same Family, and Stand in the Same relation to him.

Sir, if these are Sentiments of which you are fully persuaded, I hope you cannot but acknowledge, that it is the indispensable duty of those who maintain for themselves the rights of human nature, and who profess the obligations of Christianity, to extend their power and influence to the relief of every part of the human race, from whatever burthen or oppression they may unjustly labor under; and this I apprehend a full conviction of the truth and obligation of these principles should lead all to.

Sir, I have long been convinced, that if your love for your Selves and for those inesteemable laws which preserve to you the rights of human nature, was founded on Sincerity, you could not but be Solicitous, that every Individual of whatsoever rank or distinction, might with you equally enjoy the blessings thereof, neither could you rest Satisfyed, short of the most active diffusion of your exertions, in order to their promotion from any State of degradation, to which the unjustifiable cruelty and barbarism of men may have reduced them.

Sir I freely and Chearfully acknowledge, that I am of the African race, and in that color which is natural to them of the deepest dye,[1] and it is under a Sense of the most profound gratitude to the Supreme Ruler of the universe, that I now confess to you, that I am not under that State of tyrannical thraldom, and inhuman captivity, to which too many of my brethren are doomed; but that I have abundantly tasted of the fruition of those blessings which proceed from that free and unequaled liberty with which you are favored and which I hope you will willingly allow you have received from the immediate Hand of that Being from whom proceedeth every good and perfect gift.

Sir, Suffer me to recall to your mind that time in which the Arms and tyranny of the British Crown were exerted with every powerful effort in order to reduce you to a State of Servitude; look back I intreat you on the variety of dangers to which you were exposed, reflect on that time in which every human aid appeared unavailable, and in which even hope and fortitude wore the aspect of inability to the Conflict, and you cannot but be led to a Serious and grateful Sense of your miraculous and providential preservation; you cannot but acknowledge, that the present freedom and

---

[1]My Father was brought here a Slave from Africa. — BB

tranquility which you enjoy you have mercifully received, and that it is the peculiar blessing of Heaven.

This Sir, was a time in which you clearly saw into the injustice of a State of Slavery, and in which you had just apprehensions of the horrors of its condition, it was now Sir, that your abhorrence thereof was so excited, that you publicly held forth this true and invaluable doctrine, which is worthy to be recorded and remembered in all Succeeding ages. "We hold these truths to be Self evident, that all men are created equal, and that they are endowed by their creator with certain unalienable rights, that amongst these are life, liberty, and the pursuit of happiness."

Here Sir, was a time in which your tender feelings for yourselves engaged you thus to declare, you were then impressed with proper ideas of the great valuation of liberty, and the free possession of those blessings to which you were entitled by nature; but Sir how pitiable is it to reflect, that altho you were so fully convinced of the benevolence of the Father of mankind, and of his equal and impartial distribution of those rights and privileges which he had conferred upon them, that you should at the Same time counteract his mercies, in detaining by fraud and violence so numerous a part of my brethren under groaning captivity and cruel oppression, that you should at the Same time be found guilty of that most criminal act, which you professedly detested in others, with respect to yourselves.

Sir, I suppose that your knowledge of the situation of my brethren is too extensive to need a recital here; neither shall I presume to prescribe methods by which they may be relieved; otherwise than by recommending to you, and all others, to wean yourselves from those narrow prejudices which you have imbibed with respect to them, and as Job proposed to his friends "Put your Souls in their Souls stead,"[2] thus shall your hearts be enlarged with kindness and benevolence towards them, and thus shall you need neither the direction of myself or others in what manner to proceed herein.

And now, Sir, altho my Sympathy and affection for my brethren hath caused my enlargement thus far, I ardently hope that your candour and generosity will plead with you in my behalf, when I make known to you, that it was not originally my design; but that having taken up my pen in order to direct to you as a present, a copy of an Almanac which I have calculated for the Succeeding year, I was unexpectedly and unavoidably led thereto.

This calculation, Sir, is the production of my arduous study, in this my advanced Stage of life; for having long had unbounded desires to become Acquainted with the Secrets of nature, I have had to gratify my curiosity herein thro my own assiduous application to Astronomical Study, in which I need not to recount to you the many difficulties and disadvantages which I have had to encounter.

---

[2]In the Bible Job was afflicted with terrible losses and illness. Friends urged him to repent the sins that, they claimed, must have caused God to bring on his sufferings. Job steadfastly denied any wrongdoing and reproached his friends, telling them that instead of blaming him, they should be comforting him and trying to imagine the pain he felt. — EDS.

And altho I had almost declined to make my calculation for the ensuing year, in consequence of that time which I had allotted therefor being taking up at the Federal Territory by the request of Mr. Andrew Ellicott,[3] yet finding myself under Several engagements to printers of this state to whom I had communicated my design, on my return to my place of residence, I industriously apply'd myself thereto, which I hope I have accomplished with correctness and accuracy, a copy of which I have taken the liberty to direct to you, and which I humbly request you will favorably receive, and altho you may have the opportunity of perusing it after its publication, yet I chose to send it to you in manuscript previous thereto, that thereby you might not only have an earlier inspection, but that you might also view it in my own hand writing.

And now Sir, I Shall conclude and Subscribe myself with the most profound respect, your most Obedient humble Servant

BENJAMIN BANNEKER

READING CRITICALLY

1. Underline places in the letter where the language sounds like that of the Declaration of Independence. What effect do you think Banneker is trying to achieve with these echoes?

2. Banneker charges Jefferson with a serious inconsistency at the time of the Revolution. What is it?

3. What is Banneker asking Jefferson to do?

WRITING ANALYTICALLY

1. Banneker's rhetorical situation here is difficult. A private citizen, he undertakes to write to the famous political leader Thomas Jefferson and to accuse him of serious hypocrisy. Overall, Banneker's approach to this task could be described as cautious and conciliatory. He works hard to make himself sound credible and to avoid offending Jefferson, even as he presses his point. How does Banneker accomplish this task? Is his approach effective, in your opinion? Write a paper in which you describe and evaluate his rhetorical strategies.

2. Write your own letter to Jefferson on the inconsistency Banneker addresses. You may write as if you were Banneker (that is, write the letter you think Banneker should have written), or create some other eighteenth-century role for yourself (a fellow plantation owner, perhaps), or write in your own identity as a twentieth-century person (what you'd say to Jefferson if you could).

3. Banneker's rhetorical style is clearly very different from that of David Walker (p. 193). Write a letter from Banneker to Walker, commenting on the rhetorical

---

[3]Banneker refers to his work assisting in the surveying of land for the national capital at Washington, D.C. He was recommended for the work by his white neighbor Ellicott. — EDS.

strategies of Walker's *Appeal;* or write the same kind of letter from Walker to Banneker, commenting on Banneker's approach to Jefferson.

DAVID WALKER

From *Walker's Appeal* (1829)

David Walker (1785–1830) was born a free African American in North Carolina. He traveled widely as a young man and then settled in Boston, where he ran a clothing business. Essentially self-made, Walker became a leader in Boston's African American community and a chief instigator of abolitionist activism there at the time he published his *Appeal* in 1829. (Two years later William Lloyd Garrison [p. 270] began publishing the important Boston abolitionist newspaper *The Liberator,* in which the *Appeal* was reviewed at length.) Walker addresses the *Appeal* to African Americans and urges them to act to remedy the "wretchedness" of their people, which he says derives from slavery, ignorance, lack of aid from Christian ministers, and colonization schemes. (Each of the four "articles," or sections, of the appeal discusses one of these four sources of wretchedness.) Walker indeed had to argue that slavery was evil, for slavery's defenders often argued (see George Fitzhugh [p. 239] and Albert Bledsoe [p. 250]) that slavery was the best possible condition for African Americans.

Walker's *Appeal* rapidly went through three editions and remained in print late in the nineteenth century, in spite of the outrage it aroused among white southerners. Some attempted legal measures to suppress the *Appeal,* while others offered a bounty for Walker's death. Walker died suddenly in 1830, amid suspicion that he was poisoned by a bounty seeker. Excerpted here from the third edition (1830) of the *Appeal,* the last Walker produced before his death, are brief sections from the preamble and articles 1, 2, and 4, including passages denouncing the negative views of African Americans expressed by Thomas Jefferson in his *Notes on Virginia* (p. 180).

PREAMBLE

MY DEARLY BELOVED BRETHREN AND FELLOW CITIZENS.

Having traveled over a considerable portion of these United States, and having, in the course of my travels, taken the most accurate observations of things as they exist — the result of my observations has warranted the full

David Walker, *Walker's Appeal in Four Articles; Together with a Preamble, to the Coloured Citizens of the World, but in Particular, and Very Expressly, to Those of the United States of America,* edited with an introduction by Charles M. Wiltse (1829, 1830; reprint, New York: Hill and Wang, 1965), 1–2, 14–16, 26–28, 74–76.

In the notes, DW = David Walker, EDS. = Patricia Bizzell and Bruce Herzberg.

and unshaken conviction, that we, (colored people of these United States,) are the most degraded, wretched, and abject set of beings that ever lived since the world began; and I pray God that none like us ever may live again until time shall be no more. They tell us of the Israelites in Egypt, the Helots in Sparta, and of the Roman Slaves, which last were made up from almost every nation under heaven, whose sufferings under those ancient and heathen nations, were, in comparison with ours, under this enlightened and Christian nation, no more than a cypher — or, in other words, those heathen nations of antiquity, had but little more among them than the name and form of slavery; while wretchedness and endless miseries were reserved, apparently in a phial, to be poured out upon our fathers, ourselves and our children, by *Christian* Americans!

These positions I shall endeavor, by the help of the Lord, to demonstrate in the course of this *Appeal,* to the satisfaction of the most incredulous mind — and may God Almighty, who is the Father of our Lord Jesus Christ, open your hearts to understand and believe the truth.

The *causes,* my brethren, which produce our wretchedness and miseries, are so very numerous and aggravating, that I believe the pen only of a Josephus or a Plutarch,[1] can well enumerate and explain them. Upon subjects, then, of such incomprehensible magnitude, so impenetrable, and so notorious, I shall be obliged to omit a large class of, and content myself with giving you an exposition of a few of those, which do indeed rage to such an alarming pitch, that they cannot but be a perpetual source of terror and dismay to every reflecting mind.

I am fully aware, in making this appeal to my much afflicted and suffering brethren, that I shall not only be assailed by those whose greatest earthly desires are, to keep us in abject ignorance and wretchedness, and who are of the firm conviction that Heaven has designed us and our children to be slaves and *beasts of burden* to them and their children. I say, I do not only expect to be held up to the public as an ignorant, impudent and restless disturber of the public peace, by such avaricious creatures, as well as a mover of insubordination — and perhaps put in prison or to death, for giving a superficial exposition of our miseries, and exposing tyrants. But I am persuaded, that many of my brethren, particularly those who are ignorantly in league with slave-holders or tyrants, who acquire their daily bread by the blood and sweat of their more ignorant brethren — and not a few of those too, who are too ignorant to see an inch beyond their noses, will rise up and call me cursed — Yea, the jealous ones among us will perhaps use more abject subtlety, by affirming that this work is not worth perusing, that we are well situated, and there is no use in trying to better our condition, for we cannot. I will ask one question here. — Can our condition be any worse? — Can it be more mean and abject? If there are any changes, will they not be for the better, though they may appear for the worst at first? Can they get us any lower? Where can they get us? They are afraid to treat us worse, for they know well, the day they do it they are

---

[1]Josephus and Plutarch were historians of the classical Roman era. — EDS.

gone. But against all accusations which may or can be preferred against me, I appeal to Heaven for my motive in writing — who knows that my object is, if possible, to awaken in the breasts of my afflicted, degraded and slumbering brethren, a spirit of inquiry and investigation respecting our miseries and wretchedness in this *Republican*[2] *Land of Liberty! ! ! ! ! . . .*

ARTICLE I

. . . The world knows, that slavery as it existed among the Romans, (which was the primary cause of their destruction) was, comparatively speaking, no more than a *cypher*, when compared with ours under the Americans. Indeed I should not have noticed the Roman slaves, had not the very learned and penetrating Mr. Jefferson said, "when a master was murdered, all his slaves in the same house, or within hearing, were condemned to death."[3] — Here let me ask Mr. Jefferson, (but he is gone to answer at the bar of God, for the deeds done in his body while living,) I therefore ask the whole American people, had I not rather die, or be put to death, than to be a slave to any tyrant, who takes not only my own, but my wife and children's lives by the inches? Yea, would I meet death with avidity far! far! ! in preference to such *servile submission* to the murderous hands of tyrants. Mr. Jefferson's very severe remarks on us have been so extensively argued upon by men whose attainments in literature, I shall never be able to reach, that I would not have meddled with it, were it not to solicit each of my brethren, who has the spirit of a man, to buy a copy of Mr. Jefferson's "Notes on Virginia," and put it in the hand of his son. For let no one of us suppose that the refutations which have been written by our white friends are enough — they are *whites* — we are *blacks*. We, and the world wish to see the charges of Mr. Jefferson refuted by the blacks *themselves*, according to their chance; for we must remember that what the whites have written respecting this subject, is other men's labors, and did not emanate from the blacks. I know well, that there are some talents and learning among the colored people of this country, which we have not a chance to develop, in consequence of oppression; but our oppression ought not to hinder us from acquiring all we can. For we will have a chance to develop them by and by. God will not suffer us, always to be oppressed. Our sufferings will come to an *end,* in spite of all the Americans this side of *eternity.* Then we will want all the learning and talents among ourselves, and perhaps more, to govern ourselves. — "Every dog must have its day," the American's is coming to an end.

But let us review Mr. Jefferson's remarks respecting us some further. Comparing our miserable fathers, with the learned philosophers of Greece,

---

[2]That is, a country supposedly governed by representatives of the people; no reference to a particular political party is meant. — EDS.

[3]Walker quotes throughout from Jefferson's *Notes on Virginia* (p. 180); the passages he cites are included in our excerpt of the *Notes.* — EDS.

he says: "Yet notwithstanding these and other discouraging circumstances among the Romans, their slaves were often their rarest artists. They excelled too, in science, insomuch as to be usually employed as tutors to their master's children; Epictetus, Terence and Phaedrus, were slaves, — but they were of the race of whites. It is not their *condition* then, but *nature,* which has produced the distinction." See this, my brethren! ! Do you believe that this assertion is swallowed by millions of the whites? Do you know that Mr. Jefferson was one of as great characters as ever lived among the whites? See his writings for the world, and public labors for the United States of America. Do you believe that the assertions of such a man, will pass away into oblivion unobserved by this people and the world? If you do you are much mistaken — See how the American people treat us — have we souls in our bodies? Are we men who have any spirits at all? I know that there are many *swell-bellied* fellows among us, whose greatest object is to fill their stomachs. Such I do not mean — I am after those who know and feel, that we are MEN, as well as other people; to them, I say, that unless we try to refute Mr. Jefferson's arguments respecting us, we will only establish them.

But the slaves among the Romans. Every body who has read history, knows, that as soon as a slave among the Romans obtained his freedom, he could rise to the greatest eminence in the State, and there was no law instituted to hinder a slave from buying his freedom. Have not the Americans instituted laws to hinder us from obtaining our freedom? Do any deny this charge? Read the laws of Virginia, North Carolina, &c. Further: have not the Americans instituted laws to prohibit a man of color from obtaining and holding any office whatever, under the government of the United States of America? Now, Mr. Jefferson tells us, that our condition is not so hard, as the slaves were under the Romans! ! ! ! ! ! . . .

ARTICLE II

. . . Oh! colored people of these United States, I ask you, in the name of that God who made us, have we, in consequence of oppression, nearly lost the spirit of man, and, in no very trifling degree, adopted that of brutes? Do you answer, no? — I ask you, then, what set of men can you point me to, in all the world, who are so abjectly employed by their oppressors, as we are by our *natural enemies?* How can, Oh! how can those enemies but say that we and our children are not of the HUMAN FAMILY, but were made by our Creator to be an inheritance to them and theirs for ever? How can the slaveholders but say that they can bribe the best colored person in the country, to sell his brethren for a trifling sum of money, and take that atrocity to confirm them in their avaricious opinion, that we were made to be slaves to them and their children? How could Mr. Jefferson but say, "I advance it therefore as a suspicion only, that the blacks, whether originally a distinct race, or made distinct by time and circumstances, are *inferior* to the whites in the endowments both of body and mind?" — "It," says he, "is not against experience to suppose, that different species of the same genius, or varieties of the same species, may possess different qualifications." [Here, my brethren, listen to him.] "Will not a lover of natural history, then, one who views the gradations in all the races of *animals* with the eye of philosophy, excuse an effort to keep those in the department of MAN as *distinct* as nature has formed them?" — I hope you will try to find out the meaning of this verse — its widest sense and all its bearings: whether you do or not, remember the whites do. This very verse, brethren, having emanated from Mr. Jefferson, a much greater philosopher the world never afforded, has in truth injured us more, and has been as great a barrier to our emancipation as any thing that has ever been advanced against us. I hope you will not let it pass unnoticed. He goes on further, and says: "This *unfortunate* difference of color, and *perhaps* of *faculty,* is a powerful obstacle to the emancipation of these people. Many of their advocates, while they wish to vindicate the liberty of human nature are anxious also to preserve its *dignity* and *beauty.* Some of these, embarrassed by the question, 'What further is to be done with them?' join themselves in opposition with those who are actuated by sordid avarice only." Now I ask you candidly, my suffering brethren in time, who are candidates for the eternal worlds, how could Mr. Jefferson but have given the world these remarks respecting us, when we are so submissive to them, and so much servile deceit prevail among ourselves — when we so *meanly* submit to their murderous lashes, to which neither the Indians nor any other people under Heaven would submit? No, they would die to a man, before they would suffer such things from men who are no better than themselves, and *perhaps not so good.* Yes, how can our friends but be embarrassed, as Mr. Jefferson says, by the question, "What further is to be done with these people?" For while they are working for our emancipation, we are, by our treachery, wickedness and deceit, working against ourselves and our children — helping ours, and the enemies of God, to keep us and our dear little children in their infernal chains of slavery! ! ! Indeed, our friends cannot but relapse and join themselves "with those who are actuated by *sordid avarice* only! ! ! !" For my own part, I am glad Mr. Jefferson has advanced his positions for your sake; for you will either have to contradict or confirm him by your own actions, and not by what our friends have said or done for us; for those things are other men's labors, and do not satisfy the Americans, who are waiting for us to prove to them ourselves, that we are MEN, before they will be willing to admit the fact; for I pledge you my sacred word of honor, that Mr. Jefferson's remarks respecting us, have sunk deep into the hearts of millions of the whites, and never will be removed this side of eternity. — For how can they, when we are confirming him every day, by our *groveling submissions* and *treachery?* I aver, that when I look over these United States of America, and the world, and see the ignorant deceptions and consequent wretchedness of my brethren, I am brought oftimes solemnly to a stand, and in the midst of my reflections I exclaim to my God, "Lord didst thou make us to be slaves to our brethren, the whites?" But when I reflect that God is just, and that millions of my wretched brethren would meet death with glory — yea, more, would plunge into the very mouths of cannons and be torn into particles as minute as the atoms which compose the elements of the earth, in preference to a mean submission to the lash of tyrants, I am with streaming eyes, compelled to shrink back into nothingness before my Maker, and exclaim again, thy will be done, O Lord God Almighty. . . .

ARTICLE IV

. . . In conclusion, I ask the candid and unprejudiced of the whole world, to search the pages of historians diligently, and see if the Antideluvians — the Sodomites — the Egyptians — the Babylonians — the Ninevites — the Carthagenians — the Persians — the Macedonians — the Greeks — the Romans — the Mahometans — the Jews — or devils,[4] ever treated a set of human beings, as the white Christians of America do us, the blacks, or Africans. I also ask the attention of the world of mankind to the declaration of these very American people, of the United States.

A Declaration Made July 4, 1776

It says, "When in the course of human events, it becomes necessary for one people to dissolve the political bands which have connected them with another, and to assume among the Powers of the earth, the separate and equal station to which the laws of nature and of nature's God entitle them. A decent respect for the opinions of mankind requires, that they should declare the causes which impel them to the separation. — We hold these truths to be self evident — that all men are created equal, that they are endowed by their Creator with certain unalienable rights: that among these, are life, liberty, and the pursuit of happiness that, to secure these rights, governments are instituted among men, deriving their just powers from the consent of the governed; that when ever any form of government becomes destructive of these ends, it is the right of the people to alter or to abolish it, and to institute a new government laying its foundation on such principles, and organizing its powers in such form, as to them shall seem most likely to effect their safety and happiness. Prudence, indeed, will dictate, that governments long established should not be changed for light and transient causes; and accordingly all experience hath shown, that mankind are more disposed to suffer, while evils are sufferable, than to right themselves by abolishing the forms to which they are accustomed. But when a long train of abuses and usurpations, pursuing invariably the same object, evinces a design to reduce them under absolute despotism, it is their right it is their duty to throw off such government, and to provide new guards for their future security." See your Declaration Americans! ! ! Do you understand your own language? Hear your language, proclaimed to the world, July 4th, 1776 — "We hold these truths to be self evident — that ALL MEN

---

[4]Walker here gives a rather mixed list of ancient peoples; some, like the Greeks, kept slaves, and others, like the Sodomites, were noted for cruel behavior to everyone. — EDS.

ARE CREATED EQUAL! ! that they *are endowed by their Creator with certain un-alienable rights;* that among these are life, *liberty,* and the pursuit of happiness! !" Compare your own language above, extracted from your Declaration of Independence, with your cruelties and murders inflicted by your cruel and unmerciful fathers and yourselves on our fathers and on us — men who have never given your fathers or you the least provocation! ! ! ! !

Hear your language further! "But when a long train of abuses and usurpation, pursuing invariably the same object, evinces a design to reduce them under absolute despotism, it is their *right,* it is their *duty,* to throw off such government, and to provide new guards for their future security."

Now, Americans! I ask you candidly, was your sufferings under Great Britain, one hundredth part as cruel and tyranical as you have rendered ours under you? Some of you, no doubt, believe that we will never throw off your murderous government and "provide new guards for our future security." If Satan has made you believe it, will he not deceive you?[5] Do the whites say, I being a black man, ought to be humble, which I readily admit? I ask them, ought they not to be as humble as I? or do they think that they can measure arms with Jehovah? Will not the Lord yet humble them? or will not these very colored people whom they now treat worse than brutes, yet under God, humble them low down enough? Some of the whites are ignorant enough to tell us, that we ought to be submissive to them, that they may keep their feet on our throats. And if we do not submit to be beaten to death by them, we are bad creatures and of course must be damned, &c. If any man wishes to hear this doctrine openly preached to us by the American preachers, let him go into the Southern and Western sections of this country — I do not speak from hear say — what I have written, is what I have seen and heard myself. No man may think that my book is made up of conjecture — I have traveled and observed nearly the whole of those things myself, and what little I did not get by my own observation, I received from those among the whites and blacks, in whom the greatest confidence may be placed.

The Americans may be as vigilant as they please, but they cannot be vigilant enough for the Lord, neither can they hide themselves, where he will not find and bring them out.

READING CRITICALLY

1. According to Walker, what groups are likely to oppose or attack him?

2. Why does Walker exhort African American readers to give copies of Jefferson's *Notes on Virginia* to their children?

3. According to Walker, why is American slavery worse than Roman slavery?

4. Why does Walker believe it is important for blacks to publicly refute Jefferson's ideas?

---

[5]The Lord has not taught the Americans that we will not some day or other throw off their chains and hand-cuffs, from our hands and feet, and their devilish lashes (which some of them shall have enough of yet) from off our backs. — DW

5. What point does Walker make with his long quotations from the Declaration of Independence?

6. What does Walker threaten at the end of his *Appeal?*

WRITING ANALYTICALLY

1. Walker's rhetorical style is decidedly confrontational. He doesn't seem to care if he offends his African American audience, so long as he also moves them to action. What is Walker's attitude toward this audience? What techniques does he use for getting them to listen to him and to do what he wants? Write a paper in which you explain his rhetorical strategies, evaluating whether or not you think they would have been effective. Option: Walker was well aware that white people would read his *Appeal;* he even addresses them directly at the end, where he quotes the Declaration of Independence. What is his attitude toward this audience, and what strategies does he use for moving them? Write a paper in which you compare and contrast his rhetorical strategies for white versus black audiences, saying which you feel would have been more effective.

2. Walker's approach to ending slavery is clearly very different from that of William Lloyd Garrison (p. 270). Write a letter from Walker to Garrison, in which Walker comments on the forms of resistance recommended in Garrison's "Declaration of Sentiments"; or write the same kind of letter from Garrison to Walker, commenting on the *Appeal.*

3. Walker says nothing about query 18 in Jefferson's *Notes* (p. 186), where Jefferson condemns slavery. What do you think Walker would say about this passage? Write a paper in which you imitate Walker's style and provide his response to Jefferson's passage.

MARIA STEWART

An Address Delivered at the African Masonic Hall (February 27, 1833)

Maria W. Stewart (1803–79) née Miller, was born to free African American parents in Hartford, Connecticut, and grew up as a servant in the home of a minister. In 1826 she married James W. Stewart, an African American businessman in Boston and an associate of David Walker (p. 193). After her husband's death in 1829, Maria Stewart became one of the first American women to speak in public for any cause and the first African American

Maria Stewart, An Address Delivered at the African Masonic Hall, *The Liberator,* March 2, 1833, reprinted in *Maria Stewart: America's First Black Woman Political Writer,* ed. Marilyn Richardson (Bloomington: Indiana University Press, 1987), 56–64.

In the notes, MR = Marilyn Richardson, EDS. = Patricia Bizzell and Bruce Herzberg.

woman to work publicly for African American civil rights and women's rights. Between 1831 and 1834 she published articles frequently in William Lloyd Garrison's (p. 270) abolitionist newspaper, *The Liberator,* as well as a political pamphlet and two collections of essays. She gave speeches to primarily black audiences consisting of both men and women, a mix that was then considered highly improper (see Unit Three). The address printed here was delivered at the Masonic lodge founded by Prince Hall (p. 261) and published in *The Liberator* three days later.

Stewart left Boston for New York in 1834 to find work as a teacher. She continued to work for African American causes throughout her life, although she stopped speaking and writing for the public after she left Boston. In 1879 she published an edition of her earlier work along with an autobiographical introduction and testimonial letters from fellow Boston antislavery activists. Stewart spent the last ten years of her life as matron of the Freedman's Hospital and Asylum in Washington, D.C., a sort of refugee camp for freed slaves and their families.

AFRICAN RIGHTS AND LIBERTY IS A SUBJECT that ought to fire the breast of every free man of color in these United States, and excite in his bosom a lively, deep, decided and heart-felt interest. When I cast my eyes on the long list of illustrious names that are enrolled on the bright annals of fame among the whites, I turn my eyes within, and ask my thoughts, "Where are the names of our illustrious ones?" It must certainly have been for the want of energy on the part of the free people of color, that they have been long willing to bear the yoke of oppression. It must have been the want of ambition and force that has given the whites occasion to say that our natural abilities are not as good, and our capacities by nature inferior to theirs. They boldly assert that did we possess a natural independence of soul, and feel a love for liberty within our breasts, some one of our sable race, long before this, would have testified it, notwithstanding the disadvantages under which we labor. We have made ourselves appear altogether unqualified to speak in our own defence, and are therefore looked upon as objects of pity and commiseration. We have been imposed upon, insulted and derided on every side; and now, if we complain, it is considered as the height of impertinence. We have suffered ourselves to be considered as dastards, cowards, mean, faint-hearted wretches; and on this account (not because of our complexion) many despise us, and would gladly spurn us from their presence.

These things have fired my soul with a holy indignation, and compelled me thus to come forward, and endeavor to turn their attention to knowledge and improvement; for knowledge is power. I would ask, is it blindness of mind, or stupidity of soul, or the want of education that has caused our men who are sixty or seventy years of age, never to let their voices be heard, nor their hands be raised in behalf of their color? Or has it been for the fear of offending the whites? If it has, O ye fearful ones, throw off your fearfulness, and come forth in the name of the Lord, and in the strength of the God of Justice, and make yourselves useful and active members in society; for they admire a noble and patriotic spirit in others; and should they not admire it in us? If you are men, convince them that you possess the spirit of men; and as your day, so shall your strength be. Have the sons of Africa no souls? Feel they no ambitious desires? Shall the chains of ignorance forever confine them? Shall the insipid appellation of "clever negroes," or "good creatures," any longer content them? Where can we find among ourselves the man of science, or a philosopher, or an able statesman, or a counsellor at law? Show me our fearless and brave, our noble and gallant ones. Where are our lecturers in natural history, and our critics in useful knowledge? There may be a few such men among us, but they are rare. It is true our fathers bled and died in the revolutionary war, and others fought bravely under the command of Jackson, in defence of liberty.[1] But where is the man that has distinguished himself in these modern days by acting wholly in the defence of African rights and liberty? There was one, although he sleeps, his memory lives.[2]

I am sensible that there are many highly intelligent men of color in these United States, in the force of whose arguments, doubtless, I should discover my inferiority; but if they are blessed with wit and talent, friends and fortune, why have they not made themselves men of eminence, by striving to take all the reproach that is cast upon the people of color, and in endeavoring to alleviate the woes of their brethren in bondage? Talk, without effort, is nothing; you are abundantly capable, gentlemen, of making yourselves men of distinction; and this gross neglect, on your part, causes my blood to boil within me. Here is the grand cause which hinders the rise and progress of people of color. It is their want of laudable ambition and requisite courage.

Individuals have been distinguished according to their genius and talents, ever since the first formation of man, and will continue to be while the world stands. The different grades rise to honor and respectability as their merits may deserve. History informs us that we sprung from one of the most learned nations of the whole earth; from the seat, if not the parent, of science. Yes, poor despised Africa was once the resort of sages and legislators of other nations, was esteemed the school for learning, and the most illustrious men in Greece flocked thither for instruction. But it was our gross sins and abominations that provoked the Almighty to frown thus heavily upon us, and give our glory unto others. Sin and prodigality have caused the downfall of nations, kings and emperors; and were it not that God in wrath remembers mercy, we might indeed despair; but a promise is left us; "Ethiopia shall again stretch forth her hands unto God."[3]

[1] African American soldiers fought in the War of 1812 under the command of General Andrew Jackson, who was president of the United States (1829–37) at the time Stewart gave this speech. — EDS.

[2] Stewart refers here to her Boston abolitionist colleague David Walker, (p. 193), who died under suspicious circumstances in 1830. — EDS.

[3] Stewart paraphrases Psalm 68: "Princes shall come out of Egypt; Ethiopia shall soon stretch out her hands unto God." — EDS.

But it is of no use for us to boast that we sprung from this learned and enlightened nation, for this day a thick mist of moral gloom hangs over millions of our race. Our condition as a people has been low for hundreds of years, and it will continue to be so, unless by true piety and virtue, we strive to regain that which we have lost. White Americans, by their prudence, economy, and exertions, have sprung up and become one of the most flourishing nations in the world, distinguished for their knowledge of the arts and sciences, for their polite literature. While our minds are vacant and starve for want of knowledge, theirs are filled to overflowing. Most of our color have been taught to stand in fear of the white man from their earliest infancy, to work as soon as they could walk, and to call "master" before they could scarce lisp the name of mother. Continual fear and laborious servitude have in some degree lessened in us that natural force and energy which belong to man; or else, in defiance of opposition, our men, before this, would have nobly and boldly contended for their rights. But give the man of color an equal opportunity with the white from the cradle to manhood, and from manhood to the grave, and you would discover the dignified statesman, the man of science, and the philosopher. But there is no such opportunity for the sons of Africa, and I fear that our powerful ones are fully determined that there never shall be. Forbid, ye Powers on high, that it should any longer be said that our men possess no force. O ye sons of Africa, when will your voices be heard in our legislative halls, in defiance of your enemies, contending for equal rights and liberty? How can you, when you reflect from what you have fallen, refrain from crying mightily unto God, to turn away from us the fierceness of his anger, and remember our transgressions against us no more forever? But a god of infinite purity will not regard the prayers of those who hold religion in one hand, and prejudice, sin and pollution in the other; he will not regard the prayers of self-righteousness and hypocrisy. Is it possible, I exclaim, that for the want of knowledge we have labored for hundreds of years to support others, and been content to receive what they chose to give us in return? Cast your eyes about, look as far as you can see; all, all is owned by the lordly white, except here and there a lowly dwelling which the man of color, midst deprivations, fraud, and opposition has been scarce able to procure. Like King Solomon, who put neither nail nor hammer to the temple, yet received the praise; so also have the white Americans gained themselves a name, like the names of the great men that are in the earth, while in reality we have been their principal foundation and support. We have pursued the shadow, they have obtained the substance; we have performed the labor, they have received the profits; we have planted the vines, they have eaten the fruits of them.

I would implore our men, and especially our rising youth, to flee from the gambling board and the dance-hall; for we are poor, and have no money to throw away. I do not consider dancing as criminal in itself, but it is astonishing to me that our fine young men are so blind to their own interest and the future welfare of their children as to spend their hard

earnings for this frivolous amusement; for it has been carried on among
us to such an unbecoming extent that it has become absolutely disgusting. "Faithful are the wounds of a friend, but the kisses of an enemy are
deceitful."[4] Had those men among us who had an opportunity, turned
their attention as assiduously to mental and moral improvement as they
have to gambling and dancing, I might have remained quietly at home
and they stood contending in my place. These polite accomplishments
will never enroll your names on the bright annals of fame who admire
the belle void of intellectual knowledge, or applaud the dandy that talks
largely on politics, without striving to assist his fellow in the revolution,
when the nerves and muscles of every other man forced him into the
field of action. You have a right to rejoice, and to let your hearts cheer
you in the days of your youth; yet remember that for all these things God
will bring you into judgment. Then, O ye sons of Africa, turn your mind
from these perishable objects, and contend for the cause of God and the
rights of man. Form yourselves into temperance societies.[5] There are
temperate men among you; then why will you any longer neglect to
strive, by your example, to suppress vice in all its abhorrent forms? You
have been told repeatedly of the glorious results arising from temperance, and can you bear to see the whites arising in honor and
respectability without endeavoring to grasp after that honor and respectability also?

But I forbear. Let our money, instead of being thrown away as heretofore, be appropriated for schools and seminaries of learning for our children and youth. We ought to follow the example of the whites in this respect. Nothing would raise our respectability, add to our peace and
happiness, and reflect so much honor upon us, as to be ourselves the pro-
moters of temperance, and supporters, as far as we are able, of useful and
scientific knowledge. The rays of light and knowledge have been hid from
our view; we have been taught to consider ourselves as scarce superior to
the brute creation; and have performed the most laborious part of American drudgery. Had we as a people received one-half the early advantages
the whites have received, I would defy the government of these United
States to deprive us any longer of our rights.

I am informed that the agent of the Colonization Society has recently
formed an association of young men for the purpose of influencing those
of us to go to Liberia who may feel disposed. The colonizationists are blind
to their own interest, for should the nations of the earth make war with
America, they would find their forces much weakened by our absence; or
should we remain here, can our "brave soldiers" and "fellow citizens," as

[4]Proverbs 27:6. — MR
[5]Temperance societies aimed to persuade people to abstain from drinking alcoholic bev-
erages and to limit the sale and distribution of alcohol. Alcohol abuse was the most serious
nineteenth-century drug problem and was connected with crime and brutality against children, women family members, servants, and slaves. — EDS.

they were termed in time of calamity, condescend to defend the rights of whites and be again deprived of their own, or sent to Liberia in return? Or, if the colonizationists are the real friends to Africa, let them expend the money which they collect in erecting a college to educate her injured sons in this land of gospel, light, and liberty; for it would be most thankfully received on our part, and convince us of the truth of their professions, and save time, expense, and anxiety. Let them place before us noble objects worthy of pursuit, and see if we prove ourselves to be those unambitious negroes they term us. But, ah, methinks their hearts are so frozen toward us they had rather their money should be sunk in the ocean than to administer it to our relief: and I fear, if they dared, like Pharaoh, king of Egypt, they would order every male child among us to be drowned.[6] But the most high God is still as able to subdue the lofty pride of these white Americans as He was the heart of that ancient rebel. They say, though we are looked upon as things, yet we sprang from a scientific people. Had our men the requisite force and energy they would soon convince them by their efforts, both in public and private, that they were men, or things in the shape of men. Well may the colonizationists laugh us to scorn for our negligence; well may they cry: "Shame to the sons of Africa." As the burden of the Israelites was too great for Moses to bear, so also is our burden too great for our noble advocate to bear. You must feel interested, my brethren, in what he undertakes, and hold up his hands by your good works, or in spite of himself his soul will become discouraged and his heart will die within him; for he has, as it were, the strong bulls of Bashan to contend with.[7]

It is of no use for us to wait any longer for a generation of well educated men to arise. We have slumbered and slept too long already; the day is far spent; the night of death approaches; and you have sound sense and good judgment sufficient to begin with, if you feel disposed to make a right use of it. Let every man of color throughout the United States, who possesses the spirit and principles of a man, sign a petition to Congress to abolish slavery in the District of Columbia,[8] and grant you the rights and privileges of common free citizens; for if you had had faith as a grain of mustard seed, long before this the mountain of prejudice might have been re-

---

[6]Stewart alludes to a measure that the Egyptian Pharaoh took against his Hebrew slaves when he feared they were becoming too numerous and powerful (Exodus 1). The baby Moses was set adrift on the Nile in a basket to protect him from this edict (Exodus 2). In the next sentence, Stewart alludes to the ten plagues God sent on Egypt when Pharaoh refused to let the Hebrews go free; the final plague was the deaths of the firstborn children of all the Egyptians, including Pharaoh's (Exodus 7–12). — EDS.

[7]Bashan, a region in Palestine, was noted for producing fat cattle. In Psalm 22, "strong bulls of Bashan" threaten David: "they open wide their mouths at me, like a ravening and roaring lion." — EDS.

[8]At this time, antislavery activists attempted to publicize their cause by focusing on the evil of allowing slavery in the nation's capital. — EDS.

moved.[9] We are all sensible that the Anti-Slavery Society has taken hold of the arm of our whole population, in order to raise them out of the mire. Now all we have to do is, by a spirit of virtuous ambition, to strive to raise ourselves; and I am happy to have it in my power thus publicly to say that the colored inhabitants of this city, in some respects, are beginning to improve. Had the free people of color in these United States nobly and freely contended for their rights, and showed a natural genius and talent, although not so brilliant as some; had they held up, encouraged and patronized each other, nothing could have hindered us from being a thriving and flourishing people. There has been a fault among us. The reason why our distinguished men have not made themselves more influential, is because they fear that the strong current of opposition through which they must pass would cause their downfall and prove their overthrow. And what gives rise to this opposition? Envy. And what has it amounted to? Nothing. And who are the cause of it? Our whited sepulchres,[10] who want to be great, and don't know how; who love to be called of men "Rabbi, Rabbi"; who put on false sanctity, and humble themselves to their brethren for the sake of acquiring the highest place in the synagogue and the uppermost seat at the feast. You, dearly beloved, who are the genuine followers of our Lord Jesus Christ — the salt of the earth, and the light of the world — are not so culpable. As I told you in the very first of my writing, I will tell you again, I am but as a drop in the bucket — as one particle of the small dust of the earth.[11] God will surely raise up those among us who will plead the cause of virtue and the pure principles of morality more eloquently than I am able to do.

It appears to me that America has become like the great city of Babylon, for she has boasted in her heart: "I sit a queen and am no widow, and shall see no sorrow!"[12] She is, indeed, a seller of slaves and the souls of men; she has made the Africans drunk with the wine of her fornication; she has put them completely beneath her feet, and she means to keep them there; her right hand supports the reins of government and her left hand the wheel of power, and she is determined not to let go her grasp. But many powerful sons and daughters of Africa will shortly arise, who will put down vice and immorality among us, and declare by Him that sitteth upon the throne that they will have their rights; and if refused, I am afraid they will spread horror and devastation around. I believe that the oppression of in-

---

[9]In the Bible, Jesus tells his disciples, "If you have faith as a grain of mustard seed, you will say to this mountain, 'Move hence to yonder place,' and it will move; and nothing will be impossible to you" (Matthew 17:20). — EDS.

[10]"Whited sepulchres" are whitewashed tombs, appearing clean and pure outside but full of rottenness within. In the Bible, Jesus uses this image to condemn community leaders who use their position only for their own gain (Matthew 23:27). — EDS.

[11]Isaiah 40:15. — MR

[12]Babylon was an ancient city located near the site of present-day Baghdad. It was the center of the powerful Babylonian empire and was often invoked in the Bible as an image of corrupt power and decadent living. Stewart indicts the United States as a "Babylon" for making African Americans stagger, as if drunk, with the weight of oppression. Her quotation is from Revelations 18:7. — EDS.

jured Africa has come up before the majesty of Heaven; and when our cries shall have reached the ears of the Most High, it will be a tremendous day for the people of this land; for strong is the hand of the Lord God Almighty.

Life has almost lost its charms for me; death has lost its sting, and the grave its terrors;[13] and at times I have a strong desire to depart and dwell with Christ, which is far better. Let me entreat my white brethren to awake and save our sons from dissipation and our daughters from ruin. Lend the hand of assistance to feeble merit; plead the cause of virtue among our sable race; so shall our curses upon you be turned into blessings; and though you should endeavor to drive us from these shores, still we will cling to you the more firmly; nor will we attempt to rise above you; we will presume to be called your equals only.

The unfriendly whites first drove the native American from his much loved home. Then they stole our fathers from their peaceful and quiet dwellings, and brought them hither, and made bond-men and bond-women of them and their little ones. They have obliged our brethren to labor; kept them in utter ignorance; nourished them in vice, and raised them in degradation; and now that we have enriched their soil, and filled their coffers, they say that we are not capable of becoming like white men, and that we can never rise to respectability in this country. They would drive us to a strange land. But before I go, the bayonet shall pierce me through. African rights and liberty is a subject that ought to fire the breast of every free man of color in these United States, and excite in his bosom a lively, deep, decided, and heartfelt interest.

READING CRITICALLY

1. Stewart begins by suggesting that African Americans have brought prejudice on themselves. How?

2. According to Stewart, why is it not really in whites' best interests to promote colonization schemes? What does she think should be done with the money raised for colonization?

3. Go through Stewart's speech and note all the references to white people. Then try to group these references into categories.

WRITING ANALYTICALLY

1. Although Stewart does not refer directly to the Declaration of Independence, she makes frequent use of Declaration language on liberty and equality. Her thinking could certainly be considered in line with the ideas in the Declaration, or a sort of new Declaration of Independence for African Americans. Write a paper in which you analyze the parallels between Stewart's speech and the Declara-

---

[13] 1 Corinthians 15:55. — MR

tion. You can argue for how this speech is (or is not) a sort of African American Declaration of Independence.

2. Stewart makes only a few, indirect references to her own gender. For example, she asserts that if African American men had achieved their potential, she would not have had to emerge from woman's proper domestic sphere to exhort them but "might have remained quietly at home" (p. 204). Nevertheless, Stewart must be quite conscious of the unusual and, to many, scandalous position she is in, as a woman speaking in public to a mixed male and female audience. Write a paper in which you explain and evaluate Stewart's strategies for dealing with this problem. Option: You may write your paper in the form of a letter from Stewart to a younger woman who wants to become an activist, advising her on how to manage her public persona.

3. We can expect to find some similarities in the rhetorical strategies of Maria Stewart and David Walker (p. 193) since they knew each other well and frequently addressed the same African American audience. Both, it's clear, addressed this audience aggressively. Write a paper in which you compare and contrast the rhetorical strategies Stewart and Walker use to address African American audiences. You may argue that one or the other is the better persuader; you may argue that some of the differences may be attributed to Stewart's need to overcome public disapproval of a woman political activist.

FREDERICK DOUGLASS

"What to the Slave Is the Fourth of July?" (July 5, 1852)

Frederick Douglass (1818–95) was born Frederick Bailey, a slave in Maryland; he later suspected that his father was the white plantation overseer. After growing up in Baltimore, where he learned to read and write, he escaped slavery in 1838 with the help of a free African American woman. The two were married after they arrived in the North. Douglass renamed himself to thwart pursuit, ironically choosing the name of a hero in a popular historical novel by Sir Walter Scott. In 1841, Douglass took the platform for the first time at a Massachusetts antislavery meeting to denounce the evils of slavery, which he had experienced firsthand. He quickly became not only one of the most powerful abolitionist speakers but also one of the most important African American intellectuals of the nineteenth century. The first edition of his autobiography, published in 1845, became an instant best-seller, and subsequent versions (1855, 1892) were also well received. In 1847 Douglass began to publish his own abolitionist newspaper, which also endorsed other

Frederick Douglass, "What to the Slave Is the Fourth of July?, " in *The Frederick Douglass Papers, Series One, Speeches, Debates, and Interviews,* vol. 2, *1847—54,* ed. John W. Blassingame et al. (New Haven: Yale University Press, 1982), 359–88.

In the notes, JWB = John W. Blassingame et al., EDS. = Patricia Bizzell and Bruce Herzberg.

reform causes such as women's rights; Douglass sat on the dais at the important 1848 Seneca Falls women's rights convention (see Unit Three).

After the Civil War, Douglass was active in the national Republican Party, then best known as the antislavery party of Abraham Lincoln. He also continued his leadership role in the African American community. Printed here is an address he delivered to a largely white audience in Rochester, New York. The July Fourth speech or sermon on the ideals of the Declaration of Independence was a powerful antebellum African American genre.

MR. PRESIDENT,[1] FRIENDS AND FELLOW CITIZENS: He who could address this audience without a quailing sensation, has stronger nerves than I have. I do not remember ever to have appeared as a speaker before any assembly more shrinkingly, nor with greater distrust of my ability, than I do this day. A feeling has crept over me, quite unfavorable to the exercise of my limited powers of speech. The task before me is one which requires much previous thought and study for its proper performance. I know that apologies of this sort are generally considered flat and unmeaning. I trust, however, that mine will not be so considered. Should I seem at ease, my appearance would much misrepresent me. The little experience I have had in addressing public meetings, in country school houses, avails me nothing on the present occasion.

The papers and placards say, that I am to deliver a Fourth [of] July oration. This certainly sounds large, and out of the common way, for me. It is true that I have often had the privilege to speak in this beautiful Hall, and to address many who now honor me with their presence. But neither their familiar faces, nor the perfect gage I think I have of Corinthian Hall, seems to free me from embarrassment.

The fact is, ladies and gentlemen, the distance between this platform and the slave plantation, from which I escaped, is considerable — and the difficulties to be overcome in getting from the latter to the former, are by no means slight. That I am here today is, to me, a matter of astonishment as well as of gratitude. You will not, therefore, be surprised, if in what I have to say, I evince no elaborate preparation, nor grace my speech with any high sounding exordium. With little experience and with less learning, I have been able to throw my thoughts hastily and imperfectly together; and trusting to your patient and generous indulgence, I will proceed to lay them before you.

This, for the purpose of this celebration, is the Fourth of July. It is the birthday of your National Independence, and of your political freedom. This, to you, is what the Passover was to the emancipated people of God.[2] It

---

[1]"Mr. President" is the head of the antislavery society that invited Douglass to give this address. — EDS.

[2]The Jewish holiday of Passover commemorates God's liberation of the Hebrews from slavery in Egypt. According to the account in Exodus 12, God sent plagues on Egypt when Pharaoh refused to let the Hebrews go free. — EDS.

carries your minds back to the day, and to the act of your great deliverance; and to the signs, and to the wonders, associated with that act, and that day. This celebration also marks the beginning of another year of your national life; and reminds you that the Republic of America is now seventy-six years old. I am glad, fellow-citizens, that your nation is so young. Seventy-six years, though a good old age for a man, is but a mere speck in the life of a nation. Three score years and ten is the allotted time for individual men; but nations number their years by thousands. According to this fact, you are, even now, only in the beginning of your national career, still lingering in the period of childhood. I repeat, I am glad this is so. There is hope in the thought, and hope is much needed, under the dark clouds which lower above the horizon. The eye of the reformer is met with angry flashes, portending disastrous times; but his heart may well beat lighter at the thought that America is young, and that she is still in the impressible stage of her existence. May he not hope that high lessons of wisdom, of justice and of truth, will yet give direction to her destiny? Were the nation older, the patriot's heart might be sadder, and the reformer's brow heavier. Its future might be shrouded in gloom, and the hope of its prophets go out in sorrow. There is consolation in the thought that America is young. Great streams are not easily turned from channels, worn deep in the course of ages. They may sometimes rise in quiet and stately majesty, and inundate the land, refreshing and fertilizing the earth with their mysterious properties. They may also rise in wrath and fury, and bear away, on their angry waves, the accumulated wealth of years of toil and hardship. They, however, gradually flow back to the same old channel, and flow on as serenely as ever. But, while the river may not be turned aside, it may dry up, and leave nothing behind but the withered branch, and the unsightly rock, to howl in the abyss-sweeping wind, the sad tale of departed glory. As with rivers so with nations.

Fellow-citizens, I shall not presume to dwell at length on the associations that cluster about this day. The simple story of it is that, seventy-six years ago, the people of this country were British subjects. The style and title of your "sovereign people" (in which you now glory) was not then born. You were under the British Crown. Your fathers esteemed the English Government as the home government; and England as the fatherland. This home government, you know, although a considerable distance from your home, did, in the exercise of its parental prerogatives, impose upon its colonial children, such restraints, burdens and limitations, as, in its mature judgment, it deemed wise, right and proper.

But, your fathers, who had not adopted the fashionable idea of this day, of the infallibility of government, and the absolute character of its acts, presumed to differ from the home government in respect to the wisdom and the justice of some of those burdens and restraints. They went so far in their excitement as to pronounce the measures of government unjust, unreasonable, and oppressive, and altogether such as ought not to be quietly submitted to. I scarcely need say, fellow-citizens, that my opinion of those measures fully accords with that of your fathers. Such a declaration of agreement on my part would not be worth much to anybody. It would, certainly, prove nothing, as to what part I might have taken, had I lived during the great controversy of 1776. To say *now* that America was right, and England wrong, is exceedingly easy. Everybody can say it; the dastard, not less than the noble brave, can flippantly discant on the tyranny of England towards the American Colonies. It is fashionable to do so; but there was a time when to pronounce against England, and in favor of the cause of the colonies, tried men's souls.[3] They who did so were accounted in their day, plotters of mischief, agitators and rebels, dangerous men. To side with the right, against the wrong, with the weak against the strong, and with the oppressed against the oppressor! *here* lies the merit, and the one which, of all others, seems unfashionable in our day. The cause of liberty may be stabbed by the men who glory in the deeds of your fathers. But, to proceed.

Feeling themselves harshly and unjustly treated by the home government, your fathers, like men of honesty, and men of spirit, earnestly sought redress. They petitioned and remonstrated; they did so in a decorous, respectful, and loyal manner. Their conduct was wholly unexceptionable. This, however, did not answer the purpose. They saw themselves treated with sovereign indifference, coldness and scorn. Yet they persevered. They were not the men to look back.

As the sheet anchor takes a firmer hold, when the ship is tossed by the storm, so did the cause of your fathers grow stronger, as it breasted the chilling blasts of kingly displeasure. The greatest and best of British statesmen admitted its justice, and the loftiest eloquence of the British Senate came to its support. But, with that blindness which seems to be the unvarying characteristic of tyrants, since Pharaoh and his hosts were drowned in the Red Sea,[4] the British Government persisted in the exactions complained of.

The madness of this course, we believe, is admitted now, even by England; but we fear the lesson is wholly lost on our present rulers.

Oppression makes a wise man mad. Your fathers were wise men, and if they did not go mad, they became restive under this treatment. They felt themselves the victims of grievous wrongs, wholly incurable in their colonial capacity. With brave men there is always a remedy for oppression. Just here, the idea of a total separation of the colonies from the crown was born! It was a startling idea, much more so, than we, at this distance of time, regard it. The timid and the prudent (as has been intimated) of that day, were, of course, shocked and alarmed by it.

Such people lived then, had lived before, and will, probably, ever have a

---

[3]Douglass alludes to the opening line of a Revolutionary-era pamphlet by agitator Thomas Paine: "These are the times that try men's souls." Paine meant to underscore both the danger and the nobility involved in coming out for the Revolutionary cause. Douglass suggests that similar patriotic courage is now required to support abolition. — EDS.

[4]This is another reference to the biblical Exodus story (see note 2). As the Egyptian Pharaoh and his soldiers pursued the departing Hebrew slaves, God parted the waters of the Red Sea so the fleeing slaves could pass and then brought the waters together and drowned the Egyptians (Exodus 14). — EDS.

place on this planet; and their course, in respect to any great change, (no matter how great the good to be attained, or the wrong to be redressed by it), may be calculated with as much precision as can be the course of the stars. They hate all changes, but silver, gold and copper change! Of this sort of change they are always strongly in favor.

These people were called tories in the days of your fathers; and the appellation, probably, conveyed the same idea that is meant by a more modern, though a somewhat less euphonious term, which we often find in our papers, applied to some of our old politicians.

Their opposition to the then dangerous thought was earnest and powerful; but, amid all their terror and affrighted vociferations against it, the alarming and revolutionary idea moved on, and the country with it.

On the second of July, 1776, the old Continental Congress, to the dismay of the lovers of ease, and the worshippers of property, clothed that dreadful idea with all the authority of national sanction. They did so in the form of a resolution; and as we seldom hit upon resolutions, drawn up in our day, whose transparency is at all equal to this, it may refresh your minds and help my story if I read it.

> "Resolved, That these united colonies *are,* and of right, ought to be free and
> Independent States; that they are absolved from all allegiance to the British
> Crown; and that all political connection between them and the State of
> Great Britain *is,* and ought to be, dissolved."

Citizens, your fathers made good that resolution. They succeeded; and today you reap the fruits of their success. The freedom gained is yours; and you, therefore, may properly celebrate this anniversary. The Fourth of July is the first great fact in your nation's history — the very ring-bolt in the chain of your yet undeveloped destiny.

Pride and patriotism, not less than gratitude, prompt you to celebrate and to hold it in perpetual remembrance. I have said that the Declaration of Independence is the RING-BOLT to the chain of your nation's destiny; so, indeed, I regard it. The principles contained in that instrument are saving principles. Stand by those principles, be true to them on all occasions, in all places, against all foes, and at whatever cost.

From the round top of your ship of state, dark and threatening clouds may be seen. Heavy billows, like mountains in the distance, disclose to the leeward huge forms of flinty rocks! That *bolt* drawn, that *chain* broken, and all is lost. *Cling to this day — cling to it,* and to its principles, with the grasp of a storm-tossed mariner to a spar at midnight.

The coming into being of a nation, in any circumstances, is an interesting event. But, besides general considerations, there were peculiar circumstances which make the advent of this republic an event of special attractiveness.

The whole scene, as I look back to it, was simple, dignified and sublime.

The population of the country, at the time, stood at the insignificant number of three millions. The country was poor in the munitions of war. The population was weak and scattered, and the country a wilderness unsubdued. There were then no means of concert and combination, such as exist now. Neither steam nor lightning had then been reduced to order and discipline. From the Potomac to the Delaware was a journey of many days. Under these, and innumerable other disadvantages, your fathers declared for liberty and independence and triumphed.

Fellow Citizens, I am not wanting in respect for the fathers of this republic. The signers of the Declaration of Independence were brave men. They were great men too — great enough to give fame to a great age. It does not often happen to a nation to raise, at one time, such a number of truly great men. The point from which I am compelled to view them is not, certainly, the most favorable; and yet I cannot contemplate their great deeds with less than admiration. They were statesmen, patriots and heroes, and for the good they did, and the principles they contended for, I will unite with you to honor their memory.

They loved their country better than their own private interests; and, though this is not the highest form of human excellence, all will concede that it is a rare virtue, and that when it is exhibited, it ought to command respect. He who will, intelligently, lay down his life for his country, is a man whom it is not in human nature to despise. Your fathers staked their lives, their fortunes, and their sacred honor, on the cause of their country. In their admiration of liberty, they lost sight of all other interests.

They were peace men; but they preferred revolution to peaceful submission to bondage. They were quiet men; but they did not shrink from agitating against oppression. They showed forbearance; but that they knew its limits. They believed in order; but not in the order of tyranny. With them, nothing was *"settled"* that was not right. With them, justice, liberty and humanity were *"final";* not slavery and oppression. You may well cherish the memory of such men. They were great in their day and generation. Their solid manhood stands out the more as we contrast it with these degenerate times.

How circumspect, exact and proportionate were all their movements! How unlike the politicians of an hour! Their statesmanship looked beyond the passing moment, and stretched away in strength into the distant future. They seized upon eternal principles, and set a glorious example in their defence. Mark them!

Fully appreciating the hardship to be encountered, firmly believing in the right of their cause, honorably inviting the scrutiny of an on-looking world, reverently appealing to heaven to attest their sincerity, soundly comprehending the solemn responsibility they were about to assume, wisely measuring the terrible odds against them, your fathers, the fathers of this republic, did, most deliberately, under the inspiration of a glorious patriotism, and with a sublime faith in the great principles of justice and freedom, lay deep the corner-stone of the national superstructure, which has risen and still rises in grandeur around you.

Of this fundamental work, this day is the anniversary. Our eyes are met with demonstrations of joyous enthusiasm. Banners and pennants wave exultingly on the breeze. The din of business, too, is hushed. Even Mammon seems to have quitted his grasp on this day.5 The ear-piercing fife and the stirring drum unite their accents with the ascending peal of a thousand church bells. Prayers are made, hymns are sung, and sermons are preached in honor of this day; while the quick martial tramp of a great and multitudinous nation, echoed back by all the hills, valleys and mountains of a vast continent, bespeak the occasion one of thrilling and universal interest — a nation's jubilee.

Friends and citizens, I need not enter further into the causes which led to this anniversary. Many of you understand them better than I do. You could instruct me in regard to them. That is a branch of knowledge in which you feel, perhaps, a much deeper interest than your speaker. The causes which led to the separation of the colonies from the British Crown have never lacked for a tongue. They have all been taught in your common schools, narrated at your firesides, unfolded from your pulpits, and thundered from your legislative halls, and are as familiar to you as household words. They form the staple of your national poetry and eloquence.

I remember, also, that, as a people, Americans are remarkably familiar with all facts which make in their own favor. This is esteemed by some as a national trait — perhaps a national weakness. It is a fact, that whatever makes for the wealth or for the reputation of Americans, and can be had *cheap*! will be found by Americans. I shall not be charged with slandering Americans, if I say I think the American side of any question may be safely left in American hands.

I leave, therefore, the great deeds of your fathers to other gentlemen whose claim to have been regularly descended will be less likely to be disputed than mine!

THE PRESENT

My business, if I have any here today, is with the present. The accepted time with God and his cause is the ever-living now.

> Trust no future, however pleasant,
> Let the dead past bury its dead;
> Act, act in the living present,
> Heart within, and God overhead.6

We have to do with the past only as we can make it useful to the present and to the future. To all inspiring motives, to noble deeds which can be

---

5"Mammon" originally meant "property." In Matthew 6:24, Jesus personifies Mammon as a god of narrowly material and earthly interests, whom people are tempted to worship in place of the true God. Douglass's allusion confirms the sense in his own day that the Fourth of July was more than a secular holiday. It was a day to thank God for the blessings of freedom — a grinding irony, of course, from Douglass's point of view. — EDS.

6The stanza quoted is from Henry Wadsworth Longfellow's "A Psalm of Life." *Poems*, 22. — JWB gained from the past, we are welcome. But now is the time, the important time. Your fathers have lived, died, and have done their work, and have done much of it well. You live and must die, and you must do your work. You have no right to enjoy a child's share in the labor of your fathers, unless your children are to be blest by your labors. You have no right to wear out and waste the hard-earned fame of your fathers to cover your indolence. Sydney Smith[7] tells us that men seldom eulogize the wisdom and virtues of their fathers, but to excuse some folly or wickedness of their own. This truth is not a doubtful one. There are illustrations of it near and remote, ancient and modern. It was fashionable, hundreds of years ago, for the children of Jacob to boast, we have "Abraham to our father," when they had long lost Abraham's faith and spirit. That people contented themselves under the shadow of Abraham's great name, while they repudiated the deeds which made his name great.[8] Need I remind you that a similar thing is being done all over this country today? Need I tell you that the Jews are not the only people who built the tombs of the prophets, and garnished the sepulchres of the righteous? Washington could not die till he had broken the chains of his slaves.[9] Yet his monument is built up by the price of human blood, and the traders in the bodies and souls of men, shout — "We have Washington to *our father.*" Alas! that it should be so; yet so it is.

> The evil that men do, lives after them,
> The good is oft' interred with their bones.[10]

Fellow-citizens, pardon me, allow me to ask, why am I called upon to speak here today? What have I, or those I represent, to do with your national independence? Are the great principles of political freedom and of natural justice, embodied in that Declaration of Independence, extended to us? and am I, therefore, called upon to bring our humble offering to the national altar, and to confess the benefits and express devout gratitude for the blessings resulting from your independence to us?

Would to God, both for your sakes and ours, that an affirmative answer could be truthfully returned to these questions! Then would my task be light, and my burden easy and delightful. For *who* is there so cold, that a nation's sympathy could not warm him? Who so obdurate and dead to the claims of gratitude, that would not thankfully acknowledge such priceless benefits? Who so stolid and selfish, that would not give his voice to swell the hallelujahs of a nation's jubilee, when the chains of servitude had been

---

[7]Sydney Smith (1771–1845) was an English minister and satirical essayist. — EDS.

[8]In Luke 3:8, Jesus reproaches his Jewish audience with bragging about their heritage of piety — "We have Abraham to [as] our father" — while neglecting to perform good deeds themselves. Similarly, Douglass says, George Washington is often called the father of his country, yet white Americans invoke his name without emulating his good deed of freeing his slaves (see note 9). — EDS.

[9]George Washington's will provided that his slaves should be freed after the death of his wife, who outlived him. This was done. — EDS.

[10]William Shakespeare, *Julius Caesar*, 3.2.76. — EDS.

torn from his limbs? I am not that man. In a case like that, the dumb might eloquently speak, and the "lame man leap as an hart."

But, such is not the state of the case. I say it with a sad sense of the disparity between us. I am not included within the pale of this glorious anniversary! Your high independence only reveals the immeasurable distance between us. The blessings in which you, this day, rejoice, are not enjoyed in common. The rich inheritance of justice, liberty, prosperity and independence, bequeathed by your fathers, is shared by you, not by me. The sunlight that brought life and healing to you, has brought stripes and death to me. This Fourth [of] July is *yours,* not *mine. You* may rejoice, *I* must mourn. To drag a man in fetters into the grand illuminated temple of liberty, and call upon him to join you in joyous anthems, were inhuman mockery and sacrilegious irony. Do you mean, citizens, to mock me, by asking me to speak today? If so, there is a parallel to your conduct. And let me warn you that it is dangerous to copy the example of a nation whose crimes, towering up to heaven, were thrown down by the breath of the Almighty, burying that nation in irrecoverable ruin![11] I can today take up the plaintive lament of a peeled and woe-smitten people!

"By the rivers of Babylon, there we sat down. Yea! we wept when we remembered Zion. We hanged our harps upon the willows in the midst thereof. For there, they that carried us away captive, required of us a song; and they who wasted us required of us mirth, saying, Sing us one of the songs of Zion. How can we sing the Lord's song in a strange land? If I forget thee, O Jerusalem, let my right hand forget her cunning. If I do not remember thee, let my tongue cleave to the roof of my mouth."[12]

Fellow-citizens; above your national, tumultuous joy, I hear the mournful wail of millions! whose chains, heavy and grievous yesterday, are, today, rendered more intolerable by the jubilee shouts that reach them. If I do forget, if I do not faithfully remember those bleeding children of sorrow this day, "may my right hand forget her cunning, and may my tongue cleave to the roof of my mouth!" To forget them, to pass lightly over their wrongs, and to chime in with the popular theme, would be treason most scandalous and shocking, and would make me a reproach before God and the world. My subject, then fellow-citizens, is AMERICAN SLAVERY. I shall see, this day, and its popular characteristics, from the slave's point of view. Standing, there, identified with the American bondman, making his wrongs mine, I do not hesitate to declare, with all my soul, that the character and conduct of this nation never looked blacker to me than on this Fourth of July! Whether we turn to the declarations of the past, or to the professions of the present, the conduct of the nation seems equally

[11]Douglass alludes to the story of the biblical hero Samson. Captured, blinded, and enslaved by his enemies the Philistines, Samson was led into their temple on a holiday so they could mock him. He seized the pillars and with his enormous strength pulled down the whole building on himself and his tormentors. (Judges 17:23–31). — EDS.

[12]Douglass quotes Psalms 137:1–6, which describes the sorrow of the Jewish captives taken away to Babylon after the fall of the city of Jerusalem in 587 B.C.E. — EDS.

hideous and revolting. America is false to the past, false to the present, and solemnly binds herself to be false to the future. Standing with God and the crushed and bleeding slave on this occasion, I will, in the name of humanity which is outraged, in the name of liberty which is fettered, in the name of the constitution and the Bible, which are disregarded and trampled upon, dare to call in question and to denounce, with all the emphasis I can command, everything that serves to perpetuate slavery — the great sin and shame of America! "I will not equivocate; I will not excuse;"[13] I will use the severest language I can command; and yet not one word shall escape me that any man, whose judgment is not blinded by prejudice, or who is not at heart a slaveholder, shall not confess to be right and just.

But I fancy I hear some one of my audience say, it is just in this circumstance that you and your brother abolitionists fail to make a favorable impression on the public mind. Would you argue more, and denounce less, would you persuade more, and rebuke less, your cause would be much more likely to succeed. But, I submit, where all is plain there is nothing to be argued. What point in the antislavery creed would you have me argue? On what branch of the subject do the people of this country need light? Must I undertake to prove that the slave is a man? That point is conceded already. Nobody doubts it. The slaveholders themselves acknowledge it in the enactment of laws for their government. They acknowledge it when they punish disobedience on the part of the slave. There are seventy-two crimes in the State of Virginia, which, if committed by a black man, (no matter how ignorant he be), subject him to the punishment of death; while only two of the same crimes will subject a white man to the like punishment. What is this but the acknowledgment that the slave is a moral, intellectual and responsible being? The manhood of the slave is conceded. It is admitted in the fact that Southern statute books are covered with enactments forbidding, under severe fines and penalties, the teaching of the slave to read or to write. When you can point to any such laws, in reference to the beasts of the field, then I may consent to argue the manhood of the slave. When the dogs in your streets, when the fowls of the air, when the cattle on your hills, when the fish of the sea, and the reptiles that crawl, shall be unable to distinguish the slave from a brute, *then* will I argue with you that the slave is a man!

For the present, it is enough to affirm the equal manhood of the negro race. Is it not astonishing that, while we are ploughing, planting and reaping, using all kinds of mechanical tools, erecting houses, constructing bridges, building ships, working in metals of brass, iron, copper, silver and gold; that, while we are reading, writing and cyphering, acting as clerks, merchants and secretaries, having among us lawyers, doctors, ministers, poets, authors, editors, orators and teachers; that, while we are engaged in

---

[13]Douglass quotes from the first issue of *The Liberator,* in which William Lloyd Garrison promised, "I am in earnest — I will not equivocate — I will not excuse — I will not retreat a single inch — and *I will be heard." Lib.,* 1 January 1831; John L. Thomas, *The Liberator: William Lloyd Garrison* (Boston, 1963), 128. — JWB

all manner of enterprises common to other men, digging gold in California, capturing the whale in the Pacific, feeding sheep and cattle on the hillside, living, moving, acting, thinking, planning, living in families as husbands, wives and children, and, above all, confessing and worshipping the Christian's God, and looking hopefully for life and immortality beyond the grave, we are called upon to prove that we are men!

Would you have me argue that man is entitled to liberty? that he is the rightful owner of his own body? You have already declared it. Must I argue the wrongfulness of slavery? Is that a question for Republicans?[14] Is it to be settled by the rules of logic and argumentation, as a matter beset with great difficulty, involving a doubtful application of the principle of justice, hard to be understood? How should I look today, in the presence of Americans, dividing, and subdividing a discourse, to show that men have a natural right to freedom? speaking of it relatively, and positively, negatively, and affirmatively. To do so, would be to make myself ridiculous, and to offer an insult to your understanding. There is not a man beneath the canopy of heaven, that does not know that slavery is wrong *for him.*

What, am I to argue that it is wrong to make men brutes, to rob them of their liberty, to work them without wages, to keep them ignorant of their relations to their fellow men, to beat them with sticks, to flay their flesh with the lash, to load their limbs with irons, to hunt them with dogs, to sell them at auction, to sunder their families, to knock out their teeth, to burn their flesh, to starve them into obedience and submission to their masters? Must I argue that a system thus marked with blood, and stained with pollution, is *wrong?* No! I will not. I have better employments for my time and strength, than such arguments would imply.

What, then, remains to be argued? Is it that slavery is not divine; that God did not establish it; that our doctors of divinity are mistaken? There is blasphemy in the thought. That which is inhuman, cannot be divine! *Who* can reason on such a proposition? They that can, may; I cannot. The time for such argument is past.

At a time like this, scorching irony, not convincing argument, is needed. O! had I the ability, and could I reach the nation's ear, I would, today, pour out a fiery stream of biting ridicule, blasting reproach, withering sarcasm, and stern rebuke. For it is not light that is needed, but fire; it is not the gentle shower, but thunder. We need the storm, the whirlwind, and the earthquake. The feeling of the nation must be quickened; the conscience of the nation must be roused; the propriety of the nation must be startled; the hypocrisy of the nation must be exposed; and its crimes against God and man must be proclaimed and denounced.

What, to the American slave, is your Fourth of July? I answer: a day that reveals to him, more than all other days in the year, the gross injustice and

---

[14]By "Republicans," Douglass probably means adherents to a republican, or representative, form of government, not members of a particular political party. The national Republican Party, however, was formed shortly after Douglass gave this speech; promoting antislavery, this party won the presidential election of 1860 with Abraham Lincoln. — EDS.

cruelty to which he is the constant victim. To him, your celebration is a sham; your boasted liberty, an unholy license; your national greatness, swelling vanity; your sounds of rejoicing are empty and heartless; your denunciations of tyrants, brass fronted impudence; your shouts of liberty and equality, hollow mockery; your prayers and hymns, your sermons and thanksgivings, with all your religious parade, and solemnity, are, to him, mere bombast, fraud, deception, impiety, and hypocrisy — a thin veil to cover up crimes which would disgrace a nation of savages. There is not a nation on the earth guilty of practices, more shocking and bloody, than are the people of these United States, at this very hour.

Go where you may, search where you will, roam through all the monarchies and despotisms of the old world, travel through South America, search out every abuse, and when you have found the last, lay your facts by the side of the everyday practices of this nation, and you will say with me, that, for revolting barbarity and shameless hypocrisy, America reigns without a rival.

THE INTERNAL SLAVE TRADE

Take the American slave-trade, which, we are told by the papers, is especially prosperous just now. Ex-Senator Benton[15] tells us that the price of men was never higher than now. He mentions the fact to show that slavery is in no danger. This trade is one of the peculiarities of American institutions. It is carried on in all the large towns and cities in one-half of this confederacy; and millions are pocketed every year, by dealers in this horrid traffic. In several states, this trade is a chief source of wealth. It is called (in contradistinction to the foreign slave-trade) *"the internal slave-trade."* It is, probably, called so, too, in order to divert from it the horror with which the foreign slave-trade is contemplated. That trade has long since been denounced by this government, as piracy. It has been denounced with burning words, from the high places of the nation, as an execrable traffic. To arrest it, to put an end to it, this nation keeps a squadron, at immense cost, on the coast of Africa. Everywhere, in this country, it is safe to speak of this foreign slave-trade, as a most inhuman traffic, opposed alike to the laws of God and of man. The duty to extirpate and destroy it, is admitted even by our DOCTORS OF DIVINITY. In order to put an end to it, some of these last have consented that their colored brethren (nominally free) should leave this country, and establish themselves on the western coast of Africa! It is, however, a notable fact that, while so much execration is poured out by Americans upon those engaged in the foreign slave-trade, the men engaged in the slave-trade between the states pass without condemnation, and their business is deemed honorable.

---

[15]Thomas Hart Benton, a native of North Carolina, served as U.S. senator from Missouri from 1821 to 1851. — EDS.

Behold the practical operation of this internal slave-trade, the American slave-trade, sustained by American politics and American religion. Here you will see men and women reared like swine for the market. You know what is a swine-drover? I will show you a man-drover. They inhabit all our Southern States. They perambulate the country, and crowd the highways of the nation, with droves of human stock. You will see one of these human flesh-jobbers, armed with pistol, whip and bowie-knife, driving a company of a hundred men, women, and children, from the Potomac to the slave market at New Orleans. These wretched people are to be sold singly, or in lots, to suit purchasers. They are food for the cotton-field, and the deadly sugar-mill. Mark the sad procession, as it moves wearily along, and the inhuman wretch who drives them. Hear his savage yells and his blood-chilling oaths, as he hurries on his affrighted captives! There, see the old man, with locks thinned and gray. Cast one glance, if you please, upon that young mother, whose shoulders are bare to the scorching sun, her briny tears falling on the brow of the babe in her arms. See, too, that girl of thirteen, weeping, *yes!* weeping, as she thinks of the mother from whom she has been torn! The drove moves tardily. Heat and sorrow have nearly consumed their strength; suddenly you hear a quick snap, like the discharge of a rifle; the fetters clank, and the chain rattles simultaneously; your ears are saluted with a scream, that seems to have torn its way to the centre of your soul! The crack you heard, was the sound of the slave-whip; the scream you heard, was from the woman you saw with the babe. Her speed had faltered under the weight of her child and her chains! that gash on her shoulder tells her to move on. Follow this drove to New Orleans. Attend the auction; see men examined like horses; see the forms of women rudely and brutally exposed to the shocking gaze of American slave-buyers. See this drove sold and separated forever; and never forget the deep, sad sobs that arose from that scattered multitude. Tell me citizens, WHERE, under the sun, you can witness a spectacle more fiendish and shocking. Yet this is but a glance at the American slave-trade, as it exists, at this moment, in the ruling part of the United States.

I was born amid such sights and scenes. To me the American slave-trade is a terrible reality. When a child, my soul was often pierced with a sense of its horrors. I lived on Philpot Street, Fell's Point, Baltimore, and have watched from the wharves, the slave ships in the Basin, anchored from the shore, with their cargoes of human flesh, waiting for favorable winds to waft them down the Chesapeake. There was, at that time, a grand slave mart kept at the head of Pratt Street, by Austin Woldfolk. His agents were sent into every town and county in Maryland, announcing their arrival, through the papers, and on flaming *"hand-bills,"* headed CASH FOR NE-GROES. These men were generally well dressed men, and very captivating in their manners. Ever ready to drink, to treat, and to gamble. The fate of many a slave has depended upon the turn of a single card; and many a child has been snatched from the arms of its mother by bargains arranged in a state of brutal drunkenness.

The flesh-mongers gather up their victims by dozens, and drive them, chained, to the general depot at Baltimore. When a sufficient number have been collected here, a ship is chartered, for the purpose of conveying the forlorn crew to Mobile, or to New Orleans. From the slave prison to the ship, they are usually driven in the darkness of night; for since the anti-slavery agitation, a certain caution is observed.

In the deep still darkness of midnight, I have been often aroused by the dead heavy footsteps, and the piteous cries of the chained gangs that passed our door. The anguish of my boyish heart was intense; and I was often consoled, when speaking to my mistress in the morning, to hear her say that the custom was very wicked; that she hated to hear the rattle of the chains, and the heart-rending cries. I was glad to find one who sympathised with me in my horror.

Fellow-citizens, this murderous traffic is, today, in active operation in this boasted republic. In the solitude of my spirit, I see clouds of dust raised on the highways of the South; I see the bleeding footsteps; I hear the doleful wail of fettered humanity, on the way to the slave-markets, where the victims are to be sold like *horses, sheep,* and *swine,* knocked off to the highest bidder. There I see the tenderest ties ruthlessly broken, to gratify the lust, caprice and rapacity of the buyers and sellers of men. My soul sickens at the sight.

> Is this the land your Fathers loved,
>   The freedom which they toiled to win?
>
> Is this the earth whereon they moved?
>   Are these the graves they slumber in?[16]

But a still more inhuman, disgraceful, and scandalous state of things remains to be presented.

By an act of the American Congress, not yet two years old, slavery has been nationalized in its most horrible and revolting form. By that act, Mason & Dixon's line has been obliterated;[17] New York has become as Virginia; and the power to hold, hunt, and sell men, women, and children as slaves remains no longer a mere state institution, but is now an institution of the whole United States. The power is co-extensive with the star-spangled banner and American Christianity. Where these go, may also go the merciless slave-hunter. Where these are, man is not sacred. He is a bird for the sportsman's gun. By that most foul and fiendish of all human decrees, the liberty and person of every man are put in peril. Your broad republican domain is hunting ground for *men. Not* for thieves and robbers, enemies of society, merely, but for men guilty of no crime. Your

---

[16]Douglass slightly alters the first four lines of John Greenleaf Whittier's "Stanzas for the Times." Whittier, *Poetical Works,* 3:35. — JWB

[17]Charles Mason and Jeremiah Dixon surveyed the boundary between Maryland and Pennsylvania from 1763 to 1767. In popular usage this "Mason-Dixon line" was extended west to the Ohio River and along that river to the Mississippi. During the debate over the Missouri Compromise of 1820, the Mason-Dixon line became known as the line separating the slave and free states. — EDS.

law-makers have commanded all good citizens to engage in this hellish sport. Your President, your Secretary of State, your *lords, nobles,* and ecclesiastics, enforce, as a duty you owe to your free and glorious country, and to your God, that you do this accursed thing. Not fewer than forty Americans have, within the past two years, been hunted down and, without a moment's warning, hurried away in chains, and consigned to slavery and excruciating torture. Some of these have had wives and children, dependent on them for bread; but of this, no account was made. The right of the hunter to his prey stands superior to the right of marriage, and to *all* rights in this republic, the rights of God included! For black men there are neither law, justice, humanity, nor religion. The Fugitive Slave *Law* makes MERCY TO THEM, A CRIME; and bribes the judge who tries them. An American JUDGE GETS TEN DOLLARS FOR EVERY VICTIM HE CONSIGNS to slavery, and five, when he fails to do so. The oath of any two villains is sufficient, under this hell-black enactment, to send the most pious and exemplary black man into the remorseless jaws of slavery! His own testimony is nothing. He can bring no witnesses for himself. The minister of American justice is bound by the law to hear but *one* side; and *that* side, is the side of the oppressor.[18] Let this damning fact be perpetually told. Let it be thundered around the world, that, in tyrant-killing, king-hating, people-loving, democratic, Christian America, the seats of justice are filled with judges, who hold their offices under an open and palpable *bribe,* and are bound, in deciding in the case of a man's liberty, *to hear only his accusers!*

In glaring violation of justice, in shameless disregard of the forms of administering law, in cunning arrangement to entrap the defenseless, and in diabolical intent, this Fugitive Slave Law stands alone in the annals of tyrannical legislation. I doubt if there be another nation on the globe, having the brass and the baseness to put such a law on the statute-book. If any man in this assembly thinks differently from me in this matter, and feels able to disprove my statements, I will gladly confront him at any suitable time and place he may select.

RELIGIOUS LIBERTY

I take this law to be one of the grossest infringements of Christian Liberty, and, if the churches and ministers of our country were not stupidly blind, or most wickedly indifferent, they, too, would so regard it.

At the very moment that they are thanking God for the enjoyment of

---

[18]Although the 1850 Fugitive Slave Law did not specify the number of witnesses needed to establish that an individual was a fugitive slave, it did provide that "in no trial or hearing . . . shall the testimony of such alleged fugitive be admitted in evidence." No provision was made for the alleged fugitive to bring forth witnesses who might dispute the claims of the court transcript or warrant, but the commissioner or judge did have to be convinced that the person brought before him was indeed the escaped slave described in the transcript. *The Public Statutes at Large and Treaties of the United States of America, 1789–1873,* 17 vols. (Boston, 1845–73), 9:462–65; Campbell, *Slave Catchers,* 110–15. — JWB

civil and religious liberty, and for the right to worship God according to the dictates of their own consciences, they are utterly silent in respect to a law which robs religion of its chief significance, and makes it utterly worthless to a world lying in wickedness. Did this law concern the *"mint, anise and cummin"*[19] — abridge the right to sing psalms, to partake of the sacrament, or to engage in any of the ceremonies of religion, it would be smitten by the thunder of a thousand pulpits. A general shout would go up from the church, demanding *repeal, repeal, instant repeal!* And it would go hard with that politician who presumed to solicit the votes of the people without inscribing this motto on his banner. Further, if this demand were not complied with, another Scotland would be added to the history of religious liberty, and the stern old Covenanters would be thrown into the shade. A John Knox would be seen at every church door, and heard from every pulpit, and Fillmore would have no more quarter than was shown by Knox, to the beautiful, but treacherous Queen Mary of Scotland.[20] The fact that the church of our country, (with fractional exceptions), does not esteem "the Fugitive Slave Law" as a declaration of war against religious liberty, implies that that church regards religion simply as a form of worship, an empty ceremony, and *not* a vital principle, requiring active benevolence, justice, love and good will towards man. It esteems sacrifice above mercy; psalm-singing above right doing; solemn meetings above practical righteousness. A worship that can be conducted by persons who refuse to give shelter to the houseless, to give bread to the hungry, clothing to the naked, and who enjoin obedience to a law forbidding these acts of mercy, is a curse, not a blessing to mankind. The Bible addresses all such persons as "scribes, pharisees, hypocrites, who pay tithe of *mint, anise,* and *cummin,* and have omitted the weightier matters of the law, judgment, mercy and faith."

THE CHURCH RESPONSIBLE

But the church of this country is not only indifferent to the wrongs of the slave, it actually takes sides with the oppressors. It has made itself the bulwark of American slavery, and the shield of American slave-hunters. Many of its most eloquent Divines, who stand as the very lights of the church, have shamelessly given the sanction of religion and the Bible to the whole slave system. They have taught that man may, properly, be a slave; that the relation of master and slave is ordained of God; that to send back an es-

---

[19]Matt. 23:23: "Woe unto you, scribes and Pharisees, hypocrites! For ye pay tithe of mint, anise and cummin, and have omitted the weightier *matters* of the law, judgment, mercy and faith; these ought ye to have done, and not to leave the other undone." — JWB

[20]John Knox was a sixteenth-century leader of Calvinist Protestantism in Scotland. His fellow believers forced Roman Catholic Mary Stuart, queen of Scotland, to abdicate when she tried to suppress their form of religion. She was later executed by Elizabeth I, queen of England. Millard Fillmore (1800–74) was president in 1852; as the American head of state he corresponds to Mary in Douglass's example. — EDS.

caped bondman to his master is clearly the duty of all the followers of the Lord Jesus Christ; and this horrible blasphemy is palmed off upon the world for Christianity.

For my part, I would say, welcome infidelity! welcome atheism! welcome anything! in preference to the gospel, *as preached by those Divines!* They convert the very name of religion into an engine of tyranny, and barbarous cruelty, and serve to confirm more infidels, in this age, than all the infidel writings of Thomas Paine, Voltaire, and Bolingbroke,[21] put together, have done! These ministers make religion a cold and flinty-hearted thing, having neither principles of right action, nor bowels of compassion. They strip the love of God of its beauty, and leave the throne of religion a huge, horrible, repulsive form. It is a religion for oppressors, tyrants, man-stealers, and *thugs.* It is not that *"pure and undefiled religion"* which is from above, and which is *"first pure, then peaceable, easy to be entreated,* full of mercy and good fruits, *without partiality,* and *without hypocrisy."*[22] But a religion which favors the rich against the poor; which exalts the proud above the humble; which divides mankind into two classes, tyrants and slaves; which says to the man in chains, *stay there;* and to the oppressor, *oppress on;* it is a religion which may be professed and enjoyed by all the robbers and enslavers of mankind; it makes God a respecter of persons, denies his fatherhood of the race, and tramples in the dust the great truth of the brotherhood of man. All this we affirm to be true of the popular church, and the popular worship of our land and nation — a religion, a church, and a worship which, on the authority of inspired wisdom, we pronounce to be an abomination in the sight of God. In the language of Isaiah, the American church might be well addressed, "Bring no more vain oblations; incense is an abomination unto me: the new moons and Sabbaths, the calling of assemblies, I cannot away with; it is iniquity, even the solemn meeting. Your new moons and your appointed feasts my soul hateth. They are a trouble to me; I am weary to bear them; and when ye spread forth your hands I will hide mine eyes from you. Yea! when ye make many prayers, I will not hear. YOUR HANDS ARE FULL OF BLOOD; cease to do evil, learn to do well; seek judgement; relieve the oppressed; judge for the fatherless; plead for the widow."[23]

The American church is guilty, when viewed in connection with what it is doing to uphold slavery; but it is superlatively guilty when viewed in connection with its ability to abolish slavery.

---

[21]The American Paine (1737–1809), also known for his Revolutionary War writings; the Frenchman Voltaire (1694–1778); and the Englishman Bolingbroke (1678–1751) were all essayists noted for their attacks on accepted forms of Christianity, both Protestant and Catholic. Douglass calls these men "infidels" ironically because they were unfaithful to the dominant but repressive religion of their day. — EDS.

[22]Douglass quotes from James 1:27: "Pure religion and undefiled . . . is this . . . ," and 3:17, "But the wisdom that is from above is first pure, then peaceable, gentle, *and* easy to be intreated, full of mercy and good fruits, without partiality and without hypocrisy." — JWB

[23]Isa. 1:13–17. — JWB

The sin of which it is guilty is one of omission as well as of commission. Albert Barnes,[24] but uttered what the common sense of every man at all observant of the actual state of the case will receive as truth, when he declared that "There is no power out of the church that could sustain slavery an hour, if it were not sustained in it."

Let the religious press, the pulpit, the Sunday school, the conference meeting, the great ecclesiastical, missionary, Bible and tract associations of the land array their immense powers against slavery and slave-holding; and the whole system of crime and blood would be scattered to the winds; and that they do not do this involves them in the most awful responsibility of which the mind can conceive.

In prosecuting the antislavery enterprise, we have been asked to spare the church, to spare the ministry; but *how*, we ask, could such a thing be done? We are met on the threshold of our efforts for the redemption of the slave, by the church and ministry of the country, in battle arrayed against us; and we are compelled to fight or flee. From what *quarter*, I beg to know, has proceeded a fire so deadly upon our ranks, during the last two years, as from the Northern pulpit? As the champions of oppressors, the chosen men of American theology have appeared — men, honored for their so-called piety, and their real learning. The LORDS of Buffalo, the SPRINGS of New York, the LATHROPS of Auburn, the COXES and SPENCERS of Brooklyn, the GANNETS and SHARPS of Boston, the DEWEYS of Washington, and other great religious lights of the land, have, in utter denial of the authority of *Him*, by whom they professed to be called to the ministry, deliberately taught us, against the example of the Hebrews and against the remonstrance of the Apostles, they teach *"that we ought to obey man's law before the law of God."*[25]

My spirit wearies of such blasphemy; and how such men can be supported, as the "standing types and representatives of Jesus Christ," is a mystery which I leave others to penetrate. In speaking of the American church, however, let it be distinctly understood that I mean the *great mass* of the religious organizations of our land. There are exceptions, and I thank God that there are. Noble men may be found, scattered all over these Northern States, of whom Henry Ward Beecher of Brooklyn, Samuel J. May of Syracuse, and my esteemed friend on the platform, are shining examples;[26] and

[24]Albert Barnes was a Presbyterian minister and well-known opponent of slavery. — EDS.

[25]The men named in this list were all Protestant ministers who, in Douglass's view, did not oppose slavery vigorously enough. While some defended it, others condemned it but still opposed immediate emancipation, urged compliance with the Fugitive Slave Law, and so on. Douglass names them in the plural (for example, "LORDS," to refer to one man, John Chase Lord) to suggest that they represent types of Christian clergy, that there are many others like them. — EDS.

[26]Henry Ward Beecher was the brother of Harriet Beecher Stowe, author of the well-known antislavery novel *Uncle Tom's Cabin;* Robert Raymond was Douglass's "esteemed friend" on the speakers' platform. Raymond's contribution to the event was to read the text of the Declaration of Independence just before Douglass spoke. Both men, along with Rev. May, were staunchly antislavery ministers. — EDS.

let me say further, that upon these men lies the duty to inspire our ranks with high religious faith and zeal, and to cheer us on in the great mission of the slave's redemption from his chains.

RELIGION IN ENGLAND AND RELIGION IN AMERICA

One is struck with the difference between the attitude of the American church towards the antislavery movement, and that occupied by the churches in England towards a similar movement in that country. There, the church, true to its mission of ameliorating, elevating, and improving the condition of mankind, came forward promptly, bound up the wounds of the West Indian slave, and restored him to his liberty. There, the question of emancipation was a high[ly] religious question. It was demanded, in the name of humanity, and according to the law of the living God. The Sharps, the Clarksons, the Wilberforces, the Buxtons, and Burchells and the Knibbs, were alike famous for their piety, and for their philanthropy.[27] The antislavery movement *there* was not an anti-church movement, for the reason that the church took its full share in prosecuting that movement: and the antislavery movement in this country will cease to be an anti-church movement, when the church of this country shall assume a favorable, instead of a hostile position towards that movement.

Americans! your republican politics, not less than your republican religion, are flagrantly inconsistent. You boast of your love of liberty, your superior civilization, and your pure Christianity, while the whole political power of the nation (as embodied in the two great political parties), is solemnly pledged to support and perpetuate the enslavement of three millions of your countrymen. You hurl your anathemas at the crowned headed tyrants of Russia and Austria, and pride yourselves on your Democratic institutions, while you yourselves consent to be the mere *tools* and *body-guards* of the tyrants of Virginia and Carolina. You invite to your shores fugitives of oppression from abroad, honor them with banquets, greet them with ovations, cheer them, toast them, salute them, protect them, and pour out your money to them like water; but the fugitives from your own land you advertise, hunt, arrest, shoot and kill. You glory in your refinement and your universal education; yet you maintain a system as barbarous and dreadful as ever stained the character of a nation — a system begun in avarice, supported in pride, and perpetuated in cruelty. You shed tears over fallen Hungary, and make the sad story of her wrongs the theme of your poets, statesmen and orators, till your gallant sons are ready to fly to arms

---

[27]Douglass uses a similar technique here as in his catalog of slavery defenders, naming these antislavery English clergy in the plural so as to suggest that they are representative of the many English Christians who opposed slavery and succeeded, in 1834, in abolishing it in the countries under English rule. — EDS.

to vindicate her cause against her oppressors;[28] but, in regard to the ten thousand wrongs of the American slave, you would enforce the strictest silence, and would hail him as an enemy of the nation who dares to make those wrongs the subject of public discourse! You are all on fire at the mention of liberty for France or for Ireland; but are as cold as an iceberg at the thought of liberty for the enslaved of America. You discourse eloquently on the dignity of labor; yet, you sustain a system which, in its very essence, casts a stigma upon labor. You can bare your bosom to the storm of British artillery to throw off a threepenny tax on tea; and yet wring the last hard-earned farthing from the grasp of the black laborers of your country. You profess to believe "that, of one blood, God made all nations of men to dwell on the face of all the earth,"[29] and hath commanded all men, everywhere to love one another; yet you notoriously hate, (and glory in your hatred), all men whose skins are not colored like your own. You declare, before the world, and are understood by the world to declare, that you *"hold these truths to be self evident, that all men are created equal; and are endowed by their Creator with certain inalienable rights; and that, among these are, life, liberty, and the pursuit of happiness;"* and yet, you hold securely, in a bondage which, according to your own Thomas Jefferson, *"is worse than ages of that which your fathers rose in rebellion to oppose,"*[30] *a seventh part* of the inhabitants of your country.

Fellow-citizens! I will not enlarge further on your national inconsistencies. The existence of slavery in this country brands your republicanism as a sham, your humanity as a base pretence, and your Christianity as a lie. It destroys your moral power abroad; it corrupts your politicians at home. It saps the foundation of religion; it makes your name a hissing, and a byword to a mocking earth. It is the antagonistic force in your government, the only thing that seriously disturbs and endangers your *Union*. It fetters your progress; it is the enemy of improvement, the deadly foe of education; it fosters pride; it breeds insolence; it promotes vice; it shelters crime; it is a curse to the earth that supports it; and yet, you cling to it, as if it were the sheet anchor of all your hopes. Oh! be warned! be warned! a horrible reptile is coiled up in your nation's bosom; the venomous creature is nursing at the tender breast of your youthful republic; *for the love of God, tear away,* and fling from you the hideous monster, and *let the weight of twenty millions crush and destroy it forever!*

---

[28]In 1848 Hungarian patriot Louis Kossuth led an attempt to establish an independent Hungarian government, which was then crushed by the invasion of Austrian troops in 1849. — EDS.

[29]A paraphrase of Acts 17–26: "And [God] hath made of one blood all nations of men for to dwell on all the face of the earth." — JWB

[30]Writing to Jean Nicholas Démeunier on 26 June 1786, Thomas Jefferson observed: "What a stupendous, what an incomprehensible machine is man! Who can endure toil, famine, stripes, imprisonment or death itself in vindication of his own liberty, and the next moment be deaf to all those motives whose power supported him thro' his trial, and inflict on his fellow men a bondage, one hour of which is fraught with more misery than ages of that which he rose in rebellion to oppose." Boyd, *Papers of Thomas Jefferson*, 10:63. — JWB

THE CONSTITUTION

But it is answered in reply to all this, that precisely what I have now denounced is, in fact, guaranteed and sanctioned by the Constitution of the United States; that the right to hold and to hunt slaves is a part of that Constitution framed by the illustrious Fathers of this Republic.

Then, I dare to affirm, notwithstanding all I have said before, your fathers stooped, basely stooped

> To palter with us in a double sense:
> And keep the word of promise to the ear,
> But break it to the heart.[31]

And instead of being the honest men I have before declared them to be, they were the veriest imposters that ever practised on mankind. *This* is the inevitable conclusion, and from it there is no escape. But I differ from those who charge this baseness on the framers of the Constitution of the United States. *It is a slander upon their memory,* at least, so I believe. There is not time now to argue the constitutional question at length; nor have I the ability to discuss it as it ought to be discussed. The subject has been handled with masterly power by Lysander Spooner, Esq., by William Goodell, by Samuel E. Sewall, Esq., and last, though not least, by Gerritt Smith, Esq. These gentlemen have, as I think, fully and clearly vindicated the Constitution from any design to support slavery for an hour.

Fellow-citizens! there is no matter in respect to which, the people of the North have allowed themselves to be so ruinously imposed upon, as that of the proslavery character of the Constitution. In *that* instrument I hold there is neither warrant, license, nor sanction of the hateful thing; but, interpreted as it *ought* to be interpreted, the Constitution is a GLORIOUS LIBERTY DOCUMENT. Read its preamble, consider its purposes. Is slavery among them? Is it at the gateway? or is it in the temple? It is neither. While I do not intend to argue this question on the present occasion, let me ask, if it be not somewhat singular that, if the Constitution were intended to be, by its framers and adopters, a slave-holding instrument, why neither *slavery, slaveholding,* nor *slave* can anywhere be found in it. What would be thought of an instrument, drawn up, *legally* drawn up, for the purpose of entitling the city of Rochester to a track of land, in which no mention of land was made? Now, there are certain rules of interpretation, for the proper understanding of all legal instruments. These rules are well established. They are plain, common-sense rules, such as you and I, and all of us, can understand and apply, without having passed years in the study of law. I scout the idea that the question of the Constitutionality or unconstitutionality of slavery is not a question for the people. I hold that every American citizen has a right to form an opinion of the Constitution, and to propagate that opinion, and to use all honorable means to make his opinion the prevailing one. Without this right, the liberty of an American

---

[31]See William Shakespeare, *Macbeth,* 5.8.20–22. — EDS.

citizen would be as insecure as that of a Frenchman. Ex-Vice-President Dallas[32] tells us that the Constitution is an object to which no American mind can be too attentive, and no American heart too devoted. He further says, the Constitution, in its words, is plain and intelligible, and is meant for the home-bred, unsophisticated understandings of our fellow-citizens. Senator Berrien tells us that the Constitution is the fundamental law, that which controls all others. The charter of our liberties, which every citizen has a personal interest in understanding thoroughly. The testimony of Senator Breese, Lewis Cass, and many others that might be named, who are everywhere esteemed as sound lawyers, so regard the Constitution. I take it, therefore, that it is not presumption in a private citizen to form an opinion of that instrument.[33]

Now, take the Constitution according to its plain reading, and I defy the presentation of a single proslavery clause in it. On the other hand it will be found to contain principles and purposes, entirely hostile to the existence of slavery.

I have detained my audience entirely too long already. At some future period I will gladly avail myself of an opportunity to give this subject a full and fair discussion.

Allow me to say, in conclusion, notwithstanding the dark picture I have this day presented of the state of the nation, I do not despair of this country. There are forces in operation, which must inevitably work the downfall of slavery. *"The arm of the Lord is not shortened,"*[34] and the doom of slavery is certain. I, therefore, leave off where I began, with *hope*. While drawing encouragement from the Declaration of Independence, the great principles it contains, and the genius of American Institutions, my spirit is also cheered by the obvious tendencies of the age. Nations do not now stand in the same relation to each other that they did ages ago. No nation can now shut itself up from the surrounding world, and trot round in the same old path of its fathers without interference. The time *was* when such could be done. Long established customs of hurtful character could formerly fence themselves in, and do their evil work with social impunity. Knowledge was then confined and enjoyed by the privileged few, and the multitude walked on in mental darkness. But a change has now come over the affairs of mankind. Walled cities and empires have become unfashionable. The arm of commerce has borne away the gates of the strong city. Intelligence is penetrating the darkest corners of the globe. It makes its pathway over and under the sea, as well as on the earth. Wind, steam, and lightning are its chartered agents. Oceans no longer divide, but link nations together.

[32]George Mifflin Dallas (1792–1864) was vice president from 1845 to 1849 under President James Polk. — EDS.

[33]Douglass assumes that his audience knows that in addition to being experts on constitutional law, the men he has just named — Dallas, Berrien, Breese, and Cass — were also to varying degrees defenders of slavery. Douglass thus employs the irony of citing his opponents on his own side. — EDS.

[34]Douglass paraphrases Isa. 59:1: "Behold, the Lord's hand is not shortened, that it cannot save, neither His ear heavy, that it cannot hear." — JWB

From Boston to London is now a holiday excursion. Space is comparatively annihilated. Thoughts expressed on one side of the Atlantic are distinctly heard on the other.

The far off and almost fabulous Pacific rolls in grandeur at our feet. The Celestial Empire, the mystery of ages, is being solved. The fiat of the Almighty, *"Let there be Light,"* has not yet spent its force. No abuse, no outrage whether in taste, sport or avarice, can now hide itself from the all-pervading light. The iron shoe, and crippled foot of China must be seen, in contrast with nature.[35] *Africa must rise and put on her yet unwoven garment. "Ethiopia shall stretch out her hand unto God."*[36] In the fervent aspirations of William Lloyd Garrison, I say, and let every heart join in saying it:

> God speed the year of jubilee
>   The wide world o'er!
> When from their galling chains set free,
> Th' oppress'd shall vilely bend the knee,
> And wear the yoke of tyranny
>   Like brutes no more.
> That year will come, and freedom's reign,
> To man his plundered rights again
>   Restore.
>
> God speed the day when human blood
>   Shall cease to flow!
> In every clime be understood,
> The claims of human brotherhood,
> And each return for evil, good,
>   Not blow for blow;
> That day will come all feuds to end,
> And change into a faithful friend
>   Each foe.
>
> God speed the hour, the glorious hour,
>   When none on earth
> Shall exercise a lordly power,
> Nor in a tyrant's presence cower;
> But all to manhood's stature tower,
>   By equal birth!
> THAT HOUR WILL COME, to each, to all,
> And from his prison-house, the thrall
>   Go forth.
>
> Until that year, day, hour, arrive,
> With head, and heart, and hand I'll strive,
> To break the rod, and rend the gyve,

[35]The "Celestial Empire" is China, being visited (or invaded) in comparatively large numbers by European and American missionaries and traders for the first time in Douglass's day. Douglass refers to Chinese customs that he regards as barbaric, such as the binding of women's feet. — EDS.

[36]An allusion to Ps. 68:31: "Princes shall come out of Egypt; Ethiopia shall soon stretch out her hands unto God." — JWB

The spoiler of his prey deprive —
So witness Heaven!
And never from my chosen post,
Whate'er the peril or the cost,
Be driven.[37]

READING CRITICALLY

1. What traits of the Revolutionary leaders does Douglass emphasize?

2. Why does Douglass cite opposition to the foreign slave trade as a key example of American hypocrisy?

3. Why does the Fugitive Slave Law violate religious freedom, according to Douglass?

4. In his concluding paragraphs, Douglass hints about punishments that will come upon the United States if slavery is not abolished. What are they?

WRITING ANALYTICALLY

1. In his first three paragraphs, Douglass says that he feels "a quailing sensation," "embarrassment," and other discomfort in front of his audience. Yet we know that at this time, Douglass was an experienced public speaker who had addressed large, predominantly European American audiences before. What, then, could be his rhetorical purpose in beginning with this emphasis on his own discomfort? Write an explanation of this strategy in which you also evaluate its effectiveness. If you wish, you may compare Douglass's use of this strategy with Benjamin Banneker's or other examples of it that you may know.

2. On page 217, Douglass asserts that there is nothing to be "argued" concerning the antislavery position, and in the next few paragraphs he catalogs the issues that don't need to be argued. This is an unusual strategy, since speakers usually wish to argue for their positions. Write a paper in which you explain the rhetorical effect of Douglass's strategy and then evaluate its effectiveness.

3. Like Frederick Douglass, Charles Langston (p. 232) has to persuade a largely white audience to act on behalf of African American civil rights when he speaks in opposition to the Fugitive Slave Law. Write a paper in which you compare and contrast the two men's rhetorical strategies, arguing for which one you think is the more effective persuader.

---

[37]William Lloyd Garrison, "The Triumph of Freedom," in *The Liberator,* 10 January 1845.
— JWB

CHARLES LANGSTON

Address to the Court (1859)

Charles Langston, who came from an important old Virginia family of free African Americans, was an active abolitionist. In September 1858 while living in Cleveland, he heard about the capture in Oberlin, Ohio, of a fugitive slave named John Price. Langston led a group of white and black people to rescue Price and convey him to Canada, which banned slavery and would not extradite fugitive slaves. For this violation of the 1850 Fugitive Slave Law, Langston and other leaders of the rescue group were arrested. Reprinted here is the speech Langston made at his trial, taken from an account published by his brother John Mercer Langston, a lawyer who was later a professor of law at Howard University and a congressional representative from Virginia. Charles Langston was sentenced to spend twenty days in the county jail and to pay a fine of one hundred dollars. Since these penalties were smaller than those imposed on some of the other rescue leaders, perhaps Langston's speech did move the judge to reduce his sentence, in spite of Langston's doubts that his words would have any affect. When he was released from jail, Langston resumed his abolitionist activities.

I AM FOR THE FIRST TIME IN MY LIFE before a court of Justice, charged with the violation of law, and am now about to be sentenced. But before receiving that sentence, I propose to say one or two words in regard to the mitigation of that sentence, if it may be so construed. I cannot of course, and do not expect, that which I may say, will, in any way, change your predetermined line of action. I ask no such favor at your hands.

I know that the courts of this country, that the laws of this country, that the governmental machinery of this country, are so constituted as to oppress and outrage colored men, men of my complexion. I cannot then, of course, expect, judging from the past history of the country, any mercy from the laws, from the constitution, or from the courts of the country.

Some days prior to the thirteenth day of September, 1858, happening to be in Oberlin on a visit, I found the country round about there, and the village itself, filled with alarming rumors as to the fact that slave-catchers, kidnappers, Negro-stealers were lying hidden and skulking about, waiting some opportunity to get their bloody hands on some helpless creature to drag him back — or for the first time, into helpless and life-long bondage. These reports becoming current all over that neighborhood, old men and

Charles Langston, Address to the Court, in *A Documentary History of the Negro People in the United States,* ed. Herbert Aptheker, vol. 1, *From Colonial Times through the Civil War* (Secaucus: Citadel Press, 1951), 427–32, and *The Voice of Black America: Major Speeches by Negroes in the United States, 1797–1971,* ed. Philip Foner (New York: Simon and Schuster, 1972), 212–13.

In the notes, EDS. = Patricia Bizzell and Bruce Herzberg.

innocent women and children became exceedingly alarmed for their safety. It was not uncommon to hear mothers say that they dare not send their children to school, for fear they would be caught and carried off by the way. Some of these people had become free by long and patient toil at night, after working the long, long day for cruel masters, and thus at length getting money enough to buy their liberty. Others had become free by means of the good will of their masters. And there were others who had become free — by the intensest exercise of their God-given powers; — by escaping from the plantations of their masters, eluding the bloodthirsty patrols and sentinels so thickly scattered all along their path, outrunning blood-hounds and horses, swimming rivers and fording swamps, and reaching at last, through incredible difficulties, what they, in their delusion, supposed to be free soil. These three classes were in Oberlin, trembling alike for their safety, because they well knew their fate, should those men-hunters get their hands on them.

In the midst of such excitement the thirteenth day of September was ushered in — a day ever to be remembered in the history of that place, and I presume no less in the history of this Court — on which those men, by lying devices, decoyed into a place where they could get their hands on him — I will not say a slave, for I do not know that — but a *man,* a *brother,* who had a right to his liberty under the laws of God, under the laws of Nature, and under the Declaration of American Independence.

In the midst of all this excitement, the news came to us like a flash of lightning that an actual seizure under and by means of fraudulent pretences had been made!

Being identified with that man by color, by race, by manhood, by sympathies, such as God had implanted in us all, I felt it my duty to go and do what I could toward liberating him. I had been taught by my Revolutionary father — and I say this with all due respect to him — and by his honored associates, that the fundamental doctrine of this government was that *all* men have a right, to life and liberty, and coming from the Old Dominion[1] I brought into Ohio these sentiments, deeply impressed upon my heart; I went to Wellington, and hearing from the parties themselves by what authority the boy was held in custody, I conceived from what little knowledge I had of law, that they had no right to hold him. And as your Honor has repeatedly laid down the law in this Court, a man is free until he is proven to be legally restrained of his liberty, and I believed that upon the principle of law those men were bound to take their prisoner before the very first magistrate they found, and there establish the facts set forth in their warrant, and that until they did this, every man should presume that their claim was unfounded, and to institute such proceedings for the purpose of securing an investigation as they might find warranted by the laws of this State. Now, sir, if that is not the plain, common sense and correct view of the law, then I have been misled by your Honor, and by the prevalent received opinion.

It is said that they had a warrant. Why then should they not establish its

[1]Virginia. — EDS.

validity before the proper officers? And I stand here today, sir, to say that with an exception of which I shall soon speak, *to procure such a lawful investigation of the authority under which they claimed to act, was the part I took in that day's proceedings, and the only part.* I supposed it to be my duty as a citizen of Ohio — excuse me for saying that, sir — as an *outlaw of the United States* (much sensation), to do what I could to secure at least this form of Justice to my brother whose liberty was in peril. *Whatever more than that has been sworn to on this trial, as an act of mine, is false, ridiculously false.* When I found these men refusing to go, according to the law, as I apprehended it, and subject their claim to an official inspection, and that nothing short of a *habeas corpus*[2] would oblige such an inspection, I was willing to go even thus far, supposing in that county a Sheriff might, perhaps, be found with nerve enough to serve it. In this I again failed. Nothing then was left me, nothing to the boy in custody, but the confirmation of my first belief that the pretended authority was worthless, and the employment of those means of liberation which belong to us. With regard to the part I took in the forcible rescue, which followed, I have nothing to say, further than I have already said. The evidence is before you. It is alleged that I said, "We will have him anyhow." *This I never said.* I did say to Mr. Lowe, what I honestly believed to be the truth, that the crowd were very much excited, many of them averse to longer delay, and bent upon a rescue at all hazards; and that he being an old acquaintance and friend of mine, I was anxious to extricate him from the dangerous position he occupied, and therefore advised that he urge Jennings to give the boy up.[3] Further than this I did not say, either to him or any one else.

The law under which I am arraigned is an unjust one, one made to crush the colored man, and one that outrages every feeling of humanity, as well as every rule of right. I have nothing to do with its constitutionality; about that I care but little. I have often heard it said by learned and good men that it was unconstitutional; I remember the excitement that prevailed throughout all the free States when it was passed; and I remember how often it has been said by individuals, conventions, legislatures, and even *Judges,* that it never could be, never should be, and never was meant to be enforced. I had always believed, until contrary appeared in the actual institution of proceedings, that the provisions of this odious statute would never be enforced within the bounds of this State.

But I have another reason to offer why I should not be sentenced, and one that I think pertinent to the case. I have not had a trial before a jury of my peers. The common law of England — and you will excuse me for referring to that, since I am but a private citizen — was that every man should be tried before a jury of men occupying the same position in the social scale with himself. That lords should be tried before a jury of lords; that peers of the realm should be tried before peers of the realm; vassals

---

[2] *"Habeas corpus"* is a legal writ compelling the presentation of evidence for why someone should be detained. In this case, Langston wanted to use such a writ to compel the slave catchers to demonstrate before a judge that they had a legal right to the man they had captured, that is, that he was indeed a slave. — EDS.

[3] Lowe was one of the slave catchers, and Jennings was their leader. — EDS.

before vassals, and *aliens before aliens,* and they must not come from the district where the crime was committed, lest the prejudices of either personal friends or foes should affect the accused. The Constitution of the U.S. guarantees, not merely to its citizens, but *to all persons,* a trial before an *impartial* jury. I have had no such trial.

The colored man is oppressed by certain universal and deeply fixed *prejudices.* Those jurors are well known to have shared largely in these prejudices, and I therefore consider that they were neither impartial, nor were they a jury of my peers. And the prejudices which white people have against colored men grow out of the facts that we have as a people *consented* for two hundred years to be *slaves* of the whites. We have been scourged, crushed and cruelly oppressed, and have submitted to it all tamely, meekly, peaceably — I mean as a people, and with rare individual exceptions — and today you see us thus, meekly submitting to the penalties of an infamous law. Now the Americans have this feeling, and it is an honorable one, that they will respect those who will rebel at oppression but despise those who tamely submit to outrage and wrong; and while our people, as people, submit, they will as a people be despised. Why, they will hardly meet on terms of equality with us in a whisky shop, in a car, at a table, or even at the altar of God — so thorough and hearty a contempt have they for those who will meekly *lie still* under the heel of the oppressor. The jury came into the box with that feeling. They know they had that feeling, and so the court knows now and knew then. The gentleman who prosecuted me, the court itself, and even the counsel who defended me, have that feeling.

I was tried by a jury who were prejudiced; before a Court that was prejudiced; prosecuted by an officer who was prejudiced, and defended, though ably, by counsel that were prejudiced. And therefore, it is, your Honor, that I urge by all that is good and great in manhood, that I should not be subjected to the pains and penalties of this oppressive law, when I have *not* been tried, either by a jury of my peers, or by a jury that were impartial.

One more word, sir, and I have done. I went to Wellington, knowing that colored men have no rights in the United States, which white men are bound to respect;[4] that the Courts had so decided; that Congress had so enacted; that the people had so decreed.

There is not a spot in this wide country, not even by the altars of God, nor in the shadow of the shafts that tell the imperishable fame and glory of the heroes of the Revolution; no, nor in the old Philadelphia Hall, where any colored man may dare to ask a mercy of a white man. Let me stand in that Hall and tell a United States Marshal that my father was a Revolutionary soldier; that he served under Lafayette,[5] and fought through the whole war, and that he fought for *my* freedom as much as for his own; and he

[4]Langston paraphrases here and in the following paragraph the most inflammatory phrase from the United States Supreme Court's decision in the *Dred Scott* case (see p. 172). — EDS.

[5]The Marquis de Lafayette (1757–1834) was a French nobleman who volunteered to fight on the side of the colonists in the American Revolution. He became an important general and was one of the first to recruit black troops. — EDS.

would sneer at me, and clutch me with his bloody fingers, and say he has a *right* to make me a slave! And when I appeal to Congress, they say he has a right to make me a slave; when I appeal to your Honor, *your Honor* says he has a right to make me a slave, and if any man, white or black, seeks an investigation of that claim, they make themselves amenable to the pains and penalties of the Fugitive Slave Act, for BLACK MEN HAVE NO RIGHTS WHICH WHITE MEN ARE BOUND TO RESPECT. (Great Applause.) I, going to Wellington with the full knowledge of all this, knew that if that man was taken to Columbus, he was hopelessly gone, no matter whether he had ever been in slavery before or not. I knew that I was in the same situation myself, and that by the decision of your Honor, if any man whatever were to claim me as his slave and seize me, and my brother, being a lawyer, should seek to get out a writ of *habeas corpus* to expose the falsity of the claim, he would be thrust into prison under one provision of the Fugitive Slave Law, for interfering with the man claiming to be in pursuit of a fugitive, and I, by the perjury of a solitary wretch, would by another of its provisions be helplessly doomed to life-long bondage, without the possibility of escape.

Some may say that there is no danger of free persons being seized and carried off as slaves. No one need labor under such a delusion. Sir, *four* of the eight persons who were first carried back under the act of 1850, were afterwards proved to be *free men*. They were free persons, but wholly at the mercy of the oath of one man. And but last Sabbath afternoon, a letter came to me from a gentleman in St. Louis, informing me that a young lady who was formerly under my instructions at Columbus, a free person, is now lying in the jail at that place, claimed as the slave of some wretch who never saw her before, and waiting for testimony from relatives at Columbus to establish her freedom. I could stand here by the hour and relate such instances. In the very nature of the case they must be constantly occurring. A letter was not long since found upon the person of a counterfeiter when arrested, addressed to him by some Southern gentleman, in which the writer says:

"Go among the Negroes; find out their marks and scars; make good descriptions and send to me, and I'll find masters for 'em."

That is the way men are carried "back" to slavery.

But in view of all the facts, I say that if ever again a man is seized near me, and is about to be carried southward as a slave, before any legal investigation has been had, I shall hold it to be my duty, as I held it that day, to secure for him, if possible, a legal inquiry into the character of the claim by which he is held. And I go further: I say that if it is adjudged illegal to procure even such an investigation, then we are thrown back upon those last defences of our rights which cannot be taken from us, and which God gave us that we need not be slaves. I ask your Honor, while I say this, to place yourself in my situation, and you will say with me that if your brother, if your friend, if your wife, if your child, had been seized by men who claimed them as fugitives, and the law of the land forbade you to ask any investigation and precluded the possibility of any legal protection or redress, then you will say with me, that you would not only demand the protection of the law, but you would call in your neighbors and your friends, and would ask them to say with you that these, your friends, *could not* be taken into slavery.

And now I thank you for this leniency, this indulgence, in giving a man unjustly condemned by a tribunal before which he is declared to have no rights, the privilege of speaking in his own behalf. I know that it will do nothing towards mitigating your sentence, but it is a privilege to be allowed to speak, and I thank you for it. I shall submit to the penalty, be it what it may. But I stand here to say, that if, for doing what I did on that day at Wellington, I am to go in jail six months and pay a fine of a thousand dollars, according to the Fugitive Slave Law — and such is the protection the laws of this country afford me — I must take upon myself the responsibility of self-protection; when I come to be claimed by some perjured wretch as his slave, I shall never be taken into slavery. And as in that trying hour I would have others do to me, as I would call upon my friends to help me, as I would call upon you, your Honor, to help me, as I would call upon you (to the District Attorney) to help me, and upon you (to Judge Bliss), and upon you (to his counsel), *so help me* God I stand here to say that I will do all I can for any man thus seized and held, though the inevitable penalty of six months' imprisonment and one thousand dollars fine for each offence hangs over me! We have all a common humanity, and you all would do that; your manhood would require it, and no matter what the laws might be, you would honor yourself for doing it, while your friends and your children to all generations would honor you for doing it, and every good and honest man would say you had done *right!* (Great and prolonged applause, in spite of the efforts of Court and Marshal.)

READING CRITICALLY

1. According to Langston, what are the reasons that it is unjust for him to be sentenced?

2. Why, in Langston's opinion, are white people prejudiced against African Americans?

3. How does Langston use references to Revolutionary documents and events for his own defense?

WRITING ANALYTICALLY

1. Langston opens by telling the judge that while he hopes his words will lead to the "mitigation" of his sentence, he does "not expect, that which I may say, will, in any way, change your pre-determined line of action" (p. 232). This is an odd opening, since Langston seems to undercut the speech he is about to give by predicting that it will be ineffective. What is the rhetorical effect of this opening? Write an explanation and evaluation of Langston's strategy. If you wish, you may compare this opening with Frederick Douglass's opening expressions of discomfort (p. 209).

2. Langston's speech is officially addressed to the European American judge presiding over his trial. Langston knows, however, that as a martyr to the cause of abolition, he will be heard by African American people as well. What in this speech seems particularly directed to an African American audience? What effect on this audience do you think Langston is trying to have? Do you think his strategies are effective? Write an explanation and evaluation of his strategies, in which you argue that he is or is not an effective political activist.

3. Langston's rhetorical style is similar to that of David Walker (p. 193). Both men seem quite willing to address both African American and white audiences aggressively. Write a paper in which you compare and contrast their rhetorical strategies for either a white or an African American audience, arguing for the one you think is the more effective speaker. Alternative 1: Compare and contrast Langston with Maria Stewart on how each speaker addresses a black audience. Alternative 2: Imagine that you could bring Langston, Walker, or Stewart to your school to give a speech. Write a letter to the campus speakers' group arguing for bringing one of these people.

THE PROSLAVERY DEFENSE

GEORGE FITZHUGH

From *Sociology for the South,*
or the Failure of Free Society (1854)

George Fitzhugh (1806–81) was a Virginia lawyer who also owned a small plantation. He held several minor political offices but was not well known or prosperous until he began to publish. His work was very widely read in his own day, even though southern intellectuals such as Albert Taylor Bledsoe (p. 250) regarded him as something of an upstart and a poor scholar — charges that, reportedly, bothered Fitzhugh not at all. Fitzhugh's defenses of slavery have attracted much attention from twentieth-century scholars, and until very recently he was virtually the only defender of slavery to receive such notice. Fitzhugh may be of particular interest to contemporary scholars because he often couches his arguments in terms of criticism of the industrialized North. In his best-known work, *Cannibals All! or, Slaves without Masters* (1857), for instance, he argues that southern slave owners were less materialistic and treated their workers better than northern factory owners. His earlier work *Sociology for the South, or the Failure of Free Society* (1854) is one of the first studies to use the term "sociology" in anything like its modern sense, as a way of looking at how all the parts of a society fit together. In this excerpt, Fitzhugh attempts to undermine arguments that use the Declaration of Independence to attack slavery, and he directly attacks Declaration principles of equality.

AN ESSAY ON THE SUBJECT OF SLAVERY would be very imperfect, if it passed over without noticing these instruments.[1] The abstract principles which they enunciate, we candidly admit, are wholly at war with slavery; we shall attempt to show that they are equally at war with all government, all subordination, all order. Men's minds were heated and blinded when they were written, as well by patriotic zeal, as by a false philosophy, which, beginning with Locke, in a refined materialism, had ripened on the Continent into open infidelity. In England, the doctrine of prescriptive government, of the divine right of kings, had met with signal overthrow, and in France

George Fitzhugh, *Sociology for the South, or the Failure of Free Society* (1854; reprint, New York: Burt Franklin Research and Source Work Series 102, n.d.), 175–82.
   In the notes, EDS. = Patricia Bizzell and Bruce Herzberg.
   [1]The "instruments" are the two documents Fitzhugh discusses in this chapter, the Declaration of Independence and the Virginia Bill of Rights, both written by Thomas Jefferson. We have excerpted the part of the chapter where he discusses the Declaration. — EDS.

there was faith in nothing, speculation about everything.[2] The human mind became extremely presumptuous, and undertook to form governments on exact philosophical principles, just as men make clocks, watches or mills. They confounded the moral with the physical world, and this was not strange, because they had begun to doubt whether there was any other than a physical world. Society seemed to them a thing whose movement and action could be controlled with as much certainty as the motion of a spinning wheel, provided it was organized on proper principles. It would have been less presumptuous in them to have attempted to have made a tree, for a tree is not half so complex as a society of human beings, each of whom is fearfully and wonderfully compounded of soul and body, and whose aggregate, society, is still more complex and difficult of comprehension than its individual members. Trees grow and man may lop, trim, train and cultivate them, and thus hasten their growth, and improve their size, beauty and fruitfulness. Laws, institutions, societies, and governments grow, and men may aid their growth, improve their strength and beauty, and lop off their deformities and excrescences, by punishing crime and rewarding virtue. When society has worked long enough, under the hand of God and nature, man observing its operations, may discover its laws and constitution. The common law of England and the constitution of England, were discoveries of this kind. Fortunately for us, we adopted, with little change, that common law and that constitution. Our institutions and our ancestry were English. Those institutions were the growth and accretions of many ages, not the work of legislating philosophers.

The abstractions contained in the various instruments on which we professed, but professed falsely, to found our governments, did no harm, because, until abolition arose, they remained a dead letter. Now, and not till now, these abstractions have become matters of serious practical importance, and we propose to give some of them a candid, but fearless examination. We find these words in the preamble and Declaration of Independence,

"We hold these truths to be self-evident, that all men are created equal; that they are endowed by their Creator with certain inalienable rights, that among them, are life, liberty, and the pursuit of happiness; that to secure these rights governments are instituted among men, deriving their just powers from the consent of the governed; that whenever any form of government becomes destructive of these ends it is the right of the people to alter or abolish it, and to institute a new government, laying its founda-

---

[2]Fitzhugh blames John Locke (1632–1704), an English philosopher, for fostering atheism ("infidelity") by his theory that humans gain knowledge of the world through the senses only, not by divine revelation. Locke also believed that people have an innate right to rule themselves and to change their government if it does not serve their interests. This philosophy was opposed to the "divine right of kings"; embraced by the populace, Locke's ideas led to reforms in England and revolutions in France and the American colonies that replaced monarchies with democracies. — EDS.

tions on such principles, and organizing its powers in such form, as to them shall seem most likely to effect their safety and happiness."

It is, we believe, conceded on all hands, that men are not born physically, morally or intellectually equal, — some are males, some females, some from birth, large, strong and healthy, others weak, small and sickly — some are naturally amiable, others prone to all kinds of wickednesses — some brave, others timid. Their natural inequalities beget inequalities of rights. The weak in mind or body require guidance, support and protection; they must obey and work for those who protect and guide them — they have a natural right to guardians, committees, teachers or masters. Nature has made them slaves; all that law and government can do, is to regulate, modify and mitigate their slavery. In the absence of legally instituted slavery, their condition would be worse under that natural slavery of the weak to the strong, the foolish to the wise and cunning. The wise and virtuous, the brave, the strong in mind and body, are by nature born to command and protect, and law but follows nature in making them rulers, legislators, judges, captains, husbands, guardians, committees and masters. The naturally depraved class, those born prone to crime, are our brethren too; they are entitled to education, to religious instruction, to all the means and appliances proper to correct their evil propensities, and all their failings; they have a right to be sent to the penitentiary, — for there, if they do not reform, they cannot at least disturb society. Our feelings, and our consciences teach us, that nothing but necessity can justify taking human life.

We are but stringing together truisms, which every body knows as well as ourselves, and yet if men are created unequal in all these respects, what truth or what meaning is there in the passage under consideration? Men are not created or born equal, and circumstances, and education, and association, tend to increase and aggravate inequalities among them, from generation to generation. Generally, the rich associate and intermarry with each other, the poor do the same; the ignorant rarely associate with or intermarry with the learned, and all society shuns contact with the criminal, even to the third and fourth generations.

Men are not "born entitled to equal rights"! It would be far nearer the truth to say, "that some were born with saddles on their backs, and others booted and spurred to ride them," — and the riding does them good. They need the reins, the bit and the spur. No two men by nature are exactly equal or exactly alike. No institutions can prevent the few from acquiring rule and ascendency over the many. Liberty and free competition invite and encourage the attempt of the strong to master the weak; and insure their success.

"Life and liberty" are not "inalienable"; they have been sold in all countries, and in all ages, and must be sold so long as human nature lasts. It is an inexpedient and unwise, and often unmerciful restraint, on a man's liberty of action, to deny him the right to sell himself when starving, and again to buy himself when fortune smiles. Most countries of antiquity, and some, like China at the present day, allowed such sale and purchase. The great object of government is to restrict, control and punish man "in the pursuit of happiness." All crimes are committed in its pursuit. Under the free or competitive system, most men's happiness consists in destroying the happiness of other people. This, then, is no inalienable right.

The author of the Declaration may have, and probably did mean, that all men were created with an equal title to property. Carry out such a doctrine, and it would subvert every government on earth.

In practice, in all ages, and in all countries, men had sold their liberty either for short periods, for life, or hereditarily; that is, both their own liberty and that of their children after them. The laws of all countries have, in various forms and degrees, in all times recognised and regulated this right to *alien* or sell liberty. The soldiers and sailors of the revolution had aliened both liberty and life, the wives in all America had aliened their liberty, so had the apprentices and wards at the very moment this verbose, newborn, false and unmeaning preamble was written.

Mr. Jefferson was an enthusiastic speculative philosopher;[3] Franklin was wise, cunning and judicious;[4] he made no objection to the Declaration, as prepared by Mr. Jefferson, because, probably, he saw it would suit the occasion and supposed it would be harmless for the future. But even Franklin was too much of a physical philosopher, too utilitarian and material in his doctrines, to be relied on in matters of morals or government. We may fairly conclude, that liberty is alienable, that there is a natural right to alien it, first, because the laws and institutions of all countries have recognized and regulated its alienation; and secondly, because we cannot conceive of a civilized society, in which there were no wives, no wards, no apprentices, no sailors and no soldiers; and none of these could there be in a country that practically carried out the doctrine, that liberty is inalienable.

The soldier who meets death at the cannon's mouth, does so because he has aliened both life and liberty. Nay, more, he has aliened the pursuit of happiness, else he might desert on the eve of battle, and pursue happiness in some more promising quarter than the cannon's mouth. If the pursuit of happiness be inalienable, men should not be punished for crime, for all crimes are notoriously committed in the pursuit of happiness. If these abstractions have some hidden and cabalistic meaning, which none but the initiated can comprehend, then the Declaration should have been accompanied with a translation, and a commentary to fit it for common use, — as it stands, it deserves the tumid yet appropriate epithets which Major Lee[5] somewhere applies to the writings of Mr. Jefferson, it is, "exuberantly false, and arborescently fallacious."

---

[3]"Enthusiastic" here means excessively committed to foolish ideas; and "speculative" means willing to base philosophical conclusions on questionable chains of reasoning. Fitzhugh means both words in a negative sense. — EDS.

[4]Benjamin Franklin (1706–90) was a member of the committee for which Jefferson wrote the draft Declaration (see p. 174). Franklin was a longtime opponent of slavery. — EDS.

[5]This is probably Richard Henry Lee, a major in the American army during the Revolutionary War; Lee introduced the resolution for independence in the Continental Congress, prompting the composition of the Declaration of Independence, which he signed. — EDS.

READING CRITICALLY

1. Explain the difference between seeing human society as a clock and as a tree, according to Fitzhugh's opening discussion.

2. To whom is Fitzhugh referring when he says, "Nature has made them slaves" (p. 241)? What does he mean by "slaves"?

3. What are the rights of the weak, according to Fitzhugh?

4. What reasons does Fitzhugh give for denying that "life and liberty" are "inalienable" rights?

5. According to Fitzhugh, how did such false ideas as that "all men are created equal" find their way into the Declaration? What influenced Jefferson to put them there? What influenced Benjamin Franklin to leave them there?

WRITING ANALYTICALLY

1. Fitzhugh opposes revolutionary change in society. He seems to think that people are not able to plan changes in their society but rather must wait and let social change evolve naturally. What do you think of this viewpoint, leaving aside the fact that Fitzhugh uses it to discredit abolitionism? Do you agree or disagree? Write an essay in which you respond to Fitzhugh's ideas. You may discuss these ideas only in general terms, not applying them to any specific example such as slavery; or you may illustrate your argument with references to contemporary events.

2. Fitzhugh opposes radical individualism, or a society in which each person can do pretty much as he or she pleases; rather, he seems to prefer a vision of society in which people have responsibilities to one another based on their abilities. These relationships also define people's social positions. Of course, this is a convenient argument for someone who wants to justify the superior position of slave owners over their slaves — Fitzhugh can claim that this arrangement benefits the slaves, so long as the slave owners live up to their responsibilities. What do you think of this view of society in general? Do you prefer a vision of society in which everyone is basically independent, or one in which everyone is basically interdependent? Write an essay in which you respond to Fitzhugh's ideas. You may discuss these ideas only in general terms, not applying them to any specific example such as slavery; or you may illustrate your argument with references to contemporary events.

3. Like Fitzhugh, Albert Bledsoe (p. 250) faces the difficult rhetorical task of discrediting a widely respected document, the Declaration of Independence, and a revered national leader, Thomas Jefferson. Compare and contrast Bledsoe's strategies for discrediting the Declaration and Jefferson with Fitzhugh's, arguing for which man is the better persuader.

DAVID CHRISTY

From *Cotton Is King* (1855, 1860)

David Christy (1802–67), although the author of one of the most famous defenses of slavery, was not a native of a slave state. He was a journalist in Cincinnati, Ohio, a city torn by controversy over slavery because it was just across the Ohio River from the slave states and was a depot for trade from the South and for escaping slaves. Christy was active in the colonization movement and favored the gradual emancipation and deportation of all African Americans, including those born free. In 1855, he published *Cotton Is King*, intended to counter abolitionist "extremism" with an argument for the economic inevitability and invincibility of slavery.

The book's central argument is threefold: one, that the health of the world economic market depends on the export of cotton from the South, especially to Great Britain; two, that the ability to produce cotton for export is dependent on slavery; and therefore, three, that the institution of slavery cannot be abolished without bringing on worldwide economic collapse. The economic power of "King Cotton" keeps slavery in existence, says Christy, in spite of any moral arguments the abolitionists might mount against it. Christy's argument quickly became a staple of many defenders of slavery and convinced many people, North and South, that a belligerent South would not be left to stand alone, especially by Great Britain. For example, South Carolina Senator James Henry Hammond defied northern resistance to the spread of slavery by asserting, "No, you dare not make war on cotton. No power on earth dares to make war upon it. Cotton *is* king" (emphasis in original).

Christy sold his copyright in his book to E. N. Elliott for inclusion in Elliott's 1860 anthology *Cotton Is King and Pro-Slavery Arguments*. Although Christy's original text had included a few references to slavery as an evil, Elliott edited these out of the version he published. We have included here the chapter from Elliott's edition in which Christy deals with the issue of whether the Declaration of Independence contradicts slavery.

THE OPINION THAT THE AFRICAN RACE would become a growing burden had its origin before the revolution, and led the colonists to oppose the introduction of slaves; but failing in this, through the opposition of England, as soon as they threw off the foreign yoke many of the States at once crushed the system — among the first acts of sovereignty by Virginia, being the prohibition of the slave trade.[1] In the determination to suppress this

David Christy, *Cotton Is King,* in *Cotton Is King and Pro-Slavery Arguments,* ed. E. N. Elliott (1860; reprint, New York: Negro Universities Press, 1969), 41–47.

In the notes, DC = David Christy, EDS. = Patricia Bizzell and Bruce Herzberg.

[1]What was banned was the *foreign* slave trade, the importation of slaves from Africa. Slaves could still be bought and sold within and among the states. — EDS.

traffic all the States united — but in emancipation their policy differed. It was found easier to manage the slaves than the free blacks — at least it was claimed to be so — and, for this reason, the slave States, not long after the others had completed their work of manumission, proceeded to enact laws prohibiting emancipations, except on condition that the persons liberated should be removed.[2] The newly organized free States, too, taking alarm at this, and dreading the influx of the free colored people, adopted measures to prevent the ingress of this proscribed and helpless race.

These movements, so distressing to the reflecting colored man, be it remembered, were not the effect of the action of colonizationists, but took place, mostly, long before the organization of the American Colonization Society; and, at its first annual meeting, the importance and humanity of colonization was strongly urged, on the very ground that the slave States, as soon as they should find that the persons liberated could be sent to Africa, would relax their laws against emancipation.

The slow progress made by the great body of the free blacks in the North, or the absence, rather, of any evidences of improvement in industry, intelligence, and morality, gave rise to the notion, that before they could be elevated to an equality with the whites, slavery must be wholly abolished throughout the Union. The constant ingress of liberated slaves from the South, to commingle with the free colored people of the North, it was claimed, tended to perpetuate the low moral standard originally existing among the blacks; and universal emancipation was believed to be indispensable to the elevation of the race. Those who adopted this view, seem to have overlooked the fact, that the Africans, of savage origin, could not be elevated at once to an equality with the American people, by the mere force of legal enactments. More than this was needed, for their elevation, as all are now, reluctantly, compelled to acknowledge. Emancipation, unaccompanied by the means of intellectual and moral culture, is of but little value. The savage, liberated from bondage, is a savage still.

The slave States adopted opinions, as to the negro character, opposite to those of the free States, and would not risk the experiment of emancipation. They said, if the free States feel themselves burdened by the few Africans they have freed, and whom they find it impracticable to educate and elevate, how much greater would be the evil the slave States must bring upon themselves by letting loose a population nearly twelve times as numerous. Such an act, they argued, would be suicidal — would crush out all progress in civilization; or, in the effort to elevate the negro with the white man, allowing him equal freedom of action, would make the more energetic Anglo-Saxon the slave of the indolent African. Such a task, onerous in the highest degree, they could not, and would not undertake; such an experiment, on their social system, they dared not hazard; and in this determination they were encouraged to persevere, not only by the results of emancipation, then wrought out at the North, but by the settled convictions

---

[2]That is, forcibly resettled outside the United States; Christy refers here to colonization schemes. — EDS.

which had long prevailed at the South, in relation to the impropriety of freeing the negroes. This opinion was one of long standing, and had been avowed by some of the ablest statesmen of the Revolution. Among these Mr. Jefferson stood prominent. He was inclined to consider the African inferior "in the endowments both of body and mind" to the European; and, while expressing his hostility to slavery earnestly, vehemently, he avowed the opinion that it was impossible for the two races to live equally free in the same government — that "nature, habit, opinion, had drawn indelible lines of distinction between them" — that, accordingly, emancipation and "deportation" (colonization) should go hand in hand — and that these processes should be gradual enough to make proper provisions for the blacks in a new country, and fill their places in this with free white laborers.[3]

Another point needs examination. Notwithstanding the well-known opinions of Mr. Jefferson, it has been urged that the Declaration of Independence was designed, by those who issued it, to apply to the negro as well as to the white man; and that they purposed to extend to the negro, at the end of the struggle, then begun, all the privileges which they hoped to secure for themselves. Nothing can be further from the truth, and nothing more certain than that the rights of the negro never entered into the questions then considered. That document was written by Mr. Jefferson himself, and, with the views which he entertained, he could not have thought, for a moment, of conferring upon the negro the rights of American citizenship. Hear him further upon this subject and then judge:

"It will probably be asked, why not retain and incorporate the blacks into the State, and thus save the expense of supplying by importation of white settlers, the vacancies they will leave? Deep-rooted prejudices entertained by the whites; ten thousand recollections, by the blacks, of the injuries they have sustained; new provocations; the real distinctions which nature has made; and many other circumstances, will divide us into parties, and produce convulsions, which will probably never end, but in the extermination of the one or the other race. To these objections, which are political, may be added others, which are physical and moral."

Now it is evident, from this language, that Mr. Jefferson was not only opposed to allowing the negroes the rights of citizenship, but that he was opposed to emancipation also, except on the condition that the freedmen should be removed from the country. He could, therefore, have meant nothing more by the phrase, "all men are created equal," which he employed in the Declaration of Independence, than the announcement of a general principle, which, in its application to the colonists, was intended most emphatically to assert their equality, before God and the world, with the imperious Englishmen who claimed the divine right of lording it over them. This was undoubtedly the view held by Mr. Jefferson, and the extent

---

[3]Christy refers to ideas expressed in Jefferson's *Notes on Virginia;* he quotes briefly from the *Notes* in this paragraph and extensively later. The passages he cites are included in our excerpt from the *Notes* (p. 180). — EDS.

to which he expected the language of the Declaration to be applied.[4] Nor could the signers of that instrument, or the people whom they represented, ever have intended to apply its principles to any barbarous or semi-barbarous people, in the sense of admitting them to an equality with themselves in the management of a free government. Had this been their design, they must have enfranchised both Indians and Africans, as both were within the territory over which they exercised jurisdiction.

But testimony of a conclusive character is at hand, to show that quite a different object was to be accomplished, than negro equality, in the movements of the colonists which preceded the outbreak of the American Revolution. They passed resolutions upon the subject of the slave trade, it is true, but it was to oppose it, because it increased the colored population, a result they deprecated in the strongest language. The checking of this evil, great as the people considered it, was not the principal object they had in view, in resolving to crush out the slave trade. It was one of far greater moment, affecting the prosperity of the mother country, and designed to force her to deal justly with the colonies.

This point can only be understood by an examination of the history of that period, so as to comprehend the relations existing between Great Britain and her several colonies. Let us, then, proceed to the performance of this task.

The whole commerce of Great Britain, in 1704, amounted, in value, to thirty-two and a half millions of dollars. In less than three quarters of a century thereafter, or three years preceding the outbreak of the American Revolution, it had increased to eighty millions annually. More than thirty millions of this amount, or over one-third of the whole, consisted of exports to her West Indian and North American colonies and to Africa. The yearly trade with Africa, alone, at this period — 1772 — was over four and a third millions of dollars: a significant fact, when it is known that this African traffic was in slaves.

But this statement fails to give a true idea of the value of North America and the West Indies to the mother country. Of the commodities which she imported from them — tobacco, rice, sugar, rum — ten millions of dollars worth, annually, were re-exported to her other dependencies, and five

---

[4]That Mr. Jefferson was considered as having no settled plans or views in relation to the disposal of the blacks, and that he was disinclined to risk the disturbance of the harmony of the country for the sake of the negro, appears evident from the opinions entertained of him and his schemes by John Quincy Adams. After speaking of the zeal of Mr. Jefferson, and the strong manner in which, at times, he had spoken against slavery, Mr. Adams says: "But Jefferson had not the spirit of martyrdom. He would have introduced a flaming denunciation of slavery into the Declaration of Independence, but the discretion of his colleagues struck it out. He did insert a most eloquent and impassioned argument against it in his *Notes on Virginia;* but, on that very account, the book was published almost against his will. He projected a plan of general emancipation, in his revision of the Virginia laws, but finally presented a plan leaving slavery precisely where it was; and, in his Memoir, he leaves a posthumous warning to the planters that they must, at no distant day, emancipate their slaves, or that worse will follow; but he withheld the publication of his prophecy till he should himself be in the grave." — *Life of J. Q. Adams,* page 177, 178. — DC

millions to foreign countries — thus making her indebted to these colonies, directly and indirectly, for more than one-half of all her commerce.

If England was greatly dependent upon these colonies for her increasing prosperity, they were also dependent upon her, and upon each other, for the mutual promotion of their comfort and wealth. This is easily understood. The colonies were prohibited from manufacturing for themselves. This rendered it necessary that they should be supplied with linen and woolen fabrics, hardware and cutlery, from the looms and shops of Great Britain; and, in addition to these necessaries, they were dependent upon her ships to furnish them with slaves from Africa. The North American colonies were dependent upon the West Indies for coffee, sugar, rum; and the West Indies upon North America, in turn, for their main supplies of provisions and lumber. The North Americans, if compelled by necessity, could do without the manufactures of England, and forego the use of the groceries and rum of the West Indies; but Great Britain could not easily bear the loss of half her commerce, nor could the West India planters meet a sudden emergency that would cut off their usual supplies of provisions.

Such were the relations existing between Great Britain and the colonies, and between the colonies themselves, when the Bostonians cast the tea overboard.[5] This act of resistance to law, was followed by the passage, through Parliament, of the Boston Port Bill, closing Boston Harbor to all commerce whatsoever. The North American colonies, conscious of their power over the commerce of Great Britain, at once obeyed the call of the citizens of Boston, and united in the adoption of peaceful measures, to force the repeal of the obnoxious act. Meetings of the people were held throughout the country, generally, and resolutions passed, recommending the non-importation and non-consumption of all British manufactures and West India products; and resolving, also, that they would not export any provisions, lumber, or other products, whatever, to Great Britain or any of her colonies. These resolutions were accompanied by another, in many of the counties of Virginia, in some of the State conventions, and, finally, in those of the Continental Congress, in which the slave trade, and the purchase of additional slaves, were specially referred to as measures to be at once discontinued. These resolutions, in substance, declare, as the sentiment of the people: That the African trade is injurious to the colonies; that it obstructs the population of them by freemen; that it prevents the immigration of manufacturers and other useful emigrants from Europe from settling among them; that it is dangerous to virtue and the welfare of the population; that it occasions an annual increase of the balance of trade against them; that they most earnestly wished to see an entire stop put to such a wicked, cruel, and unlawful traffic; that they would not

---

[5]The so-called Boston Tea Party took place on December 16, 1773. A group of colonists, thinly disguised as Mohawks, dumped a cargo of tea into Boston Harbor to protest import duties assessed by England. Their action brought severe retaliation from the British and greatly escalated the tensions leading to the Revolutionary War. — EDS.

purchase any slaves hereafter to be imported, nor hire their vessels, nor sell their commodities or manufactures to those who are concerned in their importation.

From these facts it appears evident, that the primary object of all the resolutions was to cripple the commerce of England. Those in relation to the slave trade, especially, were expected, at once, when taken in connection with the determination to withhold all supplies of provisions from the West India planters — to stop the slave trade, and deprive the British merchants of all further profits from that traffic. But it would do more than this, as it would compel the West India planters, in a great degree, to stop the cultivation of sugar and cotton, for export, and force them to commence the growing of provisions for food — thus producing ruinous consequences to British manufactures and commerce. But, in the opposition thus made to the slave trade, there is no act warranting the conclusion that the negroes were to be admitted to a position of equality with the whites. The sentiments expressed, with a single exception,[6] are the reverse, and their increase viewed as an evil. South Carolina and Georgia did not follow the example of Virginia and North Carolina in resolving against the slave trade, but acquiesced in the non-intercourse policy, until the grievances complained of should be remedied. Another reason existed for opposing the slave trade; this was the importance of preventing the increase of a population that might be employed against the liberties of the colonies. That negroes were thus employed, during the Revolution, is a matter of history; and that the British hoped to use that population for their own advantage, is clearly indicated by the language of the Earl of Dartmouth, who declared, as a sufficient reason for turning a deaf ear to the remonstrances of the colonists against the further importation of slaves, that "Negroes cannot become Republicans — they will be a power in our hands to restrain the unruly colonists."[7]

And, now, will any one say, that the fathers of the Revolution ever intended to declare the negro the equal of the white man, in the sense that he was entitled to an equality of political privileges under the constitution of the United States!

READING CRITICALLY

1. How does Christy explain the meaning of the phrase "all men are created equal"?

2. What reasons does Christy give for white Americans' opposition to the slave trade from Africa?

3. What evidence does Christy present to show that Jefferson agrees with his

---

[6]Providence, Rhode Island. — DC

[7]William Leggy (1731–1801), second Earl of Dartmouth, was Great Britain's secretary of state for the colonies, which included the American and the Caribbean colonies, at the beginning of the Revolutionary War. — EDS.

views about African Americans? Why do you think he is so eager to have Jefferson on his side?

WRITING ANALYTICALLY

1. Christy emphasizes that slavery is a means to care for African Americans until they can be returned to Africa — that is, that slavery is both benevolent and temporary. He seems to be aiming this line of argument at white readers who are undecided about slavery. Write a paper in which you explain why he might want to use this line of argument with this audience, and evaluate whether it is convincing. Option: You can also consider how this line of argument might strike another of Christy's audiences, namely whites who are already strong supporters of slavery.

2. Christy deals with the apparent contradiction between the Declaration of Independence and slavery by arguing that the signers of the Declaration, particularly Jefferson himself, never intended to include African Americans in the Declaration's promises. Thus Christy avoids the difficult rhetorical task of attacking a revered document and respected national leaders. But he sets up another difficult task for himself, that of convincing readers of the intentions of people who cannot be consulted to verify his interpretation. Write a paper in which you explain how Christy attempts to convince readers that Jefferson and the Declaration are on his side, and evaluate whether his arguments and interpretations are convincing. In your paper, be sure to refer to the excerpts from Jefferson's *Autobiography* and *Notes on Virginia* (pp. 174 and 180).

3. Consider the Revolutionary-era material in the "Proclamations and Public Statements" section (beginning on p. 260) as evidence of the feelings of people about African Americans and slavery around the time of the signing of the Declaration. Make an argument that this evidence does or does not support Christy's contention that the signers never intended the Declaration to apply to everyone.

ALBERT TAYLOR BLEDSOE

From *Liberty and Slavery* (1857)

Albert Taylor Bledsoe began his career as a lawyer on the Illinois frontier, where he worked with Abraham Lincoln. A devoted southerner, however, he spent most of his professional life as a professor of mathematics at the Universities of Virginia and Mississippi, with time out for two stints as a Protestant minister. Throughout his career Bledsoe published widely on both secular and religious subjects. He was well connected in the circle of southern

Albert Taylor Bledsoe, *Liberty and Slavery*, in *Cotton Is King and Pro-Slavery Arguments*, ed. E. N. Elliott (1860; reprint, New York: Negro Universities Press, 1969), 319–31.

In the notes, AB = Albert Taylor Bledsoe, EDS. = Patricia Bizzell and Bruce Herzberg.

intellectuals who took on the task of defending slavery. Bledsoe was also a friend of Confederacy President Jefferson Davis, held a position in the Confederate government, and, after the Civil War, wrote a well-known defense of the Confederacy's right to secede. In his own day and now, he has been regarded as one of the sharpest theorists writing in defense of slavery in nineteenth-century America, and his work is beginning to get broader scholarly attention. His widely influential *Essay on Liberty and Slavery*, first published in 1857, was chosen for reissue by E. N. Elliott in his 1860 anthology *Cotton Is King and Pro-Slavery Arguments.* In this excerpt, Bledsoe attacks those who use the Declaration of Independence to condemn slavery.

XI. THE SEVENTEENTH FALLACY OF THE ABOLITIONIST; OR THE ARGUMENT FROM THE DECLARATION OF INDEPENDENCE

THIS ARGUMENT IS REGARDED BY THE ABOLITIONISTS as one of their great strongholds; and no doubt it is so in effect, for who can bear a superior? Lucifer himself, who fell from heaven because he could not acknowledge a superior, seduced our first parents by the suggestion that in throwing off the yoke of subjection, they should become "as gods."[1] We need not wonder, then, if it should be found, that an appeal to the absolute equality of all men is the most ready way to effect the ruin of States. We can surely conceive of none better adapted to subvert all order among us of the South, involving the two races in a servile war, and the one or the other in utter extinction. Hence we shall examine this argument from the equality of all men, or rather this appeal to all men's abhorrence of inferiority. This appeal is usually based on the Declaration of Independence: "We hold these truths to be self-evident: that all men are created equal; that they are endowed by their Creator with certain inalienable rights; that among these are life, liberty, and the pursuit of happiness." We do not mean to play upon these words; we intend to take them exactly as they are understood by our opponents. As they are not found in a metaphysical document or discussion, so it would be unfair to suppose — as is sometimes done — that they inculcate the wild dream of Helvétius,[2] that all men are created with equal natural capacities of mind. They occur in a declaration of independence; and as the subject is the doctrine of human rights, so we suppose they mean to declare that all men are created equal with respect to natural rights.

---

[1]According to biblical stories, Lucifer was an angel who rebelled against God and was thrown out of heaven. He then became known as Satan. In the book of Genesis he is identified with the serpent who tempted, or "seduced," Adam and Eve, "our first parents" (that is, parents of the whole human race) into disobeying God by eating the forbidden fruit that would supposedly make them equal to God. — EDS.

[2]Helvétius (1715–71) was a French philanthropist and philosopher, strongly influenced by John Locke (see note on p. 240). — EDS.

Nor do we assert that there is no truth in this celebrated proposition or maxim; for we believe that, if rightly understood, it contains most important and precious truth. It is not on this account, however, the less dangerous as a maxim of political philosophy. Nay, falsehood is only then the more dangerous, when it is so blended with truth that its existence is not suspected by its victims. Hence the unspeakable importance of dissecting this pretended maxim, and separating the precious truth it contains from the pernicious falsehood by which its followers are deceived. Its truth is certainly very far from being self-evident, or rather its truth is self-evident to some, while its falsehood is equally self-evident to others, according to the side from which it is viewed. We shall endeavor to throw some light both upon its truth and its falsehood, and, if possible, draw the line which divides them from each other.

This maxim does not mean, then, that all men have, by nature, an equal right to political power or to posts of honor. No doubt the words are often understood in this sense by those who, without reflection, merely echo the Declaration of Independence; but, in this sense, they are utterly untenable. If all men had, by nature, an equal right to any of the offices of government, how could such rights be adjusted? How could such a conflict be reconciled? It is clear that all men could not be President of the United States; and if all men had an equal natural right to that office, no one man could be elevated to it without a wrong to all the rest. In such case, all men should have, at least, an equal chance to occupy the presidential chair. Such equal chance could not result from the right of all men to offer themselves as candidates for the office; for, at the bar of public opinion, vast multitudes would not have the least shadow of a chance. The only way to effect such an object would be by resorting to the lot.[3] We might thus determine who, among so many equally just claimants, should actually possess the power of the supreme magistrate. This, it must be confessed, would be to recognize in deed, as well as in word, the equal rights of all men. But what more absurd than such an equality of rights? It is not without example in history; but it is to be hoped that such example will never be copied. The democracy of Athens, it is well known, was, at one time, so far carried away by the idea of equal rights, that her generals and orators and poets were elected by the lot. This was an equality, not in theory merely, but in practice. Though the lives and fortunes of mankind were thus intrusted to the most ignorant and depraved, or to the most wise and virtuous, as the lot might determine, yet this policy was based on an equality of rights. It is scarcely necessary to add that this idea of equality prevailed, not in the better days of the Athenian democracy, but only during its imbecility and corruption.

If all men, then, have not a natural right to fill an office of government, who has this right? Who has the natural right, for example, to occupy the office of President of the United States? Certainly some men have no such right. The man, for example, who has no capacity to govern himself, but

[3]A lottery or other system of chance for selecting the winner randomly. — EDS.

needs a guardian, has no right to superintend the affairs of a great nation. Though a citizen, he has no more right to exercise such power or authority than if he were a Hottentot, or an African, or an ape. Hence, in bidding such a one to stand aside and keep aloof from such high office, no right is infringed and no injury done. Nay, right is secured, and injury prevented.

Who has such a right, then? — such natural right, or right according to the law of nature or reason? The man, we answer, who, all things considered, is the best qualified to discharge the duties of the office. The man who, by his superior wisdom, and virtue, and statesmanship, would use the power of such office more effectually for the good of the whole people than would any other man. If there be one such man, and only one, he of *natural right* should be our President. And all the laws framed to regulate the election of President are, or should be, only so many means designed to secure the services of that man, if possible, and thereby secure the rights of all against the possession of power by the unworthy or the less worthy. This object, it is true, is not always attained, these means are not always successful; but this is only one of the manifold imperfections which necessarily attach to all human institutions; one of the melancholy instances in which natural and legal right run in different channels. All that can be hoped, indeed, either in the construction or in the administration of human laws, is an approximation, more or less close, to the great principles of natural justice.

What is thus so clearly true in regard to the office of President, is equally true in regard to all the other offices of government. It is contrary to reason, to natural right, to justice, that either fools, or knaves, or demagogues should occupy seats in Congress; yet all of these classes are sometimes seen there, and by the law of the land are entitled to their seats. Here, again, that which is right and fit in itself is different from that which exists under the law.

The same remarks, it is evident, are applicable to governors, to judges, to sheriffs, to constables, and to justices of the peace. In every instance, he who is best qualified to discharge the duties of an office, and who would do so with greatest advantage to all concerned, has the natural right thereto. And no man who would fill any office, or exercise any power so as to injure the community, has any right to such office or power.

There is precisely the same limitation to the exercise of the elective franchise. Those only should be permitted to exercise this power who are qualified to do so with advantage to the community; and all laws which regulate or limit the possession of this power should have in view, not the equal rights of all men, but solely and exclusively the public good. It is on this principle that foreigners are not allowed to vote as soon as they land upon our shores, and that native Americans can do so only after they have reached a certain age. And if the public good required that any class of men, such as free blacks or slaves, for example, should be excluded from the privilege altogether, then no doubt can remain the law excluding them would be just. It might not be equal, but would be *just*. Indeed, in the high and holy sense of the word, it would be equal; for, if it excluded some from a privilege or power which it conferred upon others, this is because they were not included within the condition on which alone it should be extended to any. Such is not an equality of rights and power, it is true; but it is an equality of justice, like that which reigns in the divine government itself. In the light of that justice, it is clear that no man, and no class of men, can have a natural right to exercise a power which, if intrusted to them, would be wielded for harm, and not for good.

This great truth, when stripped of the manifold sophistications of a false logic, is so clear and unquestionable, that it has not failed to secure the approbation of abolitionists themselves. Thus, after all his wild extravagancies about inherent, inalienable, and equal rights, Dr. Channing[4] has, in one of his calmer moods, recognized this great fundamental truth. "The slave," says he, "cannot rightfully, and should not, be owned by the individual. But, like every citizen, *he is subject to the community,* AND THE COMMUNITY HAS A RIGHT AND IS BOUND TO CONTINUE ALL SUCH RESTRAINTS AS ITS OWN SAFETY AND THE WELL-BEING OF THE SLAVE DEMANDS." Now this is all we ask in regard to the question of equal rights. All we ask is, that each and every individual may be in such wise and so far restrained as the public good demands and no further. All we ask is . . . that the right of the individual, whether real or imaginary, may be held in subjection to the undoubted right of the community to protect itself and to secure its own highest good. This solemn right, so inseparably linked to a sacred duty, is paramount to the rights and powers of the individual. Nay, . . . the individual can have no right that conflicts with this; because it is his *duty* to cooperate in the establishment of the general good. Surely he can have no right which is adverse to duty. Indeed, if for the general good, he would not cheerfully lay down both liberty and life, then both may be rightfully taken from him. We have, it is true, inherent and *inalienable rights,* but among these is neither liberty nor life. For these, upon our country's altar, may be sacrificed; but conscience, truth, honor may not be touched by man.

Has the community, then, after all, the right to compel "a man," a "rational and immortal being," to work? Let Dr. Channing answer: "If he (the slave) cannot be induced to work by rational and natural motives, *he should be obliged to labor, on the same principle on which the vagrant in other communities is confined and compelled to earn his bread.*" Now, if a man be "confined, and compelled" to work in his confinement, what becomes of his "inalienable right to liberty"? We think there must be a slight mistake somewhere. Perhaps it is in the Declaration of Independence itself. Nay, is it not evident, indeed, that if all men have an "inalienable right to liberty," then is this sacred right trampled in the dust by every government on earth? Is it not as really disregarded by the enlightened Commonwealth of Massachusetts,

---

[4]William Ellery Channing (1780—1842), a New England minister who was one of the founders of Unitarianism. Bledsoe quotes from his book *Slavery* (1835), one of several antislavery works by Channing. — EDS.

which "confines and compels" vagrants to earn their bread, as it is by the Legislature of Virginia, which has taken the wise precaution to prevent the rise of a swarm of vagrants more destructive than the locusts of Egypt?[5] The plain truth is, that although this notion of the "inalienable right" of all to liberty may sound very well in a declaration of independence, and may be most admirably adapted to stir up the passions of men and produce fatal commotions in a commonwealth, yet no wise nation ever has been or ever will be guided by it in the construction of her laws. It may be a brand of discord in the hands of the abolitionist and the demagogue. It will never be an element of light, or power, or wisdom, in the bosom of the statesman. . . .

It were much nearer the truth to say that all men have an equal right, not to act as "one wills," but to have their wills restrained by law. No greater want is known to man, indeed, than the restraints of law and government. Hence, all men have an equal right to these, but not to the same restraints, to the same laws and governments. All have an equal right to that government which is the best for them. But the same government is not the best for all. A despotism is best for some; a limited monarchy is best for others; while, for a third people, a representative republic is the best form of government.

This proposition is too plain for controversy. It has received the sanction of all the great teachers of political wisdom, from an Aristotle down to a Montesquieu, and from a Montesquieu down to a Burke.[6] It has become, indeed, one of the commonplaces of political ethics; and, however strange the conjunction, it is often found in the very works which are loudest in proclaiming the universal equality of human rights. Thus, for example, says Dr. Wayland:[7] "The best form of government for any people *is the best that its present moral condition renders practicable. A people may be so entirely surrendered to the influence of passion, and so feebly influenced by moral restraints, that a government which relied upon moral restraint could not exist for a day.* In this case, a subordinate and inferior principle remains — *the principle of fear, and the only resort is to a government of force* or a military despotism. And such do we see to be the fact." What, then, becomes of the equal and in-

---

[5]The "swarm of vagrants" is what Virginia's slaves would become if freed, according to Bledsoe. He compares the slaves to the biblical swarm of locusts that ate up Egypt's crops so that "not a green thing remained" (Exodus 10:12–15). Ironically, this locust swarm was one of the plagues sent upon Egypt by God to force Pharaoh to free his Hebrew slaves. — EDS.

[6]Aristotle (384–322 B.C.E.) was an ancient Greek philosopher who wrote on almost every subject, including politics. Montesquieu (1689–1755) was a French nobleman and philosopher who deplored despotism but favored hierarchical social orders based on hereditary privilege. Edmund Burke (1729–97), an English political thinker and younger contemporary of Montesquieu's, was strongly influenced by the Frenchman. Because all three philosophers accepted the value of social hierarchies, Bledsoe sees them as sources of political "wisdom" to defend slavery, an extreme form of hereditary social hierarchy. — EDS.

[7]Francis Wayland (1796–1865, a Baptist minister and longtime president of Brown University. Bledsoe quotes Wayland's *The Elements of Moral Science* (1853), from a section in which Wayland discusses people's general duties as members of civil society. Elsewhere in the *Elements,* Wayland condemns slavery. — EDS.

alienable right of all men to freedom? Has it vanished with the occasion which gave it birth?

But this is not all. "Anarchy," continues Wayland, "always ends in this form of government.[8] After this has been established, and habits of subordination have been formed, while the moral restraints are too feeble for self-government, an hereditary government, which addresses itself to the imagination, and strengthens itself by the influence of domestic connections, may be as good a form as a people can sustain. As they advance in intellectual and moral cultivation, it may advantageously become more and more elective, and, in a suitable moral condition, it may be wholly so. For beings who are willing to govern themselves by moral principles, there can be no doubt that a government relying upon moral principle is the true form of government. There is no reason why a man should be oppressed by taxation and subjected to fear who is willing to govern himself by the law of reciprocity. It is surely better for an intelligent and moral being to do right from his own will, than *to pay another to force him to do right.* And yet, as it is better that he should do right than wrong, even though he be forced to do it, it is well that he should pay others to force him, if there be no other way of insuring his good conduct. God has rendered the blessing of freedom inseparable from moral restraint to the individual; and hence it is vain for a people to expect to be free unless they are first willing to be virtuous." Again, "There is no self-sustaining power in any form of social organization. The only self-sustaining power is in individual virtue.

"And the form of a government will always adjust itself to the moral condition of a people. A virtuous people will, by their own moral power, frown away oppression, and, under any form of constitution, become essentially free. A people surrendered up to their own licentious passions must be held in subjection by force; for every one will find that force alone can protect him from his neighbors; and he will submit to be oppressed, if he can only be protected. Thus, in the feudal ages, the small independent landholders frequently made themselves slaves of one powerful chief to shield themselves from the incessant oppression of twenty."

Now all this is excellent sense. One might almost imagine that the author had been reading Aristotle, or Montesquieu, or Burke. It is certain he was not thinking of equal rights. It is equally certain that his eyes were turned away from the South; for he could see how even "independent landholders" might rightfully make slaves of themselves. After such concessions, one would think that all this clamor about inherent and *inalienable* rights ought to cease.

In a certain sense, or to a certain extent, all men have equal rights. All men have an equal right to the air and light of heaven; to the same air and the same light. In like manner, all men have an equal right to food and raiment, though not to the same food and raiment. That is, all men have an equal right to food and raiment, provided they will earn them. And if they will not earn them, choosing to remain idle, improvident, or nuisances to

[8]A military despotism. — AB

society, then they should be placed under a government of force, and compelled to earn them.

Again, all men have an equal right to serve God according to the dictates of their own consciences. The poorest slave on earth possesses this right — this inherent and inalienable right; and he possesses it as completely as the proudest monarch on his throne. He may choose his own religion, and worship his own God according to his own conscience, provided always he seek not in such service to interfere with the rights of others. But neither the slave nor the freeman has any right to murder, or instigate others to murder, the master, even though he should be ever so firmly persuaded that such is a part of his religious duty. He has, however, the most absolute and perfect right to worship the Creator of all men in all ways not inconsistent with the moral law. And wo be to the man by whom such right is denied or set at naught! Such a one we have never known; but whosoever he may be, or wheresoever he may be found, let all the abolitionists, we say, hunt him down. He is not fit to be a man, much less a Christian master.

But, it will be said, the slave has also a right to religious instruction, as well as to food and raiment. So plain a proposition no one doubts. But is this right regarded at the South? No more, we fear, than in many other portions of the so-called Christian world. Our children, too, and our poor, destitute neighbors, often suffer, we fear, the same wrong at our remiss hands and from our cold hearts. Though we have done much and would fain do more, yet, the truth must be confessed, this sacred and imperious claim has not been fully met by us.

It may be otherwise at the North. There, children and poor neighbors, too, may all be trained and taught to the full extent of the moral law. This godlike work may be fully done by our Christian brethren of the North. They certainly have a large surplus of benevolence to bestow on us. But if this glorious work has not been fully done by them, then let him who is without sin cast the first stone. This simple thought, perhaps, might call in doubt their right to rail at us, at least with such malignant bitterness and gall. This simple thought, perhaps, might save us many a pitiless pelting of philanthropy.

But here lies the difference — here lies our peculiar sin and shame. This great, primordial right is, with us, denied by law. The slave shall not be taught to read. Oh! that he might be taught! What floods of sympathy, what thunderings and lightnings of philanthropy, would then be spared the world! But why, we ask, should the slave be taught to read? That he might read the Bible, and feed on the food of eternal life, is the reply; and the reply is good.

Ah! if the slave would only read his Bible, and drink its very spirit in, we should rejoice at the change; for he would then be a better and a happier man. He would then know his duty, and the high ground on which his duty rests. He would then see, in the words of Dr. Wayland, *"That the duty of slaves is explicitly made known in the Bible.* They are bound to obedience, fidelity, submission, and respect to their masters — not only to the good and kind, but also the unkind and froward; not, however, on the ground of duty to man, but *on the ground of duty to God.*" But, with all, we have some little glimpse of our dangers, as well as some little sense of our duties.

The tempter is not asleep. His eye is still, as ever of old, fixed on the forbidden tree; and thither he will point his hapless victims.[9] Like certain senators, and demagogues, and doctors of divinity, he will preach from the Declaration of Independence rather than from the Bible. He will teach, not that submission, but that *resistance,* is a duty. To every evil passion his inflammatory and murder-instigating appeals will be made. Stung by these appeals and maddened, the poor African, it is to be feared, would have no better notions of equality and freedom, and no better views of duty to God or man, than his teachers themselves have. Such, then, being the state of things, ask us not to prepare the slave for his own utter undoing. Ask us not — O most kind and benevolent Christian teacher! — ask us not to lay the train beneath our feet, that *you* may no longer hold the blazing torch in vain!

READING CRITICALLY

1. According to Bledsoe, how should political offices be distributed? How does he justify denying some people the right to vote?

2. Bledsoe says that "the right of the individual" should "be held in subjection to the undoubted right of the community to protect itself and to secure its own highest good" (p. 254). How does Bledsoe apply this general principle to the particular case of slavery?

3. Bledsoe says, "All have an equal right to that government which is the best for them" (p. 255). How does Bledsoe apply this second general principle to the particular case of slavery?

4. Under what circumstances is government by force, or a "military despotism" (p. 256), the best form of government, according to Bledsoe?

5. What reasons does Bledsoe give for not teaching slaves to read?

WRITING ANALYTICALLY

1. Choose the general principle stated in either reading question 2 or 3, and write an essay on whether you think this principle is correct. Try to forget for a moment that Bledsoe uses this principle to defend slavery, and evaluate it on its own merits. Illustrate your evaluation with one specific example, as Bledsoe does with the example of slavery.

2. Bledsoe is faced with a difficult rhetorical situation here, in that his oppo-

---

[9]Bledsoe here returns to his opening image of Lucifer, the "tempter," who still seeks to lead sinners, his "victims," to disobey God (as Adam and Eve did by eating the fruit of the "forbidden tree" at his suggestion). Bledsoe compares abolitionist activists with this evil "tempter." — EDS.

nents, the abolitionists, appear to have a very strong case that a revered national document, the Declaration of Independence, agrees with them. What strategies do you see Bledsoe employing in his opening paragraphs to deal with this dilemma? Do you think they are effective? Overall, what do you think of Bledsoe's handling of opposing arguments (for example, the way he deals with Channing and Wayland)? Do you think he sounds fair? Write a paper in which you explain and evaluate his strategies.

3. Like Bledsoe, George Fitzhugh (p. 239) attacks the Declaration of Independence and Thomas Jefferson. Compare and contrast his strategies with Bledsoe's, arguing for which writer you think is the better persuader.

PROCLAMATIONS AND PUBLIC STATEMENTS

JONATHAN JACKSON

Manumission Paper (June 19, 1776)

Jonathan Jackson, a well-to-do resident of Newburyport, Massachusetts, was the first collector of the port of Boston and later treasurer of the state for many years. He died in 1810. Jackson's slave Pomp took his former master's surname after he was emancipated, as freed slaves often did. He then enlisted in the army and fought for the American side throughout the Revolutionary War. Pomp later settled in Andover, Massachusetts.

A manumission paper legally freed a slave from the powers of the master (described on p. 168). Manumission did not, however, guarantee that the former slave would be regarded as a citizen, nor did it automatically free other members of the slave's family. For example, if a slave woman was manumitted, her children were not necessarily also freed. Any children born to her after manumission, however, were free. Manumission papers were precious because they usually protected their possessors from the many penalties inflicted on runaway slaves. Manumission papers were also often contested in the courts by white people who wanted to return a freed person to slavery.

KNOW ALL MEN BY THESE PRESENTS, that I, Jonathan Jackson, of Newburyport, in the county of Essex, gentleman, in consideration of the impropriety I feel, and have long felt, in beholding any person in constant bondage, — more especially at a time when my country is so warmly contending for the liberty every man ought to enjoy, — and having sometime since promised my negro man, Pomp, that I would give him his freedom, and in further consideration of five shillings, paid me by said Pomp, I do hereby liberate, manumit, and set him free; and I do hereby remise and release unto said Pomp, all demands of whatever nature I have against said Pomp.

In witness whereof, I have hereunto set my hand and seal, this 19th June, 1776.

JONATHAN JACKSON [Seal.]

Witness — MARY COBURN,
WILLIAM NOYES.

Jonathan Jackson, Manumission Paper, in *Colored Patriots of the American Revolution*, ed. William C. Nell (1855; reprint, New York: Arno Press, 1968), 42–43.

READING CRITICALLY

What reasons does Jackson give for manumitting Pomp?

WRITING ANALYTICALLY

1. Write a paper in which you explain the extent to which this document could be said to reflect the idea that "all men are created equal," that is, the extent to which it reflects what we now like to think of as Revolutionary-era idealism. You may frame your analysis in the form of a response to the question of whether or not this document could be used as evidence that people in Revolutionary times saw the political ideals of the day as applying to African Americans as well as European Americans.

2. This document could be said to present an argument against slavery, in the form of the reasons Jackson gives for manumitting Pomp (see your response to the reading question). Jefferson also included an argument against slavery in the draft of the Declaration (p. 174), in a section taken out of the final version. Write a paper in which you compare and contrast the arguments against slavery in the manumission paper and the draft of the Declaration. Option: You may discuss the extent to which each is true to what we now regard as the spirit of the phrase "all men are created equal."

PRINCE HALL, ET AL.

Petition on behalf of Massachusetts Slaves (January 13, 1777)

Prince Hall (c. 1735–1807) grew up in the household of a Boston leather maker, where he served as a slave until he was manumitted in 1770. Then he supported himself as a leather maker and small businessman. He fought for Massachusetts in the Revolutionary War, was an active member of a predominantly white Congregational church, and was also an important leader of the free African American community. He is best known for founding an African American Masonic lodge, officially chartered in 1787. Hall's lodge became the nucleus of an important African American fraternal organization, which today has more than half a million members worldwide. It was at the lodge Hall founded that later African American abolitionists Maria Stewart (p. 200) and David Walker (p. 193) often spoke.

Prince Hall et al., Petition on behalf of Massachusetts Slaves, in *Colored Patriots of the American Revolution,* ed. William C. Nell (1855; reprint, New York: Arno Press, 1968), 47–48.

Hall was also a prolific writer on racial issues, addressing both white and African American communities. He organized many petitions to the Massachusetts government, such as the one requesting public school education for the children of taxpaying free African Americans. In the petition reprinted here, Hall speaks on behalf of African American slaves, calling for the immediate emancipation of adult slaves and the gradual emancipation of slave children (who would be freed at age twenty-one). The petition was addressed to the Council and House of Representatives of Massachusetts.

TO THE HONORABLE COUNCIL & HOUSE OF REPRESENTATIVES FOR THE STATE OF MASSACHUSETTS-BAY IN GENERAL COURT ASSEMBLED JANUARY 13TH 1777

The Petition of a Great Number of Negroes,
Who Are Detained in a State of Slavery in
the Very Bowels of a Free and Christian Country,
Humbly Showing

THAT YOUR PETITIONERS APPREHEND that they have, in common with all other men, a natural and inalienable right to that freedom, which the great Parent of the universe hath bestowed equally on all mankind, and which they have never forfeited by any compact or agreement whatever. But they were unjustly dragged by the cruel hand of power from their dearest friends, and some of them even torn from the embraces of their tender parents, — from a populous, pleasant and plentiful country, and in violation of the laws of nature and of nations, and in defiance of all the tender feelings of humanity, brought hither to be sold like beasts of burthen, and, like them, condemned to slavery for life — among a people possessing the mild religion of Jesus — a people not insensible of the sweets of national freedom, nor without a spirit to resent the unjust endeavors of others to reduce them to a state of bondage and subjection.

Your Honors need not to be informed that a life of slavery like that of your petitioners, deprived of every social privilege, of every thing requisite to render life even tolerable, is far worse than nonexistence.

In imitation of the laudable example of the good people of these States, your petitioners have long and patiently waited the event of petition after petition, by them presented to the legislative body of this State, and cannot but with grief reflect that their success has been but too similar.

They cannot but express their astonishment that it has never been considered, that every principle from which America has acted, in the course of her unhappy difficulties with Great Britain, bears stronger than a thousand arguments in favor of your humble petitioners. They therefore humbly beseech Your Honors to give their petition its due weight and consideration, and cause an act of the legislature to be passed, whereby they may be restored to the enjoyment of that freedom, which is the natural right of all men, and their children (who were born in this land of liberty) may not be held as slaves after they arrive at the age of twenty-one years. So may the inhabitants of this State (no longer chargeable with the inconsistency of acting themselves the part which they condemn and oppose in others) be prospered in their glorious struggles for liberty, and have those blessings secured to them by Heaven, of which benevolent minds cannot wish to deprive their fellow-men.

And your Petitioners, as in Duty Bound shall ever pray.

Lancaster Hill	Negroes Petition to the Honble
Peter Bess	Genl Assembly — Mass.
Brister Slenten	March 18
Prince Hall	Judge Sargeant
Jack Purpont *his mark*	M. Balton
	M. Appleton
	Coll. Brooks
Nero Suneto *his mark*	M. Stony
	W. Lowell
Newport Symner *his mark*	Matter Atlege
	W. Davis
Job Lock	

READING CRITICALLY

Underline places in the petition where the language sounds like that of the Declaration of Independence (p. 174). What effect do you think Hall is trying to have on his Massachusetts government audience with these echoes? Do you imagine that this strategy would have been effective?

WRITING ANALYTICALLY

What contradiction is Hall pointing out when he says, "Every principle from which America has acted in the course of her unhappy difficulties with Great-Britain, pleads stronger than a thousand arguments in favor of your Petitioners"? Write an explanation of his argument here and your assessment of its effectiveness.

Rhode Island Resolution for the
Formation of a Colored Regiment (February 1778)

This document is reproduced by William Nell in his 1855 *Colored Patriots of the American Revolution* to help bolster his claim that African Americans fought as regular troops for the Revolutionary cause as well as participated in battle along with men whose servants or slaves they were. The resolution did indeed pass. The fact that African Americans fought for the Revolution was emphasized in the rhetoric of many African American abolitionists, such as Charles Langston (p. 232). African Americans also fought for the British side, some accompanying British-sympathizing colonial employers or owners into battle. Other slaves ran away to join the British troops in response to promises that the British, if victorious, would free them and end slavery in the colonies.

STATE OF RHODE ISLAND AND PROVIDENCE PLANTATIONS, IN GENERAL ASSEMBLY, FEBRUARY SESSION, 1778

WHEREAS, FOR THE PRESERVATION OF the rights and liberties of the United States, it is necessary that the whole power of Government should be exerted in recruiting the Continental battalions; and, whereas, His Excellency, General Washington, hath inclosed to this State a proposal made to him by Brigadier General Varnum, to enlist into the two battalions raising by this State such slaves as should be willing to enter into the service; and, whereas, history affords us frequent precedents of the wisest, the freest and bravest nations having liberated their slaves and enlisted them as soldiers to fight in defence of their country; and also, whereas, the enemy have, with great force, taken possession of the capital and of a great part of this State, and this State is obliged to raise a very considerable number of troops for its own immediate defence, whereby it is in a manner rendered impossible for this State to furnish recruits for the said two battalions without adopting the said measures so recommended, —

It is Voted and Resolved, That every able-bodied negro, mulatto, or Indian man-slave in this State may enlist into either of the said two battalions, to serve during the continuance of the present war with Great Britain; — That every slave so enlisting shall be entitled to and receive all the bounties, wages and encouragements allowed by the Continental Congress to any soldiers enlisting into this service.

It is further Voted and Resolved, That every slave so enlisting shall, upon his passing muster by Col. Christopher Greene, be immediately discharged from the service of his master or mistress, and be absolutely free,

Rhode Island Resolution for the Formation of a Colored Regiment, in *Colored Patriots of the American Revolution*, ed. William C. Nell (1855; reprint, New York: Arno Press, 1968), 50–51.

as though he had never been incumbered with any kind of servitude or slavery. And in case such slave shall, by sickness or otherwise, be rendered unable to maintain himself, he shall not be chargeable to his master or mistress, but shall be supported at the expense of the State.

And, whereas, slaves have been by the laws deemed the property of their owners, and therefore compensation ought to be made to the owners for the loss of their service, —

It is further Voted and Resolved, That there be allowed and paid by this State to the owners, for every such slave so enlisting, a sum according to his worth, at a price not exceeding one hundred and twenty pounds for the most valuable slave, and in proportion for a slave of less value, — provided the owner of said slave shall deliver up to the officer who shall enlist him the clothes of the said slave, or otherwise he shall not be entitled to said sum.

And for settling and ascertaining the value of such slaves, — It is further Voted and Resolved, That a committee of five shall be appointed, to wit, — one from each county, any three of whom to be a quorum, — to examine the slaves who shall be so enlisted, after they shall have passed muster, and to set a price upon each slave, according to his value as aforesaid.

It is further Voted and Resolved, That upon any able-bodied negro, mulatto or Indian slave enlisting as aforesaid, the officer who shall so enlist him, after he has passed muster as aforesaid, shall deliver a certificate thereof to the master or mistress of said negro, mulatto, or Indian slave, which shall discharge him from the service of said master or mistress.

It is further Voted and Resolved, That the committee who shall estimate the value of the slave aforesaid, shall give a certificate of the sum at which he may be valued to the owner of said slave, and the general treasurer of this State is hereby empowered and directed to give unto the owner of said slave his promissory note for the sum of money at which he shall be valued as aforesaid, payable on demand, with interest, — which shall be paid with the money from Congress.

A true copy, examined,

HENRY WARD, *Sec'y.*

READING CRITICALLY

1. What reasons are given for forming a "colored" regiment?

2. What will be given to slaves who enlist, and what will be given to their former owners?

WRITING ANALYTICALLY

To what extent do you think this document can be considered as evidence that people in Revolutionary times saw African Americans as included in the promise of freedom for which the colonial rebels fought? Write a paper in which you respond to this question, also considering the extent to which this document can be interpreted as opposing slavery (drawing on your responses to the reading questions). Alternative: Compare and contrast this document with either the Prince Hall petition (p. 261) or the Jackson manumission paper (p. 260) as documents evincing Revolutionary-era opposition to slavery and promotion of African American rights.

DR. BLOOMFIELD

Fourth of July Manumission Speech (1783)

The *Eagle*, a Newark, New Jersey, newspaper, published this account of a manumission speech given by Dr. Bloomfield as part of a ceremony in which he freed his slaves. Bloomfield chose the Fourth of July, presumably, because he felt that his actions harmonized with the spirit of the Declaration of Independence, whose signing is celebrated on that day and which he quotes. July Fourth was often associated with opposition to slavery, as a day for freeing slaves or giving abolitionist speeches. African American abolitionist William Nell included this account in his 1855 *Colored Patriots of the American Revolution* to support his contention that at the time of the Revolution, slavery was generally regarded as inimical to the ideas expressed in the Declaration, particularly in regions such as New Jersey and northward, where slavery was relatively less important to the local economy than it was in the deep South.

THE NEWARK *EAGLE* PUBLISHED, some time ago, the following account of a consistent celebration of the Fourth of July, in Woodbridge: —

"We have recently had an interview with a person who was present at the first abolition meeting ever held in the United States. It took place in the township of Woodbridge, County of Middlesex, in this State, on the Fourth of July, 1783, being the first anniversary of our Independence, after the close of the Revolutionary War. Great preparations had been made — an ox was roasted, and an immense number had assembled on the memorable occasion. A platform was erected, just above the heads of the spectators, and, at a given signal, Dr. Bloomfield, father of the late Governor Bloomfield, of this State, mounted the platform, followed by his fourteen slaves, male and female, seven taking their stations on his right hand, and seven on his left. Being thus arranged, he advanced somewhat in front of his slaves, and addressed the multitude on the subject of slavery and its evils, and, in conclusion, pointing to those on his right and left, 'As a nation,' said he, 'we are free and independent, — all men are created

Dr. Bloomfield, Fourth of July Manumission Speech, in *Colored Patriots of the American Revolution*, ed. William C. Nell (1855; reprint, New York: Arno Press, 1968), 164–65.

equal, and why should these, my fellow citizens, my equals, be held in bondage? From this day, they are emancipated; and I here declare them free, and absolved from all servitude to me or my posterity.' Then, calling up before him one somewhat advanced in years — 'Hector,' said the Doctor, 'whenever you become too old or infirm to support yourself, you are entitled to your maintenance from me or my property. How long do you suppose it will be before you will require that maintenance?' Hector held up his left hand, and, with his right, drew a line across the middle joints of his fingers, saying — 'Never, never, massa, so long as any of these fingers remain below these joints.' Then, turning to the audience, the Doctor remarked, — 'There, fellow-citizens, you see that liberty is as dear to the man of color as to you or me.' The air now rung with shouts of applause, and thus the scene ended.

"Dr. Bloomfield immediately procured for Hector, either by purchase or setting off from his own farm, three acres of land, and built him a small house, where he resided and cultivated his little farm until the day of his death; and it was a common remark with the neighbors, that Hector's hay, when he took it to Amboy to sell, would always command a better price than their own."

READING CRITICALLY

1. Why does Bloomfield say he is freeing his slaves?

2. Why do you think both Bloomfield and the news article conclude with evidence that the freed slaves will be self-supporting?

WRITING ANALYTICALLY

1. Clearly, by freeing his slaves on the Fourth of July, Bloomfield intends to express his opposition to slavery and his sense that slavery conflicts with American ideals. Historian William Nell, who preserved this account, also apparently thinks that the story illustrates Revolutionary-era abolitionist attitudes. But even if Bloomfield opposes slavery, do you think he truly sees African Americans as his equals? What indications of his views do you find both in Bloomfield's words and in the ceremony itself? Write a personal response paper in which you explain your answer to this question.

2. The Bloomfield speech, the Jackson manumission paper (p. 260), and the Hall petition (p. 261) all illustrate Revolutionary-era attitudes against slavery. Using these three pieces of evidence, write a paper in which you explain what you think these Revolutionary-era attitudes were. You do not have to claim that they were widely held; you may simply argue that those who did oppose slavery tended to have certain views (illustrated by the three documents). Option: You may distinguish between the attitudes expressed by European Americans Bloomfield and Jackson and those expressed by African American Hall.

Petition Supporting Slavery

(November 10, 1785)

A number of northern states banned slavery in the years immediately following the Revolution. Antislavery sentiment was strong enough that even some southern states considered making this move. Among these, Virginia came the closest to abolishing slavery, perhaps because the state economy was not then as dependent on it as were the economies of Georgia and South Carolina, for example, and perhaps because many Revolutionary leaders from Virginia, such as Thomas Jefferson, seemed convinced that slavery was indeed a violation of the political principles on which the new nation had just been founded. In the end, however, views such as those expressed in this proslavery petition, presented to the Virginia legislature with 261 signatures, prevailed; and slavery would not be ended in Virginia until after the Civil War.

TO THE HONOURABLE THE GENERAL ASSEMBLY OF VIRGINIA THE REMONSTRANCE AND PETITION OF THE FREE INHABITANTS OF HALIFAX COUNTY

GENTLEMEN,

When the British Parliament usurped a Right to dispose of our Property without our Consent, we dissolved the Union with our Parent Country, and established a Constitution and Form of Government of our own, that our Property might be secure in Future. In Order to effect this, we risked our Lives and Fortunes, and waded through Seas of Blood. Divine Providence smiled on our Enterprise, and crowned it with Success. And our Rights of Liberty and Property are now as well secured to us, as they can be by any human Constitution and Form of Government.

But notwithstanding this, we understand, a very subtle and daring Attempt is on Foot to deprive us of a very important Part of our Property. An Attempt carried on by the Enemies of our Country, Tools of the British Administration, and supported by a Number of deluded Men among us, to wrest from us our Slaves by an Act of the Legislature for a general Emancipation of them. They have the Address, indeed to cover their Design, with the Veil of Piety and Liberality of Sentiment. But it is unsupported by the Word of God, and will be ruinous to Individuals and to the Public.

It is unsupported by the Word of God. Under the Old Testament Dispensation, Slavery was permitted by the Deity himself. Thus it is

Petition Supporting Slavery, in "Early Proslavery Petitions in Virginia," Frederika Teute Schmidt and Barbara Ripel Wilhelm, William and Mary Quarterly, 3rd. ser., vol. 30 (Jan. 1973): 133–46.

recorded, Levit. Chap. 25. Ver. 44, 45, 46. "Both thy Bond-men, and Bond-maids, which thou shalt have, shall be of the Heathen that are round about you; of them shall ye buy Bond-men and Bond-maids. Moreover, of the Children of the Strangers, that do sojourn among you of them shall ye buy, and of their Families that are with you, which they beget in your Land, and they shall be your Possession, and ye shall take them, as an Inheritance for your Children after you, to inherit them for a Possession; they shall be your Bond-men forever." This Permission to possess and inherit Bond Servants, we have Reason to conclude, was continued through all the Revolutions of the Jewish Government, down to the Advent of our Lord. And we do not find, that either he or his Apostles abridged it. On the Contrary, the Freedom which the Followers of Jesus were taught to expect, was a Freedom from the Bondage of Sin and Satan, and from the Dominion of their Lusts and Passions; but as to their outward Condition, whatever that was, whether Bond or Free, when they embraced Christianity, it was to remain the same afterwards. This Saint Paul hath expressly told us 1 Cor. Chap. 7. Ver. 20th. where he is speaking directly to this very Point; "Let every Man abide in the same Calling, wherein he is called;" and at Ver. 24. "Let every Man wherein he is called therein abide with God." Thus it is evident the above Attempt is unsupported by the Divine Word.

It is also ruinous to Individuals and to the Public. For it involves in it, and is productive of Want, Poverty, Distress, and Ruin to the Free Citizen; Neglect, Famine, and Death to the helpless black Infant and superannuated Parent; the Horrors of all the Rapes, Murders, and Outrages, which a vast Multitude of unprincipled, unpropertied, vindictive, and remorseless Banditti are capable of perpetrating; inevitable Bankruptcy to the Revenue, and consequently Breach of public Faith, and Loss of Credit with foreign Nations; and lastly Ruin to this now free and flourishing Country.

We therefore your Remonstrants and Petitioners do solemnly adjure and humbly pray you, that you will discountenance and utterly reject every Motion and Proposal for emancipating our Slaves; that as the Act lately made, empowering the Owners of Slaves to liberate them, has been and is still productive, in some Measure, of sundry of the above pernicious Effects, you will immediately and totally repeal it; and that as many of the Slaves, liberated by the said Act, have been guilty of Thefts and Outrages, Insolences and Violences destructive to the Peace, Safety, and Happiness of Society, you will make effectual Provision for the due Government of them.

And your Remonstrants and Petitioners shall ever pray, etc.

READING CRITICALLY

1. According to the petitioners, who supports emancipation?
2. What results do the petitioners forecast if the emancipation law is passed?

WRITING ANALYTICALLY

According to the petitioners, what was the main purpose of both the Revolutionary War and the new American government? What does this supposed purpose have to do with slavery? Write an explanation of the argument presented in this petition along with your own assessment of its persuasiveness.

WILLIAM LLOYD GARRISON

"Declaration of Sentiments of the American Anti-Slavery Convention"
(December 6, 1833)

William Lloyd Garrison (1805–79) was born in Newburyport, Massachusetts, to an impoverished white family. He went to work at an early age as an apprentice printer. A sincere Christian motivated by the religious urgency of nineteenth-century Protestant revivalism, Garrison worked for various reform causes. While still a young man he became convinced that slavery was the greatest national evil, the sin most in need of correction, and devoted his career, very effectively, to opposing it. In 1831 in Boston, he began publishing *The Liberator,* an antislavery newspaper that became the most influential abolitionist journal in the country. He was a colleague of African American abolitionists David Walker (p. 193) and Maria Stewart (p. 200). Stewart published frequently in *The Liberator,* and Garrison was influenced strongly by Walker's thinking as expressed in his *Appeal,* although Garrison deplored Walker's call to oppose slavery with force. In spite of vocal opposition and occasional threats of violence, Garrison continued to publish *The Liberator* until 1865, when the Civil War, and slavery, ended. He then retired from public life.

Garrison helped found the American Anti-Slavery Society in 1833; the document included here is the declaration he prepared for the first meeting of that organization, in Philadelphia. Garrison's insistence on women's rights led to a split in the American Anti-Slavery Society in 1840, when members who wished to deny equal participation to women were forced to leave the group to form their own organization, The American and Foreign Anti-Slavery Society.

Frequently basing his stand on the ideals expressed in the Declaration of Independence, as he does here, Garrison called for immediate abolition, opposing gradual emancipation and colonization schemes. A committed pacifist, he also opposed violent resistance to slavery, even though this stance eventually led to a rift between him and Frederick Douglass (p. 208). Garri-

William Lloyd Garrison, "Declaration of Sentiments of the American Anti-Slavery Convention," in *Selections from the Writings and Speeches of William Lloyd Garrison* (Boston: R. F. Wallcut, 1852), 66–71.

In the notes, EDS. = Patricia Bizzell and Bruce Herzberg.

son developed a reform perspective that linked oppressions: He was an early advocate of women's rights, and he welcomed the contributions of women as active abolitionists (see Unit Three).

THE CONVENTION ASSEMBLED IN THE CITY of Philadelphia, to organize a National Anti-Slavery Society, promptly seize the opportunity to promulgate the following Declaration of Sentiments, as cherished by them in relation to the enslavement of one-sixth portion of the American people.

More than fifty-seven years have elapsed, since a band of patriots convened in this place, to devise measures for the deliverance of this country from a foreign yoke. The corner-stone upon which they founded the Temple of Freedom was broadly this — "that all men are created equal; that they are endowed by their Creator with certain inalienable rights; that among these are life, LIBERTY, and the pursuit of happiness." At the sound of their trumpet-call, three millions of people rose up as from the sleep of death, and rushed to the strife of blood; deeming it more glorious to die instantly as freemen, than desirable to live one hour as slaves. They were few in number — poor in resources; but the honest conviction that Truth, Justice and Right were on their side, made them invincible.

We have met together for the achievement of an enterprise, without which that of our fathers is incomplete; and which, for its magnitude, solemnity, and probable results upon the destiny of the world, as far transcends theirs as moral truth does physical force.

In purity of motive, in earnestness of zeal, in decision of purpose, in intrepidity of action, in steadfastness of faith, in sincerity of spirit, we would not be inferior to them.

Their principles led them to wage war against their oppressors, and to spill human blood like water, in order to be free. Ours forbid the doing of evil that good may come, and lead us to reject, and to entreat the oppressed to reject, the use of all carnal weapons for deliverance from bondage; relying solely upon those which are spiritual, and mighty through God to the pulling down of strong holds.

Their measures were physical resistance — the marshalling in arms — the hostile array — the mortal encounter. Ours shall be such only as the opposition of moral purity to moral corruption — the destruction of error by the potency of truth — the overthrow of prejudice by the power of love — and the abolition of slavery by the spirit of repentance.

Their grievances, great as they were, were trifling in comparison with the wrongs and sufferings of those for whom we plead. Our fathers were never slaves — never bought and sold like cattle — never shut out from the light of knowledge and religion — never subjected to the lash of brutal taskmasters.

But those, for whose emancipation we are striving — constituting at the present time at least one-sixth part of our countrymen — are recognized by law, and treated by their fellow-beings, as marketable commodities, as goods and chattels, as brute beasts; are plundered daily of the fruits of their toil without redress; really enjoy no constitutional nor legal protection from licentious and murderous outrages upon their persons; and are ruthlessly torn asunder — the tender babe from the arms of its frantic mother — the heart-broken wife from her weeping husband — at the caprice or pleasure of irresponsible tyrants. For the crime of having a dark complexion, they suffer the pangs of hunger, the infliction of stripes, the ignominy of brutal servitude. They are kept in heathenish darkness by laws expressly enacted to make their instruction a criminal offence.

These are the prominent circumstances in the condition of more than two millions of our people, the proof of which may be found in thousands of indisputable facts, and in the laws of the slaveholding States.

Hence we maintain — that, in view of the civil and religious privileges of this nation, the guilt of its oppression is unequalled by any other on the face of the earth; and, therefore, that it is bound to repent instantly, to undo the heavy burdens, and to let the oppressed go free.

We further maintain — that no man has a right to enslave or imbrute his brother — to hold or acknowledge him, for one moment, as a piece of merchandize — to keep back his hire by fraud — or to brutalize his mind, by denying him the means of intellectual, social and moral improvement.

The right to enjoy liberty is inalienable. To invade it is to usurp the prerogative of Jehovah. Every man has a right to his own body — to the products of his own labor — to the protection of law — and to the common advantages of society. It is piracy to buy or steal a native African, and subject him to servitude. Surely, the sin is as great to enslave an American as an African.

Therefore we believe and affirm — that there is no difference, in principle, between the African slave trade and American slavery:

That every American citizen, who detains a human being in involuntary bondage as his property, is, according to Scripture, (Ex. xxi. 16,) a man-stealer:[1]

That the slaves ought instantly to be set free, and brought under the protection of law:

That if they had lived from the time of Pharaoh down to the present period, and had been entailed through successive generations, their right to be free could never have been alienated, but their claims would have constantly risen in solemnity:

That all those laws which are now in force, admitting the right of slavery, are therefore, before God, utterly null and void; being an audacious usurpation of the Divine prerogative, a daring infringement on the law of nature, a base overthrow of the very foundations of the social compact, a complete extinction of all the relations, endearments and obligations of

---

[1]Exodus 21:16 forms part of the law code delivered by God to the Jewish people along with the Ten Commandments at Mount Sinai. It prescribes the death penalty for anyone who "steals a man." It does not condemn slavery outright, however, only someone who forces another into bondage without observing the legal limitations on this practice. — EDS.

mankind, and a presumptuous transgression of all the holy commandments; and that therefore they ought instantly to be abrogated.

We further believe and affirm — that all persons of color, who possess the qualifications which are demanded of others, ought to be admitted forthwith to the enjoyment of the same privileges, and the exercise of the same prerogatives, as others; and that the paths of preferment, of wealth, and of intelligence, should be opened as widely to them as to persons of a white complexion.

We maintain that no compensation should be given to the planters emancipating their slaves:

Because it would be a surrender of the great fundamental principle, that man cannot hold property in man:

Because slavery is a crime, and therefore is not an article to be sold:

Because the holders of slaves are not the just proprietors of what they claim; freeing the slave is not depriving them of property, but restoring it to its rightful owner; it is not wronging the master, but righting the slave — restoring him to himself:

Because immediate and general emancipation would only destroy nominal, not real property; it would not amputate a limb or break a bone of the slaves, but by infusing motives into their breasts, would make them doubly valuable to the masters as free laborers; and

Because, if compensation is to be given at all, it should be given to the outraged and guiltless slaves, and not to those who have plundered and abused them.

We regard as delusive, cruel and dangerous, any scheme of expatriation which pretends to aid, either directly or indirectly, in the emancipation of the slaves, or to be a substitute for the immediate and total abolition of slavery.[2]

We fully and unanimously recognise the sovereignty of each State, to legislate exclusively on the subject of the slavery which is tolerated within its limits; we concede that Congress, under the present national compact, has no right to interfere with any of the slave States, in relation to this momentous subject:

But we maintain that Congress has a right, and is solemnly bound, to suppress the domestic slave trade between the several States, and to abolish slavery in those portions of our territory which the Constitution has placed under its exclusive jurisdiction.

We also maintain that there are, at the present time, the highest obligations resting upon the people of the free States to remove slavery by moral and political action, as prescribed in the Constitution of the United States. They are now living under a pledge of their tremendous physical force, to fasten the galling fetters of tyranny upon the limbs of millions in the Southern States; they are liable to be called at any moment to suppress a

---

[2]Garrison refers here to schemes that would tie emancipation to colonization, that is, the forced resettlement of freed slaves outside the United States. — EDS.

general insurrection of the slaves; they authorize the slave owner to vote for three-fifths of his slaves as property, and thus enable him to perpetuate his oppression;[3] they support a standing army at the South for its protection; and they seize the slave, who has escaped into their territories, and send him back to be tortured by an enraged master or a brutal driver. This relation to slavery is criminal, and full of danger: IT MUST BE BROKEN UP.

These are our views and principles — these our designs and measures. With entire confidence in the overruling justice of God, we plant ourselves upon the Declaration of our Independence and the truths of Divine Revelation, as upon the Everlasting Rock.

We shall organize Anti-Slavery Societies, if possible, in every city, town and village in our land.

We shall send forth agents to lift up the voice of remonstrance, of warning, of entreaty, and of rebuke.

We shall circulate, unsparingly and extensively, antislavery tracts and periodicals.

We shall enlist the pulpit and the press in the cause of the suffering and the dumb.

We shall aim at a purification of the churches from all participation in the guilt of slavery.

We shall encourage the labor of freemen rather than that of slaves, by giving a preference to their productions: and

We shall spare no exertions nor means to bring the whole nation to speedy repentance.

Our trust for victory is solely in God. We may be personally defeated, but our principles never! Truth, Justice, Reason, Humanity, must and will gloriously triumph. Already a host is coming up to the help of the Lord against the mighty, and the prospect before us is full of encouragement.

Submitting this Declaration to the candid examination of the people of this country, and of the friends of liberty throughout the world, we hereby affix our signatures to it; pledging ourselves that, under the guidance and by the help of Almighty God, we will do all that in us lies, consistently with this Declaration of our principles, to overthrow the most execrable system of slavery that has ever been witnessed upon earth; to deliver our land from its deadliest curse; to wipe out the foulest stain which rests upon our national escutcheon; and to secure to the colored population of the United States, all the rights and privileges which belong to them as men, and as Americans — come what may to our persons, our interests, or our reputation — whether we live to witness the triumph of Liberty, Justice and Humanity, or perish untimely as martyrs in this great, benevolent, and holy cause.

---

[3]The Constitution provided that each slave counted as three-fifths of a white person in tallying the population of slave states. The effect was to enlarge the slave states' representation in Congress. — EDS.

READING CRITICALLY

1. What are the main points in Garrison's opening, two-part, extended comparison between "our fathers" (p. 271) — those who founded the United States — and both the abolitionists and the slaves?

2. What are the "carnal weapons" (p. 271) that Garrison rejects? What actions against slavery does he recommend?

3. Why does Garrison reject the idea of compensating former slave owners once slavery is abolished?

4. "This relation to slavery is criminal, and full of danger: IT MUST BE BROKEN UP," says Garrison (p. 274). What relation is he talking about? What does he appear to mean by "IT MUST BE BROKEN UP"?

WRITING ANALYTICALLY

1. Garrison makes many references to God throughout the "Declaration." How does he use these references? In your opinion, do they add to the persuasive power of the document? Write a paper in which you respond to these questions.

2. Drawing on your response to reading question 1, write a paper in which you evaluate Garrison's handling of Jefferson's Declaration of Independence and other Revolutionary references. Explain whether you think this material enhances the persuasiveness of the document. Option: Compare Garrison's handling of this material with that of either Charles Langston (p. 232) or Frederick Douglass (p. 208); argue for which writer uses the material more effectively.

ASSIGNMENT SEQUENCES

SEQUENCE 1
Does the Declaration of Independence contradict slavery?

- Thomas Jefferson, Draft of the Declaration of Independence
- Thomas Jefferson, From *Notes on Virginia*
- Benjamin Banneker, Letter to Thomas Jefferson
- Frederick Douglass, "What to the Slave Is the Fourth of July?"
- George Fitzhugh, From *Sociology for the South, or the Failure of Free Society*
- David Christy, From *Cotton Is King*
- Jonathan Jackson, Manumission Paper
- Prince Hall et al., Petition on behalf of Massachusetts Slaves
- Dr. Bloomfield, Fourth of July Manumission Speech
- Petition Supporting Slavery

1. One way to answer the question that forms the title of this sequence would be to try to determine what the principal author of the Declaration of Independence, Thomas Jefferson, intended for the document to mean. Of course, it is extremely difficult to determine the intentions of someone long dead; in fact, it might be difficult even if Jefferson were alive to be interviewed about the document today. To get a sense of what can and cannot be accomplished by an argument about a person's intentions, write a paper in which you argue that Jefferson probably intended the Declaration to be interpreted in a particular way concerning slavery — you will have to decide on the way. Support your argument with references to the Declaration, the explanation surrounding it in Jefferson's *Autobiography,* and the excerpts from Jefferson's *Notes on Virginia.*

2. Another way to answer the question in the title of this sequence would be to try to determine how people interpreted the Declaration at the time it was written. Of course, if it is hard to figure out what one person — the author — meant, as suggested in question 1, it may be even harder to determine the meanings assigned by most people in an era, even with the help of far more historical research than we can do here. To get a taste of what this research problem is like, though, you can consider the Declaration (draft and final version), the Jackson manumission paper, the Bloomfield manumission ceremony, and the Hall and proslavery petitions as evidence of the views of Revolutionary-era people on slavery. Given this evidence, write a paper in which you agree or disagree with the contention that the spirit of the times worked to exclude African Americans from the promises of the Declaration.

3. How do Fitzhugh and Christy explain the Declaration's implications concerning slavery? Write a paper in which you compare and contrast their approaches, arguing for which one (if either) is the better persuader.

4. Banneker and Douglass both point out a contradiction between the Declaration and slavery, and they argue that this contradiction should lead to the abolition

of slavery. Write a paper in which you compare and contrast the arguments they use to make this case, evaluating their effectiveness as persuaders.

5. Banneker, Douglass, Fitzhugh, Christy: choose one. Write a version of the "all men are created equal" paragraph of the Declaration as you think this man would have written it; attach to your paragraph a paper in which you explain why you think he would have written it as you imagine.

6. Drawing on your responses to questions 1–5, write a paper in which you argue for your own interpretation of what the Declaration means in its "all men are created equal" paragraph. You should make clear whether you think your interpretation goes along with the interpretation of Jefferson and/or the people of the times (and if so, how you know that it does) or whether your interpretation departs from them (and if so, why your interpretation is valid). Support your position with reference to at least three readings for this sequence in addition to the Declaration.

SEQUENCE 2
What power should society have over the individual?

- Thomas Jefferson, Draft of the Declaration of Independence
- Frederick Douglass, "What to the Slave Is the Fourth of July?"
- Charles Langston, Address to the Court
- George Fitzhugh, From *Sociology for the South, or the Failure of Free Society*
- Albert Taylor Bledsoe, From *Liberty and Slavery*
- Rhode Island Resolution for the Formation of a Colored Regiment
- Petition Supporting Slavery
- William Lloyd Garrison, "Declaration of Sentiments of the American Anti-Slavery Convention"

1. What powers of society over individuals are illustrated in the resolution for forming the Rhode Island African American regiment? In the proslavery petition? List. What powers of individuals to resist larger social trends or practices are illustrated in these documents? List them.

2. What relationship between the individual and society is implied by the first paragraph of the Declaration of Independence? Write an argument in which you answer this question. Option: Put your response in the form of a political pamphlet that might have been published in Revolutionary times as people debated the course the new nation would follow about slavery. If you wish, you can imagine your audience as the signers of the 1785 proslavery petition.

3. How do Douglass and Langston defend African Americans from the charge that they need to be enslaved, that they can't take care of themselves? Write a paper in which you compare and contrast their explicit and implicit arguments and evaluate their effectiveness. Alternative: After studying the arguments in Douglass and Langston, use some of them in writing your own defense of another group that seems to be overly controlled by society.

4. How do Fitzhugh and Bledsoe justify society's taking control over individuals to the point of enslaving them? Write a paper in which you compare and contrast their arguments and evaluate their effectiveness, both the points dealing with general principles and those applying the principles specifically to a defense of slavery. Alternative: Although no one today would want to use the arguments in Fitzhugh and Bledsoe to justify slavery, these arguments might be used in discussing a group supposedly in need of more control or assistance from society. Write a paper using some of these arguments in relation to this kind of contemporary issue.

5. How does William Lloyd Garrison develop the responsibility of the individual to society when the individual wishes to protest a widely accepted social practice? What is the individual allowed to do or not to do, according to Garrison? You may write a paper in which you simply argue that Garrison answers these questions in certain ways; or you may expand your argument to include your own evaluation of his recommendations. In either case, support your argument with specific references to his text.

6. How do you think Americans today should understand the relationship between individuals and society? Argue your case using at least four readings from this sequence. Option: Illustrate with a contemporary issue or conflict.

SEQUENCE 3
How can a hostile audience be persuaded?

- Thomas Jefferson, Draft of the Declaration of Independence
- Thomas Jefferson, From *Notes on Virginia*
- David Walker, From *Walker's Appeal*
- Maria Stewart, An Address Delivered at the African Masonic Hall
- Frederick Douglass, "What to the Slave Is the Fourth of July?"
- Charles Langston, Address to the Court
- George Fitzhugh, From *Sociology for the South, or the Failure of Free Society*
- David Christy, From *Cotton Is King*

1. Write a personal narrative that tells about a time when you had to persuade a hostile audience (the audience might be a group or only one or two people). How did you go about it? How effective were you?

2. Classify the changes made in the draft Declaration according to what group each change seems intended to please: colonists (or some subgroup of colonists); British people; onlookers from other countries. You may classify simply by making lists; some changes may belong on more than one list.

3. Walker, Douglass, Langston: List the rhetorical strategies these writers employ to appeal to a white audience that is resistant to supporting African American rights. You may make four lists: one for common strategies and one each for strategies that are unique to each writer. Pay special attention to how each writer deals with Jefferson, his writings, and Revolutionary references generally. Option: Write a brief paper drawing on these lists to argue for which of these writers (if any) is the best persuader of the specified audience.

4. Walker, Stewart, Langston: List the rhetorical strategies these writers employ to appeal to an African American audience that needs encouragement to support African American rights. You may make four lists: one for common strategies and one each for strategies unique to each writer. Pay special attention to how each writer deals with Jefferson, his writings, and Revolutionary references generally. Pay attention to how Stewart deals with her particular rhetorical situation as a woman speaker. Option: Write a brief paper drawing on these lists to argue for which of these writers (if any) is the best persuader of the specified audience.

5. Fitzhugh, Christy: These writers attempt to persuade a white audience that, while not ardently abolitionist, is reluctant to support slavery. What rhetorical strategies do you see them using to appeal to this audience? Make three lists: one for each writer and one for strategies they have in common. Pay special attention to how each writer deals with Jefferson, his writings, and Revolutionary references generally. Option: Write a brief paper drawing on these lists to argue for which of these writers (if either) is the better persuader of the specified audience.

6. Explain the problems a writer or speaker faces when addressing two audiences at the same time. One of these audiences is composed of "outsiders," that is, people who largely disagree with the writer or speaker, who may not know much about the issues, and who may be downright hostile. The other audience is composed of "insiders," people who largely agree with the writer or speaker, who are better informed about the issues, and who may be anxious for the writer or speaker to represent their case well. Write your answer in the form of advice to activists who will need to address such mixed audiences, illustrating what to do (or not to do) by referring to at least four of the readings in this sequence. (Evidence can be found in your responses to the previous questions in the sequence.)

RESEARCH KIT

Negotiating Difference is an unfinished book: There are many other stories to tell in the history of "negotiating difference" in the United States. This Research Kit is intended to help you expand on the readings provided in this unit. In "Ideas from the Unit Readings," we include more perspectives on the Declaration of Independence and slavery. In "Branching Out," we add perspectives on other uses of the Declaration of Independence in other battles for equal rights in the United States. You can pursue these research ideas individually or as group or class projects.

To compile materials, you can start with the short bibliography included in this unit and with standard library search techniques that your teacher or a librarian can explain. Here are some other places where you can inquire for materials (not all regions will have all of these resources):

• Local chapters of the National Association for the Advancement of Colored People, other African American political action groups, and political action groups representing other people who have suffered discrimination

- African American churches, social clubs, and other community organizations; similar institutions for other groups who have suffered discrimination (some of these organizations may have archives, records of minutes of past meetings, in-house publications on the history of the organization or biographies of leading members and so on)
- Town and state historical societies, antiquarian societies, and the like
- Museums and historic sites related to colonial times generally or to the Revolutionary War, Thomas Jefferson, slavery, or African Americans

Keep your work focused by your research question. Remember that you are not writing a history of slavery, the Revolutionary War, the Declaration of Independence, or race relations in the United States. In keeping with the overall theme of *Negotiating Difference,* the focus of your research should be on how *contact between different groups* has shaped the interpretation of a founding document, the Declaration of Independence.

IDEAS FROM THE UNIT READINGS

1. The following people attacked slavery and defended African American civil rights. Find out more about the life and work of Benjamin Banneker; Lydia Maria Child; Paul Cuffe; Frederick Douglass; James Forten; William Lloyd Garrison; Angelina and Sarah Grimké; Prince Hall; Harriet Jacobs; Charles Langston; Maria Stewart; Sojourner Truth; Harriet Tubman; David Walker.

2. Find out more about the proslavery work of John C. Calhoun or George Fitzhugh or the antislavery work of David Christy.

3. Research the history of the Fugitive Slave Law and civil disobedience directed against it.

4. Research the history of the *Dred Scott* case, noting in particular the arguments concerning the Declaration of Independence in the Supreme Court's decision.

5. Find out more about Thomas Jefferson's views on slavery and African Americans, including the most current scholarly thinking on whether he did indeed have children by an African American slave woman.

6. Find out more about African American participation in the Revolutionary War or the Civil War. Option: Compile a bibliography of visual materials depicting African American war participation — paintings, drawings, and photographs from the time period and also twentieth-century representations such as the film *Glory* (see Kaplan and Kaplan in the bibliography).

7. Explore the unit readings for arguments concerning Christianity's stance on slavery: Does it condemn or condone slavery? Research Christian churches' positions on slavery in antebellum America.

8. Find out more about how the Fourth of July holiday was celebrated in antebellum America by both white and African American communities.

9. Find other examples of the African American July Fourth sermon or address (in addition to the example by Frederick Douglass included in this unit), and

develop an analysis of this genre's typical characteristics. Note especially whether and how the genre varies when the principal audience is African American instead of white.

BRANCHING OUT

1. Find out how the Declaration of Independence has been used by activists for African American civil rights since World War II. In pursuing this question, choose one of these alternatives: You may research this topic by focusing on the career of a nationally known activist, such as Malcolm X, Martin Luther King Jr., or Jesse Jackson, or by focusing on African American civil rights activism in your region and uses of Declaration language or ideas by local leaders.

2. Find out how Declaration ideas and language have been used in the struggle for women's rights in either the nineteenth century (see Unit Three) or the twentieth century. Choose one of the alternatives from question 1, substituting an activist in women's rights.

3. Find out how Declaration ideas and language have been used in the struggle for Japanese American civil rights from 1940 to the present (see Unit Five). Choose one alternative from question 1, substituting an activist in Japanese American civil rights.

4. Explore the civil rights struggles of any other group that has suffered discrimination, such as Latinos, Native Americans, gay people, deaf people, working-class people (see Unit Four), and others (see Foner, *We, the Other People,* in the bibliography). Find out how Declaration ideas and language have been used by that group. Choose one of the alternatives from question 1, substituting an activist in the area you selected.

5. Find out about the antislavery movement in eighteenth-century America, before the Revolutionary War (see Bruns in the bibliography).

6. Find out about efforts to return freed slaves and other African Americans to Africa—the colonization plans—including the founding of the African state of Liberia. You may focus on antebellum colonization schemes; or you may explore some twentieth-century African American–sponsored "Back to Africa" movements, comparing them with nineteenth-century colonization thinking.

7. Find out how Declaration ideas and language and patriotic themes of other kinds have been used in white supremacist rhetoric either nationally or in your region and in either 1850–1900, 1900–1950, or 1950–present.

BIBLIOGRAPHY

Works Included or Excerpted

Banneker, Benjamin. Letter to Thomas Jefferson. 1791. Reprinted in *The Black Presence in the Era of the American Revolution, 1770–1800,* edited by Sidney Kaplan and Emma Nogrady Kaplan. Amherst: University of Massachusetts Press, 1989.

Bledsoe, Albert Taylor. *Liberty and Slavery.* 1857. Reprinted in Elliott, *Cotton Is King.*

Bloomfield, Dr. Fourth of July Manumission Speech. 1783. Reprinted in Nell, *Colored Patriots.*

Christy, David. *Cotton Is King.* 1855. Reprinted in Elliott, *Cotton Is King.*

Douglass, Frederick. "What to the Slave Is the Fourth of July?" In *The Frederick Douglass Papers. Series One, Speeches, Debates, and Interviews.* Vol. 2, *1847–54,* edited by John W. Blassingame et al. New Haven: Yale University Press, 1982.

Elliott, E. N., ed. *Cotton Is King and Pro-Slavery Arguments.* 1860. Reprint, New York: Negro Universities Press, 1969.

Fitzhugh, George. *Sociology for the South, or the Failure of Free Society.* 1854. Reprint, New York: Burt Franklin Research and Source Work Series 102, n.d.

Garrison, William Lloyd. "Declaration of Sentiments of the American Anti-Slavery Convention." 1833. Reprinted in *Selections from the Writings and Speeches of William Lloyd Garrison.* Boston: R. F. Wallcut, 1852.

———. "Declaration of Sentiments of the American Anti-Slavery Convention." 1833. In *Selections from the Writings and Speeches of William Lloyd Garrison.* 1852. New York: Negro Universities Press, 1968.

Hall, Prince, et al. Petition against Slavery. 1777. Reprinted in Nell, *Colored Patriots.*

Jackson, Jonathan. Manumission Paper for Pomp. 1776. Reprinted in Nell, *Colored Patriots.*

Jefferson, Thomas. *Autobiography.* 1829. Reprinted in *The Writings of Thomas Jefferson,* edited by Andrew A. Lipscomb and Albert Ellery Bergh. Vol. 1. Washington, D.C.: Thomas Jefferson Memorial Society, 1903.

———. *Notes on Virginia.* 1788. Reprinted in *The Writings of Thomas Jefferson,* edited by Andrew A. Lipscomb and Albert Ellery Bergh. Vol. 2. Washington, D.C.: Thomas Jefferson Memorial Society, 1903.

Langston, Charles. Address to the Court. 1859. Excerpted in *A Documentary History of the Negro People in the United States,* edited by Herbert Aptheker. Vol. 1, *From Colonial Times through the Civil War.* Secaucus: Citadel Press, 1951. *The Voice of Black America: Major Speeches by Negroes in the United States, 1797–1971,* edited by Philip Foner. New York: Simon and Schuster, 1972.

Nell, William C. *Colored Patriots of the American Revolution.* 1855. Reprint, New York: Arno Press, 1968.

Petition Supporting Slavery. 1785. Reprinted in "Early Proslavery Petitions in Virginia," by Fredrika Teute Schmidt and Barbara Ripel Wilhelm. *William and Mary Quarterly,* 3rd ser., vol. 30 (January 1973): 133–46.

Rhode Island Resolution for the Formation of a Colored Regiment. 1778. Reprinted in Nell, *Colored Patriots.*

Stewart, Maria. An Address Delivered at the African Masonic Hall. Reprinted in *Maria Stewart: America's First Black Woman Political Writer,* edited by Marilyn Richardson. Bloomington: Indiana University Press, 1987.

Walker, David. *Walker's Appeal in Four Articles; Together with a Preamble, to the Coloured Citizens of the World, but in Particular, and Very Expressly, to Those of the United States of America.* 1829. Reprint (3rd ed.), 1830, edited with an introduction by Charles M. Wiltse. New York: Hill and Wang, 1965.

Other Sources

Bruns, Roger, ed. *Am I Not a Man and a Brother: The Antislavery Crusade of Revolutionary America, 1688–1788.* New York: R. R. Bowker, Chelsea House, 1977.

Calhoun, John C. *Disquisition on Government.* 1853. Reprint, edited with an introduction by C. Gordon Post. New York: Liberal Arts Press, 1953.

Condit, Celeste Michelle, and John Louis Lucaites. *Crafting Equality: America's Anglo-African Word.* Chicago: University of Chicago Press, 1993.

Davis, David Brion. *The Problem of Slavery in the Age of Revolution, 1770–1823.* Ithaca: Cornell University Press, 1975.

Detweiler, Philip F. "The Changing Reputation of the Declaration of Independence: The First Fifty Years." *William and Mary Quarterly,* 3rd ser., vol. 19 (October 1962): 557–74.

Fitzhugh, George. *Cannibals All! or, Slaves without Masters.* 1857. Reprint, edited by C. Vann Woodward. Cambridge: Harvard University Press, 1960.

Foner, Philip, ed. *We, the Other People: Alternative Declarations of Independence by Labor Groups, Farmers, Women's Rights Advocates, Socialists, and Blacks, 1829–1975.* Urbana: University of Illinois Press, 1976.

Forten, James. *A Series of Letters by a Man of Color.* 1813. Excerpted in *The Voice of Black America: Major Speeches by Negroes in the United States, 1797—1971,* edited by Philip Foner. New York: Simon and Schuster, 1972.

Genovese, Eugene D. *The Slaveholders' Dilemma: Freedom and Progress in Southern Conservative Thought, 1820–1860.* Columbia: University of South Carolina Press, 1992.

Hamilton, Alexander, James Madison, and John Jay. *The Federalist: A Commentary on the Constitution of the United States.* 1788–89. Reprinted with an introduction by E. G. Bourne. New York: Tudor Publishing Company, 1937.

Jordan, Winthrop. *White over Black: American Attitudes toward the Negro, 1550–1812.* Chapel Hill: University of North Carolina Press, 1968.

Kaplan, Sidney, and Emma Nogrady Kaplan. *The Black Presence in the Era of the American Revolution, 1770—1800.* Amherst: University of Massachusetts Press, 1989.

McKitrick, Eric L., ed. *Slavery Defended: The Views of the Old South.* Englewood Cliffs: Prentice-Hall, 1963.

Miller, Floyd J. *The Search for a Black Nationality: Black Emigration and Colonization, 1787–1863.* Urbana: University of Illinois Press, 1975.

Miller, John Chester. *The Wolf by the Ears: Thomas Jefferson and Slavery.* New York: Free Press, 1977.

Nelson, Truman, ed. *Documents of Upheaval.* New York: Hill and Wang, 1966.

Porter, Dorothy, ed. *Negro Protest Pamphlets.* New York: Arno Press, 1969.

Quarles, Benjamin. *The Negro in the American Revolution.* Chapel Hill: University of North Carolina Press, 1961.

Defining "Woman's Sphere" in Nineteenth-Century American Society

NEGOTIATIONS

How do we learn the "proper" way to behave in our roles as male and female? Who writes the rules about what men are supposed to do and what women are supposed to do? Often, it is not possible to point to some actual written text that spells out these conventions of behavior, yet virtually every culture has distinct ideas about gender roles. Whatever the rules, when we violate them we invite criticism or even punishment.

American women in the nineteenth century were criticized when they attempted to take public action against a variety of social evils, especially slavery. They were attacked by ministers and other leaders for violating the proper "woman's sphere" of action. They were told that women were not supposed to engage in any political or charitable activity outside the home — at least, not "respectable" white women.

Of course, we know that the conventions of behavior for men and women (or for other groups) do not remain the same always. They tend to change over time, in response to pressure from people who want to do things that the rules don't appear to permit. Many women did not accept the limitations that nineteenth-century leaders wished to impose on them. In particular, many felt a moral obligation to act against slavery, even if it meant stepping outside woman's "proper" sphere.

Therefore, heated debates arose on such issues as: What is woman's proper sphere of action? How can women best fulfill their duties as American citizens? How should the relationship between women's rights and African American rights be understood? These debates attempted to spell out what women should be and do and to argue against other conceptions of women's "proper" behavior.

Through these debates, which we explore in Unit Three, new opportunities for action by women were negotiated. The discussions were heated because the issues affected people's personal lives so directly. For example, in defining the proper sphere for women, married men were defining what their own home life should be like; in contesting this definition, women were risking being branded as unfeminine or, worse, unchaste. Therefore, in the texts of these debates, emotional appeals were as important as reasoned arguments, and speakers had to attend carefully to the kind of image of themselves that they were creating by taking the positions that they did. We have included a variety of voices in Unit Three, both male and female, both European American and African American, who addressed this sensitive rhetorical problem as they spoke up in these debates.

OVERVIEW OF THE SELECTIONS

The readings are arranged in three groups. The first, entitled "Circumscribing Woman's Sphere," includes writers who advocated women's devotion to purely domestic activities. While these writers sometimes seem to be taking positions that treat women as inferior to men and in need of protection or even confinement, sometimes the pro-domestic arguments have a feminist undertone.

For example, Catharine Beecher seems to be treating women as inferior when she argues that women best fulfill their duties as citizens by allowing themselves to be secluded at home, subordinate to men. At the same time, however, Beecher argues that women need advanced education to prepare them for this domestic role, a position that implicitly accords women equal or nearly equal intellectual status with men. Many modern scholars view Beecher as trying to expand opportunities for women under cover of the acceptable domestic ideology.

Less ambiguously pro-domesticity are Protestant clergy such as Jonathan Stearns and Albert Folsom and the authors of an 1837 Massachusetts "Pastoral Letter." These writers use biblical authority to insist on women's subordination to men and their confinement to the domestic sphere. Folsom, Louisa Cheves McCord, and an editorial writer for the *New York Herald* also heap special scorn on women who depart from the domestic sphere to support the abolition of slavery. McCord argues that all women — and all African Americans — are by nature inferior to white men and should remain in positions of subordination to them.

In the second group of readings, "Contesting Woman's Sphere," we present voices that argue forthrightly for an enlarged realm of activity for women. Sarah Grimké explicitly rebuts the gender-based arguments of the "Pastoral Letter" and argues that women's public duties should be the same as men's, especially in working to abolish slavery. Reviewing a book by Catharine Beecher, Margaret Fuller agrees with Beecher's advocacy of teaching as a profession for women, but Fuller argues that this and other careers should not be the resort of only those women who can't be wives and mothers, as Beecher implies. Rather, Fuller rejects restricting women to a narrow domestic sphere.

Women's rights activists also argued that women needed an enlarged range of civil rights. This argument is developed by African Americans Sojourner Truth and Frederick Douglass, both of whom assert that all women, like African Americans, deserve full rights. Elizabeth Cady Stanton compares the rights of European American women and African American men, arguing that women deserve "at least" equal rights with men. Ralph Waldo Emerson and Anna Julia Cooper detect special spiritual powers in women that will benefit society if women are given the right to vote and allowed to pursue higher education. Cooper, an African American, insists that African American women must be included in any education reform program.

The third section in this unit, "Laws, Contracts, and Proclamations on Women's Rights," begins with the famous "Declaration of Sentiments and Resolutions." Issued by the participants in the first American women's rights convention in 1848, this statement argues against domestic restrictions and for full civil rights for women, including the right to vote. The texts of two New York State married women's property laws show attempts to broaden married women's sphere of economic power. In marriage agreements, two couples attempt to begin their lives together by setting aside the legal subordination of wife to husband. The course of constitutional attempts to guarantee the vote to African Americans and to women can be traced through the texts of the Fourteenth, Fifteenth, and Nineteenth Amendments to the United States Constitution and the excerpt from the Supreme Court decision in *Minor v. Happersett.* Resolutions from an 1898 woman suffrage convention show the focus on civil rights but also some disturbing traces of racism and other prejudices.

HISTORICAL BACKGROUND

Legal Status of Women in Early America

In the debates over defining "woman's sphere," those who would circumscribe it could count for support on American laws that tended to treat all women as needing restriction and protection. A young unmarried girl living at home was essentially her father's "property." A daughter had scant legal identity except as represented by her father or other male guardian. Moreover, when a woman married, her legal identity was transferred from her father to her husband. She became what was legally termed a "feme coverte," (an English corruption of the French *femme couverte,* meaning "veiled or covered woman.") Her legal identity was swallowed up in her husband's just as a little stream is swallowed when it flows into a mighty river, to use a popular metaphor taken from English law.

This legal situation meant that the husband had complete control over the family's financial resources. For example, any property that a woman brought into a marriage, including even her clothes, became her husband's. The only way a wife could keep her property separate from her husband's was to have a male trustee hold her property. Any property a woman acquired while she was married, including wages she earned, also belonged to her husband. A married woman could not make a contract or even sign her own will.

The husband also had control over the person of his wife. He had the right to determine where the family lived and what church they attended. He had the right to physically restrain his wife and to physically punish her if she disobeyed him. He had the right to sexual intercourse with her on demand; a man could not be charged with raping a woman to whom he was legally married. He had custody of all children born to the married union and the right to make all decisions concerning them. If his wife left him, taking the children, he could enlist the law to recover them. The husband's power over his wife, in short, was very similar to the power of the slave owner over slaves.

The rationale for giving the husband this power over his wife was that he would thus be enabled to protect her. If he controlled her property and person, he could prevent either one from falling into unscrupulous hands. He, in turn, was legally required to provide for his wife, to feed and clothe her. He was also expected, under pressure of public opinion, to consult her in making all the decisions that the law empowered him to make. Redress was difficult for a woman to obtain, however, if her husband did not live up to these obligations. Divorce was only occasionally granted to men, by special petition to the legislature, and even more rarely to women.

The law did recognize that not all women were married. As an adult, an unmarried woman, whether widow or spinster, was designated as a "feme sole," from the French *femme seule,* for woman alone, to distinguish her from a woman united with a man. An unmarried woman could own property, make contracts, participate in lawsuits on her own behalf, and so on. Also, she could not be legally compelled to marry against her will.

The question of expanding women's rights in the legal structures of the new nation was widely debated during and after the American Revolution (1775–83). Ultimately, however, the country turned away from liberalizing laws for women. For example, divorce laws were not modified in women's favor, as they had been in France after the French Revolution. By 1844 all state constitutions explicitly banned granting the vote to women. Political activity came to be defined more and more as a male preserve.

Changes in "Woman's Sphere," in the Early Nineteenth Century

If women's legal status did not change for the better in the early nineteenth century, other changes produced new opportunities for women, although these opportunities were also sometimes mixed blessings. For example, as the United States industrialized, the increasing demand for cheap labor drew women of the lower social classes out of the home to earn wages. Thus a mother and her daughters might work in a mill to produce cloth, which they would then buy with their wages to make their clothing, instead of continuing to spin and weave in their home as they had done in the past. In addition to the new factories, work opportunities for women were found in occupations most closely associated with women's traditional domestic tasks, such as nursing and teaching. African American slave women, of course, had always worked, both at domestic jobs and in the fields. But these opportunities were mixed blessings because working conditions for many of these occupations were very bad.

At the same time, women of the middle and upper social classes obtained increased opportunities for education. Little coeducation existed, but the number of schools for girls dramatically increased. Typically the girls' curriculum was not as rigorous as the boys' or as obviously attuned to preparation for public careers: The girls studied reading and writing, but not speaking; French, but not Latin or Greek; history and mathematics, but not philosophy or theology. In addition, many girls' schools offered training in needlework, painting, music, and dance, which were not featured at boys' schools. Parents favored this kind of education for their daughters in the hopes that it would enable them to move up the social ladder by marrying well.

Some advocates of increased education for women, however, advanced greater reforms. Catharine Beecher advocated the "professionalization" of motherhood, seeing it as women's profession on a par with the male professions of law, medicine, and the ministry. If motherhood is indeed a profession, she argued, then it deserves professional preparation as serious as that accorded to the male professions. Beecher thus found an acceptably domestic rationale for a curriculum for young women that was almost the same as that for young men, though without Greek and Latin. Beecher even included many scientific and technical subjects, such as anatomy and architecture, in her ideal curriculum, on the grounds that girls needed them to be homemakers. Beecher's work paved the way for young women to do college-level academic work previously restricted to men, for example at Oberlin, the first coeducational (and multiracial) college in America, from which the first college degree was awarded to a woman in 1841.

Beecher's educational reforms still put all a woman's learning in the service of her family (or the community as an extended family, through schoolteaching, if she was unmarried). Thus Beecher adhered to the central tenet of the domestic ideology (although she was regarded as a women's rights proponent by many of her contemporaries), and she attacked more radical thinkers such as Sarah Grimké. For these reasons, we place her in the "Circumscribing" section of Unit Three.

The "Cult of True Womanhood" and Social Reform

While changes were occurring in women's activities and opportunities in society, explicit domestic ideologies emerged that argued for women's confinement to the home. Then and now, these ideologies have been called the "Cult of True Womanhood." As described by both male and female advocates, the True Woman's main task was not to provide rational instruction, such as Catharine Beecher wanted to equip educated women to offer, but rather to lead her family to virtue by means of her emotionally affecting and spiritually elevated example. The True Woman was expected to be sexually pure, without strong passions except devotion to her family, meekly submissive to her husband, and, above all, pious. She benefited society by influencing her male relatives to behave morally.

The True Woman's understanding of spiritual matters was supposedly almost mystical, springing from some mysterious capability of her inner being rather than stimulated by preaching or religious study. Thus the True Woman had a source of spiritual power that was inaccessible to men, including male ministers. She might be presumed to be just as good a spiritual guide as a minister, although she used other means to promote piety — for example, influence rather than direct teaching. She might also be presumed to have special insight into social evils and their remedies. For this reason, the True Woman's piety actually developed into a pathway out of the strictest confines of her role.

New England writers Ralph Waldo Emerson, Margaret Fuller, and Henry David Thoreau, adherents of Transcendentalism, a philosophical movement that emphasized spiritual insights gained from nature, encouraged this notion of the superior spiritual powers of women. Later thinkers such as Anna Julia Cooper followed suit. Fighting the restriction of the True Woman to the home, these writers saw that the claim for women's spiritual superiority could be used as a wedge to drive open the locked door of the homestead and let women out to wider possibilities. They argued that women needed more opportunities, for example through charitable work, to exercise their spiritual influence on society.

Women began to take the lead in church-sponsored charitable activities, even venturing far outside the domestic sphere under the protection of such projects. These activities sharpened women's awareness of the need for social reform but also sometimes made them uncomfortable working through religious institutions, which remained officially in the control of males. Women formed their own social reform organizations addressing a variety of issues, such as providing care for orphans and prostitutes, banning the use of alcohol (the "temperance movement"), and more. The controversy over slavery, however, was the reform issue that galvanized women as political actors. We are focusing on it for that reason and also because ideas on sex and race intersected in both abolition and anti-abolition discourse. Thus the differences negotiated in this period were complicated in interesting ways.

Women and Abolitionism

Historians usually date the beginning of the American abolition movement from January 1, 1831, when European American activist William Lloyd Garrison began publishing the antislavery newspaper *The Liberator*. (See Unit Two, p. 270). *The Liberator* called for the immediate end of slavery and the elevation of the freed people to full status as American citizens. In 1833, these views were endorsed by the founders of the American

Anti-Slavery Society. Membership in the AASS grew steadily in the 1830s, as did violent opposition to the abolition movement (for more information on abolition and its foes, see the introduction to Unit Two).

The abolition movement attracted many women. The constitution of the AASS provided that all "persons" who opposed slavery could be members of the organization, and male and female members alike engaged in the society's tasks of rousing popular opinion against slavery, publishing newspaper articles, collecting signatures on antislavery petitions, raising money to support the society's activities, and more. Women performed their work for the society in sex-segregated divisions. But when the AASS held regional and national meetings, all members, male and female, attended and had a vote in the proceedings.

Sarah and Angelina Grimké unintentionally provided the test case that disrupted this state of affairs. Women's divisions of the AASS invited the Grimké sisters to address their meetings as a typical part of the society's educational activities against slavery. In keeping with the custom of the day, these speeches, even those in public halls, were supposed to be addressed to exclusively female audiences. Disapproval of women's public social reform activity remained so strong that women who addressed mixed crowds immediately became morally suspect and were branded unchaste.

Angelina Grimké, especially, was such a powerful orator, however, that when the sisters were speaking in Massachusetts in 1837, men were drawn to attend their public lectures. This created an "improper" situation, and some counseled the Grimké sisters to stop speaking in public. The Congregational clergy of Massachusetts issued a "Pastoral Letter" inveighing against all public political activity by women, and Catharine Beecher attacked the Grimkés directly. They refused to be silenced. As abolitionist Lydia Maria Child noted, the ministers now found themselves in the position of the sorcerer's apprentice: Having awakened women to their moral duty, they "have changed the household utensil to a living, energetic being; and they have no spell to turn it into a broom again."[1]

The controversy over the Grimké sisters created a bitter division within the AASS. Some members agreed with the Massachusetts clergy that women had no business acting publicly on behalf of the cause. Other members believed that the oppression of women and slaves was similar in form, cause, and remedy and that both evils should be attacked together. These disagreements could not be resolved and created a split within the movement in 1840.

The Women's Rights Movement

In 1840, Lucretia Mott was sent as a delegate from her local antislavery society to an international antislavery convention in London, but because of her sex, she was not allowed to take her place on the convention floor.

---

[1] Quoted in Aileen Kraditor, *Means and Ends in American Abolitionism* (New York: Pantheon, 1967), 47. — EDS.

Also relegated to the balcony was Elizabeth Cady Stanton, attending with her delegate husband. Stanton and Mott vowed to do something about such discrimination against women.

Historians usually date the beginning of the American women's movement from the 1848 Seneca Falls Women's Rights Convention that Stanton and Mott organized. Like the abolition movement, the women's rights movement grew quickly, as did aggressive opposition to it. Women's rights activists followed strategies similar to those of the abolitionists (indeed, many of the women had learned these strategies as abolitionists), attempting to arouse public opinion in their favor and petitioning state legislatures for reforms. Women and men spoke before a mixed audience at Seneca Falls, thus establishing the precedent for women's rights conventions; and women's rights activists continued to speak in front of mixed, and even largely male, audiences, such as legislatures.

An important focus of the women's rights movement before the Civil War (pre–1861) was the effort to reform restrictive "feme coverte" legislation and give married women more control over their property and their children. In 1848, the state of New York passed a reform bill that gave married women control over the personal property and real estate they brought into marriage. More substantial gains were provided by an 1860 New York reform bill. This act gave married women control of their own wages, joint custody of their children, and the right to enter into legal proceedings in their own names. Not all states passed such laws, however, and a married woman's legal status remained "feme coverte" in many places.

African American women were active in the antebellum (pre–Civil War) women's movement, just as European American women were active in abolition. Sojourner Truth, freed when New York State abolished slavery in 1827, became one of the most powerful speakers on behalf of women's rights, commanding the attention even of the aggressive male hecklers who often tried to break up the meetings. Her famous speech, now called "A'n't I a Woman?," was delivered in just such circumstances at a convention in Akron, Ohio, in 1851.

After the Civil War (post–1865), with slavery abolished, Congress passed the Fourteenth and Fifteenth Amendments to the United States Constitution, granting African American men the right to vote. Women's rights activists urged former abolitionists to help them fight for female suffrage, just as the women wished to fight for broader African American civil rights, but the coalition broke down. Denied the support of African American rights groups such as the AASS, European American activists such as Stanton and others focused their efforts exclusively on women's rights, particularly the right to vote, and even sometimes exploited racist rhetoric on behalf of the franchise for white women.

The Cult of True Womanhood and other domestic ideologies did not die after the Civil War. Such ideas continued to be supported by more conservative women's groups. Also, many European American and African American advocates for women's rights continued to exploit these domestic ideologies by arguing that the special powers they granted to women justified giving women a larger sphere of action. Efforts to achieve the vote for all women in national elections were finally successful in 1920, with the passage of the Nineteenth Amendment to the Constitution. But debates over the proper place of women in society have continued to this day, and evidence that many people still consider the place of women to be different from that of men may be found in the defeat of the Equal Rights Amendment to the Constitution in 1982.

Catharine Beecher

From *A Treatise on Domestic Economy* (1842)

Catharine Beecher (1800–78) was the oldest daughter of Lyman Beecher, a nationally renowned Presbyterian minister. Among her younger siblings, for whom she had considerable domestic responsibility as a teenager, was Harriet Beecher Stowe, author of the nineteenth-century best-seller and major American novel *Uncle Tom's Cabin*. Remaining unmarried after the accidental death of her fiancé, Beecher devoted herself to the cause of women's education, taking a position in 1824 as head of a high school for women in Hartford and later helping to establish colleges for women in several midwestern states. Throughout her life, she also published extensively on women's education and women's place in society.

Although Beecher insisted that a woman's place was in the home and opposed abolitionist activism by women, she was considered by many of her contemporaries (and by many twentieth-century scholars) to be a feminist because she insisted that women needed a substantial education to fulfill their domestic responsibilities. For example, she argued that women needed to study anatomy and physiology in order to be properly trained to preserve their families' health. Beecher's *A Treatise on Domestic Economy* (1842), one of the first texts in the field we would now call home economics, was a best-seller, that was reprinted in many editions. Excerpted here is a passage from the opening section of the work, in which Beecher lays out the theory behind her approach to women's education.

THERE ARE SOME REASONS, why American women should feel an interest in the support of the democratic institutions of their Country, which it is important that they should consider. The great maxim, which is the basis of all our civil and political institutions, is, that "all men are created equal," and that they are equally entitled to "life, liberty, and the pursuit of happiness."[1]

But it can readily be seen, that this is only another mode of expressing the fundamental principle which the Great Ruler of the Universe has established, as the law of His eternal government. "Thou shalt love thy

Catharine Beecher, *A Treatise on Domestic Economy*, reprinted in *Root of Bitterness: Documents of the Social History of American Women*, ed. Nancy Cott (New York: Dutton, 1972), 171–75.

In the notes, EDS. = Patricia Bizzell and Bruce Herzberg.

[1]Beecher quotes here from the Declaration of Independence (p. 174). — EDS.

neighbor as thyself"; and "Whatsoever ye would that men should do to you, do ye even so to them," are the Scripture forms, by which the Supreme Lawgiver requires that each individual of our race shall regard the happiness of others, as of the same value as his own; and which forbid any institution, in private or civil life, which secures advantages to one class, by sacrificing the interests of another.

The principles of democracy, then, are identical with the principles of Christianity.

But, in order that each individual may pursue and secure the highest degree of happiness within his reach, unimpeded by the selfish interests of others, a system of laws must be established, which sustain certain relations and dependencies in social and civil life. What these relations and their attending obligations shall be, are to be determined, not with reference to the wishes and interests of a few, but solely with reference to the general good of all; so that each individual shall have his own interest, as well as the public benefit, secured by them.

For this purpose, it is needful that certain relations be sustained, which involve the duties of subordination. There must be the magistrate and the subject, one of whom is the superior, and the other the inferior. There must be the relations of husband and wife, parent and child, teacher and pupil, employer and employed, each involving the relative duties of subordination. The superior, in certain particulars, is to direct, and the inferior is to yield obedience. Society could never go forward, harmoniously, nor could any craft or profession be successfully pursued, unless these superior and subordinate relations be instituted and sustained.

But who shall take the higher, and who the subordinate, stations in social and civil life? This matter, in the case of parents and children, is decided by the Creator. He has given children to the control of parents, as their superiors, and to them they remain subordinate, to a certain age, or so long as they are members of their household. And parents can delegate such a portion of their authority to teachers and employers, as the interests of their children require.

In most other cases, in a truly democratic state, each individual is allowed to choose for himself, who shall take the position of his superior. No woman is forced to obey any husband but the one she chooses for herself; nor is she obliged to take a husband, if she prefers to remain single. So every domestic, and every artisan or laborer, after passing from parental control, can choose the employer to whom he is to accord obedience, or, if he prefers to relinquish certain advantages, he can remain without taking a subordinate place to any employer.

Each subject, also, has equal power with every other, to decide who shall be his superior as a ruler. The weakest, the poorest, the most illiterate, has the same opportunity to determine this question, as the richest, the most learned, and the most exalted.

And the various privileges that wealth secures, are equally open to all classes. Every man may aim at riches, unimpeded by any law or institution which secures peculiar privileges to a favored class, at the expense of another. Every law, and every institution, is tested by examining whether it secures equal advantages to all; and, if the people become convinced that any regulation sacrifices the good of the majority to the interests of the smaller number, they have power to abolish it. . . .

The tendencies of democratic institutions, in reference to the rights and interests of the female sex, have been fully developed in the United States; and it is in this aspect, that the subject is one of peculiar interest to American women. In this Country, it is established, both by opinion and by practice, that woman has an equal interest in all social and civil concerns; and that no domestic, civil, or political, institution, is right, which sacrifices her interest to promote that of the other sex. But in order to secure her the more firmly in all these privileges, it is decided, that, in the domestic relation, she take a subordinate station, and that, in civil and political concerns, her interests be intrusted to the other sex, without her taking any part in voting, or in making and administering laws. . . .

It appears, then, that it is in America, alone, that women are raised to an equality with the other sex; and that, both in theory and practice, their interests are regarded as of equal value. They are made subordinate in station, only where a regard to their best interests demands it, while, as if in compensation for this, by custom and courtesy, they are always treated as superiors. Universally, in this Country, through every class of society, precedence is given to woman, in all the comforts, conveniences, and courtesies, of life.

In civil and political affairs, American women take no interest or concern, except so far as they sympathize with their family and personal friends; but in all cases, in which they do feel a concern, their opinions and feelings have a consideration, equal, or even superior, to that of the other sex.

In matters pertaining to the education of their children, in the selection and support of a clergyman, in all benevolent enterprises, and in all questions relating to morals or manners, they have a superior influence. In such concerns, it would be impossible to carry a point, contrary to their judgement and feelings; while an enterprise, sustained by them, will seldom fail of success.

If those who are bewailing themselves over the fancied wrongs and injuries of women in this Nation, could only see things as they are, they would know, that, whatever remnants of a barbarous or aristocratic age may remain in our civil institutions, in reference to the interests of women, it is only because they are ignorant of them, or do not use their influence to have them rectified; for it is very certain that there is nothing reasonable, which American women would unite in asking, that would not readily be bestowed.

The preceding remarks, then, illustrate the position, that the democratic institutions of this Country are in reality no other than the principles of Christianity carried into operation, and that they tend to place woman in her true position in society, as having equal rights with the other sex; and that, in fact, they have secured to American women a lofty and fortunate position, which, as yet, has been attained by the women of no other nation. . . .

The success of democratic institutions, as is conceded by all, depends upon the intellectual and moral character of the mass of the people. If they are intelligent and virtuous, democracy is a blessing; but if they are ignorant and wicked, it is only a curse, and as much more dreadful than any other form of civil government, as a thousand tyrants are more to be dreaded than one. It is equally conceded, that the formation of the moral and intellectual character of the young is committed mainly to the female hand. The mother forms the character of the future man; the sister bends the fibres that are hereafter to be the forest tree; the wife sways the heart, whose energies may turn for good or for evil the destinies of a nation. Let the women of a country be made virtuous and intelligent, and the men will certainly be the same. The proper education of a man decides the welfare of an individual; but educate a woman, and the interests of a whole family are secured.

If this be so, as none will deny, then to American women, more than to any others on earth, is committed the exalted privilege of extending over the world those blessed influences, which are to renovate degraded man, and "clothe all climes with beauty."

No American woman, then, has any occasion for feeling that hers is an humble or insignificant lot. The value of what an individual accomplishes, is to be estimated by the importance of the enterprise achieved, and not by the particular position of the laborer. The drops of heaven which freshen the earth, are each of equal value, whether they fall in the lowland meadow, or the princely parterre. The builders of a temple are of equal importance, whether they labor on the foundations, or toil upon the dome.

Thus, also, with those labors which are to be made effectual in the regeneration of the Earth. And it is by forming a habit of regarding the apparently insignificant efforts of each isolated laborer, in a comprehensive manner, as indispensable portions of a grand result, that the minds of all, however humble their sphere of service, can be invigorated and cheered. The woman, who is rearing a family of children; the woman, who labors in the schoolroom; the woman, who, in her retired chamber, earns, with her needle, the mite, which contributes to the intellectual and moral elevation of her Country; even the humble domestic, whose example and influence may be moulding and forming young minds, while her faithful services sustain a prosperous domestic state; — each and all may be animated by the consciousness, that they are agents in accomplishing the greatest work that ever was committed to human responsibility. It is the building of a glorious temple, whose base shall be coextensive with the bounds of the earth, whose summit shall pierce the skies, whose splendor shall beam on all lands; and those who hew the lowliest stone, as much as those who carve the highest capital, will be equally honored, when its top-stone shall be laid, with new rejoicings of the morning stars, and shoutings of the sons of God. . . .

READING CRITICALLY

1. Although Beecher affirms that equality is sanctioned not only by American political traditions, but also by the Christian religion, she argues that relations of "subordination" are necessary in domestic and social life. What are these relations and why are they necessary?

2. Beecher says that American women "take no interest or concern" in "civil and political affairs," but that there are certain areas in which they are engaged and in which they have "superior influence" (p. 296). What are these areas?

3. Beecher concludes this excerpt with a dramatic picture of the "glorious temple" that is the democratic state. What part do women play in the erection and maintenance of this state, according to Beecher, and why is it important that they be well educated for the task?

WRITING ANALYTICALLY

1. Catharine Beecher's rhetorical problem might be described as follows: She wants to greatly expand educational opportunities for women, but she knows that her audience resists the idea and wants to see women kept in subordinate domestic roles. What rhetorical strategies does Beecher employ here to persuade such resistant readers to accept her suggestions about women's education? Do you think these strategies are effective? Write a paper in which you describe and evaluate them.

2. In contrast to writing question 1, we might describe Catharine Beecher's rhetorical problem as follows: She wants to persuade women to accept a restricted domestic sphere while maintaining their self-esteem, but she knows that many women in her audience long for greater opportunities for self-development. What rhetorical strategies does Beecher employ here to persuade such readers to accept her view of women's place in American society? Do you think these strategies are effective? Write a paper in which you describe and evaluate them.

3. According to what Beecher says here about relations of subordination in marriage, evidently she would not have approved of the prenuptial agreements signed by Owen and Robinson and by Blackwell and Stone (p. 394). Draft the sort of marriage agreement you think Beecher would be willing to sign, using one of these as your model but altering it as necessary. Attach an explanation of why you wrote it the way you did.

JONATHAN F. STEARNS

From *"Female Influence, and the True Christian Mode of Its Exercise"* (1837)

Jonathan F. Stearns (1808–89) was a Presbyterian minister in Newburyport, Massachusetts. On July 30, 1837, at the height of the controversy over abolition activism by the Grimké sisters and other women in Massachusetts, he delivered a sermon entitled "Female Influence, and the True Christian Mode of Its Exercise," which was published in pamphlet form later the same year. What follows are excerpts from that sermon.

THE INFLUENCE OF WOMAN IN FORMING the character of her relatives, gentle and unobserved as it is, is one which can never be adequately appreciated, till the great day of revelation shall disclose the secret springs of human action and feeling. We all know, by experience, what a charm there is in the word HOME, and how powerful are the influences of domestic life upon the character. It is the province of woman to make home, *whatever it is.* If she makes that delightful and salutary — the abode of order and purity, though she may never herself step beyond the threshold, she may yet send forth from her humble dwelling, a power that will be felt round the globe. She may at least save some souls that are dear to her from disgrace and punishment, present some precious ornaments to her country and the church, and polish some jewels, to shine brightly in the Saviour's crown. . . .

But the influence of woman is not limited to the domestic circle. *Society* is her empire, which she governs almost at will. . . . It is her province to *adorn* social life, to throw a *charm* over the intercourse of the world, by making it lovely and attractive, pure and improving. . . .

The cause of benevolence is peculiarly indebted to the agency of woman. She is fitted by nature to cheer the afflicted, elevate the depressed, minister to the wants of the feeble and diseased, and lighten the burden of human misery, in all its varied and trying forms. God has endowed her with qualities peculiarly adapted to these offices; and the history of benevolence will testify how well she has fulfilled her trust. The friendless orphan blesses her. The homeless sailor, the wandering exile, the child of affliction, and even the penitent outcast, find in her a patroness and friend.

Reverend Jonathan F. Stearns, "Female Influence, and the True Christian Mode of Its Exercise," reprinted in *Up from the Pedestal: Selected Writings in the History of American Feminism,* ed. Aileen Kraditor (Chicago: Quadrangle Books, 1968), 47–50.

In the notes, AK = Aileen Kraditor.

But the highest merit of all is yet to be mentioned. *Religion* seems almost to have been entrusted by its author to her particular custody. . . . It is the standing sneer of the infidel, and his last resort when arguments fail, that the religion of Christ is chiefly prevalent among women, and chiefly indebted to them for its spread. . . .

Nor is it strange that such should be the fact. In thus devoting her heart to the cause of Christianity, she does but attempt to requite, in some humble measure, the peculiar benefits she herself has received from this religion. . . . When we consider what woman was in classic Greece, and what she still is, in barbarous and savage lands, darkened and degraded, without knowledge, without influence, without honor, the mere drudge of society, or still worse, the miserable slave of sensual passion; and contrast with this dark picture, the happier scenes which Christianity presents, where she stands forth in her true dignity, as the *companion* and *equal* of man, his helper on earth, and co-heir of immortal felicity, we cannot wonder that *she* should exhibit peculiar attachment to a faith which has bestowed upon her such blessings. . . .

Much dispute has arisen in modern times in regard to the comparative intellectual ability of the sexes. . . . Now the whole debate, as it seems to me, proceeds from a mistake. The truth is, there is a natural *difference,* in the mental as well as physical constitution of the two classes — a difference which implies not *inferiority* on the one part, but only *adaptation to a different sphere.* Cultivate as highly as you will the mind of a female, and you do not deprive it of its distinguishing peculiarities. On the other hand, deprive man of his advantages, keep him in ignorance and intellectual depression, and you make him a kind of *brute beast,* but you do not approximate his character to the character of a woman. . . .

Let us turn to the Bible for a moment, and see what we can gather from the teachings of inspiration.[1] . . . I am confident no virtuous and delicate female, who rightly appreciates the design of her being, and desires to sustain her own influence and that of her sex, and fulfil the high destiny for which she is formed, would desire to abate one jot or tittle from the seeming restrictions imposed upon her conduct in these and the like passages. They are designed, not to *degrade,* but to *elevate* her character, — not to cramp, but to afford a *salutary* freedom, and give a useful direction to the energies of the feminine mind. . . . Let her lay aside delicacy, and her influence over our sex is gone.

And for what object should she make such sacrifices? That she may do good more extensively? Then she sadly mistakes her vocation. But why then? That she may see her name blazoned on the rolls of fame, and hear the shouts of delighted assemblies, applauding her eloquence? That she may place her own sex on a fancied equality with men, obtain the satisfaction of calling herself *independent,* and occupy a station in life which she can never adorn? For this would she sacrifice the almost magic power, which, in her own proper sphere, she now wields over the destinies of the

---

[1]Stearns here quotes and discusses passages from the New Testament, such as those commanding women to be silent in church and to be in subjection to their husbands. — AK

world? Surely *such privileges,* obtained at *such cost,* are unworthy of a wise and virtuous woman's ambition. . . .

That there are ladies who are capable of public debate, who could make their voice heard from end to end of the church and the senate house, that there are those who might bear a favorable comparison with others as eloquent orators, and who might speak to better edification than most of those on whom the office has hitherto devolved, I am not disposed to deny. The question is not in regard to *ability,* but to *decency,* to order, to Christian *propriety.* . . .

My hearers must pardon me for speaking thus explicitly. The advocates of such principles and measures have, in times past, been confined principally to the ranks of unbelievers, whom no pious and respectable female would desire to encourage. But when popular female writers, and women professing godliness, begin to take the same ground, it is time for the pulpit as well as the press to speak plainly. I verily believe, that should the practice I have censured become *prevalent,* and the consequent change in the treatment of females, already anticipated by some of its advocates, take place in the community, the influence of ladies, now so important to the cause of philanthropy and piety, would very speedily be crushed, and religion, morality and good order, suffer a wound from which they would not soon nor easily recover. . . .

On you, ladies, depends, in a most important degree, the destiny of our country. In this day of disorder and turmoil, when the foundations of the great deep seem fast breaking up, and the flood of desolation threatening to roll over the whole face of society, it peculiarly devolves upon you to say what shall be the result. Yours it is to determine, whether the beautiful order of society . . . shall continue as it has been, to be a source of blessings to the world; or whether, despising all forms and distinctions, all boundaries and rules, society shall break up and become a chaos of disjointed and unsightly elements. Yours it is to decide, under God, whether we shall be a nation of refined and high minded Christians, or whether, rejecting the civilities of life, and throwing off the restraints of morality and piety, we shall become a fierce race of semi-barbarians, before whom neither order, nor honor, nor chastity can stand.

And be assured, ladies, if the hedges and borders of the social garden be broken up, the lovely vine, which now twines itself so gracefully upon the trellis, and bears such rich clusters, will be the first to fall and be trodden under foot. . . .

READING CRITICALLY

1. What does Stearns appear to mean by women's "influence" in the opening paragraphs of this excerpt? Where and how is it exercised?

2. According to Stearns, what motivates women to become active outside the domestic sphere, and what do they sacrifice for that activity? What does he mean by "delicacy" on page 300?

3. Stearns concludes with a multipart metaphor about a "lovely vine" with "clusters" on a "trellis," which might "fall and be trodden." What is this metaphor all about?

WRITING ANALYTICALLY

1. Stearns's rhetorical problem might be described as follows: He wants to encourage women to remain within the domestic sphere primarily by making that sphere and its activities attractive, rather than by attacking them for leaving it. Write a paper in which you describe and evaluate his strategies.

2. If you can call to mind specific examples of negative portrayals of contemporary feminists, consider them next to Stearns's portrayal of the typical woman social activist. Compare and contrast the rhetorical strategies used by Stearns and those used by contemporary speakers or writers to make the woman activist an unattractive figure. Use the details of this comparison to support an argument on the effectiveness of such strategies. Do they succeed in making women activists unattractive to you? Why or why not? Option: Also include in this comparison the image of the woman activist to be found in the excerpt from Albert Folsom's sermon (below).

ALBERT A. FOLSOM

From *"Abolition Women"* (1837)

Albert Folsom was the minister of the Universalist Church in Hingham, Massachusetts. On August 27, 1837, he preached a sermon titled "Abolition Women," evidently directed against activism by the Grimké sisters and other women in Massachusetts. Excerpts from this sermon were printed in William Lloyd Garrison's abolitionist newspaper *The Liberator* on September 22, 1837, in a front-page column entitled "Refuge of Oppression"; the column was devoted to printing views that Garrison's readers would likely find outrageous. We have reprinted two of those excerpts.

THE LEGITIMATE EFFECT OF BEING CONVERTED to the popular measures of the Abolitionists, (popular, I mean, among a certain class — not with the great mass of people, — God forbid,) is a neglect of some of the appropriate duties of woman. She seeks relaxation too often from her domestic obligation, and in fine, looks upon family affairs as of secondary importance. Her time, she is apt to think, can be better employed than to devote

Reverend Albert A. Folsom, "Abolition Women," *The Liberator,* September 22, 1837, 1.
In the notes, EDS. = Patricia Bizzell and Bruce Herzberg.

it to her own peculiar household concerns, and therefore, she becomes a sort of travelling agent for those who make it a business to lead captive "silly women." She leaves her own children to become slaves to their "appetites and passions," while she interests herself with wonderful zeal in the cause of the Southern negro. She is, then,

> Bred only, and completed to the taste
> Of fretful appetence[1] — to sing — to dance,
> To dress, and troll the tongue, and roll the eye,
> Yet empty of all good wherein consists
> Women's domestic honor and chief grace.

But the effect of this corruption extends still further, and poisons the soul, embitters the affections, and exasperates the feelings. She, who is naturally amiable and modest, by having her mind filled with the peculiar spirit which characterizes the most clamorous among the Abolitionists, is imperceptibly transformed into a bigoted, rash, and morose being. Nor is this all. Self-sufficiency, arrogance and masculine boldness follow naturally in the train.

As Eve experienced to her sorrow the consequences of disobedience,[2] so will you, who step aside from that simplicity, and those modest manners, which ornament your sex, reap the bitter fruits of folly. The respect of the wise and good you cannot have, but their pity and contempt you must unavoidably incur, while out of your sphere — the willing dupes of crafty men. . . .

If it is not permitted unto women to speak publicly upon the subject of religion,[3] it verily is *no part of their right or privilege to be heard on the subject of slavery.* If it is a shame for a woman to speak in the church upon one topic, it is no less shameful for her to raise her voice *upon any other theme.* And in all instances of the kind, females go counter to the established opinion of the world, and the express commands of Holy Writ. Hence they ought to be looked upon as "busy bodies, speaking things which they ought not."

The "simplicity of Christ" peremptorily forbids those practices, to which we have alluded, as it does all interference in the concerns of state, on the part of the female portion of the community. It is unbecoming the dignity of the feminine class of society to importune the National Court, year after year, upon the difficult subject of slavery. Still more irreverent and unbecoming is it to threaten incessant application, until Congress shall grant

---

[1]"Appetence" means "appetite, craving." — EDS.

[2]Eve's "disobedience" was eating the forbidden fruit of the Tree of Knowledge in the Garden of Eden, for which her punishment was to be expelled from the Garden and to experience pain in childbirth (Genesis 3:1–16). — EDS.

[3]Folsom alludes to the common interpretation of the apostle Paul's words in 1 Corinthians 14:34–35: " . . . the women should keep silence in the churches. For they are not permitted to speak, but should be subordinate, even as the law says. If there is anything they desire to know, let them ask their husbands at home. For it is shameful for a woman to speak in church." These verses were often used against women's public social and religious reform efforts. — EDS.

the *stale prayer of the misguided petitioners,* who are made up of all classes, characters, and *colors.*

From such improprieties, may reason and good sense deliver you all. May a suitable regard to your own characters and sex deter you from entering upon the inappropriate and unlawful duties of public life, or from seeking unenviable notoriety after the way and manner of some.

READING CRITICALLY

1. According to Folsom, why do women become abolition activists?

2. When women become activists, how are they harmed, according to Folsom?

3. Is Folsom talking about all women here, or only European American middle-class women? How can you tell?

WRITING ANALYTICALLY

1. In attempting to persuade women to avoid activism, Folsom not only denounces public activity and public speaking as evil in themselves for women; he also says or suggests that other evils will follow from women's activism. What are these other stated or implied evils? What sort of social cause-and-effect argument is Folsom implying ("if women do thus and so, thus and so will follow")? Write a paper in which you explain this larger argument.

2. Compare and contrast the specific strategies Folsom and Jonathan Stearns (p. 299) use to persuade women. Use the details you collect from the comparison to evaluate the two men's effectiveness as persuaders, considering yourself or your class as the audience.

MASSACHUSETTS CONGREGATIONALIST CLERGY

From *"Pastoral Letter"* (1837)

The General Association of Massachusetts (Orthodox), an organization of Congregationalist clergy, issued a "Pastoral Letter" in August 1837 on the topic of social activism by Christian laypeople. (Sermons on women's activism preached around the same time by the Reverends Stearns and Folsom, who were probably members of this organization, are excerpted on pp. 299 and 302.) The letter is addressed to all Congregationalist churches in Massachusetts and would probably have been read from the pulpit.

The "Pastoral Letter" seems to have been prompted by the ministers' resistance to pressure from abolitionist congregants to take the lead in denouncing slavery as a moral evil. The ministers apparently were especially disturbed by the public role that the Grimké sisters and other women were playing in antislavery agitation. Nevertheless, no names are mentioned in the letter, and neither slavery nor abolitionism is mentioned specifically.

The "Pastoral Letter" has four parts. In part 1, the ministers argue that laypeople should not force discussion of "perplexed and agitating subjects" (such as slavery, presumably), which cause "alienation and division" within congregations. In part 2, the ministers affirm that "respect and deference" should be given to "the pastoral office." Both of these sections appear to slap at laypeople who were insisting that the ministers take up the issue of slavery. part 3, on the role of women in social activism, is reprinted in full here. Part 4 exhorts all laypeople, men and women, to concentrate on "private efforts for the spiritual good of individuals," especially children, which the ministers viewed as more important than public activism.

WE INVITE YOUR ATTENTION TO THE DANGERS which at present seem to threaten the female character with wide-spread and permanent injury.

The appropriate duties and influence of woman are clearly stated in the New Testament. Those duties and that influence are unobtrusive and private, but the source of mighty power. When the mild, dependent, softening influence of woman upon the sternness of man's opinions is fully exercised, society feels the effects of it in a thousand forms. The power of woman is in her dependence, flowing from the consciousness of that weakness which God has given her for her protection, and which keeps her in those departments of life that form the character of individuals and of the

Massachusetts Congregationalist Clergy, "Pastoral Letter," *The Liberator*, August 11, 1837, 1, reprinted in *Up from the Pedestal: Selected Writings in the History of American Feminism*, ed. Aileen Kraditor (Chicago: Quadrangle Books, 1968), 51–52.
In the notes, AK = Aileen Kraditor.

nation. There are social influences which females use in promoting piety and the great objects of Christian benevolence which we cannot too highly commend. We appreciate the unostentatious prayers and efforts of woman in advancing the cause of religion at home and abroad; in Sabbath-schools; in leading religious inquirers to the pastors for instruction; and in all such associated effort as becomes the modesty of her sex; and earnestly hope that she may abound more and more in these labors of piety and love.

But when she assumes the place and tone of man as a public reformer, our care and protection of her seem unnecessary; we put ourselves in self-defence against her; she yields the power which God has given her for protection, and her character becomes unnatural. If the vine, whose strength and beauty is to lean upon the trellis-work and half conceal its clusters, thinks to assume the independence and the overshadowing nature of the elm, it will not only cease to bear fruit, but fall in shame and dishonor into the dust. We cannot, therefore, but regret the mistaken conduct of those who encourage females to bear an obtrusive and ostentatious part in measures of reform, and countenance any of that sex who so far forget themselves as to itinerate in the character of public lecturers and teachers. — We especially deplore the intimate acquaintance and promiscuous conversation of females with regard to things "which ought not to be named";[1] by which that modesty and delicacy which is the charm of domestic life, and which constitutes the true influence of woman in society, is consumed, and the way opened, as we apprehend, for degeneracy and ruin. We say these things, not to discourage proper influences against sin, but to secure such reformation as we believe is Scriptural, and will be permanent.

READING CRITICALLY

1. The ministers begin by speaking of the influence of women. What do they mean by woman's influence, and how do they believe it is exercised?

2. What do the ministers mean when they say that God has given women "weakness" for their "protection" (p. 305)? How can someone be protected by being weak?

3. Look at the sentence in the third paragraph that begins with the words "If the vine, whose strength." What is the meaning of the extended metaphor here?

4. Who are "those who encourage females to bear an obtrusive and ostentatious part in measures of reform" (p. 306)?

---

[1]The reference is to the fact that the Grimké sisters included, in the list of outrages common in the South, the facts that slaves were forbidden to marry and that slave women were powerless to protect themselves against the lusts of overseers and masters. — AK

1. Consider the rhetorical problem of a minister or other religious leader who wants to persuade people to act in a particular way. You may have seen this problem addressed in pastoral letters in your own religion, or you may be acquainted with other methods that religious leaders use — for example, sermons, lessons, and forms of holiday observance (rituals, pageants, and so on). Choose one contemporary example with which you are familiar and compare and contrast its persuasive strategies with those in the "Pastoral Letter." Which strategies do you find more effective, and why?

2. Using the "Pastoral Letter" and the excerpts from Stearns's (p. 299) and Folsom's (p. 302) sermons as sources, describe an image of the ideal woman or the evil woman (choose one), illustrated from their work.

LOUISA CHEVES McCORD

From *"Enfranchisement of Women"* (1852)

Louisa Cheves McCord (1810–79) was born in Charleston, South Carolina. Her father was a wealthy lawyer and political leader. As a girl, McCord showed considerable aptitude for mathematics and for the discussions of politics and economics that often raged among her father and older brothers, and her father allowed her to study these subjects with her brothers' tutors. In 1840 she married David McCord, a banker, lawyer, and political activist.

In her lifelong, prolific career as a writer, McCord consistently supported laissez-faire economics (a doctrine advocating minimal government intervention) and states' rights politics, both associated with the defense of slavery in antebellum America. She also supported the subordination of women to men as a "natural" order similar to the "natural" subordination of slaves to masters. McCord was championed as a "brilliant anomaly" by one southern journal in which her writing frequently appeared: brilliant in her defense of southern values, anomalous because the defense was mounted by a woman. Reprinted here are substantial portions of "Enfranchisement of Women," McCord's review of the proceedings of the third session of the Woman's Rights Convention held in Worcester, Massachusetts, in October 1851.

. . . IN EVERY ERROR THERE IS its shadow of truth. Error is but truth turned awry, or looked at through a wrong medium. As the straightest rod will, in appearance, curve when one half of it is placed under water, so God's

Louisa Cheves McCord, "Enfranchisement of Women," *Southern Quarterly Review* (April 1852): 322–41.

In the notes, EDS. = Patricia Bizzell and Bruce Herzberg.

truths, leaning down to earth, are often distorted to our view. Woman's condition certainly admits of improvement, (but when have the strong forgotten to oppress the weak?) but never can any amelioration result from the guidance of her prophets in this present move. Here, as in all other improvements, the good must be brought about by working with, not against — by seconding, not opposing — Nature's laws. Woman, seeking as a woman, may raise her position, — seeking as a man, we repeat, she but degrades it. Every thing contrary to Nature, is abhorrent to Nature, and the mental aberrations of woman, which we are now discussing, excite at once pity and disgust, like those revolting physical deformities which the eye turns from with involuntary loathing, even while the hand of charity is extended to relieve them.[1]

We are no undervaluer of woman; rather we profess ourselves her advocate. Her mission is, to our seeming, even nobler than man's, and she is, in the true fulfillment of that mission, certainly the higher being. Passion governed, suffering conquered, self forgotten, how often is she called upon, as daughter, wife, sister, and mother, to breathe in her half-broken but loving heart, the whispered prayer, that greatest, most beautiful, most self-forgetting of all prayers ever uttered, — "Father, forgive them, they know not what they do."[2] Woman's duty, woman's nature, is to love, to sway by love; to govern by love, to teach by love, to civilize by love! Our reviewer[3] may sneer, — already does sneer, — about "animal functions" and the "maternity argument." We fear not to meet him, or rather her; (for we do not hesitate to pronounce this article to be the production of one of the *third* sex; that, viz. of the Worcester Convention petticoated would-be's;) true woman's love is too beautiful a thing to be blurred by such sneers. It is a love such as man knoweth not, and Worcester Conventionists cannot imagine. Pure and holy, self-devoted and suffering, woman's love is the breath of that God of love, who, loving and pitying, has bid *her* learn to love and to suffer, implanting in her bosom the one single comfort that she is the watching spirit, the guardian angel of those she loves.

We say not that all women are thus; we say not that most women are thus. Alas! no; for thus would man's vices be shamed from existence, and the world become perfect. But we do say, that such is the type of woman, such her moral formation, such her perfection, and in so far as she comes not up to this perfection, she falls short of the model type of her nature. Only in aiming at this type, is there any use for her in this world, and only in proportion as she nears it, each according to the talent which God has given her, can she contribute to bring forward the world in that glorious career of progress which Omniscience has marked out for it. Each can labor, each can strive, lovingly and earnestly, in her own sphere. "Life is real! Life

---

[1]We have inserted occasional paragraph breaks in McCord's text. — EDS.

[2]This is the prayer Jesus uttered as he hung dying on the cross (Luke 23:34). — EDS.

[3]The "reviewer" is Harriet Martineau, noted writer and women's rights activist, who transcribed the Worcester woman's rights conference proceedings that McCord reviews here. — EDS.

is earnest!"[4] Not less for her than for man. She has no right to bury her talent beneath silks or ribands, frippery or flowers; nor yet has she the right, because she fancies not her task, to grasp at another's, which is, or which she imagines is, easier. This is baby play. "Life is real! Life is earnest!" Let woman so read it — let woman so learn it — and she has no need to make her influence felt by a stump speech, or a vote at the polls; she has no need for the exercise of her intellect (and woman, we grant, may have a great, a longing, a hungering intellect, equal to man's) to be gratified with a seat in Congress, or a scuffle for the ambiguous honor of the Presidency.

Even at her own fireside, may she find duties enough, cares enough, troubles enough, thought enough, wisdom enough, to fit a martyr for the stake, a philosopher for life, or a saint for heaven. There are, there have been, and there will be, in every age, great hero-souls in woman's form, as well as man's. It imports little whether history notes them. The hero-soul aims at its certain duty, heroically meeting it, whether glory or shame, worship or contumely, follow its accomplishment. Laud and merit is due to such performance. *Fulfill* thy destiny; *oppose* it not. Herein lies thy track. Keep it. Nature's signposts are within thee, and it were well for thee to learn to read them. Poor fool! canst thou not spell out thy lesson, that ever thus thou fightest against Nature? Not there! not there! Nothing is done by *that* track. Never; from the creation of the world, never. Hero-souls will not try it. It is the mock-hero, the dissatisfied, the grasping, the selfish, the low-aspiring, who tries that track. Turn aside from it, dear friends — there is no heaven-fruit there; only hell-fruit and sorrow. . . .

What first do these reformers ask? "Admission in law and in fact, to equality in all rights, political, civil, and social, with the male citizens of the community." "Women are entitled to the right of suffrage, and to be considered eligible to office." "Civil and political rights acknowledge no sex, and therefore the word 'male' should be struck from every state constitution." "A co-equal share in the formation and administration of laws, — municipal, state, and national, — through legislative assemblies, courts and executive offices." Then follows the memorable quotation from the "memorable document" about all men being created free and equal, the ladies arguing, with some reason, that "men" here, certainly stands for human beings, and thereby prove their right at least equal to Cuffee's.[5] In fact, the reviewer remarks, that such being American principles,

the contradiction between principle and practice cannot be explained away. A like dereliction of the fundamental maxims of their political creed, has

---

[4]McCord quotes from a poem by American poet Henry Wadsworth Longfellow entitled "A Psalm of Life" (1839). The complete stanza is as follows:

Life is real! Life is earnest!
    And the grave is not its goal;
Dust thou art, to dust returnest,
    Was not spoken of the soul. — EDS.

[5]"Cuffee" is a derogatory name for an African American man, like "Sambo." — EDS.

been committed by the Americans in the flagrant instance of the negroes; but of this (she charitably remarks) they are learning to recognize the turpitude. After a struggle, which, by many of its incidents, deserves the name of heroic, the abolitionists are now so strong in numbers and influence, that they hold the balance of parties in the United States. It was fitting that the men whose names will remain associated with the extirpation, from the democratic soil of America, of the aristocracy of color, should be among the originators, for America, and for the rest of the world, of the first collective protest against the aristocracy of sex; a distinction as accidental as that of color, and fully as irrelevant to all questions of government.[6]

This is certainly taking a position, and we are glad to see that the advocates of this move class themselves exactly where they should be, cheek by jowl with the abolitionists. We thank them, at least, for saving us the trouble of proving this position.

Of the first Worcester Convention, that of 1850, (which is, in fact, the second Woman's Rights Convention, the first having been held somewhere in Ohio,)[7] "the president was a woman, and nearly all the chief speakers women, — numerously reinforced, however, by men, among whom were some of the most distinguished leaders in the *kindred cause* of negro emancipation." One of the resolutions of this meeting declares "that every party which claims to represent the humanity, the civilization, and the progress of the age, is bound to inscribe upon its banners, equality before the law, *without distinction of sex or color.*" Oh! there are things so horrible that man, in sheer terror, will mock at what he hates, and think to sneer the scoffing fiend away. We laugh at this, but it is frightful; — frightful to think that thousands of women, in these United States, have signed, and thousands more, if these accounts be correct, are willing to sign their names to such a document. Oh! woman, thou the ministering angel of God's earth, to what devil's work art thou degrading thyself!

But, their reasoning in all this? for they have an argument. First, then, as we have just seen, they claim that the distinctions of *sex and color are accidental and irrelevant to all questions of government.* This is certainly clinching the argument, and that by an assumption which is so extremely illogical, that we are forced to say, if this reforming sisterhood can advance no better ground for their pretensions, it shows them but ill-fitted for the reins of state which they propose taking in hand. The distinction of color has for many years been a point in discussion, and science has now settled that, so far from being accidental, it is an immutable fact of creation, that the black skin and woolly head are distinctive marks of race, which no age, climate, nor circumstance, has ever been able to efface; and there is no more accident in a negro's not being born a white man, than there is in his not being born a baboon, a mouse, or an elephant.

---

[6]McCord is quoting from the convention proceedings. — EDS.

[7]The first American woman's rights convention actually took place at Seneca Falls, New York, in 1848. See page 387 for the "Declaration of Sentiments and Resolutions" voted by this convention. — EDS.

As to the distinction of sex being accidental, this is a remarkable discovery of the present enlightened and progressive age. Sex and color are severally so essential to the being of a woman and a negro, that it is impossible to imagine the existence of either, without these distinctive marks. We have hitherto understood that the sex of a human being was fixed long before its entrance into this world, by rules and causes, which, entirely unknown to man, were equally beyond *his* reach, and that of accident. Such has, we believe, been the received opinion of the learned; but Miss Martineau (who is, we take it, our reviewer) has determined to assume the position of vice regent to Deity, (a power, by the way, which she seems inclined entirely to depose,) and, like *Sganarelle,* in Molière's witty play of the "*Médecin malgré lui,*" she arranges things to suit her own ignorance. Sganarelle having assumed the fact that the heart was on the right side of the human system, has the suggestion made by one of his bewildered admired admirers, that the generally received opinion of science and experience has universally placed it on the left. Oh! answers the ready quack, "*celà était autrefois ainsi: mais nous avons changé tout celà.*"[8] If Miss Martineau and her sisterhood should prove powerful enough to depose *Le Bon Dieu,*[9] and perfect their democratic system, by reducing *His* influence to a *single vote,* we do not doubt that, according to the approved majority system, it will be clearly and indisputably proved that Cuffee is Sir Isaac Newton, and Mrs. Cuffee, Napoleon Buonaparte, and Miss Martineau herself may stand for Cuffee, unless, indeed, she should prefer (as some of her recent works seem to indicate) to have it decided that she is *Le Bon Dieu* himself. She could probably carry the votes, with equal ease either way, and get rid of these little accidental distinctions.

We, however, must, at this point of the question, be old-fashioned enough to declare ourselves conservatives. We cannot entirely shake off old prejudices, and still, spite of Dr. Sganarelle and Miss Martineau, are inclined to look for our hearts on the left side of our bodies, and for our God in the glorious works of his creation. We prefer His rule to Miss Martineau's, and believe that He has given the distinctions of race and sex, not accidentally, (with Omniscience there is no accident,) but distinctively, to mark the unchanging order of His creation — certain beings to certain ends. . . .

"The speakers at the Convention in America, have (says the reviewer) done wisely and right, in refusing to entertain the question of the peculiar aptitudes, either of women or of men, or the limits within which this or that occupation may be supposed to be more adapted to the one or the other." In the name of all that is foolish, what shall we consider, if not the aptitude of a person or thing to his or its uses? It is fortunate that Miss Martineau has

[8]"That used to be true, but we have changed all that." McCord quotes from *Le Médecin malgré lui* (The Doctor in spite of Himself), a comedy by the French playwright Molière (1622–73), known for his satirical attacks on pretentions to wisdom. Sganarelle is the main character in several of Molière's comedies. — EDS.

[9] *"Le Bon Dieu"* means "the good God", or simply, "God." — EDS.

never descended from her high sphere, to allow herself to be burthened with the cares of a family; for had she, in that capacity, forgotten to consult the aptitudes of things to their uses, she might, in some inauspicious fit of philosophic experiment, have committed the unlucky blunder of packing her children in December ice to warm them, or, perchance, cast the little unfortunates into the fire, by way of cleansing their dirty faces. And what might the philosophical and reforming world have thus lost! The ignorant mob, who persist in judging of the uses of things by their aptitudes, might have committed the egregious mistake of taking this doubty philosopher — this Wilberforce of women[10] — this *petit bon Dieu* — for a murderess, and hung her for the interesting little experiment of burning her brats.

We, of the conservatives, who judge of the uses of things by their aptitudes, can read woman's duties anywhere better than in an election crowd, scuffling with Cuffee for a vote. Imagine the lovely Miss Caroline, the fascinating Miss Martha, elbowing Sambo for the stump! All being equals, and no respect for persons to be expected, the natural conclusion is, that Miss Caroline or Martha, being indisputably (even the Worcester conventionalists allow that) corporeally weaker than Sambo, would be thrust into the mud. "Hello da! Miss Caroline git two teet knock out, and Miss Marta hab a black eye and bloody nose!" "Well, wha' faw I stop fa dat? Ebery man must help hisself. I git de stump anyhow, and so, fellow-citizens, Sambo will show how Miss Marta desarve what she git." Or, let us suppose them hoisted through this dirty work. The member is chaired — some fair lady, some Mrs. or Miss Paulina Davis, who, we see, figures as President of the last convention, or one of her vices, Angelina Grimké Weld, or Lucretia Mott[11] — let us imagine the gentle Paulina, Angelina, or Lucretia fairly pitted, in the Senate, against Mr. Foote, for instance, or Mr. Benton, or the valorous Houston, or any other mere patriot, whom luck and electioneering have foisted there.[12] We do not doubt their feminine power, in the war of words — and again we beg to defer a little the question of intellect — but are the ladies ready for a boxing match? Such things happen sometimes; and though it is not impossible that the fair Paulina, Angelina, and Lucretia might have the courage to face a pistol, have they the strength to resist a blow? La Fontaine tells us a fable of a wax candle, which, being ambitiously desirous of immortality, and seeing a handful of clay, that, hardened by the fire into a brick, was enabled to resist time and the elements, turned the matter over for a while in its waxen brains, and finally deter-

---

[10]McCord compares Martineau to William Wilberforce (1759–1833), an English clergyman and leader in the successful fight to abolish slavery in Great Britain and its colonies. Of course, since he was an abolitionist, the proslavery McCord considers any comparison with him to be an insult. — EDS.

[11]Davis, Weld, and Mott were nineteenth-century women's rights activists. Angelina Grimké Weld, initially known for her eloquent denunciations of slavery, was the sister of Sarah Grimké (p. 321). Mott, also a longtime abolitionist, worked with Elizabeth Cady Stanton to convene the 1848 Seneca Falls woman's rights convention. — EDS.

[12]Henry S. Foote, Thomas Hart Benton, and Samuel Houston were senators with belligerent dispositions who had all been involved in physical confrontations in Congress. — EDS.

mined to try the experiment in its own person. A fire being conveniently near, and concluding, we presume, like the lady conventionalists, that all arguments on aptitudes and uses was quite *de trop*,[13] in so clear a case of logical induction,

> "Par sa propre et pure folie
> Il se lança dedans. Ce fut mal raisonné.
> Ce cièrge ne savait grain de philosophie."[14]

The fact, that women have been queens and regents, and filled well these positions, as cited by the reviewer in the cases of Elizabeth, Isabella, Maria Theresa, Catharine of Russia, Blanche, etc., proves that woman, as a woman and a monarch — with the double difference, that the habits of the civilized world accord to these positions — has had the intellect to fill the position well; but it does not prove, and rather goes to disprove, her power of struggling with the masses. As woman and queen, doubly isolated from those masses, she kept her position, simply because of such isolation — because, supported by the laws and habits of society, none dared insult or resist her. But, suppose those laws and habits abrogated, what would have become of the virago, Elizabeth, when she gave the lordly Essex a blow on the ear? If ever it should happen to the fair Paulina, Angelina, or Lucretia to try, under the new *regime*, a similar experiment on any of their male coadjutors or opponents, it is rather probable that they may receive, upon the subject of aptitudes and uses, a somewhat striking lesson. Of the combatant ladies, similarly cited, the same remark is to be made.[15] Ladies of the feudal ages, they generally were petty monarchs: that is to say, defending their strongholds. These were always supported and strengthened, rather than impeded by their sex, the *prestige* of sex seconding and doubling the admiration accorded to their remarkable actions. Joan of Arc, (decidedly the most remarkable of heroines, and, strange to say, not cited by the reviewer,) was a wonderful woman; great as a woman; a phenomenon in her way, certainly, but still a woman-phenomenon. Her deeds were unusual for woman, but, nevertheless, done as a woman, and claiming, for their sanction, not the rights and habits of manhood, but divine inspiration. She never levelled herself to man, or, so doing, must have sunk to the rank of the coarse *femmes de la Halle*[16] of the French Revolution.

Such, too, would of necessity be the case with the man-woman that our conventionists would manufacture. Deprived of all which has hitherto, in separating her from man, wrapped her, as it were, in a veil of deity; naked

---

[13] *"De trop"* is French for "superfluous." — EDS.

[14]"In accord with his own complete foolishness, / the candle threw himself into the fire. His reasoning was faulty. / That candle knew nothing of philosophy." Jean de La Fontaine (1621–95) was a French poet and author of fables. — EDS.

[15]McCord refers to Martineau's citation of medieval noblewomen who directed the military defense of their castles, perhaps while their husbands were absent on the Crusades. — EDS.

[16]La Halle was a marketplace in Paris (now known as Les Halles). The women *("femmes")* who worked there participated actively in the mob violence accompanying the French Revolution (1789–95). — EDS.

of all those observances and distinctions which have been, if not always her efficient, still her only shield; turned out upon the waste common of existence, with no distinctive mark but corporeal weakness; she becomes the inevitable victim of brutal strength. The reviewer acknowledges (or rather, remarks, for she does not seem to be conscious that it is an acknowledgment) that to account for the subjection of woman, "no other explanation is needed than physical force." Setting aside, then, for the moment, all other differences, we would be glad to have the lady explain how she would do away with the difficulty arising from this acknowledged physical inferiority? Man is corporeally stronger than woman, and because he, in the unjust use of his strength, has frequently, habitually, (we will allow her the full use of her argument,) even invariably, oppressed and misused woman, how does she propose to correct the abuse?

Strangely, by pitting woman against man, in a direct state of antagonism; by throwing them into the arena together, stripped for the strife; by saying to the man, this woman is a man like yourself, your equal and similar, possessing all rights which you possess, and (of course she must allow) possessing none others. In such a strife, what becomes of corporeal weakness? Perhaps we will be told how man conquers the wild beast, and, by knowledge and intellect, holds in sway the mighty elephant and the forest's king. True, by *intellect*. He has the superiority of intellect, and he uses it. It is God's and nature's law, that he should use it. Man, generally, uses it to subdue his inferior, the beast. The white man uses it to subdue his inferior, the negro. Both are right, for both are according to God's law. The same argument has been used, to prove the necessity of woman's subjection. This, we think, is taking mistaken ground, and unnecessarily assuming a doubtfully tenable position. Woman's bodily frame is enough to account for her position. The differences of mind between the sexes, we are, ourselves, inclined to regard rather as differences than inequalities. More of this anon, however. Granting, for the moment, exact mental equality, how will the conventionists redeem corporeal deficiencies? They do not pretend that woman is the superior mind, only the equal. Still, then, man — where they are matched against each other — where woman assumes manhood, and measures herself hand to hand with him — has, of necessity, the superiority — a brutal superiority, if you please, but still the superiority — and, in proportion as it is brutal, will the triumph it gives be brutal. Woman throws away her strength, when she *brings herself down* to man's level. She throws away that moral strength, that shadow of divinity, which nature has given her to keep man's ferocity in curb. Grant her to be his equal, and instantly she sinks to his inferior, which, as yet, we maintain she has never been. . . .

As regards the question of intellect, it is a most difficult one to argue. We are ourselves inclined to believe that the difference of intellect in the sexes exists, as we have said, rather in kind than degree. There is much talk of the difference of education and rearing bestowed upon individuals of either sex, and we think too much stress is laid upon it. Education, no doubt, influences the intellect in each individual case; but it is as logically certain, that intellect, in its kind and degree, influences education *en masse;* — that is to say, Thomas, the individual man, may be better suited to woman's duties, than Betty, the individual woman, and *vice versa.* Thomas might make a capital child's nurse, in which Betty succeeds but badly; while Betty might be quite competent to beat Thomas hollow in a stump oration; and yet we have a fair right to argue, that Thomas and Betty are but individual exceptions to a general rule, which general rule is plainly indicated by the universal practice of mankind. The fact that such relative positions of the sexes, and such habits of mind, have existed, more or less modified, in all ages of the world, and under all systems of government, goes far to prove that these are the impulses of instinct and teachings of Nature. It is certainly a little hard upon Mrs. Betty to be forced from occupations for which she feels herself particularly well qualified, and to make way for Mr. Thomas, who, although particularly *ill-*qualified for them, will be certain to assert his right; but laws cannot be made for exceptional cases, and if Mrs. Betty has good sense, as well as talent, she will let the former curb the latter; she will teach her woman-intellect to curb her man-intellect, and will make herself the stronger woman thereby.

The fact that less effort has been made to teach woman certain things, is a strong argument that she has (taking her as a class) less aptitude for being taught those certain things. It is difficult to chain down mind by any habit or any teaching, and if woman's intellect had the same turn as man's, it is most unlikely that so many myriads should have passed away and "made no sign." In the field of literature, how many women have enjoyed all the advantages which men can command, and yet how very few have distinguished themselves; and how far behind are even those few from the great and burning lights of letters! Who ever hopes to see a woman Shakespeare? And yet a greater than Shakespeare may she be.

It may be doubtful whether the brilliant intellect, which, inspiring noble thoughts, leaves still the great thinker grovelling in the lowest vices and slave of his passions, without the self-command to keep them in sway, is superior to that which, knowing good and evil, grasps almost instinctively at the first. Such, in its uncorrupted nature, is woman's intellect — such her inspiration. While man *writes,* she *does;* while he imagines the hero-soul, she is often performing its task; while he is painting, she is acting. The heart, it is sometimes argued, and not the brain, is the priceless pearl of womanhood, "the oracular jewel, the Urim and Thummim,[17] before which gross man can only inquire and adore." This is fancy and not reasoning. The heart is known to be only a part of our anatomical system, regulating the currents of the blood, and nothing more. It has, by an allegory based upon exploded error, been allowed to stand for a certain class of feelings which every body now knows to be, equally with other classes, dependent upon the brain; and, in a serious argument, not the heart and

[17]The Urim and Thummim were objects that adorned the breastplate of the high priest of the Temple in Jerusalem (see Exodus 28:30). Some biblical scholars believe that they were jewels and that they were used like lots to determine the will of God. — EDS.

the brain, but the difference of brain; not the feeling and the intellect, but the varieties of intellect, should be discussed. We consider, therefore, the question of pre-eminence as simply idle. We have already endeavored to prove that, whatever the intellect of woman, it would have no influence in altering the relative position of the sexes; we now go farther, and maintain that the nature of her intellect confirms this position. The higher her intellect, the better is she suited to fulfill that heaviest task of life which makes her the "martyr to the pang without the palm." If she suffers, — what is this but the fate of every higher grade of humanity, which rises in suffering as it rises in dignity? for, is not all intellect suffering? . . .

Woman is not what she might be, not what she ought to be. Half persuaded, as she is, that her position is one of degradation and inferiority, she becomes, as a matter of necessity, degraded to that opinion, just in so far as she is convicted of its truth; and hence, too often, folly becomes her pleasure, vanity her pride. But this is man's blotting of God's fair work. Woman is neither man's equal nor inferior, but only his different. It would indeed be well if man, convinced of this, could, in his relations with her, "throw aside his instruments of torture," and aid rather than oppress her. Thus, we firmly believe, it will be, in the perfection of time, worked out by woman's endurance and patient laboring in her own sphere; but never, certainly, by her assumption of another, equally ill-adapted to her mental and her bodily faculties. For her it is (God's apostle of love) to pass through life with "the cross, that emblem of self-sacrifice, in her hand, while her pathway across the desert is marked by the flowers which spring beneath her steps." Life's devoted martyr she may be — man's ministering angel she may be; but, for heaven's sake, mesdames, the conventionists, — not Cuffee's rival candidate for the Presidency!

READING CRITICALLY

1. In the first paragraph, McCord outlines woman's "mission" or "duty". What is it?

2. According to McCord, what is the first request of the women's rights "reformers"? What is the "memorable document" to which they refer in making this claim? What is the "aristocracy of color," which (in the passage McCord quotes) is being opposed along with the "aristocracy of sex," or oppression of women (p. 309–10)?

3. Women's rights proponents resist distinctions based on race or sex because they say that these distinctions are "accidental," meaning that they have nothing to do with the person's essential humanity by which he or she should be guaranteed a part in "questions of government." How does McCord refute this argument?

4. McCord reports that the women's rights activists refused to consider the question of whether men and women may have different "aptitudes" for different occupations, that is, whether they may be better suited for some jobs than for others on the basis of sex. Why do you think the activists set this question aside? Why does McCord think this question must be addressed?

5. What is McCord attempting to illustrate with the examples of political activism on page 312?

6. McCord asserts that women are not inferior to men in intellect but are simply "different." How does she refute the argument that any observed differences in men's and women's intellectual abilities are due to differences in the education available to them?

WRITING ANALYTICALLY

1. McCord adheres to a general principle — that people must take the stations in society to which their innate abilities suit them. She further believes that these innate abilities are largely determined by one's race and sex (although she admits that there may be exceptions in the case of sex). List and analyze her arguments supporting these two related principles, either refuting her where you can or explaining why you agree.

2. Consider McCord's rhetorical problem: She wants to make the domestic role attractive to women. Two of the primary strategies she employs to accomplish this are to stress the saintly suffering of woman in the domestic role and to emphasize the high intellectual challenges she faces. What can you infer about McCord's imagined audience from her choice of these tactics? What does she think these women want? Write a paper in which you describe the characteristics and attitudes that McCord assumes her audience possesses.

3. Both McCord and Catharine Beecher (p. 294) argue that women should remain within the domestic sphere; but they both emerge from the domestic sphere to make that argument — that is, they publish their views. Although publishing violated domestic ideologies less seriously than public speaking did, it still risked damaging the writer's credibility (she would not emerge in public at all if she were a proper woman, according to McCord and Beecher). Compare and contrast the strategies these two women writers employ to make themselves sound like strong, credible arguers. Describe and evaluate their strategies. You may make an argument simply on whether or not either of them is effective in establishing her credibility; or you may consider whether either is so effective as to be a "feminist in spite of herself" (both women were considered to be feminists of a sort by their contemporaries).

NEW YORK HERALD

"The Woman's Rights Convention: The Last Act of the Drama"

(September 12, 1852)

This editorial concerns an 1852 women's rights convention in Syracuse, New York. Notice that the writer, although presumably a northerner and a man, has views of the women's rights activists that are similar to those of southern critic Louisa Cheves McCord (p. 307).

THE FARCE AT SYRACUSE HAS been played out. . . .

Who are these women? What do they want? What are the motives that impel them to this course of action? The *dramatis personae* of the farce enacted at Syracuse present a curious conglomeration of both sexes. Some of them are old maids, whose personal charms were never very attractive, and who have been sadly slighted by the masculine gender in general; some of them women who have been badly mated, whose own temper, or their husbands', has made life anything but agreeable to them, and they are therefore down upon the whole of the opposite sex; some, having so much of the virago in their disposition, that nature appears to have made a mistake in their gender — mannish women, like hens that crow; some of boundless vanity and egotism, who believe that they are superior in intellectual ability to "all the world and the rest of mankind," and delight to see their speeches and addresses in print; and man shall be consigned to his proper sphere — nursing the babies, washing the dishes, mending stockings, and sweeping the house. This is "the good time coming." Besides the classes we have enumerated, there is a class of wild enthusiasts and visionaries — very sincere, but very mad — having the same vein as the fanatical Abolitionists, and the majority, if not all of them, being, in point of fact, deeply imbued with the antislavery sentiment. Of the male sex who attend these Conventions for the purpose of taking part in them, the majority are henpecked husbands, and all of them ought to wear petticoats. . . .

How did woman first become subject to man as she now is all over the world? By her nature, her sex, just as the negro is and always will be, to the end of time, inferior to the white race, and, therefore, doomed to subjection; but happier than she would be in any other condition, just because it is the law of her nature. The women themselves would not have this law reversed. . . .

New York Herald, "The Woman's Rights Convention: The Last Act of the Drama," September 12, 1852, reprinted in *Up from the Pedestal: Selected Writings in the History of American Feminism,* ed. Aileen Kraditor (Chicago: Quadrangle Books, 1968), 189–91.

In the notes, EDS. = Patricia Bizzell and Bruce Herzberg.

What do the leaders of the Woman's Rights Convention want? They want to vote, and to hustle with the rowdies at the polls. They want to be members of Congress, and in the heat of debate to subject themselves to coarse jests and indecent language. . . . They want to fill all other posts which men are ambitious to occupy — to be lawyers, doctors, captains of vessels, and generals in the field. How funny it would sound in the newspapers, that Lucy Stone, pleading a cause, took suddenly ill in the pains of parturition, and perhaps gave birth to a fine bouncing boy in court! Or that Rev. Antoinette Brown was arrested in the middle of her sermon in the pulpit from the same cause, and presented a "pledge" to her husband and the congregation;[1] or, that Dr. Harriot K. Hunt,[2] while attending a gentleman patient for a fit of the gout or *fistula in ano,*[3] found it necessary to send for a doctor, there and then, and to be delivered of a man or woman child — perhaps twins. A similar event might happen on the floor of Congress, in a storm at sea, or in the raging tempest of battle, and then what is to become of the woman legislator?

READING CRITICALLY

1. The editorial opens with a description of the different types of women who the writer claims are attracted to woman's rights conventions. Describe each of these types in your own words.

2. According to the editorial writer, who are the men who support women's rights? Describe them in your own words.

3. The editorial writer claims that the subordination of women is based on the same general principle as the subordination of "the negro." Summarize that principle.

4. The editorial concludes with supposedly humorous images of women giving birth in the midst of their professional activities as lawyer, minister, or doctor. What argument against women's emergence from the domestic sphere do these images imply?

WRITING ANALYTICALLY

1. The editorial writer attempts to discredit the ideas of the women's rights activists by using various rhetorical strategies for making the women themselves look ridiculous and unworthy to be listened to. Consider what these strategies are, and compare and contrast them with the strategies employed by some present-day

---

[1] The *Herald* writer is using "pledge" here in the sense of a "token of friendship," ironic understatement for a baby. — EDS.

[2] Stone, Brown, and Hunt were all well-known nineteenth-century women's rights activists. Stone's marriage agreement is on page 394. Although Stone was never admitted to the bar, in spite of her depiction here as a practicing lawyer, Brown was indeed one of the first American women to be ordained as a minister (Unitarian), and Hunt was one of the first American female physicians. — EDS.

[3] *"Fistula in ano"* is an abscess in the anus. — EDS.

newspaper columnist or television or radio commentator (such as Rush Limbaugh) who also attempts to discredit people holding views that he or she opposes. Describe and evaluate the strategies of the editorialist and your present-day example. To what extent do you think such strategies are effective?

2. Compare and contrast the images of women activists given here and in either Folsom (p. 302) or McCord (p. 307). All of these writers intend to make the women activists look bad. Describe and evaluate their strategies, arguing for whether or not they are effective. Pay particular attention to the use of race in these strategies, such as the association of the activists with abolitionism, social and physical contact between the races, and so on.

3. The Seneca Falls "Declaration of Sentiments and Resolutions" (p. 387) was produced by a woman's rights convention very similar to the one the *Herald* editorial writer attacks. Write a paper in which you refute the editorial writer's charges against male and female women's rights activists, using the text of the "Declaration" as evidence that these people are not what the editorial writer represents them to be.

CONTESTING WOMAN'S SPHERE

SARAH GRIMKÉ

From *Letters on the Equality of the Sexes and the Condition of Women* (1838)

Sarah Grimké (1792–1873), like Louisa Cheves McCord (p. 307), was born in Charleston, South Carolina. Her father, a Revolutionary War veteran, was a wealthy judge and plantation owner. Grimké's father allowed her to supplement her girls' school education in art and music by studying history, politics, and argumentative rhetoric with her brothers' tutors. On a trip to Philadelphia with her father, she became interested in the Society of Friends (Quakers), which had promoted abolitionism from pre-Revolutionary times. She moved to Philadelphia and became a Quaker in 1823 and was joined by her younger sister Angelina in 1829. Both became active in Philadelphia's vigorous abolitionist community and spoke frequently against the evils of slavery that they had witnessed.

At first, the Grimké sisters addressed only women, but men soon began attending the women's meetings to hear their powerful testimony. They thus became the first "respectable" American women to speak to mixed groups of women and men, a highly disreputable activity in antebellum times. In 1837, their speaking tour in Massachusetts brought to a head the controversy over their public role. Catharine Beecher (p. 294) denounced them, and the Massachusetts Congregationalist clergy published a "Pastoral Letter" (p. 305) that was critical of their activities without naming them. Sarah Grimké rebuts the "Pastoral Letter" in her *Letters on the Equality of the Sexes and the Condition of Women;* three of her letters are reprinted or excerpted here. These letters, addressed to Mary Parker, president of the Boston Female Anti-Slavery Society and an important supporter of the Grimkés' speaking tour, were first published in a Boston newspaper and later in book form.

In 1838, the hall where the sisters had just spoken was burned to the ground by an angry mob whom they barely escaped. Although undeterred by verbal denunciations, after this violence the sisters agreed to abolitionist Theodore Weld's request that they retire rather than risk harm to the cause or themselves. Angelina Grimké married Weld that year, and Sarah lived with them. The sisters and Weld supported themselves by teaching and in later years sought out and aided their father's African American children by one of his slaves.

Sarah Grimké, *Letters on the Equality of the Sexes and the Condition of Women,* ed. Elizabeth A. Bartlett (New Haven: Yale University Press, 1988), 37–44, 85–88.

In the notes, EAB = Elizabeth A. Bartlett, EDS. = Patricia Bizzell and Bruce Herzberg.

LETTER III

The Pastoral Letter of the General Association of Congregationalist Ministers of Massachusetts

Haverhill, 7th Mo. 1837

Dear Friend,

When I last addressed thee, I had not seen the Pastoral Letter of the General Association. It has since fallen into my hands, and I must digress from my intention of exhibiting the condition of women in different parts of the world, in order to make some remarks on this extraordinary document. I am persuaded that when the minds of men and women become emancipated from the thraldom of superstition and "traditions of men," the sentiments contained in the Pastoral Letter will be recurred to with as much astonishment as the opinions of Cotton Mather and other distinguished men of his day, on the subject of witchcraft;[1] nor will it be deemed less wonderful, that a body of divines should gravely assemble and endeavor to prove that woman has no right to "open her mouth for the dumb," than it now is that judges should have sat on the trials of witches, and solemnly condemned nineteen persons and one dog to death for witchcraft.

But to the letter. It says, "We invite your attention to the dangers which at present seem to threaten the FEMALE CHARACTER with widespread and permanent injury." I rejoice that they have called the attention of my sex to this subject, because I believe if woman investigates it, she will soon discover that danger is impending, though from a totally different source from that which the Association apprehends, — danger from those who, having long held the reins of *usurped* authority, are unwilling to permit us to fill that sphere which God created us to move in, and who have entered into league to crush the immortal mind of woman. I rejoice, because I am persuaded that the rights of woman, like the rights of slaves, need only be examined to be understood and asserted, even by some of those, who are now endeavoring to smother the irrepressible desire for mental and spiritual freedom which glows in the breast of many, who hardly dare to speak their sentiments.

"The appropriate duties and influence of women are clearly stated in the New Testament. Those duties are unobtrusive and private, but the sources of *mighty power.* When the mild, *dependent,* softening influence of woman upon the sternness of man's opinions is fully exercised, society feels the effects of it in a thousand ways." No one can desire more earnestly than I do, that woman may move exactly in the sphere which her Creator has assigned her; and I believe her having been displaced from that sphere has introduced confusion into the world. It is, therefore, of vast importance to herself and to all the rational creation, that she should ascertain what are her duties and her privileges as a responsible and im-

---

[1]Cotton Mather (1663–1728), clergyman, theologian, and author, is reputed to be the fomenter of the witchcraft hysteria in New England in the late seventeenth century. — EAB

mortal being. The New Testament has been referred to, and I am willing to abide by its decisions, but must enter my protest against the false translation of some passages by the MEN who did that work, and against the perverted interpretation by the MEN who undertook to write commentaries thereon. I am inclined to think, when we are admitted to the honor of studying Greek and Hebrew, we shall produce some various readings of the Bible a little different from those we now have.

The Lord Jesus defines the duties of his followers in his Sermon on the Mount. He lays down grand principles by which they should be governed, without any reference to sex or condition. — "Ye are the light of the world. A city that is set on a hill cannot be hid. Neither do men light a candle and put it under a bushel, but on a candlestick, and it giveth light unto all that are in the house. Let your light so shine before men, that they may see your good works, and glorify your Father which is in Heaven" [Matt. 5:14–16]. I follow him through all his precepts, and find him giving the same directions to women as to men, never even referring to the distinction now so strenuously insisted upon between masculine and feminine virtues: this is one of the anti-Christian "traditions of men" which are taught instead of the "commandments of God." Men and women were CREATED EQUAL; they are both moral and accountable beings, and whatever is *right* for man to do, is *right* for woman.

But the influence of woman, says the Association, is to be private and unobtrusive; her light is not to shine before man like that of her brethren; but she is passively to let the lords of the creation, as they call themselves, put the bushel over it, lest peradventure it might appear that the world has been benefitted by the rays of *her* candle. So that her quenched light, according to their judgment, will be of more use than if it were set on the candlestick. "Her influence is the source of mighty power." This has ever been the flattering language of man since he laid aside the whip as a means to keep woman in subjection. He spares her body; but the war he has waged against her mind, her heart, and her soul, has been no less destructive to her as a moral being. How monstrous, how anti-Christian, is the doctrine that woman is to be dependent on man! Where, in all the sacred Scriptures, is this taught? Alas! she has too well learned the lesson, which MAN has labored to teach her. She has surrendered her dearest RIGHTS, and been satisfied with the privileges which man has assumed to grant her; she has been amused with the show of power, whilst man has absorbed all the reality into himself. He has adorned the creature whom God gave him as a companion, with baubles and gewgaws, turned her attention to personal attractions, offered incense to her vanity, and made her the instrument of his selfish gratification, a plaything to please his eye and amuse his hours of leisure. "Rule by obedience and by submission sway," or in other words, study to be a hypocrite, pretend to submit, but gain your point, has been the code of household morality which woman has been taught. The poet has sung, in sickly strains, the loveliness of woman's dependence upon man, and now we find it reechoed by those who profess to teach the religion of the Bible. God says, "Cease ye from man whose breath is in his nostrils, for wherein is he to be accounted of?" Man says, depend upon me. God says, "HE will teach us of his ways." Man says, believe it not, I am to be your teacher. This doctrine of dependence upon man is utterly at variance with the doctrine of the Bible. In that book I find nothing like the softness of woman, nor the sternness of man: both are equally commanded to bring forth the fruits of the Spirit, love, meekness, gentleness, &c.

But we are told, "the power of woman is in her dependence, flowing from a consciousness of that weakness which God has given her for her protection." If physical weakness is alluded to, I cheerfully concede the superiority; if brute force is what my brethren are claiming, I am willing to let them have all the honor they desire; but if they mean to intimate, that mental or moral weakness belongs to woman, more than to man, I utterly disclaim the charge. Our powers of mind have been crushed, as far as man could do it, our sense of morality has been impaired by his interpretation of our duties; but no where does God say that he made any distinction between us, as moral and intelligent beings.

"We appreciate," say the Association, "the *unostentatious* prayers and efforts of woman in advancing the cause of religion at home and abroad, in leading religious inquirers TO THE PASTOR for instruction." Several points here demand attention. If public prayers and public efforts are necessarily ostentatious, then "Anna the prophetess, (or preacher,) who departed not from the temple, but served God with fastings and prayers night and day," "and spake of Christ to all them that looked for redemption in Israel," was ostentatious in her efforts.[2] Then, the apostle Paul encourages women to be ostentatious in their efforts to spread the gospel, when he gives them directions how they should appear, when engaged in praying, or preaching in the public assemblies. Then, the whole association of Congregational ministers are ostentatious, in the efforts they are making in preaching and praying to convert souls.

But woman may be permitted to lead religious inquirers to the PASTORS for instruction. Now this is assuming that all pastors are better qualified to give instruction than woman. This I utterly deny. I have suffered too keenly from the teaching of man, to lead any one to him for instruction. The Lord Jesus says, — "Come unto me and learn of me" [Matt. 11:29]. He points his followers to no man; and when woman is made the favored instrument of rousing a sinner to his lost and helpless condition, she has no right to substitute any teacher for Christ; all she has to do is, to turn the contrite inquirer to the "Lamb of God which taketh away the sins of the world" [John 1:29]. More souls have probably been lost by going down to Egypt for help, and by trusting in man in the early stages of religious expe-

---

[2]Anna was an aged widow and woman of faith who lived in the Temple at Jerusalem. Seeing Jesus as an infant at the ceremonial service of his mother's repurification, she was the first to proclaim him the Christ. She was likened to Miriam, Deborah, and Huldah in her prophetic powers (Luke 2:36–38). — EAB On Miriam, Deborah, and Huldah, see note 5, page 329. — EDS.

rience, than by any other error. Instead of the petition being offered to God, — "Lead me in thy truth, and TEACH me, for thou art the God of my salvation" [Ps. 25:5], — instead of relying on the precious promises — "What man is he that feareth the Lord? him shall HE TEACH in the way that he shall choose" [Ps. 25:12] — "I will instruct thee and TEACH thee in the way which thou shalt go — I will guide thee with mine eye" [Ps. 27:11] — the young convert is directed to go to man, as if he were in the place of God, and his instructions essential to an advancement in the path of righteousness. That woman can have but a poor conception of the privilege of being taught of God, what he alone can teach, who would turn the "religious inquirer aside" from the fountain of living waters, where he might slake his thirst for spiritual instruction, to those broken cisterns which can hold no water, and therefore cannot satisfy the panting spirit. The business of men and women, who are ORDAINED OF GOD to preach the unsearchable riches of Christ to a lost and perishing world, is to lead souls to Christ, and not to Pastors for instruction.

The General Association say, that "when woman assumes the place and tone of man as a public reformer, our care and protection of her seem unnecessary; we put ourselves in self-defence against her, and her character becomes unnatural." Here again the unscriptural notion is held up, that there is a distinction between the duties of men and women as moral beings; that what is virtue in man, is vice in woman; and women who dare to obey the command of Jehovah, "Cry aloud, spare not, lift up thy voice like a trumpet, and show my people their transgression" [Isa. 58:1], are threatened with having the protection of the brethren withdrawn. If this is all they do, we shall not even know the time when our chastisement is inflicted; our trust is in the Lord Jehovah, and in him is everlasting strength. The motto of woman, when she is engaged in the great work of public reformation should be, — "The Lord is my light and my salvation; whom shall I fear? The Lord is the strength of my life; of whom shall I be afraid?" [Ps. 27:1]. She must feel, if she feels rightly, that she is fulfilling one of the important duties laid upon her as an accountable being, and that her character, instead of being "unnatural," is in exact accordance with the will of Him to whom, and to no other, she is responsible for the talents and the gifts confided to her. As to the pretty simile, introduced into the "Pastoral Letter," "If the vine whose strength and beauty is to lean upon the trellis work, and half conceal its clusters, thinks to assume the independence and the overshadowing nature of the elm," &c. I shall only remark that it might well suit the poet's fancy, who sings of sparkling eyes and coral lips, and knights in armor clad; but it seems to me utterly inconsistent with the dignity of a Christian body, to endeavor to draw such an antiscriptural distinction between men and women. Ah! how many of my sex feel in the dominion, thus unrighteously exercised over them, under the gentle appellation of *protection*, that what they have leaned upon has proved a broken reed at best, and oft a spear.

Thine in the bonds of womanhood,

Sarah M. Grimké

LETTER IV

Social Intercourse of the Sexes

Andover, 7th Mo. 27th, 1837

My Dear Friend,

Before I proceed with the account of that oppression which woman has suffered in every age and country from her *protector,* man, permit me to offer for your consideration, some views relative to the social intercourse of the sexes. Nearly the whole of this intercourse is, in my apprehension, derogatory to man and woman, as moral and intellectual beings. We approach each other, and mingle with each other, under the constant pressure of a feeling that we are of different sexes; and, instead of regarding each other only in the light of immortal creatures, the mind is fettered by the idea which is early and industriously infused into it, that we must never forget the distinction between male and female. Hence our intercourse, instead of being elevated and refined, is generally calculated to excite and keep alive the lowest propensities of our nature. Nothing, I believe, has tended more to destroy the true dignity of woman, than the fact that she is approached by man in the character of a female. The idea that she is sought as an intelligent and heaven-born creature, whose society will cheer, refine, and elevate her companion, and that she will receive the same blessings she confers, is rarely held up to her view. On the contrary, man almost always addresses himself to the weakness of woman. By flattery, by an appeal to her passions, he seeks access to her heart; and when he has gained her affections, he uses her as the instrument of his pleasure — the minister of his temporal comfort. He furnishes himself with a housekeeper, whose chief business is in the kitchen, or the nursery. And whilst he goes abroad and enjoys the means of improvement afforded by collision of intellect with cultivated minds, his wife is condemned to draw nearly all her instruction from books, if she has time to peruse them; and if not, from her meditations, whilst engaged in those domestic duties which are necessary for the comfort of her lord and master.

Surely no one who contemplates, with the eye of a Christian philosopher, the design of God in the creation of woman, can believe that she is now fulfilling that design. The literal translation of the word "help-meet" is a helper like unto himself; it is so rendered in the Septuagint,[3] and manifestly signifies a companion. Now I believe it will be impossible for woman to fill the station assigned her by God, until her brethren mingle with her as an equal, as a moral being; and lose, in the dignity of her immortal nature, and in the fact of her bearing like himself the image and superscription of her God, the idea of her being a female. The apostle beautifully remarks, "As many of you as have been baptized into Christ, have put on Christ. There is neither Jew nor Greek, there is neither bond nor free, there is neither *male* nor *female;* for ye are all one in Christ Jesus" [Gal. 3:28]. Until our intercourse is purified by the forgetfulness of sex, — until

---

[3]The Septuagint is the oldest Greek version of the Bible. — EAB

we rise above the present low and sordid views which entwine themselves around our social and domestic interchange of sentiment and feelings, we never can derive that benefit from each other's society which it is the design of our Creator that we should. Man has inflicted an unspeakable injury upon woman, by holding up to her view her animal nature, and placing in the back ground her moral and intellectual being. Woman has inflicted an injury upon herself by submitting to be thus regarded; and she is now called upon to rise from the station where *man,* not God, has placed her, and claim those sacred and inalienable rights, as a moral and responsible being, with which her Creator has invested her.

What but these views, so derogatory to the character of woman, could have called forth the remark contained in the Pastoral Letter? "We especially deplore the intimate acquaintance and promiscuous conversation of *females* with regard to things 'which ought not to be named,' by which that modesty and delicacy, which is the charm of domestic life, and which constitutes the true influence of woman, is consumed." How wonderful that the conceptions of man relative to woman are so low, that he cannot perceive that she may converse on any subject connected with the improvement of her species, without swerving in the least from that modesty which is one of her greatest virtues! Is it designed to insinuate that woman should possess a greater degree of modesty than man? This idea I utterly reprobate. Or is it supposed that woman cannot go into scenes of misery, the necessary result of those very things, which the Pastoral Letter says ought not to be named, for the purpose of moral reform, without becoming contaminated by those with whom she thus mingles?

This is a false position; and I presume has grown out of the never-forgotten distinction of male and female. The woman who goes forth, clad in the panoply of God, to stem the tide of iniquity and misery, which she beholds rolling through our land, goes not forth to her labor of love as a female. She goes as the dignified messenger of Jehovah, and all she does and says must be done and said irrespective of sex. She is in duty bound to communicate with all, who are able and willing to aid her in saving her fellow creatures, both men and women, from that destruction which awaits them.

So far from woman losing any thing of the purity of her mind, by visiting the wretched victims of vice in their miserable abodes, by talking with them, or of them, she becomes more and more elevated and refined in her feelings and views. While laboring to cleanse the minds of others from the malaria of moral pollution, her own heart becomes purified, and her soul rises to nearer communion with her God. Such a woman is infinitely better qualified to fulfill the duties of a wife and a mother, than the woman whose *false delicacy* leads her to shun her fallen sister and brother, and shrink from *naming those sins* which she knows exist, but which she is too fastidious to labor by deed and by word to exterminate. Such a woman feels, when she enters upon the marriage relation, that God designed that relation not to debase her to a level with the animal creation, but to increase the happiness and dignity of his creatures. Such a woman comes to the important task of training her children in the nurture and admonition of the Lord, with a soul filled with the greatness of the beings committed to her charge. She sees in her children, creatures bearing the image of God; and she approaches them with reverence, and treats them at all times as moral and accountable beings. Her own mind being purified and elevated, she instills into her children that genuine religion which induces them to keep the commandments of God. Instead of ministering with ceaseless care to their sensual appetites, she teaches them to be temperate in all things. She can converse with her children on any subject relating to their duty to God, can point their attention to those vices which degrade and brutify human nature, without in the least defiling her own mind or theirs. She views herself, and teaches her children to regard themselves as moral beings; and in all their intercourse with their fellow men, to lose the animal nature of man and woman, in the recognition of that immortal mind wherewith Jehovah has blessed and enriched them.

   Thine in the bonds of womanhood,

Sarah M. Grimké

LETTER XIV

Ministry of Women

Brookline, 9th Mo. 1837

My Dear Sister,
According to the principle which I have laid down, that man and woman were created equal, and endowed by their beneficent Creator with the same intellectual powers and the same moral responsibilities, and that consequently whatever is *morally* right for a man to do, is *morally* right for a woman to do, it follows as a necessary corollary, that if it is the duty of man to preach the unsearchable riches of Christ, it is the duty also of woman.

   I am aware, that I have the prejudices of education and custom to combat, both in my own and the other sex, as well as "the traditions of men," which are taught for the commandments of God. I feel that I have no sectarian views to advance; for although among the Quakers, Methodists, and Christians,[4] women are permitted to preach the glad tidings of peace and salvation, yet I know of no religious body, who entertain the Scripture doctrine of the perfect equality of man and woman, which is the fundamental principle of my argument in favor of the ministry of women. I wish simply to throw my views before thee. If they are based on the immutable foundation of truth, they cannot be overthrown by unkind insinuations, bitter sarcasms, unchristian imputations, or contemptuous ridicule. These are

---

[4]By "Christians," Grimké means a particular Protestant denomination, the Christian Church, which was formed in the late eighteenth century from independent groups of Methodists, Presbyterians, and Baptists. She does not mean *all* Christians. Women were not permitted to preach in most Protestant denominations of her day. — EDS.

weapons which are unworthy of a good cause. If I am mistaken, as truth only can prevail, my supposed errors will soon vanish before her beams; but I am persuaded that woman is not filling the high and holy station which God allotted to her, and that in consequence of her having been driven from her "appropriate sphere," both herself and her brethren have suffered an infinity of evils. . . .

That women were called to the prophetic office, I believe is universally admitted. Miriam, Deborah, and Huldah[5] were prophetesses. The judgments of the Lord are denounced by Ezekiel on false prophetesses, as well as false prophets [Ezek. 13:17–18]. And if Christian ministers are, as I apprehend, successors of the prophets, and not of the priests,[6] then of course, women are now called to that office as well as men, because God has no where withdrawn from them the privilege of doing what is the great business of preachers, viz. to point the penitent sinner to the Redeemer. "Behold the Lamb of God, which taketh away the sins of the world" [John 1:29].

It is often triumphantly inquired, why, if men and women are on an equality, are not women as conspicuous in the Bible as men? I do not intend to assign a reason, but I think one may readily be found in the fact, that from the days of Eve to the present time, the aim of man has been to crush her. He has accomplished this work in various ways; sometimes by brute force, sometimes by making her subservient to his worst passions, sometimes by treating her as a doll, and while he excluded from her mind the light of knowledge, decked her person with gewgaws and frippery which he scorned for himself, thus endeavoring to render her like unto a painted sepulchre.

It is truly marvellous that any woman can rise above the pressure of circumstances which combine to crush her. Nothing can strengthen her to do this in the character of a preacher of righteousness, but a call from Jehovah himself. And when the voice of God penetrates the deep recesses of her heart, and commands her to go and cry in the ears of the people, she is ready to exclaim, "Ah, Lord God, behold I cannot speak, for I am a woman." I have known women in different religious societies, who have felt like the prophet. "His word was in my heart as a burning fire shut up in my bones, and I was weary with forbearing." But they have not dared to open their lips, and have endured all the intensity of suffering, produced by disobedience to God, rather than encounter heartless ridicule and injurious suspicions. I rejoice that we have been the oppressed, rather than the oppressors. God thus prepared his people for deliverance from outward bondage; and I hope our sorrows have prepared us to fulfill our high and

---

[5]Miriam (Exod. 2:4–10), sister of Moses, led women in song when they were crossing the Red Sea (Exod. 15:20–21). Deborah, a Hebrew prophetess and judge, was called the "Mother of Israel" (Judges 4:5). Huldah, the Hebrew prophetess to whom King Josiah sent his high priest for counsel, prophesied that Jerusalem would be destroyed, though Josiah would be spared (2 Kings 22:14; 2 Chron. 34:22). — EAB

[6]The Israelite priests who served in the Temple in Jerusalem before its final destruction in 70 C.E. — EDS.

holy duties, whether public or private, with humility and meekness; and that suffering has imparted fortitude to endure trials, which assuredly await us in the attempt to sunder those chains with which man has bound us, galling to the spirit, though unseen by the eye.

Surely there is nothing either astonishing or novel in the gifts of the Spirit being bestowed on woman: nothing astonishing, because there is no respect of persons with God; the soul of the woman in his sight is as the soul of the man, and both are alike capable of the influence of the Holy Spirit. Nothing novel, because, as has been already shown, in the sacred records there are found examples of women, as well as of men, exercising the gift of prophecy. . . .

READING CRITICALLY

Letter 3

1. How does Grimké rebut the argument of the "Pastoral Letter" (p. 305) that the Bible requires a different sphere of activity for women than for men?

2. How does Grimké deal with the claim in the "Pastoral Letter" that women work best by using private "influence" and remaining "dependent" on men? How does she deal with the claims that women are physically, mentally, and morally inferior to men?

Letter 4

1. What does Grimké mean when she says that the constant emphasis on distinctions between men and women "keep[s] alive the lowest propensities of our nature" (p. 326)?

2. How does man appeal to "the weakness of woman," according to Grimké (p. 326)?

Letter 14

1. Grimké echoes the Declaration of Independence (p. 174) in her opening paragraph. What is the rhetorical effect of this allusion?

2. According to Grimké, why are women not "as conspicuous in the Bible as men" (p. 329)?

3. According to Grimké, why are women moved to speak in public on moral issues?

WRITING ANALYTICALLY

1. Grimké clearly has a different idea of "woman's sphere" than that of writers in the first section of Unit Three. Write a paper in which you summarize her views on what women should be and do, supporting your description with evidence from her *Letters*. If you wish, you may agree or disagree with her views.

2. How would Grimké respond to Catharine Beecher's (p. 294) argument that women best perform their duties as citizens by remaining in the home, in relations of "subordination"? Write a paper in the form of a letter from Grimké to Beecher, in which Grimké comments on Beecher's views (and perhaps also on the propriety of Beecher's denunciation of her and her sister for their public abolitionist activity).

3. Consider the negative portraits of female abolitionists presented in Folsom (p. 302) and McCord (p. 307). One of Grimké's rhetorical problems in her *Letters* is to combat such negative images — to appear in a different guise herself and to deny that such images apply to activist women. How does she address this problem? What rhetorical strategies does she employ, and what kind of portrait of activist women (including herself) does she seem to want to create? Write a paper in which you describe and evaluate her strategies. Do you think they work to combat the negative images? Option: In your discussion, compare and contrast Grimké's rhetorical strategies for dealing with negative images of women activists with those of a contemporary feminist whose work you are familiar with.

MARGARET FULLER

"The Wrongs of American Women, the Duty of American Women" (1845)

Margaret Fuller (1810–50) was born in Cambridgeport, Massachusetts. Her father was a prosperous lawyer and important local politician who tried to give his daughter an education equivalent in every way to a young man's of her class. She made a career for herself as an intellectual and person of letters, one of the first American women to do so. In the 1830s she became associated with Transcendentalism, a philosophical movement that emphasized self-reliance and spiritual insights gained from nature. Other members of the Transcendentalist circle were Ralph Waldo Emerson (p. 346) and Henry David Thoreau. Fuller edited the Transcendentalist journal *The Dial* for two years. Meanwhile she supported herself by giving what we would now call adult education classes for women in Boston on topics in literature, philosophy, and politics. In 1844 she moved to New York to work as the first female correspondent for the *New York Tribune*. The paper sent her to Europe in 1846, and she soon became caught up in events leading to uprisings all over Europe in 1848 on behalf of representative government. In Italy, Fuller linked herself to the revolution both by her sympathetic news reports and by her liaison with rebel Giovanni Ossoli, with whom she had a son. Returning home in 1850, she was drowned with her husband and child in a shipwreck.

Margaret Fuller, "The Wrongs of American Women, the Duty of American Women," *New York Tribune*, September 30, 1845, reprinted in *The Essential Margaret Fuller*, ed. Jeffrey Steele (New Brunswick: Rutgers University Press, 1992), 393–400.
    In the notes, JS = Jeffrey Steele.

Although Fuller's fellow Transcendentalists mourned her loss when she died, their later memoirs diminished her reputation by presenting her as foolishly self-important and unpleasantly aggressive. Consequently, her work was neglected until recently when twentieth-century feminists have given it some attention. Her best-known work, *Woman in the Nineteenth Century* (1845), is a long, dense essay examining many aspects of American women's lives from a feminist perspective. Reprinted here is a book review Fuller wrote for the *Tribune* concerning a report by a Mr. Burdett on the condition of working-class women in New York and a "circular" (or appeal for funds) based on recommendations put forward by Catharine Beecher.

THE SAME DAY BROUGHT US A COPY of Mr. Burdett's little book, in which the sufferings and difficulties that beset the large class of women who must earn their subsistence in a city like New York are delineated with so much simplicity, feeling, and exact adherence to the facts — and a printed circular containing proposals for immediate practical adoption of the plan more fully described in a book published some weeks since under the title "The Duty of American Women to Their Country," which was ascribed alternately to Mrs. Stone and Miss Catharine Beecher, but of which we understand both those ladies decline the responsibility.[1] The two matters seemed linked with one another by natural piety. Full acquaintance with the wrong must call forth all manner of inventions for its redress.

The Circular, in showing the vast want that already exists of good means for instructing the children of this nation, especially in the West, states also the belief that among women, as being less immersed in other cares and toils, from the preparation it gives for their task as mothers, and from the necessity in which a great proportion stand of earning a subsistence somehow, at least during the years which precede marriage, if they *do* marry, must the number of teachers wanted be found, which is estimated already at *sixty thousand.*

We cordially sympathize with these views.

Much has been written about Woman's keeping within her sphere, which is defined as the domestic sphere. As a little girl she is to learn the lighter family duties, while she acquires that limited acquaintance with the realm of literature and science that will enable her to superintend the instruction of children in their earliest years. It is not generally proposed that she should be sufficiently instructed and developed to understand the pursuits or aims of her future husband; she is not to be a helpmeet to him, in the way of companionship or counsel, except in the care of his house and children. Her youth is to be passed partly in learning to keep house

---

[1]This review is of Charles Burdett, *Wrongs of American Women. First Series. The Elliott Family; or the Trials of New York Seamstresses* (1845) and of Catharine Beecher, *The Duty of American Women to Their Country* (1845). Lucy Stone (1818–93), prominent American woman suffragist; Catharine Beecher (1800–78), author of *Treatise on Domestic Economy* (1841) and *Letters to Persons Who Are Engaged in Domestic Service* (1842), sister of Harriet Beecher Stowe. — JS

and the use of the needle, partly in the social circle where her manners may be formed, ornamental accomplishments perfected and displayed, and the husband found who shall give her the domestic sphere for which exclusively she is to be prepared.

Were the destiny of Woman thus exactly marked out, did she invariably retain the shelter of a parent's or a guardian's roof till she married, did marriage give her a sure home and protector, were she never liable to be made a widow, or, if so, sure of finding immediate protection from a brother or new husband, so that she might never be forced to stand alone one moment, and were her mind given for this world only, with no faculties capable of eternal growth and infinite improvement, we would still demand for her a far wider and more generous culture than is proposed by those who so anxiously define her sphere. We would demand it that she might not ignorantly or frivolously thwart the designs of her husband, that she might be the respected friend of her sons no less than her daughters, that she might give more refinement, elevation, and attraction to the society which is needed to give the characters of *men* polish and plasticity — no less so than to save them from vicious and sensual habits. But the most fastidious critic on the departure of Woman from her sphere, can scarcely fail to see at present that a vast proportion of the sex, if not the better half, do not, CANNOT have this domestic sphere. Thousands and scores of thousands in this country no less than in Europe are obliged to maintain themselves alone. Far greater numbers divide with their husbands the care of earning a support for the family. In England, now, the progress of society has reached so admirable a pitch that the position of the sexes is frequently reversed, and the husband is obliged to stay at home and "mind the house and bairns" while the wife goes forth to the employment she alone can secure.

We readily admit that the picture of this is most painful — that Nature made entirely an opposite distribution of functions between the sexes. We believe the natural order to be the best, and that, if it could be followed in an enlightened spirit, it would bring to Woman all she wants, no less for her immortal than her mortal destiny. We are not surprised that men, who do not look deeply or carefully at causes or tendencies, should be led by disgust at the hardened, hackneyed characters which the present state of things too often produces in women to such conclusions as they are. We, no more than they, delight in the picture of the poor woman digging in the mines in her husband's clothes. We, no more than they, delight to hear their voices shrilly raised in the market-place, whether of apples or celebrity. But we see that at present they must do as they do for bread. Hundreds and thousands must step out of that hallowed domestic sphere, with no choice but to work or steal, or belong to men, not as wives, but as the wretched slaves of sensuality.

And this transition state, with all its revolting features, indicates, we do believe, the approach of a nobler era than the world has yet known. We trust that by the stress and emergencies of the present and coming time, the minds of women will be formed to more reflection and higher purposes than heretofore — their latent powers developed, their characters strengthened and eventually beautified and harmonized. Should the state of society then be such that each may remain, as Nature seems to have intended, the tutelary genius of a home, while men manage the outdoor business of life, both may be done with a wisdom, a mutual understanding and respect unknown at present. Men will be no less the gainers by this than women, finding in pure and more religious marriages the joys of friendship and love combined — in their mothers and daughters better instruction, sweeter and nobler companionship, and in society at large an excitement to their finer powers and feelings unknown at present except in the region of the fine arts.

Blest be the generous, the wise among them who seek to forward hopes like these, instead of struggling against the fiat of Providence and the march of Fate to bind down rushing Life to the standard of the Past. Such efforts are vain, but those who make them are unhappy and unwise.

It is not, however, to such that we address ourselves, but to those who seek to make the best of things as they are, while they also strive to make them better. Such persons will have seen enough of the state of things in London, Paris, New York, and manufacturing regions every where, to feel that there is an imperative necessity for opening more avenues of employment to women, and fitting them better to enter them, rather than keeping them back. Women have invaded many of the trades and some of the professions. Sewing, to the present killing extent, they cannot long bear. Factories seem likely to afford them permanent employment. In the culture of fruit, flowers, and vegetables, even in the sale of them, we rejoice to see them engaged. In domestic service they will be aided, but can never be supplanted, by machinery. As much room as there is here for woman's mind and woman's labor will always be filled. A few have usurped the martial province, but these must always be few; the nature of woman is opposed to war. It is natural enough to see "Female Physicians," and we believe that the lace cap and workbag are as much at home here as the wig and gold-headed cane. In the priesthood they have from all time shared more or less — in many eras more than at the present. We believe there has been no female lawyer, and probably will be none. The pen, many of the fine arts they have made their own, and, in the more refined countries of the world, as writers, as musicians, as painters, as actors, women occupy as advantageous ground as men. Writing and music may be esteemed professions for them more than any other.

But there are two others where the demand must invariably be immense, and for which they are naturally better fitted than men, for which we should like to see them better prepared and better rewarded than they are. These are the profession of nurse to the sick and of teacher. The first of these professions we have warmly desired to see dignified. It is a noble one, now most unjustly regarded in the light of menial service. It is one which no menial, no servile nature can fitly occupy. We were rejoiced when an intelligent lady of Massachusetts made the refined heroine of a little romance select that calling. This lady (Mrs. George Lee) has looked on society with unusual largeness of spirit and healthiness of temper. She is well acquainted with the world of conventions, but sees beneath it the world of nature. She is a generous writer and unpretending, as the generous are wont to be. We do not recall the name of the tale, but the circumstance above mentioned marks its temper. We hope to see the time when the refined and cultivated will choose this profession and learn it, not only through experience under the direction of the doctor, but by acquainting themselves with the laws of matter and of mind, so that all they do shall be intelligently done, and afford them the means of developing intelligence as well as the nobler, tenderer feelings of humanity; for even the last part of the benefit they cannot receive if their work be done in a selfish or mercenary spirit.

The other profession is that of teacher, for which women are particularly adapted by their nature, superiority in tact, quickness of sympathy, gentleness, patience, and a clear and animated manner in narration or description. To form a good teacher should be added to this sincere modesty combined with firmness, liberal views with a power and will to liberalize them still further, a good method and habits of exact and thorough investigation. In the two last requisites women are generally deficient, but there are now many shining examples to prove that if they are immethodical and superficial as teachers it is because it is the custom so to teach them, and that when aware of these faults they can and will correct them.

The profession is of itself an excellent one for the improvement of the teacher during that interim between youth and maturity when the mind needs testing, tempering, and to review and rearrange the knowledge it has acquired. The natural method of doing this for one's self is to attempt teaching others; those years also are the best of the practical teacher. The teacher should be near the pupil both in years and feelings — no oracle, but the elder brother or sister of the pupil. More experience and years form the lecturer and the director of studies, but injure the powers as to familiar teaching.

These are just the years of leisure in the lives even of those women who are to enter the domestic sphere, and this calling most of all compatible with a constant progress as to qualifications for that.

Viewing the matter thus it may well be seen that we should hail with joy the assurance that sixty thousand *female* teachers are wanted, and more likely to be, and that a plan is projected which looks wise, liberal and generous, to afford the means of those whose hearts answer to this high calling obeying their dictates.

The plan is to have Cincinnati for a central point, where teachers shall be for a short time received, examined, and prepared for their duties. By mutual agreement and cooperation of the various sects funds are to be raised and teachers provided according to the wants and tendencies of the various locations now destitute. What is to be done for them centrally, is for suitable persons to examine into their various kinds of fitness, communicate some general views whose value has been tested, and counsel adapted to the difficulties and advantages of their new positions. The

Central Committee are to have the charge of raising funds and finding teachers and places where teachers are wanted.

The passage of thoughts, teachers, and funds will be from East to West, the course of sunlight upon this earth.

The plan is offered as the most extensive and pliant means of doing a good and preventing ill to this nation, by means of a national education, whose normal school shall have an invariable object in the search after truth and the diffusion of the means of knowledge, while its form shall be plastic according to the wants of the time. This normal school promises to have good effects, for it proposes worthy aims through simple means, and the motive for its formation and support seems to be disinterested philanthropy.

It promises to eschew the bitter spirit of sectarianism and proselytism, else we, for one party, could have nothing to do with it. Men, no doubt, have been oftentimes kept from absolute famine by the wheat with which such tares are mingled; but we believe the time is come when a purer and more generous food is to be offered to the people at large. We believe the aim of all education to be [to] rouse the mind to action, show it the means of discipline and of information; then leave it free, with God, Conscience, and the love of Truth for its guardians and teachers. Wo be to those who sacrifice these aims of universal and eternal value to the propagation of a set of opinions. But on this subject we can accept such doctrine as is offered by Rev. Calvin Stowe,[2] one of the committee, in the following passage:

> "In judicious practice, I am persuaded there will seldom be any very great difficulty, especially if there be excited in the community anything like a whole-hearted honesty and enlightened sincerity in the cause of public instruction.
>
> "It is all right for people to suit their own taste and convictions in respect to sect; and by fair means and at proper times to teach their children and those under their influence to prefer the denominations which they prefer; but farther than this no one has any right to go. It is all wrong to hazard the well being of the soul, to jeopardize great public interests for the sake of advancing the interests of a sect. People must learn to practice some self-denial, on Christian principles, in respect to their denominational preferences, as well as in respect to other things, before pure Religion can ever gain a complete victory over every form of human selfishness."

The persons who propose themselves to the examination and instruction of the teachers at Cincinnati, till the plan shall be sufficiently under weigh to provide regularly for the office, are Mrs. Stowe[3] and Miss Catharine Beecher, ladies well known to fame, as possessing unusual qualifications for the task.

[2]Rev. Calvin Ellis Stowe (1802–86), husband of Harriet Beecher Stowe, was influential in founding the College of Teachers in Cincinnati (1833). — JS

[3]The novelist Harriet Beecher Stowe (1811–96) lived in Cincinnati from 1833 to 1850. — JS

As to finding abundance of teachers, who that reads this little book of Mr. Burdett's, or the account of the compensation of female labor in New York, and the hopeless, comfortless, useless, pernicious lives those who have even the advantage of getting work must live with the sufferings and almost inevitable degradation to which those who cannot are exposed, but must long to snatch such as are capable of this better profession, and among the multitude there must be many who are or could be made so, from their present toils and make them free and the means of freedom and growth to others.

To many books on such subjects, among others to "Woman in the Nineteenth Century," the objection has been made that they exhibit ills without specifying any practical means for their remedy. The writer of the last named essay does indeed think that it contains one great rule which, if laid to heart, would prove a practical remedy for many ills, and of such daily and hourly efficacy in the conduct of life that any extensive observance of it for a single year would perceptibly raise the tone of thought, feeling, and conduct throughout the civilized world. But to those who ask not only such a principle, but an external method for immediate use, we say, here is one proposed that looks noble and promising, the proposers offer themselves to the work with heart and hand, with time and purse: Go ye and do likewise.

Those who wish details as to this plan, will find them in the "Duty of American Women to Their Country," published by Harper & Brothers, Cliff-st. The publishers may, probably, be able to furnish also the Circular to which we have referred. At a leisure day we shall offer some suggestions and remarks as to the methods and objects there proposed.

READING CRITICALLY

1. What reasons does Fuller give for rejecting the idea that women should be educated only to perform within a narrow domestic sphere?

2. Fuller briefly describes a "nobler era" of relations between the sexes that she hopes is soon to be (p. 333–34). Summarize her vision.

3. Fuller reviews various professions that women have filled or may fill and especially recommends the work of teachers and nurses. According to her, why are women well suited to be teachers?

4. Fuller suggests that her own book *Woman in the Nineteenth Century* (then just published) contains "one great rule" that would serve as a guide for the remedy of many social ills (p. 337). She doesn't say what this rule is. What do you think it is?

WRITING ANALYTICALLY

1. In this essay, Fuller clearly sees herself as advancing a project on behalf of women's rights. Would you call her a feminist by your own definition of the term? Write a review of this essay for your local campus newspaper or women's newsletter, using the essay as the basis for your recommendation that contemporary feminists should, or should not, be interested in Fuller's work.

2. Fuller appears to give full support in this essay to the ideas of Catharine Beecher (p. 294), but the two writers also seem to disagree in some areas, such as in their ideas of what women should do with their education. To compare and contrast their views, write a letter from Beecher to Fuller commenting on Fuller's review of her work.

3. Fuller clearly opposes the views of Louisa Cheves McCord (p. 307) and the Jonathan F. Stearns (p. 299). Write an essay in which you compare and contrast the views of Fuller and either Stearns or McCord. Alternative: Write a letter from McCord or Stearns to Fuller, commenting on her review.

FREDERICK DOUGLASS

Editorials on Women's Rights
(July 28, 1848 and October 30, 1851)

Frederick Douglass (1818–95) né Frederick Bailey, was born a slave in Maryland; he later suspected that his father was the white plantation overseer. A European American woman who owned him taught him his letters, and after her husband forbade her to instruct him any further, at great risk he learned to read and write. Douglass escaped slavery in 1838 with the help of a free African American woman, Anna Murray, whom he married once they were in the North. Douglass renamed himself to thwart pursuit, ironically choosing the name of a hero in a popular historical novel by Sir Walter Scott.

In 1841, Douglass spoke for the first time at an antislavery meeting, denouncing the evils that he had experienced firsthand. He quickly became not only one of the most powerful abolitionist speakers but also one of the most important African American intellectuals of the nineteenth century. (For an example of his antislavery oratory, see Unit Two, p. 208.) The first edition of his autobiography, published in 1845, became an instant bestseller, and subsequent versions (1855, 1892) were also well received. In 1847 Douglass began to publish his own abolitionist newspaper, which went under various titles such as *The North Star, The Watch-Tower,* and *Frederick Douglass' Paper.* Douglass endorsed other reform causes besides abolition and was an early supporter of women's rights, advertising the 1848 Seneca Falls convention in his paper and sitting on the dais at the meeting. After the Civil War, Douglass was active in the national Republican Party (known then as the antislavery party of Abraham Lincoln), held several important posts, and continued his leadership in the African American community.

Frederick Douglass, "The Rights of Women," *The North Star,* July 28, 1848, "Woman's Rights Convention at Worcester, Mass.," *Frederick Douglass' Paper,* October 30, 1851, reprinted in *Frederick Douglass on Women's Rights,* ed. Philip Foner (Westport, Conn.: Greenwood, 1976), 49–51, 55.
In the notes, EDS. = Patricia Bizzell and Bruce Herzberg.

Reprinted here are Douglass's editorials on the 1848 Seneca Falls convention (see the convention's "Declaration of Sentiments and Resolutions" on p. 387) and on the 1851 woman's rights convention at Worcester, Massachusetts, which was denounced by Louisa Cheves McCord (p. 307).

THE RIGHTS OF WOMEN

ONE OF THE MOST INTERESTING EVENTS of the past week, was the holding of what is technically styled a Woman's Rights Convention at Seneca Falls. The speaking, addresses, and resolutions of this extraordinary meeting was wholly conducted by women; and although they evidently felt themselves in a novel position, it is but simple justice to say that their whole proceedings were characterized by marked ability and dignity. No one present, we think, however much he might be disposed to differ from the views advanced by the leading speakers on that occasion, will fail to give them credit for brilliant talents and excellent dispositions. In this meeting, as in other deliberative assemblies, there were frequent differences of opinion and animated discussion; but in no case was there the slightest absence of good feeling and decorum. Several interesting documents setting forth the rights as well as the grievances of women were read. Among these was a Declaration of Sentiments, to be regarded as the basis of a grand movement for attaining the civil, social, political, and religious rights of women. We should not do justice to our own convictions, or to the excellent persons connected with this infant movement, if we did not in this connection offer a few remarks on the general subject which the Convention met to consider and the objects they seek to attain. In doing so, we are not insensible that the bare mention of this truly important subject in any other than terms of contemptuous ridicule and scornful disfavor, is likely to excite against us the fury of bigotry and the folly of prejudice. A discussion of the rights of animals would be regarded with far more complacency by many of what are called the "wise" and the "good" of our land, than would a discussion of the rights of women. It is, in their estimation to be guilty of evil thoughts, to think that woman is entitled to equal rights with man. Many who have at last made the discovery that the negroes have some rights as well as other members of the human family, have yet to be convinced that women are entitled to any. Eight years ago a number of persons of this description actually abandoned the antislavery cause, lest by giving their influence in that direction they might possibly be giving countenance to the dangerous heresy that woman, in respect to rights, stands on an equal footing with man.[1] In the judgment of such persons the American slave system, with all its concomitant horrors, is less to be de-

---

[1]Douglass is referring to the 1840 split in the ranks of the American Anti-Slavery Society in the wake of the Grimké controversy, over what women's roles in the organization should be (see the introduction, p. 291). — EDS.

plored than this "wicked" idea. It is perhaps needless to say, that we cherish little sympathy for such sentiments or respect for such prejudices. Standing as we do up on the watch-tower of human freedom, we cannot be deterred from an expression of our approbation of any movement, however humble, to improve and elevate the character of any members of the human family. While it is impossible for us to go into this subject at length, and dispose of the various objections which are often urged against such a doctrine as that of female equality, we are free to say that in respect to political rights, we hold woman to be justly entitled to all we claim for man. We go farther, and express our conviction that all political rights which it is expedient for man to exercise, it is equally so for woman. All that distinguishes man as an intelligent and accountable being, is equally true of woman, and if that government only is just which governs by the free consent of the governed, there can be no reason in the world for denying to woman the exercise of the elective franchise, or a hand in making and administering the laws of the land. Our doctrine is that "right is of no sex." We therefore bid the women engaged in this movement our humble God-speed.

WOMAN'S RIGHTS CONVENTION AT WORCESTER, MASS.

Absorbed as we are in these perilous times, with the great work of unchaining the American bondman, and assisting the hapless and hunted fugitive in his flight from his merciless pursuers to a place of safety, we have little time to consider the inequalities, wrongs and hardships endured by woman. Our silence, however, must not be set down either to indifference or to a want of independence. In our eyes, the rights of woman and the rights of man are identical — We ask no rights, we advocate no rights for ourselves, which we would not ask and advocate for woman. Whatever may be said as to a division of duties and avocations, the rights of man and the rights of woman are one and inseparable, and stand upon the same indestructible basis. If, for the well-being and happiness of man, it is necessary that he should hold property, have a voice in making the laws which he is expected to obey, be stimulated by his participation in government to cultivate his mental faculties, with a view to an honorable fulfillment of his social obligations, precisely the same may be said of woman.

We advocate woman's rights, not because she is an angel, but because she is a woman, having the same wants, and being exposed to the same evils as man.

Whatever is necessary to protect him, is necessary to protect her. Holding these views, and being profoundly desirous that they should universally prevail, we rejoice at every indication of progress in their dissemination.

READING CRITICALLY

The Rights of Women

1. What is the first point that Douglass makes about the Seneca Falls convention?

2. How does Douglass use abolitionism to support the cause of women's rights?

3. What rights for women does Douglass claim at the end of this editorial?

Woman's Rights Convention at Worcester, Mass.

1. According to Douglass, why hasn't he done much recently to support the cause of women's rights?

2. What rights for women does Douglass claim here?

WRITING ANALYTICALLY

1. Douglass is in a sensitive rhetorical position. His first commitment is to abolitionism and the rights of African Americans. He also wants to support rights for all women, but, presumably, not at the expense of his first commitment. Write an essay analyzing and evaluating Douglass's rhetorical strategies for handling this delicate situation. Alternative: Write a letter as if you were a nineteenth-century women's rights activist to another activist, commenting on how well you think Douglass is supporting your cause and balancing this support with his primary support for abolitionism. Or write a letter as if you were a nineteenth-century abolitionist to another abolitionist, commenting on how well you think Douglass is supporting your cause and balancing this support with his additional support for women's rights. In either case, defend the position you take in your letter with references to specific passages in Douglass's editorials.

2. In his editorial on the Worcester convention, Douglass could almost seem to be setting aside the question of what woman's sphere should be when he dismisses discussion of "a division of duties and avocations" between men and women (p. 340). In neither of these editorials does he explicitly give a full picture of his views on woman's sphere. Nevertheless, you may infer from what he does say that he has an idea of what woman's sphere should be. Write a paper in which you argue for what you take to be Douglass's particular view of woman's sphere, basing your argument on evidence from these two editorials. If you wish, you may also comment on the extent to which Douglass fits your own definition of "feminist."

3. Imagine either that Albert A. Folsom (p. 302) has read Douglass's editorial "The Rights of Women" or that Louisa Cheves McCord (p. 307) has read the editorial "Woman's Rights Convention" (as they may well have done), and write a "letter to the editor" that he or she might have sent Douglass in reply.

SOJOURNER TRUTH,
RECORDED BY FRANCES D. GAGE

"A'n't I a Woman?" (1851)

Sojourner Truth (c. 1797–1883), originally named Isabella, was born to slave parents held by a family in a Dutch-speaking community of upstate New York. As an adult, she was owned by John Dumont, as were her husband and five children. When Dumont reneged on a promise to free her, Truth left his farm with her youngest child and took refuge with neighbors, the Van Wagenen family, who bought her and the baby out of slavery. Meanwhile, her five-year-old son had been sold into Alabama by Dumont. This sale was illegal because the boy, although still an indentured servant whose labor contract could be sold, had been freed from slavery by New York's laws for gradual emancipation, which also provided that a person in his situation could not be sent out of state. Illiterate and impoverished as she was, Truth nevertheless took Dumont to court to recover the boy and succeeded.

In 1829 Truth moved to New York City and found work as a domestic servant. She became active in evangelical Christian circles and in 1843 had a vision in which a divine voice commanded her to go forth and preach against slavery and other social ills. She gave herself the name Sojourner Truth to represent her mission of traveling exhortation. Throughout the 1840s and 1850s Truth was a frequent speaker at abolitionist and women's rights conventions in the East and Midwest, sharing the platform with such notables as Frederick Douglass (p. 338). During the Civil War, she helped gather supplies for African American soldiers, and after the war she worked as an adviser to emancipated slaves through the National Freedman's Relief Association. A national figure in the latter part of her life, Sojourner Truth continued to speak out for African American and women's rights.

Sojourner Truth was a powerful speaker, tall and commanding, with a ringing voice. Her fame came mainly from the effect of her oral performances; because of her lack of education, her literacy skills were such that she was able to leave few written records of her ideas (her 1850 autobiography was dictated to Olive Gilbert, a white abolitionist friend). In studying her work, then, we are faced with the difficulty of having to rely on transcriptions of her performances made by members of her audience.

A case in point is her famous speech, now known as "A'n't I a Woman?," delivered at an 1851 woman's rights convention in Akron, Ohio. The best-known version of this speech is the one reprinted here, in an account published twelve years after the fact by white abolitionist and women's rights activist Frances D. Gage, who presided at the Akron meeting. In spite of this version's renown, especially among twentieth-century feminists, contempo-

Sojourner Truth, recorded by Frances D. Gage, "A'n't I a Woman?," in *History of Woman Suffrage,* ed. Elizabeth Cady Stanton, Susan B. Anthony, and Matilda Joslyn Gage, vol. 1, 2nd ed. (1889; reprint, New York: Source Book Press, 1970), 115–17.

In the notes, EDS. = Patricia Bizzell and Bruce Herzberg

rary scholars have faulted it on a number of grounds. For example, the broad southern dialect Gage ascribes to Truth is unlikely for a person whose first language was Dutch and who lived her whole life in the North. Truth did not have thirteen children and saw only one sold away from her, whom she recovered. The famous refrain "A'n't I a Woman?" may even have been an invention of Gage's, who was an amateur poet.

Rendering Gage's version of the speech into standard English, as some modern editors have done, fails to do justice to Sojourner Truth's unique, pithy vernacular style. Some scholars recommend a newspaper account of the speech published shortly after the Akron convention. Though it is more accurate than Gage's version in representing Truth's ideas (the discrepancies between the two versions are minor), as a paraphrase it presents the same problem with respect to style. Gage at least has made the attempt, however faulty, to capture the immediate, powerful effect of Truth's oral performances. Sojourner Truth herself must have felt that Gage represented her well, for she chose Gage's version of her Akron speech for inclusion in a later edition of her autobiography (1875).

THE LEADERS OF THE MOVEMENT TREMBLED on seeing a tall, gaunt black woman in a gray dress and white turban, surmounted with an uncouth sun-bonnet, march deliberately into the church, walk with the air of a queen up the aisle, and take her seat upon the pulpit steps. A buzz of disapprobation was heard all over the house, and there fell on the listening ear, "An abolition affair!" "Woman's rights and niggers!" "I told you so!" "Go it, darkey!"

I chanced on that occasion to wear my first laurels in public life as president of the meeting. At my request order was restored, and the business of the Convention went on. Morning, afternoon, and evening exercises came and went. Through all these sessions old Sojourner, quiet and reticent as the "Lybian Statue,"[1] sat crouched against the wall on the corner of the pulpit stairs, her sun-bonnet shading her eyes, her elbows on her knees, her chin resting upon her broad, hard palms. At intermission she was busy selling the "Life of Sojourner Truth," a narrative of her own strange and adventurous life. Again and again, timorous and trembling ones came to me and said with earnestness, "Don't let her speak, Mrs. Gage, it will ruin us. Every newspaper in the land will have our cause mixed up with abolition and niggers, and we shall be utterly denounced." My only answer was, "We shall see when the time comes."

The second day the work waxed warm. Methodist, Baptist, Episcopal, Presbyterian, and Universalist ministers came in to hear and discuss the resolutions presented. One claimed superior rights and privileges for man, on the ground of "superior intellect"; another, because of the "manhood

---

[1]The "Lybian Statue" was a sculpture by American artist William Wetmore Story (1819–95), entitled *The Libyan Sybil*. It depicts a beautiful, powerfully built African woman, seated in a contemplative pose and holding a scroll. It was often invoked in descriptions of Sojourner Truth. — EDS.

of Christ; if God had desired the equality of woman, He would have given some token of His will through the birth, life, and death of the Savior." Another gave us a theological view of the "sin of our first mother."[2]

There were very few women in those days who dared to "speak in meeting"; and the august teachers of the people were seemingly getting the better of us, while the boys in the galleries, and the sneerers among the pews, were hugely enjoying the discomfiture, as they supposed, of the "strong-minded." Some of the tender-skinned friends were on the point of losing dignity, and the atmosphere betokened a storm. When, slowly from her seat in the corner rose Sojourner Truth, who, till now, had scarcely lifted her head. "Don't let her speak!" gasped half a dozen in my ear. She moved slowly and solemnly to the front, laid her old bonnet at her feet, and turned her great speaking eyes to me. There was a hissing sound of disapprobation above and below. I rose and announced "Sojourner Truth," and begged the audience to keep silence for a few moments.

The tumult subsided at once, and every eye was fixed on this almost Amazon form, which stood nearly six feet high, head erect, and eyes piercing the upper air like one in a dream. At her first word there was a profound hush. She spoke in deep tones, which, though not loud, reached every ear in the house, and away through the throng at the doors and windows.

"Wall, chilern, whar dar is so much racket dar must be somethin' out o' kilter. I tink dat 'twixt de niggers of de Souf and de womin at de Norf, all talkin' 'bout rights, de white men will be in a fix pretty soon. But what's all dis here talkin' 'bout?

"Dat man ober dar say dat womin needs to be helped into carriages, and lifted ober ditches, and to hab de best place everywhar. Nobody eber helps me into carriages, or ober mud-puddles, or gibs me any best place!" And raising herself to her full height, and her voice to a pitch like rolling thunder, she asked, "And a'n't I a woman? Look at me! Look at my arm! (and she bared her right arm to the shoulder, showing her tremendous muscular power). I have ploughed, and planted, and gathered into barns, and no man could head me! And a'n't I a woman? I could work as much and eat as much as a man — when I could get it — and bear de lash as well! And a'n't I a woman? I have borne thirteen chilern, and seen 'em mos' all sold off to slavery, and when I cried out with my mother's grief, none but Jesus heard me! And a'n't I a woman?

"Den dey talks 'bout dis ting in de head; what dis dey call it?" ("Intellect," whispered some one near.) "Dat's it, honey. What's dat got to do wid womin's rights or nigger's rights? If my cup won't hold but a pint, and yourn holds a quart, wouldn't ye be mean not to let me have my little half-measure full?" And she pointed her significant finger, and sent a keen glance at the minister who had made the argument. The cheering was long and loud.

"Den dat little man in black dar, he say women can't have as much rights as men 'cause Christ wan't a woman! Whar did your Christ come

---

[2]Eve, whose "sin" was eating the forbidden fruit in the Garden of Eden (Genesis 3). — EDS.

from?" Rolling thunder couldn't have stilled that crowd, as did those deep, wonderful tones, as she stood there with outstretched arms and eyes of fire. Raising her voice still louder, she repeated, "Whar did your Christ come from? From God and a woman! Man had nothin' to do wid Him." Oh, what a rebuke that was to that little man.

Turning again to another objector, she took up the defense of Mother Eve. I can not follow her through it all. It was pointed, and witty, and solemn; eliciting at almost every sentence deafening applause; and she ended by asserting: "If de fust woman God every made was strong enough to turn de world upside down all alone, dese women togedder (and she glanced her eye over the platform) ought to be able to turn it back, and get it right side up again! And now dey is asking to do it, de men better let 'em." Long-continued cheering greeted this. " 'Bleeged[3] to ye for hearin' on me, and now ole Sojourner han't got nothin' more to say."

Amid roars of applause, she returned to her corner, leaving more than one of us with streaming eyes, and hearts beating with gratitude. She had taken us up in her strong arms and carried us safely over the slough of difficulty turning the whole tide in our favor. I have never in my life seen anything like the magical influence that subdued the mobbish spirit of the day, and turned the sneers and jeers of an excited crowd into notes of respect and admiration. Hundreds rushed up to shake hands with her, and congratulate the glorious old mother, and bid her Godspeed on her mission of "testifyin' agin concerning the wickedness of this 'ere people."

READING CRITICALLY

1. In her address, how does Sojourner Truth refute the argument that women need to be protected by being confined to the domestic sphere?

2. How does Sojourner Truth refute the argument that women do not deserve equal rights with men because their intellectual abilities are not equal to men's?

3. How does Frances Gage present Sojourner Truth as she dramatizes the scene of the convention? What does Gage emphasize? Make a list, illustrated with specific passages in the text.

WRITING ANALYTICALLY

1. Write a paper in which you explain how Sojourner Truth connects the causes of women's rights and abolition. Cite specific passages in her address to support your explanation. Option: You may describe the balance you see in her thinking between these two issues. Do you think she really does treat them as equal, or does she appear to favor one over the other?

2. Many scholars have been disturbed by the way Gage presents Sojourner Truth in this memoir. These scholars claim that Gage, while praising her, treats Truth as

---

[3]Obliged. — EDS.

an exotic oddity, not a "serious" activist like herself, and that she patronizes her in a racist fashion. Write a paper in which you argue for your own idea of how Gage represents Sojourner Truth, indicating the extent to which you agree or disagree with the scholars (your response to reading question 3 can help you here).

3. Write a paper in which you compare and contrast both the views of Frederick Douglass (p. 338) and of Sojourner Truth on African American rights and women's rights, and their rhetorical strategies for promoting those views. Option: You may respond to this question by writing a dialogue between Douglass and Truth, in which *what* they say presents their views and *how* they say it illustrates their rhetorical strategies.

RALPH WALDO EMERSON

"Woman" (1855)

Ralph Waldo Emerson (1803–82) was born in Boston to an eminently respectable Puritan family. As a young man, he ran a school for girls and then entered Harvard Divinity School to prepare to become a Unitarian minister. In 1832, however, he resigned his pastorate at the prestigious Second Church of Boston because of religious doubts. Settling in Concord, Massachusetts, he became the leader of the Transcendentalist movement, which emphasized social self-reliance and nonsectarian spiritual insights gained from nature. The Transcendentalists, including Emerson's friends Henry David Thoreau and Margaret Fuller (p. 331), were most noted for their thoughtful essays on ethical issues pertaining to education, adult spiritual development, and civic responsibility. They are widely regarded as establishing a uniquely American type of philosophy, put forward most notably in Emerson's essays. His important publications include *Nature* (1836), *The American Scholar* (1837), *Essays* (1841), and *Representative Men* (1850); these works brought him an international reputation that persisted even as he entered a long period of mental decline in the 1870s.

Emerson was not a political activist, although he nominally supported both abolitionism and women's rights. He was both an early supporter and a posthumous detractor of Margaret Fuller. Reprinted here is an address he gave at a Boston woman's rights convention in 1855.

AMONG THOSE MOVEMENTS WHICH SEEM TO BE, now and then, endemic in the public mind, — perhaps we should say, sporadic, — rather than the single inspiration of one mind, is that which has urged on society the ben-

Ralph Waldo Emerson, "Woman," in *Miscellanies*, vol. 11 of *The Works of Ralph Waldo Emerson*, ed. James Elliot Cabot (Boston: Houghton Mifflin, 1883), 337–56.

In the notes, EDS. = Patricia Bizzell and Bruce Herzberg.

efits of action having for its object a benefit to the position of Woman. And none is more seriously interesting to every healthful and thoughtful mind.

In that race which is now predominant over all the other races of men,[1] it was a cherished belief that women had an oracular nature. They are more delicate than men, — delicate as iodine to light,[2] — and thus more impressionable. They are the best index of the coming hour. I share this belief. I think their words are to be weighed; but it is their inconsiderate word, — according to the rule, "take their first advice, not their second": as Coleridge[3] was wont to apply to a lady for her judgment in questions of taste, and accept it; but when she added — "I think so, because" — "Pardon me, madam," he said, "leave me to find out the reasons for myself." In this sense, as more delicate mercuries of the imponderable and immaterial influences, what they say and think is the shadow of coming events. Their very dolls are indicative. Among our Norse ancestors, Frigga was worshipped as the goddess of women. "Weirdes all," said the Edda,[4] "Frigga knoweth, though she telleth them never." That is to say, all wisdoms Woman knows; though she takes them for granted, and does not explain them as discoveries, like the understanding of man. Men remark figure: women always catch the expression. They inspire by a look, and pass with us not so much by what they say or do, as by their presence. They learn so fast and convey the result so fast as to outrun the logic of their slow brother and make his acquisitions poor. 'Tis their mood and tone that is important. Does their mind misgive them, or are they firm and cheerful? 'Tis a true report that things are going ill or well. And any remarkable opinion or movement shared by woman will be the first sign of revolution.

Plato said, Women are the same as men in faculty, only less in degree. But the general voice of mankind has agreed that they have their own strength; that women are strong by sentiment; that the same mental height which their husbands attain by toil, they attain by sympathy with their husbands. Man is the will, and Woman the sentiment. In this ship of humanity, Will is the rudder, and Sentiment the sail: when Woman affects to steer, the rudder is only a masked sail. When women engage in any art or trade, it is usually as a resource, not as a primary object. The life of the affections is primary to them, so that there is usually no employment or career which they will not with their own applause and that of society quit for a suitable marriage. And they give entirely to their affections, set their whole fortune on the die,[5] lose themselves eagerly in

---

[1]The "predominant" race that Emerson refers to is what was commonly called the Anglo-Saxon — a term not as broad as "Caucasian," as tending to exclude the peoples of southern Europe and the Mediterranean. — EDS.

[2]The chemical iodine oxidizes rapidly when exposed to light and loses its potency as an antiseptic. — EDS.

[3]Samuel Taylor Coleridge (1772–1834) was an English poet. — EDS.

[4]The *Poetic Edda* is a collection of Old Norse myths, most of which were composed from c. 800 to c. 1200. — EDS.

[5]The roll of the die; Emerson imagines women gambling their entire happiness on the success of their marriage, a gamble he admires. — EDS.

the glory of their husbands and children. Man stands astonished at a magnanimity he cannot pretend to. Mrs. Lucy Hutchinson, one of the heroines of the English Commonwealth, who wrote the life of her husband, the Governor of Nottingham, says, "If he esteemed her at a higher rate than she in herself could have deserved, he was the author of that virtue he doted on, while she only reflected his own glories upon him. All that she was, was *him,* while he was hers, and all that she is now, at best, but his pale shade."

As for Plato's opinion, it is true that, up to recent times, in no art or science, not in painting, poetry, or music, have they produced a masterpiece. Till the new education and larger opportunities of very modern times, this position, with the fewest possible exceptions, has always been true. Sappho, to be sure, in the Olympic Games, gained the crown over Pindar.[6] But, in general, no mastery in either of the fine arts — which should, one would say, be the arts of women — has yet been obtained by them, equal to the mastery of men in the same. The part they play in education, in the care of the young and the tuition of older children, is their organic office in the world. So much sympathy as they have, makes them inestimable as the mediators between those who have knowledge and those who want it: besides, their fine organization, their taste, and love of details, makes the knowledge they give better in their hands.

But there is an art which is better than painting, poetry, music, or architecture, — better than botany, geology, or any science; namely, Conversation. Wise, cultivated, genial conversation is the last flower of civilization and the best result which life has to offer us, — a cup for gods, which has no repentance. Conversation is our account of ourselves. All we have, all we can, all we know, is brought into play, and as the reproduction, in finer form, of all our havings.

Women are, by this and their social influence, the civilizers of mankind. What is civilization? I answer, the power of good women. It was Burns's[7] remark when he first came to Edinburgh that between the men of rustic life and the polite world he observed little difference; that in the former, though unpolished by fashion and unenlightened by science, he had found much observation and much intelligence; but a refined and accomplished woman was a being almost new to him, and of which he had formed a very inadequate idea. "I like women," said a clear-headed man of the world, "they are so finished." They finish society, manners, language. Form and ceremony are their realm. They embellish trifles. All these ceremonies that hedge our life around are not to be despised, and when we have become habituated to them cannot be dispensed with. No woman can despise them with impunity. Their genius delights in ceremonies, in forms, in decorating life with manners, with proprieties, order and grace. They are, in their nature, more relative; the circumstance must always be

---

[6]Sappho, a woman poet of ancient Greece, won a poetry prize over the male poet Pindar. — EDS.

[7]Robert Burns (1759–96) was a Scottish poet. — EDS.

fit; out of place they lose half their weight, out of place they are disfranchised. Position, Wren[8] said, is essential to the perfecting of beauty; — a fine building is lost in a dark lane; a statue should stand in the air; much more true is it of woman.

We commonly say that easy circumstances[9] seem somehow necessary to the finish of the female character: but then it is to be remembered that they create these with all their might. They are always making that civilization which they require; that state of art, of decoration, that ornamental life in which they best appear.

The spiritual force of man is as much shown in taste, in his fancy and imagination — attaching deep meanings to things and to arbitrary inventions of no real value, — as in his perception of truth. He is as much raised above the beast by this creative faculty as by any other. The horse and ox use no delays; they run to the river when thirsty, to the corn when hungry, and say no thanks but fight down whatever opposes their appetite. But man invents and adorns all he does with delays and degrees, paints it all over with forms, to please himself better; he invented majesty and the etiquette of courts and drawing-rooms; architecture, curtains, dress, all luxuries and adornments, and the elegance of privacy, to increase the joys of society. He invented marriage; and surrounded by religion, by comeliness, by all manner of dignities and renunciations, the union of the sexes.

And how should we better measure the gulf between the best intercourse of men in old Athens, in London, or in our American capitals, — between this and the hedgehog existence of diggers of worms, and the eaters of clay and offal, — than by signalizing just this department of taste or comeliness? Herein woman is the prime genius and ordainer. There is no grace that is taught by the dancing-master, no style adopted into the etiquette of courts, but was first the whim and mere action of some brilliant woman, who charmed beholders by this new expression, and made it remembered and copied. And I think they should magnify their ritual of manners. Society, conversation, decorum, flowers, dances, colors, forms, are their homes and attendants. They should be found in fit surroundings — with fair approaches, with agreeable architecture, and with all advantages which the means of man collect: —

> The far-fetched diamond finds it home
> Flashing and smouldering in her hair.
> For her the seas their pearls reveal,
> Art and strange lands her pomp supply
> With purple, chrome and cochineal,
> Ochre and lapis lazuli.
> The worm its golden woof presents.
> Whatever runs, flies, dives or delves
> All doff for her their ornaments,
> Which suit her better than themselves.

[8]Christopher Wren (1632–1723) was an English architect. — EDS.
[9]"Easy circumstances," that is, at least moderate wealth. — EDS.

There is no gift of nature without some drawback. So, to women, this exquisite structure could not exist without its own penalty. More vulnerable, more infirm, more mortal than men, they could not be such excellent artists in this element of fancy if they did not lend and give themselves to it. They are poets who believe their own poetry. They emit from their pores a colored atmosphere, one would say, wave upon wave of rosy light, in which they walk evermore, and see all objects through this warm-tinted mist that envelops them.

But the starry crown of woman is in the power of her affection and sentiment, and the infinite enlargements to which they lead. Beautiful is the passion of love, painter and adorner of youth and early life: but who suspects, in its blushes and tremors, what tragedies, heroisms and immortalities are beyond it? The passion, with all its grace and poetry, is profane to that which follows it. All these affections are only introductory to that which is beyond, and to that which is sublime.

We men have no right to say it, but the omnipotence of Eve is in humility. The instincts of mankind have drawn the Virgin Mother —

> Created beings all in lowliness
> Surpassing, as in height above them all.

This is the Divine Person whom Dante and Milton saw in vision. This is the victory of Griselda, her supreme humility.[10] And it is when love has reached this height that all our pretty rhetoric begins to have meaning. When we see that, it adds to the soul a new soul, it is honey in the mouth, music in the ear and balsam in the heart.

> Far have I clambered in my mind,
> But nought so great as Love I find.
> What is thy tent, where dost thou dwell?
>
> "My mansion is humility,
> Heaven's vastest capability."
> The further it doth downward tend,
> The higher up it doth ascend.

The first thing men think of, when they love, is to exhibit their usefulness and advantages to the object of their affection. Women make light of these, asking only love. They wish it to be an exchange of nobleness.

There is much in their nature, much in their social position which gives them a certain power of divination. And women know, at first sight, the characters of those with whom they converse. There is much that tends to give them a religious height which men do not attain. Their sequestration

---

[10]The "Virgin Mother" is Mary, mother of Jesus and a model of feminine modesty. Dante (1265–1321) was an Italian poet whose *Divine Comedy* offered visions of hell, purgatory, and heaven. John Milton (1608–74) was an English poet who depicted Adam and Eve's fall in *Paradise Lost*, from which these lines on Mary are taken, and humanity's redemption from their sin through the birth of Jesus in *Paradise Regained*. Griselda is the heroine of a European folktale who patiently endures much abuse by her husband. — EDS.

from affairs[11] and from the injury to the moral sense which affairs often inflict, aids this. And in every remarkable religious development in the world, women have taken a leading part. It is very curious that in the East, where Woman occupies, nationally, a lower sphere, where the laws resist the education and emancipation of women, — in the Mohammedan faith,[12] Woman yet occupies the same leading position, as a prophetess, that she has among the ancient Greeks, or among the Hebrews, or among the Saxons. This power, this religious character, is everywhere to be remarked in them.

The action of society is progressive. In barbarous society the position of women is always low — in the Eastern nations lower than in the West. "When a daughter is born," says the Shiking, the old Sacred Book of China, "she sleeps on the ground, she is clothed with a wrapper, she plays with a tile; she is incapable of evil or of good." And something like that position, in all low society, is the position of woman; because, as before remarked, she is herself its civilizer. With the advancements of society the position and influence of woman bring her strength or her faults into light. In modern times, three or four conspicuous instrumentalities may be marked. After the deification of Woman in the Catholic Church, in the sixteenth or seventeenth century, — when her religious nature gave her, of course, new importance, — the Quakers have the honor of having first established, in their discipline, the equality in the sexes. It is even more perfect in the later sect of the Shakers,[13] wherein no business is broached or counselled without the intervention of one elder and one elderess.

A second epoch for Woman was in France, — entirely civil; the change of sentiment from a rude to a polite character, in the age of Louis XIV., — commonly dated from the building of the Hôtel de Rambouillet.[14] I think another important step was made by the doctrine of Swedenborg,[15] a sublime genius who gave a scientific exposition of the part played severally by man and woman in the world, and showed the difference of sex to run through nature and through thought. Of all Christian sects this is at this moment the most vital and aggressive.

Another step was the effect of the action of the age in the antagonism to Slavery. It was easy to enlist Woman in this; it was impossible not to enlist her. But that Cause turned out to be a great scholar. He was a terrible metaphysician. He was a jurist, a poet, a divine. Was never a University of

---

[11]Business affairs, or the activities of the public sphere generally. — EDS.

[12]Islam. — EDS.

[13]A religious sect that originated in England in 1747 and spread to the United States in 1774. Among its tenets were celibacy, equality between the sexes, separation from the world, and ascetic communal living. — EDS.

[14]The Hôtel de Rambouillet was the domain of the Marquise de Rambouillet (1588–1665), generally credited with refining the manners of the French court during the reign of Louis XIV (1643–1715). — EDS.

[15]Emmanuel Swedenborg (1688–1772), a Swedish theologian whose work greatly influenced Emerson. The Church of the New Jerusalem, founded by Swedenborg's followers, attracted many adherents in the northeastern United States in the nineteenth century; but it has greatly dwindled in influence today. — EDS.

Oxford or Göttingen that made such students. It took a man from the plough and made him acute, eloquent, and wise, to the silencing of the doctors. There was nothing it did not pry into, no right it did not explore, no wrong it did not expose. And it has, among its other effects, given Woman a feeling of public duty and an added self-respect.

One truth leads in another by the hand; one right is an accession of strength to take more. And the times are marked by the new attitude of Woman; urging, by argument and by association, her rights of all kinds, — in short, to one-half of the world; — as the right to education, to avenues of employment, to equal rights of property, to equal rights in marriage, to the exercise of the professions and of suffrage.

Of course, this conspicuousness had its inconveniences. But it is cheap wit that has been spent on this subject; from Aristophanes,[16] in whose comedies I confess my dullness to find good joke, to Rabelais,[17] in whom it is monstrous exaggeration of temperament, and not borne out by anything in nature, — down to English Comedy, and, in our day, to Tennyson,[18] and the American newspapers. In all, the body of the joke is one, namely, to charge women with temperament; to describe them as victims of temperament; and is identical with Mahomet's[19] opinion that women have not a sufficient moral or intellectual force to control the perturbations of their physical structure. These were all drawings of morbid anatomy, and such satire as might be written on the tenants of a hospital or on an asylum for idiots. Of course it would be easy for women to retaliate in kind, by painting men from the dogs and gorillas that have worn our shape. That they have not, is an eulogy on their taste and self-respect. The good easy world took the joke which it liked. There is always the want of thought; there is always credulity. There are plenty of people who believe women to be incapable of anything but to cook, incapable of interest in affairs. There are plenty of people who believe that the world is governed by men of dark complexions,[20] that affairs are only directed by such, and do not see the use of contemplative men, or how ignoble would be the world that wanted them. And so without the affection of women.

But for the general charge: no doubt it is well founded. They are victims of the finer temperament. They have tears, and gaieties, and faintings, and glooms, and devotion to trifles. Nature's end, of maternity for twenty years, was of so supreme importance that it was to be secured at all events, even to the sacrifice of the highest beauty. They are more personal. Men taunt them that, whatever they do, say, read, or write, they are thinking of themselves and their set. Men are not to the same degree temperamented, for there are

[16]Aristophanes (c. 448 B.C.E.–c. 338 B.C.E.) was a Greek comic playwright. — EDS.

[17]François Rabelais (c. 1490–1553) was a French satirical writer. — EDS.

[18]Alfred, Lord Tennyson (1809–92) was an English poet. — EDS.

[19]The prophet Mohammed (c. 570–632) was the founder of the religion of Islam. — EDS.

[20]Emerson means men whose vitality gives them a ruddy skin tone, not what we would call "men of color." He refers to the popular belief that men who are effective leaders will have a ruddy complexion, in contrast with the pale cheeks of "contemplative" men who take little part in public affairs. Evidently both types of men are European American. — EDS.

multitudes of men who live to objects quite out of them, as to politics, to trade, to letters or an art, unhindered by any influence of constitution.

The answer that lies, silent or spoken, in the minds of well-meaning persons, to the new claims, is this: that, though their mathematical justice is not to be denied, yet the best women do not wish these things; they are asked for by people who intellectually seek them, but who have not the support or sympathy of the truest women; and that, if the laws and customs were modified in the manner proposed, it would embarrass and pain gentle and lovely persons with duties which they would find irksome and distasteful. Very likely. Providence is always surprising us with new and unlikely instruments. But perhaps it is because these people have been deprived of education, fine companions, opportunities, such as they wished, — because they feel the same rudeness and disadvantage which offends you, — that they have been stung to say, "It is too late for us to be polished and fashioned into beauty, but, at least, we will see that the whole race of women shall not suffer as we have suffered."

They have an unquestionable right to their own property. And if a woman demand votes, offices, and political equality with men, as among the Shakers an Elder and Elderess are of equal power, — and among the Quakers, — it must not be refused. It is very cheap wit that finds it so droll that a woman should vote. Educate and refine society to the highest point, — bring together a cultivated society of both sexes, in a drawing-room, and consult and decide by voices on a question of taste or on a question of right, and is there any absurdity or any practical difficulty in obtaining their authentic opinions? If not, then there need be none in a hundred companies, if you educate them and accustom them to judge. And, for the effect of it, I can say, for one, that all my points would sooner be carried in the state if women voted. On the questions that are important; — whether the government shall be in one person, or whether representative, or whether democratic; whether men shall be holden in bondage, or shall be roasted alive and eaten, as in Typee,[21] or shall be hunted with bloodhounds, as in this country; whether men shall be hanged for stealing, or hanged at all; whether the unlimited sale of cheap liquors shall be allowed; — they would give, I suppose, as intelligent a vote as the voters of Boston or New York.

We may ask, to be sure, — Why need you vote? If new power is here, of a character which solves old tough questions, which puts me and all the rest in the wrong, tries and condemns our religion, customs, laws, and opens new careers to our young receptive men and women, you can well leave voting to the old dead people. Those whom you teach, and those whom you half teach, will fast enough make themselves considered and strong with their new insight, and votes will follow from all the dull.

---

[21]The Typees were cannibal inhabitants of a South Seas island in American writer Herman Melville's (1819–91) first novel, *Typee: A Peep at Polynesian Life* (1846). — EDS.

The objection to their voting is the same as is urged, in the lobbies of legislatures, against clergymen who take an active part in politics; — that if they are good clergymen they are unacquainted with the expediencies of politics, and if they become good politicians they are worse clergymen. So of women, that they cannot enter this arena without being contaminated and unsexed.

Here are two or three objections; first, a want of practical wisdom; second, a too purely ideal view; and third, danger of contamination. For their want of intimate knowledge of affairs, I do not think this ought to disqualify them from voting at any town-meeting which I ever attended. I could heartily wish the objection were sound. But if any man will take the trouble to see how our people vote, — how many gentlemen are willing to take on themselves the trouble of thinking and determining for you, and, standing at the door of the polls, give every innocent citizen his ticket as he comes in, informing him that this is the vote of his party; and how the innocent citizen, without further demur, goes and drops it in the ballot-box, — I cannot but think he will agree that most women might vote as wisely.

For the other point, of their not knowing the world, and aiming at abstract right without allowance for circumstances, — that is not a disqualification, but a qualification. Human society is made up of partialities. Each citizen has an interest and a view of his own, which, if followed out to the extreme, would leave no room for any other citizen. One man is timid and another rash; one would change nothing, and the other is pleased with nothing; one wishes schools, another armies, one gunboats, another public gardens. Bring all these biases together and something is done in favor of them all.

Every one is a half vote, but the next elector behind him brings the other or corresponding half in his hand: a reasonable result is had. Now there is no lack, I am sure, of the expediency, or of the interests of trade or of imperative class-interests being neglected. There is no lack of votes representing the physical wants; and if in your city the uneducated emigrant vote numbers thousands, representing a brutal ignorance and mere animal wants, it is to be corrected by an educated and religious vote, representing the wants and desires of honest and refined persons. If the wants, the passions, the vices, are allowed a full vote through the hands of a half-brutal intemperate population, I think it but fair that the virtues, the aspirations should be allowed a full vote, as an offset, through the purest part of the people.

As for the unsexing and contamination, — that only accuses our existing politics, shows how barbarous we are, — that our policies are so crooked, made up of things not to be spoken, to be understood only by wink and nudge; this man to be coaxed, that man to be bought, and that other to be duped. It is easy to see that there is contamination enough, but it rots the men now, and fills the air with stench. Come out of that: it is like a dance-cellar.[22] The fairest names in this country in literature, in

---

[22]A dance hall in a basement room. Men paid to dance with the women who worked there; liquor was also sold. Even without the casual sexual contact that often characterized such places, Emerson would have regarded them as degrading to both women and men. — EDS.

law, have gone into Congress and come out dishonored. And when I read the list of men of intellect, of refined pursuits, giants in law, or eminent scholars, or of social distinction, leading men of wealth and enterprise in the commercial community, and see what they have voted for and suffered to be voted for, I think no community was ever so politely and elegantly betrayed.

I do not think it yet appears that women wish this equal share in public affairs. But it is they and not we that are to determine it. Let the laws be purged of every barbarous remainder, every barbarous impediment to women. Let the public donations for education be equally shared by them, let them enter a school as freely as a church, let them have and hold and give their property as men do theirs; — and in a few years it will easily appear whether they wish a voice in making the laws that are to govern them. If you do refuse them a vote, you will also refuse to tax them, — according to our Teutonic principle, No representation, no tax.[23]

All events of history are to be regarded as growths and offshoots of the expanding mind of the race, and this appearance of new opinions, their currency and force in many minds, is itself the wonderful fact. For whatever is popular is important, shows the spontaneous sense of the hour. The aspiration of this century will be the code of the next. It holds of high and distant causes, of the same influences that make the sun and moon. When new opinions appear, they will be entertained and respected, by every fair mind, according to their reasonableness, and not according to their convenience, or their fitness to shock our customs. But let us deal with them greatly; let them make their way by the upper road, and not by the way of manufacturing public opinion, which lapses continually into expediency, and makes charlatans. All that is spontaneous is irresistible, and forever it is individual force that interests. I need not repeat to you, — your own solitude will suggest it, — that a masculine woman is not strong, but a lady is. The loneliest thought, the purest prayer, is rushing to be the history of a thousand years.[24]

Let us have the true woman, the adorner, the hospitable, the religious heart, and no lawyer need be called in to write stipulations, the cunning clauses of provision, the strong investitures; — for woman moulds the lawgiver and writes the law. But I ought to say, I think it impossible to separate the interests and education of the sexes. Improve and refine the men, and you do the same by the women, whether you will or no. Every woman being the wife or the daughter of a man, — wife, daughter, sister, mother, of a man, she can never be very far from his ear, never not of his counsel,

[23]"Teutonic" means Germanic or, more generally, Anglo-Saxon. Emerson continues his practice of ascribing the highest American ideals, such as the familiar Revolutionary-era slogan, to the culture of northern Europe (see also note 1). — EDS.

[24]Emerson asserts that a "lady," one who makes full use of the oracular power Emerson has ascribed to women, is stronger in making social change than a "masculine woman" who discards the special powers of her sex. The lady's "loneliest thought" or "purest prayer," which seem unpopular now, will become influential in the future and shape the course of history. — EDS.

if she has really something to urge that is good in itself and agreeable to nature. Slavery it is that makes slavery; freedom, freedom. The slavery of women happened when the men were slaves of kings. The melioration of manners brought their melioration of course. It could not be otherwise, and hence the new desire of better laws. For there are always a certain number of passionately loving fathers, brothers, husbands, and sons who put their might into the endeavor to make a daughter, a wife, or a mother happy in the way that suits best. Woman should find in man her guardian. Silently she looks for that, and when she finds that he is not, as she instantly does, she betakes her to her own defences, and does the best she can. But when he is her guardian, fulfilled with all nobleness, knows and accepts his duties as her brother, all goes well for both.

The new movement is only a tide shared by the spirits of man and woman; and you may proceed in the faith that whatever the woman's heart is prompted to desire, the man's mind is simultaneously prompted to accomplish.

READING CRITICALLY

1. What does Emerson mean when he says that women have an "oracular nature" (p. 347)?

2. Emerson says that "the life of the affections is primary" to women. What does this mean? How does Emerson feel that this focus affects women's lives (p. 347)?

3. What does Emerson mean by calling women the "civilizers of mankind" (p. 348)?

4. According to Emerson, how did the battle against slavery begin to change women?

5. How does Emerson refute the argument that no further change in the situation of women is needed because most women do not want it?

6. What reasons does Emerson give for wanting women to be allowed to vote, and how does he handle arguments against their voting?

WRITING ANALYTICALLY

1. Emerson calls for women to have the vote; and at the end of his essay, he also calls for them to have control of their own property, to have access to education equal with men's, and so on. Nevertheless, throughout his essay Emerson talks about men and women as if he believes they are fundamentally different. Write a paper in which you describe the essential nature of women as presented by Emerson. Illustrate your description with reference to specific passages in the text. Option 1: You may also assess the degree to which Emerson's picture of woman is limited by social class — that is, the extent to which it is necessary to be a member of the middle or upper classes in order to be the woman Emerson describes. Option 2: You may add an evaluation of the extent to which Emerson is a feminist, according to your own definition of the term.

2. Compare and contrast Emerson's views on women with those of his fellow New England ministers such as Jonathan F. Stearns (p. 299). You may develop the comparison by writing a letter from Stearns to Emerson, commenting on Emerson's essay.

3. Compare and contrast Emerson's views on the relations between the sexes with those of Sarah Grimké (p. 321). You may develop the comparison by writing a letter from Grimké to Emerson, commenting on Emerson's essay (much as she comments on the "Pastoral Letter").

ELIZABETH CADY STANTON

"A Slave's Appeal" (1860)

Elizabeth Cady Stanton (1815–1902) was born in upstate New York. Her father, Daniel Cady, was a judge and, according to Stanton, an archconservative. Nevertheless, Elizabeth became an abolitionist, and she married fellow activist Henry Stanton in 1840. They spent their honeymoon in England, where Henry Stanton attended a world antislavery convention while his wife was forced to sit in the balcony because of a prohibition on women's participation. Here Stanton met an excluded delegate, Lucretia Coffin Mott, a Quaker leader from Philadelphia who had inspired Sarah and Angelina Grimké, among many others. Upon returning home, Stanton was soon involved in the cares of raising a family (she had seven children). She relates in her autobiography (1898) that her family concerns at this time both educated her in the need for women's rights and prevented her from acting until her children were somewhat older. Nevertheless, Stanton and Mott were able to organize the first American women's rights convention in Seneca Falls, New York, in 1848, and the "Declaration of Sentiments" promulgated at this convention (p. 387) became a pattern for women's rights activism throughout the century.

Stanton herself became the prototype of the women's rights activist. An eloquent, engaging speaker and an accomplished writer, she was a major leader of the nineteenth-century women's movement. She headed a number of national organizations, including the National Woman Suffrage Association (president, 1869–90). Among her important publications were the three-volume *History of Woman Suffrage* (1881–87), coedited with activist Susan B. Anthony, and the two-volume commentary *Woman's Bible* (1895, 1898). Although Stanton was both an active abolitionist and a women's rights activist before the Civil War, after the war she concentrated her efforts more on women's rights, particularly on obtaining European American women's right to vote in national elections.

Elizabeth Cady Stanton, "A Slave's Appeal," reprinted in *Man Cannot Speak for Her,* vol. 2 of *Key Texts of the Early Feminists,* ed. Karlyn Kohrs Campbell (New York: Greenwood, Praeger, 1989), 168–86.

In the notes, KKC = Karlyn Kohrs Campbell, EDS. = Patricia Bizzell and Bruce Herzberg.

Stanton gave her first public address at the 1848 convention at Seneca Falls. Reprinted here is "A Slave's Appeal," a speech she gave before the all-male New York state legislature in February 1860, requesting liberalization of married women's property laws. Stanton herself considered this to be one of her best speeches, and it was successful — the legislature did modify the law as she requested.

GENTLEMEN OF THE JUDICIARY: — There are certain natural rights as inalienable to civilization as are the rights of air and motion to the savage in the wilderness. The natural rights of the civilized man and woman are government, property, the harmonious development of all their powers, and the gratification of their desires. There are a few people we now and then meet, who, like Jeremy Bentham,[1] scout the idea of natural rights in civilization, and pronounce them mere metaphors, declaring there are no rights aside from those the law confers. If the law made man too, that might do, for then he could be made to order, to fit the particular niche he was designed to fill. But inasmuch as God made man in his own image, with capacities and powers as boundless as the universe, whose exigencies no mere human law can meet, it is evident that the man must ever stand first — the law but the creature of his wants — the law-giver but the mouthpiece of humanity. If, then, the nature of a being decides its rights, every individual comes into this world with rights that are not transferable. He does not bring them like a pack on his back, that may be stolen from him, but they are a component part of himself — the laws which insure his growth and development. The individual may be put in the stocks, body and soul, he may be dwarfed, crippled, killed outright, but his rights can no man get — they live and die with him.

Though the atmosphere be forty miles deep all round the globe, no man can do more than fill his own lungs. No man can see, or hear, or smell, but just so far; and though hundreds are deprived of these senses, his are not the more acute. Though rights have been abundantly supplied by the good Father, no man can appropriate to himself those that belong to another. A citizen can have but one vote, fill but one office, though thousands are not permitted to do either. These axioms prove that woman's poverty does not add to man's wealth, and if, in the plenitude of his power, he should secure to her the exercise of all her God-given rights, her wealth could not bring poverty to him. There is a kind of nervous unrest always manifested by those in power, whenever new claims are started by those out of their own immediate class. The philosophy of this is very plain. They imagine that if the rights of this new class be granted, they must, of necessity, sacrifice something of what they already possess. They cannot divest themselves of the idea that rights are very much like lands, stocks, bonds, and mortgages, and that if every new claimant be satisfied,

---

[1]Jeremy Bentham (1748–1832) was an English philosopher, jurist, and political theorist. — EDS.

the supply of human rights must in time run low. You might as well carp at the birth of every child, lest there should not be enough air left to inflate your lungs; at the success of every scholar, for fear that your draughts at the fountain of knowledge, could not be so long and deep; at the glory of every hero, lest there be no glory left for you.

"If the citizens of the United States should not be free and happy, the fault," says Washington, "will be entirely their own." Yes, gentlemen, the basis of our government is broad enough and strong enough to securely hold the rights of all its citizens, and should we pile up rights ever so high, and crown the pinnacle with those of the weakest woman, there is no danger that it will totter to the ground. Yes, it is woman's own fault that she is where she is. Why has she not claimed all those rights, long ago guaranteed by our own declaration[2] to all the citizens of this Republic? Why does she not this day stand in our Senate Chamber and House of Representatives, to look after her own interests?[3]

A citizen is defined to be a person, native or naturalized, who has the privilege of exercising the elective franchise, or the qualifications which enable him to vote for rulers, and to purchase and hold real estate. With this definition, a woman can hardly be called a citizen of this State, and if not, her position is a singularly anomalous one. She is a native and naturalized, yet has not the privilege of exercising the elective franchise. She has all the necessary qualifications to vote for rulers, and to govern herself, — yet she is denied the right. She may hold real estate, but cannot protect her property by law. She is taxed to support government, pays the penalty of her own crimes, and suffers the consequences of all man's false legislation, but she is not permitted to say what her taxes shall be, what civil acts shall be criminal, and she has no appeal from man's administration of law. She is, in fine, honored with all the duties and responsibilities of a citizen, and at the same time is denied all his rights and privileges.

It is declared that every citizen has a right to life, liberty, and the pursuit of happiness. Can woman be said to have a right to life, if all means of self-protection are denied her, — if, in case of life and death, she is not only denied the right of trial by a jury of her own peers, but has no voice in the choice of judge or juror, her consent has never been given to the criminal code by which she is judged? Can she be said to have a right to liberty, when another citizen may have the legal custody of her person; the right to shut her up and administer moderate chastisement; to decide when and how she shall live, and what are the necessary means for her support?[4] Can any citizen be said to have a right to the pursuit of happiness, whose inalienable rights are denied; who is disfranchised from all the privileges of citizenship; whose person is subject to the control and absolute will of another?

[2]The Declaration of Independence (p. 174). Other allusions to this document occur throughout Stanton's speech. — EDS.

[3]We have inserted occasional paragraph breaks in Stanton's text. — EDS.

[4]"Another citizen" who possesses these powers over a woman is her father or, if she is married, her husband, according to nineteenth-century law (see the Introduction, pp. 287—88). — EDS.

Now, why is it, gentlemen, that woman stands at this day wholly unrepresented in this government? Why is it that the mass of laws affecting her special interests remain in their original barbarism at this hour, whilst all others have been undergoing change and improvement? Simply because she has never exercised her right to the elective franchise. The grant of this right would secure all others, but the grant of every other, whilst this is denied, is a mockery! What is the right to property without the right to protect it? The enjoyment of that right today is no security it will be continued tomorrow, so long as it is granted to her as a favor by a privileged class, and not secured as a sacred right.

It is folly to urge woman's claims on the broad platform of human rights, or from the grand basis of republicanism, upon which this government rests, for by your laws you deny her humanity, her citizenship, her identity with yourself. Justice, common sense, sound logic, all point to equality, to a full and perfect recognition of all her God-given rights. But as you are not yet prepared for any thing more than a partial legislation, believing, as you do, that womanhood is such a subtle essence of frivolities and contradictions that it needs some special code of laws to meet its exigencies, on the low ground of expediency and precedent must we plead our cause.

Man having denied woman's identity with himself, has no data to go upon in judging of her interests. If the sexes are alike in their mental structure, then there is no reason why woman should not have a voice in making the laws which govern her. But if they are not alike, most certainly woman must make laws for herself, for who else can understand her wants and needs? If it be admitted in this government, that all men and women are free and equal, then must women claim a place in our Senate Chambers and Houses of Representatives. But if it be found that even here, we have classes and castes, not Lord and Commons,[5] but Lords and Ladies, then must woman claim a lower house, where her representatives may watch the passage of all bills affecting her own welfare, and the good of the country. Surely you should have as much respect for the rights of different classes as monarchical England. Experience taught her that the nobility could not legislate for the peasantry, and experience teaches us that man cannot legislate for woman.

If the object of government is to protect the weak against the strong, how unwise to place the power wholly in the hands of the strong? Yet that is the history of all governments, even the model republic of these United States. You who have read the history of nations, from Moses down to our last election, where have you ever seen one class looking after the interests of another? Any of you can readily see the defects in other governments, and pronounce sentence against those who have sacrificed the masses to themselves; but when we come to our own case, we are blinded by custom

---

[5]The English Parliament is divided into a House of Lords and a House of Commons. Those who have inherited positions in the nobility sit in Lords; those elected to represent everyone else sit in Commons. — EDS.

and self-interest. Some of you who have no capital can see the injustice which the laborer suffers; some of you who have no slaves, can see the cruelty of his oppression; but who of you appreciate the galling humiliation, the refinements of degradation, to which women (the mothers, wives, sisters, and daughters of freemen) are subject, in this the last half of the nineteenth century? How many of you have ever read even the laws concerning her that now disgrace your statute-books? In cruelty and tyranny, they are not surpassed by any slaveholding code in the Southern States; in fact they are worse, by just so far as woman, from her social position, refinement, and education, is on a more equal ground with the oppressor.

Allow me just here to call the attention of that party now so much interested in the slave of the Carolinas, to the similarity in his condition and that of the mothers, wives, and daughters of the Empire State. The negro has no name. He is Cuffy Douglas or Cuffy Brooks, just whose Cuffy he may chance to be.[6] The woman has no name. She is Mrs. Richard Roe or Mrs. John Doe, just whose Mrs. she may chance to be. Cuffy has no right to his earnings; he cannot buy or sell, or lay up anything that he can call his own. Mrs. Roe has no right to her earnings; she can neither buy nor sell, make contracts, nor lay up anything that she can call her own. Cuffy has no right to his children; they can be sold from him at any time. Mrs. Roe has no right to her children; they may be bound out to cancel a father's debts of honor. The unborn child, even by the last will of the father, may be placed under the guardianship of a stranger and a foreigner. Cuffy has no legal existence; he is subject to restraint and moderate chastisement. Mrs. Roe has no legal existence; she has not the best right to her own person. The husband has the power to restrain, and administer moderate chastisement.

Blackstone[7] declares that the husband and wife are one, and learned commentators have decided that that one is the husband. In all civil codes, you will find them classified as one. Certain rights and immunities, such and such privileges are to be secured to white male citizens. What have women and negroes to do with rights? What know they of government, war, or glory?

The prejudice against color, of which we hear so much, is no stronger than that against sex. It is produced by the same cause, and manifested very much in the same way. The negro's skin and the woman's sex are both *prima facie* evidence[8] that they were intended to be in subjection to the white Saxon man. The few social privileges which the man gives the woman, he makes up to the negro in civil rights. The woman may sit at the same table and eat with the white man; the free negro may hold property and vote. The woman may sit in the same pew with the white man, in

---

[6]"Cuffy" is a derogatory name for an African American man, like Sambo. — Eds.

[7]Sir William Blackstone (1723–80) was an English jurist whose codification of English law widely influenced the formation of laws in the colonies that became the United States. He is a principal source of the "feme covert" concept (see p. 287), which claims that a wife's legal identity is subsumed in her husband's. — Eds.

[8]Evidence that is obvious at first sight. — Eds.

church; the free negro may enter the pulpit and preach. Now, with the right to suffrage, the right unquestioned, even by Paul, to minister at the altar, it is evident that the prejudice against sex is more deeply rooted and more unreasonably maintained than that against color.[9] As citizens of a republic, which should we most highly prize, social privileges or civil rights? The latter, most certainly.

To those who do not feel the injustice and degradation of the condition, there is something inexpressibly comical in man's "citizen woman." It reminds me of those monsters I used to see in the old world, head and shoulders woman, and the rest of the body sometimes fish, and sometimes beast. I used to think, What a strange conceit! but now I see how perfectly it represents man's idea! Look over all his laws concerning us, and you will see just enough of woman to tell of her existence; all the rest is submerged, or made to crawl upon the earth. Just imagine an inhabitant of another planet entertaining himself some pleasant evening in searching over our great national compact, our Declaration of Independence, our Constitutions, or some of our Statute-books; what would he think of those *"women and negroes"* that must be so fenced in, so guarded against? Why, he would certainly suppose we were monsters, like those fabulous giants or Brobdingnagians of olden times, so dangerous to civilized man, from our size, ferocity, and power.[10]

Then let him take up our poets, from Pope down to Dana;[11] let him listen to our Fourth of July toasts, and some of the sentimental adulations of social life, and no logic could convince him that this creature of the law, and this angel of the family altar, could be one and the same being. Man is in such a labyrinth of contradictions with his marital and property rights; he is so befogged on the whole question of maidens, wives, and mothers, that from pure benevolence we should relieve him from this troublesome branch of legislation. We should vote, and make laws for ourselves. Do not be alarmed, dear ladies! You need spend no time reading Grotius, Coke, Puffendorf [*sic*], Blackstone, Bentham, Kent, and Story[12] to find out what you need. We may safely trust the shrewd selfishness of the white man, and consent to live under the same broad code where he has so comfortably ensconced himself. Any legislation that will do for man, we may abide by most cheerfully.

[9]Stanton points out that the "free negro" may vote and may serve as a Christian minister, whereas women may not; thus, she asserts, the prejudice against women is stronger than that against African Americans. Even the apostle Paul, says Stanton, who in his New Testament letters placed so many strictures on women's speaking in church, did not feel compelled to silence men of color. (For more information on Paul's views on women, see p. 303, note 3). — EDS.

[10]The Brobdingnagians were giants, twelve times the size of humans, in Jonathan Swift's *Gulliver's Travels* (1726). They are basically benevolent — no more ferocious, Stanton implies, than "women and negroes" are. — EDS.

[11]Alexander Pope (1688–1744) was an English poet; Richard Henry Dana (1787–1879) was an American poet and editor.

[12]Named here are noted European and American male writers on law and political theory. — EDS.

"Governments derive their just powers from the consent of the governed." "Taxation and representation are inseparable." These glorious truths were uttered for some higher purpose than to decorate holiday flags, or furnish texts for Fourth of July orations. If they mean any thing, by what right do you try woman by your civil code, or tax her to support this government? Do you claim that she is represented by her father, husband, brother, son? Your statute-books testify against you. They show but too well how faithless you have been to the high and holy trust you have assumed. A proper self-respect forbids such an admission. If those to whom woman is bound, by all the ties of blood and affection, have made, and do now sanction, such laws as disgrace your whole code, may Heaven save her from her friends! But if man claims to be her representative, let him pay her taxes. Instead of sending his tax-gatherer round to poor widows, let him look up their fathers, brothers, sons, or some negro that they have helped to emancipate, or some clergyman they have helped to educate. Get it out of some one crowned with the glory of manhood.

But for consistency's sake; for the respect you bear to republican principles; as you honor the memory of those who settled this question for you, by the veneration we all feel for the sufferings and glory of those who sent forth that grand declaration of rights which made every crowned head in Europe tremble on his throne; for the memory of all those mighty words and deeds of the past, do not hold one half of the people of this State beyond the limits of justice. Our State Treasury reports show thousands of dollars collected every year from the one-house and lot of poor widows and maidens. Taxation without representation was the theme for many a hot debate in the parliaments of the old world, and for many an eloquent oration in the forests of the new. We but re-echo those undying truths uttered by the heroes of American liberty, scarce one century ago. It must strike every mind as just, that if man is not willing to have woman represented in this government, then she should not be subject to taxation.

Your Constitution regards the negro, so unjustly degraded, with far more consideration than your wives and mothers. If he is possessed of a certain amount of property, then is he permitted to vote, and pay taxes, too. If he has not that amount, then he is not permitted to vote, neither is he taxed. But woman — no matter how rich, how noble, how virtuous, she shall have no voice in the government; and no matter how weak or ignorant, how wretched or worn out with life's struggles, if, by unwearied industry, she has made a home for herself and children, she must be subject to taxation. Talk not of chivalry, men of New York, so long as feeble women, who own but one house and lot, are legal subjects of taxation! Talk not of justice, so long as sex is made a badge of oppression!

I am better educated than the Irishman who saws my wood. I read and write his letters for him to the Emerald Isle, and in conversation, I find myself better posted than he is on law and politics, and with a far higher appreciation of the blessings of a republican form of government. Yet he suffers none of the injustice I do, but is in the full possession of all his civil and political rights, equally with any member of your honorable body. In standing before grave and reverend senators, full of years, experience, and wisdom, I might find in their vast superiority sufficient ground for their superior rights. But when I contrast myself with the ignorant alien, the gambler, the drunkard, the prize-fighter, the licentious profligate, the silly stripling of twenty-one, the fool, the villain, I see no ground for these broad distinctions.

But, say you, we would not have woman exposed to the grossness and vulgarity of public life, or encounter what she must at the polls. When you talk, gentlemen, of sheltering woman from the rough winds and revolting scenes of real life, you must be either talking for effect, or wholly ignorant of what the facts of life are. The man, whatever he is, is known to the woman. She is the companion, not only of the accomplished statesman, the orator, and the scholar, but the vile, vulgar, brutal man has his mother, his wife, his sister, his daughter. Yes, delicate, refined, educated women are in daily life with the drunkard, the gambler, the licentious man, the rogue, and the villain; and if man shows out what he is any where, it is at his own hearthstone. There are over forty thousand drunkards in this State. All these are bound by the ties of family to some woman. Allow but a mother and a wife to each, and you have over eighty thousand women. All these have seen their fathers, brothers, husbands, sons, in the lowest and most debased stages of obscenity and degradation. In your own circle of friends, do you not know refined women, whose whole lives are darkened and saddened by gross and brutal associations?

Now, gentlemen, do you talk to woman of a rude jest or jostle at the polls, where noble, virtuous men stand ready to protect her person and her rights, when, alone in the darkness and solitude and gloom of night, they have trembled on their own thresholds, awaiting the return of husbands from their midnight revels? — when, stepping from her chamber, she has beheld her royal monarch, her lord and master, — her legal representative, — the protector of her property, her home, her children, and her person, down on his hands and knees slowly crawling up the stairs? Behold him in her chamber — *in her bed!* The fairy tale of Beauty and the Beast is far too often realized in life.

Gentlemen, such scenes as woman has witnessed at her own fireside, where no eye save Omnipotence could pity, no strong arm could help, can never be realized at the polls, never equalled elsewhere, this side the bottomless pit. No, woman has not hitherto lived in the clouds, surrounded by an atmosphere of holiness and divinity, ignorant of vice and impurity, — but she has been the companion of man in health, in sickness, and in death, in his highest and in his lowest moments. She has worshipped him as a saint and an orator, and pitied him as madman and a fool. In Paradise, man and woman were placed together, and so they must ever be. They must sink or rise together. If man is low and wretched and vile, woman cannot escape the contagion, and any atmosphere that is unfit for woman to breathe, is not fit for man. Verily, the sins of the fathers shall be visited upon the children to the third and fourth generation.[13]

[13]Exod. 20:5; Num. 14:18. — KKC

You, by your unwise legislation, have crippled and dwarfed woman-hood, by closing to her all honorable and lucrative means of employment, have driven her into the garrets and dens of our cities, where she now revenges herself on your innocent sons, sapping the very foundations of national virtue and strength. Alas! for the young men just coming on the stage of action, who soon shall fill your vacant places — our future senators, our presidents, the expounders of our constitutional law! Terrible are the penalties we are now suffering for the ages of injustice done to woman.

But, say you, God has appointed woman's sphere; it is His will that she is as she is. Well, if that be so, then woman will be kept in her sphere by God's laws. It is folly, said Daniel Webster,[14] to reenact God's laws. Wherever God has placed woman, there must she ever be. You might as well pass laws to keep Venus, the beautiful morning star, from refreshing herself by an occasional promenade on the broad belt of Saturn. Nature's laws are immutable; no planet or immortal being can ever get out of its prescribed orbit. Again, the condition of woman, in all ages, has differed materially, and differs at this moment, among the various nations of the earth. Now, which of all these conditions, think you, is in accordance with the will of God? Enervated and voluptuous by confinement, as she is in the Turkish harem, or exhausted by toil and outdoor labor, as she is in Switzerland and Germany, — with her feet compressed in iron boots to the smallest possible dimensions, depending on man to carry her about, as she is in China, or standing all day in the intense heat of a summer's sun in the cotton field and rice plantation, as she is in Christian America, — with the crown and sceptre ruling the mightiest nation on the globe,[15] or burning on the funeral pile of her husband, a useless relic of her lordly dead, as she is in India, — who can decide which of all these is the woman's true sphere?

Ever and anon, through the long ages, great emergencies have called forth the true, the individual woman, and multitudes have always greeted her with joy, and proudly welcomed her success. On the war-horse, bearing the flag of conquest, she has led the armies of mighty nations. With telescopic vision, she has prescribed the orbit of planetary worlds. In the midst of peril, mutiny, and death, she has seized the command of the lonely ship, and brought it safely to its destined port. With the mild gospel of Jesus, she has passed, unscathed, through all earthly dangers. What depths of pollution and vice have been unwatched and unpitied by the eye of woman? An angel of mercy, she has walked up and down the solitary places, by-lanes and dark prison-houses of our modern Babylons, ministering to the children of suffering and want, cheering the trembling criminal, the depraved and the profligate with bright hopes of the future! Amid all

[14]Daniel Webster (1782–1852), trained as a lawyer, served for many years in the U.S. Congress and Senate and as secretary of state. He was known for his oratory, particularly in the legislature and the courts. — EDS.

[15]Stanton refers to Queen Victoria, then the reigning monarch of Great Britain, "the mightiest nation on the globe." — EDS.

the horrors of the French Revolution, in the gloomy Bastille,[16] at the guillotine, through all the tragic scenes of the Crimea,[17] amid all the dangers and sudden emergencies of everyday life, self-poised and self-sustained, tell me,

> Can she be too great, too grand,
> To fill the place where she can
>   stand,
> To do and dare what she has done
> Before all Israel and the sun?

Again, it is said that the majority of women do not ask for any change in the laws, that it is time enough to give them the elective franchise when they, as a class, demand it.

Wise statesmen legislate for the best interests of the nation; the State, for the highest good of its citizens; the Christian, for the conversion of the world. Where would have been our railroads, our telegraphs, our ocean steamers, our canals and harbors, our arts and sciences, if government had withheld the means from the far-seeing minority? This State established our present system of common schools, fully believing that educated men and women would make better citizens than ignorant ones. In making this provision for the education of its children, had they waited for a majority of the urchins of this State to petition for schools, how many, think you, would have asked to be transplanted from the street to the schoolhouse? Does the State wait for the criminal to ask for his prison-house? the insane, the idiot, the deaf and dumb for his asylum? Does the Christian, in his love to all mankind, wait for the majority of the benighted heathen to ask him for the gospel? No; unasked and unwelcomed, he crosses the trackless ocean, rolls off the mountain of superstition that oppresses the human mind, proclaims the immortality of the soul, the dignity of manhood, the right of all to be free and happy. No, gentlemen, if there is but one woman in this State who feels the injustice of her position, she should not be denied her inalienable rights, because the common household drudge and the silly butterflies of fashion are ignorant of all laws, both human and Divine. Because they know nothing of governments, or rights, and therefore ask nothing, shall my petitions be unheard?

I stand before you the rightful representative of woman, claiming a share in the halo of glory that has gathered round her in the ages, and by the wisdom of her past words and works, her peerless heroism and self-sacrifice, I challenge your admiration, and, moreover, claiming, as I do, a share in all her outrages and sufferings, in the cruel injustice, contempt and ridicule now heaped upon her, in her deep degradation, hopeless

---

[16]The Bastille was a French prison and fortress that was stormed on July 14, 1789, at the beginning of the French Revolution. Bastille Day, July 14, is celebrated as the national holiday of France. — EDS.

[17]A reference to Florence Nightingale (1820–1910), the founder of modern nursing, who in 1854 organized a unit of 38 women nurses for service in the Crimean War; by the end of the war, she had become a legend. — KKC

wretchedness, by all that is helpless in her present condition, that is false in law and public sentiment, I urge your generous consideration; for as my heart swells with pride to behold woman in the highest walks of literature and art, it grows big enough to take in those who are bleeding in the dust.

Now do not think, gentlemen, we wish you to do a great many troublesome things for us, that you need spend a whole session in fixing up a code of laws to satisfy a class of most unreasonable women. We ask no more than the poor devils in the Scripture asked, "Let us alone" [Mark 1:24]. In mercy, let us take care of ourselves, our property, our children, and our homes. True, we are not so strong, so wise, so crafty as you are, but if any kind friend leaves us a little money, or we can by great industry earn fifty cents a day, we would rather buy bread and clothes for our children, than cigars and champagne for our legal protectors.[18]

There has been a great deal written and said about protection. We, as a class, are tired of one kind of protection, that which leaves us everything to do, to dare and to suffer, and strips us of all means for its accomplishment. We would not tax man to take care of us. No, the Great Father has endowed all his creatures with the necessary powers for self-support, self-defence, and protection. We do not ask man to represent us, it is hard enough in times like these for man to carry back-bone enough to represent himself. So long as the mass of men spend most of their time on the fence, not knowing which way to jump, they are surely in no condition to tell us where we had better stand. In pity for man, we would no longer hang like a millstone round his neck. Undo what man did for us in the dark ages, and strike out all special legislation for us; strike out the name, *woman,* from all your constitutions, and then, with fair sailing, let us sink or swim, live or die, survive or perish together.

At Athens, an ancient apologue tells us, on the completion of the temple of Minerva, a statue of the goddess was wanted to occupy the crowning point of the edifice.[19] Two of the greatest artists produced what each deemed his master-piece. One of these figures was the size of life, admirably designed, exquisitely finished, softly rounded, and beautifully refined. The other was of Amazonian stature, and so boldly chiselled that it looked more like masonry than sculpture. The eyes of all were attracted by the first, and turned away in contempt from the second. That, therefore, was adopted, and the other rejected, almost with resentment, as though an insult had been offered to a discerning public. The favored statue was accordingly borne in triumph to the place for which it was designed, in the presence of applauding thousands, but as it receded from their up-turned eyes, all, all at once agaze upon it, the thunders of applause unaccountably died away, — a general misgiving ran through every bosom, — the mob themselves stood like statues, as silent and as petrified, for as it slowly went up, and up, the soft expression of those chiselled features, the delicate

---

[18]At the time, a woman's wages legally belonged to her husband, to spend as he saw fit. — EDS.

[19]Minerva was the widely worshipped Roman goddess of handicrafts with whom the Greek Athena was regularly identified. — KKC

curves and outlines of the limbs and figure, became gradually fainter and fainter, and when at last it reached the place for which it was intended, it was a shapeless ball, enveloped in mist. Of course, the idol of the hour was now clamored down as rationally as it had been cried up, and its dishonored rival, with no good will and no good looks on the part of the chagrined populace, was reared in its stead. As it ascended, the sharp angles faded away, the rough points became smooth, the features full of expression, the whole figure radiant with majesty and beauty. The rude hewn mass, that before scarcely appeared to bear even the human form, assumed at once the divinity which it represented, being so perfectly proportioned to the dimensions of the building, and to the elevation on which it stood, that it seemed as though Pallas[20] herself had alighted upon the pinnacle of the temple in person, to receive the homage of her worshippers.

The woman of the nineteenth century is the shapeless ball in the lofty position which she was designed fully and nobly to fill. The place is not too high, too large, too sacred for woman, but the type that you have chosen is far too small for it. The woman we declare unto you is the rude, misshapen, unpolished object of the successful artist. From your stand-point, you are absorbed with the defects alone. The true artist sees the harmony between the object and its destination. Man, the sculptor, has carved out his ideal, and applauding thousands welcome his success. He has made a woman that from his low standpoint looks fair and beautiful, a being without rights, or hopes, or fears but in him — neither noble, virtuous, nor independent.

Where do we see, in Church or State, in schoolhouse or at the fireside, the much talked-of moral power of woman? Like those Athenians, we have bowed down and worshiped in woman, beauty, grace, the exquisite proportions, the soft and beautifully rounded outline, her delicacy, refinement, and silent helplessness — all well when she is viewed simply as an object of sight, never to rise one foot above the dust from which she sprung. But if she is to be raised up to adorn a temple, or represent a divinity — if she is to fill the niche of wife and counsellor to true and noble men, if she is to be the mother, the educator of a race of heroes or martyrs, of a Napoleon, or a Jesus — then must the type of womanhood be on a larger scale than that yet carved by man.

In vain would the rejected artist have reasoned with the Athenians as to the superiority of his production; nothing short of the experiment they made could have satisfied them. And what of your experiment, what of your wives, your homes? Alas! for the folly and vacancy that meet you there! But for your clubhouses and newspapers, what would social life be to you? Where are your beautiful women? your frail ones, taught to lean lovingly and confidingly on man? Where are the crowds of educated dependents — where the long line of pensioners on man's bounty? Where all the young girls, taught to believe that marriage is the only legitimate object of a woman's pursuit — they who stand listlessly on life's shores,

[20]Another name for Athena. — EDS.

waiting, year after year, like the sick man at the pool of Bethesda, for some one to come and put them in?[21] These are they who by their ignorance and folly curse almost every fireside with some human specimen of deformity or imbecility. These are they who fill the gloomy abodes of poverty and vice in our vast metropolis. These are they who patrol the streets of our cities, to give our sons their first lessons in infamy. These are they who fill our asylums, and make night hideous with their cries and groans.

The women who are called masculine, who are brave, courageous, self-reliant, and independent, are they who, in the face of adverse winds, have kept one steady course upward and onward in the paths of virtue and peace — they who have taken their gauge of womanhood from their own native strength and dignity — they who have learned for themselves the will of God concerning them. This is our type of womanhood. Will you help us raise it up, that you too may see its beautiful proportions — that you may behold the outline of the goddess who is yet to adorn your temple of Freedom? We are building a model republic; our edifice will one day need a crowning glory. Let the artists be wisely chosen. Let them begin their work. Here is a temple to Liberty, to human rights, on whose portals behold the glorious declaration, "All men are created equal." The sun has never yet shone upon any of man's creations that can compare with this. The artist who can mould a statue worthy to crown magnificence like this, must be godlike in his conceptions, grand in his comprehensions, sublimely beautiful in his power of execution. The woman — the crowning glory of the model republic among the nations of the earth — what must she not be? *(Loud applause.)*

READING CRITICALLY

1. Stanton does not believe that men and women are fundamentally different. But, she says, if they are, then women must have their own representatives in government. Why?

2. According to Stanton, why are the laws oppressing women more cruel than southern slave laws? What women does she seem to have in mind?

3. Stanton says that sex prejudice is worse than race prejudice because white men deny only "social privileges" to blacks, while they deny to (white) women their "civil rights." Exactly what is the distinction between "social privileges" and "civil rights"?

4. How does Stanton refute the argument that women cannot be allowed to participate in political life (such as by voting) because they must be protected from male vulgarity?

5. What does Stanton say about the argument that God requires women to be confined to a narrow domestic sphere?

6. What is the point of Stanton's concluding story of the two statues?

[21]John 5:2–7. — KKC

WRITING ANALYTICALLY

1. The "slave" in the title of Stanton's speech is the white woman, enslaved by restrictive laws. Throughout her speech, Stanton draws a number of comparisons and contrasts between the condition of white women and that of African American men, both slave and free. Clearly her primary commitment is to attacking sexism, but as an abolitionist she also wants to attack racism. How does Stanton relate the issues of sexism and racism in this speech? Do you think she promotes antisexism at the expense of antiracism? Write a paper in which you respond to these questions, supporting your analysis with specific references to her text. Option: You may argue that she does, or does not, successfully attack both sexism and racism.

2. Stanton addresses a number of issues that you may have encountered in your other reading in Unit Three. For example, McCord (p. 307) argues that women will be exposed to male vulgarity and, worse, violence if they become politically active (see reading question 4). Stearns (p. 299), Folsom (p. 302), and the authors of the "Pastoral Letter" (p. 305) suggest that woman's place in the home is divinely ordained (see reading question 5). Emerson (p. 346) agrees with Stanton that the fact that many women do not want change does not mean that change is not needed. Choose one of these issues, and write a paper in which you compare and contrast the authors' views and the rhetorical strategies they employ for promoting those views. Option: You may also evaluate the writers' effectiveness as persuaders, considering yourself or your class as the audience.

3. The "Laws, Contracts, and Proclamations" section includes the text of two New York state laws governing married women's rights to property and guardianship of their children (p. 392). The second of these laws is the one Stanton successfully persuaded the legislature to pass with her speech "A Slave's Appeal." Write a paper in the form of a letter from Stanton to another women's rights activist after the passage of the 1860 law. In the letter have Stanton explain why the 1848 law was unsatisfactory, why the changes embodied in the 1860 law are good, and what further changes she might now want to work for.

ANNA JULIA COOPER

"The Higher Education of Women" (1892)

Anna Julia Cooper (1858–1964) was born in Raleigh, North Carolina, to a slave woman, Hannah, and her owner, George Washington Haywood, a successful lawyer. With emancipation, Cooper was sent to good schools, and in 1877 she married a young African American minister, George Cooper, who died two years later. Cooper then continued her education at Oberlin College, earning a B.A. and M.A., and went to work as a teacher. In 1902 she was appointed principal of what would become a noted Washington, D.C., school for African Americans, Dunbar High School, and here she spent most of the rest of her life. She quickly changed the school's policy of educating its students only for trades and prepared many of them for study at prestigious colleges. In 1925 Cooper earned a Ph.D. from the Sorbonne in Paris, one of the first African American women to attain this degree. Her acquaintances among African American intellectuals included Frederick Douglass and W. E. B. Du Bois, who once quoted her, anonymously, in an essay on women.

Cooper spoke frequently on African American rights, women's rights, and education issues and published frequently in the black press well into the 1940s; her major work is a collection of essays published in 1892, *A Voice from the South*. The essays are grouped into two sections, the first addressing women's issues generally, although infused with race consciousness, and the second focusing on African American rights. Reprinted here is an essay from the first section.

IN THE VERY FIRST YEAR OF OUR CENTURY, the year 1801, there appeared in Paris a book by Silvain Maréchal, entitled "Shall Woman Learn the Alphabet." The book proposes a law prohibiting the alphabet to women, and quotes authorities weighty and various, to prove that the woman who knows the alphabet has already lost part of her womanliness. The author declares that woman can use the alphabet only as Molière predicted they would, in spelling out the verb *amo;* that they have no occasion to peruse Ovid's *Ars Amoris,* since that is already the ground and limit of their intuitive furnishing;[1] that Madame Guion would have been far more adorable had she remained a beautiful ignoramus as nature made her; that Ruth,

Anna Julia Cooper, "The Higher Education of Women," in *A Voice from the South* (1892); reprinted with an introduction by Mary Helen Washington (New York: Oxford University Press, 1988), 48–79.

In the notes, AJC = Anna Julia Cooper, EDS. = Patricia Bizzell and Bruce Herzberg.

[1]Pierre-Sylvain Maréchal (1750–1803) was a French intellectual known for his scorn of religion — not, perhaps, the most trustworthy authority on what women should be and do. He refers to the French playwright Molière (1622–73) and also to the classical Roman poet Ovid (43 B.C.E–C.E.17?). *"Amo"* means "love" in Latin, and *"Ars Amoris"* is "The Art of Love." — EDS.

Naomi, the Spartan woman, the Amazons, Penelope, Andromache, Lucretia, Joan of Arc, Petrarch's Laura, the daughters of Charlemagne, could not spell their names; while Sappho, Aspasia, Madame de Maintenon, and Madame de Stael could read altogether too well for their good;[2] finally, that if women were once permitted to read Sophocles and work with logarithms, or to nibble at any side of the apple of knowledge, there would be an end forever to their sewing on buttons and embroidering slippers.[3]

Please remember this book was published at the *beginning* of the Nineteenth Century. At the end of its first third, (in the year 1833) one solitary college in America decided to admit women within its sacred precincts, and organized what was called a "Ladies' Course" as well as the regular B.A. or Gentlemen's course.[4]

It was felt to be an experiment — a rather dangerous experiment — and was adopted with fear and trembling by the good fathers, who looked as if they had been caught secretly mixing explosive compounds and were guiltily expecting every moment to see the foundations under them shaken and rent and their fair superstructure shattered into fragments.

But the girls came, and there was no upheaval. They performed their tasks modestly and intelligently. Once in a while one or two were found choosing the gentlemen's course. Still no collapse; and the dear, careful, scrupulous, frightened old professors were just getting their hearts out of their throats and preparing to draw one good free breath, when they found they would have to change the names of those courses; for there were as many ladies in the gentlemen's course as in the ladies', and a distinctively Ladies' Course, inferior in scope and aim to the regular classical course, did not and could not exist.

Other colleges gradually fell into line, and today there are 198 colleges for women, and 207 coeducational colleges and universities in the United States alone offering the degree of B. A. to women, and sending out yearly into the arteries of this nation a warm, rich flood of strong, brave, active, energetic, well-equipped, thoughtful women — women quick to see and eager to help the needs of this needy world — women who can think as well as feel, and who feel none the less because they think — women who are none the less tender and true for the parchment scroll they bear in their hands — women who have given a deeper, richer, nobler, and grander meaning to the word "womanly" than any

---

[2]Madame Guion was a seventeenth-century French woman of letters who was jailed repeatedly on charges of heresy. In Maréchal's list of illiterates are women from the Bible, ancient Greece and Rome, and more recent European history, all of whom are presumably admirable role models. Those who could read "too well" are ancient and modern women noted not only for their learning but also for their questionable sexual morality. — EDS.

[3]Like many other nineteenth-century essayists, Cooper alludes to historical and contemporary people, the work of other writers, the Bible, and so on. We provide explanatory footnotes only for allusions that are crucial for your understanding of Cooper's point. Otherwise, Cooper's own context is usually sufficient. (See writing question 3 on p. 386, where we invite you to consider the rhetorical technique of allusion in Cooper). — EDS.

[4]The college was Oberlin, in Ohio, from which Cooper herself graduated. — EDS.

one-sided masculine definition could ever have suggested or inspired — women whom the world has long waited for in pain and anguish till there should be at last added to its forces and allowed to permeate its thought the complement of that masculine influence which has dominated it for fourteen centuries.

Since the idea of order and subordination succumbed to barbarian brawn and brutality in the fifth century,[5] the civilized world has been like a child brought up by his father. It has needed the great mother heart to teach it to be pitiful, to love mercy, to succor the weak, and care for the lowly.

Whence came this apotheosis of greed and cruelty? Whence this sneaking admiration we all have for bullies and prize-fighters? Whence the self-congratulation of "dominant" races, as if "dominant" meant "righteous" and carried with it a title to inherit the earth? Whence the scorn of so-called weak or unwarlike races and individuals, and the very comfortable assurance that it is their manifest destiny to be wiped out as vermin before this advancing civilization? As if the possession of the Christian graces of meekness, nonresistance, and forgiveness, were incompatible with a civilization professedly based on Christianity, the religion of love! Just listen to this little bit of Barbarian brag:

> "As for Far Orientals, they are not of those who will survive. Artistic attractive people that they are, their civilization is like their own tree flowers, beautiful blossoms destined never to bear fruit. If these people continue in their old course, their earthly career is closed. Just as surely as morning passes into afternoon, so surely are these races of the Far East, if unchanged, destined to disappear before the advancing nations of the West. Vanish, they will, off the face of the earth, and leave our planet the eventual possession of the dwellers where the day declines. Unless their newly imported ideas really take root, it is from this whole world that Japanese and Koreans, as well as Chinese, will inevitably be excluded. Their Nirvana is already being realized; already, it has wrapped Far Eastern Asia in its winding sheet."
>
> — *Soul of the Far East* — P. Lowell

Delightful reflection for "the dwellers where day declines."[6] A spectacle to make the gods laugh, truly, to see the scion of an upstart race by one sweep of his generalizing pen consigning to annihilation one-third the inhabitants of the globe — a people whose civilization was hoary headed before the parent elements that begot his race had advanced beyond nebulosity.

---

[5]In the fifth century C.E., the civilization of ancient Rome was invaded by northern Europeans, commonly termed "barbarians" for their lack of Greco-Roman culture and of Christianity. Later in her essay, Cooper identifies these conquerors with the Anglo-Saxon "race," often deemed in the literature of the day to be the world's superior "race" (see notes 1 and 23 on pp. 347 and 355). — EDS.

[6]That is, where the sun sets — the "West," as Europeans and Americans often refer to their part of the earth, as opposed to the "East" of Asia. — EDS.

How like Longfellow's Iagoo,[7] we Westerners are, to be sure! In the few hundred years, we have had to strut across our allotted territory and bask in the afternoon sun, we imagine we have exhausted the possibilities of humanity. Verily, we are the people, and after us there is none other. Our God is power; strength, our standard of excellence, inherited from barbarian ancestors through a long line of male progenitors, the Law Salic permitting no feminine modifications.[8]

Says one, "The Chinaman is not popular with us, and we do not like the Negro. It is not that the eyes of the one are set bias, and the other is dark-skinned; but the Chinaman, the Negro is weak — *and Anglo Saxons don't like weakness.*"

The world of thought under the predominant man-influence, unmollified and unrestrained by its complementary force, would become like Daniel's fourth beast:[9] "dreadful and terrible, and *strong* exceedingly"; "it had great iron teeth; it devoured and brake in pieces, and stamped the residue with the feet of it"; and the most independent of us find ourselves ready at times to fall down and worship this incarnation of power.

Mrs. Mary A. Livermore, a woman whom I can mention only to admire, came near shaking my faith a few weeks ago in my theory of the thinking woman's mission to put in the tender and sympathetic chord in nature's grand symphony, and counteract, or better, harmonize the diapason of mere strength and might.

She was dwelling on the Anglo-Saxon genius for power and his contempt for weakness, and described a scene in San Francisco which she had witnessed.

The incorrigible animal known as the American small-boy, had pounced upon a simple, unoffending Chinaman, who was taking home his work, and had emptied the beautifully laundried contents of his basket into the ditch. "And," said she, "when that great man stood there and blubbered before that crowd of lawless urchins, to any one of whom he might have taught a lesson with his two fists, *I didn't much care.*"

This is said like a man! It grates harshly. It smacks of the worship of the beast. It is contempt for weakness, and taken out of its setting it seems to contradict my theory. It either shows that one of the highest exponents of the Higher Education can be at times untrue to the instincts I have ascribed to the thinking woman and to the contribution she is to add to the civilized world, or else the influence she wields upon our civilization may be potent without being necessarily and always direct and conscious. The latter is the case. Her voice may strike a false note, but her whole being is musical with the vibrations of human suffering. Her

---

[7]Iagoo is a teller of fanciful tales who entertains at Hiawatha's wedding in *The Song of Hiawatha* (1855) by Henry Wadsworth Longfellow (1807–82). — EDS.

[8]The "Law Salic," possibly derived from the code of an ancient tribe in France, provided that the throne could neither be inherited by a woman nor passed on to a man through the female line. — EDS.

[9]An apocalyptic monster, the fourth to emerge in the prophet's vision as described in the book of Daniel in the Bible. — EDS.

tongue may parrot over the cold conceits that some man has taught her, but her heart is aglow with sympathy and loving kindness, and she cannot be true to her real self without giving out these elements into the forces of the world.

No one is in any danger of imagining Mark Antony "a plain blunt man," nor Cassius a sincere one — whatever the speeches they may make.[10]

As individuals, we are constantly and inevitably, whether we are conscious of it or not, giving out our real selves into our several little worlds, inexorably adding our own true ray to the flood of starlight, quite independently of our professions and our masquerading; and so in the world of thought, the influence of thinking woman far transcends her feeble declamation and may seem at times even opposed to it.

A visitor in Oberlin once said to the lady principal, "Have you no rabble in Oberlin? How is it I see no police here, and yet the streets are as quiet and orderly as if there were an officer of the law standing on every corner."

Mrs. Johnston replied, "Oh, yes; there are vicious persons in Oberlin just as in other towns — *but our girls are our police.*"

With from five to ten hundred pure-minded young women threading the streets of the village every evening unattended, vice must slink away, like frost before the rising sun: and yet I venture to say there was not one in a hundred of those girls who would not have run from a street brawl as she would from a mouse, and who would not have declared she could never stand the sight of blood and pistols.

There is, then, a real and special influence of woman. An influence subtle and often involuntary, an influence so intimately interwoven in, so intricately interpenetrated by the masculine influence of the time that it is often difficult to extricate the delicate meshes and analyze and identify the closely clinging fibers. And yet, without this influence — so long as woman sat with bandaged eyes and manacled hands, fast bound in the clamps of ignorance and inaction, the world of thought moved in its orbit like the revolutions of the moon; with one face (the man's face) always out, so that the spectator could not distinguish whether it was disc or sphere.

Now I claim that it is the prevalence of the Higher Education among women, the making it a common everyday affair for women to reason and think and express their thought, the training and stimulus which enable and encourage women to administer to the world the bread it needs as well as the sugar it cries for; in short it is the transmitting the potential forces of her soul into dynamic factors that has given symmetry and completeness to the world's agencies. So only could it be consummated that Mercy, the lesson she teaches, and Truth, the task man has set himself, should meet together: that righteousness, or *rightness,* man's ideal, — and *peace,* its necessary "other half," should kiss each other.

---

[10]Mark Antony and Cassius were Roman statesmen around the time of Julius Caesar, probably best known to Cooper and her contemporary audience as characters in Shakespeare's play *Julius Caesar.* They plot Caesar's assassination and cover their violence with speeches that hide their true natures. — EDS.

We must thank the general enlightenment and independence of woman (which we may now regard as a *fait accompli*)[11] that both these forces are now at work in the world, and it is fair to demand from them for the twentieth century a higher type of civilization than any attained in the nineteenth. Religion, science, art, economics, have all needed the feminine flavor; and literature, the expression of what is permanent and best in all of these, may be gauged at any time to measure the strength of the feminine ingredient. You will not find theology consigning infants to lakes of unquenchable fire long after women have had a chance to grasp, master, and wield its dogmas. You will not find science annihilating personality from the government of the Universe and making of God an ungovernable, unintelligible, blind, often destructive physical force; you will not find jurisprudence formulating as an axiom the absurdity that man and wife are one, and that one the man — that the married woman may not hold or bequeath her own property save as subject to her husband's direction;[12] you will not find political economists declaring that the only possible adjustment between laborers and capitalists is that of selfishness and rapacity — that each must get all he can and keep all that he gets, while the world cries *laissez faire*[13] and the lawyers explain, "it is the beautiful working of the law of supply and demand"; in fine, you will not find the law of love shut out from the affairs of men after the feminine half of the world's truth is completed.

Nay, put your ear now close to the pulse of the time. What is the key-note of the literature of these days? What is the banner cry of all the activities of the last half decade? What is the dominant seventh which is to add richness and tone to the final cadences of this century and lead by a grand modulation into the triumphant harmonies of the next? Is it not compassion for the poor and unfortunate, and, as Bellamy[14] has expressed it, "indignant outcry against the failure of the social machinery as it is, to ameliorate the miseries of men!" Even Christianity is being brought to the bar of humanity and tried by the standard of its ability to alleviate the world's suffering and lighten and brighten its woe. What else can be the meaning of Matthew Arnold's saddening protest, "We cannot do without Christianity," cried he, " and we cannot endure it as it is."

When went there by an age, when so much time and thought, so much money and labor were given to God's poor and God's invalids, the lowly and unlovely, the sinning as well as the suffering — homes for inebriates and homes for lunatics, shelter for the aged and shelter for babes, hospi-

---

[11] *"Fait accompli"* is a French phrase meaning "an accomplished fact"—that is, something generally regarded to be true or complete. — EDS.

[12] By Cooper's day, these restrictive laws governing married women (see the introduction, pp. 287–88) had been liberalized in many states, although at this date (1892) women still were not able to vote in national elections. — EDS.

[13] *"Laissez faire"* a French phrase used for the economic doctrine that calls for minimal government intervention in free competition. — EDS.

[14] Edward Bellamy (1850–98) was an American writer and author of the utopian novel *Looking Backward: 2000–1887* (1888), which is excerpted in Unit Four (p. 477).

tals for the sick, props and braces for the falling, reformatory prisons and prison reformatories, all show that a "mothering" influence from some source is leavening the nation.

Now please understand me. I do not ask you to admit that these bene-factions and virtues are the exclusive possession of women, or even that women are their chief and only advocates. It may be a man who formulates and makes them vocal. It may be, and often is, a man who weeps over the wrongs and struggles for the amelioration: but that man has imbibed those impulses from a mother rather than from a father and is simply materializing and giving back to the world in tangible form the ideal love and tenderness, devotion and care that have cherished and nourished the helpless period of his own existence.

All I claim is that there is a feminine as well as a masculine side to truth; that these are related not as inferior and superior, not as better and worse, not as weaker and stronger, but as complements — complements in one necessary and symmetric whole. That as the man is more noble in reason, so the woman is more quick in sympathy. That as he is indefatigable in pursuit of abstract truth, so is she in caring for the interests by the way — striving tenderly and lovingly that not one of the least of these "little ones" should perish. That while we not unfrequently see women who reason, we say, with the coolness and precision of a man, and men as considerate of helplessness as a woman, still there is a general consensus of mankind that the one trait is essentially masculine and the other is peculiarly feminine. That both are needed to be worked into the training of children, in order that our boys may supplement their virility by tenderness and sensibility, and our girls may round out their gentleness by strength and self-reliance. That, as both are alike necessary in giving symmetry to the individual, so a nation or a race will degenerate into mere emotionalism on the one hand, or bullyism on the other, if dominated by either exclusively; lastly, and most emphatically, that the feminine factor can have its proper effect only through woman's development and education so that she may fitly and intelligently stamp her force on the forces of her day, and add her modicum to the riches of the world's thought.

> For woman's cause is man's: they rise or sink
> Together, dwarfed or godlike, bond or free:
> For she that out of Lethe scales with man
> The shining steps of nature, shares with man
> His nights, his days, moves with him to one goal.
> If she be small, slight-natured, miserable,
> How shall men grow?
> . . . Let her make herself her own
> To give or keep, to live and learn and be
> All that not harms distinctive womanhood.
> For woman is not undeveloped man
> But diverse: could we make her as the man
> Sweet love were slain; his dearest bond is this,
> Not like to like, but like in difference.

> Yet in the long years liker must they grow;
> The man be more of woman, she of man;
> He gain in sweetness and in moral height,
> Nor lose the wrestling thews that throw the world;
> She mental breadth, nor fail in childward care,
> Nor lose the childlike in the larger mind;
> Till at the last she set herself to man,
> Like perfect music unto noble words.

Now you will argue, perhaps, and rightly, that higher education for women is not a modern idea, and that, if that is the means of setting free and invigorating the long desired feminine force in the world, it has already had a trial and should, in the past, have produced some of these glowing effects. Sappho, the bright, sweet singer of Lesbos, "the violet-crowned, pure, sweetly smiling Sappho" as Alcaeus calls her, chanted her lyrics and poured forth her soul nearly six centuries before Christ, in notes as full and free, as passionate and eloquent as did ever Archilochus or Anacreon.

Aspasia, that earliest queen of the drawing room, a century later ministered to the intellectual entertainment of Socrates and the leading wits and philosophers of her time. Indeed, to her is attributed, by the best critics, the authorship of one of the most noted speeches ever delivered by Pericles.

Later on, during the Renaissance period, women were professors in mathematics, physics, metaphysics, and the classic languages in Bologna, Pavia, Padua, and Brescia. Olympia Fulvia Morata, of Ferrara, a most interesting character, whose magnificent library was destroyed in 1553 in the invasion of Schweinfurt by Albert of Brandenburg, had acquired a most extensive education. It is said that this wonderful girl gave lectures on classical subjects in her sixteenth year, and had even before that written several very remarkable Greek and Latin poems, and what is also to the point, she married a professor at Heidelberg, and became a *help-meet for him.*

It is true then that the higher education for women — in fact, the highest that the world has ever witnessed — belongs to the past; but we must remember that it was possible, down to the middle of our own century, only to a select few; and that the fashions and traditions of the times were before that all against it. There were not only no stimuli to encourage women to make the most of their powers and to welcome their development as a helpful agency in the progress of civilization, but their little aspirations, when they had any, were chilled and snubbed in embryo, and any attempt at thought was received as a monstrous usurpation of man's prerogative.

Lessing declared that "the woman who thinks is like the man who puts on rouge — ridiculous"; and Voltaire in his coarse, flippant way used to say, "Ideas are like beards — women and boys have none." Dr. Maginn remarked, "We like to hear a few words of sense from a woman sometimes, as we do from a parrot — they are so unexpected!" and even the pious

Fenelon taught that virgin delicacy is almost as incompatible with learning as with vice.

That the average woman retired before these shafts of wit and ridicule and even gloried in her ignorance is not surprising. The Abbé Choisi, it is said, praised the Duchesse de Fontanges as being pretty as an angel and silly as a goose, and all the young ladies of the court strove to make up in folly what they lacked in charms. The ideal of the day was that "women must be pretty, dress prettily, flirt prettily, and not be too well informed"; that it was the *summum bonum*[15] of her earthly hopes to have, as Thackeray puts it, "all the fellows battling to dance with her"; that she had no God-given destiny, no soul with unquenchable longings and inexhaustible possibilities — no work of her own to do and give to the world — no absolute and inherent value, no duty to self, transcending all pleasure-giving that may be demanded of a mere toy; but that her value was purely a relative one and to be estimated as are the fine arts — by the pleasure they give. "Woman, wine, and song," as "the world's best gifts to man," were linked together in praise with as little thought of the first saying, "What doest thou," as that the wine and the song should declare, "We must be about our Father's business."[16]

Men believed, or pretended to believe, that the great law of self development was obligatory on their half of the human family only; that while it was the chief end of man to glorify God and put his five talents to the exchangers, gaining thereby another five, it was, or ought to be, the sole end of woman to glorify man and wrap her one decently away in a napkin[17] retiring into "Hezekiah Smith's lady during her natural life and Hezekiah Smith's relict on her tombstone"; that higher education was incompatible with the shape of the female cerebrum, and that even if it could be acquired it must inevitably unsex woman destroying the lisping, clinging, tenderly helpless, and beautifully dependent creatures whom men would so heroically think for and so gallantly fight for, and giving in their stead a formidable race of blue stockings with cork-screw ringlets and other spinster propensities.

But these are eighteenth century ideas.

We have seen how the pendulum has swung across our present century. The men of our time have asked with Emerson, "that woman only show us

[15]Latin for "supreme good." — EDS.

[16]Cooper alludes here to Luke 2:48–49. Upon finding the boy Jesus deep in discussion with the rabbis in the Temple, his mother questions him by saying, "What doest thou?" Jesus replies, "I must be about my Father's business." Cooper playfully uses this allusion to make a point about woman's status as pleasure object, comparable to "wine and song." According to Cooper, man would be just as surprised to hear woman question her status (by saying, "What doest thou?") as to hear "wine and song" start answering back (by declaring, "We must be about our Father's business"). — EDS.

[17]Cooper alludes here to Jesus' parable of the talents, or pieces of money, given by a rich man to his servants. The man praises the servants who used their talents to make more money and condemns the one who hid his piece away, supposedly to keep it safe (Matthew 25:14–30). Jesus suggests that God wants us to use our "talents," or abilities, to the fullest for good. — EDS.

how she can best be served"; and woman has replied: the chance of the seedling and of the animalcule is all I ask — the chance for growth and self development, the permission to be true to the aspirations of my soul without incurring the blight of your censure and ridicule.

Audetque viris concurrere virgo.[18]

In soul-culture woman at last dares to contend with men, and we may cite Grant Allen (who certainly cannot be suspected of advocating the unsexing of woman) as an example of the broadening effect of this contest on the ideas at least of the men of the day. He says in his *Plain Words on the Woman Question*, recently published:

> The position of woman was not [in the past] a position which could bear the test of nineteenth-century scrutiny. Their education was inadequate, their social status was humiliating, their political power was nil, their practical and personal grievances were innumerable; above all, their relations to the family — to their husbands, their children, their friends, their property — was simply insupportable.

And again:

> As a body we "Advanced men" are, I think, prepared to reconsider, and to reconsider fundamentally, without prejudice or misconception, the entire question of the relation between the sexes. We are ready to make any modifications in those relations which will satisfy the woman's just aspiration for personal independence, for intellectual and moral development, for physical culture, for political activity, and for a voice in the arrangement of her own affairs, both domestic and national.

Now this is magnanimous enough, surely; and quite a step from eighteenth century preaching, is it not? The higher education of Woman has certainly developed the men; — let us see what it has done for the women.

Matthew Arnold during his last visit to America in '82 or '83, lectured before a certain coeducational college in the West. After the lecture he remarked, with some surprise, to a lady professor, that the young women in his audience, he noticed, paid as close attention as the men, *all the way through.*" This led, of course, to a spirited discussion of the higher education for women, during which he said to his enthusiastic interlocutor, eyeing her philosophically through his English eyeglass: "But — eh — don't you think it — eh — spoils their *chawnces,* you know!"

Now, as to the result to women, this is the most serious argument ever used against the higher education. If it interferes with marriage, classical training has a grave objection to weigh and answer.

For I agree with Mr. Allen at least on this one point, that there must be marrying and giving in marriage even till the end of time.

I grant you that intellectual development, with the self-reliance and capacity for earning a livelihood which it gives, renders woman less depen-

---

[18]"And the virgin associates with the men." — EDS.

dent on the marriage relation for physical support (which, by the way, does not always accompany it). Neither is she compelled to look to sexual love as the one sensation capable of giving tone and relish, movement and vim to the life she leads. Her horison is extended. Her sympathies are broadened and deepened and multiplied. She is in closer touch with nature. Not a bud that opens, not a dew drop, not a ray of light, not a cloudburst or a thunderbolt, but adds to the expansiveness and zest of her soul. And if the sun of an absorbing passion be gone down, still 'tis night that brings the stars. She has remaining the mellow, less obtrusive, but none the less enchanting and inspiring light of friendship, and into its charmed circle she may gather the best the world has known. She can commune with Socrates about the *daimon*[19] he knew and to which she too can bear witness; she can revel in the majesty of Dante, the sweetness of Virgil, the simplicity of Homer, the strength of Milton. She can listen to the pulsing heart throbs of passionate Sappho's encaged soul, as she beats her bruised wings against her prison bars and struggles to flutter out into Heaven's aether, and the fires of her own soul cry back as she listens. "Yes; Sappho, I know it all; I know it all." Here, at last, can be communion without suspicion; friendship without misunderstanding; love without jealousy.[20]

We must admit then that Byron's picture, whether a thing of beauty or not, has faded from the canvas of today.

> "Man's love," he wrote, "is of man's life a thing apart,
> 'Tis woman's whole existence.
> Man may range the court, camp, church, the vessel and the mart,
> Sword, gown, gain, glory offer in exchange.
> Pride, fame, ambition, to fill up his heart —
> And few there are whom these cannot estrange.
> Men have all these resources, we *but one* —
> *To love again and be again undone.*"

This may have been true when written. *It is not true today.* The old, subjective, stagnant, indolent, and wretched life for woman has gone. She has as many resources as men, as many activities beckon her on. As large possibilities swell and inspire her heart.

Now, then, does it destroy or diminish her capacity for loving?

Her standards have undoubtedly gone up. The necessity of speculating in "chawnces" has probably shifted. The question is not now with the woman "How shall I so cramp, stunt, simplify, and nullify myself as to make me eligible to the honor of being swallowed up into some little man?" but the problem, I trow, now rests with the man as to how he can so develop his God-given powers as to reach the ideal of a generation of women who

---

[19]The *"daimon"* of the ancient Greek philosopher Socrates was an attendant spirit whom he spoke of as inspiring his thoughts. — EDS.

[20]Cooper here imagines the educated woman enriching her life with enjoyment of the writings of classical and Renaissance poets and philosophers. — EDS.

demand the noblest, grandest, and best achievements of which he is capable; and this surely is the only fair and natural adjustment of the chances. Nature never meant that the ideals and standards of the world should be dwarfing and minimizing ones, and the men should thank us for requiring of them the richest fruits which they can grow. If it makes them work, all the better for them.

As to the adaptability of the educated woman to the marriage relation, I shall simply quote from that excellent symposium of learned women that appeared recently under Mrs. Armstrong's signature in answer to the "Plain Words" of Mr. Allen, already referred to. "Admitting no longer any question as to their intellectual equality with the men whom they meet, with the simplicity of conscious strength, they take their place beside the men who challenge them, and fearlessly face the result of their actions. They deny that their education in any way unfits them for the duty of wifehood and maternity or primarily renders these conditions any less attractive to them than to the domestic type of woman. On the contrary, they hold that their knowledge of physiology makes them better mothers and housekeepers; their knowledge of chemistry makes them better cooks; while from their training in other natural sciences and in mathematics, they obtain an accuracy and fair-mindedness which is of great value to them in dealing with their children or employees."

So much for their willingness. Now the apple may be good for food and pleasant to the eyes, and a fruit to be desired to make one wise. Nay, it may even assure you that it has no aversion whatever to being tasted. Still, if you do not like the flavor all these recommendations are nothing. Is the intellectual woman *desirable* in the matrimonial market?

This I cannot answer. I confess my ignorance. I am no judge of such things. I have been told that strong-minded women could be, when they thought it worth their while, quite endurable, and, judging from the number of female names I find in college catalogues among the alumnae with double patronymics, I surmise that quite a number of men are willing to put up with them.

Now I would that my task ended here. Having shown that a great want of the world in the past has been a feminine force; that that force can have its full effect only through the untrammelled development of woman; that such development, while it gives her to the world and to civilization, does not necessarily remove her from the home and fireside; finally, that while past centuries have witnessed sporadic instances of this higher growth, still it was reserved for the latter half of the nineteenth century to render it common and general enough to be effective; I might close with a glowing prediction of what the twentieth century may expect from this heritage of twin forces — the masculine battered and toil-worn as a grim veteran after centuries of warfare, but still strong, active, and vigorous, ready to help with his hard-won experience the young recruit rejoicing in her newly found freedom, who so confidently places her hand in his with mutual pledges to redeem the ages.

> And so the twain upon the skirts of Time,
> Sit side by side, full-summed in all their powers,
> Dispensing harvest, sowing the To-be,
> Self-reverent each and reverencing each.

Fain would I follow them, but duty is nearer home. The high ground of generalities is alluring but my pen is devoted to a special cause: and with a view to further enlightenment on the achievements of the century for THE HIGHER EDUCATION OF COLORED WOMEN, I wrote a few days ago to the colleges which admit women and asked how many colored women had completed the B. A. course in each during its entire history. These are the figures returned: Fisk leads the way with twelve; Oberlin next with five; Wilberforce, four; Ann Arbor and Wellesley three each, Livingstone two, Atlanta one, Howard, as yet, none.

I then asked the principal of the Washington High School how many out of a large number of female graduates from his school had chosen to go forward and take a collegiate course. He replied that but one had ever done so, and she was then in Cornell.[21]

Others ask questions too, sometimes, and I was asked a few years ago by a white friend, "How is it that the men of your race seem to outstrip the women in mental attainment?" "Oh," I said, "so far as it is true, the men, I suppose, from the life they lead, gain more by contact; and so far as it is only apparent, I think the women are more quiet. They don't feel called to mount a barrel and harangue by the hour every time they imagine they have produced an idea."

But I am sure there is another reason which I did not at that time see fit to give. The atmosphere, the standards, the requirements of our little world do not afford any special stimulus to female development.

It seems hardly a gracious thing to say, but it strikes me as true, that while our men seem thoroughly abreast of the times on almost every other subject, when they strike the woman question they drop back into sixteenth century logic. They leave nothing to be desired generally in regard to gallantry and chivalry, but they actually do not seem sometimes to have outgrown that old contemporary of chivalry — the idea that women may stand on pedestals or live in doll houses, (if they happen to have them) but they must not furrow their brows with thought or attempt to help men tug at the great questions of the world. I fear the majority of colored men do not yet think it worth while that women aspire to higher education. Not many will subscribe to the "advanced" ideas of Grant Allen already quoted. The three R's, a little music and a good deal of dancing, a first rate dressmaker and a bottle of magnolia balm, are quite enough generally to render charming any woman possessed of tact and the capacity for worshipping masculinity.

[21]Graduated from Scientific Course, June, 1890, the first colored woman to graduate from Cornell. — AJC

My readers will pardon my illustrating my point and also giving a reason for the fear that is in me, by a little bit of personal experience. When a child I was put into a school near home that professed to be normal and collegiate, i.e., to prepare teachers for colored youth, furnish candidates for the ministry, and offer collegiate training for those who should be ready for it. Well, I found after a while that I had a good deal of time on my hands. I had devoured what was put before me, and, like Oliver Twist, was looking around to ask for more. I constantly felt (as I suppose many an ambitious girl has felt) a thumping from within unanswered by any beckoning from without. Class after class was organized for these ministerial candidates (many of them men who had been preaching before I was born). Into every one of these classes I was expected to go, with the sole intent, I thought at the time, of enabling the dear old principal, as he looked from the vacant countenances of his sleepy old class over to where I sat, to get off his solitary pun — his never-failing pleasantry, especially in hot weather — which was, as he called out "Any one!" to the effect that "*any* one" then meant "*Annie* one."

Finally a Greek class was to be formed. My inspiring preceptor informed me that Greek had never been taught in the school, but that he was going to form a class *for the candidates for the ministry,* and if I liked I might join it. I replied — humbly I hope, as became a female of the human species — that I would like very much to study Greek, and that I was thankful for the opportunity, and so it went on. A boy, however meager his equipment and shallow his pretentions, had only to declare a floating intention to study theology and he could get all the support, encouragement and stimulus he needed, be absolved from work and invested beforehand with all the dignity of his far away office. While a self-supporting girl had to struggle on by teaching in the summer and working after school hours to keep up with her board bills, and actually to fight her way against positive discouragements to the higher education; till one such girl one day flared out and told the principal "the only mission opening before a girl in his school was to marry one of those candidates." He said he didn't know but it was. And when at last that same girl announced her desire and intention to go to college it was received with about the same incredulity and dismay as if a brass button on one of those candidate's coats had propounded a new method for squaring the circle or trisecting the arc.

Now this is not fancy. It is a simple unvarnished photograph, and what I believe was not in those days exceptional in colored schools, and I ask the men and women who are teachers and co-workers for the highest interests of the race, that they give the girls a chance! We might as well expect to grow trees from leaves as hope to build up a civilization or a manhood without taking into consideration our women and the home life made by them, which must be the root and ground of the whole matter. Let us insist then on special encouragement for the education of our women and special care in their training. Let our girls feel that we expect something more of them than that they merely look pretty and appear well in society. Teach them that there is a race with special needs which they and only they can help; that the world needs and is already asking for their trained, efficient forces. Finally, if there is an ambitious girl with pluck and brain to take the higher education, encourage her to make the most of it. Let there be the same flourish of trumpets and clapping of hands as when a boy announces his determination to enter the lists; and then, as you know that she is physically the weaker of the two, don't stand from under and leave her to buffet the waves alone. Let her know that your heart is following her, that your hand, though she sees it not, is ready to support her. To be plain, I mean let money be raised and scholarships be founded in our colleges and universities for self-supporting, worthy young women, to offset and balance the aid that can always be found for boys who will take theology.

The earnest well trained Christian young woman, as a teacher, as a homemaker, as wife, mother, or silent influence even, is as potent a missionary agency among our people as is the theologian; and I claim that at the present stage of our development in the South she is even more important and necessary.

Let us then, here and now, recognize this force and resolve to make the most of it — not the boys less, but the girls more.

READING CRITICALLY

1. Cooper claims that men have dominated Western civilization since the fifth century. What does she say has resulted from this domination?

2. According to Cooper, how will civilization benefit from the increased feminine influence that college-educated women will be able to exert on it?

3. How does Cooper explain the fact that few women have attained higher education at the time of her writing (the end of the nineteenth century)?

4. How does Cooper answer the objection that higher education will make women unfit for marriage?

5. According to Cooper, why do women of color lag behind men of color in their educational accomplishments? How is this illustrated by the story of her own struggle to be educated?

WRITING ANALYTICALLY

1. Although Cooper clearly wants women to enter all areas of public life and all professions, she also talks continually as if she believed that men and women were fundamentally different. Write a paper in which you explain what Cooper's view of women's essential nature is, supporting your analysis with references to her text. Option: You may assess the extent to which Cooper is a feminist according to your own definition of the term. Alternative: Compare and contrast Cooper's view of the essential nature of women with that put forward by Ralph Waldo Emerson (p. 346).

2. Although Cooper does not address the education of women of color until the end of her essay, how could race consciousness be said to influence her earlier

analysis of Western civilization and its need for feminine influence? Write a paper in which you explain how Cooper's awareness of the evils of white supremacist racism influences her argument. If you wish, you may consider the evidence of this influence as a deliberate rhetorical strategy employed by Cooper to attract white, women's rights activists to the cause of civil rights for people of color; in that case, you should describe and evaluate how these references work as strategies for this purpose.

3. Reading Emerson (p. 346), Stanton (p. 357), and Cooper, you have discovered that nineteenth-century authors like to illustrate their discussions with frequent allusions to other writers, brief quotations, snippets of poetry, and the like. We find more of this technique in Cooper than in any other writer in Unit Three. Write a paper in which you explain how you think the frequent allusions change Cooper's essay (for better or worse) and why you think she makes such heavy use of this rhetorical strategy. Alternative: As a class, make a list of all the names Cooper mentions. Try to put them into groups according to country of origin, time period, and so on (you will have to make some guesses). Then have small groups of students divide the lists of names and find out who they are. Your teacher or a reference librarian can suggest places to look. The groups should report back to the whole class on what they have discovered. Finally, provided with this information, the whole class may discuss — or each student may write a brief response to — the question of what these references reveal about Cooper, her education, her sense of her audience, and so on.

LAWS, CONTRACTS, AND PROCLAMATIONS ON WOMEN'S RIGHTS

SENECA FALLS WOMEN'S RIGHTS CONVENTION

"Declaration of Sentiments and Resolutions" (1848)

The "Declaration of Sentiments and Resolutions" was written by Mary Ann McClintock, Lucretia Coffin Mott, Elizabeth Cady Stanton (also see p. 357), and Martha Coffin Wright for the first American women's rights convention, which took place in Seneca Falls, New York, on July 19 and 20, 1848. The convention was organized by Stanton and Mott, who had met in London in 1840 when they were excluded from a world abolitionist conference because they were women.

After discussing the document, the convention participants voted on the resolutions, number 12 being added by Mott from the convention floor. All but number 9, on women's suffrage, passed unanimously; 9 did pass, in part due to vigorous support from Frederick Douglass (p. 338). About one hundred participants then signed the document, but when it was published it excited so much negative criticism that many asked to have their names removed. Nevertheless, the "Declaration" became a model for ongoing efforts to remedy women's legal inequities and to reduce gender-based discrimination.

WHEN, IN THE COURSE OF HUMAN EVENTS, it becomes necessary for one portion of the family of man to assume among the people of the earth a position different from that which they have hitherto occupied, but one to which the laws of nature and of nature's God entitle them, a decent respect to the opinions of mankind requires that they should declare the causes that impel them to such a course.

We hold these truths to be self-evident: that all men and women are created equal; that they are endowed by their Creator with certain inalienable rights, that among these are life, liberty, and the pursuit of happiness; that to secure these rights governments are instituted, deriving their just powers from the consent of the governed. Whenever any form of government becomes destructive of these ends, it is the right of those who suffer from

Seneca Falls Women's Rights Convention, "Declaration of Sentiments and Resolutions," reprinted in *Man Cannot Speak for Her*, vol. 2 of *Key Texts of the Early Feminists*, ed. Karlyn Kohrs Campbell (New York: Greenwood, Praeger, 1989), 34–39.

In the notes, EDS. = Patricia Bizzell and Bruce Herzberg.

it to refuse allegiance to it, and to insist upon the institution of a new government, laying its foundation on such principles, and organizing its powers in such form as to them shall seem most likely to effect their safety and happiness. Prudence, indeed, will dictate that governments long established should not be changed for light and transient causes; and accordingly, all experience hath shown that mankind are more disposed to suffer, while evils are sufferable, than to right themselves by abolishing the forms to which they were accustomed. But when a long train of abuses and usurpations, pursuing invariably the same object evinces a design to reduce them under absolute despotism, it is their duty to throw off such government and to provide new guards for their future security. Such has been the patient sufferance of the women under this government, and such is now the necessity which constrains them to demand the equal station to which they are entitled.

The history of mankind is a history of repeated injuries and usurpations on the part of man toward woman, having in direct object the establishment of an absolute tyranny over her. To prove this, let facts be submitted to a candid world.

He has never permitted her to exercise her inalienable right to the elective franchise.

He has compelled her to submit to laws, in the formation of which she had no voice.

He has withheld from her rights which are given to the most ignorant and degraded men — both natives and foreigners.

Having deprived her of this first right of a citizen, the elective franchise, thereby leaving her without representation in the halls of legislation, he has oppressed her on all sides.

He has made her, if married, in the eye of the law, civilly dead.

He has taken from her all right in property, even to the wages she earns.

He has made her, morally, an irresponsible being, as she can commit many crimes with impunity, provided they be done in the presence of her husband. In the covenant of marriage, she is compelled to promise obedience to her husband, he becoming, to all intents and purposes, her master — the law giving him power to deprive her of her liberty, and to administer chastisement.

He has so framed the laws of divorce, as to what shall be the proper causes of divorce; in case of separation, to whom the guardianship of the children shall be given; as to be wholly regardless of the happiness of women — the law, in all cases, going upon a false supposition of the supremacy of man, and giving all power into his hands.

After depriving her of all rights as a married woman, if single and the owner of property, he has taxed her to support a government which recognizes her only when her property can be made profitable to it.

He has monopolized nearly all the profitable employments, and from those she is permitted to follow, she receives but a scanty remuneration.

He closes against her all the avenues to wealth and distinction, which he considers most honorable to himself. As a teacher of theology, medicine, or law, she is not known.

He has denied her the facilities for obtaining a thorough education — all colleges being closed against her.[1]

He allows her in Church, as well as State, but a subordinate position, claiming Apostolic authority for her exclusion from the ministry, and, with some exceptions, from any public participation in the affairs of the Church.

He has created a false public sentiment, by giving to the world a different code of morals for men and women, by which moral delinquencies which exclude women from society, are not only tolerated but deemed of little account in man.[2]

He has usurped the prerogative of Jehovah himself, claiming it as his right to assign for her a sphere of action, when that belongs to her conscience and to her God.

He has endeavored, in every way that he could, to destroy her confidence in her own powers, to lessen her self-respect, and to make her willing to lead a dependent and abject life.

Now, in view of this entire disfranchisement of one-half the people of this country, their social and religious degradation, — in view of the unjust laws above mentioned, and because women do feel themselves aggrieved, oppressed, and fraudulently deprived of their most sacred rights, we insist that they have immediate admission to all the rights and privileges which belong to them as citizens of the United States.

In entering upon the great work before us, we anticipate no small amount of misconception, misrepresentation, and ridicule; but we shall use every instrumentality within our power to effect our object. We shall employ agents, circulate tracts, petition the state and national legislatures, and endeavor to enlist the pulpit and the press in our behalf. We hope this Convention will be followed by a series of Conventions, embracing every part of the country.

Firmly relying upon the final triumph of the Right and True, we do this day affix our signatures to this declaration. [*Names followed.*]

RESOLUTIONS

Whereas, The great precept of nature is conceded to be, "that man shall pursue his own true and substantial happiness." Blackstone,[3] in his *Commentaries* remarks, that this law of Nature being coeval with mankind, and

---

[1] In fact, by 1848 Oberlin College admitted women. — EDS.

[2] The "delinquencies" referred to here are sexual misconduct. This double standard of sexual morality is attacked in resolution 6, which calls for men to behave as chastely as women are required to do. — EDS.

[3] Sir William Blackstone (1723–80) was an English jurist whose codification of English law widely influenced the formation of laws in the colonies that became the United States. No more respected legal authority could be cited. — EDS.

dictated by God himself, is of course superior in obligation to any other. It is binding over all the globe, in all countries, and at all times; no human laws are of any validity if contrary to this, and such of them as are valid, derive all their force, and all their validity, and all their authority, mediately and immediately, from this original; therefore,

1. Resolved, That such laws as conflict, in any way, with the true and substantial happiness of woman, are contrary to the great precept of nature, and of no validity; for this is "superior in obligation to any other."

2. Resolved, That all laws which prevent woman from occupying such a station in society as her conscience shall dictate, or which place her in a position inferior to that of man, are contrary to the great precept of nature, and therefore of no force or authority.

3. Resolved, That woman is man's equal — was intended to be so by the Creator, and the highest good of the race demands that she should be recognized as such.

4. Resolved, That the women of this country ought to be enlightened in regard to the laws under which they live, that they may no longer publish their degradation, by declaring themselves satisfied with their present position, nor their ignorance, by asserting that they have all the rights they want.

5. Resolved, That inasmuch as man, while claiming for himself intellectual superiority, does not accord to woman moral superiority, it is preeminently his duty to encourage her to speak, and teach, as she has an opportunity, in all religious assemblies.

6. Resolved, That the same amount of virtue, delicacy, and refinement of behavior, that is required of woman in the social state, should also be required of man, and the same transgressions should be visited with equal severity on both man and woman.

7. Resolved, That the objection of indelicacy and impropriety, which is so often brought against woman when she addresses a public audience, comes with a very ill grace from those who encourage, by their attendance, her appearance on the stage, in the concert, or in feats of the circus.

8. Resolved, That woman has too long rested satisfied in the circumscribed limits which corrupt customs and a perverted application of the Scriptures have marked out for her, and that it is time she should move in the enlarged sphere which her great Creator has assigned her.

9. Resolved, That it is the duty of the women of this country to secure to themselves their sacred right to the elective franchise.

10. Resolved, That the equality of human rights results necessarily from the fact of the identity of the race in capabilities and responsibilities.

11. Resolved, therefore, That, being invested by the Creator with the same capabilities, and the same consciousness of responsibility

for their exercise, it is demonstrably the right and duty of woman, equally with man, to promote every righteous cause, by every righteous means; and especially in regard to the great subjects of morals and religions, it is self-evidently her right to participate with her brother in teaching them, both in private and in public, by writing and by speaking, by any instrumentalities proper to be used, and in any assemblies proper to be held; and this being a self-evident truth, growing out of the divinely implanted principles of human nature, any custom or authority adverse to it, whether modern or wearing the hoary sanction of antiquity, is to be regarded as a self-evident falsehood, and at war with mankind.

12. Resolved, That the speedy success of our cause depends upon the zealous and untiring efforts of both men and women, for the overthrow of the monopoly of the pulpit, and for the securing to woman an equal participation with men in the various trades, professions, and commerce.

READING CRITICALLY

1. The first two paragraphs of the "Declaration" imitate the Declaration of Independence, but with some changes. Compare this text with the text of the Declaration of Independence (p. 174) and list all actual changes. Make a second list of phrases that are identical in wording in the two documents but seem to mean one thing in the Declaration of Independence and something else in the "Declaration of Sentiments."

2. On pages 388–89, the "Declaration" lists the grievances of women against men, imitating the Declaration of Independence and the way it lists the colonists' grievances against the English king. Make a list of the women's grievances, putting them in your own words.

3. Examine the resolutions and list, in your own words, those that demand action from women.

WRITING ANALYTICALLY

1. The repeated references to the Declaration of Independence within the "Declaration of Sentiments" could be said to constitute a kind of implied argument in favor of women's rights. Write a paper in which you explain the argument implied by these references and evaluate the effectiveness of the references as a rhetorical strategy for advancing this argument.

2. One of woman's grievances against man, according to the "Declaration," is that he has assigned her to an overly limited "sphere of action" (p. 389). The "Declaration" never explicitly states what woman's sphere should be, but you can make an inference based on what the "Declaration" requests or demands for women's activities. Write an essay in which you explain the idea of woman's sphere that operates in the "Declaration," citing evidence from the text to support your answer.

3. Write a speech that might have been given at the Seneca Falls convention by either Catharine Beecher (p. 294) or Jonathan F. Stearns (p. 299), supposing that they attended in order to oppose the convention's "sentiments and resolutions."

New York State Married Women's Property Laws (1848, 1860)

Mississippi in 1839 and New York in 1848 passed the first laws modifying married women's legal inability to hold property (see the introduction to Unit Three, pp. 287–88 and 292–93, on this issue). Some historians argue that male legislatures were influenced to pass these laws by men who wished to protect inheritances that they might leave to their daughters. The Mississippi law explicitly protected the married woman's right to own slaves independently of her husband.

The first New York law (1848) protected only personal property, such as clothing and real property — what we would call real estate. The second New York law (1860) enlarged the married woman's legal capabilities, frequently paralleling her with the "sole," or unmarried, woman. Notably, the 1860 law allowed a woman to be the legal guardian of her children, meaning that she could manage their financial assets if her husband was absent or dead. As you will see, these laws corrected some of the abuses attacked in the Seneca Falls "Declaration" (p. 387). Historians generally credit activism like that of the convention with helping to promote a climate for change.

1848

THE REAL AND PERSONAL PROPERTY of any female [now married and] who may hereafter marry, and which she shall own at the time of marriage, and the rents, issues, and profits thereof shall not be subject to the disposal of her husband, nor be liable for his debts, and shall continue her sole and separate property, as if she were a single female. . . .

It shall be lawful for any married female to receive, by gift, grant, devise, or bequest, from any person other than her husband and hold to her sole and separate use, as if she were a single female, real and personal property, and the rents, issues, and profits thereof, and the same shall not be subject to the disposal of her husband, nor be liable for his debts. . . .

New York State Married Women's Property Laws, in *Women's America: Refocusing the Past,* ed. Linda K. Kerber and Jane De Hart (New York: Oxford University Press, 1991), 434.
In the notes, EDS. = Patricia Bizzell and Bruce Herzberg.

1860

[The provisions of the law of 1848 were retained, and others were added:]

A married woman may bargain, sell, assign, and transfer her separate personal property, and carry on any trade or business, and perform any labor or services on her sole and separate account, and the earnings of any married woman from her trade . . . shall be her sole and separate property, and may be used or invested by her in her own name. . . .

Any married woman may, while married, sue and be sued in all matters having relation to her . . . sole and separate property . . . in the same manner as if she were sole.[1] And any married woman may bring and maintain an action in her own name, for damages, against any person or body corporate, for any injury to her person or character, the same as if she were sole; and the money received upon the settlement . . . shall be her sole and separate property.

No bargain or contract made by any married woman, in respect to her sole and separate property . . . shall be binding upon her husband, or render him or his property in any way liable therefor.

Every married woman is hereby constituted and declared to be the joint guardian of her children, with her husband, with equal powers, rights, and duties in regard to them, with the husband. . . .

READING CRITICALLY

1. The 1848 law talks about a woman's real and personal property. As far as you can tell from the text of the law itself, how is the woman supposed to get this property?

2. What does the 1848 law seem most concerned to prevent a husband from doing?

3. The 1860 law also talks about a married woman's financial assets. What sources of income are treated in this law?

4. How does the 1860 law control a husband's behavior?

WRITING ANALYTICALLY

1. Write a brief description of the woman whose activities are described in these laws, basing your portrait on what the laws allow married women to do. Then explain what, if anything, you think is missing from this portrait. That is, what economic activities might you imagine a woman legitimately wanting to do that are not permitted or protected by these laws? To come up with what's missing, share your portraits in small groups.

---

[1]"Sole" here means "single, unmarried"; but in the earlier phrase "sole and separate property," it means belonging to the woman only, not to her husband. — EDS.

2. Take your portrait from writing question 1 and write a paper in which you explain how one of the following people would react to it: Catharine Beecher (p. 294), Louisa Cheves McCord (p. 307), Sarah Grimké (p. 321), or Margaret Fuller (p. 331). Option: You may write your paper in the form of a newspaper article written by your chosen author, reporting on the passage of the laws and commenting on them.

Marriage Agreements:
Robert Dale Owen and Mary Jane Robinson (1832)
Henry B. Blackwell and Lucy Stone (1855)

With agreements such as these, couples who supported women's rights took a public stand against laws giving husbands power over wives even though such agreements were not legally binding. Robert Dale Owen, son of the socialist philosopher and political activist Robert Owen, was active in a number of social reform causes. Henry Blackwell was a noted worker for women's rights, though not as well known as his wife, Lucy Stone, who was one of the leaders of the national women's movement and one of its most powerful public speakers. She is named and ridiculed in the *New York Herald* editorial on page 318.

THIS AFTERNOON I ENTER INTO a matrimonial engagement with Mary Jane Robinson, a young person whose opinions on all important subjects, whose mode of thinking and feeling, coincide more intimately with my own than do those of any other individual with whom I am acquainted. . . . We have selected the simplest ceremony which the laws of this State recognize. . . . This ceremony involves not the necessity of making promises regarding that over which we have no control, the state of human affections in the distant future, nor of repeating forms which we deem offensive, inasmuch as they outrage the principles of human liberty and equality, by conferring rights and imposing duties unequally on the sexes. The ceremony consists of a simply written contract in which we agree to take each other as husband and wife according to the laws of the State of New York, our signatures being attested by those friends who are present.

Of the unjust rights which in virtue of this ceremony an iniquitous law tacitly gives me over the person and property of another, I can not legally, but I can morally divest myself. And I hereby distinctly and emphatically declare that I consider myself, and earnestly desire to be considered by others, as utterly divested, now and during the rest of my life, of any such

Marriage Agreements, reprinted in *Up from the Pedestal: Selected Writings in the History of American Feminism,* ed. Aileen Kraditor (Chicago: Quadrangle Books, 1968), 148–50.

In the notes, EDS. = Patricia Bizzell and Bruce Herzberg.

rights, the barbarous relics of a feudal, despotic system, soon destined, in the onward course of improvement, to be wholly swept away; and the existence of which is a tacit insult to the good sense and good feeling of this comparatively civilized age.

ROBERT DALE OWEN.

I concur in this sentiment.
MARY JANE ROBINSON.

PROTEST

While acknowledging our mutual affection by publicly assuming the relationship of husband and wife, yet in justice to ourselves and a great principle, we deem it a duty to declare that this act on our part implies no sanction of, nor promise of voluntary obedience to such of the present laws of marriage, as refuse to recognize the wife as an independent, rational being, while they confer upon the husband an injurious and unnatural superiority, investing him with legal powers which no honorable man would exercise, and which no man should possess. We protest especially against the laws which give to the husband:

1. The custody of the wife's person.
2. The exclusive control and guardianship of their children.
3. The sole ownership of her personal,[1] and use of her real estate, unless previously settled upon her, or placed in the hands of trustees, as in the case of minors, lunatics, and idiots.
4. The absolute right to the product of her industry.
5. Also against laws which give to the widower so much larger and more permanent an interest in the property of his deceased wife, than they give to the widow in that of the deceased husband.
6. Finally, against the whole system by which "the legal existence of the wife is suspended during marriage," so that in most States, she neither has a legal part in the choice of her residence, nor can she make a will, nor sue or be sued in her own name, nor inherit property.

We believe that personal independence and equal human rights can never be forfeited, except for crime; that marriage should be an equal and permanent partnership, and so recognized by law; that until it is so recognized, married partners should provide against the radical injustice of present laws, by every means in their power.

We believe that where domestic difficulties arise, no appeal should be made to legal tribunals under existing laws, but that all difficulties should be submitted to the equitable adjustment of arbitrators mutually chosen.

---

[1]"Personal" means "personal property," such as clothes. — EDS.

Thus reverencing law, we enter our protest against rules and customs which are unworthy of the name, since they violate justice, the essence of law.

(Signed), HENRY B. BLACKWELL,
LUCY STONE.

READING CRITICALLY

1. The Owen-Robinson agreement announces that this couple has refused to engage in a wedding ceremony that involves "making promises regarding that over which we have no control, the state of human affections in the distant future," and "conferring rights and imposing duties unequally on the sexes." Drawing on your own knowledge of traditional Christian wedding ceremonies, or knowledge supplied by your classmates, explain what aspects of the traditional ceremony are being rejected here.

2. In the Blackwell-Stone agreement, what do you think is the "great principle" on which these two people base their protest against the existing legal inequities of married women?

3. What does the Blackwell-Stone agreement suggest should be done in a case where the husband and wife disagree?

WRITING ANALYTICALLY

1. These two documents both clearly intend to create more egalitarian marriages than were recommended by prevailing domestic ideologies and laws. Write a paper in which you describe the kind of marriage these two documents seek to create, illustrating with specific references to the texts. You may emphasize the similarities between the two documents and draw a composite picture of the egalitarian marriage; or you may compare and contrast them and, if you wish, argue for which one you think is more egalitarian.

2. Many twentieth-century couples sign prenuptial agreements or design portions of their wedding ceremonies to reflect the values they hope will be expressed in their married life. In Jewish weddings, such values are formalized in the *ketubah*, the marriage contract that the groom gives the bride. If you plan to write anything for your own wedding or have already done so, or if you know about what friends or family members have written, what values would you say are expressed in these writings? What kind of marriage do they aim to create, and what kinds of problems do they try to avert? How would you compare your twentieth-century example with the goals of the Owen-Robinson and Blackwell-Stone agreements? Write a paper in which you respond to these questions.

3. Consider the picture of marriage that these two documents present (and that you may have described in some detail, if you completed writing question 1). Now write a paper in which you explain how one of the following people would react to this picture: Jonathan F. Stearns (p. 299), Louisa Cheves McCord (p. 307), Sarah Grimké (p. 321), or Elizabeth Cady Stanton (p. 357). Option: You may present this reaction in the form of a letter from your chosen writer to one of the brides.

From the *Fourteenth Amendment to the United States Constitution* (1868)

This amendment was intended to frustrate southern attempts to bar freed African American men from voting. Note that section 2 provides a penalty for barring any eligible male from voting. This is the first use of the word *male* in the Constitution. Women's suffrage advocates hoped, however, that section 1 of this amendment might permit women to vote. That hope was destroyed by the Supreme Court decision in *Minor v. Happersett* (p. 399).

SECTION 1. ALL PERSONS BORN or naturalized in the United States, and subject to the jurisdiction thereof, are citizens of the United States and of the State wherein they reside. No State shall make or enforce any law which shall abridge the privileges or immunities of citizens of the United States; nor shall any State deprive any person of life, liberty, or property, without due process of law; nor deny to any person within its jurisdiction the equal protection of the laws.

Section 2. Representatives shall be apportioned among the several States according to their respective numbers, counting the whole number of persons in each State, excluding Indians not taxed. But when the right to vote at any election for the choice of electors for President and Vice President of the United States, Representatives in Congress, the executive and judicial officers of a State, or the members of the legislature thereof, is denied to any of the male inhabitants of such State, being twenty-one years of age and citizens of the United States, or in any way abridged, except for participation in rebellion, or other crime, the basis of representation therein shall be reduced in the proportion which the number of such male citizens shall bear to the whole number of male citizens twenty-one years of age in such State.

READING CRITICALLY

1. According to section 1 of this amendment, who counts as a "citizen" of the United States? What protections are given to citizens here?

2. In section 2, what penalty is placed on a state that prevents a male citizen age twenty-one or older from voting?

WRITING ANALYTICALLY

1. Write a paper arguing that this amendment should allow women to vote; now write another paper arguing that this amendment does not support the vote

for women. For a third part of this assignment, write an evaluation of both of your arguments and explain which one you find more persuasive.

2. In "A Slave's Appeal," Elizabeth Cady Stanton (p. 357) argues that white men treat women worse than they treat black men, because they take away black men's mere "social privileges" but deny women their precious "civil rights." Write a paper in which you explain how you think Stanton would regard the Fourteenth Amendment. Is this another example of the unequal treatment she complains about? Or is it a step in the direction of correcting that unequal treatment? Option: You may write your response in the form of a speech given by Stanton at a women's rights convention, urging the people to support (or not to support) ratification of this amendment.

Fifteenth Amendment to the United States Constitution (1870)

This amendment was meant to plug the loopholes in the Fourteenth Amendment, passed less than two years earlier. Since the focus here is on banning discrimination on the basis of race, the two amendments together provide a strong argument that the intention of the Fourteenth was to protect male former slaves only. Advocates of women's suffrage had hoped that this amendment would specifically ban discrimination on the basis of sex as well, but it does not.

SECTION 1. THE RIGHT OF CITIZENS of the United States to vote shall not be denied or abridged by the United States or by any State on account of race, color, or previous condition of servitude.

Section 2. The Congress shall have power to enforce this article by appropriate legislation.

READING CRITICALLY

1. What does the phrase "previous condition of servitude" refer to? What kind of discrimination is being banned here?

WRITING ANALYTICALLY

1. This amendment does not appear to have anything to do with defining "woman's sphere," the announced theme of Unit Three. Women's issues are most significant by the fact that they do *not* appear in the amendment. Race is the focus. But Unit Three includes several writers who are strongly committed to both

women's rights and African American rights, such as Frederick Douglass (p. 338), Sojourner Truth (p. 342), and Anna Julia Cooper (p. 371). Choose one of these thinkers and explain how he or she would react to this amendment. Option: You may present the reaction in the form of a speech your chosen person would give at a women's rights convention, urging the audience to support (or not support) this amendment and giving reasons for his or her position.

From *Minor v. Happersett* (1875)

Excerpted here is the U.S. Supreme Court decision in a case that tested whether the Fourteenth Amendment to the United States Constitution (p. 397) guaranteed the vote to women. Virginia Minor, president of the Woman Suffrage Association of Missouri, attempted to vote in St. Louis in 1872 and was turned away from the polls by the registrar of voters, Mr. Happersett. Minor and her husband then sued Happersett for denying her one of her rights as a citizen. The Supreme Court found that while Minor was indeed a citizen, the right to vote was not a right guaranteed to all citizens, and specifically not guaranteed to women. After this decision was handed down, it became clear to supporters of women's suffrage that a new amendment to the Constitution would be needed to legally permit women to vote.

Mr. Chief Justice Morrison R. Waite delivered the opinion of the Court:

THE QUESTION IS PRESENTED IN THIS CASE, whether, since the adoption of the fourteenth amendment, a woman, who is a citizen of the United States and of the State of Missouri, is a voter in that State, notwithstanding the provision of the constitution and laws of the State, which confine the right of suffrage to men alone. . . . The argument is, that as a woman, born or naturalized in the United States and subject to the jurisdiction thereof, is a citizen of the United States and of the State in which she resides, she has the right of suffrage as one of the privileges and immunities of her citizenship, which the State cannot by its laws or constitution abridge.

There is no doubt that women may be citizens. They are persons, and by the fourteenth amendment "all persons born or naturalized in the United States and subject to the jurisdiction thereof" are expressly declared to be "citizens of the United States and of the State wherein they reside." But, in our opinion, it did not need this amendment to give them

Minor v. Happersett, in *Women's America: Refocusing the Past*, ed. Linda K. Kerber and Jane De Hart (New York: Oxford University Press, 1991).
In the notes, EDS. = Patricia Bizzell and Bruce Herzberg.

that position . . . sex has never been made one of the elements of citizenship in the United States. In this respect men have never had an advantage over women. The same laws precisely apply to both. The fourteenth amendment did not affect the citizenship of women any more than it did of men. . . . Mrs. Minor . . . has always been a citizen from her birth, and entitled to all the privileges and immunities of citizenship. . . .

If the right of suffrage is one of the necessary privileges of a citizen of the United States, then the constitution and laws of Missouri confining it to men are in violation of the Constitution of the United States, as amended, and consequently void. The direct question is, therefore, presented whether all citizens are necessarily voters.

The Constitution does not define the privileges and immunities of citizens. For that definition we must look elsewhere. In this case we need not determine what they are, but only whether suffrage is necessarily one of them.

It certainly is nowhere made so in express terms. The United States has no voters in the States of its own creation. The elective officers of the United States are all elected directly or indirectly by state voters. . . . it cannot for a moment be doubted that if it had been intended to make all citizens of the United States voters, the framers of the Constitution would not have left it to implication. . . .

It is true that the United States guarantees to every State a republican form of government. . . . No particular government is designated as republican, neither is the exact form to be guaranteed, in any manner especially designated. . . . When the Constitution was adopted . . . all the citizens of the States were not invested with the right of suffrage. In all, save perhaps New Jersey,[1] this right was only bestowed upon men and not upon all of them. . . . Under these circumstances it is certainly now too late to contend that a government is not republican, within the meaning of this guaranty in the Constitution, because women are not made voters. . . . If suffrage was intended to be included within its obligations, language better adapted to express that intent would most certainly have been employed. . . .

. . . For nearly ninety years the people have acted upon the idea that the Constitution, when it conferred citizenship, did not necessarily confer the right of suffrage. If uniform practice long continued can settle the construction of so important an instrument as the Constitution of the United States confessedly is, most certainly it has been done here. Our province is to decide what the law is, not to declare what it should be.

We have given this case the careful consideration its importance demands. If the law is wrong, it ought to be changed; but the power for that is not with us. . . . No argument as to woman's need of suffrage can be considered. We can only act upon her rights as they exist. . . .

---

[1]Women did vote in New Jersey in colonial times. — EDS.

READING CRITICALLY

1. The Supreme Court gives a number of reasons for its contention that the Constitution does not guarantee the right to vote to women citizens. List these reasons in your own words.

2. Why does the Court refuse to consider arguments on whether women need or deserve the vote?

WRITING ANALYTICALLY

1. Write a paper in which you evaluate the reasons you listed in reading question 1. Do you find the Court's argument persuasive? Why or why not?

2. Clearly, the Court feels that women can function as citizens without the right to vote. Write a paper in which you explain how either Catharine Beecher (p. 294) or Elizabeth Cady Stanton (p. 357) would evaluate this assumption. If you choose Beecher, pay particular attention to the means she advocates for women to affect civic life, not including voting. If you choose Stanton, pay particular attention to her arguments for why the vote is necessary. Option: You may write your paper in the form of a newspaper column by your chosen author, reporting on the *Minor v. Happersett* decision and advising women on how they ought to respond to it.

Resolutions of the American Woman Suffrage Association Convention (1893)

These resolutions exemplify the direction that white women's rights activists took after the Civil War. The union between women's rights activism and action on behalf of African American rights began to weaken once slavery was abolished. Statistical arguments, alluded to in the first resolution here, were used to support the vote for literate, native-born white women. Henry B. Blackwell, a women's rights activist whose marriage agreement is included on page 394, was one of the first to develop these statistical techniques.

Note that women gradually gained various kinds of voting rights during this period, granted by individual states or cities. For example, many states extended school suffrage to women, allowing them to vote in school board elections. Although it was now clear that an amendment to the United States Constitution would be necessary to guarantee all women the right to vote in all elections, such an amendment is not requested here. These resolutions take a more gradual approach and seek the many forms of local suffrage that could be granted without constitutional change.

Resolutions of the American Woman Suffrage Association Convention, reprinted in *Up from the Pedestal: Selected Writings in the History of American Feminism,* ed. Aileen Kraditor (Chicago: Quadrangle Books, 1968), 260–61.

RESOLVED, THAT WITHOUT EXPRESSING any opinion on the proper qualifications for voting, we call attention to the significant facts that in every State there are more women who can read and write than the whole number of illiterate male voters; more white women who can read and write than all negro voters; more American women who can read and write than all foreign voters; so that the enfranchisement of such women would settle the vexed question of rule by illiteracy, whether of home-grown or foreign-born production.

Resolved, That as all experience proves that the rights of the laboring man are best preserved in governments where he has possession of the ballot, we therefore demand on behalf of the laboring woman the same powerful instrument, that she may herself protect her own interests; and we urge all organized bodies of working women, whether in the field of philanthropy, education, trade, manufacture, or general industry, to join our association in the endeavor to make woman legally and politically a free agent, as the best means for furthering any and every line of woman's work.

Resolved, That in all States possessing School Suffrage for women, suffragists are advised to organize in each representative district thereof, for the purpose of training and stimulating women voters to exercise regularly this right, using it as a preparatory school for the coming work of full-grown citizenship with an unlimited ballot. We also advise that women everywhere work for the election of an equal number of women and men upon school boards, that the State in taking upon itself the education of children may provide them with as many official mothers as fathers.

Whereas, Many forms of woman suffrage may be granted by State Legislatures without change in existing constitutions; therefore,

Resolved, That the suffragists in every State should petition for Municipal, School, and Presidential Suffrage by statute, and take every practicable step toward securing such legislation.

Resolved, That we urge all women to enter protest, at the time of paying taxes, at being compelled to submit to taxation without representation.

READING CRITICALLY

1. What reason for giving women the vote does the first resolution urge? What women are being spoken for here, and what women are not included in this argument?

2. How is this constituency enlarged by the second resolution, or is it?

3. Why do the suffragists appear to be concerned with providing children with "as many official mothers as fathers"?

4. What is the historical allusion in the last resolution, where the suffragists protest "being compelled to submit to taxation without representation"? Do you think this reference is effective?

WRITING ANALYTICALLY

1. Throughout the nineteenth century, the women's rights movement attempted to serve as broad a constituency as possible and to ally itself with other social reform movements, such as abolitionism and the fight for African American rights. In spite of this tradition of social advocacy, however, the women's rights movement was never perfectly democratic or egalitarian in its membership or political agenda. Write a paper in which you analyze the degree to which these resolutions reflect an egalitarian social agenda.

2. Compare and contrast these resolutions and Elizabeth Cady Stanton's "A Slave's Appeal" (p. 357) in their treatment of the civil rights claims of women and of African Americans. Option: You may write this paper in the form of a speech given by Stanton at the Woman Suffrage Convention urging the delegates to approve (or reject) the resolutions and giving reasons for her position.

3. Criticism of racism within the women's rights movement can be found in Anna Julia Cooper's "The Higher Education of Women" (p. 371). Compare and contrast her essay with these resolutions in their treatment of the civil rights claims of women and of African Americans. Option: You may write this paper in the form of a speech given by Cooper at the Woman Suffrage Convention, urging the delegates to approve (or reject) the resolutions and giving reasons for her position.

Nineteenth Amendment to the United States Constitution (1920)

Before this amendment passed, women could vote in a number of elections at the local and state levels (see p. 401). The Nineteenth Amendment, however, guaranteed them the right to vote in national elections, as well as preventing discrimination against them on the basis of sex in local and state elections. Votes both in Congress and among the states to ratify this amendment were very close, but it passed in time for women to vote in the 1920 presidential election. Many of the key participants in nineteenth-century struggles over women's rights, including Catharine Beecher (p. 294), Sarah Grimké (p. 321), Elizabeth Cady Stanton (p. 357), and Sojourner Truth (p. 342), did not live to see this day. One of the few who did was Anna Julia Cooper (p. 371).

SECTION 1. THE RIGHT OF THE CITIZENS of the United States to vote shall not be denied or abridged by the United States or by any State on account of sex.

Section 2. Congress shall have power to enforce this article by appropriate legislation.

READING CRITICALLY

In *Minor v. Happersett,* the Supreme Court found that the right to vote was not guaranteed to all citizens. After the passage of the Nineteenth Amendment, which citizens are guaranteed the right to vote?

WRITING ANALYTICALLY

Taking the Fourteenth, Fifteenth, and Nineteenth Amendments together, make a list of the ways they protect the vote for citizens. Now consider what the amendments do not cover: Are there still citizens not entitled to vote? Are some citizen voting rights not protected? Are there groups of United States residents not protected by the focus on citizens here? In your opinion, are there people who are correctly banned or who should be banned from voting? Note your responses to these questions in a second list (compiling these lists would be a good activity to do in class, perhaps in small groups). In your opinion, is another amendment needed to further define and protect the right to vote and, if so, how would you word it? Write a paper in which you argue for your response to this question, drawing on the lists you've compiled.

Alternative 1: You may know that the civil rights movement of the 1960s, which focused on civil rights for African Americans, had as a major focus overcoming barriers to suffrage. If you know something about this movement, you might add to your written responses such considerations as these: How is it that African Americans were still confronted with barriers to suffrage after passage of the Fourteenth, Fifteenth, and Nineteenth Amendments? Could a new amendment help to prevent such situations from developing again?

Alternative 2: You may know that an amendment to the Constitution called the Equal Rights Amendment was proposed in 1970, was debated throughout the 1970s, was almost ratified, but finally was defeated in 1982. Its principal text reads, "Equality of rights under the law shall not be denied or abridged by the United States or by any State on account of sex." If you know something about the campaign for the ERA, you might add to your written responses such considerations as these: Why do you think the ERA was seen by some as necessary even though the Fourteenth and Nineteenth Amendments were already on the books? Why do you think it didn't pass? Should it have passed?

ASSIGNMENT SEQUENCES

SEQUENCE 1
What is woman's proper sphere of activity?

- Jonathan F. Stearns, From "Female Influence, and the True Christian Mode of Its Exercise"
- Massachusetts Congregationalist Clergy, From "Pastoral Letter"
- Louisa Cheves McCord, From "Enfranchisement of Women"
- Sarah Grimké, Letters III and IV from *Letters on the Equality of the Sexes and the Condition of Women*
- Margaret Fuller, "The Wrongs of American Women, the Duty of American Women"
- Ralph Waldo Emerson, "Woman"
- New York State Married Women's Property Laws
- Marriage Agreements

1. Write a story (which could be fictional or autobiographical) that illustrates your own idea of a good woman and that you would be willing for other women to read as a model.

2. Describe the good or "True Woman" as depicted in Stearns and McCord, illustrating your composite portrait with specific references to their texts. Pay particular attention to how they represent the good woman dealing with suffering. Option: In presenting this description, also argue that Stearns and McCord do, or do not, make the portrait attractive to you.

3. Stearns and the "Pastoral Letter" place heavy emphasis on the good woman's affecting society through her benign influence. Emerson speaks of woman as the "civilizer" of the human race. Write a paper in which you explain these concepts of "influence" and "civilizer," and then compare and contrast them. Explain the extent (if any) to which Emerson's ideas differ from the doctrine of "influence" put forward by the other ministers.

4. Take the portrait of the "True Woman" from your response to question 2 and the account of "influence" from your response to question 3, and combine them to make a more complete composite picture of the nineteenth-century good woman confined to the domestic sphere, illustrated with specific references to the four sources. Now write a paper in which you explain how Sarah Grimké would critique this portrait, supporting your analysis with reference to Grimké's letters 3 and 4. Option: You may write this paper in the form of a book review by Grimké discussing the other four sources.

5. Grimké, Fuller, and Emerson all appear to be on the side of an enlarged sphere of activity for women. The New York State married women's property laws and the marriage agreements also envision greater activity for women. Taking these sources together, describe a composite portrait of the good woman as imagined by these sources, in opposition to the traditionally domestic portrait you compiled in response to question 4. At the same time, though, consider whether there may still be traces of "True Womanhood" thinking in these supposedly progressive

sources. Point out such traces where you find them. Your paper may compare and contrast the portrait drawn from these sources with the one you prepared for question 4; or you may argue that the portrait drawn from these sources does or does not fit your own model of the good woman.

6. Based on all your work for this sequence, write a paper in which you describe and argue for your own model of twentieth-century women's behavior. Cite at least four of the readings assigned for this sequence, which you may use as illustrations, points of agreement or disagreement, and so on. Alternative: Answer this question by writing a new response to assignment 1, accompanying it with an appendix in which you explain why you wrote the story as you did.

SEQUENCE 2
What are the responsibilities of women as American citizens?

- Catharine Beecher, From *A Treatise on Domestic Economy*
- Louisa Cheves McCord, From "Enfranchisement of Women"
- Sarah Grimké, Letters III, IV, and XIV from *Letters on the Equality of the Sexes and the Condition of Women*
- Frederick Douglass, Editorials on Women's Rights
- Elizabeth Cady Stanton, "A Slave's Appeal"
- Anna Julia Cooper, "The Higher Education of Women"
- Seneca Falls Women's Rights Convention, "Declaration of Sentiments and Resolutions"
- *Minor v. Happersett*
- Nineteenth Amendment to the United States Constitution

1. Make a list of all the duties of an American citizen that you can think of (this would be a good activity to do with your whole class or with your small group). You may include not only civic duties, such as voting, but also other responsibilities that contribute to the public good, such as rearing a healthy, law-abiding child or practicing a useful trade or profession. Next to each duty, indicate whether it is the responsibility equally of men and women or whether it falls more on one sex than the other. If you are unsure about the application of some civic duty, such as responding to the military draft, do a little research to find out how men and women are obligated.

2. Exactly what public responsibilities and civil rights are requested for women in the "Declaration of Sentiments and Resolutions" and by Douglass and Stanton? Make three lists.

3. Beecher supports the confinement of women to a domestic sphere but argues that by accepting this confinement and performing the duties that the domestic sphere requires or permits, women are actually doing their part as American citizens. While presumably agreeing, McCord places greater emphasis in her argument on the evils that will ensue if women do not remain within the domestic sphere but instead attempt to perform duties McCord would restrict to male citizens. The decision in *Minor v. Happersett* asserts that women can be citizens without

voting. Write a paper in which you explain the ideas expressed in these three sources and draw from them a composite picture of the domestic woman as citizen. Option: You may argue that this is, or is not, a good model for twentieth-century women.

4. Grimké, Stanton, and Cooper argue for a wider sphere of action for women, and they assert that this enlargement of women's activities is necessary for the good of society. In other words, in their view, women would not be fulfilling their responsibilities as citizens if they remained within the domestic sphere. The Nineteenth Amendment also implies that women need to vote in order to fulfill their responsibilities as citizens. Write a paper in which you explain the ideas in these three sources and draw from them a composite picture of the politically active woman as citizen. Option: You may argue that this is, or is not, a good model for twentieth-century women.

5. In arguing for increased public responsibilities for women, Grimké, Stanton, and Cooper face a sensitive rhetorical situation. One of their strongest arguments is that it is only fair to give women the same opportunities as men. The problem with this argument, however, is that it can seem selfish, as if they are arguing for these opportunities for women only for the benefit of women. The three writers also want to argue that giving women increased public responsibilities will benefit society as a whole — a seemingly less selfish, more altruistic argument. Write a paper in which you compare and contrast the ways in which these three writers balance attention to the "benefits for women" and the "benefits for society" arguments. Option: You may argue that one of these writers deals with this sensitive rhetorical situation more successfully and persuasively than the others.

6. Based on all your work for this sequence, write a paper in which you explain your own ideas about how women can best fulfill their responsibilities as citizens. The lists constructed for questions 1 and 2 can help you here, as well as the portraits compiled for questions 3 and 4. Cite at least four of the readings assigned for this sequence, using them as illustrations, points of agreement or disagreement, and so on. Alternative: Express your ideas on this topic by rewriting the "Declaration of Sentiments and Resolutions" as you think it should be today; accompany the text with an appendix explaining why you wrote it as you did.

SEQUENCE 3
How are women's rights and African Americans' rights connected?

- Albert A. Folsom, From "Abolition Women"
- Louisa Cheves McCord, From "Enfranchisement of Women"
- *New York Herald*, "The Woman's Rights Convention"
- Frederick Douglass, Editorials on Women's Rights
- Sojourner Truth, Recorded by Frances D. Gage, "A'n't I a Woman?"
- Elizabeth Cady Stanton, "A Slave's Appeal"
- Anna Julia Cooper, "The Higher Education of Women"
- From the Fourteenth Amendment to the United States Constitution

- Fifteenth Amendment to the United States Constitution
- Resolutions of the American Woman Suffrage Association Convention

---

1. Write a personal narrative about a time when you were part of a group that was seeking particular benefits in a climate of competition with other groups. Perhaps different clubs were contending for financial aid from your school, different sports teams were contending over the use of facilities, different political groups were vying for people's support, and so on. Tell how the conflict was defined, what the issues were, and how it was resolved (if it was).

2. The principal agenda of the Fourteenth and Fifteenth Amendments to the United States Constitution may be interpreted as promoting voting rights for African American males. Write a magazine article on these two amendments as you imagine it might be written by either Stanton or Cooper. Your article should comment on whether or not readers should have supported these two amendments, giving reasons for the position that are consistent with the ideas of Stanton or Cooper.

3. Consider the negative images of white women's rights activists put forward in Folsom, McCord, and the *Herald* editorial, and write a paper in which you draw a composite portrait of an activist, making specific references to these sources. Pay special attention to the part played in the negative images by the activists' involvement in abolitionism and in relations with African Americans. Option: Compare this negative portrait with contemporary negative portrayals of women activists that you may know about.

4. Frederick Douglass puts forward an abstract argument for the linkage of women's rights and African Americans' rights. What is it? Sojourner Truth uses her experience as an African American woman to refute arguments against equal treatment for all women. How does she do this? Write a paper in which you respond to both of these questions, illustrating your analysis with specific references to the text and comparing and contrasting both the political views and the rhetorical strategies of these two writers.

5. In arguing for increased civil rights for women, Cooper, Stanton, and the resolutions connect the issue with that of rights for African Americans. Write a paper in which you compare and contrast the ways that they make these connections. Consider the extent to which each text argues either for promoting women's rights and African Americans' rights simultaneously or for giving (white) women's rights priority over African Americans' rights.

6. McCord opposes increasing both women's rights and African Americans' rights as specific instances of a single general principle, namely, that people's rights should be suited to their innate abilities; she further assumes that these abilities are determined by sex and race and that white women and all African Americans are innately inferior to white men. Write a paper in which you explain McCord's views, illustrating your analysis with references to her text. Then explain how you think either Douglass or Stanton would respond to McCord on this issue, again drawing on specific references to the texts.

7. Drawing on all your work for this sequence, including your own experiences as you related them in question 1, write a paper in which you argue that white women and African Americans should work together to advance civil rights for

both groups or, alternatively, that each group would be better off working alone. Cite at least four readings from this sequence as illustrations, points of agreement or disagreement, and so on.

RESEARCH KIT

Negotiating Difference is an unfinished book: There are many other stories to tell in the history of "negotiating difference" in the United States. This Research Kit is intended to help you expand the readings provided in this unit. In "Ideas from the Unit Readings," we include more perspectives on the debate over "woman's sphere" in nineteenth-century America. In "Branching Out," we add perspectives on other struggles over women's rights in different regions of the country from Revolutionary times to the present day. You can pursue these research ideas individually or as group or class projects.

To compile materials, you can start with the short bibliography included in this unit and with standard library search techniques that your teacher or a librarian can explain. Here are some other places where you can inquire for materials (not all regions will have all of these resources):

- Town and state historical societies, antiquarian societies, and local historical museums.
- Records kept by local women's groups, such as the League of Women Voters, which may tell about the history of the group.
- State university presses (which often publish local histories that may include works on women's issues).
- Records kept by houses of worship, schools, hospitals, museums, or other institutions that draw major support from private charitable donors. Women have been important contributors to, and directors of, many such institutions, and finding out who these women were might give you leads to other aspects of women's activism in your region; if possible, consult the institution's development officer (he or she raises money for the institution), who might have an institutional history that includes the information you want; if any buildings are named after women, find out who these women were.

Keep your work focused by your research question. Remember that whenever possible, you want to use primary source material, that is, texts written by actual participants in the negotiation of gender roles that you are studying. The temptation to use a contemporary historian's summary of what happened may be strong, but you should resist it. You may, however, find bibliographic leads to useful primary sources embedded in the accounts of contemporary historians. Photocopy copiously, even items that you doubt you will use. Be sure to keep *complete* bibliographic records of *everything* you find — page numbers of all quotations or bits of information as well as publication information recommended by the MLA citation style.

Try to represent as many as possible of the contending voices that emerge in the history you are studying. Seek out not only sources that speak for women's rights, but also sources that oppose them or that express feelings of exclusion from the debate. Seek out men as well as women.

Remember that you are not telling a single-minded story of either victimization or triumph in your account of struggles over gender roles. You want to focus on efforts to *negotiate* gender roles among parties with different ideas of what men and women should be and do. You will need to sift through your material accordingly.

IDEAS FROM THE UNIT READINGS

1. Find out about the life of one of these people, with a special focus on her or his involvement in women's issues: Catharine Beecher, Lydia Maria Child, Anna Julia Cooper, Frederick Douglass, Margaret Fuller, Angelina Grimké, Sarah Grimké, Frances E. W. Harper, Elizabeth Cady Stanton, Harriet Beecher Stowe, Sojourner Truth.

2. Read Lucy Larcom's *A New England Girlhood,* the autobiography of a Lowell, Massachusetts, mill worker, and develop a description of working-class women's lives in the early nineteenth century based on this book and other sources on the New England mills.

3. Find out more about nineteenth-century American women's humor writing, such as that of Fanny Fern and Marietta Holley. You will find that these authors are often explicitly feminist in their orientation; consider the effectiveness of arguments on gender roles advanced via humor.

4. Find out more about European American men's and women's involvement in the abolition movement, with special emphasis on the relation between abolitionism and women's rights activism. Tracing the history of the American Anti-Slavery Society will tell you something about how debates over women's rights became involved in abolitionism.

5. Read Karlyn Kohrs Campbell's *Man Cannot Speak for Her,* volume 1, *A Critical Study of Early Feminist Rhetoric,* and read several of the speeches included in volume 2, *Man Cannot Speak for Her* (the source of the Elizabeth Cady Stanton speech included here). Respond to Campbell's characterizations of the rhetorical strategies of early women's rights activists — you might consider the extent to which these women denounced or exploited domestic ideologies on "woman's sphere."

6. Explore the connection between Quakerism or Methodism and the rise of women's rights activism in the early nineteenth century (see the bibliography for several places to start).

BRANCHING OUT

1. Find out what one of these thinkers from the late 1700s (Revolutionary War era) and early 1800s said about women's rights: Abigail Adams, John Adams, Charles Brockden Brown, Alexis de Tocqueville, Benjamin Franklin, Thomas Jefferson, Thomas Paine, Judith Sergeant Murray, Mercy Otis Warren.

2. Find out more about African American men's and women's involvement in women's rights activism after the Civil War, including the efforts of Anna Julia Cooper, W. E. B. Du Bois, Frederick Douglass, Frances E. W. Harper, and others.

3. Examine the alleged white supremacist racism of European American women's activism for female suffrage. Why were activists for women's rights and for African American rights not able to cooperate after the Civil War as well as they were before the Civil War? Compare this situation with contemporary conflicts among different group interests, such as tension over racism in the women's movement today.

4. Trace the history of women's rights activism in the twentieth century. This might be a class project with teams working in different areas: how the vote for women was finally won (in the Nineteenth Amendment to the U.S. Constitution, 1920); what happened in efforts for women's rights from 1920 to 1945; what happened in efforts for women's rights from 1945 to 1982 (defeat of the Equal Rights Amendment).

5. Read Nina Baym's literary-critical study *Women's Fiction: A Guide to Novels by and about Women in America, 1820—1870* and read several of the novels she discusses. Respond to her characterization of the typical "women's fiction" plot — you might consider the extent to which it supports or undermines domestic ideologies on "woman's sphere."

6. What might "feminist architecture" or home design be? See the unit bibliography for several places to start finding answers to this question as they developed in nineteenth-century America.

7. Research the specific role played in women's activism in your region by nineteenth-century women and men who were Native Americans, Asian Americans, Hispanic Americans — members of any ethnic group except African American or European American.

8. Find out about the temperance movement, the efforts for temperance legislation, and the relationship of that movement to other women's issues.

BIBLIOGRAPHY

Works Included or Excerpted

Beecher, Catharine. *A Treatise on Domestic Economy.* 1842, 1847. Reprinted in Cott, *Root of Bitterness.*

Campbell, Karlyn Kohrs, ed. *Man Cannot Speak for Her.* Vol. 2 of *Key Texts of the Early Feminists.* New York: Greenwood, Praeger, 1989.

Cooper, Anna Julia. "The Higher Education of Women." In *A Voice from the South.* 1892. Reprinted with an introduction by Mary Helen Washington. New York: Oxford University Press, 1988.

Cott, Nancy, ed. *Root of Bitterness: Documents of the Social History of American Women.* New York: Dutton, 1972.

"Declaration of Sentiments and Resolutions," Seneca Falls Convention. 1848. In Campbell, *Man Cannot Speak for Her.*

Douglass, Frederick. Editorials. Reprinted in *Frederick Douglass on Women's Rights,* edited by Philip Foner. Westport, Conn.: Greenwood, 1976.

Emerson, Ralph Waldo. "Woman." In *Miscellanies.* Vol. 11 of *The Works of Ralph Waldo Emerson,* edited by James Elliot Cabot. Boston: Houghton Mifflin, 1883.

Folsom, Reverend Albert A. "Abolition Women." *The Liberator,* September 22, 1837, 1.

Fuller, Margaret. "The Wrongs of American Women, the Duty of American Women." *New York Tribune,* September 30, 1845. Reprinted in *The Essential Margaret Fuller,* ed. Jeffrey Steele. New Brunswick: Rutgers University Press, 1992, 393–400.

Grimké, Sarah. *Letters on the Equality of the Sexes and the Condition of Women.* Edited by Elizabeth A. Bartlett. New Haven: Yale University Press, 1988.

Kerber, Linda K., and Jane De Hart. *Women's America: Refocusing the Past.* New York: Oxford University Press, 1991.

Kraditor, Aileen, ed. *Up from the Pedestal: Selected Writings in the History of American Feminism.* Chicago: Quadrangle Books, 1968.

Marriage Agreements. In Kraditor, *Up from the Pedestal.*

Massachusetts Congregationalist Clergy. "Pastoral Letter." *The Liberator,* August 11, 1837, 1. Reprinted in Kraditor, *Up from the Pedestal.*

McCord, Louisa Cheves. "Enfranchisement of Women." *Southern Quarterly Review* (April 1852): 322–41.

Minor v. Happersett. In Kerber and De Hart, *Women's America.*

New York Herald. Editorial. "The Woman's Rights Convention: The Last Act of the Drama." September 12, 1852. Reprinted in Kraditor, *Up from the Pedestal.*

New York State Married Women's Property Laws. In Kerber and De Hart, *Women's America.*

Resolutions of the American Woman Suffrage Association Convention. In Kraditor, *Up from the Pedestal.*

Seneca Falls Women's Rights Convention. "Declaration of Sentiments and Resolutions." 1848. Reprinted in Campbell, *Man Cannot Speak for Her.*

Stanton, Elizabeth Cady. "A Slave's Appeal." 1860. Reprinted in Campbell, *Man Cannot Speak for Her.*

Stearns, Reverend Jonathan F. "Female Influence, and the True Christian Mode of Its Exercise." 1837. Reprinted in Kraditor, *Up from the Pedestal.*

Truth, Sojourner, recorded by Frances D. Gage. "A'n't I a Woman?" In *History of Woman Suffrage,* edited by Elizabeth Cady Stanton, Susan B. Anthony, and Matilda Joslyn Gage. Vol. 1. 2nd ed. 1889. Reprint, New York: Source Book Press, 1970.

Other Sources

Andolsen, Barbara Hilkert. *"Daughters of Jefferson, Daughters of Bootblacks": Racism and American Feminism.* Macon, Ga.: Mercer University Press, 1986.

Bacon, Margaret. *Mothers of Feminism: The Story of Quaker Women in America.* New York: Harper and Row, 1986.

Beecher, Catharine, Isabella Beecher Hooker, and Harriet Beecher Stowe. *The Limits of Sisterhood: The Beecher Sisters on Women's Rights and Women's Sphere.* Edited by Jeanne Boydston, Mary Kelley, and Anne Margolis. Chapel Hill: University of North Carolina Press, 1988.

Berg, Barbara. *The Remembered Gate: Origins of American Feminism, The Woman and the City, 1800—1860.* New York: Oxford University Press, 1978.

Campbell, Karlyn Kohrs. *Man Cannot Speak for Her.* Vol. 1 of *A Critical Study of Early Feminist Rhetoric.* New York: Greenwood, Praeger, 1989.

Clinton, Catherine. *The Other Civil War: American Women in the Nineteenth Century.* New York: Hill and Wang, 1984.

Conrad, Susan P. *Perish the Thought: Intellectual Women in Romantic America, 1830—1860.* New York: Oxford University Press, 1976.

Cott, Nancy. *The Bonds of Womanhood: "Woman's Sphere" in New England, 1780—1835.* New Haven: Yale University Press, 1977.

Douglas, Ann. *The Feminization of American Culture.* New York: Knopf, 1977.

DuBois, Ellen. *Feminism and Suffrage: The Emergence of an Independent Women's Movement in America, 1848—1869.* Ithaca: Cornell University Press, 1978.

Epstein, Barbara. *The Politics of Domesticity: Women, Evangelism, and Temperance in 19th-Century America.* Middletown: Wesleyan University Press, 1981.

Flexner, Eleanor. *Century of Struggle: The Woman's Rights Movement in the United States.* 1959. Rev. ed., Cambridge: Harvard University Press, 1975.

Fuller, Margaret. "Woman in the Nineteenth Century." 1845. Reprinted in *The Woman and the Myth: Margaret Fuller's Life and Writings,* edited by Bell Gale Chevigny. Old Westbury, N.Y.: Feminist Press, 1976.

Harper, Frances E. W. "We Are All Bound Up Together." 1866. Reprinted in *A Brighter Coming Day,* edited by F. S. Foster. New York: Feminist Press, 1990.

Hayden, Delores. *The Grand Domestic Revolution: A History of Feminist Designs for American Homes, Neighborhoods, and Cities.* Cambridge: MIT Press, 1982.

Holley, Marietta. *Samantha Rastles the Woman Question.* Edited by Jane Curry. Urbana: University of Illinois Press, 1983.

Karcher, Caroline. *The First Woman of the Republic: A Cultural Biography of Lydia Maria Child.* Durham: Duke University Press, 1994.

Kerber, Linda. *Women of the Republic: Intellect and Ideology in Revolutionary America.* Chapel Hill: University of North Carolina Press, 1980.

Kraditor, Aileen. *Means and Ends in American Abolitionism.* New York: Pantheon, 1967.

Larcom, Lucy. *A New England Girlhood.* 1883. Reprint, New York: Corinth Books, 1961.

Lerner, Gerda. "The Lady and the Mill Girl: Changes in the Status of Women in the Age of Jackson." *American Studies Journal* 10 (Spring 1969): 5–14.

Mabee, Carlton, with Susan Mabee Newhouse. *Sojourner Truth: Slave, Prophet, Legend.* New York: New York University Press, 1993.

Paine, Thomas. "An Occasional Letter on the Female Sex." In *Life and Writings of Thomas Paine,* edited by Daniel Edwin Wheeler. New York: Vincent Parke, 1908.

Rosenberg, Rosalind. *Beyond Separate Spheres: Intellectual Roots of Modern Feminism.* New Haven: Yale University Press, 1982.

Ryan, Mary P. *Women in Public.* Baltimore: Johns Hopkins University Press, 1990.

Tocqueville, Alexis de. *Democracy in America.* 1835, 1840. Reprint, edited by Richard D. Heffner. New York: New American Library, 1956.

Welter, Barbara. "The Cult of True Womanhood: 1820–1860." In *Dimity Convictions: The American Woman in the Nineteenth Century.* Athens: Ohio University Press, 1976.

Yellin, Jean Fagan. *Women and Sisters: Anti-Slavery Feminists.* New Haven: Yale University Press, 1989.

Unit Four

Wealth, Work,
and Class Conflict
in the Industrial Age

Negotiations

I am the master of my fate;
I am the captain of my soul.

— *William Ernest Henley, "Invictus"* (1888)

Are we the masters of our own fates? The sentiment in Henley's poem could be a motto for Americans: We believe, or want to believe, that we are responsible for our own successes in life, that we are self-made. After all, in a free country with universal education and boundless opportunities, who is to blame but ourselves if we fail to take advantage of opportunities and make a good life for ourselves? Americans have used this principle of personal responsibility to defend the justice of our economic system: As long as there are no formal barriers such as race or gender that artificially prevent people from competing, we can argue that the free enterprise system is right and proper. Those who achieve have earned their success and those who fail have only themselves to blame.

So we say, so we say. But is it really true? And if so, is it true for all Americans or only some? How much are we responsible for our own successes and failures and how much is due to the accidents of birth: who our parents are, how wealthy or poor they are, where we grow up, what race we are, the opportunities that come to us, and the impediments we must face? The rules of the game may seen fair, but it may be that they favor some over others. Americans have been negotiating these issues since the middle of the nineteenth century.

In the years after the Civil War, it seemed that the American promise of limitless prosperity would certainly come true, that anyone could rise from rags to riches. It was in this world that Henley wrote "I am the master of my fate." American industry took off like a rocket — actually, like a railroad train, for the growing network of transportation and communication made it possible to produce goods in huge quantities and then sell them to distant markets. Machines replaced and extended human labor. In the rapidly expanding economy, huge corporations were formed and huge fortunes were made.

But one result of the changing economy was the growth of economic and social inequality in the United States. There were rich and poor people before the Civil War, to be sure, but the gap did not seem wide. In a local, agricultural economy, there were opportunities to start farms and businesses and accumulate some property. After the Civil War, such independence became harder and harder to achieve and more and more men, women, and children worked for wages. This was a precarious position, for wages could be cut and workers could be fired.

In this new world, a few became wealthy, many became comfortable, but a depressingly large proportion of Americans lived in or close to poverty. The unequal distribution of wealth that began after the Civil War has continued as a general trend right up to the present. Was the idea of equal opportunity then a lie, or so partial a truth as to be almost a lie? The debate over this question raged in the United States during the last half of the nineteenth century (and has by no means ceased today). Those who preached the "Gospel of Wealth" believed that any American with energy and incentive could become rich. Of course this would lead to differences in wealth, but, they argued, such differences were a sign of true freedom and a necessary condition of material progress, which benefited everyone. Others argued that the large class of wage earners had lost their freedom and equality. While workers were "free" to quit a job, the critics argued, that amounted to the freedom to choose to starve. A few might succeed, but the vast majority could not. Thus, they said, the Gospel of Wealth was nothing more than a myth and a false hope, a way of pacifying the vast majority of workers who were exploited by the captains of industry — the only ones who were truly captains of their own souls.

Negotiating economic differences in the nineteenth century eventually led to government policies in the twentieth century that protected workers and regulated some business practices: unemployment insurance, a minimum wage, business and income taxes, and job safety rules. But the questions about wealth, work, and class conflict that were raised in the nineteenth century are still with us today: Does the Gospel of Wealth reflect the ideals of freedom and equality? Does working for someone else remove one's freedom and dignity? Is the right to own property unlimited? Can workers form unions to protect their rights or does the formation of unions violate the principle of individual responsibility? Should wealth be redistributed by the government? Is capitalism inherently unfair? Should the government protect business from strikes and boycotts or protect workers from exploitation? And, of course, to what extent is economic opportunity really equal?

"The Gospel of Wealth" is the theme of the first set of readings. Horatio Alger was a minister-turned-author who wrote many books and stories about rising from rags to riches. His name has become synonymous with the idea of rapid success through individual effort. His novel *Ragged Dick* was the bible from which many read the Gospel of Wealth. The successful industrialist Andrew Carnegie seemed to be a character from an Alger novel come to life. His enormous financial success made him a living symbol of the gospel he preached in his essay "Wealth." African American leader William Councill urged the recently freed slaves to follow the advice of Alger and Carnegie if they wished to share in the opportunities and wealth of the country. Finally, Rev. Russell Conwell, founder of Temple University, actually made his own fortune by giving his sermon on the success ethic, "Acres of Diamonds," all around the country.

The Gospel of Wealth was a popular topic, and many more examples of it can be found in the literature of the day. But there are far fewer examples of critics of the Gospel of Wealth. Three notable critics, included in the unit's second section, are Edward Bellamy, Henry Demarest Lloyd, and Henry George, each of whom wrote about the greed and oppression that came with the drive for wealth. Bellamy's science fiction novel *Looking Backward: 2000—1887* criticizes capitalism by imagining a utopian socialist community in the United States in the year 2000. Lloyd criticizes the outright rapaciousness of the railroad and oil barons who, along with others who controlled big industry, advanced their own ends without regard to the good of others or of the country as a whole. George argues that the monopolization of land by industry and speculators deprived individuals of the opportunity to go off and make their own way in life, thus subjecting them to their employers' pressure to reduce wages.

What was life like for the workers in this world? The next section, "Working Conditions," examines this question, beginning with a look at the dreadful working conditions in a New England mill. In Elizabeth Stuart Phelps's novel *The Silent Partner*, a wealthy young woman inherits a share of a mill and attempts to improve the lives of the workers. The second selection presents the testimony of eight witnesses who appeared before the Senate Committee on the Relations between Capital and Labor in 1883. The accounts describe the way that workers lived, their low wages, their lack of protection against wage reductions and layoffs, their health problems and so-called vices, the indifference of employers, and the merits of unions. One witness, an African American bricklayer, tells how he managed to succeed on his own. The next selection in this section is from the autobiography of William Z. Foster, a union activist, who describes in vivid detail some of his work experiences. The last selection in this section is the "Declaration of Independence" issued by the Workingmen's Party of Illinois on July 4, 1876. This declaration demands that

American principles of freedom and equality under the law be extended to workers.

HISTORICAL BACKGROUND

Economic Changes and Social Reorganization

The changes in American society brought about by industrialization began shortly before the Civil War, when railroads first created mass markets and new technology increased production. Industrialization brought vast changes in demography, gender roles, family structure, culture, and the types of work people did. Many people moved from the country into expanding cities and from farms to factories and shops. Men worked outside the home, often for long shifts of twelve hours or more each day, six or seven days a week. Women who were once able to contribute to the domestic economy by tending kitchen gardens and making clothes were torn between a middle-class ideal of homemaking they could ill afford and the rigors of industrial labor or domestic service. These dislocations were profoundly unsettling to American families who were forced to move and adjust to new conditions.

Immigrants who came in increasing numbers to the United States often endured even greater distress, for they faced not only dislocation but discrimination and the poorest jobs, working conditions, and living arrangements. Moreover, many Americans resented the post–Civil War immigrants. Workers hated them for swelling the labor pool, and the press reviled them as bestial. Many citizens' groups sought to suppress immigration. In the meantime, industrial leaders promoted immigration precisely because it did increase the labor pool and drove down wages. They also welcomed the strife it caused between workers, which disrupted efforts to form unions.

The African Americans recently liberated from slavery were in an even worse state. Many worked in near-slavery conditions on the farms and plantations of the South as hands or sharecroppers. Those who sought work in the cities found little. As labor historian William H. Harris says, the history of black workers is "not so much how blacks got along on their jobs but whether they got jobs at all" (3). African Americans were also largely excluded from the protection of the unions that grew in numbers and power after the Civil War.

The middle class at midcentury was made up of merchants, professionals, manufacturing employers, and master craftsmen. Women of the middle class contributed to the household economy by controlling purchases: Careful shopping was an essential element of home management. Middle-class women became responsible for providing a pleasant home, a home that was now separate from the scene of work and a refuge from it. Working-class women, however, were unable to conform to the ideal of female domesticity (see Unit Three). Women and children of working-class families needed to work at industrial jobs, a situation that exacerbated social differences and made the role of women in society an element of conflict between the classes.

The Gospel of Wealth

The appearance of many successful "self-made" businessmen — men who had risen from poverty to wealth by their own efforts — bolstered the Gospel of Wealth, which held that hard work was a virtue that had its reward in earthly wealth. Many church leaders argued that salvation came through self-discipline and endorsed the lives of the successful, for worldly success was evidence of self-control, effort, initiative, and so on. In short, the qualities that ensured spiritual salvation also ensured earthly riches. "By their fruits shall ye know them" referred to both spiritual and material success.

If getting rich was the result of virtue, poverty must be the result of vice. Proponents of the Gospel of Wealth blamed the poor for their own poverty. Consequently, many writers, including clergymen, opposed individual charity because it was a counterincentive to virtue: Poverty was supposed to teach people to be frugal and hardworking. As Henry Ward Beecher put it, "How blessed, then, is the stroke of disaster, which sets the children free, and gives them over to the hard but kind bosom of Poverty, who says to them, 'Work!' and, working, makes them men" (quoted in Wyllie, 23). Those who learned the lesson of poverty would be successes, while those who didn't would continue to be poor, the sign and punishment of their laziness. The poor had been given an incentive to virtue and a punishment for vice. Thus, charity was not called for. The wealthy should build churches, museums, libraries, and other institutions that would benefit those who took the initiative to better themselves. Later in the century, the idea of social Darwinism contributed to the critical view of the poor. Espousing Darwin's theory of the survival of the fittest, social Darwinists argued that the successful were the more fit in terms of evolution and that nature should be left to weed out the unsuccessful — namely, the poor. According to this argument, public or private charity was unnatural.

As the Gospel of Wealth claimed, many wealthy businessmen were indeed born poor, at least during the middle years of the century. Within a single generation, though, the number of wealthy men who had been born in poverty dropped sharply. The owners of new businesses and managers of old ones came increasingly from the already-established upper and middle classes. But the myth of the self-made man did not respond to statistics. The Protestant clergy continued to promote the idea that godliness was in league with riches and that wealth was a sign of spiritual election.

Critics of the Gospel of Wealth pointed out the flaws in the argument that virtue led to success: Hard workers frequently stayed poor and patently bad men became millionaires. Henry Demarest Lloyd argued that the Gospel of Wealth was a crass rationalization of the greed of those who held a virtual monopoly on American capital. Henry George asked how the wealth of the nation had become so inequitably distributed in the first place. George argued that the monopolization of land by corporations and speculators was to blame.

Westward Expansion

Large tracts of public land in western territories were sold after the Civil War. Many private citizens bought land for farms, but most of the land was purchased by speculators — wealthy individuals, banks and land companies, lumber and mining interests — all to be resold at a profit, often mortgaged and foreclosed as farms failed, as they frequently did because of declining agricultural prices. However, government land policies did nothing to decrease the number of industrial workers and reduce unemployment and underemployment. Augustine Duganne captured the problem in these lines in 1855:

> A billion of acres of unsold land
> Are lying in grievous dearth;
> And millions of men in the image of God
> Are starving all over the earth!
> Oh! Tell, ye sons of America!
> How much men's lives are worth! . . .
> Who hath ordained that a parchment scroll
> Shall fence round miles of lands, —
> When millions of hands want acres
> And millions of acres want hands.

In addition to the public land that was sold to individuals and businesses following the Civil War, 100 million acres of public land were given outright to the railroads, which also received $64 million in government loans and tax breaks. The railroad became a huge industry; the Pennsylvania Railroad alone employed twenty thousand by 1870. But railroad equipment and interest on loans represented a large fixed expense for the railroads, and because it was important to run full loads, rate wars broke out in competitive markets. Smaller railroads were bankrupted, leaving a few large companies with monopolies in many markets. The personal fortunes of the remaining railroad magnates soared, and the power of the railroads was maintained by an army of lobbyists who secured federal land grants, subsidies, favorable regulations, and tax protection.

Small farms — which had been the basis not only of the economy of the country but also of Americans' sense of self-sufficiency — became less and less viable. Land prices rose with expansion and speculation, while transportation and distribution costs and high interest rates depressed producers' profits and raised prices. Marginal farmers went under and new immigrants could not hope to survive by starting farms. By the middle of the nineteenth century, wage-workers constituted 40 percent of the workforce, up from 12 percent in 1800. Between 1860 and 1880, the number of industrial workers doubled from two million to four million. At the same time, the worker's position in society deteriorated rapidly. Workers resented their loss of independence, the lack of dignity in factory labor, and the absence of control over their lives at work. Workers in the North were often compared with the slaves of the old South to make the point that employers cared far less for their workers than masters for their slaves. Industrial workers were simply wage-slaves.

Workers and Unions

As early as the 1820s, workers were forming unions to protect themselves from the arbitrary authority of their employers. One important issue was working hours: In several trades, workers sought a reduction of their daily work hours from twelve to ten, arguing that they needed more time to read, think, and exercise their rights as citizens. The first unions were craft unions, organizations of workers by trade — carpenters, cigarmakers, and teamsters, for example. During and after the Civil War, as the number of factory workers and other industrial laborers increased, the less-skilled workers joined industrial unions, organizations of all the workers in a particular industry — railroad workers, steelworkers, and so on. By 1872, some 300,000 workers — out of a labor force of about 3 million — belonged to unions. The unions tried to increase wages (averaging about $1 a day in the 1860s, $1.50 thereafter), reduce hours (which were still ten to twelve per day), and improve working conditions. Historian Melvyn Dubofsky notes that "long hours and intensive labor practices combined to produce in the United States one of the highest industrial accident rates in the Western world. From 1880 to 1900, 35,000 workers were killed annually and another 536,000 were injured" (22).

The eight-hour movement was one of the unions' primary concerns through the latter half of the nineteenth century. A popular song of the period put the unions' case this way:

> We mean to make things over,
> We're tired of toil for naught,
> With bare enough to live upon
> And never an hour for thought;
> We want to feel the sunshine,
> And we want to smell the flowers,
> We're sure that God has willed it,
> And we mean to have Eight Hours.
> We're summoning our forces
> From shipyard, shop, and mill;
> Eight hours for work, eight hours for rest,
> Eight hours for what we will!

The Federation of Organized Trades and Labor Unions called for a general strike on May 1, 1886, if the eight-hour day was not instituted by that time. It wasn't, and the strike began as threatened. Nearly 1,500 strikes involving 400,000 workers took place by the end of 1886.

Unions and working-class political parties debated the problem of whether to encourage or resist the development of a working-class consciousness: Should workers regard themselves as a class with a relatively fixed social position or as individuals rising steadily in a society without rigid class barriers? Was there still any hope that most Americans could become well-off? The great fortunes made in industry deepened class divisions and increased the inequality both of wealth and of opportunity. It was becoming less and less possible for a skilled worker to become an entrepreneur, to save enough to open his own shop. Class mobility for most workers came to mean the hope of advancing to a supervisory position, buying a house, and perhaps seeing a child move into a white-collar job. While workers were willing to recognize the relatively fixed position of the individual worker, most refused to accept the idea that the United States had anything like the old European class structure with its assumption of a permanent working class. This attitude often made it difficult for unions to take strong positions to benefit the working class.

Unions adopted various strategies to respond to this difficulty. On the one hand, craft unions sought conditions that would allow skilled workers, the aristocrats of the working class, to maintain their relatively high status, if not to become entrepreneurs. Such unions clung to the doctrine of individualism and fostered further class divisions. On the other hand, some unions sought collective improvement for the working class as a whole and enrolled workers of all skill levels and all industries. Politically oriented unions looked for legislative reform to demand decent wages and safe working conditions. The most radical unions and political parties worked for the elimination of class distinctions, both of wealth and of dignity, through socialism or other means of abolishing the wage system.

Depressions and Poverty

A great national depression began in 1873 and lasted until late in 1878. Terrible depressions also occurred in 1883–85 and 1893–97. In these depressions, unemployment was widespread. As Melvyn Dubofsky says, "For many working people in the late nineteenth and early twentieth centuries, poverty was an inescapable fact of life. In an economy blighted by recurrent business slumps, seasonal patterns of production, and rapid technological changes and in a society without guaranteed forms of social insurance, unemployment and part-time employment spelled material disaster" (24).

The long depression of 1873–78 had devastating effects. Wall Street closed for a week; railroad construction stopped; railroads and banks and tens of thousands of businesses went bankrupt; over a million workers lost their jobs and a great many of them were evicted from their homes. Labor unions called for public relief programs and public spending for jobs. The unemployed demonstrated to call attention to their plight, but their rallies were suppressed, often violently, by the police. Unemployed men became tramps, traveling from place to place looking for work — and then were reviled for being dirty, homeless, and unemployed. Business and government leaders blamed the unemployed for their own problems — indolence, immorality, and ignorance were the causes of unemployment, they said. Public works projects were rejected as "communistic." The unemployed did not deserve charity: "Free soup must be prohibited," proclaimed the free-market ideologue E. L. Godkin, "and all classes must learn that soup of any kind, beef or turtle, can be had only by being paid for" (quoted in Levine, 1:548–49). The Chicago Relief and Aid Society refused to disburse its $600,000, claiming that there was work to be had for those who were not too lazy to look for it. Social Darwinists pointed out that depressions, like other calamities, weeded out those who were unfit for society. To give them charity would be to preserve the unfit.

For workers who retained their jobs during depressions, wage cuts were frequent. With a huge pool of unemployed workers available, little could be done to stop wage cuts and work rules that forced workers to pay for job-related expenses. On many railroads, for example, engineers who drove trains to distant cities had to stay overnight in company hotels at high rates and pay for their own return passage at regular fares. Rents of company-owned housing in the coal and steel "company towns" rarely dropped along with wage cuts. At the time, there was no national currency. Big companies paid wages in "scrip" — which could not be redeemed for bank notes and was good only in company stores. The powerlessness of workers also meant that safety measures could be ignored: There was simply no incentive for companies to invest in them. The courts declared that risk was part of the job, and so companies were not responsible for injuries.

Strikes and the Government's Response

These desperate conditions led to a widespread general strike, the Great Uprising of 1877. Following a joint wage cut by four major railroads — all of which had already announced their profitability by declaring a stock dividend — workers shut down a B&O railroad yard in West Virginia. A few days later, President Rutherford Hayes sent federal troops to put down the strike and run the lines. Workers elsewhere in the country demonstrated to protest the use of federal troops, sparking more confrontations. Eleven people were killed by militia in Baltimore. Striking railroad workers in Pittsburgh were supported by the ironworkers and much of the rest of the city's population, and the city militia refused to attack the strikers. When federal troops called in from Philadelphia arrived, they were assaulted with rocks. They fired on the crowd, killing twenty. Infuriated workers set fire to the railroad cars and buildings and chased the troops out of town. President Hayes again sent federal troops to restore order.

Rail strikes spread to fourteen states. In Chicago, strikers were attacked by police, while middle-class vigilantes patrolled the streets in what was nearly an all-out class war. In San Francisco, the strikes turned to violence against the Chinese community. The main target of the Great Uprising, however, was the uncontrolled corporate power represented by the railroads. Workers invoked the principles of liberty and equality as the basis of their demands for reasonable pay and decent treatment. Businessmen claimed, however, that the strikes were the work of foreign agitators and Communists; they were attempts to interfere with the fundamental right to private property and an outrageous ploy by tramps presuming to tell them how to run their businesses. Before the strikes ended, more than one hundred people had died and millions of dollars in property had been destroyed. Though the strikes were unsuccessful in achieving the workers' immediate demands, they preserved the union movement and refocused the problem of labor and capital in the nation. The strikes were part of a negotiation between workers and those of the middle and upper classes to define the meaning of liberty and equality.

Strategies of the Corporations

Industrialists, meanwhile, sought opportunities to reduce competition and get more control over markets. Those who could, like John D. Rockefeller in the oil industry, secured near-monopolies by buying out their competitors. Andrew Carnegie tried "vertical integration" in the steel industry, buying up or finding ways to control his suppliers. Railroads overbuilt to drive out competition (a tactic that led to the depression of 1893). Reducing labor costs, however, remained a tried and true method of increasing profits. "Scientific management" was introduced as a way to speed up operations and increase production by timing and regulating all work. This practice further reduced workers' control over the conditions of labor, chaining them to the clock (indeed, the time clock was introduced at this time) and making them behave more like machines.

Another form of control came through quite blatant manipulation of legislatures and the courts. Businessmen supported both national political parties, openly buying votes and maintaining extensive and unrestrained lobbyists. By this means, legislation limiting business could be stopped or vitiated. For example, in 1890 a growing popular fear of business monopolies pressured Congress into passing the Sherman Antitrust Act, which outlawed every "contract, combination in the form of trust or otherwise, or conspiracy" in restraint of interstate or foreign trade. Despite the intention of the act, however, it was rarely enforced against big businesses. Instead, it was invoked to prevent "conspiracies" by labor unions and to break strikes.

Middle-class Americans were divided in their views of the class war. They might well believe in acquisitive individualism in both its practical and intellectual forms. But they could also sympathize with struggling workers and the poor. Many workers, too, saw the promise of wealth as an optimistic ideal and were reluctant to reject it. The debate touched on many points: many wealthy men were public benefactors, endowing libraries, museums, and universities because, they said, these institutions would help people raise themselves up through education. These same benefactors, though, mercilessly cut wages, maintained unsafe working conditions, and regarded charity as immoral. And the universities they endowed were attended, at the time, by a tiny percentage of Americans — about 2 percent of the population, nearly all of them white men of the upper and middle classes. The Gospel of Wealth demanded religious behavior and philanthropy, and while some wealthy philanthropists were undoubtedly following deeply felt Christian principles, others just as clearly were simply rationalizing their own greed.

Throughout this period in America, the roles of worker and capitalist and the meaning of freedom and equality in the economic sphere were endlessly contested. Freedom of property ownership, individualism, the Gospel of Wealth, and the scientific forces of natural selection formed the matrix of principles that supported laissez-faire capitalism — the right of business to operate unhindered by conspiracies of workers and government regulation. On the other side, the right to the fruits of one's labor, equal access to natural resources, freedom from monopolies, and freedom from wage-slavery were the principles that workers invoked when claiming the right to create unions and receive government protection. The clashes between these sets of rights form the backdrop to the selections in this unit.

THE GOSPEL OF WEALTH

HORATIO ALGER

From *Ragged Dick* (1867)

Horatio Alger (1832–99) entered Harvard Divinity School with the intention of following his father into the ministry. While at Harvard, Alger helped his landlord out of financial difficulty by giving him forty dollars that he had won in a school essay contest. The landlord died two years later, leaving Alger two thousand dollars. This experience would find its way into *Ragged Dick* and many other Alger stories in a variety of forms: The upright hero earns a small amount of money on his merit and hard work, invests it in a worthy fellow man, and finds his generosity repaid manyfold.

Alger served in the ministry for two years, during which time he wrote several children's stories and the novel *Ragged Dick*. The success of the novel brought him fame and wealth. He moved to New York from rural Massachusetts and became a public figure, serving on commissions on vice, crime, and other urban problems. Alger wrote more than 120 books, which sold millions of copies during his lifetime. These novels of self-made men inspired many who hoped to follow the example of Dick and the other Alger heroes. The novels were also a comfort to those who believed that they had risen through the virtues of courage, frugality, industry, and wise charity.

CHAPTER 1

Ragged Dick Is Introduced to the Reader

"WAKE UP THERE, YOUNGSTER," said a rough voice.

Ragged Dick opened his eyes slowly, and stared stupidly in the face of the speaker, but did not offer to get up.

"Wake up, you young vagabond!" said the man, a little impatiently; "I suppose you'd lay there all day, if I hadn't called you."

"What time is it?" asked Dick.

"Seven o'clock."

"Seven o'clock! I oughter 've been up an hour ago. I know what 'twas made me so precious sleepy. I went to the Old Bowery last night, and didn't turn in till past twelve."

"You went to the Old Bowery? Where'd you get your money?" asked the man, who was a porter in the employ of a firm doing business on Spruce Street.

Horatio Alger, *Ragged Dick* (1867; reprint, New York: Collier, 1962).
  In the notes EDS. = Patricia Bizzell and Bruce Herzberg.

"Made it by shines, in course. My guardian don't allow me no money for theatres, so I have to earn it."

"Some boys get it easier than that," said the porter significantly.

"You don't catch me stealin', if that's what you mean," said Dick.

"Don't you ever steal, then?"

"No, and I wouldn't. Lots of boys does it, but I wouldn't."

"Well, I'm glad to hear you say that. I believe there's some good in you, Dick, after all."

"Oh, I'm a rough customer!" said Dick. "But I wouldn't steal. It's mean."

"I'm glad you think so, Dick," and the rough voice sounded gentler than at first. "Have you got any money to buy your breakfast?"

"No, but I'll soon get some."

While this conversation had been going on, Dick had got up. His bed-chamber had been a wooden box half full of straw, on which the young bootblack had reposed his weary limbs, and slept as soundly as if it had been a bed of down. He dumped down into the straw without taking the trouble of undressing. Getting up too was an equally short process. He jumped out of the box, shook himself, picked out one or two straws that had found their way into the rents of his clothes, and, drawing a well-worn cap over his uncombed locks, he was all ready for the business of the day.

Dick's appearance as he stood beside the box was rather peculiar. His pants were torn in several places, and had apparently belonged in the first instance to a boy two sizes larger than himself. He wore a vest, all the buttons of which were gone except two, out of which peeped a shirt which looked as if it had been worn a month. To complete his costume he wore a coat too long for him, dating back, if one might judge from its general appearance, to a remote antiquity.

Washing the face and hands is usually considered proper in commencing the day, but Dick was above such refinement. He had no particular dislike to dirt, and did not think it necessary to remove several dark streaks on his face and hands. But in spite of his dirt and rags there was something about Dick that was attractive. It was easy to see that if he had been clean and well dressed he would have been decidedly good-looking. Some of his companions were sly, and their faces inspired distrust; but Dick had a frank, straight-forward manner that made him a favorite.

Dick's business hours had commenced. He had no office to open. His little blacking-box was ready for use, and he looked sharply in the faces of all who passed, addressing each with, "Shine yer boots, sir?"

"How much?" asked a gentleman on his way to his office.

"Ten cents," said Dick, dropping his box, and sinking upon his knees on the sidewalk, flourishing his brush with the air of one skilled in his profession.

"Ten cents! Isn't that a little steep?"

"Well, you know 'taint all clear profit," said Dick, who had already set to work. "There's the *blacking* costs something, and I have to get a new brush pretty often."

"And you have a large rent too," said the gentleman quizzically, with a glance at a large hole in Dick's coat.

"Yes, sir," said Dick, always ready to joke; "I have to pay such a big rent for my manshun up on Fifth Avenoo, that I can't afford to take less than ten cents a shine. I'll give you a bully shine, sir."

"Be quick about it, for I am in a hurry. So your house is on Fifth Avenue, is it?"

"It isn't anywhere else," said Dick, and Dick spoke the truth there.

"What tailor do you patronize?" asked the gentleman, surveying Dick's attire.

"Would you like to go to the same one?" asked Dick, shrewdly.

"Well, no; it strikes me that he didn't give you a very good fit."

"This coat once belonged to General Washington," said Dick comically. "He wore it all through the Revolution, and it got torn some, 'cause he fit so hard. When he died he told his widder to give it to some smart young feller that hadn't got none of his own; so she gave it to me. But if you'd like it, sir, to remember General Washington by, I'll let you have it reasonable."

"Thank you, but I wouldn't want to deprive you of it. And did your pants come from General Washington too?"

"No, they was a gift from Lewis Napoleon.[1] Lewis had outgrown 'em and sent 'em to me, — he's bigger than me, and that's why they don't fit."

"It seems you have distinguished friends. Now, my lad, I suppose you would like your money."

"I shouldn't have any objection," said Dick.

"I believe," said the gentleman, examining his pocketbook, "I haven't got anything short of twenty-five cents. Have you got any change?"

"Not a cent," said Dick. "All my money's invested in the Erie Railroad."

"That's unfortunate."

"Shall I get the money changed, sir?"

"I can't wait; I've got to meet an appointment immediately. I'll hand you twenty-five cents, and you can leave the change at my office any time during the day."

"All right, sir. Where is it?"

"No. 125 Fulton Street. Shall you remember?"

"Yes, sir. What name?"

"Greyson, — office on second floor."

"All right, sir; I'll bring it."

"I wonder whether the little scamp will prove honest," said Mr. Greyson to himself, as he walked away. "If he does, I'll give him my custom regularly. If he don't, as is most likely, I shan't mind the loss of fifteen cents."

Mr. Greyson didn't understand Dick. Our ragged hero wasn't a model boy in all respects. I am afraid he swore sometimes, and now and then he played tricks upon unsophisticated boys from the country or gave a wrong direction to honest old gentlemen unused to the city. A clergyman in

[1]Louis (mispronounced "Lewis" by Dick) Napoleon (1808–73) was nephew of Napoleon Bonaparte and emperor of France (1852–71). — EDS.

search of the Cooper Institute[2] he once directed to the Tombs Prison, and, following him unobserved, was highly delighted when the unsuspicious stranger walked up the front steps of the great stone building on Centre Street, and tried to obtain admission.

"I guess he wouldn't want to stay long if he did get in," thought Ragged Dick, hitching up his pants. "Leastways I shouldn't. They're so precious glad to see you that they won't let you go, but board you gratooitous, and never send in no bills."

Another of Dick's faults was his extravagance. Being always wide awake and ready for business, he earned enough to have supported him comfortably and respectably. There were not a few young clerks who employed Dick from time to time in his professional capacity, who scarcely earned as much as he, greatly as their style and dress exceeded his. Dick was careless of his earnings. Where they went he could hardly have told himself. However much he managed to earn during the day, all was generally spent before morning. He was fond of going to the Old Bowery Theatre, and to Tony Pastor's, and if he had any money left afterwards, he would invite some of his friends in somewhere to have an oyster stew; so it seldom happened that he commenced the day with a penny.

Then I am sorry to add that Dick had formed the habit of smoking. This cost him considerable, for Dick was rather fastidious about his cigars, and wouldn't smoke the cheapest. Besides, having a liberal nature, he was generally ready to treat his companions. But of course the expense was the smallest objection. No boy of fourteen can smoke without being affected injuriously. Men are frequently injured by smoking, and boys always. But large numbers of the newsboys and bootblacks form the habit. Exposed to the cold and wet they find that it warms them up, and the self-indulgence grows upon them. It is not uncommon to see a little boy, too young to be out of his mother's sight, smoking with all the apparent satisfaction of a veteran smoker.

There was another way in which Dick sometimes lost money. There was a noted gambling house on Baxter Street, which in the evening was sometimes crowded with these juvenile gamesters, who staked their hard earnings, generally losing of course, and refreshing themselves from time to time with a vile mixture of liquor at two cents a glass. Sometimes Dick strayed in here, and played with the rest.

I have mentioned Dick's faults and defects, because I want it understood, to begin with, that I don't consider him a model boy. But there were some good points about him nevertheless. He was above doing anything mean or dishonorable. He would not steal, or cheat, or impose upon younger boys, but was frank and straightforward, manly and self-reliant. His nature was a noble one, and had saved him from all mean faults. I hope my young readers will like him as I do, without being blind to his

---

[2]Later known as the Cooper Union for the Advancement of Science and Art, the Cooper Institute was founded in 1859 by Peter Cooper (1791–1883). The institute provided free lectures and cultural events for the working poor. For more information, see note 6 on page 457. — Eds.

faults. Perhaps, although he was only a bootblack, they may find something in him to imitate.

And now, having fairly introduced Ragged Dick to my young readers, I must refer them to the next chapter for his further adventures.

[*Dick walks the streets of New York plying his trade. We rejoin him as he is walking uptown.* — EDS.]

CHAPTER 3

Dick Makes a Proposition

. . . Dick shouldered his box and walked up as far as the Astor House. He took his station on the sidewalk, and began to look about him.

Just behind him were two persons, — one, a gentleman of fifty; the other, a boy of thirteen or fourteen. They were speaking together, and Dick had no difficulty in hearing what was said.

"I am sorry, Frank, that I can't go about, and show you some of the sights of New York, but I shall be full of business today. It is your first visit to the city too."

"Yes, sir."

"There's a good deal worth seeing here. But I'm afraid you'll have to wait till next time. You can go out and walk by yourself, but don't venture too far, or you may get lost."

Frank looked disappointed.

"I wish Tom Miles knew I was here," he said. "He would go around with me."

"Where does he live?"

"Somewhere uptown, I believe."

"Then, unfortunately, he is not available. If you would rather go with me than stay here, you can, but as I shall be most of the time in merchants' counting rooms, I am afraid it would not be very interesting."

"I think," said Frank, after a little hesitation, "that I will go off by myself. I won't go very far, and if I lose my way, I will inquire for the Astor House."

"Yes, anybody will direct you here. Very well, Frank, I am sorry I can't do better for you."

"Oh, never mind, uncle, I shall be amused in walking around, and looking at the shop windows. There will be a great deal to see."

Now Dick had listened to all this conversation. Being an enterprising young man, he thought he saw a chance for a speculation, and determined to avail himself of it.

Accordingly he stepped up to the two just as Frank's uncle was about leaving, and said, "I know all about the city, sir; I'll show him around, if you want me to."

The gentleman looked a little curiously at the ragged figure before him.

"So you are a city boy, are you?"

"Yes, sir," said Dick, "I've lived here ever since I was a baby."

"And you know all about the public buildings, I suppose?"

"Yes, sir."

"And the Central Park?"

"Yes, sir. I know my way all round."

The gentleman looked thoughtful.

"I don't know what to say, Frank," he remarked after a while. "It is rather a novel proposal. He isn't exactly the sort of guide I would have picked out for you. Still he looks honest. He has an open face, and I think can be depended upon."

"I wish he wasn't so ragged and dirty," said Frank, who felt a little shy about being seen with such a companion.

"I'm afraid you haven't washed your face this morning," said Mr. Whitney, for that was the gentleman's name.

"They didn't have no wash bowls at the hotel where I stopped," said Dick.

"What hotel did you stop at?"

"The Box Hotel."

"The Box Hotel?"

"Yes, sir, I slept in a box on Spruce Street."

Frank surveyed Dick curiously.

"How did you like it?" he asked.

"I slept bully."

"Suppose it had rained?"

"Then I'd have wet my best clothes," said Dick.

"Are these all the clothes you have?"

"Yes, sir."

Mr. Whitney spoke a few words to Frank, who seemed pleased with the suggestion.

"Follow me, my lad," he said.

Dick in some surprise obeyed orders, following Mr. Whitney and Frank into the hotel, past the office, to the foot of the staircase. Here a servant of the hotel stopped Dick, but Mr. Whitney explained that he had something for him to do, and he was allowed to proceed.

They entered a long entry, and finally paused before a door. This being opened a pleasant chamber was disclosed.

"Come in, my lad," said Mr. Whitney.

Dick and Frank entered.

CHAPTER 4

Dick's New Suit

"Now," said Mr. Whitney to Dick, "my nephew here is on his way to a boarding school. He had a suit of clothes in his trunk about half worn. He is willing to give them to you. I think they will look better than those you have on."

Dick was so astonished that he hardly knew what to say. Presents were something that he knew very little about, never having received any to his knowledge. That so large a gift should be made to him by a stranger seemed very wonderful.

The clothes were brought out, and turned out to be a neat gray suit.

"Before you put them on, my lad, you must wash yourself. Clean clothes and a dirty skin don't go very well together. Frank, you may attend to him. I am obliged to go at once. Have you got as much money as you require?"

"Yes, uncle."

"One more word, my lad," said Mr. Whitney, addressing Dick; "I may be rash in trusting a boy of whom I know nothing, but I like your looks, and I think you will prove a proper guide for my nephew."

"Yes, I will, sir," said Dick, earnestly. "Honor bright!"

"Very well. A pleasant time to you."

The process of cleansing commenced. To tell the truth Dick needed it, and the sensation of cleanliness he found both new and pleasant. Frank added to his gift a shirt, stockings, and an old pair of shoes. "I am sorry I haven't any cap," he said.

"I've got one," said Dick.

"It isn't so new as it might be," said Frank, surveying an old felt hat, which had once been black, but was now dingy, with a large hole in the top and a portion of the rim torn off.

"No," said Dick; "my grandfather used to wear it when he was a boy, and I've kep' it ever since out of respect for his memory. But I'll get a new one now. I can buy one cheap on Chatham Street."

"Is that near here?"

"Only five minutes' walk."

"Then we can get one on the way."

When Dick was dressed in his new attire, with his face and hands clean, and his hair brushed, it was difficult to imagine that he was the same boy.

He now looked quite handsome, and might readily have been taken for a young gentleman, except that his hands were red and grimy.

"Look at yourself," said Frank, leading him before the mirror.

"By gracious!" said Dick, staring back in astonishment, "that isn't me, is it?"

"Don't you know yourself?" asked Frank, smiling.

"It reminds me of Cinderella," said Dick, "when she was changed into a fairy princess. I see it one night at Barnum's.[3] What'll Johnny Nolan say when he sees me? He won't dare to speak to such a young swell as I be now. Ain't it rich?" and Dick burst into a loud laugh. His fancy was tickled by the anticipation of his friend's surprise. Then the thought of the valuable gifts he had received occurred to him, and he looked gratefully at Frank.

"You're a brick," he said.

[3]Barnum's American Museum, a vast collection of oddities, was owned and operated by entrepreneur and showman Phineas Taylor (P. T.) Barnum (1810–91), later of circus fame. — EDS.

"A what?"

"A brick! You're a jolly good fellow to give me such a present."

"You're quite welcome, Dick," said Frank, kindly. "I'm better off than you are, and I can spare the clothes just as well as not. You must have a new hat though. But that we can get when we go out. The old clothes you can make into a bundle." . . .

"But what shall I do with my brush and blacking?" he asked.

"You can leave them here till we come back," said Frank. "They will be safe."

"Hold on a minute," said Dick, surveying Frank's boots with a professional eye, "you ain't got a good shine on them boots. I'll make 'em shine so you can see your face in 'em."

And he was as good as his word.

"Thank you," said Frank; "now you had better brush your own shoes."

This had not occurred to Dick, for in general the professional boot-black considers his blacking too valuable to expend on his own shoes or boots, if he is fortunate enough to possess a pair.

The two boys now went downstairs together. They met the same servant who had spoken to Dick a few minutes before, but there was no recognition.

"He don't know me," said Dick. "He thinks I'm a young swell like you."

"What's a swell?"

"Oh, a feller that wears nobby clothes like you."

"And you, too, Dick."

"Yes," said Dick, "who'd ever have thought as I should have turned into a swell?"

They had now got out on Broadway, and were slowly walking along the west side by the Park, when who should Dick see in front of him, but Johnny Nolan?

Instantly Dick was seized with a fancy for witnessing Johnny's amazement at his change in appearance. He stole up behind him, and struck him on the back.

"Hallo, Johnny, how many shines have you had?"

Johnny turned round expecting to see Dick, whose voice he recognized, but his astonished eyes rested on a nicely dressed boy (the hat alone excepted) who looked indeed like Dick, but so transformed in dress that it was difficult to be sure of his identity.

"What luck, Johnny?" repeated Dick.

Johnny surveyed him from head to foot in great bewilderment.

"Who be you?" he said.

"Well, that's a good one," laughed Dick; "so you don't know Dick?"

"Where'd you get all them clothes?" asked Johnny. "Have you been stealin'?"

"Say that again, and I'll lick you. No, I've lent my clothes to a young feller as was goin' to a party, and didn't have none fit to wear, and so I put on my second-best for a change."

Without deigning any further explanation, Dick went off, followed by the astonished gaze of Johnny Nolan, who could not quite make up his mind whether the neat-looking boy he had been talking with was really Ragged Dick or not. . . .

[*Dick shows Frank some of his haunts in New York. Soon, Frank asks Dick about himself.* — EDS.]

CHAPTER 8

Dick's Early History

"Have you always lived in New York, Dick?" asked Frank, after a pause.

"Ever since I can remember."

"I wish you'd tell me a little about yourself. Have you got any father or mother?"

"I ain't got no mother. She died when I wasn't but three years old. My father went to sea; but he went off before mother died, and nothin' was ever heard of him. I expect he got wrecked, or died at sea."

"And what became of you when your mother died?"

"The folks she boarded with took care of me, but they was poor, and they couldn't do much. When I was seven the woman died, and her husband went out West, and then I had to scratch for myself."

"At seven years old!" exclaimed Frank, in amazement.

"Yes," said Dick, "I was a little feller to take care of myself, but," he continued with pardonable pride, "I did it."

"What could you do?"

"Sometimes one thing, and sometimes another," said Dick. "I changed my business accordin' as I had to. Sometimes I was a newsboy, and diffused intelligence among the masses, as I heard somebody say once in a big speech he made in the Park. Them was the times when Horace Greeley and James Gordon Bennett[4] made money."

"Through your enterprise?" suggested Frank.

"Yes," said Dick; "but I give it up after a while."

"What for?"

"Well, they didn't always put news enough in their papers, and people wouldn't buy 'em as fast as I wanted 'em to. So one morning I was stuck on a lot of *Herald*s, and I thought I'd make a sensation. So I called out 'GREAT NEWS! QUEEN VICTORIA[5] ASSASSINATED!' All my *Herald*s went off like hot cakes, and I went off, too, but one of the gentlemen what got sold remembered me, and said he'd have me took up, and that's what made me change my business."

"That wasn't right, Dick," said Frank.

"I know it," said Dick; "but lots of boys does it."

[4]Greeley (1811–72) founded the *New York Tribune;* Bennett (1795–1872) founded the *New York Herald.* — EDS.

[5]Victoria was queen of Great Britain and Ireland from 1837 to 1901. — EDS.

"That don't make it any better."

"No," said Dick, "I was sort of ashamed at the time, 'specially about one poor old gentleman, — a Englishman he was. He couldn't help cryin' to think the queen was dead, and his hands shook when he handed me the money for the paper."

"What did you do next?"

"I went into the match business," said Dick; "but it was small sales and small profits. Most of the people I called on had just laid in a stock, and didn't want to buy. So one cold night, when I hadn't money enough to pay for a lodgin', I burned the last of my matches to keep me from freezin'. But it cost too much to get warm that way, and I couldn't keep it up."

"You've seen hard times, Dick," said Frank, compassionately.

"Yes," said Dick, "I've knowed what it was to be hungry and cold, with nothin' to eat or to warm me; but there's one thing I never could do," he added, proudly.

"What's that?"

"I never stole," said Dick. "It's mean and I wouldn't do it."

"Were you ever tempted to?"

"Lots of times. Once I had been goin' round all day, and hadn't sold any matches, except three cents' worth early in the mornin'. With that I bought an apple, thinkin' I should get some more bimeby.[6] When evenin' come I was awful hungry. I went into a baker's just to look at the bread. It made me feel kind o' good just to look at the bread and cakes, and I thought maybe they would give me some. I asked 'em wouldn't they give me a loaf, and take their pay in matches. But they said they'd got enough matches to last three months; so there wasn't any chance for a trade. While I was standin' at the stove warmin' me, the baker went into the back room, and I felt so hungry I thought I would take just one loaf, and go off with it. There was such a big pile I don't think he'd have known it."

"But you didn't do it?"

"No, I didn't, and I was glad of it, for when the man came in ag'in, he said he wanted some one to carry some cake to a lady in St. Mark's Place. His boy was sick, and he hadn't no one to send; so he told me he'd give me ten cents if I would go. My business wasn't very pressin' just then, so I went, and when I come back, I took my pay in bread and cakes. Didn't they taste good, though?"

"So you didn't stay long in the match business, Dick?"

"No, I couldn't sell enough to make it pay. Then there was some folks that wanted me to sell cheaper to them; so I couldn't make any profit. There was one old lady — she was rich, too, for she lived in a big brick house — beat me down so, that I didn't make no profit at all; but she wouldn't buy without, and I hadn't sold none that day; so I let her have them. I don't see why rich folks should be so hard upon a poor boy that wants to make a livin'."

"There's a good deal of meanness in the world, I'm afraid, Dick."

---

[6]Dick's pronunciation of "by and by." — EDS.

"If everybody was like you and your uncle," said Dick, "there would be some chance for poor people. If I was rich I'd try to help 'em along."

"Perhaps you will be rich sometime, Dick."

Dick shook his head. . . .

"That depends very much on yourself, Dick," said Frank. "Stewart[7] wasn't always rich, you know."

"Wasn't he?"

"When he first came to New York as a young man he was a teacher, and teachers are not generally very rich. At last he went into business, starting in a small way, and worked his way up by degrees. But there was one thing he determined in the beginning: that he would be strictly honorable in all his dealings, and never overreach any one for the sake of making money. If there was a chance for him, Dick, there is a chance for you."

"He knowed enough to be a teacher, and I'm awful ignorant," said Dick.

"But you needn't stay so."

"How can I help it?"

"Can't you learn at school?"

"I can't go to school 'cause I've got my livin' to earn. It wouldn't do me much good if I learned to read and write, and just as I'd got learned I starved to death."

"But are there no night schools?"

"Yes."

"Why don't you go? I suppose you don't work in the evenings."

"I never cared much about it," said Dick, "and that's the truth. But since I've got to talkin' with you, I think more about it. I guess I'll begin to go."

"I wish you would, Dick. You'll make a smart man if you only get a little education."

"Do you think so?" asked Dick, doubtfully.

"I know so. A boy who has earned his own living ever since he was seven years old must have something in him. I feel very much interested in you, Dick. You've had a hard time of it so far in life, but I think better times are in store. I want you to do well, and I feel sure you can if you only try."

"You're a good fellow," said Dick, gratefully. "I'm afraid I'm a pretty rough customer, but I ain't as bad as some. I mean to turn over a new leaf, and try to grow up 'spectable."

"There've been a great many boys begin as low down as you, Dick, that have grown up respectable and honored. But they had to work pretty hard for it."

"I'm willin' to work hard," said Dick.

"And you must not only work hard, but work in the right way."

"What's the right way?"

[7]Alexander Turney Stewart (1803–76) turned his dry-goods store into a giant department store and wholesale business and then invested in real estate. He built Garden City, New York. — EDS.

"You began in the right way when you determined never to steal, or do anything mean or dishonorable, however strongly tempted to do so. That will make people have confidence in you when they come to know you. But, in order to succeed well, you must manage to get as good an education as you can. Until you do, you cannot get a position in an office or counting room, even to run errands."

"That's so," said Dick, soberly. "I never thought how awful ignorant I was till now."

"That can be remedied with perseverance," said Frank. "A year will do a great deal for you."

"I'll go to work and see what I can do," said Dick, energetically.

CHAPTER 11

Dick as a Detective

. . . The two boys walked up to Broadway, just where the tall steeple of Trinity faces the street of bankers and brokers, and walked leisurely to the hotel. When they arrived at the Astor House, Dick said, "Good-by, Frank."

"Not yet," said Frank; "I want you to come in with me."

Dick followed his young patron up the steps. Frank went into the reading room, where, as he had thought probable, he found his uncle already arrived, and reading a copy of *The Evening Post*, which he had just purchased outside.

"Well, boys," he said, looking up, "have you had a pleasant jaunt?"

"Yes, sir," said Frank. "Dick's a capital guide."

"So this is Dick," said Mr. Whitney, surveying him with a smile. "Upon my word, I should hardly have known him. I must congratulate him on his improved appearance."

"Frank's been very kind to me," said Dick, who, rough street boy as he was, had a heart easily touched by kindness, of which he had never experienced much. "He's a tip-top fellow."

"I believe he is a good boy," said Mr. Whitney. "I hope, my lad, you will prosper and rise in the world. You know in this free country poverty in early life is no bar to a man's advancement. I haven't risen very high myself," he added, with a smile, "but have met with moderate success in life; yet there was a time when I was as poor as you."

"Were you, sir?" asked Dick, eagerly.

"Yes, my boy, I have known the time when I have been obliged to go without my dinner because I didn't have enough money to pay for it."

"How did you get up in the world?" asked Dick, anxiously.

"I entered a printing office as an apprentice, and worked for some years. Then my eyes gave out and I was obliged to give that up. Not knowing what else to do, I went into the country, and worked on a farm. After a while I was lucky enough to invent a machine, which has brought me in a great deal of money. But there was one thing I got while I was in the print-ing office which I value more than money."

"What was that, sir?"

"A taste for reading and study. During my leisure hours I improved my-self by study, and acquired a large part of the knowledge which I now pos-sess. Indeed, it was one of my books that first put me on the track of the in-vention, which I afterwards made. So you see, my lad, that my studious habits paid me in money, as well as in another way."

"I'm awful ignorant," said Dick, soberly.

"But you are young, and, I judge, a smart boy. If you try to learn, you can, and if you ever expect to do anything in the world, you must know something of books."

"I will," said Dick, resolutely. "I ain't always goin' to black boots for a livin'."

"All labor is respectable, my lad, and you have no cause to be ashamed of any honest business; yet when you can get something to do that promises better for your future prospects, I advise you to do so. Till then earn your living in the way you are accustomed to, avoid extravagance, and save up a little money if you can."

"Thank you for your advice," said our hero. "There ain't many that takes an interest in Ragged Dick."

"So that's your name," said Mr. Whitney. "If I judge you rightly, it won't be long before you change it. Save your money, my lad, buy books, and de-termine to be somebody, and you may yet fill an honorable position."

"I'll try," said Dick. "Good night, sir."

"Wait a minute, Dick," said Frank. "Your blacking box and old clothes are upstairs. You may want them." . . .

They went into the reading room. Dick had wrapped up his blacking brush in a newspaper with which Frank had supplied him, feeling that a guest of the Astor House should hardly be seen coming out of the hotel displaying such a professional sign.

"Uncle, Dick's ready to go," said Frank.

"Good-by, my lad," said Mr. Whitney. "I hope to hear good accounts of you sometime. Don't forget what I have told you. Remember that your fu-ture position depends mainly upon yourself, and that it will be high or low as you choose to make it."

He held out his hand, in which was a five-dollar bill. Dick shrunk back.

"I don't like to take it," he said. "I haven't earned it."

"Perhaps not," said Mr. Whitney; "but I give it to you because I remem-ber my own friendless youth. I hope it may be of service to you. Sometime when you are a prosperous man, you can repay it in the form of aid to some poor boy, who is struggling upward as you are now."

"I will, sir," said Dick, manfully.

He no longer refused the money, but took it gratefully, and, bidding Frank and his uncle good-by, went out into the street. A feeling of loneli-ness came over him as he left the presence of Frank, for whom he had formed a strong attachment in the few hours he had known him.

[*His adventures with Frank and his new clothes leave Dick thoughtful. He decides to try to improve himself and begins by renting a room for seventy-five cents a week.* — EDS.]

CHAPTER 14

A Battle and a Victory

. . . In the course of the next morning, in pursuance of his new resolutions for the future, he called at a savings bank, and held out four dollars in bills besides another dollar in change. There was a high railing, and a number of clerks busily writing at desks behind it. Dick, never having been in a bank before, did not know where to go. He went, by mistake, to the desk where money was paid out.

"Where's your book?" asked the clerk.

"I haven't got any."

"Have you any money deposited here?"

"No sir, I want to leave some here."

"Then go to the next desk."

Dick followed directions, and presented himself before an elderly man with gray hair, who looked at him over the rims of his spectacles.

"I want you to keep that for me," said Dick, awkwardly emptying his money out on the desk.

"How much is there?"

"Five dollars."

"Have you got an account here?"

"No, sir."

"Of course you can write?"

The "of course" was said on account of Dick's neat dress.

"Have I got to do any writing?" asked our hero, a little embarrassed.

"We want you to sign your name in this book," and the old gentleman shoved round a large folio volume containing the names of depositors.

Dick surveyed the book with some awe.

"I ain't much on writin'," he said.

"Very well; write as well as you can."

The pen was put into Dick's hand, and, after dipping it in the inkstand, he succeeded after a hard effort, accompanied by many contortions of the face, in inscribing upon the book of the bank the name

DICK HUNTER

"Dick! — that means Richard, I suppose," said the bank officer, who had some difficulty in making out the signature.

"No; Ragged Dick is what folks call me."

"You don't look very ragged."

"No, I've left my rags at home. They might get wore out if I used 'em too common."

"Well, my lad, I'll make out a book in the name of Dick Hunter, since you seem to prefer Dick to Richard. I hope you will save up your money and deposit more with us."

Our hero took his bank book, and gazed on the entry "Five Dollars" with a new sense of importance. He had been accustomed to joke about Erie shares; but now, for the first time, he felt himself a capitalist; on a small scale, to be sure, but still it was no small thing for Dick to have five dollars which he could call his own. He firmly determined that he would lay by every cent he could spare from his earnings towards the fund he hoped to accumulate.

But Dick was too sensible not to know that there was something more than money needed to win a respectable position in the world. He felt that he was very ignorant. Of reading and writing he only knew the rudiments, and that, with a slight acquaintance with arithmetic, was all he did know of books. Dick knew he must study hard, and he dreaded it. He looked upon learning as attended with greater difficulties than it really possesses. But Dick had good pluck. He meant to learn, nevertheless, and resolved to buy a book with his first spare earnings.

When Dick went home at night he locked up his bank book in one of the drawers of the bureau. It was wonderful how much more independent he felt whenever he reflected upon the contents of that drawer, and with what an important air of joint ownership he regarded the bank building in which his small savings were deposited.

CHAPTER 15

Dick Secures a Tutor

The next morning Dick was unusually successful, having plenty to do, and receiving for one job twenty-five cents, — the gentleman refusing to take change. Then flashed upon Dick's mind the thought that he had not yet returned the change due to the gentleman whose boots he had blacked on the morning of his introduction to the reader.

"What'll he think of me?" said Dick to himself. "I hope he won't think I'm mean enough to keep the money."

Now Dick was scrupulously honest, and though the temptation to be otherwise had often been strong, he had always resisted it. He was not willing on any account to keep money which did not belong to him, and he immediately started for 125 Fulton Street (the address which had been given him) where he found Mr. Greyson's name on the door of an office on the first floor.

The door being open, Dick walked in.

"Is Mr. Greyson in?" he asked of a clerk who sat on a high stool before a desk.

"Not just now. He'll be in soon. Will you wait?"

"Yes," said Dick.

"Very well; take a seat then."

Dick sat down and took up the morning *Tribune*, but presently came to a word of four syllables, which he pronounced to himself a "sticker," and laid it down. But he had not long to wait, for five minutes later Mr. Greyson entered.

"Did you wish to speak to me, my lad?" said he to Dick, whom in his new clothes he did not recognize.

"Yes, sir," said Dick. "I owe you some money."

"Indeed!" said Mr. Greyson, pleasantly; "that's an agreeable surprise. I didn't know but you had come for some. So you are a debtor of mine, and not a creditor?"

"I b'lieve that's right," said Dick, drawing fifteen cents from his pocket, and placing in Mr. Greyson's hand.

"Fifteen cents!" repeated he, in some surprise. "How do you happen to be indebted to me in that amount?"

"You gave me a quarter for a-shinin' your boots, yesterday mornin', and couldn't wait for the change. I meant to have brought it before, but I forgot all about it till this mornin'."

"It had quite slipped my mind also. But you don't look like the boy I employed. If I remember rightly he wasn't as well dressed as you."

"No," said Dick. "I was dressed for a party, then, but the clo'es was too well ventilated to be comfortable in cold weather."

"You're an honest boy," said Mr. Greyson. "Who taught you to be honest?"

"Nobody," said Dick. "But it's mean to cheat and steal. I've always knowed that."

"Then you've got ahead of some of our businessmen. Do you read the Bible?"

"No," said Dick. "I've heard it's a good book, but I don't know much about it."

"You ought to go to some Sunday School. Would you be willing?"

"Yes," said Dick, promptly. "I want to grow up 'spectable. But I don't know where to go."

"Then I'll tell you. The church I attend is at the corner of Fifth Avenue and Twenty-first Street."

"I've seen it," said Dick.

"I have a class in the Sunday School there. If you'll come next Sunday, I'll take you into my class, and do what I can to help you."

"Thank you," said Dick, "but p'r'aps you'll get tired of teaching me. I'm awful ignorant."

"No, my lad," said Mr. Greyson, kindly. "You evidently have some good principles to start with, as you have shown by your scorn for dishonesty. I shall hope good things of you in the future."

"Well, Dick," said our hero, apostrophizing himself, as he left the office; "you're gettin' up in the world. You've got money invested, and are goin' to attend church, by partic'lar invitation, on Fifth Avenue. I shouldn't wonder much if you should find cards, when you get home, from the Mayor, requestin' the honor of your company to dinner, along with other distinguished guests."

Dick felt in very good spirits. He seemed to be emerging from the world in which he had hitherto lived, into a new atmosphere of respectability, and the change seemed very pleasant to him. . . .

[*Dick befriends another bootblack, a timid boy named Henry Fosdick. Fosdick has had some schooling, and Dick engages him as his tutor, sharing his room with Fosdick by way of payment. Dick studies diligently and is soon on his way to literacy. Fosdick improves, too, taking a job in a hat store.* — EDS.]

CHAPTER 20

Nine Months Later

. . . Fosdick was still at the hat store, having succeeded in giving perfect satisfaction to Mr. Henderson. His wages had just been raised to five dollars a week. He and Dick still kept house together at Mrs. Mooney's lodging house, and lived very frugally, so that both were able to save up money. Dick had been unusually successful in business. He had several regular patrons, who had been drawn to him by his ready wit, and quick humor, and from two of them he had received presents of clothing, which had saved him an expense on that score. His income had averaged quite seven dollars a week in addition to this. Of this amount he was now obliged to pay one dollar weekly for the room which he and Fosdick occupied, but he was still able to save half the remainder. At the end of nine months therefore, or thirty-nine weeks, it will be seen that he had accumulated no less a sum than one hundred and seventeen dollars. Dick may be excused for feeling like a capitalist when he looked at the long row of deposits in his little bank book. There were other boys in the same business who had earned as much money, but they had had little care for the future, and spent as they went along, so that few could boast a bank account, however small.

"You'll be a rich man some time, Dick," said Henry Fosdick, one evening.

"And live on Fifth Avenoo," said Dick.

"Perhaps so. Stranger things have happened."

"Well," said Dick, "if such a misfortin' should come upon me I should bear it like a man. When you see a Fifth Avenoo manshun for sale for a hundred and seventeen dollars, just let me know and I'll buy it as an investment."

"Two hundred and fifty years ago you might have bought one for that price, probably. Real estate wasn't very high among the Indians."

"Just my luck," said Dick; "I was born too late. I'd orter have been an Indian, and lived in splendor on my present capital."

"I'm afraid you'd have found your present business rather unprofitable at that time."

But Dick had gained something more valuable than money. He had studied regularly every evening, and his improvement had been marvelous. He could now read well, write a fair hand, and had studied arithmetic as far as Interest. Besides this he had obtained some knowledge of grammar and geography. If some of my boy readers, who have been studying for years, and got no farther than this, should think it incredible that Dick, in less than a year, and studying evenings only, should have accomplished it, they must remember that our hero was very much in earnest in his desire to improve. He knew that, in order to grow up respectable, he must be well advanced, and he was willing to work. But then the reader must not forget that Dick was naturally a smart boy. His street education had sharpened his faculties, and taught him to rely upon himself. He knew that it would take him a long time to reach the goal which he had set before him, and he had patience to keep on trying. He knew that he had only himself to depend upon, and he determined to make the most of himself, — a resolution which is the secret of success in nine cases out of ten.

"Dick," said Fosdick, one evening, after they had completed their studies, "I think you'll have to get another teacher soon."

"Why?" asked Dick, in some surprise. "Have you been offered a more loocrative position?"

"No," said Fosdick, "but I find I have taught you all I know myself. You are now as good a scholar as I am."

"Is that true?" said Dick, eagerly, a flush of gratification coloring his brown cheek.

"Yes," said Fosdick. "You've made wonderful progress. I propose, now that evening schools have begun, that we join one, and study together through the winter."

"All right," said Dick. "I'd be willin' to go now; but when I first began to study I was ashamed to have anybody know that I was so ignorant. Do you really mean, Fosdick, that I know as much as you?"

"Yes, Dick, it's true."

"Then I've got you to thank for it," said Dick, earnestly. "You've made me what I am."

"And haven't you paid me, Dick?"

"By payin' the room rent," said Dick, impulsively. "What's that? It isn't half enough. I wish you'd take half my money; you deserve it."

"Thank you, Dick, but you're too generous. You've more than paid me. Who was it took my part when all the other boys imposed upon me? And who gave me money to buy clothes, and so got me my situation?"

"Oh, that's nothing!" said Dick.

"It's a great deal, Dick. I shall never forget it. But now it seems to me you might try to get a situation yourself."

"Do I know enough?"

"You know as much as I do."

"Then I'll try," said Dick, decidedly. . . .

A few days later, as Dick was looking about for customers in the neighborhood of the Park, his attention was drawn to a fellow bootblack, a boy about a year younger than himself, who appeared to have been crying.

"What's the matter, Tom?" asked Dick. "Haven't you had luck today?"

"Pretty good," said the boy; "but we're havin' hard times at home.

Mother fell last week and broke her arm, and tomorrow we've got to pay the rent, and if we don't the landlord says he'll turn us out."

"Haven't you got anything except what you earn?" asked Dick.

"No," said Tom, "not now. Mother used to earn three or four dollars a week; but she can't do nothin' now, and my little sister and brother are too young."

Dick had quick sympathies. He had been so poor himself, and obliged to submit to so many privations, that he knew from personal experience how hard it was. Tom Wilkins he knew as an excellent boy, who never squandered his money, but faithfully carried it home to his mother. In the days of his own extravagance and shiftlessness he had once or twice asked Tom to accompany him to the Old Bowery or Tony Pastor's, but Tom had always steadily refused.

"I'm sorry for you, Tom," he said. "How much do you owe for rent?"

"Two weeks now," said Tom.

"How much is it a week?"

"Two dollar a week — that makes four."

"Have you got anything towards it?"

"No; I've had to spend all my money for food for mother and the rest of us. I've had pretty hard work to do that. I don't know what we'll do. I haven't any place to go to, and I'm afraid mother'll get cold in her arm."

"Can't you borrow the money somewhere?" asked Dick.

Tom shook his head despondingly.

"All the people I know are as poor as I am," said he. "They'd help me if they could, but it's hard work for them to get along themselves."

"I'll tell you what, Tom," said Dick impulsively, "I'll stand your friend."

"Have you got any money?" asked Tom, doubtfully.

"Got any money!" repeated Dick. "Don't you know that I run a bank on my own account? How much is it you need?"

"Four dollars," said Tom. "If we don't pay that before tomorrow night, out we go. You haven't got as much as that, have you?"

"Here are three dollars," said Dick, drawing out his pocketbook. "I'll let you have the rest tomorrow, and maybe a little more."

"You're a right down good fellow, Dick," said Tom; "but won't you want it yourself?"

"Oh, I've got some more," said Dick.

"Maybe I'll never be able to pay you."

"'Spose you don't," said Dick; "I guess I won't fail."

"I won't forget it, Dick. I hope I'll be able to do somethin' for you some-time."

"All right," said Dick. "I'd ought to help you. I haven't got no mother to look out for. I wish I had."

There was a tinge of sadness in his tone, as he pronounced the last four words; but Dick's temperament was sanguine, and he never gave way to un-availing sadness. Accordingly he began to whistle as he turned away, only adding, "I'll see you tomorrow, Tom."

The three dollars which Dick had handed to Tom Wilkins were his savings for the present week. It was now Thursday afternoon. His rent, which amounted to a dollar, he expected to save out of the earnings of Friday and Saturday. In order to give Tom the additional assistance he had promised, Dick would be obliged to have recourse to his bank savings. He would not have ventured to trench upon it for any other reason but this. But he felt that it would be selfish to allow Tom and his mother to suffer when he had it in his power to relieve them. . . .

CHAPTER 26

An Exciting Adventure

Dick now began to look about for a position in a store or counting room. Until he should obtain one he determined to devote half the day to blacking boots, not being willing to break in upon his small capital. He found that he could earn enough in half a day to pay all his necessary expenses, including the entire rent of the room. Fosdick desired to pay his half; but Dick steadily refused, insisting upon paying so much as compensation for his friend's services as instructor.

It should be added that Dick's peculiar way of speaking and use of slang terms had been somewhat modified by his education and his intimacy with Henry Fosdick. Still he continued to indulge in them to some extent, especially when he felt like joking, and it was natural to Dick to joke, as my readers have probably found out by this time. Still his manners were considerably improved, so that he was more likely to obtain a situation than when first introduced to our notice.

Just now, however, business was very dull, and merchants, instead of hiring new assistants, were disposed to part with those already in their employ. After making several ineffectual applications, Dick began to think he should be obliged to stick to his profession until the next season. But about this time something occurred which considerably improved his chances of preferment.

This is the way it happened.

As Dick, with a balance of more than a hundred dollars in the savings bank, might fairly consider himself a young man of property, he thought himself justified in occasionally taking a half holiday from business, and going on an excursion. On Wednesday afternoon Henry Fosdick was sent by his employer on an errand to that part of Brooklyn near Greenwood Cemetery. Dick hastily dressed himself in his best, and determined to accompany him.

The two boys walked down to the South Ferry, and, paying their two cents each, entered the ferryboat. They remained at the stern, and stood by the railing, watching the great city, with its crowded wharves, receding from view. Beside them was a gentleman with two children, — a girl of eight and a little boy of six. The children were talking gaily to their father. While he was pointing out some object of interest to the little girl, the boy managed to creep, unobserved, beneath the chain that extends across the boat, for the protection of passengers, and, stepping incautiously to the edge of the boat, fell over into the foaming water.

At the child's scream, the father looked up, and, with a cry of horror, sprang to the edge of the boat. He would have plunged in, but, being unable to swim, would only have endangered his own life, without being able to save his child.

"My child!" he exclaimed in anguish, — "who will save my child? A thousand — ten thousand dollars to any one who will save him!"

There chanced to be but few passengers on board at the time, and nearly all these were either in the cabins or standing forward. Among the few who saw the child fall was our hero.

Now Dick was an expert swimmer. It was an accomplishment which he had possessed for years, and he no sooner saw the boy fall than he resolved to rescue him. His determination was formed before he heard the liberal offer made by the boy's father. Indeed, I must do Dick the justice to say that, in the excitement of the moment, he did not hear it at all, nor would it have stimulated the alacrity with which he sprang to the rescue of the little boy.

Little Johnny had already risen once, and gone under for the second time, when our hero plunged in. He was obliged to strike out for the boy, and this took time. He reached him none too soon. Just as he was sinking for the third and last time, he caught him by the jacket. Dick was stout and strong, but Johnny clung to him so tightly, that it was with great difficulty he was able to sustain himself.

"Put your arms round my neck," said Dick.

The little boy mechanically obeyed, and clung with a grasp strengthened by his terror. In this position Dick could bear his weight better. But the ferryboat was receding fast. It was quite impossible to reach it. The father, his face pale with terror and anguish, and his hands clasped in suspense, saw the brave boy's struggles, and prayed with agonizing fervor that he might be successful. But it is probable, for they were now midway of the river, that both Dick and the little boy whom he had bravely undertaken to rescue would have been drowned, had not a rowboat been fortunately near. The two men who were in it witnessed the accident, and hastened to the rescue of our hero.

"Keep up a little longer," they shouted, bending to their oars, "and we will save you."

Dick heard the shout, and it put fresh strength into him. He battled manfully with the treacherous sea, his eyes fixed longingly upon the approaching boat.

"Hold on tight, little boy," he said. "There's a boat coming."

The little boy did not see the boat. His eyes were closed to shut out the fearful water, but he clung the closer to his young preserver. Six long, steady strokes, and the boat dashed along side. Strong hands seized Dick and his youthful burden, and drew them into the boat, both dripping with water.

"God be thanked!" exclaimed the father, as from the steamer he saw the child's rescue. "That brave boy shall be rewarded, if I sacrifice my whole fortune to compass it." . . .

The boat at once headed for the ferry wharf on the Brooklyn side. The captain of the ferryboat, seeing the rescue, did not think it necessary to stop his boat, but kept on his way. The whole occurrence took place in less time than I have occupied in telling it.

The father was waiting on the wharf to receive his little boy, with what feeling of gratitude and joy can be easily understood. With a burst of happy tears he clasped him to his arms. Dick was about to withdraw modestly, but the gentleman perceived the movement, and, putting down the child, came forward, and, clasping his hand, said with emotion, "My brave boy, I owe you a debt I can never repay. But for your timely service I should now be plunged into an anguish which I cannot think of without a shudder."

Our hero was ready enough to speak on most occasions, but always felt awkward when he was praised.

"It wasn't any trouble," he said, modestly. "I can swim like a top."

"But not many boys would have risked their lives for a stranger," said the gentleman. "But," he added with a sudden thought, as his glance rested on Dick's dripping garments, "both you and my little boy will take cold in wet clothes. Fortunately I have a friend living close at hand, at whose house you will have an opportunity of taking off your clothes, and having them dried."

Dick protested that he never took cold; but Fosdick, who had now joined them, and who, it is needless to say, had been greatly alarmed at Dick's danger, joined in urging compliance with the gentleman's proposal, and in the end our hero had to yield. His new friend secured a hack, the driver of which agreed for extra recompense to receive the dripping boys into his carriage, and they were whirled rapidly to a pleasant house in a side street, where matters were quickly explained, and both boys were put to bed.

"I ain't used to goin' to bed quite so early," thought Dick. "This is the queerest excursion I ever took."

Like most active boys Dick did not enjoy the prospect of spending half a day in bed; but his confinement did not last as long as he anticipated.

In about an hour the door of his chamber was opened, and a servant appeared, bringing a new and handsome suit of clothes throughout.

"You are to put on these," said the servant to Dick; "but you needn't get up till you feel like it."

"Whose clothes are they?" asked Dick.

"They are yours."

"Mine! Where did they come from?"

"Mr. Rockwell sent out and bought them for you. They are the same size as your wet ones."

"Is he here now?"

"No. He bought another suit for the little boy, and has gone back to New York. Here's a note he asked me to give you."

Dick opened the paper, and read as follows, —

Please accept this outfit of clothes as the first installment of a debt which I can never repay. I have asked to have your wet suit dried, when you can reclaim it. Will you oblige me by calling tomorrow at my counting room, No. —, Pearl Street.

Your friend,

JAMES ROCKWELL.

CHAPTER 27

Conclusion

When Dick was dressed in his new suit, he surveyed his figure with pardonable complacency. It was the best he had ever worn, and fitted him as well as if it had been made expressly for him.

"He's done the handsome thing," said Dick to himself; "but there wasn't no 'casion for his givin' me these clothes. My lucky stars are shinin' pretty bright now. Jumpin' into the water pays better than shinin' boots; but I don't think I'd like to try it more'n once a week."

About eleven o'clock the next morning Dick repaired to Mr. Rockwell's counting room on Pearl Street. He found himself in front of a large and handsome warehouse. The counting room was on the lower floor. Our hero entered, and found Mr. Rockwell sitting at a desk. No sooner did that gentleman see him than he arose, and, advancing, shook Dick by the hand in the most friendly manner.

"My young friend," he said, "you have done me so great a service that I wish to be of some service to you in return. Tell me about yourself, and what plans or wishes you have formed for the future."

Dick frankly related his past history, and told Mr. Rockwell of his desire to get into a store or counting room, and of the failure of all his applications thus far. The merchant listened attentively to Dick's statement, and, when he had finished, placed a sheet of paper before him, and, handing him a pen, said, "Will you write your name on this piece of paper?"

Dick wrote, in a free, bold hand, the name Richard Hunter. He had very much improved his penmanship . . . and now had no cause to be ashamed of it.

Mr. Rockwell surveyed it approvingly.

"How would you like to enter my counting room as clerk, Richard?" he asked.

Dick was about to say "Bully," when he recollected himself, and answered, "Very much."

"I suppose you know something of arithmetic, do you not?"

"Yes, sir."

"Then you may consider yourself engaged at a salary of ten dollars a week. You may come next Monday morning."

"Ten dollars!" repeated Dick, thinking he must have misunderstood.

"Yes; will that be sufficient?"

"It's more than I can earn," said Dick, honestly.

"Perhaps it is at first," said Mr. Rockwell, smiling; "but I am willing to pay you that. I will besides advance you as fast as your progress will justify it."

Dick was so elated that he hardly restrained himself from some demonstration which would have astonished the merchant; but he exercised self-control, and only said, "I'll try to serve you so faithfully, sir, that you won't repent having taken me into your service."

"And I think you will succeed," said Mr. Rockwell, encouragingly. "I will not detain you any longer, for I have some important business to attend to. I shall expect to see you on Monday morning."

Dick left the counting room, hardly knowing whether he stood on his head or his heels, so overjoyed was he at the sudden change in his fortunes. Ten dollars a week was to him a fortune, and three times as much as he had expected to obtain at first. Indeed he would have been glad, only the day before, to get a place at three dollars a week. He reflected that with the stock of clothes which he had now on hand, he could save up at least half of it, and even then live better than he had been accustomed to do; so that his little fund in the savings bank, instead of being diminished, would be steadily increasing. Then he was to be advanced if he deserved it. It was indeed a bright prospect for a boy who, only a year before, could neither read nor write, and depended for a night's lodging upon the chance hospitality of an alleyway or old wagon. Dick's great ambition to "grow up 'spectable" seemed likely to be accomplished after all. . . .

Although it was yet only noon, Dick did not go out again with his brush. He felt that it was time to retire from business. He would leave his share of the public patronage to other boys less fortunate than himself. That evening Dick and Fosdick had a long conversation. Fosdick rejoiced heartily in his friend's success, and on his side had the pleasant news to communicate that his pay had been advanced to six dollars a week.

"I think we can afford to leave Mott Street now," he continued. "This house isn't as neat as it might be, and I should like to live in a nicer quarter of the city."

"All right," said Dick. "We'll hunt up a new room tomorrow. I shall have plenty of time, having retired from business. I'll try to get my reg'lar customers to take Johnny Nolan in my place. That boy hasn't any enterprise. He needs somebody to look out for him."

"You might give him your box and brush, too, Dick."

"No," said Dick; "I'll give him some new ones, but mine I want to keep, to remind me of the hard times I've had, when I was an ignorant boot-black, and never expected to be anything better."

"When, in short, you were 'Ragged Dick.' You must drop that name, and think of yourself now as" —

"Richard Hunter, Esq.," said our hero, smiling.

"A young gentleman on the way to fame and fortune," added Fosdick.

READING CRITICALLY

1. Name the qualities that lead to Dick's success. What accounts for Dick's many good qualities — where, in other words, does Alger suggest that people's characteristics come from?

2. What particular events lead Dick to change his old habits of spending for new ones of saving?

3. What part does luck play in Dick's success? List specific incidents in which luck is a factor.

4. Describe the way Dick talks. Why does he wisecrack so much? What is the basis of his jokes and clever remarks?

WRITING ANALYTICALLY

1. What stories about admirable characters do you remember from your own experience? What qualities were held up to you for admiration and imitation? Write a personal essay about these stories and qualities. Discuss whether they affected you in any way or if you believe they were good models. What models of virtue (or other idealized behavior) are now available to young people (if these are different from the ones you remember)?

2. *Ragged Dick* was an enormously popular book during a time of economic and social upheaval. Its readers found in it some advice or solace or praise as they struggled to make their way in the new industrial world. Write an essay in which you describe the kind of world pictured in *Ragged Dick*. What advice does the book give? What does it invite its readers to believe about the way the world works? What does it ignore or exclude? Does it encourage readers to blame the poor for lacking the qualities necessary for success? In the last part of your essay, speculate about why you think the book was so popular with Americans in the nineteenth century.

ANDREW CARNEGIE

"Wealth" (1889)

Andrew Carnegie (1835–1919) was born in Scotland, the son of a handloom weaver who was falling into poverty as weaving became mechanized. Carnegie's family was well read and politically active. His mother was devoted to his education and he early became a voracious reader and eager writer. In 1848 the family immigrated to the United States, where young Andrew worked as a bobbin boy in a cotton factory and wrote many letters to

Andrew Carnegie, "Wealth," *North American Review,* June 1889, 653–64; reprinted in *Democracy and the Gospel of Wealth,* edited with an introduction by Gail Kennedy (Boston: Heath, 1949), 1–8.
In the notes, EDS. = Patricia Bizzell and Bruce Herzberg.

the *New York Tribune* opposing slavery. Later, working as a messenger in a telegraph office, he taught himself telegraphy and moved into a relatively high-paying job in that important field. His skill and personal charm landed him a position at the Pennsylvania Railroad, and by the time of the Civil War he was superintendent of the Pittsburgh division.

After the war he started an iron company, using his railroad contacts to get jobs building railroad bridges. In 1873 Carnegie recognized the superiority of steel over iron as a building material for the railroads and moved into steel production. He was known as a canny bond trader as well as an excellent salesman, but he excelled at industrial organization, developing the talents of many high-energy and creative managers. This was his true genius: designing efficient production systems, managing costs, controlling quality, and organizing people.

As for his personal development, Carnegie intended to complete his education and become a journalist. He vowed at one point not to allow business to take up all of his time, to return to England, go to college, and start a magazine. He didn't fulfill his vow, but he did write prolifically for magazines and completed one book. "Wealth," the essay printed here, won instant popularity when published in 1889. It was reprinted in England under the title "The Gospel of Wealth." In it Carnegie expounds his theory about the responsibilities of the wealthy person to society.

Carnegie retired in 1901 to become the kind of philanthropist he describes in his gospel. In all, he distributed $350 million — $125 million to the Carnegie Foundation and the rest to libraries, colleges, and the Carnegie Fund for the Advancement of Teaching.

THE PROBLEM OF OUR AGE is the proper administration of wealth, so that the ties of brotherhood may still bind together the rich and poor in harmonious relationship. The conditions of human life have not only been changed, but revolutionized, within the past few hundred years. In former days there was little difference between the dwelling, dress, food, and environment of the chief and those of his retainers. The Indians are today where civilized man then was. When visiting the Sioux, I was led to the wigwam of the chief. It was just like the others in external appearance, and even within the difference was trifling between it and those of the poorest of his braves. The contrast between the palace of the millionaire and the cottage of the laborer with us today measures the change which has come with civilization.

This change, however, is not to be deplored, but welcomed as highly beneficial. It is well, nay, essential for the progress of the race, that the houses of some should be homes for all that is highest and best in literature and the arts, and for all the refinements of civilization, rather than that none should be so. Much better this great irregularity than universal squalor. Without wealth there can be no Maecenas.[1] The "good old times"

---

[1]Gaius Maecenas (70–8 B.C.E.) was a wealthy Roman politician and patron of the arts. — EDS.

were not good old times. Neither master nor servant was as well situated then as today. A relapse to old conditions would be disastrous to both — not the least so to him who serves — and would sweep away civilization with it. But whether the change be for good or ill, it is upon us, beyond our power to alter, and therefore to be accepted and made the best of. It is a waste of time to criticize the inevitable.

It is easy to see how the change has come. One illustration will serve for almost every phase of the cause. In the manufacture of products we have the whole story. It applies to all combinations of human industry, as stimulated and enlarged by the inventions of this scientific age. Formerly articles were manufactured at the domestic hearth or in small shops which formed part of the household. The master and his apprentices worked side by side, the latter living with the master, and therefore subject to the same conditions. When these apprentices rose to be masters, there was little or no change in their mode of life, and they, in turn, educated in the same routine succeeding apprentices. There was, substantially, social equality, and even political equality, for those engaged in industrial pursuits had then little or no political voice in the State.

But the inevitable result of such a mode of manufacture was crude articles at high prices. Today the world obtains commodities of excellent quality at prices which even the generation preceding this would have deemed incredible. In the commercial world similar causes have produced similar results, and the race is benefited thereby. The poor enjoy what the rich could not before afford. What were the luxuries have become the necessaries of life. The laborer has now more comforts than the farmer had a few generations ago. The farmer has more luxuries than the landlord had, and is more richly clad and better housed. The landlord has books and pictures rarer, and appointments more artistic, than the King could then obtain.

The price we pay for this salutary change is, no doubt, great. We assemble thousands of operatives in the factory, in the mine, and in the counting-house, of whom the employer can know little or nothing, and to whom the employer is little better than a myth. All intercourse between them is at an end. Rigid Castes are formed, and, as usual, mutual ignorance breeds mutual distrust. Each Caste is without sympathy for the other, and ready to credit anything disparaging in regard to it. Under the law of competition, the employer of thousands is forced into the strictest economies, among which the rates paid to labor figure prominently, and often there is friction between the employer and the employed, between capital and labor, between rich and poor. Human society loses homogeneity.

The price which society pays for the law of competition, like the price it pays for cheap comforts and luxuries, is also great; but the advantages of this law are also greater still, for it is to this law that we owe our wonderful material development, which brings improved conditions in its train. But, whether the law be benign or not, we must say of it, as we say of the change in the conditions of men to which we have referred: It is here; we cannot evade it; no substitutes for it have been found; and while the law may be sometimes hard for the individual, it is best for the race, because it insures the survival of the fittest in every department. We accept and welcome, therefore, as conditions to which we must accommodate ourselves, great inequality of environment, the concentration of business, industrial and commercial, in the hands of a few, and the law of competition between these, as being not only beneficial, but essential for the future progress of the race. Having accepted these, it follows that there must be great scope for the exercise of special ability in the merchant and in the manufacturer who has to conduct affairs upon a great scale. That this talent for organization and management is rare among men is proved by the fact that it invariably secures for its possessor enormous rewards, no matter where or under what laws or conditions. The experienced in affairs always rate the MAN whose services can be obtained as a partner as not only the first consideration, but such as to render the question of his capital scarcely worth considering, for such men soon create capital; while, without the special talent required, capital soon takes wings. Such men become interested in firms or corporations using millions; and estimating only simple interest to be made upon the capital invested, it is inevitable that their income must exceed their expenditures, and that they must accumulate wealth. Nor is there any middle ground which such men can occupy, because the great manufacturing or commercial concern which does not earn at least interest upon its capital soon becomes bankrupt. It must either go forward or fall behind: to stand still is impossible. It is a condition essential for its successful operation that it should be thus far profitable, and even that, in addition to interest on capital, it should make profit. It is a law, as certain as any of the others named, that men possessed of this peculiar talent for affairs, under the free play of economic forces, must, of necessity, soon be in receipt of more revenue than can be judiciously expended upon themselves; and this law is as beneficial for the race as the others.

Objections to the foundations upon which society is based are not in order, because the condition of the race is better with these than it has been with any others which have been tried. Of the effect of any new substitutes proposed we cannot be sure. The Socialist or Anarchist[2] who seeks to overturn present conditions is to be regarded as attacking the foundation upon which civilization itself rests, for civilization took its start from the day that the capable, industrious workman said to his incompetent and lazy fellow, "If thou dost not sow, thou shalt not reap," and thus ended primitive Communism by separating the drones from the bees. One who studies this subject will soon be brought face to face with the conclusion that upon the sacredness of property civilization itself depends — the right of the laborer to his hundred dollars in the savings bank, and equally the legal right of the millionaire to his millions. To those who propose to sub-

---

[2]Socialists seek a radically democratic economic system in which the means of production are owned collectively. Anarchism is a form of socialism that seeks the elimination of government. Some nineteenth-century anarchists advocated the use of violence against capitalists and government officials. Communism (later in paragraph) is an advanced form of socialism in which all property is held in common. — EDS.

stitute Communism for this intense Individualism the answer, therefore, is: The race has tried that. All progress from that barbarous day to the present time has resulted from its displacement. Not evil, but good, has come to the race from the accumulation of wealth by those who have the ability and energy that produce it. But even if we admit for a moment that it might be better for the race to discard its present foundation, Individualism, — that it is a nobler ideal that man should labor, not for himself alone, but in and for a brotherhood of his fellows, and share with them all in common, realizing Swedenborg's[3] idea of Heaven, where, as he says, the angels derive their happiness, not from laboring for self, but for each other, — even admit all this, and a sufficient answer is, This is not evolution, but revolution. It necessitates the changing of human nature itself — a work of aeons, even if it were good to change it, which we cannot know. It is not practicable in our day or in our age. Even if desirable theoretically, it belongs to another and long-succeeding sociological stratum. Our duty is with what is practicable now; with the next step possible in our day and generation. It is criminal to waste our energies in endeavoring to uproot, when all we can profitably or possibly accomplish is to bend the universal tree of humanity a little in the direction most favorable to the production of good fruit under existing circumstances. We might as well urge the destruction of the highest existing type of man because he failed to reach our ideal as to favor the destruction of Individualism, Private Property, the Law of Accumulation of Wealth, and the Law of Competition; for these are the highest results of human experience, the soil in which society so far has produced the best fruit. Unequally or unjustly, perhaps, as these laws sometimes operate, and imperfect as they appear to the Idealist, they are, nevertheless, like the highest type of man, the best and most valuable of all that humanity has yet accomplished.

We start, then, with a condition of affairs under which the best interests of the race are promoted, but which inevitably gives wealth to the few. Thus far, accepting conditions as they exist, the situation can be surveyed and pronounced good. The question then arises, — and, if the foregoing be correct, it is the only question with which we have to deal, — What is the proper mode of administering wealth after the laws upon which civilization is founded have thrown it into the hands of the few? And it is of this great question that I believe I offer the true solution. It will be understood that *fortunes* are here spoken of, not moderate sums saved by many years of effort, the returns from which are required for the comfortable maintenance and education of families. This is not *wealth*, but only *competence*, which it should be the aim of all to acquire.

There are but three modes in which surplus wealth can be disposed of. It can be left to the families of the descedents; or it can be bequeathed for public purposes; or, finally, it can be administered during their lives by its

[3]Emanuel Swedenborg (1688–1772) was a Swedish theologian. The Church of the New Jerusalem, founded by Swedenborg's followers, attracted many adherents in the northeastern United States in the nineteenth century. — EDS.

possessors. Under the first and second modes most of the wealth of the world that has reached the few has hitherto been applied. Let us in turn consider each of these modes. The first is the most injudicious. In monarchical countries, the estates and the greatest portion of the wealth are left to the first son, that the vanity of the parent may be gratified by the thought that his name and title are to descend to succeeding generations unimpaired. The condition of this class in Europe today teaches the futility of such hopes or ambitions. The successors have become impoverished through their follies or from the fall in the value of land. Even in Great Britain the strict law of entail[4] has been found inadequate to maintain the status of an hereditary class. Its soil is rapidly passing into the hands of the stranger. Under republican institutions the division of property among the children is much fairer, but the question which forces itself upon thoughtful men in all lands is: Why should men leave great fortunes to their children? If this is done from affection, is it not misguided affection? Observation teaches that, generally speaking, it is not well for the children that they should be so burdened. Neither is it well for the state. Beyond providing for the wife and daughters moderate sources of income, and very moderate allowances indeed, if any, for the sons, men may well hesitate, for it is no longer questionable that great sums bequeathed oftener work more for the injury than for the good of the recipients. Wise men will soon conclude that, for the best interests of the members of their families and of the state, such bequests are an improper use of their means.

It is not suggested that men who have failed to educate their sons to earn a livelihood shall cast them adrift in poverty. If any man has seen fit to rear his sons with a view to their living idle lives, or, what is highly commendable, has instilled in them the sentiment that they are in a position to labor for public ends without reference to pecuniary considerations, then, of course, the duty of the parent is to see that such are provided for *in moderation*. There are instances of millionaires' sons unspoiled by wealth, who, being rich, still perform great services in the community. Such are the very salt of the earth, as valuable as, unfortunately, they are rare; still it is not the exception, but the rule, that men must regard, and, looking at the usual result of enormous sums conferred upon legatees, the thoughtful man must shortly say, "I would as soon leave to my son a curse as the almighty dollar," and admit to himself that it is not the welfare of the children, but family pride, which inspires these enormous legacies.

As to the second mode, that of leaving wealth at death for public uses, it may be said that this is only a means for the disposal of wealth, provided a man is content to wait until he is dead before it becomes of much good in the world. Knowledge of the results of legacies bequeathed is not calculated to inspire the brightest hopes of much posthumous good being accomplished. The cases are not few in which the real object sought by the testator is not attained, nor are they few in which his real wishes are thwarted. In many cases the bequests are so used as to become only monu-

---

[4]Inheritance by a specified succession of heirs. — EDS.

ments of his folly. It is well to remember that it requires the exercise of not less ability than that which acquired the wealth to use it so as to be really beneficial to the community. Besides this, it may fairly be said that no man is to be extolled for doing what he cannot help doing, nor is he to be thanked by the community to which he only leaves wealth at death. Men who leave vast sums in this way may fairly be thought men who would not have left it at all, had they been able to take it with them. The memories of such cannot he held in grateful remembrance, for there is no grace in their gifts. It is not to be wondered at that such bequests seem so generally to lack the blessing.

The growing disposition to tax more and more heavily large estates left at death is a cheering indication of the growth of a salutary change in public opinion. The State of Pennsylvania now takes — subject to some exceptions — one-tenth of the property left by its citizens. The budget presented in the British Parliament the other day proposes to increase the death duties; and, most significant of all, the new tax is to be a graduated one. Of all forms of taxation, this seems the wisest. Men who continue hoarding great sums all their lives, the proper use of which for public ends would work good to the community, should be made to feel that the community, in the form of the state, cannot thus be deprived of its proper share. By taxing estates heavily at death the state marks its condemnation of the selfish millionaire's unworthy life.

It is desirable that nations should go much further in this direction. Indeed, it is difficult to set bounds to the share of a rich man's estate which should go at his death to the public through the agency of the state, and by all means such taxes should be graduated, beginning at nothing upon moderate sums to dependents, and increasing rapidly as the amounts swell, until of the millionaire's hoard, as of Shylock's, at least

——— The other half
Comes to the privy coffer of the state.[5]

This policy would work powerfully to induce the rich man to attend to the administration of wealth during his life, which is the end that society should always have in view, as being that by far most fruitful for the people. Nor need it be feared that this policy would sap the root of enterprise and render men less anxious to accumulate, for to the class whose ambition it is to leave great fortunes and be talked about after their death, it will attract even more attention, and, indeed, be a somewhat nobler ambition to have enormous sums paid over to the state from their fortunes.

There remains, then, only one mode of using great fortunes; but in this we have the true antidote for the temporary unequal distribution of wealth, the reconciliation of the rich and the poor — a reign of harmony — another ideal, differing, indeed, from that of the Communist in requiring only the further evolution of existing conditions, not the total overthrow of our civilization. It is founded upon the present most intense indi-

[5]Shakespeare, *The Merchant of Venice*, 4.1.352–53, spoken by Shylock. — EDS.

vidualism, and the race is prepared to put it in practice by degrees whenever it pleases. Under its sway we shall have an ideal state, in which the surplus wealth of the few will become, in the best sense, the property of the many, because administered for the common good, and this wealth, passing through the hands of the few, can be made a much more potent force for the elevation of our race than if it had been distributed in small sums to the people themselves. Even the poorest can be made to see this, and to agree that great sums gathered by some of their fellow citizens and spent for public purposes, from which the masses reap the principal benefit, are more valuable to them than if scattered among them through the course of many years in trifling amounts.

If we consider what results flow from the Cooper Institute,[6] for instance, to the best portion of the race in New York not possessed of means, and compare these with those which would have arisen for the good of the masses from an equal sum distributed by Mr. Cooper in his lifetime in the form of wages, which is the highest form of distribution, being for work done and not for charity, we can form some estimate of the possibilities for the improvement of the race which lie embedded in the present law of the accumulation of wealth. Much of this sum, if distributed in small quantities among the people, would have been wasted in the indulgence of appetite, some of it in excess, and it may be doubted whether even the part put to the best use, that of adding to the comforts of the home, would have yielded results for the race, as a race, at all comparable to those which are flowing and are to flow from the Cooper Institute from generation to generation. Let the advocate of violent or radical change ponder well this thought.

We might even go so far as to take another instance, that of Mr. Tilden's bequest of five millions of dollars for a free library in the city of New York, but in referring to this one cannot help saying involuntarily, How much better if Mr. Tilden had devoted the last years of his own life to the proper administration of this immense sum; in which case neither legal contest nor any other cause of delay could have interfered with his aims. But let us assume that Mr. Tilden's millions finally became the means of giving to this city a noble public library, where the treasures of the world contained in books will be open to all forever, without money and without price. Considering the good of that part of the race which congregates in and around Manhattan Island, would its permanent benefit have been better promoted had these millions been allowed to circulate in small sums through the hands of the masses? Even the most strenuous advocate of Communism must entertain a doubt upon this subject. Most of those who think will probably entertain no doubt whatever.

Poor and restricted are our opportunities in this life; narrow our horizon; our best work most imperfect; but rich men should be thankful for

---

[6]Now known as the Cooper Union, the Cooper Institute was founded in 1859 by Peter Cooper (1791–1883), who built the first American locomotive, grew wealthy, and became a philanthropist. The Cooper Institute was a free, coeducational college open to all races and established to provide educational opportunities for the working poor. Cooper, himself illiterate, aimed to help others gain an education. — EDS.

one inestimable boon. They have it in their power during their lives to busy themselves in organizing benefactions from which the masses of their fellows will derive lasting advantage, and thus dignify their own lives. The highest life is probably to be reached, not by such imitation of the life of Christ as Count Tolstoi[7] gives us, but, while animated by Christ's spirit, by recognizing the changed conditions of this age, and adopting modes of expressing this spirit suitable to the changed conditions under which we live; still laboring for the good of our fellows, which was the essence of his life and teaching, but laboring in a different manner.

This, then, is held to be the duty of the man of Wealth: First, to set an example of modest, unostentatious living, shunning display or extravagance; to provide moderately for the legitimate wants of those dependent upon him; and after doing so to consider all surplus revenues which come to him simply as trust funds which he is called upon to administer, and strictly bound as a matter of duty to administer in the manner which, in his judgment, is best calculated to produce the most beneficial results for the community — the man of wealth thus becoming the mere agent and trustee for his poorer brethren, bringing to their service his superior wisdom, experience, and ability to administer, doing for them better than they would or could do for themselves. . . .

The best uses to which surplus wealth can be put have already been indicated. Those who would administer wisely must, indeed, be wise, for one of the serious obstacles to the improvement of our race is indiscriminate charity. It were better for mankind that the millions of the rich were thrown into the sea than so spent as to encourage the slothful, the drunken, the unworthy. Of every thousand dollars spent in so called charity today, it is probable that $950 is unwisely spent; so spent, indeed, as to produce the very evils which it proposes to mitigate or cure. A well-known write of philosophic books admitted the other day that he had given a quarter of a dollar to a man who approached him as he was coming to visit the house of his friend. He knew nothing of the habits of this beggar; knew not the use that would be made of this money, although he had every reason to suspect that it would be spent improperly. This man professed to be a disciple of Herbert Spencer;[8] yet the quarter-dollar given that night will probably work more injury than all the money which its thoughtless donor will ever be able to give in true charity will do good. He only gratified his own feelings, saved himself from annoyance — and this was probably one of the most selfish and very worst actions of his life, for in all respects he is most worthy.

In bestowing charity, the main consideration should be to help those who will help themselves; to provide part of the means by which those who desire to improve may do so; to give those who desire to rise the aids by

[7]Count Leo Tolstoy (1828–1910), author of *War and Peace* and *Anna Karenina*, was also an influential spiritual leader who opposed organized religion. — EDS.

[8]Herbert Spencer (1820–1903) was a British philosopher who applied the principles of Darwinian evolution to all disciplines as well as to ethics. Spencer was associated with social Darwinism, which opposed charity. — EDS.

which they may rise; to assist, but rarely or never to do all. Neither the individual nor the race is improved by alms-giving. Those worthy of assistance, except in rare cases, seldom require assistance. The really valuable men of the race never do, except in cases of accident or sudden change. Everyone has, of course, cases of individuals brought to his own knowledge where temporary assistance can do genuine good, and these he will not overlook. But the amount which can be wisely given by the individual for individuals is necessarily limited by his lack of knowledge of the circumstances connected with each. He is the only true reformer who is as careful and as anxious not to aid the unworthy as he is to aid the worthy, and, perhaps, even more so, for in alms-giving more injury is probably done by rewarding vice than by relieving virtue.

The rich man is thus almost restricted to following the examples of Peter Cooper, Enoch Pratt of Baltimore, Mr. Pratt of Brooklyn, Senator Stanford,[9] and others, who know that the best means of benefiting the community is to place within its reach the ladders upon which the aspiring can rise — parks, and means of recreation, by which men are helped in body and mind; works of art, certain to give pleasure and improve the public taste, and public institutions of various kinds, which will improve the general condition of the people; — in this manner returning their surplus wealth to the mass of their fellows in the forms best calculated to do them lasting good.

Thus is the problem of Rich and Poor to be solved. The laws of accumulation will be left free; the laws of distribution free. Individualism will continue, but the millionaire will be but a trustee for the poor; intrusted for a season with a great part of the increased wealth of the community, but administering it for the community far better than it could or would have done for itself. The best minds will thus have reached a stage in the development of the race in which it is clearly seen that there is no mode of disposing of surplus wealth creditable to thoughtful and earnest men into whose hands it flows save by using it year by year for the general good. This day already dawns. But a little while, and although, without incurring the pity of their fellows, men may die sharers in great business enterprises from which their capital cannot be or has not been withdrawn, and is left chiefly at death for public uses, yet the man who dies leaving behind him millions of available wealth, which was his to administer during life, will pass away "unwept, unhonored, and unsung," no matter to what uses he leaves the dross which he cannot take with him. Of such as these the public verdict will then be: "The man who dies thus rich dies disgraced."

Such, in my opinion, is the true Gospel concerning Wealth, obedience to which is destined some day to solve the problem of the Rich and the Poor, and to bring "Peace on earth, among men Good-Will."

[9]Enoch Pratt (1808–96) founded the Baltimore Public Library, the House of Reformation and Instruction for Colored Children, and the Maryland School for the Deaf and Dumb. Charles Pratt (1830–91) founded Pratt Institute in New York City and a free library in Brooklyn. Leland Stanford (1824–93) founded Leland Stanford Junior University (now Stanford University) in memory of his son. (He was a U.S. senator from 1885 to 1893.) — EDS.

READING CRITICALLY

1. Why, according to Carnegie, is it in "the best interests of the race" to support a system that "inevitably gives wealth to the few" (p. 454)?

2. What does Carnegie claim is the "price which society pays" for the benefits of "cheap comforts and luxuries" (p. 454)? In what sense does "society" pay this price?

3. What does Carnegie mean by "individualism"?

4. Why does Carnegie oppose the inheritance of fortunes?

5. According to Carnegie, why is it wrong to give charity?

WRITING ANALYTICALLY

1. Carnegie says that individualism, property, wealth, and competition are "the highest results of human experience" (p. 454). An unequal distribution of wealth and power is the necessary — and, Carnegie says, desirable — consequence of a system that embodies these principles. Yet Carnegie recognizes that there is some unfairness in this arrangement, which he addresses by urging the wealthy to engage in certain kinds of philanthropy.

Write an essay in which you analyze Carnegie's attempt to reach an accommodation between individualism (and its related principles of property, wealth, and competition) on the one hand and fairness on the other. Begin by summarizing Carnegie's thesis as succinctly as you can. Then evaluate his arguments and assess whether the whole scheme is likely to achieve the results that Carnegie himself sets as his goal. Review reading questions 1, 3, 4, and 5 before writing this essay. Consider also how Carnegie decides what is "fair."

2. Carnegie says that by endowing the Cooper Institute, Peter Cooper used his wealth in a way that would benefit the poor more than raising his workers' wages would have done. Carnegie regards this use of wealth as the finest example of his thesis about wealth. Carnegie himself endowed many libraries and universities in imitation of Cooper. Write an essay evaluating Carnegie's argument that concentrated wealth is more beneficial to the poor than higher wages. How well do the examples of Cooper, Enoch and Charles Pratt, and Stanford support his argument?

3. To what audience does "Wealth" seem to be addressed? How might people in different economic classes respond to it? Read some of the Senate testimony on the condition of workers (p. 553) and consider how Carnegie's own wage-workers might have responded. Imagine that you are a worker in one of Carnegie's steel mills, and write him a letter in response to the essay "Wealth." Alternative: Write a dialogue between Carnegie and one of his critics — Edward Bellamy, Henry Demarest Lloyd, or Henry George — on the merits of the Gospel of Wealth.

WILLIAM H. COUNCILL

From *The Negro Laborer: A Word to Him* (1887)

William H. Councill (1849–1909) was born a slave in Fayetteville, North Carolina. Shortly after his father escaped to Canada in 1854, William and his brother were sold and taken to Alabama. In 1863, during the Civil War, William was able to escape to the Union lines. He attended a freedman's school for three years and then began teaching in schools for African Americans and working in hotels while continuing his studies — in science, Latin, and law — at night. In 1883, Councill was admitted to the bar in Alabama. He held several government jobs and was appointed head of a college for African Americans, the State Normal and Industrial School in Huntsville.

Councill was not a militant defender of the rights of African Americans. Instead, he sought to gain favor from white people as a way to help black people improve their condition. This was also, to some extent, the strategy of Booker T. Washington, head of the rival Tuskegee Institute. Both Councill and Washington preached self-reliance rather than conflict with whites. But Councill was regarded, even by Washington, as going too far in making statements about the "blessings" of segregation and the inferior capacities of African Americans. Washington accused him openly of "toadying to white people." Later historians have tried to be more generous. Councill took some radical positions — successfully suing a railroad for refusing to seat him in the first-class section, for example, and, late in his life, endorsing the black nationalist movement and its call for an African homeland. His defenders argue that his accommodationism was an expedient, a bitter pill that Councill felt obliged to swallow to achieve greater ends.

The excerpt printed here is from a long essay of advice directed to black workers twenty-two years after emancipation.

YOU OFTEN HEAR LAWYERS AND DOCTORS speak about the ethics of their professions. This means nothing more than those rules which should govern the lawyers and doctors in their relation to each other and to their clients and patients. Now, every occupation has its ethics. The workingmen are bound by moral obligations to have regard for the interests of one another; i.e., they are morally bound to give one another equal chance in the great race for bread. Then they must observe all the rules for the government of their relations to the employer. This is very important, as the good of society depends entirely upon the faithful observance of the laws of reciprocity. The Great Teacher has laid down one infallible rule which is ample for all

William H. Councill, *The Negro Laborer: A Word to Him*, excerpted in *The Black Worker during the Era of the Knights of Labor*, edited by Philip S. Foner and Ronald L. Lewis, vol. 3 of *The Black Worker: A Documentary History from Colonial Times to the Present* (1887; Philadelphia: Temple University Press, 1978), 45–48.

In the notes, EDS. = Patricia Bizzell and Bruce Herzberg.

the transactions of life, viz: "Whatsoever ye would that men should do to you, do ye even so to them." I would like for you to regard this divine injunction as your constitution, and then adopt the following by-laws:

1. Decide what you are going to follow for a living.
2. Select an occupation in keeping with your abilities and capabilities.
3. Thoroughly qualify yourself for that calling.
4. Always have a plain understanding with your employer as to wages and hours of work.
5. Carry out your part of the contract "though the heavens fall."
6. Be at the place at the time appointed, do faithfully your work in good spirit, not grumblingly, and then your employer will meet you in a like spirit, and your life will be one of happiness.
7. Consider that for the time being you are the property of your employer, and faithfully obey his instructions and requests.
8. It is better — more honest — to give him an hour or two of labor than to cheat him by idling or work poorly performed.
9. Avoid intoxicants, especially while you are at work, for as your time belongs to your employer, you should strive to render faithful, intelligent service, which cannot be done under the influence of liquor. Besides, you endanger your own life and the safety of the property you are paid to protect.
10. Be frank, and never under any circumstances deceive your employer. If you have done wrong, or made a mistake, own it like a man. He will respect you more for it.
11. Treat your employer's property as you would your own; and if you are a careless man, treat it better.
12. To be polite and gentle to your fellow workmen and your employer, as coarse jests and ill temper are out of place even on the rock pile, as well as in the parlor. Remember the street scavenger can be a Chesterfield[1] as well as the gentleman of fashion who graces the Richest drawing room.

True politeness is to do and say
The noblest things in the kindest way.

I shall next consider Labor, Capital, and Wealth. . . .

Society can no more be in a healthful state without the harmonious working of these three elements, governed by ethics, than the human body could without the united action of heart, arteries, and veins influenced by the lungs. Let me go a step further and say that labor is capital, or labor and capital are one. Labor is power. That power produces wealth. That wealth in action is called capital, and thus the work of labor, capital and wealth goes on subduing the earth. Every individual with all the powers and capacities of his constitution sound, is a capitalist to the extent of the

---

[1]The Fourth Earl of Chesterfield (1694–1773) was well known for *Letters to His Son* (1774), in which he described proper behavior for a gentleman. — EDS.

exercise of those powers. That which such exercise produces and he accumulates is wealth, and if he wish to employ it to produce other wealth, it becomes capital.

The peanut vendor is a capitalist to the extent of his investment in earth nuts, roaster, pans, baskets, etc. The little girl who peddles laces, or newspapers, or pins around the streets, is as much a capitalist to the extent of her investment as Mr. Vanderbilt or Mr. Gould.[2] Mr. Gould and Mr. Vanderbilt have simply by the exercise of more economy, sagacity, and energy accumulated more wealth than she. But the peanut vendor may become a greater capitalist as he accumulates more wealth and employs it. It is folly to go point the finger of prejudice and envy at the very rich people and cry: "These men oppress us; these capitalists are sharks; these wealthy people have our earnings." It is not only folly, but it is unjust. I see many of you with watches and chains, rings on your fingers, and pins on your breasts. These articles are wealth. They represent so much capital — labor or money — at rest. The man who owns the watch worth $8 and the one with the $100 watch, are men of wealth to the valuation of those useful articles. The poor laborer, who, by industry and frugality, after the exercise of his capital — his muscle — accumulates enough to buy an acre of land and erect a small cottage for his faithful wife and little ones, was in turn a laborer, capitalist, and is now a man of wealth to the value of that happy little home, where peace and virtue reign and upon which the blessings of God rest. Mr. Vanderbilt is a man of greater wealth than this man, but it is because he operated a larger capital. Sometimes a spirit of envy creeps in between these two capitalists and then both suffer — each in proportion to his wealth. This brings me to consider Agrarianism.[3]

This form of ownership originated in bloody Rome. It was tried among the early Christians. Wherever it has been introduced failure and crime followed. The population of the United States and Territories is 50,155,783; the value of real estate and personal property is $16,902,993,443. Divide this according to agrarianism and each person would get $337, which by trade and speculation would soon again be in the hands of a few. And thus with each day we should have to re-collect and re-distribute. Out of such a system no good could possibly come. Nature everywhere teaches that differences and distinctions must exist. Why has she been more lavish with the peafowl than with the crow? Why has she bedecked the goldfinch or the bird of paradise more gorgeously than the snowbird or the hawk? Why the lily more fragrant than the sunflower? Why the difference in the magnitude of the twinkling stars? Why the dissimilarity in the talents of men? Why are some men born idiots and others with the sparkling gems of genius shining in their souls? Why do some mountains possess millions of dollars of the precious or useful minerals and others only sandstone or lime rock? The

[2]Cornelius Vanderbilt (1794–1877) and Jay Gould (1836–92) were wealthy financiers and railroad barons. — EDS.

[3]"Agrarianism" was a movement that advocated equal distribution of land (as Councill explains in the next two paragraphs). — EDS.

answers are secrets locked up in the mystery of the Almighty. The man of talent, of push, of energy, frugality, and sagacity cannot help accumulating more of the results of labor than the individual of opposite qualities. Agrarianism is a foe to thrift and activity, and encourages idleness and stagnation. It would paralyze business and cause the wheels of industry to hang dry and still over the stream of progress.

Agrarianism is a hydra-headed monster. It has presented itself in many forms and at various times. Today it breeds discontent among the common people which tomorrow bursts into rebellion and revolution. Lawlessness prevails, property is destroyed, and bloody murder stalks boldly abroad. Is anything gained? No! as loud as heaven's loudest artillery can sound it. All classes of capitalists are weakened, wealth is destroyed, and fond Hope, the bright anchor of the soul, sits dark and gloomy in the ashes of ruin.

Communism. Saint-Simonianism, nihilism, anarchy, socialism, Henry Georgeism,[4] are all dangerous forms of that hideous monster, agrarianism. Every capitalist — every man of wealth — whether his muscle is his only stock in trade or not, or whether he counts his capital and wealth by dimes or by millions — should seize the bludgeon of reason and justice and strike the monster — the common foe to the progress and happiness of man — a deadly blow. It is true that laboring men have their grievances, but strikes are not the means by which these wrongs may be set right. The appeal to strikes is an appeal from reason to error, from justice to injustice, from order to disorder, from law to riot, from morality to immorality, from virtue to sin, from innocence to murder. The strike is a foe to the infant at the mother's breast; it is an enemy to the happiness of home; it is the howling wolf at the door of the humble cottage; it is hostile to personal liberty; it is an enemy to religion, it is the embodiment of riot and murder striding through the land stamping out the life of the nation, crushing out the manhood of the citizens, setting a premium upon crime and outlawing virtue and honesty. I wish I had the power to represent it in its true light. A mass of grumbling, dissatisfied men who will not work, by desperation and lawlessness deterring others from honest toil. Business is paralyzed and millions of dollars sunk. But this is small compared to the suffering and misery and want in the homes of these frantic men. Could we but lift the curtain which hides their dark homes, a picture would be presented which would cause the blood to chill and sicken the soul. These man hang around the saloons and stifle the cries for bread from their homes by liquor and beer — a morsel of cheese or a cracker answering for food. But what about the wretched wife and starving child?

But they do not stop there. The torch, pistol, the knife, the bomb, and infernal machines[5] are brought into play their deadly parts. Then the fire

---

[4]All of the political movements named here advocated the redistribution of wealth and political power in a more equitable way. For "Henry Georgeism," see the selection by Henry George on page 511. — EDS.

[5]"Infernal machines" are bombs or incendiary devices. — EDS.

fiend with his angry tongue laps up wealth and happy homes, the knife and the pistol start streams of human gore down the gutters of the streets, and the hellish bomb brings massive edifices cracking, crumbling to the earth.

The fiend having sated himself in gore and ruin, surveys the field of desolation. What has been gained? Nothing. If permitted he returns to work with a weakened constitution, less respect of his family, kept under the watch of the law, without the confidence of his employer and with the curse of his own conscience. You ask: "If strikes are not the remedy, what is the remedy?" Have a clear understanding with your employer. Try to enter into his interests and feelings. Tell him plainly that you cannot afford to work for him at present rates. If he cannot or does not raise your wages, give him notice that you will quit at a certain time, and then do not interfere with the person engaged in your place. All parties will feel better, and your employer may soon be able to grant your request and recall you. You certainly have no right to interfere with others who are willing to work for him.

The colored laborer can neither afford to strike nor encourage strikes. He has felt the baneful effects of them. He has time and time again seen white labor organizations resort to this method of getting colored men out of employment. If it is right against the employer for higher wages, it is right against a fellow workman on account of race or color. But it is not right at all. This is a country of law and order, and the negro's salvation lies in his willing obedience to law — fairly and impartially administered. . . .

READING CRITICALLY

1. Reread Councill's list of twelve "by-laws" for workers. What sort of relationship between employer and employee do they assume or advocate? Does Councill seem to favor one side or the other?

2. Why, according to Councill, is Vanderbilt richer than the little girl who peddles pins on the streets? What conclusion does Councill draw from his reasoning?

3. Councill argues against "Agrarianism," by which he means the proposal to distribute land more or less equally among all the citizens. What evidence does he present in arguing that inequality is natural?

4. What is Councill's view of labor strikes? In what way might his view be based on consideration of the African American worker's place in the labor force?

WRITING ANALYTICALLY

1. In a short essay, summarize Councill's positions on the four issues he discusses here: behavior at work, capital and labor, land reform, and strikes. Following your summary, explain the premises (such as religious principle, political ideology, or economic theory) that seem to underlie his arguments or link them together.

2. Expand your essay from writing question 1 by considering the following: Why does Councill, an African American writing to other African Americans, take

the positions that he does? He is not, presumably, simply trying to keep black people from annoying whites with their complaints. What, then, is his motive? How might the situation of the ex-slaves lead Councill to give this particular advice? (See the Senate testimony by N. R. Fielding on p. 573 for some insight into their conditions.) How do you think Councill's nineteenth-century African American readers might have reacted to his advice? Do you think that his advice to them is good? If not, what would you have advised?

RUSSELL H. CONWELL

From *Acres of Diamonds* (1888–1915)

Russell Conwell (1843–1925) was known during the Civil War as a great recruiter, raising a volunteer militia in central Massachusetts in 1862 and then serving as recruiting officer in Virginia and North Carolina. After the war, he was admitted to the bar but preferred to work as a journalist. In 1872, he became interested in religion and was ordained a Baptist minister in 1879. He accepted the pulpit of the deteriorating Grace Baptist Church in Philadelphia, where his recruiting and fundraising skills rebuilt the church on a vast scale. In 1888, Conwell founded Temple University, which began as a night school for working people in the basement of his church. He earned the money to endow the university and the huge Baptist church with his phenomenally popular sermon "Acres of Diamonds," which he delivered more than six thousand times. Conwell also founded three hospitals and wrote several books on Civil War generals and other prominent American men. "Acres of Diamonds," excerpted here, is written with Philadelphia as the location of the lecture; to get the proper effect, read the name of your hometown in place of "Philadelphia" wherever it appears.

WHEN GOING DOWN THE TIGRIS AND EUPHRATES rivers[1] many years ago with a party of English travelers I found myself under the direction of an old Arab guide whom we hired up at Baghdad, and I have often thought how that guide resembled our barbers in certain mental characteristics. He thought that it was not only his duty to guide us down those rivers, and do what he was paid for doing, but also to entertain us with stories curious and weird, ancient and modern, strange and familiar. Many of them I have forgotten, and I am glad I have, but there is one I shall never forget.

Russell H. Conwell, *Acres of Diamonds* (c. 1890; Westwood, N.J.: Fleming H. Revell Co., 1960), 9–37, 64

In the notes, EDS. = Patricia Bizzell and Bruce Herzberg.
[1]The Tigris and Euphrates, major rivers in Iraq, are mentioned in the book of Genesis in the Bible as the location of the Garden of Eden. — EDS.

The old guide was leading my camel by its halter along the banks of those ancient rivers, and he told me story after story until I grew weary of his storytelling and ceased to listen. I have never been irritated with that guide when he lost his temper as I ceased listening. But I remember that he took off his Turkish cap and swung it in a circle to get my attention. I could see it through the corner of my eye, but I determined not to look straight at him for fear he would tell another story. But although I am not a woman, I did finally look, and as soon as I did he went right into another story.

Said he, "I will tell you a story now which I reserve for my particular friends." When he emphasized the words "particular friends," I listened, and I have ever been glad I did. I really feel devoutly thankful that there are 1,674 young men who have been carried through college by this lecture who are also glad that I did listen. The old guide told me that there once lived not far from the River Indus an ancient Persian by the name of Ali Hafed. He said that Ali Hafed owned a very large farm, that he had orchards, grain fields, and gardens; that he had money at interest, and was a wealthy and contented man. He was contented because he was wealthy, and wealthy because he was contented. One day there visited the old Persian farmer one of those ancient Buddhist priests, one of the wise men of the East. He sat down by the fire and told the old farmer how this world of ours was made. He said that this world was once a mere bank of fog, and that the Almighty thrust His finger into this bank of fog, and began slowly to move His finger around, increasing the speed until at last He whirled this bank of fog into a solid ball of fire. Then it went rolling through the universe, burning its way through other banks of fog, and condensed the moisture without, until it fell in floods of rain upon its hot surface, and cooled the outward crust. Then the internal fires bursting outward through the crust threw up the mountains and hills, the valleys, the plains and prairies of this wonderful world of ours. If this internal molten mass came bursting out and cooled very quickly it became granite; less quickly copper, less quickly silver, less quickly gold, and, after gold, diamonds were made.

Said the old priest, "A diamond is a congealed drop of sunlight." Now that is literally scientifically true, that a diamond is an actual deposit of carbon from the sun. The old priest told Ali Hafed that if he had one diamond the size of this thumb he could purchase the county, and if he had a mine of diamonds he could place his children upon thrones through the influence of their great wealth.

Ali Hafed heard all about diamonds, how much they were worth, and went to bed that night a poor man. He had not lost anything, but he was poor because he was discontented, and discontented because he feared he was poor. He said, "I want a mine of diamonds," and he lay awake all night.

Early in the morning he sought out the priest. I know by experience that a priest is very cross when awakened early in the morning, and when he shook that old priest out of his dream, Ali Hafed said to him:

"Will you tell me where I can find diamonds?"

"Diamonds! What do you want with diamonds?" "Why, I wish to be immensely rich." "Well, then, go along and find them. That is all you have to do; go and find them, and then you have them." "But I don't know where to go." "Well, if you will find a river that runs through white sands, between high mountains, in those white sands you will always find diamonds." "I don't believe there is any such river." "Oh yes, there are plenty of them. All you have to do is to go and find them, and then you have them." Said Ali Hafed, "I will go."

So he sold his farm, collected his money, left his family in charge of a neighbor, and away he went in search of diamonds. He began his search, very properly to my mind, at the Mountains of the Moon.[2] Afterward he came around into Palestine, then wandered on into Europe, and at last when his money was all spent and he was in rags, wretchedness, and poverty, he stood on the shore of that bay at Barcelona, in Spain, when a great tidal wave came rolling in between the pillars of Hercules, and the poor, afflicted, suffering, dying man could not resist the awful temptation to cast himself into that incoming tide, and he sank beneath its foaming crest, never to rise in this life again.

When that old guide had told me that awfully sad story he stopped the camel I was riding on and went back to fix the baggage that was coming off another camel, and I had an opportunity to muse over his story while he was gone. I remember saying to myself, "Why did he reserve that story for his 'particular friends'?" There seemed to be no beginning, no middle, no end, nothing to it. That was the first story I had ever heard told in my life, and would be the first one I ever read, in which the hero was killed in the first chapter. I had but one chapter of that story, and the hero was dead.

When the guide came back and took up the halter of my camel, he went right ahead with the story, into the second chapter, just as though there had been no break. The man who purchased Ali Hafed's farm one day led his camel into the garden to drink, and as that camel put its nose into the shallow water of that garden brook, Ali Hafed's successor noticed a curious flash of light from the white sands of the stream. He pulled out a black stone having an eye of light reflecting all the hues of the rainbow. He took the pebble into the house and put it on the mantel which covers the central fires, and forgot all about it.

A few days later this same old priest came in to visit Ali Hafed's successor, and the moment he opened that drawing-room door he saw that flash of light on the mantel, and he rushed up to it, and shouted: "Here is a diamond! Has Ali Hafed returned?" "Oh no, Ali Hafed has not returned, and that is not a diamond. That is nothing but a stone we found right out here in our own garden." "But," said the priest, "I tell you I know a diamond when I see it. I know positively that is a diamond."

Then together they rushed out into that old garden and stirred up the

---

[2]The Greek astronomer-mathematician Ptolemy (2nd century C.E.) identified the Mountains of the Moon as the source of the Nile. They are in the Ruwenzori range bordering Uganda and Zaire. — EDS.

white sands with their fingers, and lo! there came up other more beautiful and valuable gems than the first. "Thus," said the guide to me, and, friends, it is historically true, "was discovered the diamond mine of Golcanda, the most magnificent diamond mine in all the history of mankind, excelling the Kimberly itself. The Kohinoor, and the Orloff of the crown jewels of England and Russia, the largest on earth, came from that mine."[3]

When that old Arab guide told me the second chapter of his story, he then took off his Turkish cap and swung it around in the air again to get my attention to the moral. Those Arab guides have morals to their stories, although they are not always moral. As he swung his hat, he said to me, "Had Ali Hafed remained at home and dug in his own cellar, or underneath his own wheat fields, or in his own garden, instead of wretchedness, starvation, and death by suicide in a strange land, he would have had 'acres of diamonds.' For every acre of that old farm, yes, every shovelful, afterward revealed gems which since have decorated the crowns of monarchs."

When he had added the moral to his story I saw why he reserved it for "his particular friends." But I did not tell him I could see it. It was that mean old Arab's way of going around a thing like a lawyer, to say indirectly what he did not dare say directly, that "in his private opinion there was a certain young man then traveling down the Tigris River that might better be at home in America." I did not tell him I could see that, but I told him his story reminded me of one, and I told it to him quickly, and I think I will tell it to you.

I told him of a man out in California in 1847, who owned a ranch. He heard they had discovered gold in southern California, and so with a passion for gold he sold his ranch to Colonel Sutter, and away he went, never to come back. Colonel Sutter put a mill upon a stream that ran through that ranch, and one day his little girl brought some wet sand from the raceway into their home and sifted it through her fingers before the fire, and in that falling sand a visitor saw the first shining scales of real gold that were ever discovered in California. The man who had owned that ranch wanted gold, and he could have secured it for the mere taking. Indeed, thirty-eight millions of dollars have been taken out of a very few acres since then. About eight years ago I delivered this lecture in a city that stands on that farm, and they told me that a one-third owner for years and years had been getting one hundred and twenty dollars in gold every fifteen minutes, sleeping or waking, without taxation. You and I would enjoy an income like that — if we didn't have to pay an income tax. . . .

As I come here tonight and look around this audience I am seeing again what through these fifty years I have continually seen — men that are making precisely that same mistake. I often wish I could see the younger people, and would that the Academy had been filled tonight with

---

[3]Kimberley, in South Africa, is a rich diamond mine. Kohinoor is a huge diamond (109 carats) that became one of the British crown jewels. Count Orlov purchased the famous 200-carat diamond that now bears his name for Catharine the Great of Russia. — EDS.

our high school scholars and our grammar school scholars, that I could have them to talk to. While I would have preferred such an audience as that, because they are most susceptible, as they have not grown up into their prejudices as we have, they have not gotten into any custom that they cannot break, they have not met with any failures as we have; and while I could perhaps do such an audience as that more good than I can do grown-up people, yet I will do the best I can with the material I have. I say to you that you have "acres of diamonds" in Philadelphia right where you now live. "Oh," but you will say, "you cannot know much about our city if you think there are any 'acres of diamonds' here."

I was greatly interested in that account in the newspaper of the young man who found that diamond in North Carolina. It was one of the purest diamonds that has ever been discovered, and it has several predecessors near the same locality. I went to a distinguished professor in mineralogy and asked him where he thought those diamonds came from. The professor secured the map of the geologic formations of our continent, and traced it. He said it went either through the underlying carboniferous strata adapted for such production, westward through Ohio and the Mississippi, or in more probability came eastward through Virginia and up the shore of the Atlantic Ocean. It is a fact that the diamonds were there, for they have been discovered and sold; and that they were carried down there during the drift period, from some northern locality. Now who can say but some person going down with his drill in Philadelphia will find some trace of a diamond mine yet down here? Oh, friends! you cannot say that you are not over one of the greatest diamond mines in the world, for such a diamond as that only comes from the most profitable mines that are found on earth. . . .

Now then, I say again that the opportunity to get rich, to attain unto great wealth, is here in Philadelphia now, within the reach of almost every man and woman who hears me speak tonight, and I mean just what I say. I have not come to this platform even under these circumstances to recite something to you. I have come to tell you what in God's sight I believe to be the truth, and if the years of life have been of any value to me in the attainment of common sense, I know I am right; that the men and women sitting here, who found it difficult perhaps to buy a ticket to this lecture or gathering tonight, have within their reach "acres of diamonds," opportunities to get largely wealthy. There never was a place on earth more adapted than the city of Philadelphia today, and never in the history of the world did a poor man without capital have such an opportunity to get rich quickly and honestly as he has now in our city. I say it is the truth, and I want you to accept it as such; for if you think I have come to simply recite something, then I would better not be here. I have no time to waste in any such talk, but to say the things I believe, and unless some of you get richer for what I am saying tonight my time is wasted.

I say that you ought to get rich, and it is your duty to get rich. How many of my pious brethren say to me, "Do you, a Christian minister, spend your time going up and down the country advising young people to get rich, to get money?" "Yes, of course I do." They say, "Isn't that awful! Why don't you preach the gospel instead of preaching about man's making money?" "Because to make money honestly is to preach the gospel." That is the reason. The men who get rich may be the most honest men you find in the community.

"Oh," but says some young man here tonight, "I have been told all my life that if a person has money he is very dishonest and dishonorable and mean and contemptible." My friend, that is the reason why you have none, because you have that idea of people. The foundation of your faith is altogether false. Let me say here clearly, and say it briefly, though subject to discussion which I have not time for here, ninety-eight out of one hundred of the rich men of America are honest. That is why they are rich. That is why they are trusted with money. That is why they carry on great enterprises and find plenty of people to work with them. It is because they are honest men.

Says another young man, "I hear sometimes of men that get millions of dollars dishonestly." Yes, of course you do, and so do I. But they are so rare a thing in fact that the newspapers talk about them all the time as a matter of news until you get the idea that all the other rich men got rich dishonestly.

My friend, you take and drive me — if you furnish the auto[4] — out into the suburbs of Philadelphia, and introduce me to the people who own their homes around this great city, those beautiful homes with gardens and flowers, those magnificent homes so lovely in their art, and I will introduce you to the very best people in character as well as in enterprise in our city, and you know I will. A man is not really a true man until he owns his own home, and they that own their homes are made more honorable and honest and pure, and true and economical and careful, by owning the home.

For a man to have money, even in large sums, is not an inconsistent thing. We preach against covetousness, and you know we do, in the pulpit, and oftentimes preach against it so long and use the terms about "filthy lucre" so extremely that Christians get the idea that when we stand in the pulpit we believe it is wicked for any man to have money — until the collection basket goes around, and then we almost swear at the people because they don't give more money. Oh, the inconsistency of such doctrines as that!

Money is power, and you ought to be reasonably ambitious to have it. You ought because you can do more good with it than you could without it. Money printed your Bible, money builds your churches, money sends your missionaries, and money pays your preachers, and you would not have many of them, either, if you did not pay them. I am always willing that my church should raise my salary, because the church that pays the largest salary always raises it the easiest. You never knew an exception to it in your life. The man who gets the largest salary can do the most good with the

---

[4]Automobiles were rare and expensive until after World War I. — EDS.

power that is furnished to him. Of course he can if his spirit be right to use it for what it is given to him.

I say, then, you ought to have money. If you can honestly attain unto riches in Philadelphia, it is your Christian and godly duty to do so. It is an awful mistake of these pious people to think you must be awfully poor in order to be pious.

Some men say, "Don't you sympathize with the poor people?" Of course I do, or else I would not have been lecturing these years. I won't give in but what I sympathize with the poor, but the number of poor who are to be sympathized with is very small. To sympathize with a man whom God has punished for his sins, thus to help him when God would still continue a just punishment, is to do wrong, no doubt about it, and we do that more than we help those who are deserving. While we should sympathize with God's poor — that is, those who cannot help themselves — let us remember there is not a poor person in the United States who was not made poor by his own shortcomings, or by the shortcomings of someone else. It is all wrong to be poor, anyhow. Let us give in to that argument and pass that to one side.

A gentleman gets up back there, and says, "Don't you think there are some things in this world that are better than money?" Of course I do, but I am talking about money now. Of course there are some things higher than money. Oh yes, I know by the grave that has left me standing alone that there are some things in this world that are higher and sweeter and purer than money. Well do I know there are some things higher and grander than gold. Love is the grandest thing on God's earth, but fortunate the lover who has plenty of money. Money is power, money is force, money will do good as well as harm. In the hands of good men and women it could accomplish, and it has accomplished, good.

I hate to leave that behind me. I heard a man get up in a prayer meeting in our city and thank the Lord he was "one of God's poor." Well, I wonder what his wife thinks about that? She earns all the money that comes into that house, and he smokes a part of that on the veranda. I don't want to see any more of the Lord's poor of that kind, and I don't believe the Lord does. And yet there are some people who think in order to be pious you must be awfully poor and awfully dirty. That does not follow at all. While we sympathize with the poor, let us not teach a doctrine like that.

Yet the age is prejudiced against advising a Christian man (or, as a Jew would say, a godly man) from attaining unto wealth. The prejudice is so universal and the years are far enough back, I think, for me to safely mention that years ago up at Temple University there was a young man in our theological school who thought he was the only pious student in that department. He came into my office one evening and sat down by my desk, and said to me: "Mr. President, I think it is my duty sir, to come in and labor with you." "What has happened now?" Said he, "I heard you say at the Academy, at the Peirce School commencement, that you thought it was an honorable ambition for a young man to desire to have wealth, and that you thought it made him temperate, made him anxious to have a good name, and made him industrious. You spoke about man's ambition to have money helping to make him a good man. Sir, I have come to tell you the Holy Bible says that 'money is the root of all evil.'"

I told him I had never seen it in the Bible, and advised him to go out into the chapel and get the Bible, and show me the place. So out he went for the Bible, and soon he stalked into my office with the Bible open, with all the bigoted pride of the narrow sectarian, or of one who founds his Christianity on some misinterpretation of Scripture. He flung the Bible down on my desk, and fairly squealed into my ear: "There it is, Mr. President; you can read it for yourself." I said to him: "Well, young man, you will learn when you get a little older that you cannot trust another denomination to read the Bible for you. You belong to another denomination. You are taught in the theological school, however, that emphasis is exegesis. Now, will you take that Bible and read it yourself, and give the proper emphasis to it?"

He took the Bible, and proudly read, "'The love of money is the root of all evil.'"

Then he had it right, and when one does quote aright from that same old Book he quotes the absolute truth. I have lived through fifty years of the mightiest battle that old Book has ever fought, and I have lived to see its banners flying free; for never in the history of this world did the great minds of earth so universally agree that the Bible is true — all true — as they do at this very hour.

So I say that when he quoted right, of course he quoted the absolute truth. "The love of money is the root of all evil." He who tries to attain unto it too quickly, or dishonestly, will fall into many snares, no doubt about that. The love of money. What is that? It is making an idol of money, and idolatry pure and simple everywhere is condemned by the Holy Scriptures and by man's common sense. The man that worships the dollar instead of thinking of the purposes for which it ought to be used, the man who idolizes simply money, the miser that hoards his money in the cellar, or hides it in his stocking, or refuses to invest it where it will do the world good, that man who hugs the dollar until the eagle squeals has in him the root of all evil.

I think I will leave that behind me now and answer the question of nearly all of you who are asking, "Is there opportunity to get rich in Philadelphia?" Well, now, how simple a thing it is to see where it is, and the instant you see where it is it is yours. Some old gentleman gets up back there and says, "Mr. Conwell, have you lived in Philadelphia for thirty-one years and don't know that the time has gone by when you can make anything in this city?" "No, I don't think it is." "Yes, it is; I have tried it." "What business are you in?" "I kept a store here for twenty years, and never made over a thousand dollars in the whole twenty years."

"Well, then, you can measure the good you have been to this city by what this city has paid you, because a man can judge very well what he is worth by what he receives; that is, in what he is to the world at this time. If you have not made over a thousand dollars in twenty years in Philadelphia, it would have been better for Philadelphia if they had kicked you out of the city nineteen years and nine months ago. A man has no right to keep a store in

Philadelphia twenty years and not make at least five hundred thousand dollars, even though it be a corner grocery uptown." You say, "You cannot make five thousand dollars in a store now." Oh, my friends, if you will just take only four blocks around you, and find out what the people want and what you ought to supply and set them down with your pencil, and figure up the profits you would make if you did supply them, you would very soon see it. There is wealth right within the sound of your voice.

Someone says: "You don't know anything about business. A preacher never knows a thing about business." Well, then, I will have to prove that I am an expert. I don't like to do this, but I have to do it because my testimony will not be taken if I am not an expert. My father kept a country store, and if there is any place under the stars where a man gets all sorts of experience in every kind of mercantile transactions, it is in the country store. I am not proud of my experience, but sometimes when my father was away he would leave me in charge of the store, though fortunately for him that was not very often. But this did occur many times, friends: A man would come in the store and say to me, "Do you keep jackknives?" "No, we don't keep jackknives," and I went off whistling a tune. What did I care about that man, anyhow? Then another farmer would come in and say, "Do you keep jackknives?" "No, we don't keep jackknives." Then I went away and whistled another tune. Then a third man came right in the same door and said, "Do you keep jackknives?" "No. Why is everyone around here asking for jackknives? Do you suppose we are keeping this store to supply the whole neighborhood with jackknives?" Do you carry on your store like that in Philadelphia? The difficulty was I had not then learned that the foundation of godliness and the foundation principle of success in business are both the same precisely. The man who says, "I cannot carry my religion into business" advertises himself either as being an imbecile in business, or on the road to bankruptcy, or a thief, one of the three, sure. He will fail within a very few years. He certainly will if he doesn't carry his religion into business. If I had been carrying on my father's store on a Christian plan, godly plan, I would have had a jackknife for the third man when he called for it. Then I would have actually done him a kindness, and I would have received a reward myself, which it would have been my duty to take. . . .

But another young man gets up over there and says, "I cannot take up the mercantile business." (While I am talking of trade it applies to every occupation.) "Why can't you go into the mercantile business?" "Because I haven't any capital." Oh, the weak and dudish creature that can't see over its collar! It makes a person weak to see these little dudes standing around the corners and saying, "Oh, if I had plenty of capital, how rich I would get." "Young man, do you think you are going to get rich on capital?" "Certainly." Well, I say, "Certainly not." If your mother has plenty of money, and she will set you up in business, you will "set her up in business," supplying you with capital.

The moment a young man or woman gets more money than he or she has grown to by practical experience, that moment he has gotten a curse. It is no help to a young man or woman to inherit money. It is no help to your children to leave them money, but if you leave them education, if you leave them Christian and noble character, if you leave them a wide circle of friends, if you leave them an honorable name, it is far better than that they should have money. It would be worse for them, worse for the nation, that they should have any money at all. Oh, young man, if you have inherited money, don't regard it as a help. It will curse you through your years, and deprive you of the very best things of human life. There is no class of people to be pitied so much as the inexperienced sons and daughters of the rich of our generation. I pity the rich man's son. He can never know the best things in life.

One of the best things in our life is when a young man has earned his own living, and when he becomes engaged to some lovely young woman, and makes up his mind to have a home of his own. Then with that same love comes also that divine inspiration toward better things, and he begins to save his money. He begins to leave off his bad habits and put money in the bank. When he has a few hundred dollars he goes out in the suburbs to look for a home. He goes to the savings bank, perhaps, for half of the value, and then goes for his wife, and when he takes his bride over the threshold of that door for the first time he says in words of eloquence my voice can never touch: "I have earned this home myself. It is all mine, and I divide with thee." That is the grandest moment a human heart may ever know.

But a rich man's son can never know that. He takes his bride into a finer mansion, it may be, but he is obliged to go all the way through it and say to his wife, "My mother gave me that, my mother gave me that, and my mother gave me this," until his wife wishes she had married his mother. I pity the rich man's son. . . .

. . . Greatness consists not in the holding of some future office, but really consists in doing great deeds with little means and the accomplishment of vast purposes from the private ranks of life. To be great at all one must be great here, now, in Philadelphia. He who can give to this city better streets and better sidewalks, better schools and more colleges, more happiness and more civilization, more of God, he will be great anywhere. Let every man or woman here, if you never hear me again, remember this, that if you wish to be great at all, you must begin where you are and with what you are, in Philadelphia, now. He who can give to his city any blessing, he who can be a good citizen while he lives here, he who can make better homes, he who can be a blessing whether he works in the shop or sits behind the counter or keeps house, whatever be his life, he who would be great anywhere must first be great in his own Philadelphia.

READING CRITICALLY

1. Why, according to Conwell, should people be rich? Why are poor people poor? Why is it important to own a house?

2. What reaction does Conwell seem to want to elicit from his audience with the story of the farmer who sold his farm?

3. What connection does Conwell make between basic marketing principles and basic Christian morality?

4. How does Conwell distinguish between the desire to get money and the love of money itself?

5. What distinction does Conwell draw between making money and having money?

WRITING ANALYTICALLY

1. In a brief essay, answer two questions: What is Conwell arguing *for*, and what is he arguing *against*? The answer to the first question seems fairly obvious, though it is worth examining this issue carefully (see reading question 1). The answer to the second question may be less obvious. He is ostensibly refuting the Christian argument that it is better to be poor than rich. What other arguments does he seem to be refuting or responding to?

2. Evaluate the validity of Conwell's arguments — spelled out in your essay on writing question 1 — for people today. Do you know of anyone who makes such arguments nowadays? How do you think people would respond to them? Alternative: As a way of answering these questions, imagine that Conwell has delivered an updated version of his speech at your school, and write a response to it that might appear in the school newspaper.

EDWARD BELLAMY

From *Looking Backward: 2000–1887* (1888)

Edward Bellamy (1850–98) became a lawyer but abandoned this career after his first case. He found the practice of law so distasteful that he eliminated the profession from the utopian society of his novel *Looking Backward*. He became a journalist and novelist, and in 1888 *Looking Backward* became his greatest success. The book spawned more than 150 Bellamy Clubs and Nationalist Clubs and two periodicals, *The Nationalist* and *The New Nation* (founded by Bellamy himself), which advocated the modified form of socialism, called Nationalism, described in the novel. A Nationalist political party also arose whose principles were close to those of the Populist Party, a powerful force at the end of the century. (The Populists advocated such anti-elitist policies as nationalizing the railroads and imposing a graduated income tax.) Bellamy's last book, *Equality* (1897), is an economic treatise that develops his ideas in more detail. Bellamy Clubs are still in existence today, testifying to the enduring appeal of his vision of the future.

Looking Backward, like many other examples of utopian fiction, has a science fiction–like plot and a great deal of explanation and argument presented as a dialogue between characters. The main character, Julian West, is hypnotized one night in 1887 so that he can overcome insomnia. His house burns down that night — but Julian, asleep in an underground room that he has constructed as part of his attempt to defeat his insomnia, remains safe, in a hypnotic trance, until he is finally discovered in the year 2000. In *Looking Backward*, Julian narrates his own story and engages in lengthy discussions with Dr. Leete, the man who cares for him when he first awakens.

The excerpts here skirt most of the staging and focus on discussions in the early chapters in which Julian compares the past and the present. They tell of the organization of work, wages, and the distribution of resources. Later chapters describe the methods of international commerce, shipping and storage of products, publishing and artistic production, pricing, the political system, the activities of retirees, crime and the justice system, and education; they also contain an extended discussion of the philosophical and practical differences between the individualistic capitalism of the nineteenth century and the utopian socialism of the year 2000.

Edward Bellamy, *Looking Backward: 2000–1887* (1888; reprint, New York: Bantam, 1983), 1–4, 23–52, 66–74.
In the notes, EDS. = Patricia Bizzell and Bruce Herzberg.

CHAPTER 1

I FIRST SAW THE LIGHT IN THE CITY of Boston in the year 1857. "What!" you say, "eighteen fifty-seven? That is an odd slip. He means nineteen fifty-seven, of course." I beg pardon, but there is no mistake. It was about four in the afternoon of December the 26th, one day after Christmas, in the year 1857, not 1957, that I first breathed the east wind of Boston, which, I assure the reader, was at that remote period marked by the same penetrating quality characterizing it in the present year of grace, 2000.

These statements seem so absurd on their face, especially when I add that I am a young man apparently of about thirty years of age, that no person can be blamed for refusing to read another word of what promises to be a mere imposition upon his credulity. Nevertheless I earnestly assure the reader that no imposition is intended, and will undertake, if he shall follow me a few pages, to entirely convince him of this. If I may, then, provisionally assume, with the pledge of justifying the assumption, that I know better than the reader when I was born, I will go on with my narrative. As every schoolboy knows, in the latter part of the nineteenth century the civilization of today, or anything like it, did not exist, although the elements which were to develop it were already in ferment. Nothing had, however, occurred to modify the immemorial division of society into the four classes, or nations, as they may be more fitly called, since the differences between them were far greater than those between any nations nowadays, of the rich and the poor, the educated and the ignorant. I myself was rich and also educated, and possessed, therefore, all the elements of happiness enjoyed by the most fortunate in that age. Living in luxury, and occupied only with the pursuit of the pleasures and refinements of life, I derived the means of my support from the labor of others, rendering no sort of service in return. My parents and grandparents had lived in the same way, and I expected that my descendants, if I had any, would enjoy a like easy existence.

But how could I live without service to the world? you ask. Why should the world have supported in utter idleness one who was able to render service? The answer is that my great-grandfather had accumulated a sum of money on which his descendants had ever since lived. The sum, you will naturally infer, must have been very large not to have been exhausted in supporting three generations in idleness. This, however, was not the fact. The sum had been originally by no means large. It was, in fact, much larger now that three generations had been supported upon it in idleness, than it was at first. This mystery of use without consumption, of warmth without combustion, seems like magic, but was merely an ingenious application of the art now happily lost but carried to great perfection by your ancestors, of shifting the burden of one's support on the shoulders of others. The man who had accomplished this, and it was the end all sought, was said to live on the income of his investments. To explain at this point how the ancient methods of industry made this possible would delay us too much. I shall only stop now to say that interest on investments was a species of tax in perpetuity upon the product of those engaged in industry which a person possessing or inheriting money was able to levy. It must not be supposed that an arrangement which seems so unnatural and preposterous according to modern notions was never criticized by your ancestors. It had been the effort of lawgivers and prophets from the earliest ages to abolish interest, or at least to limit it to the smallest possible rate. All these efforts had, however, failed, as they necessarily must so long as the ancient social organizations prevailed. At the time of which I write, the latter part of the nineteenth century, governments had generally given up trying to regulate the subject at all.

By way of attempting to give the reader some general impression of the way people lived together in those days, and especially of the relations of the rich and poor to one another, perhaps I cannot do better than to compare society as it then was to a prodigious coach which the masses of humanity were harnessed to and dragged toilsomely along a very hilly and sandy road. The driver was hunger, and permitted no lagging, though the pace was necessarily very slow. Despite the difficulty of drawing the coach at all along so hard a road, the top was covered with passengers who never got down, even at the steepest ascents. These seats on top were very breezy and comfortable. Well up out of the dust, their occupants could enjoy the scenery at their leisure, or critically discuss the merits of the straining team. Naturally such places were in great demand and the competition for them was keen, everyone seeking as the first end in life to secure a seat on the coach for himself and to leave it to his child after him. By the rule of the coach a man could leave his seat to whom he wished, but on the other hand there were many accidents by which it might at any time be wholly lost. For all that they were so easy, the seats were very insecure, and at every sudden jolt of the coach persons were slipping out of them and falling to the ground, where they were instantly compelled to take hold of the rope and help to drag the coach on which they had before ridden so pleasantly. It was naturally regarded as a terrible misfortune to lose one's seat, and the apprehension that this might happen to them or their friends was a constant cloud upon the happiness of those who rode.

But did they think only of themselves? you ask. Was not their very luxury rendered intolerable to them by comparison with the lot of their brothers and sisters in the harness, and the knowledge that their own weight added to their toil? Had they no compassion for fellow beings from whom fortune only distinguished them? Oh, yes; commiseration was frequently expressed by those who rode for those who had to pull the coach, especially when the vehicle came to a bad place in the road, as it was constantly doing, or to a particularly steep hill. At such times, the desperate straining of the team, their agonized leaping and plunging under the pitiless lashing of hunger, the many who fainted at the rope and were trampled in the mire, made a very distressing spectacle, which often called forth highly creditable displays of feeling on the top of the coach. At such times the passengers would call down encouragingly to the toilers of the rope, exhorting them to patience, and holding out hopes of possible compensation in another world for the hardness of their lot, while others contributed to buy salves and liniments for the crippled and injured. It was agreed that it was a great pity that the coach should be so hard to pull, and there was a sense of general relief when the specially bad piece of road was gotten over. This relief was not, indeed, wholly on account of the team, for there was always some danger at these bad places of a general overturn in which all would lose their seats.

It must in truth be admitted that the main effect of the spectacle of the misery of the toilers at the rope was to enhance the passengers' sense of the value of their seats upon the coach, and to cause them to hold on to them more desperately than before. If the passengers could only have felt assured that neither they nor their friends would ever fall from the top, it is probable that, beyond contributing to the funds for liniments and bandages, they would have troubled themselves extremely little about those who dragged the coach.

I am well aware that this will appear to the men and women of the twentieth century an incredible inhumanity, but there are two facts, both very curious, which partly explain it. In the first place, it was firmly and sincerely believed that there was no other way in which Society could get along, except the many pulled at the rope and the few rode, and not only this, but that no very radical improvement even was possible, either in the harness, the coach, the roadway, or the distribution of the toil. It had always been as it was, and it always would be so. It was a pity, but it could not be helped, and philosophy forbade wasting compassion on what was beyond remedy.

The other fact is yet more curious, consisting in a singular hallucination which those on the top of the coach generally shared, that they were not exactly like their brothers and sisters who pulled at the rope, but of finer clay, in some way belonging to a higher order of beings who might justly expect to be drawn. This seems unaccountable, but, as I once rode on this very coach and shared that very hallucination, I ought to be believed. The strangest thing about the hallucination was that those who had but just climbed up from the ground, before they had outgrown the marks of the rope upon their hands, began to fall under its influence. As for those whose parents and grandparents before them had been so fortunate as to keep their seats on the top, the conviction they cherished of the essential difference between their sort of humanity and the common article was absolute. The effect of such a delusion in moderating fellow feeling for the sufferings of the mass of men into a distant and philosophical compassion is obvious. To it I refer as the only extenuation I can offer for the indifference which, at the period I write of, marked my own attitude toward the misery of my brothers. . . .

[*The narrator of the story, Julian West, describes how, one night in 1887, he is hypnotized as a treatment for his insomnia. His house burns down that night — but Julian, asleep in an underground room that he has constructed as part of his insomnia therapy, remains safe, in a hypnotic trance, until the year 2000. Julian is awakened by Dr. Leete, who has discovered and cared for him. Julian takes several days to recover, to explain who he is and figure out what has happened to him. Soon, though, he and Dr. Leete begin to discuss the past and the present. —* EDS.]

CHAPTER 5

When, in the course of the evening the ladies retired, leaving Dr. Leete and myself alone, he sounded me as to my disposition for sleep, saying that if I felt like it my bed was ready for me; but if I was inclined to wakefulness nothing would please him better than to bear me company. "I am a late bird, myself," he said, "and, without suspicion of flattery, I may say that a companion more interesting than yourself could scarcely be imagined. It is decidedly not often that one has a chance to converse with a man of the nineteenth century."

Now I had been looking forward all the evening with some dread to the time when I should be alone, on retiring for the night. Surrounded by these most friendly strangers, stimulated and supported by their sympathetic interest, I had been able to keep my mental balance. Even then, however, in pauses of the conversation I had had glimpses, vivid as lightning flashes, of the horror of strangeness that was waiting to be faced when I could no longer command diversion. I knew I could not sleep that night, and as for lying awake and thinking, it argues no cowardice, I am sure, to confess that I was afraid of it. When, in reply to my host's question, I frankly told him this, he replied that it would be strange if I did not feel just so, but that I need have no anxiety about sleeping; whenever I wanted to go to bed, he would give me a dose which would insure me a sound night's sleep without fail. Next morning, no doubt, I would awake with the feeling of an old citizen.

"Before I acquire that," I replied, "I must know a little more about the sort of Boston I have come back to. You told me . . . that though a century only had elapsed since I fell asleep, it had been marked by greater changes in the conditions of humanity than many a previous millennium. With the city before me I could well believe that, but I am very curious to know what some of the changes have been. To make a beginning somewhere, for the subject is doubtless a large one, what solution, if any, have you found for the labor question? It was the Sphinx's riddle[1] of the nineteenth century, and when I dropped out the Sphinx was threatening to devour society, because the answer was not forthcoming. It is well worth sleeping a hundred years to learn what the right answer was, if, indeed, you have found it yet."

"As no such thing as the labor question is known nowadays," replied Dr. Leete, "and there is no way in which it could arise, I suppose we may claim to have solved it. Society would indeed have fully deserved being devoured

---

[1]In Greek mythology, the Sphinx is a winged female monster with a woman's head and a lion's body who devours travelers who cannot solve the riddle it poses. — EDS.

if it had failed to answer a riddle so entirely simple. In fact, to speak by the book, it was not necessary for society to solve the riddle at all. It may be said to have solved itself. The solution came as the result of a process of industrial evolution which could not have terminated otherwise. All that society had to do was to recognize and cooperate with that evolution, when its tendency had become unmistakable. . . .

". . . Since you are in the humor to talk rather than to sleep, as I certainly am, perhaps I cannot do better than to try to give you enough idea of our modern industrial system to dissipate at least the impression that there is any mystery about the process of its evolution. The Bostonians of your day had the reputation of being great askers of questions, and I am going to show my descent by asking you one to begin with. What should you name as the most prominent feature of the labor troubles of your day?"

"Why, the strikes, of course," I replied.

"Exactly; but what made the strikes so formidable?"

"The great labor organizations."

"And what was the motive of these great organizations?"

"The workmen claimed they had to organize to get their rights from the big corporations," I replied.

"That is just it," said Dr. Leete; "the organization of labor and the strikes were an effect, merely, of the concentration of capital in greater masses than had ever been known before. Before this concentration began, while as yet commerce and industry were conducted by innumerable petty concerns with small capital, instead of a small number of great concerns with vast capital, the individual workman was relatively important and independent in his relations to the employer. Moreover, when a little capital or a new idea was enough to start a man in business for himself, workingmen were constantly becoming employers and there was no hard and fast line between the two classes. Labor unions were needless then, and general strikes out of the question. But when the era of small concerns with small capital was succeeded by that of the great aggregations of capital, all this was changed. The individual laborer, who had been relatively important to the small employer, was reduced to insignificance and powerlessness over against the great corporation, while at the same time the way upward to the grade of employer was closed to him. Self-defense drove him to union with his fellows.

"The records of the period show that the outcry against the concentration of capital was furious. Men believed that it threatened society with a form of tyranny more abhorrent than it had ever endured. They believed that the great corporations were preparing for them the yoke of a baser servitude than had ever been imposed on the race, servitude not to men but to soulless machines incapable of any motive but insatiable greed. Looking back, we cannot wonder at their desperation, for certainly humanity was never confronted with a fate more sordid and hideous than would have been the era of corporate tyranny which they anticipated.

"Meanwhile, without being in the smallest degree checked by the clamor against it, the absorption of business by ever larger monopolies continued. In the United States there was not, after the beginning of the last quarter of the century, any opportunity whatever for individual enterprise in any important field of industry, unless backed by a great capital. During the last decade of the century, such small businesses as still remained were fast-failing survivals of a past epoch, or mere parasites on the great corporations, or else existed in fields too small to attract the great capitalists. Small businesses, as far as they still remained, were reduced to the condition of rats and mice, living in holes and corners, and counting on evading notice for the enjoyment of existence. The railroads had gone on combining till a few great syndicates controlled every rail in the land. In manufactories, every important staple was controlled by a syndicate. These syndicates, pools, trusts, or whatever their name, fixed prices and crushed all competition except when combinations as vast as themselves arose. Then a struggle, resulting in a still greater consolidation, ensued. The great city bazaar crushed its country rivals with branch stores, and in the city itself absorbed its smaller rivals till the business of a whole quarter was concentrated under one roof, with a hundred former proprietors of shops serving as clerks. Having no business of his own to put his money in, the small capitalist, at the same time that he took service under the corporation, found no other investment for his money but its stocks and bonds, thus becoming doubly dependent upon it.

"The fact that the desperate popular opposition to the consolidation of business in a few powerful hands had no effect to check it proves that there must have been a strong economical reason for it. The small capitalist, with their innumerable petty concerns, had in fact yielded the field to the great aggregations of capital, because they belonged to a day of small things and were totally incompetent to the demands of an age of steam and telegraphs and the gigantic scale of its enterprises. To restore the former order of things, even if possible, would have involved returning to the day of stagecoaches. Oppressive and intolerable as was the regime of the great consolidations of capital, even its victims, while they cursed it, were forced to admit the prodigious increase of efficiency which had been imparted to the national industries, the vast economies effected by concentration of management and unity of organization, and to confess that since the new system had taken the place of the old the wealth of the world had increased at a rate before undreamed of. To be sure this vast increase had gone chiefly to make the rich richer, increasing the gap between them and the poor; but the fact remained that, as a means merely of producing wealth, capital had been proved efficient in proportion to its consolidation. The restoration of the old system with the subdivision of capital, if it were possible, might indeed bring back a greater equality of conditions, with more individual dignity and freedom, but it would be at the price of general poverty and the arrest of material progress.

"Was there, then, no way of commanding the services of the mighty wealth-producing principle of consolidated capital without bowing down to a plutocracy like that of Carthage?[2] As soon as men began to ask themselves these questions, they found the answer ready for them. The movement toward the conduct of business by larger and larger aggregations of capital, the tendency toward monopolies, which had been so desperately and vainly resisted, was recognized at last, in its true significance, as a process which only needed to complete its logical evolution to open a golden future to humanity.

"Early in the last century the evolution was completed by the final consolidation of the entire capital of the nation. The industry and commerce of the country, ceasing to be conducted by a set of irresponsible corporations and syndicates of private persons at their caprice and for their profit, were entrusted to a single syndicate representing the people, to be conducted in the common interest for the common profit. The nation, that is to say, organized as the one great business corporation in which all other corporations were absorbed; it became the one capitalist in the place of all other capitalists, the sole employer, the final monopoly in which all previous and lesser monopolies were swallowed up, a monopoly in the profits and economies of which all citizens shared. The epoch of trusts had ended in The Great Trust. In a word, the people of the United States concluded to assume the conduct of their own business, just as one hundred odd years before they had assumed the conduct of their own government, organizing now for industrial purposes on precisely the same grounds that they had then organized for political purposes. At last, strangely late in the world's history, the obvious fact was perceived that no business is so essentially the public business as the industry and commerce on which the people's livelihood depends, and that to entrust it to private persons to be managed for private profit is a folly similar in kind, though vastly greater in magnitude, to that of surrendering the functions of political government to kings and nobles to be conducted for their personal glorification."

"Such a stupendous change as you describe," said I, "did not, of course, take place without great bloodshed and terrible convulsions."

"On the contrary," replied Dr. Leete, "there was absolutely no violence. The change had been long foreseen. Public opinion had become fully ripe for it, and the whole mass of the people was behind it. There was no more possibility of opposing it by force than by argument. On the other hand the popular sentiment toward the great corporations and those identified with them had ceased to be one of bitterness, as they came to realize their necessity as a link, a transition phase, in the evolution of the true industrial system. The most violent foes of the great private monopolies were now forced to recognize how invaluable and indispensable had been their office in educating the people up to the point of assuming

---

[2]Carthage was an ancient city-state in northern Africa, northeast of modern Tunis. Like many ancient Greek states, it was ruled by the wealthy, a form of government called "plutocracy." — EDS.

control of their own business. Fifty years before, the consolidation of the industries of the country under national control would have seemed a very daring experiment to the most sanguine. But by a series of object lessons, seen and studied by all men, the great corporations had taught the people an entirely new set of ideas on this subject. They had seen for many years syndicates handling revenues greater than those of states, and directing the labors of hundreds of thousands of men with an efficiency and economy unattainable in smaller operations. It had come to be recognized as an axiom that the larger the business the simpler the principles that can be applied to it; that, as the machine is truer than the hand, so the system, which in a great concern does the work of the master's eye in a small business, turns out more accurate results. Thus it came about that, thanks to the corporations themselves, when it was proposed that the nation should assume their functions, the suggestion implied nothing which seemed impracticable even to the timid. To be sure it was a step beyond any yet taken, a broader generalization, but the very fact that the nation would be the sole corporation in the field would, it was seen, relieve the undertaking of many difficulties with which the partial monopolies had contended."

CHAPTER 6

Dr. Leete ceased speaking, and I remained silent, endeavoring to form some general conception of the changes in the arrangements of society implied in the tremendous revolution which he had described.

Finally I said, "The idea of such an extension of the functions of government is, to say the least, rather overwhelming."

"Extension!" he repeated. "Where is the extension?"

"In my day," I replied, "it was considered that the proper functions of government, strictly speaking, were limited to keeping the peace and defending the people against the public enemy, that is, to the military and police powers."

"And, in heaven's name, who are the public enemies?" exclaimed Dr. Leete. "Are they France, England, Germany, or hunger, cold, and nakedness? In your day governments were accustomed, on the slightest international misunderstanding, to seize upon the bodies of citizens and deliver them over by hundreds of thousands to death and mutilation, wasting their treasures the while like water; and all this oftenest for no imaginable profit to the victims. We have no wars now, and our governments no war powers, but in order to protect every citizen against hunger, cold, and nakedness, and provide for all his physical and mental needs, the function is assumed of directing his industry for a term of years. No, Mr. West, I am sure on reflection you will perceive that it was in your age, not in ours, that the extension of the functions of governments was extraordinary. Not even for the best ends would men now allow their governments such powers as were then used for the most maleficent."

"Leaving comparisons aside," I said, "the demagoguery and corruption of our public men would have been considered, in my day, insuperable objections to any assumption by government of the charge of the national industries. We should have thought that no arrangement could be worse than to entrust the politicians with control of the wealth-producing machinery of the country. Its material interests were quite too much the football of parties as it was."

"No doubt you were right," rejoined Dr. Leete, "but all that is changed now. We have no parties or politicians, and as for demagoguery and corruption, they are words having only an historical significance."

"Human nature itself must have changed very much," I said.

"Not at all," was Dr. Leete's reply, "but the conditions of human life have changed, and with them the motives of human action. The organization of society with you was such that officials were under a constant temptation to misuse their power for the private profit of themselves or others. Under such circumstances it seems almost strange that you dared entrust them with any of your affairs. Nowadays, on the contrary, society is so constituted that there is absolutely no way in which an official, however ill-disposed, could possibly make any profit for himself or anyone else by a misuse of his power. Let him be as bad an official as you please, he cannot be a corrupt one. There is no motive to be. The social system no longer offers a premium on dishonesty. But these are matters which you can only understand as you come, with time, to know us better."

"But you have not yet told me how you have settled the labor problem. It is the problem of capital which we have been discussing," I said. "After the nation had assumed conduct of the mills, machinery, railroads, farms, mines, and capital in general of the country, the labor question still remained. In assuming the responsibilities of capital the nation had assumed the difficulties of the capitalist's position."

"The moment the nation assumed the responsibilities of capital those difficulties vanished," replied Dr. Leete. "The national organization of labor under one direction was the complete solution of what was, in your day and under your system, justly regarded as the insoluble labor problem. When the nation became the sole employer, all the citizens, by virtue of their citizenship, became employees, to be distributed according to the needs of industry."

"That is," I suggested, "you have simply applied the principle of universal military service, as it was understood in our day, to the labor question."

"Yes," said Dr. Leete, "that was something which followed as a matter of course as soon as the nation had become the sole capitalist. The people were already accustomed to the idea that the obligation of every citizen, not physically disabled, to contribute his military services to the defense of the nation was equal and absolute. That it was equally the duty of every citizen to contribute his quota of industrial or intellectual services to the maintenance of the nation was equally evident, though it was not until the nation became the employer of labor that citizens were able to render this sort of service with any pretense either of universality or equity. No organization of labor was possible when the employing power was divided among hundreds or thousands of individuals and corporations, between which concert of any kind was neither desired, nor indeed feasible. It constantly happened then that vast numbers who desired to labor could find no opportunity, and on the other hand, those who desired to evade a part or all of their debt could easily do so."

"Service, now, I suppose, is compulsory upon all," I suggested.

"It is rather a matter of course than of compulsion," replied Dr. Leete. "It is regarded as so absolutely natural and reasonable that the idea of its being compulsory has ceased to be thought of. He would be thought to be an incredibly contemptible person who should need compulsion in such a case. Nevertheless, to speak of service being compulsory would be a weak way to state its absolute inevitableness. Our entire social order is so wholly based upon and deduced from it that if it were conceivable that a man could escape it, he would be left with no possible way to provide for his existence. He would have excluded himself from the world, cut himself off from his kind, in a word, committed suicide."

"Is the term of service in this industrial army for life?"

"Oh, no; it both begins later and ends earlier than the average working period in your day. Your workshops were filled with children and old men, but we hold the period of youth sacred to education, and the period of maturity, when the physical forces begin to flag, equally sacred to ease and agreeable relaxation. The period of industrial service is twenty-four years, beginning at the close of the course of education at twenty-one and terminating at forty-five. After forty-five, while discharged from labor, the citizen still remains liable to special calls, in case of emergencies causing a sudden great increase in the demand for labor, till he reaches the age of fifty-five, but such calls are rarely, in fact almost never, made. The fifteenth day of October of every year is what we call Muster Day, because those who have reached the age of twenty-one are then mustered into the industrial service, and at the same time those who, after twenty-four years' service, have reached the age of forty-five, are honorably mustered out. It is the great day of the year with us, whence we reckon all other events, our Olympiad, save that it is annual."

CHAPTER 7

"It is after you have mustered your industrial army into service," I said, "that I should expect the chief difficulty to arise, for there its analogy with a military army must cease. Soldiers have all the same thing, and a very simple thing, to do, namely, to practice the manual of arms, to march, and stand guard. But the industrial army must learn and follow two or three hundred diverse trades and avocations. What administrative talent can be equal to determining wisely what trade or business every individual in a great nation shall pursue?"

"The administration has nothing to do with determining that point."

"Who does determine it, then?" I asked.

"Every man for himself in accordance with his natural aptitude, the utmost pains being taken to enable him to find out what his natural aptitude really is. The principle on which our industrial army is organized is that a man's natural endowments, mental and physical, determine what he can work at most profitably to the nation and most satisfactorily to himself. While the obligation of service in some form is not to be evaded, voluntary election, subject only to necessary regulation, is depended on to determine the particular sort of service every man is to render. . . . "

"Surely," I said, "it can hardly be that the number of volunteers for any trade is exactly the number needed in that trade. It must be generally either under or over the demand."

"The supply of volunteers is always expected to fully equal the demand," replied Dr. Leete. "It is the business of the administration to see that this is the case. The rate of volunteering for each trade is closely watched. If there be a noticeably greater excess of volunteers over men needed in any trade, it is inferred that the trade offers greater attractions than others. On the other hand, if the number of volunteers for a trade tends to drop below the demand, it is inferred that it is thought more arduous. It is the business of the administration to seek constantly to equalize the attractions of the trades, so far as the conditions of labor in them are concerned, so that all trades shall be equally attractive to persons having natural tastes for them. This is done by making the hours of labor in different trades to differ according to their arduousness. The lighter trades, prosecuted under the most agreeable circumstances, have in this way the longest hours, while an arduous trade, such as mining, has very short hours. . . . Of course you will see that dependence on the purely voluntary choice of avocations involves the abolition in all of anything like unhygienic conditions or special peril to life and limb. Health and safety are conditions common to all industries. The nation does not maim and slaughter its workmen by thousands, as did the private capitalists and corporations of your day." . . .

"How is this class of common laborers recruited?" I asked. "Surely nobody voluntarily enters that."

"It is the grade to which all new recruits belong for the first three years of their service. It is not till after this period, during which he is assignable to any work at the discretion of his superiors, that the young man is allowed to elect a special avocation. These three years of stringent discipline none are exempt from, and very glad our young men are to pass from this severe school into the comparative liberty of the trades. If a man were so stupid as to have no choice as to occupation, he would simply remain a common laborer; but such cases, as you may suppose, are not common." . . .

"As an industrial system, I should think this might be extremely efficient," I said, "but I don't see that it makes any provision for the professional classes, the men who serve the nation with brains instead of hands. Of course you can't get along without the brain workers. How, then, are they selected from those who are to serve as farmers and mechanics? That must require a very delicate sort of sifting process, I should say."

"So it does," replied Dr. Leete; "the most delicate possible test is needed here, and so we leave the question whether a man shall be a brain or hand worker entirely to him to settle. At the end of the term of three years as a common laborer, which every man must serve, it is for him to choose, in accordance to his natural tastes, whether he will fit himself for an art or profession, or be a farmer or mechanic. If he feels that he can do better work with his brains than his muscles, he finds every facility provided for testing the reality of his supposed bent, of cultivating it, and if fit of pursuing it as his avocation. The schools of technology, of medicine, of art, of music, of histrionics, and of higher liberal learning are always open to aspirants without condition."

"Are not the schools flooded with young men whose only motive is to avoid work?"

Dr. Leete smiled a little grimly.

"No one is at all likely to enter the professional schools for the purpose of avoiding work, I assure you," he said. "They are intended for those with special aptitude for the branches they teach, and anyone without it would find it easier to do double hours at his trade than try to keep up with the classes. Of course many honestly mistake their vocation, and, finding themselves unequal to the requirements of the schools, drop out and return to the industrial service; no discredit attaches to such persons, for the public policy is to encourage all to develop suspected talents which only actual tests can prove the reality of. The professional and scientific schools of your day depended on the patronage of their pupils for support, and the practice appears to have been common of giving diplomas to unfit persons, who afterwards found their way into the professions. Our schools are national institutions, and to have passed their tests is a proof of special abilities not to be questioned." . . .

A question which had a dozen times before been on my lips now found utterance, a question which touched upon what, in my time, had been regarded the most vital difficulty in the way of any final settlement of the industrial problem. "It is an extraordinary thing," I said, "that you should not yet have said a word about the method of adjusting wages. Since the nation is the sole employer, the government must fix the rate of wages and determine just how much everybody shall earn, from the doctors to the diggers. All I can say is, that this plan would never have worked with us, and I don't see how it can now unless human nature has changed. In my day, nobody was satisfied with his wages or salary. Even if he felt he received enough, he was sure his neighbor had too much, which was as bad. If the universal discontent on this subject, instead of being dissipated in curses and strikes directed against innumerable employers, could have been concentrated upon one, and that the government, the strongest ever devised would not have seen two paydays."

Dr. Leete laughed heartily.

"Very true, very true," he said, "a general strike would most probably have followed the first payday, and a strike directed against a government is a revolution."

"How, then, do you avoid a revolution every payday?" I demanded. "Has some prodigious philosopher devised a new system of calculus satisfactory to all for determining the exact and comparative value of all sorts of service, whether by brawn or brain, by hand or voice, by ear or eye? Or has human nature itself changed, so that no man looks upon his own things but 'every man on the things of his neighbor'? One or the other of these events must be the explanation."

"Neither one nor the other, however, is," was my host's laughing response. "And now, Mr. West," he continued, "you must remember that you are my patient as well as my guest, and permit me to prescribe sleep for you before we have any more conversation. It is after three o'clock."

"The prescription is, no doubt, a wise one," I said; "I only hope it can be filled."

"I will see to that," the doctor replied, and he did, for he gave me a wineglass of something or other which sent me to sleep as soon as my head touched the pillow.

[*Julian awakens early the next morning and takes a walk around the city. When he returns to the Leetes' house, he shares his adventures with his hosts.* — EDS.]

CHAPTER 9

Dr. and Mrs. Leete were evidently not a little startled to learn, when they presently appeared, that I had been all over the city alone that morning, and it was apparent that they were agreeably surprised to see that I seemed so little agitated after the experience.

"Your stroll could scarcely have failed to be a very interesting one," said Mrs. Leete, as we sat down to table soon after. "You must have seen a good many new things."

"I saw very little that was not new," I replied. "But I think what surprised me as much as anything was not to find any stores on Washington Street, or any banks on State. What have you done with the merchants and bankers? Hung them all, perhaps, as the anarchists wanted to do in my day?"[3]

"Not so bad as that," replied Dr. Leete. "We have simply dispensed with them. Their functions are obsolete in the modern world."

"Who sells you things when you want to buy them?" I inquired.

"There is neither selling nor buying nowadays; the distribution of goods is effected in another way. As to the bankers, having no money we have no use for those gentry. . . .

---

[3]Anarchism is a form of socialism that seeks the elimination of government. Some nineteenth-century anarchists advocated the use of violence against capitalists and government officials. — EDS.

"You were surprised," he said, "at my saying that we got along without money or trade, but a moment's reflection will show that trade existed and money was needed in your day simply because the business of production was left in private hands, and that, consequently, they are superfluous now."

"I do not at once see how that follows," I replied.

"It is very simple," said Dr. Leete. "When innumerable different and independent persons produced the various things needful to life and comfort, endless exchanges between individuals were requisite in order that they might supply themselves with what they desired. These exchanges constituted trade, and money was essential as their medium. But as soon as the nation became the sole producer of all sorts of commodities, there was no need of exchanges between individuals that they might get what they required. Everything was procurable from one source, and nothing could be procured anywhere else. A system of direct distribution from the national storehouses took the place of trade, and for this money was unnecessary."

"How is this distribution managed?" I asked.

"On the simplest possible plan," replied Dr. Leete. "A credit corresponding to his share of the annual product of the nation is given to every citizen on the public books at the beginning of each year, and a credit card issued him with which he procures at the public storehouses, found in every community, whatever he desires whenever he desires it. This arrangement, you will see, totally obviates the necessity for business transactions of any sort between individuals and consumers. Perhaps you would like to see what our credit cards are like."

"You observe," he pursued as I was curiously examining the piece of pasteboard he gave me, "that this card is issued for a certain number of dollars. We have kept the old word, but not the substance. The term, as we use it, answers to no real thing, but merely serves as an algebraical symbol for comparing the values of products with one another. For this purpose they are all priced in dollars and cents, just as in your day. The value of what I procure on this card is checked off by the clerk, who pricks out of these tiers of squares the price of what I order."

"If you wanted to buy something of your neighbor, could you transfer part of your credit to him as consideration?" I inquired.

"In the first place," replied Dr. Leete, "our neighbors have nothing to sell us, but in any event our credit would not be transferable, being strictly personal. Before the nation could even think of honoring any such transfer as you speak of, it would be bound to inquire into all the circumstances of the transaction, so as to be able to guarantee its absolute equity. It would have been reason enough, had there been no other, for abolishing money, that its possession was no indication of rightful title to it. In the hands of the man who had stolen it or murdered for it, it was as good as in those which had earned it by industry. People nowadays interchange gifts and favors out of friendship, but buying and selling is considered absolutely inconsistent with the mutual benevolence and disinterestedness which should prevail between citizens and the sense of community of interest which supports our social system. According to our ideas, buying and selling is essentially antisocial in all its tendencies. It is an education in self-seeking at the expense of others, and no society whose citizens are trained in such a school can possibly rise above a very low grade of civilization."

"What if you have to spend more than your card in any one year?" I asked.

"The provision is so ample that we are more likely not to spend it all," replied Dr. Leete. "But if extraordinary expenses should exhaust it, we can obtain a limited advance on the next year's credit, though this practice is not encouraged, and a heavy discount is charged to check it. Of course if a man showed himself a reckless spendthrift he would receive his allowance monthly or weekly instead of yearly, or if necessary not be permitted to handle it all."

"If you don't spend your allowance, I suppose it accumulates?"

"That is also permitted to a certain extent when a special outlay is anticipated. But unless notice to the contrary is given, it is presumed that the citizen who does not fully expend his credit did not have occasion to do so, and the balance is turned into the general surplus."

"Such a system does not encourage saving habits on the part of citizens," I said.

"It is not intended to," was the reply. "The nation is rich, and does not wish the people to deprive themselves of any good thing. In your day, men were bound to lay up goods and money against coming failure of the means of support and for their children. This necessity made parsimony a virtue. But now it would have no such laudable object, and, having lost its utility, it has ceased to be regarded as a virtue. No man anymore has any care for the morrow, either for himself or his children, for the nation guarantees the nurture, education, and comfortable maintenance of every citizen from the cradle to the grave."

"That is a sweeping guarantee!" I said. "What certainty can there be that the value of a man's labor will recompense the nation for its outlay on him? On the whole, society may be able to support all its members, but some must earn less than enough for their support, and others more; and that brings us back once more to the wages question, on which you have hitherto said nothing. It was at just this point, if you remember, that our talk ended last evening; and I say again, as I did then, that here I should suppose a national industrial system like yours would find its main difficulty. How, I ask once more, can you adjust satisfactorily the comparative wages or remuneration of the multitude of avocations, so unlike and so incommensurable, which are necessary for the service of society? In our day the market rate determined the price of labor of all sorts, as well as of goods. The employer paid as little as he could, and the worker got as much. It was not a pretty system ethically, I admit; but it did, at least, furnish us a rough and ready formula for settling a question which must be settled ten thousand times a day if the world was ever going to get forward. There seemed to us no other practicable way of doing it."

"Yes," replied Dr. Leete, "it was the only practicable way under a system which made the interests of every individual antagonistic to those of every other; but it would have been a pity if humanity could never have devised a better plan, for yours was simply the application to the mutual relations of men of the devil's maxim, 'Your necessity is my opportunity.' The reward of any service depended not upon its difficulty, danger, or hardship, for throughout the world it seems that the most perilous, severe, and repulsive labor was done by the worst-paid classes; but solely upon the strait of those who needed the service."

"All that is conceded," I said. "But, with all its defects, the plan of settling prices by the market rate was a practical plan; and I cannot conceive what satisfactory substitute you can have devised for it. The government being the only possible employer, there is of course no labor market or market rate. Wages of all sorts must be arbitrarily fixed by the government. I cannot imagine a more complex and delicate function than that must be, or one, however performed, more certain to breed universal dissatisfaction." . . .

". . . You ask me how we regulate wages; I can only reply that there is no idea in the modern social economy which at all corresponds with what was meant by wages in your day."

"I suppose you mean that you have no money to pay wages in," said I. "But the credit given the worker at the government storehouse answers to his wages with us. How is the amount of the credit given respectively to the workers in different lines determined? By what title does the individual claim his particular share? What is the basis of allotment?"

"His title," replied Dr. Leete, "is his humanity. The basis of his claim is the fact that he is a man."

"The fact that he is a man!" I repeated, incredulously. "Do you possibly mean that all have the same share?"

"Most assuredly."

The readers of this book never having practically known any other arrangement, or perhaps very carefully considered the historical accounts of former epochs in which a very different system prevailed, cannot be expected to appreciate the stupor of amazement into which Dr. Leete's simple statement plunged me.

"You see," he said, smiling, "that it is not merely that we have no money to pay wages in, but, as I said, we have nothing at all answering to your idea of wages."

By this time I had pulled myself together sufficiently to voice some of the criticisms which, man of the nineteenth century as I was, came uppermost in my mind, upon this to me astounding arrangement. "Some men do twice the work of others!" I exclaimed. "Are the clever workmen content with a plan that ranks them with the indifferent?"

"We leave no possible ground for any complaint of injustice," replied Dr. Leete, "by requiring precisely the same measure of service from all."

"How can you do that, I should like to know, when no two men's powers are the same?"

"Nothing could be simpler," was Dr. Leete's reply. "We require of each that he shall make the same effort; that is, we demand of him the best service it is in his power to give."

"And supposing all do the best they can," I answered, "the amount of the product resulting is twice greater from one man than from another."

"Very true," replied Dr. Leete; "but the amount of the resulting product has nothing whatever to do with the question, which is one of desert. Desert is a moral question, and the amount of the product a material quantity. It would be an extraordinary sort of logic which should try to determine a moral question by a material standard. The amount of the effort alone is pertinent to the question of desert. All men who do their best, do the same. A man's endowments, however godlike, merely fix the measure of his duty. The man of great endowments who does not do all he might, though he may do more than a man of small endowments who does his best, is deemed a less deserving worker than the latter, and dies a debtor to his fellows. The Creator sets men's tasks for them by the faculties he gives them; we simply exact their fulfillment."

"No doubt that is very fine philosophy," I said; "nevertheless it seems hard that the man who produces twice as much as another, even if both do their best, should have only the same share."

"Does it, indeed, seem so to you?" responded Dr. Leete. "Now, do you know, that seems very curious to me? The way it strikes people nowadays is, that a man who can produce twice as much as another with the same effort, instead of being rewarded for doing so, ought to be punished if he does not do so. In the nineteenth century, when a horse pulled a heavier load than a goat, I suppose you rewarded him. Now, we should have whipped him soundly if he had not, on the ground that, being much stronger, he ought to. It is singular how ethical standards change." The doctor said this with such a twinkle in his eye that I was obliged to laugh.

"I suppose," I said, "that the real reason that we rewarded men for their endowments, while we considered those of horses and goats merely as fixing the service to be severally required of them, was that the animals, not being reasoning beings, naturally did the best they could, whereas men could only be induced to do so by rewarding them according to the amount of their product. That brings me to ask why, unless human nature has mightily changed in a hundred years, you are not under the same necessity."

"We are," replied Dr. Leete. "I don't think there has been any change in human nature in that respect since your day. It is still so constituted that special incentives in the form of prizes, and advantages to be gained, are requisite to call out the best endeavors of the average man in any direction."

"But what inducement," I asked, "can a man have to put forth his best endeavors when, however much or little he accomplishes, his income remains the same? High characters may be moved by devotion to the common welfare under such a system, but does not the average man tend to rest back on his oar, reasoning that it is of no use to make a special effort, since the effort will not increase his income, nor its withholding diminish it?"

"Does it then really seem to you," answered my companion, "that human nature is insensible to any motives save fear of want and love of luxury, that you should expect security and equality of livelihood to leave them without possible incentives to effort? Your contemporaries did not really think so, though they might fancy they did. When it was a question of the grandest class of efforts, the most absolute self-devotion, they depended on quite other incentives. Not higher wages, but honor and the hope of men's gratitude, patriotism and the inspiration of duty, were the motives which they set before their soldiers when it was a question of dying for the nation, and never was there an age of the world when those motives did not call out what is best and noblest in men. And not only this, but when you come to analyze the love of money which was the general impulse to effort in your day, you find that the dread of want and desire of luxury was but one of several motives which the pursuit of money represented; the others, and with many the more influential, being desire of power, of social position, and reputation for ability and success. So you see that though we have abolished poverty and the fear of it, and inordinate luxury with the hope of it, we have not touched the greater part of the motives which underlay the love of money in former times, or any of those which prompted the supremer sorts of effort. The coarser motives, which no longer move us, have been replaced by higher motives wholly unknown to the mere wage earners of your age. Now that industry of whatever sort is no longer self-service, but service of the nation, patriotism, passion for humanity, impel the worker as in your day they did the soldier. The army of industry is an army, not alone by virtue of its perfect organization, but by reason also of the ardor of self-devotion which animates its members.

"But as you used to supplement the motives of patriotism with the love of glory, in order to stimulate the valor of your soldiers, so do we. Based as our industrial system is on the principle of requiring the same unit of effort from every man, that is, the best he can do, you will see that the means by which we spur the workers to do their best must be a very essential part of our scheme. With us, diligence in the national service is the sole and certain way to public repute, social distinction, and official power. The value of a man's services to society fixes his rank in it. Compared with the effect of our social arrangements in impelling men to be zealous in business, we deem the object lessons of biting poverty and wanton luxury on which you depended a device as weak and uncertain as it was barbaric. The lust of honor even in your sordid day notoriously impelled men to more desperate effort than the love of money could." . . .

CHAPTER 12

The questions which I needed to ask before I could acquire even an outline acquaintance with the institutions of the twentieth century being endless, and Dr. Leete's good nature appearing equally so, we sat up talking for several hours after the ladies left us. Reminding my host of the point at which our talk had broken off that morning, I expressed my curiosity to learn how the organization of the industrial army was made to afford a sufficient stimulus to diligence in the lack of any anxiety on the worker's part as to his livelihood.

"You must understand in the first place," replied the doctor, "that the supply of incentives to effort is but one of the objects sought in the organization we have adopted for the army. The other, and equally important, is to secure for the file leaders and captains of the force, and the great officers of the nation, men of proven abilities, who are pledged by their own careers to hold their followers up to their highest standard of performance and permit no lagging. With a view to these two ends the industrial army is organized. First comes the unclassified grade of common laborers, men of all work, to which all recruits during their first three years belong. This grade is a sort of school, and a very strict one, in which the young men are taught habits of obedience, subordination, and devotion to duty. While the miscellaneous nature of the work done by this force prevents the systematic grading of the workers which is afterwards possible, yet individual records are kept, and excellence receives distinction corresponding with the penalties that negligence incurs. It is not, however, policy with us to permit youthful recklessness or indiscretion, when not deeply culpable, to handicap the future careers of young men, and all who have passed through the unclassified grade without serious disgrace have an equal opportunity to choose the life employment they have most liking for. Having selected this, they enter upon it as apprentices. The length of the apprenticeship naturally differs in different occupations. At the end of it the apprentice becomes a full workman, and a member of his trade or guild. Now not only are the individual records of the apprentices for ability and industry strictly kept, and excellence distinguished by suitable distinctions, but upon the average of his record during apprenticeship the standing given the apprentice among the full workmen depends.

"While the internal organizations of different industries, mechanical and agricultural, differ according to their peculiar conditions, they agree in a general division of their workers into first, second, and third grades, according to ability, and these grades are in many cases subdivided into first and second classes. According to his standing as an apprentice a young man is assigned his place as a first, second, or third grade worker. Of course only young men of unusual ability pass directly from apprenticeship into the first grade of the workers. The most fall into the lower grades, working up as they grow more experienced, at the periodical regradings. These regradings take place in each industry at intervals corresponding with the length of the apprenticeship to that industry, so that merit never need wait long to rise, nor can any rest on past achievements unless they would drop into a lower rank. One of the notable advantages of a high grading is the privilege it gives the worker in electing which of the various branches or processes of his industry he will follow as his specialty. Of course it is not intended that any of these processes shall be disproportionately arduous, but there is often much difference between them, and the privilege of election is accordingly highly prized. So far as possible, indeed, the preferences even of the poorest workmen are considered in assigning them their line of work, because not only their happiness but their usefulness is thus enhanced. While, however, the wish of the lower grade man is consulted so far as the exigencies of the service permit, he is considered only after the upper grade men have been provided for, and often he has to put up with second or third choice, or even with an arbitrary assignment when help is needed. This privilege of election attends every regrading, and when a man loses his grade he also risks having to exchange the sort of work he likes for some other less to his taste. The results of each regrading, giving the standing of every man in his industry, are gazetted in the public prints, and those who have won promotion since the last regrading receive the nation's thanks and are publicly invested with the badge of their new rank."

"What may this badge be?" I asked.

"Every industry has its emblematic device," replied Dr. Leete, "and this, in the shape of a metallic badge so small that you might not see it unless you knew where to look, is all the insignia which the men of the army wear, except where public convenience demands a distinctive uniform. This badge is the same in form for all grades of industry, but while the badge of the third grade is iron, that of the second grade is silver, and that of the first is gilt.

"Apart from the grand incentive to endeavor afforded by the fact that the high places in the nation are open only to the highest class men, and that rank in the army constitutes the only mode of social distinction for the vast majority who are not aspirants in art, literature, and the professions, various incitements of a minor, but perhaps equally effective, sort are provided in the form of special privileges and immunities in the way of discipline, which the superior class men enjoy. These, while intended to be as little as possible invidious to the less successful, have the effect of keeping constantly before every man's mind the great desirability of attaining the grade next above his own. . . .

"I should not fail to mention," resumed the doctor, "that for those too deficient in mental or bodily strength to be fairly graded with the main body of workers, we have a separate grade, unconnected with the others — a sort of invalid corps, the members of which are provided with a light class of tasks fitted to their strength. All our sick in mind and body, all our deaf and dumb, and lame and blind and crippled, and even our insane, belong to this invalid corps, and bear its insignia. The strongest often do nearly a man's work, the feeblest, of course, nothing; but none who can do anything are willing quite to give up. In their lucid intervals, even our insane are eager to do what they can."

"That is a pretty idea of the invalid corps," I said. "Even a barbarian from the nineteenth century can appreciate that. It is a very graceful way of disguising charity, and must be grateful to the feelings of its recipients."

"Charity!" repeated Dr. Leete. "Did you suppose that we consider the incapable class we are talking of objects of charity?"

"Why, naturally," I said, "inasmuch as they are incapable of self-support."

But here the doctor took me up quickly.

"Who is capable of self-support?" he demanded. "There is no such thing in a civilized society as self-support. In a state of society so barbarous as not even to know family cooperation, each individual may possibly support himself, though even then for a part of his life only; but from the moment that men begin to live together, and constitute even the rudest sort of society, self-support becomes impossible. As men grow more civilized, and the subdivision of occupations and services is carried out, a complex mutual dependence becomes the universal rule. Every man, however solitary may seem his occupation, is a member of a vast industrial partnership, as large as the nation, as large as humanity. The necessity of mutual dependence should imply the duty and guarantee of mutual support; and that it did not in your day constituted the essential cruelty and unreason of your system."

"That may all be so," I replied, "but it does not touch the case of those who are unable to contribute anything to the product of industry."

"Surely I told you this morning, at least I thought I did," replied Dr. Leete, "that the right of a man to maintenance at the nation's table depends on the fact that he is a man, and not on the amount of health and strength he may have, so long as he does his best."

"You said so," I answered, "but I supposed the rule applied only to the workers of different ability. Does it also hold of those who can do nothing at all?"

"Are they not also men?"

"I am to understand, then, that the lame, the blind, the sick, and the impotent, are as well off as the most efficient, and have the same income?"

"Certainly," was the reply.

"The idea of charity on such a scale," I answered, "would have made our most enthusiastic philanthropists gasp."

"If you had a sick brother at home," replied Dr. Leete, "unable to work, would you feed him on less dainty food, and lodge and clothe him more poorly, than yourself? More likely far, you would give him the preference; nor would you think of calling it charity. Would not the word, in that connection, fill you with indignation?"

"Of course," I replied; "but the cases are not parallel. There is a sense, no doubt, in which all men are brothers; but this general sort of brotherhood is not to be compared, except for rhetorical purposes, to the brotherhood of blood, either as to its sentiment or its obligations."

"There speaks the nineteenth century!" exclaimed Dr. Leete. "Ah, Mr. West, there is no doubt as to the length of time that you slept. If I were to give you, in one sentence, a key to what may seem the mysteries of our civilization as compared with that of your age, I should say that it is the fact that the solidarity of the race and the brotherhood of man, which to you were but fine phrases, are, to our thinking and feeling, ties as real and as vital as physical fraternity.

"But even setting that consideration aside, I do not see why it so surprises you that those who cannot work are conceded the full right to live on the produce of those who can. Even in your day, the duty of military service for the protection of the nation, to which our industrial service corresponds, while obligatory on those able to discharge it, did not operate to deprive of the privileges of citizenship those who were unable. They stayed at home, and were protected by those who fought, and nobody questioned their right to be, or thought less of them. So, now, the requirement of industrial service from those able to render it does not operate to deprive of the privileges of citizenship, which now implies the citizen's maintenance, him who cannot work. The worker is not a citizen because he works, but works because he is a citizen. As you recognize the duty of the strong to fight for the weak, we, now that fighting is gone by, recognize his duty to work for him.

"A solution which leaves an unaccounted-for residuum is no solution at all; and our solution of the problem of human society would have been none at all had it left the lame, the sick, and the blind outside with the beasts, to fare as they might. Better far have left the strong and well unprovided for than these burdened ones, toward whom every heart must yearn, and for whom ease of mind and body should be provided, if for no others. Therefore it is, as I told you this morning, that the title of every man, woman, and child to the means of existence rests on no basis less plain, broad, and simple than the fact that they are fellows of one race — members of one human family. The only coin current is the image of God, and that is good for all we have.

"I think there is no feature of the civilization of your epoch so repugnant to modern ideas as the neglect with which you treated your dependent classes. Even if you had no pity, no feeling of brotherhood, how was it that you did not see that you were robbing the incapable class of their plain right in leaving them unprovided for?"

"I don't quite follow you there," I said. "I admit the claim of this class to our pity, but how could they who produced nothing claim a share of the product as a right?"

"How happened it," was Dr. Leete's reply, "that your workers were able to produce more than so many savages would have done? Was it not wholly on account of the heritage of the past knowledge and achievements of the race, the machinery of society, thousands of years in contriving, found by you ready-made to your hand? How did you come to be possessors of this knowledge and this machinery, which represent nine parts to one contributed by yourself in the value of your product? You inherited it, did you not? And were not these others, these unfortunate and crippled brothers whom you cast out, joint inheritors, co-heirs with you? What did you do with their share? Did you not rob them when you put them off with crusts, who were entitled to sit with the heirs, and did you not add insult to robbery when you called the crusts charity?

"Ah, Mr. West," Dr. Leete continued, as I did not respond, "what I do not understand is, setting aside all considerations either of justice or brotherly feeling toward the crippled and defective, how the workers of your day could have had any heart for their work, knowing that their children, or grandchildren, if unfortunate, would be deprived of the comforts and even necessities of life. It is a mystery how men with children could favor a system under which they were rewarded beyond those less endowed with bodily strength or mental power. For, by the same discrimination by which the father profited, the son, for whom he would give his life, being perchance weaker than others, might be reduced to crusts and beggary. How men dared leave children behind them, I have never been able to understand." . . .

READING CRITICALLY

1. What is the allegory of the coach about?

2. What, according to Julian West, is the function of government? How does Dr. Leete explain the government's role in managing the economy in the year 2000?

3. What is Dr. Leete's objection to the idea of self-support? Why is he so vehement about the idea that supporting nonproducers is not charity? What is Dr. Leete's argument that nonproducers have a *right* to equal maintenance?

WRITING ANALYTICALLY

1. What are your motives for doing your best? In a personal essay, describe a time when you worked primarily for money or some material reward. Compare it with a time when you worked for some other kind of reward. Does the type of reward affect your performance? Option: Consider further: If all jobs paid the same, would your career plans be different? What do you think of the idea of national service? Of retirement at age forty-five? Of equalizing pay for all jobs as in Bellamy's utopia?

2. Bellamy describes the motives that would lead people to do their best even if pay were not an incentive and if poverty and luxury were both eliminated. In a short essay, summarize Bellamy's argument and discuss whether, from your experience and observation, you think the system he proposes would be likely to work.

3. Dr. Leete claims that individual freedom exists in the world of 2000. Do you think this is so? Write an essay evaluating the way that the system in the year 2000 works: How does it preserve or violate individual freedom? What elements of individualism does the system deliberately try to suppress? Which does it try to preserve? Compared with the social and economic order today, is Bellamy's utopia an improvement?

4. Bellamy says that fear of poverty and desire for luxury are "barbaric" motives, yet the Gospel of Wealth says that these are good motives. Write an essay comparing and contrasting Bellamy's position with that of Andrew Carnegie, and then argue for your own position on this issue.

HENRY DEMAREST LLOYD

From *Wealth against Commonwealth* (1894)

Henry Demarest Lloyd (1847–1903) was a lawyer, political reformer, and journalist. As a financial writer for the *Chicago Tribune* beginning in 1872, he immersed himself in research on the business dealings of the great corporations of the day — railroads, steel, and oil — and soon began to write about the interconnections among these industries. In 1881, Lloyd published an enormously popular article in the *Atlantic Monthly* detailing the collusion between Standard Oil and several railroads to fix prices and drive out competitors. This piece was followed by a series of articles on the efforts of big industries to gain monopolies on essential products and services, to fix prices, and to profit from stock and land speculation.

Lloyd also engaged in direct political activity. Though not a supporter of socialism, he worked on behalf of the Haymarket defendants — socialists who were sentenced to death for a bombing in Haymarket Square, Chicago, on May 4, 1886, that they clearly had no hand in — and was able to help get some of the sentences commuted. (Four defendants were hanged and all were pardoned — posthumously for the executed four — a few years later.) Lloyd wrote a book about the Spring Valley coal strike, criticizing the "industrial oppression" of the miners, and then in 1894 published *Wealth against Commonwealth*, an elaborately detailed follow-up account of the collusion between Standard Oil and the railroads and the failure or unwillingness of the government and courts to intervene. Though widely popular, like his earlier articles on the same subject, the book did not cause a public demand for reform, and no reforms followed. In the excerpt printed here, from chapter 34, "The Old Self-Interest," Lloyd speaks in general about the problem of wealth and society.

THE CORN OF THE COMING HARVEST is growing so fast that, like the farmer standing at night in his fields, we can hear it snap and crackle. We have been fighting fire on the well-worn lines of old-fashioned politics and political economy, regulating corporations, and leaving competition to regulate itself. But the flames of a new economic evolution run around us, and we turn to find that competition has killed competition, that corporations are grown greater than the State and have bred individuals greater than themselves, and that the naked issue of our time is with property becoming master instead of servant, property in many necessaries of life becoming monopoly of the necessaries of life.

Henry Demarest Lloyd, *Wealth against Commonwealth*, edited with an introduction by Thomas C. Cochran (1894; reprint, Englewood Cliffs, N.J.: Prentice-Hall, 1963), 159–70.
   In the notes, EDS. = Patricia Bizzell and Bruce Herzberg.

We are still, in part, as Emerson[1] says, in the quadruped state. Our industry is a fight of every man for himself. The prize we give the fittest is monopoly of the necessaries of life, and we leave these winners of the powers of life and death to wield them over us by the same "self-interest" with which they took them from us. In all this we see at work a "principle" which will go into the records as one of the historic mistakes of humanity. Institutions stand or fall by their philosophy, and the main doctrine of industry since Adam Smith[2] has been the fallacy that the self-interest of the individual was a sufficient guide to the welfare of the individual and society. . . .

"It is a law of business for each proprietor to pursue his own interest," said the committee of Congress which in 1893 investigated the coal combinations. "There is no hope for any of us, but the weakest must go first," is the golden rule of business. There is no other field of human associations in which any such rule of action is allowed. The man who should apply in his family or his citizenship this "survival of the fittest" theory as it is practically professed and operated in business would be a monster, and would be speedily made extinct, as we do with monsters. To divide the supply of food between himself and his children according to their relative powers of calculation, to follow his conception of his own self-interest in any matter which the self-interest of all has taken charge of, to deal as he thinks best for himself with foreigners with whom his country is at war, would be a short road to the penitentiary or the gallows. In trade men have not yet risen to the level of the family life of the animals. The true law of business is that all must pursue the interest of all. In the law, the highest product of civilization, this has long been a commonplace. The safety of the people is the supreme law. We are in travail to bring industry up to this. Our century of the caprice of the individual as the lawgiver of the common toil, to employ or disemploy, to start or stop, to open or close, to compete or combine, has been the disorder of the school while the master slept. The happiness, self-interest, or individuality of the whole is not more sacred than that of each, but it is greater. They are equal in quality, but in quantity they are greater. In the ultimate which the mathematician, the poet, the reformer projects the two will coincide.

Meanwhile, we who are the creators of society have got the times out of joint,[3] because, less experienced than the Creator of the balanced matter of earth, we have given the precedence to the powers on one side. As gods we are but half-grown. For a hundred years or so our economic theory has been one of industrial government by the self-interest of the individual.

[1]Ralph Waldo Emerson (1803–82), the great American writer and philosopher. (See selection from Emerson in Unit Three, p. 346.) — EDS.

[2]The economist Adam Smith (1723–90) wrote *Wealth of Nations* (1776), in which he developed the theory of free-market economics. — EDS.

[3]Lloyd is alluding to *Hamlet:* "The time is out of joint. O cursed spite, / That ever I was born to set it right" (1.5.196–97). — EDS.

Political government by the self-interest of the individual we call anarchy.[4] It is one of the paradoxes of public opinion that the people of America, least tolerant of this theory of anarchy in political government, lead in practicing it in industry. Politically, we are civilized; industrially, not yet. Our century, given to this *laissez-faire*[5] — "leave the individual alone; he will do what is best for himself, and what is best for him is best for all" — has done one good: It has put society at the mercy of its own ideals, and has produced an actual anarchy in industry which is horrifying us into a change of doctrines.

The true *laissez-faire* is, let the individual do what the individual can do best, and let the community do what the community can do best. The *laissez-faire* of social self-interest, if true, cannot conflict with the individual self-interest, if true, but it must outrank it always. What we have called "free competition" has not been free, only freer than what went before. The free is still to come. . . .

Where the self-interest of the individual is allowed to be the rule both of social and personal action, the level of all is forced down to that of the lowest. Business excuses itself for the things it does — cuts in wages, exactions in hours, tricks of competition — on the plea that the merciful are compelled to follow the cruel. . . . When the self-interest of society is made the standard the lowest must rise to the average. The one pulls down, the other up. That men's hearts are bad and that bad men will do bad things has a truth in it. But whatever the general average of morals, the anarchy which gives such individuals their head and leaves them to set the pace for all will produce infinitely worse results than a policy which applies mutual checks and inspirations. Bad kings make bad reigns, but monarchy is bad because it is arbitrary power, and that, whether it be political or industrial, makes even good men bad.

A partial truth universally applied as this of self-interest has been is a universal error. Everything goes to defeat. Highways are used to prevent travel and traffic. Ownership of the means of production is sought in order to "shut down" production, and the means of plenty make famine. All follow self-interest to find that though they have created marvelous wealth it is not theirs. We pledge "our lives, our fortunes, and our sacred honor"[6] to establish the rule of the majority, and end by finding that the minority — a minority in morals, money, and men — are our masters whichever way we turn. We agonize over "economy," but sell all our grain and pork and oil and cotton at exchanges where we pay brokerage on a hundred or a thousand barrels or bushels or bales of wind to get one real one sold. These intolerabilities — sweatshops where model merchants buy and sell the cast-off scarlet-fever skins of the poor, factory and mine where childhood is forbidden to become manhood and manhood is forbidden to

[4]Anarchy is a form of socialism that seeks the elimination of government. — EDS.

[5] *"Laissez-faire"* (from the French "allow it to do") is the economic theory that government should not regulate the market but should allow it to do as it will. — EDS.

[6]Lloyd is quoting the Declaration of Independence (see p. 174). — EDS.

die a natural death, mausoleums in which we bury the dead rich, slums in which we bury the living poor, coal pools with their manufacture of artificial winter — all these are the rule of private self-interest arrived at its destination. . . .

We are very poor. The striking feature of our economic condition is our poverty, not our wealth. We make ourselves "rich" by appropriating the property of others by methods which lessen the total property of all. Spain took such riches from America and grew poor. Modern wealth more and more resembles the winnings of speculators in bread during famine — worse, for to make the money it makes the famine. What we call cheapness shows itself to be unnatural fortunes for a very few, monstrous luxury for them and proportionate deprivation for the people, judges debauched, trustees dishonored, Congress and State legislatures insulted and defied, when not seduced, multitudes of honest men ruined and driven to despair. . . .

Syndicates,[7] by one stroke, get the power of selling dear on one side, and producing cheap on the other. Thus they keep themselves happy, prices high, and the people hungry. What model merchant could ask more? The dream of the king who wished that all his people had but one neck that he might decapitate them at one blow is realized today in this industrial garrote. The syndicate has but to turn its screw, and every neck begins to break. Prices paid to such intercepters are not an exchange of service; they are ransom paid by the people for their lives. The ability of the citizen to pay may fluctuate; what he must pay remains fixed, or advances like the rent of the Irish tenant to the absentee landlord until the community interfered. Those who have this power to draw the money from the people — from every railroad station, every streetcar, every fireplace, every saltcellar, every breadpan, washboard, and coal scuttle — to their own safes have the further incentive to make this money worth the most possible. By contracting the issue of currency and contracting it again by hoarding it in their banks, safe-deposit vaults, and the government treasury, they can depress the prices of all that belongs to the people. Their own prices are fixed. These are "regular prices," established by price lists. Given, as a ruling motive, the principles of business—to get the most and give the least; given the legal and economic, physical and mechanical control, possible under our present social arrangements, to the few over the many, and the certain end of all this, if unarrested, unreversed, can be nothing less than a return to chattel slavery. There may be some finer name, but the fact will not be finer. Between our present tolerance and our completed subjection the distance is not so far as that from the equality and simplicity of our Pilgrim Fathers to ourselves.

Everything withers — even charity. Aristocratic benevolence spends a shrunken stream in comparison with democratic benevolence. In an ad-

---

[7]Syndicates are combinations of companies that control all or most of a single industry from production to distribution in an attempt to impede outside competition; also known as *cartels.* — EDS.

dress to the public, soliciting subscriptions, the Committee of the United Hospitals Association of New York said, in December, 1893: "The committee have found that, through the obliteration of old methods of individual competition by the establishment of large corporations and trusts in modern times, the income of such charitable institutions as are supported by the individual gifts of the benevolent has been seriously affected."

In the worst governments and societies that have existed one good can be seen — so good that the horrors of them fall back into secondary places as extrinsic, accidental. That good is the ability of men to lead the life together. The more perfect monopoly makes itself the more does it bring into strong lights the greatest fact of our industry, of far more permanent value than the greed which has for the moment made itself the cynosure of all eyes. It makes this fair world more fair to consider the loyalties, intelligences, docilities of the multitudes who are guarding, developing, operating with the faithfulness of brothers and the keen interest of owners properties and industries in which brotherhood is not known and their title is not more than a tenancy at will. One of the largest stones in the arch of "consolidation," perhaps the keystone, is that men have become so intelligent, so responsive and responsible, so cooperative that they can be entrusted in great masses with the care of vast properties owned entirely by others and with the operation of complicated processes, although but a slender cost of subsistence is awarded them out of fabulous profits. The spectacle of the million and more employees of the railroads of this country despatching trains, maintaining tracks, collecting fares and freights, and turning over hundreds of millions of net profits to the owners, not one in a thousand of whom would know how to do the simplest of these things for himself, is possible only where civilization has reached a high average of morals and culture. More and more the mills and mines and stores, and even the farms and forests, are being administered by others than the owners. The virtue of the people is taking the place Poor Richard[8] thought only the eye of the owner could fill. If mankind, driven by their fears and the greed of others, can do so well, what will be their productivity and cheer when the "interest of all" sings them to their work?

This new morality and new spring of wealth have been seized first by the appropriating ones among us. But, as has been in government, their intervention of greed is but a passing phase. Mankind belongs to itself, not to kings or monopolists, and will supersede the one as surely as the other with the institutions of democracy. Yes, Callicles, said Socrates, the greatest are usually the bad, for they have the power.[9] If power could continue paternal and benign, mankind would not be rising through one emancipation after another into a progressive communion of equalities. The individual and society will always be wrestling with each other in a composition of forces. But to just the extent to which civilization prevails, society will be

---

[8]Benjamin Franklin used the pseudonym "Poor Richard" to give economic and ethical advice in his journal *Poor Richard's Almanac.* — EDS.

[9]Plato, *Gorgias,* 526. — EDS.

held as inviolable as the individual; not subordinate — indeed inaudible — as now in the counting room and corporation office. We have overworked the self-interest of the individual. The line of conflict between individual and social is a progressive one of the discovery of point after point in which the two are identical. Society thus passes from conflict to harmony, and on to another conflict. Civilization is the unceasing accretion of these social solutions. We fight out to an equilibrium, as in the abolition of human slavery; then upon this new level thus built up we enter upon the struggle for a new equilibrium, as now in the labor movement. The man for himself destroys himself and all men; only society can foster him and them.

Children yet, we run everything we do — love or war, work or leisure, religion or liberty — to excess. Every possibility of body and mind must be played upon till it is torn to pieces, as toys by children. Priests, voluptuaries, tyrants, knights, ascetics — in the long procession of fanatics a newcomer takes his place; he is called "the model merchant" — the cruelest fanatic in history. He is the product of ages given to progressive devotion to "trading." He is the high priest of the latest idolatry, the self-worship of self-interest. Whirling dervish of the market, self, friends, and family, body and soul, loves, hopes, and faith, all are sacrificed to seeing how many "turns" he can make before he drops dead. Trade began, Sir Henry Sumner Maine[10] tells us, not within the family or community, but without. Its first appearances are on the neutral borderland between hostile tribes. There, in times of peace, they meet to trade, and think it no sin that "the buyer must beware" since the buyer is an enemy. Trade has spread thence, carrying with itself into family and State the poison of enmity. From the fatherhood of the old patriarchal life, where father and brother sold each other nothing, the world has chaffered along to the anarchy of a "free" trade which sells everything. One thing after another has passed out from under the regime of brotherhood and passed in under that of bargainhood. . . .

Conceptions of duty take on a correspondingly unnatural complexion. The main exhortations the world gives beginners are how to "get on" — the getting on so ardently inculcated being to get, like the old-man-of-the-sea,[11] on somebody's back. "If war fails you in the country where you are, you must go where there is war," said one of the successful men of the fourteenth century to a young knight who asked him for the Laws of Life. "I shall be perfectly satisfied with you," I heard one of the great business geniuses of America say to his son, "if you will only always go to bed at night worth more than when you got up in the morning." The system grows, as all systems do, more complicated, and gets further away from its first purposes of barter of real things and services. It goes more under the hands of men of apt selfishness, who push it further away from general

---

[10]Sir Henry Sumner Maine (1822–88) was an English historian. — EDS.

[11]Nereus, one of the Greek gods of the sea and father of the Nereids, was called the "Old Man of the Sea." He is often depicted wrestling with Hercules. — EDS.

comprehension and the general good. Tariffs, currencies, finances, freight-rate sheets, the laws, become instruments of privilege, and just in proportion become puzzles no people can decipher. "I have a right to buy my labor where I can buy it cheapest" — beginning as a protest against the selfish exclusions of antiquated trade guilds outgrown by the new times — has at last come to mean, "I have a right to do anything to cheapen the labor I want to buy, even to destroying the family life of the people."

When steaming kettles grew into beasts of burden and public highways dwindled into private property administered by private motives for private ends, all previous tendencies were intensified into a sudden whirl redistributing wealth and labors. It appears to have been the destiny of the railroad to begin and of oil to lubricate to its finish the last stage of this crazy commercialism. Business colors the modern world as war reddened the ancient world. Out of such delirium monsters are bred, and their excesses destroy the system that brought them forth. There is a strong suggestion of moral insanity in the unrelieved sameness of mood and unvarying repetition of one act in the life in the model merchant. Sane minds by an irresistible law alternate one tension with another. Only a lunatic is always smiling or always weeping or always clamoring for dividends. Eras show their last stages by producing men who sum up individually the morbid characteristics of the mass. When the crisis comes in which the gathering tendencies of generations shoot forward in the avalanche, there is born some group of men perfect for their function — good be it or bad. They need to take time for no second thought, and will not delay the unhalting reparations of nature by so much as the time given to one tear over the battlefield or the bargain. With their birth their mission is given them, whether it be the mission of Lucifer or Gabriel.[12] This mission becomes their conscience. The righteous indignation that other men feel against sin these men feel against that which withstands them. Sincere as rattlesnakes, they are selfish with the unconsciousness possible to only the entirely commonplace, without the curiosity to question their times or the imagination to conceive the pain they inflict, and their every ideal is satisfied by the conventionalities of church, parlor, and counting room. These men are the touchstones to wither the cant of an age.

We preach "Do as you would be done by" in our churches, and "A fair exchange no robbery" in our counting rooms, and "All citizens are equal as citizens" in courts and Congress. Just as we are in danger of believing that to say these things is to do them and be them, there come unto us these men, practical as granite and gravitation. Taking their cue not from our lips, but from our lives, they better the instruction, and, passing easily to the high seats at every table, prove that we are liars and hypocrites. Their only secret is that they do, better than we, the things we are all trying to do, but of which in our morning and evening prayers, seen of all men, we are continually making believe to pray: Good Lord, deliver us! When the hour strikes for such leaders, they come and pass as by a law of nature

---

[12]Lucifer is one of the names of Satan; Gabriel is an angel. — Eds.

to the front. All follow them. It is their fate and ours that they must work out to the end the destiny interwoven of their own insatiate ambition and the false ideals of us who have created them and their opportunity.

If our civilization is destroyed, as Macaulay[13] predicted, it will not be by his barbarians from below. Our barbarians come from above. Our great moneymakers have sprung in one generation into seats of power kings do not know. The forces and the wealth are new, and have been the opportunity of new men. Without restraints of culture, experience, the pride, or even the inherited caution of class or rank, these men, intoxicated, think they are the wave instead of the float, and that they have created the business which has created them. To them science is but a never-ending repertoire of investments stored up by nature for the syndicates, government but a fountain of franchises, the nations but customers in squads, and a million the unit of a new arithmetic of wealth written for them. They claim a power without control, exercised through forms which make it secret, anonymous, and perpetual. The possibilities of its gratification have been widening before them without interruption since they began, and even at a thousand millions they will feel no satiation and will see no place to stop. They are gluttons of luxury and power, rough, unsocialized, believing that mankind must be kept terrorized. Powers of pity die out of them, because they work through agents and die in their agents, because what they do is not for themselves.

Of gods, friends, learnings, of the uncomprehended civilization they overrun, they ask but one question: How much? What is a good time to sell? What is a good time to buy? The Church and the Capitol, incarnating the sacrifices and triumphs of a procession of martyrs and patriots since the dawn of freedom, are good enough for a money changer's shop[14] for them, and a market and shambles. Their heathen eyes see in the law and its consecrated officers nothing but an intelligence office and hired men to help them burglarize the treasures accumulated for thousands of years at the altars of liberty and justice, that they may burn their marbles for the lime of commerce.[15]

Business motivated by the self-interest of the individual runs into monopoly at every point it touches the social life — land monopoly, transportation monopoly, trade monopoly, political monopoly in all its forms, from contraction of the currency to corruption in office. The society in which in half a lifetime a man without a penny can become a hundred times a millionaire is as overripe, industrially, as was, politically, the Rome in which the most popular bully could lift himself from the ranks of the legion on to the throne of the Caesars. Our rising issue is with business. Monopoly is business at the end of its journey. It has got there. The irrepress-

---

[13]Thomas Babington Macaulay (1800–59), a respected English critic, historian, and statesman, referred to the fall of civilization in several of his essays and books. — EDS.

[14]See the biblical story of Jesus chasing the money-changers from the Temple (Matthew 21:12, Mark 11:15, Luke 19:45, John 2:14). — EDS.

[15]Marble is a form of limestone. Lloyd means that it would be barbaric to destroy marble statues to get the limestone needed for industry. — EDS.

ible conflict is now as distinctly with business as the issue so lately met was with slavery. Slavery went first only because it was the cruder form of business.

Our tyrants are our ideals incarnating themselves in men born to command. What these men are we have made them. All governments are representative governments; none of them more so than our government of industry. We go hopelessly astray if we seek the solution of our problems in the belief that our business rulers are worse men in kind than ourselves. Worse in degree; yes. It is a race to the bad, and the winners are the worst. A system in which the prizes go to meanness invariably marches with the meanest men at the head. But if any could be meaner than the meanest it would be they who run and fail and rail.

Every idea finds its especially susceptible souls. These men are our most susceptible souls to the idea of individual self-interest. They have believed implicitly what we have taught, and have been the most faithful in trying to make the talent given them grow into ten talents.[16] They rise superior to our halfhearted social corrections: publicity, private competition, all devices of market opposition, private litigation, public investigation, legislation, and criminal prosecution — all. Their power is greater today than it was yesterday, and will be greater tomorrow. The public does not withhold its favor, but deals with them, protects them, refuses to treat their crimes as it treats those of the poor, and admits them to the highest places. The predominant mood is the more or less concealed regret of the citizens that they have not been able to conceive and execute the same lucky stroke or some other as profitable. The conclusion is irresistible that men so given the lead are the representatives of the real "spirit of the age," and that the protestants against them are not representative of our times — are at best but intimators of times which may be.

Two social energies have been in conflict, and the energy of reform has so far proved the weaker. We have chartered the self-interest of the individual as the rightful sovereign of conduct; we have taught that the scramble for profit is the best method of administering the riches of earth and the exchange of services. Only those can attack this system who attack its central principle, that strength gives the strong in the market the right to destroy his neighbor. Only as we have denied that right to the strong elsewhere have we made ourselves as civilized as we are. And we cannot make a change as long as our songs, customs, catchwords, and public opinion tell all to do the same thing if they can. Society, in each person of its multitudes, must recognize that the same principles of the interest of all being the rule of all, of the strong serving the weak, of the first being the last — "I am among you as one that serves"[17] — which have given us the home where the weakest is the one surest of his rights and of the fullest service of

---

[16]A talent is an ancient coin. Lloyd alludes to the biblical parable of the talents in Matthew 25:14–30. — EDS.

[17]"The first shall be last": see Matthew 19:30. "I am among you as one who serves": see Luke 22:27. — EDS.

the strongest, and have given us the republic in which all join their labor that the poorest may be fed, the weakest defended, and all educated and prospered, must be applied where men associate in common toil as wherever they associate. Not until then can the forces be reversed which generate those obnoxious persons — our fittest.

Our system, so fair in its theory and so fertile in its happiness and prosperity in its first century, is now, following the fate of systems, becoming artificial, technical, corrupt; and, as always happens in human institutions, after noon, power is stealing from the many to the few. Believing wealth to be good, the people believed the wealthy to be good. But, again in history, power has intoxicated and hardened its possessors, and Pharaohs[18] are bred in counting rooms as they were in palaces. Their furniture must be banished to the world garret, where lie the outworn trappings of the guilds and slavery and other old lumber of human institutions.

READING CRITICALLY

1. How does Lloyd refute the argument that "survival of the fittest" is the rule by which the economy must run? What effect does he wish to achieve by saying that "in trade men have not yet risen to the level of the family life of the animals" (p. 502)?

2. What contrast does Lloyd draw between the political and economic principles that guide the United States? How does he connect political anarchy and laissez-faire economics?

3. Lloyd quotes a report from a charitable foundation to the effect that the concentration of wealth has reduced total charitable giving (p. 505). How does Lloyd account for this phenomenon?

4. Lloyd comments extensively on the fact that workers take good care of the property of the owners and carry out complicated processes in cooperation. To what does he attribute this behavior?

WRITING ANALYTICALLY

1. "We go hopelessly astray if we seek the solution of our problems in the belief that our business rulers are worse men in kind than ourselves. Worse in degree; yes. It is a race to the bad, and the winners are the worst" (p. 509). Write an essay explaining what Lloyd means by this statement. Begin by summarizing, first, the problems he identifies and, second, what he regards as the main cause or causes of those problems. Finally, consider the point he is trying to make in the quoted passage (a point he develops through the last four paragraphs of his essay). What is he saying? What kinds of argument or evidence does he use to support this contention? Do you find his argument convincing?

[18]The pharaohs were the kings of Egypt. See Exodus 1–15. — EDS.

2. Lloyd uses a large number of biblical references in his essay, most of which are identified in footnotes. Write an essay in which you analyze Lloyd's use of these biblical allusions. In what passages is he explicitly refuting the "Gospel of Wealth" arguments? In your opinion, is the use of biblical allusions an effective rhetorical strategy? How much familiarity with the Bible must a reader have to be affected by these allusions?

3. In what way is Lloyd answering Carnegie's argument in "Wealth"? Write an essay contrasting Lloyd's arguments with Carnegie's.

HENRY GEORGE

From *Progress and Poverty* (1879)

Henry George (1839–97) worked as a sailor, a gold hunter in California, a printer, and a journalist. He was struck, in all his travels, by the great wealth being produced by the new technologies of the time and the great contrast between that wealth and the grinding poverty of those who worked — or were unable to get work — in the new industries. In a pamphlet called *Our Land and Land Policies* (1871), George calls for an end to land speculation through a land tax that would supplant all other taxes. He develops these ideas at greater length in *Progress and Poverty* (1879), written while he himself was living in poverty in New York. The book was a best-seller, surprising the many publishers who had turned down the manuscript because they believed that books on economics didn't sell. George elaborated the ideas in *Progress and Poverty* in six more books and a weekly periodical, *The Standard*. He was supported by the organized labor movement in two campaigns for mayor of New York, lectured extensively in the United States and Europe, and inspired the creation of many single-tax societies and clubs, but his ideas never influenced land or tax policy in the United States. His supporters founded the Henry George School of Social Science in Chicago.

In the excerpts here, George analyzes the economic ideas that led, in his view, to the creation of poverty during a period when the wealth of industrial nations was expanding rapidly. The root problem, George argues, is the private ownership of land. The landowner charges rent but does not contribute to production. Rent simply eats up profits that should go to wages and interest on capital investments. To achieve the effect of making land common property, George proposes to tax land at 100 percent of its rental value and to eliminate all other taxes entirely. As George explains, no one could then afford to keep land for speculation only. If the land were not being used productively (for a house or a business), there would be no point in having it at all. He argues that imposing a single tax would thus benefit both capitalists

Henry George, *Progress and Poverty* (1879; reprint, New York: Robert Schalkenbach Foundation, 1992), 221–24, 294–96, 313, 328, 333–42, 388–94.
    In the notes, HG = Henry George, EDS. = Patricia Bizzell and Bruce Herzberg.

and laborers, drive away speculators, allow more businesses and farms to operate, and thereby distribute more sensibly the fruits of a vast system of production.

INTRODUCTORY: THE PROBLEM

THE PRESENT CENTURY HAS BEEN MARKED by a prodigious increase in wealth-producing power. The utilization of steam and electricity, the introduction of improved processes and labor-saving machinery, the greater subdivision and grander scale of production, the wonderful facilitation of exchanges, have multiplied enormously the effectiveness of labor.

At the beginning of this marvelous era it was natural to expect, and it was expected, that labor-saving inventions would lighten the toil and improve the condition of the laborer; that the enormous increase in the power of producing wealth would make real poverty a thing of the past. Could a man of the last century — a Franklin or a Priestley[1] — have seen, in a vision of the future, the steamship taking the place of the sailing vessel, the railroad train of the wagon, the reaping machine of the scythe, the threshing machine of the flail; could he have heard the throb of the engines that in obedience to human will, and for the satisfaction of human desire, exert a power greater than that of all the men and all the beasts of burden of the earth combined; could he have seen the forest tree transformed into finished lumber — into doors, sashes, blinds, boxes, or barrels, with hardly the touch of a human hand; the great workshops where boots and shoes are turned out by the case with less labor than the old-fashioned cobbler could have put on a sole; the factories where, under the eye of a girl, cotton becomes cloth faster than hundreds of stalwart weavers could have turned it out with their hand looms; could he have seen steam hammers shaping mammoth shafts and mighty anchors, and delicate machinery making tiny watches; the diamond drill cutting through the heart of the rocks, and coal oil sparing the whale; could he have realized the enormous saving of labor resulting from improved facilities of exchange and communication — sheep killed in Australia eaten fresh in England, and the order given by the London banker in the afternoon executed in San Francisco in the morning of the same day; could he have conceived of the hundred thousand improvements which these only suggest, what would he have inferred as to the social condition of mankind?

It would not have seemed like an inference; further than the vision went it would have seemed as though he saw; and his heart would have

---

[1]Benjamin Franklin (1706–90), American statesman, philosopher, and inventor, and Joseph Priestley (1733–1804), English clergyman and chemist, were scientists who would have seen the significance of the technological advances George describes in the rest of the paragraph. — EDS.

leaped and his nerves would have thrilled, as one who from a height beholds just ahead of the thirst-stricken caravan the living gleam of rustling woods and the glint of laughing waters. Plainly, in the sight of the imagination, he would have beheld these new forces elevating society from its very foundations, lifting the very poorest above the possibility of want, exempting the very lowest from anxiety for the material needs of life; he would have seen these slaves of the lamp of knowledge taking on themselves the traditional curse, these muscles of iron and sinews of steel making the poorest laborer's life a holiday, in which every high quality and noble impulse could have scope to grow.

And out of these bounteous material conditions he would have seen arising, as necessary sequences, moral conditions realizing the golden age of which mankind have always dreamed. Youth no longer stunted and starved; age no longer harried by avarice; the child at play with the tiger; the man with the muck rake drinking in the glory of the stars. Foul things fled, fierce things tame; discord turned to harmony! For how could there be greed where all had enough? How could the vice, the crime, the ignorance, the brutality, that spring from poverty and the fear of poverty, exist where poverty had vanished? Who should crouch where all were freemen; who oppress where all were peers?

More or less vague or clear, these have been the hopes, these the dreams born of the improvements which give this wonderful century its preeminence. They have sunk so deeply into the popular mind as radically to change the currents of thought, to recast creeds, and displace the most fundamental conceptions. The haunting visions of higher possibilities have not merely gathered splendor and vividness, but their direction has changed — instead of seeing behind the faint tinges of an expiring sunset, all the glory of the daybreak has decked the skies before.

It is true that disappointment has followed disappointment, and that discovery upon discovery, and invention after invention, have neither lessened the toil of those who most need respite, nor brought plenty to the poor. But there have been so many things to which it seemed this failure could be laid, that up to our time the new faith has hardly weakened. We have better appreciated the difficulties to be overcome; but not the less trusted that the tendency of the times was to overcome them.

Now, however, we are coming into collision with facts which there can be no mistaking. From all parts of the civilized world come complaints of industrial depression; of labor condemned to involuntary idleness; of capital massed and wasting; of pecuniary distress among businessmen; of want and suffering and anxiety among the working classes. All the dull, deadening pain, all the keen, maddening anguish, that to great masses of men are involved in the words "hard times," afflict the world today. This state of things, common to communities differing so widely in situation, in political institutions, in fiscal and financial systems, in density of population and in social organization, can hardly be accounted for by local causes. There is distress where large standing armies are maintained, but there is also distress where the standing armies are nominal; there is distress where protective tariffs stupidly and wastefully hamper trade, but there is also distress where trade is nearly free; there is distress where autocratic government yet prevails, but there is also distress where political power is wholly in the hands of the people; in countries where paper is money, and in countries where gold and silver are the only currency. Evidently, beneath all such things as these, we must infer a common cause.

That there is a common cause, and that it is either what we call material progress or something closely connected with material progress, becomes more than an inference when it is noted that the phenomena we class together and speak of as industrial depression are but intensifications of phenomena which always accompany material progress, and which show themselves more clearly and strongly as material progress goes on. Where the conditions to which material progress everywhere tends are most fully realized — that is to say, where population is densest, wealth greatest, and the machinery of production and exchange most highly developed — we find the deepest poverty, the sharpest struggle for existence, and the most of enforced idleness.

It is to the newer countries — that is, to the countries where material progress is yet in its earlier stages — that laborers emigrate in search of higher wages, and capital flows in search of higher interest. It is in the older countries — that is to say, the countries where material progress has reached later stages — that widespread destitution is found in the midst of the greatest abundance. Go into one of the new communities where Anglo-Saxon vigor is just beginning the race of progress; where the machinery of production and exchange is yet rude and inefficient; where the increment of wealth is not yet great enough to enable any class to live in ease and luxury; where the best house is but a cabin of logs or a cloth and paper shanty, and the richest man is forced to daily work — and though you will find an absence of wealth and all its concomitants, you will find no beggars. There is no luxury, but there is no destitution. No one makes an easy living, nor a very good living; but every one *can* make a living, and no one able and willing to work is oppressed by the fear of want.

But just as such a community realizes the conditions which all civilized communities are striving for, and advances in the scale of material progress — just as closer settlement and a more intimate connection with the rest of the world, and greater utilization of labor-saving machinery, make possible greater economies in production and exchange, and wealth in consequence increases, not merely in the aggregate, but in proportion to population — so does poverty take a darker aspect. Some get an infinitely better and easier living, but others find it hard to get a living at all. The "tramp" comes with the locomotive, and almshouses and prisons are as surely the marks of "material progress" as are costly dwellings, rich warehouses, and magnificent churches. . . .

This fact — the great fact that poverty and all its concomitants show themselves in communities just as they develop into the conditions toward which material progress tends — proves that the social difficulties existing wherever a certain stage of progress has been reached, do not arise from local circumstances, but are, in some way or another, engendered by progress itself.

And, unpleasant as it may be to admit it, it is at last becoming evident that the enormous increase in productive power which has marked the present century and is still going on with accelerating ratio, has no tendency to extirpate poverty or to lighten the burdens of those compelled to toil. It simply widens the gulf between Dives and Lazarus,[2] and makes the struggle for existence more intense. The march of invention has clothed mankind with powers of which a century ago the boldest imagination could not have dreamed. But in factories where labor-saving machinery has reached its most wonderful development, little children are at work; wherever the new forces are anything like fully utilized, large classes are maintained by charity or live on the verge of recourse to it; amid the greatest accumulations of wealth, men die of starvation, and puny infants suckle dry breasts; while everywhere the greed of gain, the worship of wealth, shows the force of the fear of want. The promised land flies before us like the mirage. The fruits of the tree of knowledge turn as we grasp them to apples of Sodom[3] that crumble at the touch.

It is true that wealth has been greatly increased, and that the average of comfort, leisure, and refinement has been raised; but these gains are not general. In them the lowest class do not share.[4] I do not mean that the condition of the lowest class has nowhere nor in anything been improved; but that there is nowhere any improvement which can be credited to increased productive power. I mean that the tendency of what we call material progress is in nowise to improve the condition of the lowest class in the essentials of healthy, happy human life. Nay, more, that it is still further to depress the condition of the lowest class. The new forces, elevating in their nature though they be, do not act upon the social fabric from underneath, as was for a long time hoped and believed, but strike it at a point intermediate between top and bottom. It is as though an immense wedge were being forced, not underneath society, but through society. Those who are above the point of separation are elevated, but those who are below are crushed down. . . .

This association of poverty with progress is the great enigma of our

---

[2]In the biblical story, Lazarus is a poor man who is refused food by a wealthy man (traditionally called Dives). When the two men die, Lazarus goes to heaven and the rich man goes to hell. (See Luke 16:19–31.) — EDS.

[3]The tree of knowledge was in the Garden of Eden (Genesis 2). The wicked city of Sodom was destroyed by God (Genesis 19). — EDS.

[4]It is true that the poorest may now in certain ways enjoy what the richest a century ago could not have commanded, but this does not show improvement of condition so long as the ability to obtain the necessaries of life is not increased. The beggar in a great city may enjoy many things from which the backwoods farmer is debarred, but that does not prove the condition of the city beggar better than that of the independent farmer. — HG

times. It is the central fact from which spring industrial, social, and political difficulties that perplex the world, and with which statesmanship and philanthropy and education grapple in vain. From it come the clouds that overhang the future of the most progressive and self-reliant nations. It is the riddle which the Sphinx of Fate[5] puts to our civilization and which not to answer is to be destroyed. So long as all the increased wealth which modern progress brings goes but to build up great fortunes, to increase luxury and make sharper the contrast between the House of Have and the House of Want, progress is not real and cannot be permanent. The reaction must come. The tower leans from its foundations, and every new story but hastens the final catastrophe. To educate men who must be condemned to poverty, is but to make them restive; to base on a state of most glaring social inequality political institutions under which men are theoretically equal, is to stand a pyramid on its apex.

All-important as this question is, pressing itself from every quarter painfully upon attention, it has not yet received a solution which accounts for all the facts and points to any clear and simple remedy. . . .

I propose in the following pages to attempt to solve by the methods of political economy the great problem I have outlined. I propose to seek the law which associates poverty with progress, and increases want with advancing wealth. . . .

. . . If the conclusions that we reach run counter to our prejudices, let us not flinch; if they challenge institutions that have long been deemed wise and natural, let us not turn back.

[*In the next several chapters, George asks why, if productive power is increasing, wages tend to fall to the minimum necessary for subsistence. He rebuts the common answer, which is that wages are taken out of capital that is invested for the purpose of paying wages. First, George defines "wages" as any recompense for labor of any kind (for example, the food one grows for oneself to eat), not just pay to an employee. "Capital" he defines as the part of wealth that is used to produce more wealth. Labor acts upon capital — in the form of raw material and tools — and adds value to the raw material. Wages come from the added value, not from capital itself. The return on capital also comes from the added value. Labor thus pays for itself as well as the return on capital.*

How is it then, George asks, that as productivity increases, wages tend to fall? The answer is that rent charged on land takes away most of the added value. George defines "rent" as both payment for the use of land and the value of land even when it is used by the owner (calculated as the rent that might be charged or as the selling price). In the following section, George argues that rising rent consumes the wealth that would otherwise go to wages or to the legitimate return on investment. — EDS.]

---

[5]In Greek mythology, the Sphinx is a winged female monster with a woman's head and a lion's body who devours travelers who cannot solve the riddle it poses. — EDS.

BOOK III

Chapter 8: The Statics of the Problem
Thus Explained

. . . Nothing can be clearer than the proposition that the failure of wages to increase with increasing productive power is due to the increase of rent.

Three things unite to production — labor, capital, and land.

Three parties divide the produce — the laborer, the capitalist, and the landowner.

If, with an increase of production the laborer gets no more and the capitalist no more, it is a necessary inference that the landowner reaps the whole gain.

And the facts agree with the inference. Though neither wages nor interest anywhere increase as material progress goes on, yet the invariable accompaniment and mark of material progress is the increase of rent — the rise of land values.

The increase of rent explains why wages and interest do not increase. The cause which gives to the landholder is the cause which denies to the laborer and capitalist. That wages and interest are higher in new than in old countries is not, as the standard economists say, because nature makes a greater return to the application of labor and capital, but because land is cheaper, and, therefore, as a smaller proportion of the return is taken by rent, labor and capital can keep for their share a larger proportion of what nature does return. It is not the total produce, but the net produce, after rent has been taken from it, that determines what can be divided as wages and interest. Hence, the rate of wages and interest is everywhere fixed, not so much by the productiveness of labor as by the value of land. Wherever the value of land is relatively low, wages and interest are relatively high; wherever land is relatively high, wages and interest are relatively low.

If production had not passed the simple stage in which all labor is directly applied to the land and all wages are paid in its produce, the fact that when the landowner takes a larger portion the laborer must put up with a smaller portion could not be lost sight of.

But the complexities of production in the civilized state, in which so great a part is borne by exchange, and so much labor is bestowed upon materials after they have been separated from the land, though they may to the unthinking disguise, do not alter the fact that all production is still the union of the two factors, land and labor, and that rent (the share of the landholder) cannot be increased except at the expense of wages (the share of the laborer) and interest (the share of capital). Just as the portion of the crop, which in the simpler forms of industrial organization the owner of agricultural land receives at the end of the harvest as his rent, lessens the amount left to the cultivator as wages and interest, so does the rental of land on which a manufacturing or commercial city is built lessen the amount which can be divided as wages and interest between the laborer and capital there engaged in the production and exchange of wealth.

In short, the value of land depending wholly upon the power which its ownership gives of appropriating wealth created by labor, the increase of land values is always at the expense of the value of labor. And, hence, that the increase of productive power does not increase wages, is because it does increase the value of land. Rent swallows up the whole gain and pauperism accompanies progress.

It is unnecessary to refer to facts. They will suggest themselves to the reader. It is the general fact, observable everywhere, that as the value of land increases, so does the contrast between wealth and want appear. It is the universal fact, that where the value of land is highest, civilization exhibits the greatest luxury side by side with the most piteous destitution. To see human beings in the most abject, the most helpless and hopeless condition, you must go, not to the unfenced prairies and the log cabins of new clearings in the backwoods, where man single-handed is commencing the struggle with nature, and land is yet worth nothing, but to the great cities, where the ownership of a little patch of ground is a fortune.

[*George goes on to argue that the monopoly or virtual monopoly of land is the real cause of poverty in the midst of progress. There is, he continues, no legal or moral justification for private ownership of land. George then proposes his remedy: to make land common property.* — EDS.]

BOOK V

Chapter 2: The Persistence of Poverty

In all our long investigation we have been advancing to this simple truth: That as land is necessary to the exertion of labor in the production of wealth, to command the land which is necessary to labor, is to command all the fruits of labor save enough to enable labor to exist. We have been advancing as through an enemy's country, in which every step must be secured, every position fortified, and every bypath explored; for this simple truth, in its application to social and political problems, is hid from the great masses of men partly by its very simplicity, and in greater part by widespread fallacies and erroneous habits of thought which lead them to look in every direction but the right one for an explanation of the evils which oppress and threaten the civilized world. And back of these elaborate fallacies and misleading theories is an active, energetic power, a power that in every country, be its political forms what they may, writes laws and molds thought — the power of a vast and dominant pecuniary interest.

But so simple and so clear is this truth, that to see it fully once is always to recognize it. There are pictures which, though looked at again and again, present only a confused labyrinth of lines or scroll work — a landscape, trees, or something of the kind — until once the attention is called to the fact that these things make up a face or a figure. This relation once recognized, is always afterward clear. It is so in this case. In the light of this truth all social facts group themselves in an orderly relation, and the most diverse phenomena are seen to spring from one great principle. It is not in the relations of capital and labor; it is not in the pressure of population against subsistence,[6] that an explanation of the unequal development of our civilization is to be found. The great cause of inequality in the distribution of wealth is inequality in the ownership of land. The ownership of land is the great fundamental fact which ultimately determines the social, the political, and consequently the intellectual and moral condition of a people. And it must be so. For land is the inhabitation of man, the storehouse upon which he must draw for all his needs, the material to which his labor must be applied for the supply of all his desires; for even the products of the sea cannot be taken, the light of the sun enjoyed, or any of the forces of nature utilized, without the use of land or its products. On the land we are born, from it we live, to it we return again — children of the soil as truly as is the blade of grass or the flower of the field. Take away from man all that belongs to land, and he is but a disembodied spirit. Material progress cannot rid us of our dependence upon land; it can but add to the power of producing wealth from land; and hence, when land is monopolized, it might go on to infinity without increasing wages or improving the condition of those who have but their labor. It can but add to the value of land and the power which its possession gives. Everywhere, in all times, among all peoples, the possession of land is the base of aristocracy, the foundation of great fortunes, the source of power. As said the Brahmins, ages ago —

> To whomsoever the soil at any time belongs, to him belong the fruits of it. White parasols and elephants mad with pride are the flowers of a grant of land.

BOOK VI

Chapter 2: The True Remedy

We have traced the unequal distribution of wealth which is the curse and menace of modern civilization to the institution of private property in land. We have seen that so long as this institution exists no increase in productive power can permanently benefit the masses; but, on the contrary, must tend still further to depress their condition. . . .

There is but one way to remove an evil — and that is, to remove its cause. Poverty deepens as wealth increases, and wages are forced down

---

[6]In a previous section (book 2, chapter 1), George has refuted the popular theory of population proposed by Thomas Malthus (1766–1834) in his *Essay on the Principle of Population* (1798). The Malthusian theory is "that population naturally tends to increase faster than subsistence" — in other words, that the growth of population constantly tends to outstrip food production, which leads to poverty and vice, which in turn holds down excess population. According to George, it is people's mistaken acceptance of Malthus that leads them to believe another false theory: that wages fall because the number of workers increases faster than available capital. (See note 7, p. 523) — EDS.

while productive power grows, because land, which is the source of all wealth and the field of all labor, is monopolized. To extirpate poverty, to make wages what justice commands they should be, the full earnings of the laborer, we must therefore substitute for the individual ownership of land a common ownership. Nothing else will go to the cause of the evil — in nothing else is there the slightest hope.

This, then, is the remedy for the unjust and unequal distribution of wealth apparent in modern civilization, and for all the evils which flow from it:

> *We must make land common property.*

. . .

BOOK VII

Chapter 1: The Injustice of Private Property in Land

When it is proposed to abolish private property in land the first question that will arise is that of justice. Though often warped by habit, superstition, and selfishness into the most distorted forms, the sentiment of justice is yet fundamental to the human mind, and whatever dispute arouses the passions of men, the conflict is sure to rage, not so much as to the question "Is it wise?" as to the question "Is it right?" . . .

What constitutes the rightful basis of property? What is it that enables a man justly to say of a thing, "It is mine!" From what springs the sentiment which acknowledges his exclusive right as against all the world? Is it not, primarily, the right of a man to himself, to the use of his own powers, to the enjoyment of the fruits of his own exertions? Is it not this individual right, which springs from and is testified to by the natural facts of individual organization — the fact that each particular pair of hands obey a particular brain and are related to a particular stomach; the fact that each man is a definite, coherent, independent whole — which alone justifies individual ownership? As a man belongs to himself, so his labor when put in concrete form belongs to him.

And for this reason, that which a man makes or produces is his own, as against all the world — to enjoy or to destroy, to use, to exchange, or to give. No one else can rightfully claim it, and his exclusive right to it involves no wrong to any one else. Thus there is to everything produced by human exertion a clear and indisputable title to exclusive possession and enjoyment, which is perfectly consistent with justice, as it descends from the original producer, in whom it vested by natural law. The pen with which I am writing is justly mine. No other human being can rightfully lay claim to it, for in me is the title of the producers who made it. It has become mine, because transferred to me by the stationer, to whom it was transferred by the importer, who obtained the exclusive right to it by transfer from the manufacturer, in whom, by the same process of purchase, vested the rights of those who dug the material from the ground and shaped it into a pen. Thus, my exclusive right of ownership in the pen springs from the natural right of the individual to the use of his own faculties.

Now, this is not only the original source from which all ideas of exclusive ownership arise — as is evident from the natural tendency of the mind to revert to it when the idea of exclusive ownership is questioned, and the manner in which social relations develop — but it is necessarily the only source. There can be to the ownership of anything no rightful title which is not derived from the title of the producer and does not rest upon the natural right of the man to himself. There can be no other rightful title, because (1st) there is no other natural right from which any other title can be derived, and (2d) because the recognition of any other title is inconsistent with and destructive of this.

For (1st) what other right exists from which the right to the exclusive possession of anything can be derived, save the right of a man to himself? With what other power is man by nature clothed, save the power of exerting his own faculties? How can he in any other way act upon or affect material things or other men? Paralyze the motor nerves, and your man has no more external influence of power than a log or stone. From what else, then, can the right of possessing and controlling things be derived? If it spring not from man himself, from what can it spring? Nature acknowledges no ownership or control in man save as the result of exertion. In no other way can her treasures be drawn forth, her powers directed, or her forces utilized or controlled. She makes no discriminations among men, but is to all absolutely impartial. She knows no distinction between master and slave, king and subject, saint and sinner. All men to her stand upon an equal footing and have equal rights. She recognizes no claim but that of labor, and recognizes that without respect to the claimant. If a pirate spread his sails, the wind will fill them as well as it will fill those of a peaceful merchantman or missionary bark; if a king and a common man be thrown overboard, neither can keep his head above water except by swimming; birds will not come to be shot by the proprietor of the soil any quicker than they will come to be shot by the poacher; fish will bite or will not bite at a hook in utter disregard as to whether it is offered them by a good little boy who goes to Sunday school, or a bad little boy who plays truant; grain will grow only as the ground is prepared and the seed is sown; it is only at the call of labor that ore can be raised from the mine; the sun shines and the rain falls, alike upon just and unjust. The laws of nature are the decrees of the Creator. There is written in them no recognition of any right save that of labor; and in them is written broadly and clearly the equal right of all men to the use and enjoyment of nature; to apply to her by their exertions, and to receive and possess her reward. Hence, as nature gives only to labor, the exertion of labor in production is the only title to exclusive possession.

(2d) This right of ownership that springs from labor excludes the possibility of any other right of ownership. If a man be rightfully entitled to the produce of his labor, then no one can be rightfully entitled to the ownership of anything which is not the produce of his labor, or the labor of some one else from whom the right has passed to him. If production give to the producer the right to exclusive possession and enjoyment, there can rightfully be no exclusive possession and enjoyment of anything not the production of labor, and the recognition of private property in land is a wrong. For the right to the produce of labor cannot be enjoyed without the right to the free use of the opportunities offered by nature, and to admit the right of property in these is to deny the right of property in the produce of labor. When nonproducers can claim as rent a portion of the wealth created by producers, the right of the producers to the fruits of their labor is to that extent denied.

There is no escape from this position. To affirm that a man can rightfully claim exclusive ownership in his own labor when embodied in material things, is to deny that anyone can rightfully claim exclusive ownership in land. To affirm the rightfulness of property in land, is to affirm a claim which has no warrant in nature, as against a claim founded in the organization of man and the laws of the material universe.

What most prevents the realization of the injustice of private property in land is the habit of including all the things that are made the subject of ownership in one category, as property, or, if any distinction is made, drawing the line, according to the unphilosophical distinction of the lawyers, between personal property and real estate, or things movable and things immovable. The real and natural distinction is between things which are the produce of labor and things which are the gratuitous offerings of nature; or, to adopt the terms of political economy, between wealth and land.

These two classes of things are in essence and relations widely different, and to class them together as property is to confuse all thought when we come to consider the justice or the injustice, the right or the wrong of property.

A house and the lot on which it stands are alike property, as being the subject of ownership, and are alike classed by the lawyers as real estate. Yet in nature and relations they differ widely. The one is produced by human labor, and belongs to the class in political economy styled wealth. The other is a part of nature, and belongs to the class in political economy styled land.

The essential character of the one class of things is that they embody labor, are brought into being by human exertion, their existence or nonexistence, their increase or diminution, depending on man. The essential character of the other class of things is that they do not embody labor, and exist irrespective of human exertion and irrespective of man; they are the field or environment in which man finds himself; the storehouse from which his needs must be supplied, the raw material upon which and the forces with which alone his labor can act.

The moment this distinction is realized, that moment is it seen that the sanction which natural justice gives to one species of property is denied to the other; that the rightfulness which attaches to individual property in the produce of labor implies the wrongfulness of individual property in land; that, whereas the recognition of the one places all men upon equal terms, securing to each the due reward of his labor, the recognition of the other is the denial of the equal rights of men, permitting those who do not labor to take the natural reward of those who do.

Whatever may be said for the institution of private property in land, it is therefore plain that it cannot be defended on the score of justice.

The equal right of all men to the use of land is as clear as their equal right to breathe the air — it is a right proclaimed by the fact of their existence. For we cannot suppose that some men have a right to be in this world and others no right.

If we are all here by the equal permission of the Creator, we are all here with an equal title to the enjoyment of his bounty — with an equal right to the use of all that nature so impartially offers.[7] This is a right which is natural and inalienable; it is a right which vests in every human being as he enters the world, and which during his continuance in the world can be limited only by the equal rights of others. . . . There is on earth no power which can rightfully make a grant of exclusive ownership in land. If all existing men were to unite to grant away their equal rights, they could not grant away the right of those who follow them. For what are we but tenants for a day? Have we made the earth, that we should determine the rights of those who after us shall tenant it in their turn? The Almighty, who created the earth for man and man for the earth, has entailed it upon all the generations of the children of men by a decree written upon the constitution of all things — a decree which no human action can bar and no prescription determine. Let the parchments be ever so many, or possession ever so long, natural justice can recognize no right in one man to the possession and enjoyment of land that is not equally the right of all his fellows. Though his titles have been acquiesced in by generation after generation,

---

[7]In saying that private property in land can, in the ultimate analysis, be justified only on the theory that some men have a better right to existence than others, I am stating only what the advocates of the existing system have themselves perceived. What gave to Malthus his popularity among the ruling classes — what caused his illogical book to be received as a new revelation, induced sovereigns to send him decorations, and the meanest rich man in England to propose to give him a living, was the fact that he furnished a plausible reason for the assumption that some have a better right to existence than others — an assumption which is necessary for the justification of private property in land, and which Malthus clearly states in the declaration that the tendency of population is constantly to bring into the world human beings for whom nature refuses to provide, and who consequently "have not the slightest right to any share in the existing store of the necessaries of life"; whom she tells as interlopers to begone, "and does not hesitate to extort by force obedience to her mandates," employing for that purpose "hunger and pestilence, war and crime, mortality and neglect of infantine life, prostitution and syphilis." And today this Malthusian doctrine is the ultimate defense upon which those who justify private property in land fall back. In no other way can it be logically defended. — HG

to the landed estates of the Duke of Westminster the poorest child that is born in London today has as much right as has his eldest son.[8] Though the sovereign people of the state of New York consent to the landed possessions of the Astors, the puniest infant that comes wailing into the world in the squalidest room of the most miserable tenement house, becomes at that moment seized of an equal right with the millionaires. And it is robbed if the right is denied.

Our previous conclusions, irresistible in themselves, thus stand approved by the highest and final test. Translated from terms of political economy into terms of ethics they show a wrong as the source of the evils which increase as material progress goes on.

The masses of men, who in the midst of abundance suffer want; who, clothed with political freedom, are condemned to the wages of slavery; to whose toil labor-saving inventions bring no relief, but rather seem to rob them of a privilege, instinctively feel that "there is something wrong." And they are right.

The widespreading social evils which everywhere oppress men amid an advancing civilization spring from a great primary wrong — the appropriation, as the exclusive property of some men, of the land on which and from which all must live. From this fundamental injustice flow all the injustices which distort and endanger modern development, which condemn the producer of wealth to poverty and pamper the nonproducer in luxury, which rear the tenement house with the palace, plant the brothel behind the church, and compel us to build prisons as we open new schools.

There is nothing strange or inexplicable in the phenomena that are now perplexing the world. It is not that material progress is not in itself a good; it is not that nature has called into being children for whom she has failed to provide; it is not that the Creator has left on natural laws a taint of injustice at which even the human mind revolts, that material progress brings such bitter fruits. That amid our highest civilization men faint and die with want is not due to the niggardliness of nature, but to the injustice of man. Vice and misery, poverty and pauperism, are not the legitimate results of increase of population and industrial development; they only follow increase of population and industrial development because land is treated as private property — they are the direct and necessary results of the violation of the supreme law of justice, involved in giving to some men the exclusive possession of that which nature provides for all men.

---

[8] This natural and inalienable right to the equal use and enjoyment of land is so apparent that it has been recognized by men wherever force or habit has not blunted first perceptions. To give but one instance: The white settlers of New Zealand found themselves unable to get from the Maoris what the latter considered a complete title to land, because, although a whole tribe might have consented to a sale, they would still claim with every new child born among them an additional payment on the ground that they had parted with only their own rights, and could not sell those of the unborn. The government was obliged to step in and settle the matter by buying land for a tribal annuity, in which every child that is born acquires a share. — HG

The recognition of individual proprietorship of land is the denial of the natural rights of other individuals — it is a wrong which *must* show itself in the inequitable division of wealth. For as labor cannot produce without the use of land, the denial of the equal right to the use of land is necessarily the denial of the right of labor to its own produce. If one man can command the land upon which others must labor, he can appropriate the produce of their labor as the price of his permission to labor. The fundamental law of nature, that her enjoyment by man shall be consequent upon his exertion, is thus violated. The one receives without producing; the others produce without receiving. The one is unjustly enriched; the others are robbed. . . .

[*In the next few chapters, George argues that ownership of land effectively creates slavery for workers. He asks why the users of land should perpetually pay for its purchase, which is what they do by paying rent. He offers examples of societies past and present that held land in common and resumes with a discussion of land ownership in the United States. —* EDS.]

BOOK VII

Chapter 5: Property in Land in the United States

. . . And so it has come to pass that the great republic of the modern world has adopted at the beginning of its career an institution that ruined the republics of antiquity; that a people who proclaim the inalienable rights of all men to life, liberty, and the pursuit of happiness have accepted without question a principle which, in denying the equal and inalienable right to the soil, finally denies the equal right to life and liberty; that a people who at the cost of a bloody war have abolished chattel slavery, yet permit slavery in a more widespread and dangerous form to take root.

The continent has seemed so wide, the area over which population might yet pour so vast, that familiarized by habit with the idea of private property in land, we have not realized its essential injustice. For not merely has this background of unsettled land prevented the full effect of private appropriation from being felt, even in the older sections, but to permit a man to take more land than he could use, that he might compel those who afterwards needed it to pay him for the privilege of using it, has not seemed so unjust when others in their turn might do the same thing by going further on. And more than this, the very fortunes that have resulted from the appropriation of land, and that have thus really been drawn from taxes levied upon the wages of labor, have seemed, and have been heralded, as prizes held out to the laborer. In all the newer States, and even to a considerable extent in the older ones, our landed aristocracy is yet in its first generation. Those who have profited by the increase in the value of land have been largely men who began life without a cent. Their great fortunes, many of them running up high into the millions, seem to them, and to many others, as the best proofs of the justice of existing social conditions in rewarding prudence, foresight, industry, and thrift; whereas, the truth is that these fortunes are but the gains of monopoly, and are necessarily made at the expense of labor. But the fact that those thus enriched started as laborers hides this, and the same feeling which leads every ticket holder in a lottery to delight in imagination in the magnitude of the prizes has prevented even the poor from quarreling with a system which thus made many poor men rich.

In short, the American people have failed to see the essential injustice of private property in land, because as yet they have not felt its full effects. This public domain — the vast extent of land yet to be reduced to private possession, the enormous common to which the faces of the energetic were always turned, has been the great fact that, since the days when the first settlements began to fringe the Atlantic Coast, has formed our national character and colored our national thought. It is not that we have eschewed a titled aristocracy and abolished primogeniture;[9] that we elect all our officers from school director up to president; that our laws run in the name of the people, instead of in the name of a prince; that the State knows no religion, and our judges wear no wigs — that we have been exempted from the ills that Fourth of July orators[10] used to point to as characteristic of the effete despotisms of the Old World. The general intelligence, the general comfort, the active invention, the power of adaptation and assimilation, the free, independent spirit, the energy and hopefulness that have marked our people, are not causes, but results — they have sprung from unfenced land. This public domain has been the transmuting force which has turned the thriftless, unambitious European peasant into the self-reliant Western farmer; it has given a consciousness of freedom even to the dweller in crowded cities, and has been a wellspring of hope even to those who have never thought of taking refuge upon it. The child of the people, as he grows to manhood in Europe, finds all the best seats at the banquet of life marked "taken," and must struggle with his fellows for the crumbs that fall, without one chance in a thousand of forcing or sneaking his way to a seat. In America, whatever his condition, there has always been the consciousness that the public domain lay behind him; and the knowledge of this fact, acting and reacting, has penetrated our whole national life, giving to it generosity and independence, elasticity and ambition. All that we are proud of in the American character; all that makes our conditions and institutions better than those of older countries, we may trace to the fact that land has been cheap in the United States, because new soil has been open to the emigrant.

But our advance has reached the Pacific. Further west we cannot go, and increasing population can but expand north and south and fill up

---

[9]"Primogeniture" is inheritance by the oldest child, usually the oldest son. — EDS.

[10]The Fourth of July holiday was (and in some places still is) the occasion for speeches about the American Revolution extolling U.S. freedom from the tyrannies of European monarchy and aristocracy. — EDS.

what has been passed over. North, it is already filling up the valley of the Red River, pressing into that of the Saskatchewan and preempting Washington Territory; south, it is covering western Texas and taking up the arable valleys of New Mexico and Arizona.

The republic has entered upon a new era, an era in which the monopoly of the land will tell with accelerating effect. The great fact which has been so potent is ceasing to be. The public domain is almost gone — a very few years will end its influence, already rapidly failing. . . .

But the evil effects of making the land of a whole people the exclusive property of some do not wait for the final appropriation of the public domain to show themselves. It is not necessary to contemplate them in the future; we may see them in the present. They have grown with our growth, and are still increasing.

We plow new fields, we open new mines, we found new cities; we drive back the Indian and exterminate the buffalo; we girdle the land with iron roads and lace the air with telegraph wires; we add knowledge to knowledge, and utilize invention after invention; we build schools and endow colleges; yet it becomes no easier for the masses of our people to make a living. On the contrary, it is becoming harder. The wealthy class is becoming more wealthy; but the poorer class is becoming more dependent. The gulf between the employed and the employer is growing wider; social contrasts are becoming sharper; as liveried carriages appear, so do barefooted children. We are becoming used to talk of the working classes and the propertied classes; beggars are becoming so common that where it was once thought a crime little short of highway robbery to refuse food to one who asked for it, the gate is now barred and the bulldog loosed, while laws are passed against vagrants which suggest those of Henry VIII.[11]

We call ourselves the most progressive people on earth. But what is the goal of our progress, if these are its wayside fruits?

These are the results of private property in land — the effects of a principle that must act with increasing and increasing force. It is not that laborers have increased faster than capital; it is not that population is pressing against subsistence; it is not that machinery has made "work scarce"; it is not that there is any real antagonism between labor and capital — it is simply that land is becoming more valuable; that the terms on which labor can obtain access to the natural opportunities which alone enable it to produce are becoming harder and harder. The public domain is receding and narrowing. Property in land is concentrating. The proportion of our people who have no legal right to the land on which they live is becoming steadily larger. . . .

The harder times, the lower wages, the increasing poverty perceptible in the United States are but results of the natural laws we have traced — laws as universal and as irresistible as that of gravitation. We did not establish the republic when, in the face of principalities and powers, we flung

[11]Henry VIII (1491–1547), king of England (1509–47), issued many laws that harassed the poor. — EDS.

the declaration of the inalienable rights of man; we shall never establish the republic until we practically carry out that declaration by securing to the poorest child born among us an equal right to his native soil! We did not abolish slavery when we ratified the Fourteenth Amendment;[12] to abolish slavery we must abolish private property in land! Unless we come back to first principles, unless we recognize natural perceptions of equity, unless we acknowledge the equal right of all to land, our free institutions will be in vain; our common schools will be in vain; our discoveries and inventions will but add to the force that presses the masses down!

READING CRITICALLY

1. Why would "a man of the last century" who could have seen the industrial progress of George's time think that in such a world there would be no poverty?

2. According to George, what is the basis of ownership? What distinction does George draw between ownership of land and ownership of other things?

3. According to George, how does the elimination of open land in the United States lead to gross inequities between the wealthy and the poor?

4. George says that the open land to the west was more important than political democracy in forming the American character and sense of freedom. How does he defend this idea?

5. What appeals does George make to typical American ideals? List them.

WRITING ANALYTICALLY

1. George argues that land is a natural resource that cannot be withheld from humans by private ownership any more than air can be withheld by ownership. This argument is used today to support efforts to protect the environment: We have no right to use up or ruin the air, the water, the rain forest, or the ozone layer, the argument goes, and leave the consequences to future generations. In your opinion, is George correct in placing land ownership in this category? Write an essay explaining and evaluating George's "environmental" arguments against land ownership. Consider, in your essay, how his arguments could be refuted. What arguments could be advanced in favor of private ownership of land? Where do you stand on the question? Alternative: Do you agree with George's argument that the very notion of freedom on which the United States is based demands that private ownership of land be abolished? Write an essay exploring and evaluating George's political arguments against private ownership of land. Consider, in your essay, how his arguments could be refuted. What political arguments could be advanced in favor of private ownership of land? Where do you stand on the question?

---

[12]In fact, the Thirteenth Amendment (1865) abolished slavery. The Fourteenth Amendment (1868) declared all Americans to be citizens not only of their states but also of the United States and was intended to frustrate southern attempts to prevent freed male slaves from voting. (See p. 397.) — EDS.

2. George begins with the observation that industrial capitalism creates tremendous wealth but permits vast disparities in the distribution of that wealth. He then analyzes this situation in two ways: moral and economic. Before proceeding with this question, reread the selection and note where he engages in each kind of analysis.

George asks why workers make the lowest possible wages while capitalists live in luxury. The simplest answer would seem to be that capitalists have the power to keep wages down and enrich themselves — in other words, they are greedy. This, for George, is only part of the answer. The other part is the dilemma of private ownership of land. Write an essay in which you assess the validity and effectiveness of the way George combines a technical analysis of economics (the land issue) with a moral argument (the greed issue), focusing on one or two examples of each.

3. George uses both a highly technical style and a more discursive or literary style to argue his points. Select a passage in which he uses technical explanations and another in which he uses stories, literary references, biblical references, or philosophical reflection to make his case. Compare and contrast the two passages and their relative persuasiveness. Why do you think George uses these two different styles to make his argument?

WORKING CONDITIONS

ELIZABETH STUART PHELPS

From *The Silent Partner* (1871)

Elizabeth Stuart Phelps (1844–1911) wrote a number of novels about women's status in society. The best known today is *The Story of Avis* (1877), which describes a woman's frustrated attempts to develop a career as a painter. Phelps sought social justice not only for women but also for others who faced discriminatory treatment. In *The Silent Partner*, Phelps tells the story of Perley Kelso, a wealthy and frivolous young woman who decides after her father's death that she would like to become a partner in his Massachusetts textile business, called Hayle and Kelso Mills. Her father's partner, Mr. Hayle, and the partner's son, Maverick (to whom Perley is engaged), laugh at her aspirations. Perley becomes a "silent partner," an investor with little influence on the business. She turns her attention to the workers at the mills, becoming friendly with Sip Garth, a young woman who guides Perley into the inner lives of the working class. With growing frustration, Perley realizes that the mill owners do not know or care about the workers' lives. As the silent partner, she tries to redress some of the wrongs done by the business, inviting the workers to her luxurious house for lectures and social events and working to improve their lives as best she can.

In the book's opening chapter, Perley meets Sip Garth by accident in Boston. That night, Perley's father dies. In chapter 2, a month later, Perley has moved to the mill town of Five Falls and encounters Sip Garth again. Sip, it turns out, is employed at the Hayle and Kelso Mills. Sip reveals some of the difficulties of such work and mentions her deaf sister, Catty, for whom she is responsible. In chapter 3, Perley asks to take her father's place as an active partner in the firm but is rebuffed by Maverick and his father. She then reveals her incipient desire to improve the lives of the mill hands, which only provokes their further scorn. Our excerpt begins with chapter 4.

CHAPTER IV

The Stone House

IF YOU ARE ONE OF "THE HANDS" in the Hayle and Kelso Mills, you go to your work, as is well known, from the hour of half past six to seven, according to the turn of the season. Time has been when you went at half past

Elizabeth Stuart Phelps, *The Silent Partner* (1871; reprint, New York: Feminist Press, 1983), 70–115, 126–42.

In the notes, ESP = Elizabeth Stuart Phelps, EDS. = Patricia Bizzell and Bruce Herzberg.

four. The Senior forgot this the other day in a little talk which he had with his silent partner, — very naturally, the time having been so long past; but the time has been, is now, indeed, yet in places. Mr. Hayle can tell you of mills he saw in New Hampshire last vacation, where they ring them up, if you'll believe it, winter and summer, in and out, at half past four in the morning. O no, never let out before six, of course. Mr. Hayle disapproves of this. Mr. Hayle thinks it not humane. Mr. Hayle is confident that you would find no mission Sunday school connected with that concern.

If you are one of "the hands" in the Hayle and Kelso Mills — and again, in Hayle and Kelso, — you are so dully used to this classification, "the hands," that you were never known to cultivate an objection to it, are scarcely found to notice its use or disuse. Being surely neither head nor heart, what else remains? Conscious scarcely, from bell to bell, from sleep to sleep, from day to dark, of either head or heart, there seems even a singular appropriateness in the chance of the word with which you are dimly struck. Hayle and Kelso label you. There you are. The world thinks, aspires, creates, enjoys. There you are. You are the fingers of the world. You take your patient place. The world may have need of you, but only that it may think, aspire, create, enjoy. It needs your patience as well as your place. You take both, and you are used to both, and the world is used to both, and so, having put the label on for safety's sake, lest you be mistaken for a thinking, aspiring, creating, enjoying compound, and so someone be poisoned, shoves you into your place upon its shelf, and shuts its cupboard door upon you.

If you are one of "the hands," then, in Hayle and Kelso, you have a breakfast of bread and molasses probably; you are apt to eat it while you dress; somebody is heating the kettle, but you cannot wait for it; somebody tells you that you have forgotten your shawl, you throw it over one shoulder, and step out, before it is fastened, into the sudden raw air; you left lamplight indoors; you find moonlight without; the night seems to have overslept itself; you have a fancy for trying to wake it, would like to shout at it or cry through it, but feel very cold, and leave that for the bells to do by and by. You and the bells are the only waking things in life. The great brain of the world is in serene repose. The great heart of the world lies warm to the core with dreams. The great hands of the world, the patient, perplexed, one almost fancies at times, just for the fancy, seeing you here by the morning moon, the dangerous hands, alone are stirring in the dark.

You hang up your shawl and your crinoline, and understand, as you go shivering by gaslight to your looms, that you are chilled to the heart, and that you were careless about your shawl, but do not consider carefulness worth your while by nature or by habit; a little less shawl means a few less winters in which to require shawling. You are a godless little creature, but you cherish a stolid leaning, in these morning moons, towards making an experiment of death and a wadded coffin.

By the time that gas is out, you cease, perhaps, though you cannot depend upon that, to shiver and incline less and less to the wadded coffin, and more to a chat with your neighbor in the alley. Your neighbor is of either sex and any description, as the case may be. In any event, warming a little with the warming day, you incline more and more to chat. If you chance to be a cotton weaver, you are presently warm enough. It is quite warm enough in the weaving room. The engines respire into the weaving room; with every throb of their huge lungs you swallow their breath. The weaving room stifles with steam. The windowsills of this room are guttered to prevent the condensed steam from running in streams along the floor; sometimes they overflow, and water stands under the looms; the walls perspire profusely; on a damp day, drops will fall from the roof.

The windows of the weaving room are closed; the windows must be closed; a stir in the air will break your threads. There is no air to stir. You inhale for a substitute motionless, hot moisture. If you chance to be a cotton weaver, it is not in March that you think most about your coffin.

Being "a hand" in Hayle and Kelso, you are used to eating cold luncheon in the cold at noon, or you walk, for the sake of a cup of soup or coffee, half a mile, three-quarters, a mile and half, and back. You are allowed three-quarters of an hour in which to do this. You come and go upon the jog-trot.

You grow moody, being "a hand" at Hayle and Kelso's, with the growing day; are inclined to quarrel or to confidence with your neighbor in the alley; find the overseer out of temper, and the cotton full of flaws; find pains in your feet, your back, your eyes, your arms; feel damp and sticky lint in your hair, your neck, your ears, your throat, your lungs; discover a monotony in the process of breathing hot moisture, lower your window at your risk; are bidden by somebody whose threads you have broken at the other end of the room to put it up, and put it up; are conscious that your head swims, your eyeballs burn, your breath quickens; yield your preference for a wadded coffin, and consider whether the river would not be the comfortable thing; cough a little, cough a great deal, lose your balance in a coughing fit, snap a thread, and take to swearing roundly.

From swearing you take to singing; both perhaps are equal relief, active and diverting. There is something curious about that singing of yours. The time, the place, the singers, characterize it sharply, — the waning light, the rival din, the girls with tired faces. You start some little thing with a refrain and a ring to it; a hymn, it is not unlikely; something of a River and of Waiting, and of Toil and Rest, or Sleep, or Crowns, or Harps, or Home, or Green Fields, or Flowers, or Sorrow, or Repose, or a dozen things, but always, it will be noticed, of simple, spotless things, such as will surprise the listener who caught you at your oath of five minutes past. You have other songs, neither simple nor spotless, it may be; but you never sing them at your work, when the waning day is crawling out from spots between your looms, and the girls lift up their tired faces to catch and keep the chorus in the rival din.

You like to watch the contest between the chorus and the din; to see — you seem almost to see — the struggle of the melody from alley to alley, from loom to loom, from darkening wall to darkening wall, from lifted face to lifted face; to see — for you are very sure you see — the machinery fall into a fit of rage. That is a sight! You would never guess, unless you had watched it just as many times as you have, how that machinery will rage. How it throws its arms about, what fists it can clench, how it shakes at the elbows and knees, what teeth it knows how to gnash, how it writhes and roars, how it clutches at the leaky, strangling gaslights, and how it bends its impotent black head, always, at last, without fail, and your song sweeps triumphant, like an angel, over it! With this you are very much pleased, though only "a hand," to be sure, in Hayle and Kelso.

You are singing when the bell strikes, and singing still when you clatter down the stairs. Something of the simple spotlessness of the little song is on your face, when you dip into the wind and dusk. Perhaps you have only pinned your shawl, or pulled your hat over your face, or knocked against a stranger on the walk; but it passes; it passes and is gone. It is cold and you tremble, direct from the morbid heat in which you have stood all day; or you have been cold all day, and it is colder, and you shrink; or you are from the weaving room, and the wind strikes you faint, or you stop to cough and the girls go on without you. The town is lighted, and people are out in their best clothes. You pull your dingy veil about your eyes. You are weak and heartsick all at once. You don't care to go home to supper. The pretty song creeps, wounded, back for the engines in the deserted dark to crunch. You are a miserable little factory girl with a dirty face.

A broken chatter falls in pieces about you; all the melody of the voices that you hear has vanished with the vanquished song; they are hoarse and rough.

"Goin' to the dance tonight, Bet?"

"Nynee Mell! yer alway speerin' awa' after some young mon. Can't yer keep yer een at home like a decint lassie?"

"An' who gave *you* lave to hoult a body's hand onasked an' onrequested, Pathrick Donnavon?"

"Sip Garth, give us 'Champagne Charley'; can't you?"

"Do you think the mules[1] will strike?"

"More mules they, if they do. Did ye never see a mouse strike a cat?"

"There's Bub beggin' tobacco yet! How old is that little devil?"

"The Lord knows!"

"Pity the Lord don't know a few more things as one would suppose might fall in his line."

"A tract?"

"A tract. Bless you, four pages long. Says I, What in ———'s this? for I was just going in to the meetin' to see the fun. So he stuffs it into my hand, and I clears out."

"Sip, I say! Priscilla! Sip Garth — "

But Sip Garth breaks out of sight as the chatter breaks out of hearing; turns a corner; turns another; walks wearily fast, and wearily faster; pushes her stout way through a dirty street and a dirtier street; stops at shadowy corners to look for something which she does not find; stops at lighted

---

[1]Here the "mules" are the workers who operate the mule-spinners, the machines that make the thread from raw cotton or wool. — EDS.

doors to call for something that does not answer; hesitates a moment at the dismal gate of a dismal little stone house by the water, and, hesitating still and with a heavy sigh, goes in.

It is a damp house, and she rents the dampest room in it; a tenement boasting of the width of the house, and a closet bedroom with a little cupboard window in it; a low room with cellar smells and river smells about it, and with gutter smells and drain smells and with unclassified smells of years settled and settling in its walls and ceiling. Never a cheerful room; never by any means a cheerful room, when she and Catty — or she without Catty — come home from work at night.

Something has happened to the forlorn little room tonight. Sip stops with the door latch in her hand. A fire has happened, and the kerosene lamp has happened, and drawn curtains have happened; and Miss Kelso has happened, — down on her knees on the bare floor, with her kid gloves off, and a poker in her hands.

So, original in Perley! Maverick would say; Maverick not being there to say it, Perley spoke for herself, with the poker in her hand, and still upon her knees.

"I beg your pardon, Sip, but they told me, the other side of the house, that you would be in in five minutes, and the room was dark and so I took the liberty. If you wouldn't mind me, and would go right on as if I hadn't come, I should take it very kindly."

"All right," said Sip.

"The fact is," said Miss Kelso, meditatively twirling her poker, "that that is the first fire I ever made in my life. Would you believe it, to look at it?"

"I certainly shouldn't," said Sip.

"And you're quite sure that you wouldn't mind me?"

"No, not quite sure. But if you'll stay awhile, I'll find out and tell you."

"Very well," said Miss Kelso.

"See how dirty I am," said Sip, stopping in the full light on her way to the closet bedroom.

"I hadn't seen," said Miss Kelso to the poker.

"O, well. No matter. I didn't know but *you*'d mind."

There was dust about Sip, and oil about her, and a consciousness of both about her, that gave her a more miserable aspect than either. In the full light she looked like some half-cleared Pompeian statue just dug against the face of day.

"We can't help it, you see," said poor Sip; "mill folks can't. Dust we are and to dust do we return. I've got a dreadful sore throat tonight."

"Have you taken cold?"

"O no. I have it generally. It comes from sucking filling through the shuttle. But I don't think much of it. There's girls I know, weavers, can't even talk beyond a whisper; lost their voices some time ago."

Sip washed and dressed herself after this in silence. She washed herself in the sink; there was no pump to the sink; she went out bareheaded, and brought water in from a well in the yard; the pail was heavy, and she walked wearily, with her head and body bent to balance it, over the slippery path.

She coughed while she walked and when she came in, — a peculiar, dry, rasping cough, which Perley learned afterwards to recognize as the "cotton cough." She washed herself in a tin basin, which she rinsed carefully and hung up against the wall. While she was dressing in the closet bedroom, Perley still knelt, thoughtfully playing with the poker beside the fire.

"I don't suppose," said Sip, coming out presently in her plaid dress, with her hair in a net, and speaking as if she had not been interrupted, — "I don't suppose you'd ever guess how much difference the dirt makes. I don't suppose you ever *could.* Cotton ain't so bad, though. Once I worked to a flax mill. *That* was dirt."

"What difference?"

"Hush!" said Sip, abruptly. "I thought I heard — " She went to the window and looked out, raising her hands against her eyes, but came back with a disappointed face.

"Catty hasn't come in," she said, nervously. "There's times she slips away from me; she works in the Old Stone, and I can't catch her. There's times she doesn't come till late. Will you stay to tea?" with a quick change of voice.

"Thank you. I don't understand about Catty," with another.

Sip set her table before she spoke again; bustled about, growing restless; put the kettle on and off the hob; broke one of her stone-china plates; stopped to sweep the floor a little and to fill her coal hod; the brown tints of her rugged little face turning white and pinched in spots about the mouth.

She came, presently, and stood by the fire by Miss Kelso's side, in the full sweep of the light. "Miss Kelso," her hands folding and unfolding restlessly, "there's many things you don't understand. There's things you *could*n't understand."

"Why?"

"I don't know why. I never did quite know why."

"You may be right; you may be wrong. How can you tell till you try me?"

"How can I tell whether I can skate on running water till I try it? — I wish Catty would come!"

Sip walked to the window again, and walked back again, and took a look at the teapot, and cut a slice or two of bread.

"So you've left the Company board," observed Miss Kelso, quite as if they had been talking about the Company board. "You didn't like it?"

"I liked well enough."

"You left suddenly?"

"I left sudden." Sip threw her bread knife down, with an aimless, passionate gesture. "I suppose it's no good to shy off. I might as well tell o't first as last. They turned us off!"

"Turned you off?"

"On account of Catty."

Miss Kelso raised a confused face from the poker and the fire.

"You see," said Sip, "I *told* you there's things you couldn't understand. Now there ain't one of my own kind of folks, your age, wouldn't have understood half an hour ago, and saved me the trouble of telling. Catty's queer, don't you see? She runs away, don't you see? Sometimes she drinks, don't you understand? Drinks herself the dead kind. That ain't so often. Most times she just runs away about streets. There's sometimes she does — worse."

"Worse?" The young lady's pure, puzzled face dropped suddenly. "O, I was very dull! I am sorry. I am not used — " And so broke off, with a sick look about the lips, — a look which did not escape the notice of the little brown, pinched face in the firelight, for it was curving into a bitter smile when the door opened, banging back against the wall as if the opener had either little consciousness or little care of the noise it made.

"There's Catty," said Sip, doggedly. "Come and get warm, Catty." This in their silent language on her rapid, work-worn fingers.

"If you mind me now, I'll go," said Miss Kelso, in a low voice.

"That's for you to say, whether I shall mind you now."

"Poor Catty!" said Perley, still in a very low voice. "Poor, poor Catty!"

Sip flushed, — flushed very sweetly and suddenly all over her dogged face. "*Now* I don't mind you. Stay to supper. We'll have supper right away. Come here a minute, Catty dear." . . .

Catty sat down to supper without washing her face. This troubled Sip more than it did her visitor. Her visitor, indeed, scarcely noticed it. Her face wore yet something of the solemn fright which had descended on it with Catty's coming in.

She noticed, however, that she had bread and butter for her supper, and that she was eating from a stone-china plate, and with a steel fork and with a pewter spoon. She noticed that the bread was toasted, it seemed in deference to the presence of a guest, and that the toasting had feverishly flushed Sip's haggard face. She noticed that Sip and Catty ate no butter, but dipped their bread into a little blue bowl of thick black molasses. She noticed that there was a kind of coarse black tea upon the table, and noticed that she found a single pewter spoonful of it quite sufficient for her wants. She noticed that Sip made rather a form than a fact of playing with her toasted bread in the thick black molasses, and that she drained her dreadful teacup thirstily, and that she then leaned, with a sudden sick look, back into her chair.

Everything tasted of oil, she said. She could not eat. There were times that she could not eat day nor night for a long time. How long? She was not sure. It had been often two days that nothing passed her lips. Sometimes, with the tea, it was longer. There were times that she came home and got right into bed, dirt and all. She couldn't undress, no, not if it was to save her soul, nor eat. But, generally, she managed to cook for Catty. Besides, there was the work.

"What work?" asked Miss Kelso, innocently.

"Washing. Ironing. Baking. Sweeping. Dusting. Sewing. Marketing. Pumping. Scrubbing. Scouring," said Sip, drumming out her periods on a teaspoon with her hard, worn fingers.

"Oh!" said Miss Kelso.

"For two, you see," said Sip.

"But all this, — you cannot have all this to do after you have stood eleven hours and a half at your loom?"

"When should I have it to do! There's Sunday, to be sure; but I don't do so much now Sundays, except the washing and the brushing up. I like," with a gentle, quick look at the deaf and dumb girl, who still sat dipping bread crusts into black molasses, absorbed and still, "to make it a kind of a comfortable day for Catty, Sunday. I don't bother Catty so much to help me, you know," added Sip, cheerfully. "I like," with another very pleasant look, "to make it comfortable for Catty."

"I went into the mills today," said Miss Kelso, in reply. It was not very much to the point as a reply, and was said with an interrogatory accent, which lessened its aptness.

"Yes?" said Sip, in the same tone.

"I never was in a mill before."

"No?"

"No."

There was a pause, in which the young lady seemed to be waiting for a leading question, like a puzzled scholar. If she were, she had none. Sip sat with her dogged smile, and snapped little paper balls into the fire.

"I thought it rather close in the mills."

"Yes?"

"And — dirty. And — there was one very warm room; the overseer advised me not to go in."

"It was very good advice."

"I went into the Company boardinghouse too."

"For the first time?"

"For the first time. I went to inquire after you. The landlady took me about. Now I think of it, she invited me to tea."

"Why didn't you stay?"

"Why, to tell the truth, the — tablecloth was — rather dirty."

"Oh!"

"And I saw her wipe her face on — the dishtowel. Do the girls often sleep six in a room? They had no washstands. I saw some basins set on trunks. They carried all the water up and down stairs themselves; there were two or three flights. There wasn't a ventilator in the house. I saw a girl there sick."

"Sick? O, Bert Bush. Yes. Pleurisy. She's going to work her notice when she gets about again. Given out."

"She coughed while I was there. I thought her room was rather cold. I thought all the rooms were rather cold. I didn't seem to see any fire for anybody, except in the common sitting room. But the bread was sweet."

"Yes, the bread was sweet."

"And the gingerbread."

"Very sweet."

"And, I suppose, the board —

"The board is quarter of a dollar cheaper than in other places."

Sip stopped snapping paper balls into the fire, and snapped instead one of her shrewd, sidewise glances at her visitor's face.

The fine, fair, finished face! How puzzled it looked! Sip smiled. . . .

Catty had crept around while they were talking, and sat upon the floor by Miss Kelso's chair. She was still amusing herself with the young lady's dress, passing her wise fingers to and fro across its elegant surface, and nodding to herself in her dull way. Miss Kelso's hand, the one with the rings, lay upon her lap, and Catty, attracted suddenly by the blaze of the jewels, took it up. She took it up as she would a novel toy, examined it for a few moments with much pleasure, then removed the rings and dropped them carelessly, and laid her cheek down upon the soft flesh. It was such a dusty cheek, and such a beautiful, bare, clean hand, that Sip started anxiously to speak to Catty, but saw that Perley sat quite still, and that her earnest eyes were full of sudden tears.

"You will not let me say, you know, that I am sorry for you. I have been trying all the evening. I can't come any nearer than this." This she said smiling.

"Look here!" said Sip; her brown face worked and altered. She said, "Look here!" again, and stopped. "That's nigh enough. I'll take that. I like that. I like you. Look here! I never said that to one of your kind of folks before; I like you. Generally I hate your kind of folks."

"Now that," said Miss Kelso, musing, "perplexes me. We feel no such instinct of aversion to you. As far as I understand 'my kind of folks,' they have kindly hearts, and they have it in their hearts to feel very sorry for the poor."

"Who wants their pity? And who cares what's in their hearts?"

Sip had hardened again like a little growing prickly nut. The subject and her softer mood dropped away together.

"Sip," said Perley, fallen into another revery, "you see how little I know — "

Sip nodded.

"About — people who work and — have a hard time."

"They don't none of 'em know. That's why I hate your kind of folks. It ain't because they don't care, it's because they don't *know;* nor they don't care enough *to* know."

"Now I have always been brought up to believe," urged Miss Kelso, "that our factory people, for instance, had good wages."

"I never complained of the wages. Hayle and Kelso couldn't get a cotton weaver for three dollars a week, like a paper factory I know about in Cincinnati. I knew a girl as worked to Cincinnati. Three dollars a week, and board to come out of it! Cotton weaving's no play, and cotton weavers are no fools."

"And I always thought," continued Miss Kelso, "that such people were — why, happy and comfortable, you know. Of course, I knew they must economize, and that, but — "

She looked vaguely over at the supper table; such uncertain conceptions as she might hitherto be said to have had of "economizing" acquiring suddenly the form of thick, black molasses, a little sticky, to be sure, but tangible.

Sip made no reply, and Perley, suddenly aware of the lateness of the hour, started in dismay to take her leave. It occurred to her that the sticky stone-china dishes were yet to be washed, and that she had done a thoughtless thing in imposing, for a novel evening's entertainment, upon the scanty leisure of a worn-out factory girl. . . .

CHAPTER V

Bub Mell

It was a March night, and a gray night, and a wild night; Perley Kelso stepped out into it, from the damp little stone house, with something of the confusion of the time upon her. Her head and heart both ached. She felt like a stranger setting foot in a strange land. Old, homelike boundary lines of things to which her smooth young life had rounded, wavered before her. It even occurred to her that she should never be very happy again, for knowing that factory girls ate black molasses and had the cotton cough.

She meant to tell Maverick about it. She might have meant many other things, but for being so suddenly and violently jerked by the elbow that she preserved herself with difficulty from a smart fall into the slushy street. Striking out with one hand to preserve her balance, she found herself in the novel position of collaring either a very old young child or a very young old man, it was impossible at first sight to tell which. Whatever he was, it was easy at first sight to tell that he was filthy and ragged.

"Le' go!" yelled the old young creature, writhing. "Le' go, I say, dern yer! Le' me be!"

Perley concluded, as her eyes wonted to the dark street, that the old young creature was by right a child.

"If yer hadn't le' go I'd 'a' made yer, yer bet," said the boy, gallantly. "Pretty way to treat a cove[2] as doin' yer a favor. You bet. Hi-igh!"

This, with a cross between a growl of defiance and a whine of injury.

"Guess what I've got o' yourn? You couldn't. You bet."

"But I don't bet," said Perley, with an amused face.

"Yer don't? *I* do. Hi-igh! Don't I though? *You* bet! Now what do you call that? Say!"

"I call that my glove. I did not miss it till this minute. Did you pick it up? Thank you."

"You needn't thank me till you've got it, *you* needn't," said the child. "*I*'m a cove as knows a thing or two. I want ten cents. You bet I do."

[2]Nineteenth-century slang for "fellow." — EDS.

"Where do you live?" asked Perley.

He lived down to East Street. Fust Tenement. No. 6. What business was it of hern, he'd like to know.

"Have you a father and mother?"

Lor yes! Two of 'em. Why shouldn't he?

"I believe I will go home with you," said Perley, "it is so nearby; and — I suppose you are poor?"

Lor, yes. She might bet.

"And I can make it right about the recovery of the glove when I get there?"

"No-n-oo you don't!" promptly, from the cove as knew a thing or two. "You'll sling over to the old folks, I'll bet. You don't come that!"

"But," suggested Perley, "I can, perhaps, give your father and mother a much larger sum of money than I should think it best to give you. If they are poor, I should think you would be glad that they should have it. And I can't walk in, you know, and give your father and mother money for nothing."

"You give *me* ten cents," said this young old man, stoutly, "or what do you s'pose I'll do with this 'ere glove? Guess now!"

Perley failed to guess now.

"I'll cut 'n' run with it. I'll cut 'n' run like mad. *You* bet. I'll snip it up with a pair of shears I know about. I'll jab holes in it with a jackknife I've got. No, I won't. I'll swop it off with my sister, for a yaller yaggate[3] I've got my eye on in the 'pothecarry's winder. My sister's a mill gal. She'll wear it on one hand to meetin', an' stick the t'other in her muff. That's what I'll do. How'll you like that? Hi-igh! You bet!"

"At least, I can go home with you," said Perley, absently effecting an exchange between her glove and a fresh piece of ten-cent scrip, which the boy held up in the light from a shop window, and tested with the air of a middle-aged counterfeiter; "you ought to have been at home an hour ago."

"Lor now," said this promising youth, "I was just thinkin' so ought you."

"What is your name?" asked Perley, as they turned their two faces (one would have been struck, seeing them together, with thinking how much younger the woman looked than the child), toward East Street, the First Tenement, and No. 6.

"My name's Bub. Bub Mell. They used to call me Bubby, for short, till I got so large they give it up."

"How old are you?"

"Eight last Febiverry."

"What do you do?"

"Work to the Old Stone."

"But I thought no children under ten years of age were allowed to work in the mills."

"You must be green!" said Bub.

"But you go to school?"

---

[3]"Agate," that is, a marble. — EDS.

"I went to school till I got so large they give it up."

"But you go a part of the time, of course?"

"No, I don't neither. Don't you s'pose I knows?"

"What is that you have in your mouth?" asked Perley, suddenly.

Bub relieved himself of a quid of fabulous size, making quite superfluous the concise reply, "Terbaccer."

"I never saw such a little boy as you chew tobacco before," said Perley, gasping.

"You must be green! I took my fust swag a year and a half ago. We all does. I'm just out, it happens," said Bub, with a candid smile. "That's what I wanted your ten cents for. I smokes too," added Bub, with an air of having tried not to mention it, for modesty's sake, but of being tempted overmuch. "You bet I do! Sometimes it's pipes, and sometimes it's ends. As a gener'l thing, give me a pipe."

"What else do you do?" demanded Perley, faintly.

"What else?" Bub reflected, with his old, old head on one side. He bet on marbles. He knew a tip-top gin-sling,[4] when he see it, well as most folks. He could pitch pennies. He could ketch a rat ag'in any cove on East Street. Lor! couldn't he?

"But what else?" persisted Perley.

Bub was puzzled. He thought there warn't nothin' else. After that he had his supper.

"And after that?"

Lor. After that he went to bed.

"And after that?"

After that he got up and went in.

"Went in where?"

She must be green. Into the Old Stone. Spoolin', you know.

Did he go to church?

She might bet he didn't! Why, when should he ketch the rats?

Nor Sunday school?

He went to the Mission once. Had a card with a green boy onto it. Got so old he give it up.

What did he expect, asked Perley, in a sudden, severe burst of religious enthusiasm, would become of him when he died?

Eh?

When he died, what would become of him?

Lor.

Could he read?

Fust Primer. Never tried nothin' else.

Could he write?

No.

Was he going to school again?

Couldn't say.

Why didn't his parents send him?

[4]An obscure term, possibly a drink made of sweetened gin. — Eds.

Couldn't say that. Thought they was too old; no, thought he was too old; well, he didn't know; thought somebody was too old, and give it up.

Was this where he lived?

She must be green! Of course he did. Comin' in?

Perley was coming in. With hesitation she came in.

She came into what struck her as a very unpleasant place; a narrow, crumbling place; a place with a peculiar odor; a very dark place. Bub cheerfully suggested that she'd better look out.

For what?

Holes.

Where?

Holes in the stairs. *He* used to step into 'em and sprain his ankles, you bet, till he got so old he give it up. She'd better look out for the plaster too. She'd bump her head. She never saw nothin' break like that plaster did; great cakes of it. Here, this way. Keerful now!

By this way and that way, by being careful now and patient then and quite persistent at all times, Perley contrived to follow Bub in safety up two flights of villainous stairs and into the sudden shine of a low, little room, into which he shot rather than introduced her, with the unembarrasing remark that he didn't know what she'd come for, but there she was.

There were six children, a cooking stove, a bed, a table, and a man with stooped shoulders in the room. There was an odor in the room like that upon the stairs. The man, the children, the cooking stove, the bed, the table, and the odor quite filled the room.

The room opened into another room, in which there seemed to be a bureau, a bed, and a sick woman.

Miss Kelso met with but a cool reception in these rooms. The man, the children, the cooking stove, the bed, the odor, and the woman thrust her at once, she could not have said how, into the position of an intruder. The sick woman, upon hearing her errand, flung herself over to the wall with an impatient motion. The man sullenly invited her to sit down; gave her to understand — again she could hardly have told how — that he wanted no money of her; no doubt the boy had had more than he deserved; but that, if she felt inclined, she might sit down.

"To tell the truth," said Perley, in much confusion, "I did not come so much on account of the glove as on account of the boy."

What had the boy been up to now? The sullen man darted so fierce a look at the boy, who sat with his old, old smile, lighting an old pipe behind the cooking stove, that Perley hastened to explain that she did not blame the boy. Who could blame the boy?

"But he was out so late about the streets, Mr. Mell. He uses tobacco as most children use candy. And a child of that age ought not to be in the mills, sir," said Perley, warming, "he ought to be at school!"

O, that was all, was it? Mr. Mell pushed back his stooped shoulders into his chair with an air of relief, and Bub lighted his pipe in peace. But he had a frowning face, this Mr. Mell, and he turned its frown upon his visitor. He would like to know what business it was of hers what he did with his boy, and made no scruple of saying so.

"It ought to be some of my business," said the young lady, growing bolder, "when a child of eight years works all the year round in these mills. I have no doubt that I seem very rude, sir; but I have in fact come out, and come out alone as you see me, to see with my own eyes and to hear with my own ears how people live who work in these mills."

Had she? Mr. Mell smiled grimly. Not a pleasant job for a lady he should think; and uncommon.

"It's a job I mean to finish," said Miss Kelso, firmly. "The stairs in this house are in a shocking condition. What is — excuse me — the very peculiar odor which I notice on these premises? It must be poisonous to the sick woman, — your wife?"

It was his wife. Yes; consumption; took it weaving; had been abed this four month; couldn't say how long she'd hold out. Doctor said, five month ago, as nothin' would save her but a change. So he sits and talks about Florida and the South sun, and the folks as had been saved down there. It was a sort of a fretful thing to hear him. Florida! Good God! How was the likes of him to get a dyin' wife to Florida?

She didn't like strangers overmuch; better not go nigh her; she was kind of fretful; the childern was kind of fretful too; sometimes they cried like as his head would split; he kept the gell home to look after 'em; not the first gell; he couldn't keep her to home at all; she made seven; he didn't know's he blamed her; it was a kind of a fretful place, let alon' the stairs and the smell. It come from the flood, the smell did.

"The flood?"

Yes, the cellar flooded up every spring from the river; it might be drained, he should think; but it never was as he heard of. There was the offal from the mills floated in; it left a smell pretty much the year round; and a kind of chill. Then they hadn't any drain, you see. There was that hole in the wall where they threw out dishwater and such. So it fell into the yard under the old woman's window, and made her kind of fretful. It made her fretful to see the children ragged too. She greeted over it odd times. She had a clean way about her, when she was up and about, the old woman had.

"Who owns this house?" asked Miss Kelso, with burning eyes.

The man seemed unaccountably reluctant to reply; he fixed the fire, scolded Bub, scolded a few other children, and shook the baby, but was evidently unwilling to reply.

Upon Perley's repeating her question, the sick woman, with another impatient fling against the wall, cried out sharply, What was the odds? Do tell the girl. It couldn't harm her, could it? Her husband, very ill at ease, believed that young Mr. Hayle owned the house; though they dealt with his lessee; Mr. Hayle had never been down himself.

For a sullen man, with a stoop in the shoulders, a frown in the face, seven children, a sick wife, and no drain spout, Mr. Mell did very well about this. He grew even communicative, when the blaze in Miss Kelso's eyes went out, paled by the sudden fire in her cheek.

He supposed he was the more riled up by this and that, he said, for being English; Scotch by breed, you know; they'd named the first gell after her grandma, — Nynee; quite Scotch, ye see; she was a Hielander, grandma, — but married to England, and used to their ways. Now there was ways and ways, and *one* way was a ten-hour bill.[5] There was no mistaking that, one way was a ten-hour bill, and it was a way they did well by in England, and it was a way they'd have to walk in this side the water yet — *w-a-l-k in y-e-t!* He'd been turned out o' mills in this country twice for goin' into a ten-hour strike; once to Lawrence and once up to New Hampshire. He'd given it up. It didn't pay. Since the old woman was laid up, he must get steady work or starve.

He'd been a factory operative[6] thirty-three years; twenty-three years to home, and ten years to the United States, only one year as he was into the army; he was forty-three years old. Why didn't he send that boy to school? Why didn't he drive a span of grays! He couldn't send the boy to school, nor none of the other boys to school, except as mayhap they took their turn occasional. He made it a point to send them till they was eight if he could; he didn't like to put a young un to spoolin' before he was eight, if he could help it. The law? O yes, there was a law, and there was ways of getting round a law, bless you! Ways enough. There was parties as had it in their hands to make it none so easy, and again to make it none so hard.

"What parties?"

"Parties as had an interest in spoolin' in common with the parent."

"The child's employers?"

Mr. Mell suddenly upon his guard. Mr. Mell trusted to the good feelin' of a young lady as would have a heart for the necessities of poverty, and changed the subject.

"But you cannot mean," persisted Perley, "that a healthy man like you, with his grown children earning, finds it impossible to support his family without the help of a poor baby like Bub over there?"

Mr. Mell quite meant it. Didn't know what other folks could do; he couldn't; not since the rise in prices, and the old woman givin' out. Why, look at here. There was the gell, twenty year old; she worked to weaving; there was the boy as was seventeen, him reading the picture paper over to the table there, he draws and twists; there was another gell of fifteen, you might say, hander at the harnesses into the dressing room; then there was Bub, and the babies.

---

[5] A central issue for unions and labor parties at this time was the effort to pass laws to restrict the working day to ten or even eight hours. Even when such bills were passed, employers generally ignored the laws, which were rarely enforced. (See the discussion of the eight-hour movement in the Introduction, p. 421) — EDS.

[6] Mr. Mell's "testimony" may be found in the reports of the Massachusetts Bureau of Labor. — ESP

Counting in the old woman and the losses, he must have Bub. The old woman ate a powerful sight of meat. He went without himself whensoever he could; but his work was hard; it made him kind of deathly to the stomach if he went without his meat.

What losses did he speak of? Losses enough. High water. Low water. Strikes. Machinery under repair. Besides the deathly feelin' to the stomach. He'd been out for sickness off and on, first and last, a deal; though he looked a healthy man, as she said, and you wouldn't think it. Fact was, he'd never worked but *one whole* month in six year; nor he'd never taken a week's vacation at a time, of his own will an' pleasure, for six year. Sometimes he lost two days and a half a week, right along, for lack of work.7 Sometimes he give out just for the heat. He'd often seen it from 110° to 116° Fahrenheit in the dressing room. He wished he was back to England. He wouldn't deny but there was advantages here, but he wished he was back.

(This man had worked in England from 6 A.M. to 8 o'clock P.M., with no time allowed for dinner; he paid threepence a week to an old woman who brought hot water into the mills at noon, with which she filled the tin pot in which he had brought tea and sugar from home. He had, besides, a piece of bread. He ate with one hand and worked with the other.)

He warn't complainin' of nobody in particular, *to* nobody in particular, but he thought he had a kind of a fretful life. He hadn't been able to lay by a penny, not by this way nor that, considerin' his family of nine and the old woman, and the feelin' to the stomach. Now that made him fretful sometimes. He was a temperate man, he'd like to have it borne in mind. He was a member of a ten-hour society, of the Odd Fellows, Good Templars, and Orthodox Church.

Anything for him? No; he didn't know of anything she could do for him. He'd never taken charity from nobody's hands yet. He might, mayhap, come to it some day. He supposed it was fretful of him, but he'd rather lay in his grave. The old woman she wouldn't never know nothing of that; it was a kind of a comfort, that was. He was obliged to her for wishing him kindly. Sorry the old woman was so fretful tonight; she was oncommon noisy; and the children. He'd ask her to call again, if the old woman wasn't so fretful about strangers. Hold the door open for the lady, Bub. Put down your pipe, sir! Haven't ye no more manners than to smoke in a lady's face? There. Now, hold the door open wide.

Wide, very wide, the door flung that Bub opened to Perley Kelso. As wide it seemed to her as the gray, wild, March night itself. At the bottom of the stairs, she stood still to take its touch upon her burning face.

Bub crept down after her, and knocked the ashes out of his pipe against the door.

"Ain't used to the dark, be ye?"

No; not much used to the dark.

7"We may here add that our inquiries will authorize us to say that three out of every five laboring men were out of employ." — *Statistics of Labor.* — ESP.

"Afraid?"

Not at all afraid.

Lor. He was goin' to offer to see her home, — for ten cents. *He* used to be afraid. Got so old he give it up. . . .

[Perley meets Sip on her way home from the Mells'. As they pass through town, Sip gives Perley thumbnail sketches of the people they see, all of them workers whose lives are difficult. Reaching home, Perley invites Sip in. — EDS.]

The lofty, luxurious house was lighted and still. Sip held her breath when the heavy front door shut her into it. Her feet fell on a carpet like thick, wild moss, as she crossed the warm wide hall. Miss Kelso took her, scarcely aware, it seemed, that she did so, into the parlors, and shut their oaken doors upon their novel guest. She motioned the girl to a chair, and flung herself upon another.

Now, for a young lady who had had a season ticket to the Opera every winter of her life, it will be readily conjectured that she had passed an exciting evening. In her way, even the mill girl felt this. But in her way, the mill girl was embarassed and alarmed by the condition in which she found Miss Kelso.

The young lady sat, white to the lips, and trembled violently; her hands covered and re-covered each other, with a feeble motion, as they lay upon her lap; the eyes had burned to a still white heat; her breath came as if she were in pain.

Suddenly she rose with a little crouch like a beautiful leopardess and struck the gray and green chess table with her soft hand; the blow snapped one of her rings.

"You do not understand," she cried, "you people who work and suffer, how it is with us! We are born in a dream, I tell you! Look at these rooms! Who would think — in such a room as this — except he dreamed it, that the mothers of very little children died for want of a few hundreds and a change of climate? Why, the curtains in this room cost six! See how it is! You touch us — in such a room — but we dream; we shake you off. If you cry out to us, we only dream that you cry. We are not cruel, we are only asleep. Sip Garth, when we have clear eyes and a kind heart, and perhaps a clear head, and are waked up, for instance, without much warning, it is *nature* to spring upon our wealth, to hate our wealth, to feel that we have no right to our wealth; no more moral right to it than the opium eater has to his drug!

"Why, Sip," rising to pick up the chess table, "I never knew until tonight what it was like to be poor. It wasn't that I didn't care, as you said. I didn't *know.* I thought it was a respectable thing, a comfortable thing; a thing that couldn't be helped; a clean thing, or a dirty thing, a lazy thing, or a drunken thing; a thing that must be, just as mud must be in April; a thing to put on overshoes for."

And now what did she think?

"Who knows what to think," said Perley Kelso, "that is just waked up?"

"Miss Kelso?" said Sip.

"Yes," said Miss Kelso.

"I never knew in all my life how grand a room could be till I come into this grand room tonight. Now, you see, if it was mine — "

"What would you do, if this grand room were yours?" asked Miss Kelso, curiously.

"Just supposing it, you know, — am I very saucy?"

"Not very, Sip."

"Why," said Sip, "the fact is, I'd bring Nynee Mell in to spend an evening!"

An engraving that lay against a rich easel in a corner of the room attracted the girl's attention presently. She went down on her knees to examine it. It chanced to be Lemude's dreaming Beethoven. Sip was very still about it.

"What is that fellow doing?" she asked, after a while, — "him with the stick in his hand."

She pointed to the leader of the shadowy orchestra, touching the *baton* through the glass, with her brown finger.

"I have always supposed," said Perley, "that he was only floating with the rest; you see the orchestra behind him."

"Floating after those women with their arms up? No, he isn't!"

"What is he doing?"

"It's riding over him, — the orchestra. He can't master it. Don't you see? It sweeps him along. He can't help himself. They come and come. How fast they come! How he fights and falls! O, I know how they come. That's the way things come to me; things I could do, things I could say, things I could get rid of if I had the chance; they come in the mills mostly; they tumble over me just so; I never have the chance. How he fights! I didn't know there was any such picture as that in the world. I'd like to look at that picture day and night. See! O, I know how they come."

"Miss Kelso — " after another silence and still upon her knees before the driving Dream and the restless dreamer. "You see, that's it. That's like your pretty things. I'd keep your pretty things if I was you. It ain't that there shouldn't be music anywhere. It's only that the music shouldn't ride over the master. Seems to me it is like that."

CHAPTER VI

Mouldings and Bricks

"Maverick!"

"At your service."

"But Maverick — "

"What then?"

"Last year, at Saratoga,[8] I paid fifteen dollars apiece for having my dresses done up!"

---

[8]Saratoga, New York, with its famous racetrack, was and is a resort for the wealthy. — EDS.

"Thus supporting some pious and respectable widow for the winter, I have no doubt."

"Maverick! how much did *I* think about the widow?"

"I should say, from a cursory examination of the subject, that your thoughts would be of less consequence — excuse me — to a pious and respectable widow, than — how many times fifteen? Without doubt, a serious lack of taste on the part of a widow; but, I fear, a fatal fact."

"But, Maverick! I know a man on East Street whom I never could make up my mind to look in the face again, if he should see the bill for santalina[9] in those carriage cushions!"

The bill was on file, undoubtedly, suggested Maverick. Allow her friend an opportunity to see it, by all means.

"Maverick! do you see that shawl on the arm of the *tête-à-tête?*[10] It cost me three thousand dollars."

Why not? Since she did the thing the honor to become it, she must in candor admit, amazingly.

"And there's lace up stairs in my bureau drawer for which I paid fifty dollars a yard. And, Maverick! I believe the contents of any single jewel case in that same drawer would found a free bed in a hospital. And my bill for Farina cologne and kid gloves last year would supply a sick woman with beefsteak for this. And Maverick!"

"And what?" very languidly from Maverick.

"Nothing, only — why, Maverick! I am a member of a Christian church. It has just occurred to me."

"Maverick!" again, after a pause, in which Maverick had languished quite out of the conversation, and had entertained himself by draping Perley in the shawl from the *tête-à-tête*, as if she had been a lay figure[11] for some crude and gorgeous design which he failed to grasp. Now he made a Sibyl of her, now a Deborah, now a Maid of Orleans, a priestess, a princess, a Juno; after some reflection, a Grace Darling;[12] after more, a prophetess at prayer.

"Maverick! we must have a library in our mills."

"Must we?" mused Maverick, extinguishing his prophetess in a gorgeous turban.

"There; how will that do? What a Nourmahal[13] you are!"

"And relief societies, and halftime schools, and lectures, and reading rooms, and, I hope, a dozen better things. Those will only do to start with."

---

[9]"Santalina" is a perfume made from sandalwood. — EDS.

[10]A *"tête-à-tête"* (French for "head to head") is a love seat with two seats side by side but facing in opposite directions. — EDS.

[11]A "lay figure" is a mannequin often used by artists to demonstrate the arrangement of drapery. — EDS.

[12]"Sibyl" is a prophetess in Greek mythology. "Deborah" is a judge and prophet in the Bible (Judges 4–5). "Maid of Orleans" refers to Joan of Arc. "Juno" is the chief goddess in Roman mythology. "Grace Darling" is an Englishwoman who saved six people from a shipwreck. — EDS.

[13]"Nourmahal" was the wife of the Mogul emperor Jehangir (reigned 1605–27) and heroine of a popular nineteenth-century poem, "The Light of the Harem." — EDS.

"A modest request — for Cophetua,[14] for instance," said Maverick, dropping the shawl in a blazing heap at her feet.

"Maverick! I've been a lay figure in life long enough, if you please. Maverick, Maverick! I cannot play any longer. I think you will be sorry if you play with me any longer."

Cophetua said this with knitted brows. Maverick tossed the shawl away, and sat down beside her. The young man's face also had a wrinkle between the placid eyes.

"Those will only do to start with," repeated Perley, "but start with those we must. And, Maverick," with rising color, "some tenement houses, if you please, that are fit for human beings to inhabit; more particularly human beings who pay their rentals to Christian people."

"It seems to me, Perley," said her lover, pleasantly, "a great blunder in the political economy of Hayle and Kelso that you and I should quarrel over the business. Why *should* we quarrel over the business? It is the last subject in the world that collectively, and as comfortable and amiable engaged people, *can* concern us. If you must amuse yourself with these people, and must run athwart the business, go to father. Have you been to father?"

"I had a long talk with your father," said Perley, "yesterday."

"What did he say to you?"

"He said something about Political Economy; he said something else about Supply and Demand. He said something, too, about the State of the Market."

"He said, in short, that we cannot afford any more experiments in philanthropy on this town of Five Falls?"

"He said, in short, just that."

"He said, undoubtedly, the truth. It would be out of the question. Why, we ran the works at a dead loss half of last year; kept the hands employed, and paid their wages regularly, when the stock was a drug in the market and lay like lead on our hands. Small thanks we get for that from the hands, or — you."

"Your machinery, I suppose, would not have been improved by lying unused?" observed Perley, quietly.

"It would have been injured, I presume."

"And it *has* been found worthwhile, from a business point of view, to retain *employees* even at a loss, rather than to scatter them?"

"It has been, perhaps," admitted Maverick, uneasily. "One would think, however, Perley, that you thought me destitute of common humanity, just because you *cannot* understand the ins and outs of the thousand and one questions which perplex a businessman. I own that I do not find these people as much of a diversion as you do, but I protest that I do not abuse them. They go about their business, and I go about mine. Master and man meet on business grounds, and business grounds alone. Bub Mell and a

[14]"Cophetua" is a fictional African king in the ballad "Cophetua and the Beggar Maid." — EDS.

young lady with nothing else to do may meet, without doubt, upon religious grounds; upon the highest religious grounds."

"These improvements which I suggest," pursued Perley, waving Maverick's last words away with her left hand (it was without ornament and had a little bruise upon one finger), "have been successful experiments, all of them, in other mills; most of them in the great Pacific. Look at the great Pacific!"

"The great Pacific can afford them," said Maverick, shortly. "That's the way with our little country mills always. If we don't bankrupt ourselves by reflecting every risk that the great concerns choose to run, some soft-hearted and soft-headed philanthropist pokes his finger into our private affairs, and behold, there's a hue and cry over us directly."

"For a little country mill," observed Perley, making certain figures in the air with her bruised white finger, "I think, if I may judge from my own income, that a library and a reading room would not bankrupt us, at least this year. However, if Hayle and Kelso cannot afford some few of these little alterations, I think their silent partner can."

"Very well," laughed Maverick; "we'll make the money and you may spend it."

"Maverick Hayle," said Perley, after a silence, "do you know that every law of this State which regulates the admission of children into factories is broken in your mills?"

"Ah?" said Maverick.

"I ask," insisted Perley, "if you know it?"

"Why, no," said Maverick, with a smile; "I cannot say that I know it exactly. I know that nobody not behind the scenes can conceive of the dodges these people invent to scrape and screw a few dollars, more or less, out of their children. As a rule, I believe the more they earn themselves the more they scrape and screw. I know how they can lie about a child's age. Turn a child out of one mill for his three months' schooling, and he's in another before night, half the time. Get him fairly to school, and I've known three months' certificates begged or bribed out of a schoolmistress at the end of three weeks. Now, what can I do? You can't expect a mill master to have the time, or devote it to running round the streets compelling a few Irish babies to avail themselves of the educational privileges of this great and glorious country!"

"That is a thing," observed Perley, "that I can look after in some measure, having, as you noticed, nothing else to do."

"That is a thing," said Maverick, sharply, "which I desire, Perley, that you will let alone. I must leave it to the overseers, or we shall be plunged into confusion worse confounded. That is a thing which I must insist upon it that you do not meddle with."

Perley flushed vividly. The little scar upon her finger flushed too. She raised it to her lips as if it pained her.

"There is reason," urged Maverick, — "there is reason in all things, even in a young lady's fancies. Just look at it! You run all over Five Falls alone on a dark night, very improperly, to hear mill people complain of their drains, and — unrebuked by you — of their master. You come home and break your engagement ring and cut your finger. Forthwith you must needs turn my mill hands into lapdogs, and feed them on — what was it? roast beef? — out of your jewelry box!"

"I do not think," said Perley, faintly smiling, "that you understand, Maverick."

"I do *not* think I understand," said Maverick.

"You do not understand," repeated Perley, firmly but faintly still. "Maverick! Maverick! if you cannot understand, I am afraid we shall both be very sorry!"

Perley got up and crossed the room two or three times. There was a beautiful restlessness about her which Maverick, leaning back upon the *tête-à-tête*, with his mustache between his fingers, noted and admired.

"I cannot tell you," pursued Perley in a low voice, "how the world has altered to me, nor how I have altered to myself, within the past few weeks. I have no words to say how these people seem to me to have been thrust upon my hands, — as empty, idle, foolish hands, God knows, as ever he filled with an unsought gift!"

"Now I thought," mentioned Maverick, gracefully, "that both the people and the hands did well enough as they were."

Perley spread out the shining hands, as if in appeal or pain, and cried out, as before, "Maverick! Maverick!" but hardly herself knowing, it seemed, why she cried.

"One would think," pursued Maverick, with a jerk at his mustache, "to hear and to see you, Perley, that there were no evils in the country but the evils of the factory system; that there was no poverty but among weavers earning ten dollars a week. Questions which political economists spend life in disputing, you expect a mill master — "

"Who doesn't care a fig about them," interrupted Perley.

"Who doesn't care a fig about them," admitted the mill master, "you are right; between you and me, you are right; who doesn't care a fig about them — to settle. Now there's father; he is *au fait*[15] in all these matters; has a theory for every case of whooping cough, — and a mission school. Once for all, I must beg to have it understood that I turn you and the State committees over to father. You should hear him talk to a State committee!"

"And yet," said Perley, sadly, "your father and you tie my hands to precisely the same extent by different methods."

"No?" said Maverick. "Really?"

"He with Adam Smith,[16] and you with a *tête-à-tête*. He is too learned, and you are too lazy. I have not been educated to reason with him, and I suppose I am too fond of you to deal with you," said the young lady. "But, Maverick, there *is* something in this matter which neither of you touch. There is *something* about the relations of rich and poor, of master and man,

---

[15] *"Au fait"* is French for "conversant with." — EDS.

[16] The economist Adam Smith (1723–90) wrote *Wealth of Nations* (1776), in which he developed the theory of free-market economics. — EDS.

with which the state of the market has nothing whatever to do. There is *something*, — a claim, a duty, a puzzle, it is all too new to me to know what to call it, — but I am convinced that there is *something* at which a man cannot lie and twirl his mustache forever."

Being a woman, and having no mustache to twirl, urged Maverick, nothing could well be more natural than that she should think so. An appropriate opinion, and very charmingly expressed. Should he order the horses at half past ten?

"Maverick!" cried Perley, thrusting out her hands as before, and as before hardly knowing, it seemed, why she cried, — "Maverick, Maverick!" . . .

READING CRITICALLY

1. Characterize Perley Kelso's attitude toward the mills and the workers at the beginning of the selection.

2. Phelps tells the rather horrifying story of Bub Mell in a comic tone (somewhat in the style of Charles Dickens). What is the effect of writing the story this way? How does it make you feel about Bub?

3. What seem to be Perley's motives in visiting Sip Garth and Bub Mell's family? How does she treat them?

4. Sip Garth says that she doesn't complain about the wages. What are her complaints?

WRITING ANALYTICALLY

1. *The Silent Partner* attempts to portray the way a member of the wealthy class comes to see the working class. Write a brief essay in which you identify the stages through which Perley Kelso passes as she changes her attitude toward the workers. Considering your own experiences in coming to understand people who are different from you, do you find the description of Perley's experience realistic?

2. Perley attempts to explain to Sip the view that her class takes of the working class (p. 546). Why does Perley have this view? Does Maverick share the view she expresses? What reasons do Maverick and Mr. Hayle give for rejecting her ideas about helping the mill workers? Do Perley's ideas seem appropriate given what she has learned about the workers? Does Phelps seem to be endorsing Perley's personal response to the dilemma of class difference? Write an essay answering these questions and then evaluating Perley's reactions, based on your own response to the situation Phelps describes.

3. Phelps used reports from the Bureau of Labor Statistics as the basis of her descriptions of workers' conditions. Look at the Senate testimony on working conditions (p. 553) to get a sense of what Phelps was referring to. In your opinion, has she presented the material fairly? How effective do you think it is to present such testimony in the form of a novel? If Phelps sought reform, should she have written something other than a novel? Write an essay in which you argue that Phelps's use of fiction is or is not a more effective way of moving you to social action than a nonfiction essay would be. Support your answer by referring, if you can, to other novels

(such as *Looking Backward,* p. 477) or to movies or TV shows that present fictional accounts of real social issues. Are these forms more or less effective than documentaries? Why, or why not?

TESTIMONY BEFORE THE SENATE COMMITTEE ON THE RELATIONS BETWEEN CAPITAL AND LABOR (1883)

The material in this selection comes primarily from John A. Garraty's compilation of excerpts from the Senate Committee hearings, *Labor and Capital in the Gilded Age.* Much of the information about the witnesses also comes from Garraty.

The Senate Committee on the Relations between Capital and Labor was formed in 1883 to investigate the causes of labor strikes and industrial relations generally. The committee convened in several cities to bring in local witnesses, and the hearings generated thousands of pages of testimony. The testimony was published in 1885, but the only apparent result of the committee's work was the establishment of a federal Bureau of Labor Statistics.

Note: Reading questions follow the testimony of each witness, and writing questions follow all of the testimony.

SAMUEL GOMPERS

Samuel Gompers (1850–1924) was born in London and immigrated with his family to New York City in 1863. Gompers's father was a cigarmaker and the son followed him into the same calling. Cigarmakers were traditionally working-class intellectuals and political activists. In the quiet workshops, one worker would be elected to read aloud from newspapers and magazines purchased from a common fund while the others would produce the reader's quota of cigars. Young Gompers proved to be a good reader and pursued his own education through voracious reading. Attracted to socialist philosophy, Gompers taught himself German so that he could read Marx in the original. He never joined a socialist party, however, preferring the role of union organizer.

All testimony, except that of N. R. Fielding, is from John A. Garraty, *Labor and Capital in the Gilded Age: Testimony Taken by the Senate Committee upon the Relations between Labor and Capital —* *1883* (Boston: Little, Brown, 1968), 8–18, 26–29, 30–33, 66–72, 118–23, 133–36. The Fielding testimony is from *The Black Worker during the Era of the Knights of Labor,* edited by Philip S. Foner and Ronald L. Lewis, vol. 3 of *The Black Worker: A Documentary History from Colonial Times to the Present* (Philadelphia: Temple University Press, 1978), 23–24.

In the notes, EDS. = Patricia Bizzell and Bruce Herzberg.

Gompers reorganized the Cigarmakers Union, setting up a national office, a dues structure, and unemployment benefits. In 1886, he was elected to the Constitution Committee of the newly created American Federation of Labor (AFL), an association of autonomous craft unions (see Introduction p. 421) that organized skilled workers by craft rather than by industry. (A craft union consists of workers from a single occupation, while an industrial union consists of all the workers in a particular industry.) Thereafter, Gompers was elected president of the Federation and was reelected every year but one until his death. He operated on the principle of providing "moral" leadership, using persuasion, encouraging mutual support among unions, and attempting to improve the lives and civic involvement of workers.

The Witness: The condition of the working people appears to be coming to what may rightly be termed a focus. On the one hand it would be well to note the underlying motives that frequently break out in what are generally termed strikes. Strikes are the result of a condition, and are not, as is generally or frequently understood, the cause. For instance, in the State of Massachusetts they have a ten-hour law,[1] intended to benefit the female and child operatives there, yet the employers (and the same is true in Cohoes, in this State [New York], and other places where the hours of labor are recognized as settled) or their agents start up the mills several minutes, sometimes seven, eight, nine, or ten minutes, before the time for commencing to work according to rule and law. In other instances they close them at "noon" several minutes after twelve o'clock and open them again several minutes before the hour, or half hour rather, has elapsed, closing again for the day several minutes after the rule requires. These employers are pretty well described by some of the English economists and labor advocates — not labor advocates, but men who have made economic questions a study; they call them "minute thieves." . . .

In the branch of industry in which I work we have a bane to contend with, a curse, known as the manufacturing of cigars in tenement houses, in which the employer hires a row of tenements four or five stories high, with two, three, or four families living on each floor, occupying a room and bedroom, or a room, bedroom, and an apology for a kitchen. The tobacco for the work is given out by the manufacturer or his superintendent to the operatives who work there, the husband and wife, and they seldom work without one or more of their children, if they have any. Even their parents, if they have any, work also in the room, and any indigent relative that may live with them also helps along. I myself made an investigation of these houses about two years ago; went through them and made measurements of them, and found that however clean the people might desire to be they could not be so. The bedroom is generally dark, and contains all

---

[1]A law restricting the working day to ten hours. Even when such bills existed, however, employers generally ignored them and they were rarely enforced. (See the discussion of the eight-hour movement in the Introduction, p. 421.) — EDS.

the wet tobacco that is not intended for immediate use, but perhaps for use on the following day; while in the front room (or back room, as the case may be) the husband and wife and child, or any friend or relative that works with them, three or four or five persons, are to be found. Each has a table at which to work. The tobacco which they work and the clippings or cuttings, as they are termed, are lying around the floor, while the scrap or clip that is intended to be used immediately for the making of cigars is lying about to dry. Children are playing about, as well as their puny health will permit them, in the tobacco. I have found, I believe, the most miserable conditions prevailing in those houses that I have seen at any time in my life.

Sen. Blair: How many families are thus engaged in the manufacture of cigars in this city [New York City]? — A. Between 1,900 and 2,000. The lowest ascertained number was 1,920 families. That was about five or six months ago.

Q. About 10,000 people, taking the average to a family of five? — A. Probably. These rooms I found to be, the main room, in which they work, about 12 feet by 8 or 9; the height of ceiling generally about 7 feet 6 inches to 8 feet 2 inches. . . .

Sen. George: What was the size of the bedrooms? — A. The bedrooms were generally 6 feet by 8, or, in some instances, less. The kitchen was generally what is known in New York tenements as "dark" — an intermediate room. There is, first, the front or back room, as the case may be, then the kitchen, which has no light, and then another room in the back, which has no ventilation whatever except an aperture about 2 feet square in the side, and leading into a hall which leads into the street or the yard.

Q. The kitchen is not so large as the front room? — A. Not so long; it is as wide, generally.

Q. There is a narrow hall, making four families on each floor? — A. Four families on each floor.

Q. In what condition were the yards? — A. I made an investigation into that also, and found that the yards were all dirty. The halls were kept very dirty with tobacco stems and refuse that accumulates from the tobacco. In one instance it bordered on the ludicrous. There was a sign, "Keep off the grass!" The only "grass" that I could see was the green paint on the walls and the tobacco stems lying around by the hundred weight. The water closets are all vaults, in very few places connected with sewers, vaults in the backyard, around which a few boards have been nailed and the places termed "water closets."[2] The water supply is very meager indeed.

Q. How many stories high are the buildings? — A. Four, generally; sometimes higher.

Q. Is there a water closet for each family? — A. No; there are generally two or three private closets, which are locked and keys given to, probably, one closet for two, three, or four families, there being not more than three or four water closets for all the families in the building. On the lower floor

---

[2]The "water closets" were outhouses, simply holes in the ground. — EDS.

or basement generally in those houses there are stores, sometimes grocery stores or lager-beer saloons, or secondhand furniture stores, or Chinese laundries.

Q. Do you mean to say that about 1,900 families, engaged in the manufacture of cigars, live in the manner which you have just described? — *A.* Four-fifths of them, I think. Within this last year one of the manufacturers has endeavored to build a row of houses that are an improvement upon the old ones; but notwithstanding all attempts to keep these places clean, that is impossible, in consequence of the long hours of toil and the fact that all of the family are employed right at the work of cigar-making. . . .

The Cigarmakers' International Union adopted a system of agitation against the tenement-house cigar manufacture some years ago, believing that it was a public nuisance, and the press of the city of New York, together with that of the entire country, took this matter in hand, discussed it ably, exposed the iniquity of the system and the greed and avarice to which many men will resort in unfair competition, even with their fairer rivals in the trade. The opinions of the press, several of them, were extracted and printed by us and spread broadcast. I do not know that they may be of any importance, but this one from the *New York Sun* says, speaking of certain of these tenements:

> From cellar to attic the business carried on is the stripping of tobacco or the manufacture of cigars; women as well as men, girls as well as boys, toiling for life in an atmosphere thick with tobacco dust and reeking with odors too foul to be described. All this illustrates how one may start an extensive cigar and tobacco factory without investing in buildings and appliances.

The New York *Staats Zeitung*[3] said:

> The manufacture of cigars is one of the most important industries in our city, and tens of thousands of our working population make, directly or indirectly, their living in the tobacco industry. Circumstances impeding this industry must therefore affect also the prosperity of the city in general.
>
> That the manufacturer in tenement houses can underbid other tobacco manufacturers is in the first place possible by compelling their workmen to pay the rent for factory rooms. Every other manufacturer has to pay high rents, taxes, etc., for his factory rooms; while the manufacturer in tenement houses not only pays nothing therefor, but the subletting of the rooms yields him perhaps a surplus income. In addition to saving his expense he makes additional extra profits by means of low wages. He is not, like other manufacturers, confined to certain working hours; the law against the employment of children under fourteen years of age is a dead letter for his tenement-house factories; the workingman, whose landlord he is at the same time, is much more dependent upon him. The workingman cannot quit work without being thrown into the street; when he is refractory, the manufacturer raises the rent, or assigns him to poorer rooms; in short, he has a great many more

---

[3]The New York *Staats-Zeitung* ("City Times") was one of several German-English papers published by German immigrants in the nineteenth century. — EDS.

means to oppress the workingman. The wages are so regulated that the whole family must assist in working; that women, young girls, and children, without regard to age, bodily development, mental education, must year after year, on Sunday and weekday, work hard in an atmosphere pestered by poisonous tobacco dust to earn the money necessary for the high rent and the direct necessities of life.

The manufacturer is getting rich, though he sells cheaper than his competitors. But he obtains his favorable position at the expense of the health, morals, and manliness of his workingmen, and the system thereby becomes an aggravated nuisance. The system is not only a pecuniary injury to a great many; to enrich a few it is a social as well as an economical evil. Hundreds of medical testimonials prove the injurious effects which the work has in ill-ventilated factories upon workingmen, and all these consequences are much stronger in tenement houses where the working room is at the same time used for dwelling purposes. This kind of work is especially injurious to the health of women. Out of 100 girls of the age of twelve to sixteen years, 72 in the average become sick after six months' work. In tenement houses where cigars are manufactured there are only 1.09 to 1.63 children to every married couple, and the mortality is about twenty percent greater than in other tenement houses. Surely this evil ought to be remedied. It endangers the whole society, inasmuch as infectious diseases, as scarlet fever, etc., when occurring in such houses, may be spread all over the city by means of cigars manufactured in the room of sick cigarmakers. One physician states from his own experience that in the same room where persons were suffering from smallpox the manufacture of cigars was continued until the board of health interfered. Other physicians have seen that persons suffering from diptheria continue to make cigars. This is a direct danger to all citizens. . . .

I will proceed now to another branch of inquiry, in reference to one of the most hardworked class of people under the sun, the freight handlers of the city of New York. They are a body of men, very sinewy, working for $.17 an hour for the railroad corporations. Last year they had the hardihood to ask for three cents more an hour, making $.20 an hour, when the railroads informed them that they would not pay it. The freight handlers were, after a struggle, starved into submission, and are working now for $.17 an hour.

Sen. Blair: Now, you are here and see these people: What sort of life does a freight handler have on $.17 an hour? — *A.* He generally lives in very poor quarters; his home is but scantily furnished; he can eat only of the coarsest food; his children, like too many others, are frequently brought into the factories at a very tender age; in some instances his wife takes in sewing and does chores for other people, while in other instances that I know of they work in a few of the remaining laundries where women are still engaged, the work not having been absorbed by the Chinese. By this means the home, of course, is broken up; indeed there is hardly the semblance of a home, and in these instances where the wife goes out to work no meal is cooked. Many of the stores have for sale dried meats or herrings, cheese, or some other article which does not require any cooking. Of course, when the wife is at home although the living is very poor, it is cooked; she cooks what can be purchased with the portion of the $.17 per hour remaining after the payment of rent, and the cost of light, fuel, etc. . . .

The car drivers of the city of New York are working from fourteen to sixteen hours a day in all weathers, and receive $1.75 a day.

Q. Now, why is not that enough? — *A.* Because it will not purchase the commonest necessaries of life.

Q. You understand, of course, that my question is designed to draw you out fully in regard to that class of workmen, their condition, etc. I understand your assertion to be that it is not enough; it does not seem to me, either, that it is enough; but I want to know from you what chance a man has to live on $1.75 a day? — *A.* He has this chance: His meals are served to him by his wife or friend or child, as the case may be, in a kettle, while he is driving his team, and at the end of the route he may possibly have two or three minutes to swallow his food. It is nothing more than swallowing it, and when he comes home he is probably too tired or perhaps too hungry to eat.

Q. There is no cessation in his work during the day of any consequence, then? — *A.* If there is, that which is termed relays or switches, he has still the same number of hours to work.

Q. Do you mean that that is deducted from his fourteen or sixteen hours? — *A.* Yes, sir.

Q. Then, if the relays amounted to an hour, he would be absent from his home seventeen hours? — *A.* Yes, sir.

Q. And if two hours, eighteen? — *A.* Yes, sir. And in the matter of these relays, in some instances men who do not and cannot live, on account of the meagerness of their wages, on the route of the railroad, are compelled to live at some distance, and when they have these relays or switches it takes them sometimes twenty or thirty minutes to reach their homes, and to return again takes another half or three-quarters of an hour.

Q. Then, do I understand you that these relays and the time occupied morning and evening going to and returning from their work are to be added to the fourteen or sixteen hours of actual service required? — *A.* The actual service is from fourteen to fifteen hours. Then there is the looking after their horses and cleaning the car besides. . . .

Q. Have you any knowledge with regard to those who operate the elevated railways? — *A.* The men who work at ticket collecting or at the boxes where the tickets are deposited receive $1.25 a day, I think. I would rather wait until I can give you information definitely. I think I can do so now, but I prefer to wait.

Sen. George: Are the car drivers allowed to have seats? — *A.* They are not. They have to stand all the time.

Sen. Call: How many hours do they stand? — *A.* Fourteen or fifteen.

Q. Do you mean fourteen hours' standing without intermission? — *A.* Very little intermission. They sometimes rest back against the door of the car for a while. They also, in some instances, have to act as conductors; that is, give change, count the passengers, and register the number of passengers on an indicator. And then they are sometimes held responsible when somebody is run over on account, perhaps, of their having to perform two men's work. The greed of the horse-railroad companies has been such that they have introduced on several lines what is known as the bobtailed car, and have dispensed with the services of a conductor.

Sen. Blair: Don't you think that is because they cannot afford to pay any more? — *A.* I hardly believe that. Judging from the traffic, they are capable of paying it, and judging from what is currently reported as their dividends, they are more than capable of paying it. I must acknowledge, though, that so far as their dividends are concerned, I am personally uninformed. I take merely current rumor and the appearance of the traffic, the number of passengers I see on the cars.

Among some of the tailoresses in the city I have made a personal investigation. They make a regular heavy pantaloon, working pants, for $.07 a pair. They are capable of making ten pairs per day of twelve hours. Boys' pantaloons they make for $.05 to $.06 per pair, making fourteen to sixteen pairs per day of twelve hours. They work mostly seven full days in the week; sometimes they will stop on Sunday afternoon, but all work on Sunday, and their average weekly wages is about $3.81, providing no time is lost.

They are compelled to provide their own cotton out of this, and their own needles and thimbles, and other small things that are necessary in the work. Overalls and jumpers (a kind of calico jacket used by laborers in warm weather sometimes, to prevent the dirt getting to the shirt or underclothing) they make for $.30 to $.35 per dozen. They generally work in "teams" of two, and they make about three dozen per day, or in a working day of thirteen to fifteen hours they earn from $.45 to $.52$\frac{1}{2}$ each. They work generally in the shop, but usually finish some work at home on Sunday.

In the manufacture of cigars in shops there is a branch termed "stripping." I am not sure as to these statistics that I am going to give you, but I believe them to be correct. Nine-tenths of these strippers, or about that proportion, are females. Their average hours of labor are ten per day. Their wages range between $3 and $7 a week when at work. About one-half of these girls are employed at the former wage, but two-thirds at $5 a week, and the remaining third at a higher wage.

They lose days and weeks' work frequently, or have lost them in the past more than at present, and in very rare instances are they paid for loss of time, even when it is caused by national or other holidays. In the shops, more especially the larger ones, they are prohibited from holding any conversation under pain of fine or dismissal. Even if they were disposed to converse they could not. The very positions in which they work, or are placed to work (which are not necessary to the work), in long rows, in which each faces the back of the girl in front of her, precludes them from holding conversation. They suffer in every way the disciplinary measures of imprisonment at hard labor. They cannot hold conversation. One sits with her face to the back of the other, and that is the rule in almost all the factories. Where there are only a few of them of course it makes very little difference. It is believed that this plan of placing them gets more work out of them. . . .

Q. Now, about the newsboys and the other little fellows that we see around the streets, the bootblacks. Those little waifs seem to be pretty busy doing something all the time. What pay do they get out of their labors — how do they live? — *A.* Well, the newsboys earn very small sums. I do not believe more than one-half of them live at home with their parents. The others, out of the papers they sell or earn, try to purchase a ticket for some variety show, and buy cigarettes, of course, and keep just sufficient to get a meal in a five-cent restaurant and to pay their lodging in a newsboys' lodging house, which costs about half a dollar a week.

Q. What chance is there of their attending school? — *A.* Without answering that question I would like to make a statement that I read in one of the papers (and the paper said that the superintendent of the Newsboys' Home acknowledged it to be true) that the newsboys were required to pay for one week's lodging in advance; that one boy was taken sick while in the lodging house, and sent to the hospital after the second night of the week for which he had paid, and when he came out of the hospital he thought that he had five nights good yet to sleep in the lodging house, but when he came there he was informed that he had forfeited that money by not sleeping in the lodging house during the week. . . .

Q. Are the newsboys employed by the newspapers, or do they just get so much for every paper they sell? — *A.* They get so much for every paper they sell, and sometimes a man can buy two-cent papers for a penny. Some will offer you two papers for a cent.

Q. When they have a supply left which they do not sell what becomes of it? — *A.* It is their own loss.

Sen. George: They buy the papers themselves and make what they can? — *A.* Yes, sir; and it is quite a sight to see some of the boys running after the wagons that contain the papers, the evening papers more especially; to see one hundred or two hundred of them, and as one drops off that has been served with his papers another one takes his place, the others coming up continually and keeping up the crowd. If the poor boys were on the point of starvation and their only hope of life was in that wagon I do not believe they could run much faster or risk their lives much more than they do sometimes. . . .

Q. Does the newsboy get a chance for school at all? — *A.* I do not see where that comes in, except that possibly one here and there may have an opportunity of going to a night school, and that, I think, is not generally taken advantage of by them. The boy fails to see the importance of an education himself, and there are very few who are willing to lend a hand to guide him. . . .

Sen Pugh: What is your opinion as to whether that idea of regarding the laborer as a machine exists more now than it has existed in the past? — *A.* I think it exists now in a greater degree than it did formerly. Not only do I think that, but I am forced to the opinion that it is increasing and intensifying even as we go along.

Q. Anyhow, that, you say, is the view that the employees take of the sentiments entertained towards them by their employers? — *A.* Yes, sir. They find that employers are no longer — when I speak of employers I speak of them generally — that they are no longer upon the same footing with them that they were on formerly. They find that where a man who may have worked at the bench with them employs one or two hands they and he may have full social intercourse together, but as that man increases his business and employs a larger number of hands they find that his position has been removed so far above that of his old friends that they meet no more socially. Probably they may meet occasionally in the factory, when there will be a passing remark of "Good morning" or "Good day"; and then, after a while, the employer fails to see the employees at all; the superintendent does all the business and the employer does not bother himself any more about the men. That is how the position of the two has been changed since both were workingmen at the bench. The difference is considerably greater when the employer and the employee did not know each other before, and when the employer's resources are already large. In such cases he and the men do not know each other at all, and in most such instances the employees are not known as men at all, but are known by numbers — "1," "2," "3," or "4," and so on. . . .

READING CRITICALLY

1. What attempts does Gompers make to give a sense of workers as people? What does he say about family relations, dignity, morality, and so on?

2. How does Gompers explain the attitude of employers to employees? In what way does the view that laborers are machines help to explain the wages and conditions that Gompers describes here?

JOHN HILL

This information about Hill comes from Garraty: "In 1872 John Hill, an Illinois woolens manufacturer, migrated to Columbus, Georgia, to become a manager of the woolens division of the Eagle and Phoenix Mills. In 1883 he was in charge of the company's cotton division, which processed nearly fifty 500-pound bales of cotton daily."

Sen. Blair: I would like to have you state the wages actually paid in the construction of the mill which you superintended, and then the pay which the operatives receive? — *A.* The labor question in this portion of the South, in fact in the whole South, has radically changed within the last ten years. Ten years ago, and previous to that, back to the close of the war, there was an enormous percent of unemployed labor. That was the case, first, because there was little demand for labor; and, secondly, because, from the results of the war and the changed conditions and necessities of labor, it was not appreciated, because there was a lack of capital and of enterprise which would call for the employment of large amounts of labor. Owing to the changes that have taken place, this condition of things does not now exist. There is no able-bodied man, woman, or child, who desires employment, permanently unemployed in the city of Columbus. Everybody that desires employment may obtain it at fair, reasonable, and profitable rates; the demand being about equal to the supply. The construction of our new mill in 1876 was the first step in the movement which has resulted in a radical change in this respect; and that, together with improved conditions all round, has changed the question of the price of labor, and the question of supply and demand here. In 1876, at the commencement of the construction of this mill, the supply of labor was so great that the price paid for it could have been made anything within reason that we chose. For some time after the commencement we employed several hundred laborers at $.50 a day. The river banks were lined black with men every morning seeking employment at that price, and we had probably one hundred applications every morning.

Q. From laborers of both races? — *A.* Yes, sir; from both races. We employed them both together at that time. We didn't know any better then. We found, however, that low wages did not pay, and that while an abundance of labor could be procured at that price, the remuneration was too small an inducement to call out the best men so we found our labor very irregular. Sometimes we would have twenty, thirty, or forty hands who had worked yesterday who would not be at work today, and while we were able to fill their places without any trouble, yet we found that these continued changes were undesirable. Therefore, for the purpose of securing the most desirable labor and rendering it more permanent, we advanced the wages to $.60 a day, which was then considered a high figure.

Q. Did that remedy the evil of irregularity and instability? — *A.* Yes, sir; we were then able to secure the best labor, and it became comparatively permanent, with very few changes. Labor here today is very much more proficient than it used to be. We have no vagabonds or loafers now, comparatively speaking, and at present, unlike that time, when a man hires a man to do a day's labor, he expects to perform the labor. At that time he expected to get his pay without working if he could. The men are the same now that they were then. The average price today is probably on the same basis as before, $.75 a day; but, owing to experience and to other causes, the labor has become much more intelligent and in many instances $.90 and $1.00 and $1.25 a day are paid. It is not really, however, an advance in wages, but an advance in capability and in general proficiency which renders the labor more valuable. The laborers are smarter now, and they are worth more money than they were then. . . .

Q. Now, what have you to say to us in regard to child labor in factories?
— *A.* Well, the child labor question is different here from what it is in the
North, for sundry reasons. In the first place, it is a lamentable fact that parents here do not recognize the necessity of education to the extent that
they do in the North. In the North all the people, including all the laboring classes, think it a duty to have their children educated, and the facilities which the free-school system gives them for that purpose are very
largely used. Perhaps the laws of the northern states regulate the matter
somewhat; but laws are second to facts, and if the sentiment of the people
did not justify such laws they would not be made. Then, too, a law that
would be good in that regard in Massachusetts would not be good for anything in Alabama. You must adapt your laws to the state and conditions of
society. Suppose you should pass a law in Alabama that, up to a certain
age, children should not work because they must go to school; it wouldn't
be good for anything; for the reason that, in the first place, even if they did
not work, they would not go to school, because the parents would not want
to send them, and also because if they did there are no schools to which
they could send them generally. . . .

In regard to the small children, more especially those in our spinning
room, they are worth all they are paid, and the fact is that the wages they
earn are a necessity for the support of the families from which the children come; so that if they were turned out there would be suffering upon
the part of those families for want of that income. We do not really employ
those children as a matter of preference, but as a matter of necessity.
When a family comes here and a portion of them go to work in the mill
they are sure to make application for employment for all their children
who are of sufficient age to go to work in the mill, and they persist in those
applications until those children are employed.

Q. At what ages are the children employed? — *A.* About ten years, I believe, is the youngest age at which we employ them.

Q. What do children of ten years and upward do? — *A.* They do this
very light work, attending the spinning and winding machinery — very
light work. There is no work that those children do that is sufficiently arduous to overtax them or to interfere with their health or development.
Their work is all light, and the only thing that can tax them is perhaps the
hours of labor.

Q. Are they generally as healthy as other children of the same age? — *A.*
I think they are. Of course, the dust and all that kind of thing in a cotton
mill is not quite so healthy as the air that comes unpolluted from the Gulf,
but still, I think, their health generally is very good.

Q. Does their health average well compared with that of other children
who are not employed in the mills? — *A.* Yes, sir; I think their health is, if
anything, a little better, for the reason that they are not exposed in cold
weather so much as other children, but work in the mill where it is warm
and pleasant. They are better housed and better regulated than those outside as a general rule. . . .

READING CRITICALLY

1. Hill says that at one time, his mill employed men of both races together, but "we didn't know any better then." What does Hill imply that they didn't know?

2. Why did the mill raise wages from fifty cents to sixty cents a day?

3. Who, according to Hill, is responsible for the fact that children work in the mills? What is Hill's own opinion on the question of child labor?

TIMOTHY D. STOW

Timothy D. Stow, a physician in Fall River, Massachusetts, told the committee about the physical and mental condition of the industrial workers whom he treated. He also gave his opinion of the reasons for their poor health and morals.

Sen. Blair: You are a physician? — A. Yes.

Q. You live at Fall River? — A. Yes.

Q. Won't you state how you happen to appear before the committee, what your object is in coming here, and at whose request you come; and then give us the benefit of any observations you choose to lay before us? — A. Mr. Robert Howard, of our city, called on me yesterday, and desired me to appear here today before your committee to give whatever testimony I could relating particularly to the physical and mental and perhaps the moral condition of the operatives and laboring classes of Fall River. I have made no notes, and I hardly know what your plan is; but I would as soon answer questions as to make any detailed statement.

Q. We want to find out how the working people of Fall River are living and doing. You can tell us that in the way in which one gentleman would talk to another, the one understanding the subject and the other not understanding it. Just tell us the condition of the operatives there, in your own way, bearing in mind that we would rather have it without premeditation than as a prepared statement. — A. I have been in Fall River about eleven years, though I have been one year absent during that time. As a physician and surgeon, of course, I have been brought into contact with all classes of people there, particularly the laboring classes, the operatives of the city.

With regard to the effect of the present industrial system upon their physical and moral welfare, I should say it was of such a character as to need mending, to say the least. It needs some radical remedy. Our laboring population is made up very largely of foreigners, men, women, and children, who have either voluntarily come to Fall River, or who have been induced to come there by the manufacturers.

As a class they are dwarfed physically. Of course there are exceptions to that; some notable ones. On looking over their condition and weighing it as carefully as I have been able to, I have come to the conclusion that the character and quality of the labor which they have been doing in times past, and most of them from childhood up, has been and is such as to bring this condition upon them slowly and steadily.

They are dwarfed, in my estimation, sir, as the majority of men and women who are brought up in factories must be dwarfed under the present industrial system; because by their long hours of indoor labor and their hard work they are cut off from the benefit of breathing fresh air, and from the sights that surround a workman outside a mill. Being shut up all day long in the noise and in the high temperature of these mills, they become physically weak.

Then, most of them are obliged to live from hand to mouth, or, at least, they do not have sufficient food to nourish them as they need to be nourished. Those things, together with the fact that they have to limit their clothing supply — this constant strain upon the operative — all tend to make him on the one hand uneasy and restless, or on the other hand to produce discouragement and recklessness. They make him careless in regard to his own condition. All those things combined tend to produce what we have in Fall River.

Now, first, as to the moral condition of the operatives of Fall River. I think so far as crime is concerned we have quite as little crime there as in any city of its size. We have a population rising on 50,000. There is a disposition at times, and under certain pressure, for some operatives to violate the law, to pilfer, or something of that kind, and I think it grows out of not what is called "pure cussedness," but a desire to relieve some physical want. For instance, a man wants a coat and has not the means of earning it, and he is out of employment, and being pinched with the cold, and with no prospect of getting employment, or of getting a coat by honest means, he steals one. Or perhaps he steals food on the same principle.

But so far as crime is concerned, we have comparatively little. But what I do say, and what has been on my mind ever since I came to Fall River, with reference to operatives there, is the peculiar impress they seem to bear, a sort of dejected, tired, worn-out, discouraged appearance, growing out of the bad influences of long hours of labor, the close confinement of the mills, the din of the machinery, their exclusion from social intercourse, except at night.

And I think we can look for a solution of the problem which the country at large is endeavoring to solve — that with reference to the intemperate habits of the laboring classes and the operatives — in those facts that I have mentioned.

I have questioned many thoughtful men and women in regard to that. I have said, "Why is it that at night particularly you frequent the dram shops?[4] Why is it that by day you drink; that you store enough even for the day in your houses?" The answer is, "Well, doctor, I tell you the fact is this, there is a sense of fatigue over us which we do not know how to overcome, and which we must overcome for the time being if we are to have any social qualities of an evening, and we can't do it without taking something which will bridge over the time and make us equal to the emergency of the evening or the occasion.". . . But I have said, "How does this make you feel? You say you have been feeling fatigued in the evening and discouraged; that your future does not look bright; how do you feel when you get the liquor?" "Why," he will say, "it covers that all up; we lose all thought of that, and for the time being we feel well." And so they go on from day to day, and from night to night.

Now, after all, I do not know of many drunkards in Fall River, but this is true: the operative spends his five, ten, or fifteen, or twenty-five cents a night for liquor, and it is so much lost money to him, and yet he feels impelled to it, because he does not know how otherwise to adapt himself to the circumstances of the evening. . . .

Now, it is invariably the testimony of the more intelligent men and women in answer to the question, "Why do you persist in drinking?" "It makes us feel better; we are relieved of the ennui of life; we are relieved of mental depression for the time being, and after the evening's social engagements are over we get home and go to bed, and think nothing of it, and next day resume our day's work." And so it goes on from day to day.

Now, there are other things which hinge upon low wages and long hours of labor to demoralize the operative. For instance, his food. I think it is safe to say that the great mass of operatives there are forced to buy the cheapest food. They go to the meat stores and purchase joints, which, of course, made up into a soup, generally makes good food, but it does not do to have soup all the time. Then they purchase the cheapest vegetables and endeavor to make the money go as far as it possibly will to supply their wants. But all that produces this condition: They lack that sort of nutrition which is essential to an increase of fiber and flesh, and to maintain that elasticity which they ought to have for the performance of a fair amount of labor. I think if the food of the operatives could be increased it would be better.

Q. You mean increased in quantity, in quality, or both? — *A.* I mean both.

Q. You mean that they do not have enough to eat? — *A.* Many of them do not, they are limited in amount. I have occasion almost every day to see the manner in which the average operative has his table spread, and certainly it seems to me eminently proper that if it be within the scope of human legislation, or within the scope of the religion which men and women profess, to alleviate the condition of the laboring classes who are our producers, it should be done. . . .

---

[4]"Dram shops" were bars or taverns. — EDS.

READING CRITICALLY

1. What does Stow mean by "the effect of the present industrial system upon their [the workers'] . . . moral welfare" (p. 564)? What are the moral effects? How does Stow relate these to physical effects?

2. According to Stow, why do the workers drink? What point do you think he is trying to make by recounting his discussions with the workers about drinking?

CHARLES F. WINGATE

This information about Wingate comes from Garraty: "Charles F. Wingate was a New York sanitary engineer whose work, he told the committee, provided 'very unusual advantages for studying this problem of the condition of the working classes.'"

The Witness: I suppose a small library has been published on the subject of the tenement-house problem in New York City. I do not propose to talk mere sentiment on this matter, or to exaggerate its evils; I wish simply to state some facts, and rather to soften them down than to exaggerate them; and while I shall speak specifically of tenement houses in New York, I must repeat that these conditions are to be found in Boston, in Philadelphia to a less extent, in Savannah, Georgia, which I lately visited, and even in the smaller places like, Newark, Paterson, and manufacturing towns generally where there is a large operative population. . . .

It is impossible to ventilate the ordinary tenement house, because they call a ventilator a shaft which is open simply at the top. They build a skylight or light shaft and put an opening at the top, which is not always open, and then allow the tenants to close all the windows connected with it. Then the halls are closed in on all sides, so that there is no possibility of any fresh air getting in. Then there is always a "living room" for such families, which is an interior room, and it is impossible to secure a draft of air through it. Yet, by securing air below and having an opening at the top of the shaft, you would secure a great deal of air, and sufficient ventilation, or by making the shaft larger you would get more air.

Damp cellars are also a great trouble, yet that is entirely curable. It is nearly fifty years since cellar occupation was forbidden in this city. Yet you see many people living in cellars today, and business carried on in them. It is perfectly feasible to have dry cellars, and if you had them you would win half the battle. From my experience I should say that damp cellars are the chief cause of sickness in cities. While a large number of the tenements of New York have plumbing in the house a large portion have not, and the people are compelled, if they are going to be cleanly or decent, to carry up all the water they use from a hydrant in the yard, which, in the winter time, is apt to be frozen. It is manifestly unjust to expect that with such labor anybody can be cleanly. The mere fact of carrying water up four or five stories for cooking purposes is as much as can be expected — if they have to carry all the waste water back, four or five stories. Furthermore, these four or five stories representing eighty or ninety persons, there is sometimes nothing in the way of sanitary conveniences except four or five or six water closets, or "privies," in the yard. . . .

Another evil is that the rooms of the poor are so contracted that they can do nothing. When a woman wants to do anything, or carry on any little occupation, there is no room in which to do it. If you can supply homes where the people can carry on labor, washing or sewing, or a little light manufacturing, you assist the tenants or workingmen very much. It is considered one of the great reasons of the prosperity of the workingmen of Philadelphia that they have small homes and can carry on such industries; and even in this city, as I notice in hot weather, when people leave their windows open, as you ride along the Third Avenue Elevated Road, you will see scores, if not hundreds, of places with one, two, or three mechanics at work at some small industry. . . .

The New York Association for Improving the Condition of the Poor employs a special inspector to visit the houses of the poor. The first put an advertisement in the *Daily News* offering to examine any place having bad smells. But the poor tenant is afraid to make a complaint, even if he sees death staring him in the face, because of the fear of being turned out of his place. And when the inspectors go to these places — and they visit thousands of them frequently — it is with great difficulty that they can get information. People will point to the sink, and say, "There is where the smell is, but don't you mention my name." Some of the letters written by people on this subject are of the most pitiable character. I will read a few extracts from the thirty-eighth annual report of the board of health, in which some of these letters are quoted:

> . . . Last spring the following advertisement was inserted in an evening newspaper — one which is read chiefly by the working classes:
>
> "A notice sent to John Browne, secretary of the New York Association for Improving the Condition of the Poor, 79 Fourth Avenue, of any defect in a tenement house, will receive prompt attention. Communications confidential."
>
> The above appeared for six weeks, and was responded to by complaints — chiefly anonymous — relating to upwards of two hundred houses, and indirectly to about one hundred more.
>
> The complaints, in many instances, left the story only half told, generally referring to one particular nuisance, inspection revealing other defects.
>
> A perusal of all the letters received would repay anyone desirous of gaining a knowledge of tenement-house life, and of the struggle against adverse circumstances which render the lives of the poor of New York so pitiable.

The following quotations will serve to reflect truthfully, but only partially, a picture of the condition in which so many of our fellow-beings and near neighbors live:

"The privies of ——— Forsyth Street are in a horribly filthy condition."

"Will you please to try and do something to relieve the poor tenants of ——— Tenth Avenue; the stench today is beyond everything; it can be traced a block away; you will be doing an everlasting gratitude to the ——— (Poor People.)" ...

"The cellar is overrun by water; . . . it seems useless to talk to the agent; you can see through the flooring in the basement, and the children there are always sick with colds. — (A Neighbor, ——— W. Thirty-third Street.)"

"The filth (of the privies) oozes out all over the yard, and the stench is intolerable. . . . The stench that was coming up through the front grating was horrible. — (A Sufferer, ——— W. Fortieth Street.)"

"There is a terrible bad smell from the water closets, . . . the yard flags are loose and the smell comes up . . . I see in the News you will help us poor men. — (——— E. Thirty-eighth Street.)" ...

" . . . Manure is thrown into our yard every day; our children have no other place to play in. — (——— E. Sixteenth Street.)"

"I was glad to see your advertisement. . . . I have reported to the board of health three or four times; . . . the sewer pipe is broken, it is making the people in the house sick. — (——— Roosevelt Street.)"

"The privies are full to overflowing, the flooring is all broken, to give the odors better ventilation. — (——— Third Avenue.)"

"The stink (from the cellar) is enough to knock you down. . . . If you will look after this the whole house will be greatly obliged to you. — (——— E. Seventy-fourth Street.)" ...

" . . . There has been in house No. ——— several deaths since last January of diphtheria, I myself lost two children this last month, and one death occurred last night in the same house . . . and others are sick in No. ——— with diphtheria; . . . you will receive the blessings of myself and others. — (——— to ——— Third Avenue.)"

"See to leaky hydrant and water closet that empties its filth into the cellar. . . . The house belongs to Trinity Church. — (——— Washington Street.)"

"We ask the agent for water, and he says we must move out or pay the rent, water or no water. — (——— Third Avenue.)" ...

"The ceiling is all down and the rain comes in, and the waste pipe runs through the room, so that when it rains we cannot stand the smell, and the roof and roof stairs are in a terrible state; the roof had no door on all winter. We spoke to the landlady several times about it, and she paid no attention to it. — (——— Third Avenue.)"

" . . . After reading your kind notice . . . visit the defective sinks in tenement house, No. ———. The landlord does not seem to care. . . . Please do not say there is complaint made; if the landlord would know I am the person he would have me put out, therefore I will not give my name. — (——— Second Avenue.)"

I have here a report on the tenement-house system of New York by a committee of gentlemen, at the head of which was Rev. Henry C. Potter, D.D., which I wish to submit:

THE TENEMENT-HOUSE SYSTEM IN NEW YORK

. . . The total number of arrests made by the police in 1878 was 76,484, of which 30,373, or 19,538 males and 10,835 females, were for drunkenness, and 15,628 for disorderly conduct, chiefly the effect of drink. About 12,000 of these were made in the three crowded tenement-house wards, the Eleventh, Fourteenth, and Seventeenth. . . .

Mr. Charles L. Brace, of the Children's Aid Society, says: "After twenty-five years' experience among the children of the poor in this city, I can truly say that there is no one cause so fruitful of crime, vagrancy, and bad habits among them as the condition of the tenement houses. How they ever grow up to purity, honesty, and decency is a wonder when one knows how they live. The enormous number of vagrant children in this city, our lodging houses alone reaching some 15,000 different homeless boys and girls in the course of the year, arises from the influence of the tenement houses."

A citizen specially interested in the temperance movement writes: "The discomforts of close, gloomy quarters, and above all the discouragement from the sickness and consequent wretchedness sure to prevail in such dwellings, do more to fill the dram shops than any other material cause whatever." . . .

Here is a picture from life of three tenement houses of the *worst* class:

No. 1. Down in the basement, a resort for vagrants of the worst class, at midday were nine men and three women, all sodden with stale beer; the passageway was obstructed by a helpless wretch who had been ejected from the adjacent room. A little later this same man, after he had been revived by fresh air, was fiercely assaulted and beaten by a woman. In another room where rags and bones, not devoid of putrid flesh, were being sorted, the air was so vile the visitor could not remain. In this building but four [water] closets were provided for the 182 inmates. An attic room here, lighted by one small window, is occupied by 4 men and 4 women, almost certainly not married, at a monthly rent of four dollars. In another room 3 men and 4 women live — all rag pickers. Here was a young girl, who was represented as "stopping for a few days." She looked as if she might be saved, for she was obviously ashamed of herself and her friends. In this entire tenement were 182 persons; of these 122 were men, 37 women, and 23 children.

No. 2. A structure of the poorest class. A basement room was unfurnished except with a stove, a keg of stale beer, and boxes used for seats. Around the former were huddled 4 men and 3 women, 4 others being in the room. Humanity gets no lower than these people are, and they are looked down upon by the other denizens of the place. The proprietor of this room (which is 14½ by 10 feet in extent) takes from 8 to 12 lodgers at night. Stale beer is sold at two cents a pint or three cents a quart. Another room, the darkest in the house, is occupied by 2 Italian men and 3 women. In only 4 rooms was there anything like a family organization. The police report the arrests for assault and battery in this house to average one a week. In this house are 14 rooms, occupied by 72 persons; of these 19 are men, 24 women, 12 children, and 17 lodgers.

No. 3. In the court are four closets, used by the 118 inhabitants of the house, all in a sickening state. The water leaks from the roof to the ground below through the two intervening floors. In one of the second-story rooms live 1 woman, 6 men, 2 large boys (18 or 20 years old). The woman is un-

married. On the third story in a small room live 3 men and 3 women, all unmarried Irish and Italians; 118 people live in this tenement; of these 87 are
men, 18 women, 13 children.

Sen. Pugh: The sole power to remedy these evils is with the city authorities, and it is amazing to me that they have not been remedied. It seems
most extraordinary.

The Witness: Let me answer that remark briefly. Our board of health is a
good body. They have certain funds. They receive six thousand, or more,
complaints in a year from all sorts of buildings, from the best to the worst.
They send their inspector to examine the buildings. He comes back and
makes a report, and a notice is sent to the landlord of the character of
that report and of the difficulty existing at the house, with instructions to
remedy the difficulty. The inspector goes there a second time, and reports again, and if the remedy is not applied another notice is sent to the
landlord. The same thing is done again and if the third notice is not attended to proceedings will be taken to sue the man. This requires a great
deal of labor, and you cannot expect officials to do any more than they
can. . . .

Sen. Blair: Why is that? I do not understand that statement. — A. I state
it, then, as a fact, that buildings have existed in this city, held up by nothing but the elements, you may say; buildings notoriously unfit for human
habitation, and only after months have they been condemned by the
board.

Q. Why is it? What is the trouble? Have the people no courage to condemn such a thing, and remedy it? — A. The board of health was stated
some years ago to have arbitrary power. It was stated, for example, as a
joke, that the Shah of Persia was going to have a board of health like ours,
established in his government, to carry on the affairs of his Kingdom. They
have ample power, but they cannot rise above public opinion. And, if they
find $200,000,000 of capital invested in tenement houses to combat them
and only half a dozen men to sustain them, what are they going to do?

Q. Can they not say that such a building is unfit for habitation? — A.
Well, I do not wish to criticize the board of health, but I can take you to
buildings which are unfit for human beings to enter, in which you could
not cross the halls without having your feet covered with filth.

Q. Does anybody live in those buildings? — A. Yes.

Q. Where are they? — A. In this city.

Q. Where? — A. One in Fifty-fourth Street.

Q. When did you see it? — A. Two of my associates inspected it within
thirty days, and reported it to the board of health. There are buildings in
this city, of the better class, not tenement houses — where people paying
as much rent as I pay myself — bookkeepers and clerks and middle-class
of people — in Yorkville and Harlem, "skin buildings," as they are called,
without any party wall between the cellars, the houses supported by
wooden braces, which are splitting with the weight of the buildings — in
which the coping of the roof is built with mortar which has nothing but

sand in it, and buildings where the sewer pipe has burst and its contents have come up into the room that a poor washerwoman lives in. These are facts. In fact, this whole city, from a sanitary point of view, is simply rotten.

Q. Do you mean to say that the board of health, knowing these facts, do not state them? — *A.* I mean to say that the board of health, from want of courage, or from some cause that I will not state too explicitly, is either ignorant of them, or has ignored them, or has delayed attending to them. . . .

Sen. Blair: Colonel Clark, the secretary of the board of health, testified about this matter, and said that there were difficulties; but he denied quite emphatically the existence of such facts as you testify to. I am sure those facts cannot be in the possession of the board of health.

The Witness: This very report that I have submitted to you has been in the hands of the board of health for a year or more. It is a notorious fact, which has been published broadcast, that buildings in New York City, which were condemned by the citizens' sanitary committee in 1865, for being in a bad sanitary condition, are in that same condition today. . . .

Sen. Pugh: You say that these facts which you have stated are open to the eyes of anybody who will go where they are? — *A.* They are.

Sen. Pugh: Then it seems to me they are physical facts, about which there can be no mistake, and the truth or falsehood of what the witness swears about them can be ascertained by ocular demonstration.

The Witness: That is so.

Sen. Blair: You have seen them? — *A.* I have seen them; I can bring you column after column of description in the New York papers of the last two months — the *Sun,* the *Post,* and the *Tribune* — which are simply duplicates of things that have been published in the same papers every summer within my knowledge, till I got tired of reading them; they are facts. The reporters find them out and state them, and that is all the good it does. For instance, one reporter says, "I find a whole family of Jewish tailors living in a cellar, working 10 or 12 hours a day, tumbling off their benches and going to sleep on the floor, and getting up and going to work again — in a cellar condemned by law, and unfit for any human being to live in." Another says he found "a woman who had lived in a cellar for 20 years, and a stable 20 feet away, and she said she was very healthy, and had a large family there." It is a question involving no dispute. . . .

READING CRITICALLY

1. Use Wingate's testimony to draw a diagram of the kind of tenement he describes. What does this diagram reveal about the living conditions of the workers?

2. Examine the exchange among Senator Pugh, Senator Blair, and Wingate. What are they arguing about? Why? Do you think this is the key issue or is there a more basic problem?

N. R. FIELDING

This testimony comes from *The Black Worker during the Era of the Knights of Labor,* edited by Philip S. Foner and Ronald L. Lewis. N. R. Fielding told the committee that he was a fairly successful bricklayer and contractor in Birmingham, Alabama.

Chairman: You live in Birmingham?

The Witness: Yes, sir.

Q. What is your business? — *A.* I am a bricklayer.

Q. Are you a good one? — *A.* Well, you know I might say so without other people believing it. I pass for one, anyhow.

Q. Do you get plenty of work? — *A.* Yes, sir.

Q. Do you ever take contracts and employ others to help you? — *A.* Yes, sir.

Q. How many men have you had in your employ at one time? — *A.* I have had six or eight bricklayers, apart from laborers. Probably I have had twenty-five men altogether employed, including laborers.

Q. Then you have yourself superintended the labor of twenty-five men in your business? — *A.* Yes, sir.

Q. It is skilled work that you do? — *A.* Yes.

Q. You understand the general subject of our inquiry. If you have any ideas that you think would be useful to the committee, just make your own statement of them. — *A.* Well, I have not given the subject much thought. I was just caught up and asked to meet this committee, and I did not know what they wanted with me.

Q. Well, we want to know, in a general way, how you colored people, and other laboring people, are getting along here, and how you think you are getting along — whether you feel that your condition is improving or is getting worse, and generally how you are situated in this part of the country. — *A.* A question like that I will answer first in regard to myself, and then, perhaps, I can branch out a little about other people. My circumstances are very good. Since I have been in business I have made quite a success as a bricklayer, while others that have been more advanced and better workmen than I am, have not made as much as I have. There is a great many men, you know, that will make a dollar today and spend a dollar, and there is others that will make only fifty cents, but will save it. Wherever I made any money I saved a part of it.

Q. Have you a family? — *A.* Yes, sir; I have two children.

Q. You have got a home? — *A.* Yes, sir.

Q. Do you send your children to school? — *A.* My oldest girl is going to school, but not in this county. She is going to school at Limestone.

Q. How old is she? — *A.* She is fourteen.

Q. How old is your other child? — *A.* He is going on two years of age.

Q. Is your house in this city? — *A.* Yes, sir.

Q. Do you own it? — *A.* Yes.

Q. Have you any objection to telling us what your place is worth? — *A.* Well, I can get $2,500 cash for it, if I want to sell it.

Q. Is it in a good situation? — *A.* Yes, sir; I have got a good two-story house of thirteen rooms.

Q. A brick house? — *A.* No, sir; it is a frame house.

Q. What did it cost you? — *A.* It cost me about $900, the way I built it. I paid $250 for the lot, and now the same lot, with nothing on it, would be worth $500.

Q. You have made that by saving and managing a little? — *A.* Yes, sir.

Q. Tell us now about the rest of the colored folks. — *A.* Well, the rest suffers themselves to be oppressed in some instances, but in others they do not. What they earn in the week most of them go on Saturday and spend it in rowdiness, and don't have anything left on Monday morning. In old times, you know, we always used to have a living from our master's smoke-house, and if the master did not have anything for us to eat we waited until he got it for us, and a good many of the colored people are of that opinion still — they wait for some one else to provide for them without trying to provide for themselves. But there is others that do better, and there is some others that would probably do better only that they are somewhat oppressed in their labor.

Q. What do you mean by "oppressed"? — *A.* Well, they are not permitted to get the value of their labor.

Q. In what way does that come about? — *A.* Suppose I was a journeyman, working for a contractor, he would give me $2.50 a day, and a white man would come along, and if the contractor wanted another man and employed him he might give him $3.50 or $4 a day.

Q. For doing the same work? — *A.* Yes, sir; and sometimes the white man might not be as good a workman as I was. The highest wages a colored man gets now is $2.50 a day, while the white men get $3 or $4 a day. They always get 50 cents or $1 a day more than colored men, even though the colored man be a better workman.

Q. How does that come to be so? — *A.* Well, we look at it that it is all on account of color.

Q. They discount your color? — *A.* Yes, sir; it is not worth a great deal to be black.

Q. There is no compound interest on that? — *A.* No, sir; not a bit.

Q. The main question, after all, is whether you are not improving under all these difficulties; whether things are not getting better. We have had a big war and lots of trouble all around, but now the question is whether we are improving all over the country? — *A.* If we are getting along at all, it must be better than it used to be, because it is impossible for us to be in a worse condition than we were then. If there is any change at all it must be to the better. All the condition wherein we are not better is this being oppressed in our labor, in our work, and deprived of being advanced in skilled labor as we might be. We have no opportunities to learn trades as the whites have.

Q. Do you take any apprentices? — *A.* Yes, sir; but I do not have work enough to keep them. I have had one.

Q. Do you think that the white man has the preference over the black man as a skilled laborer? — *A.* Oh, yes; two to one in every respect, in any kind of work from a sawmill up.

Q. In what they call common labor, the lowest paid labor, which will get most wages, the white or the colored? — *A.* If there is any difference at all in that, the white man will get from 10 cents to 25 cents a day more than the colored man. On the railroads they will pay a colored man 80 cents or 90 cents a day and a white man $1 a day.

Q. Where the work is the same? — *A.* Yes, sir; the same thing. Take the same tools and the same work, and the men working side by side.

Q. What reason do they give for that discrimination? — *A.* Some give the reason that it takes more for the white man to live on than the colored man, and that, consequently, they pay him higher wages, so that he may live better. The colored man, they say, gets board for $2.50 a week, while the white man has to pay $3.50, and they have to make up the difference in wages to make the men even.

Q. Do you think that is so? — *A.* I have some doubt about it. I think the board bill depends upon where the man boards and what he demands for his subsistence.

Q. Have you thought of anything which the general government ought to do, or that you would like to have it do, for the improvement of your condition here? — *A.* I really don't know of anything that you could do for us. I have never given much time to matters outside of what comes directly in my business of bricklaying. I don't profess to know everything connected with that, but I don't know whether the government could improve that or not. It seems to be a matter left entirely to the contractors. . . .

READING CRITICALLY

1. To what does Fielding attribute his own success and others' failures?

2. How does Fielding explain the difference between the wages paid to black and white workers?

JOHN ROACH

John Roach (1813–87) was born in Ireland and immigrated to the United States with his family at age sixteen. He worked as an iron molder for a few years and then, with a group of fellow workers, opened an iron works. The works thrived, and eventually he bought out the other owners. His operation prospered during the Civil War and in 1868, after studying iron shipbuilding, he converted his iron works to that business. He won many contracts to build naval vessels and came to be known as "the father of iron shipbuilding in the United States."

John Garraty (editor of the collection from which our excerpt is taken) points out that Roach was controversial because he was accused of garnering contracts as a result of his heavy political contributions and friends in the government. Moreover, his detractors claimed that he defrauded the government in carrying out the contracts. Roach was, by any account, a self-made man. In the testimony here, he argues that unions are bad for workers.

The Witness: It must not be understood here that I am opposed to trade unions. The true way to convince any man is to let him have his own way, after you have reasoned with him. I am going to make a statement now, and if any man can contradict it, I wish him to do so. That statement is that no one has ever heard me ask a man what his politics or what his religion was; and not only that, but there is a standing order in my shops that any foreman who may become the tool of any political party, and who undertakes to use his influence with the men to help any political party, will be discharged when proper complaint is made of such action on his part and proper proof offered. I am quite willing to open my shop to the trades union men, and I have done it. I say to the men, "You may enjoy yourselves with your unions just as you do with your religion or your politics, but while you are in my workshop you must conform to my rules." Now, what are those rules? One rule is that every man has got to speak for himself. I say to the men, "When you came to seek employment of me, you came in your own individual capacity, you presented yourself on your own individual merits, and it was upon that condition that I hired you. Now, if you have any complaint to make, make it for yourself. I will hear it, and try to treat you fairly; but you must not attempt to take the control of my workshop out of my hands." I do not care how many union men come into my shop. No man shall be denied employment by me simply because he is a union man, I am satisfied that wherever coercive measures have been used to make men do this or that — for instance, to vote this ticket or that ticket — not one percent of them could be relied upon to vote as they were required or as they might have promised. . . .

Now, with regard to strikes, there is probably no employer in the country who has had less trouble with his labor in that respect than I have had. I take a great deal of pains to encourage and reason with my workmen. I will give you an illustration of that. Very often I have a man come to see me about his wages. Three or four months ago a very enterprising man, a good talker, came to me and said, "Mr. Roach, I want more wages." "Well," said I, "why do you want more wages? You know I am paying you double what you got on the other side of the water" (the man is a foreigner). "Well," said he, "but it costs me double the amount to live here that it cost me there, so I am no better off." Said I, "Do you get no more for the amount you pay here than you got for what you paid there?" "Oh, yes," said he, "I do." "Then," said I, "why don't you do with less expense here and save more?" The principal difficulty with this man was his rent; and, by the way, this rent question is a very sore one in New York. I asked the man, "What wages do you get?" Said he, "I get $15.00 a week, $60.00 a month, if I work every day, and I pay $12.50, or nearly 20 percent of my whole income, for the bare walls of the place I live in; 20 percent of all my toil goes for a place to shelter my family." "Well," I said, "what kind of a place is that? How much did you pay for your house on the other side?" "Oh," said he, "a great deal less than that." "What accommodations did you have there?" I asked him. He said that the accommodations were poor, and he went on to describe them. "Well," said I, "there are plenty of those places where the Chinese live downtown in New York that you can rent for the same price that you paid on the other side of the water; now why don't you go down there and get rooms?" "Oh," said he, "what position would I occupy in your shop among the other mechanics if I did that? And besides, my family don't want to live there. My landlord is" (to use the man's own language) "a damned hog."

Now, I am not a landlord, and I have no interest as a landlord, but I have some workmen who are landlords, and I said to this man, "Well, we have some men that are landlords, you know, here among ourselves. There are Jim Brown and Tom Burns; they are just as gentle and kind men as I ever saw; their children go to Sunday school, and they are very nice men, and you can't call such men as they are hogs." He scratched his head.

I thought I would bring him face to face with one of these landlords, and I sent for Tom Burns, and I said, "Here, Tom, is one of your fellow workmen. He says that out of regard for you as a fellow workman he won't call *you* a hog; but he does call everybody else that is a landlord a hog; what have you got to say about this matter, and how came you to own a house?" "Well," said Tom, "I had a little money in the savings bank, where I was getting 5 or 6 percent interest on it, and I took it out and I bought a house, and I mortgaged the house and I pay 7 percent interest on the mortgage and when I pay that interest and pay my taxes and keep the house in repair, and take into account the time that it is empty occasionally, and also sometimes when the tenant is sick and does not work and cannot pay the rent — when I sum these things all up, why I wish I had never seen the house. It is not very profitable to me as it is." . . .

Now, if we are to have cheaper rents we can only have them by reducing the price of American capital or else reducing the wages of labor. The workingmen cry out about the high rents, but when you call together the carpenter and the mason and the plumber and the man who makes the brick and ask them, "Are you willing to hold up your hands for a policy that will reduce your wages, so as to enable Tom Burns to afford to rent his house cheap?" they will answer you, "No!" There seems to be a strong disposition nowadays to excite discontent among working people, and the worst enemies of the workingman are those who try to deceive him, for political purposes or in the interest of foreign competition, who try to make the poor man believe that he is injured because he pays so much for his coat, and tell him that that coat could be bought on the other side of the water so much cheaper if this tariff were taken off. The proper way to settle that question is to ask the tailor what he gets for making that coat here, and to compare that price with what the tailor gets in Europe. That tells the tale. And why do those people come here and never go back to stay again where clothes and rent are cheap? It is a small and petty thing to be arraying one class of labor against another, and trying to excite discontent in the mind of the American workingman, upon the ground that he could get his coat or his boots or something else a little cheaper only for what is called "protection." My observation and my experience lead me to the conviction that there is no country in the world in which the people are so well off or so happy as they are here. When you look back at the condition of this nation at the close of the Civil War, without credit, buried in debt, not one among the nations of the earth believing that within the lifetime of any man then living it would be able to restore its credit; when you look back at that condition of things and then look at this nation today, feeding not only itself but also helping to feed the rest of the world; when you see our population at the same time enjoying comforts which no other population existing on God's earth enjoy; and when you see still further that we have now a credit inferior to that of no nation in the world, everybody must admit that we have certainly been making mighty strides. There never was, in my opinion, a better opportunity for the workingman than there is in this country today. . . .

There is a great outcry among certain classes of workingmen for higher wages and for uniform wages for men engaged in the same kinds of work; but how can you harmonize, how can you average men in that way? Take my own case, for instance. I am content to put myself down as a man who is willing to get as much out of labor as can be got out of it fairly, but I am paying one man nearly double the wages I pay to another, though they both belong to the same trade and are working side by side. I do not say that the difference in all cases results entirely from the superiority as a workman of the one who gets the higher wages, but as a general rule it does result from that to a great extent. One man is more wasteful than another, or is less regular at his work than another, or something of that kind; and of course there are many other reasons in many cases why we pay one man more than we do another in the same occupation. I have men in my employ who have worked for me for thirty-five years. Of two men in the same trade and working in the same shop one will be a moral man, a good man, a faithful man, who does not require to be watched; he will be faithful no matter whether the boss is present or not; whenever the bell rings he will be at the shop ready to go to work. Or, to take another illustration, one man is more careful and economical than another; and the man who cannot be faithful and economical for the boss will seldom be so for himself. A careful man sees a piece of timber, for example, and he thinks of some place that that will fit, and he takes it up carefully and uses it for that purpose, while the other fellow throws it away and goes and gets a board and puts a saw into it and saws out a portion and spoils the board, when he might just as well have taken that loose piece of timber. Then, again, some men are very good workmen when they are at work, but they are never to be relied upon. Such a man is often absent from the shop. Perhaps he drinks, or perhaps he spends his time on excursions, or gunning, or something of that kind. I have no sympathy with that man in his demand for higher wages, because I have come to the conclusion that the more money he gets the worse he is off; and when such a man makes big wages one week, generally he will not work the next week. I think he would be better off if he had to work all the time, and I have no sympathy with him. Now, this being the state of the case as we know it actually to exist, how are you going, by any legislation, or by any trades union organizations, to force an employer to pay men of this latter class as much as he pays good, trustworthy men?

I will give you an illustration of how that thing works sometimes, and how it is met. I had a strike about a year ago at the Chester shipyard, the first in a long time; for, as I have said, I am about as little troubled in that way as any man. A deputation of seven men came from the wooden shipbuilders to represent them and confer with me. I said to them, "I cannot hear you as a deputation; you must come in your individual capacity if I am to deal with you." "That will take too much time," they said. "Very well," said I, "I will give you the time; I will be at the loss of time." I would not recognize them as a deputation, and they said they had to go back to see whether my suggestion was in accordance with the will of the organization, and to consult as to how they should act. I said to them, "I have got no time now. Be kind enough to postpone this matter until next Saturday." In the meantime I called the foreman (sometimes a great deal of the difficulty in these cases exists with the foreman himself), and I said to him before I went away, "Have for me on next Saturday the names of all the men that this deputation came to represent, the wages that each is receiving, and the time that each is making with reference to regularity of work, and so forth. Find out for me, if you can, how many of these men send their children to church or to school, how their families are clothed, how many of the men are drunkards; classify them as fully as you can."

He classified them into three classes, and when I came down the next Saturday I notified these men that I would give them half a day out of my own time and I would talk to them in regular order, but that I insisted that each man must represent himself without reference to what his neighbor had to say. When they came I had them separated into these three classes, and they stood there classified in that way. There were about one-fifth of them who were really very valuable men, and to whom it was a pleasure to pay money, because they made a good use of it, and you knew when the money went into their hands that it was going to be used to make their homes happy and give their families the comforts of life. When this class of men came up I asked them what they wanted. "Well," said the first man, "I want more wages." I asked him, "How much more do you want?" Said he,

"I want so much." I said, "Timekeeper, mark these men down with that increase of wages, to go to work." Then the next class came up, and of
course the best talker, the man who could make the most noise and talk
the loudest, stepped up first. He began to talk, and the next man began to
talk, and the next man began to talk, but I said to them, "I will not give you
one dollar more. You are getting more money now than you are entitled
to. You are getting more than is good for you. There is not a man in this
line who is in the habit of making a full week's pay. My shop and my tools
are standing there idle while you are off hunting, or something else, and
the capital that I have invested in these tools is idle and the plant is suffering while you are idling in that way. I will not give you one cent advance."
Then the next class came up, and the spokesman began to talk. To that
class I said, "I do not want you at all; you are only wanted here when there
is a surplus of work. Some of you men, as I am informed, do not pay your
board, nor do you pay your landlords; the widows that some of you board
with have to come here and ask that your pay be stopped to pay for your
board. I do not want you at all. There may come a time that I may want
you, but I do not want you now at all." Now when these men separated, the
question was put by the inferior men to the men of the better class, "Are
you going to desert us?" And there was quite a tussle over that question,
and a delegation of the first-class men came to me and said, "Mr. Roach,
can you not do so and so?" I said, "I have no change to make. There are
some of those men who are as good workmen as you are, and when they
do as you do I will leave instructions here to have their wages advanced."
And in fact I have now in my workshops men who are receiving certain
wages upon condition that if they shall make full time and continue sober,
at the end of a certain time they shall be paid the advance. There is one
man in my employ, an excellent man, moral in every other way except that
he will drink liquor, a man that I am paying $2,500 a year to, a man whose
services are invaluable, but he has this fault, he will drink; and if you were
to know of the thousand and one means I have resorted to to cure that
good man they would astonish you. The last plan I attempted with that
man was this: I said to him, "I will not cast upon you the odious reputation
of having been discharged because you are a drunkard. I will not bring
that disgrace upon your family. I will not discharge you. If it is done you
have got to do it yourself." I wrote a letter for him, addressed to myself,
running about in this way: "Mr. John Roach: I hereby hand you my resignation. I prefer to be a drunkard rather than to be a sober man and to retain your respect and confidence." "Now," said I, "when you want to take
the next glass of liquor, just sign that letter and hand it to me." That was
several months ago, and I have not got the letter yet. So you see, as I said
before, that if I appear to have better luck in dealing with my men than
other employers have, it is because I take a great deal of pains to talk with
them and reason with them. Now, when you ask me whether the workingmen are as well off in other employments as they are in mine, I can only
say I do not know. I do not pay any more wages than others pay; in fact, I
am charged with paying less; but there is a reason for that. However, I

exact as much from my men as other employers do, and I do not see why every other employer cannot produce a record equal to that of myself and my workmen. . . . .

READING CRITICALLY

1. What reason does Roach give for insisting on individual rather than collective bargaining?
2. To what does Roach attribute high rents?
3. What is Roach's reason for paying different workers different rates?

JOSEPH MEDILL

Joseph Medill (1823–99) was born in Canada to a family of successful shipbuilders. He moved to the United States and was admitted to the bar in 1846. He decided, however, to be a journalist and helped establish several influential papers. Heavily involved in national politics, he was a friend of Lincoln and, in 1854, came up with the name "Republican" for the new antislavery party. He later bought an interest in the *Chicago Tribune* and held several civil service commissions under President Grant. In 1871, he was elected mayor of Chicago. In 1874, he gained a controlling interest in the *Tribune* and set the editorial policy of that influential newspaper.

The Witness: The chief cause of the impecunious condition of millions of the wage classes of this country is due to their own improvidence and misdirected efforts. Too many are trying to live without labor — that is, industrial or productive labor, and too many squander their earnings on intoxicating drinks, cigars, and amusements, who cannot afford it. While they continue to spend their surplus earnings on these things they will not get on in the world and will fail to accumulate property. The possession of property among the masses is really due more to saving than to earning; on small earnings a man may still save something, while no amount of earnings will improve his bank account without economy. The power of waste is vastly greater than the power of production. The wisest politician and the most original thinker on social subjects which this country has yet produced, laid it down as an axiom that "a penny saved is better than two pennies earned." It was the habit of saving which he inculcated as absolutely essential to success in life. I refer, of course, to Dr. Benjamin Franklin. It was to the working classes that he addressed his wise maxims, his suggestions, and advice. I have rarely known a steady, sober, industrious man, who saved his surplus earnings and prudently invested them but attained independence before old age.

And I have never known a workman, no matter what might be his wages, who freely indulged his appetite for liquor and nicotine, that ever made much headway. And that observation covers a good many thousand workmen with whom I have come in contact during my life — of all classes. This sort of people always remain poor and dissatisfied — complain of their "bad luck," denounce the tyranny of capital, and allege that they are cheated in the division of the profits produced by capital and labor.

Those who have closely investigated the subject estimate that the money spent by the wage classes of our cities and towns on intoxicating drinks exceeds $400,000,000 per annum. Of course, the total consumption of liquors is a great deal more, taking in the remainder of the population, which I do not include under this head; and to this enormous sum must be added at least $100,000,000 for cigars, and $100,000,000 for useless amusement, and gambling, making a total of $600,000,000 a year absolutely squandered by the discontented employee classes of this country. I have understated the waste of wages on those injurious indulgences in order to be safe in my estimate. The money thrown away on liquor by the wage workers for the last ten years would have provided each family with a comfortable home free of rent, thereby emancipating all of them from servitude to landlords. If that squandered money has been loaned out at interest it would now amount to the enormous sum of $5,000,000,000 — at a moderate rate of interest, say 5 percent — multiplied into the last ten years. And if invested in railroad stocks and bonds during that period, it would have transferred the ownership of every mile of railway in the United States to the possession of the laboring classes who have wasted their wages in drink. Drink is the evil progenitor of most of the ills which the poor man encounters and is the cause of the "bad luck" which keeps him in poverty. I have used that term "bad luck" several times because it is a stereotyped phrase in every household that has a hard struggle in life.

The wage classes cannot support in idleness a quarter of a million saloon keepers, and their bartenders and families, and pay the rent of their dram shops, and at the same time hope to prosper themselves. No trade union combinations, or Knights of Labor[5] "strikes," to force up wages or shorten the hours of work will enable them to do it; and no relief that political legislation can give will essentially improve their condition in the absence of the virtues of temperance and economy, the cornerstones of prosperity and independence. . . .

It is a standard belief in trades union lodges that the ills of labor would be relieved in great degree by shortening the day's work to six or eight hours, as it would cut down production per man 25 or 40 percent, thus cre-

---

[5]Originally a tailors' union founded in 1869, the Knights of Labor in 1878 became a national industrial union as well as a central organizing body for unions in all trades and industries. Highly successful in mounting strikes in the 1880s, the Knights folded in the 1890s because of internal politics and external pressures. — EDS.

ating a great demand for extra labor, which, in turn, would force up wages to a high point, say, twelve hours' pay for eight hours' work or fourteen hours' pay for six hours' work. And it is alleged and contended that nothing stands in the way of the adoption of this scheme of long pay for short work except the unfeeling selfishness of employing capitalists. In my opinion, this idea to get a "corner" on the labor market would prove delusive, and fail utterly, if tried; and for these reasons: increased wages for short work would instantly attract to this country countless multitudes of foreign workmen. They would rush hither as fast as fleets of steamers could bring them, and quickly swamp the demand for extra labor caused by short work. In a little while they would be soliciting employment at reduced wages, and offering to work for ten hours a day for probably half the pay that had at first been demanded for six hours' work, and for this by reason of the oversupply of labor. But the panacea would fail to cure from the operation of another cause. It is an axiom that "dear labor makes dear goods." The effect of large wages and small work would be to greatly increase the cost of production and the price of manufactures in proportion to the enhancement of labor prices; the demand for such goods would necessarily decline, because the remainder of the community cannot afford to buy as large a quantity of artificially dear fabrics. Rents, too, would advance to the same degree that the cost of building houses increased, and the number of new structures would greatly decline, and that would cut off labor. Merchants would refuse to buy the excessively dear domestic goods produced under these circumstances, but would import what merchandise they needed, and if the trades unionists undertook to double up the tariff in order to prohibit importation, the great agricultural masses would sternly resist being thus fleeced for the benefit of any city class of producers. . . .

Sen. Blair: We are required to inquire into the relations between labor and capital, and we have construed that as implying that we should try to learn something of the personal feelings that exist between laborers, as a body, and the employing class, and have taken some testimony in that direction. Now, as you have observed it, what attitude or feeling do you think these two classes occupy with reference to each other? — *A.* Well, I suppose a feeling generally of distrust and dissatisfaction. They are not amicable, as a general thing.

Q. Is that feeling that you refer to on the increase or decrease in this country? — *A.* I think it is on the increase steadily.

Q. Do you think it of a character sufficiently serious to occasion any alarm or require attention? — *A.* Well, it is a serious question. Yes, sir; it is a growing dissatisfaction. The trades unions of this country are feeling more and more dissatisfied with their position, and they are developing more of what might be called a communistic feeling — a tendency or desire to resort to what may be called revolutionary and chaotic methods of rectifying things. They are not satisfied with their division of the profits of business, and they look at the enormous and sudden acquirement of fortunes by a few speculators with feelings of dissatisfaction and anger. I think that expression is not too strong. . . .

READING CRITICALLY

1. How does Medill view the workers' drinking problem?

2. Medill summarizes one view of the movement to reduce working hours from twelve or more down to ten or even eight. His summary is essentially correct: The idea was to give the same day's pay for fewer hours' work. What arguments does he make against the proposal?

3. Medill implies that the unions propose to reduce working hours to six. What effect is he striving for by exaggerating the proposal?

ROBERT S. HOWARD

This information about Howard comes from Garraty: "Robert S. Howard, a Fall River, Massachusetts, textile worker, was secretary of the local union and a former member of the Massachusetts legislature. Before migrating to the United States he had worked for seventeen years in English textile factories."

The Witness: Now there is one remarkable thing in Massachusetts, and that is that if ever a bill is brought before our legislature for the redress of some grievance which may exist, or if the workingmen come to the legislature asking for some law which may be beneficial to their interests as workingmen, such as a law providing that they shall be paid weekly, or a law providing for boards of arbitration, or a law to make the ten-hour rule more stringent — if ever there is a bill of any of these kinds brought before our legislature you will always see the corporation detectives there, particularly from Lowell and from Lawrence. Lowell wishes itself to be looked upon as the workingman's Paradise of Massachusetts, but it is the worst place in Massachusetts, and pays the lowest prices to its workingmen. The Lowell manufacturers always have a ring of men down at the State House, and they always wish to make it appear that their city is a Paradise and an Eden. It was that Merrimac corporation that got us reduced 10 percent in 1880. When the Board of Trade met the others said to us, "You make that Merrimac company pay the same as we are paying; they can undersell us as things are." There are men there running 1,500 spindles for about $9.50 a week, while in the other New England mills they can get $12.00 a week. They have a man named Moses Sargent who is there at the State House every week, and when I was on the legislative committee I used to see him watching every man that came in; so that a Lowell man that had to earn his bread in the mills dare not put his head into the committee room. The same is true in Lawrence. They had a detective named Filbrook always watching to see if any Lawrence men came before the committee to give testimony. Then, after the meetings were over, they would say, "There are those Fall River fellows; they are a turbulent set." It is not that we in Fall River are turbulent; it is because we had manhood enough and nerve enough to go and ask and demand what was our right that they say that about us. There are no Fall River detectives at the State House. I went to a meeting of the mule-spinners[6] at Lawrence some six or seven weeks ago. I wanted to get all the mule-spinners out from the Pacific Mills where the wages was reduced about a year ago, and I called a meeting by circular and had the circular distributed through the Pacific and the Atlantic and the Pemberton Mills. When the time came that was appointed for the meeting, there across the road stood Filbrook, the corporation detective, and Russell, the overseer, watching every man that came in. There was one man at that meeting who was looking out of the window at them, and he said, "I never belonged to a union in my life, Howard, but nothing does so much as the presence of those men there to convince me that there must be some good for the workingmen in unions, for unless there was, those men would not stand there spying us as we come in." That is the condition of affairs. Those manufacturers have their detectives employed permanently. I will not vouch for the statement I am going to make, but I have been told that Filbrook gets a salary of $6,000 a year from the Pacific Mills alone. However, I do not vouch for that as true. . . .

Sen. Blair: In regard to the actual physical condition of the operatives in Fall River and elsewhere, can you give us any information? — A. The condition of the operative in our city is a very unenviable one. The work there is very hard and the wages are very low — low in proportion to what they used to be some ten years ago, before the financial depression set in. Our females in particular are overworked; their strength is entirely overtaxed by the labors they have to perform. I have often argued myself that if our manufacturers would give over preaching so much about temperance and other things and try to bring about a reform in the condition of their operatives, it would be better than all the many thousand temperance lectures and temperance tales. . . .

The work is too severe. Nobody would credit the amount of labor that a cotton operative has to perform. You may take a girl, boy, or man, from outside and put him in there to walk by the side of one who is employed in those mills, and I tell you that unless he has a very good constitution you will soon perceive a failure — that is, on account of the mere traveling, irrespective of the peculiar labor they have to perform. It is dreadful to see those girls, stripped almost to the skin, wearing only a kind of loose wrapper, and running like a racehorse from the beginning to the end of the day; and I can perceive that it is bringing about both a moral and physical decay in them. I do not want to say a word that would reflect disagreeably on my city or its people, because I think others are quite as bad, but I must say that I have noticed that the hard, slavish overwork is driving those girls into the saloons after they leave the mills in the evenings; and you might as

---

[6]Mule-spinners make thread from raw fiber. The term here refers to the people who do the work. The machines on which they work have the same name. — EDS.

well try to deprive them of their suppers; after they leave the mills you will see them going into saloons, looking scared and ashamed, and trying to go in without anyone seeing them — good respectable girls, too, but they come out so tired, and so thirsty, and so exhausted, especially in the summer months, from working along steadily from hour to hour and breathing the noxious effluvia from the grease and other ingredients that are used in the mills, and they are so exhausted when the time comes to quit, that you will find that all their thoughts are concentrated on something to drink to allay their thirst. I know of one girl in particular that lived close by me; her father died in the war and she lives with her widowed mother, who is receiving a pension from the state. The girl's health began to fail her some time ago and she had to go round the country trying to recruit her strength, and finally the doctor told her that the work was too hard and tried to keep her out of the mills, but the mother found it hard to get along, because it is so difficult to get occupation outside of the mills, and the doctor advised the mother to tell the girl to get a glass of beer or something to stimulate her appetite, as she could not eat anything; for beer, with all its bad faults — and I do not believe it is a good thing for anybody, still it has an effect sometimes in stimulating the stomach and creating the desire for something to eat, and without they do eat they won't work long in the mills. I would not put a child of mine in to be a mule-spinner for anything — I think I would sooner put it to a chimney sweep to learn his trade. It is a trade and it is no trade, mule-spinning, and if the manufacturers would only try it a little they would think so too, because it is a continual race from morning till night, and there is not one man in twenty not brought up in the business who could follow a mule-spinner from the beginning of his day's work to the end, even considering nothing but the walking. . . .

It is a constant race from morning to night after this machinery; and you may know as well as I can tell you, how a man must feel in this hot weather following such an occupation as that. He just feels no manhood about him. He can only take a glass of beer to stimulate him, to give him a little appetite so that he may eat, in order to be able to go through his daily drudgery. I have been there and I know it. From the time I was very young I was fond of reading, and I remember many occasions when I have gone to my supper and taken my daily paper and have fallen asleep with the paper in my hand, and have slept there until about eleven o'clock. Then I have been determined to read it, and have put my lamp beside me when I went to bed, and have gone to sleep again with the paper in my hand and lain there just as I put myself down, without stirring, until morning, the result of exhaustion.

Now we can never expect to advance civilization among such a class of people until we get a reform of this miserable condition of affairs. We must get our people to read and think, and to look for something higher and nobler in life than working along in that wretched way from day to day and from week to week and from year to year. . . .

But there is one thing that needs rectifying in Massachusetts, and that is the blacklisting system — the system of blacklisting men who have the courage to speak their opinions. In Lowell some two years ago I went to start the men to ask for more wages, because we in Fall River could not do anything until Lowell made some advance. I went down there and we had a petition drawn up. No name was signed to it, because all of the men were afraid, but the petition was sent in asking for an advance in wages. In about two weeks after that petition was presented to the Lowell manufacturers the three men that had had the drawing up of the petition were discharged from the mills. That is a fact. I made this same statement before the legislature of Massachusetts; I told it to Mr. Ludlam and the representatives of the three corporations and they could not deny it. Then their detective came walking across and said to me, "If you have any charges you should make them in writing"; and I turned to him and said, "It was you that tracked those men." One of those three men is now dead; another is tending bar, and the other we do not know where he is. The same practice exists in Lawrence. I know a man who left the Arlington Mills. They had an imported superintendent from England and he wanted to show our Americans that he could make people do anything he pleased, and he sent down to one of our mills to have the man blacklisted, and that man is now working in the city under an assumed name. I may say also in the same connection, that in my own city we had thirty-three men discharged about two years ago for asking for an advance of wages, and they are working now under assumed names. The bosses hired a detective in our city (for they have adopted the Lowell and Lawrence system), and I am told that he goes around with his list to see if he can find those men.

Q. What do you say those men were blacklisted for? — *A.* Merely for having courage enough to ask for an advance of wages when the state of the trade warranted it. . . .

READING CRITICALLY

1. How does Howard explain the drinking habits of women mill workers?

2. What does Howard mean by saying of the worker who drinks, "He just feels no manhood about him" (p. 586)?

3. According to Howard, how did the blacklisting system work?

WRITING ANALYTICALLY

1. The central issues raised in the Senate testimony concern (a) hours of labor, (b) wages, (c) working conditions and rules, (d) child labor, (e) living conditions, (f) physical health, (g) the social or moral condition of the workers, (h) alcohol, (i) racism, and (j) unions. Choose one of these issues and collect information on it from all of the testimony, keeping careful track of who said what. Write an essay synthesizing this information. From the small sample of witnesses here, what observations can you make about the issue you chose?

2. Contrast the ways that Stow, Medill, and Howard explain the workers' drinking problem. What possible correctives or solutions to the problem are implied by the explanation of each witness? Which approach do you find most convincing? Write an essay evaluating these explanations and implied solutions, either supporting the one you agree with or proposing your own.

3. Write an essay evaluating John Roach's philosophy of employment. Do you find it admirable or not? Do you believe that Roach is truly concerned about the moral welfare of his employees? Does he have the right as an employer to be concerned about the moral welfare of his employees or, more important, to do anything about it? Use the testimony of Gompers, Stow, Medill, and Howard to support your answer.

4. What attitudes about work and unions underlie the opinions of Roach and Medill? Make a compendium of their ideas about work and workers (an exercise that might be done in a group or class discussion). Looking at your list, consider what general principles about people and society account for these ideas. Following this exercise, write an essay explaining Roach's and Medill's philosophies of work and employment. Explain how their principles lead Roach and Medill to reject unionism.

5. How would supporters of unionism respond to the criticisms of Roach and Medill? Consider first what attitudes about work underlie the opinions of union supporters such as Gompers and Howard. Write either an essay or a series of position-and-response statements on unionism, explaining how each side would answer the other's arguments and advocating your own position on the issues raised here. Alternative: Write the script of a panel discussion among Roach, Medill, Gompers, and Howard, with you as moderator, on the question "How should employers treat workers?"

WILLIAM Z. FOSTER

From *Pages from a Worker's Life* (1939)

William Z. Foster (1881–1961) was born in eastern Massachusetts and in 1888 moved with his family to Philadelphia, where his father sought work. This excerpt from chapter 1 of his 1939 autobiography tells of his early experiences as an industrial worker and graphically reveals the working conditions in a variety of industries at the end of the nineteenth and beginning of the twentieth centuries. In the last part of the excerpt, Foster begins to think about unions and political action. In 1901, he joined the Socialist Party. He became a successful organizer for the American Federation of Labor (AFL) and was exceptionally good at overcoming racial and ethnic strife in the locals. He helped win an important strike for the eight-hour day in the Chicago stockyards in 1917. Foster worked to politicize and radicalize the

William Z. Foster, *Pages from a Worker's Life* (International Publishers, 1939), 15, 20–40.
In the notes, EDS. = Patricia Bizzell and Bruce Herzberg.

AFL and hoped, for some time, to promote a labor revolution. He joined the Communist Party of the United States in 1921 and was its candidate for president in the elections of 1924, 1928, and 1932. Foster remained in the party through the anti-Communist "red scare" after 1948, and though he escaped conviction during the McCarthy era, he was unable to prevent the American party's disintegration. In this section of his autobiography, Foster eschews political and economic analysis to paint a vivid picture of his experience as an industrial worker.

I BEGAN WORK AT THE AGE OF SEVEN, selling newspapers — the old Philadelphia *Evening Star, News, Item,* and *Call,* all four of which have long since expired. At nine I applied for a job at Wanamaker's store, but the man told me to grow up first. At ten I finally managed to "go to work." This was the beginning of twenty-six years (from 1891 to 1917) in lumber, agriculture, building, chemical, metal, mining, transport, etc. — during which time I rambled all over the country. The following are true pictures from this industrial experience.

. . .

FERTILIZER

NEARLY EVERY INDUSTRY FESTERS with occupational diseases, and these reap a harvest of suffering and death among the workers. I have seen much of workers being ruthlessly ruined in health for the sake of employers' profits. . . . I worked three years for the American Type Founders Company, where I got myself saturated with lead. Next I got work as a fireman at the Harrison White Lead works in Philadelphia. One department in this plant, where they mixed pulverized lead, was so destructive to health that the workers called it the "death house." The most dangerous work was done by green immigrants, unaware of the menace to their lives. The other workers used to say that if a man working in the "death house" saved his money diligently he could buy himself a coffin by the time the lead poisoning finished him.

But the most unhealthy conditions I ever experienced were in fertilizer. I worked in this industry during the years 1898–1900, in various plants and localities, as laborer, steamfitter, fireman, engineer, and skilled fertilizer mixer.

One of the most noisome[1] and unhealthy phases of the fertilizer industry was the disposal of city garbage. The plant of the American Reduction Company at West Reading, Pennsylvania, was a typical example. In this place some of the garbage was burned in furnaces and the rest was boiled in huge kettles, then dried, mixed, and sold for fertilizer.

---

[1]Foul-smelling. — EDS.

The plant was indescribably filthy, a menace to the health of its workers and the whole community. Within the place garbage was indiscriminately littered about and allowed to decompose, and I often saw whole sections of the dumping floor a living, creeping carpet of maggots. In summer, when garbage collections were heaviest, the plant was swamped, and hundreds of tons of rotting swill, besprinkled with decaying cats, dogs, etc., was left to fester outside in the blazing sun. With the stench, flies, and maggots it was a sickening mess. The plant stank to the high heavens for a mile in all directions, and it sent forth millions of filthy, disease-laden flies to endanger the population round about.

Another sweet flower of the fertilizer industry was the disposal of dead animals. I also worked at this, in Wyomissing, Pennsylvania. The plant was owned by a veterinary. This doctor got paid for treating sick horses, cows, and pigs, collected fees for removing them when they were dead, and, finally, made fat profits in selling their remains to farmers as fertilizer. The workers believed that the old doctor, in tending sick animals, carefully developed his other activities as a remover of dead animals and fertilizer manufacturer. The fertilizer was a glaring fake. It was composed of at least fifty percent yellow clay, and the half dozen brands, differing only in their fancy names, coloring, and prices, all came out of the same bin.

In this plant horses and other dead animals were skinned, hacked to pieces, boiled down into tankage, their bones ground, and the whole business mixed with guano, kainit, potash,[2] sheep manure, phosphate rock, lime, clay (especially clay), and other chemicals that go to make up fertilizer. The dead animals in summer were usually in a high stage of "ripeness" when they reached the factory. This plant, with its own special unspeakable smells and unaccountable myriads of flies, outdid in noisomeness, if possible, the West Reading beauty rose garbage plant.

The dead animals were prepared for the boiling tanks by men working in a room filled with stifling steam and crawling with maggots. The horrible odor of the cooking, putrefying flesh would gag a skunk. The men ran grave danger of contracting diseases of which the animals had died. Shortly before my time, one man died from glanders[3] caught from an infected horse. The butcher, although young, was a weazened, sickly man from his disgusting occupation. He was so saturated with the stench that, bathe as he might, he could not get rid of the sickening odor. In the streetcar people shied away from him as though he had the plague. For his dangerous and unhealthy work he received ten dollars a week and his helper got seven-fifty.

The machinery in these two plants was quite unprotected, and many workers were mangled and crippled. At Wyomissing there was an epileptic who should not have been permitted into such a plant, as he would collapse

---

[2]"Tankage" is dried animal residues, used as fertilizer and feed. "Guano" is bird dung. "Kainit" (or kainite) and "potash" are potassium-rich minerals. — EDS.

[3]"Glanders" is a horse disease, usually fatal. — EDS.

in a fit without a second's warning. But as he worked for almost nothing he was given a job. One day he had a sudden seizure and fell onto a whirling emory wheel. This ground half his face away before he could be rescued.

The most deadly menace to health in the fertilizer industry, however, was the terrible dust. The various grinding mills, mixers, conveyors, baggers, and chutes, totally unequipped with ventilators, blowers, covers, or other health-protection devices, constantly threw huge clouds of dust into the air. From a distance a plant often appeared to be on fire, with the volume of dust pouring out of the windows and doors. So dense was this dust at times that, in daylight and with lanterns in our hands, we would stumble into posts and piles of stock while trying to make our way about. All the plants I worked in were very bad for dust, especially the big factory of Armour & Company in Jacksonville, then the largest in the South.

Most of the fertilizer dust consisted of chemicals highly injurious to health. One dust we particularly feared came from dry bones. The rapidly revolving mills threw out dense clouds of it, much of it doubtlessly germ-laden. It produced heavy chills in the men, and for hours after a bone-grinding they would shiver and shake. Another deadly dust arose from the milling of dry tobacco stems. This dangerous dust produced eye burning, sore throats, and violent coughing. The Negro workers dreaded this most of all and called it "Old King Tobacco Dust."

We had no masks to protect ourselves. Some workers used handkerchiefs over their faces, but about the only effect was to incommode breathing. Nose, throat, and lung troubles were widespread in the industry. Deaths from tuberculosis were common. After three years of it, I also began to develop tuberculosis. Fortunately, however, I took myself in hand in time. I quit the deadly fertilizer industry and went to sea. Three years of knocking over the world in windjammers finally put me back on my feet again. At the Kremlin hospital in Moscow, thirty years later, physicians X-raying me found traces of healed-over tuberculosis scars.

PEONAGE IN FLORIDA

In the winter of 1900 I pulled up stakes in Pennsylvania and worked my way to Havana, Cuba. The Spanish American War was just ended, and conditions for work were none too good; so, after a short stay, I returned to the States.

Arriving in Tampa broke, I aimed to get a job in the backcountry, to make a "road stake" before going North. Florida was (and still is) a tough country for workers. Wage rates were low and the employers used the police power and a system of peonage to get workers. Unemployed men were arrested and sentenced as vagrants and then farmed out in chain gangs to the turpentine camps and phosphate mines, where the greedy contractors mercilessly exploited them. The Negroes especially were victims of this persecution.

Conditions on the county prison farms and in the prison-operated turpentine and phosphate industries were terrible — brutal discipline, exhausting labor, garbage as food, unsanitary conditions. A man guilty of nothing but being out of work would be sentenced to work out a fine of say fifteen dollars at a few cents a day. This was bad enough, but from time to time he was furnished shoes, shirts, etc., at high prices and compelled to work out their cost at the regular rate. In consequence, it usually took a year or more before a man, often broken in health, finally succeeded in paying the State his original fine of a few dollars. A similar system prevailed in nearly all the Southern states.

I was soon to learn that Florida's "free" industries were not much better than her chain gangs and prison camps. I took a Seaboard Air Line freight out of Tampa and dropped off a few miles out at a place called Turkey Creek. There I got a job with a railroad grading outfit ten miles back in the woods. I arrived in camp just at supper time. There were about fifty workers, all whites. It was the night before the monthly payday, and the men had just received their pay statements. Complaints and lamentations rose on all sides. Practically all the men were in debt to the contractor. Just as in the prison camps, they had been charged with various objects at high prices, and these were checked off against the wage of eighty cents a day. Only a few had any money coming, and these were local people.

I remember the plight of the donkey engine fireman. He was a youth with a broad Southern accent who had lived "away up north in Georgia." His wage was a dollar a day and he had twenty-one days' pay coming. But against his twenty-one dollars total wages, they had charged off, besides the regular board of three-fifty a week, a canthook, mattress, blanket, tobacco, and doctor fee, amounting in all to twenty-seven dollars. Thus, after three weeks' hard work, the fireman was six dollars in debt, and nearly all the men were in the same boat.

I sounded out a few of the more discontented men about the possibility of a strike; but they were too badly demoralized to take any action. One told me that on the previous payday, confronted by a similar payless situation, four men had quit. But when they reached Turkey Creek they were picked up by the police as "vags" and sent to prison camps. The bosses used the threat of imprisonment in the medieval Florida chain gangs to force the men to work practically for nothing. The line between "free" and prison labor was a thin one in the Florida backwoods.

Evidently I could not pick up my "road stake" at Turkey Creek; so I decided to "blow" in the morning. But I dared not tell the boss, as that would have invited a prison sentence. I ate breakfast after the rest, being delayed by the hiring-on process. The timekeeper directed me how to get to the "works." But at the forks of the road, where I should turn to the right, I went to the left instead and hotfooted the ten miles back to Turkey Creek. Fortunately the bosses did not check up on me until noon, and by that time I had already hit a freight and was gone. Otherwise I would have surely had a trip to the turpentine camps.

Still job hunting, I dropped off the freight train a few miles from Turkey Creek at a sawmill, owned by one Bramlitt. This man, a typical, raw-boned Florida "cracker,"[4] immediately gave me a job with a partner felling trees. Our wages were a dollar a day, minus three dollars a week board, and we worked from daylight to dark.

Bramlitt had four sons, all yellow-faced and gaunt from constant quinine dosing in their never-ending war against malaria. There were eight white workers and half a dozen Negroes. The Negroes were Jim-Crowed[5] in a nearby tumble-down shanty, while the whites bunked in a pine board shack. We were fed on the typical Southern workers' diet of sow-belly, beans, grits, and corn pone.

One night the quiet air of our camp was broken by a medley of yells, pistol shots, and the clatter of galloping horses. We whites piled out of the bunkhouse to learn what was up; but the Negroes, taught discretion by years of terrorism, fled into the nearby timber. About a dozen mounted men came riding boisterously into the mill yard. It was a raid such as the "night-riders" and "white-caps" of that period often made in the Southern states. The raiders were armed, but did not wear masks or other regalia. Several were drunk and all displayed the traditional violent Ku Klux Klan spirit.

Bramlitt and the horsemen hailed each other in friendly fashion. But we workers were lined up, questioned singly, and bawled out collectively. The leader informed me that in southern Florida "if a Yankee minds his own business he is almost as good as a dog."

Finally, the night-riders rode off, leaving us unmolested. Several complained loudly, however, because the "niggers" had escaped them. In talking about it later, the workers stated that such raids were not unusual and that their purpose was to terrorize the working crews. The frightened Negroes stayed out in the woods all night.

After two weeks' work at Bramlitt's mill I figured that, with all due allowance for commissary robbery, I should have at least three dollars for my "road stake." So I told Bramlitt one night that I was quitting and wanted my time. He "flew off the handle" and told me that I could not quit. I was astounded. He was actually trying to keep me on the job by force. All argument was fruitless. Bramlitt simply refused to pay me and warned me not to quit.

In the bunkhouse the men sympathized with me but said they could do nothing. My partner earnestly advised me not to go to the authorities with the matter. If I did, said he, I would be arrested as a vagrant. Anyhow, even if by some miracle I could force Bramlitt to pay, all I would get would be a typical statement showing me to be in debt to him. They told me to "beat it while my shoes were good," by hopping a northbound freight train.

[4]Here, a poor Southern white person; frequently used disparagingly. — EDS.

[5]"Jim Crow" is the title character in a minstrel song that came to be used as a derogatory name for African Americans. The term also came to refer to the post-Civil War system of racial segregation in the South. Used as a verb, "Jim Crow" meant to segregate and discriminate against. — EDS.

Next morning I refused to work. The Bramlitt clan were on hand to prevent my going into the dining room. Bramlitt, violently angry, shouted that if I did not go to work he would have me arrested. The workers assured me it was no mere threat and they warned me I was heading for a turpentine camp. Nothing could be done about it; so that night I jumped a "rattler" into Jacksonville and saw no more of Bramlitt and his peonage camp.

THE NEW YORK STREETCARS

Returning from Florida, I worked several months in 1901 as a motorman on the Third Avenue lines in New York. The electric trolley car, now on its last legs, was then in its heyday. The old horse cars had almost died out, there were as yet no subways, the automobile was just being born, and the elevated trains were still being hauled by slow, chugging steam locomotives.

Our wages were only twenty-two cents per hour and we worked ten hours per day, seven days a week. The men were unorganized and the bosses ruled with an iron hand, abusing and discharging workers on the slightest pretext.

The motorman's work was hard and nerve-wracking. New York streets were then jammed with slow-moving, horse-drawn trucks, and to pilot a streetcar through this maze, and not fall behind, was a real task. We had no airbrakes, seats, or vestibules. We had to stand up all day twisting heavy hand brakes and being fully exposed to the weather. Many's the time I was soaked with driving rain and half frozen from cold. It was a man-killing job.

The workers thoroughly hated the company. As for the conductors, many of them helped themselves freely, with no twinges of conscience, to the fares they took in. There were no pay-as-you-enter cars, and with the conductors collecting in the densely packed cars even the army of company "spotters" could not keep tab on them. The "nickelers" and "short-arm artists," as they were called, were located mostly by bookkeeping methods. That is, when a run failed to bring in the regular average of receipts the conductor was fired forthwith for "nickeling."

We motormen deeply resented our unnecessarily hard work and exposure to severe weather conditions. We demanded airbrakes, seats, and vestibules. But the company bosses and engineers assured us that these things, although in use elsewhere, were impossible in the dense traffic conditions of New York: The airbrakes would speedily wear out from incessant use, the seats would lessen our alertness, the vestibules would obscure our vision, and all three together would make for more accidents. But this was only a hypocritical, profit-grabbing defense. Years later the company was compelled to introduce these much-needed improvements, and the service was thereby greatly improved.

Determined to end the abuses from which we suffered, some of us younger workers began to organize. We set up groups of platform men in the several barns of the Third Avenue lines and also those of other companies. Then I contacted an AFL organizer, Herman Robinson. All he gave us was sympathy and a promise to "take in" the men if we would line them up. It was my first experience with AFL armchair organizing methods.

A few others and myself managed to become members of the union, and we were making considerable headway, when one day the half dozen of us in the 66th Street barn were called into the Super's office and given our walking papers. In those days of the brazen open shop[6] the boss made no bones about telling us we were fired for union activity. He took a similar course the same day in the other barns, and our nascent union was killed. It was more than thirty years later when, after many fruitless struggles, New York's army of transport workers finally got organized into the CIO[7] Transport Workers Union. . . .

THE CLASS POINT OF VIEW

The IWW[8] free speech fight in Spokane, Washington, in 1909, was just over. It had been a very bitter struggle, with hundreds of arrests and beatings, but it ended victoriously for the workers. Now our problem was to find jobs for those just released from jail. Harry Black had a suggestion.

Black had been through the fight and had conducted himself well. He was a Western floating worker, a ranch-hand, miner, logger, construction worker. Alive and energetic, he voiced the typical IWW bitter hatred of the bosses.

Black's idea was this: A contractor had offered him some sewer digging on a subcontracting basis. Black proposed that he take the subcontract, which involved no financial outlay for him, and that we Wobblies be his workers. As a good IWW, Black said he opposed exploitation of the workers, so he would make the sewer-digging job a "home" for us. He, himself, would be satisfied to make merely regular day wages. Nobody but Wobblies would be given work.

We had nothing to lose, so we took it on. For a few days everything went fine. Black worked in the ditch with us; and we joked, smoked, and talked of the revolution as we dug. This easygoing arrangement did not slow the job; if anything, we did more than a usual day's work.

Soon, however, Black began to change. He became impatient with our talk; he complained that it interfered with the work; he spent more and more time on the top, "looking down our collars" as we worked. In short, he started to "rawhide" us.

---

[6]An "open shop" is a business in which employees are hired without regard to union membership. In practice, as Foster implies, it meant a nonunion shop. — EDS.

[7]The CIO (Congress of Industrial Organizations) was founded in 1935 as a militant offshoot of the AFL, with which it merged in 1955. — EDS.

[8]The Industrial Workers of the World (IWW), whose members were known as Wobblies, was a national labor union founded in 1905 to offer a radical socialist alternative to the American Federation of Labor. The Wobblies sought to organize all workers together, unlike the AFL, which was an association of existing trade unions. — EDS.

Black was fast taking on the typical employer's psychology. He was one of those who are quick to seek personal emancipation by climbing out of their class over the shoulders of their fellow workers. It is the type that gives birth to spies, strike breakers, and corrupt labor leaders. Lurking beneath his thin veneer of working-class revolutionary phrases had lain the seed of petty-bourgeois greed, planted there by his capitalist environment. Black was giving just one more illustration of the truth of Marx's great principle that the way people get their living determines their social outlook.

Black's progress capitalist-wards was swift. In the third week of our job he fired one of our gang for not doing enough work. Then he gave up eating dinner with us, and no more did he join in our revolutionary talk. He even complained against the union and hired two non-Wobblies.

Meanwhile, we were boiling higher and higher with resentment. Things came to an open break when he took on the nonunionists. We struck. Whereupon Black denounced the union like any capitalist and called in the police to help smash our strike. He did not succeed, however, as the IWW in Spokane was strong and militant. The general contractor, who had urgent need of the work, stepped in, eliminated the subcontractor, Black, and reinstated the discharged workers. Then we returned to work. Thus ended Black's experiment at combing IWW-ism and capitalism.

But Black had had a taste of exploiting workers. The capitalist tiger instinct in him was roused. No more working for wages, no more revolution, no more IWW for him. He was now out to "get his." Years later I ran across him, a nonunion contractor in that haven of open-shoppers, Los Angeles. The capitalist class had recruited another bitter labor hater. . . .

READING CRITICALLY

1. What was the "system of peonage" employed in Florida? Why was Foster unable to leave the job he took there? How did he finally get away?

2. Foster begins to think about union organizing when he works on the New York streetcars. How did the company discourage unions?

3. How does Foster account for Harry Black's change in views?

WRITING ANALYTICALLY

1. What is your own work history? Write a narrative describing the kinds of work you have done. Discuss working conditions, pay, hours, bosses' characters, and so on. Did you (or do you) feel any group solidarity with fellow workers or with any group based on your position or your income?

2. In what way does Foster seem like a self-made man? Write an essay in which you judge Foster by the characteristics of the "self-made man" discussed at the beginning of this unit.

3. Foster says that he agrees with "Marx's great principle that the way people get their living determines their social outlook" (p. 596). Write an essay in which you argue for or against this proposition. Support your argument with an explanation of how Foster came to have this view and how your own experiences or observations have led you to your own view. Be sure to define "social outlook" early on in your essay. Consider, too, whether there might be conditions that would allow people to take a "social outlook" that is not based on the way they make their living.

WORKINGMEN'S PARTY OF ILLINOIS

"Declaration of Independence" (July 4, 1876)

The Workingmen's Party, established in 1828, was the first labor party in the United States. While unions worked to secure better economic conditions for workers, labor parties sought to improve the workers' lot through social reforms. Labor parties supported the movements for shorter hours, for women's rights, and for the rights of African American workers. Some, like the Workingmen's Party of Illinois, sought revolutionary change in American society and advocated socialism. But all such parties reflected the desire of workers to engage in political affairs as an expression of their rights as American citizens.

July 4, 1876, the hundredth birthday of the United States, was the occasion of nationwide celebration. The Workingmen's Party of Illinois organized a parade and rally, with drill teams and bands, a parade queen, and groups representing each trade union. At the end of the parade, there were several speeches, capped by a reading of the party's alternative Declaration of Independence.

The declaration was first published on July 15, 1876, in *The Socialist,* a New York newspaper.

WHEN IN THE COURSE OF HUMAN EVENTS, it becomes necessary for a class of men to repudiate the social and political relations which they have hitherto sustained towards another class, and to assume among their fellow creatures the equal station to which the laws of nature entitle them, a decent respect to the opinions of mankind requires that they should declare the causes which compel them to such action.

We hold these truths to be self-evident: that all men are created equal, that they are endowed with certain inalienable rights; that among these are life, liberty, and the full benefit of their labor. That to secure these rights, governments are instituted among men, deriving their just powers from the consent of the governed; that whenever any form of government or system of production becomes destructive of these ends, it is the right of the people to alter or to abolish it, and to institute a new system laying its foundations on such principles, and organizing its powers in such form as to them shall seem most likely to effect their safety and happiness.

Prudence, indeed, will dictate that systems, long established, should not be changed for light and transient causes, and accordingly all experience hath shown that mankind are more disposed to suffer while evils are sufferable, than to right themselves by abolishing the forms to which they are accustomed.

But when a long train of abuses and impositions pursing invariably the same object, evinces a design to reduce them under absolute slavery, it is their right, it is their duty to throw off such system, and to provide new guards for their future security. Such has been the patient sufferance of the workingmen, and such is now the necessity which constrains them to alter their former systems of government and production.

The history of the present competitive system, extending back to the middle ages, is a history of oppression, robbery, and despotism, compelling the great mass of producers to waste their lives in misery and degradation, toiling for the benefit of the few, who by taking advantage of their necessities, enforced ignorance and obtained control of all means of production, and through pretended competition with each other, in which the suffering workers are the real competitors, have put a premium upon selfishness and crime.

To prove this, let facts be exhibited to a candid world.

The present system has enabled capitalists to make laws in their own interests to the injury and oppression of the workers.

It has made the name Democracy, for which our forefathers fought and died, a mockery and a shadow, by giving to property an unproportionate amount of representation and control over Legislation.

It has enabled capitalists, through their control over legislation, to secure government aid, in land grants and money loans, to selfish railroad corporations, who, by monopolizing the means of transportation are enabled to swindle both the producer and the consumer, and who, through corrupt and fraudulent management, have become involved in bankruptcy, thus evading their obligations and robbing the public.

It has presented to the world the absurd spectacle of a deadly civil war for the abolition of negro slavery while the majority of the white population, those who have created all the wealth of the nation, are compelled to suffer under a bondage infinitely more galling and humiliating, as their education and habits create wants and tastes which the unnatural competition for bread with the pauperized labor of the world, prevents them from gratifying.

It has allowed capitalists to interfere with the free operation of the law of supply and demand, by conspiring to reduce the wages of the workers, and thus crushing down the demand which encourages production, by robbing the product of the benefit of his labor.

It has allowed capitalists to trample on the most sacred rights of American Citizens, by dispersing and shooting down the workingmen when they have peaceably assembled together to discuss their wrongs and the means of redress.

It has allowed the capitalists, as a class, to appropriate annually 5/6 of the entire production of the country — the amount annually paid to Labor, as shown by the United States statistics, being but 1/6 of the total amount produced, while the number of employers in proportion to that of employees stands in the relation of 3/10: 7/10.

It has allowed capitalists to rob mankind of the benefits of progress, by using the grand inventions in labor-saving machinery to still further en-slave us, instead of reducing the hours of labor in proportion to the time saved by its use, and thereby giving employment to the thousands whose labor is superseded by this machinery.

It has made men's *actual necessities* alone the basis for compensation of labor, instead of their natural and educated wants.

It has therefore prevented mankind from fulfilling their natural des-tinies on earth — crushed out ambition, prevented marriages, or caused false and unnatural ones — has shortened human life, destroyed morals and fostered crime, corrupted judges, ministers, and statesmen, shat-tered confidence, love, and honor among men, and made life a selfish, merciless struggle for existence instead of a noble and generous struggle for perfection, in which equal advantages should be given to all, and human lives relieved from an unnatural and degrading competition for bread.

In every stage of these oppressions we have petitioned for justice in the most reasonable and humble terms; we have asked in the name of human-ity, for the sake of our starving wives and children and our own manhood, only a fair allowance of life's necessities; our repeated prayers have been answered only by sneers and cold denials.

We have elected officials to represent us in legislative bodies, hoping for a partial alleviation of our sufferings, but the power of capital has invari-ably corrupted them, and our efforts have been fruitless.

We must, therefore, acquiesce in the necessity which demands a radical reform throughout our entire social and political system.

We, therefore, the representatives of the workers of Chicago, in mass-meeting assembled, do in the name and by the authority of the working-men of this city, solemnly publish and declare, that the workers are, and of right ought to be, free and independent producers.

That we are absolved from all allegiance to the existing political par-ties of this country, and that as free and independent producers we shall endeavor to acquire the full power to make our own laws, manage our own production, and govern ourselves, acknowledging *no rights without duties, no duties without rights*. And for the support of this declaration, with a firm reliance on the assistance and cooperation of all working-men, we mutually pledge to each other our lives, our means, and our sacred honor.

READING CRITICALLY

1. Compare this Declaration of Independence with the original (p. 174). What new element is introduced here?

2. Paraphrase the paragraph on page 598 beginning, "It has presented to the world the absurd spectacle of a deadly civil war for the abolition of negro slavery. . . ."

3. What does this declaration actually declare? What sort of freedom does it call for? Identify and list the arguments it uses.

WRITING ANALYTICALLY

Is this a legitimate use of the *arguments* in the original Declaration or just a clever use of the *language* of that Declaration? Write an essay in which you argue both sides of this issue before explaining your final position. In other words, take this assignment in three steps: (1) Defend this declaration as a true cousin to the original Declaration. (2) Criticize it for imitating the language but not the substance of the original Declaration. (3) Finally, explain which side you come out on and why. Option: If there is class time for an extra step, it might be helpful to stage a debate between advocates of the two positions. Since the essay should have both sides represented, it is more important to pay attention to both sets of arguments than to decide the winner.

ASSIGNMENT SEQUENCES

SEQUENCE 1
What kind of society is envisioned by the Gospel of Wealth?

- Horatio Alger, From *Ragged Dick*
- Andrew Carnegie, "Wealth"
- William H. Councill, From *The Negro Laborer: A Word to Him*
- Russell H. Conwell, From "Acres of Diamonds"
- Edward Bellamy, From *Looking Backward: 2000—1887*
- Henry Demarest Lloyd, From *Wealth against Commonwealth*
- Henry George, From *Progress and Poverty*

1. Write a brief personal statement on the place of material wealth in your own aspirations. Do you think that becoming wealthy is regarded as an admirable goal by your family, your friends, your culture, or your social group? Why or why not? After each class member writes an informal essay on this question, class members should share ideas — anonymously — and try to decide collectively if there is still a Gospel of Wealth at work in society today.

2. Explain the Gospel of Wealth, drawing on the arguments and images presented by Alger, Carnegie, Councill, and Conwell. Your essay should address three questions that are critical to understanding the Gospel of Wealth: (1) What are the principles of this gospel? (2) Why is it put forward as a model of virtue for individuals and society? (3) How do these writers defend the idea that the accumulation of wealth is sanctioned by Christianity (or religion in a general sense)? Your task here is not to evaluate the Gospel of Wealth but to explain it in detail.

3. What criticisms of the Gospel of Wealth are leveled by Bellamy, Lloyd, and George? Before writing your essay, list the arguments made by each writer and divide the arguments into categories: economic, political, and moral. Then organize the essay according to those categories (don't, in other words, summarize Bellamy, Lloyd, and George sequentially). As with question 2, your task is not to evaluate the arguments but to explain them in detail.

4. What sort of society do the critics of the Gospel of Wealth imagine, and how is it different from the one imagined by its defenders? Which do you find more attractive? Using the answers you generated to questions 2 and 3, write an essay describing the kind of society promoted by the writers in each question and argue for the world you would prefer to live in. In your preferred world, what social role would you like to fill? Would your choice of preferred world be different if you could not choose the social position into which you'd be born?

5. Who should be in charge of the production of wealth? Is it better to have individuals own the means of production (as in capitalism) or to have the means of production owned collectively by the workers or by the nation (as in socialism)? Carnegie argues explicitly for individual ownership, and Councill and Conwell take the same position implicitly. Bellamy argues explicitly for a form of socialism and receives some implicit support from George. Write an essay comparing and contrasting — and ultimately evaluating — the arguments on both sides of this issue,

arguing for your own position. Alternative: Write an imaginary debate between Carnegie and Bellamy and their supporters on the question of who should own the means of production.

SEQUENCE 2

Is the "self-made man" a myth?

- Horatio Alger, From *Ragged Dick*
- Andrew Carnegie, "Wealth"
- Russell H. Conwell, From "Acres of Diamonds"
- Edward Bellamy, From *Looking Backward: 2000—1887*
- Henry Demarest Lloyd, From *Wealth against Commonwealth*
- Senate Committee on the Relations between Capital and Labor: N. R. Fielding, John Roach

1. What stories about "self-made" people do you know? Are there any members of your family, acquaintances, or public figures you can think of who are regarded or regard themselves as self-made? Write a memoir or informal essay about one or more of these people and why they might be called "self-made."

2. What is a self-made person? Drawing on the ideas and images presented in Alger, Carnegie, and Conwell, define the self-made person and his or her philosophy. You may include, if you wish, an example of a self-made person you know about. Your goal in this essay is not to evaluate the philosophy of self-making, but to explain it in as much detail as you can based on the selections.

3. What personal and social attitudes are promoted by Carnegie and Conwell in their advice about how to become a self-made person? Begin with the definition called for in question 2. Then distinguish between the characteristics of the self-made person that are specifically identified (such as hardworking and thrifty) and those that are unstated. Use Carnegie and Conwell as sources for the positive view and Bellamy or Lloyd as a source for a critical view. (If you wish, use Ragged Dick, Fielding, and Roach as examples of self-made men.) Your essay should analyze and describe the model or ideal of self-making and then evaluate the model: Is it, finally, a good or a bad thing to promote?

4. The idea of self-making depends on several beliefs about America: that everyone has an equal opportunity to develop himself or herself, that there are no formal barriers to advancement based on accidents of birth (such as race, religion, or gender) and that America is a "meritocracy" — a society in which advancement is based on ability. Begin this assignment by having a group brainstorming session to look for the ways that these beliefs are expressed and supported in Alger, Carnegie, Conwell, Fielding, and Roach. Describe other related beliefs about society that you find expressed or exemplified in these selections. Continue this exercise, this time looking for arguments and evidence in Bellamy and Lloyd that oppose these ideas.

Now write an essay explaining the beliefs that support the idea of self-making. In this essay, you may take the historian's view and explain what Americans believed in the late nineteenth century, or you may take a position on the validity of these beliefs and — after explaining them — defend your view that self-making is or is not a valuable American ideal.

5. Does human nature determine the economic structure of society, or is it the other way around? Write an essay in which you carefully consider both sides of this question and then take a position and defend it. Begin by defining "human nature," drawing on the explicit and implicit ideas in five or more of the selections. Then contrast the different positions to answer the main question. Follow the advice in question 4 about brainstorming and structuring the essay.

SEQUENCE 3
How can we understand class conflict in the United States?

- Andrew Carnegie, "Wealth"
- Elizabeth Stuart Phelps, From *The Silent Partner*
- William Z. Foster, From *Pages from a Worker's Life*
- Senate Committee on the Relations between Capital and Labor
- Workingmen's Party of Illinois, "Declaration of Independence"

1. Write a personal narrative telling when and how you first became aware of the differences between the social and economic classes in the United States or other countries. Discuss specific incidents, things you learned at home or at school, or attitudes of people around you. The informal essays or memoirs that class members produce on this question should be shared, if possible, either in oral reports or in a booklet (anonymously, if everyone prefers).

2. Carnegie asserts that inequality is not only good but inevitable. How would the Workingmen's Party of Illinois answer that argument? Write a letter from the members of the party to Carnegie responding to his arguments on inequality in the essay "Wealth."

3. The primary difference between social classes in the United States is, of course, money. Once economic differences are set, what other differences follow? How are these compounded by racial differences? Write an essay describing these differences, illustrating them with material from Phelps, Foster, the Senate testimony, the Workingmen's "Declaration," and, if you wish, your own observations and experiences.

4. The Gospel of Wealth maintained that inequality was natural and necessary. How would the Gospel of Wealth — represented by Carnegie, Roach, and Medill in these selections — answer the complaints about inequality made by Gompers, Wingate, Foster, and the Workingmen's Party of Illinois? Write an analytical essay in which you examine the philosophical and practical arguments on both sides of this issue. In evaluating the arguments, you need not be concerned about social changes that have occurred since these arguments were put forward. Evaluate the arguments, to the extent you can, on their own merits.

5. How should class conflict in the United States be addressed? Perley Kelso, the main character in *The Silent Partner,* attempts to bridge the gulf between the classes. Is her solution likely to work? Is there any support for this kind of approach from Carnegie or the other voices in these selections? Write an essay in which you analyze the solutions to class conflict that are imagined in these selections. Use all of the selections in this sequence, grouping them by the position they take —

maintaining the status quo, seeking revolutionary change, or suggesting other ways of dealing with class differences. After explaining the contending views, give your own answer to the opening question: How should class conflict be addressed? Defend your answer and indicate the extent to which you agree or disagree with the writers you have summarized.

RESEARCH KIT

Negotiating Difference is an unfinished book: There are many other stories to tell in the history of "negotiating difference" in the United States. This Research Kit is intended to help you expand the readings provided in this unit. In "Ideas from the Unit Readings," we include more perspectives on the problems of wealth, work, and class conflict during the Industrial Age. In "Branching Out," we expand the focus of research to include work and class issues in other periods in U.S. history, as well as in your own family and community. You can pursue these research ideas individually or as group or class projects.

To compile materials, you can start with the short bibliography included in this unit and with standard library search techniques that your teacher or a librarian can explain. Here are some other places where you can inquire for materials (not all regions will have all materials):

- Labor unions or federations, like the AFL-CIO, which will provide information about workers, working conditions, labor issues, and other sources of information.
- The National Association of Manufacturers, which provides information on the owners' side of labor issues.
- Museums and libraries devoted to work (some communities have converted old factories for this purpose) or dedicated to industrialist benefactors.
- Town and state historical societies, antiquarian societies, and museums, which often have exhibits on work and workers.
- State university presses, which often have a list of local history titles that include works on capitalists and laborers, on local industries, and on different groups of workers — immigrants, women, and minority groups, for example.

Also, see other units in this book for suggestions about researching related topics (for example, see Unit Three for more ideas on how to research women's issues).

In collecting your material, always consider how a writer's account may be influenced by definite motives. For example, many of the successful nineteenth-century industrialists had official biographers who were completely uncritical. Similarly, many histories of unions and class conflict have been written by labor leaders. The issues raised in this chapter have strong political implications, so be aware that you may find many one-sided stories.

Also, keep your work focused by your research question or thesis. Remember that you cannot write an entire history of wealth, work, and class conflict in America.

IDEAS FROM THE UNIT READINGS

1. Investigate the Gospel of Wealth. This idea has its roots in colonial days with the sermons of Cotton Mather and Benjamin Franklin's *Poor Richard's Almanac*. It flourished in the latter half of the nineteenth century and then slowly declined, but it never quite went away. Who were its proponents? What literature (in addition to Alger) did it inspire? How powerful has it been as an American philosophy?

2. Look into the lives of the early industrialists such as Carnegie, John D. Rockefeller, and Peter Cooper. How did they gain their wealth? What did they do with it? How did they see themselves? An interesting approach to this project is to investigate the way others have seen them. Some writers have treated the pioneering capitalists as heroes, while others have reviled them as the "robber barons." It is important to be aware of these differences in looking at the material on any of the industrialists of this period.

3. Find out more about Edward Bellamy, Henry Demarest Lloyd, Henry George, and other opponents of capitalism as it was practiced in the United States in the nineteenth century. Some critics, like William Z. Foster, advocated socialism or communism, but Bellamy, Lloyd, and George did not (though Bellamy came close). Both Bellamy and George had large followings, and their ideas were the basis of political parties and movements.

4. William Z. Foster and Samuel Gompers were early union leaders, and both wrote autobiographies as well as many articles on labor issues. Research into their experiences and the development of the labor movement in this period will open many worthwhile questions. How, for example, did unions address the problem of trying to develop solidarity among workers when workers seemed xenophobic, sexist, and downright racist? How could a working-class movement be sustained when workers tended to believe the Gospel of Wealth and hoped to leave the working class behind?

5. Many stories and novels were written about self-made men, work, unions, and workers in the nineteenth and early twentieth centuries. Find several such stories or novels and report on them. There are a number of bibliographies that list labor novels, arranged by date and subject, and even give brief annotations. Your librarian can help you find them. To sort through the many available novels, it is best to choose a theme — a region of the country, an industry or kind of work, the experience of women or an immigrant group. Authors of these works take different points of view: pro- or antiworker, reformist, or mixed (like Phelps). Novels of this sort — like *Looking Backward* and *The Silent Partner* — play a role in sorting out public attitudes, promoting certain points of view, or advocating positions. What are the goals (aside from telling an entertaining story) of the novels and stories you find?

6. Research one of the famous labor conflicts of this period: the Homestead strike (against Carnegie), the Pullman strike, the Great Uprising of 1877, the Haymarket incident, or the eight-hour movement.

7. Nativism (the movement to keep immigrants out of the country) was rampant in the late nineteenth century. Immigrants (particularly the Irish and Eastern Europeans), children, and women were discriminated against and exploited in special ways. With this in mind, investigate a particular group from the point of view of work.

8. In what ways were the African American ex-slaves and their descendents able to enter the workforce in the years after the Civil War? What sorts of occupations and class affiliations were open to them in different periods and regions of the country? How were African Americans received in unions?

BRANCHING OUT

1. Study your family work history. Use what you have learned from this unit to be critical about the working conditions your family has faced and the class affiliations that resulted from the work they have done and their relative success. Your library work for this project is to fill in their history by investigating the economic conditions that existed for them — in the kind of work they did, the place or places they lived, their social advantages or disadvantages, and so on.

2. Study a type of work in your community (city, state, or region, as the case may be). Interview workers, observe working conditions if you can, find out about qualifications required, expectations for advancement, attitudes of workers toward management, and so on. Focus on nonprofessional and nonmanagerial types of work for this project.

3. Investigate the development of women's occupations and women's participation in unions. See the film *Union Maids* and look more deeply into the forms of activism, the forms of discrimination, and the levels of commitment presented by the women interviewed.

4. Investigate how child labor laws and compulsory education laws have interacted to redefine the nature of family life and the roles of mothers, fathers, and children over the period from the Civil War to the present. This is a large project that lends itself to group work.

5. In the late nineteenth century, what did the government do about labor unrest in this country? What legislation was passed? What policies were implemented? How did the public respond to labor unrest and the military suppression of strikes?

6. When did the government finally begin to pass and enforce labor reform laws? What caused that to happen? How effective has such legislation been? This is a big task, so focus on a particular period, a type of legislation (for example, When did ten hours and then eight hours become the standard workday? When were child labor laws enforced?), or — even better — do this as a group project.

7. How has Hollywood depicted work and workers? Look at a film like *Matewan*, *The Molly Maguires*, *Norma Rae*, or *Silkwood* and compare it with historical accounts of the incidents depicted or to documentaries like *Harlan County, USA*. Is the Hollywood version realistic or idealized? How might you explain the reasons for the way work and workers are depicted in different films?

8. What are the issues confronting unions today? What concerns seem to be the same as (or similar to) those faced by unions and workers a century ago? What concerns are different? There are three possible orientations to this question:

a. What are the internal concerns of the unions (for example, setting policy and organizing)?

b. What are the labor-management issues that are the subject of contracts, negotiations, and strikes?

c. What are the legal and social issues that unions face (crime and corruption, shrinking membership, right-to-work laws)?

Pick one of these and then focus on a manageable number of problems. For your research, use books and articles, but also see films like *Roger and Me* and *Harlan County, USA*; look for labor-oriented publications like *In These Times,* the *Progressive,* and *Mother Jones;* write to unions; write to the National Association of Manufactures and read the *Wall Street Journal* to get the management side of the picture. This is a large project that might be done by a group.

9. What happened to the labor and socialist political parties that sprang up in the late nineteenth century? What success did they have? Why did they finally not become major players in the United States as they did in other countries?

BIBLIOGRAPHY

Works Included or Excerpted

Alger, Horatio. *Ragged Dick.* 1867. Reprint, New York: Collier, 1962.

Bellamy, Edward. *Looking Backward: 2000—1887.* 1888. Reprint, New York: Bantam, 1983. Reprint, edited by Daniel H. Borus, Boston: Bedford Books, 1995.

Carnegie, Andrew. "Wealth." *North American Review,* June 1889, 653–64. Reprinted in *Democracy and the Gospel of Wealth,* edited with an introduction by Gail Kennedy. Boston: Heath, 1949.

Conwell, Russell H. "Acres of Diamonds." c. 1890. Westwood, N.J.: Fleming H. Revell Co., 1960.

Councill, William H. *The Negro Laborer: A Word to Him.* 1887. Excerpted in *The Black Worker during the Era of the Knights of Labor,* edited by Philip S. Foner and Ronald L. Lewis. Vol. 3 of *The Black Worker: A Documentary History from Colonial Times to the Present.* Philadelphia: Temple University Press, 1978.

Foster, William Z. *Pages from a Worker's Life.* International Publishers, 1939.

Garraty, John A. *Labor and Capital in the Gilded Age: Testimony Taken by the Senate Committee upon the Relations between Labor and Capital — 1883.* Boston: Little, Brown, 1968.

George, Henry. *Progress and Poverty.* 1879. Reprint, New York: Robert Schalkenbach Foundation, 1992.

Lloyd, Henry Demarest. *Wealth against Commonwealth.* 1894. Reprint, edited with an introduction by Thomas C. Cochran. Englewood Cliffs, N.J.: Prentice-Hall, 1963.

Phelps, Elizabeth Stuart. *The Silent Partner.* 1871. Reprint, New York: Feminist Press, 1983.

Workingmen's Party of Illinois. "Declaration of Independence." 1876. In *We, the Other People: Alternative Declarations of Independence by Labor Groups, Farmers,*

Woman's Rights Advocates, Socialists, and Blacks, 1829—1975, edited by Philip S. Foner. Urbana, Ill.: University of Illinois Press, 1976.

Other Sources

Blewett, Mary H. *We Will Rise in Our Might: Workingwomen's Voices from Nineteenth-Century America.* Ithaca, N.Y.: Cornell University Press, 1991.

Brewer, Thomas B. *The Robber Barons: Saints or Sinners?* Huntington, N.Y.: Krieger, 1976.

Dubofsky, Melvyn. *Industrialism and the American Worker, 1865—1920.* Arlington Heights, Ill.: Harlan Davidson, 1975.

Foner, Philip S., and Ronald L. Lewis, eds. *The Black Worker* Vol. II: *The Black Worker during the Era of the National Labor Union: A Documentary History from Colonial Times to the Present.* Philadelphia: Temple University Press, 1978.

Grob, Gerald. *Workers and Utopia: A Study of Ideological Conflict in the American Labor Movement, 1865—1900.* Evanston, Ill.: Northwestern University Press, 1961.

Gutman, Herbert. *Work, Culture, and Society in Industrializing America.* New York: Vintage, 1976.

Harris, William H. *The Harder We Run: Black Workers since the Civil War.* New York: Oxford University Press, 1982.

Kessler-Harris, Alice. *Out to Work: A History of Wage-Earning Women in the United States.* New York: Oxford University Press, 1982.

Levine, Bruce, et al. *Who Built America?* 2 vols. New York: Pantheon, 1989.

Painter, Nell Irvin. *Standing at Armageddon: The United States, 1877—1919.* New York: Norton, 1987.

Sennett, Richard. *The Hidden Injuries of Class.* New York: Vintage, 1973.

Thomas, John L. *Alternative America: Henry George, Edward Bellamy, Henry Demarest Lloyd, and the Adversary Tradition.* Cambridge: Harvard University Press, 1983.

Wyllie, Irvin G. *The Self-Made Man in America: The Myth of Rags to Riches.* New York: Free Press, 1954.

Yellowitz, Irwin. *The Position of the Worker in American Society, 1865—1896.* Englewood Cliffs, N.J.: Prentice-Hall, 1969.

UNIT FIVE

Japanese American Internment
and the Problem
of Cultural Identity

NEGOTIATIONS

During World War II, 120,000 Japanese American men, women, and children were forcibly removed from their homes on the West Coast of the United States and interned in ramshackle "camps" farther inland. Why? They were considered to be dangerous to the American war effort against Japan. Most of these people lost everything they had worked for and all they possessed — homes, businesses, savings. They were dispossessed and detained solely because they were of Japanese ancestry. Some historians feel that this internment process might more properly be called "incarceration," and the camps "concentration camps" (although the inmates were not killed). It is now acknowledged that this internment was a terrible injustice. The survivors have been given a formal apology and monetary redress by the United States government.

Open to exploration, however, is the great variety of reactions to this injustice among the Japanese Americans themselves. To assume that all responded with righteous indignation and resistance is to oversimplify the complex reactions that suffering injustice brings, as well as to erase the nuances in the Japanese Americans' reactions that reflect their unique culture. How is a member of a racially and culturally distinct group to understand the experience of such injustice? How are other Americans to understand it? How does this experience affect whether a racially and culturally distinct group can, or should, assimilate into mainstream American culture? These are the negotiations of difference we address in Unit Five.

OVERVIEW OF THE SELECTIONS

In the first section of the unit, "Official Documents Establishing the Internment," we print President Roosevelt's Executive Order 9066, which gave the U.S. Army the authority to proceed with the internment. The "Instructions" document typifies army orders issued to begin the internment process.

The second section, "Opinions on the Japanese 'Threat,'" illustrates some of the arguments, pro and con, about whether the internment was necessary. Montaville Flowers, writing in 1917, of course does not mention the internment, but the excerpt from his *Japanese Conquest of American Opinion* illustrates the kind of racism that had been building on the West Coast since the late nineteenth century and that created a climate of public opinion favorable to internment. Next, moving to the time of World War II, we excerpt the official U.S. War Department *Final Report,* which cites national security as the primary reason for the removal and internment of the Japanese Americans. During the war, the internment was legally challenged in several cases brought by Japanese Americans, and we have printed an excerpt from a brief submitted in one of these cases by the Japanese American Citizens League, which attacks specific points in the army report. Also refuting the army report point by point is the last selection in this section, an excerpt from *Personal Justice Denied,* the 1982 U.S. government report officially vindicating the Japanese Americans and calling for monetary redress for the interned.

The third section of the unit, "Testimony of the Interned," includes a selection of works by Japanese American writers who have told their own stories of the internment in both memoirs and fiction. Each presents his or her own personal experience as representative, negotiating a difficult rhetorical path: trying to narrate a personal account that is emotionally powerful without seeming self-indulgent. In the process of recounting their autobiographical stories, the writers raise questions about the nature of race, assimilation, and civil justice. They hold up a mirror in which all Americans can view the national ideals of equal treatment for all before the law against the real experiences of the internment.

In an excerpt from his memoir *They Call Me Moses Masaoka,* Mike Masaoka, a wartime leader of the Japanese American Citizens League, explains why he counseled Japanese Americans to cooperate with the internment process. Michi Nishiura Weglyn, although not a professional historian, has written one of the first critical histories of the internment — *Years of Infamy: The Untold Story of America's Concentration Camps.* We have excerpted her description of the indignities and injustices accompanying the initial evacuation to the camps. In our first excerpt from *Farewell to Manzanar,* Jeanne Wakatsuki Houston has written a memoir of her childhood experience of the internment, describing the losses attending the evacuation and the stresses dividing the community of the interned. In an interview in John Tateishi's *And Justice for All,* Minoru Yasui remembers his legal challenge to the internment, which resulted in a jail term, and explains why, after his release, he decided to recruit other Japanese American men to fight in the U.S. Army.

The interned suffered not only the pains of adjusting to camp life, but also the pains of reentering American society when the internment ended. In an excerpt from her memoir *Nisei Daughter,* Monica Sone describes this process as a time when she finally achieved peace with her dual Japanese and American identity and stopped feeling like a "two-headed monster." In contrast, our second excerpt from *Farewell to Manzanar* describes the emotional breakdown that Jeanne Wakatsuki Houston's father suffered after the internment as well as her own desperate efforts to win the acceptance of her European American teenage peers by exploiting what they regarded as her "exotic" sexuality. In an excerpt from *No-No Boy,* novelist John Okada describes the homecoming of a "No-No Boy," as interned men who refused military service came to be called. After spending time in prison for his resistance, Ichiro Yamada returns home feeling alienated both from mainstream American society, which condemns his decision, and from his family, who support it. In the last selection in Unit Five, the essay "A Fire in Fontana," Hisaye Yamamoto discovers that, long after the internment, the experience has caused her to feel powerful solidarity with African Americans' experience of racism.

HISTORICAL BACKGROUND

Japanese Immigration to the United States

Japanese people first came to the United States in 1868, but not in large numbers until after 1886, when the Japanese government lifted a ban on emigration, partly in response to requests from the United States for laborers. Most of the Japanese coming to the United States at this time were men who intended to work for a few years and then return to their families in Japan. They settled in Hawaii, then a U.S. territory, and on the West Coast. But as "a few years" stretched into many for some, Japanese women too were encouraged to emigrate to marry the earlier settlers.

European Americans showed distrust of Asian immigrants early on. Indeed, the work opportunities that first brought Japanese in large numbers were created by earlier restrictions on Chinese immigration and settlement. In 1870, the U.S. Congress passed a bill, directed against Asian immigrants, that allowed only immigrants of Caucasian or African descent to become U.S. citizens. Thus the Japanese immigrants could not become citizens, no matter how long they remained in the United States. In 1913, California passed a law forbidding Japanese aliens (noncitizens) from owning land in the state. Finally, after other attempts to limit immigration from Japan, the U.S. Congress passed the Immigration Act of 1924, banning immigration by anyone not eligible to become a citizen. This act set quotas on immigration by country, with a zero quota for Japan. For this provision, it became commonly known as the Oriental Exclusion Act.

This law virtually halted all immigration from Japan and created a distinctive generation in the United States of people who had grown up in Japan but who were raising their own families in the United States. The Japanese term for this group is "Issei." The children of the Issei were U.S. citizens because they were born here; the Japanese term for them is "Nisei." Because many of the Issei still intended to return to Japan one day, some sent their children back to Japan to be educated. These children were the "Kibei," and they usually returned to the United States as young adults. Today the Japanese American community uses the term "Nikkei" to refer to all Japanese Americans; we will use this term unless we mean to refer specifically to one subgroup.

Nikkei Life in the United States before World War II

More than half of the Issei worked in agriculture and related trades, such as transporting and selling produce, and they were quite successful in spite of the limitations placed on them, in part because they were adept at forming mutually beneficial collective organizations. Most mainstream U.S. unions would not accept them as members. In 1930, the young adult Nisei formed the Japanese American Citizens League (JACL) for the purpose of organizing political resistance both to the legal burdens placed on the Issei and to the prejudice from which all Nikkei, including those who were U.S. citizens, suffered.

Always a tiny minority (one percent) of the West Coast population, the Issei tended to stay in rural areas and to belong to their own social organizations as well as Buddhist and Christian churches (they were excluded from many European American churches and organizations). They did send many of their children to American public schools, however, while often supplementing this education with Japanese afternoon schools that taught the Japanese language (which many Nisei did not speak fluently), culture, and religion. By the late 1930s, Nisei were entering American high schools and colleges, and the Nikkei population had a slightly higher percentage of college graduates than did the European American population.

World War II and the Decision to Intern

Japan entered World War II against the United States on December 7, 1941, with a surprise attack on the naval base at Pearl Harbor, Hawaii. In that same month, Lieutenant General John L. DeWitt became the commanding officer of the Western Defense Command, in charge of military security on the West Coast. Although personally racist, DeWitt was initially undecided about whether internment was necessary. But U.S. military reverses in the Pacific alarmed him about the possibility of a Japanese attack on California, and he finally recommended interning adult Japanese, Italian, and German citizens residing in the United States. However, at that time, the Justice Department, not the military, was responsible for the control of aliens, including those from enemy countries.

DeWitt's proposal was taken up by the provost marshal general, Major General Allen W. Gullion, who enlisted DeWitt's aid in persuading the War Department to push for taking jurisdiction over alien residents away from the Justice Department. Military leaders were already envisioning mass internment and wanted jurisdiction so that the process could be carried out with the legal justification of military necessity. Major Karl R. Bendetsen, Gullion's chief of the Aliens Division, urged DeWitt to modify his internment proposal to include Nikkei of all ages (and to intern nationals from other enemy countries only after individual hearings). Pressured also by rising anti-Japanese bigotry on the West Coast, DeWitt agreed. In fact, DeWitt helped inflame bigotry with exaggerated estimates of the threat of sabotage by West Coast Nikkei. Finally, with Secretary of War Henry L. Stimson and Assistant Secretary John McCloy insisting, Attorney General Francis Biddle agreed to hand over control of aliens to the military, and shortly thereafter President Roosevelt signed Executive Order 9066, permitting the U.S. Army to define military security areas anywhere in the United States and to exclude from these areas anyone deemed to be a security risk.

DeWitt used Executive Order 9066 to define very large security areas, encompassing much of the states of California, Oregon, and Washington and portions of Arizona, and to exclude from those areas about 120,000 Nikkei men, women, and children, including many who were U.S. citizens. In comparison, about 10,000 German and Italian adults, residents of the United States but not naturalized citizens, were arrested as security risks in the early days of the war, and about 6,000 of them were interned.

DeWitt claimed, in the *Final Report,* that the mass evacuation and internment of Nikkei were necessary because the Nikkei had been aiding the imperial Japanese war effort, for example by signaling ships off the California coast to direct them to targets, and because he feared massive sabotage. Subsequent investigations have shown that Nikkei gave no aid to the Japanese war effort. Nevertheless, DeWitt's decision was supported by President Roosevelt. It was also supported by many citizens' groups, including the American Civil Liberties Union.

In contrast to the treatment of West Coast Nikkei, very few Hawaiian residents of Japanese ancestry were interned, even though Hawaii had in fact been attacked by the Japanese. Hawaii had been placed under martial law after the attack on Pearl Harbor, so no special areas or rules of exclusion were deemed necessary there. Mass internment would have been difficult in any case, since Nikkei made up about one-third of the population of Hawaii, and the local economy would have been devastated by their removal. Moreover, the military governor of Hawaii, General Delos Emmons, argued against mass internment, praising the Hawaiian Nikkei for their exemplary behavior during the Pearl Harbor attack. The great majority of Japanese Americans who volunteered to serve in the United States military during World War II came from Hawaii.

The Internment Process and Life in the Camps

The army moved people out of their homes with no more than a few days' notice, collected them in grimy "assembly centers" at such places as fairgrounds and racetracks, and then shipped them by train to shabby "relocation centers" — in reality detention camps — in desolate areas of California, Arizona, Utah, and other states. The camps were run by a civilian War Relocation Authority (WRA), headed by Dillon Myer. While some of the interned were allowed out of the camps to work, attend school, or join the army, most could not leave unless their loyalty to the U.S. government had been established by means determined by the WRA.

The first detention camp, Manzanar, opened for use as an assembly center in March 1942 and was turned over to the WRA in June of that year. By August 1942, the Japanese Americans had all been moved out of their homes to assembly centers, and by September they were detained in a total of ten camps. The JACL leaders decided to encourage people to cooperate with the relocation process, for which some internees reviled them. Life in the camps was grim. Families were divided as fathers who held supposedly suspicious positions, such as the heads of community organizations, were interned separately and interrogated by the army; some returned later to their families.

At the time of the forced relocation, most of the Issei were middle-aged or older — especially the fathers — and most had been living in the United States for at least twenty years. Few Nisei, by contrast, were older than their twenties, and most were much younger. (This generation began to marry and have children as World War II ended and their children, the third generation, are called "Sansei.")

Nikkei Service in the United States Military

Early in 1943, the U.S. government decided to allow interned men to volunteer for military service, a move advocated by the JACL. Already, in Hawaii, where there was no mass internment, an all-Nisei National Guard unit had been transformed into the 100th Battalion, which by June 1943 was fighting in Italy. The 100th Battalion fought for a year, losing half its men and winning the title "Purple Heart Battalion."

Understandably, few men from the camps wished to volunteer for the army — so few, in fact, that a draft would later have to be instituted. Nevertheless, some did enlist, and the all-Nisei 442nd Regimental Combat Team was formed, to include volunteers from the camps as well as more from Hawaii. The 442nd's motto was "Go for Broke," an exclamation used by Hawaiian crapshooters. The 442nd went into combat in Italy in August 1943 and continued in heavy fighting until May 1945, when the war in Europe ended, losing more than three times its original strength and becoming the most decorated unit in the war. Nisei men also fought against Japan directly, for example in the Military Intelligence Service as translators, propagandists, and infiltrators in the Pacific theater. Nisei women served in the United States military as nurses and in other roles. All in all, about 25,000 Nikkei entered the military.

Loyalty Oaths and "No-No Boys"

Interned men who volunteered for the army still had to complete a loyalty questionnaire before they could be released from the camps. At this time the WRA decided to give the same loyalty questionnaire to all internees, male and female, aged seventeen or older, so that some might be released to attend school or to seek work outside the West Coast military security areas. The call for army volunteers, coupled with the loyalty questionnaire, caused tremendous stress for many of those interned — primarily because of two questions on the questionnaire: One asked male internees to agree to serve "on combat duty, wherever ordered" (women might be asked to serve in other military capacities), and another asked the respondent to "forswear any form of allegiance" to Japan and "swear unqualified allegiance" to the United States.

Although the Nikkei had complied peacefully with the evacuation and relocation process and generally lived peacefully in the camps, there was a great undercurrent of resentment at the way they had been treated, particularly among the Nisei. Even men who wanted to volunteer for the army felt that they could not call their allegiance to the United States "unqualified" after what had happened to them and their families. Some who did not want to volunteer, perhaps because they were tending aged parents, feared that if they answered yes to those two questions, they would be drafted. Older Issei men were reluctant to answer yes for the same reason, while also wondering what would happen to them if they appeared to give up the only citizenship, Japanese, that they were then legally allowed to hold and to swear allegiance to a government that barred them from citizenship. The overwhelming majority, however, did finally answer yes to the two difficult questions.

A small minority, almost all of them Nisei and Kibei, insisted on answering no to both questions because of their anger at the unfair treatment. They were called "No-No Boys" and were segregated from the rest of the internees and urged by WRA camp officials to renounce their American citizenship. Due to defiant pressure to renounce from some angry members of the segregated group, many did so, and of these, some returned to Japan at war's end. Others later won the legal right to reapply for citizenship, although processing all such cases was not completed until 1968. When interned men were subjected to the military draft in January 1944, some refused to enlist, were sentenced as draft resisters, and served time in prison.

The End of Internment and the Process of Redress

A series of court cases mounted by resisting Nikkei attempted to test the constitutionality of the internment. In 1942 Gordon Hirabayashi, a Quaker who condemned what he saw as the blatant racism of the internment, attempted to challenge its legality by refusing to report for evacuation. In ruling on the *Hirabayashi* case in 1943, the U.S. Supreme Court, which really did not want to touch the politically explosive issue of the constitutionality of the internment, managed to consider only Hirabayashi's conviction (which it upheld) on the charge of violating the curfew imposed on all Nikkei just before the internment. By its decision, the Court justified placing special restrictions on a group of people solely because of their race.

In 1944 the Supreme Court handed down more substantive decisions in the *Korematsu* and *Endo* cases. Fred Korematsu had attempted to hide from evacuation by disguising himself. When caught, he decided to test the legality of the Nikkei's exclusion from the West Coast. The court upheld Korematsu's conviction, finding that excluding an entire group of people was legal on grounds of military necessity. Mitsuye Endo, while complying fully with the internment, had planned from the moment it began to challenge the legality of her detention in an internment camp. The court found that Endo's detention was illegal, since she had not been proved to be disloyal. Once the *Endo* decision was handed down, even though the constitutionality of the internment process had not been fully established and the loyalty of the Nikkei had not been fully vindicated, the government announced that people of Japanese ancestry were free to return to the West Coast and that all the camps would be closed within a year. They could not be closed immediately because many of the older people still living in the camps had lost everything in the relocation and had nowhere to go. Internees' financial losses have been estimated at from $1.2 to $3.1 billion (adjusted for inflation in 1980s dollars and including interest and so on).

In 1948 the Evacuation Claims Act promised some compensation to those interned, but a total of only $38 million was paid out by 1965. Meanwhile, in 1952 the U.S. Congress passed a bill allowing Issei (and members of any other racial group) to become American citizens. In 1965 the Immigration Reform Act eased restrictions on immigration from Japan. In the early 1970s, Nikkei activists began to press for more compensation for the interned. Their call for redress was opposed for many different reasons within the Japanese American community. For example, some felt that monetary payments could never compensate for the injustice done; others feared that forcing the U.S. government to admit wrongdoing would harm relations with Japan. Although some JACL leaders opposed redress, the national organization voted in 1978 to request a formal apology and $25,000 to be paid to each surviving internee. After the publication of *Personal Justice Denied* (1982), pressure grew in support of redress. Finally, in 1988 the Civil Liberties Act officially denounced the internment as unjust and called for payment of $20,000 to each surviving internee — an appropriation of about $1.25 billion for the approximately 70,000 survivors. The first checks, along with a presidential apology, were distributed in 1990.

OFFICIAL DOCUMENTS ESTABLISHING THE INTERNMENT

FRANKLIN DELANO ROOSEVELT

Executive Order 9066 (February 19, 1942)

This executive order gave the army authority to set up security zones anywhere in the United States and to exclude from these zones any people deemed to be security risks. This order set in motion the evacuation and internment of the Nikkei.

WHEREAS, THE SUCCESSFUL PROSECUTION of the war requires every possible protection against espionage and against sabotage to national-defense material, national-defense premises and national-defense utilities as defined in Section 4, Act of April 20, 1918, 40 Stat. 533, as amended by the Act of November 30, 1940, 54 Stat. 1220, and the Act of August 21, 1941, 55 Stat. 655 (U.S.C., Title 50, Sec. 104):

Now therefore, by virtue of the authority vested in me as President of the United States, and Commander in Chief of the Army and Navy, I hereby authorize and direct the Secretary of War, and the Military Commanders whom he may from time to time designate, whenever he or any designated Commander deems such action necessary or desirable, to prescribe military areas in such places and of such extent as he or the appropriate Military Commander may determine, from which any or all persons may be excluded, and with respect to which, the right of any person to enter, remain in, or leave shall be subject to whatever restriction the Secretary of War or the appropriate Military Commander may impose in his discretion. The Secretary of War is hereby authorized to provide for residents of any such area who are excluded therefrom, such transportation, food, shelter, and other accommodations as may be necessary, in the judgment of the Secretary of War or the said Military Commander, and until other arrangements are made, to accomplish the purpose of this order. The designation of military areas in any region or locality shall supersede designations of prohibited and restricted areas by the Attorney General under the Proclamations of December 7 and 8,

Franklin Delano Roosevelt, Executive Order 9066 (1942), reprinted in U.S. Department of War, *Final Report: Japanese Evacuation from the West Coast, 1942* (Washington, D.C.: Government Printing Office, 1943; reprint, New York: Arno Press, 1978).

1941, and shall supersede the responsibility and authority of the Attorney General under the said Proclamations in respect of such prohibited and restricted areas.

I hereby further authorize and direct the Secretary of War and the said Military Commanders to take such other steps as he or the appropriate Military Commander may deem advisable to enforce compliance with the restrictions applicable to each Military area hereinabove authorized to be designated, including the use of Federal troops and other Federal Agencies, with authority to accept assistance of state and local agencies.

I hereby further authorize and direct all Executive Departments, independent establishments, and other Federal Agencies, to assist the Secretary of War or the said Military Commanders in carrying out this Executive Order, including the furnishing of medical aid, hospitalization, food, clothing, transportation, use of land, shelter, and other supplies, equipment, utilities, facilities, and services.

This order shall not be construed as modifying or limiting in any way the authority heretofore granted under Executive Order No. 8972, dated December 12, 1941, nor shall it be construed as limiting or modifying the duty and responsibility of the Federal Bureau of Investigation, with respect to the investigations of alleged acts of sabotage or the duty and responsibility of the Attorney General and the Department of Justice under the Proclamations of December 7 and 8, 1941, prescribing regulations for the conduct and control of alien enemies, except as such duty and responsibility is superseded by the designation of military areas hereunder.

READING CRITICALLY

1. What reasons are given in the first paragraph for the issuing of this executive order?

2. What responsibilities remain with the Federal Bureau of Investigation, according to the last paragraph of the order?

WRITING ANALYTICALLY

Historians generally agree that this executive order was aimed at the Nikkei and was intended to give the army the power to intern them. Yet the order mentions "any or all persons," rather than specifying the Nikkei. Also, it makes no mention of what is to be done with these "persons" once they are "excluded" from the security areas — that is, it makes no mention of internment. If the intent was to confine the Nikkei, why do you think the order was written in such vague terms? Write an argumentative paper in which you answer this question. You should consider Executive Order 9066 as an example of a government proclamation of a controversial action and frame your argument in terms of general guidelines for how such an announcement should, or should not, be handled.

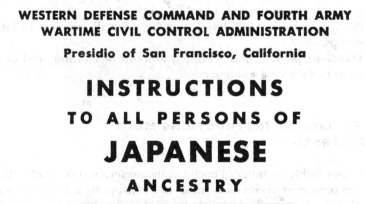

JOHN L. DEWITT

"Instructions to All Persons of Japanese Ancestry"

April 30, 1942

John L. DeWitt (1880–1962), the son of an army general, entered the army himself at age eighteen and served in France during World War I. He was a lieutenant general when he took charge of the Western Defense Command in December 1941. DeWitt played an important role in bringing about the internment (see introduction, p. 609), and he supervised its initial stages. The "Instructions" typify orders he gave to assemble the Nikkei for evacuation. DeWitt retired in 1947 and was later appointed full general along with other retired officers who had attained the lieutenant general rank during World War II.

WESTERN DEFENSE COMMAND AND FOURTH ARMY
WARTIME CIVIL CONTROL ADMINISTRATION

Presidio of San Francisco, California

INSTRUCTIONS
TO ALL PERSONS OF
JAPANESE
ANCESTRY
LIVING IN THE FOLLOWING AREA:

All of that portion of the County of Alameda, State of California, within that boundary beginning at the point at which the southerly limits of the City of Berkeley meet San Francisco Bay; thence easterly and following the southerly limits of said city to College Avenue; thence southerly on College Avenue to Broadway; thence southerly on Broadway to the southerly limits of the City of Oakland; thence following the limits of said city westerly and northerly, and following the shoreline of San Francisco Bay to the point of beginning.

Pursuant to the provisions of Civilian Exclusion Order No. 27, this Headquarters, dated April 30, 1942, all persons of Japanese ancestry, both

John L. DeWitt, "Instructions to All Persons of Japanese Ancestry" (1942), reprinted in U.S. Department of War, *Final Report: Japanese Evacuation from the West Coast, 1942* (Washington, D.C.: Government Printing Office, 1943; reprint, New York: Arno Press, 1978).

alien and nonalien, will be evacuated from the above area by 12 o'clock noon, P.W.T., Thursday May 7, 1942.

No Japanese person living in the above area will be permitted to change residence after 12 o'clock noon, P.W.T., Thursday, April 30, 1942, without obtaining special permission from the representative of the Commanding General, Northern California Sector, at the Civil Control Station located at:

> 530 Eighteenth Street,
> Oakland, California.

Such permits will only be granted for the purpose of uniting members of a family, or in cases of grave emergency.

The Civil Control Station is equipped to assist the Japanese population affected by this evacuation in the following ways:

1. Give advice and instructions on the evacuation.
2. Provide services with respect to the management, leasing, sale, storage, or other disposition of most kinds of property, such as real estate, business and professional equipment, household goods, boats, automobiles, and livestock.
3. Provide temporary residence elsewhere for all Japanese in family groups.
4. Transport persons and a limited amount of clothing and equipment to their new residence.

THE FOLLOWING INSTRUCTIONS MUST BE OBSERVED:

1. A responsible member of each family, preferably the head of the family, or the person in whose name most of the property is held, and each individual living alone, will report to the Civil Control Station to receive further instructions. This must be done between 8:00 A.M. and 5:00 P.M. on Friday, May 1, 1942, or between 8:00 A.M. and 5:00 P.M. on Saturday, May 2, 1942.

2. Evacuees must carry with them on departure for the Assembly Center, the following property:

> (a) Bedding and linens (no mattress) for each member of the family;
> (b) Toilet articles for each member of the family;
> (c) Extra clothing for each member of the family;
> (d) Sufficient knives, forks, spoons, plates, bowls, and cups for each member of the family;
> (e) Essential personal effects for each member of the family.

All items carried will be securely packaged, tied, and plainly marked with the name of the owner and numbered in accordance with instructions obtained at the Civil Control Station. The size and number of packages is limited to that which can be carried by the individual or family group.

3. No pets of any kind will be permitted.

4. No personal items and no household goods will be shipped to the Assembly Center.

5. The United States Government through its agencies will provide for the storage at the sole risk of the owner of the more substantial household items, such as iceboxes, washing machines, pianos, and other heavy furniture. Cooking utensils and other small items will be accepted for storage if crated, packed, and plainly marked with the name and address of the owner. Only one name and address will be used by a given family.

6. Each family and individual living alone will be furnished transportation to the Assembly Center or will be authorized to travel by private automobile in a supervised group. All instructions pertaining to the movement will be obtained at the Civil Control Station.

Go to the Civil Control Station between the hours of 8:00 A.M. and 5:00 P.M., Friday, May 1, 1942, or between the hours of 8:00 A.M. and 5:00 P.M., Saturday, May 2, 1942, to receive further instructions.

J. L. DEWITT
Lieutenant General, U.S. Army
Commanding

April 30, 1942
See Civilian Exclusion Order No. 27.

READING CRITICALLY

1. How much time is to elapse from the issuing of these instructions to the evacuation of all Nikkei from the designated area?

2. Who are the "non-aliens" referred to in the second paragraph of the instructions?

3. What do the instructions say and what can you infer about the kinds of things people could *not* take with them to the camps?

4. What services do the instructions promise will be provided by the Civil Control Station to people being evacuated?

WRITING ANALYTICALLY

1. Presumably the army did not want to have to use force to remove the Nikkei unless absolutely necessary. The instructions, then, can be assumed to be a document that intends to persuade people to comply peacefully with the evacuation and internment. Write a paper in which you explain what strategies you see in the document that seem intended to reassure and induce compliance. Use this evidence to support a thesis concerning whether you think the document is actually

reassuring. Alternative: Respond to this question in the form of a letter that you, as a Nisei, are writing to a non-Nisei friend, having just read the instructions.

2. If we read only these instructions, it is difficult to get a clear picture of what happened when the Nikkei were moved out. Write a paper in which you use Michi Nishiura Weglyn (p. 689) or Jeanne Wakatsuki Houston and James D. Houston (pp. 715 and 757) to provide details to illustrate some of the provisions of the instructions. Comparing these details with what the instructions lead you to believe should have happened, write an argumentative essay on the extent to which the instructions gave the Nikkei a sense of what to expect. Alternative: Respond to this question in the form of a letter that you, as a Nisei, are writing to a non-Nisei friend shortly after your arrival at Manzanar.

MONTAVILLE FLOWERS

From *The Japanese Conquest of American Opinion* (1917)

Montaville Flowers (1868–1934) was a leading proponent of anti-Japanese racism in early-twentieth-century California. Anti-Asian racism in California had grown since the mid-nineteenth century, when it was directed initially at the Chinese. After Chinese immigration was restricted in 1882, this racism was increasingly directed against the small but growing number of Japanese immigrants. Initially, anti-Japanese agitation was led by labor unions, which feared the competition of workers willing to do undesirable jobs for low pay. After World War I, however, anti-Japanese racism spread among farmers, shopkeepers, and groups such as the American Legion and the Native Sons of the Golden West. Various groups joined in 1919 to form the Japanese Exclusion League. Its activities diminished with the passage of the 1924 Immigration Act, also known as the Oriental Exclusion Act, forbidding Japanese immigration. But a stereotype of the Japanese immigrants as cunning, treacherous, ambitious, and militantly loyal to Japan had been built up over the years. This stereotype reemerged virulently after the bombing of Pearl Harbor.

Flowers, who had come to California from the Midwest shortly after the turn of the century, lectured widely on the Japanese "threat" and wrote a column for *Grizzly Bear,* the newspaper published by the Native Sons of the Golden West. He wrote *The Japanese Conquest of American Opinion* primarily to attack *The American Japanese Problem* (1914), which recommended racially nondiscriminatory immigration laws, and to vilify its author, Reverend Sidney L. Gulick, a missionary in Japan (for more information on Gulick, see note 2, p. 625). Flowers's ideas gained wide credence among right-wing politicians of his day and apparently convinced even military intelligence and the FBI that Gulick was a paid agent of the Japanese government. Flowers himself dropped from sight after an unsuccessful bid for a Republican congressional seat in 1918.

We have reprinted an excerpt from chapter 18, "The Dead Soul in the Pot," from the last section of *The Japanese Conquest of American Opinion.* In this section, Flowers analyzes what he considers to be the misguided ideals that make Americans susceptible to what he depicts as a rising tide of pro-Japanese propaganda. In the previous chapter he especially condemns the notion that the United States can and should be a racial melting pot. Later in the chapter

Montaville Flowers, *The Japanese Conquest of American Opinion* (New York: George H. Doran, 1917), 209–14.

In the notes, EDS. = Patricia Bizzell and Bruce Herzberg.

we excerpt, Flowers argues that the melting pot idea puts the "soul" of the nation at risk by polluting it with the "dead soul" of "Asiatic blood."

WHAT IS A NATION? In common usage the word nation has two distinct ideas. One refers to a group of people, the other to the land they live in. A true nation is like a great family living in one home; its members are one in blood, one in language, one in government, equal in rank, mutual in interest, dwelling in peace. The best technical definition of nation is: "A nation is an ethnographical unit occupying a geographical unit"; that is, a race unit living in a land unit. Nation therefore has two units, race and land. Whatever disturbs these two units causes trouble. When two different racial units are bound within one land unit, or when one land extends its boundaries over two racial units, the causes of war are laid down. Albert Bushnell Hart, of Harvard, sums up the causes of the World War as follows: "The military spirit, commercial expansion, the desire for territory, the self-assertion of great states, these are things that, in the long run, may overcome all the checks of parliaments and statesmen and Hague Conference.[1] But none of these could have brought about the fearful conditions of 1914. The strongest and determining reason of the war is the growth of race antipathies. Europe is a mosaic of races. And at last the world has realized that the political boundaries of Europe cut across more persistent lines of race, language, and religion, and thus have brought about this conflict between the nations." Race mixture has been not only a fundamental cause of war, involving as it does internal convulsions and external complications, but the crossing of races has always resulted in a change of civilization and lowering of the rank of higher civilizations.

Of all the efforts made by the Japanese themselves, and by their champions, the Gulicks and Scudders and Griffiths, the most extraordinary and dangerous one is the effort to establish several propositions concerning mixed races, all of which are without basis in fact. One is that all of the leading civilizations of the present have been produced by peoples of mixed races; another, that there really are no peoples of pure race; another, that greater civilizations will be produced by greater mixtures; and then that the Mongolians and Malays are not Yellow Races, but White Races; and finally that the Japanese are the whitest of all the White-Yellow Races. Doremus E. Scudder, of Hawaii, in a preface to *Asia at the Door,* by Kawakami, definitely states that the Japanese are the most mixed of Oriental races, and the Americans are the most mixed of Occidental races; that therefore there should be a fellow feeling of similarity between the two

[1]International conferences took place at The Hague, Netherlands, in 1899 and 1907. They were unsuccessful at resolving the tensions that resulted in World War I (1914–18), which was in progress as Flowers wrote. Nevertheless, they did succeed in establishing international laws of war and a court where violations of these laws — what we now call "war crimes" — could be tried. — EDS.

mixtures, and that the greatest results in race will be obtained by a mixture of the mixtures.

Mr. Gulick[2] makes a most extraordinary effort, in furtherance of his general theory of the benefits of race mixture, to prove that Japanese and other Asiatics readily blend with the white stocks and are highly assimilable by the white race. The general arguments he produces are a budget of discarded theories that grew out of a theological hypothesis, which is now disproved by science and all its applications are abandoned by educated men. That hypothesis was that all the peoples of the earth came from one pair of parents created by one divine act. It is now generally conceded that the various human races have originated under different conditions, in different places, from widely different Simian ancestors, *and that whatever the origin was it has no bearing on the affairs of modern nations.* Theology also gave the cue that a new and better man should be evolved, and fancy created the notion that the melting pot is the ideal — the only — process to produce him.

Mr. Gulick's treatment of "social assimilation" makes the fundamental blunder of assuming that the evolutionary processes — variation, selection, transmission, adaptation — which obtain in physical life cease entirely and do not continue with equal determinative power in psychic and social evolution. This theory of social inheritance is based on the premise that each psychic is born without inherent tendency or direction; that physical inheritance carries with it no basis for psychic traits.[3] All of this is absolutely disproved by historical experience. Opposed to these notions are the best psychologists and sociologists of America and Europe — Summer and Keller and Fairchild of Yale and Le Bon of France, Weale of England have exploded these theories. Professor Keller says, "The case of societal variation reduces ultimately, then, to the mental reaction of individuals. It must not be forgotten that they (social phenomena) probably go back to physical change in the individual brain *and so root in organic processes and in the resultant 'race-character' or temperament.*"

The arguments of Mr. Gulick, therefore, are the hypotheses of an amicable gentleman of the Old School in a great effort to harmonize the theology to which he must adhere with a fragmentary knowledge of some truths of modern science that he cannot ignore, to the especial end of getting the Japanese into the United States and into social relations with the white race.

---

[2]Sidney L. Gulick was the author of *The American Japanese Problem* (1914), which urged that immigration laws be made racially nondiscriminatory and that the Nikkei be admitted to full citizenship. Gulick (1860–1945) was a Congregational minister who went to Japan in 1887 as a missionary, advised Japanese leaders on relations with the United States, and became an active proponent of peace and friendship between the two countries. From Hawaii during World War II, Gulick supported efforts to halt the West Coast internment of the Nikkei, though he advocated peaceful compliance once internment became inevitable. — EDS.

[3]"Psychic" here means "psyche" or "individual mentality." "Psychic traits" are what we would call "psychological traits." — EDS.

The particular instance which Mr. Gulick cites to sustain these general arguments (and it is a fair sample of what is cited by all who stand for race-mixtures) for the assimilation and cross breeding of Asiatics and Europeans proves nothing. He tells of a half white and half Asiatic child whom his parents, then missionaries in the Marshall Islands, adopted in infancy, and whom he regarded as his sister through all the years of childhood. He avers that her mental habits and moral character were of the highest type of the white child. From such instances as this he makes the sweeping general conclusion that the United States can adopt, rear, and assimilate the Asiatic peoples.

The illustration entirely fails because the conditions are not parallel, indeed they are and always will be wholly absent. If the white families of the United States could and would adopt the newly born babes of Asiatic parents, and isolate them, each one, from the Oriental environment and ensconce them within the soul of our social inheritance, it might be possible to develop from many such Asiatic infants adults evidencing a similarity, in grosser aspects, to the white race. But these conditions do not exist, nor will they ever exist. The Japanese children in the United States are raised by Japanese parents whom Mr. Kawakami, in a recent pronouncement which entirely contradicts former declarations as well as his own practice, says are as proud of their race and their social inheritance as the Americans are of theirs. These parents give to their children the Oriental character and social inheritance. The more numerous these families become, the more they segregate themselves in larger communities; and the more then their Oriental civilization becomes encysted in white lands; and the more fully then will be preserved their Oriental nature and their character.

But there are other aspects to be noted in this special instance of Mr. Gulick's foster sister. The child died in early life and there was no chance to finish the experiment either in herself or in her progeny. Mr. Gulick, himself, also a child, was the only observer, and the accuracy of his observations is discounted by his own admission that he thought her so like himself that he never knew until she died that she was not his sister. Is it likely that any one who could not detect the essential physical differences between a white child and a half-Mongolian child could detect the more subtle, yet real differences, that may have existed (and undoubtedly did exist) in the mental and moral constitutions of the two?

We cannot take the Asiatic immigrants as babes and adopt them into our families, one or two to a family. There are not one-fourth enough families to go round. The Japanese will not give up their babes, nor can the adults become babes themselves. How absurd this illustration becomes! The facts are the Asiatics come here by thousands with their racial characteristics set forever. They raise their own babes in their own way, imparting to them the soul of their race. Even in cases of intermarriage, in every instance that has come under my observation, the Japanese himself is the dominant and controlling force in the family, because his whole civilization proclaims that he must be such. Thus every feature of Mr. Gulick's case fades away, and his conclusion, based upon it, is more than worthless. It is mischievous because it leads to error that can never be corrected.

No intelligent observer or traveler will deny that from the crossing of races there is produced occasionally a fine individual, but that one individual produced under the finest conditions cannot be taken as a type of what is produced generally by such race crosses. When they cite the fact that a Burbank, in the crossing of plants, has produced marvelous fruits and marvelous plants and "astonishing variants," they fail to recognize the largest fact in that process of production; for Mr. Burbank says that to produce one plant of worthy type from cross-breeding, he has often been obliged to destroy one hundred thousand other plants that are utter failures, because they were worse in quality than the stocks which he attempted to improve. This is a fatal condition in race mixture, for in the case of human beings it is utterly impossible to destroy the one hundred thousand abnormal, degenerate, and wretched beings that result from race crosses, but each must be permitted to live and to reproduce his stock until its own degeneracy obliterates it from the earth.

The limits of this book will not permit a refutation of all the material used by Mr. Gulick and Kawakami, as if in scientific proof to establish their positions upon race mixtures.

After one has read their books and pamphlets he is impressed with the fact that they have but one practical end — to secure for the Japanese the rights of entrance, citizenship, intermarriage. To achieve that end they turn architects and lay down a broad chart of foundation theories, diagram the floors into apartments for all the races, design the bedchambers with the morals of Oriental men, draw beautiful facades of conglomerate civilizations, and cover it all with the canopy of religious appeals — in order to leave the main entrance open to the Japanese. . . .

READING CRITICALLY

1. How does Flowers define *nation* in his opening paragraph?

2. At the end of his opening paragraph, Flowers mentions his fears for the "lowering of the rank of higher civilizations." What does he appear to mean by "higher civilizations"?

3. Flowers argues that Japanese immigrants can never become part of the American nation. What arguments does he make against Scudder's concept of "racial mixture"?

4. How does Flowers argue against Gulick's concept of "social assimilation"?

WRITING ANALYTICALLY

1. Flowers is trying to persuade a particular audience to action. Who is his main intended audience, what is he trying to get them to do, and how can you tell? Look at your responses to the reading questions for evidence that can be used to address these questions — that is, details on the kinds of arguments and other rhetorical

strategies that Flowers is using. Write a paper in which you argue that Flowers is or is not likely to be effective in moving his target audience. Option: Compare and contrast the effect you think he would have had on his intended audience with his effect on you.

2. In reading Flowers, you may recognize arguments and other rhetorical strategies that you have seen used in discussions that attack other immigrant groups. If you have access to another such discussion (perhaps concerning a group of which you are a member), write a paper in which you compare and contrast Flowers's approach with the one used in the discussion of the other group. You should aim to develop a thesis on how attacks on immigrant groups may typically be handled.

3. The Japanese American Citizens League brief (p. 647) contends that Nikkei are assimilated into American culture. This position is a direct challenge to Flowers, who reviews and rebuts several arguments on the possibility of assimilation. Write a paper in the form of a letter from Flowers to the Supreme Court, explaining why the Court should not believe the arguments of the Japanese American Citizens League brief.

U.S. DEPARTMENT OF WAR

From *Final Report: Japanese Evacuation from the West Coast, 1942* (1943)

In December 1941, Lieutenant General John L. DeWitt became the commanding officer of the U.S. Army's Western Defense Command, in charge of military security for the West Coast. He helped bring about the decision to intern the Nikkei and supervised the initial stages of the internment (for more on this process, see the Introduction, p. 612).

Incorporating some of DeWitt's own writings, the *Final Report* was prepared for him by a U.S. Department of War team under the direction of Colonel Karl R. Bendetsen. It was intended to show DeWitt's superiors, politicians, and concerned private citizens that DeWitt had acted responsibly and that the Nikkei were being treated neither too harshly nor too leniently. This sort of report was typically prepared as part of record keeping in the military bureaucracy, but this particular report came under close scrutiny in the War Department because its leaders knew that it might become a key document in the event of legal challenges to the internment. (In fact, it did — see point-by-point refutations of the report in other selections in this unit, pp. 647 and 661.) Assistant Secretary of War John McCloy even ordered that the original draft be rewritten to eliminate some of its most overt racism.

U.S. Department of War, *Final Report: Japanese Evacuation from the West Coast, 1942* (Washington, D.C.: Government Printing Office, 1943; reprint, New York: Arno Press, 1978), 7–19, 33–38.

In the notes, USDOW = U.S. Department of War, EDS. = Patricia Bizzell and Bruce Herzberg.

We have excerpted chapter 2, "Need for Military Control and Evacuation," and the appendix to chapter 3, "Establishment of Military Control" (a memo written by DeWitt), as best representing the kinds of arguments made at the time for the military necessity for internment. These arguments were powerful enough to convince even liberal thinkers such as California Attorney General Earl Warren (later chief justice of the U.S. Supreme Court), who would express regret in his memoirs for his complicity in the internment.

CHAPTER 2

Need for Military Control and for Evacuation

THE COMMANDING GENERAL [DEWITT], meantime, prepared and submitted recommendations for the establishment of prohibited zones in Arizona, Oregon, and Washington, similar to those he had prepared for California. Upon receipt of these supplemental recommendations, forwarded by the Secretary of War, the Attorney General declined to act until further study. In the case of Washington State, the recommended prohibited zone included virtually all of the territory lying west of the Cascades. A general enemy alien evacuation from this area would have been required. More than 9,500 persons would have been affected. No agency was then prepared to supervise or conduct a mass movement, and the Attorney General was not convinced of the necessity.

As early as January 5, in a memorandum of that date to Mr. Rowe,[1] during the initial conferences at San Francisco, the Commanding General pointed to the need for careful advanced planning to provide against such economic and social dislocations which might ensue from such mass evacuation. The point was also established that the Army had no wish to assume any aspects of civil control if there were any means by which the necessary security measures could be taken through normal civilian channels. . . .

The Department of Justice had indicated informally that it did not consider itself in a position to direct any enforced migrations. The Commanding General's recommendations for prohibited zones in Washington and Oregon were therefore viewed with particular concern by the Department. Not only did it feel that such action should be predicated on convincing evidence of the military necessity, it regarded the responsibility for collective evacuation as one not within its functions.

The Attorney General, on February 9, 1942, formally advised the Secretary of War, by letter, that he could not accept the recommendation of the Commanding General for the establishment of a zone prohibited to enemy aliens in the States of Washington and Oregon of the extent proposed by him. He stated in part:

---

[1] James Rowe Jr., aide to Attorney General Francis Biddle. — EDS.

Your recommendation of prohibited areas for Oregon and Washington include the cities of Portland, Seattle, and Tacoma and therefore contemplate a mass evacuation of many thousands. . . . No reasons were given for this mass evacuation . . . I understood that . . . Lieutenant General DeWitt has been requested to supply the War Department with further details and further material before any action is taken on these recommendations. I shall, therefore, await your further advice.

. . . The evacuation . . . from this area would, of course, present a problem of very great magnitude. The Department of Justice is not physically equipped to carry out any mass evacuation. It would mean that only the War Department has the equipment and personnel to manage the task.

The proclamations directing the Department of Justice to apprehend, and where necessary, evacuate alien enemies, do not, of course, include American citizens of the Japanese race. If they have to be evacuated, I believe that this would have to be done as a military necessity in these particular areas. Such action, therefore, should in my opinion, be taken by the War Department and not by the Department of Justice.

The Commanding General thereafter submitted a résumé of the military considerations which prompted his recommendation for a prohibited zone in Washington and Oregon embracing virtually the westerly half of those states. The Department of Justice, however, concluded that it was not in a position to undertake any mass evacuation, and declined in any event to administer such general civil control measures.

Meanwhile, the uncertainties of the situation became further complicated. The enforcement of contraband provisions was impeded by the fact that many Japanese aliens resided in premises owned by American-born persons of Japanese ancestry. The Department of Justice had agreed to authorize its special field agents of the Federal Bureau of Investigation to undertake spot raids without warrant to determine the possession of arms, cameras, and other contraband by Japanese, but only in those premises occupied *exclusively* by enemy aliens. The search of mixed occupancy premises or dwellings had not been authorized except by warrant only. . . .

In the Monterey area in California a Federal Bureau of Investigation spot raid made about February 12, 1942, found more than 60,000 rounds of ammunition and many rifles, shotguns, and maps of all kinds. These raids had not succeeded in arresting the continuance of illicit signaling. Most dwelling places were in the mixed occupancy class and could not be searched promptly upon receipt of reports. It became increasingly apparent that adequate security measures could not be taken unless the Federal Government placed itself in a position to deal with the whole problem.

The Pacific Coast had become exposed to attack by enemy successes in the Pacific. The situation in the Pacific theater had gravely deteriorated. There were hundreds of reports nightly of signal lights visible from the coast, and of intercepts of unidentified radio transmissions. Signaling was often observed at premises which could not be entered without a warrant because of mixed occupancy. The problem required immediate solution. It called for the application of measures not then in being.[2]

Further, the situation was fraught with danger to the Japanese population itself. The combination of spot raids revealing hidden caches of contraband, the attacks on coastwise shipping, the interception of illicit radio transmissions, the nightly observation of visual signal lamps from constantly changing locations, and the success of the enemy offensive in the Pacific, had so aroused the public along the West Coast against the Japanese that it was ready to take matters into its own hands. Press and periodical reports of the public attitudes along the West Coast from December 7, 1941, to the initiation of controlled evacuation clearly reflected the intensity of feeling. Numerous incidents of violence involving Japanese and others occurred; many more were reported but were subsequently either unverified or were found to be cumulative.

The acceptance by the Attorney General of the Washington and Oregon recommendations would not have provided the security which the military situation then required. More than two-thirds of the total Japanese population on the West Coast were not subject to alien enemy regulations. The action ultimately taken was based upon authority not then existing. It had become essential to provide means which would remove the potential menace to which the presence of this group under all the circumstances subjected the West Coast. It is pertinent now to examine the situation with which the military authorities were then confronted.

Because of the ties of race, the intense feeling of filial piety, and the strong bonds of common tradition, culture, and customs, this population presented a tightly knit racial group. It included in excess of 115,000 persons deployed along the Pacific Coast. Whether by design or accident, virtually always their communities were adjacent to very vital shore installations, war plants, etc. While it was believed that some were loyal, it was known that many were not. To complicate the situation no ready means existed for determining the loyal and the disloyal with any degree of safety. It was necessary to face the realities — a positive determination could not have been made.

It could not be established, of course, that the location of thousands of Japanese adjacent to strategic points verified the existence of some vast conspiracy to which all of them were parties. Some of them doubtless resided there through mere coincidence. It seemed equally beyond doubt, however, that the presence of others was not mere coincidence. It was difficult to explain the situation in Santa Barbara County, for example, by coincidence alone.

Throughout the Santa Maria Valley in that County, including the cities of Santa Maria and Guadalupe, every utility, air field, bridge, telephone and power line, or other facility of importance was flanked by Japanese.

[2]It is interesting to note that following the evacuation, interceptions of suspicious or unidentified radio signals and shore-to-ship signal lights were virtually eliminated and attacks on outbound shipping from West Coast ports appreciably reduced. — USDOW

They even surrounded the oil fields in this area. Only a few miles south, however, in the Santa Ynez Valley, lay an area equally as productive agriculturally as the Santa Maria Valley and with lands equally available for purchase and lease, but without any strategic installations whatever. There were no Japanese in the Santa Ynez Valley.

Similarly, along the coastal plain of Santa Barbara County from Gaviota south, the entire plain, though narrow, had been subject to intensive cultivation. Yet, the only Japanese in this area were located immediately adjacent to such widely separated points as the El Capitan Oil Field, Elwood Oil Field, Summerland Oil Field, Santa Barbara airport, and Santa Barbara lighthouse and harbor entrance. There were no Japanese on the equally attractive lands between these points. In the north end of the county is a stretch of open beach ideally suited for landing purposes, extending for fifteen or twenty miles, on which almost the only inhabitants were Japanese.

Such a distribution of the Japanese population appeared to manifest something more than coincidence. In any case, it was certainly evident that the Japanese population of the Pacific Coast was, as a whole, ideally situated with reference to points of strategic importance, to carry into execution a tremendous program of sabotage on a mass scale should any considerable number of them have been inclined to do so.

There were other very disturbing indications that the Commanding General could not ignore. He was forced to consider the character of the Japanese colony along the coast. While this is neither the place nor the time to record in detail significant pro-Japanese activities in the United States, it is pertinent to note some of these in passing. Research has established that there were over 124 separate Japanese organizations along the Pacific Coast engaged, in varying degrees, in common pro-Japanese purposes. This number does not include local branches of parent organizations, of which there were more than 310.

Research and coordination of information had made possible the identification of more than 100 parent fascistic or militaristic organizations in Japan which have had some relation, either direct or indirect, with Japanese organizations or individuals in the United States. Many of the former were parent organizations of subsidiary or branch organizations in the United States and in that capacity directed organizational and functional activities. There was definite information that the great majority of activities followed a line of control from the Japanese government, through key individuals and associations to the Japanese residents in the United States.

That the Japanese associations, as organizations, aided the military campaigns of the Japanese Government is beyond doubt. The contributions of these associations towards the Japanese war effort had been freely published in Japanese newspapers throughout California.

The extent to which Emperor worshiping ceremonies were attended could not have been overlooked. Many articles appearing in issues of Japanese language newspapers gave evidence that these ceremonies had been directed toward the stimulation of "burning patriotism" and "all-out support of the Japanese Asiatic Co-Prosperity Program."

Numerous Emperor worshiping ceremonies had been held. Hundreds of Japanese attended these ceremonies, and it was an objective of the sponsoring organization to encourage one hundred percent attendance. For example, on February 11, 1940, at 7:00 P.M., the Japanese Association of Sacramento sponsored an Emperor worshiping ceremony in commemoration of the 2,600th anniversary of the founding of Japan. Three thousand attended.

Another group of Japanese met on January 1, 1941, at Lindsay, California. They honored the 2,601st Year of the Founding of the Japanese Empire and participated in the annual reverence to the Emperor, and bowed their heads toward Japan in order to indicate that they would be ". . . *ready to respond to the call of the mother country with one mind. Japan is fighting to carry out our program of Greater Asiatic co-prosperity. Our fellow Japanese countrymen must be of one spirit and should endeavor to unite our Japanese societies in this country. . . .*"

Evidence of the regular occurrence of Emperor worshiping ceremonies in almost every Japanese populated community in the United States had been discovered.

A few examples of the many Japanese associations extant along the Pacific Coast are described in the following passages:

The Hokubei Butoku Kai. The Hokubei Butoku Kai or Military Virtue Society of North America was organized in 1931 with headquarters in Alvarado, Alameda County, California, and a branch office in Tokyo. One of the purposes of the organization was to instill the Japanese military code of Bushido among the Japanese throughout North America. This highly nationalistic and militaristic organization was formed primarily to teach Japanese boys "military virtues" through Kendo (fencing), Judo (Jiujitsu), and Sumo (wrestling). The manner in which this society became closely integrated with many other Japanese organizations, both business and social, is well illustrated by the postal address of some of these branches.

The Heimusha Kai. The Heimusha Kai was organized for the sole purpose of furthering the Japanese war effort. The intelligence services (including the Federal Bureau of Investigation, the Military Intelligence Service, and the Office of Naval Intelligence) had reached the conclusion that this organization was engaged in espionage. Its membership contained highly militaristic males eligible for compulsory military service in Japan. Its prime function was the collection of war funds for the Japanese army and navy. In more than one thousand translated articles in which Heimusha Kai was mentioned, there was no evidence of any function save the collection of war relief funds.

A prospectus was issued to all Japanese in the United States by the Sponsor Committee for Heimusha Kai in America. That prospectus is quoted as follows:

The world should realize that our military action in China is based upon the significant fact that we are forced to fight under realistic circumstances. *As a matter of historical fact, whenever the Japanese government begins a military campaign, we, Japanese, must be united and every one of us must do his part.*

As far as our patriotism is concerned, the world knows that we are superior to any other nation. However, as long as we are staying on foreign soil, what can we do for our mother country? All our courageous fighters are fighting at the front today, forgetting their parents, wives, and children in their homes! It is beyond our imagination, the manner in which our imperial soldiers are sacrificing their lives at the front line, bomb after bomb, deaths after deaths! Whenever we read and hear this sad news, who can keep from crying in sympathy? Therefore, we, the Japanese in the United States, have been contributing a huge amount of money for war relief funds and numerous comforting bags for our imperial soldiers.

Today, we, Japanese in the United States, who are not able to sacrifice our lives for our National cause are now firmly resolved to stand by to settle the present war as early as possible. *We are proud to say that our daily happy life in America is dependent upon the protective power of Great Japan. We are facing a critical emergency, and we will take strong action as planned. We do hope and beg you all to cooperate with us for our National cause.* (Italics supplied.)

The Heimusha Kai was organized on October 24, 1937, in San Francisco. The meeting took place at the Golden Gate Hall, and there were more than two hundred members present. The following resolution was passed:

We, the members of the Japanese Reserve Army Corps in America are resolved to do our best in support of the Japanese campaign in China and to set up an Army Relief Department for Our Mother Country.

According to reliable sources there were more than ten thousand members of Heimusha Kai in 1940. . . .

One extremely important obstacle in the path of Americanization of the second-generation Japanese was the widespread formation, and increasing importance, of the Japanese language schools in the United States. The purposes and functions of these Japanese language schools are well known. They employed only those textbooks which had been edited by the Department of Education of the Japanese Imperial Government.

In order to assist the Japanization of the second generation, the Zaibei Ikuei Kai (Society for Education of the Second Generation in America) was organized in Los Angeles in April, 1940. "With the grace of the Emperor, the ZAIBEI IKUEI KAI is being organized in commemoration of the 2,600th Anniversary of the Founding of the Japanese Empire to Japanize the second and third generations in this country for the accomplishment of establishing a greater Asia in the future. . . ."

In California alone there were over 248 schools with an aggregate faculty of 454 and a student body of 17,800.

The number of American-born Japanese who had been sent to Japan for education and who were now in the United States could not be overlooked. For more than twenty-five years American-born progeny of alien Japanese had been sent to Japan by their parents for education and indoctrination. There they remained for extended periods, following which they ordinarily returned to the United States. The extent of their influence upon other Nisei Japanese could not be accurately calculated. But it could not be disregarded.

The Kibei Shimin movement was sponsored by the Japanese Association of America. Its objective for many years had been to encourage the return to America from Japan of American-born Japanese. When the movement started it was ascertained that there were about twenty thousand American-born Japanese in Japan. The Japanese Association of America sent representatives to Japan to confer with Prefectural officials on the problems of financing and transportation. The Association requested all Japanese associations to secure employment for returning American-born Japanese, and arranged with steamship companies for special rates for groups of ten or more.

During 1941 alone more than 1,573 American-born Japanese entered West Coast ports from Japan. Over 1,147 Issei, or alien Japanese, reentered the United States from Japan during that year.

The 557 male Japanese less than twenty-five years of age who entered West Coast ports from Japan during 1941 had an average age of 18.2 years and had spent an average of 5.2 years in Japan. Of these, 239 had spent more than three years there. This latter group had spent an average of 10.2 years in Japan.

Of the 239 males who spent three years or more abroad, 180 were in the age group fifteen to nineteen (with an assumed average age of 17.5 years) and had spent 10.7 years abroad. In other words, these 180 Kibei lived, on the average, 6.8 years at the beginning of their life in the United States and the next 10.7 years in Japan. Forty of the 239 who had spent three or more years abroad were in the age group twenty to twenty-four, with an assumed average age 22.5. These were returning to the United States after having lived here, on the average, for their first 13 years and having spent the last 9.5 years in Japan, including one or more years when they were of compulsory (Japanese) military age.

The table (p. 636) indicates the nearest relative in Japan for the age groups fifteen to nineteen, and twenty to twenty-four years of age.

It will be noted that 42.3 percent of those in the fifteen to nineteen year group lived with a father or mother in Japan, and that 13.2 lived with a grandparent. In other words, more than 50 percent of this group of Kibei had a parent of grandparent in Japan, and it is reasonable to assume that in most instances these Kibei lived with this nearest relative.

Combining this information with that from the . . . table, it is seen that in a group with an average age of 17.5 years who were returning to the United States after having spent an average of 7.4 years abroad continuously (in other words, from the time they were ten years of age) one-half had lived with their parent or grandparent in Japan. Yet, this group consists entirely of American citizens.

Of the Kibei in Hawaii, Andrew W. Lind, professor of sociology, University of Hawaii, says: "Finally, there is the rather large Kibei group of the

	Age Group			
Nearest Relative in Japan	*15 to 19 years*		*20 to 24 years*	
	Number	*Percent*	*Number*	*Percent*
All	**272**	**100.0**	**163**	**100.0**
Father or mother	115	42.3	66	40.5
Father	67	24.6	46	28.2
Mother	48	17.7	20	12.3
Grandparent	36	13.2	18	11.0
Uncle or aunt	95	34.9	42	25.8
Other relative	16	5.9	30	18.4
No relative indicated	10	3.7	7	4.3
Nonrelative	4	1.5	7	4.3
Unknown	6	2.2	–	–

second generation who, although citizens of the United States by virtue of birth within the Territory, are frequently more fanatically Japanese in their disposition than their own parents. Many of these individuals have returned from Japan so recently as to be unable to speak the English language and some are unquestionably disappointed by the lack of appreciation manifested for their Japanese education." . . .

It was, perforce, a combination of factors and circumstances with which the Commanding General had to deal. Here was a relatively homogenous, unassimilated element bearing a close relationship through ties of race, religion, language, custom, and indoctrination to the enemy.

The mission of the Commanding General was to defend the West Coast from enemy attack, both from within and without. The Japanese were concentrated along the coastal strip. The nature of this area and its relation to the national war effort had to be carefully considered.

The areas ultimately evacuated of all persons of Japanese ancestry embraced the coastal area of the Pacific slope. In the States of Washington and Oregon to the north, Military Area No. 1 contains all that portion lying westerly of the eastern bases of the Cascade Mountains. In other words, the coastal plain, the forests, and the mountain barrier. In California the evacuation program encompassed the entire State — that is to say, not only Military Area No. 1 but also Military Area No. 2. Military Area No. 2 in California was evacuated because (1) geographically and strategically the eastern boundary of the State of California approximates the easterly limit of Military Area No. 1 in Washington and Oregon . . . and because (2) the natural forests and mountain barriers, from which it was determined to exclude all Japanese, lie in Military Area No. 2 in California, although these lie in Military Area No. 1 of Washington and Oregon. A brief reference to the relationship of the coastal states to the national war effort is here pertinent.

That part of the States of Washington, Oregon, and California which lies west of the Cascade and Sierra Nevada Ranges, is dominated by many waterways, forests, and vital industrial installations. Throughout the Puget Sound area there are many military and naval establishments as well as shipyards, airplane factories and other industries essential to total war. In the vicinity of Whidby Island, Island County, Washington, at the north end of the island, is the important Deception Pass bridge. This bridge provides the only means of transit by land from important naval installations, facilities, and properties in the vicinity of Whidby Island. This island afforded an ideal rendezvous from which enemy agents might communicate with enemy submarines in the Strait of Juan de Fuca or with other agents on the Olympic Peninsula. From Whidby and Camano Islands, comprising Island County, the passages through Admiralty Inlet, Skagit Bay, and Saratoga Passage from Juan de Fuca Strait to the vital areas of the Bremerton Navy Yard and Bainbridge Island can be watched. The important city of Seattle with its airplane plants, airports, waterfront facilities, Army and Navy transport establishments, and supply terminals required that an unassimilated group of doubtful loyalty be removed a safe distance from these critical areas. . . . [There is] a high concentration of persons of Japanese ancestry in the Puget Sound area. Seattle is the principal port in the Northwest; it is the port from which troops in Alaska are supplied; its inland water route to Alaska passes the north coast of Washington into the Straits of Georgia on its way to Alaska.

The lumber industry is of vital importance to the war effort. The State of Washington, with Oregon and California close seconds, produces the bulk of sawed lumber in the United States. The large area devoted to this industry afforded saboteurs unlimited freedom of action. The danger from forest fires involved not only the destruction of valuable timber but also threatened cities, towns, and other installations in the affected area. The entire coastal strip from Cape Flattery south to Lower California is particularly important from a protective viewpoint. There are numerous naval installations with such facilities constantly under augmentation. The coastline is particularly vulnerable. Distances between inhabited areas are great and enemy activities might be carried on without interference.

The petroleum industry of California and its great centers of production for aircraft and shipbuilding, are a vital part of the lifeblood of a nation at war. The crippling of any part of this would seriously impede the war effort. Through the ports of Seattle, Portland, San Francisco, Los Angeles, and San Diego, flow the sinews of war — the men, equipment, and supplies for carrying the battle against the enemy in the Pacific. . . . [A] high concentration of this segment of the population surround[s] nearly all these key installations.

In his estimate of the situation, then, the Commanding General found a tightly knit, unassimilated racial group, substantial numbers of whom were engaged in pro-Japanese activities. He found them concentrated in great numbers along the Pacific Coast, an area of the utmost importance to the national war effort. These considerations were weighed against the progress of the Emperor's Imperial Japanese forces in the Pacific. This chapter would be incomplete without a brief reference to the gravity of the external situation obtaining in the Pacific theater. It is necessary only to state the chronology of war in the Pacific to show this.

At 8:05 A.M., the 7th of December, the Japanese attacked the United States naval base at Pearl Harbor without warning. Simultaneously they struck against Malaysia, Hong Kong, the Philippines, and Wake and Midway Islands.

On the day following, the Japanese Army invaded Thailand. Two days later the British battleships H.M.S. *Wales* and H.M.S. *Repulse* were sunk off the Malay Peninsula. The enemy's successes continued without interruption. On the 13th of December, Guam was captured and on successive days the Japanese captured Wake Island and occupied Hong Kong, December 24th and 25th, respectively. On January 2nd Manila fell and on the 27th of February the battle of the Java Sea resulted in a crushing naval defeat to the United Nations.[3] Thirteen United Nations' warships were sunk and one damaged. Japanese losses were limited to two warships sunk and five damaged.

On the 9th of March the Japanese Imperial forces established full control of the Netherlands East Indies; Rangoon and Burma were occupied. Continuing during the course of evacuation, on the 9th of April, Bataan was occupied by the Japanese and on May 6th Corregidor surrendered.

On June 3rd, Dutch Harbor, Alaska, was attacked by Japanese carrier-based aircraft and, with the occupation by the Japanese on June 7th of Attu and Kiska Islands, United States territory in continental Northern America had been invaded.

As already stated, there were many evidences of the successful communication of information to the enemy, information regarding positive knowledge on his part of our installations. The most striking illustrations of this are found in three of the several incidents of enemy attacks on West Coast points.

On February 23, 1942, a hostile submarine shelled Goleta, near Santa Barbara, California, in an attempt to destroy vital oil installations there. On the preceding day the shore battery in position at this point had been withdrawn to be replaced by another. On the succeeding day, when the shelling occurred, it was the only point along the coast where an enemy submarine could have successfully surfaced and fired on a vital installation without coming within the range of coast defense guns.

In the vicinity of Brookings (Mt. Emily), Oregon, an enemy submarine-based plane dropped incendiary bombs in an effort to start forest fires. At that time it was the only section of the Pacific Coast which could have been approached by enemy aircraft without interception by aircraft warning devices.

Similarly, a precise knowledge of the range of coast defense guns at Astoria, Oregon, was in the possession of the enemy. A hostile submarine surfaced and shelled shore batteries there from the only position at which

---

[3]"United Nations" refers to the United States and its allies; no reference is meant to the international organization of that name today. — EDS.

a surfaced submarine could have approached the coastline close enough to shell a part of its coast defenses without being within range of the coastal batteries.

In summary, the Commanding General was confronted with the Pearl Harbor experience, which involved a positive enemy knowledge of our patrols, our naval dispositions, etc., on the morning of December 7th; with the fact that ships leaving West Coast ports were being intercepted regularly by enemy submarines; and with the fact that an enemy element was in a position to do great damage and substantially to aid the enemy nation. Time was of the essence.

The Commanding General, charged as he was with the mission of providing for the defense of the West Coast, had to take into account these and other military considerations. He had no alternative but to conclude that the Japanese constituted a potentially dangerous element from the viewpoint of military security — that military necessity required their immediate evacuation to the interior. The impelling military necessity had become such that any measures other than those pursued along the Pacific Coast might have been "too little and too late." . . .

APPENDIX TO CHAPTER 3

Final Recommendation of the Commanding General, Western Defense Command and Fourth Army, Submitted to the Secretary of War

HEADQUARTERS WESTERN DEFENSE COMMAND AND
FOURTH ARMY
Presidio of San Francisco, California
Office of the Commanding General

February 14, 1942

MEMORANDUM FOR: The Secretary of War,[4]
(Thru: The Commanding General,
Field Forces, Washington, D.C.)

SUBJECT: Evacuation of Japanese and Other Subversive Persons from the Pacific Coast.

1. In presenting a recommendation for the evacuation of Japanese and other subversive persons from the Pacific Coast, the following facts have been considered:
   A. Mission of the Western Defense Command and Fourth Army.
      1. Defense of the Pacific Coast of the Western Defense Command, as extended, against attacks by sea, land, or air;

---

[4]Henry L. Stimson was the secretary of war. This memo was written before the signing of Executive Order 9066 (see p. 617) and it helped to convince Roosevelt that the order was necessary. — EDS.

    2. Local protection of establishments and communications vital to the National Defense for which adequate defense cannot be provided by local civilian authorities.

B. Brief Estimate of the Situation.

    1. Any estimate of the situation indicates that the following are possible and probable enemy activities:

       a. Naval attack on shipping in coastal waters;

       b. Naval attack on coastal cities and vital installations;

       c. Air raids on vital installations, particularly within two hundred miles of the coast;

       d. Sabotage of vital installations throughout the Western Defense Command.

       Hostile Naval and air raids will be assisted by enemy agents signaling from the coastline and the vicinity thereof; and by supplying and otherwise assisting enemy vessels and by sabotage.

       Sabotage, (for example, of airplane factories), may be effected not only by destruction within plants and establishments, but by destroying power, light, water, sewer, and other utility and other facilities in the immediate vicinity thereof or at a distance. Serious damage or destruction in congested areas may readily be caused by incendiarism.

    2. The area lying to the west of the Cascade and Sierra Nevada Mountains in Washington, Oregon, and California, is highly critical not only because the lines of communication and supply to the Pacific theater pass through it, but also because of the vital industrial production therein, particularly aircraft. In the war in which we are now engaged racial affinities are not severed by migration. The Japanese race is an enemy race and while many second and third generation Japanese born on United States soil, possessed of United States citizenship, have become "Americanized," the racial strains are undiluted. To conclude otherwise is to expect that children born of white parents on Japanese soil sever all racial affinity and become loyal Japanese subjects, ready to fight and, if necessary, to die for Japan in a war against the nation of their parents. That Japan is allied with Germany and Italy in this struggle is no ground for assuming that any Japanese, barred from assimilation by convention as he is, though born and raised in the United States, will not turn against this nation when the final test of loyalty comes. It, therefore, follows that along the vital Pacific Coast over 112,000 potential enemies, of Japanese extraction, are at large today. There are indications that these are organized and ready for concerted action at a favorable opportunity. The very fact that no sabotage has taken place to date is a disturbing and confirming indication that such action will be taken.

C. Disposition of the Japanese.

1. *Washington.* As the term is used herein, the word "Japanese" includes alien Japanese and American citizens of Japanese ancestry. In the State of Washington the Japanese population, aggregating over 14,500, is disposed largely in the area lying west of the Cascade Mountains and south of an east-west line passing through Bellingham, Washington, about seventy miles north of Seattle and some fifteen miles south of the Canadian border. The largest concentration of Japanese is in the area, the axis of which is along the line Seattle, Tacoma, Olympia, Willapa Bay, and the mouth of the Columbia River, with the heaviest concentration in the agricultural valleys between Seattle and Tacoma, viz., the Green River and the Puyallup Valleys. The Boeing Aircraft factory is in the Green River Valley. The lines of communication and supply including power and water which feed this vital industrial installation, radiate from this plant for many miles through areas heavily populated by Japanese. Large numbers of Japanese also operate vegetable markets along the Seattle and Tacoma waterfronts, in Bremerton, near the Bremerton Navy Yard, and inhabit islands in Puget Sound opposite vital naval ship building installations. Still others are engaged in fishing along the southwest Washington Pacific Coast and along the Columbia River. Many of these Japanese are within easy reach of the forests of Washington State, the stockpiles of seasoning lumber and the many sawmills of southwest Washington. During the dry season these forests, mills, and stockpiles are easily fired. . . .

2. *Oregon.* There are approximately four thousand Japanese in the State of Oregon, of which the substantial majority reside in the area in the vicinity of Portland along the south bank of the Columbia River, following the general line Bonneville, Oregon City, Astoria, Tillamook. Many of these are in the northern reaches of the Willamette Valley and are engaged in agricultural and fishing pursuits. Others operate vegetable markets in the Portland metropolitan area and still others reside along the northern Oregon seacoast. Their disposition is in intimate relationship with the northwest Oregon sawmills and lumber industry, near and around the vital electric power development at Bonneville and the pulp and paper installations at Camas (on the Washington State side of the Columbia River) and Oregon City, directly south of Portland. . . .

3. *California.* The Japanese population in California aggregates approximately 93,500 people. Its disposition is so widespread and so well known that little would be gained by setting it forth in detail here. They live in great numbers along the coastal strip, in and around San Francisco and the Bay Area, the Salinas Valley, Los Angeles, and San Diego. Their truck farms are

contiguous to the vital aircraft industry concentration in and around Los Angeles. They live in large numbers in and about San Francisco, now a vast staging area for the war in the Pacific, a point at which the nation's lines of communication and supply converge. Inland they are disposed in the Sacramento, San Joaquin, and Imperial Valleys. They are engaged in the production of approximately 38 percent of the vegetable produce of California. Many of them are engaged in the distribution of such produce in and along the waterfronts at San Francisco and Los Angeles. Of the 93,500 in California, about 25,000 reside inland in the mentioned valleys where they are largely engaged in vegetable production cited above, and 54,600 reside along the coastal strip, that is to say, a strip of coastline varying from eight miles in the north to twenty miles in width in and around the San Francisco bay area, including San Francisco, in Los Angeles and its environs, and in San Diego. Approximately 13,900 are dispersed throughout the remaining portion of the state. In Los Angeles City the disposition of vital aircraft industrial plants covers the entire city. Large numbers of Japanese live and operate markets and truck farms adjacent to or near these installations. . . .

D. Disposition of Other Subversive Persons.

Disposed within the vital coastal strip already mentioned are large numbers of Italians and Germans, foreign and native born, among whom are many individuals who constitute an actual or potential menace to the safety of the nation.

2. Action recommended.

    a. Recommendations for the designation of prohibited areas, described as "Category A" areas in California, Oregon, and Washington, from which are to be excluded by order of the Attorney General all alien enemies, have gone forward from this headquarters to the Attorney General through the Provost Marshal General and the Secretary of War. These recommendations were made in order to aid the Attorney General in the implementation of the Presidential Proclamations of December 7 and 8, 1941, imposing responsibility on him for the control of alien enemies as such. These recommendations were for the exclusion of all alien enemies from Category "A." The Attorney General has adopted these recommendations in part, and has the balance under consideration. Similarly, recommendations were made by this headquarters, and adopted by the Attorney General, for the designation of certain areas as Category "B" areas, within which alien enemies may be permitted on pass or permit.

    b. I now recommend the following:

        1. That the Secretary of War procure from the President

direction and authority to designate military areas in the combat zone of the Western Theater of Operations (if necessary to include the entire combat zone), from which, in his discretion, he may exclude all Japanese, all alien enemies, and all other persons suspected for any reason by the administering military authorities of being actual or potential saboteurs, espionage agents, or fifth columnists.[5] Such executive order should empower the Secretary of War to requisition the services of any and all other agencies of the Federal Government, with express direction to such agencies to respond to such requisition, and further empowering the Secretary of War to use any and all federal facilities and equipment, including Civilian Conservation Corps Camps, and to accept the use of State facilities for the purpose of providing shelter and equipment for evacuees. Such executive order to provide further for the administration of military areas for the purposes of this plan by appropriate military authorities acting with the requisitioned assistance of the other federal agencies and the cooperation of State and local agencies. The executive order should further provide that by reason of military necessity the right of all persons, whether citizens or aliens, to reside, enter, cross, or be within any military areas shall be subject to revocation and shall exist on a pass and permit basis at the discretion of the Secretary of War and implemented by the necessary legislation imposing penalties for violation.[6]

2. That, pursuant to such executive order, there be designated as military areas all areas in Washington, Oregon, and California, recommended by me to date for designation by the Attorney General as Category "A" areas and such additional areas as it may be found necessary to designate hereafter.

3. That the Secretary of War provide for the exclusion from such military areas, in his discretion, of the following classes of persons, viz:

   a. Japanese aliens.

   b. Japanese-American citizens.

   c. Alien enemies other than Japanese aliens.

   d. Any and all other persons who are suspected for any reason by the administering military authorities

---

[5] "Fifth columnists" are members of a secret organization that supports an enemy's military and political objectives by sabotage, misinformation, and so on. — EDS.

[6] Five days after this memo was issued, Roosevelt's signing of Executive Order 9066 granted the powers requested here. — EDS.

to be actual or potential saboteurs, espionage agents, fifth columnists, or subversive persons.

4. That the evacuation of classes (a), (b), and (c) from such military areas be initiated on a designated evacuation day and carried to completion as rapidly as practicable.

   That prior to evacuation day all plans be complete for the establishment of initial concentration points, reception centers, registration, rationing, guarding, transportation to internment points, and the selection and establishment of internment facilities in the Sixth, Seventh, and Eighth Corps Areas.

   That persons in class (a) and (c) above be evacuated and interned at such selected places of internment, under guard.

   That persons in class (b) above, at the time of evacuation, be offered an opportunity to accept voluntary internment, under guard, at the place of internment above mentioned.

   That persons in class (b) who decline to accept voluntary internment, be excluded from all military areas, and left to their own resources, or, in the alternative, be encouraged to accept resettlement outside of such military areas with such assistance as the State governments concerned or the Federal Security Agency may be by that time prepared to offer.

   That the evacuation of persons in class (d) be progressive and continuing, and that upon their evacuation persons in class (d) be excluded from all military areas and left in their own resources outside of such military areas, or, in the alternative, be offered voluntary internment or encouraged to accept voluntary resettlement as above outlined, unless the facts in a particular case shall warrant other action.

5. The Commanding General, Western Defense Command and Fourth Army [DeWitt], to be responsible for the evacuation, administration, supply, and guard, to the place of internment; the Commanding Generals of the Corps Areas concerned to be responsible for guard, supply, and administration at the places of internment.

6. That direct communication between the Commanding General, Western Defense Command and Fourth Army and the Corps Area Commanders concerned for the purpose of making necessary arrangements be authorized.

7. That the Provost Marshal General coordinate all

phases of the plan between the Commanding General, Western Defense Command and Fourth Army, on the one hand, and the Corps Area Commanders on the other hand.

8. That all arrangements be accomplished with the utmost secrecy.

9. That adult males (above the age of fourteen years) be interned separately from all women and children until the establishment of family units can be accomplished.

10. No change is contemplated in Category "B" areas.

3. Although so far as the Army is concerned, such action is not an essential feature of the plan, but merely incidental thereto, I, nevertheless, recommend that mass internment be considered as largely a temporary expedient pending selective resettlement, to be accomplished by the various Security Agencies of the Federal and State Governments.

4. The number of persons involved in the recommended evacuation will be approximately 133,000. (This total represents all enemy aliens and Japanese-American citizens in Category "A" areas recommended to date.)

5. If these recommendations are approved detailed plans will be made by this headquarters for the proposed evacuation. The number evacuated to be apportioned by the Provost Marshal General among the Corps Area Commanders concerned as the basis for formulating their respective plans. It is possible that the State of California, and perhaps the State of Washington, will be able to offer resettlement facilities for a given number of evacuees who may be willing to accept resettlement.

6. Pending further and detailed study of the problem, it is further recommended: (1) That the Commanding General, Western Defense Command and Fourth Army, coordinate with the local and State authorities, in order to facilitate the temporary physical protection by them of the property of evacuees not taken with them; (2) That the Commanding General, Western Defense Command and Fourth Army, determine the quantity and character of property which the adult males, referred to in paragraph 2b(9), may be permitted to take with them; and (3) That the Treasury Department or other proper Federal agency be responsible for the conservation, liquidation, and proper disposition of the property of evacuees if it cannot be cared for through the usual and normal channels.

J. L. DeWitt,
Lieutenant General, U.S. Army
Commanding

READING CRITICALLY

1. The *Final Report* attempts in chapter 2 to give reasons supporting its recommendation that all Nikkei be evacuated from the West Coast. What Nikkei actions directly helping the Japanese war effort against the United States does the report list? What kinds of evidence does the report give that these actions actually took place?

2. The report also cites as reasons for evacuation some Nikkei activities that the War Department regards as suspicious even though not directly aiding the enemy war effort. What are these activities? What kinds of evidence of these activities does the report give?

3. The appendix to chapter 3 — a long memo by DeWitt — summarizes the report's arguments that the Nikkei have committed acts aiding the enemy and are likely to commit more such acts. What reasons does DeWitt give here?

4. In his memo, DeWitt also discusses Italians, Germans, Italian Americans, and German Americans living on the West Coast. How does he propose to treat these groups? What reasons does he give for this treatment?

WRITING ANALYTICALLY

1. Consider the cultural activities you listed in your response to reading question 2. Do you know of any similar activities performed by other ethnic groups today? What are they? Could they be considered suspicious? Write a paper in which you use as examples the Nikkei activities described by the *Final Report* and the activities of one other group known to you. Argue for a two-part thesis: that it is, or is not, reasonable to regard such activities as suspicious; and that such activities do, or do not, in fact encourage divided loyalties and a lack of proper American patriotism.

2. What, if anything, do you find convincing in the case the *Final Report* makes for the need to evacuate all Japanese Americans? Write a paper in which you evaluate its arguments. You may write this paper in the form of a letter to the editor of a major California newspaper, to be published early in 1943, after the internment process has been completed and the report has been published. Address your fellow California citizens on how they ought to be thinking about the internment now.

3. The *Final Report* was intended to show DeWitt's superiors, politicians, and concerned private citizens that DeWitt had acted responsibly and that the Japanese Americans were not receiving excessive treatment. Using the evidence you collected in response to the reading questions, write a paper in which you argue that his rhetorical strategies are, or are not, effective to attain these goals. Option: You may write this paper in the form of a general argument on how a government official ought to inform the public about a controversial decision, using DeWitt as a good, or bad, example.

JAPANESE AMERICAN CITIZENS LEAGUE

From *The Case for the Nisei* (1945?)

The following selection is from a brief filed in the U.S. Supreme Court by the Japanese American Citizens League (JACL) in support of Fred Korematsu's challenge to the legality of the evacuation that preceded detention in the internment camps. The JACL brief is included in the book The Case for the Nisei, along with the opinions of the Supreme Court justices in the Korematsu and Endo cases (see the Unit Five introduction, p. 615).

As Saburo Kido, then president of the JACL and one of the two signers of the brief, explains in the book's foreword, the JACL decided to publish and distribute the book to refute the "charges and innuendos" in the War Department's *Final Report* (p. 628). Kido explains that American citizens need to study this material because by ruling in the *Korematsu* decision that special restrictions could be placed on a group on the basis of race alone, the Supreme Court set "a dangerous precedent . . . to make every minority group dubious of its security in a national war emergency."

Born in Hawaii, Kido was a lawyer in San Francisco and a founding member of the JACL. An elderly man at the time of the internment, he was sent to the camp at Poston, Arizona. After the JACL came out strongly in favor of allowing Nikkei men to serve in the U.S. military, he was severely beaten by fellow internees opposed to the move. He continued as JACL president through the war years, until 1946.

The other signer of the JACL brief was A. L. Wirin, a European American lawyer who served as special counsel to the American Civil Liberties Union and often advised the JACL leadership on legal matters.

The JACL was founded in 1930, admitting only Nisei to membership. Issei could not belong because they were not citizens (until 1952, when the ban on their applying for citizenship was lifted). The JACL is still active nationwide today.

Excerpted here is the section of the JACL brief that challenges the *Final Report's* assertions about Nikkei unwillingness to assimilate.

Contrary to Unsubstantiated Assumptions and Assertions, Americans of Japanese Ancestry Are Well Assimilated and Loyal. Abundant and Reliable Information Was on Hand to Prove This at the Time of Evacuation.

SINCE AMERICANS OF JAPANESE ANCESTRY have been treated differently from all other citizens, those who favor this discriminatory treatment and those who uphold it are logically forced to assert or to assume that these young

Japanese American Citizens League, amicus curiae brief, *Fred Toyosaburo Korematsu v. United States*, U.S. Supreme Court, October term, 1944, reprinted in *The Case for the Nisei* (Salt Lake City, Utah: Japanese American Citizens League, 1945?), 82–97.

In the notes, EDS. = Patricia Bizzell and Bruce Herzberg.

people are in fact different from all other elements of our population. And since variations of race or physical type are not legitimate grounds for discriminatory treatment under our Constitution, they must argue that the differences are social or cultural as well as biological. The racists and divisionists among us do not hesitate to use this argument. They are eager to convince the country that those who are physically distinct from the majority are also separate in customs and mentality, and therefore should be barred from coming to our shores or eliminated if they are already here. But it is a dark day for liberty when this doctrine of vast social and psychological gulfs between groups in our population becomes dignified and implemented by favorable mention in the decisions of this Court. Persecution has become so common in our day and the rationalizations for persecution so specious that the grounds on the basis of which discrimination against any group of citizens is urged should be weighed on the most sensitive scales of justice that free men can devise. If this Court upholds discriminatory treatment of certain citizens on the basis of "ethnic affiliations" with an enemy of our country, its thrice solemn responsibility is to ascertain that so serious a contention is actually true and is not asserted merely because it is the only legally supportable assumption that will excuse what was done in haste and folly.

The credo of democracy is that men of all races, colors, and faiths can be molded to common ideals and a common national devotion by the institutions which they inherit and share. The alacrity with which a General, some politicians, and some judges are ready, in spite of a rich store of reassuring evidence, to abandon this conception for the assumption that our young people are motivated, not by the social dynamics and values of America, not by her schools, churches, and athletic fields, but by considerations of race or dim parental memories of a distant land, is grim and disillusioning indeed.

Every argument for evacuation expresses or implies the conviction that Americans of Japanese ancestry are not assimilated into American life and therefore could not be expected to be as loyal and devoted as other elements of the population. Those who advance these arguments ordinarily know very little about culture, about assimilation, or about Americans of Japanese ancestry. They always confuse the concept of "intermingling" with the concept of "assimilation." The Negroes of Harlem participate in American culture. Certainly they have no knowledge of the African tribal life of their remote ancestors. They listen to, dance to, and create American music. They eat American-type foods. They speak English. In all important aspects of behavior they conform closely to common American standards. Yet they dwell by themselves in a special section of the city. In the same way, because of property restrictions, persons of Japanese ancestry often lived together in certain sections of West Coast cities. But this is no more reason than it is in the case of the Negro to assume that they were not there conforming to genuine American habits of thought and action. After all they were attending the same kind of American schools, they were listening to the same radio programs, they were singing the same popular tunes, and were using the same slang as were boys and girls who lived elsewhere. The 100th battalion and the 442nd battalion are formed almost entirely of Americans of Japanese ancestry. But this does not prevent them from facing America's enemies, wearing American uniforms, using American weapons and tactics, fighting America's fight, and shedding American blood. The unrestricted intermingling of races and peoples may be ideal in itself, but it is by no means necessary for assimilation. We protest against the narrow and superficial assumption which we find in every statement of General DeWitt and every brief of the Government on this subject, namely, that because people of Japanese ancestry lived together, they must have been carrying on mysterious and un-American customs of oriental origin.

In extenuation of his orders General DeWitt has called the persons whom he banished, most of them American citizens, "a large, unassimilated, tightly knit racial group, bound to an enemy nation by strong ties of race, culture, custom, and religion." This theme he repeats over and over. In another place he says, "Because of the ties of race, the intense feeling of filial piety, and the strong bonds of common tradition, culture, and customs, this population presented a tightly knit racial group." (*Final Report:* page 9.) Further on he returns to this refrain to state, "In his estimate of the situation, then, the Commanding General found a tightly knit, assimilated racial group. . . ." (*Final Report:* page 17.)[1]

General DeWitt is the author, or at least the popularizer of the most un-American slogan used in the United States during the present conflict, "A Jap's a Jap." We know his opinion of Americans of Japanese ancestry. But what do those who are somewhat more qualified by training and contacts to speak on this subject, have to say? It is impossible to reconcile General DeWitt's dicta with this statement of Monroe E. Deutsch, Vice President and Provost of the University of California:

> As one who has lived almost all his life in California and has seen a great deal of the Japanese population, I feel able to express a considered judgment on them. I have never had occasion to doubt the loyalty of any of those with whom I have been in contact; I have found them hard working, devoted, and law-abiding. On the Berkeley campus of the University of California we have had some four hundred American Japanese; they have acquitted themselves well, not only in their studies, but in their conduct, also. It has been a joy to me to see how in the days preceding the war these students were accepted more and more as part of the student life on the campus.

The General's view also seems to be diametrically opposed to that of so experienced and trustworthy a guide as Bishop Baker, who has written:

---

[1]The JACL's quotations from the War Department's *Final Report* can be found in our excerpt from the *Final Report,* pages 631 and 637. — EDS.

I have known intimately many Japanese American citizens. I am proud of them as *fellow citizens* and should count it a privilege to have them as my neighbors. They are persons of character and are devoted to the ideals of American democracy.

In December, after the start of the conflict, Governor Olson saw no lack of loyalty or assimilation to disturb him, even among the aliens:

I have every confidence that the FBI and other agencies are fully capable of handling the problems presented by the presence of disloyal persons, whether they be Japanese or Germans or Italians.

They have been watching these persons a long time; therefore they were ready to act promptly and effectively in the first few days of hostilities.

I am reminding the citizens of California that the vast majority of Japanese in California are native born American citizens and completely loyal to the government of the United States; also, that the noncitizen Japanese, for the most part, are likewise loyal and anxious to serve our country, although they themselves are not eligible for citizenship.

Dr. Floyd Schmoe of the University of Washington, on the basis of rather substantial evidence, argues that the citizens were entering business successfully into every aspect of American life and work:

Because they work hard and are serious they make good grades. Year in and year out a much larger percentage of the valedictorians and salutatorians of West Coast high schools are Nisei students than the total percentage of such students would ever indicate. Many also are leaders in student affairs, athletics, and other extracurricular activities. Since December 7th a Nisei student was elected president of the student body of an Oregon high school. Last year in a Seattle high school a Nisei girl held elective offices in seven different school organizations.

At institutions of higher learning Japanese American students are equally quick to take advantage of the opportunities offered them. Although they come from an economic level appreciably lower than that of the white American students, a much higher percentage of them attend the universities and colleges. At the University of Washington in Seattle, where some eight thousand students are enrolled from a community of approximately half a million people, there are nearly four hundred Nisei students from a Japanese community of about ten thousand — a ratio of three to one.

Until recently more than one thousand held state civil service appointments. Capable Japanese lawyers, doctors, dentists, and optometrists were practicing in some twenty-five cities of the Pacific area. Every large educational institution on the West Coast and in Hawaii had Japanese professors and scientists on its staff. A few were employed by the Federal Government, and many were trusted executives of banks, transportation companies, and commercial firms. In Hawaii five members of the Territorial Legislature were Hawaiian Japanese.

In the testimony before the Tolan Committee of Seattle's Mayor Earl Millikin, the DeWitt charges of poor citizenship are strangely absent:

In the main, the American-born Japanese, and even the aliens are fine, good citizens — hard working. They contribute nothing to our juvenile delinquency; they are out of our courts almost entirely; they are very fine citizenry. It is just a situation developed by Japan herself. . . .

A frank citizen who has had considerable experience with children of Japanese ancestry gives information which directly controverts the assertions of General DeWitt, moreover.

Now, as to these Japanese, I have had pretty close contact with them for the past thirty years, and I consider that they are loyal. If I and my son have to go across the water to fight — he is in his teens — I am not afraid of those boys failing to produce back on the soil, at the home place. As to students in our schools — I have been on the school board for years and have handled boys and worked in the Boy Scout group, and the Japanese boys in the Scout group have been excellent citizens. The girls and boys in the school have ranked above my child and most of her race, so far as scholarships went. I think that it would be safe to say that 75 percent on the honor roll are Japanese. Morally, the Japanese children rank — even outrank our white children. We have around 925 or something like that, in our valley, and the big share of them there are farmers.

If the Americans of Japanese ancestry were as isolated and unassimilated as General DeWitt alleges, their Caucasian friends and classmates were curiously unaware of it, as this eloquent statement of a University of Washington student representative attests:

I wish to testify to this committee in an unofficial capacity and merely as an individual student speaking for an informal group of students who feel that the Japanese students should be allowed to continue their studies at the University of Washington and not be evacuated from the area. There are over 250 Japanese Americans, 70 of them girls, who are at present studying at the university so as to prepare themselves to become useful American citizens. I know many of these students personally, am pleased to count some of them as my intimate friends, have gone to school with them, studied with them, participated in student activities with them, gone to the same parties, and visited their homes and so I feel at least partially qualified to speak in their behalf.

What are the Nisei students like? I am convinced that the majority of university students will agree with me when I say that the answer can be given in just one word — American. Aside from the superficial differences of skin color, you would be unable to tell them from the average American college student. They dress the same, talk the same, and most importantly they think and believe the same. . . .

Another student, a young woman, gave similar convincing testimony:

. . . It has been said that these people are as dangerous to our country as if they had grown up in Japan. I do not believe this to be true, for they have learned our way of life and have grown up thinking of America as their country. They have learned our *mores*, often teaching their parents our traditions and customs. Even those who have visited Japan, just as many of us have visited the homes of our ancestors in England or Norway, have returned saying they could not agree with the Japanese philosophy of life, and were proud that America was their country.

These students who have grown up loving America, unless ruthlessly treated, so that their ideals and faiths are considerably shaken, are not likely to change a lifetime philosophy in the course of a few months. They are the first generation of Japanese Americans born in this area, and the first really to learn our customs and language. They have learned more in school than book knowledge; they have learned the American way of doing things, and have taken it back to their parents. This assimilation process has been taking place for twenty years, and the new generation — the third-generation Japanese Americans — is just beginning in the Seattle area. Must we spoil that long process now by prejudice and isolation?

The evidence introduced by an official of the University of Washington is shockingly at variance with the sweeping charges of General DeWitt:

> The second-generation Japanese have made a good adjustment to the educational institutions in this area. At the University of Washington alone there are over four hundred students from this group, and there are some twenty Nisei in the employ of the university. One, a veteran of the first World War, is an assistant professor; another is an instructor in nursing; one each are associates in Far Eastern studies and sociology; five others are teaching fellows; and the rest hold research and clerical positions. Students of Japanese ancestry hold offices in student organizations, and represent the university in athletic and nonathletic competition.
>
> This opportunity to participate fully in campus life has resulted in the development of close ties between students of Japanese parentage and other undergraduates. When the Seattle public schools recently considered accepting the resignations of their Nisei employees, over a thousand university students of white parentage petitioned the board on behalf of the Americans of Japanese ancestry.
>
> So integrated are many of the campus Nisei that they refuse to celebrate the Japanese victories over China, and in a few cases American Japanese even joined the boycott against shipping war supplies to Japan two years ago. . . .
>
> Objective standards for measuring loyalty are virtually impossible to set up. However, there are a number of overt reactions of the Nisei at the University of Washington which can be recorded. As the official in charge of recommending draft deferment in the college of arts and sciences, I have had the opportunity to interview hundreds of men regarding Selective Service. Last spring (before Pearl Harbor) I had noticed that practically none of the Americans of Japanese ancestry asked either for deferment or "special" jobs. After the treacherous attack on Hawaii, over a dozen Nisei called in my office to find out how to volunteer to fight for the United States. In checking over the recent members of the Japanese Students Club, I find eighty-three who have either volunteered or are serving under Selective Service in the American Army.

Many more statements of prominent and informed Caucasians attesting to the achievements, the Americanism, the loyalty, and the assimilation of citizens of Japanese ancestry could be introduced, but perhaps a sufficient number have been presented to establish that every trained, competent, and impartial witness directly challenges the basic assumption upon which the General ordered evacuation.

If assimilation means anything it connotes participating in and contributing to the intellectual, artistic, and recreational life of the society of which one is a part. And when a person's achievements and contributions along these lines are recognized and rewarded, despite the fact that he is of a minority group and is distinct in a physical sense, assimilation can be said to be complete. Let us apply this standard to Americans of Japanese ancestry whom General DeWitt decided to evacuate because he considered them to be unassimilated.

In February, 1942, *after* the beginning of the war, four Nisei girls were elected to offices in the honor-scholarship society of a large Los Angeles high school. One of them was named the school's representative to the city's second annual Youth Conference. In March, 1942, two Nisei girls who were attending Hollywood High School not only received recognition for outstanding scholarship but were elected to the school's Citizenship Honorary Society. Perhaps this is the answer of the young people of Hollywood, California, to the absurdities of General DeWitt and his kind. Two young people of Japanese ancestry also received scholarship recognition at the Los Angeles City College. In May the person who had been voted the most distinguished student in the 1942 graduating class and who had been awarded the University Medal for highest scholastic standing, Harvey Itano, was not at the University of California Graduation exercises. General DeWitt, who looks in strange places for the enemies of this nation, had discovered him to be unassimilated and to be a member of a "close-knit racial group" and had ordered him from the area! In June, 1942, a Nisei boy was nominated for the office of president of the student body at Lincoln Junior High School in Salt Lake City. Though he seemed assured of election he withdrew from the contest. Honors and awards earned by twenty-two Nisei students were announced at the University of Washington in June. Of these four were Phi Beta Kappa memberships and two were memberships in Sigma Xi. Many other high school and college students of Japanese ancestry were honored by election to class offices, and by awards at this time. At Tacoma, Washington, in late June, the Berkeley episode was repeated. When nearly seven hundred students graduated from the Lincoln High School the prize for highest scholarship had to be awarded in absentia. The recipient, whom General DeWitt had singled out for attention according to other criteria, was behind barbed wire and under armed guard.

In 1943 and 1944 citizens of Japanese ancestry, driven from California schools by General DeWitt's decrees, began to find havens in colleges elsewhere. It did not take the vital and observant young people of this country long to appraise the newcomers and to thoroughly discredit the General's judgment.

Kenji Okuda was soon elected president of the student council at Oberlin College in Ohio. Paul Tani was elected president of his class at Heidelberg College. William Marutani, Masamori Kojima, and Thomas Hayashi were honored by class presidencies at South Dakota Wesleyan, Haverford, and Bard College respectively. At South Dakota Wesleyan, too, Oliver Takaichi came out best in a selection based on scholarship, personality, and participation in school activities. Girls have been honored with class offices as well. For example, Naomi Nakano was chosen vice president of the graduating class of the University of Pennsylvania. At least fourteen other Nisei have been elected class officers in colleges over the country. And the recognition is by no means limited to political office. At Baylor University in Texas Miss Toyoko Hayashi was voted "Most Popular Girl" and Queen of the Junior Prom. The list of fellowships, scholarships, and other honors, many of them elective, which have come in wartime America to these strange representatives of a "close-knit racial group" is a long one and has only been suggested by what has been given.

The contributions of persons of Japanese ancestry to the graphic and fine arts brought some embarrassing moments at evacuation time. The winner of Seattle's annual traffic safety poster contest won a cash reward and a set of encyclopedia for his school. But he no longer could attend the school and the cash award had to be delivered to him at an assembly center. At the very time that the famous sculptor and onetime Guggenheim Fellow, Isamu Noguchi, was evacuated to Poston, his work was being placed on exhibit at the San Francisco Museum. The work of Chiura Obata, noted artist and long a faculty member of the University of California, was on exhibit at Mills College in Oakland in July of 1942. This American artist, however, was in detention. In the spring of 1943 the watercolors of Henry Fukuhara were receiving favorable notice at an exhibition at the Otis Art Institute in Los Angeles. The artist, however, was confined in the Manzanar Relocation Center. Other painters of Japanese descent, most of them American citizens, who have been and continue to be a vital force in the art of this country are Mitsu Iwamatsu, Teru Masumoto, Chuzo Tamotsu, Taro Yashima, Robert Kuwahara, Sueo Serisawa, Kenneth Nishi, Henry Sugimoto, Shizu Matsuda, and, best known of all, Yasuo Kuniyoshi. Many of these artists have been violently anti-Fascist. Kuniyoshi broadcasts to Japan and paints anti-Axis posters for our government. The proceeds of an exhibit of his work went to United China Relief. Chuzo Tamotsu was selling paintings for the relief of the free Chinese long before Pearl Harbor. Kenneth Nishi, who was evacuated from California, is now a Corporal in the United States Army as well as a promising young American artist. Of such as these does General DeWitt's unassimilated group consist!

In the field of music there is Lewis Izumi who was a piano soloist with the Los Angeles Philharmonic Orchestra at the age of seven and who now, at the age of eleven, has been awarded a Curtis Institute scholarship. His older brother, John, incidentally, is serving with the United States Army. Kay Sadanaga of the San Francisco Conservatory of Music had won several music competitions on the West Coast. General DeWitt decided that she could play there no more. But that did not prevent her from winning a piano scholarship at the Juilliard School of Music in New York City. Teruko Akagi has received a scholarship to attend the Oberlin Conservatory of Music, and Mari Taniguchi, Nisei soprano, was recently granted the artist's diploma, highest award of the Eastman School of Music.

Even the dance and ballet have their Nisei representatives. Yuriko Amemiya, who has appeared with the Martha Graham dance company, received a scholarship to attend the dance school at Bennington College in Vermont. Sono Osato, who is part Japanese and would therefore have been evacuated by General DeWitt, has taken the country by storm. Dorothy Maruki, whose study of the ballet in San Francisco and Sacramento was interrupted by General DeWitt's blanket orders, has lately been awarded a ballet dancing scholarship from the Metropolitan Opera Company of New York.

Athletics is an important aspect of American life and we find that Americans of Japanese ancestry have made a place for themselves in this field, too. We have only to mention the names of Chet Maeda, Colorado State football player who was mentioned for all-American honors; Peter Mitsuo Ida, the former Stanford track star; Kenneth Furuya who ranks high among the nation's golf players; Kiyoshi Nakama, captain of the Ohio State University swimming team who broke the world's record for the one-mile swim in August, 1942, and was named on the 1942 all-American swimming team; Joseph Nagata, Salt Lake University football star who is credited with leading his team to victory over Fordham; Harry Osaki who was cocaptain of Washington State's intercollegiate championship archery team, badminton champion of the college, and ranking tennis and golf player when he was evacuated, and who followed his brother into the United States Army as soon as he was permitted to volunteer (his two sisters volunteered for the WACs); William Kajikawa who was a star athlete and later a coach at State Teachers College, Tempe, Arizona, and who is now in the army; Watson Misaka who starred on the University of Utah basketball team which this year won the National Collegiate Athletic Association basketball championship; Jack Yoshihara, University of Utah half-back; Jim Yagi, who plays in the backfield of the same eleven; and Jim Nagata who calls the signals for the Louisiana State football team.

Boxing, too, has its Nisei performers. Richard Miyagawa, who was forced to leave San Jose State College by evacuation, was unanimously chosen captain of the 1944 University of Wisconsin boxing team by his teammates. Two Nisei, one a soldier in training at Fort Sheridan, Illinois, were finalists for the 118 pound championship in the Chicago Golden Glove tournament last February. The best-known Nisei boxer, a man who turned professional and lost a close decision to the world's featherweight champion, is probably dead. He was Henry Nakamura, who volunteered for the army in 1941 and now has been reported missing in action.

Americans of Japanese ancestry have scored brilliantly in the field of science, too. Dr. Eben T. Takamine, the son of the scientist who discovered adrenalin, is working on a new process for the production of penicillin. His work is considered by authorities to be particularly vital to the war effort. Another Nisei, Dr. Henry Tsuchiya, is credited with a part in the discovery of a new bacteria-killer, a substance allied to penicillin. With other scientists he ran hundreds of experiments in the laboratories of the University of Minnesota to make this significant advance. Then there is Dr. William N. Takahashi who had to relinquish a teaching position at the University of California to accommodate General DeWitt's racial phobia. He has been awarded a Guggenheim Fellowship for the study of virus reproduction and is now carrying on his important studies at Cornell University. It is no wonder that Joseph C. Grew has called Americans of Japanese ancestry "an invaluable element in our population" and praised "the contributions of loyal Americans of Japanese ancestry."

To detail the evidences of loyalty and patriotism of Americans of Japanese ancestry before and after Pearl Harbor would be an almost endless task. Before Pearl Harbor persons of Japanese ancestry pledged their help in any crisis, increased their food production if they were farmers, bought defense bonds, cheerfully answered each selective service call, and supported to the fullest extent the Red Cross, the USO, and all other drives and measures related to national defense. After Pearl Harbor they condemned Japan's action in the most scathing terms and matched their words by volunteering for the army, and by gathering funds to buy bombers, anti-aircraft guns and Red Cross ambulances for the United States forces. They acted as blood donors and increased their contributions to all wartime appeals. They pledged themselves to prevent and to report any subversive activity within the Japanese community. The women busied themselves with knitting and with other services for the Red Cross, and the children salvaged scrap iron and old paper. Antifascist forces among the Nisei, such as the Nisei Democratic Club of Oakland, California, which had supported an embargo on war materials to Japan and an embargo on oil shipments to Japan long before Pearl Harbor, redoubled their efforts on behalf of the cause of the democracies. Even after evacuation, when a war poster contest was announced, Nisei confined at Santa Anita sent in a number of entries. And from behind barbed wire, too, they called for a second front in Europe, an opportunity to aid in the war effort, and they continued to contribute money and blood. American Legion Posts formed anew within the assembly and relocation centers and Nisei at Manzanar and Poston manufactured camouflage nets for the army. Men and women, some of whom had never done agricultural work before, went out in unrestricted regions to pick and save vital crops. Those who had been living in the East and who had never been evacuated gave ample evidence of their patriotism, too. On the 12th anniversary of the start of the Japanese drive on Manchuria, twenty-five persons of Japanese ancestry, members of the Japanese American Committee for Democracy, appeared in New York at the Chinese Blood Bank, and donated blood for the soldiers of Free China. When the Bataan atrocities were announced, the reply of the American Japanese was the most eloquent of all. They came in numbers to the Red Cross Banks to offer their blood in protest.

The greatest and sometimes the final proof of loyalty to a country during a time of war is cheerful and heroic military service. At the time of

Pearl Harbor there were over three thousand young Americans of Japanese ancestry in the armed services. The officer who commanded and trained many of them has testified to their excellent conduct and ability. Today there are over ten thousand Americans of Japanese ancestry in service. Their exploits and brave victories have since shamed and softened the most hardened critics of the group. Recently William P. Haughton, Commander of the California Department of the American Legion, said:

> Numerous persons of Japanese ancestry are now serving with the armed forces of our country on the battlefronts, and according to all reports, are serving valiantly and well.
> We salute all men and women who love this country enough to fight, and, if need be, die for it. Every person good enough to fight for us is entitled to our respect and equal protection under our Constitution.

It is not unusual for parents and sisters who are detained behind barbed wire in relocation centers to have three, four, five, and even six sons and brothers in the United States Army. When in February, 1943, the call came for volunteers for a United States Army combat unit, 1,300 young men volunteered for service from the centers despite all that had happened to them and to their families. The Nisei 100th and 442nd Infantry Battalions are best known for their gallant and important battles in Italy and for the citations and awards these have brought, but it is now recognized that Japanese Americans have fought for the United States on every battlefield of the war, and in the Pacific as well as in Europe. Americans of Japanese ancestry were at Pearl Harbor on December 7, 1941, where Private Tadao Migita died while defending Wheeler Field from enemy attack, and where a Nisei National Guardsman, as Colonel E. W. Wilson has revealed, captured the first enemy soldier who fell into American hands in this war. Sergeant Arthur Komori participated in the defense of the Philippines and was evacuated from Bataan at the last moment, escaping to Australia with some of General MacArthur's forces. Sergeant Frank Fujita Jr. fought the Japanese in Java, and his mother has been notified that he is a prisoner of the Japanese. Sergeant Fred Nishitsuji, formerly of Los Angeles, is known to have participated in the bloody Buna campaign. It is also known that Sergeant Ralph Kimoto has been on active duty in the jungles of New Guinea, and the War Department announced on August 15, 1943, that Sergeant Kazuo Komoto had been wounded in action in the Southwest Pacific. It is a commentary on the DeWitt method of determining loyalty that Sergeant Komoto's mother had to receive this news at the Gila Relocation Center to which she had been evacuated from California. Sergeant Ben Moriwaki and Sergeant Roy Ashizawa are Nisei soldiers who landed at Attu looking for the Japanese enemy, and Sergeant Kuni Nakao has been on duty in the Alaskan war theater. On August 19, 1944, it was disclosed that American soldiers of Japanese ancestry had taken part in the capture of Saipan. Six of them, including a former resident of Marysville, California, and another from Los Angeles, California, were cited and decorated for meritorious service in action there. In a letter which has been made public, H. V. Kaltenborn, well-known radio commentator, has written:

> I have just returned from a comprehensive, although brief, tour of our Pacific fighting areas.
>
> On the basis of first-hand information I can tell you that American citizens of Japanese ancestry are performing some of the most valuable work that is being done by our Armed Forces in the Pacific. These American citizens of Japanese ancestry have not only proved their loyalty, but in many cases they have voluntarily risked their lives in order to perform important front-line services.

It has been necessary to present the evidence concerning the assimilation, loyalty, and contributions of Americans of Japanese ancestry because, under the stress of war, a tendency has set in to accept uncritically anything derogatory that is said about a group which can be somehow associated, if only by means of a name or label, with the enemy Japanese. Actually the subject of the assimilation and Americanism of the citizens of Japanese ancestry has been intensively studied a number of times by impartial and able investigators, and there is little excuse for the gullibility and misinformation that surrounds the topic today.

As long ago as 1928, Dr. Robert E. Park, chairman of the Department of Sociology of the University of Chicago, directed a large-scale study of resident Orientals which was called "Survey of Race Relations of the Pacific Coast." A number of publications resulted, and the large body of materials which were gathered were placed in a depository of the Survey at Stanford University. The undertaking was ambitious and extensive, being supported by a $55,000 budget. Scholars and leading citizens of the West Coast as well as from other parts of the country participated in the research. Dr. Park and his associates, to sum up their findings as far as assimilation is concerned, determined that the American of Japanese ancestry "born in America and educated in our Western schools is culturally an Occidental, even though he be racially an Oriental, and this is true to an extent that no one who has investigated the matter disinterestedly and at first hand is ever likely to imagine."

In 1929 a substantial grant was made to Stanford University by the Carnegie Corporation, for a study of Americans of Japanese ancestry on the West Coast. The work was carried out under the direction of Professor E. K. Strong and resulted in the appearance of four volumes, the first published in 1933. A large staff of trained workers cooperated to gather and analyze the materials. Every device known to social science was employed. The general conclusion, to use Professor Strong's own words, was that:

> The word "assimilation" has two meanings — interbreeding and comprehension of political and social conditions. In the latter sense, the young Japanese are more readily assimilated than people of several European races. . . .

Through the years there have been a number of other studies and investigations by impartial and competent students and they all support the findings of Strong and Park.

In all the loose talk about "lack of assimilation" and "close-knit racial groups" there is no hint that the trained investigators who have pursued the subject for years were even consulted. The Tolan Committee called politicians and sheriffs before it to testify concerning questions of assimilation and acculturation. The men who had made a life study of these questions, Professors Strong, Bell, and Farnsworth of Stanford and Professor Bogardus of the University of Southern California, among others, were never consulted or approached. We talk a great deal about the irrationality and anti-intellectualism of the Nazis and Fascists, of their appeal to violent prejudice and emotion instead of to knowledge. The Nazi pattern was never better exemplified than in this particular crisis. With good reason has Professor Freeman written:

> When the final history of the Japanese evacuation is written, it will almost certainly appear that decisions were made on misinformation, assumptions, prejudices, half-truths, when excellent, scientifically accurate material was available.

There is little need to deal at length with the argument that Americans of Japanese ancestry would have turned upon the country of their birth because of past discrimination and mistreatment. The argument itself is a twisted and peculiar one, implying that the cure for injustice is more injustice. It gives to racists a powerful weapon to use at some future time against any minority which has experienced local prejudice — against Negroes, Jews, Catholics, Mexicans, and Orientals other than Japanese. If this conception is accepted by the Courts, no minority group can ever "be above suspicion." The facts we have reviewed dispose of this argument as far as Americans of Japanese ancestry are concerned. As we have shown, these citizens were making rapid and remarkable progress in educational, artistic, scientific, and economic endeavors. They had reason to be proud of their achievements and they were proud of their achievements. If they had their enemies among Caucasians they also had many kind and powerful friends. To the question of whether they would aid an enemy for *any* reason, history has given an unequivocal answer. The reaction of those of Japanese ancestry in Hawaii when the attack came and the services which have since been rendered to the country's cause in all theaters of war by Americans of Japanese ancestry is the complete rejoinder to this unworthy rationalization.

We ask this Court to review the evidence we have submitted with particular care, because in the *Hirabayashi* case[2] it accepted much too easily the assumptions and broad charges that we have gone to some trouble to answer here. The Opinion of the Court in the *Hirabayashi* decision refers to conditions which "have in a large measure prevented their assimilation as an integral part of the white population." It accepts without question the assertion that "there has been relatively little social intercourse between them and the

---

[2]For more information on the *Hirabayashi* case, see the introduction to Unit Five (p. 615). — Eds.

white population." It speaks of their "isolation" and, most disturbing of all, it justifies the imposition of a curfew by reference to "ethnic affiliations with an invading enemy." We contend that whatever affiliation citizens of Japanese ancestry may have with the Pacific enemy is of a general biological nature. We contend that the ethnic affiliations of these people are solidly with America. To assert otherwise is to ignore the rich store of evidence that scholarship and history have heaped high for us, and is to imply the Nazi doctrine that race and physical type determine loyalty and "ethnic affiliations."

READING CRITICALLY

1. This section of the JACL brief quotes and attempts to refute the *Final Report*'s claim that everyone of Japanese ancestry is "unassimilated." List the kinds of evidence presented here that Nisei are assimilated to the American way of life.

2. To what extent does the JACL brief treat Issei differently from Nisei? List differences and similarities.

3. How does the JACL brief distinguish between "assimilation" and "intermingling"? How does the brief use African Americans to illustrate this distinction?

WRITING ANALYTICALLY

1. This section of the JACL brief says nothing about the afternoon schools in Japanese language and culture cited in the *Final Report* as evidence of probable disloyalty. The brief also makes several distinctions between Issei and Nisei. These two points could be considered examples of places where the writers of the brief cut corners to make their case more convincing; that is, it could be argued that it is deceptive of them not to mention the afternoon schools and cruel not to stand up for the Issei as well as the Nisei. What do you think of these objections to the brief's rhetorical strategies? Write a paper in which you evaluate these two strategies in light of the brief's difficult rhetorical situation — trying to speak up for a group, the Nikkei, that has already been judged as a whole to be disloyal, at least potentially. Your paper should have a two-part thesis: that these strategies are, or are not, effective in helping to persuade a skeptical audience that the Nikkei are mostly loyal and that these strategies are justified or fair to use in order to persuade.

2. Write a paper in which you explain the brief's definition of *assimilation* (drawing on evidence you assembled to answer the reading questions). Option: You may also argue for whether this notion of assimilation points to a social process that is good, or bad, in your opinion; you may wish to offer an alternative definition of assimilation that accords better with your own views.

3. Imagine that either Monica Sone (p. 748) or Jeanne Wakatsuki Houston (p. 715 and 757) has been invited by the JACL lawyers to appear in court as an example of an assimilated Japanese American such as they describe in their brief. The lawyers are hoping that the appearance of such an exemplary Nisei woman will help persuade the Court that the internment was unnecessary. Now imagine that you are Sone or Houston, and write a letter to the JACL lawyers replying to their invitation. Tell them whether or not you are willing to appear in court as a "model" assimilated person, and why.

U.S. Commission on Wartime Relocation and Internment of Civilians

From *Personal Justice Denied* (1982)

In the 1970s, a movement grew to provide redress for victims of the internment (see the introduction to Unit Five, p. 616). Its leaders felt that American public opinion had to be awakened to the enormous injustice of the internment if the government was ever to be persuaded to grant significant monetary compensation. The movement's efforts resulted in the appointment of the U.S. Commission on Wartime Relocation and Internment of Civilians, which held extensive hearings, interviewing hundreds of internees, and published a report in 1982 called *Personal Justice Denied*. The report concludes in no uncertain terms that the Nikkei internment was a grave injustice. (It also contains sections on the treatment of Nikkei in Hawaii; the deportation of Japanese, Italian, and German nationals from Latin American countries for internment in the United States; and the evacuation of the Aleut people from the Aleutian Islands.)

Shortly after publishing the report, the commission also recommended that Congress issue a formal apology for the Nikkei internment and authorize the payment of $20,000 to every surviving internee. These recommendations were enacted by the Civil Liberties Act of 1988, and payments began in 1990.

Chairing the commission was federal official Joan Z. Bernstein. The vice chair was Daniel E. Lundgren, then a member of Congress from California. Former federal legislators on the commission were Edward W. Brooke, Hugh B. Mitchell, and Robert F. Drinan, who was also a Jesuit priest. Former Supreme Court Justice Arthur J. Goldberg and former Secretary of Health, Education, and Welfare Arthur S. Fleming also served. The commission's only Japanese American member was William M. Marutani, then a federal judge. Ishmael Gromoff, a priest of the Russian Orthodox Church, to which most of the surviving Aleut people belonged, represented them on the commission. Angus Macbeth, special counsel to the commission, headed the research team that prepared *Personal Justice Denied*.

We have excerpted the portion of the report's opening summary that establishes the commission's conclusions concerning the internment, often directly contradicting claims in the War Department's *Final Report* (p. 628).

U.S. Commission on Wartime Relocation and Internment of Civilians, *Personal Justice Denied* (Washington, D.C.: Government Printing Office, 1982), 2–16.

In the notes, EDS. = Patricia Bizzell and Bruce Herzberg.

PART I: NISEI AND ISSEI

ON FEBRUARY 19, 1942, ten weeks after the Pearl Harbor attack, President Franklin D. Roosevelt signed Executive Order 9066, which gave to the Secretary of War and the military commanders to whom he delegated authority, the power to exclude any and all persons, citizens and aliens, from designated areas in order to provide security against sabotage, espionage, and fifth column activity.[1] Shortly thereafter, all American citizens of Japanese descent were prohibited from living, working, or traveling on the West Coast of the United States. The same prohibition applied to the generation of Japanese immigrants who, pursuant to federal law and despite long residence in the United States, were not permitted to become American citizens. Initially, this exclusion was to be carried out by "voluntary" relocation. That policy inevitably failed, and these American citizens and their alien parents were removed by the army, first to "assembly centers" — temporary quarters at racetracks and fairgrounds — and then to "relocation centers" — bleak barrack camps mostly in desolate areas of the West. The camps were surrounded by barbed wire and guarded by military police. Departure was permitted only after a loyalty review on terms set, in consultation with the military, by the War Relocation Authority, the civilian agency that ran the camps. Many of those removed from the West Coast were eventually allowed to leave the camps to join the army, go to college outside the West Coast, or to whatever private employment was available. For a larger number, however, the war years were spent behind barbed wire; and for those who were released, the prohibition against returning to their homes and occupations on the West Coast was not lifted until December 1944.

This policy of exclusion, removal, and detention was executed against 120,000 people without individual review, and exclusion was continued virtually without regard for their demonstrated loyalty to the United States. Congress was fully aware of and supported the policy of removal and detention; it sanctioned the exclusion by enacting a statute which made criminal the violation of orders issued pursuant to Executive Order 9066. The United States Supreme Court held the exclusion constitutionally permissible in the context of war, but struck down the incarceration of admittedly loyal American citizens on the ground that it was not based on statutory authority.

All this was done despite the fact that not a single documented act of espionage, sabotage, or fifth column activity was committed by an American citizen of Japanese ancestry or by a resident Japanese alien on the West Coast.

No mass exclusion or detention, in any part of the country, was ordered against American citizens of German or Italian descent. Official actions

---

[1]A "fifth column" is a secret organization that supports an enemy's military and political objectives by sabotage, misinformation, and so on. — EDS.

against enemy aliens of other nationalities were much more individualized and selective than those imposed on the ethnic Japanese.

The exclusion, removal, and detention inflicted tremendous human cost. There was the obvious cost of homes and businesses sold or abandoned under circumstances of great distress, as well as injury to careers and professional advancement. But, most important, there was the loss of liberty and the personal stigma of suspected disloyalty for thousands of people who knew themselves to be devoted to their country's cause and to its ideals but whose repeated protestations of loyalty were discounted — only to be demonstrated beyond any doubt by the record of Nisei soldiers, who returned from the battlefields of Europe as the most decorated and distinguished combat unit of World War II, and by the thousands of other Nisei who served against the enemy in the Pacific, mostly in military intelligence. The wounds of the exclusion and detention have healed in some respects, but the scars of that experience remain, painfully real in the minds of those who lived through the suffering and deprivation of the camps.

The personal injustice of excluding, removing, and detaining loyal American citizens is manifest. Such events are extraordinary and unique in American history. For every citizen and for American public life, they pose haunting questions about our country and its past. It has been the Commission's task to examine the central decisions of this history — the decision to exclude, the decision to detain, the decision to release from detention, and the decision to end exclusion. The Commission has analyzed both how and why those decisions were made, and what their consequences were. And in order to illuminate those events, the mainland experience was compared to the treatment of Japanese Americans in Hawaii and to the experience of other Americans of enemy alien descent, particularly German Americans.

The Decision to Exclude

The Context of the Decision. First, the exclusion and removal were attacks on the ethnic Japanese which followed a long and ugly history of West Coast anti-Japanese agitation and legislation. Antipathy and hostility toward the ethnic Japanese was a major factor of the public life of the West Coast states for more than forty years before Pearl Harbor. Under pressure from California, immigration from Japan had been severely restricted in 1908 and entirely prohibited in 1924. Japanese immigrants were barred from American citizenship, although their children born here were citizens by birth. California and the other western states prohibited Japanese immigrants from owning land. In part the hostility was economic, emerging in various white American groups who began to feel competition, particularly in agriculture, the principal occupation of the immigrants. The anti-Japanese agitation also fed on racial stereotypes and fears: the "yellow peril" of an unknown Asian culture achieving substantial influence on the

Pacific Coast or of a Japanese population alleged to be growing far faster than the white population. This agitation and hostility persisted, even though the ethnic Japanese never exceeded three percent of the population of California, the state of greatest concentration.

The ethnic Japanese, small in number and with no political voice — the citizen generation was just reaching voting age in 1940 — had become a convenient target for political demagogues, and over the years all the major parties indulged in anti-Japanese rhetoric and programs. Political bullying was supported by organized interest groups who adopted anti-Japanese agitation as a consistent part of their program: the Native Sons and Daughters of the Golden West, the Joint Immigration Committee, the American Legion, the California State Federation of Labor, and the California State Grange.

This agitation attacked a number of ethnic Japanese cultural traits or patterns which were woven into a bogus theory that the ethnic Japanese could not or would not assimilate or become "American." Dual citizenship, Shinto,[2] Japanese language schools, and the education of many ethnic Japanese children in Japan were all used as evidence. But as a matter of fact, Japan's laws on dual citizenship went no further than those of many European countries in claiming the allegiance of the children of its nationals born abroad. Only a small number of ethnic Japanese subscribed to Shinto, which in some forms included veneration of the emperor. The language schools were not unlike those of other first-generation immigrants, and the return of some children to Japan for education was as much a reaction to hostile discrimination and an uncertain future as it was a commitment to the mores, much less the political doctrines, of Japan. Nevertheless, in 1942 these popular misconceptions infected the views of a great many West Coast people who viewed the ethnic Japanese as alien and unassimilated.

Second, Japanese armies in the Pacific won a rapid, startling string of victories against the United States and its allies in the first months of World War II. On the same day as the attack on Pearl Harbor, the Japanese struck the Malay Peninsula, Hong Kong, Wake and Midway Islands and attacked the Philippines. The next day the Japanese Army invaded Thailand. On December 13 Guam fell; on December 24 and 25 the Japanese captured Wake Island and occupied Hong Kong. Manila was evacuated on December 27, and the American army retreated to the Bataan Peninsula. After three months the troops isolated in the Philippines were forced to surrender unconditionally — the worst American defeat since the Civil War. In January and February 1942, the military position of the United States in the Pacific was perilous. There was fear of Japanese attacks on the West Coast.

Next, contrary to the facts, there was a widespread belief, supported by a statement by Frank Knox, Secretary of the Navy, that the Pearl Harbor at-

---

[2]Shinto is the ancient religion native to Japan (still practiced today), which includes veneration of nature spirits and ancestors. — EDS.

tack had been aided by sabotage and fifth column activity by ethnic Japanese in Hawaii. Shortly after Pearl Harbor the government knew that this was not true, but took no effective measures to disabuse public belief that disloyalty had contributed to massive American losses on December 7, 1941. Thus the country was unfairly led to believe that both American citizens of Japanese descent and resident Japanese aliens threatened American security.

Fourth, as anti-Japanese organizations began to speak out and rumors from Hawaii spread, West Coast politicians quickly took up the familiar anti-Japanese cry. The Congressional delegations in Washington organized themselves and pressed the War and Justice Departments and the President for stern measures to control the ethnic Japanese — moving quickly from control of aliens to evacuation and removal of citizens. In California, Governor Olson, Attorney General Warren, Mayor Bowron of Los Angeles, and many local authorities joined the clamor. These opinions were not informed by any knowledge of actual military risks, rather they were stoked by virulent agitation which encountered little opposition. Only a few churchmen and academicians were prepared to defend the ethnic Japanese. There was little or no political risk in claiming that it was "better to be safe than sorry" and, as many did, that the best way for ethnic Japanese to prove their loyalty was to volunteer to enter detention. The press amplified the unreflective emotional excitement of the hour. Through late January and early February 1942, the rising clamor from the West Coast was heard within the federal government as its demands became more draconian.

Making and Justifying the Decision. The exclusion of the ethnic Japanese from the West Coast was recommended to the Secretary of War, Henry L. Stimson, by Lieutenant General John L. DeWitt, Commanding General of the Western Defense Command with responsibility for West Coast security. President Roosevelt relied on Secretary Stimson's recommendations in issuing Executive Order 9066.

The justification given for the measure was military necessity. The claim of military necessity is most clearly set out in three places: General DeWitt's February 14, 1942, recommendation to Secretary Stimson for exclusion; General DeWitt's *Final Report: Japanese Evacuation from the West Coast, 1942;* and the government's brief in the Supreme Court defending the Executive Order in *Hirabayashi v. United States.*[3] General DeWitt's February 1942 recommendation presented the following rationale for the exclusion:

> In the war in which we are now engaged racial affinities are not severed by migration. The Japanese race is an enemy race and while many second- and third-generation Japanese born on United States soil, possessed of United States citizenship, have become "Americanized," the racial strains are undi-

[3]For more information on the *Hirabayashi* case, see the introduction to Unit Five, p. 615. — EDS.

luted. To conclude otherwise is to expect that children born of white parents on Japanese soil sever all racial affinity and become loyal Japanese subjects, ready to fight and, if necessary, to die for Japan in a war against the nation of their parents. That Japan is allied with Germany and Italy in this struggle is no ground for assuming that any Japanese, barred from assimilation by convention as he is, though born and raised in the United States, will not turn against this nation when the final test of loyalty comes. It, therefore, follows that along the vital Pacific Coast over 112,000 potential enemies, of Japanese extraction, are at large today. There are indications that these are organized and ready for concerted action at a favorable opportunity. The very fact that no sabotage has taken place to date is a disturbing and confirming indication that such action will be taken.4

There are two unfounded justifications for exclusion expressed here: first, that ethnicity ultimately determines loyalty; second, that "indications" suggest that ethnic Japanese "are organized and ready for concerted action" — the best argument for this being the fact that it hadn't happened.

The first evaluation is not a military one but one for sociologists or historians. It runs counter to a basic premise on which the American nation of immigrants is built — that loyalty to the United States is a matter of individual choice and not determined by ties to an ancestral country. In the case of German Americans, the First World War demonstrated that race did not determine loyalty, and no negative assumption was made with regard to citizens of German or Italian descent during the Second World War. The second judgment was, by the General's own admission, unsupported by any evidence. General DeWitt's recommendation clearly does not provide a credible rationale, based on military expertise, for the necessity of exclusion.

In his 1943 *Final Report,* General DeWitt cited a number of factors in support of the exclusion decision: signaling from shore to enemy submarines; arms and contraband found by the FBI during raids on ethnic Japanese homes and businesses; dangers to the ethnic Japanese from vigilantes; concentration of ethnic Japanese around or near militarily sensitive areas; the number of Japanese ethnic organizations on the coast which might shelter pro-Japanese attitudes or activities such as emperor-worshipping Shinto; and the presence of the Kibei, who had spent some time in Japan.

The first two items point to demonstrable military danger. But the reports of shore-to-ship signaling were investigated by the Federal Communications Commission, the agency with relevant expertise, and no identifiable cases of such signaling were substantiated. The FBI did confiscate arms and contraband from some ethnic Japanese, but most were items normally in the possession of any law-abiding civilian, and the FBI concluded that these searches had uncovered no dangerous persons that "we

---

4This quotation can be found in the context of DeWitt's entire recommendation, included in our excerpt from the War Department's *Final Report* on page 628. — EDS.

could not otherwise know about." Thus neither of these "facts" militarily justified exclusion.

There had been some acts of violence against ethnic Japanese on the West Coast and feeling against them ran high, but "protective custody" is not an acceptable rationale for exclusion. Protection against vigilantes is a civilian matter that would involve the military only in extreme cases. But there is no evidence that such extremity had been reached on the West Coast in early 1942. Moreover, "protective custody" could never justify exclusion and detention for months and years.

General DeWitt's remaining points are repeated in the *Hirabayashi* brief, which also emphasizes dual nationality, Japanese language schools, and the high percentage of aliens (who, by law, had been barred from acquiring American citizenship) in the ethnic population. These facts represent broad social judgments of little or no military significance in themselves. None supports the claim of disloyalty to the United States and all were entirely legal. If the same standards were applied to other ethnic groups, as Morton Grodzins, an early analyst of the exclusion decision, applied it to ethnic Italians on the West Coast, an equally compelling and meaningless case for "disloyalty" could be made. In short, these social and cultural patterns were not evidence of any threat to West Coast military security.

In sum, the record does not permit the conclusion that military necessity warranted the exclusion of ethnic Japanese from the West Coast.

The Conditions Which Permitted the Decision. Having concluded that no military necessity supported the exclusion, the Commission has attempted to determine how the decision came to be made.

First, General DeWitt apparently believed what he told Secretary Stimson: Ethnicity determined loyalty. Moreover, he believed that the ethnic Japanese were so alien to the thought processes of white Americans that it was impossible to distinguish the loyal from the disloyal. On this basis he believed them to be potential enemies among whom loyalty could not be determined.

Second, the FBI and members of Naval Intelligence who had relevant intelligence responsibility were ignored when they stated that nothing more than careful watching of suspicious individuals or individual reviews of loyalty were called for by existing circumstances. In addition, the opinions of the Army General Staff that no sustained Japanese attack on the West Coast was possible were ignored.

Third, General DeWitt relied heavily on civilian politicians rather than informed military judgments in reaching his conclusions as to what actions were necessary, and civilian politicians largely repeated the prejudiced, unfounded themes of anti-Japanese factions and interest groups on the West Coast.

Fourth, no effective measures were taken by President Roosevelt to calm the West Coast public and refute the rumors of sabotage and fifth column activity at Pearl Harbor.

Fifth, General DeWitt was temperamentally disposed to exaggerate the measures necessary to maintain security and placed security far ahead of any concern for the liberty of citizens.

Sixth, Secretary Stimson and John J. McCloy, Assistant Secretary of War, both of whose views on race differed from those of General DeWitt, failed to insist on a clear military justification for the measures General DeWitt wished to undertake.

Seventh, Attorney General Francis Biddle, while contending that exclusion was unnecessary, did not argue to the President that failure to make out a case of military necessity on the facts would render the exclusion constitutionally impermissible or that the Constitution prohibited exclusion on the basis of ethnicity given the facts on the West Coast.

Eighth, those representing the interests of civil rights and civil liberties in Congress, the press, and other public forums were silent or indeed supported exclusion. Thus there was no effective opposition to the measures vociferously sought by numerous West Coast interest groups, politicians, and journalists.

Finally, President Roosevelt, without raising the question to the level of Cabinet discussion or requiring any careful or thorough review of the situation, and despite the Attorney General's arguments and other information before him, agreed with Secretary Stimson that the exclusion should be carried out.

The Decision to Detain

With the signing of Executive Order 9066, the course of the President and the War Department was set: American citizens and alien residents of Japanese ancestry would be compelled to leave the West Coast on the basis of wartime military necessity. For the War Department and the Western Defense Command, the problem became primarily one of method and operation, not basic policy. General DeWitt first tried "voluntary" resettlement: The ethnic Japanese were to move outside restricted military zones of the West Coast but otherwise were free to go wherever they chose. From a military standpoint this policy was bizarre, and it was utterly impractical. If the ethnic Japanese had been excluded because they were potential saboteurs and spies, any such danger was not extinguished by leaving them at large in the interior where there were, of course, innumerable dams, power lines, bridges, and war industries to be disrupted or spied upon. Conceivably sabotage in the interior could be synchronized with a Japanese raid or invasion for a powerful fifth column effect. This raises serious doubts as to how grave the War Department believed the supposed threat to be. Indeed, the implications were not lost on the citizens and politicians of the interior western states, who objected in the belief that people who threatened wartime security in California were equally dangerous in Wyoming and Idaho.

The War Relocation Authority (WRA), the civilian agency created by the President to supervise the relocation and initially directed by Milton

Eisenhower, proceeded on the premise that the vast majority of evacuees were law-abiding and loyal, and that, once off the West Coast, they should be returned quickly to conditions approximating normal life. This view was strenuously opposed by the people and politicians of the mountain states. In April 1942, Milton Eisenhower met with the governors and officials of the mountain states. They objected to California using the interior states as a "dumping ground" for a California "problem." They argued that people in their states were so bitter over the voluntary evacuation that unguarded evacuees would face physical danger. They wanted guarantees that the government would forbid evacuees to acquire land and that it would remove them at the end of the war. Again and again, detention camps for evacuees were urged. The consensus was that a plan for reception centers was acceptable so long as the evacuees remained under guard within the centers.

In the circumstances, Milton Eisenhower decided that the plan to move the evacuees into private employment would be abandoned, at least temporarily. The War Relocation Authority dropped resettlement and adopted confinement. Notwithstanding WRA's belief that evacuees should be returned to normal productive life, it had, in effect, become their jailer. The politicians of the interior states had achieved the program of detention.

The evacuees were to be held in camps behind barbed wire and released only with government approval. For this course of action no military justification was proffered. Instead, the WRA contended that these steps were necessary for the benefit of evacuees and that controls on their departure were designed to assure they would not be mistreated by other Americans on leaving the camps.

It follows from the conclusion that there was no justification in military necessity for the exclusion, that there was no basis for the detention.

The Effect of the Exclusion and Detention

The history of the relocation camps and the assembly centers that preceded them is one of suffering and deprivation visited on people against whom no charges were, or could have been, brought. The Commission hearing record is full of poignant, searing testimony that recounts the economic and personal losses and injury caused by the exclusion and the deprivations of detention. No summary can do this testimony justice.

Families could take to the assembly centers and the camps only what they could carry. Camp living conditions were Spartan. People were housed in tar-papered barrack rooms of no more than 20 by 24 feet. Each room housed a family, regardless of family size. Construction was often shoddy. Privacy was practically impossible and furnishings were minimal. Eating and bathing were in mass facilities. Under continuing pressure from those who blindly held to the belief that evacuees harbored disloyal intentions, the wages paid for work at the camps were kept to the minimal level of $12 a month for unskilled labor, rising to $19 a month for professional employees. Mass living prevented normal family communication and activities. Heads of families, no longer providing food and shelter, found their authority to lead and to discipline diminished.

The normal functions of community life continued but almost always under a handicap — doctors were in short supply; schools which taught typing had no typewriters and worked from hand-me-down school books; there were not enough jobs.

The camp experience carried a stigma that no other Americans suffered. The evacuees themselves expressed the indignity of their conditions with particular power:

> On May 16, 1942, my mother, two sisters, niece, nephew, and I left . . . by train. Father joined us later. Brother left earlier by bus. We took whatever we could carry. So much we left behind, but the most valuable thing I lost was my freedom.

> Henry went to the Control Station to register the family. He came home with twenty tags, all numbered 10710, tags to be attached to each piece of baggage, and one to hang from our coat lapels. From then on, we were known as Family #10710.

The government's efforts to "Americanize" the children in the camps were bitterly ironic:

> An oft-repeated ritual in relocation camp schools . . . was the salute to the flag followed by the singing of "My country, 'tis of thee, sweet land of liberty" — a ceremony Caucasian teachers found embarrassingly awkward if not cruelly poignant in the austere prison-camp setting.

> In some ways, I suppose, my life was not too different from a lot of kids in America between the years of 1942 and 1945. I spent a good part of my time playing with my brothers and friends, learned to shoot marbles, watched sandlot baseball, and envied the older kids who wore Boy Scout uniforms. We shared with the rest of America the same movies, screen heroes and listened to the same heart-rending songs of the forties. We imported much of America into the camps because, after all, we were Americans. Through imitation of my brothers, who attended grade school within the camp, I learned the salute to the flag by the time I was five years old. I was learning, as best one could learn in Manzanar, what it meant to live in America. But, I was also learning the sometimes bitter price one has to pay for it.

After the war, through the Japanese American Evacuation Claims Act, the government attempted to compensate for the losses of real and personal property; inevitably that effort did not secure full or fair compensation. There were many kinds of injury the Evacuation Claims Act made no attempt to compensate: the stigma placed on people who fell under the exclusion and relocation orders; the deprivation of liberty suffered during detention; the psychological impact of exclusion and relocation; the breakdown of family structure; the loss of earnings or profits; physical injury or illness during detention.

The Decision to End Detention

By October 1942, the government held over 100,000 evacuees in relocation camps. After the tide of war turned with the American victory at Midway in June 1942, the possibility of serious Japanese attack was no longer credible; detention and exclusion became increasingly difficult to defend. Nevertheless, other than an ineffective leave program run by the War Relocation Authority, the government had no plans to remedy the situation and no means of distinguishing the loyal from the disloyal. Total control of these civilians in the presumed interest of state security was rapidly becoming the accepted norm.

Determining the basis on which detention would be ended required the government to focus on the justification for controlling the ethnic Japanese. If the government took the position that race determined loyalty or that it was impossible to distinguish the loyal from the disloyal because "Japanese" patterns of thought and behavior were too alien to white Americans, there would be little incentive to end detention. If the government maintained the position that distinguishing the loyal from the disloyal was possible and that exclusion and detention were required only by the necessity of acting quickly under the threat of Japanese attack in early 1942, then a program to release those considered loyal should have been instituted in the spring of 1942 when people were confined in the assembly centers.

Neither position totally prevailed. General DeWitt and the Western Defense Command took the first position and opposed any review that would determine loyalty or threaten continued exclusion from the West Coast. Thus, there was no loyalty review during the assembly center period. Secretary Stimson and Assistant Secretary McCloy took the second view, but did not act on it until the end of 1942 and then only in a limited manner. At the end of 1942, over General DeWitt's opposition, Secretary Stimson, Assistant Secretary McCloy, and General George C. Marshall, Chief of Staff, decided to establish a volunteer combat team of Nisei soldiers. The volunteers were to come from those who had passed a loyalty review. To avoid the obvious unfairness of allowing only those joining the military to establish their loyalty and leave the camps, the War Department joined WRA in expanding the loyalty review program to all adult evacuees.

This program was significant, but remained a compromise. It provided an opportunity to demonstrate loyalty to the United States on the battlefields; despite the human sacrifice involved, this was of immense practical importance in obtaining postwar acceptance for the ethnic Japanese. It opened the gates of the camps for some and began some reestablishment of normal life. But, with no apparent rationale or justification, it did not end exclusion of the loyal from the West Coast. The review program did not extend the presumption of loyalty to American citizens of Japanese descent, who were subject to an investigation and review not applied to other ethnic groups.

Equally important, although the loyalty review program was the first major government decision in which the interests of evacuees prevailed, the program was conducted so insensitively, with such lack of understanding of the evacuees' circumstances, that it became one of the most divisive and wrenching episodes of the camp detention.

After almost a year of what the evacuees considered utterly unjust treatment at the hands of the government, the loyalty review program began with filling out a questionnaire which posed two questions requiring declarations of complete loyalty to the United States. Thus, the questionnaire demanded a personal expression of position from each evacuee — a choice between faith in one's future in America and outrage at present injustice. Understandably most evacuees probably had deeply ambiguous feelings about a government whose rhetorical values of liberty and equality they wished to believe, but who found their present treatment in painful contradiction to those values. The loyalty questionnaire left little room to express that ambiguity. Indeed, it provided an effective point of protest and organization against the government, from which more and more evacuees felt alienated. The questionnaire finally addressed the central question of loyalty that underlay the exclusion policy, a question which had been the predominant political and personal issue for the ethnic Japanese over the past year; answering it required confronting the conflicting emotions aroused by their relation to the government. Evacuee testimony shows the intensity of conflicting emotions:

> I answered both questions number 27 and 28 [the loyalty questions] in the negative, not because of disloyalty but due to the disgusting and shabby treatment given us. A few months after completing the questionnaire, U.S. Army officers appeared at our camp and gave us an interview to confirm our answers to the questions 27 and 28, and followed up with a question that in essence asked: "Are you going to give up or renounce your U.S. citizenship?" to which I promptly replied in the affirmative as a rebellious move. Sometime after the interview, a form letter from the Immigration and Naturalization Service arrived saying if I wanted to renounce my U.S. citizenship, sign the form letter and return. Well, I kept the Immigration and Naturalization Service waiting.

> Well, I am one of those that said "no, no" on it, one of the "no, no" boys, and it is not that I was proud about it, it was just that our legal rights were violated and I wanted to fight back. However, I didn't want to take this sitting down. I was really angry. It just got me so damned mad. Whatever we do, there was no help from outside, and it seems to me that we are a race that doesn't count. So therefore, this was one of the reasons for the "no, no" answer.

Personal responses to the questionnaire inescapably became public acts open to community debate and scrutiny within the closed world of the camps. This made difficult choices excruciating:

> After I volunteered for the [military] service, some people that I knew refused to speak to me. Some older people later questioned my father for letting me volunteer, but he told them that I was old enough to make up my own mind.

The resulting infighting, beatings, and verbal abuses left families torn apart, parents against children, brothers against sisters, relatives against relatives, and friends against friends. So bitter was all this that even to this day, there are many amongst us who do not speak about that period for fear that the same harsh feelings might arise up again to the surface.

The loyalty review program was a point of decision and division for those in the camps. The avowedly loyal were eligible for release; those who were unwilling to profess loyalty or whom the government distrusted were segregated from the main body of evacuees into the Tule Lake [California] camp, which rapidly became a center of disaffection and protest against the government and its policies — the unhappy refuge of evacuees consumed by anger and despair.

The Decision to End Exclusion

The loyalty review should logically have led to the conclusion that no justification existed for excluding loyal American citizens from the West Coast. Secretary Stimson, Assistant Secretary McCloy, and General Marshall reached this position in the spring of 1943. Nevertheless, the exclusion was not ended until December 1944. No plausible reason connected to any wartime security has been offered for this eighteen to twenty month delay in allowing the ethnic Japanese to return to their homes, jobs, and businesses on the West Coast, despite the fact that the delay meant, as a practical matter, that confinement in the relocation camps continued for the great majority of evacuees for another year and a half.

Between May 1943 and May 1944, War Department officials did not make public their opinion that exclusion of loyal ethnic Japanese from the West Coast no longer had any military justification. If the President was unaware of this view, the plausible explanation is that Secretary Stimson and Assistant Secretary McCloy were unwilling, or believed themselves unable, to face down political opposition on the West Coast. General DeWitt repeatedly expressed opposition until he left the Western Defense Command in the fall of 1943, as did West Coast anti-Japanese factions and politicians.

In May 1944 Secretary Stimson put before President Roosevelt and the Cabinet his position that the exclusion no longer had a military justification. But the President was unwilling to act to end the exclusion until the first Cabinet meeting following the Presidential election of November 1944. The inescapable conclusion from this factual pattern is that the delay was motivated by political considerations.

By the participants' own accounts, there is no rational explanation for maintaining the exclusion of loyal ethnic Japanese from the West Coast for the eighteen months after May 1943 — except political pressure and fear. Certainly there was no justification arising out of military necessity. . . .

The promulgation of Executive Order 9066 was not justified by military necessity, and the decisions which followed from it — detention, ending detention, and ending exclusion — were not driven by analysis of military conditions. The broad historical causes which shaped these decisions were race prejudice, war hysteria, and a failure of political leadership. Widespread ignorance of Japanese Americans contributed to a policy conceived in haste and executed in an atmosphere of fear and anger at Japan. A grave injustice was done to American citizens and resident aliens of Japanese ancestry who, without individual review or any probative evidence against them, were excluded, removed, and detained by the United States during World War II.

In memoirs and other statements after the war, many of those involved in the exclusion, removal, and detention passed judgment on those events. While believing in the context of the time that evacuation was a legitimate exercise of the war powers, Henry L. Stimson recognized that "to loyal citizens this forced evacuation was a personal injustice." In his autobiography, Francis Biddle reiterated his beliefs at the time: "the program was ill-advised, unnecessary, and unnecessarily cruel." Justice William O. Douglas, who joined the majority opinion in *Korematsu* which held the evacuation constitutionally permissible, found that the evacuation case "was ever on my conscience." Milton Eisenhower described the evacuation to the relocation camps as "an inhuman mistake." Chief Justice Earl Warren, who had urged evacuation as Attorney General of California, stated, "I have since deeply regretted the removal order and my own testimony advocating it, because it was not in keeping with our American concept of freedom and the rights of citizens." Justice Tom C. Clark, who had been liaison between the Justice Department and the Western Defense Command, concluded, "Looking back on it today [the evacuation] was, of course, a mistake."

READING CRITICALLY

1. The commission report aims to prove that the government was wrong to evacuate and intern the Nikkei. How does the report refute DeWitt's arguments that Nikkei committed acts aiding the enemy on the West Coast? List the points.

2. The report argues that since no true military need required the evacuation, other reasons were really behind the decision. What were these reasons?

3. According to the report, what were the Nikkei losses resulting from the internment? How does the report document these losses?

4. When internment camp inmates were asked to answer questions on a loyalty review questionnaire, some gave answers that could be considered as showing disloyalty to the United States. But the report aims to give the impression that very few inmates really were disloyal. It does this primarily by explaining the circumstances in which the loyalty questionnaire was designed and administered. What were these circumstances?

WRITING CRITICALLY

1. Write a paper in which you explain the ways white supremacist racism contributed to the decision to intern the Nikkei, according to *Personal Justice Denied*.

2. The report says that the Nikkei's greatest loss was the loss of "personal justice" — greater than their lost time, money, and possessions. What exactly does this phrase mean? Why might "personal justice" be considered the greatest loss they suffered? Write a paper in which you speculate on answers to these questions. You will have to infer support from the report for your ideas, because nowhere in it will you find the nature of "personal justice" spelled out.

3. *Personal Justice Denied* argues that the Nikkei did not in fact present a security risk to the United States and that a reasonable inspection of the evidence available at the time of the internment would have shown that they did not present a risk. Write a paper in which you evaluate how convincing you find the commission report's argument on this point. Your responses to reading questions 1, 2, and 4 should help you here. You will notice that to make its case, the commission report must cite and refute the War Department's *Final Report* on the internment. If you wish to include the *Final Report* in your response to this question, write your paper in the form of a comparison of the credibility of the two reports; you may also include some discussion of what a historian should do when confronted with two sources that contradict each other.

MIKE MASAOKA WITH BILL HOSOKAWA

From *They Call Me Moses Masaoka: An American Saga* (1987)

Mike Masaoka (b. 1915) was born in California but grew up in Salt Lake City, Utah, where his father had a fish and produce business. In 1941, at the age of twenty-six, he became the Japanese American Citizens League (JACL) executive secretary and was its most dynamic leader throughout the war years. After the internment began in 1942, Masaoka was sent by the JACL to lobby in Washington, D.C., while the rest of his family, who had been living in Los Angeles, were interned at Manzanar. He helped bring about the U.S. government decision to organize the all-Nisei 442nd Regimental Combat Team, which four of his five brothers served in (one died in combat) and to which Masaoka was attached as a communications specialist. He was never interned. After the war, Masaoka developed a career as a professional lobbyist for Japanese and Nikkei interests in Washington. His JACL leadership was controversial — and still is — because he counseled cooperation with the internment. Excerpted here is chapter 5, "Decision to Cooperate," from Masaoka's autobiography, which he wrote at least in part as an attempt to answer his critics. The book's title emphasizes the nickname given to him by those who approved of his actions, suggesting that, like the biblical Moses, he led his people through the tribulations of discrimination to within sight, at least, of a "promised land" of social equality.

SOMETIME DURING THE EARLY PART of February 1942, John H. Tolan, an obscure Democratic congressman from Oakland, California, announced formation of what was grandiosely called the Select Committee Investigating National Defense Migration of the House of Representatives, Seventy-seventh Congress, Second Session. As it turned out, its primary function was not to investigate "migration" but to provide a platform for those advocating the removal of Japanese Americans from the West Coast.

At first, however, it appeared the committee was established in a genuine effort to determine the facts about a confused situation. I thought it was the best news we had heard in a long time, and our advisers, Nisei and Caucasian alike, agreed. The Tolan Committee, as it became known, seemed to offer us a forum before which we could make our case for fair

Mike Masaoka with Bill Hosokawa, *They Call Me Moses Masaoka: An American Saga* (New York: William Morrow, 1987), 85–100.
    In the notes, EDS. = Patricia Bizzell and Bruce Herzberg.

treatment and marshal witnesses to testify as to their faith in our loyalty, to give us a direct pipeline to members of Congress, and to provide an opportunity to get the kind of media treatment we needed to rally public support. I arranged for JACL representatives to appear before the committee and urged JACL chapters in other cities to present testimony when Tolan and his cohorts arrived for hearings. Kido as national president was the logical spokesman for JACL, but he insisted that I could make a more eloquent presentation and would be a better witness than he.

I believed my appearance before the committee was critical to JACL's hopes of forestalling further evacuation talk. No extemporaneous speech would do. I dropped all other activities and set to work to write a statement. Drafts were read and criticized by our advisers as I edited and rewrote and polished the text.

All of us were concentrating so intensely on preparing for the Tolan hearings that an event of far greater significance almost escaped our notice. That was the signing, on February 19, of Executive Order 9066 by President Roosevelt. The first we knew of EO 9066[1] was when Lawrence Davies of the *New York Times* called to get our reaction. It was all news to me, and I had to ask what it was all about. Davies said he understood Roosevelt had given the secretary of war authority to designate military areas "from which any and all persons may be excluded."

My first impression was that it had been a predictable move, something we had expected, and nothing to be really concerned about. There had been considerable agitation for removing enemy aliens from sensitive areas adjacent to aircraft factories, airports, military installations, power plants, and the like. The Justice Department had pressed for authority to get the job done, and we assumed EO 9066 simply provided it. At the time it was only mildly disturbing to us that the army had received the assignment rather than a civilian agency.

What the army then proceeded to do was to use EO 9066 as a device for overriding the constitutional rights of citizens. Within weeks the army's Western Defense Command under Lieutenant General John L. DeWitt employed its new power to incarcerate Japanese Americans en masse on the basis of their ethnicity, depriving them of rights guaranteed even petty criminals.

The press failed to catch the alarming significance of EO 9066. This assault on the Bill of Rights passed virtually unnoticed and provoked little if any editorial comment. Civil libertarians, what few there were in those days, were silent. Imagine what the press would do today if a president attempted to issue such an order.

What we had no way of knowing was that on February 11, eight days before the president signed EO 9066, Secretary of War Henry Stimson had received Roosevelt's approval to prepare for a general evacuation of Japanese and Japanese Americans from the West Coast. That same day General DeWitt was notified and told to be prepared to get the job done.

[1]See page 628. — EDS.

Thus the decision on mass evacuation had been made a full ten days before Congressman Tolan opened his hearings in San Francisco on February 21. As the book *Nisei* has stated, "the hearings were a sham, a forum for expressions of opinions and prejudices, for the voicing of pleas for justice as well as the cries of bigotry, none of which could have any effect on the issue."[2] We had approached the hearings in the belief that the democratic system was working. In reality we were participants in an exercise in futility.

A parade of city and state officials appeared to dredge up tired old myths to justify their fears that Japanese Americans were a security risk and should be moved off the West Coast for the nation's and — voiced piously — their own safety. Significantly, no one said anything about detention; the entire focus was on removal, although no one seemed to have any idea where the displaced should go or what they should do to support themselves.

I was the first Japanese American witness, and I took the stand still firm in the belief that what I was about to say would have an influence on the government's decisions. Congressman John Sparkman of Alabama took a prominent part in the questioning. I felt he was more sympathetic than the others.

(Elected to the Senate years later, Sparkman headed both the Foreign Relations and Banking committees before Adlai Stevenson picked him for his running mate in the 1952 presidential race. I happened to meet Sparkman during the campaign. He recalled the Tolan Committee hearings, then asked for my backing. Even though it appeared Dwight Eisenhower would win over Stevenson, I gave Sparkman a letter of support.)

The members of the Tolan Committee obviously were unfamiliar with Nisei, displaying the kind of ignorance that was to make the evacuation acceptable to the American public. They appeared surprised that I could speak English without an accent, that I was a Mormon and not something they considered "subversive" like a Buddhist, that I had never been to Japan to fall under the evil spell of militarism and emperor worship, that I understood virtually no Japanese, that I was solely the product of the American educational system. The essence of my testimony was that we as loyal Americans had no choice but to bow to military necessity if that was the case, but would resist evacuation demands based on political opportunism or economic greed. I said:

> With any policy of evacuation definitely arising from reasons of military
> necessity and national safety, we are in complete agreement. As American
> citizens we cannot and should not take any other stand. But, also, as Ameri-
> can citizens believing in the integrity of our citizenship, we feel that any evac-
> uation enforced on grounds violating that integrity should be opposed. If, in
> the judgment of military and federal authorities, evacuation of Japanese resi-
> dents from the West Coast is a primary step toward assuring the safety of this

[2]Bill Hosokawa, *Nisei: The Quiet Americans* (New York: William Morrow, 1969), 291. —
EDS.

nation, we will have no hesitation in complying with the necessities implicit in that judgment. But if, on the other hand, such evacuation is primarily a measure whose surface urgency cloaks the desires of political or other pressure groups who want us to leave merely from motives of self-interest, we feel that we have every right to protest and to demand equitable judgment on our merits as American citizens.

I concluded with these words:

> In this emergency, as in the past, we are not asking for special privileges or concessions. We ask only for the opportunity and the right of sharing the common lot of all Americans, whether it be in peace or in war.

Although I spoke in broad terms, at this point in history the only real issue was removal of persons, primarily aliens, from militarily sensitive areas. There were rumors of wholesale evacuation of all Japanese Americans from the entire West Coast, but no one with the administration had said anything publicly about that possibility. Certainly there was no responsible reference to imprisonment of Japanese Americans in detention camps.

We know now that there was no military necessity to justify any of these possibilities. As I have noted earlier, the congressional Commission on Wartime Relocation and Internment of Civilians found after lengthy inquiry that "racial prejudice, war hysteria, and a failure of political leadership" were responsible for what it termed a "gross injustice."[3] In 1942 we sensed this to be true, but how could we prove it when we knew nothing more than what was published in the newspapers and broadcast by radio? Congressmen on the Tolan Committee insisted there were photographs proving Japanese Americans had sabotaged defense efforts in Honolulu during the enemy attack. We Nisei didn't believe it, but had no way of disproving such stories. Only much later did we learn that Nisei in Hawaii had responded magnificently in defense of their homeland. At the time there was little we could do other than try to make our case before forums like the Tolan Committee, where, without our knowledge, the cards were stacked.

The situation was so confused that even federal officials weren't sure of policy. About the time EO 9066 was being drawn up, Kido and I met with Richard M. Neustadt, regional director of the Federal Security Agency, which had been made responsible for the welfare of those who might be forced to move by government order. He told us that the government did not contemplate either wholesale or indiscriminate evacuation of Japanese from the West Coast. Curtis Munson had given us similar information. Neustadt said only Japanese nationals living in areas specified by the Justice Department, if it came to that, would have to move out. He also assured us that Japanese nationals would be treated no differently from other enemy aliens like Germans and Italians, and that American citizens of Japanese descent would not be involved in any of the contemplated

---

[3]An excerpt from this commission's report, *Personal Justice Denied*, begins on page 661. — EDS.

evacuation movements. Tom Clark of the Justice Department, later to become a Supreme Court justice, told us much the same thing.

Their assurances did not hold up, of course. I have no reason to believe that Neustadt and Clark were other than sincere, speaking on the basis of information available to them at the moment. And we had no reason not to believe them. At the worst, we thought martial law might be declared on the West Coast as had been done in Hawaii, placing some restrictions on a few civilians living in particularly sensitive areas. Even that seemed to be a remote possibility so far from the war zone. Under the circumstances the terrible danger to constitutional rights inherent in EO 9066 was not apparent.

Some time later, when at last we saw the text of EO 9066, we were amazed by the sweeping powers granted the military. EO 9066 was posed as a military measure, declaring that "the successful prosecution of the war requires every possible protection against espionage and against sabotage." Authority was given "any designated commander," when he "deems such action necessary or desirable," to designate military areas "from which any or all persons may be excluded." The key words in that infamous document were "any or all persons." Roosevelt by a stroke of his pen granted the military the power to disrupt the lives and violate the rights — if it alone deemed it "necessary or desirable" — of any or all persons be they civilians or soldiers, citizens or aliens. In the absence of a declaration of martial law this was a clear violation of guarantees specified in the Bill of Rights.

There is no way now to tell what Stimson and Roosevelt had in mind when the first devised and the second approved EO 9066. I would like to believe they intended cautious use of its powers. However, the fact that General DeWitt was alerted to carry out a mass evacuation before that document was made public indicates that the president and his secretary of war had a clear idea of how the power would be used. DeWitt took advantage of the broad language of EO 9066 to force the wholesale *removal* of an entire racial minority and, in two subsequent steps not specified in the order, *imprisoned* them and *continued to exclude* them from the West Coast long after there was any possible necessity. There was nothing in EO 9066 to indicate that the government was contemplating other than removal. Not once in the many conversations Kido and I had with military officials was detention suggested.

When legal tests finally reached the Supreme Court, the justices were troubled by the arbitrary extension of military power. Frank Chuman writes in *The Bamboo People*, his legal history of Japanese Americans:

> Justice William O. Douglas declared that "detention in relocation centers was no part of the original program of evacuation." He pointed out that the legislative history of the act establishing the War Relocation Authority and the Executive Order 9066 authorizing the evacuation was silent on the power of WRA to detain the evacuees. He delineated Executive Order 9066 and Executive Order 9102, and all the public proclamations including the 108 civilian exclusion orders issued by General DeWitt, as being war mea-

sures put into effect only to "remove from designated areas . . . persons whose removal is necessary in the interests of national security."

Yet, somewhere along the line, the army changed its objective and mission from simple removal to confinement, and a civilian agency, the War Relocation Authority, was given the job of jailkeeper. The army reinterpreted its powers under EO 9066 to mean it had total authority over the freedom of Japanese American civilians. The nation, and later the courts, sanctioned that action without really acknowledging the terrible precedent it established.

Late in February, even as the Tolan Committee continued its hearings, Kido and I were summoned to Western Defense Command headquarters in the San Francisco Presidio. We were ushered into the presence of General DeWitt, a short, stocky, gray-haired man with the three stars of a lieutenant general on his shoulders. DeWitt was surrounded by a bevy of lesser officers, all cold and stern. He did not introduce them. DeWitt made a brief statement making it clear that we had been called in to hear what the army had to say, not for discussion or negotiation. With that he left the room.

Another officer broke the news. In a few days the Western Defense Command would issue Public Proclamation No. 1 announcing that "all persons of Japanese ancestry" — we were referred to as "aliens" and "nonaliens" — would be required to get out of the western half of California, Oregon, and Washington and the southern one-third of Arizona. The Japanese Americans would be urged to move out "voluntarily." If "voluntary" departure didn't work, the alternative would be transfer to temporary havens until the government could map the next move. It was obvious no one had any idea what that would be. But there was no doubt that the army intended to proceed without delay; the removal of 115,000 men, women, and children, citizens and aliens alike, voluntarily or otherwise, would begin just as soon as arrangements could be made.

I heard all this in utter disbelief. I cannot remember ever feeling so desperately let down. What we in moments of doubt had feared might happen was about to take place, and there was nothing more we could do to try to prevent it. There was no more room for argument or reason, only the cold reality of military orders. On top of it all, the Nisei were being lumped together with enemy aliens. We had been prepared for drastic restrictions on the freedom of the Issei generation. But we had remained confident in the sanctity of our rights as citizens. I felt I had failed JACL and its members. What made it even worse was that the generals now were asking JACL to cooperate with them — to cooperate like Judas goats — in the incarceration of our own people. I gagged at the thought.

But in my desperation I could see another side. If mass evacuation was inevitable, the army's request also confronted JACL with the responsibility to help minimize the pain and trauma of the ordeal ahead.

For the moment, Kido and I could not go beyond saying that we represented only our membership and that we had no authority or right to speak for the entire Japanese American community. Even as representatives of JACL the decision as to its role was too important to be made by just the two of us. We asked for and received permission to call a conference of league leaders to discuss our response.

Kido and I left the Presidio in silence, but that was a prelude to many agonizing discussions about principles involved, the leadership obligations to the people that we had assumed involuntarily, and the new obligations the army was asking us to accept. What an anomalous position we were in. Our government was asking us to cooperate in the violation of what we considered to be our fundamental rights. The first impulse was to refuse, to stand up for what we knew to be right.

But on the other hand there were persuasive reasons for working with the government.

First of all was the matter of loyalty. In a time of great national crisis the government, rightly or wrongly, fairly or unfairly, had demanded a sacrifice. Could we as loyal citizens refuse to respond? The answer was obvious. We had to reason that to defy our government's orders was to confirm its doubts about our loyalty.

There was another important consideration. We had been led to believe that if we cooperated with the army in the projected mass movement, the government would make every effort to be as helpful and as humane as possible. Cooperation as an indisputable demonstration of loyalty might help to speed our return to our homes. Moreover, we feared the consequences if Japanese Americans resisted evacuation orders and the army moved in with bayonets to eject the people forcibly. JACL could not be party to any decision that might lead to violence and bloodshed. At a time when Japan was still on the offensive, the American people could well consider us saboteurs if we forced the army to take drastic action against us. This might place our future — and the future of our children and our children's children — as United States citizens in jeopardy. As the involuntary trustees of the destiny of Japanese Americans, Kido and I agreed that we could do no less than whatever was necessary to protect that future. I was determined that JACL must not give a doubting nation further cause to confuse the identity of Americans of Japanese origin with the Japanese enemy.

The officers had made it clear to us that we could cooperate or they would do it the army way. Anxious to avoid panic, the military did not make that threat public, nor were we in position to do so. Only when the evacuation was well under way did Colonel Karl R. Bendetsen, who has been described by the army's official historian as the "most industrious advocate of mass evacuation," reveal in a blood-chilling speech to the Commonwealth Club of San Francisco that he had been prepared to complete the evacuation "practically overnight" in an emergency.

Reluctantly, we concluded there was no choice but to cooperate. We talked over the decision with friends and advisers, who, once over their shock, agreed we had no other choice. The few Issei community elders who hadn't been imprisoned counseled cooperation.

For several nights, after Kido had gone home to his family, I could not sleep. I tried to read and was drawn time and again to the Bill of Rights, particularly the due-process and equal-protection provisions in the Fifth and Fourteenth Amendments to the Constitution. "No person shall be deprived of life, liberty, or property without due process of law," the Fifth Amendment says. Due process meant the right to be presumed innocent until tried and found guilty by a jury of one's peers. Yet, the government was presuming our guilt without ever filing charges and putting us away until we could prove our innocence. Could anything be more wrong?

And the Fourteenth promises this: "No state shall make or enforce any law which shall abridge the privileges or immunities of citizens of the United States; nor shall any state deprive any person of life, liberty, or property, without due process of law; nor deny to any person within its jurisdiction the equal protection of the laws." Generations of Americans had fought and died to defend those rights. Now we were being asked to yield them peacefully in the name of national defense. I would toss and turn for hours until exhaustion claimed me.

The army had taken the racist position that because we were not white, it was impossible to tell the loyal from the disloyal. Earl Warren endorsed this position in his Tolan Committee testimony. In England, at the beginning of the war with Germany, 117 hearing boards were set up. In six months more than seventy-four thousand enemy aliens were summoned before these boards. Some two thousand were interned, eight thousand were made subject to special restrictions, and the rest were allowed to go their way. My suggestion for similar boards to clear the loyalty of Nisei fell on deaf ears.

By contrast, hearing boards were established for Issei who had been picked up as possible security risks, and virtually all of them were cleared. A member of one of the boards was a young professor from Montana State University named Mike Mansfield who was destined to go on to a long and distinguished career in Congress followed by appointment as U.S. ambassador to Japan. He found nothing in the background of the Japanese he interviewed to justify continued detention. Recalling this experience, he once told me he wondered why similar boards hadn't been established to investigate Nisei instead of simply letting them sit in camps.

Because of the emphasis being put on loyalty and the difficulty of demonstrating it, I designed a JACL membership card which included a loyalty oath. It had no official or legal standing, but at least it would be a visible assertion of our fealty. Hundreds of Nisei joined JACL to get the cards.

Once Kido and I had determined that cooperation was the proper course, we went to work to convince others. The reality of the situation was that virtually every element of the Japanese American community was looking to JACL for leadership. Buddhist and Christian churches, the only other organizations with more than local affiliates, sent telegrams to headquarters expressing support.

Kido summoned JACL representatives to a conference in San Francisco on March 8, 9, and 10. The discussions were unexpectedly subdued. I realized that everyone was in a state of shock, hardly able to comprehend that the justice they had believed in had been destroyed. Public officials who had called for fair play the week after the Pearl Harbor attack were now joining the clamor for our ouster.

Without dissent the National Board voted JACL officers extraordinary powers for the duration of the war to carry out these objectives:

1. To urge all JACL members to cooperate with the duly constituted authorities in the struggle for victory, and to recommend the same course for others.
2. To assist Japanese Americans in every way possible, help maintain morale, and ease the impact of the evacuation.
3. To keep in touch with federal authorities to ensure just and humane treatment for the evacuees.
4. To carry on a public relations program to demonstrate that Japanese Americans are good citizens.

On my recommendation, the board voted to move headquarters to Salt Lake City, which was out of the evacuation zone and where we had friends. Then the board instructed me to go to Washington, where I would have access to federal decision-makers and could lobby for justice as the evacuation program proceeded. In view of the ignorance about Japanese Americans in the nation's capital, I knew I had my work cut out for me. Kido gave an emotional and moving concluding address:

> It has been our constant fear that race prejudice would be fanned by the various elements which have been constantly watching for an opening to destroy us. They included many of our economic competitors and those who believe this country belongs to the whites alone. Many of them wanted to indulge in the unpatriotic pastime of using us as a political football in this hour of America's greatest peril. . . . We were counting on the better understanding we thought we had created. We all had expected that the public officials, at least, would serve as a buffer against possible mass hysteria. We never dreamed that such a large number of them would ride on the bandwagon, to reap political benefit out of this abnormal condition. . . . When we hear our erstwhile friends of peaceful days, those who praised us to the skies as model citizens, brand us more dangerous than the so-called enemy aliens, we cannot help but wonder if this is all but a bad dream.

Kido went on to say:

> No matter whatever we may do, wherever we may go, always retain your faith in our government and maintain your self-respect. . . . We are going into exile as our duty to our country because the president and the military commander of this area have deemed it a necessity. We are gladly cooperating because this is one way of showing that our protestations of loyalty are sincere. We have pledged our full support to President Roosevelt and

to the nation. This is a sacred promise which we shall keep as good patriotic citizens.

It is significant that while Kido spoke of exile, not once did he mention the possibility that we were going into detention. Nor did anyone else. Kido and I were surprised and relieved that there was practically no outcry from the Japanese American community against the decision to cooperate in the evacuation. We had to believe the lack of adverse reaction indicated general agreement that cooperation was indeed proper under the conditions we faced. Many besides me must have hoped that if we demonstrated our ultimate faith in the nation, the people of the United States after the heat and hysteria of war was over would somehow more than make up for what we had sacrificed.

Kido and I never doubted the necessity of JACL's decision. Yet there were times in private when we discussed violating the military's edicts, first as a gesture of outrage, and second to provoke a court test of the constitutionality of the orders. Kido had an unshakable faith in the sanctity of law and had no doubt that a challenge would be upheld. There were other JACLers who felt the same way. Walter Tsukamoto was prepared to go to jail to test the order but decided against it when he was warned he would jeopardize his captain's commission in the Army Reserve and perhaps face a court-martial on charges of disloyalty.

I was a logical candidate for a legal test, being without dependents. However, Kido insisted I would be of greater use to Japanese Americans outside of prison. Besides, Kido pointed out, any court test surely would be dragged out for months and perhaps years, and while a decision on constitutional issues was critical in the overall picture, it was not likely to be rendered until long after the immediate crisis was over. In short, there was no prospect of winning a judicial judgment in time to do anybody any good. In view of the urgencies of the moment he saw a court challenge at that time as little more than a futile, quixotic gesture that would demand more of our resources than JACL could spare. Thus we put aside thoughts of provoking a test and focused on the immediate problems. JACL, however, did become involved in a basic court challenge involving a young lady named Mitsuye Endo. . . .

The government lost no time in demonstrating that it meant business. On February 27 it ordered the evacuation on two days' notice of several hundred Japanese Americans remaining in the fishing village of Terminal Island in Los Angeles Harbor.[4] The result was near-panic, heartbreak, and heavy economic loss. This action was dramatic warning of difficulties to come. Less than a week later, when the evacuation zones were announced,

---

[4]See the excerpt by Jeanne Wakatsuki Houston and James D. Houston from *Farewell to Manzanar* on page 715; some members of Jeanne Wakatsuki Houston's family lived on Terminal Island, and her father fished out of this port before the internment. — EDS.

the army simultaneously urged Japanese Americans to move out of them voluntarily.

Many Nisei did their best to comply. Henry Mitarai, a prosperous farmer from Mountain View near San Jose, was ready to buy land in Nevada or Utah to which he and his friends could move their operations. I accompanied Henry and several others on a scouting trip. Few landowners would even talk to us, and we came back empty-handed. Fred Wada of Los Angeles was a bit more successful. He found some land near Keatley, Utah, and settled a dozen families there in a "Food for Freedom" farming colony. Jimmie Sakamoto and other Seattleites entertained serious thoughts of moving into the Moses Lake district of eastern Washington with anyone willing to break the sod of a new area. But there was neither enough time nor enough capital to get projects like these under way, much less to meet the needs of tens of thousands of persons. The federal government, which was spending millions to train women for war work and opening up job opportunities for minorities other than Japanese Americans, failed to lift a finger on our behalf. In Congressman Tolan's words, we were part of the national defense migration program, but all it meant for us was that we had to get out.

DeWitt's voluntary removal plan was in reality a tragic farce. Most Japanese Americans had never been east of the coastal states. Few had friends inland on whom to depend for shelter, jobs, and other help. Moreover, the federal government and the army guaranteed the failure of voluntary evacuation by doing nothing to explain to residents of interior areas why they should accept people considered too much of a security threat to be left on the West Coast. Many of the hardy souls who loaded cars with family and possessions and headed east ran into hostility. JACL headquarters heard reports that in some towns they were denied food, gasoline, and shelter. They encountered armed vigilantes and roadside signs ordering them to move on. Some had windshields smashed and tires slashed. Local law enforcement officials were getting calls that "Japs" were "escaping" from California and ought to be apprehended at the state line. It was only too obvious that unrestricted and unsupervised movement inland was fraught with danger.

I must also fault the general body of the Christian churches, including my own Mormon Church, for failing us in a time of need. Understandably they did not speak out when the issue was relocation of aliens from militarily sensitive areas. But with few exceptions, churchmen continued their silence when citizen rights were being trampled. Except for a handful of notable exceptions, West Coast churches did nothing to prepare their inland brethren to assist voluntary evacuees seeking only to obey military orders. So rampant was the fear and hysteria that some Christian ministers said that while they could vouch for most Japanese members of their denominations, they would have nothing to do with Buddhists. In time the churches became strong supporters of Japanese Americans attempting to start new lives in the interior, but that was much later.

DeWitt's headquarters ignored my pleas for protection for the voluntary evacuees. There was a war to be fought, an officer reminded me harshly, and there was no way he would detach troops to escort a bunch of Japs. I was relieved when the army ordered voluntary evacuation halted on March 24. DeWitt thus made it illegal for Japanese Americans to leave their homes, and soon it would be illegal for them to remain.

March 24 also was the date that an 8:00 P.M. to 6:00 A.M. curfew on enemy aliens was extended to all Japanese Americans. It was a further erosion of our rights, given legitimacy by Congress a few days earlier when by simple voice vote it passed Public Law 503, making it a misdemeanor to violate orders of military commanders prescribed under Executive Order 9066. In that august body, where in the memorable past great debates about freedom had been heard, citizen rights were casually suspended. A routine, little-noticed voice vote had put our future in cold storage.

It was this sort of unthinking and outrageously callous action by the government that caused Joe Shinoda, a well-to-do nursery operator from Southern California, to offer to pay my expenses if JACL would dispatch me to Washington immediately to lobby Congress. That we turned down the proposal is a measure of our naiveté. Everyone we consulted said that in view of the national temper it would be a waste of time to go to Washington in hopes of influencing Congress.

Now it is obvious we were wrong, because of two things we didn't realize. In the Midwest and East there was relatively little concern about the Japanese Americans, little knowledge about what was going on. If the American public had been aware of the lasting constitutional implications of a hasty wartime measure, we might have been able to stir up enough concern to blunt the injustice. Second, we didn't need to influence a majority in Congress to have an impact. It did not occur to any of us that if one senator, just one, could be persuaded that we were being treated unjustly, he could bring Congress up short with a filibuster that would focus national media attention on our plight.

Under the circumstances, could we have found such a person? Would an old friend like Senator Thomas have risked his career to come to our aid? We will never know, because we didn't try to find out. But in retrospect it is difficult to believe there wasn't at least one member of Congress who would have had the courage to stand up and stir the conscience of the nation. For an example, we need only to look at Congresswoman Jeanette Rankin, the Montana Republican. She voted her conscience and alone among all the members of Congress cast a ballot against a declaration of war on Japan. When it was time to act against Germany and Italy, she voted only "present." While she was an ineffective minority of one in the House, a dissident could delay action in the Senate by the filibuster, a frequently used tactic. If I or someone had come up with the idea of convincing some senator that the principles involved in our cause were important enough to filibuster for, history might have taken a different course. We had so much to learn in 1942.

One morning abut this time I read that Minoru Yasui, a young Nisei attorney in Portland, Oregon, had violated the curfew to invite arrest so that he could provoke a court test.5 Yasui ultimately took his case to the Supreme Court in an unsuccessful appeal. He has become a genuine Japanese American folk hero, a tireless fighter for human rights, and a JACL stalwart who deservedly won its two most prestigious awards, Nisei of the Biennium in 1952 and JACLer of the Biennium thirty years later. In 1942 I knew nothing of Yasui except that he was considered an important JACL leader in the Pacific Northwest. The news stories about Yasui's arrest made it appear that he was just a maverick publicity-seeker. There was nothing to indicate Yasui's genuine concern for constitutional safeguards or the deep thought that had preceded his decision to defy the government order. Without this knowledge I was profoundly disturbed by what seemed to be his unwise and unwarranted action.

Many years later, Yasui told me he had written to express his feelings and outline his intentions. I never received that letter. Completely in the dark and fearful that Yasui was endangering the delicate unwritten understanding we had with federal authorities, I issued a strong statement criticizing him.

Even today that statement is cited as proof of my shortsightedness in failing to oppose the army's evacuation order. I do not apologize for it. Under the circumstances that existed in 1942 — and it is important not to judge long-past decisions by contemporary values — I could not have done otherwise. There is no doubt in my mind that even had I known Yasui's thinking I would have opposed his action, morally defensible as it was, because of my conviction that it would hurt the majority. Today, Yasui is hailed for his courage. At the time he was a Lone Ranger widely criticized by his peers. Realistically, he was not the best possible candidate for a test case, since he had been an employee of the Japanese consulate in Chicago until war broke out. In the final analysis, my disagreement with Yasui was less over policy than timing. He wanted an immediate challenge. I had been convinced the challenge must come later. Over the years Yasui and I were good friends and coworkers in behalf of many good causes until his death in 1986. I respected his dedication, integrity, and talent, just as I'm sure he respected me.

Yasui was no more successful in stemming the tide of evacuation than anybody else. As Kido had prophesied, the evacuation was a *fait accompli*6 long before the courts reached a final determination on Yasui's challenge, and on the suits involving Gordon Hirabayashi, Fred Korematsu, and Mitsuye Endo, which also went to the Supreme Court.7

5Excerpts from Yasui's account of his experiences begin on page 729. — Eds.

6French for "accomplished fact," something already completed. — Eds.

7For more information on the *Hirabayashi, Endo,* and *Korematsu* cases, see the introduction to Unit Five, page 615. — Eds.

READING CRITICALLY

1. Masaoka's aim in this chapter is to explain the JACL's decision to cooperate with the evacuation of the Nikkei and to defend himself against charges that he should have led resistance to the evacuation order instead. What reasons does he give for the JACL's and his own decisions?

2. What views of the U.S. government does Masaoka convey, and how?

3. How does Masaoka explain the fact that he was never interned? What does he seem to be defending himself against here?

4. How does Masaoka explain his reaction to Minoru Yasui's resistance to the internment?

WRITING ANALYTICALLY

1. Throughout this excerpt, Masaoka attempts to prove that he acted only for the good of his people, the Nikkei, and not for hope of personal gain or advantage. He wants to argue that actions of his that might seem self-serving have actually been misinterpreted. Using the evidence you collected in response to the reading questions, explain how Masaoka goes about defending himself here and evaluate his defense. Are his rhetorical strategies effective? What does he do to make you think he acted unselfishly, or how does he fail to convince you? Argue for a thesis in which you respond to these questions.

2. Write a review of Masaoka's book (based on this one excerpt) as you imagine the review would be written by either Minoru Yasui (p. 729) or Michi Nishiura Weglyn (below).

MICHI NISHIURA WEGLYN

From *Years of Infamy: The Untold Story of America's Concentration Camps* (1976)

Michiko Nishiura Weglyn (b. 1926) was born in California and was interned in the Gila Camp in Arizona as a teenager. After the war, she became a very successful theatrical costume designer. Weglyn once said that she was inspired to write *Years of Infamy,* even though she had no formal training as a historian, to refute a claim by Ramsey Clark, U.S. attorney general from 1967 to 1969, that there had never been any concentration camps in America. Although earlier historical work on the internment had been done, and although Weglyn's

Michi Nishiura Weglyn, *Years of Infamy: The Untold Story of America's Concentration Camps* (New York: William Morrow, 1976), 67–92.

In the notes, MNW = Michi Nishiura Weglyn, EDS. = Patricia Bizzell and Bruce Herzberg.

book shows some inaccuracies, her book was one of the first revisionist histories of the internment — one of the first to clearly call it an injustice and to attract public attention to that injustice. We reprint chapters 3 and 4.

CHAPTER 3: "SO THE ARMY COULD HANDLE THE JAPS"

Has the Gestapo come to America? Have we not risen in righteous anger at Hitler's mistreatment of the Jews? Then, is it not incongruous that citizen Americans of Japanese descent should be similarly mistreated and persecuted?
                                              — James M. Omura
                                              Testimony before Tolan Committee Hearings, February 1942

I

The wartime incarceration of Japanese Americans has been characterized by historian James J. Martin as "a breach of the Bill of Rights on a scale so large as to beggar the sum total of all such violations from the beginnings of the United States down to that time." It was this veritable descent to despotism which Francis Biddle, an eminent "practicing liberal," was obliged to defend as national policy in his position as FDR's wartime attorney general.

According to his former aide, James Rowe, Jr., Biddle's "only failure," and one that was to burden his soul to his dying day, was the part he reluctantly played in this mass repression through his failure to deal more firmly with the then august secretary of war and with his willful collegemate-turned-president, both of whom were of the opinion that the "Japanese problem" was strictly a military one — that Biddle and the Justice Department were not to intrude upon their sovereignty.

Though constitutional bounds had been flagrantly overstepped by the attorney general's office in its wholesale seizure of Issei suspects against whom there had been little or no evidence of wrongdoing, and despite the increasingly harsh security measures being imposed on Japanese residents under the prodding of the War Department, the wrath of West Coast pressure groups was relentlessly concentrated on Biddle for what they derided as "pussyfooting" — his unwillingness to negate the rights of citizens.

"A great many West Coast people distrust the Japanese [and] various special interests would welcome their removal from good farmland and the elimination of their competition," the attorney general wrote the president on February 17, 1942, to assert for the record what he plainly believed were racist and economic motivations behind all the public and political proevacuation hysterics. Biddle, moreover, made a last-ditch try at slowing down at least the large-scale, and hurried, removals which he suspected were under army consideration — over and beyond the stepped-up activities of his own department, then busily engaged in removing enemy aliens from around strategically important areas recommended by the military. Though pleading conciliatorily that "there is no dispute between the War, Navy and Justice Departments," the attorney general called the president's attention to the "legal limits" of his own department's authority and the fact that "under the Constitution, sixty thousand of these Japanese are American citizens."

Biddle then lashed out in severe criticism of journalists who, he felt, were "acting with dangerous irresponsibility" (he compared their inciting utterances to "shouting FIRE! in a crowded theater") in arousing sentiment for speedy arbitrary action on the ground that an enemy attack and concerted sabotage were imminent. "My last advice from the War Department is that there is no evidence of imminent attack and from the FBI that there is no evidence of planned sabotage,"[1] Biddle assured the president.

Had the attorney general vigorously lashed out against the obvious un-Americanism of singling out for especially cruel treatment a colored minority, the president, in turn, might conceivably have had to face up to his nobler libertarian instincts. But Biddle, like the president — though championing the rights of downtrodden minorities abroad — lacked the driving, down-reaching commitment against racism within America's own borders, and the opportunity to assert the very principles for which Americans were then fighting and dying was lost. "Only a great outcry of protest on the highest moral grounds would have stopped the drift toward evacuation," declares James MacGregor Burns in *Roosevelt: The Soldier of Freedom*, "and Biddle was neither temperamentally nor politically capable of it."

With sadness and regret, the attorney general was to recall in his postwar memoirs:

> American citizens of Japanese origin were not even handled like aliens of the other enemy nationalities — Germans and Italians — on a selective basis, but as untouchables, a group who could not be trusted and had to be shut up only because they were of Japanese descent. . . .
>
> Their constitutional rights were the same as those of the men who were responsible for the program: President Roosevelt, Secretary of War Stimson, and the Assistant Secretary of War, John J. McCloy . . . , Lieutenant General John L. DeWitt, commanding officer of the Pacific Coast area, and Colonel Karl Robin Bendetsen of the General Staff, who was brought into the provost marshal's office in Washington from a successful law practice on the West Coast, where a strong anti-Japanese prejudice prevailed.[2]

It was the West Coast–born, Stanford-educated Karl R. Bendetsen who catapulted himself into veritable immortality by coming up with the legally

[1]Memorandum, Francis Biddle to Roosevelt, February 17, 1942, OF 18, FDR Library. — MNW. Weglyn extensively documents the information in this excerpt. To avoid overburdening the pages with footnotes, we have reproduced only her footnotes citing sources quoted directly. — EDS.

[2]Francis Biddle, *In Brief Authority* (New York: Doubleday, 1962), 212–13. — MNW

— and constitutionally — airtight plan enabling the incarceration en masse of a citizen Nisei without too obvious an appearance of discrimination. Bendetsen's achievement was considerable in that it wrested the entire "Japanese problem" away from justice [department], enabling army advocates of drastic action to rid themselves of the irksome "constitutional conscience" represented by Biddle, with public opinion fully on their side.

The Bendetsen formula, which earned its architect an immediate promotion, later one of the nation's highest military decorations, was simple but sweepingly effective. It involved the following:

- the issuance of an Executive Order which would authorize the secretary of war to designate "military areas" from which all persons who did not have permission to enter and remain to be excluded as a "military necessity"
- the designation of military areas (as per General DeWitt)
- the immediate evacuation from these areas of all persons lacking licenses to reenter or remain.

The army stratagem, which makes no mention of the "Japanese" for whom it was intended, was to become the basis of the now famed Executive Order 9066, issued by the president on February 19, 1942, also under the authorship of Bendetsen. It enabled the military, in absence of martial law, to immediately circumvent the constitutional safeguards of over seventy thousand American citizens and to treat the Nisei like aliens. Although the order theoretically affected German and Italian nationals, more of whom lived in the restricted area than Japanese Americans, all considered suspect were given individual hearings and very few were interned.

By virtue of coming up with the adroit proposal, Bendetsen thereafter soared to instant national prominence. The thirty-five-year-old major, who had been promoted to lieutenant colonel on February 4, 1942, was tendered another promotion within a remarkable ten-day period: to the position of full colonel (on February 14), in order that he might personally supervise the execution of the presidential mandate.

"We will not under any threat, or in face of any danger, surrender the guarantees of liberty our forefathers framed for us in the Bill of Rights," the president had loftily proclaimed after the United States entry into the war. But that was before the grim days and weeks of spirit-shattering reverses in the Pacific War; before Bendetsen's remarkable blueprint made simple and expedient a procedure which would undoubtedly be a rousing morale booster for the public at large — a public then in desperate need to give vent to their frustrations, to lash out at the nearest, most visible target.

II

The decision for collective evacuation and internment was made on February 11, 1942, a veritable "Pearl Harbor" for the Nisei, many of whom had felt reasonably confident that those of greater wisdom and charity in

Washington would ultimately reject the regional clamor of bigots and self-serving greed interests. Even as the attorney general was putting the finishing touches to a *Collier's* article eulogizing the administration's determination that it would be "wiser and more humane to hold only those who were dangerous to our safety, or who might become so . . . America is too big and generous, too open of heart and hand, to allow petty persecutions," other forces were at work. Biddle's personal recollection of events, as recorded in his memoirs, also points to the eleventh of February as the day of betrayal for the Nisei and Issei — the day when the president figuratively tossed the Munson certification of loyalty into the trash heap:[3]

> Apparently the War Department's course of action had been tentatively charted by Mr. McCloy and Colonel Bendetsen in the first ten days of February. General DeWitt's final recommendation to evacuate was completed on February 13, and forwarded to Washington with a covering letter the next day. Mr. Stimson and Mr. McCloy did not, however, wait for this report, which contained the "finding" on which their "military necessity" argument to the president was based, but obtained their authority before the recommendation was received. On February 11 the president told the War Department to prepare a plan for wholesale evacuation, specifically including citizens. . . . After the conference the assistant secretary reported to Bendetsen: "We have *carte blanche* to do what we want to as far as the president is concerned."[4]

The wartime diary of Secretary of War Stimson provides additional insight into the tenor of high-level thinking at that critical moment for the Nisei in America. When the question of evacuating American citizens was forthrightly put to the president (Stimson diary entry for February 11), he "fortunately found that he [the president] was very vigorous about it."

In this amazingly private conduct of affairs on the part of the secretary of war and the president, not only Biddle but also Congress had been bypassed. The impatient exclusion demands of the West Coast congressional delegation calling for the "immediate evacuation of all persons of Japanese lineage" thus landed on the president's desk two days *after* such a plan had already been set in motion.

---

[3]Curtis B. Munson was a California businessman recruited to investigate the Nikkei for a secret information-gathering unit reporting directly to President Roosevelt. In 1941 Munson reported that the overwhelming majority of Nisei and Issei were completely loyal to the United States but that there might be a few who would be willing to commit acts of sabotage on behalf of the Imperial Japanese war effort. Weglyn interprets this report as a wholesale "certification of loyalty" and suggests that the internment might have been avoided if the report had not been suppressed and ignored. Other historians disagree, however; Roger Daniels argues that the Munson report was not in fact ignored and that Munson's warning of the potential for sabotage may have helped convince the president and his military advisers that internment was necessary. — EDS.

[4]Biddle, *In Brief Authority*, p. 218. After receiving carte blanche powers to proceed, Bendetsen had "prepared Franklin Roosevelt's executive order that . . . started the evacuation program," according to *Time* magazine, November 30, 1942. — MNW. A person who has "carte blanche" (a French phrase meaning "white ticket") has unrestricted authority. — EDS.

Once the attorney general had decided not to oppose the evacuation further, however, the drastic wartime forfeiture of constitutional principles was far less troubling to Biddle at the time than his postwar memoirs would indicate. Biddle capitulated without a murmur to the army grab of power for removing citizens as well as aliens and, in fact, had given the draft of Executive Order 9066 a quick once-over prior to its submission to the president. And on February 20 — the day after Executive Order 9066 had been promulgated — a memorandum reassuring the president and the military of their wartime powers and immunities was sent to the White House by Biddle. A covering letter explained: "I thought that you might have questions asked you with reference to the order at a press conference and that this memorandum would therefore, be convenient." It read:

> This authority gives very broad powers to the secretary of war and the military commanders. These powers are broad enough to permit them to exclude any particular individual from military areas. They could also evacuate groups of persons based on a reasonable classification. The order is not limited to aliens but includes citizens so that it can be exercised with respect to Japanese, irrespective of their citizenship.
>
> The decision of safety of the nation in time of war is necessarily for the military authorities. Authority over the movement of persons, whether citizens or noncitizens, may be exercised in time of war. . . .
>
> The president is authorized in acting under his general war powers without further legislation. The exercise of the power can meet the specific situation and, of course, cannot be considered as any punitive measure against any particular nationalities. It is rather a precautionary measure to protect the national safety. It is not based on any legal theory but on the facts [*sic*] that the unrestricted movement of certain racial classes, whether American citizens or aliens, in specified defense areas may lead to serious disturbances. These disturbances cannot be controlled by police protection and have the threat of injury to our war effort. A condition and not a theory confronts the nation.[5]

On the same day that Biddle informed the president of the sweeping extension of his war powers by virtue of Order 9066, which also passed on near-carte-blanche power to the military, Secretary of War Stimson designated General John L. DeWitt to be the military commander who would carry out the evacuation. On March 11, DeWitt, in turn, designated Colonel Karl Robin Bendetsen as Director of the Wartime Civil Control Administration (established as a "Civilian Affairs" branch of the Western Defense Command), to supervise the actual removal and roundup of the evacuees under the terms of Executive Order 9066.

Though there was little likelihood of opposition to the grim surgical removal of a minority about to be precipitated, army lawyers took special care to obtain the implied sanction of Congress before issuing the exclusion orders. Public Law No. 503 (77th Congress), which made it a federal offense to violate any and all restrictions issued by a military commander

[5]Memorandum, Francis Biddle to Roosevelt, February 20, 1942, OF 4805, FDR Library. — MNW

in a "military area" (under authority of Executive Order 9066), and which provided for enforcement in the federal courts, passed both houses of Congress on March 19 by unanimous voice vote. It was signed into law by the president on March 21, 1942.[6]

The only lawmaker in Congress to take issue with the legislation intended to ratify and give legal clout to Executive Order 9066 was Senator Robert Taft of Ohio. Taft objected specifically to the wording of the measure, calling it "probably the sloppiest criminal law I have ever read or seen anywhere." It was not that Taft opposed the intent of the legislation: "I do not want to object, because I understand the pressing character of this kind of legislation for the Pacific Coast today." But with apparent concern that the penal sanctions provided for could perversely affect persons other than those for whom it was intended, Taft recommended that the measure be "redrafted in some kind of legal form, instead of in the form of a military order."[7]

Many lawmakers may have been led to believe that the anticipated army restrictions and removals, and the penalties provided under Public Law No. 503, would affect only noncitizens since Senator Robert Reynolds, who had been requested by Stimson to introduce the bill in the Senate, had done so describing the emergency measure "to deal with the peril" as one dealing "primarily with the activities of aliens and alien enemies." Only once did the Senator mention that the act could apply to citizens.

In the House, Congressman Robert F. Rich asked if military zones were plainly marked "so that citizens of this country cannot get into them without their knowledge and then be penalized." Congressman Andrew J. May, who had introduced the measure in the House, replied that "citizens of this country will never be questioned about them, as a matter of fact. This is intended for a particular situation about which the gentleman knows." (All relocation centers were in time designated as "military areas.")

Though Public Law 503 passed both houses overwhelmingly, Congress had not gone so far as to expressly authorize the impending mass exclusion; but in the failure of the nation's lawmakers to repudiate, even question, the clearly totalitarian aspects of a law which gave unbridled "teeth" to the military, Congress had unwittingly placed itself in the role of accomplice.

III

That Roosevelt himself had been motivated by racial bias in authorizing the evacuation is a fact inadvertently laid bare in a letter left by the troubled attorney general, who had never ceased to entertain the gravest doubts about the legality of this highly authoritarian move on the part of the president.

---

[6]This is the law Minoru Yasui violated in an attempt to test the constitutionality of the discriminatory treatment of the Nikkei; see Yasui's account on page 729. — EDS.

[7]*Congressional Record*, vol. 88, part 2 (1942), 2726. Public Law 503 provided a penalty of $5,000 or one year's imprisonment, or both, for individuals disobeying military orders "in any military area or military zone . . . it if appears that he knew or should have known of the existence and extent of the restrictions or order. . . ." — MNW

The circumstance which prompted Biddle's letter was the sharply intensified conflict between Justice and the War Department — one which had had its origin in the "Japanese problem," once the exclusive province of justice. Biddle, who at the time of the evacuation had been new to the cabinet, was now stubbornly standing his ground, unwilling to bow to the whims of the secretary of war, of whom he had once stood in awe.

Following the West Coast evacuation, Biddle's disinclination to prosecute a number of cases involving Germans and Italians against whom exclusion orders had been issued by military commanders of the Eastern, Western, and Southern commands had become exceedingly irksome to the military; and on March 31, 1943, Secretary of War Stimson importuned the president:

> The attorney general should not be permitted to thwart the military commanders. . . . I request that you direct the attorney general to enforce these orders in accordance with the provisions of Public Law 503. . . .[8]

Biddle's acid response to this continued army "pushing" is singularly revealing. On April 17, he wrote the president:

> I have your memorandum of April 7th, suggesting that I talk to the secretary of war about these cases. I shall, of course, be glad to do so, and so informed him sometime ago. Conferences have already been going on for several months; and I have talked personally to McCloy (and others) for several hours.
>
> The secretary's letter [Stimson to FDR] misses the points at issue, which are:
>
> 1. Whatever the military do, as attorney general I should decide what criminal cases to bring and what not to bring. *I shall not institute criminal proceedings on exclusion orders which seem to me unconstitutional.*
> 2. You signed the original Executive Order permitting the exclusions *so the army could handle the Japs. It was never intended to apply to Italians and Germans.* Your order was based on "protection against espionage and sabotage." There is absolutely no evidence in the case of ADRIANO, who has been a leading citizen of San Francisco for thirty years, that he ever had anything to do either with espionage or sabotage. He was merely pro-Mussolini before the war. He is harmless, and I understand is now living in the country outside of San Francisco.
> 3. KRAUS was connected before Pearl Harbor with German propaganda in this country. She turned state's evidence. The order of exclusion is so broad that I am of the opinion the courts would not sustain it. As I have said before to you, *such a decision might well throw doubt* on your powers as Commander in Chief. . . .[9] [Italics Weglyn's]

[8]Memorandum, Henry Stimson to Roosevelt, March 31, 1943, OF 10 1943 (Justice), FDR Library. — MNW

[9]Memorandum, Francis Biddle to Roosevelt, April 17, 1943, OF 10 1943 (Justice), FDR Library. — MNW

In short, Roosevelt's Executive Order 9066 — and the exclusion-internment program which grew out of it — represented nothing less than a rash, deliberate violation of the Constitution by the president himself, the attorney general's letter suggesting that racism more than national security had motivated the decision.

As it turned out, decisions handed down by the lower courts (in cases involving Caucasians who refused to obey exclusion orders) varied widely. In one suit brought by Kenneth Alexander, an excludee from the Los Angeles area, the Ninth District Court of Appeals went on to declare on March 10, 1944, that orders excluding citizens from the military area were not orders legally but merely notices, that they "commanded nothing and prohibited nothing."[10] Biddle had had good reason to be emphatic in his recommendation to the president (memo of April 17) that no more prosecutory action be taken — until the nation's highest tribunal pass judgment on the "power to exclude the Japanese."

Yet, in what has been referred to as "the most suppressive opinion in the history of the Court," the Supreme Court of the United States was to go on in a case involving a Nisei who refused to submit to evacuation (*Korematsu v. U.S.* 323 U.S. 214 [1944]) to uphold the validity and constitutionality of such spurious orders against the strong dissenting opinions of three justices: Owen J. Roberts, Robert H. Jackson, and Frank Murphy. Justice Roberts saw through the Bendetsen-devised strategy aimed only at those of Japanese ancestry as "a cleverly designed trap to accomplish the real purpose of military authority, which was to lock him [Korematsu] in a concentration camp." Justice Jackson: ". . . we may as well say that any military order will be constitutional and be done with it." Justice Murphy: "Being an obvious racial discrimination, the order deprives all those within its scope of equal protection of the laws as guaranteed by the Fifth Amendment."

Speaking for the majority, Justice Hugo Black was to reject as nonsense the charges of race prejudice: "Our task would be simple, our duty clear, were this a case involving the imprisonment of a loyal citizen in a concentration camp because of racial prejudice. . . . To cast this case into outlines of racial prejudice, without reference to the real military dangers which were present, merely confuses the issue."

Clearly, the lofty judiciary, like Congress, was totally unaware of the Munson certification of loyalty then in careful wartime impoundment. By the High Court's majority decision (6–3) vindicating the mass forcible removals on the basis of a fictitious military necessity, the Supreme Court, the Congress, and the president had coalesced as "accomplices" in one of history's most remarkable legalizations of official illegality.

"Those who now most oppose our methods will ultimately adopt them." Hitler had given this prophetic warning. In the Supreme Court's sanctification of this "legalization of racism," as bluntly charged by Justice Murphy in his *Korematsu* dissent, there was chilling irony. It was a decision to be cited repeatedly in defense of Nazi war criminals at the Nuremberg Tribunal.

[10]*Pacific Citizen,* March 18, 1944. — MNW

CHAPTER 4: OUTCASTS

> The watch-tower
> Stands where
> Escape is impossible.
> — *Senryu,* by Tule Lake inmate

I

Repression was applied, one small step at a time. First came the roundup of suspect enemy aliens; the freezing of bank accounts, the seizure of contraband, the drastic limitation on travel, curfew, and other restrictive measures of increasing severity. Executive Order 9066, of February 19, 1942, then authorized the establishment of military areas and the exclusion therefrom of "any or all persons." A March 2 army proclamation finally made clear that not only aliens but also the American-born of Japanese ancestry would be affected, the restricted military areas defined as the western halves of the Pacific Coast states, including the southern half of Arizona. Then in quick succession came the posters on telephone poles carrying the same terse notice: . . . ALL PERSONS OF JAPANESE ANCESTRY, BOTH ALIEN AND NONALIEN, WILL BE EVACUATED FROM THE ABOVE DESIGNATED AREA BY 12:00 O'CLOCK NOON. . . .

The army had not anticipated some of the resulting confusions. Among them: What was meant by "all Japanese persons"? Were these to include people of mixed blood, some of them mere infants abandoned in orphanages?

Taken aback by the Third Reich harshness of the commandant presiding over the uprooting was the late Father Hugh T. Lavery of the Catholic Maryknoll Center in Los Angeles:

> Colonel Bendetsen showed himself to be a little Hitler. I mentioned that we had an orphanage with children of Japanese ancestry, and that some of these children were half Japanese, others one-fourth or less. I asked which children should we send. . . . Bendetsen said: "I am determined that if they have one drop of Japanese blood in them, they must go to camp."[11]

Upon registration at one of the sixty-four Civil Control stations established near centers of Japanese American concentration, individuals and families were turned overnight into numbers on tags. Instructions laid down by the army were explicit and absolute: On an appointed time and date, evacuees were to assemble themselves voluntarily for internment with bedrolls and baggage, no more than could be carried by hand, properly tagged. A week to ten days was usually given for winding up their businesses.

[11] Letter, Father Hugh T. Lavery to President Harry S. Truman (sent in protest previous to Bendetsen's confirmation as under secretary of army in 1949), *Pacific Citizen,* September 24, 1949. — MNW

The suddenness of the removal edict, and bureaucratic inertia in making provisions for the sale or safeguarding of property, precipitated a condition of utter chaos as evacuees sought frantically to dispose of their life accumulations in any way they knew how in hopes of salvaging what cash they could. Few dared to take advantage of governmental storage facilities offered "at the sole risk" of the evacuees. Widespread suspicion and mistrust, moreover, hampered the efforts of government agents who offered assistance in the transfer of land into Caucasian hands.

In the few days allowed the evacuees before their eviction, bargain hunters and junk dealers descended in hordes. The frightened and confused became easy prey to swindlers who threatened to "arrange" for the confiscation of their property if they would not agree to a forced sale at the pittance offered.

Some permitted hopefully trustworthy white friends to move into their homes as overseers — often rent-free — or to take over the care of their land, sometimes with a power of attorney mandate. There were many who turned over possessions for storage in local Japanese temples and churches, others who simply boarded them up in garages or vacant sheds belonging to kindly disposed neighbors. But pilfering and vandalism often began before they were hardly out of their homes. A postwar survey was to reveal that 80 percent of goods privately stored were "rifled, stolen, or sold during absence."

For the majority of the Issei who had helped to make the California desert bloom, the rewards of a lifetime of zealous perseverance evaporated within a frenzied fortnight.

II

True to their cultural imperative of unquestioning obedience, the evacuees turned themselves in at the appointed time and place with such orderliness as to astound the army. Only if one were tubercular, critically ill in the hospital, or hopelessly mad and institutionalized was one exempt from the roundup.

A solitary Nisei was found in hiding and near starvation three weeks later. A page-one story in the *San Francisco News* of June 1, 1942, declared: "No Food since May 9 — Jap Found Hiding in Cellar."

Two Issei had chosen suicide to being evacuated. One had hanged himself because of a condition of uncontrollable trembling which he knew caused people to draw away from him. According to the statements of a friend, fear that he would bring shame and disgrace to his attractive sixteen-year-old daughter had driven him to the desperate act.

To explain his actions, he left a concise note. . . . In it he explained to the daughter why he had done such a thing, and he asked her to forgive him . . . that if he went to camp, his beloved daughter would be ridiculed by thoughtless children and made miserable for something that was not her fault. He knew, he said, that she loved him, and that she wouldn't mind, but the mothers and fathers of the other children perhaps would not let her be friends with them, on account of her father. Her chances of marriage, in such a confined place, would be almost hopeless if his condition were generally known. In everything, he was thinking of her first and foremost. . . . He couldn't give her material things, he said, but maybe this last action of his would, in some way, help her achieve his dreams for her.

This is just one personal tragedy in many, but that was the state of mind of many people during those trying days of evacuation . . . the hopelessness of these people was astounding. To them their world had come to an end, and they really felt they had nothing more to live for.[12]

Another Issei, Hideo Murata of Pismo Beach, was found with a bullet through his head, an Honorary Citizenship Certificate grasped in his hand. The testimonial, which had been bestowed on Murata at an Independence Day celebration the year before, read in part:

Monterey County presents this testimony of heartfelt gratitude, of honor and respect for your loyal and splendid service to the country in the Great World War. Our flag was assaulted and you gallantly took up its defense.[13]

Otherwise, the evacuation proceeded "without mischance, with minimum hardship, and almost without incident," according to its coordinator, Colonel Karl Bendetsen. It had begun with the issuing, on March 24, of Exclusion Order No. 1 calling for the March 30 evacuation of Bainbridge Island near Seattle, Washington — about which an editorial writer of a Seattle paper was moved to comment:

If anything ever illustrated the repute of these United States as a melting pot of diverse races, it was the recent evacuation of Japanese residents, American and foreign-born, from the pleasant countryside of Bainbridge Island. . . . The Japanese departed their homes cheerfully, knowing full well, most of them, that the measures was [sic] designed to help preserve the precious, kindly camaraderie among divergent races which is one of this country's great contributions to humanity.[14]

From the various evacuation depots, evacuees were transported by army-commandeered trains or buses to assigned "reception centers," one of the several army euphemisms for the initial camps of detention. Officially referred to as "assembly centers," twelve of these temporary detention compounds had been established within the state of California alone. Only one was located in the state of Oregon — at the Portland Livestock Pavilion. In the neighboring state of Washington, the Puyallup Assembly

---

[12]"Suicide during Evacuation," Manzanar Community Analysis Report No. 104, December 14, 1943, RG 210, National Archives. — MNW

[13]Carey McWilliams, *Prejudice: Japanese Americans: Symbol of Racial Intolerance* (Boston: Little, Brown, 1944), 133. — MNW

[14]*Seattle Times*, December 7, 1969. — MNW

Center — or "Camp Harmony" — was the only camp set up for its Japanese American population. The smallest of all the assembly centers was the one erected in Mayer, Arizona, which accommodated 260 evacuees.

All centers (except the Arizona-based one) were still within the forbidden military zone (Zone A) and had been improvised within a remarkable twenty-eight-day period with such dispatch that the Japanese community had no idea of the concentrated activity taking place, some of it in their own backyards. Assurance was given by way of propaganda channels that these reception and assembly centers were by no means concentration camps and that the inmates were not prisoners. But the sense of being debased human beings was inescapable for a people being guarded night and day by soldiers up in guard towers. As one Nisei put it: "This evacuation did not seem too unfair until we got right to the camp and were met by soldiers with guns and bayonets. Then I almost started screaming."

The assembly centers were under continual close supervision from both the Presidio[15] and the War Department, but were administered by a WPA staff at a per diem cost per evacuee which varied from twenty-five cents in the Salinas Center to seventy-three cents at the Mayer Assembly Center. From the word "go," speed and economy had been overriding factors in the construction of these camps, so building them on racetracks, fairgrounds, and livestock pavilions had substantially minimized the need for establishing electrical, water, and sewage systems. At the same time, stadiums, livestock stalls, and stables provided instant — though odoriferous — housing for thousands.

The shortage of critical building material also had much to do with the crudeness of the hastily thrown-up shacks which made up the balance of the housing. Obvious labor- and lumber-saving efforts at the Puyallup Assembly Center had resulted in near-windowless shacks resembling chicken coops, they had been built so low.

Generally, a bare room comprised a "family apartment," provided only with cots, blankets, and mattresses (often straw-filled sacks). The apartment's only fixture was a hanging light bulb. Each family unit was separated from the adjoining one by a thin dividing partition which, "for ventilation purpose," only went partway up.

Under a declared policy of the "preservation of the family unit," camp authorities tried to keep parents, grandparents, and the children together — all of them packed together, wherever possible, in a single room. In camps where housing facilities fell drastically short of the intake, couples with few children (or none at all) were often forced to double up with other couples.

I was rather disappointed at the barracks which we evacuees were to live in. I thought at least each individual family would be assigned to a separate apart-

---

[15]The Presidio was the building housing U.S. military headquarters in San Francisco. — EDS.

ment. Instead, two or three families were crowded into a six beam apartment, offering no privacy. It didn't matter so much with the bachelors or the single girls if they slept in quarters together. But when two or three families were placed in one apartment to make the quota for the barrack, it was terrible.[16]

At the Tanforan (Race Track) Assembly Center, the lower grandstand area was converted into a mammoth dormitory which housed four hundred bachelors, who, according to artist Mine Okubo, then documenting her camp experiences, "slept and snored, dressed and undressed, in one continuous performance."

Evacuees ate communally, showered communally, defecated communally. Again with an eye toward economy, no partitions had been built between toilets — a situation which everywhere gave rise to camp-wide cases of constipation. Protests from Caucasian church groups led, in time, to the building of partial dividing walls, but doors were never installed. Equally abhorred by the Issei, for whom scalding baths were a nightly fatigue-relieving ritual, were the Western-style showers, from which they usually walked away unsatisfied and shivering, for the hot water supply was never dependable.

In interior California camps, the hot summer sun beating down on paper-thin roofs turned living quarters into sizzling ovens, sometimes causing the floors to melt. Alan Taniguchi, whose family was assigned to a converted horse stable, recently recalled "falling on the cot and going to sleep and finding myself sleeping on the floor — the legs of the cot had penetrated the asphalt topping and sunk. The bed frame had ended up resting on the floor."

Notwithstanding concerned efforts of humanitarian groups, the Public Health Service could not be moved to condemn the stables as unfit for human habitation though the stench became oppressive in the summer heat, especially in stables which had been merely scraped out and no floors put in. At the largest of the assembly centers, the Santa Anita Race Track outside of Los Angeles, then housing over eighteen thousand evacuees, hospital records show that 75 percent of the illnesses came from the horse stalls.

Insight into conditions prevailing at Tanforan, another well-known racetrack (located south of San Francisco in San Bruno), is provided by hospital notes recorded during the early days of the center intake:

> Pregnancy cases — Dr. Fujita says there are many of them but she has had no time to contact them or get them registered for care. . . .
> Many cases of German measles are coming into camp as new evacuees arrive — It is almost uncontrollable. Doctor said she asked for an isolation

---

[16]A Heart Mountain report also noted the gross overcrowding: "The breakdown of persons assigned to units showed wide discrepancies; to relate an extreme case, the same size unit is being quartered by from one to thirteen persons. It is noted that there was leniency in housing families at first; as the camp began to fill, overcrowded assignments began." Heart Mountain Reports Division, May 1943, Heart Mountain Documents, Box 50, RG 210, National Archives. — MNW

building but none was given. Dr. Harrison of U.S. Public Health Service told the doctor, "Well, they all have to get measles some time so let them get it."

Morale: Is high so far among young people but not among older ones. Older people who have poor memories, etc., get up at night and try to get out — Doctor says she has to bandage and sew up heads in the mornings of the old people who try to get thru the gates and have been struck on head by soldiers.[17]

During the first ten days of Tanforan, only one woman doctor attended the needs of thousands. Equipment and medicine were in short supply, and newborn babies slept in cardboard cartons. The report noted inadequacies in the mess hall diet:

Food No milk for any one over 5 years of age
Had eggs only once (1 egg each) in first ten days
No meat at all until 12th day when very small portions were served
NO BUTTER AT ALL
There is both white and brown bread served with meals
Coffee for breakfast, cocoa made with water completely is served for lunch, tea for dinner . . .
Anyone doing heavy or outdoor work states they are not getting nearly enough to eat and are hungry all the time. This includes the doctor . . .

In the early days of the army-controlled assembly centers, camp fare consisted largely of canned goods: hash, pork and beans, canned weiners, beans of infinite variety. Conspicuous by their absence were the fresh fruits and vegetables which the Issei had once raised in succulent profusion. Following the mass dislocation of farm specialists, prices had skyrocketed.

At the Santa Anita Assembly Center, some eight hundred Nisei who had patriotically volunteered to work on the army's camouflage net-making project suddenly announced a sit-down strike, complaining, among other things, of weakness from an insufficiency of food. Hunger drove restless adolescents into invading neighboring mess halls, eventually bringing about the wearing of regulatory badges at mealtime. A teenager chronicled his personal escapades:

One day I and some friends went to messhall One and saw on a table reserved for doctors and nurses a lot of lettuce and tomatoes, fresh. We just went wild and grabbed at it like animals. When it gets down here [the stomach] they can't get it back. It was the best treat I ever had. . . . One day we went to messhall Two and they had three kinds of beans with bread for lunch.[18]

Mess halls in most of these centers served thousands. One thus learned to eat rapidly in deference to the multitude waiting patiently in lines which

[17]"Tanforan Hospital Report," May 18, 1942, University Research Library, UCLA. There is one recorded case of an evacuee who did manage to "get out." According to the *San Francisco News* of May 13, 1942, a twenty-one-year-old Nisei, Clarence Sadamune, whose two brothers were then in the army, escaped from Tanforan and then attempted suicide. — MNW

[18]Undated document, University Research Library, UCLA. — MNW

stretched endlessly. With little else to look forward to, food assumed a place of supreme importance for the young and old, and the queuing up which began well before the meal hour turned into an accepted ritual of camp life. In the driving rain and mud, in whipping sandstorms and under the blistering midday sun, the line leading to food was always doggedly held. Observed a Nisei:

> In a camp, it can be said that food, above all things, is the center and the pleasure of life. It's natural to want to eat something good. I cannot help thinking about the old men standing with plates in their hands. Residents in America for forty or fifty years, they pursued gigantic dreams and crossed an expansive ocean to America to live. The soil they tilled was a mother to them, and their life was regulated by the sun. They were people who had worked with all they had, until on their foreheads wave-like furrows were harrowed. Every time I see these oldsters with resigned, peaceful expressions meekly eating what is offered them, I feel my eyes become warm.[19]

III

Life behind these bleak detention pens, however, was not all deprivation and Dostoevskian gloom. The Issei who had relentlessly driven themselves without thought of self were now enjoying their first real vacation. If losses had been heart-rending, there were others who had suffered incalculably more. There was consolation in misery being mutually shared; there was the balm of newfound friendship. Mothers and grandmothers inured to dawn-to-dusk drudgery were, all of a sudden, ladies of leisure, no longer confronted by the day-to-day struggle for survival. For many, there was an all-pervasive feeling of relief in not being continually rebuffed and humiliated by the larger society, in suddenly feeling equal — if only to one another.

> In my heart I secretly welcomed the evacuation because it was a total escape from the world I knew. Even when the men took me away to the tar-papered barracks I felt for the first time in my life a complete sense of relief. The struggle against a life which seemed so futile and desperate was ended.[20]

Before long, dainty patches of flowers broke the virgin sod. Serenely tasteful Japanese-style rock gardens began to transform cheerless barrack fronts under the loving ministration of earnest ubiquitous landscape artists. Needed articles of furniture were ingeniously handcrafted, and drab interiors underwent colorful "Sears Roebuck" transformations. One saw everywhere a remarkable yearning for beauty and neatness assert itself even in temporary refuge.

A strong sense of community was also evidenced among a people to whom indolence was foreign. However little the remuneration ("salaries," when they finally came through, amounted to around five cents an hour),

---

[19]From "Wartime Diary," by Hatsuye Egami, published in *All Aboard* (Topaz), spring edition, 1944. — MNW

[20]Paul Jacobs, Saul Landau, and Eve Pell, *To Serve the Devil*, vol. 2 (New York: Random House, 1971), 185. — MNW

many volunteered their services as recreational directors, doctors, dentists, mess hall workers, garbage collectors, stenographers, clerks, block wardens, sign painters, reporters, and sketchers on the camp newsletter. Informal grade school classes were organized so youngsters would not be entirely deprived of an education; hobby groups were begun for adults. But meetings, classes, or lectures could not be conducted in the Japanese language (unless by a Caucasian), and all books written in Japanese, except religious ones, were confiscated.

In this caged-in government-made ghetto without privacy or permanence, the adolescent Nisei also experienced their first exhilarating sense of release — from the severe parental restraint placed upon them. Until their camp experience, such phenomena as youth gangs and social workers, for example, were virtually unheard of in Japanese communities. In the free-and-easy contacts now available to the army of teenagers involved, the carefully inculcated discipline, the traditional solidarity of the Japanese family and its extremely rigorous moral code all underwent a steady weakening.

IV

While order was gradually being established in the assembly centers, work crews under the supervision of army engineers were toiling at a feverish pace to meet the near-impossible governmental deadline on relocation camps in the far interior. While most of these sprawling encampments were located on hot desert acres or on drought-parched flatlands, two of the relocation projects (Rohwer and Jerome) were taking shape on swampland areas in distant Arkansas.

Again, with scant regard for the elderly in fragile health, rough-hewn wooden barracks — the flimsy "theater-of-operations" kind meant for the temporary housing of robust fighting men — had been speedily hammered together, providing only the minimum protection from the elements. Though lined on the inside with plasterboard and almost totally wrapped with an overlay of black tar paper, they afforded far from adequate protection against the icy wintry blast that swept through the warped floor boards in such northerly centers of relocation as Heart Mountain, Minidoka, Topaz, and Tule Lake, where the mercury dipped, on occasion, to a numbing minus 30 degrees in the winter.

A degree of uniformity existed in the physical makeup of all the centers. A bare room measuring 20 feet by 24 feet was again referred to as a "family apartment"; each accommodated a family of five to eight members; barrack end-rooms measuring 16 feet by 20 feet were set aside for smaller families. A barrack was made up of four to six such family units. Twelve to fourteen barracks, in turn, comprised a community grouping referred to as a "block." Each block housed from 250 to 300 residents and had its own mess hall, laundry room, latrines, and recreation hall.

The construction "is so very cheap that, frankly, if it stands up for the duration we are going to be lucky," testified Milton Eisenhower before a

Senate appropriations committee, noting that the Arizona camps were in areas which could be "as high as 130 degrees in summertime." On March 18, 1942 (the same day that the War Relocation Authority was established by Executive Order 9102), the youngest brother of the famous wartime general had been appointed by the president to become the first national director of the WRA, a nonmilitary agency.

Mindful that evacuees were capable of effecting soil improvements which would turn into postwar public assets, hitherto worthless parcels of real estate were purposely chosen for the WRA campsites — an idea which had been pushed with vigorous persistence by one Thomas D. Campbell, a name lost to history despite the considerable impetus and direction he appears to have given the evolving program at the time. Campbell, an agricultural engineer and top expert on available private and federally owned farm lands, saw in "the emergency" a tremendous opportunity for the wartime exploitation of Japanese American manpower and their farming wizardry. His ambitious, wide-ranging proposals for an expeditious solution to a "national problem" had momentarily caught the imagination of War Department officials, then in urgent need of such expertise. Campbell, in fact, had called for the colonization of the raw, unexploited Indian land which would later become the site of Poston.

In a recent letter to the author, then Assistant War Secretary John J. McCloy commented: "I remember that Tom Campbell had a very provocative, energetic mind and I was disposed to take his ideas seriously."[21] Campbell believed that an "army officer of rank must be in full charge." And that the first order of business was to gather up the West Coast minority in army-established concentration camps with an eye to "the big movement" later: i.e., seeing to their orderly transfer, with the cooperation of other governmental agencies, to potentially self-supporting federal projects involving such activities as food production, land subjugation, soil conservation, irrigation, road building, etc., which he believed would be less costly than prison camps.

Campbell cautioned against having anyone of Japanese extraction left "near any factory, dock, warehouse, public utility, railroad, bridge, or reservoir," and suggested that the "safest place for these people is in that part of the United States west of the Mississippi and east of the Rocky Mountains."[22] He envisioned the seasonal use of internees as migratory harvesters in sugar beets, cotton, and perishable crops ("beet growers alone can use twenty-five thousand men"), utilizing CCC camps[23] as way stations or by the utilization of "trailers which can be moved from place to place." In his memorandum of February 25, 1942, to McCloy, Campbell called for a meeting of the governors "of all Western States."

---

[21] Letter, John J. McCloy to author, January 6, 1975. — MNW

[22] Memorandum, Thomas D. Campbell to McCloy, February 25, 1942, OF 133, FDR Library. — MNW

[23] CCC camps were rustic campsites set up to house workers in the Civilian Conservation Corps, a Depression-era government organization designed to provide jobs for some of the many unemployed, who performed tasks such as building trails and shelters in national parks. — EDS.

On March 11, Campbell met with President Roosevelt over dinner. A follow-up letter sent the following day to the president stressed once more:

> There are many and various projects between the Mississippi Valley and the Rocky Mountains, publicly and privately owned which have been abandoned or are in receivership, in poor financial condition, or partially used. . . .
> The various governors, who are opposing the movement, can be shown that, in addition to being a military necessity, it can become an asset. Land in Southern California has its high value today, to a great extent, as a result of the ability and industry of the Japanese. . . . [24]

Campbell's paranoiac misconception of the minority was typical of prevailing racial attitudes:

> We probably can place the men in camps or at gainful jobs, but how about the wives and children? It is better for us to err on the safe side and place many foreigners in camps, some of which foreigners may be loyal, than to be less careful and let just one remain free who might do great damage.[25]

Though Milton Eisenhower (whose advice and expertise as land use coordinator with the Department of Agriculture was then also being sought) ended up being tapped for the unprecedented job which Campbell had described to the president as one in which "we can write a new chapter in the care and utilization of aliens and war prisoners," some of Thomas D. Campbell's proposals had been passed on to Eisenhower, for McCloy had been roundly impressed: "I think some of the ideas are excellent, and perhaps Campbell himself could be useful in this connection, but since the president has already appointed Mr. Eisenhower, who seems to me to be an excellent man, I think that Mr. Campbell could only be useful if Mr. Eisenhower desired his services."[26] Campbell, who operated ninety-five thousand acres of Montana wheat and flax land, chose not to serve under Eisenhower and ended up in the Pentagon as a colonel in the Army Air Force.

Yet doubtlessly on some of the barren, unexploited acreage to which Campbell had early called attention, barbed-wire-ringed communities bearing the following names took shape during the spring and summer of 1942:

Poston Relocation Center (Arizona)
Gila Relocation Center (Arizona)
Jerome Relocation Center (Arkansas)
Rohwer Relocation Center (Arkansas)
Topaz Relocation Center (Utah)

[24]Letter, Thomas D. Campbell to Roosevelt, March 12, 1942. — MNW

[25]From memorandum, Thomas D. Campbell to McCloy, February 25, 1942. Campbell had sent along this memorandum (which he had earlier sent to McCloy) with his March 12 letter to the president. — MNW

[26]Memorandum, John J. McCloy to General Watson, March 22, 1942, OF 133, FDR Library. — MNW

Granada Relocation Center (Colorado)
Heart Mountain Relocation Center (Wyoming)
Minidoka Relocation Center (Idaho)
Tule Lake Relocation Center (California)
Manzanar Relocation Center (California)

The switch-over of the army-operated Owens Valley Reception Center (subsequently renamed "Manzanar") and the Colorado River Project (Poston) to WRA jurisdiction in July 1942 had resulted in ten "relocation centers" then in partial readiness for the mass deportation inland. Known only to high-level planners, at the time, this was to include the intake of around fifteen thousand from Hawaii "in family groups, from among the United States citizens of Japanese ancestry who may be considered as potentially dangerous to national security." There had been remarkably little agitation locally or on the mainland demanding such a move, and few people were aware of the one exception in this regard: the strong, steady proevacuation pressure emanating from the Western Defense Command. WRA National Director Dillon Myer would declare after the war: ". . . after the evacuation order was issued here on the mainland, he [Colonel Bendetsen] tried for weeks to get a large group of people evacuated from Hawaii with the idea, I am sure, of justifying their West Coast evacuation."[27]

V

Though under constant pressure from Washington to carry out the March 13, 1942, directive calling for wide-scale removal of Hawaii's Japanese community to U.S. mainland camps beginning with fifteen thousand to twenty thousand of the "most dangerous," the Hawaiian Department made it crystal-clear on July 1, 1942, that it "does not want to arbitrarily select fifteen thousand Japanese," and that the "present situation was highly satisfactory."[28] For months the severe lack of shipping and transportation had precluded the sending in of troops, munitions, and replacement labor believed necessary before the movement could begin. Considered essential also was the prior evacuation of twenty thousand wives and children of servicemen, for the possibility of a retaliatory enemy attack had to be considered.

What finally contravened to prevent removals on a massive scale were the legal difficulties which developed: ACLU[29] action had forced, at once, the return of thirteen citizens earlier shipped off to mainland internment camps. The legal setback portended annoying complications inherent "in

[27]From "Typescript of Unpublished Autobiography" of Dillon Myer (which is part of interviews conducted from 1968 to 1970), FDR Library. Hereafter cited as "Unpublished Autobiography." — MNW

[28]"Memorandum for Record." See Article 3: Radio No. 1182 CM IN 0177 (7/1/42), ASW 014.311 Hawaii, RG 107, National Archives. — MNW

[29]The ACLU is the American Civil Liberties Union, a nonprofit organization dedicated to preserving the freedoms outlined in the Bill of Rights (the first ten amendments to the United States Constitution). Although the national headquarters of the ACLU endorsed the internment, some local offices, as here, took action on behalf of internees. — EDS.

placing American citizens, even of Japanese ancestry, in concentration camps"; and it led to a total recision of the March directive, which had called for the transfer to mainland camps of 100,000 Japanese Americans, both citizens and aliens.

The new Chiefs of Staff directive of July 15, 1942 (approved by the president on July 17), called for a vastly reduced withdrawal of no more than fifteen thousand individuals considered "potentially dangerous to national security." The directive specified that the evacuees be "in family groups, from among the United States citizens of Japanese ancestry" and that they were being sent to the mainland "for resettlement rather than internment." Individuals who constituted "a source of danger to our national security" — if citizens — were to be interned locally (under martial law) rather than be removed to mainland camps since "it has been found that this procedure is not feasible as through application for a writ of habeas corpus any United States citizen can obtain release from custody."[30]

But once again the authorized removal, still pressingly demanded by Secretary of Navy Knox and the president, never got off the ground. The number targeted for transplantation in mainland relocation centers dwindled precipitously — 15,000 to 5,000, then to 1,500 — with the factor of "dangerousness" eventually getting lost in the shuffle. To designate anyone as even *potentially* dangerous had become exceedingly difficult for the team of three G-2 officers responsible for selecting the individuals and families to be removed, as others in the island population were hard put to match the exemplary loyalty demonstration of the Hawaiian Japanese.

The hard-line Knox-FDR team nevertheless kept up its evacuation demands far into 1942 despite the near-total lack of political and economic pressure on the local level calling for such a move, and in dynamic opposition to recommendations of Hawaiian authorities who preferred to "treat the Japanese in Hawaii as citizens of an occupied country."[31] Following an on-the-spot assessment, even Secretary McCloy joined local authorities in discouraging the called-for transplantation which could topple the island economy if undertaken without sending in an equivalent labor force of comparable skill and experience. Yet mindful of existing pressures, McCloy had put it squarely to General Emmons [military governor of Hawaii] that "he had better work out some alternative evacuation plan . . . to satisfy the president and Mr. Knox."[32]

The military governor subsequently organized a "voluntary evacuation" for which a total of 1,037 evacuees were netted — 912 of them citizens. Included in the group were Nisei suspects then being held in the Sand Island Concentration Camp, along with family members "persuaded" into accompanying them. (A conference permitted between internee and wife

---

[30]Memorandum, Ernest J. King (Commander in Chief, U.S. Fleet) and George C. Marshall to Roosevelt, July 15, 1942, PSF (S) FDR Library. — MNW

[31]Stetson, Conn, Rose C. Engelman, and Byron Fairchild, *The United States Army in World War II: The Western Hemisphere: Guarding the United States and Its Outposts* (Washington: Government Printing Office, 1964), 211. — MNW

[32]Ibid., 212. — MNW

usually settled the matter.) Also fetched up in the net of "voluntary" exiles — generally individuals considered nonproductive and "a drain on the economy" — were wives and children of alien husbands and fathers who had been sent earlier to the mainland for internment (the "welfare group").33

Included, too, were individuals the island authorities considered "potentially dangerous" in Hawaii but harmless on the mainland: alien and citizen fishermen with knowledge of the waters; persons who had requested repatriation; a number of Kibei and released detainees under surveillance, all of whom (including accompanying family members) were considered to be harmless, but a group the military preferred not to have at large. As Colonel Fielding of G-2, Hawaiian Department, explained to General DeWitt and his aide over the trans-Pacific hotline, "the evacuation is merely a matter of relieving pressure. . . . They really aren't dangerous and not bad at all."34

On the departure of the Hawaiian contingent, beginning in November 1942, Governor Emmons appealed to the public: "No stigma or suspicion should be attached to the individual."

Contrary to the mythology of decent and admirably restrained treatment of the Hawaiian Japanese built up over the years, the Hawaiian evacuation was a surrealistic tale of chicanery and duress, deplorable for its official use of mendacity to abrogate the rights of ordinary citizens blameless of wrongdoing. With slight variation, the curious experience recounted below was one shared by numerous evacuees from Hawaii who unsuspectingly ended up in the mosquito-infested, fenced-in muddy compounds of Jerome and Topaz.

> One day a Caucasian who talked fluent Japanese came into the [Sand Island] center and told them that they had good news for them. He said the citizens could evacuate to the mainland with their families and that they would be free over here. Before leaving the center they had to sign a statement that they would not sue the government for arrest or detention. On the ship coming over here, they were told that they were coming to the mainland where they would be free citizens and would get employment. Most of them anticipated doing some farm work. Women and children were told that they would be united with their husbands who were interned on the mainland.
>
> The relocation center was somewhat of a shock to the people in several respects. In the first place, the guard towers and the barbed wire fences did not seem consistent with their being free citizens. Furthermore, they found they were unable to engage in regular employment. . . . Those who had expected to be reunited with their husbands or fathers were also disappointed.

33Memorandum for the Officer in Charge, by Frank O. Blake (Captain, Infantry), December 1, 1942 (attached to memo to Director, WRA, 12/16/42), Headquarters Security Classified Files (hereafter cited as Washington Central File), RG 210, National Archives. — MNW

34Phone conversation, Lieutenant Colonel W. F. Durbin and Colonel Fielding, November 9, 1942, Hawaii File of Washington Central File, RG 210, National Archives. — MNW

Furthermore, aliens and some of the citizens had their assets frozen in Hawaii. At the center they have found that they are spending their capital continuously in order to provide necessities. . . . [35]

A theme widely exploited by U.S. propaganda channels, including the army's own public relations setup, was that relocation centers were wartime "resettlement communities" and "havens of refuge," so it is little wonder that the public — and even those who ended up in them — were easily misled. Assembly center internees resentful of searchlights, machine-gun-manned watchtowers, and other repressive paraphernalia were generally reassured that it was all "a temporary measure," that their freedom would be largely restored to them after the move to civilian-controlled "permanent camps" in the hinterland.

VI

The midsummer of 1942 saw the activation of the second phase of the mass withdrawal. This involved the herding off daily of approximately five hundred deportees from each of the assembly centers to unfinished barrack communities, some of them so geographically remote that the train trip sometimes took from four to five days.

Tubercular patients (hundreds were discovered during the uprooting) and their families were thoughtfully diverted from the Siberia-like winter clime of the more northerly camps of resettlement to the dry Arizona desert compound of Gila. Considered less suitable for individuals weakened by respiratory dysfunction was Poston, the larger of the sprawling sun-baked Arizona stockades, which became known for its choking dust-storms of such merciless ferocity that they sometimes tore away roofs.

To travel-weary refugees, the spectacle of guard towers and gun-toting sentries in the middle of a vast, primitive expanse of nothingness came as a rude shock, especially to evacuees who had been assured in the assembly centers that the relocation centers were to be resettlement communities, not prison camps, and that the evacuees would be free to go to the neighboring villages to shop. Evacuees who, after their arrival, found themselves being caged in by degrees were hotly indignant; for at camps Minidoka and Heart Mountain, as had been the case in the early days of Manzanar, the construction of the spectacularly useless guard towers and fence began *after* the start of the intake. In the Idaho-based camp of Minidoka, feelings soared to a dangerous degree of intensity when residents discovered the fence to be electrified. The camp community analyst (one was assigned to each relocation center to analyze and interpret evacuee moods) reported back to his Washington superiors:

On November 12, the contractor became so incensed by the continual sabo-tage on the fence by the residents that an electric generator was hooked up

[35]"Interview with a Hawaiian Kibei," by Edgar C. McVoy, Jerome Community Analyst Report No. 113, September 8, 1943, RG 210, National Archives. — MNW

and the fence charged. This was done without knowledge or consent of either army or local WRA authorities. . . .

The removal of portions of the fence early in April, 1943, was an occasion of deep satisfaction for the workers involved. It is reported that never on the project was a job attacked so willingly. It may be significant to note that the residents believe the fence in these areas to be permanently out. As one resident phrased it, "There will be revolution if the fence is put back again." This is exaggeration but illustrates the depth of feeling with respect to the fence. . . . The bitter feeling about the fence runs through the entire resident group from children in school to the oldest Issei. It crops out in school children's themes, in artwork, in letters written by the residents. Everywhere the feeling is found that the fence has and will have a deep psychological effect on the younger people.

Here in Minidoka, it is impossible to point out any practical value of the fence. True, there is a canal and there is danger of small children drowning. To defend the fence in this area on those grounds is to have the answer flung back: "Safety for children is fine, but it is a funny way to protect small children with barbed wire on which they can cut themselves." . . . The residents put it this way: "Who would want to go over the fence anyway? There are no Seattles or Portlands on the other side. Besides there are ticks and rattlesnakes all over the place."[36]

There was no mistaking, however, that internment — not refuge — was the intent and purpose of the military personnel charged with guarding a people who, in all too many fired-up minds, were somehow connected with the Pearl Harbor perfidy. It was therefore fortunate that authorities had early determined that troops be restricted to patrolling the outer perimeter and the gates because of attempts made by a few of them to seduce female evacuees. "The M.P.s are mostly Limited Service men, some of whom are not too intelligent," wrote back Jerome's community analyst to Washington, adding, "and they are trying to make their work appear dangerous and exciting." An alarming trigger-minded proclivity on the part of army sentries had, indeed, come to light at Manzanar. A WRA investigation conducted in the summer of 1942 had revealed:

The guards have been instructed to shoot anyone who attempts to leave the center without a permit, and who refuses to halt when ordered to do so. The guards are armed with guns that are effective at a range of up to 500 yards. I asked Lt. Buckner if a guard ordered a Japanese who was out of bounds to halt and the Jap did not do so, would the guard actually shoot him. Lt. Buckner's reply was that he only hoped the guard would bother to ask him to halt. He explained that the guards were finding guard service very monotonous, and that nothing would suit them better than to have a little excitement, such as shooting a Jap.

Sometime ago, a Japanese [Nisei] was shot for being outside of a center. . . . The guard said that he ordered the Japanese to halt — that the Japanese started to run away from him, so he shot him. The Japanese was seriously injured, but recovered. He said that he was collecting scrap lumber to make

[36]"The Fence at Minidoka," by John de Young, Project Analysis Series No. 4, April 1943, RG 210, National Archives. — MNW

shelves in his house, and that he did not hear the guard say halt. The guard's story does not appear to be accurate, inasmuch as the Japanese was wounded in the front and not in the back.[37]

In more vigilantly guarded assembly centers, children were instructed to stay within twenty feet of the fence since pot shots had been taken at a few who strayed, one child suffering a gunshot wound. News of such incidents, however, was kept discreetly suppressed.

It was a bewildering, unreal world for youngsters. And for parents and elders, the problem of how best to explain to them that this is "still America" and why soldiers had to patrol about with rifles ("Mommy, who are they afraid of?") was a continuing dilemma which all parents of small children grappled with and devised solutions for in the best way they knew how. But however much the internees strove corporately to maintain a lofty image of America for the sake of a whole generation growing up behind stockades, little could be done to erase from impressionable minds the all too pervasive evidence that much of the treatment which cast them as separate and inferior people had to do with the color of their skin.

> A Nisei mother once told me with tears in her eyes of her six-year-old son who insisted on her "taking him back to America." The little boy had been taken to Japan about two years ago but was so unhappy there that she was compelled to return to California with him. Soon afterwards they were evacuated to Santa Anita, and the little boy in the absence of his Caucasian playmates was convinced that he was still in Japan and kept on entreating his mother to "take him back to America." To reassure him that he was in America she took him to the information center in her district and pointed to the American flag but he could not be consoled because Charlie and Jimmie, his Caucasian playmates, were not there with him in camp.[38]

An oft-repeated ritual in relocation camp schools (where "Americanization" was constantly stressed, as demanded by congressional lawmakers in their unfailing patriotic zeal) was the salute to the flag followed by the singing of "My country, 'tis of thee, sweet land of liberty" — a ceremony Caucasian teachers found embarrassingly awkward if not cruelly poignant in the austere prison-camp setting. After a speaking visit of five of the far-flung citizen detention camps, the famous missionary to India and Methodist Bishop, E. Stanley Jones (who, with his spiritual colleague, Toyohiko Kagawa, had sought in vain to deter Japan and America from their collision course), wrote movingly in the *Christian Century* of November 24, 1943:

> Their spirits are unbroken. They took the pledge of allegiance to the flag in a high school assembly, and my voice broke as I joined with them in the promise of loyalty "to one nation, undivisible, with liberty and justice for all."

---

[37]"Report of Investigation at Manzanar Relocation Center," by Philip Webster, August 31 to September 2, 1942, University Research Library, UCLA. On May 16, 1942, Hikoji Takeuchi had been shot by Private Phillips, Co. B747 MP Battalion. — MNW

[38]Jacobs, Landau, and Pell, *To Serve the Devil*, 259. — MNW

"Liberty and justice for all" — how could they say it? But they did and they meant it. Their faith in democracy is intact. Their faith in God holds too, in spite of everything.

READING CRITICALLY

1. What evidence does Weglyn present that President Roosevelt and others who approved the evacuation were motivated by racism?

2. Near the beginning of her chapter on the evacuation process (chapter 4), why do you think Weglyn quotes Father Hugh T. Lavery (p. 698)?

3. Weglyn describes a number of conditions at the assembly centers that made the evacuees feel like criminals or that dehumanized them. What were these conditions? What rhetorical strategies does Weglyn use to present this information?

4. Weglyn also describes conditions at the relocation centers, or detention camps. How are these conditions similar to those in the assembly centers? What new conditions are found at the camps? What rhetorical strategies does Weglyn use to present this information?

5. How does Weglyn present the reactions of the Issei and Nisei to the evacuation process? What are her strategies here? In particular, how does she handle the reactions of young Japanese American children to the relocation?

WRITING ANALYTICALLY

1. Weglyn clearly wishes to dramatize the physical and mental suffering caused to the Nikkei by the evacuation and internment process. Consider the strategies she uses to create this impression, drawing on your responses to the reading questions. Do you think Weglyn is effective in dramatizing the process in this way? Does she make you feel sympathetic to the interned people? Do you think that her efforts to enlist your sympathy undermine her effectiveness as a historian? Write a paper in which you argue for a thesis that addresses these questions.

2. Write a review of Weglyn's book (based on the chapters excerpted here) as you think it might be written by either Mike Masaoka (p. 676) or Jeanne Wakatsuki Houston (pp. 715 and 757).

3. Using Weglyn and the commission report *Personal Justice Denied* (p. 661) as your sources, write a paper in which you answer this question: How could the internment have happened in the United States? Make the argument that you think is best supported by these two sources. Then add an appendix to your paper in which you comment on what you have written: How complete an answer to this question do you think you have been able to piece together just from these two sources? Do you see any problems with the position that these sources lead you to take? If so, how would you solve these problems? If not, how would you convince a critic that your answer is in fact complete?

JEANNE WAKATSUKI HOUSTON AND
JAMES D. HOUSTON

From *Farewell to Manzanar* (1973)

Jeanne Wakatsuki Houston (b. 1934), the youngest of ten children, was born near Inglewood, California, where her father was a farmer. When he became a commercial fisherman, the family moved to Ocean Park. Shortly after the Japanese attack on Pearl Harbor, her father was arrested because his seafaring activities were regarded as suspicious by military authorities looking for spies feeding information to the Imperial Japanese Navy. Her mother then moved the family to be near several of her married siblings on Terminal Island, a fishing port in Long Beach Harbor and one of the first locations from which the Nikkei were removed as the internment began. Wakatsuki Houston and her large extended family were interned in Manzanar, from which her brother Woody volunteered to serve in the 442nd Regimental Combat Team.

After the war, Wakatsuki Houston attended San Jose State University, where she met and married fellow student and California native James D. Houston (b. 1933). She and her husband wrote *Farewell to Manzanar* about her internment experience and also collaborated on a prize-winning screenplay of the book that was televised in 1976. The following excerpts (from chapters 1, 8, 9, and 11) describe reaction in the Nikkei community to the attack on Pearl Harbor and life in the relocation camps. Emphasizing the way the stresses of internment caused tension within the Nikkei community, the authors describe camp uprisings and the controversial loyalty questionnaire. (Later in the unit, p. 757, we have reprinted a second excerpt dealing with the Wakatsuki family's life after being released from Manzanar.)

CHAPTER 1

"What Is Pearl Harbor?"

ON THAT FIRST WEEKEND IN DECEMBER there must have been twenty or twenty-five boats getting ready to leave. I had just turned seven. I remember it was Sunday because I was out of school, which meant I could go down to the wharf and watch. In those days — 1941 — there was no smog around Long Beach. The water was clean, the sky a sharp Sunday blue, with all the engines of that white sardine fleet puttering up into it, and a lot of yelling, especially around Papa's boat. Papa loved to give orders. He

Jeanne Wakatsuki Houston and James D. Houston, *Farewell to Manzanar* (1973; reprint, New York: Bantam Books, 1974), 3–7, 47–65.

In the notes, JWH/JDH = Jeanne Wakatsuki Houston and James D. Houston, EDS. = Patricia Bizzell and Bruce Herzberg.

had attended military school in Japan until the age of seventeen, and part of him never got over that. My oldest brothers, Bill and Woody, were his crew. They would have to check the nets again, and check the fuel tanks again, and run back to the grocery store for some more cigarettes, and then somehow everything had been done, and they were easing away from the wharf, joining the line of boats heading out past the lighthouse, into the harbor.

Papa's boat was called *The Nereid* — long, white, low-slung, with a fore-deck wheel cabin. He had another smaller boat, called *The Waka* (a short version of our name), which he kept in Santa Monica, where we lived. But *The Nereid* was his pride. It was worth about $25,000 before the war, and the way he stood in the cabin steering toward open water you would think the whole fleet was under his command. Papa had a mustache then. He wore knee-high rubber boots, a rust-colored turtleneck Mama had knitted him, and a black skipper's hat. He liked to hear himself called "Skipper."

Through one of the big canneries he had made a deal to pay for *The Nereid* with percentages of each catch, and he was anxious to get it paid off. He didn't much like working for someone else if he could help it. A lot of fishermen around San Pedro Harbor had similar contracts with the canneries. In typical Japanese fashion, they all wanted to be independent commercial fishermen, yet they almost always fished together. They would take off from Terminal Island, help each other find the schools of sardine, share nets and radio equipment — competing and cooperating at the same time.

You never knew how long they'd be gone, a couple of days, sometimes a week, sometimes a month, depending on the fish. From the wharf we waved good-bye — my mother, Bill's wife, Woody's wife Chizu, and me. We yelled at them to have a good trip, and after they were out of earshot and the sea had swallowed their engine noises, we kept waving. Then we just stood there with the other women, watching. It was a kind of duty, perhaps a way of adding a little good luck to the voyage, or warding off the bad. It was also marvelously warm, almost summery, the way December days can be sometimes in southern California. When the boats came back, the women who lived on Terminal Island would be rushing to the canneries. But for the moment there wasn't much else to do. We watched until the boats became a row of tiny white gulls on the horizon. Our vigil would end when they slipped over the edge and disappeared. You had to squint against the glare to keep them sighted, and with every blink you expected the last white speck to be gone.

But this time they didn't disappear. They kept floating out there, suspended, as if the horizon had finally become what it always seemed to be from shore: the sea's limit, beyond which no man could sail. They floated awhile, then they began to grow, tiny gulls becoming boats again, a white armada cruising toward us.

"They're coming back," my mother said.

"Why would they be coming back?" Chizu said.

"Something with the engine."

"Maybe somebody got hurt."

"But they wouldn't *all* come back," Mama said, bewildered.

Another woman said, "Maybe there's a storm coming."

They all glanced at the sky, scanning the unmarred horizon. Mama shook her head. There was no explanation. No one had ever seen anything like this before. We watched and waited, and when the boats were still about half a mile off the lighthouse, a fellow from the cannery came running down to the wharf shouting that the Japanese had just bombed Pearl Harbor.

Chizu said to Mama, "What does he mean? What is Pearl Harbor?"

Mama yelled at him, "What is Pearl Harbor?"

But he was running along the docks, like Paul Revere, bringing the news, and didn't have time to explain.

That night Papa burned the flag he had brought with him from Hiroshima thirty-five years earlier. It was such a beautiful piece of material, I couldn't believe he was doing that. He burned a lot of papers too, documents, anything that might suggest he still had some connection with Japan. These precautions didn't do him much good. He was not only an alien; he held a commercial fishing license, and in the early days of the war the FBI was picking up all such men, for fear they were somehow making contact with enemy ships off the coast. Papa himself knew it would only be a matter of time.

They got him two weeks later, when we were staying overnight at Woody's place, on Terminal Island. Five hundred Japanese families lived there then, and FBI deputies had been questioning everyone, ransacking houses for anything that could conceivably be used for signaling planes or ships or that indicated loyalty to the emperor. Most of the houses had radios with a short-wave band and a high aerial on the roof so that wives could make contact with the fishing boats during these long cruises. To the FBI every radio owner was a potential saboteur. The confiscators were often deputies sworn in hastily during the turbulent days right after Pearl Harbor, and these men seemed to be acting out the general panic, seeing sinister possibilities in the most ordinary household items: flashlights, kitchen knives, cameras, lanterns, toy swords.

If Papa were trying to avoid arrest, he wouldn't have gone near that island. But I think he knew it was futile to hide out or resist. The next morning two FBI men in fedora hats and trench coats — like out of a thirties movie — knocked on Woody's door, and when they left, Papa was between them. He didn't struggle. There was no point to it. He had become a man without a country. The land of his birth was at war with America; yet after thirty-five years here he was still prevented by law from becoming an American citizen. He was suddenly a man with no rights who looked exactly like the enemy.

About all he had left at this point was his tremendous dignity. He was tall for a Japanese man, nearly six feet, lean and hard and healthy-skinned from the sea. He was over fifty. Ten children and a lot of hard luck had worn him down, had worn away most of the arrogance he came to this country with. But he still had dignity, and he would not let those deputies push him out the door. He led them.

Mama knew they were taking all the alien men first to an interrogation center right there on the island. Some were simply being questioned and released. In the beginning she wasn't too worried; at least she wouldn't let herself be. But it grew dark and he wasn't back. Another day went by and we still had heard nothing. Then word came that he had been taken into custody and shipped out. Where to, or for how long? No one knew. All my brothers' attempts to find out were fruitless.

What had they charged him with? We didn't know that either, until an article appeared the next day in the Santa Monica paper, saying he had been arrested for delivering oil to Japanese submarines offshore.

My mother began to weep. It seems now that she wept for days. She was a small, plump woman who laughed easily and cried easily, but I had never seen her cry like this. I couldn't understand it. I remember clinging to her legs, wondering why everyone was crying. This was the beginning of a terrible, frantic time for all my family. But I myself didn't cry about Papa, or have any inkling of what was wrenching Mama's heart, until the next time I saw him, almost a year later.

[*The Wakatsuki family is interned at Camp Manzanar — minus the father, who has been taken to Fort Lincoln, North Dakota, with other Issei men accused of subversive activities. They are given a two-room apartment: one room for two of the older siblings, their spouses, and one couple's infant girl; the other room for the grandmother, the mother, and five younger siblings (including Jeanne). After nine months of imprisonment, Jeanne's father is allowed to rejoin his family in Manzanar. As he steps off the bus, the author recalls, "he had aged ten years." The psychological damage he has suffered becomes apparent as chapter 8 opens.* — EDS.]

CHAPTER 8

Inu

With Papa back our cubicle was filled to overflowing. Woody brought in another army bunk and tick mattress, up next to Mama's. But that was not what crowded the room. It was Papa himself, his dark, bitter, brooding presence. Once moved in, it seemed he didn't go outside for months. He sat in there, or paced, alone a great deal of the time, and Mama had to bring his meals from the mess hall.

He made her bring him extra portions of rice, or cans of the syrupy fruit they served. He would save this up and concoct brews in a homemade still he kept behind the door, brews that smelled so bad Mama was ashamed to let in any visitors. Day after day he would sip his rice wine or his apricot brandy, sip till he was blind drunk and passed out. In the morning he would wake up groaning like the demon in a kabuki drama; he would vomit and then start sipping again. He terrified all of us, lurching around the tiny room, cursing in Japanese and swinging his bottles wildly. No one could pacify him. Mama got nothing but threats and abuse for her attempts to comfort him.

I turned eight that fall. I remember telling myself that he never went out and never associated with others because he thought he was better than they were and was angry at being forced to live so close to them for the first time in his life. I told myself they whispered about him because he brewed his own foul-smelling wine in our barracks.

All of this was partly true. But there were deeper, uglier reasons for his isolation. I first sensed it one night when Mama and I went to the latrine together. By this time the stalls were partitioned. Two Terminal Island women about Mama's age were leaving just as we walked in. They lingered by the doorway, and from inside my stall I could hear them whispering about Papa, deliberately, just loud enough for us to hear. They kept using the word "inu." I knew it meant "dog," and I thought at the time they were backbiting him because he never socialized.

Spoken Japanese is full of disrespectful insult words that can be much more cutting than mere vulgarity. They have to do with bad manners, or worse, breaches of faith and loyalty. Years later I learned that *inu* also meant collaborator or informer. Members of the Japanese American Citizens League were being called *inu* for having helped the army arrange a peaceful and orderly evacuation. Men who cooperated with camp authorities in any way could be labeled *inu,* as well as those genuine informers inside the camp who relayed information to the War Department and to the FBI.

For the women in the late-night latrine Papa was an *inu* because he had been released from Fort Lincoln earlier than most of the Issei men, many of whom had to remain up there separated from their families throughout the war. After investigating his record, the Justice Department found no reason to detain him any longer. But the rumor was that, as an interpreter, he had access to information from fellow Isseis that he later used to buy his release.

This whispered charge, added to the shame of everything that had happened to him, was simply more than he could bear. He did not yet have the strength to resist it. He exiled himself, like a leper, and he drank.

The night Mama and I came back from the latrine with this newest bit of gossip, he had been drinking all day. At the first mention of what we'd overheard, he flew into a rage. He began to curse her for listening to such lies, then he cursed her for leaving him alone and wanted to know where she had *really* gone. He cursed her for coming back and disturbing him, for not bringing him his food on time, for bringing too much cabbage and not enough rice. He yelled and shook his fists and with his very threats forced her across the cluttered room until she collided with one of the steel bed frames and fell back onto a mattress.

I had crawled under another bunk and huddled, too frightened to cry. In a house I would have run to another room, but in the tight little world of our cubicle there was no escaping this scene. I knew his wrath could turn on any one of us. Kiyo[1] was already in bed, scrunched down under the covers, hoping not to be seen. Mama began to weep, great silent tears, and Papa was now limping back and forth beside the bunk, like a caged animal, brandishing his long, polished North Dakota cane.

"I'm going to kill you this time!"

"Go ahead, if that will make you happy."

"You lie to me. You imprison me here with your lies!"

"Kill me then. I don't care. I just don't care."

"I can never go outside, because of you!"

"Here. Here is my head. My chest. Get it over with. Who wants to go on living like this?"

She was lying very still, gazing up at him. The tears had stopped.

Papa stood over her, gripping his cane in both hands, right above her head, holding it so tightly the cane and both his arms quivered. "All right!" he yelled. "All right, I will! I will! I will!"

We had watched many scenes like this since his return, with Papa acting so crazy sometimes you could almost laugh at the samurai in him, trying to cow her with sheer noise and fierce display. But these were still unfamiliar visits from a demon we had never seen when we lived in Ocean Park. There had always been doors to keep some moments private. Here there were no doors. Nothing was private. And tonight he was far too serious — he seemed to have reached some final limit.

Inside my own helplessness I cowered, sure he was going to kill her or hurt her very badly, and the way Mama lay there I believed she was actually ready to be beaten to death. Kiyo must have felt something similar, because at the height of Papa's tirade he threw his covers back, and in his underwear he jumped out of bed yelling, "Stop it, Papa! Stop it!"

With his cane in both hands high above his head, Papa turned from the waist. Kiyo sprang across the room, one arm cocked, and punched Papa square in the face.

No one had ever seen such a thing before. Papa's arms went limp. The cane fell clattering to the floor. He reached up and touched his nose. Blood was pouring onto his shirt, dripping down onto Mama's dress. Kiyo stepped back, crouching, staring at the blood. This was like bloodying the nose of God. His face, contorted, looked ready to cry, but even his tears were stopped by the knowledge of what he had done. He waited paralyzed for whatever punishment might strike him down. Papa couldn't move either. He stared at Kiyo, his eyes wide with both outrage and admiration that his son had the courage to do this. They stood like that until Papa's gaze went bleary from the drink in his veins and dropped to the damp shirt, to the blood still spattering onto Mama's dress.

Kiyo turned and bolted out the door. I ran over to Mama, whimpering with relief that this ghastly scene was over and she had been saved, yet aching with a great sadness I could not at the time find words for. I was

---

[1]Kiyo, Jeanne's brother, is ten years old here. — EDS.

proud of Kiyo and afraid for what would happen to him; but deeper than that, I felt the miserable sense of loss that comes when the center has collapsed and everything seems to be flying apart around you.

Kiyo had fled to one of my married sisters' barracks. For two weeks he hid there. When he finally returned it was to admit that he had been in the wrong and to ask Papa's forgiveness. He too wanted some order preserved in the world and in the family. Papa accepted his apology, and this settled the waters some. But that aching sadness did not go away. It was something undefinable I'd already been living with for months, now enflamed by Papa's downfall. He kept pursuing oblivion through drink, he kept abusing Mama, and there seemed to be no way out of it for anyone. You couldn't even run.

CHAPTER 9

The Mess Hall Bells

Papa never said more than three or four sentences about his nine months at Fort Lincoln. Few men who spent time there will talk about it more than that. Not because of the physical hardships: He had been through worse times on fishing trips down the coast of Mexico. It was the charge of disloyalty. For a man raised in Japan, there was no greater disgrace. And it was the humiliation. It brought him face to face with his own vulnerability, his own powerlessness. He had no rights, no home, no control over his own life. This kind of emasculation was suffered, in one form or another, by all the men interned at Manzanar. Papa's was an extreme case. Some coped with it better than he, some worse. Some retreated. Some struck back.

During that first summer and fall of sandy congestion and wind-blown boredom, the bitterness accumulated, the rage festered in hundreds of tar-papered cubicles like ours. Looking back, what they now call the December Riot seems to have been inevitable. It happened exactly a year after the Pearl Harbor attack. Some have called this an anniversary demonstration organized by militantly pro-Japan forces in the camp. It wasn't as simple as that. Everything just came boiling up at once.

In the months before the riot the bells rang often at our mess hall, sending out the calls for public meetings. They rang for higher wages, they rang for better food, they rang for open revolt, for patriotism, for common sense, and for a wholesale return to Japan. Some meetings turned into shouting sessions. Some led to beatings. One group tried to burn down the general store. Assassination threats were commonplace.

On the night of December 5, Fred Tayama, a leader in the Japanese American Citizens League and a "friend" of the administration, was badly beaten by six men and taken to the camp hospital for treatment. Tayama couldn't identify anyone precisely, but the next day three men were arrested and one of these was sent out of the camp to the county jail at Independence, ten miles away. This was a young cook well known for his defiance and contempt for the authorities. He had been trying to organize a Kitchen Workers' Union and had recently charged the camp's chief steward, a Caucasian, with stealing sugar and meat from the warehouses to sell on the black market. Since sugar and meat were both in short supply, and since it was rumored that infants had died from saccharin mixed into formulas as a sugar substitute, these charges were widely believed. The young cook's arrest became the immediate and popular cause that triggered the riot.

I was too young to witness any of it. Papa himself did not take part and he kept all of us with him in the barracks during the day and night it lasted. But I remember the deadly quiet in the camp the morning before it began, that heavy atmospheric threat of something about to burst. And I remember hearing the crowds rush past our block that night. Toward the end of it they were a lynch mob, swarming from one side of the camp to the other, from the hospital to the police station to the barracks of the men they were after, shouting slogans in English and Japanese.

"Idiots," Papa called them. *"Bakatare.* They want to go back to Japan."

"It is more than going back to Japan," Mama said. "It is the sugar. It disappears so fast . . ."

"What do they think they will find over there?"

"Maybe they would be treated like human beings," Mama said.

"You be quiet. Listen to what I am saying. These idiots won't even get to the front gate of this camp. You watch. Before this is over, somebody is going to be killed. I guarantee it. They might all be killed."

The man who emerged as leader of the rioters was Hawaiian-born Joe Kurihara. During the First World War he had served in the U.S. Army in France and in Germany, and he was so frustrated by his treatment at Manzanar he was ready to renounce his citizenship and sail to the old country. Kurihara's group set up microphones and speakers near the cook's barracks and began a round of crowd-stirring speeches, demanding his release, charging that Tayama and the administration had used this beating to cover up the sugar fraud and saying it was time to get the *inus* once and for all.

That afternoon the authorities agreed to bring the young cook back into camp. But this wasn't enough. By 6:00 P.M. two thousand people were looking for blood. The Internal Security Force, made up of internees like the demonstrators, had evaporated in the face of such a mob. For a while they had the camp to themselves.

They split into two groups, one heading for the police station to free the cook, the other heading for the hospital to finish off Tayama, who had been concealed under a hospital bed. A vigilante party searched the corridors. When they failed to find their man, this half of the crowd moved off in search of others on their "death list."

Meanwhile the mob heading for the police station had been met by a detachment of military police carrying submachine guns and M-1s. When an army captain asked them to disperse, they stoned him. Now they were hooting *"Banzai!,"* jeering threats at the MPs and singing songs in Japanese. The MPs started lobbing tear gas bombs, and then, with no announcement or command to shoot, while the mob swirled frantically to escape the gas, several soldiers opened fire.

This instantly cleared the street, and the riot was over. Only the dead and the injured remained. Ten were treated in the hospital for gunshot wounds. One young man was killed on the spot. Another nineteen-year-old died five days later.

What I recall vividly are the bells that began to toll late that night. After dispersing, some of the demonstrators organized shifts, and kept them tolling all over camp. With the bells and the MP jeeps patrolling up and down the streets, I was a long time getting to sleep. Against Papa's orders I kept sneaking looks out the window, and I saw something I had only seen once before. The searchlights. They operated every night, but I never saw them because I went to bed so early and our block was well in from the perimeter. From the guard towers the lights scanned steadily, making shadows ebb and flow among the barracks like dark, square waves.

The next morning I awoke long after sunup. The lights were gone. Shadows were sharp and fixed. But the bells were still ringing. It was the only sound in camp, the only sound in Owens Valley, the mess hall bells, their gongs echoing between the Inyo Range and the nearby Sierras, their furthest ripples soaking into dry sand. They rang till noon.

CHAPTER 11

Yes Yes No No

27. Are you willing to serve in the Armed Forces of the United States on combat duty, wherever ordered?

_____ _____
(yes)   (no)

28. Will you swear unqualified allegiance to the United States of America and faithfully defend the United States from any or all attack by foreign or domestic forces, and forswear any form of allegiance or obedience to the Japanese emperor, or any other foreign government, power, or organization?

_____ _____
(yes)   (no)

— From the *War Relocation Authority*
Application for Leave Clearance, 1943

Later in December the administration gave each family a Christmas tree hauled in from the Sierras. A new director had been appointed and this was his gesture of apology for all the difficulties that had led up to the riot, a promise of better treatment and better times to come.

It was an honest gesture, but it wasn't much of a Christmas that year. The presents were makeshift, the wind was roaring, Papa was drunk. Better times were a long way off, and the difficulties, it seemed, had just begun. Early in February the government's Loyalty Oath appeared. Everyone seventeen and over was required to fill it out. This soon became the most divisive issue of all. It cut deeper than the riot, because no one could avoid it. Not even Papa. After five months of self-imposed isolation, this debate was what finally forced him out of the barracks and into circulation again.

At the time, I was too young to understand the problem. I only knew there was no peace in our cubicle for weeks. Block organizers would come to talk to Papa and my brothers. They would huddle over the table awhile, muttering like conspirators, sipping tea or one of his concoctions. Their voices gradually would rise to shouts and threats. Mama would try to calm the men down. Papa would tell her to shut up, then Granny would interrupt and order him to quit disgracing Mama all the time. Once he just shoved Granny across the room, up against the far wall and back into her chair, and where she sat sniffling while the arguments went on.

If the organizers weren't there, Papa would argue with Woody. Or rather, Woody would listen to Papa lecture him on *true* loyalty, pacing from bunk to bunk, waving his cane.

"Listen to me, Woodrow. When a soldier goes into war he must go believing he is never coming back. This is why the Japanese are such courageous warriors. They are prepared to die. They expect nothing else. But to do that, you must *believe* in what you're fighting for. If you do not believe, you will not be willing to die. If you are not willing to die, you won't fight well. And if you don't fight well you will probably be killed stupidly, for the wrong reason, and unheroically. So tell me, how can you think of going off to fight?"

Woody always answered softly, respectfully, with a boyish and submissive smile.

"I will fight well, Papa."

"In this war? How is it possible?"

"I am an American citizen. America is at war."

"But look where they have put us!"

"The more of us who go into the army, the sooner the war will be over, the sooner you and Mama will be out of here."

"Do you think I would risk losing a son for that?"

"You want me to answer NO NO, Papa?"

"Do you think that is what I'm telling you? Of course you cannot answer NO NO. If you say NO NO, you will be shipped back to Japan with all those other *bakatare!*"

"But if I answer YES YES I will be drafted anyway, no matter how I feel about it. That is why they are giving us the oath to sign."

"No! That is not true! They are looking for volunteers. And only a fool would volunteer."

Papa stared hard at Woody, making this a challenge. Woody shrugged, still smiling his boyish smile, and did not argue. He knew that when the time came he would join the army, and he knew it was pointless to begin the argument again. It was a circle. His duty as a son was to sit and listen to Papa thrash his way around it and around it and around it.

A circle, or you might have called it a corral, like Manzanar itself, with no exit save via three narrow gates. The first led into the infantry, the second back across the Pacific. The third, called *relocation,* was just opening up: interned citizens who could find a job and a sponsor somewhere inland, away from the West Coast, were beginning to trickle out of camp. But the program was bogged down in paperwork. It was taking months to process applications and security clearances. A loyalty statement required of everyone, it was hoped, might save some time and a lot of red tape. This, together with the search for "loyal" soldiers, had given rise to the ill-fated "oath."

Two weeks before the December Riot, JACL leaders met in Salt Lake City and passed a resolution pledging Nisei to volunteer out of the camps for military service.[2] In January the government announced its plan to form an all-Nisei combat regiment. While recruiting for this unit and speeding up the relocation program, the government figured it could simultaneously weed out the "disloyal" and thus get a clearer idea of exactly how many agents and Japanese sympathizers it actually had to deal with. This part of it would have been comical if the results were not so grotesque. No self-respecting espionage agent would willingly admit he was disloyal. Yet the very idea of the oath itself — appearing at the end of that first chaotic year — became the final goad that prodded many once-loyal citizens to turn militantly anti-American.

From the beginning Papa knew his own answer would be YES YES. He agreed with Woody on this much, even though it meant swearing allegiance to the government that had sent him to Fort Lincoln and denying his connections with the one country in the world where he might still have the rights of a citizen. The alternative was worse. If he said NO NO, he could be sent to Tule Lake Camp in northern California where all the "disloyal" were to be assembled for what most people believed would be eventual repatriation to Japan. Papa had no reason to return to Japan. He was too old to start over. He believed America would win the war, and he knew, even after all he'd endured, that if he had a future it still lay in this country. What's more, a move to Tule Lake could mean a further splitting up of our family.

This was a hard choice to make, and even harder to hold to. Anti-American feeling in camp ran stronger than ever. Pro-Japan forces were trying to organize a NO NO vote by blocks, in massive resistance. Others wanted to boycott the oath altogether in a show of noncooperation or through the mistaken fear that *anyone* who accepted the form would be shipped out of camp: the NO NO back to Japan, the YES YES into an American society full of wartime hostility and racial hate.

---

[2]At the time this move was widely condemned, and *inu* charges escalated. That was, in fact, one of the causes for Tayama's beating. Since then history has proved the JACL was right. Mike Masaoka, who pushed the resolution through, understood that the most effective way Japanese Americans could combat the attitudes that put them in places like Manzanar was to shed their blood on the battlefield. The all-Nisei 442nd Regimental Combat Team was the most decorated American unit in World War II; it also suffered the highest percentage of casualties and deaths. They were much admired, and the JACL strategy succeeded. This was visible *proof* that these 110,000 people could be trusted. — JWH/JDH

A meeting to debate the matter was called in our mess hall. Papa knew that merely showing his face would draw stares and muttered comments. YES YES was just what they expected of an *inu*. But he had to speak his mind before the NO NO contingent carried the block. Saying NO NO as an individual was one thing, bullying the entire camp into it was quite another. At the very least he didn't want to be sucked into such a decision without having his own opinion heard.

Woody wanted to go with him, but Papa said it was a meeting for "heads of households" only and he insisted on going alone. From the time he heard about it he purposely drank nothing stronger than tea. He shaved and trimmed his mustache and put on a silk tie. His limp was nearly gone now, but he carried his cane and went swaggering off down the narrow walkway between the barracks, punching at the packed earth in front of him.

About four o'clock, I was playing hopscotch in the firebreak with three other girls. It was winter, the sun had already dropped behind Mount Whitney. Now a wind was rising, the kind of biting, steady wind that could bring an ocean of sand into camp at any moment with almost no warning. I was hurrying back to the barracks when I heard a great commotion inside the mess hall, men shouting wildly, as if a fire had broken out. The loudest voice was Papa's, cursing.

"*Eta!* (trash) *Eta! Bakayaro! Bakayaro!*"

The door of the mess hall flew open and a short, beefy man came tearing out. He jumped off the porch, running as his feet hit the ground. He didn't get far. Papa came through the doorway right behind him, in a flying leap, bellowing like a warrior, "Yaaaaaah!" He let go of his cane as he landed on the man's back, and they both tumbled into the dirt. The wind was rising. Half the sky was dark with a tide of sand pouring toward us. The dust billowed and spun as they kicked and pummeled and thrashed each other.

At the meeting, when Papa stood up to defend the YES YES position, murmurs of "*Inu, inu*" began to circulate around the mess hall. This man then jumped up at the speaker's table and made the charge aloud. Papa went for him. Now, outside in the dirt, Papa had him by the throat and would have strangled him, but some other men pulled them apart. I had never seen him so livid, yelling and out of his head with rage. While they pinned his arms, he kicked at the sand, sending windblown bursts of it toward the knot of men dragging his opponent out of reach.

A few moments later the sandstorm hit. The sky turned black as night. Everyone ran for cover. Two men hustled Papa to our barracks. The fighting against the wind and sand to get there calmed him down some.

Back inside he sat by the stove holding his teacup and didn't speak for a long time. One cheekbone was raw where it had been mashed into the sand. Mama kept pouring him little trickles of tea. We listened to the wind howl. When the sand died down, the sky outside stayed black. The storm had knocked out the electricity all over the camp. It was a cold, lonely night, and we huddled around our oil stove while Mama and Woody and Chizu began to talk about the day.

A young woman came in, a friend of Chizu's, who lived across the way. She had studied in Japan for several years. About the time I went to bed she and Papa began to sing songs in Japanese, warming their hands on either side of the stove, facing each other in its glow. After a while Papa sang the first line of the Japanese national anthem, *Kimi ga yo.* Woody, Chizu, and Mama knew the tune, so they hummed along while Papa and the other woman sang the words. It can be a hearty or a plaintive tune, depending on your mood. From Papa, that night, it was a deep-throated lament. Almost invisible in the stove's small glow, tears began running down his face.

I had seen him cry a few times before. It only happened when he was singing or when someone else sang a song that moved him. He played the three-stringed *samisen,* which Kiyo and I called his "pinko-pinko." We would laugh together when we heard him plucking it and whining out old Japanese melodies. We would hold our ears and giggle. It was always a great joke between us, except for those rare times when Papa began to weep at the lyrics. Then we would just stare quietly — as I did that night — from some hidden corner of the room. This was always mysterious and incomprehensible.

The national anthem, I later learned, is what he had sung every morning as a schoolboy in Japan. They still sing it there, the way American kids pledge allegiance to the flag. It is not a martial song, or a victory song, the way many national anthems are. It is really a poem, whose words go back to the ninth century:

> *Kimi ga yo wa chiyoni*
> *yachiyoni sa-za-re i-shi no i-wa-o to*
> *na-ri-te ko-ke no musu made.*
>
> May thy peaceful reign last long.
> May it last for thousands of years,
> Until this tiny stone will grow
> Into a massive rock, and the moss
> Will cover it deep and thick.

It is a patriotic song that can also be read as a proverb, as a personal credo for endurance. The stone can be the kingdom or it can be a man's life. The moss is the greenery that, in time, will spring even from a rock. In Japan, before the turn of the century, outside my father's house there stood one of those stone lanterns, with four stubby legs and a small pagoda-like roof. Each morning someone in the household would pour a bucketful of water over his lantern, and after several years a skin of living vegetation began to show on the stone. As a boy he was taught that the last line of the anthem refers to a certain type of mossy lichen with exquisitely tiny white flowers sprinkled in amongst the green.

READING CRITICALLY

1. Why was Houston's father labeled an "inu"?

2. Most of Houston's relatives cooperated with the camp authorities, as shown in chapter 9. How do you think Houston and Houston feel about those who resisted, such as the young cook or the rioters mentioned in chapter 9? How can you tell?

3. In chapter 11, the authors suggest a number of factors that entered into people's decisions about how to respond to the loyalty questionnaire, particularly the two most controversial questions. What were these various factors?

4. What is the effect of the authors' decision to end chapter 11 with a scene showing Jeanne's father singing the Japanese national anthem and weeping?

WRITING ANALYTICALLY

1. Houston and Houston offer two contrasting portraits of Jeanne's father — in chapter 1, before he is imprisoned, and in chapters 8, 9, and 11, when he rejoins his family at Manzanar. How would you describe the contrast? What is happening to her father, and how is he affected by the questioning of his loyalty by both the U.S. government and his fellow Nikkei? Your response to the reading questions may help you here. Write a paper in which you argue for a thesis concerning how Houston and Houston are attempting to depict Jeanne's father. Consider in your argument the ways in which the father's experience is offered as representative of what happened to all Nikkei during the internment.

2. In these chapters, Houston and Houston present a complicated picture of what it might mean to be loyal to a country or a culture. Drawing on your responses to reading questions 2, 3, and 4 as well as any other evidence from this reading, write a paper in which you explain what "loyalty" or "patriotism" seem to mean to Houston and Houston. You may come up with a complicated or contradictory definition. Option: To build up an even more nuanced definition, you may compare and contrast Houston and Houston's definition with your own sense of what loyalty or patriotism ought to be.

3. Who would you say is more effective in arousing your sympathy for the interned Nikkei, Houston and Houston here or Weglyn (p. 689)? Write a paper comparing and contrasting the two selections, noting in particular which rhetorical strategies, whether common to both or unique to one text, are most powerful. In making your comparison, consider the fact that one selection presents itself as an autobiography (Houston and Houston), while the other presents itself as a history (Weglyn).

MINORU YASUI

Oral History (1984)

Minoru Yasui (1916–86) was born in Hood River, Oregon. He graduated from the University of Oregon Law School in 1939 and took a job with the Japanese consulate in Chicago. After the attack on Pearl Harbor, Yasui returned to Oregon and tried unsuccessfully to prevent his father and other Issei men from being interned early on as "suspect" community leaders. In 1942, slated to be interned himself, Yasui decided to challenge the internment by violating the military curfew imposed on the Nikkei before their departure for the camps. At Yasui's first trial, the judge found that military orders imposed on civilian citizens in the absence of martial law were indeed illegal but that Yasui was not a citizen, in spite of his birth in the United States, because of actions that showed he identified with Japan. On appeal, the U.S. Supreme Court did not hear Yasui's case but directed that it be reinterpreted in accordance with the Supreme Court decision in another challenge case by Gordon Hirabayashi. (This was before the 1944 Supreme Court decisions in the *Endo* and *Korematsu* cases, which stated that while evacuation was permitted, civilians could not be interned without proof that they were disloyal. For more information on all three cases, see the introduction to Unit Five, p. 615.) Yasui was ruled to be a citizen, but his conviction was upheld. He served nine months in solitary confinement and was then interned in Minidoka Camp in Idaho. Volunteering for military service, he was rejected, but he joined Japanese American Citizens League efforts to persuade other men to enlist, working closely with Mike Masaoka's (p. 676) brother Joe Grant Masaoka. After the war, Yasui settled in Denver and continued his career as a lawyer. He was a leader in efforts to obtain government redress for the interned.

Appearing here are excerpts from an oral history of Yasui's experience that was collected for an anthology of testimony on the internment.

I WAS BORN IN HOOD RIVER, OREGON, on October 19, 1916, the third son of Masuo and Shidzuyo Yasui. The Masuo Yasui family was six boys and three girls, but my oldest brother died at age eighteen and a younger sister at age four or five. My paternal grandfather, Shinataro Yasui, had come out of the rice fields of rural Okayama, during the mid-1890s, to work on the railroads in Idaho, Montana, Washington, and Oregon. Having put aside some money from his earnings as a railroad-gang laborer, he later

Minoru Yasui, oral history, in *And Justice for All: An Oral History of the Japanese American Detention Camps,* ed. John Tateishi (New York: Random House, 1984), 62–93.
   In the notes, EDS. = Patricia Bizzell and Bruce Herzberg.

sent for his two older sons (my paternal uncles), who came to the United States before 1900, also to work on the railroads.

Grandfather Yasui returned to Japan during 1917; his eldest son (my oldest uncle) subsequently also returned to Japan to establish a textile factory in their home village in Okayama-ken.

My father, Masuo Yasui, came to the United States in 1903, at age sixteen. Because he was so slight that he could not physically perform the hard labor on the railroad gangs, he became a "school boy" in Portland, Oregon, doing domestic work, learning to cook, hand laundering clothes, working in the garden. He wanted to become a lawyer, but found out soon enough that the legal profession was barred to him because of his Japanese alienage. He also discovered that he could not become a U.S. citizen because he was an Oriental. He worked in Portland in a Caucasian's home as a houseboy for about three years.

My father used to tell the story that as a twenty-year-old, he heard about a place called *Shin-Shin-no-chi* (Cincinnati), which translated would mean "a new, new land." Enthralled by vague thoughts of such a place, he took a train out of Portland (he could use his father's railroad pass) and started to head East. However, in traveling up the Columbia River gorge and coming to a place called Hood River, the terrain reminded him so much of his home in Japan that he got off the train and decided to settle there — or so he told the story.

In 1906 he persuaded his older brother, Renichi Fujimoto — a *yoshi* ("adopted son to carry on the family name") to the Fujimoto family — to start a mercantile store in Hood River. By dint of inordinate hard work (Dad used to tell of sweeping out the old Butler Bank building early in the morning, so townsfolk would not see a businessman doing janitorial work!), the business slowly prospered. The Yasui Brothers Company began to acquire extensive interests in farm and orchard lands, and to assist newly arrived Japanese immigrants establish farms and orchards on the logged-over hills of Hood River valley.

In 1912 my mother, Shidzuyo Miyake, who grew up in the same village of Nanokaichi, Okayama-ken, Japan, came to the United States through the port of Tacoma, Washington, to marry my father. Both my father and mother were Methodists at the time of their marriage, and my father insisted that all of his children would be Americans but without forgetting their Japanese lineage. My mother was a college educated woman (which was rare in those days) and had been a teacher in a women's school in Japan, before she immigrated to this country in 1912. She was able to teach other Japanese immigrant women about *cha-no-yu* ("tea ceremony"), *ikebana* ("flower arranging"), koto, and haiku, which we, as children, absorbed to some degree.

My mother's younger brother, Saburo Miyake, also later came to the United States and joined my father and uncle in one of the farms, twenty acres in Pine Grove in the Hood River valley, at the end of World War I, to grow strawberries and to raise fruit. He stayed until about the time of the Oriental Exclusion Act and the passage of antialien land laws in Oregon, which was about 1924. I have vague memories of him and his family. He returned to Japan to fulfill responsibility to the Miyake family, who were minor local officials in the village in the early Meiji years.[1] I still remember, in 1925, my maternal grandfather with his short sword, as a symbol of his authority, when we visited Japan.

Because the Yasui Brothers Company grubstaked Japanese immigrant families to the Hood River Valley, helping them with start-up capital, negotiations, and so forth, by 1940 my father and uncle had a half or a third, or some shares in probably about a thousand acres of farm and orchard lands in the valley, besides owning outright several hundreds of acres of farms. I can still remember my father pioneering, with a number of Japanese farmers, the asparagus industry at Mosier and Viento farms, shipping carloads of asparagus back East during the 1930s. By 1940, as a successful businessman and agriculturist, Masuo Yasui was a member of the local Rotary Club, a member of the board of the Apple Growers Association, a pillar of the local Methodist church, as well as founder of the local Japanese Methodist church and the local Japanese Association. He was a friend and neighbor of the local bank president, the most prominent lawyer in town, the editor of the local newspaper, and all "important" people in Hood River, Oregon.

On December 7, 1941, Masuo Yasui, in short, was a prominent member of the Hood River community. His eldest son, Ray T. Yasui, was managing one of his larger fruit farms at Willow Flats; as the next son, I was a licensed attorney in Oregon, but was in Chicago, Illinois, at the time; his oldest daughter and another son were students at the University of Oregon, with another son at the University of Michigan in engineering; his youngest son and youngest daughter were still students at the local high school. Although many of the Japanese American community leaders in Portland, Oregon, were immediately picked up by the FBI on December 7, 1941, Masuo Yasui was not arrested and taken away as an "enemy alien" until December 13, 1941. Mother, then fifty-six, and my youngest sister did not know for weeks where they had taken my father. Meanwhile, all of the assets of Yasui Brothers Company, and personal assets of Masuo Yasui were frozen by the U.S. Treasury Department, including the mercantile store. For all Japanese American families on the West Coast, it was a bleak Christmas and New Year's season in 1941; and it was for the Yasui family in Oregon too.

I was in Chicago at the time of Pearl Harbor. I will never forget that it was about twelve o'clock noon, Sunday, December 7, 1941, when Suma Tsuboi called me when I was asleep on a couch in my apartment at the Dearborn Plaza, saying that the Japanese have bombed Pearl Harbor. I was shocked, dismayed, and at first, unbelieving. I had been out the night be-

[1]In 1868 a new imperial government was established at Edo, renamed Tokyo, ending about two centuries of rule by military leaders, or shoguns. The new government proclaimed the dawning of the "Meiji era," when Japan would return to traditional values that had decayed under the shoguns. The early Meiji period is known as a time of rapid modernization in Japan. — EDS.

fore with some of the Japanese Consulate people, and there had been no hint of such outbreak of war.

Upon graduation from the University of Oregon Law School in 1939, I took the Oregon state bar examination that June. During September 1939, I was notified that I had passed the Oregon bar exams and was admitted as a practicing attorney in Oregon. During the fall of 1939, and early spring of 1940, I had accepted a retainer from the Japanese Association of Oregon to research and write a public relations piece about the contributions (mostly agricultural) of Japanese Americans to the economy of Oregon. Also, in trying to establish a law practice, I found that a number of my law school classmates had accepted positions with established law firms in Portland but were receiving minimal pay. So, rather than working for $35 less per month than a produce clerk, I accepted a position as an attaché at the consulate general of Japan in Chicago at $125 per month. My father had known Consul General Hiroshini Akino. I commenced work at the consulate on March 1, 1940.

Because my duties were not overly onerous at the consulate, I was personally engaged in running a Boy Scouts of America troop, and I participated in various community groups. I led a hyperactive social life, carousing in the bars along North Rush Street, playing poker all night, and generally running around too much. Thus it wasn't until noon that I was awakened on December 7 by the telephone call from Suma Tsuboi. I checked with friends in regard to what would be transpiring. On the next day, December 8, I resigned by letter from the consulate.

In mid-December 1941, I received official orders to report for active duty with the United States Army at Camp Vancouver, Washington. I held a reserve commission as a second lieutenant in the U.S. Army. The instructions ordered me to report for duty on January 19, 1942. So I went down to the Union Pacific Railroad station to purchase a ticket back to Portland, Oregon. But the ticket agent wanted to know if I were a "Jap." When I foolishly answered truthfully that I was of Japanese ancestry, he responded that he could not sell transportation to a "Jap." Despite my showing him travel orders from the U.S. Army, I could not persuade him to issue me a railroad ticket. I finally had to make an appointment to see one of the attorneys in the general counsel's office for the Union Pacific Railroad in Chicago to obtain authorization for me to buy a ticket to report for active duty with the U.S. Army. I had to point to the Fourteenth Amendment to the Constitution of the United States to persuade that lawyer that I was a citizen of the United States, on the basis of my birth certificate alone.

I traveled to North Platte, Nebraska, on the first leg of my trip home to Oregon. I stopped off to see old friends and to say goodbyes, because as far as I was concerned, I would be off to the wars, in the infantry, and there was no assurance that I would ever be back. While staying overnight in North Platte, the sheriff or police chief knocked on my hotel door and demanded to know who I was and what I was doing in North Platte. This plainclothes officer asked me, "You're a Jap, aren't you?" I answered, "No,

I'm bog-Irish." And the guy answered, "Don't get smart with me! I'll throw your ass in jail if you fuck around with me."

"And who are you?" I asked him. He identified himself as a law enforcement officer. So I showed him my military travel orders, and he left. It shook me up as I wondered whether I had been followed out of Chicago and how could I have been spotted as a stranger in a town like North Platte, Nebraska? The next morning I boarded the train and returned to Oregon without further incident.

On January 19, 1942, I took my dad's car and drove to Portland, crossed the river, to report for active duty at Camp Vancouver. I do not remember the rank of the officer who received me, but it seems to me that it was a colonel who looked over my papers, referred to other papers in my files, looked up, and curtly told me, "We'll let you know when to report." I replied, "Okay," and left. Years later, in October 1944, I received official discharge papers from the U.S. War Department, stating that I was no longer a second lieutenant in the U.S. Army's Officers Reserve Corps. And so ended my military career in World War II. It occurred to me that was probably just as well because the outfit to which I would have been assigned was a detachment from Texas. If we had gone into any active combat situation, I'd probably have been shot in the back. Or so it seems to me now.

I went back to Hood River, Oregon. My mother had received word that a hearing would be held to determine whether Masuo Yasui should be held as a potentially dangerous "enemy alien." The hearings were to be held during the first part of February 1942 in Fort Missoula, Montana. As a son, and as an attorney, I felt that I had to go to try to help my father at these hearings. I knew that my father was truly loyal to the ideals and high principles of this country. Also, we learned that other hearings were being conducted by the Enemy Alien Control Unit. Later I learned this unit was headed by Edward J. Ennis,[2] but at the time I assumed that normal rules of law would apply and that unless actual conduct were shown to endanger the security of this country, the internees would be released. I knew a number of the Portland Japanese internees. I requested permission to attend the hearings of all these internees, and I talked with the wives and families of these men in Portland before leaving for Missoula, Montana, which is about eight hundred miles to the east.

With headlines screaming about the furious battles for Bataan, it was intimidating to realize that, being physically Japanese, there was no assurance of being able to get a hotel room or even being able to go to a restaurant in Missoula. In short, I was scared and alone in hostile territory. After

---

[2]Edward J. Ennis was head of the Justice Department's Aliens Division. Yasui, like many other Nikkei, clearly regards Ennis as complicit in the Justice Department's acquiescence in the internment. Ennis was also later associated with the distasteful proceedings whereby some Nisei who answered "no, no" on the crucial loyalty questionnaire were urged to renounce their U.S. citizenship (see the introduction to Unit Five, p. 615). Nevertheless, after the war Ennis assisted the Japanese American Citizens League in making claims for monetary compensation for the interned. — EDS.

arriving I was able to get a hotel room, and I hired a taxi to go out to Fort Missoula, to the internment center. There, surrounded by barbed wire, guarded by armed MPs, I went into the offices to try to arrange to see the various internees from Oregon.

I was permitted to visit with my father, Masuo Yasui, but denied permission to visit the others whom I had known for years. I was also granted permission to attend the hearing for my father and allowed to participate. The proceedings were a complete farce. The official for the Enemy Control Unit pointed out that my father was an influential leader in the Japanese community in Hood River, Oregon; that he had extensive property interests; that he had visited Japan for a summer vacation for three months in 1925; that he had been awarded a medal by the Emperor of Japan for promoting U.S.-Japan relations; and that he had been instrumental in obtaining a position with the consulate general of Japan in Chicago for me.

The most incredible thing was when they produced childlike drawings of the Panama Canal showing detailed drawings of how the locks worked. The hearing officer took these out and asked, "Mr. Yasui, what are these?" Dad looked at the drawings and diagrams and said, "They look like drawings of the Panama Canal." They were so labeled, with names of children. Then the officer asked my father to explain why they were in our home. "If they were in my home," my father replied, "it seems to me that they were drawings done by my children for their schoolwork." The officer then asked, "Didn't you have these maps and diagrams so you could direct the blowing up of the canal locks?" My father said, "Oh no! These are just schoolwork of my children." The officer said, "No, we think you've cleverly disguised your nefarious intent and are using your children merely as a cover. We believe you had intent to damage the Panama Canal." To which my father vehemently replied, "No, no, no!" And then the officer said pointedly, "Prove that you didn't intend to blow up the Panama Canal!" I can still remember so vividly the officer asking my father to prove that he didn't intend to blow up the Panama Canal!

Why a businessman and agriculturalist with an impeccable reputation, living in a far-off rural town like Hood River — two hundred miles from the ocean, and possibly three thousand miles from the Panama Canal — should have to prove that he had no intent to blow up the Panama Canal seemed to me then, and seems to me now, to be the height of absurdity.

It was on this kind of "evidence" that my father and thousands of others were confined to internment camps, operated by the U.S. Department of Justice and manned by the U.S. Army, and were kept for the duration, until the spring of 1946.

I went back to Oregon after the hearings, utterly repulsed by the kangaroo-court proceedings of the U.S. Department of Justice. I knew that no legal appeals would be of any use, because we were at war with Japan, and these men were Japanese nationals, and hence "enemy aliens" for whom judicial processes were not available in time of war. Never mind that U.S. laws prevented them from becoming U.S. citizens. Returning to Portland, Oregon, I made the rounds, visiting the wives of Portland internees, telling them the bad news of hearings in Missoula, based on my impressions of my father's "hearing." From there, I went to Hood River to finish application forms and reports in connection with my father's and uncle's businesses.

News from the battlefronts in the Pacific were disastrous. General Jonathan Wainwright's American and Filipino forces were being decimated on Bataan and Corregidor; Hong Kong had fallen, and Singapore was soon to follow; Japanese expeditionary forces were entrenched on Attu and Kiska on the Aleutian chain; all of the Dutch East Indies all the way to Australia was wide open for the Japanese invaders; and news from the European theater was equally bad.

On the home front, things for Japanese Americans were deteriorating daily. In Portland, the city council gave instructions not to issue business licenses to Japanese. Business contracts with Japanese individuals, citizens or noncitizens, were being ignored, and open-and-shut cases in court were being lost when the claimant was Japanese.

Rules and regulations were being issued by the Alien Property Custodian and the U.S. Treasury Department regarding "enemy aliens." The Nisei became ensnared in tangles of red tape because of shared interests or because equitable or beneficial ownership was retained by the Issei. Normal and ordinary business transactions were becoming chaotic if you were a person of Japanese ancestry, because you had not only to prove U.S. citizenship, but to prove also that you had no beneficial interest owed by an enemy alien, that is, an Issei.

Fraud and outright cheating of rightful owners occurred in many transactions involving persons of Japanese ancestry. In such a chaotic situation, the services of lawyers were needed. Because I was the only Japanese American lawyer in the state of Oregon and the only Oregon lawyer who could speak Japanese, and particularly since we generally had to deal with the wives of internees, it seemed appropriate for me to reopen a law office in the Foster Hotel on NW Third Avenue in Portland, Oregon. I did this, and I was promptly swamped and overwhelmed. From February to the end of April 1942, my law practice was a blur of trying to do too much in too short a time. I know that I didn't do a good job of serving my clients. There were too many, too soon, and their problems were too complex for easy solutions. But I did what I could, going without sleep for days and getting no rest during the evenings and weekends.

On February 19, 1942, President Franklin Delano Roosevelt signed Executive Order 9066, but this scarcely made a ripple in public awareness, at least in Portland. On the other hand, the newspapers and radio were beginning to hammer out an incessant barrage of anti-Jap invectives. We kept hearing that the Japanese Issei would all be interned; we heard that the Nisei would be allowed to remain at home to run the businesses and farms the Issei would have to leave behind; we heard conflicting rumors that Issei and Nisei alike would be put into work camps to labor for the war effort; we heard suggestions that all Japanese would be sterilized and, after the war, deported to Japan. We heard a hundred and one wild things, almost daily, almost hourly.

We knew that Francis Biddle, as attorney general of the United States, had counseled that evacuation and incarceration of Japanese persons who were U.S. citizens would be unconstitutional. Nevertheless, when Walter Lippmann began his series supporting evacuation, he was shrilly echoed by Westbrook Pegler, Walter Winchell, Damon Runyan, and others, as well as by politicians of every stripe, including the now revered Earl Warren of California.[3] The die seemed cast, particularly when it became clear that religious groups (except the Quakers) and civil rights organizations would not come to aid the Japanese Americans. This was the situation in spite of the protestations by military leaders such as General Mark Clark and Admiral Harold Stark, both of whom said that evacuation of all Japanese Americans was not necessary.

On March 21, 1942, the Congress passed a law imposing a penalty of one year in jail, a five-thousand-dollar fine, or both, for knowingly violating any military order. A penal clause is not a bad law, because there is always the question of whether a particular order, military or otherwise, is a valid order. Here, as events proved, the U.S. Supreme Court failed to make strict scrutiny of the validity of a particular order.

On March 23, 1942, as I recall, General John L. DeWitt issued his Military Proclamation No. 3, requiring all German enemy aliens, all Italian enemy aliens, and all persons of Japanese ancestry to conform to a curfew order. This extended from 8:00 P.M. until 6:00 A.M., and all affected were to remain within five miles of their usual place of abode or business, unless exempted by special military permission.

It was my feeling and belief, then and now, that no military authority has the right to subject any United States citizen to any requirement that does not equally apply to all other U.S. citizens.

Moreover, if a citizen believes that the sovereign state is committing an illegal act, it is incumbent upon that citizen to take measures to rectify such error, or so, at least, I believed. Finally, it seemed to me then and now that if the government unlawfully curtails the rights of any person, the damage is done not only to that individual person but to the whole society. If we believe in America, if we believe in equality and democracy, if we believe in law and justice, then each of us, when we see or believe errors are being made, has an obligation to make every effort to correct them.

Quixotic or idealistic as it may seem, I believed this in March 1942. And I still do today.

Consequently, at 8:00 P.M., March 28, 1942, after having asked Rae Shimojima, my assistant, to notify the FBI and the local Portland police, I

---

[3]Walter Lippman, Westbrook Pegler, Walter Winchell, and Damon Runyan were all influential journalists who supported the internment. Earl Warren, who was attorney general of California at the time of the internment, later became chief justice of the U.S. Supreme Court, in which position he was noted for his vigorous protection of civil liberties. — EDS.

started to walk the streets of Portland in deliberate violation of Military Proclamation No. 3. The principle involved was whether the military could single out a specific group of U.S. citizens on the basis of ancestry and require them to do something not required of other U.S. citizens. As a lawyer, I knew that unless legal protest is made at the time of injury, the doctrine of laches or indeed the statute of limitations[4] would forever bar a remedy.

I was convinced, having discussed this matter in some considerable detail with a number of constitutional lawyers in Portland, that unless a legal challenge were successful, there would be no way to stop the inexorable processes of evacuation, and that unless the courts would find that the military was exercising unlawful powers, there could never be a legal claim against the United States government.

So on March 28, 1942, I began to walk the streets of Portland, up and down Third Avenue until about 11:00 P.M., and I was getting tired of walking. I stopped a Portland police officer, and I showed him a copy of Military Proclamation No. 3, prohibiting persons of Japanese ancestry from being away from their homes after 8:00 P.M.; and I pulled out my birth certificate to show him that I was a person of Japanese ancestry. When I asked him to arrest me, he replied, "Run along home, sonny boy, or you'll get in trouble." So I had to go on down to the Second Avenue police station and argue myself into jail. I pulled this thing on a Saturday and didn't get bailed out until the following Monday.

After being released I called my mother in Hood River. Dad had been interned; she was at home alone with two of her youngest children. Earlier, the Portland *Oregonian* had come out with a front-page, two-inch headline across the top of the page, trumpeting "Jap Spy Arrested." I knew that Mom would be worried. I said, "Mom, *shimpai shiteru dessho?*" ("You are worried, aren't you?") I wanted to reassure her that I was physically okay. Her response was, and I shall never forget, *"Shimpai dokoro ka! Susumeru zo!"* ("Worry? Nonsense! I encourage you!") We have never given our Issei mothers enough credit for having brought up a generation of Nisei strong enough to endure and prevail in a hostile environment.

And so began the test case, but unfortunately, only on curfew. I know that Gordon Kiyoshi Hirabayashi also later refused to be evacuated, by refusing to report for evacuation and processing, and that the federal authorities charged him with violating the curfew as well as the exclusion orders. His case was heard by the U.S. Supreme Court only on the issue of curfew. After starting the curfew test case, I was content to let the matter lie quietly. I was indicted by a federal grand jury in April, but I don't remember when my trial began. In the meanwhile, my Uncle Ren was suffering from cataracts. He needed to see specialists in Portland, and since March was a busy season on the farms, I volunteered to take him from Hood River to Portland. I obtained appropriate military permission for

---

[4]"Laches" is negligence or delay in asserting a claim. The statute of limitations provides that legal charges cannot be brought after a certain time period has elapsed. — EDS.

him to travel more than five miles for medical reasons, and then I drove him 140 miles around Mount Hood to avoid the restricted Bonneville Dam area, because I did not want him to languish in an internment camp for violating military orders. But in returning to Portland, I deliberately drove through the restricted area, expecting almost every moment to be stopped and arrested. I figured as long as they had me for curfew, I might as well ask for a test of other aspects of military orders.

At the end of April 1942, military orders were posted for all residents of Japanese ancestry, aliens and nonaliens (a euphemism for citizen), calling for them to report for evacuation and processing at the North Portland Livestock Pavilion. There was about a five-day grace period. So again, I notified the military authorities that I had no intention of conforming or obeying what I considered to be absolutely unconstitutional, illegal, and unenforceable military orders, and that I was going home to Hood River, some sixty miles up the Columbia River. It was again my thought that since I was testing the curfew, I might as well test the validity of evacuation orders too.

So before the deadline to report to the North Portland Livestock Pavilion, I packed my files and my few belongings and left for Hood River. I had given the military my address and invited them to arrest me, should they want to stop me. In law, you really can't have a "preventive" arrest. After I was home for a few days, I received a call from the military offices in Portland saying that the MPs would be coming to get me on May 12, 1942, and that they would escort me to the North Portland Livestock Pavilion. I indicated that I would cooperate but would go under coercion only. Sure enough, on May 12, 1942, a sedan with a second lieutenant, a driver, and a jeep with four MPs came to our home in Hood River at the appointed time. The lieutenant said, "Let's go," and I complied in my 1935 Chevy. Molly Kageyama, a younger sister of my older brother's wife who was to be married, went with me. The entourage traveled down the Columbia Gorge highway, some sixty-six miles, and two and a half hours later, we were escorted into the North Portland Livestock Pavilion, which by then was filled with some three thousand Japanese Americans from Multnomah County. . . .

At the North Portland Assembly Center I put in with Ronald Shiozaki and his three younger brothers who were a "family." They invited me to join them; otherwise I would have been shunted off to the bachelors' quarters, where the single men had to live dormitory-style. I also remember Benny Higashi's and Don Sugai's families. Both men were married to local Chinese American women, and both had two small children. The wives, LaLun Higashi and Pil Sugai, endured camp with us. Even though they themselves would have been exempt, their children would not, because they were half Japanese. The children, in each case, were two and four years old.

Somehow we endured the hot summer of 1942. In September 1942, trains began pulling into the siding where meat packers used to load cattle, hogs, and sheep. We were herded into what seemed to be World War I rolling stock. The grapevine had it that we were being moved to someplace in the deserts of Idaho. But no one seemed to know for sure. We were told that we were being moved into permanent camps for the duration of the war. At least it seemed better than the cattle cars loaded with Jews in Europe, being shunted off to extermination camps. But, again, who knew for sure? The Jews were told that they were going to labor camps, and six million of them died. Was the same fate in store for us? Personally, I never wavered in my belief there would be decent treatment. But among the more disillusioned and frantic there was all kinds of speculation and fear.

I remember the train stopping from time to time, mostly in Idaho, to let fast freight roll on through towards the coast. And at such stops, some MPs would allow us to buy beer or soft drinks. Mostly, I guess, I remember we were allowed to have meals in the dining car, and the black stewards would indicate their sympathy toward us as though to say, without speaking, that they empathized with us. We arrived late afternoon, at some isolated siding in the desert area, north of Twin Falls, although we did not know where we were. No houses were in sight, no trees or anything green — only scrubby sagebrush and an occasional low cactus, and mostly dry, baked earth. There was a slight rise to the north, and one could not see to the horizon.

Baggage was unloaded and piled up next to the road, and army trucks were rolling in, kicking up huge clouds of dust. People came off the train, were lined up and loaded into the trucks, and went off into the distance. The seats were hard planks, and after riding all day on the train, most were sore and tired.

We had left the dark, dank confines of a livestock barn hoping to breathe the fresh, open air. But because the virgin desert had been bulldozed and disturbed by men and machinery, instead of fresh air, we got to breathe dust. I remember groups of women getting off the train, looking bewildered. After the lush greenness of the Willamette Valley, to see the sterile, dusty desert which was to be our home "for the duration," many sat on the baggage in the middle of nowhere and wept. As truckloads of people were delivered to Minidoka, we could see that the west end was already occupied by people from so-called Camp Harmony in Puyallup Valley in Washington, where Japanese from Seattle had been confined.

We saw again the barbed-wire fences, the watchtowers, guard houses, the MP detachments, the administration housing, warehouse areas, and block after block of black, tar-paper barracks, about 120 feet long and about 20 feet wide. I remember that at least the mess halls and kitchens were completed, and that evening we had hot meals, perhaps spam and canned vegetables. The barracks were supplied with army cots with metal springs, and we got padding-filled ticks and a couple of army blankets. There was a potbellied stove, and each block had a coal depot. One bare bulb hung from the center of the room. There were real composition-board ceilings, but the walls were unfinished with open two-by-four studs. The floor was wood, and single layered, so one could see the earth below, through the cracks. The smaller units for childless couples were on the end of the building, with two windows on each side, or a total of four windows. There was only one entrance to each unit. No chairs or tables were furnished; however, later the evacuees scrounged scrap lumber and built chairs, tables, bunk beds, dressers, and other things. But only those who were handy with tools could do this. The internee wives with small children were not always able to furnish their rooms comfortably. There was, however, a great deal of sharing and exchange going on.

The Minidoka camp was on a slight rise to the east, with an irrigation canal wending along its southern border. The camp proper was probably about a mile or more long and perhaps slightly less than a mile wide, with a wide street, unpaved, going up the middle of the living area. The hospital was down on lower ground, off a bit to the west and north, the administration section was centered almost due west, and the warehouse area was off to the south a bit. I am not certain where the MP unit was quartered, but it was obvious that access in and out of the camp was controlled by the military.

No sooner had I begun to settle in than I received word that I would be taken back to Portland, Oregon, for the decision of Judge James Alger Fee of the U.S. District Court. There were some delays caused, I learned later, by considerable discussion over whether I would be transported in the custody of the U.S. marshal or army MPs. If the judge ruled against the army orders, there was concern that I would be released to remain in Portland without supervision and under no one's control. The military suggested that if I were transported by MPs, they could physically keep me in custody, whereas a civilian U.S. marshal would have to turn me loose if the judge so ordered.

An inordinately long time was taken for the judge to arrive at his decision. We had a number of eminent constitutional law experts who had filed amicus curiae briefs,[5] and there was some indication that the judge would find the military orders to be null and void as applied to United States citizens of Japanese ancestry. Hence, all of us would be free to come and go as we pleased.

Evidently sufficient assurances were made so that on the fourteenth of November 1942, a single U.S. marshal came to Minidoka to take me into custody and to transport me back to Portland. The marshal drove an ordinary car without any special markings and signed me out at the office of the camp director, Clarence Stafford. We got into his car and drove off. I sat in the rear seat, with no restraints or handcuffs, just like an ordinary passenger. Towards evening we stopped at Bend, Oregon, and instead of going to a restaurant for an evening meal, he delivered me to the jail where I was fed and locked up for the night. That was a shocker to me, because my interpretation of the law was that, until the judge found me guilty, I was a free man, free to return to court voluntarily.

---

[5] "Amicus curiae" is Latin for "friend of the court"; an amicus curiae brief is a commentary on a legal case filed by some person or organization that is not a party to the lawsuit but that wants to provide information to help the court decide the case in a particular way. For example, the Japanese American Citizens League filed an amicus curiae brief (p. 647) attempting to persuade the U.S. Supreme Court to overturn Fred Korematsu's conviction for violating the internment. — EDS.

The next day we drove into Portland, and I was delivered to the Mult-nomah County Jail and was placed in isolation. Knowing that Portland was in Military Zone 1, I had expected to be placed in strict confinement. The next morning, I was brought out of my cell, handcuffs were placed on my wrists, a light restraint chain placed around my waist, and I was led out of the building to the street. I found it degrading to be led around the public streets like a convicted criminal when, in fact, I had under-taken this entire matter on my own initiative and was eager to stand be-fore the court.

Anyway, after entering the federal building I was taken to a room off the courtroom, and the chain and handcuffs were removed. After a short wait, I was taken before Judge James Alger Fee who announced his deci-sion, giving my attorney an opportunity to indicate his intentions to ap-peal. Then I was led back to the Multnomah County Jail, again in hand-cuffs and in chains. This time it seemed appropriate, because in fact I was now a convicted criminal. The judge had found me guilty.

The judge indicated that sentence would be pronounced at a later time and that I would be given the opportunity to make a statement. I was again led into the federal court in Portland, and the judge imposed the maxi-mum sentence on me: one year in jail and a five-thousand-dollar fine. I made a statement, expressing my fundamental faith in the United States and indicating that I believed the U.S. Supreme Court would sustain Judge James Alger Fee on the law, but would reverse his findings of fact.

Judge Fee had made an extensive analysis of constitutional law, based primarily on the old Civil War case of *ex parte* Milligan, and had ruled, in law, that the military could not impose orders against civilians in the ab-sence of martial law, which had never been declared on the West Coast. The judge's review and analysis of the law on this point is extensive and was well reasoned. However, inexplicably, in less than two pages, Judge Fee ruled that all Japanese who were born in the United States prior to 1924, under international law were dual citizens of the United States and of Japan (how Japanese nationality laws could be held to be effective within the United States, I don't know) and had to choose which citizenship they desired upon attaining majority. He ruled that I had, by my conduct, elected to be a Japanese national. To reach his conclusion, the judge cited the facts that our family had gone to Japan for a summer vacation of three months (when I was nine years old) to visit our grandparents and that I had learned to speak the Japanese language.

Acknowledging that I had attended public schools as well as the Univer-sity of Oregon, receiving both an arts degree and a law degree, he noted that I took a course in military training because it was "unquestionably compulsory," in his words. It's true that lower classmen at the University of Oregon were required to take military training for two years, but at the up-perclassman level, beginning in the junior year, advanced ROTC wasn't only optional but was fairly competitive. Having been accepted into Ad-vanced ROTC in 1935, I was sufficiently proficient that by 1937, I held the rank of cadet captain, commanding the color company.

Judge Fee noted that while I graduated with "acceptable standards" — in 1937 I was elected to Phi Beta Kappa — and received a commission as a second lieutenant in the Officers Reserve Corps and thus took an oath of allegiance to the United States, "such acts were all during minority." Since I had enrolled as a freshman at the University of Oregon in the fall of 1933 prior to my seventeenth birthday, the army wouldn't give me my commission as a second lieutenant until after October 1937 when I was fully twenty-one years of age. My taking of the Oath of Allegiance to the United States was after I had fully attained my majority. So the judge was wrong on that point too.

The judge also referred to the facts that my father had been decorated by the emperor of Japan for promoting better U.S.-Japanese relationships and that within a few months after I had been admitted to the Bar of the State of Oregon, I was, at the instigation of my father, employed by the consulate general of Japan in Chicago. Judge Fee ignored the salient fact that to be admitted to the Oregon state bar, one had to be a citizen of the United States. Incidentally, this occurred on December 9, 1939, when I was fully twenty-three years of age, and not during my minority as stated by Judge Fee.

As for working for the consulate general of Japan in Chicago, Judge Fee stated that I was "registered twice by the consulate general." The consulate general of Japan didn't register me with the U.S. State Department. I sent for, obtained, and registered papers indicating that I was a U.S. citizen employed by a foreign nation. Secondly, the laws and regulations of the United States required that *only* U.S. citizens were required to so register, so the fact that I registered twice as an agent employed by a foreign nation is further clear evidence that I did so as a United States citizen. The bases on which Judge Fee made his ruling read: "The court thus concludes from these evidences that defendant made an election and chose allegiance to the emperor of Japan, rather than citizenship in the United States at his majority." This of course is completely erroneous.

On appeal, first to the U.S. Circuit Court of Appeals in San Francisco, and later to the U.S. Supreme Court, attorneys for the Department of Justice didn't in any way claim that I wasn't a citizen of the United States, and therefore, upon plea of my attorneys, the Supreme Court in June 1943 remanded my case to the U.S. District Court of Oregon with instructions to rule in accordance with the decision in Gordon Hirabayashi's case and reimpose sentence upon me.

Judge Fee sentenced me to one year in jail and a five-thousand-dollar fine. Because of his weird decision relating to my U.S. citizenship, I instructed my attorneys to appeal in order to reestablish my citizenship. Admittedly, it was tempting to let the matter stand and urge all Nisei to come back to the western reaches of Oregon, because a federal judge had declared the military orders of the Western Defense Command to be void. But I couldn't relinquish my U.S. citizenship, and so I appealed the case.

When they first brought me to the fourth floor jail complex of the Multnomah County Jail in Portland, I had a suitcase, toilet articles including a razor, and some changes of clothes. I also had some money, perhaps twenty-five or thirty dollars. Because I was a person of Japanese ancestry, and especially because the judge had ruled that I was an "enemy alien," the jailers decided to keep me in isolation. I am persuaded that in their judgment this decision was made in my best interests — to avoid any confrontations or problems.

Consequently, I was whisked past the cellblocks and led to isolation row. The floor was concrete, and they were kind enough to put me in a corner cell that had bars and a view out on two sides. The other two walls, and the ceiling, were gray painted steel. The cell was probably about six feet wide and eight feet long. There was an uncovered toilet bowl which flushed, a washbasin with running hot and cold water, and a double-decker steel bunk. There was nothing else, except a lot of cockroaches and years of accumulated ground-in grime. When I was put into the cell, I was so keyed up for the court appearance that I don't remember whether they fed me or not, and I didn't care.

I do remember pacing back and forth, thinking of all the marvelous and eloquent things I would say in court, which I never got a chance to utter. I also remember that I could only take three steps back and forth. After the judge pronounced sentence, and after I knew that I'd be in confinement for a long time, I sat down on the edge of my bunk to take stock. I wanted my attorneys to apply for an appeal bond so I could be free pending the appeal. (They subsequently did, and it was refused.) I then thought of serving sentence at a federal work camp — at Kooskia, Idaho — but decided that serving sentence would be an admission of guilt. So I decided to sit out the appeal, still stubbornly insisting that I was right.

After the first few days in isolation, the routine of the day became fixed; I suppose one can get used to anything. It wasn't too bad, but the nights were rough, because after the lights would go out in the cells, things would become quieter and one is left alone with one's thoughts. I'd think of many things, such as what I would do after I got out of jail, where I would go, what kind of a life I'd try to lead. And always my thoughts would turn to food, and it would disgust me to be thinking about ham and eggs for breakfast, with fruit juice and toast and jam; and of shoyu, rice, and fish, or *okazu* ("entrée"), such as Mother used to make. Because the jail regulations allowed me paper and a pencil, I was always trying to write — poetry, letters, thoughts. At one point I was transcribing the Bible in shorthand, to occupy my mind, but gave up on names such as Nebuchadnezzar, or Jehoshaphat, and similar polysyllabic names.

Precious were the visits by Buddy and Cora Oliver, who would come around once a month. There was another devout Christian lady, whose name, regrettably, I have forgotten but who in the kindness of her heart would visit me from time to time. The hardest thing to bear was not knowing when I would be out of there; it was the uncertainty that was the hardest.

At first the guards would not let me out long enough to take a bath or to get a haircut or shave. At the end of several months, I was stinking dirty, although I tried to wash myself in the washbasin with rags. My hair was growing long and shaggy, unkempt and tangled. My facial hair was growing in all directions, untrimmed. And my nails were growing so long that they began to curl over on themselves, both on my hands and feet. I found I could chew off my fingernails, but the nails on my toes gave me trouble. It was not until after Christmas that I was given permission to take a bath and get a haircut and shave, and that seemed like such a luxury then. Thereafter, they permitted me monthly baths and monthly hair trims.

Isolation wasn't too bad. After a while I found that the absence of people wasn't so important to one's sense of self. I knew who I was, and I knew what I was trying to do. I suppose one could say that I found peace within myself.

Then, in June 1943, my attorney advised me that we had lost the final appeal to the U.S. Supreme Court, which had sustained General John DeWitt's military orders as valid and enforceable. But because the Department of Justice attorneys did not question my U.S. citizenship, my case was being remanded to the district court in Portland for judgment and resentencing in accordance with the decision of the U.S. Supreme Court in the *Hirabayashi* case. There was substantial delay between the time of the Supreme Court decision and the case's remand to the district court. I was beginning to chafe a bit, because I wanted to get out of my solitary cell and to begin serving my sentence. Sometime during the end of July or the beginning of August 1943, my attorney told me that the judge had considered my time already spent in the Multnomah County Jail as sufficient punishment under the law, and he suspended the five-thousand-dollar fine imposed on me.

Finally, around the nineteenth of August 1943, a U.S. marshal came to get me at the Multnomah County Jail early in the morning and drove me straight back to the Minidoka WRA camp. It's funny, but I cannot now recall anything about that car ride from Portland, Oregon, to the Minidoka WRA. One would think release from jail . . . but I can't remember now. Obviously, I was going from one kind of imprisonment to another, but at least at the Minidoka WRA camp, there were a hundred acres in which to wander and there were people. Real live people with whom one could talk and reminisce, and plan, and share ideas and thoughts and feelings.

I came out of the Multnomah County Jail pale and pasty-faced, and a bit bloated and flabby, having been confined to a space of less than forty-eight square feet for nine months. I cannot say that I remember all of the days and nights I spent in jail. Today, it seems like an unreal blur. I do remember certain things; but overall, it's almost as though my life was suspended for nine months. And, today, I think: What a waste of time!

Clarence Stafford was still project director at the camp. I was checked in through his office, and was sternly told to behave myself or else I'd find myself back in jail again. I had had enough of jail. I did not cause any particular problems for the camp administration.

I learned that during my absence the military draft had been reopened for Nisei, and further volunteers were being sought for both the 442nd Infantry Combat Team and for the Camp Savage military intelligence school in Minnesota. Because of my infantry training, I immediately volunteered for the infantry, and many months later was advised that I had been rejected. In the meantime, in returning to Minidoka I felt that I should perform some service for the camp residents, because during my absence a group of camp residents had formed a Min Yasui Support Committee, and had raised some funds for my case. Many of them had gone out on relocation, but I felt that I owed the camp residents whatever services I could do for them. . . .

[*When Yasui returned to Minidoka, he learned that his mother and younger siblings had been allowed to relocate to Denver (his father was still being held separately and at that time was incarcerated in Santa Fe). After much haggling, Yasui obtained a thirty-day temporary leave from Minidoka to visit his family in Denver.* — EDS.]

While in Denver, during October 1943, I met Joe Grant Masaoka, the older brother of Mike M. Masaoka. Joe Grant was the JACL representative for the Tri-State area (Colorado, Wyoming, and Nebraska). He was very concerned about Nisei refusing to register for the military draft. Many of the young Nisei men were being arrested and put into prisons. The JACL had been a prime mover in having the military draft reinstituted for Nisei — to give us an opportunity to prove our loyalty and patriotism to the United States of America. Because the JACL had in effect caused these Nisei young men to be caught in a situation where they felt they must defy the military draft orders, JACL felt a deep sense of responsibility to these young men.

There were a number of Nisei from the Granada WRA camp imprisoned at the Federal Correctional Institution (FCI) in Englewood, Colorado. Joe Grant obtained permission to visit them, to counsel them to obey the military draft orders and the law. I remember going with Joe Grant to the FCI and meeting a young Nisei who had just turned eighteen years of age, who had refused to register and refused to conform to draft-board orders. He had been indicted, arrested, and was being held, pending trial.

We said to him, "Son, you're ruining your life. You're still a young man, and you'll have a criminal record that will hold you back for the rest of your life. Please reconsider and cooperate with your draft board."

He replied, "Why should I when the government has taken away our rights and locked us up like a bunch of criminals anyway?"

We responded, "But, you've got to fulfill your obligations to the government. When you fulfill your responsibilities, you'll be in a much stronger position to demand your rights."

To which he said, "Look, the government took my father away, and interned him someplace. My mother is alone at the Granada camp with my younger sister who is only fourteen. If the government would take care of them here in America, I'd feel like going out to fight for my country, but this country is treating us worse than shit!"

We would talk in this vein for half an hour or more, cajoling, pleading, and reasoning until tears would be rolling down his face, and his hands

gripping the bars so hard that his knuckles would show white. It was emotionally traumatic for these young men, and for us too, because we knew
that any group of soldiers going into combat might not ever come home
again.

Joe Grant was indefatigable; we'd make trips up to the jail in Cheyenne,
Wyoming, to counsel a number of young men brought down from the
Heart Mountain WRA camp. We would confer with the U.S. attorneys,
hoping for leniency, given the impossible situations in which these young
men found themselves. We were not at all successful in either persuading
the draft protesters to reconsider or in getting the U.S. attorneys to be le-
nient. . . .

While I was reminiscing about evacuation recently with a long-time
Nisei friend, who is urbane, polished, highly intelligent, and well educated
— a "civilized" gentleman — with courtly manners and a restrained approach to life, but who had undergone the traumas of evacuation as a
teenager, he remarked,

"You know, now realizing what evacuation involved — the degradation
of the human spirit — if that happened again, now, you know what I
would do?"

"No," I replied, "what would you do?"

"I'd get a rifle, lay in plenty of supplies and ammunition, see that my
family members are safe elsewhere, and then I'd barricade myself in my
home and tell them to come and get me! And there would be plenty of
other younger Nisei and Sansei who would be doing the same."

"You mean that you'd actually shoot to kill," I asked, "to avoid being
evacuated?"

"Yes," he replied, "I'd shoot to kill. I'd kill anyone who tried to put me
into one of those camps."

I pointed out that the federal government could bring in overwhelming
manpower, all kinds of barricade-busting equipment, and that such individual resistance would be ruthlessly crushed.

"That's true, of course," he responded. "Certain numbers of us would
be killed. But I'm not sure that the government would go so far as to kill
all of us, and if they did, there would be such a feeling of revulsion, there
would be the most distasteful spilling of blood that such a process would
be stopped."

I wonder! Acknowledging that 1982 isn't 1942, and knowing that the
fervor of civil rights and human rights reached its peak during the 1960s,
nevertheless, I do wonder whether our American public has so fundamentally changed that the ruthless destruction of a few lives by the federal government would result in any sympathy for the sacrificial dead, or would
that only serve to inflame the blood lust of the people?

Although such actions would have an undoubted impact upon the
American people, both in terms of sympathy as well as in cries for more
blood, I wonder whether there would be many other Nikkei (Japanese
Americans) who would man the barricades and die, defying the govern-

ment? My feeling is that there would be precious few. It certainly isn't a matter of physical courage. The Nisei men of the 442nd and the MIS (Military Intelligence Service) amply proved the heroism of Japanese Americans. Rather, it's a question of whether our deeply ingrained sense of duty and loyalty to our nation would allow us to take such drastic action. I'm personally convinced that the Nikkei in 1942 would have gone docilely to the gas chambers if ordered to do so by competent authority.

That's a terrible thing to say, but remembering the quiet obedience of the Japanese Americans in 1942, their almost pathetic eagerness to please, the lack of anger or overwhelming feelings of injustice, I'm not convinced that any large numbers of Nikkei now would take up arms to resist the U.S. government. I don't believe that Japanese Americans would fight back with violence.

And maybe that's a sad commentary on where we are today.

As for myself, I believe I would passively resist again, protesting all the way, but I cannot possibly conceive of taking the lives of other people to protect and preserve my rights. It would be far better to be killed than to kill, because the person who might kill me might just as fervently believe that he's doing his duty as I would believe it to be wrong. Two wrongs can never make it right. Perhaps in that kind of death, rather than killing or being killed, there would be a far more principled dying.

At any rate, my good and gentle Nisei friend, in espousing violent resistance, gives us pause to think again about what we would do if this sorry sort of thing were to happen again.

Now, forty years later, we are still struggling to find means whereby this kind of thing can never happen again to any group of people. Tremendous outrages were inflicted upon us. We cannot rest, we shall not rest until we make every effort to assure that it shall never happen again — so that my good friend, a man of law and of principle, does not feel that he might have to pick up a rifle to defend his integrity as a human being.

READING CRITICALLY

1. What reasons does Yasui give for his decision to violate the curfew imposed on Japanese Americans?

2. In addition to violating the curfew, what else did Yasui do that resisted the military orders imposed on the Nikkei?

3. Yasui alludes briefly several times to the concentration camp experiences of Jews in Europe. Why do you think Yasui includes these references?

4. What reasons did Judge Fee give for saying that Yasui was not an American citizen?

5. In retrospect, what does Yasui think the Nikkei should have done about the internment? Has he changed his mind? Does he now wish he had resisted more strongly, or not at all?

WRITING ANALYTICALLY

1. One key question in Yasui's trials was whether he could be considered an American citizen. This was an issue, even though he was born in the United States, because Judge Fee in effect questioned whether he was sufficiently assimilated to American culture. Write a paper in which you explain what definition of *assimilation* seems to be operating in Judge Fee's thinking. Option: Compare and contrast this definition with the one provided either in Flowers (p. 623) or in the JACL brief (p. 647).

2. Yasui's behavior provides a range of responses to injustice other than violent resistance. Write a paper in which you discuss the options open to people who suffer injustice because of their membership in a particular group, as the Nikkei were singled out for their Japanese ancestry. Your thesis should indicate the extent to which you agree or disagree with what Yasui seems to be recommending. You should also consider which Nikkei responses (if any) might be useful to other oppressed groups. Alternative: Write a dialogue between Yasui and Mike Masaoka (p. 676) concerning what people ought to do in response to an injustice such as the internment. Write yourself into the dialogue if you wish.

MONICA SONE

From *Nisei Daughter* (1953)

Monica Sone (b. 1919) was born Kazuko Itoi in Seattle, where her father ran a hotel. Her education at the University of Washington was interrupted by the internment, and she and her family were sent to Camp Minidoka in Idaho. Sone was later allowed to leave the camp, first to work in Chicago and then to attend Hanover College (represented in this chapter as "Wendell College") in Indiana and Case Western Reserve University in Cleveland, Ohio, where she did graduate work in psychology. We are including the final chapter, "Deeper into the Land," from her autobiography, in which she discusses the impact of the internment on her own cultural identity.

I ENROLLED AT WENDELL COLLEGE in southern Indiana. The cluster of ivy-covered red brick buildings stood gathered on the edge of a thick-wooded bluff which rose almost three hundred feet, overlooking the stately Ohio River. Wendell College was a Presbyterian-affiliated liberal arts school, and the atmosphere of its campus reflected a leisurely pace of life, simplicity and friendly charm. Young people from all walks of life were there . . .

Monica Sone, *Nisei Daughter* (1953; 2nd ed., Seattle: University of Washington Press, 1979), 226–38.
In the notes, EDS. = Patricia Bizzell and Bruce Herzberg.

studying for the ministry, the teaching profession, the medical profession, and other varied fields. There was also a distinct international air with foreign students from all parts of the world: South America, China, Java, India.

Mrs. Ashford, the widow with whom I lived on the edge of the campus, was an example of the college town's friendliness. She was a comfortable, motherly woman with silky, honey-colored hair done up in a bun, and merry blue eyes. Her husband had been a minister and college official. He had died several years before, and Mrs. Ashford had been living alone ever since. In the tall, two-storied gray frame house, my new friend had prepared a cozy room for me upstairs, where I could study quietly. Despite a stiff knee, Mrs. Ashford was up at dawn to fire up the furnace and prepare breakfast. I awakened to her cheerful call and the fragrant aroma of coffee wafting up to my room. In the evenings when I returned home from school, we sat in the two wooden rocking chairs in the sitting room, chatted about the days' events, listened to a favorite radio program or two, then I went upstairs to study. And always before bedtime, Mrs. Ashford called me down to the kitchen for a light snack because she firmly believed that mental work was just as exhausting as physical labor. Thus she provided me with the companionship I needed and a wealth of enchanting memories which I could conjure up at the thought of Wendell . . . the warm fragrance of freshly baked nutbread and homemade cookies filling the house on a cold winter night, the creaking porch swing where I could relax on warm spring evenings to watch the fireflies pinpoint the dark blue night, as I breathed in the thick sweet scent of lilacs surrounding the house.

There were three other Nisei girls enrolled at Wendell. Two were from southern California, and the third from my own hometown. Faculty and students alike went out of their way to make us feel a real part of the campus life. We were swept into a round of teas and dinner parties, and invited to join the independent women's organization. The sororities included us in their rush parties, too, although because of a national ruling we could not be asked to join. I knew about this policy, and although I had ceased to feel personally hurt about it, one sorority apparently felt troubled by the restriction imposed on it. One day its officers, Alice Week, Lorraine Brown, and the faculty advisor, Miss Knight, paid me a special visit. I remember how Alice looked at Miss Knight as if she were taking a deep breath before the plunge, and then spoke gently to me. "Monica, we've enjoyed meeting you, and we hope we'll get to know a lot more of each other from now on. But there are national restrictions placed on our membership. Although many of us sincerely want to invite you into our group, we can't. I hope you understand."

After a moment of embarrassed silence, I managed to say, "Yes, Alice, I do know about this from back home. I understand."

Lorraine said, "We felt we should tell you about it, Monica, rather than say nothing. We didn't want you to think we were ignoring you for personal reasons."

"Thank you. I really appreciate your visit." I knew this call had cost them something in pride, and it took moral honesty to have come in the spirit in which they did.

In the following years I came to know and like Alice, a charming and earnest young woman, who took valedictory honors in my graduation class, and Lorraine, a talented music major. My constant companion was Marta Sanchez, a vivacious dark-eyed girl from Bogotá, Colombia, who spoke with her expressive hands whenever her English failed her. We both liked music and played the piano about the same way, loud and stormy. We were frustrated "classical" students who yearned to play jazz with the abandon of George Gershwin. Marta was studying to be a doctor because, as she said, there was a great need for them in her country. Then there was Anna Jong from Bangkok. She had been a student in China until the time Japan had pushed into its interior. Anna had fled to safety by walking long, cruel miles southward. She had come to Wendell through the auspices of the Presbyterian Mission Board. Anna wanted to be a geologist. I also became good friends with Sylvia Arnold and her brother John from Dayton, Ohio, both of whom were studying to go into the Christian service.

The professors were at once friendly and casual. Although during class hours they were distant and insistent that we study, we grew to know them, their wives and their children, well at school and church functions and from day-to-day encounters at the post office and stores. There was one distinguished-looking language professor whom I always called whenever I wanted to get a ride into town on a Saturday. Dr. Konig and his wife always went into town on weekends, taking a carload of students with them. There was another, tall, gruff-mannered economics professor whom we could sometimes persuade to move classes out to the cool green lawn under the trees on warm spring days. And whenever I was faced with a vexing personal problem, I immediately hied myself to Dr. or Mrs. Scott who diffused affection and understanding like a glowing hearth fire. It was a far cry from the dignified and austere University of Washington where I hurried alone from class to class along the sprawling pathways.

I had been intimidated by the racial barriers in the business and professional world and I wasn't brave enough to explore or develop my other interests. It seemed useless to do so in the face of closed doors. So when I entered the University of Washington, I clung to literature, my first love, saying to my friends that I wanted to teach. We all knew this was a fancy, too, destined to wither.

Now my interests exploded in a number of directions — music, history and current events, religion and philosophy, sociology. But above all, I discovered that I liked people, as individuals and unique personalities. Whatever career I chose, it would have something to do with people. And since I had to come to the Midwest and was embarked on a life more normal and happier than I had dared hope for, I gradually uncoiled and relaxed enough to take more honest stock of my real inclinations. I was attracted to psychology courses and did well in them. After talking it over with my advisor, I decided to go into clinical psychology.

The first two school years at Wendell I worked for my tuition and board, waiting on tables in the women's dormitory. Being physically inept, I never learned to hoist the huge tray over my head with one hand as most students did within the first week. Instead I staggered and groaned under the weight of the tray until at last I was offered a job as secretary to Dr. Scott, and not a day too soon, I thought, for I had worn deep dents into my sides from carrying trays on my hips. During summer vacations, I went home to the Richardsons in Chicago where I worked as a stenographer in a law firm.[1] Father's foresight in persuading me to go to business school was paying off at last.

My second year at Wendell, just before Christmas, I had a letter from Father and Mother, who were still in camp, urging me to spend the holiday with them. "It would be so nice to have at least one of you back." They enclosed a check for the railroad fare. So I packed a suitcase, kissed Mrs. Ashford "Good-by and Merry Christmas," and set off for Camp Minidoka.

At Shoshone, my last stop, I went into a crumbling old hotel and sat in its overheated lobby to wait for the bus to take me into camp. Bewhiskered, wrinkled old men lounged silently, reading every word in the newspaper, reaching around now and then to spit tobacco juice into the battered brass spittoon. I wondered if Father's hotel in Seattle was now filled with dried-up, dusty remnants of humanity like these.

At Camp Minidoka, I was startled to see an MP again, standing at the gate. I had forgotten about such things as MPs and barbed-wire fences. Mother rushed out of the gate shelter, her face beaming. "Ka-chan! It was so good of you to come. Have you been well and happy?" She looked closely into my face. I was relieved to see Mother looking well and still full of smiles, although I noticed a few gray streaks in her smooth jet-black head of hair as I hugged her.

"Where's Papa?" I asked.

"He had a bad cold, and he's resting at the hospital now. He'll be home in a day or two."

Although Mother tried to hide it, I learned that Father had had a close brush with pneumonia.

The camp was quiet and ghostly, drained of its young blood. All of the able-bodied Nisei men had been drafted into the army. The rest of the young people had relocated to the Midwest and East to jobs and schools. Some of the parents had followed them out. But the Issei who still wanted to go back West and had a home or a business to return to, remained in camp, hoping that the military restriction on the Coast would be lifted at the end of the war.

When I stepped into our old barracks room, I felt as if I had returned to a shell of a prison. The room had been stripped down to two cots, and it

---

[1]The Richardsons were a Presbyterian minister and his wife who had sponsored Sone's departure from Minidoka. She lived with them in a Chicago suburb while working as an office assistant to a dentist. The Richardsons had also used their church connections to help her enroll at Wendell College. — EDS.

yawned silent and bare. The white walls were now filmed over with a dingy gray from the coal smoke. The wall where Sumi's cot had stood, formerly plastered with movie actors' pictures, was empty and dotted with black pin-holes.[2] The dressing table, once cluttered with rows of nail polishes, lip-sticks, and bottles of cologne, stood stark and empty. Only Mother and Fa-ther's brush and comb sets lay there, neatly, side by side.

That evening Mother and I went to see Father at the hospital. From a distance down the hall I could see him sitting up in bed. What had been a firm-fleshed, nut-brown face, was now thin-chiseled and pinched. His high forehead gleamed pale. I did not have the heart to ask whether this was only the result of his illness.

I had written to Father and Mother about everything which had hap-pened to me since I left camp, but they wanted to hear about it all over again. For two hours I talked, telling them in detail about the Richardson family, how I had been able to return to school, and about my new friends at Wendell. Mother had been studying me as I talked. She said, "You've be-come a happy person, Ka-chan. I remember those days back in Seattle when the war started, I wondered when any of us would ever feel secure and happy again. We worried a great deal about our children."

Father told me that things were not going too well with his business in Seattle. From the looks of the monthly reports, Father suspected that somebody was siphoning huge sums of money into his own pockets, and juggling books to make it appear that vast improvements were being made, which Father had no way of checking. Father said that Henry was going to Seattle soon to look into the matter. Henry had given up thoughts of pursuing his medical career for the present, and he and Min-nie decided to leave St. Louis and go back to Seattle to help Father with his business comeback. Minnie's folks planned to return to their former home, too.[3]

"At least I still have the business," Father said philosophically. "I'm a lot luckier than many of my friends who lost everything."

Mr. Kato had lost his hotel lease and his entire personal property had been carted away from the hotel by men, posing as government storage men, who said they were going to move everything into the storehouse. Mr. Kato and his wife said they would probably work together as houseman and cook in a home, for a while, when they returned to Seattle until they had a better plan. For the present, they were waiting their days out, look-ing for mail from their son Jiro who was somewhere in Europe.

Mr. Oshima had been released from the internment camp in Missoula. He and his wife intended to return to the barber business provided they could find a suitable shop. They were living in suspended anxiety for their son Dunks had been taken prisoner of war by the Germans.

[2]Sumi, Sone's younger sister Sumiko, had left Minidoka to train for the Cadet Nurses Corps. — EDS.

[3]Henry, Sone's older brother, was married to another internee, Minnie, and was in Twin Falls, Idaho, on a temporary leave from Minidoka. He had attempted to enlist in the U.S. Army but was rejected on account of his poor eyesight. — EDS.

Mrs. Matsui had joined her daughter, now married, in New York. Mother said Mrs. Matsui was toying with the idea of returning to Japan where her son Dick was, but Dick had written, saying that he wanted to return to the States. She was in a dilemma. Mrs. Matsui also mentioned that she had run into Kazuo, our former Seattle childhood friend. Kazuo was now a happily married man with three children, and he was star soloist in his church choir.

I also learned that Genji, the model boy whom we had disliked so much at Nihon Gakko[4] was now studying for the ministry in the East. And Mr. Ohashi, the old schoolmaster, was operating a bookstore in Colorado. There was also a rumor that the Nihon Gakko building might be converted into apartment houses for the returning evacuees.

Father asked me to call on his best friend, Mr. Sawada, the former clothes salesman. "He's all alone here now since his daughter has left for Chicago. As you know, George was killed in Italy, and now his other son, Paul, is reported missing in action. Mr. Sawada often asks about you." I remembered long ago how hard Mr. Sawada had worked to send George to medical school, and how he straightened up whenever he talked about his children.

I found Mr. Sawada in an untidy room. Half-filled teacups stood on windowsills and a saucer overflowed with cigarette butts. An odd wired cage stood on a stool near the stove, a ragged gray sweater flung over it. Mr. Sawada grinned as he caught me staring at it. "This is where Shozo lives," he said. He pulled the sweater off to show me a disgruntled black crow. "For hours I sat out there on the prairie before I could persuade him to light on my shoulder. Since then we've become good friends. Sometimes I let him fly around in here, but he gets it so messy. I think one messy old man in the room is enough, don't you?"

I laughed. Mr. Sawada was still his cheerful, casual self. He told me he was eager to return to Seattle. When I said that I didn't want to go back there for a long, long time, he said, "You young ones feel everything so keenly. It's good, but sometimes you must suffer more for it. When you get old like me, Kazuko-san, things are not so sharply differentiated into black and white. Don't worry, I'll be happy in Seattle. The common people there won't hold grudges for long, and neither will I. All the fire and emotion will have died down. All I want is to live out my days there peacefully."

We sat silently together for a moment. Then I stood up to leave. "It was nice seeing you again, Mr. Sawada. Please take good care of yourself, and I hope you will hear good news about Paul soon."

"Hah, *arigato.* I'm praying."

"And I was terribly sorry to hear about George."

Mr. Sawada said quietly, "He walked into it, that boy of mine. Maybe you heard . . . he volunteered to go on a special mission."

---

[4]Nihon Gakko was the afternoon school in Japanese language and culture that Sone and her brother attended after their American schoolday ended. — EDS.

"Yes, Father told me about it."

I lapsed into an unhappy silence, thinking how painful it must be for him to talk about it. He spoke to me gently, as if he were trying to put me at ease. "Kazuko-san, I want to show you a letter which he wrote me when he was on the train, on his way to Camp Shelby. After you read it, you will understand why I do not feel as lonely as you think I do." He walked to a bookshelf on which stood a photograph of George in uniform. A Japanese Bible lay in front of it. From between its pages, Mr. Sawada withdrew the letter and handed it to me.

In the quiet of the little room where I heard only the loud ticking of the alarm clock and Shozo strutting up and down on his horny little feet, I read George's letter, written only a few hours after he had told his father good-by at the camp gate.

He wrote: "I feel I owe it to myself and to you to tell you some of the things I should have said and didn't when the time came for us to part. I don't know why I didn't. Perhaps, because I was overly reticent; perhaps, it was because we were Japanese, but mainly, because I think I was a little bit self-conscious."

George went on to say that as the train carried him away, he was thinking back over their happy family life. He recalled family picnics, the sorrow when his mother died, the family struggles and triumphs. "When Evacuation Day came," George wrote, "I was stricken with bitterness, and I remember how you comforted me. I could not then understand why you tried to restore my faith in this country which was now rejecting us, making us penniless. You said wisely: 'It is for the best. For the good of many, a few must suffer. This is your sacrifice. Accept it as such and you will no longer be bitter.' I listened, and my bitterness left me. You, who had never been allowed citizenship, showed me its value. That I retained my faith and emerged a loyal American citizen, I owe to your understanding. When the time came for enlistment, I was ready."

There were tears in my eyes. I heard Mr. Sawada say, "With this letter, George will comfort me always. I know that George understood and loved me well."

I thanked him for letting me read the letter. He took Shozo out of the cage and walked to the door with me. "Well, Kazuko-san, study hard. But don't forget to keep one eye out for your future husband!"

I laughed, in spite of my brimming eyes, and walked quickly away.

The days passed by too quickly and it was time to leave Camp Minidoka. Father and Mother accompanied me to the camp gate. It was one of those crisp winter mornings when the pale sky and the snow were bathed in a taut cold pink.

"Ah, well, this parting is not a sad one for us, is it, Mama?" Father said. "It isn't as if she were a young son going off to war."

"This is what happens to all parents. Children grow, and they must fly away. But it is well . . . you all seem so happy in your letters, Henry and

Minnie in St. Louis, and Sumi way out there in the East. When the war came and we were all evacuated, Papa and I were heartsick. We felt terribly bad about being your Japanese parents."

"No, don't say those things, Mama, please. If only you knew how much I have changed about being a Nisei. It wasn't such a tragedy. I don't resent my Japanese blood anymore. I'm proud of it, in fact, because of you and the Issei who've struggled so much for us. It's really nice to be born into two cultures, like getting a real bargain in life, two for the price of one. The hardest part, I guess, is the growing up, but after that, it can be interesting and stimulating. I used to feel like a two-headed monstrosity, but now I find that two heads are better than one."

Father beamed, "It makes us very happy to hear that."

"In spite of the war and the mental tortures we went through, I think the Nisei have attained a clearer understanding of America and its way of life, and we have learned to value her more. Her ideas and ideals of democracy are based essentially on religious principles and her very existence depends on the faith and moral responsibilities of each individual. I used to think of the government as a paternal organization. When it failed me, I felt bitter and sullen. Now I know I'm just as responsible as the men in Washington for its actions. Somehow it all makes me feel much more at home in America. All in all, I think the Issei's losses during this war are greater."

"If we consider material losses, maybe so, but our children's gain is our gain, too. Our deepest happiness we receive from our children," Father said.

"What are you and Mama going to do, the first thing after you return to Seattle?"

Father had a ready reply.

"Oh, first, we'll go and say 'Hello and thank you' to Joe, Sam, and Peter for looking after the hotel. After that, we will take a walk along the waterfront and maybe dine on a crab or two. Then we will buy a little house and wait for visits from you all with your little children."

Mother smiled in assent. I gave a quick hug to Father and Mother and stepped inside the bus. As I looked out of the window, I saw them standing patiently, wrapped in heavy dark winter clothes, Father in his old navy pea jacket, Mother in black wool slacks and black coat. They looked like wistful immigrants. I wondered when they would be able to leave their no-man's land, pass through the legal barrier, and become naturalized citizens. Then I thought, in America, many things are possible. When I caught Father and Mother's eyes, they smiled instantly.

I was returning to Wendell College with confidence and hope. I had discovered a deeper, stronger pulse in the American scene. I was going back into its main stream, still with my Oriental eyes, but with an entirely different outlook, for now I felt more like a whole person instead of a sadly split personality. The Japanese and the American parts of me were now blended into one.

READING CRITICALLY

1. What did Sone like about Wendell College?

2. How do you think Sone wants her readers to react to the incident with the sorority? How can you tell?

3. How do you think Sone wants her readers to react to her portrait of Mr. Sawada?

4. What do you think Sone's parents mean when they tell her, "We felt terribly bad about being your Japanese parents" (p. 755)?

5. At the end of this final chapter in her book, Sone says she no longer feels like "a two-headed monstrosity" (p. 755). What does she mean?

WRITING ANALYTICALLY

1. Sone's account of the internment is generally regarded as comparatively up-beat and positive about the consequences for her own sense of self — unlike, say, the Houston and Houston account (pp. 715 and 757). Write a paper in which you argue that Sone is, indeed, relatively upbeat or, alternatively, that she only appears to be upbeat, while actually presenting many negatives about the internment. Base your argument on an analysis of specific incidents in the narrative such as the sorority incident (reading question 2 will help you here) or the concluding conver-sation with her parents (see reading question 4).

2. Imagine that Sone has written you a letter from the internment camp, asking if you think she should come to your college. Write a letter to her in which you re-spond to this question, based on your knowledge of your school as it is today.

3. Sone discusses what it is like to feel allegiance to two cultures, the Japanese and the American. Although she says she once felt like a "two-headed monstrosity" (see reading question 5), she says at the end of her narrative that she feels comfort-ably bicultural, able to function in and maintain loyalty to both cultures. Other writers in this unit, notably Houston and Houston (pp. 715 and 757) and Okada (p. 766), also depict characters who are struggling with dual cultural identities. Using these three sources, and your own experience if appropriate, write a paper in which you describe what it is like to be bicultural. You may wish to consider the extent to which a comfortable bicultural identity is attainable and/or the extent to which the picture of biculturalism that we get from these three Nikkei sources can be generalized to apply to all bicultural people.

JEANNE WAKATSUKI HOUSTON
AND JAMES D. HOUSTON

From *Farewell to Manzanar* (1973)

Jeanne Wakatsuki Houston and her family left Manzanar in October 1945 and returned to Long Beach, California. They had lost their prewar car, two fishing boats, and all their other possessions except for a few household goods. They rented an apartment in Cabrillo Homes, a run-down housing project. Jeanne's mother soon found work in a fish cannery, but her father would not stoop to what he considered such degrading labor. Chapters 20 and 21, excerpted here, describe Jeanne's return to public school after the internment. (For more information on Jeanne Wakatsuki Houston and James D. Houston, see the headnote on p. 715.)

CHAPTER 20

A Double Impulse

WHEN THE SIXTH-GRADE TEACHER USHERED ME IN, the other kids inspected me, but not unlike I myself would study a new arrival. She was a warm, benevolent woman who tried to make this first day as easy as possible. She gave me the morning to get the feel of the room. That afternoon, during a reading lesson, she finally asked me if I'd care to try a page out loud. I had not yet opened my mouth, except to smile. When I stood up, everyone turned to watch. Any kid entering a new class wants, first of all, to be liked. This was uppermost in my mind. I smiled wider, then began to read. I made no mistakes. When I finished, a pretty blond girl in front of me said, quite innocently, "Gee, I didn't know you could speak English."

She was genuinely amazed. I was stunned. How could this have even been in doubt?

It isn't difficult, now, to explain her reaction. But at age eleven, I couldn't believe anyone could think such a thing, say such a thing about me, or regard me in that way. I smiled and sat down, suddenly aware of what being of Japanese ancestry was going to be like. I wouldn't be faced with physical attack, or with overt shows of hatred. Rather, I would be seen as someone foreign, or as someone other than American, or perhaps not be seen at all.

During the years in camp I had never really understood why we were there, nor had I questioned it much. I knew no one in my family had committed a crime. If I needed explanations at all, I conjured up vague no-

Jeanne Wakatsuki Houston and James D. Houston, *Farewell to Manzanar* (1973; reprint, New York: Bantam Books, 1974), 113–30.
In the notes, EDS. = Patricia Bizzell and Bruce Herzberg.

tions about a *war* between America and Japan. But now I'd reached an age where certain childhood mysteries begin to make sense. This girl's guileless remark came as an illumination, an instant knowledge that brought with it the first buds of true shame.

From that day on, part of me yearned to be invisible. In a way, nothing would have been nicer than for no one to see me. Although I couldn't have defined it at the time, I felt that if attention were drawn to me, people would see what this girl had first responded to. They wouldn't see me, they would see the slant-eyed face, the Oriental. This is what accounts, in part, for the entire evacuation. You cannot deport 110,000 people unless you have stopped seeing individuals. Of course, for such a thing to happen, there has to be a kind of acquiescence on the part of the victims, some submerged belief that this treatment is deserved, or at least allowable. It's an attitude easy for nonwhites to acquire in America. I had inherited it. Manzanar had confirmed it. And my feeling, at eleven, went something like this: You are going to be invisible anyway, so why not completely disappear.

But another part of me did not want to disappear. With the same sort of reaction that sent Woody into the army, I instinctively decided I would have to prove that I wasn't different, that it should not be odd to hear me speaking English. From that day forward I lived with this double impulse: the urge to disappear and the desperate desire to be acceptable.

I soon learned there were certain areas I was automatically allowed to perform in: scholarship, athletics, and school-time activities like the yearbook, the newspaper, and student government. I tried all of these and made good grades, became news editor, held an office in the Girls Athletic League.

I also learned that outside school another set of rules prevailed. Choosing friends, for instance, often depended upon whether or not I could be invited to their homes, whether their parents would allow this. And what is so infuriating, looking back, is how I accepted the situation. If refused by someone's parents, I would never say, "Go to hell!" or "I'll find other friends," or "Who wants to come to your house anyway?" I would see it as my fault, the result of my failings. I was imposing a burden on *them*.

I would absorb such rejections and keep on looking, because for some reason the scholarship society and the athletic league and the yearbook staff didn't satisfy me, were never quite enough. They were too limited, or too easy, or too obvious. I wanted to declare myself in some different way, and — old enough to be marked by the internment but still too young for the full impact of it to cow me — I wanted *in*.

At one point I thought I would like to join the Girl Scouts. A friend of mine belonged, that blond girl who had commented on my reading. Her name was Radine. Her folks had come west from Amarillo, Texas, and had made a little money in the aircraft plants but not enough yet to get out of Cabrillo Homes. We found ourselves walking partway home together every day. Her fascination with my ability to speak English had led to many other topics. But she had never mentioned the Girl Scouts to me. One day I did.

"Can I belong?" I asked, then adding as an afterthought, as if to ease what I knew her answer would have to be, "You know, I'm Japanese."

"Gee," she said, her friendly face suddenly a mask. "I don't know. But we can sure find out. Mama's the assistant troop leader."

And then, the next day, "Gee, Jeannie, no. I'm *really* sorry."

Rage may have been simmering deep within me, but my conscious reaction was, "Oh well, that's okay, Radine. I understand. I guess I'll see you tomorrow."

"Sure. I'll meet you at the stoplight."

I didn't hold this against her, any more than I associated her personally with the first remark she made. It was her mother who had drawn the line, and I was used to that. If anything, Radine and I were closer now. She felt obliged to protect me. She would catch someone staring at me as we walked home from school and she would growl, "What are *you* looking at? *She's* an American citizen. She's got as much right as anybody to walk around on the street!"

Her outbursts always amazed me. I would much rather have ignored those looks than challenged them. At the same time I wondered why my citizenship had to be so loudly affirmed, and I couldn't imagine why affirming it would really make any difference. (If so, why hadn't it kept me out of Manzanar?) But I was grateful when Radine stuck up for me. Soon we were together all the time. I was teaching her how to twirl baton, and this started a partnership that lasted for the next three years.

I hadn't forgotten what I'd learned in camp. My chubby teacher had taught me well. Radine and I would practice in the grassy plots between the buildings, much as I used to in the firebreaks near Block 28: behind the back, between the legs, over the shoulder, high into the air above the two-story rooftops, watching it, timing its fall for the sudden catch. We practiced the splits, and bending backward, the high-stepping strut, and I saw myself a sequined princess leading orchestras across a football field, the idol of cheering fans.

There happened to be a Boy Scout drum and bugle corps located in the housing project next to ours. They performed in local parades, and they were looking for some baton twirlers to march in front of the band. That fall Radine and I tried out, and we suited them just fine. They made me the lead majorette, in the center between Radine and Gloria, another girl from the seventh grade. Those two wore blue satin outfits to accent their bright blond hair. My outfit was white, with gold braid across the chest. We all wore white, calf-high boots and boat-shaped hats. We worked out trio routines and practiced every weekend with the boys, marching up and down the streets of the project. We performed with them at our junior high assemblies, as well as in the big band reviews each spring, with our batons glinting out in front of the bass drums and snares and shiny bugles, their banners, merit badges, khaki uniforms, and their squared-off military footwork.

This was exactly what I wanted. It also gave me the first sure sign of how certain intangible barriers might be crossed.

The Girl Scouts was much like a sorority, of the kind I would be excluded from in high school and later on in college. And it was run by mothers. The Boy Scouts was like a fraternity and run by fathers. Radine and I were both maturing early. The boys in the band loved having us out there in front of them all the time, bending back and stepping high, in our snug satin outfits and short skirts. Their dads, mostly navy men, loved it too. At that age I was too young to consciously use my sexuality or to understand how an Oriental female can fascinate Caucasian men, and of course far too young to see that even this is usually just another form of invisibility. It simply happened that the attention I first gained as a majorette went hand in hand with a warm reception from the Boy Scouts and their fathers, and from that point on I knew intuitively that one resource I had to overcome the war-distorted limitations of my race would be my femininity. . . .

CHAPTER 21

The Girl of My Dreams

. . . The strutting, sequined partnership I had with Radine was exactly how I wanted my life to go. My path through the next few years can be traced by its relationship to hers. It was a classic situation.

In many ways we had started even. Poor whites from west Texas, her family was so badly off sometimes she'd come to school with no lunch and no money and we would split whatever I had brought along. At the same time we were both getting all this attention together with the drum and bugle corps. After three years at our junior high school, in a ghetto neighborhood that included many Asians, Blacks, Mexicans, and other white migrants from the south, we had ended up close to being social equals.

We stayed best friends until we moved to Long Beach Polytechnic. There everything changed. Our paths diverged. She was asked to join high school sororities. The question of whether or not I should be asked was never even raised. The boys I had crushes on would not ask me out. They would flirt with me in the hallways or meet me after school, but they would ask Radine to the dances, or someone like Radine, someone they could safely be *seen* with. Meanwhile she graduated from baton twirler to song girl, a much more prestigious position in those days. It was unthinkable for a Nisei to be a song girl. Even choosing me as majorette created problems.

The band teacher knew I had more experience than anyone else competing that year. He told me so. But he was afraid to use me. He had to go speak to the board about it, and to some of the parents, to see if it was allowable for an Oriental to represent the high school in such a visible way. It had never happened before. I was told that this inquiry was being made, and my reaction was the same as when I tried to join the Girl Scouts. I was apologetic for imposing such a burden on those who had to decide. When they finally assented, I was grateful. After all, I *was* the first Oriental majorette they'd ever had. Even if my once enviable role now seemed vaguely second-rate, still I determined to try twice as hard to prove they'd made the right choice. . . .

[*After almost killing himself in a terrible drinking binge, Jeanne's father finally sobers up permanently, pulls himself together, and decides to go back into farming. The family leases a hundred acres from a strawberry grower in Santa Clara Valley, outside of San Jose.* — EDS.]

I was a senior when we moved. In those days, 1951, San Jose was a large town, but not yet a city. Coming from a big high school in southern California gave me some kind of shine, I suppose. It was a chance to start over, and I made the most of it. By the spring of that year, when it came time to elect the annual carnival queen from the graduating seniors, my homeroom chose me. I was among fifteen girls nominated to walk out for inspection by the assembled student body on voting day.

I knew I couldn't beat the other contestants at their own game, that is, look like a bobbysoxer. Yet neither could I look too Japanese-y. I decided to go exotic, with a flower-print sarong, black hair loose, and a hibiscus flower behind my ear. When I walked barefooted out onto the varnished gymnasium floor, between the filled bleachers, the howls and whistles from the boys were double what had greeted any of the other girls. It sounded like some winning basket had just been made in the game against our oldest rivals.

It was pretty clear what the outcome would be, but ballots still had to be cast and counted. The next afternoon I was standing outside my Spanish class when Leonard Rodriguez, who sat next to me, came hurrying down the hall with a revolutionary's fire in his eye. He helped out each day in the administration office. He had just overheard some teachers and a couple of secretaries counting up the votes.

"They're trying to stuff the ballot box," he whispered loudly. "They're fudging on the tally. They're afraid to have a Japanese girl be queen. They've never had one before. They're afraid of what some of the parents will say."

He was pleased he had caught them, and more pleased to be telling this to me, as if some long-held suspicion of conspiracy had finally been confirmed. I shared it with him. Whether this was true or not, I was prepared to believe that teachers would stuff the ballot box to keep me from being queen. For that reason I couldn't afford to get my hopes up.

I said, "So what?"

He leaned toward me eagerly, with final proof. "They want Lois Carson to be queen. I heard them say so."

If applause were any measure, Lois Carson wasn't even in the running. She was too slim and elegant for beauty contests. But her father had contributed a lot to the school. He was on the board of trustees. She was blond, blue-eyed. At that point her name might as well have been Radine. I was ready to capitulate without a groan.

"If she doesn't make carnival queen this year," Leonard went on smugly, "she'll never be queen of anything anywhere else for the rest of her life."

"Let her have it then, if she wants it so much."

"No! We can't do that! *You* can't do that!"

I could do that very easily. I wasn't going to be caught caring about this, or needing it, the way I had needed the majorette position. I already sensed, though I couldn't have said why, that I would lose either way, no matter how it turned out. My face was indifferent.

"How can I stop them from fudging," I said, "if that's what they want to do?"

He hesitated. He looked around. He set his brown face. My champion. "You can't," he said. "But I can."

He turned and hurried away toward the office. The next morning he told me he had gone in there and "raised holy hell," threatened to break this news to the student body and make the whole thing more trouble than it would ever be worth. An hour later the announcement came over the intercom that I had been chosen. I didn't believe it. I couldn't let myself believe it. But, for the classmates who had nominated me, I had to look overjoyed. I glanced across at Leonard and he winked, shouting and whooping now with all the others.

At home that evening, when I brought this news, no one whooped. Papa was furious. I had not told them I was running for queen. There was no use mentioning it until I had something to mention. He asked me what I had worn at the tryouts. I told him.

"No wonder those *hakajin* [Caucasian] boys vote for you!" he shouted. "It is just like those majorette clothes you wear in the street. Showing off your body. Is that the kind of queen you want to be?"

I didn't say anything. When Papa lectured, you listened. If anyone spoke up it would be Mama, trying to mediate.

"Ko," she said now, "these things are important to Jeannie. She is . . ."

"Important? I'll tell you what is important. Modesty is important. A graceful body is important. You don't show your legs all the time. You don't walk around like this."

He did an imitation of a girl's walk, with shoulders straight, an assertive stride, and lips pulled back in a baboon's grin. I started to laugh.

"Don't laugh! This is not funny. You become this kind of woman and what Japanese boy is going to marry you? Tell me that. You put on tight clothes and walk around like Jean Harlow and the *hakajin* boys make you the queen. And pretty soon you end up marrying a *hakajin* boy . . ."

He broke off. He could think of no worse end result. He began to stomp back and forth across the floor, while Mama looked at me cautiously, with a glance that said, "Be patient, wait him out. After he has spoken his piece, you and I can talk sensibly."

He saw this and turned on her. "Hey! How come your daughter is seventeen years old and if you put a sack over her face you couldn't tell she was Japanese from anybody else on the street?"

"Ko," Mama said quietly. "Jeannie's in high school now. Next year she's going to go to college. She's learning other things . . ."

"Listen to me. It's not too late for her to learn Japanese ways of movement. The Buddhist church in San Jose gives odori class[1] twice a week. Jeannie, I want you to phone the teacher and tell her you are going to start taking lessons. Mama has kimonos you can wear. She can show you things too. She used to know all the dances. We have pictures somewhere. Mama, what happened to all those pictures?"

I had seen them, photos of Mama when she lived in Spokane, twelve years old and her round face blanched with rice powder. I remember the afternoon I spent with the incomprehensible old geisha at Manzanar.

"Papa," I complained.

"Don't make faces. You want to be the carnival queen? I tell you what. I'll make a deal with you. You can be the queen if you start odori lessons at the Buddhist church as soon as school is out."

He stood there, hands on hips, glaring at me, and not at all satisfied with this ultimatum. It was far too late for odori classes to have any effect on me and Papa knew this. But he owed it to himself to make one more show of resistance. When I signed up, a few weeks later, I lasted about ten lessons. The teacher herself sent me away. I smiled too much and couldn't break the habit. Like a majorette before the ever-shifting sidewalk crowd, I smiled during performances, and in Japanese dancing that is equivalent to a concert violinist walking onstage in a bathing suit.

Papa didn't mention my queenship again. He just glared at me from time to time, with great distaste, as if I had betrayed him. Yet in that glare I sometimes detected a flicker of approval, as if this streak of independence, this refusal to be shaped by him reflected his own obstinance. At least, these glances seemed to say, she has inherited *that*.

Mama, of course, was very proud. She took charge and helped me pick out the dress I would wear for the coronation. We drove to San Jose and spent an afternoon in the shops downtown. She could take time for such things now that Papa was working again. This was one of the few days she and I ever spent together, just the two of us, and it confirmed something I'd felt since early childhood. In her quiet way, she had always supported me, alongside of or underneath Papa's demands and expectations. Now she wanted for me the same thing I thought I wanted. Acceptance, in her eyes, was simply another means for survival.

Her support and Papa's resistance had one point in common: too much exposure was unbecoming. All the other girls — my four attendants — were going strapless. Mama wouldn't allow this. By the time we finished shopping, I had begun to agree with her. When she picked out a frilly ball gown that covered almost everything and buried my legs under layers of

---

[1]Odori classes trained Nisei girls in Japanese culture, particularly in the manners and arts expected of proper young ladies. — EDS.

ruffles, I thought it was absolutely right. I had used a low-cut sarong to win the contest. But once chosen I would be a white-gowned figure out of *Gone With the Wind;* I would be respectable.

On coronation night the gym was lit like a church, with bleachers in half-dark and a throne at one end, flooded brightly from the ceiling. The throne was made of plywood, its back shaped in a fleur-de-lis all covered with purple taffeta that shone like oily water under moonlight. Bed sheets were spread to simulate a wide, white carpet the length of the gym, from the throne to the door of the girls' locker room where, with my attendants, we waited for the PA system to give us our musical cue.

Lois Carson, the trustee's daughter, was one of them. She wore a very expensive strapless gown and a huge orchid corsage. Her pool-browned shoulders glowed in the harsh bulb light above the lockers.

"Oh Jeannie," she had said, as we took off our coats. "What a marvelous idea!"

I looked at her inquisitively.

"The high *neck*," she explained, studying my dress. "You look so . . . *sedate*. Just perfect for a queen."

As the other girls arrived, she made sure they all agreed with this. "Don't you *wish* you'd thought of it," she would say. And then to me, during a silence she felt obliged to fill, "I just *love* Chinese food." The others exclaimed that they too loved Chinese food, and we talked about recipes and restaurants until the music faded in:

> *Girl of my dreams, I love you,*
> *Honest I do,*
> *You are so sweet.*

It swelled during the opening bars to cover all other sounds in the gym. I stepped out into blue light that covered the first sheet, walking very slowly, like you do at weddings, carrying against the white bodice of my gown a bouquet of pink carnations.

A burst of applause resounded beneath the music, politely enthusiastic, followed by a steady murmur. The gym was packed, and the lights were intense. Suddenly it was too hot out there. I imagined that they were all murmuring about my dress. They saw the girls behind me staring at it. The throne seemed blocks away, and now the dress was stifling me. I had never before worn such an outfit. It was not at all what I should have on. I wanted my sarong. But then thought, NO. That would have been worse. Papa had been right about the sarong. Maybe he was right about everything. What was I doing out there anyway, trying to be a carnival queen? The teachers who'd counted the votes certainly didn't think it was such a good idea. Neither did the trustees. The students wanted me though. Their votes proved that. I kept walking my processional walk, thinking of all the kids who had voted for me, not wanting to let them down, although in a way I already had. It wasn't the girl in this old-fashioned dress they had voted for. But if not her, who *had* they voted for? Somebody I wanted to be. And wasn't. Who was I then? According to the big wall speakers now saxophoning through the gym, I was the girl of somebody's dream:

> *Since you've been gone, dear,*
> *Life don't seem the same.*
> *Please come back again . . .*

I looked ahead at the throne. It was even further away, a purple carriage receding as I approached. I glanced back. My four attendants seemed tiny. Had they stopped back there? Afterward there would be a little reception in one of the classrooms, punch and cookies under fluorescent tubes. Later, at Lois Carson's house, there'd be a more intimate, less public gathering, which I'd overheard a mention of but wouldn't be invited to. Champagne in the foothills. Oyster dip. I wanted to laugh. I wanted to cry. I wanted to be ten years old again, so I could believe in princesses and queens. It was too late. Too late to be an odori dancer for Papa, too late to be this kind of heroine. I wanted the carnival to end so I could go somewhere private, climb out of my stuffy dress, and cool off. But all eyes were on me. It was too late now not to follow this make-believe carpet to its plywood finale, and I did not yet know of any truer destination.

READING CRITICALLY

1. Why is Jeanne so upset by her classmate's amazement that she can speak English?

2. Houston says that her response to prejudice as a schoolgirl was to ignore it and try harder to gain acceptance through her accomplishments, such as working on the yearbook. What explanation does she give for her response?

3. In what ways does Jeanne use her sexuality to gain acceptance?

4. Jeanne's use of her sexuality to gain acceptance is seen by her father as not only unchaste but also a rejection of her Japanese heritage. Why does he feel that way?

5. Houston suggests that certain attitudes within the Japanese Americans themselves were partly to blame for the internment (see p. 758). What are these attitudes, and how are they illustrated in this excerpt?

WRITING ANALYTICALLY

1. Jeanne's conflict with her father in this excerpt centers around the degree to which she will preserve her Japanese identity while she also integrates into the American way of life. What does Jeanne do to assimilate? What does she do to preserve her connection with Japanese culture? What does her father think she should do? Collect information in response to these questions (reading questions 1–4 can help you here). Write a paper in which you use Jeanne as an example of how the child of immigrant parents should, or should not, handle the transition to American life. If appropriate, you may compare and contrast her experience in this re-

gard with your own. Consider how your own family has dealt with issues concerning the transmission of ethnic and cultural heritages from one generation to the next. Option: Add to this paper a comparison of Jeanne as an example with either Sone (p. 748) or Ichiro in Okada's *No-No Boy* (below).

2. In depicting Jeanne's struggle to assimilate into mainstream American society after the internment, Houston and Houston suggest that she suffered from sexism as well as racism. They imply that white society rejected Jeanne because of her race but then offered her some form of acceptance (however limited) if she was willing to exploit what it considered her "exotic" sexuality. Write a paper in which you explain how Houston and Houston make the case that Jeanne did indeed suffer from this sort of double oppression. Option: Evaluate the effectiveness of their presentation — that is, their ability to convince you that Jeanne was indeed oppressed in these ways.

JOHN OKADA

From *No-No Boy* (1957)

John Okada (1923–1971) was born in Seattle and served in the U.S. armed forces during World War II. After the war, he attended the University of Washington and Columbia University and worked as a librarian and a writer. His only novel, *No-No Boy*, was published in 1957 and was not well received. After Okada died of a heart attack in 1971, his widow offered his papers, including the unfinished manuscript of a novel about Issei, to the University of California at Los Angeles. When her offer was rejected, she destroyed everything. *No-No Boy* is now considered to be an important twentieth-century American novel. Our excerpt is from chapter 1.

TWO WEEKS AFTER HIS TWENTY-FIFTH BIRTHDAY, Ichiro got off a bus at Second and Main in Seattle. He had been gone four years, two in camp and two in prison.

Walking down the street that autumn morning with a small, black suitcase, he felt like an intruder in a world to which he had no claim. It was just enough that he should feel this way, for, of his own free will, he had stood before the judge and said that he would not go in the army. At the time there was no other choice for him. That was when he was twenty-three, a man of twenty-three. Now, two years older, he was even more of a man.

Christ, he thought to himself, just a goddamn kid is all I was. Didn't know enough to wipe my own nose. What the hell have I done? What am I

John Okada, *No-No Boy* (1957; reprint, Seattle: University of Washington Press, 1979), 1–31.

doing back here? Best thing I can do would be to kill some son of a bitch and head back to prison.

He walked toward the railroad depot where the tower with the clocks on all four sides was. It was a dirty looking tower of ancient brick. It was a dirty city. Dirtier, certainly, than it had a right to be after only four years.

Waiting for the light to change to green, he looked around at the people standing at the bus stop. A couple of men in suits, half a dozen women who failed to arouse him even after prolonged good behavior, and a young Japanese with a lunch bucket. Ichiro studied him, searching in his mind for the name that went with the round, pimply face and the short-cropped hair. The pimples were gone and the face had hardened, but the hair was still cropped. The fellow wore green, army-fatigue trousers and an Eisenhower jacket — Eto Minato. The name came to him at the same time as did the horrible significance of the army clothes. In panic, he started to step off the curb. It was too late. He had been seen.

"Itchy!" That was his nickname.

Trying to escape, Ichiro urged his legs frenziedly across the street.

"Hey, Itchy!" The caller's footsteps ran toward him.

An arm was placed across his back. Ichiro stopped and faced the other Japanese. He tried to smile, but could not. There was no way out now.

"I'm Eto. Remember?" Eto smiled and extended his palm. Reluctantly, Ichiro lifted his own hand and let the other shake it.

The round face with the round eyes peered at him through silver-rimmed spectacles. "What the hell! It's been a long time, but not that long. How've you been? What's doing?"

"Well . . . that is, I'm . . ."

"Last time must have been before Pearl Harbor. God, it's been quite a while, hasn't it? Three, no, closer to four years, I guess. Lotsa Japs coming back to the Coast. Lotsa Japs in Seattle. You'll see 'em around. Japs are funny that way. Gotta have their rice and sake and other Japs. Stupid, I say. The smart ones went to Chicago and New York and lotsa places back East, but there's still plenty coming back out this way." Eto drew cigarettes from his breast pocket and held out the package. "No? Well, I'll have one. Got the habit in the army. Just got out a short while back. Rough time, but I made it. Didn't get out in time to make the quarter, but I'm planning to go to school. How long you been around?"

Ichiro touched his toe to the suitcase. "Just got in. Haven't been home yet."

"When'd you get discharged?"

A car grinding its gears started down the street. He wished he were in it. "I . . . that is . . . I never was in."

Eto slapped him good-naturedly on the arm. "No need to look so sour. So you weren't in. So what? Been in camp all this time?"

"No." He made an effort to be free of Eto with his questions. He felt as if he were in a small room whose walls were slowly closing in on him. "It's been a long time, I know, but I'm really anxious to see the folks."

"What the hell. Let's have a drink. On me. I don't give a damn if I'm late to work. As for your folks, you'll see them soon enough. You drink, don't you?"

"Yeah, but not now."

"Ahh." Eto was disappointed. He shifted his lunch box from under one arm to the other.

"I've really got to be going."

The round face wasn't smiling any more. It was thoughtful. The eyes confronted Ichiro with indecision which changed slowly to enlightenment and then to suspicion. He remembered. He knew.

The friendliness was gone as he said: "No-no boy, huh?"

Ichiro wanted to say yes. He wanted to return the look of despising hatred and say simply yes, but it was too much to say. The walls had closed in and were crushing all the unspoken words back down into his stomach. He shook his head once, not wanting to evade the eyes but finding it impossible to meet them. Out of his big weakness the little ones were branching, and the eyes he didn't have the courage to face were ever present. If it would have helped to gouge out his own eyes, he would have done so long ago. The hate-churned eyes with the stamp of unrelenting condemnation were his cross and he had driven the nails with his own hands.

"Rotten bastard. Shit on you." Eto coughed up a mouthful of sputum and rolled his words around it: "Rotten, no-good bastard."

Surprisingly, Ichiro felt relieved. Eto's anger seemed to serve as a release to his own naked tensions. As he stooped to lift the suitcase a wet wad splattered over his hand and dripped onto the black leather. The legs of his accuser were in front of him. God in a pair of green fatigues, U.S. Army style. They were the legs of the jury that had passed sentence upon him. Beseech me, they seemed to say, throw your arms about me and bury your head between my knees and seek pardon for your great sin.

"I'll piss on you next time," said Eto vehemently.

He turned as he lifted the suitcase off the ground and hurried away from the legs and the eyes from which no escape was possible.

Jackson Street started at the waterfront and stretched past the two train depots and up the hill all the way to the lake, where the houses were bigger and cleaner and had garages with late-model cars in them. For Ichiro, Jackson Street signified that section of the city immediately beyond the railroad tracks between Fifth and Twelfth Avenues. That was the section which used to be pretty much Japanese town. It was adjacent to Chinatown and most of the gambling and prostitution and drinking seemed to favor the area.

Like the dirty clock tower of the depot, the filth of Jackson Street had increased. Ichiro paused momentarily at an alley and peered down the passage formed by the walls of two sagging buildings. There had been a door there at one time, a back door to a movie house which only charged a nickel. A nickel was a lot of money when he had been seven or nine or eleven. He wanted to go into the alley to see if the door was still there.

Being on Jackson Street with its familiar storefronts and taverns and restaurants, which were somehow different because the war had left its mark on them, was like trying to find one's way out of a dream that seemed real most of the time but wasn't really real because it was still only a dream. The war had wrought violent changes upon the people, and the people, in turn, working hard and living hard and earning a lot of money and spending it on whatever was available, had distorted the profile of Jackson Street. The street had about it the air of a carnival without quite succeeding at becoming one. A shooting gallery stood where once had been a clothing store; fish and chips had replaced a jewelry shop; and a bunch of Negroes were horsing around raucously in front of a pool parlor. Everything looked older and dirtier and shabbier.

He walked past the pool parlor, picking his way gingerly among the Negroes, of whom there had been only a few at one time and of whom there seemed to be nothing but now. They were smoking and shouting and cussing and carousing and the sidewalk was slimy with their spittle.

"Jap!"

His pace quickened automatically, but curiosity or fear or indignation or whatever it was made him glance back at the white teeth framed in a leering dark brown which was almost black.

"Go back to Tokyo, boy." Persecution in the drawl of the persecuted.

The white teeth and brown-black leers picked up the cue and jigged to the rhythmical chanting of "Jap-boy, To-ki-yo; Jap-boy, To-ki-yo . . ."

Friggin' niggers, he uttered savagely to himself and, from the same place deep down inside where tolerance for the Negroes and the Jews and the Mexicans and the Chinese and the too short and too fat and too ugly abided because he was Japanese and knew what it was like better than did those who were white and average and middle class and good Democrats or liberal Republicans, the hate which was unrelenting and terrifying seethed up.

Then he was home. It was a hole in the wall with groceries crammed in orderly confusion on not enough shelving, into not enough space. He knew what it would be like even before he stepped in. His father had described the place to him in a letter, composed in simple Japanese characters because otherwise Ichiro could not have read it. The letter had been purposely repetitive and painstakingly detailed so that Ichiro should not have any difficulty finding the place. The grocery store was the same one the Ozakis had operated for many years. That's all his father had had to say. Come to the grocery store which was once the store of the Ozakis. The Japanese characters, written simply so that he could read them, covered pages of directions as if he were a foreigner coming to the city for the first time.

Thinking about the letter made him so mad that he forgot about the Negroes. He opened the door just as he had a thousand times when they had lived farther down the block and he used to go to the Ozakis' for a loaf of bread or a jar of pickled scallions, and the bell tinkled just as he knew it would. All the grocery stores he ever knew had bells which tinkled when one opened the door and the familiar sound softened his inner turmoil.

"Ichiro?" The short, round man who came through the curtains at the back of the store uttered the name preciously as might an old woman. "Ya,

Ichiro, you have come home. How good that you have come home!" The gently spoken Japanese which he had not heard for so long sounded strange. He would hear a great deal of it now that he was home, for his parents, like most of the old Japanese, spoke virtually no English. On the other hand, the children, like Ichiro, spoke almost no Japanese. Thus they communicated, the old speaking Japanese with an occasional badly mispronounced word or two of English; and the young, with the exception of a simple word or phrase of Japanese which came fairly effortlessly to the lips, resorting almost constantly to the tongue the parents avoided.

The father bounced silently over the wood flooring in slippered feet toward his son. Fondly, delicately, he placed a pudgy hand on Ichiro's elbow and looked up at his son who was Japanese but who had been big enough for football and tall enough for basketball in high school. He pushed the elbow and Ichiro led the way into the back, where there was a kitchen, a bathroom, and one bedroom. He looked around the bedroom and felt like puking. It was neat and clean and scrubbed. His mother would have seen to that. It was just the idea of everybody sleeping in the one room. He wondered if his folks still pounded flesh.

He backed out of the bedroom and slumped down on a stool. "Where's Ma?"

"Mama is gone to the bakery." The father kept his beaming eyes on his son who was big and tall. He shut off the flow of water and shifted the metal teapot to the stove.

"What for?"

"Bread," his father said in reply, "bread for the store."

"Don't they deliver?'

"Ya, they deliver." He ran a damp rag over the table, which was spotlessly clean.

"What the hell is she doing at the bakery then?"

"It is good business, Ichiro." He was at the cupboard, fussing with the tea cups and saucers and cookies. "The truck comes in the morning. We take enough for the morning business. For the afternoon, we get soft, fresh bread. Mamma goes to the bakery."

Ichiro tried to think of a bakery nearby and couldn't. There was a big Wonder Bread bakery way up on Nineteenth, where a nickel used to buy a bagful of day-old stuff. That was thirteen and a half blocks, all uphill. He knew the distance by heart because he'd walked it twice every day to go to grade school, which was a half-block beyond the bakery or fourteen blocks from home.

"What bakery?"

The water on the stove began to boil and the old man flipped the lid on the pot and tossed in a pinch of leaves. "Wonder Bread."

"Is that the one up on Nineteenth?"

"Ya."

"How much do you make on bread?"

"Let's see," he said pouring the tea. "Oh, three, four cents. Depends."

"How many loaves does Ma get?"

"Ten or twelve. Depends."

Ten loaves at three or four cents' profit added up to thirty or forty cents. He compromised at thirty-five cents and asked the next question: "The bus, how much is it?"

"Oh, let's see." He sipped the tea noisily, sucking it through his teeth in well regulated gulps. "Let's see. Fifteen cents for one time. Tokens are two for twenty-five cents. That is twelve and one-half cents."

Twenty-five cents for bus fare to get ten loaves of bread which turned a profit of thirty-five cents. It would take easily an hour to make the trip up and back. He didn't mean to shout, but he shouted: "Christ, Pa, what else do you give away?"

His father peered over the teacup with a look of innocent surprise.

It made him madder. "Figure it out. Just figure it out. Say you make thirty-five cents on ten loaves. You take a bus up and back and there's twenty-five cents shot. That leaves ten cents. On top of that, there's an hour wasted. What are you running a business for? Your health?"

Slup went the tea through his teeth, slup, slup, slup. "Mama walks." He sat there looking at his son like a benevolent Buddha.

Ichiro lifted the cup to his lips and let the liquid burn down his throat. His father had said "Mama walks" and that made things right with the world. The overwhelming simplicity of the explanation threatened to evoke silly giggles which, if permitted to escape, might lead to hysterics. He clenched his fists and subdued them.

At the opposite end of the table the father had slupped the last of his tea and was already taking the few steps to the sink to rinse out the cup.

"Goddammit, Pa, sit down!" He'd never realized how nervous a man his father was. The old man had constantly been doing something every minute since he had come. It didn't figure. Here he was, round and fat and cheerful-looking and, yet, he was going incessantly as though his trousers were crawling with ants.

"Ya, Ichiro, I forget you have just come home. We should talk." He resumed his seat at the table and busied his fingers with a box of matches.

Ichiro stepped out of the kitchen, spotted the cigarettes behind the cash register, and returned with a pack of Camels. Lighting a match, the old man held it between his fingers and waited until the son opened the package and put a cigarette in his mouth. By then the match was threatening to sear his fingers. He dropped it hastily and stole a sheepish glance at Ichiro, who reached for the box and struck his own match.

"Ichiro." There was a timorousness in the father's voice. Or was it apology?

"Yeah."

"Was it very hard?"

"No. It was fun." The sarcasm didn't take.

"You are sorry?" He was waddling over rocky ground on a pitch-black night and he didn't like it one bit.

"I'm okay, Pa. It's finished. Done and finished. No use talking about it."

"True," said the old man too heartily, "it is done and there is no use to talk." The bell tinkled and he leaped from the chair and fled out of the kitchen.

Using the butt of the first cigarette, Ichiro lit another. He heard his father's voice in the store.

"Mama. Ichiro. Ichiro is here."

The sharp, lifeless tone of his mother's words flipped through the silence and he knew that she hadn't changed.

"The bread must be put out."

In other homes mothers and fathers and sons and daughters rushed into hungry arms after weekend separations to find assurance in crushing embraces and loving kisses. The last time he saw his mother was over two years ago. He waited, seeing in the sounds of the rustling waxed paper the stiff, angular figure of the woman stacking the bread on the rack in neat, precise piles.

His father came back into the kitchen with a little less bounce and began to wash the cups. She came through the curtains a few minutes after, a small, flat-chested, shapeless woman who wore her hair pulled back into a tight bun. Hers was the awkward, skinny body of a thirteen-year-old which had dried and toughened through the many years following but which had developed no further. He wondered how the two of them had ever gotten together long enough to have two sons.

"I am proud that you are back," she said. "I am proud to call you my son."

It was her way of saying that she had made him what he was and that the thing in him which made him say no to the judge and go to prison for two years was the growth of a seed planted by the mother tree and that she was the mother who had put this thing in her son and that everything that had been done and said was exactly as it should have been and that that was what made him her son because no other would have made her feel the pride that was in her breast.

He looked at his mother and swallowed with difficulty the bitterness that threatened to destroy the last fragment of understanding for the woman who was his mother and still a stranger because, in truth, he could not know what it was to be a Japanese who breathed the air of America and yet had never lifted a foot from the land that was Japan.

"I've been talking with Pa," he said, not knowing or caring why except that he had to say something.

"After a while, you and I, we will talk also." She walked through the kitchen into the bedroom and hung her coat and hat in a wardrobe of cardboard which had come from Sears Roebuck. Then she came back through the kitchen and out into the store.

The father gave him what was meant to be a knowing look and uttered softly: "Doesn't like my not being in the store when she is out. I tell her the bell tinkles, but she does not understand."

"Hell's bells," he said in disgust. Pushing himself out of the chair violently, he strode into the bedroom and flung himself out on one of the double beds.

Lying there, he wished the roof would fall in and bury forever the anguish which permeated his every pore. He lay there fighting with his burden, lighting one cigarette after another and dropping ashes and butts purposely on the floor. It was the way he felt, stripped of dignity, respect, purpose, honor, all the things which added up to schooling and marriage and family and work and happiness.

It was to please her, he said to himself with teeth clamped together to imprison the wild, meaningless, despairing cry which was forever straining inside of him. Pa's okay, but he's a nobody. He's a goddamned, fat, grinning, spineless nobody. Ma is the rock that's always hammering, pounding, pounding, pounding in her unobtrusive, determined, fanatical way until there's nothing left to call one's self. She's cursed me with her meanness and the hatred that you cannot see but which is always hating. It was she who opened my mouth and made my lips move to sound the words which got me two years in prison and an emptiness that is more empty and frightening than the caverns of hell. She's killed me with her meanness and hatred and I hope she's happy because I'll never know the meaning of it again.

"Ichiro."

He propped himself up on an elbow and looked at her. She had hardly changed. Surely, there must have been a time when she could smile and, yet, he could not remember.

"Yeah?"

"Lunch is on the table."

As he pushed himself off the bed and walked past her to the kitchen, she took broom and dustpan and swept up the mess he had made.

There were eggs, fried with soy sauce, sliced cold meat, boiled cabbage, and tea and rice. They all ate in silence, not even disturbed once by the tinkling of the bell. . . .

No, he said to himself as he watched her part the curtains and start into the store. There was a time when I was your son. There was a time that I no longer remember when you used to smile a mother's smile and tell me stories about gallant and fierce warriors who protected their lords with blades of shining steel and about the old woman who found a peach in the stream and took it home and, when her husband split it in half, a husky little boy tumbled out to fill their hearts with boundless joy. I was that boy in the peach and you were the old woman and we were Japanese with Japanese feelings and Japanese pride and Japanese thoughts because it was all right then to be Japanese and feel and think all the things that Japanese do even if we lived in America. Then there came a time when I was only half Japanese because one is not born in America and raised in America and taught in America and one does not speak and swear and drink and smoke and play and fight and see and hear in America among Americans in American streets and houses without becoming American and loving it. But I did not love enough, for you were still half my mother and I was thereby still half Japanese and when the war came and they told me to fight for America, I was not strong enough to fight you and I was not strong enough to fight the bitterness which made the half of me which was you bigger than the half of me which was America and really the whole of me that I could not see or feel. Now that I know the truth when it is too late and the half of me which was you is no longer there, I am only half of me and the half that remains is American by law because the government was wise and strong enough to know why it was that I could not fight for America and did not strip me of my birthright. But it is not enough to be American only in the eyes of the law and it is not enough to be only half an American and know that it is an empty half. I am not your son and I am not Japanese and I am not American. I can go someplace and tell people that I've got an inverted stomach and that I am an American, true and blue and Hail Columbia, but the army wouldn't have me because of the stomach. That's easy and I would do it, only I've got to convince myself first and that I cannot do. I wish with all my heart that I were Japanese or that I were American. I am neither and I blame you and I blame myself and I blame the world which is made up of many countries which fight with each other and kill and hate and destroy but not enough, so that they must kill and hate and destroy again and again and again. It is so easy and simple that I cannot understand it at all. And the reason I do not understand it is because I do not understand you who were the half of me that is no more and because I do not understand what it was about that half that made me destroy the half of me which was American and the half which might have become the whole of me if I had said yes I will go and fight in your army because that is what I believe and want and cherish and love . . .

Defeatedly, he crushed the stub of a cigarette into an ash tray filled with many other stubs and reached for the package to get another. It was empty and he did not want to go into the store for more because he did not feel much like seeing either his father or mother. He went into the bedroom and tossed and groaned and half slept. . . .

[*Later that same evening, Ichiro's mother forces him to accompany her in visiting some friends, two families from his parents' village in Japan. The last stop is the newly purchased home of the Kumasakas.* — EDS.]

The Kumasakas had run a dry cleaning shop before the war. Business was good and people spoke of their having money, but they lived in cramped quarters above the shop because, like most of the other Japanese, they planned some day to return to Japan and still felt like transients even after thirty or forty years in America and the quarters above the shop seemed adequate and sensible since the arrangement was merely temporary. That, he thought to himself, was the reason why the Japanese were still Japanese. They rushed to America with the single purpose of making a fortune which would enable them to return to their own country and live adequately. It did not matter when they discovered that fortunes were not for the mere seeking or that their sojourns were spanning decades instead of years and it did not matter that growing families and growing bills and misfortunes and illness and low wages and just plain hard luck were constant obstacles to the realization of their dreams. They continued to maintain their dreams by refusing to learn how to speak or write the language of America and by living only among their own kind and by zealously avoiding long-term commitments such as the purchase of a house. But now, the Kumasakas, it seemed, had bought this house, and he was impressed. It could only mean that the Kumasakas had exchanged hope for reality and, late as it was, were finally sinking roots into the land from which they had previously sought not nourishment but only gold.

Mrs. Kumasaka came to the door, a short, heavy woman who stood solidly on feet planted wide apart, like a man. She greeted them warmly but with a sadness that she would carry to the grave. When Ichiro had last seen her, her hair had been pitch black. Now it was completely white.

In the living room Mr. Kumasaka, a small man with a pleasant smile, was sunk deep in an upholstered chair, reading a Japanese newspaper. It was a comfortable room with rugs and soft furniture and lamps and end tables and pictures on recently papered walls.

"Ah, Ichiro, it is nice to see you looking well." Mr. Kumasaka struggled out of the chair and extended a friendly hand. "Please, sit down."

"You've got a nice place," he said, meaning it.

"Thank you," the little man said. "Mama and I, we finally decided that America is not so bad. We like it here."

Ichiro sat down on the sofa next to his mother and felt strange in this home which he envied because it was like millions of other homes in America and could never be his own.

Mrs. Kumasaka sat next to her husband on a large, round hassock and looked at Ichiro with lonely eyes, which made him uncomfortable.

"Ichiro came home this morning." It was his mother, and the sound of her voice, deliberately loud and almost arrogant, puzzled him. "He has suffered, but I make no apologies for him or for myself. If he had given his life for Japan, I could not be prouder."

"Ma," he said, wanting to object but not knowing why except that her comments seemed out of place.

Ignoring him, she continued, not looking at the man but at his wife, who now sat with head bowed, her eyes emptily regarding the floral pattern of the carpet. "A mother's lot is not an easy one. To sleep with a man and bear a son is nothing. To raise the child into a man one can be proud of is not play. Some of us succeed. Some, of course, must fail. It is too bad, but that is the way of life."

"Yes, yes, Yamada-san," said the man impatiently. Then, smiling, he turned to Ichiro: "I suppose you'll be going back to the university?"

"I'll have to think about it," he replied, wishing that his father was like this man who made him want to pour out the turbulence in his soul.

"He will go when the new term begins. I have impressed upon him the importance of a good education. With a college education, one can go far in Japan." His mother smiled knowingly.

"Ah," said the man as if he had not heard her speak, "Bobbie wanted to go to the university and study medicine. He would have made a fine doctor. Always studying and reading, is that not so, Ichiro?"

He nodded, remembering the quiet son of the Kumasakas, who never played football with the rest of the kids on the street or appeared at dances, but could talk for hours on end about chemistry and zoology and physics and other courses which he hungered after in high school.

"Sure, Bob always was pretty studious." He knew, somehow, that it was not the right thing to say, but he added: "Where is Bob?"

His mother did not move. Mrs. Kumasaka uttered a despairing cry and bit her trembling lips.

The little man, his face a drawn mask of pity and sorrow, stammered: "Ichiro, you — no one has told you?"

"No. What? No one's told me anything."

"Your mother did not write you?"

"No. Write about what?" He knew what the answer was. It was in the whiteness of the hair of the sad woman who was the mother of the boy named Bob and it was in the engaging pleasantness of the father which was not really pleasantness but a deep understanding which had emerged from resignation to a loss which only a parent knows and suffers. And then he saw the picture on the mantel, a snapshot, enlarged many times over, of a grinning youth in uniform who had not thought to remember his parents with a formal portrait because he was not going to die and there would be worlds of time for pictures and books and other obligations of the living later on.

Mr. Kumasaka startled him by shouting toward the rear of the house: "Jun! Please come."

There was the sound of a door opening and presently there appeared a youth in khaki shirt and wool trousers, who was a stranger to Ichiro.

"I hope I haven't disturbed anything, Jun," said Mr. Kumasaka.

"No, it's all right. Just writing a letter."

"This is Mrs. Yamada and her son Ichiro. They are old family friends."

Jun nodded to his mother and reached over to shake Ichiro's hand.

The little man waited until Jun had seated himself on the end of the sofa. "Jun is from Los Angeles. He's on his way home from the army and was good enough to stop by and visit us for a few days. He and Bobbie were together. Buddies — is that what you say?"

"That's right," said Jun.

"Now, Jun."

"Yes?"

The little man looked at Ichiro and then at his mother, who stared stonily at no one in particular.

"Jun, as a favor to me, although I know it is not easy for you to speak of it, I want you to tell us about Bobbie."

Jun stood up quickly. "Gosh, I don't know." He looked with tender concern at Mrs. Kumasaka.

"It is all right, Jun. Please, just this once more."

"Well, okay." He sat down again, rubbing his hands thoughtfully over his knees. "The way it happened, Bobbie and I, we had just gotten back to the rest area. Everybody was feeling good because there was a lot of talk about the Germans' surrendering. All the fellows were cleaning their equipment. We'd been up in the lines for a long time and everything was pretty well messed up. When you're up there getting shot at, you don't worry much about how crummy your things get, but the minute you pull back, they got to have inspection. So, we were cleaning things up. Most of us were cleaning our rifles because that's something you learn to want to do no matter how anything else looks. Bobbie was sitting beside me and he was talking about how he was going to medical school and become a doctor — "

A sob wrenched itself free from the breast of the mother whose son was once again dying, and the snow-white head bobbed wretchedly.

"Go on, Jun," said the father.

Jun looked away from the mother and at the picture on the mantel. "Bobbie was like that. Me and the other guys, all we talked about was drinking and girls and stuff like that because it's important to talk about those things when you make it back from the front on your own power, but Bobbie, all he thought about was going to school. I was nodding my head and saying yeah, yeah, and then there was this noise, kind of a pinging noise right close by. It scared me for a minute and I started to cuss and said, 'Gee, that was damn close,' and looked around at Bobbie. He was slumped over with his head between his knees. I reached out to hit him, thinking he was fooling around. Then, when I tapped him on the arm, he fell over and I saw the dark spot on the side of his head where the bullet had gone through. That was all. Ping, and he's dead. It doesn't figure, but it happened just the way I've said."

The mother was crying now, without shame and alone in her grief that knew no end. And in her bottomless grief that made no distinction as to what was wrong and what was right and who was Japanese and who was not, there was no awareness of the other mother with a living son who had come to say to her you are with shame and grief because you were not Japanese and thereby killed your son but mine is big and strong and full of life because I did not weaken and would not let my son destroy himself uselessly and treacherously.

Ichiro's mother rose and, without a word, for no words would ever pass between them again, went out of the house which was a part of America.

Mr. Kumasaka placed a hand on the rounded back of his wife, who was forever beyond consoling, and spoke gently to Ichiro: "You don't have to say anything. You are truly sorry and I am sorry for you."

"I didn't know," he said pleadingly.

"I want you to feel free to come and visit us whenever you wish. We can talk even if your mother's convictions are different."

"She's crazy. Mean and crazy. Goddamned Jap!" He felt the tears hot and stinging.

"Try to understand her."

Impulsively, he took the little man's hand in his own and held it briefly. Then he hurried out of the house which could never be his own. . . .

READING CRITICALLY

1. Why does Eto spit at Ichiro?

2. How do the African Americans he meets on the street react to Ichiro?

3. Why does Ichiro's mother take him to visit the Kumasakas?

4. What are Ichiro's connections to Japanese culture? What does he do that can be considered "Japanese"?

5. What are Ichiro's connections to American culture? What does he do that can be considered "American"?

WRITING ANALYTICALLY

1. At one point Ichiro says to himself, "I am not Japanese and I am not American" (p. 774). He presents a particularly painful picture of what can happen when a person tries to be bicultural or has biculturalism forced on him or her. Write a paper in which you explain the extent to which Ichiro can be considered bicultural (your responses to reading questions 4 and 5 will help you here). Consider the extent to which he embodies both Japanese and American cultures, as you understand them, and the ways he negotiates, or fails to negotiate, links between the two — or at least a truce to tensions between the two. If you wish, you may also consider the extent to which, in your opinion, Ichiro's experience is representative of most people who try to be or can't avoid being bicultural. Option: Compare and contrast Ichiro and either Jeanne Wakatsuki Houston (pp. 715 and 757) or Monica Sone (p. 748) as bicultural people; use both examples to build up a model of biculturalism.

2. Political activists sometimes argue that all victims of oppression, such as people of color, who all suffer from white racism, ought to unite in their fight against injustice. But the encounters with both Eto and the African Americans (see reading questions 1 and 2) suggest that the experience of injustice in the internment has not created solidarity among all people of color in Ichiro's world. The African Americans do not appear to sympathize with him, and even within the Nikkei community there are sharp divisions. Write a paper in which you explain what seems to be preventing this solidarity from becoming established in Ichiro's world. Consider whether the barriers to solidarity as Okada draws them are specific to the time and place of the novel or generally applicable. Argue for a thesis on this issue, drawing also on your own experience of race relations. Options: Still working toward a thesis on solidarity and barriers to solidarity, enrich your discussion with comparison and contrast of Okada and Yamamoto (p. 779).

3. The tension in Ichiro's uncomfortable dual Japanese and American identity is mirrored in the tensions within his own family. Exactly what seems to be wrong in Ichiro's relationship with his parents? Write a paper in which you argue for a response to this question, illustrating your views with evidence from either the opening scene in the shop between Ichiro and his father, before his mother returns, or the scene in which his mother takes him to the Kumasakas. Alternative: Compare and contrast Okada's dramatization of Ichiro's relations with his parents with the ways Houston and Houston present Jeanne's relations with her parents (pp. 715 and 757). Using these two examples, frame a thesis that generalizes about the problems families are likely to encounter when the parents are recent immigrants and the children are moving toward assimilation into American society.

HISAYE YAMAMOTO

"A Fire in Fontana" (1985)

Hisaye Yamamoto (b.1921) was born in California, where she attended Japanese school as well as public school for twelve years. After she graduated from Compton Junior College with a major in languages, she and her family were interned at the camp in Poston, Arizona. During the war one of her brothers was killed in combat in Italy. Yamamoto began writing as a young teenager and wrote for the camp newspaper while in Poston. After the war, she worked for three years for an African American newspaper, the *Los Angeles Tribune.* Yamamoto was one of the few Asian American writers to win widespread recognition in the tense times after the war. In 1950 she received a one-year Whitney Foundation fellowship to develop her fiction. She then joined the Catholic Worker movement in New York. Her stories have appeared in many journals, and she won the American Book Award for Lifetime Achievement in 1986. Her short-story collection, *Seventeen Syllables and Other Stories,* was published in 1988. The autobiographical essay reprinted here, "A Fire in Fontana," describes her experiences during and after the internment, when she began to feel solidarity with African Americans.

SOMETHING WEIRD HAPPENED TO ME not long after the end of the Second World War. I wouldn't go so far as to say that I, a Japanese American, became Black, because that's a pretty melodramatic statement. But some kind of transformation did take place, the effects of which are with me still.

I remember reading a book called *Young Man with a Horn,* by Dorothy Baker, which is said to be based on the life of Bix Beiderbecke,[1] in which the narrator early wonders if his musician friend would have come to the same tragic end if he hadn't become involved with Negroes (in 1985, how odd the word has become!) and with one musician in particular.

In real life, there happened to be a young white musician in an otherwise Black band which played in such places as the Club Alabam on Central Avenue. His name was Johnny Otis, and the group became quite respected in jazz and blues circles. But his name was once Veliotis — he is of Greek heritage; in more recent years he has become the pastor of a church in Watts.[2] I suppose he, too, arrived at a place in his life from which there was no turning back. But his life, as I see it, represents a triumph.

Hisaye Yamamoto, "A Fire in Fontana," *Rafu Shrimpo,* December 21, 1985, 8–9, 16–17, 19.

In the notes, EDS. = Patricia Bizzell and Bruce Herzberg.

[1]Bix Beiderbecke was a well-known European American jazz musician who died in 1931 at age twenty-eight. — EDS.

[2]Watts is a part of Los Angeles with a large African American population. Also see note 7. — EDS.

But I don't know whether mine is or not. Because when I realized that something was happening to me, I scrambled to backtrack for a while. By then it was too late. I continued to look like the Nisei I was, with my height remaining at slightly over four feet ten, my hair straight, my vision myopic. Yet I know that this event transpired inside me; sometimes I see it as my inward self being burnt black in a certain fire.

Or perhaps the process, unbeknownst to me, had begun even earlier. Once, during the war, squeezed into a hot summer bus out of Chicago, my seatmate was a blond girl about my size or maybe a little taller, who started telling me her life story.

The young woman wore a bright-flowered jersey dress, swirling purples and reds and greens on a white background, and she chortled a lot. She said she was twenty-eight years old and married to a man in his sixties, a customer of where she'd been a waitress. Just now she had been visiting in Chicago with her married sister and she'd had a lot of fun, her brother-in-law pretending he was going to drown her in the lake where they'd all gone for a swim. She said in East St. Louis, where she lived, all the kids of the neighborhood would come around for her cookies. Her husband was very good to her, so she was quite content.

The bus was south of Springfield somewhere when suddenly, startling me, the girl sat bolt upright and began chortling. "I knew it! I knew it!" For some reason, she was filled with glee.

"See that nigger?" she asked. "He got off the bus and went into that restaurant to ask for a drink and they told him to go around outside to the faucet!"

Sure enough, the young fellow was bent awkwardly over the outside tap which protruded from the wooden building about a foot from the ground, trying to get a drink without getting his clothes sloshed.

"I knew they wouldn't give him a glass of water!" She crowed as though it were a personal victory.

Here I was on a bus going back to the camp in Arizona where my father still lived,[3] and I knew there was a connection between my seatmate's joy and our having been put in that hot and windblown place of barracks.

Even though I didn't dare shove her out the window, I must have managed to get some sign of protest across to her. After a while, she said doggedly. "Well, it's all in the way you're brought up. I was brought up this way, so that's the way I feel."

After the girl got off in East St. Louis, where (she had informed me) Negroes walked on one side of the street and white people on the other, the bus went through a bleak and dry territory where when one got off, there were large grasshoppers which clung to the walls like ivy and scrunched underfoot on the pavement like eggshells. The toilets were a new experience, too, labeled either Colored or White. I dared to try White first, and no one challenged me, so I continued this presumptuous practice at all the way stations of Texas. After I got back on the bus the first time, I was

---

[3]The camp is Poston. — EDS.

haunted by the long look given me by a cleaning woman in the restroom. I decided, for the sake of my conscience, that the Negro woman had never seen a Japanese before.

So the first job I got after coming out of camp again was with a Negro newspaper in Los Angeles. I really wanted the job badly, and was amazed when I was hired over a Nisei fellow who was more qualified, since the ad in the *Pacific Citizen* had specified a man. Moreover, the young man, already a Nisei journalist of some note, had edited his own newspaper before the war and knew athletes like Kenny Washington and Woody Strode because he'd gone to UCLA with them. The idea of hiring a Japanese on a Black newspaper was that maybe the returning Japanese businessmen would advertise and this would attract some Japanese readership, and maybe there would be the beginnings of an intercultural community.

It didn't work out that way at all, because I'm not one of your go-getters or anything. I did rewrites mostly, of stories culled from all the other Black newspapers across the country that exchanged with the *Los Angeles Tribune,* from the very professional ones like the *Chicago Defender* (with columnists like Langston Hughes and S. I. Hayakawa)[4] and the *New Amsterdam News* to smaller ones like the primly proper Bostonian sheet with elegant society notes and the smudged weeklies from small towns in Mississippi and Oklahoma that looked to have been turned out on antiquated, creaking presses. Almost every week, I toted up the number of alleged lynchings across the country and combined them into one story.

The office was on the mezzanine of the Dunbar Hotel, where people well known in the entertainment industry, as they say, would regularly stay. There was a spirited running argument going on almost every day of the week down in the foyer which the *Tribune* office overlooked. The denizens of the place, retired members of the Brotherhood of Sleeping Car Porters and such, were provoked to discussion regularly by one of the hotel owners, a Negro who looked absolutely white and whose dark eyes smoldered with a bitter fire. The inexhaustible topic was Race, always Race.

I got a snootful of it. Sometimes I got to wondering whether Negroes talked about anything else. No matter what the initial remark, if the discussion continued for any length of time, the issue boiled down to Race. Even the jokes were darkly tinged with a dash of bitters. More than once I was easily put down with a casual, "That's mighty White of you," the connotations of which were devastating.

But it was not all work. One Halloween Mrs. Preacley, the secretary, and I visited a nightclub to watch a beauty contest. Among the contestants flouncing about in their scented silks and furs across the platform were a couple of guys employed by the hotel. One young man, donning a mop of auburn curls, a pink sheath dress, and high heels, had turned into a young

[4]Langston Hughes (1902–67) was a well-known African American poet and leader of the Harlem Renaissance, a 1920s movement of African American intellectuals and artists. S. I. Hayakawa (1906–92) was born in Canada to Japanese parents; he was well known in the United States as a scholar and politician and was a U.S. senator from California from 1977 to 1983. — Eds.

matron; another competed in a simple white gown, statuesquely, regally, as though posing for an expensive fashion magazine. Another time, the bosses took a visiting fireman out for a night on the town and a couple of us Nisei were invited along. At one Sunset Strip nightclub the waiter was slow in returning with drinks and the table chitchat suddenly turned into a serious consideration of what strategy to use if the waiter failed to return. But eventually the drinks came.

The office was frequently visited by a well-to-do retired physician, the color of café-au-lait, whose everyday outfit consisted of a creamy Panama, impeccable white suit, and cane. With his distinguished-looking goatee, all that was missing was the frosted, tall, tinkling glass topped with a sprig of mint. The young eager beaver sports editor-advertising manager rushed in and out at all hours, breathlessly, bringing in a new display ad or dashing off to interview a boxing contender.

Later he was to get an appointment to West Point from Representative Helen Gahagan Douglas. There were glimpses of the sprinkling of show folk who stayed at the hotel — Billy Eckstine, the recently married Ossie Davis and Ruby Dee, the Delta Rhythm Boys; and down on Central Avenue, the theater marquee would advertise live acts like Pigmeat Markham, Mantan Moreland, Moms Mabley, and Redd Foxx. A tall young police lieutenant, later to become mayor of the city, came by to protest the newspaper's editorial on police brutality.[5]

One day when a new secretary named Miss Moten and I were in the mezzanine office, which was really three desks and two filing cabinets jammed into one end of the open mezzanine, with a counter separating the office from the subscribing and advertising public, a nice-looking young man with a mustache came up the stairs.

He said his name was Short. Urgently, he told us a disturbing story. He said he and his wife and two children had recently purchased a house in Fontana.[6] They had not been accorded a very warm welcome by the community. In fact, he said, there had been several threats of get-out-or-else, and his family was living in fear. He wanted his situation publicized so that some sentiment could be mustered in support of his right to live in Fontana. He was making the rounds of the three Negro newspapers in town to enlist their assistance.

I took down his story for the editor to handle when she got in. After he left, I noticed Miss Moten was extremely agitated. She was on the tense side to begin with, but she was a quiet, conscientious worker and always spoke in a gentle murmur.

But now her eyes were blazing with fury. She spat out the words. "I hate white people!"

"What?" I said, feeling stupid. I'd heard her all right, but I'd never seen her even halfway angry before.

---

[5]In this paragraph Yamamoto names a number of African American entertainers, some of whom are still active today. — EDS.

[6]Fontana is an eastern suburb of Los Angeles. — EDS.

"I hate white people! They're all the same!"

Then, later the same week, there was a fire in Fontana. Dead in the blaze, which appeared to have started with gasoline poured all around the house and outbuildings, were the young man who had told us his story, his comely wife, and their two lovely children, a boy and a girl (one of the other newspapers had obtained a recent portrait of the family, probably from relatives in the city).

There was an investigation, of course. The official conclusion was that probably the man had set the gasoline fire himself, and the case was closed.

Among those who doubted the police theory was a white priest who was so skeptical that he wrote a play about the fire in Fontana. *Trial by Fire,* he called it. Not long after it was presented on stage, the priest was suddenly transferred to a parish somewhere in the boondocks of Arizona.

And that was the last time I heard mention of the conflagration.

It was around this time that I felt something happening to me, but I couldn't put my finger on it. It was something like an itch I couldn't locate, or like food not being cooked enough, or something undone which should have been done, or something forgotten which should have been remembered. Anyway, something was unsettling my innards.

There was a Japanese evangelist who, before the war, used to shout on the northeast corner of First and San Pedro in Little Tokyo, his large painting of Jesus propped up against the signal pole there, and his tambourine for contributions placed on the sidewalk in front of the picture. He wore a small mustache, a uniform of navy blue, and a visored military-type cap. So regular was the cadence of his call to salvation that, from a distance, it sounded like the sharp barking of a dog. *"Wan, wan, wan! Wan, wan, wan!"* until, closer up, the man could be seen in exhortation, his face awry and purple with the passion of his message.

A fellow regular about that time on the sidewalks of Little Tokyo was a very large boy in a wheelchair which was usually pushed by a cute girl in bangs or another boy, both smaller than their charge, both of whom seemed to accept their transporting job cheerfully, as a matter of course. The large boy's usual outfit was denim overalls, his head was closely shaven, Japanese military-style, and there was a clean white handkerchief tied around his neck to catch the bit of saliva which occasionally trickled from a corner of his mouth.

It seems to me that my kinship, for all practical purposes, was with the large boy in the wheelchair, not with the admirable evangelist who was literally obeying the injunction to shout the good news from the housetops and street corners. For, what had I gone and done? Given the responsibility by the busy editor, I had written up from my notes a calm, impartial story, using "alleged" and "claimed" and other cautious journalese. Anyone noticing the story about the unwanted family in Fontana would have taken it with a grain of salt.

I should have been an evangelist at 7th and Broadway, shouting out the name of the Short family and their predicament in Fontana. But I had been as handicapped as the boy in the wheelchair, as helpless.

All my family and friends had already been feeling my displeasure when it came to certain matters anyway. I was a curmudgeon, a real pill. If they funned around or dared so much as to imitate a Southernly accent, I pounced on them like a cougar. They got so they would do their occasional sho-nuffs behind my back, hushing up suddenly when I came into the room.

And my correspondence suffered. When one fellow dared to imply that I was really unreasonable on the subject of race relations, saying that he believed it sufficient to make one's stand known only when the subject happened to come up, the exchange of letters did not continue much longer.

I even dared to engage in long-distance tilting with a university scholar who had been kind enough to notice my writing. Specifically, I objected to his admiration of Herman Melville's "Benito Cereno" as one of the most perfect short stories extant, to his citing of the slave Babo in the story as the epitome of evil. The professor replied that race was not the issue, and that, anyway, Melville was writing from assumptions prevalent in the culture of his time, and, furthermore, Negroes themselves had participated in the sealing of their fellow Blacks into bondage. These non sequiturs, coming from such a distinguished source, dismayed me.

So I guess you could say that things were coming to a head. Then, one afternoon when I was on the trolley bus heading home to Boyle Heights, there was some kind of disagreement at First and Broadway between the Negro driver of the bus I was on, turning onto First, and the white driver of the other bus turning onto Broadway. The encounter ended with the white driver waving his arms and cursing, "Why, you Black bastard!"

The Negro driver merely got back on and turned the bus onto Broadway, but I was sick, cringing from the blow of those words. My stomach was queasy with anxiety, and I knew Miss Moten's fury for my very own. I wanted to yell out the window at the other driver, but what could I have said? I thought of reporting him to management, but what could I have said?

Not long after, going to work one morning, I found myself wishing that the streetcar would rattle on and on and never stop. I'd felt the sensation before, on the way to my mother's funeral. If I could somehow manage to stay in the automobile forever, I thought, I would never have to face the fact of my mother's death. A few weeks after this incident on the street, I mumbled some excuse about planning to go back to school and left the paper.

I didn't go back to school, but after a time I got on trains and buses that carried me several thousand miles across the country and back. I guess you could say I was realizing my dream of traveling forever (escaping responsibility forever). I was in Massachusetts, New York, New Jersey, Maryland, and most of the time I didn't argue with anyone.

But once in Baltimore, I couldn't help objecting to a guest's offhand remark. This lady had been a patient in a maternity ward alongside a Negro woman and she mimicked the latter's cry, "Oh, give me something to ease the pain! Give me something to ease the pain!"

She gave me a pain, so I entered into a polite and wary fray, with the lady's husband joining in on his wife's behalf. "Edge-acated niggers," they said, what they couldn't support was the uppity airs of edge-acated niggers.

As the discussion continued, they backed down to allow as how northern Negroes might be another matter. But I knew nothing had been accomplished except the discomfiture of those whose hospitality we were enjoying.

In Baltimore, too, I admired the industry of the lady owner of the rowhouse next door. Lovely enough to be in the movies, with softly curling dark hair, she spoke a soft Marylandese that enchanted me. In the middle of winter, I could see her cleaning her upstairs windows, seated precariously on the sill so as to face the windows from the outside. But, one day, happening to walk with her to do some shopping, I saw her spewing lizards, toads, and wriggling serpents: "It's them damn niggras!"

When I finally came back to Los Angeles I was married and set about producing a passel of children. But stuff kept happening. Our son in high school reported that his classmates took delight in saying "nigger" behind the back of the Black electronics teacher. A white electronics teacher, visiting his sister in the hospital in the same room where I lay, said that he knew it was wrong, but he didn't want Blacks moving into his neighborhood in Alhambra—no Moors in Alhambra?[7] — because of the drop in property values that would ensue (I jousted feebly with him — well, I was sick — and later, on my return home, happened to be talking to someone who knew him, and found out that the teacher felt the same way about Japanese moving near him). When I objected to my children repeating a favorite word used by their playmates, one grandparent informed me that there was nothing wrong with the word nigger — she used it all the time herself. An attractive Korean lady friend and real estate agent put her children into Catholic schools because, as her daughter explained it, the public schools hereabouts were "integrated," while, on the other hand, she winsomely urged local real estate onto Black clients because, as she explained to me, "It's the coming thing," and her considerable profits ("It's been very good to me") made possible her upward mobility into less integrated areas.

So it was that, in between putting another load of clothes into the automatic washer, ironing, maybe whipping up some tacos for supper, I watched the Watts riot on television.[8] Back then I was still middle-aged, sitting safely in a house which was located on a street where panic would be

[7]The name for the Los Angeles suburb Alhambra comes from a castle built in the late Middle Ages in Grenada, Spain, by invading Moslem Moors from North Africa. Yamamoto notes the irony of excluding dark-skinned African Americans from a town named after a landmark built by dark-skinned Moors. — EDS.

[8]Yamamoto refers to a protest uprising in Watts in the summer of 1965, marked by violence, destruction, and loss of life. — EDS.

the order of the day if a Black family should happen to move in — I had come there on sufferance myself, on the coattails of a pale husband.

Appalled, inwardly cowering, I watched the burning and looting on the screen and heard the reports of the dead and wounded. But beneath all my distress, I felt something else, a tiny trickle of warmth which I finally recognized as an undercurrent of exultation. To me, the tumult in the city was the long-awaited, gratifying next chapter of an old movie that had flickered about in the back of my mind for years. In the film, shot in the dark of about three o'clock in the morning, there was this modest house out in the country. Suddenly the house was in flames and there were the sound effects of the fire roaring and leaping skyward. Then there could be heard the voices of a man and woman screaming, and the voices of two small children as well.

READING CRITICALLY

1. Yamamoto announces in the first paragraph that the topic of this essay will be a process whereby she, a Nisei, came to feel that she was African American, or, as she puts it a few paragraphs later, that "my inward self [was] burnt black" (p. 780). What are the stages in this process?

2. Yamamoto also says that she resisted the process: "I scrambled to backtrack for a while" (p. 780). Where do you see her resisting or denying a feeling of solidarity with African Americans?

3. How does Yamamoto use the contrasting pictures of the street evangelist and the "large boy in the wheelchair" (p. 783) to reproach herself for not acting vigorously enough against anti–African American racism?

4. Yamamoto senses some kind of connection between the fires during the Watts riots and the fire in Fontana that killed a black family. What is this connection, and why does it cause her to feel "exultation" (p. 786)?

WRITING ANALYTICALLY

1. Write a paper in which you explain how Yamamoto's feeling of solidarity with African Americans developed (note the stages you outlined in reading questions 1 and 2) and what the consequences of this developing solidarity were for her own actions — that is, what she did or failed to do to act on this feeling of solidarity.

2. Compare and contrast the relations between Nikkei and African Americans depicted in Yamamoto and in Okada (p. 766). From these two examples, what do you think are the chances for people of color to unite to fight injustice such as racism? Write a paper in which you argue for a response to this question. Alternative: Write a letter from Yamamoto to Okada responding to his book, or a letter from Okada to Yamamoto responding to her essay.

ASSIGNMENT SEQUENCES

SEQUENCE 1
What is "assimilation"?

- Montaville Flowers, From *The Japanese Conquest of American Opinion*
- U.S. Department of War, From *Final Report: Japanese Evacuation*
- Japanese American Citizens League, From *The Case for the Nisei*
- Jeanne Wakatsuki Houston and James D. Houston, From *Farewell to Manzanar* (both excerpts)
- Minoru Yasui, Oral History
- Monica Sone, From *Nisei Daughter*
- John Okada, From *No-No Boy*

1. State the definition of "assimilation" operating in either Flowers or the JACL brief, and explain whether, according to this definition, you are assimilated into American culture. Provide supporting evidence from your own background and experience, paying special attention to details such as languages, religions, attitudes toward "good" behavior, family legends, and so on.

2. Write a dialogue between Yasui and Okada's Ichiro on how it feels to try to be both Japanese and American. You might imagine that they are conversing from next-door jail cells.

3. Are Wakatsuki Houston's Jeanne, Yasui, Sone, and Okada's Ichiro "assimilated" into American culture? Write a paper in which you argue for an answer to this question, using your own definition of "assimilation." Compare two or more characters; you may also add yourself to the comparison, if you wish.

4. A principal reason that the Department of War's *Final Report* considers the Nikkei to be a security risk is that the *Report* regards them as unassimilated into American culture. What do you think the Nikkei would have to do to satisfy the authors of the report that they are indeed assimilated? What did they have to do to enable the writers of the JACL brief to argue that they are assimilated? Using these sources and, if appropriate, your own experience, write a paper in which you argue that it is, or is not, both possible and desirable for immigrants to become assimilated into American culture. You will have to consider whether or not American requirements for assimilation are so great that an immigrant group may not be able to meet them or may not want to make the effort and sacrifice necessary to meet them. Alternative: Write this paper in the form of a dialogue between you and either Wakatsuki Houston's Jeanne, Sone, or Okada's Ichiro on whether or not assimilation is possible and desirable.

5. Wakatsuki Houston, Okada, and Sone all deal with situations in which there are problems with the transmission of Japanese culture to children growing up in an American setting. You, too, may have had experiences with trying to keep more than one cultural heritage alive. Drawing on evidence from all these sources (and any others in this sequence you may wish to use), write an essay in which you explain the problems facing people who are trying to preserve their ethnic culture within the larger American culture. Alternative: You may write your essay in the

form of a feature article to be published in your local newspaper, in which you recommend a plan that will either help young people from diverse cultural backgrounds to assimilate into American culture as quickly and completely as possible or help them to maintain their diverse cultural heritages while also learning what they need to know to function as American citizens.

SEQUENCE 2
What is "race"?

- Montaville Flowers, From *The Japanese Conquest of American Opinion*
- U.S. Department of War, From *Final Report: Japanese Evacuation*
- Mike Masaoka, From *They Call Me Moses Masaoka*
- Jeanne Wakatsuki Houston and James D. Houston, From *Farewell to Manzanar* (both excerpts)
- Monica Sone, From *Nisei Daughter*
- John Okada, From *No-No Boy*
- Hisaye Yamamoto, "A Fire in Fontana"

1. Write a personal narrative in which you tell the story of how you first became conscious of the fact that human beings can be classified as belonging to different races. Alternative: Choose an incident from any of the readings in this sequence and comment on how it illustrates your own ideas of what racial differences mean.

2. Masaoka, Houston and Houston, Sone, Okada, and Yamamoto all describe incidents in which Asian people were made aware of their race or had their racial classification pointed out to them. Write a paper in which you compare and contrast the rhetorical strategies used in two of these sources for presenting this kind of situation.

3. Flowers and the Department of War's *Final Report* use their definitions of "race" to justify particular policies concerning the Nikkei. Write a paper in which you explain what these definitions are and how they are used. Using this evidence, argue for a thesis that one or both of these texts do or do not use a concept of "race" effectively to justify policies concerning the Nikkei.

4. Houston and Houston, Okada, and Yamamoto all allude in various ways to the possibility that different people of color, such as Asian Americans and African Americans, could get together to fight against the racism that hurts them all. Drawing on these sources and your own experience, write an argument in which you contend either that such cooperation is possible and desirable or that it is not. Support your position with references to at least three of the readings. You may either make your argument general, to cover any situation, or apply it to a particular situation in your community or on your campus where interracial cooperation is an issue. Option: You may imagine that your essay will be published in either a newspaper circulated to the general public, a campus newspaper, or a newspaper directed at a particular ethnic or racial group.

5. Masaoka, Houston and Houston, Sone, and Yamamoto all allude in various ways to the possibility that people of color can work with European Americans to fight against racism. Drawing on these sources and your own experience, write an

argument in which you contend either that such cooperation is possible and desirable or that it is not. Support your position with references to at least three of the readings. Avail yourself of the same choices for general or specific argument as in question 4 and of the same option for hypothetical publication.

6. From all your work in this sequence, develop an argument for how you think Americans should understand the concept of "race" today. Discuss how you would define the term "race" and how you think your understanding of race would affect race relations if widely adopted. Support your position with references to at least three of the readings for this sequence.

SEQUENCE 3
How could this happen in the United States?

- Executive Order 9066
- John L. DeWitt, "Instructions to All Persons of Japanese Ancestry"
- U.S. Department of War, From *Final Report: Japanese Evacuation*
- U.S. Commission on Wartime Relocation, From *Personal Justice Denied*
- Mike Masaoka, From *They Call Me Moses Masaoka*
- Michi Nishiura Weglyn, From *Years of Infamy*
- Jeanne Wakatsuki Houston and James D. Houston, From *Farewell to Manzanar* (both excerpts)
- Minoru Yasui, Oral History

1. Most historians now agree with the conclusion of *Personal Justice Denied,* that the rights of those interned were violated. National leaders decided to violate the rights of a small minority because they believed that this action would benefit the larger society (by protecting the United States from possible spying and sabotage, and so on). Do you think a country is ever justified in violating the rights of a minority in order to benefit the larger group? Write a brief opinion paper in response to this question.

2. The Commission on Wartime Relocation, Masaoka, and Weglyn all contend that racism directed against Asians played a large part in the decision to intern Japanese Americans. Write a paper in which you agree or disagree with this view. In the process, evaluate the arguments of at least two of these sources and consider the possible evidence of racism in one of the following: the Department of War's *Final Report,* Executive Order 9066, and "Instructions to All Persons."

3. Houston and Houston suggest that the Japanese Americans were partly to blame for the internment because they did not resist. Evidence relating to this issue can also be found in Masaoka, Weglyn, and Yasui. Drawing on at least two of these sources in addition to Houston and Houston, write an argument in which you indicate whether and to what extent you agree with Houston and Houston. Alternative: Respond to this question in the form of a letter you, a non-Nisei, are writing to a Nisei friend just before the internment process begins.

4. Yasui weighs the possibility of violent resistance to the internment and also describes his attempts to resist through legal challenges and passive resistance. From the information in Yasui and in Masaoka, what kinds of resistance do you

think the Nikkei should have employed? Do you think any form of resistance could have prevented or lessened the severity of the internment in the short run? What form of resistance do you believe would be most effective in the long run? Write a paper that supports a thesis responding to these questions with evidence from Yasui and Masaoka and one other source in this sequence. Option: You may add to your answer what you know about resistance to injustice mounted by other American groups. Alternative: Respond to this question by writing a panel discussion among Masaoka, Yasui, and a contemporary leader (such as Malcolm X or Nelson Mandela) on the topic of how people should resist injustice.

5. The *Final Report*, written by the U.S. Department of War to justify its own actions, gives one account of the internment. *Personal Justice Denied*, written by a U.S. commission to justify paying compensation to those interned, gives a very different account of the internment (and frequently attacks the *Final Report*). Write an essay in which you evaluate the credibility of these two sources and explain how you would use both of them to help you build a picture of what happened. If you wish, you may frame your argument in terms of general advice to historians on how to deal with conflicting sources. Option: Also include Masaoka, Houston and Houston, or Yasui, and explain how the historian should deal with personal accounts such as these. Are they valuable aids to rounding out a picture of what happened, or must they be set aside as too subjective and biased?

6. Drawing on all your work for this sequence, why do you think the internment happened? Was it wrong? If so, can we prevent such a thing from happening again? Write an argument responding to these questions, citing at least three of the readings in this sequence.

RESEARCH KIT

Negotiating Difference is an unfinished book: There are many other stories to tell in the history of "negotiating difference" in the United States. This Research Kit is intended to help you expand the readings provided in this unit. In "Ideas from the Unit Readings," we include more perspectives on the experiences of people of Japanese ancestry in the United States. In "Branching Out," we add perspectives on the experiences of other groups who have come to the United States and faced issues of assimilation, cultural preservation, and civil liberties. You can pursue these research ideas individually or as group or class projects.

To compile materials, you can start with the short bibliography included in this unit and with standard library search techniques that your teacher or a librarian can explain. Here are some other places where you can inquire for materials (not all regions will have all of these resources):

- Local chapters of the JACL or other Japanese American political action organizations, social organizations, churches, and so on.
- Museums devoted to the internment, Japanese American art and culture, or Asian American art and culture.

- Historic sites associated with the internment that have been preserved for tourist visits.
- Town and state historical societies, antiquarian societies, and so on.
- State university presses (which often have a list of local history titles that may include works on the internment, Japanese Americans, or other groups you may be studying).

Some of these same sources can be used for other groups you may be studying in answering some of the comparative questions in this Research Kit. Also, see other units in this book for suggestions for related topics (for example, Unit One has ideas on how to research Native American issues).

In collecting your material, always consider how a writer's account may be influenced by his or her motives. For example, a detention camp director may exaggerate the danger posed by the Nikkei in order to justify his use of force against them.

Also, keep your work focused by one of the research questions suggested here or by another that seems good to you. Remember that you are not writing an entire history of Japanese people in America (or of any other group); you are not going to be able to faithfully represent every aspect of Nikkei culture. In light of the overall theme of *Negotiating Difference,* you should keep your research focused in some way on Nikkei *contacts with other groups,* including the conceptual connections generated by some of the comparison questions suggested here.

IDEAS FROM THE UNIT READINGS

1. Find out more about the following people: Mike Masaoka, Jeanne Wakatsuki Houston, Minoru Yasui, Monica Sone, John Okada, Hisaye Yamamoto, Wayne Collins (a lawyer who fought for the internees who renounced their citizenship under duress), and Dillon Myer (head of the War Relocation Authority, which ran the camps).

2. Find out more about the U.S. Supreme Court cases of Mitsuye Endo, Fred Korematsu, and Gordon Hirabayashi, which challenged the legality of the evacuation and internment. What was at issue in each case? How did various American groups react to the cases?

3. What part did President Franklin D. Roosevelt play in the internment, and what should he have done? Research historians' answers, and develop your own.

4. Find out more about how the non-Nikkei American public reacted to the internment as it was happening. Your library may have archives that will enable you to see how the internment was reported in newspapers and magazines. Also, you can interview people who were teenagers or older at the time of World War II and ask about their views on the internment, both then and now.

5. Find out more about white supremacist writings and activities by groups such as the Sons and Daughters of the Golden West in early-twentieth-century California. What were the origins and the goals of these groups? Did they meet with any resistance?

6. Research the history of efforts to compensate the internees, from the 1948 Evacuation Claims Act to the present, in the wake of the 1988 Civil Liberties Act.

7. Find out more about the "No-No Boys" and other resistance movements within the camps and the government's responses to these movements. What were the different groups protesting? What became of the groups and their members during and after the internment?

8. Find out more about the activities of the 100th Battalion and the 442nd Regimental Combat Team, including Congressional Medal of Honor winner Sadao Munemori. Consider what these army units did, how their activities were reported in the American press, and how the returning Japanese American soldiers were received. If possible, see *Go for Broke!*, a film about the 442nd.

9. Trace the history of people of Japanese ancestry in Hawaii from the nineteenth century to the present, focusing especially on their experiences during World War II. You may wish to compare and contrast their experiences with those of Nikkei on the mainland and speculate on reasons for the differences. Why weren't the Hawaiian Nikkei interned? How did they contribute to the war effort?

10. Do you live in a region that was part of the military security area from which the army removed the Nikkei; that contained an assembly center or a relocation center (detention camp); that was a major destination for people leaving the camps? Research this local history, visiting sites where possible.

11. Do you have Japanese ancestry? Research your family history or, if you have already done so, prepare an account of it for an audience who knows very little about Japanese culture, the Nikkei experience, or the internment.

BRANCHING OUT

1. Find out what has happened to the Issei and their descendants since World War II. You will be studying not only the Nisei, but also the Sansei and their children, the Yonsei, as the fourth generation is called. You have two options that two different teams from the class might work on:
   a. Focus the topic broadly, on national trends.
   b. Focus the topic more narrowly, on the experiences of Nikkei in your region.

2. Find out what the Sansei, most of whom were born after the internment, think about it (one starting point is Janice Mirikitani's collection *Ayumi*). As with the reactions of those who experienced the internment, be alert to a wide variety of responses.

3. Find out more about how resident German aliens and German Americans were treated during World Wars I and II. Compare and contrast their treatment with the treatment of the Nikkei.

4. Trace the history of white racist activity in your region. You may wish to choose a time period on which to focus (or class teams can take them): before 1860; 1860–1900; 1900–1950; 1950–present. Against what groups has it been primarily directed? What kinds of resistance to it have been made?

5. Find out more about the Issei experience of coming to America: what parts of Japan they came from, when they came and why, where they settled and what

work they found, and so on. Also, unless you are a full-blooded Native American, find out more about the experiences of some of your ancestors coming to America — ask the same questions you've asked about the Issei and compare and contrast the experiences. (This could be a class project with one team working on the Issei and other teams working on other groups relevant to class members.)

6. Dillon Myer, head of the War Relocation Authority, was later head of the Bureau of Indian Affairs. Find out more about his conduct in these two offices as a way of comparing and contrasting the experiences of Native Americans and Nikkei in dealing with the federal government in the twentieth century. Another way to approach this comparison would be to find out more about the movement that led to the passage of the 1988 Civil Liberties Act and compare and contrast it with some recent effort by a Native American tribe (such as the Massachusetts Mashpees, Maine Passamaquoddies, Connecticut Mohegans, or another in your region) to settle financial claims against the federal government.

7. Create an annotated bibliography of visual materials on the Japanese experience in America. Consider artworks, photography (such as Ansel Adams's photos in John Armor and Peter Wright's *Manzanar*), video, films (such as *Go for Broke!*, about the 442nd Regimental Combat Team, or *Come See the Paradise,* about the internment experience). Weglyn's book contains a bibliographic essay on relevant films although it is somewhat dated. Your annotations should describe each entry in light of what you have learned in all your work on this unit. For example, you might comment on how No-No Boys are portrayed in *Come See the Paradise* or compare Adams's photographs with those in the War Department's *Final Report.*

BIBLIOGRAPHY

Works Included or Excerpted

DeWitt, John L. "Instructions to All Persons of Japanese Ancestry." 1942. Reprinted in U.S. Department of War, *Final Report.*

Flowers, Montaville. *The Japanese Conquest of American Opinion.* New York: George H. Doran, 1917.

Houston, Jeanne Wakatsuki, and James D. Houston. *Farewell to Manzanar.* 1973. Reprint, New York: Bantam Books, 1974.

Japanese American Citizens League. Amicus curiae brief. *Fred Toyosaburo Korematsu v. United States.* U.S. Supreme Court. October term, 1944. Reprinted in *The Case for the Nisei.* Salt Lake City, Utah: Japanese American Citizens League, 1945?.

Masaoka, Mike, with Bill Hosokawa. *They Call Me Moses Masaoka: An American Saga.* New York: William Morrow, 1987.

Okada, John. *No-No Boy.* 1957. Reprint, Seattle: University of Washington Press, 1979.

Roosevelt, Franklin Delano. Executive Order 9066. 1942. Reprinted in U.S. Department of War, *Final Report.*

Sone, Monica. *Nisei Daughter.* 1953. 2nd ed., Seattle: University of Washington Press, 1979.

U.S. Commission on Wartime Relocation and Internment of Civilians. *Personal Justice Denied.* Washington, D.C.: Government Printing Office, 1982.

U.S. Department of War. *Final Report: Japanese Evacuation from the West Coast, 1942.* Washington, D.C.: Government Printing Office, 1943. Reprint, New York: Arno Press, 1978.

Weglyn, Michi Nishiura. *Years of Infamy: The Untold Story of America's Concentration Camps.* New York: William Morrow, 1976.

Yamamoto, Hisaye. "A Fire in Fontana." *Rafu Shimpo,* December 21, 1985, 8–9, 16–17, 19.

Yasui, Minoru. Oral History. In *And Justice for All: An Oral History of the Japanese American Detention Camps,* edited by John Tateishi. New York: Random House, 1984.

Other Sources

Armor, John, and Peter Wright. *Manzanar.* Photographs by Ansel Adams. Commentary by John Hersey. New York: Random House, Times Books, 1988.

Chiasson, Lloyd. "Japanese-American Relocation during World War II: A Study of California Editorial Reactions." *Journalism Quarterly* 68 (Spring/Summer 1991): 263–68.

Daniels, Roger. *Prisoners without Trial: Japanese Americans in World War II.* New York: Hill and Wang, 1993.

Daniels, Roger, Sandra C. Taylor, and Harry H. L. Kitano, eds. *Japanese Americans: From Relocation to Redress.* Rev. ed. Seattle: University of Washington Press, 1991.

Kitano, Harry. *Japanese Americans: Evolution of a Subculture.* Englewood Cliffs, N.J.: Prentice-Hall, 1969.

Kogawa, Joy. *Iksuka.* New York: Anchor Books, 1994.

———. *Obasan.* Toronto: Lester & Orpen Dennys, 1981. Reprint, Boston: David Godine, 1982.

Ichioka, Yuji, ed. *Views from Within: The Japanese American Evacuation and Resettlement Study.* Los Angeles: Asian American Studies Center, University of California at Los Angeles, 1989.

Mirikitani, Janice, ed. *Ayumi: A Japanese American Anthology.* San Francisco: Japanese American Anthology Committee, 1980.

Mori, Toshio. *The Chauvinist and Other Stories.* Los Angeles: Asian American Studies Center, University of California at Los Angeles, 1979.

National Archives and Records Administration. Office of Public Programs. Education Branch. *Internment of Japanese Americans: Documents from the National Archives.* Dubuque, Iowa: Kendall Hunt Publishing Co., n.d.

O'Brien, David J., and Stephen S. Fugita. *The Japanese American Experience.* Bloomington: Indiana University Press, 1991.

Ota, Peter. "Peter Ota." In *"The Good War": An Oral History of World War II,* edited by Studs Terkel. New York: Pantheon Books, 1984.

Sundquist, Eric J. "The Japanese-American Internment: A Reappraisal." *American Scholar* 57 (Autumn 1988): 529–47.

Takaki, Ronald. *Strangers from a Different Shore: A History of Asian Americans.* Boston: Little, Brown, 1989.

tenBroek, Jacobus, Edward N. Barnhart, and Floyd W. Matson. *Prejudice, War, and the Constitution: Causes and Consequences of the Evacuation of the Japanese Americans in World War II.* Berkeley: University of California Press, 1954.

Tule Lake Committee. *Kinenhi: Reflections on Tule Lake.* San Francisco: n.p., 1980.

Uchida, Yoshiko. *Desert Exile: The Uprooting of a Japanese American Family.* Seattle: University of Washington Press, 1982.

Policy and Protest
over the Vietnam War

NEGOTIATIONS

On Monday, May 4, 1970, four students at Kent State University were killed and nine were wounded by the Ohio National Guard during a protest against the war in Vietnam. For years, opposition to the war had been increasing. Americans were divided not only over the justification for and conduct of the war, but also over their image of America. Was America noble and good? Could the government be trusted to do the right thing? The most acrimonious of debates and the most violent of reactions to protest often turned on the issue of whether Americans should protest at all. Protesters were condemned as traitors while supporters of the war displayed American flag stickers on their car windows. The protesters themselves, like the students at Kent State, condemned the repressive policy of sending police and National Guard troops with M-1 rifles to college campuses. The war in Vietnam had generated a conflict at home.

In every conflict that has taken place on foreign soil — wars declared or undeclared — Americans have disagreed about whether to fight. In World War I and World War II, pacifists (those who feel that wars should not be fought at all) and neutralists (those who feel that the United States should not take a role in foreign wars) protested the government's decision to go to war and often refused to serve when called. During the Korean War, neutralists and pacifists were joined by those who felt that the United States was violating international law by intervening in a civil war. Moreover, they argued, the United States was violating its own laws as well, for it had not even bothered to declare war. Still, these protests were minor compared with the upheaval that took place over the Vietnam War, a war not only undeclared but long and drawn out — longer and in many ways costlier than any other war fought in the history of the United States.

The United States is still living through the consequences of the Vietnam War. Veterans of the war are now mostly middle-aged. Many are wounded physically, many scarred psychologically by the horrors they witnessed and the atrocities they themselves committed. In Washington, D.C., the Vietnam Veterans Memorial, popularly called the Wall, and the smaller Wall that moves from city to city will continue to attract the families and friends of those who died. Questions about entering foreign conflicts are still met by the ominous warning "no more Vietnams."

But during the war itself, sentiment in the United States was split — and not along any easily marked lines such as age or political party affiliation or military status, as many people claimed. Protests at the beginning of the war were few and were often ignored by the media. Until quite late in the war, a majority of Americans polled continued to support the government's policy. Congress never declared war and was slow to restrict the president's powers or cut off funding. But between 1963, when President Lyndon B. Johnson declared his commitment to Vietnam, and 1975, when the last Americans left, protests steadily mounted. Counterprotests followed and soon there was conflict within the United States — the so-called war at home. Though popular depictions of this conflict at the time pitted the young against the old, college students against "hard hats," and "draft-dodgers" against militarists, the positions that Americans took were in fact too complex to fit those categories, as the materials assembled here show.

In the selections in this unit, the Vietnam War stands for a set of social actions and political ideas that many favored and many opposed. How do we negotiate so large a set of differences? How do we argue for and against a government policy that has so many implications in philosophical principles and individual lives? Though the war is over, it is still with us, as are the questions it raised about how our democracy ought to work.

OVERVIEW OF THE SELECTIONS

The selections are divided into four groups. The first section, "A Precursor to War," contains a single document, the "Declaration of Independence of the Democratic Republic of Vietnam," written in 1945. In that year Vietnam declared its independence from the French, who had imposed colonial rule on the country for one hundred years. The declaration document was composed by Ho Chi Minh, the legendary leader of the Vietnamese Communists. Modeled on the U.S. Declaration of Independence, this document reflected Ho's efforts to enlist the United States on the side of his nationalist movement.

The second section, "1965: Year of Escalation and Protest," presents a selection of arguments for and against the war, all from 1965. This year was a turning point, when President Johnson decided to send U.S. troops to Vietnam in large numbers. Before the escalation occurred, Senator Thomas J. Dodd gave a speech to the U.S. Senate defending the war as an appropriate and essential expression of the U.S. policy of anticommunism.

The State Department's "white paper" of 1965, *Aggression from the North,* argued that Communist North Vietnam was waging war against the democratic South and that therefore the United States was defending a free country from aggression. I. F. Stone, a well-respected progressive journalist, refuted this argument, charging that the State Department's interpretation of its evidence was based on what it wanted to see rather than what was truly there. In the same year, a group of older pacifists issued a declaration of their intent to illegally counsel young men to resist the draft. The draft-card-burning movement followed from this statement and others like it. Two poems are also included in this section — one by a twelve-year-old American girl on the deaths of Vietnamese children, the other a response by a Vietnamese poet. Following them is a speech by student leader Paul Potter attacking the government's claim that the war was about protecting the freedom of the Vietnamese people.

The next group of selections, "The War at Home," reveals the increasing conflicts among Americans about whether to support the war effort. In 1967 Martin Luther King Jr. overtly linked the civil rights movement to the Vietnam War in a speech delivered at the Riverside Church in New York City. King argued that African Americans lacked the freedoms that President Johnson hoped to gain for the Vietnamese and pointed out the irony that black American soldiers were dying in disproportionate numbers in Vietnam for Johnson's goals. In a 1968 speech Johnson confronted the divisions in the country and attempted to balance continued commitment to the war with an effort to negotiate its end. In the speech, Johnson unexpectedly and dramatically announced his withdrawal from the upcoming presidential race. A pamphlet from the antiwar movement, "A Message to GIs and to the Movement," asked soldiers and protesters to try to understand each other and see that their interests were similar. Richard M. Nixon, who succeeded Johnson as president, pursued the war for five more years under the provisions of the "plan for peace" that he outlined in the 1969 speech included in this section. Nixon called on the "youth of this nation" to understand the situation and appealed for the support of the "silent majority" — that allegedly large portion of the population Nixon claimed approved of his policy but was not as vocal or active as the liberal opponents of the war. Nixon's vice president, Spiro T. Agnew, gave a number of speeches, some of which are excerpted here, viciously attacking war protesters as traitors.

In the last selection of this group, John F. Kerry, a Vietnam War veteran who would later be elected a senator from Massachusetts, appeared before the Senate Foreign Relations Committee in 1971 as a representative of the Vietnam Veterans Against the War. Kerry's testimony revealed some of the horrors of the war that other veterans would write and talk about in later years.

The last section of the unit, "Veterans Remember," contains some of the autobiographical accounts produced by Vietnam veterans after they came home. Tim O'Brien's memoir "On the Rainy River" explores the emotions of an eighteen-year-old draftee who must decide whether to face

Vietnam or leave the country to avoid the draft. The stories of African American soldier Harold Bryant and nurse Leslie McClusky come from two of several collections of oral histories that have been published fairly recently. Both describe their wartime experiences as well as their difficult homecomings. Ron Kovic's autobiography, *Born on the Fourth of July*, is a moving account of his time in Vietnam, his paralyzing wound, the shabby way he was treated in military hospitals, and his decision to become an antiwar activist.

HISTORICAL BACKGROUND

Early History of Vietnam

The kingdom of Nam-Viet, occupying parts of what is today southern China and northern Vietnam, was founded in 208 B.C.E. One hundred years later, the kingdom was annexed by China, which governed it for the next thousand years. The Chinese called the country An Nam, meaning "pacified south." The name Vietnam, preferred by the people who lived in the kingdom, means "distant south." After many attempts to throw off the Chinese yoke, Vietnam regained its independence in 939 C.E., but China remained a threat and exacted tribute for many centuries thereafter. After regaining its independence, the country expanded steadily southward to its present borders, reaching the Gulf of Siam by the mid-eighteenth century.

Vietnam as a French Colony

In the seventeenth century, the European powers (England, France, Portugal, and the Netherlands) were trading with Vietnam and, against the opposition of the country's rulers, sending missionaries there. Christianity was outlawed and in the mid-nineteenth century, the emperor Tu Duc attempted to expel all foreigners. When some French and Spanish missionaries were killed, the French invaded and conquered the country. The French divided the country into administrative areas — Annam, Cochin China, and Tonkin — and included Laos and Thailand in a larger entity they called Indochina. Paris controlled the country through French governors, bureaucrats, and soldiers and a small class of French-educated, Christian Vietnamese. As in most colonies, the economy was organized to benefit the French, who remained largely ignorant of Vietnamese culture.

Armed opposition to the French was more or less constant. Both Communist and non-Communist nationalist parties formed in the early twentieth century to resist the French. In 1930, Ho Chi Minh united several small groups into the Indochinese Communist Party, which organized demonstrations, strikes, and armed resistance. The French continued to rule Vietnam until 1940, when France fell to the Germans in World War II. At the same time, Japan overran Indochina. The French administration, however, remained in place under Japanese control until March 1945, when the Japanese took over. Just before their surrender in August 1945, the Japanese allowed Vietnam to declare its independence and set up its own government under a Japanese puppet ruler, Emperor Bao Dai. After the Japanese surrender, Bao Dai abdicated and Ho Chi Minh, now the leader of the Viet Minh — the Vietnam Independence League — composed the "Declaration of Independence of the Democratic Republic of Vietnam" (DRV) and delivered it publicly on September 2, 1945. Ho sent a telegram to President Truman in October asking for support for the DRV, but the Truman administration refused to risk contact with a committed Communist and Ho's telegram went unanswered, as did several subsequent appeals.

Chinese troops had been assigned to disarm the Japanese at the end of the war. Vietnam agreed to replace them with French troops in 1946. Under this agreement, France recognized Vietnam as a "free state" and a member of the "French Union." The meaning of these terms was not clear and was not clarified by negotiations between Ho and the French. Late in 1946, war broke out between the French and the Viet Minh.

U.S. Policy in the 1950s

In 1949, the Viet Minh established ties with Communist China. The United States, already supporting France in its efforts to control Indochina, increased military aid to help contain communism. Between 1946 and 1954, U.S. aid totaled $2.5 billion. In 1950 the U.S. Military Assistance and Advisory Group was set up in Saigon in the south of Vietnam as part of a "mutual defense assistance pact" with France and Indochina.

In 1954, the Viet Minh defeated French forces in the decisive battle of Dien Bien Phu. France was forced to negotiate a settlement and sign the Geneva accords, which provisionally divided Vietnam at the seventeenth parallel into North and South. The North was led by Ho and the Viet Minh from Hanoi, while the South was led by Bao Dai and his prime minister, Ngo Dinh Diem, from Saigon. Nationwide elections were to be held in 1956 to determine who would lead a reunified nation. The U.S. government regarded the prospect of elections and a unified Vietnam as a disaster, sure that the elections would lead to a victory by Ho and the Viet Minh and thus to the spread of communism. Neither the United States nor South Vietnam signed the accords. The United States did, however, issue a separate declaration that it would "refrain from the threat or use of force to disturb them," and South Vietnam also publicly stated its support for them.

In 1955 Diem held fraudulent elections in South Vietnam to remove Bao Dai and had himself installed as head of state. Knowing that Diem was opposed to reunification elections, the United States fully backed and encouraged Diem. As the U.S. government hoped, Diem refused to discuss elections with the Communists in the North, repudiated the Geneva accords, and did not hold elections in 1956. These moves effectively created a separate state in the South. In the same year, the United States, ignoring the Geneva agreement, sent additional military advisers to Vietnam. Meanwhile, dissatisfaction with Diem grew. An arrogant leader who consulted with no one and issued peremptory orders, Diem was increasingly opposed by his own staff as well as the people of the country. The United States was unable to convince Diem to change his tyrannical tactics, and open insurgency broke out in 1959. In December 1960, Ho Chi Minh formed the National Front for the Liberation of South Vietnam (NLF) to drive Diem and the United States out and to bring about reunification of the country under Communist leadership. Diem called the NLF "Viet Cong," identifying them as Communists allied with the North. Diem was partly correct: The NLF was aided and largely controlled by Hanoi, but many of its members were non-Communist opponents of Diem. In 1963 Diem was overthrown and assassinated in a coup by his officers, who were supported fully by the Kennedy administration. Diem was followed by several unstable military regimes. In 1965 Nguyen Van Thieu and Nguyen Cao Ky came to power, where they remained until the end of the war.

Kennedy's War

Early in John F. Kennedy's presidency, in 1961, the Pentagon argued for a massive buildup of troops and arms in Vietnam to fend off the Communist threat. In 1961, Kennedy sent hundreds of troops and advisers to Vietnam and agreed to finance a major increase in the South Vietnamese army. Sending troops to Vietnam was not a new idea. As early as 1954, the U.S. government had contemplated armed intervention in Vietnam: "Will Indochina be lost to the Communists unless the United States commits combat resources in some form?" asked a National Security Council report of April 5, 1954. The potential threat of "losing" one Southeast Asian country after another if Vietnam "fell" — the domino theory — became a standard justification for U.S. involvement in Vietnam. The report played out several scenarios: the possibility of war with China and even another "general war"; the acceptability to the American public of various courses of action; and the need to "counteract or modify" the view that the French interest was colonialist or imperialist. Such reports, couched in terms of anticommunism, policy alternatives, and public opinion, continued to come to Washington from the National Security Council, the Pentagon, ambassadors, and special commissions from the 1950s until the end of the war. Reading them, as we can do now in several excellent collections, gives us the sense of an inexorable march of rational decisions leading to Kennedy's intervention and the escalations under Lyndon Johnson and Richard Nixon.

These reports convinced Kennedy that the United States had to support South Vietnam both financially and militarily, with troops and equipment. The U.S. government did this, despite sanctions by other nations (including, ironically, France), which pointed out that such support was a repeated violation of the Geneva accords (although the United States had not signed the accords). To avoid such attacks, Kennedy began the practice of keeping the U.S. buildup a secret. He claimed, too, that U.S. troops were not in combat, an outright lie. Kennedy and, later, Johnson hoped that minimal intervention would hold up the South Vietnamese government and shield the administration from charges of being soft on communism.

Lyndon Johnson and the Protest Movement

In early 1964, with Lyndon Johnson having assumed the presidency after Kennedy's assassination, the United States and South Vietnam made elaborate plans to attack North Vietnam directly. The Johnson administration hoped to pass a congressional resolution giving the president the power to launch such attacks without a declaration of war. But an incident in early August provided the justification Johnson needed to put his plans into action. On August 2, the U.S. destroyer *Maddox* was attacked by three North Vietnamese gunboats in the Gulf of Tonkin — well within North Vietnamese waters. The *Maddox* sank one of the boats and chased the others away. Johnson ordered the destroyer to remain in North Vietnamese waters, and two days later the destroyer reported another incident during a storm. This incident has never been completely explained — was it another attack or a false radar signal? At the time, however, Johnson and the Pentagon seized the opportunity to claim that North Vietnam had attacked a U.S. vessel in the open seas. Despite conflicting reports about the incident, Congress on August 7, 1964, passed nearly unanimously the Tonkin Gulf Resolution authorizing the use of armed force in Vietnam. Until the *Pentagon Papers* revealed otherwise, the government denied that there had been any advance planning for all of this. The *Pentagon Papers* (see p. 802) also revealed that many Pentagon experts argued the futility of trying to bomb North Vietnam into submission. Bombing of the North began early in 1965, along with significant increases in the numbers of American soldiers — to a total of nearly 200,000 by the end of the year. The numbers increased until 1969, when the total reached 543,000.

By 1965, a significant number of groups and individuals had begun sustained opposition to the war in Vietnam. In the following years, massive antiwar demonstrations were held in New York, Washington, D.C., and other major cities. The protests sparked national debate — always highly emotional — about the merits of the war and the motives of the protesters themselves. Johnson and others in the administration, as well as many members of Congress, seemed to have increasing doubts about the merits of the war, which seemed only to increase Johnson's subterfuge about the size of the U.S. force and its failing mission. In 1968, Johnson tried several versions of a "bombing halt" to accelerate negotiations. Worn down by the pressures he faced, Johnson withdrew from the upcoming presidential race.

Richard Nixon and the Final Chapters

In the 1968 presidential race, Democrats Robert Kennedy and Eugene McCarthy campaigned successfully as antiwar candidates. On June 5, 1968, just as he was declaring victory in the California primary, Kennedy was assassinated. Hubert Humphrey, Johnson's vice president, caught between his support for the administration and his own antiwar sentiment, won the Democratic nomination. In the end, the Republican candidate, Richard M. Nixon, won the presidency, having run on a promise that he had a secret plan to end the war.

A massive demonstration at the Democratic Party convention in Chicago provoked a police riot and became a focal point for protests not only against the war but against the "system" or the "establishment." The war in Vietnam had generated violent conflict at home — violence that would be repeated in other demonstrations and capped by the May 1970 killing of four Kent State students by the National Guard during a rally to protest the bombing of Cambodia. Radical groups of antiwar protesters countered with their own violence, making bombs and committing robberies in the name of protest.

By 1970, polls indicated that about half of the American population was sympathetic to the antiwar movement and the other half opposed. Nonetheless, more than half approved of President Nixon's handling of the war, which in March 1969 had expanded to include attacks on Communist forces in Cambodia and a resumption of heavy bombing of North Vietnam. The largest antiwar demonstration occurred in April 1971, with 500,000 protesters in Washington. Vice President Spiro Agnew lambasted the protest leaders as "an effete corps of impudent snobs" who were nothing but cowards and traitors. Nixon was obsessed with the protests. He ordered the FBI to infiltrate antiwar groups and composed an "enemies list" of antiwar activists and sympathizers. A presidential commission studying the protest movement reported that the division in American society was "as deep as any since the Civil War."

In June 1971, the *Pentagon Papers* were published by the *New York Times*. A Pentagon analyst, Daniel Ellsberg, had copied the papers, a collection of memoranda and analyses that were part of a secret history of United States involvement in Vietnam that was commissioned in 1967 by Secretary of Defense Robert McNamara. The papers revealed conflict within the Kennedy and Johnson administrations and a deliberate effort to conceal government decisions from Congress and the public. Nixon was furious. He assembled a staff of investigators — called the "plumbers," because their job was to "plug leaks"—to go after Ellsberg. This group soon expanded its scope to target all of Nixon's enemies, including the Democratic Party, whose headquarters at the Watergate building they bugged. These activities and their coverup by Nixon and his advisers came to be known as the Watergate scandal and eventually led to Nixon's resignation in 1974 under threat of impeachment.

As for the war itself, Nixon's plan was to reduce the number of U.S. troops in Vietnam, to keep up the bombing of North Vietnam, and to "Vietnamize" the war by building up the South Vietnamese army. All the while Henry Kissinger, Nixon's national security adviser, was engaged in negotiations with North Vietnam and various intermediaries.

In 1971, Congress attempted to take some control of the war and held extensive hearings. The testimony of Vietnam veterans was particularly powerful. Many veterans were actively protesting the war on a new set of grounds — that soldiers were being made to fight in unspeakably horrible conditions for no discernible reason. The Vietnam Veterans Against the War (VVAW) held their own hearings, the Winter Soldier Investigation, early in 1971 to begin to publicize the soldiers' stories. The VVAW's demonstration in Washington during the congressional hearings was intended to ensure that the stories were heard in high places.

It took most veterans a long time to come to terms with their war experiences. Many have not come to terms with them yet. Not only was the war itself wrenching, but when the veterans returned home, they did not receive a hero's welcome; many were spat on, called baby-killers, or simply ignored. Thinking that they had been defending their country, they came home to a country increasingly embarrassed by the war and angry at those who prosecuted it, from the administration down to the troops. U.S. atrocities were widely known and all veterans seemed suspect. Many veterans found that even their families did not want to hear their stories, their confessions, or their views. The result, for many veterans, was massive alienation, a high rate of stress, drug and alcohol use, and almost no audience for their grievances.

Through 1972 and into 1973, more than 400,000 U.S. troops were withdrawn from Vietnam, despite the inability of the South Vietnamese to hold off the Viet Cong or the North Vietnamese. In 1972 Nixon won reelection over antiwar Democrat George McGovern on the promise of "peace with honor." A peace treaty was signed at last in 1973 by the United States, North Vietnam, South Vietnam, and the NLF's provisional revolutionary government. U.S. ground troops were completely withdrawn, though 43,000 air force personnel remained to continue bombing in the hope that the South Vietnamese government would soon be able to defend itself. Finally, on April 30, 1975, Saigon fell to the Viet Cong. As the Communist forces entered the U.S. embassy compound, the last of the U.S. forces helped evacuate Vietnamese who had been employed by U.S. officials. The war in Vietnam was over, but the wounds it inflicted on the United States have yet to heal.

A PRECURSOR TO WAR

HO CHI MINH

"Declaration of Independence of the Democratic Republic of Vietnam"
(September 2, 1945)

At the end of World War I in 1919, the young Ho Chi Minh (1890–1969), already a leader in his country's fight for independence, wrote to the U.S. secretary of state asking for support for Vietnam's request for greater freedoms and, ultimately, independence from France. Ho had spent a year in the United States (1913–14) and was impressed at the freedoms enjoyed by all people, including immigrants like him. Through the years, he made repeated appeals for help to the U.S. government but was answered only once, during World War II, when the OSS (predecessor of the CIA) trained Ho's troops to help them fight the Japanese. The OSS provided Ho with a copy of the U.S. Declaration of Independence, parts of which he incorporated in the declaration of his own country's independence in 1945. Despite his deep commitment to communism, Ho still hoped for U.S. support, which never came.

"WE HOLD TRUTHS THAT ALL MEN are created equal, that they are endowed by their Creator with certain unalienable Rights, among these are Life, Liberty, and the pursuit of Happiness."

This immortal statement is extracted from the Declaration of Independence of the United States of America in 1776. Understood in the broader sense, this means: "All peoples on the earth are born equal; every person has the right to live to be happy and free."

The Declaration of Human and Civic Rights proclaimed by the French Revolution in 1791 likewise propounds: "Every man is born equal and enjoys free and equal rights."

These are undeniable truths.

Yet, during and throughout the last eighty years, the French imperialists, abusing the principles of "Freedom, equality, and fraternity,"[1] have violated the integrity of our ancestral land and oppressed our countrymen. Their deeds run counter to the ideals of humanity and justice.

Ho Chi Minh, "Declaration of Independence of the Democratic Republic of Vietnam," in *Vietnam: A History in Documents,* ed. Gareth Porter (New York: New American Library, 1981), 29–30.

In the notes, EDS. = Patricia Bizzell and Bruce Herzberg.

[1]"Liberty, equality, fraternity" was adopted as the motto of the French Revolution. — EDS.

In the political field, they have denied us every freedom. They have enforced upon us inhuman laws. They have set up three different political regimes in Northern, Central, and Southern Viet Nam (Tonkin, Annam, and Cochinchina) in an attempt to disrupt our national, historical, and ethnical unity.

They have built more prisons than schools. They have callously ill-treated our fellow-compatriots. They have drowned our revolutions in blood.

They have sought to stifle public opinion and pursued a policy of obscurantism on the largest scale; they have forced upon us alcohol and opium in order to weaken our race.

In the economic field, they have shamelessly exploited our people, driven them into the worst misery and mercilessly plundered our country.

They have ruthlessly appropriated our rice fields, mines, forests, and raw materials. They have arrogated to themselves the privilege of issuing banknotes, and monopolized all our external commerce. They have imposed hundreds of unjustifiable taxes, and reduced our countrymen, especially the peasants and petty tradesmen, to extreme poverty.

They have prevented the development of native capital enterprises; they have exploited our workers in the most barbarous manner.

In the autumn of 1940, when the Japanese Fascists, in order to fight the Allies, invaded Indochina and set up new bases of war, the French imperialists surrendered on bended knees and handed over our country to the invaders.

Subsequently, under the joint French and Japanese yoke, our people were literally bled white. The consequences were dire in the extreme. From Quang Tri up to the North, two millions of our countrymen died from starvation during the first months of this year.

On March 9, 1945, the Japanese disarmed the French troops. Again the French either fled or surrendered unconditionally. Thus, in no way have they proved capable of "protecting" us; on the contrary, within five years they have twice sold our country to the Japanese.

Before March 9, many a time did the Viet Minh League invite the French to join in the fight against the Japanese. Instead of accepting this offer, the French, on the contrary, let loose a wild reign of terror with rigor worse than ever before against Viet Minh's partisans. They even slaughtered a great number of our "*condamnés politiques*"[2] imprisoned at Yen Bay and Cao Bang.

Despite all that, our countrymen went on maintaining, vis-à-vis the French, a humane and even indulgent attitude. After the events of March 9, the Viet Minh League helped many French to cross the borders, rescued others from Japanese prisons, and, in general, protected the lives and properties of all the French in their territory.

In fact, since the autumn of 1940, our country ceased to be a French colony and became a Japanese possession.

After the Japanese surrender, our people, as a whole, rose up and pro-

[2]French for "political prisoners." — EDS.

claimed their sovereignty and founded the Democratic Republic of Viet Nam.

The truth is that we have wrung back our independence from Japanese hands and not from the French.

The French fled, the Japanese surrendered. Emperor Bao Dai[3] abdicated, our people smashed the yoke which pressed hard upon us for nearly one hundred years, and finally made our Viet Nam an independent country. Our people at the same time overthrew the monarchical regime established tens of centuries ago, and founded the Republic.

For these reasons, we, the members of the Provisional Government representing the entire people of Viet Nam, declare that we shall from now on have no more connections with imperialist France; we consider null and void all the treaties France has signed concerning Viet Nam, and we hereby cancel all the privileges that the French arrogated to themselves on our territory.

The Vietnamese people, animated by the same common resolve, are determined to fight to the death against all attempts at aggression by the French imperialists.

We are convinced that the Allies who have recognized the principles of equality of peoples at the Conferences of Teheran and San Francisco[4] cannot but recognize the Independence of Viet Nam.

A people which has so stubbornly opposed the French domination for more than eighty years, a people who, during these last years, so doggedly ranged itself and fought on the Allied side against fascism, such a people has the right to be free, such a people must be independent.

For these reasons, we, the members of the Provisional Government of the Democratic Republic of Viet Nam, solemnly declare to the world:

"Viet Nam has the right to be free and independent and, in fact, has become free and independent. The people of Viet Nam decide to mobilize all their spiritual and material forces and to sacrifice their lives and property in order to safeguard their right of Liberty and Independence."

READING CRITICALLY

1. What does the declaration accuse the French of doing?

2. What does the declaration assert about Vietnam to support its contention that it is, in effect, already an independent state?

[3]Bao Dai (b. 1913) was the last emperor of Vietnam. He cooperated with the Japanese in World War II and became their puppet ruler just before their surrender in 1945. After the surrender, he abdicated and joined the Viet Minh briefly. He lived in France from 1945 to 1949 and returned to Vietnam as a puppet head of state under the French until 1955, when he retired to France. — EDS.

[4]At the Conference of Teheran, Iran, in November 1943, U.S. President Franklin Roosevelt, British Prime Minister Winston Churchill, and Soviet Premier Joseph Stalin agreed on the military plans that would end World War II and declared the sovereignty of nations that had been conquered by Germany. The United Nations charter was drawn up at the San Francisco conference in the spring of 1945. — EDS.

WRITING ANALYTICALLY

Read the U.S. Declaration of Independence (p. 174). Find the two near-quotes from it that are included in the Vietnamese declaration, and note other similarities between the two documents in language, structure, and argument. In an essay comparing the two documents, analyze the way in which the principle that "all men are created equal" actually underlies the desire for national independence as expressed in the documents. What other principles might have been invoked to support the Vietnamese claims? Alternative: Analyze how the situation of the British colonization of America contrasts with the French colonization of Vietnam. Do the differences invalidate the links between the two documents or reinforce them?

1965: YEAR OF ESCALATION AND PROTEST

THOMAS J. DODD

From a Speech to the U.S. Senate
(February 23, 1965)

Thomas J. Dodd (1907–71) was the Democratic senator from Connecticut from 1958 to 1970. This selection consists of excerpts from a speech Dodd gave opposing American isolationism. In this speech, Dodd clearly articulates the principle of anticommunism that had guided U.S. foreign policy since the end of World War II. Dodd also makes the case that the war in Vietnam is not a civil war, but an aggression against South Vietnam by a foreign country, North Vietnam. Dodd recommends strong support for the war, though he wants to stop short of sending in a large number of U.S. ground forces, as President Johnson would do later in 1965.

Dodd's senate career ended after he was censured by the Senate for diverting campaign funds for his own use.

OVER THE PAST SEVERAL MONTHS, a number of my most respected colleagues have taken the floor to urge that we get out of Vietnam or that we enter into negotiations over Vietnam.

The propriety of our presence in Vietnam and the validity of our position has been challenged. It has even been suggested that we are the real aggressors in Vietnam. The war has been called "McNamara's War."[1] It has been suggested that we more or less ignore Asia and Africa and concentrate on Europe and the Americas.

I have listened with growing dismay to these presentations — and with all the more dismay because of the respect and affection I have for the senators who made them. . . .

I hope that the remarks I make today will contribute at least in some measure to the further unfolding of this debate. Out of this debate, let us hope, will ultimately emerge the kind of assistance and guidance that every president must have in dealing with vital issues of our foreign policy.

Thomas J. Dodd, speech before the U.S. Senate, reprinted in *The Viet-Nam Reader: Articles and Documents on American Foreign Policy and the Viet-Nam Crisis*, ed. Marcus G. Raskin and Bernard B. Fall (New York: Random House, 1965), 164–94.

In the notes, EDS. = Patricia Bizzell and Bruce Herzberg.

[1]Robert S. McNamara, secretary of defense from 1961 to 1968, directed the war under Presidents Kennedy and Johnson. In his book *In Retrospect: The Tragedy and Lessons of Vietnam* (1995), McNamara admits that the war was a terrible mistake. — EDS.

What we say here may help to guide the president. But in the final analysis the terrible responsibility of decision is his and his alone. He must listen to the exchanges which take place in this chamber. He must endure a hundred conflicting pressures from public sources, seeking to push him in this direction or that. He must also endure the impatience of those who demand answers to complex questions today, and who accuse him of not having made the American position clear when he has in fact made our position abundantly clear on repeated occasions.

And finally, when all the voices have been heard, when he has examined all the facts, when he has discussed all aspects of the situation with his most trusted advisers, the president must alone decide — for all Americans and for the entire free world — what to do about Vietnam.

No president has ever inherited a more difficult situation on coming to office. No president has ever been called upon to make a decision of greater moment. At stake may be the survival of freedom. At stake may be the peace of the world.

I believe the United States can count itself fortunate that it has found a president of the stature of Lyndon B. Johnson to meet this crisis in its history. I also believe that, whatever differences we in this chamber may have on the question of Vietnam, our feelings to a man are with the president in the ordeal of decision through which he is now passing.

I have said that I have been dismayed by the rising clamor for a negotiated settlement. In the type of war which the Communists are now waging against us, I fear that, although those who urge negotiation would be among the first to oppose an outright capitulation, their attitude may not be construed in this way by the Communists.

The Vietnamese war, in the Communist lexicon, is described as a "war of national liberation." Its strategy is based on the concept of what the Communists call "the long war." This strategy is premised upon the belief that the free world lacks the patience, the stamina, the fanatical determination to persist, which inspires the adherents of communism. It is based on the conviction that if the Communists keep on attacking and attacking and attacking in any given situation, they will ultimately be able to destroy the morale and the will to resist of those who oppose them in the name of freedom.

China affords the classic example of the long war. It took twenty years for Mao Tse-tung[2] to prevail. There were several times during this period when his entire movement seemed on the verge of collapse. But, even in his blackest days, Mao Tse-tung remained confident that, if he persevered, ultimately his enemies would crack and he would emerge as China's undisputed ruler.

There is no more cruel test of courage and staying power than "the long war" as it is waged by the Communists. Five years, ten years, twenty years,

---

[2]Mao Tse-tung, or Mao Zedong (1893–1976), was a founder of the Chinese Communist Party in 1921 and a leader of the People's Republic of China from 1949 until his death. For twenty years his forces battled those of the Nationalists, led by Chiang Kai-shek, until Mao's victory in 1949. — EDS.

means nothing to them. And if they detect any sign that those opposed to them are flagging, that their patience is growing thin or that their will to resist has weakened, the Communists can be relied upon to redouble their efforts, in the belief that victory is within their grasp.

I disagree strongly with my colleagues who have spoken up to urge negotiations.

But if there is any way in which my voice could reach to Peiping[3] and to Moscow, I would warn the Communist leaders that they should not construe the debate that is now taking place in this chamber as a sign of weakness; it is, on the contrary, a testimony to our strength.

Nor should they believe that those who speak up in favor of negotiations are the forerunners of a larger host of Americans who are prepared to accept surrender. Because there is no one here who believes in surrender or believes in capitulation. I believe the senior senator from Idaho[4] made this abundantly clear in his own presentation, in which he underscored his complete support for the retaliatory air strikes against North Vietnam.

I have been amazed by a number of letters I have received asking the question, "Why are we in Vietnam?" or "What is our policy in Vietnam?" I have been even more amazed to have the same questions put to me by sophisticated members of the press.

To me the reasons for our presence in Vietnam are so crystal clear that I find it difficult to comprehend the confusion which now appears to exist on this subject.

We are in Vietnam because our own security and the security of the entire free world demands that a firm line be drawn against the further advance of Communist imperialism — in Asia, in Africa, in Latin America, and in Europe.

We are in Vietnam because it is our national interest to assist every nation, large and small, which is seeking to defend itself against Communist subversion, infiltration, and aggression. There is nothing new about this policy; it is a policy, in fact, to which every administration has adhered since the proclamation of the Truman Doctrine.[5]

We are in Vietnam because our assistance was invited by the legitimate government of that country.

We are in Vietnam because, as the distinguished majority leader, the senator from Montana,[6] pointed out in his 1963 report, Chinese Communist hostility to the United States threatens "the whole structure of our own security in the Pacific."

We are in Vietnam not merely to help the fourteen million South Viet-

---

[3]The capital of China, later known as Peking, and now as Beijing. — EDS.

[4]Frank Church, senior senator from Idaho, consistently opposed the war. — EDS.

[5]Formulated by President Harry Truman in 1947, the Truman Doctrine provided military and economic aid to countries resisting the spread of communism. — EDS.

[6]Mike Mansfield, senator from Montana, was in favor of negotiations. — EDS.

namese defend themselves against communism, but because what is at stake is the independence and freedom of 240 million people in Southeast Asia and the future of freedom throughout the western Pacific.

These are the reasons why we are in Vietnam. There is nothing new about them and nothing very complex. They have never been obscure. They have never been concealed. I cannot, for the life of me, see why people fail to understand them.

The senior senator from Idaho and several other senators who spoke last Wednesday, repeated the proposal that we should seek negotiations for the purpose of terminating the bloodshed in Vietnam and of avoiding an enlargement of the war. We are told by some people that negotiations are the way of diplomacy and that if we reject negotiations now, we are in effect rejecting diplomacy.

The proposal that we negotiate now overlooks the fact that there does exist a negotiated agreement on Vietnam, approved by the participants of the Geneva Conference of 1954. The final declaration of this agreement read, and I think it is worthwhile reading it for the [*Congressional*] *Record* and for our own recollection:

> Each member . . . undertakes to respect the sovereignty, the independence, the unity, and the territorial integrity of the above-mentioned states and to refrain from any interference in their internal affairs.

Since there is no point to negotiating if it simply means reiterating the Geneva agreement, I cannot help wondering whether those who urge negotiations envisage rewriting the agreement so that it does not "guarantee the territorial integrity of the above-mentioned states."

The history of negotiated agreements with the Communists underscores the fact that their promises are worthless and that only those agreements have validity which are self-enforcing or which we have the power to enforce. A report issued by the Senate Subcommittee on Internal Security — on which I have the honor to serve — establishes that the Soviet Union has since its inception violated more than one thousand treaties and agreements. The Communists have repeatedly violated the terms of the Korean armistice [and] of the Geneva agreement of Vietnam. . . .

All this does not mean to say that we must not under any circumstances enter into negotiations with the Communists. I do not suggest that at all. It simply means that when we do so, we must do so with our eyes open and with a clear understanding of the ingredients required to enforce compliance with the agreement about to be entered into. That is all I have ever urged.

Moreover, there is a time to negotiate and a time not to negotiate.

The demand that we negotiate now over Vietnam is akin to asking Churchill to negotiate with the Germans at the time of Dunkirk, or asking Truman to negotiate with the Communists when we stood with our backs to the sea in the Pusan perimeter in Korea.7 In either case, the free world could have negotiated nothing but total capitulation.

The situation in Vietnam is probably not as desperate and certainly no more desperate, than Britain's plight at the time of Dunkirk or our own plight at the time of Pusan. If we are of good heart, if we refuse to listen to the counsels of despair, if we again resolve that "we will never give in" — as Churchill put it — there is every reason to be confident that a time will arrive when we can negotiate with honor and for a more acceptable objective than a diplomatic surrender.

There are those who say that the whole of Southeast Asia will, whether we like it or not, go Communist. These people are at least consistent in urging negotiations now. But anyone who believes that we can negotiate now and not lose Vietnam to communism is deluding himself in the worst possible way.

It is human to oppose the cost of staying on in Vietnam when American boys are dying in a faraway land about which we understand very little. I am conscious of this. I am sensitive to it. I share the troubled minds of all senators. But I am convinced that the great majority of those who advocate that we abandon Vietnam to communism, either by pulling out or by "negotiating" a settlement, have not taken the time to weigh the consequences of defeat.

In my opinion, the consequences of an American defeat in Vietnam would be so catastrophic that we simply cannot permit ourselves to think of it. . . .

For the Vietnamese people, the first consequence would be a bloodletting on a genocidal scale.

In the Soviet Union and in Red China, tens of millions of "class enemies" were eliminated by the victorious Communists. While it is true that there are some slightly more moderate Communist regimes in certain countries, Vietnamese communism is characterized by utter disregard for human life of Stalinism and Maoism. What will happen to the more than one million refugees from North Vietnam? What will happen to the millions of peasants who resisted or bore arms against the Viet Cong? I shudder to think of it. The massacre of innocents in Vietnam will be repeated in every Southeast Asian country that falls to communism in its wake, in a gigantic bloodletting that will dwarf the agony and suffering of the war in Vietnam.

Those who urge our withdrawal from Vietnam is the name of saving human lives have the duty to consider the record of Communist terror in every country that has fallen under the sway of this merciless ideology, with its total disregard for human life. . . .

7In May 1940, during World War II, the British retreated from Dunkirk (in northern France) in a desperate effort to avoid a horrible defeat at the hands of Germany. Winston Churchill was British prime minister at the time. In June 1950, during the Korean War, Communist North Korean forces pushed south to the vital port city of Pusan. South Korean, U.S., and UN forces set up a defensive perimeter and held the city. — EDS.

And if the administration should ever succumb to their pressure and negotiate the surrender of Vietnam, and if the Vietnamese Communists than embark on the orgy of bloodletting which has always accompanied the establishment of Communist power, let those who are pressuring for negotiations not be heard to say, "But we didn't intend it this way." Because there is today no excuse for ignorance about communism.

Our withdrawal from Vietnam would immediately confront us with an agonizing choice.

If we decide to try to defend what is left of Southeast Asia against the advance of communism, it will require far more money, far more men, and far more American blood than we are today investing in the defense of Vietnam. What is more, it would involve a far greater risk of the major escalation which we seek to avoid.

If, on the other hand, we decide to abandon the whole of Southeast Asia to communism, as some of the proponents of withdrawal have frankly proposed, it would result in the early disintegration of all our alliances, and in the total eclipse of America as a great nation. Because no nation can remain great when its assurances are considered worthless even by its friends.

Whether we decide to abandon Southeast Asia or to try to draw another line outside Vietnam, the loss of Vietnam will result in a dozen more Vietnams in different parts of the world. If we cannot cope with this type of warfare in Vietnam, the Chinese Communists will be encouraged in the belief that we cannot cope with it anywhere else.

In the Congo, the Chinese Communists have launched their first attempt at applying the Vietnamese strategy to Africa.[8]

In the Philippines, the Huk guerrillas, after being decisively defeated in the early 1950s, have now staged a dramatic comeback. According to the *New York Times,* the Huks are now active again in considerable strength, control large areas of central Luzon, and are assassinating scores of village heads and local administrators on the Viet Cong pattern.

In Thailand, Red China has already announced the formation of a patriotic front to overthrow the government and eradicate American influence. This almost certainly presages the early launching of a Thai Communist insurrection, also patterned after the Viet Cong.

An article in the *Washington Post* on January 16 pointed out that the Venezuelan Communists now have five thousand men under arms in the cities and in the countryside, and that the Venezuelan Communist Party is openly committed to "the strategy of a long war, as developed in China, Cuba, Algeria, and Vietnam."

And there are at least half a dozen other Latin American countries where the Communists are fielding guerrilla forces, which may be small today, but which would be encouraged by a Communist victory in Vietnam to believe that the West has no defense against the long war.

---

[8]Dodd refers in this and the next few paragraphs to countries where Communist insurgencies arose, supported by other Communist countries. — EDS.

It is interesting to note in this connection that, according to Cuban reports, a Viet Cong delegation which came to Havana in 1964 signed a "mutual-aid pact" with the Venezuelan guerrilla forces. In addition, Marguerite Higgins, the distinguished correspondent for the *Washington Star* and other papers, points out that Viet Cong experts have teamed up with experts from Communist China and the Soviet Union in training Latin Americans for guerrilla operations in the several schools maintained by Fidel Castro.

It has been suggested that if we abandon Southeast Asia, our seapower would make it possible for us to fall back on Japan and the Philippines and the other Pacific islands, and constitute a more realistic defense line there. This is nonsense. American seapower and American nuclear power have thus far proved impotent to cope with Communist political warfare. Cuba is the best proof of this.

If we abandon Southeast Asia, the Philippines may prove impossible to hold against a greatly stepped-up Huk insurgency.

Japan, even it if remains non-Communist, would probably, by force of circumstances, be compelled to come to terms with Red China, adding the enormous strength of its economy to Communist strategic resources. . . .

If we fail to draw the line in Vietnam, in short, we may find ourselves compelled to draw a defense line as far back as Seattle and Alaska, with Hawaii as a solitary outpost in mid-Pacific.

To all those who agree that we must carefully weigh the consequences of withdrawal before we commit ourselves to withdrawal, I would refer the recent words of the well-known Filipino political commentator, Vincente Villamin. The abandonment of Vietnam, wrote Mr. Villamin, "would be an indelible blemish on America's honor. It would reduce America in the estimation of mankind to a dismal third-rate power, despite her wealth, her culture, and her nuclear arsenal. It would make every American ashamed of his government and would make every individual American distrusted everywhere on earth."

This is strong language. But from conversations with a number of Asians, I know that it is an attitude shared by many of our best friends in Asia.

The situation in Vietnam today bears many resemblances to the situation just before Munich.

Chamberlain wanted peace. Churchill wanted peace.[9]

Churchill said that if the free world failed to draw the line against Hitler at an early stage, it would be compelled to draw the line under much more difficult circumstances at a later date.

---

[9]Dodd draws an analogy between World War II and Vietnam, contrasting the policies of British Prime Ministers Neville Chamberlain (1869–1940) and Winston Churchill (1874–1965). In a 1938 meeting in Munich, Chamberlain acceded to Adolf Hitler's demand that part of Czechoslovakia be given to Germany as a condition for preventing war. Hitler subsequently started the war anyway and took all the rest of Czechoslovakia as well. Churchill succeeded Chamberlain in 1940, completely repudiating his predecessor's policy of appeasement in favor of stout resistance. Dodd condemns the call for the United States to withdraw from Vietnam as a form of appeasement. — EDS.

Chamberlain held that a confrontation with Hitler might result in war, and that the interests of peace demanded some concessions to Hitler. Czechoslovakia, he said, was a faraway land about which we knew very little.

Chamberlain held that a durable agreement could be negotiated with Hitler that would guarantee "peace in our time."

How I remember those words.

Churchill held that the appeasement of a compulsive aggressor simply whetted his appetite for further expansion and made war more likely.

Chamberlain's policy won out, because nobody wanted war. . . .

Churchill remained a voice crying in the wilderness.

But who was right — Churchill or Chamberlain?

Who was the true man of peace?

In Vietnam today, we are again dealing with a faraway land, about which we know very little.

In Vietnam today, we are again confronted by an incorrigible aggressor, fanatically committed to the destruction of the free world, whose agreements are as worthless as Hitler's. Indeed, even while the Communist propaganda apparatus is pulling out all the stops to pressure us into a diplomatic surrender in Vietnam, the Chinese Communists are openly encouraging a new Huk insurgency in the Philippines and have taken the first step in opening a Viet Cong type insurgency in Thailand through the creation of their quisling Thai patriotic front.

In signing the Munich agreement, it was not Chamberlain's intention to surrender the whole of Czechoslovakia to Hitler. The agreement was limited to the transfer of the German-speaking Sudetenland to German sovereignty. And no one was more indignant than Chamberlain when Hitler, having deprived Czechoslovakia of her mountain defenses, proceeded to take over the entire country.

While there are some proponents of a diplomatic solution who are willing to face up to the fact that negotiations at this juncture mean surrender, there are others who apparently quite honestly believe that we can arrive at a settlement that will both end the war and preserve the freedom of the South Vietnamese people. If such negotiations should ever come to pass, I am certain that the story of Czechoslovakia would be repeated. Having deprived South Vietnam of the political and military capability to resist, the North Vietnamese Communists would not tarry long before they completely communized the country.

And, before very long, those who urge a diplomatic solution for the sake of preventing war may find themselves compelled to fight the very war that they were seeking to avoid, on a bigger and bloodier scale, and from a much more difficult line of defense.

I take it for granted that no one in this chamber and no loyal American citizen believes that we should stand by indifferently while communism takes over the rest of the world.

I take it for granted that every intelligent person realizes that America could not long survive as a free nation in a world that was completely Communist.

I take it for granted that everyone agrees that somewhere, somehow, we must draw the line against further Communist expansion.

The question that separates us, therefore, is not whether such a line should be drawn, but where such a line should be drawn.

I believe that we have been right in drawing the line in Vietnam and that President Johnson is right in trying to hold the line in Vietnam, despite the setbacks we have suffered over the past year. Because, if this line falls, let us have no illusions about the difficulty of drawing a realistic line of defense anywhere in the western Pacific.

We have been told in many statements and articles that the only alternative to withdrawal from Vietnam, with or without negotiations, is a dramatic escalation of the war against the North. And we have been warned that such an escalation might bring in both Red China and the Soviet Union and might bring about the thermonuclear holocaust that no one wants.

These are supposed to be the choices before us.

It is my belief, however, that the tide of war in Vietnam can be reversed and that this war can ultimately be won without an invasion of the North and without a significant intensification of our military effort. It is my belief that there are many measures we can take, primarily in the nonmilitary field, to strengthen our posture and the posture of South Vietnamese forces in the fight against the Viet Cong insurgency.

Before outlining some of the measures which I believe can and must be taken, I wish to deal with a number of widely accepted fallacies and misconceptions about the situation in Vietnam, because one cannot intelligently approach the problem of what to do about Vietnam without first establishing the essential facts about the present situation in that country.

The belief that the Vietnamese war is a civil war is one of the most widespread misconceptions about Vietnam. This is frequently associated with the charge that it is the United States, and not North Vietnam or Red China, which is intervening in South Vietnam.

The war in South Vietnam is not a civil war. It was instigated in the first place by the North Vietnamese Communists, with the material and moral support of both Peiping and Moscow. There is overwhelming proof that Hanoi has provided the leadership for the Viet Cong insurrection, that it has supplied them massively, and that it has served as the real command headquarters for the Viet Cong.

The present insurrection in South Vietnam goes back to the third Communist Party Congress in Hanoi in September of 1960. At this congress it was decided "to liberate South Vietnam from the ruling yoke of the U.S. imperialists and their henchmen in order to achieve national unity and complete independence." The congress also called for the creation of a broad national front in South Vietnam directed against the United States–Diem clique. Several months later the formation of the front for the liberation of the South[10] was announced.

---

[10]The National Front for the Liberation of South Vietnam (NLF). See introduction to Unit Six, p. 800. — EDS.

I understand that there is an official report, according to which the U.S. Military Assistance Command in Vietnam is in possession of reliable evidence indicating that probably as many as thirty-four thousand Viet Cong infiltrators have entered South Vietnam from the North between January 1959 and August 1964.[11]

The report indicates that the majority of hard-core Viet Cong officers and the bulk of specialized personnel such as communications and heavy weapons specialists have been provided through infiltration. Infiltrators, moreover, apparently make up the major part of Viet Cong regulars in the northern half of South Vietnam.

The infiltration from the North supplies the Viet Cong with much of its leadership, specialist personnel, key supplies such as heavy ordnance and communications equipment, and, in some cases, elite troops.

This information is derived from the interrogation of many thousands of Viet Cong captives and defectors and from captured documents.

It is this hard core that has come down from the North that has provided the leadership cadres in all major insurgent actions, including the series of sensational attacks on American installations.

The scale on which Hanoi has been supplying the Viet Cong insurgency was dramatically illustrated this weekend when an attack by an American helicopter on a ship off the coast of South Vietnam resulted in the discovery of an enormous arms cache — almost enough, in the words of one American officer, to equip an entire division. The haul included a thousand Russian-made carbines, hundreds of Russian submachine guns, and light machine guns, and Chinese burp guns, and scores of tons of ammunition. There were also a variety of sophisticated land mines and ammunition for a new type of rocket launcher used against tanks. A Communist guerrilla who was captured in the action said that the ship which delivered the weapons had made six trips to bases along the South Vietnam coast, dropping off supplies.

Finally, we would do well to consider the fact that the general offensive launched by the Communist forces in Vietnam two weeks ago was preceded by an open call by Hanoi radio for assaults throughout the country on Vietnamese and American positions. . . .

In order to understand the war in Vietnam, we have to get away from traditional concepts in which armies with their own insignias cross clearly marked national demarcation lines after their governments have duly declared war.

Communist guerrilla warfare is waged without any declaration of war. In the case of Vietnam, it is waged from external sanctuaries which claim immunity to attack because the state which harbors them has not formally declared war.

It blends military cadres who have infiltrated into the country with native dissidents and conscripts, in a manner which conceals the foreign in-

[11]See The White Paper "Aggression from the North," page 824. — EDS.

stigation of the insurgency, and which enables the Communists to pretend that it is merely a civil war.

It is time that we nail the civil war lie for what it is. It is time that we recognize it as a form of aggression as intolerable as open aggression across marked frontiers. . . .

There has been a good deal of talk about the United States escalating the war in South Vietnam. Several senators who spoke last week warned that if we escalate the war by means of air strikes against North Vietnam, the escalation may get out of hand and wind up as a war with Red China or perhaps even a world war.

But is not we who have escalated the war; it is the Communists. Peiping and Hanoi have been busy escalating the war in South Vietnam for several years now. They have sent in tens of thousands of soldiers of the North Vietnamese Army; they have trained additional tens of thousands of dissident South Vietnamese; they have supplied them with massive quantities of equipment; and they have stepped up the tempo of their attacks against the Vietnamese people.

Now we are told that if we take any action against the territory of North Vietnam, which has mounted and directed the entire attack on South Vietnam, it will entail the risk of world war.

If the Communists are always to be permitted the privilege of escalating their attempts to take over new countries, while we shrink from retaliation for fear of further escalation, we might as well throw in the sponge now and tell the Communists the world is theirs for the taking.

I find it difficult to conceive of Red China sending in her armies in response to air strikes against carefully selected military targets. After all, if they did so, they would be risking retaliation against their highly vulnerable coastal cities, where most of Red China's industry is concentrated. They would be risking setting back their economy ten or twenty years.

Moreover, both the Chinese Communists and the Hanoi Communists are aware that the massive introduction of Chinese troops would create serious popular resentment because of the traditional Vietnamese suspicion of Chinese imperialism.

That there will be no invasion of the North by Vietnamese and American forces can, I believe, be taken as axiomatic. Nor do I believe there will be any large-scale involvement of American troops on the Korean model. We will have to continue to provide the Vietnamese with logistical support and air support, as we are doing now. But on the ground, the fighting can most effectively be done by the Vietnamese armed forces, supported, I believe, by military contingents from the other free Asian countries.

It has been stated by the senior senator from Idaho and by other critics of our foreign policy in Vietnam that it is pointless to talk about fighting for freedom in Asia because the Asian people historically do not know the meaning of freedom. It has even been implied that, because of their ignorance of freedom and their indifference to it, communism exercises a genuine attraction for the peoples of Asia.

I am sure that most Asians would consider this analysis condescending and offensive. I myself would be disposed to agree with them. It is an analysis which, in my opinion, is false on almost every score.

We have grown accustomed to equating freedom with the full range of freedoms that we in the United States today enjoy. But, in the world in which we live, the word "freedom" has at least three separate and perhaps equally important connotations.

First, there is national freedom, or independence from foreign control.

Second, there is freedom of speech and press and the other freedoms inherent in parliamentary democracy, such as we enjoy.

And, third, there is the type of natural freedom that is enjoyed by primitive peasants and tribesmen in many backward countries, even under political autocracies.

It is true that most Asian governments are autocratic; and it is probably true that the Vietnamese people do not understand or appreciate freedom in the sense of parliamentary democracy. But they certainly understand the meaning of "freedom" when the word is used to mean independence from foreign rule. They are, in fact, a people with a long and proud history and a strong sense of national identity. Every Vietnamese schoolboy knows that his people fought and triumphed over the hordes of Genghis Khan[12] in defense of their freedom; and he also knows that his country was free for five centuries before the French occupation. Finally, he knows and takes pride in the fact that his people drove out the French colonialists despite their army of 400,000 men. Do not tell me that these people know nothing about freedom.

To the Westernized Saigonese intellectuals, freedom of speech and freedom of the press are certainly very real issues; and even though they may have not mastered the processes, they would unquestionably like to see some kind of parliamentary democracy in their country. It is completely understandable that they should have chafed over the political controls that existed under the Diem government, and that have existed, in one degree or another, under succeeding governments.

But in the countryside, where the great mass of the people reside, the political controls that exist in the city are meaningless. The peasant is free to own his own land, to dispose of his produce, to worship according to his beliefs, to guide the upbringing of his children, and to elect his local village officials. To him, these freedoms that touch on his everyday life are the freedoms that really count, not the abstract and remote freedoms of constitutional and federal government.

And, if on top of granting him these natural freedoms, the government assists him by building schools and dispensaries and by providing seed and fertilizer, then, from the standpoint of the Southeast Asian peasant, his life is full and he is prepared to fight to defend it against the Communists.

---

[12]Under the ruthless Genghis Khan (1162–1227), the Mongols conquered large portions of Asia, including Mongolia, Russia, and northern China, but did not conquer Southeast Asia, what is now Vietnam. — EDS.

It is, in short, completely untrue that the Vietnamese people and the other peoples of Asia do not know the meaning of freedom. And it is equally untrue that communism is acceptable to the Asian peasant because of his indifference to freedom.

Communism has never been freely accepted by any people, anywhere, no matter how primitive.

It has never been accepted for the simple reason that even primitive peoples do not enjoy being pushed around and brutalized and terrorized, and told what to do and what not to do, and having their every activity ordered and supervised by political commissars.

This is why communism must govern by means of ruthless dictatorship wherever it takes power.

This is why the primitive mountain peoples of both Laos and Vietnam have, in an overwhelming majority, sided against the Communists.

This is why there are almost eight million refugees from Communist rule in Asia today — people who have seen the reality of the so-called People's Democracy, and who have given up everything they possessed and frequently risked their lives to escape from it.

That is why there is barbed wire and iron curtains surrounding the Communist countries. The inhabitants of the Communist countries would all leave if they could.

There is one final comment I would like to make while dealing with this subject. Too often I have heard it said that the Vietnamese people are not fighting because there is nothing to choose between communism and the kind of government they now have.

To equate an authoritarian regime like that in South Vietnam, or Taiwan, or Thailand with the totalitarian rule of communism is tantamount to losing all sense of proportion. Not only have these regimes never been guilty of the massive bloodletting and total direction of personal life which has characterized Communist rule in every country, but, carefully examined, it will turn out that these regimes are a mixture of natural democracy at the bottom with political controls of varying rigidity at the top.

Even at their worst, the political autocracies that exist in certain free Asian countries are a thousand times better than communism from the standpoint of how they treat their own people. And at their best, some of these autocracies have combined control of the press and political parties with remarkably progressive social programs.

But perhaps more important from our standpoint is that these free autocracies, for lack of a better term, do not threaten the peace of their neighbors or of the world or threaten our own security, whereas world communism has now become a threat of terrifying dimensions. . . .

Over and over again in recent months I have heard it said that our position in Vietnam is impossible because the French, who knew Vietnam so much better than we do, were compelled to admit defeat after eight years of war against the Viet Minh. A recent half-page advertisement in the *New York Times* asked: "How can we win in Vietnam with less than thirty thousand advisers, when the French could not win with an army of nearly half a million?"

Our own position is entirely different from the French position in Indochina. The French were a colonial power, exploiting and imposing their will on the Indochinese people and stubbornly denying them their freedom. The French military effort in Indochina was doomed because it had against it not only the Communists but the overwhelming majority of the Indochinese people. It was a war fought by Frenchmen against Indochinese.

The United States, however, does not seek to impose its control on Vietnam or exploit Vietnam. We are not a colonial power. We seek only to help the people of South Vietnam defend their freedom against an insurgency that is inspired and directed and aided by the North Vietnamese Communists. This is understood by the Vietnamese people. And that is why hundreds of thousands of Vietnamese who fought with Ho Chi Minh against the French are today fighting for the Saigon government against the Viet Cong.

That is why the war against the Viet Cong can be won, while the war of French colonialism against the Indochinese independence movement was doomed from the outset.

There is no similarity in the two situations that has any meaning or validity.

I believe the war in Vietnam can be won without a significant increase in our military effort. There are many things that can be done to improve the performance of our side, and most of them lie essentially in the nonmilitary field. . . .

I have pointed out that the Vietnamese people have a proud history and a strong sense of national unity. All Vietnamese, whether they live in the North or South, would like to see a unified and peaceful Vietnam. But as matters now stand, only the Communists are able to hold forth the prospect of the reunification of Vietnam. To date we have not given the South Vietnamese government the green light to set up a "Committee for the Liberation of North Vietnam," as counterpart to the "Liberation Front" which the Communists have set up in the South. This places the South Vietnamese side at a grave disadvantage.

There are any number of patriotic North Vietnamese refugees who have been itching for the opportunity to set up a Liberation Committee for the North. The establishment of such a committee could, in my opinion, have an immediate and profound impact on the conduct of the war. . . .

If we decide to withdraw from Vietnam we can certainly find plenty of excuses to ease our path. We can blame it on the geography; or on the topography; or on local apathy; or on political instability; or on religious strife; or even on anti-Americanism. But that will fool no one but ourselves. These conditions make our success there difficult, but only our own timidity and vacillation can make it impossible.

It has become obvious that we cannot go on fighting this undeclared war under the rules laid down by our enemies. We have reached the point where we shall have to make a great decision, a decision as to whether we are to take the hard steps necessary to turn the tide in Vietnam or whether we are to refrain from doing so and thus lose inevitably by default.

The ultimate outcome of the Cold War depends upon an affirmative decision to do whatever is necessary to achieve victory in South Vietnam. The events of recent weeks[13] demonstrate again that the administration is not lacking in resolve and that it is rapidly approaching such a decision.

Whether that means a larger commitment of forces, or continued retaliatory strikes against the North, or carrying guerrilla warfare to the enemy homeland, or completely sealing off South Vietnam from Communist aid — I say to the administration, "Give us the plan that will do the job, and we will support you."

Whether our victory be near or far, can we, dare we, turn away or begin to turn away from the task before us, however frustrating or burdensome it may be?

Here surely is a time for us to heed Santayana's[14] maxim "Those who will not learn from the past are destined to repeat it."

And so I speak today not merely to urge that we stand fast in Vietnam, but also to urge that we meet head on the new isolationism in its incipient stages, before the long months and years of discontent, frustration, and weariness that lie ahead have swelled the chorus urging disengagement and withdrawal to a deafening roar.

Let us expound a foreign policy nurtured in our constantly growing strength, not one fed by fear and disillusionment; a policy which each year is prepared to expend more, not less, in the cause of preserving our country and the decencies of man.

Let us insist upon a defense budget based upon the dangers we face abroad, not upon the benefits we seek at home.

Let us embrace a doctrine that refuses to yield to force, ever; that honors its commitments because we know that our good faith is the cement binding the free world together; a doctrine that recognizes in its foreign aid program not only that the rich are morally obligated to help the poor, but also that prosperity cannot permanently endure surrounded by poverty, and justice cannot conquer until its conquest is universal.

Let us, above all, encourage and inspire a national spirit worthy of our history, worthy of our burgeoning, bursting strength, in our arms, in our agriculture, in industry, in science, in finance, a spirit of confidence, of optimism, of willingness to accept new risks and exploit new opportunities.

And let us remember that providence has showered upon our people greater blessings than on any other, and that, great though our works have been, much greater is expected of us.

In recent days, the free world has paid tribute to its greatest champion of our age, Winston Churchill.

It is a curious thing that though Churchill is acknowledged on all sides as the preeminent figure of our time and as the highest embodiment of Western statesmanship, he was, throughout his life, and remains today, a prophet unheeded, a statesman whom men venerate but will not emulate.

---

[13]About two weeks earlier, on February 7, the Viet Cong attacked U.S. installations, and President Johnson ordered air raids on North Vietnam. — EDS.

[14]George Santayana (1863–1952) was a Spanish-American philosopher. — EDS.

It may well be that Winston Churchill's greatest legacy will prove to be, not the legacy of his immortal deeds, but that of his example and his precepts; and that freemen of the future will pay him the homage denied by his contemporaries, the tribute of imitation and acceptance of his message.

As we ponder the passing of this heroic figure and reflect upon his career and try to draw from it lessons which we might apply to the aggressive onslaught that we face today in a hundred ways on a hundred fronts, we might take to heart this advice which he gave in the dark days of 1941 to the boys of Harrow, his old school:

> Never give in. Never, never, never, never. Never yield to force and the apparently overwhelming might of the enemy. Never yield in any way, great or small, large or petty, except to convictions of honor and good sense.

Let us resolve to nail this message to the masthead of our ship of state in this year of decision.

READING CRITICALLY

1. What is the "long war" strategy?

2. Why, according to Dodd, will the U.S. effort in Vietnam help hold back communism in other countries?

3. Why is Dodd opposed to negotiating with the Communists?

4. What steps does Dodd believe would cause the United States to lose its freedom? According to Dodd, what are the three forms of freedom?

5. What does he say is the difference between *autocratic* and *totalitarian* governments?

WRITING ANALYTICALLY

1. In 1965, memories of World War II, which had ended twenty years before, were still fresh. Dodd draws an analogy between that war and the situation in Vietnam. Before you begin writing the essay assigned here, brainstorm with your group or the whole class about the similarities and differences between World War II and the Vietnam War. It will be helpful to assign some members of the group to look up the basic facts about World War II in an encyclopedia or history textbook.

Write an essay examining Dodd's comparison of the two wars and the effect he wants to achieve with it. In what ways is the analogy between the two wars a good one? In what ways is it flawed? On balance, is the analogy strong enough to hold up?

2. Dodd points out that the National Front for the Liberation of South Vietnam was created by North Vietnam and argues that therefore the war is not a civil conflict at all. Yet he proposes that the United States instigate the formation of a similar liberation front to operate in North Vietnam. We know that Dodd's proposal was not adopted — no NLF of the North was formed. How would Dodd respond if he were accused of hypocrisy in proposing that the United States do exactly what he criticizes North Vietnam for doing? Write the response you imagine he would give.

U.S. DEPARTMENT OF STATE

From the White Paper *Aggression from the North: The Record of North Vietnam's Campaign to Conquer South Vietnam* (February 1965)

By 1965, U.S. involvement in Vietnam had escalated to full-scale war, yet war had not been (and never would be) officially declared by the Senate. Instead, the war had the status of a foreign policy initiative and was therefore under the purview of the State Department. To explain the government's official policy and the reasons for it, the State Department issued this "white paper" (a conventional term for an official document).

The sole argument of the white paper is that the conflict in Vietnam is not a civil war, but a war of Communist aggression by North Vietnam against South Vietnam.

INTRODUCTION

SOUTH VIETNAM IS FIGHTING FOR ITS LIFE against a brutal campaign of terror and armed attack inspired, directed, supplied, and controlled by the Communist regime in Hanoi. This flagrant aggression has been going on for years, but recently the pace has quickened and the threat has now become active.

The war in Vietnam is a new kind of war, a fact as yet poorly understood in most parts of the world. Much of the confusion that prevails in the thinking of many people, and even many governments, stems from this basic misunderstanding. For in Vietnam a totally new brand of aggression has been loosed against an independent people who want to make their own way in peace and freedom.

Vietnam is *not* another Greece, where indigenous guerrilla forces used friendly neighboring territory as a sanctuary.

Vietnam is *not* another Malaya, where Communist guerrillas were, for the most part, physically distinguishable from the peaceful majority they sought to control.

Vietnam is *not* another Philippines, where Communist guerrillas were physically separated from the source of their moral and physical support.[1]

U.S. Department of State, *Aggression from the North: The Record of North Vietnam's Campaign to Conquer South Vietnam*, Department of State Publication 7839, Far Eastern Series, no. 130, reprinted in *Vietnam and America: A Documented History*, ed. Marvin Gettleman et al. (New York: Grove Press, 1985), 253–65.

In the notes, EDS. = Patricia Bizzell and Bruce Herzberg.

[1]Greek Communists, supported by Yugoslavia, fomented a civil war fought from early 1947 to late 1949. The Communist insurgency in Malaya lasted from 1948 to 1960. In the Philippines, the Communist Huk rebellion began in 1946 and was not put down until 1954. — EDS.

Above all, the war in Vietnam is *not* a spontaneous and local rebellion against the established government.

There are elements in the Communist program of conquest directed against South Vietnam common to each of the previous areas of aggression and subversion. But there is one fundamental difference. In Vietnam a Communist government has set out deliberately to conquer a sovereign people in a neighboring state. And to achieve its end, it has used every resource of its own government to carry out its carefully planned program of concealed aggression. North Vietnam's commitment to seize control of the South is no less total than was the commitment of the regime in North Korea in 1950. But knowing the consequences of the latter's undisguised attack, the planners in Hanoi have tried desperately to conceal their hand. They have failed and their aggression is as real as that of an invading army.

This report is a summary of the massive evidence of North Vietnamese aggression obtained by the government of South Vietnam. This evidence has been jointly analyzed by South Vietnamese and American experts.

The evidence shows that the hard core of the Communist forces attacking South Vietnam were trained in the North and ordered into the South by Hanoi. It shows that the key leadership of the Viet Cong (VC), the officers and much of the cadre, many of the technicians, political organizers, and propagandists have come from the North and operate under Hanoi's direction. It shows that the training of essential military personnel and their infiltration into the South is directed by the Military High Command in Hanoi.

The evidence shows that many of the weapons and much of the ammunition and other supplies used by the Viet Cong have been sent into South Vietnam from Hanoi. In recent months new types of weapons have been introduced in the VC army, for which all ammunition must come from outside sources. Communist China and other Communist states have been the prime suppliers of these weapons and ammunition, and they have been channeled primarily through North Vietnam.

The directing force behind the effort to conquer South Vietnam is the Communist Party in the North, the Lao Dong (Workers) Party. As in every Communist state, the party is an integral part of the regime itself. North Vietnamese officials have expressed their firm determination to absorb South Vietnam into the Communist world. . . .

I. HANOI SUPPLIES THE KEY PERSONNEL FOR THE ARMED AGGRESSION AGAINST SOUTH VIETNAM

The hard core of the Communist forces attacking South Vietnam are men trained in North Vietnam. They are ordered into the South and remain under the military discipline of the Military High Command in Hanoi. Special training camps operated by the North Vietnamese army give political and military training to the infiltrators. Increasingly the forces sent into the South are native North Vietnamese who have never seen South Vietnam. A special infiltration unit, the 70th Transportation Group, is responsible for moving men from North Vietnam into the South via infiltration trails through Laos. Another special unit, the maritime infiltration group, sends weapons and supplies and agents by sea into the South.

The infiltration rate has been increasing. From 1959 to 1960, when Hanoi was establishing its infiltration pipeline, at least 1,800 men, and possibly 2,700 more, moved into South Vietnam from the North. The flow increased to a minimum of 3,700 in 1961 and at least 5,400 in 1962. There was a modest decrease in 1963 to 4,200 confirmed infiltrators, though later evidence is likely to raise this figure.

For 1964 the evidence is still incomplete. However, it already shows that a minimum of 4,400 infiltrators entered the South, and it is estimated more than three thousand others were sent in.

There is usually a time lag between the entry of infiltrating troops and the discovery of clear evidence they have entered. This fact, plus collateral evidence of increased use of the infiltration routes, suggests strongly that 1964 was probably the year of greatest infiltration so far.

Thus, since 1959, nearly twenty thousand VC officers, soldiers, and technicians are known to have entered South Vietnam under orders from Hanoi. Additional information indicates that an estimated seventeen thousand more infiltrators were dispatched to the South by the regime in Hanoi during the past six years. It can reasonably be assumed that still other infiltration groups have entered the South for which there is no evidence yet available.

To some the level of infiltration from the North may seem modest in comparison with the total size of the armed forces of the Republic of Vietnam. But one-for-one calculations are totally misleading in the kind of warfare going on in Vietnam. First, a high proportion of infiltrators from the North are well-trained officers, cadres, and specialists. Second, it has long been realized that in guerrilla combat the burdens of defense are vastly heavier than those of attack. In Malaya, the Philippines, and elsewhere a ratio of at least 10-to-1 in favor of the forces of order was required to meet successfully the threat of the guerrillas' hit-and-run tactics.

In the calculus of guerrilla warfare the scale of the North Vietnamese infiltration into the South takes on a very different meaning. For the infiltration of five thousand guerrilla fighters in a given year is the equivalent of marching perhaps fifty thousand regular troops across the border, in terms of the burden placed on the defenders.

Above all, the number of proved and probable infiltrators from the North should be seen in relation to the size of the VC forces. It is now estimated that the Viet Cong number approximately thirty-five thousand so-called hard-core forces, and another 60,000–80,000 local forces. It is thus apparent that infiltrators from the North — allowing for casualities — makes up the majority of the so-called hard-core Viet Cong. Personnel from the North, in short, are now and have always been the backbone of the entire VC operation.

It is true that many of the lower level elements of the VC forces are recruited within South Vietnam. However, the thousands of reported cases of

VC kidnappings and terrorism make it abundantly clear that threats and other pressures by the Viet Cong play a major part in such recruitment. . . .

II. HANOI SUPPLIES WEAPONS, AMMUNITION, AND OTHER WAR MATERIAL TO ITS FORCES IN THE SOUTH

When Hanoi launched the VC campaign of terror, violence, and subversion in earnest in 1959, the Communist forces relied mainly on stocks of weapons and ammunition left over from the war against the French. Supplies sent in from North Vietnam came largely from the same source. As the military campaign progressed, the Viet Cong depended heavily on weapons captured from the armed forces in South Vietnam. This remains an important source of weapons and ammunition for the Viet Cong. But as the pace of the war has quickened, requirements for up-to-date arms and special types of weapons have risen to a point where the Viet Cong cannot rely on captured stocks. Hanoi has undertaken a program to re-equip its forces in the South with Communist-produced weapons.

Large and increasing quantities of military supplies are entering South Vietnam from outside the country. The principal supply point is North Vietnam, which provides a convenient channel for material that originates in Communist China and other Communist countries.

An increasing number of weapons from external Communist sources have been seized in the South. These include such weapons as 57-mm. and 75-mm. recoilless rifles, dual-purpose machine guns, rocket launchers, large mortars, and antitank mines.

A new group of Chinese Communist-manufactured weapons has recently appeared in VC hands. These include the 7.62 semiautomatic carbine, 7.62 light machine gun, and the 7.62 assault rifle. These weapons and ammunition for them, manufactured in Communist China in 1962, were first captured in December 1964 in Chuong Thien Province. Similar weapons have since been seized in each of the four corps areas of South Vietnam. Also captured have been Chinese Communist antitank grenade launchers and ammunition made in China in 1963.

One captured Viet Cong told his captors that his entire company had been supplied recently with modern Chinese weapons. The re-equipping of VC units with a type of weapons that require ammunition and parts from outside South Vietnam indicates the growing confidence of the authorities in Hanoi in the effectiveness of their supply lines into the South.

Incontrovertible evidence of Hanoi's elaborate program to supply its forces in the South with weapons, ammunition, and other supplies has accumulated over the years. Dramatic new proof was exposed just as this report was being completed.

On February 16, 1965, an American helicopter pilot flying along the South Vietnamese coast sighted a suspicious vessel. It was a cargo ship of an estimated 100-ton capacity, carefully camouflaged and moored just offshore along the coast of Phu Yen Province. Fighter planes that approached the vessel met machine gun fire from the guns on the deck of the ship and from the shore as well. A Vietnamese Air Force strike was launched against the vessel, and Vietnamese government troops moved into the area. They seized the ship after a bitter fight with the Viet Cong.

The ship, which had been sunk in shallow water, had discharged a huge cargo of arms, ammunition, and other supplies. Documents found on the ship and on the bodies of several Viet Cong aboard identified the vessel as having come from North Vietnam. A newspaper in the cabin was from Haiphong and was dated January 23, 1965. The supplies delivered by the ship — thousands of weapons and more than a million rounds of ammunition — were almost all of Communist origin, largely from Communist China and Czechoslovakia, as well as North Vietnam. At least 100 tons of military supplies were discovered near the ship.

A preliminary survey of the cache near the sunken vessel from Hanoi listed the following supplies and weapons:

> approximately 1 million rounds of small-arms ammunition;
> more than 1,000 stick grenades;
> 500 pounds of TNT in prepared charges;
> 2,000 rounds of 82-mm mortar ammunition;
> 500 antitank grenades;
> 500 rounds of 57-mm. recoilless rifle ammunition;
> more than 1,000 rounds of 75-mm. recoilless rifle ammunition;
> 1 57-mm. recoilless rifle;
> 2 heavy machine guns;
> 2,000 7.92 Mauser rifles;
> more than 100 7.62 carbines;
> 1,000 submachine guns;
> 15 light machine guns;
> 500 rifles;
> 500 pounds of medical supplies (with labels from North Vietnam, Communist China, Czechoslovakia, East Germany, Soviet Union, and other sources). . . .

III. NORTH VIETNAM: BASE FOR CONQUEST OF THE SOUTH

The Third Lao Dong Party Congress in Hanoi in September 1960 set forth two tasks for its members: "to carry out the socialist revolution in North Vietnam" and "to liberate South Vietnam."

The resolutions of the congress described the effort to destroy the legal government in South Vietnam as follows: "The revolution in the South is a protracted, hard, and complex process of struggle, combining many forms of struggle of great activity and flexibility, ranging from lower to higher, and taking as its basis the building, consolidation, and development of the revolutionary power of the masses."

At the September meeting the Communist leaders in the North called for formation of "a broad national united front." Three months later Hanoi announced creation of the "Front for Liberation of the South." This is the organization that Communist propaganda now credits with guiding the forces of subversion in the South; it is pictured as an organization established and run by the people in the South themselves. At the 1960 Lao Dong Party Congress the tone was different. Then, even before the front existed, the Communist leaders were issuing orders for the group that was being organized behind the scenes in Hanoi. "This front must rally . . ."; "The aims of its struggle are . . ."; "The front must carry out . . ." — this is the way Hanoi and the Communist Party addressed the "Liberation Front" even before its founding.

The Liberation Front is Hanoi's creation; it is neither independent nor Southern, and what it seeks is not liberation but subjugation of the South. . . .

V. A Brief History of Hanoi's Campaign of Aggression against South Vietnam

While negotiating an end to the Indochina War in Geneva in 1954, the Communists were making plans to take over all former French territory in Southeast Asia. When Vietnam was partitioned, thousands of carefully selected party members were ordered to remain in place in the South and keep their secret apparatus intact to help promote Hanoi's cause. Arms and ammunition were stored away for future use. Guerrilla fighters rejoined their families to await the party's call. Others withdrew to remote jungle and mountain hideouts. The majority — an estimated ninety thousand — were moved to North Vietnam.

Hanoi's original calculation was that all of Vietnam would fall under its control without resort to force. For this purpose, Communist cadres were ordered to penetrate official and nonofficial agencies, to propagandize and sow confusion, and generally to use all means short of open violence to aggravate war-torn conditions and to weaken South Vietnam's government and social fabric.

South Vietnam's refusal to fall in with Hanoi's scheme for peaceful takeover came as a heavy blow to the Communists. Meantime, the government had stepped up efforts to blunt Viet Cong subversion and to expose Communist agents. Morale in the Communist organization in the South dropped sharply. Defections were numerous.

Among South Vietnamese, hope rose that their nation could have a peaceful and independent future, free of Communist domination. The country went to work. The years after 1955 were a period of steady progress and growing prosperity.

Food production levels of the prewar years were reached and surpassed. While per capita food output was dropping 10 percent in the North from 1956 to 1960, it rose 20 percent in the South. By 1963, it had risen 30 percent — despite the disruption in the countryside caused by intensified Viet Cong military attacks and terrorism. The authorities in the North admitted openly to continuing annual failures to achieve food production goals.

Production of textiles increased in the South more than 20 percent in one year (1958). In the same year, South Vietnam's sugar crop increased more than 100 percent. Despite North Vietnam's vastly larger industrial complex, South Vietnam's per capita gross national product in 1960 was estimated at $110 a person while it was only $70 in the North.

More than 900,000 refugees who had fled from Communist rule in the North were successfully settled in South Vietnam. An agrarian reform program was instituted. The elementary school population nearly quadrupled between 1956 and 1960. And so it went — a record of steady improvement in the lives of the people. It was intolerable for the rulers in Hanoi; under peaceful conditions, the South was outstripping the North. They were losing the battle of peaceful competition and decided to use violence and terror to gain their ends.

After 1956, Hanoi rebuilt, reorganized, and expanded its covert political and military machinery in the South. Defectors were replaced by trained personnel from party ranks in the North. Military units and political cells were enlarged and were given new leaders, equipment, and intensified training. Recruitment was pushed. In short, Hanoi and its forces in the South prepared to take by force and violence what they had failed to achieve by other means.

By 1958 the use of terror by the Viet Cong increased appreciably. It was used both to win prestige and to back up demands for support from the people, support that political and propaganda appeals had failed to produce. It was also designed to embarrass the government in Saigon and raise doubts about its ability to maintain internal order and to assure the personal security of its people. From 1959 through 1961, the pace of Viet Cong terrorism and armed attacks accelerated substantially.

The situation at the end of 1961 was so grave that the government of the Republic of Vietnam asked the United States for increased military assistance. That request was met. Meantime, the program of strategic hamlets,[2] designed to improve the peasant's livelihood and give him some protection against Viet Cong harassment and pressure, was pushed energetically.

But the Viet Cong did not stand still. To meet the changing situation, they tightened their organization and adopted new tactics, with increasing emphasis on terrorism, sabotage, and armed attacks by small groups. They also introduced from the North technicians in fields such as armor and antiaircraft. Heavier weapons were sent in to the regular guerrilla forces.

The military and insurgency situation was complicated by a quite separate internal political struggle in South Vietnam, which led in November 1963 to the removal of the Diem government and its replacement with a

[2]Strategic hamlets were planned, walled communities created by the Diem regime as a way to insulate villagers from the Viet Cong. Designed as ideal towns, with schools, power plants, and other amenities, they were hated by the peasants who had been forced to move to them from their ancestral villages. — EDS.

new one. Effective power was placed in the hands of a Military Revolutionary Council. There have been a number of changes in the leadership and
composition of the government in Saigon in the ensuing period.

These internal developments and distractions gave the Viet Cong an invaluable opportunity, and they took advantage of it. Viet Cong agents did
what they could to encourage disaffection and to exploit demonstrations
in Saigon and elsewhere. In the countryside the Communists consolidated
their hold over some areas and enlarged their military and political apparatus by increased infiltration. Increasingly they struck at remote outposts
and the most vulnerable of the new strategic hamlets and expanded their
campaign of aggressive attacks, sabotage, and terror.

Any official, worker, or establishment that represents a service to the
people by the government in Saigon is fair game for the Viet Cong.
Schools have been among their favorite targets. Through harassment, the
murder of teachers, and sabotage of buildings, the Viet Cong succeeded in
closing hundreds of schools and interrupting the education of tens of
thousands of youngsters.

Hospitals and medical clinics have often been attacked as part of the
antigovernment campaign and also because such attacks provide the Viet
Cong with needed medical supplies. The Communists have encouraged
people in rural areas to oppose the government's antimalaria teams, and
some of the workers have been killed. Village and town officers, police stations, and agricultural research stations are high on the list of preferred
targets for the Viet Cong.

In 1964, 436 South Vietnamese hamlet chiefs and other government officials were killed outright by the Viet Cong and 1,131 were kidnapped.
More than 1,350 civilians were killed in bombings and other acts of sabotage. And at least 8,400 civilians were kidnapped by the Viet Cong.

Today the war in Vietnam has reached new levels in intensity. The elaborate effort by the Communist regime in North Vietnam to conquer the
South has grown, not diminished. Military men, technicians, political organizers, propagandists, and secret agents have been infiltrating into the
Republic of Vietnam from the North in growing numbers. The flow of
Communist-supplied weapons, particularly those of large caliber, has increased. Communications links with Hanoi are extensive. Despite the
heavy casualties of three years of fighting, the hard-core VC force is considerably larger now than it was at the end of 1961.

The government in Saigon has undertaken vigorous action to meet the
new threat. The United States and other free countries have increased
their assistance to the Vietnamese government and people. Secretary of
State Dean Rusk visited Vietnam in 1964, and he promised the Vietnamese: "We shall remain at your side until the aggression from the North
has been defeated, until it has been completely rooted out and this land
enjoys the peace which it deserves."

President Johnson has repeatedly stressed that the United States' goal is
to see peace secured in Southeast Asia. But he has noted that "that will
come only when aggressors leave their neighbors in peace."

Though it has been apparent for years that the regime in Hanoi was conducting a campaign of conquest against South Vietnam, the government in Saigon and the government of the United States both hoped that the danger could be met within South Vietnam itself. The hope that any widening of the conflict might be avoided was stated frequently.

The leaders in Hanoi chose to respond with greater violence. They apparently interpreted restraint as indicating lack of will. Their efforts were pressed with greater vigor and armed attacks and incidents of terror multiplied.

Clearly the restraint of the past was not providing adequately for the defense of South Vietnam against Hanoi's open aggression. It was mutually agreed between the governments of the Republic of Vietnam and the United States that further means for providing for South Vietnam's defense were required. Therefore, air strikes have been made against some of the military assembly points and supply bases from which North Vietnam is conducting its aggression against the South. These strikes constitute a limited response fitted to the aggression that produced them.

Until the regime in Hanoi decides to halt its intervention in the South, or until effective steps are taken to maintain peace and security in the area, the governments of South Vietnam and the United States will continue necessary measures of defense against the Communist armed aggression coming from North Vietnam.

VI. CONCLUSION

The evidence presented in this report could be multiplied many times with similar examples of the drive of the Hanoi regime to extend its rule over South Vietnam.

The record is conclusive. It establishes beyond question that North Vietnam is carrying out a carefully conceived plan of aggression against the South. It shows that North Vietnam has intensified its efforts in the years since it was condemned by the International Control Commission. It proves that Hanoi continues to press its systematic program of armed aggression into South Vietnam. This aggression violates the United Nations charter. It is directly contrary to the Geneva accords of 1954 and of 1962 to which North Vietnam is a party. It shatters the peace of Southeast Asia. It is a fundamental threat to the freedom and security of South Vietnam.

The people of South Vietnam have chosen to resist this threat. At their request, the United States has taken its place beside them in their defensive struggle.

The United States seeks no territory, no military bases, no favored position. But we have learned the meaning of aggression elsewhere in the postwar world, and we have met it.

If peace can be restored in South Vietnam, the United States will be ready at once to reduce its military involvement. But it will not abandon friends who want to remain free. It will do what must be done to help them. The choice now between peace and continued and increasingly destructive conflict is one for the authorities in Hanoi to make.

READING CRITICALLY

1. According to the white paper, what is the "totally new brand of aggression" used against the people of Vietnam (p. 824)?

2. How does the white paper argue that a small number of infiltrators from North Vietnam can be regarded as evidence of aggression?

3. How, according to the white paper, did the Communists plot to take over the South in 1954?

4. What motives are attributed to North Vietnam and the Viet Cong? To the United States and South Vietnam?

5. What does the white paper say is the U.S. role in Vietnam?

WRITING ANALYTICALLY

1. The white paper takes the position that U.S. involvement in Vietnam is justified because it represents resistance to an outside aggressor. The central argument of the white paper, then, is that the war in South Vietnam is not a rebellion by the South Vietnamese but an invasion by North Vietnam, a separate country. Write an essay analyzing the white paper's defense of this argument. How does the State Department support its contention that the war is not a rebellion? What is the logical basis of its argument? What evidence does it supply? What emotional appeals does it employ? Why is it necessary to prove that the Viet Cong are aided by the North and China in order to justify U.S. war policy?

2. What sort of rhetorical effect does the white paper seek to have on U.S. citizens? What American ideals does it appeal to? What premises about American beliefs does it rely on? Write an essay evaluating the persuasive appeal of the white paper.

I. F. STONE

"A Reply to the 'White Paper'"

(March 8, 1965)

I. F. Stone (1907–89) began his career as a journalist in his sophomore year in high school when he founded a monthly called *The Progress*. He worked for daily newspapers while in high school and college and then served as Washington correspondent for several dailies and magazines. In 1953 he began *I. F. Stone's Weekly*, publishing it for the next nineteen years while continuing to contribute columns to other publications until the end of his life. The winner of many awards for his journalism and admired by others in the profession, Stone always espoused progressive causes. His sources were often public records — newspapers, government documents, committee reports, and records of hearings — to which he brought a critical eye for subterfuge and illogic. His books include histories of the Korean War, Israel, the 1950s, and the killing of four students at an antiwar protest at Kent State University in 1971. His refutation of the 1965 State Department white paper *Aggression from the North* (p. 824) has been widely reprinted as an example of excellent investigative journalism.

THAT NORTH VIETNAM SUPPORTS THE GUERRILLAS in South Vietnam is no more a secret than that the United States supports the South Vietnamese government against them. The striking thing about the State Department's new white paper is how little support it can prove. "Incontrovertible evidence of Hanoi's elaborate program to supply its forces in the South with weapons, ammunition, and other supplies," the white paper says, "has accumulated over the years." A detailed presentation of this evidence is in Appendix D; unfortunately few will see the appendices since even the *New York Times* did not reprint them, though these are more revealing than the report. Appendix D provides a list of weapons, ammunition, and other supplies of Chinese Communist, Soviet, Czech, and North Vietnamese manufacture, with the dates and place of capture from the Viet Cong guerrillas, over the eighteen-month period from June 1962 to January 29 last year [1964], when it was presented to the International Control Commission. The commission was set up by the Geneva agreements of 1954. This list provides a good point at which to begin an analysis of the white paper.

I. F. Stone, "A Reply to the 'White Paper,'" *I. F. Stone's Weekly*, March 8, 1965, reprinted in *Vietnam and America: A Documented History*, ed. Marvin Gettleman et al. (New York: Grove Press, 1985), 265–70.

In the notes, EDS. = Patricia Bizzell and Bruce Herzberg.

THE PENTAGON'S FIGURES

To put the figures in perspective, we called the Pentagon press office and obtained some figures the white paper does not supply — the number of weapons captured from the guerrillas and the number lost to them in recent years.

	Captured from Guerrillas	Lost to Them
1962	4,800	5,200
1963	5,400	8,500
1964	4,900	13,700
3-Year Total	15,100	27,400

In three years, the guerrillas captured from our side 12,300 more weapons than they lost to us.

What interests us at the moment is not this favorable balance but the number of guerrilla weapons our side captured during the past three years. The grand total was 15,100. If Hanoi has indeed engaged in an "elaborate program" to supply the Viet Cong, one would expect a substantial number of enemy-produced weapons to turn up. Here is the sum total of enemy-produced weapons and supplies in the eighteen-month tally of the Control Commission —

72 rifles (46 Soviet, 26 Czech), 64 submachine guns (40 Czech, 24 French but "modified" in North Vietnam), 15 carbines (Soviet), 8 machine guns (6 Chinese, 2 North Vietnamese), 5 pistols (4 Soviet, 1 Czech), 4 mortars (Chinese), 3 recoilless 75-mm rifles (Chinese), 3 recoilless 57-mm guns (Chinese), 2 bazookas (1 Chinese, 1 Czech), 2 rocket launchers (Chinese), 1 grenade launcher (Czech). Total 179.

This is not a very impressive total. According to the Pentagon figures, we captured on the average of 7,500 weapons each eighteen months in the past three years. If only 179 Communist-made weapons turned up in eighteen months, that is less than 2½ percent of the total. Judging by these white paper figures, our military are wrong in estimating, as they have in recent months, that 80 percent of the weapons used by guerrillas are captured from us. It looks as if the proportion is considerably higher. The material of North Vietnamese origin included only those 24 French submachine guns "modified" in North Vietnam, 2 machine guns made in North Vietnam, 16 helmets, a uniform, and an undisclosed number of mess kits, belts, sweaters, and socks. Judging by this tally, the main retaliatory blow should be at North Vietnam's clothing factories.

There is another way to judge this tally of captured Communist weapons. A Communist battalion has about 450 men. It needs 500 rifles, four 80-mm mortars, eight 60-mm mortars, and at least 4 recoilless rifles. The weapons of Communist origin captured in eighteen months would not adequately outfit one battalion. The figures in the appendix on ammunition captured provide another index. We captured 183 (Chinese) shells for a 60-mm mortar. This fires about twenty shells a minute, so that was hardly enough ammunition for ten minutes of firing. There were 100,000 (Chinese) cartridges for 7.26-mm machine guns. That looks impressive until one discovers on checking with knowledgeable military sources that these machine guns fire six hundred rounds a minute. A machine gun platoon normally has 4 machine guns. This was enough ammunition for about forty minutes of firing by one platoon. Indeed, if the ratio of Communist-made weapons captured is the same for weapons used, then only twelve and a half days of those eighteen months were fought by the guerillas on the basis of Communist-made supplies.

If these figures were being presented in a court of law, they would run up against a further difficulty: one would have to prove the arms actually came from the Communist side. There is a worldwide market in second-hand weapons. One can buy Soviet, Czech, and Chinese Communist weapons of all kinds only two miles from the Pentagon through Inter-armco, Ltd., 10 Prince Street, Alexandria, Virginia. Interarmco, one of the world's foremost dealers, can provide more Communist weapons than we picked up in eighteen months on Vietnamese battlefields. The supply of East European Communist weapons comes in large part from the huge stocks of Soviet and Czech arms captured by the Israelis in the Suez campaign [in 1956]. Many Chinese Communist weapons were captured by our side in the Korean War. There is also, of course, a wide selection of our own military surplus. This has turned up in strange places.

For example, a book on the Algerian war, *Les Algériens en guerre,* by Dominique Darbois and Philippe Vingneau, was published in Milan in 1960 by Feltrinelli. It shows pictures of FLN (National Liberation Front) Algerian rebels wearing U.S. Marine Corps uniforms from which the "USM" and the eagle and globe insignia have not even been removed. It shows Algerians carrying U.S. 80-mm mortars and U.S. 50-caliber machine guns. Such photos could have been used by France to accuse the United States of supplying the Algerian rebels.

The State Department's white paper says "dramatic new proof was exposed just as this report was being completed" in the discovery of a suspected Viet Cong arms cargo ship on February 16. The *New York Times* commented astringently on this in an editorial February 28:

> Apparently, the major new evidence of a need for escalating the war, with all the hazards that this entails, was provided by the sinking in a South Vietnamese cove earlier this month of a 100-ton cargo ship loaded with Communist-made small arms and ammunition. A ship of that size is not much above the Oriental junk class. The standard Liberty or Victory ship of World War II had a capacity of 7,150 to 7,650 tons.

The affair of the cargo ship is curious. Until now there has been little evidence of arms coming in by ship. A huge fleet of small vessels patrols the coast and there have been glowing stories in the past of its efficiency. "About twelve thousand vessels," the AP reported from Saigon (the *New York Times,* February 22), "are searched each month by the South Vietnamese coastal junk patrol force but arrests are rare and no significant amounts of incriminating goods or weapons ever have been found." This lone case of a whole shipload of arms is puzzling.

FEW NORTHERN INFILTREES CITED

The white paper's story on the influx of men from the North also deserves a closer analysis than the newspapers have given it. Appendix C [of the white paper] provides an elaborate table from 1959–1960 to 1964 inclusive, showing the number of "confirmed" military infiltrees per year from the North. The total is given at 19,550. One way to measure this number is against that of the military we have assigned to South Vietnam in the same years. These now total 23,500, or 25 percent more, and 1,000 are to be added in the near future. The number of North Vietnamese infiltrees is "based on information . . . from at least two independent sources." *Nowhere are we told how many men who infiltrated from the North have actually been captured.* There is reason to wonder whether the count of infiltrees may be as bloated as the count of Viet Cong dead; in both cases the numbers used are estimates rather than actual bodies.

The white paper claims "that as many as 75 percent of the more than 7,000 Viet Cong who are known to have entered the South in 1964 were natives of North Vietnam." But a careful reading of the text and the appendices turns up the names of only six North Vietnamese infiltrees. In Part I of the white paper, Section B gives "individual case histories of North Vietnamese soldiers" sent South by Hanoi but all nine of these are of South Vietnamese origin. The next section, C, is headed "Infiltration of Native North Vietnamese." It names five infiltrees but one of these is also from the South. That leaves four North Vietnamese natives. Then, in Appendix C, we are given the case histories and photographs of nine other Viet Cong sent South by Hanoi. The report does not explain which ones were originally from the South but it does give the names of the provinces in which they were born. When these are checked, it turns out that only two of the nine were born in North Vietnam. This gives us a total of six Northern infiltrees. It is strange that after five years of fighting, the white paper can cite so few.

None of this is discussed frankly in the white paper. To do so would be to bring the war into focus as a rebellion in the South, which may owe some men and materiel to the North but is largely dependent on popular indigenous support for its manpower, as it is on captured U.S. weapons for its supply. The white paper withholds all evidence which points to a civil war. It also fails to tell the full story of the July 1962 Special Report by the International Control Commission. Appendix A quotes that portion in which the Commission 2-to-1 (Poland dissenting) declared that the North had in specific instances sent men and materiel south in violation of the Geneva accords. But nowhere does the State Department mention that the same report also condemned South Vietnam and the United States, declaring that they had entered into a military alliance in violation of the Geneva agreements. The United States was criticized because it then had about 5,000 military advisers in South Vietnam. The Geneva accords limited the U.S. military mission to the 684 in Vietnam at the time of the 1954 cease-fire. The United States and South Vietnam were also criticized by the ICC for hamstringing the Commission's efforts to check on imports of arms in violation of the Geneva accords.

The reader would never guess from the white paper that the Geneva accords promised that elections would be held in 1956 to reunify the country. The 1961 Blue Book[1] at least mentioned the elections, though somehow managing to make them seem a plot. "It was the Communists' calculation," the Blue Book put it, "that nationwide elections scheduled in the accords for 1956 would turn all of South Vietnam over to them. . . . The authorities in South Vietnam refused to fall into this well-laid trap." The white paper omits mention of the elections altogether and says, "South Vietnam's refusal to fall in with Hanoi's scheme for peaceful takeover came as a heavy blow to the Communists." This is not the most candid and objective presentation. From the Viet Minh point of view, the failure to hold the elections promised them when they laid down their arms was the second broken promise of the West. The earlier one was in 1946 when they made an agreement to accept limited autonomy within the French union, and welcomed the returning French troops as comrades of the liberation. Most of the French military did not want to recognize even this limited form of independence, and chose instead the road which led after eight years of war to Dien Bien Phu.[2]

THAT ECONOMIC MIRACLE AGAIN

The most disingenuous part of the white paper is that in which it discusses the origins of the present war. It pictures the war as an attack from the North, launched in desperation because the "economic miracle" in the South under Diem had destroyed Communist hopes of a peaceful takeover from within. Even the strategic hamlets are described as "designed to improve the peasant's livelihood" and we are asked to believe that for the first time in history a guerrilla war spread not because the people were discontented but because their lot was improving!

The true story is a story of lost opportunities. The Communist countries acquiesced in the failure to hold elections. Diem had a chance to make his part of the country a democratic showcase. The year 1956 was a bad one in the North. There was a peasant uprising and widespread resentment among the intellectuals over the Communist Party's heavy-handed thought control. But Diem on the other side of the Seventeenth Parallel was busy erecting a dictatorship of his own. In 1956 he abolished elections

[1]The "Blue Book" of 1961 was an earlier State Department white paper (with a blue cover) on Vietnam. — EDS.

[2]After a six-month siege at the northern town of Dien Bien Phu, the French suffered a crushing defeat, withdrawing thereafter from Vietnam and agreeing to the Geneva accords. — EDS.

even for village councils. In 1957 his mobs smashed the press of the one legal opposition party, the Democratic Bloc, when it dared criticize the government. That was the beginning of a campaign to wipe out every form of opposition. It was this campaign and the oppressive exactions imposed on the peasantry, the fake land reform and the concentration camps Diem set up for political opponents of all kinds, which stirred even wider rebellion from 1958 onward in the grass roots *before* North Vietnam gave support. It was this which drove oppositionists of all kinds into alliance with the Communists in the National Liberation Front.

Long before the North was accused of interference, its government was complaining to the Control Commission of "border and air-space violations by the South and infringements of the Geneva agreements by the introduction of arms and U.S. servicemen." For four years after Geneva, both North Vietnam and China followed the "peaceful coexistence" policy while the United States turned South Vietnam into a military base and a military dictatorship. It is in this story the white paper does not tell, and the popular discontent it does not mention, that the rebellion and the aid from the North had their origins.

READING CRITICALLY

1. Which of the white paper's specific claims does Stone refute?

2. How does Stone respond to the white paper's argument about the supply of weapons?

3. How does Stone respond to its argument about infiltration from the North?

4. What is Stone's response to the claim that economic success in South Vietnam stimulated aggression from the North?

WRITING ANALYTICALLY

1. Stone argues that the war is a "rebellion in the South" (p. 837), directly contrary to the white paper's view that "above all, the war in Vietnam is *not* a spontaneous and local rebellion" (p. 825). The white paper says that the war is a form of aggression from the North, while in Stone's view the aggression argument is largely false. Write an essay lining up the two arguments, comparing and contrasting them point by point. Option: Note that Stone does not answer every claim in the white paper. Do you think this damages his refutation? What sort of statements does Stone make about the *way* the white paper argues? In your opinion, do these statements help or hurt Stone's effectiveness?

2. Part of the white paper's effectiveness comes from the fact that it is an official government document. For example, it uses information that can be obtained only by the government. It also has the authority of the State Department and, ultimately, the president behind it. Write an essay examining the issue of authority (called "ethos" in rhetoric). How does the white paper take advantage of its authority? What does I. F. Stone do in his refutation to create his own authority and reduce the effects of the white paper's authority?

DAVID DELLINGER,
A. J. MUSTE, ET AL.

"Declaration of Conscience against the War in Vietnam"

(1965)

David Dellinger (b. 1915) traces his pacifism to his days at Union Theological Seminary in New York at the start of World War II. He refused to register for the draft in 1942 and was jailed twice. After the war, Dellinger worked as an activist for the peace movement and the disarmament movement, which opposed the development and proliferation of nuclear weapons. He also joined other prominent activists like A. J. Muste in pressing for egalitarian social reforms and social justice. Dellinger was among the first to protest U.S. involvement in Vietnam: He organized the first major antiwar demonstration in New York City in 1965; he chaired the National Mobilization Committee to End the War in Vietnam (see p. 868); and, later, he traveled to North Vietnam to arrange for the release of some American prisoners of war. He was also one of the Chicago Seven, a group of antiwar activists who were tried for allegedly inciting a riot at the 1968 Democratic national convention in Chicago.

A. J. Muste (1885–1967) was ordained in the Dutch Reformed Church in 1909. He worked in the labor movement during the 1920s and 1930s and counseled conscientious objectors to the draft during World War II. After the war, Muste was a leader in the disarmament movement, and with Dellinger he was among the early and persistent Vietnam War protesters. An admirer of the nonviolence of Mahatma Gandhi, who led India to independence through nonviolent civil disobedience, Muste was often referred to as the "American Gandhi."

Dellinger, Muste, and others came together at the very beginning of the Vietnam War to organize marches and rallies, to raise people's consciousness about the war, and to urge draft resistance. No longer subject to the draft themselves, they were nonetheless breaking the law by declaring their intention, in the "Declaration of Conscience," to counsel others to refuse to serve. The document, published jointly by several antiwar groups, was delivered to the White House with more than four thousand signatures.

Because the use of the military resources of the United States in Vietnam and elsewhere suppresses the aspirations of the people for political independence and economic freedom;

Because inhuman torture and senseless killing are being carried out by forces armed, uniformed, trained, and financed by the United States;

David Dellinger, A. J. Muste, et al., "Declaration of Conscience against the War in Vietnam," reprinted in *Vietnam and America: A Documented History,* ed. Marvin Gettleman et al. (New York: Grove Press, 1985), 301–2.

Because we believe that all peoples of the earth, including both Americans and non-Americans, have an inalienable right to life, liberty, and the peaceful pursuit of happiness in their own way; and

Because we think that positive steps must be taken to put an end to the threat of nuclear catastrophe and death by chemical or biological warfare, whether these result from accident or escalation —

We hereby declare our conscientious refusal to cooperate with the United States government in the prosecution of the war in Vietnam.

We encourage those who can conscientiously do so to refuse to serve in the armed forces and to ask for discharge if they are already in.

Those of us who are subject to the draft ourselves declare our own intention to refuse to serve.

We urge others to refuse and refuse ourselves to take part in the manufacture or transportation of military equipment, or to work in the fields of military research and weapons development.

We shall encourage the development of other nonviolent acts, including acts which involve civil disobedience, in order to stop the flow of American soldiers and munitions to Vietnam.

NOTE: *Signing or distributing this Declaration of Conscience might be construed as a violation of the Universal Military Training and Service Act, which prohibits advising persons facing the draft to refuse service. Penalties of up to five years imprisonment, and/or a fine of $5,000 are provided. While prosecutions under this provision of the law almost never occur, persons signing or distributing this declaration should face the possibility of serious consequences.*

READING CRITICALLY

1. What reasons do the signers give for opposing the war?
2. What actions do they pledge to take?

WRITING ANALYTICALLY

1. Have you ever committed or contemplated committing an act of civil disobedience? If so, tell the story and the circumstances and explain why you felt that placing yourself in legal jeopardy was important. If not, are there any circumstances in which you might consider doing so?

2. What is the difference between civil disobedience and lawbreaking? Write an essay defining this difference and considering how the actions called for in the "Declaration of Conscience" might be viewed as one or the other.

3. Write an analysis of the "Declaration of Conscience," assessing its purposes, the strength of its arguments, its likely audience, and its underlying premises. Why do you think it leaves out any argument concerning communism, aggression, or any of the other arguments surrounding the Vietnam War? Why do you think it recommends illegal actions? How effective do you find this appeal?

BARBARA BEIDLER

"Afterthoughts on a Napalm-Drop on Jungle Villages near Haiphong" (1965)

HUY CAN

"Truth Blazes Even in Little Children's Hearts" (1965)

The story of these two poems is told in *Vietnam and America,* the collection of documents from which these poems are taken.

In 1965, twelve-year-old Barbara Beidler of Vero Beach, Florida, wrote a poem about the Vietnam War. When her poem was printed in the Presbyterian magazine *Venture,* the Defense Department immediately dropped *Venture* from its list of recommended publications. This brought the poem to the attention of the media. Huy Can, one of the most famous poets in Vietnam, answered Barbara's poem. Read at many programs about the war during the next few years, this pair of poems came to symbolize a bond between the Vietnamese being attacked by the U.S. government and the Americans opposed to the war.

Napalm is a highly flammable jelly used in incendiary bombs. During the Vietnam War, U.S. forces dropped tons of napalm bombs on villages and forests in attacks on suspected Viet Cong and in an attempt to defoliate areas of the country in which they might hide. Vivid descriptions and horrifying photographs of people fleeing such attacks — particularly children, their naked bodies or their clothes on fire — made napalm a symbol of American callousness.

AFTERTHOUGHTS ON A NAPALM-DROP ON JUNGLE VILLAGES NEAR HAIPHONG

All was still.
The sun rose through silver pine boughs,
Over sleeping green-straw huts,
Over cool rice ponds,
Through the emerald jungles.
Into the sky.

Barbara Beidler, "Afterthoughts on a Napalm-Drop on Jungle Villages near Haiphong," and Huy Can, "Truth Blazes Even in Little Children's Hearts," reprinted in *Vietnam and America: A Documented History,* ed. Marvin Gettleman et al. (New York: Grove Press, 1985), 299–301.

The men rose and went out to the fields and ponds.
The women set pots on the fire, boiling rice and jungle berries,
                    and some with baskets went for fish.
The children played in the streams and danced through the weeds.

Then there was the flash — silver and gold
Silver and gold,
Silver birds flying,
Golden water raining.
The rice ponds blazed with the new water.
The jungles burst into gold and sent up little birds of fire.
Little animals with fur of flame.

Then the children flamed.
Running — their clothes flying like fiery kites.
Screaming — their screams dying as their faces seared.
The women's baskets burned on their heads.
The men's blazed on the rice waters.
Then the rains came.

A rag, fire black, fluttered.
A curl of smoke rose from a lone rice stem.
The forest lay singed, seared.
A hut crumbled.

And all was still.
    Listen, Americans,
    Listen, clear and long.
    The children are screaming
    In the jungles of Haiphong.

Barbara Beidler

TRUTH BLAZES EVEN IN LITTLE CHILDREN'S HEARTS

Little Barbara
Separated from us by the ocean
And by the color of your skin
You have heard and understood.

You have heard the screams
Of the children near Haiphong
Whose clothing turns to flame
From American napalm.

You are twelve years old
And your heart speaks
For the conscience of mankind
Tormented by each rain of bombs.

America, America!
Don't you hear the screams
Of those thousands of children
Consumed by the golden fire?

Golden fire of napalm
Golden fire of dollars
Which eats the flesh
Like a cancer.

A filthy cancer
Devouring the bones
The blood and the soul
Of the United States.

America, don't you feel
The fire burning your flesh
And your conscience
Killed by your bombs?

Little Barbara,
The fire of your poem
Scorches the demons
And drives them wild.

They would ban poetry
But how can they ban
The truth that blazes
Even in little children's hearts!

Huy Can (translated from the Vietnamese)

READING CRITICALLY

1. According to Beidler's poem, what was the effect of a napalm attack? Who and what were affected?

2. In Huy Can's poem, what does the line "They would ban poetry" refer to? What is ironic about this statement?

WRITING ANALYTICALLY

1. Write a short analysis of the images in the two poems. For example, what forms of fire appear in Beidler's poem? How do these build and change in the course of the poem? How do they contribute to the poem's effect? What does Huy Can do with these images in echo of Beidler? What other strong images do you find in Huy Can's poem? What other echoes of Beidler's images?

2. Poems and songs very often play a prominent role in political movements such as elections, strikes, and especially wars. This was certainly the case in the Vietnam War. (Looking into the songs and poems of the war would make an excellent

research topic; see the Research Kit for this unit.) Though it seems perfectly natural that this should be so, it is worth considering why. What is it that songs and poems do? What is their appeal? Do they simply strike emotional chords for those who believe their message, or do they work as arguments as well, rallying those who already agree with the positions they express and attempting to persuade those who don't agree to change their minds?

Write an analysis of the Beidler and Huy poems as arguments. What arguments do they make? Do they make logical appeals with evidence, or do they make only emotional appeals?

PAUL POTTER

From *"The Incredible War"*
(April 17, 1965)

In 1965, Paul Potter (b. 1940) was president of Students for a Democratic Society (SDS), the new name given in 1960 to the Student League for Industrial Democracy, a socialist organization. With civil rights as their main concern initially, SDS members organized for social change, especially in ghettos, and also spoke out against systemic poverty, racism, and the threat of nuclear war.

In 1962, SDS issued its "Port Huron Statement" analyzing the ills of American society and sounding the themes of the youth movement of the sixties. In the mid-1960s, SDS became more focused on organizing college students, through demonstrations and "teach-ins" against the war and the draft. Potter became a member of SDS in 1962, while he was a student at Oberlin College in Ohio, and served as the group's president from June 1964 to June 1965. SDS organized the first antiwar march on Washington, on April 17, 1965, at which Potter gave the speech excerpted here. The speech galvanized the crowd and earned Potter a standing ovation.

THE INCREDIBLE WAR IN VIETNAM has provided the razor, the terrifying sharp cutting edge that has finally severed the last vestiges of illusion that morality and democracy are the guiding principles of American foreign policy. The saccharine, self-righteous moralism that promises the Vietnamese a billion dollars of economic aid at the very moment we are delivering billions for economic and social destruction and political repression is rapidly losing what power it might ever have had to reassure us about

Paul Potter, "The Incredible War," *National Guardian*, April 29, 1965, reprinted in *The New Left*, ed. Massimo Teodori (New York: Bobbs-Merrill, 1969), 246–48.
    In the notes, EDS. = Patricia Bizzell and Bruce Herzberg.

the decency of our foreign policy. The further we explore the reality of what this country is doing and planning in Vietnam the more we are driven toward the conclusion of Senator Morse[1] that the United States may well be the greatest threat to peace in the world today. . . .

The president says that we are defending freedom in Vietnam. Whose freedom? Not the freedom of the Vietnamese. The first act of the first dictator (Diem) the United States installed in Vietnam was to systematically begin the persecution of all political opposition, non-Communist as well as Communist. . . .

The pattern of repression and destruction that we have developed and justified in the war is so thorough that it can only be called "cultural genocide." I am not simply talking about napalm[2] or gas or crop destruction or torture hurled indiscriminantly on women and children, insurgent and neutral, upon the first suspicion of rebel activity. That in itself is horrendous and incredible beyond belief. But it is only part of a large pattern of destruction to the very fabric of the country. We have uprooted the people from the land and imprisoned them in concentration camps called "sunrise villages." Through conscription and direct political intervention and control we have broken or destroyed local customs and traditions, trampled upon those things of value which give dignity and purpose to life. . . .

Not even the president can say that this is war to defend the freedom of the Vietnamese people. Perhaps what the president means when he speaks of freedom is the freedom of the Americans.

What in fact has the war done for freedom in America? It has led to even more vigorous governmental efforts to control information, manipulate the press, and pressure and persuade the public through distorted or downright dishonest documents such as the white paper on Vietnam.[3] . . .

In many ways this is an unusual march, because the large majority of the people here are not involved in a peace movement as their primary basis of concern. What is exciting about the participants in this march is that so many of us view ourselves consciously as participants as well in a movement to build a more decent society. There are students here who have been involved in protest over the quality and kind of education they are receiving in growingly bureaucratized, depersonalized institutions called universities; there are Negroes from Mississippi and Alabama who are struggling against the tyranny and repression of those states; there are poor people here — Negro and white — from Northern urban areas who are attempting to build movements that abolish poverty and secure democracy; there are faculty who are beginning to question the relevance of their institutions to the critical problems facing the society. . . .

The president mocks freedom if he insists that the war in Vietnam is a defense of American freedom. Perhaps the only freedom that this war pro-

---

[1]Wayne Morse, Democratic senator from Oregon from 1945 to 1969, was the first senator to oppose the Vietnam War. He was one of only two senators to vote against the Tonkin Gulf Resolution in 1964 (see introduction to Unit Six, p. 801). — EDS.

[2]See page 842. — EDS.

[3]See page 824 for excerpts from this white paper. — EDS.

tects is the freedom of the warhawks in the Pentagon and the State Department to "experiment" with "counterinsurgency" and guerrilla warfare in Vietnam. Vietnam, we may say, is a "laboratory" run by a new breed of gamesmen who approach war as a kind of rational exercise in international power politics. . . .

Thus far the war in Vietnam has only dramatized the demand of ordinary people to have some opportunity to make their own lives, and of their unwillingness, even under incredible odds, to give up the struggle against external domination. We are told however that that struggle can be legitimately suppressed since it might lead to the development of a Communist system — and before that menace, all criticism is supposed to melt.

This is a critical point and there are several things that must be said here — not by way of celebration, but because I think they are the truth. First, if this country were serious about giving the people of Vietnam some alternative to a Communist social revolution, that opportunity was sacrificed in 1954 when we helped to install Diem and his repression of non-Communist movements. There is no indication that we were serious about that goal — that we were ever willing to contemplate the risks of allowing the Vietnamese to choose their own destinies. Second, those people who insist now that Vietnam can be neutralized are for the most part looking for a sugar coating to cover the bitter pill. We must accept the consequences that calling for an end of the war in Vietnam is in fact allowing for the likelihood that a Vietnam without war will be a self-styled Communist Vietnam. Third, this country must come to understand that the creation of a Communist country in the world today is not an ultimate defeat. If people are given the opportunity to choose their own lives it is likely that some of them will choose what we have called "Communist systems." . . . And yet the war that we are creating and escalating in Southeast Asia is rapidly eroding the base of independence of North Vietnam as it is forced to turn to China and the Soviet Union.

But the war goes on; the freedom to conduct that war depends on the dehumanization not only of Vietnamese people but of Americans as well; it depends on the construction of a system of premises and thinking that insulates the president and his advisers thoroughly and completely from the human consequences of the decisions they make. I do not believe that the president or Mr. Rusk or Mr. McNamara or even McGeorge Bundy[4] are particularly evil men. If asked to throw napalm on the back of a ten-year-old child they would shrink in horror — but their decisions have led to mutilation and death of thousands and thousands of people.

What kind of system is it that allows "good" men to make those kinds of decisions? What kind of system is it that justifies the United States or any country seizing the destinies of the Vietnamese people and using them callously for our own purpose? What kind of system is it that disenfranchises people in the South, leaves millions upon millions of people throughout

---

[4]In 1965, Robert S. McNamara was secretary of defense, Dean Rusk was secretary of state, and McGeorge Bundy was national security adviser. — EDS.

the country impoverished and excluded from the mainstream and promise of American society, that creates faceless and terrible bureaucracies and makes those the place where people spend their lives and do their work, that consistently puts material values before human values — and still persists in calling itself free and still persists in finding itself fit to police the world? . . .

We must name that system. We must name it, describe it, analyze it, understand it, and change it. For it is only when that system is changed and brought under control that there can be any hope for stopping the forces that create a war in Vietnam today or a murder in the South tomorrow. . . .

If the people of this country are to end the war in Vietnam, and to change the institutions which create it, then, the people of this country must create a massive social movement — and if that can be built around the issue of Vietnam, then that it what we must do. . . .

But that means that we build a movement that works not simply in Washington but in communities and with the problems that face people throughout the society. That means that we build a movement that understands Vietnam, in all its horror, as but a symptom of a deeper malaise, that we build a movement that makes possible the implementation of the values that would have prevented Vietnam, a movement based on the integrity of man and a belief in man's capacity to determine his own life; a movement that does not exclude people because they are too poor or have been held down; a movement that has the capacity to tolerate all of the formulations of society that men may choose to strive for; a movement that will build on the new and creative forms of protest that are beginning to emerge, such as the teach-in, and extend their efforts and intensify them; a movement that will not tolerate the escalation or prolongation of this war but will, if necessary, respond to the administration war effort with massive civil disobedience all over the country that will wrench the country into a confrontation with the issues of the war; a movement that must of necessity reach out to all those people in Vietnam or elsewhere who are struggling to find decency and control for their lives.

For in a strange way the people of Vietnam and the people on this demonstration are united in much more than a common concern that the war be ended. In both countries there are people struggling to build a movement that has the power to change their condition. The system that frustrates these movements is the same. All our lives, our destinies, our very hopes to live depend on our ability to overcome that system. . . .

READING CRITICALLY

1. According to Potter, what is the "illusion" about U.S. policy that the war has shattered (p. 845)?

2. What does Potter mean by "cultural genocide" (p. 846)?

3. How does Potter respond to the argument that the war opposes communism?

4. What is the "system" that Potter describes (p. 847)?

5. What are the characteristics of the "movement" that Potter calls for?

WRITING ANALYTICALLY

1. Potter attacks the war as symptomatic of larger social problems in the United States. On the one side is the "system" and on the other side is the "movement." What are the connotations of these terms? Write an essay explaining the nature of Potter's criticism of the war and the society that supports it. Your answers to reading questions 4 and 5 will help you here.

2. Is Potter's criticism of the United States applicable today? Answer that question in an essay based on your own observations of both the domestic and foreign policies of the nation. In formulating your answer, consider whether the "system" that Potter criticizes exists in the same form, exists in a different form, or no longer exists.

3. Write an essay describing the social issues that concern student groups today. What groups are on your campus? Who runs them? What is the scope of their concerns? Do you think that social activism is an important part of student life? Is there any "movement" today comparable to the one that Potter describes?

4. Antiwar arguments were necessarily refutations of positions taken by the U.S. government. Write an essay examining Potter's strategies for attacking the government's arguments. Compare and contrast Potter's approach with I. F. Stone's (p. 834) or Martin Luther King Jr.'s (p. 850). How does each one deflect and refute the authority and power of government pronouncements?

THE WAR AT HOME

MARTIN LUTHER KING JR.

"Declaration of Independence from the War in Vietnam" (April 4, 1967)

By 1967, when U.S. escalation of the war in Vietnam was attracting wide-scale protests across the country, the Reverend Martin Luther King Jr. (1929–68) was the preeminent leader of the civil rights movement. A charismatic presence and a powerful speaker, King had been instrumental in integrating the buses in Montgomery, Alabama, in 1954 and had founded the Southern Christian Leadership Conference (SCLC) in 1957 to campaign for desegregation, voting rights, and community development for African Americans. King advocated the nonviolent protest style of Mahatma Gandhi, who led India to its independence through nonviolent protest and civil disobedience. In 1963 the SCLC organized the March on Washington, at which 250,000 people rallied for civil rights and King gave his now famous "I Have a Dream" speech. In 1964, King was awarded the Nobel Prize for peace.

Throughout the mid-1960s, King became increasingly concerned about the diversion of funds from the government's "war on poverty" to its war in Southeast Asia. He also spoke out about the irony that African Americans were fighting and dying in disproportionate numbers in Vietnam, a war waged by white men against another oppressed people of color. The speech reprinted here was among King's first public statements on the Vietnam War, delivered at Riverside Church in New York City. While the antiwar movement recognized him as a powerful ally, other African American leaders were divided in their reactions to the speech. Some praised it, but others feared that a strong antiwar stance would alienate President Lyndon Johnson and cause him to pull back from his war on poverty and his support for civil rights legislation. King, however, never wavered. He continued to stand by the position he articulated in this speech, until his assassination a year later as he was preparing for a civil rights march and rally in Memphis, Tennessee.

OVER THE PAST TWO YEARS, as I have moved to break the betrayal of my own silences and to speak from the burnings of my own heart, as I have called for radical departures from the destruction of Vietnam, many persons have questioned me about the wisdom of my path. At the heart of

Martin Luther King Jr., "Declaration of Independence from the War in Vietnam," *Ramparts*, May 1967, 33–37, reprinted in *Vietnam and America: A Documented History*, ed. Marvin Gettleman et al. (New York: Grove Press, 1985), 306–14.

In the notes, EDS. = Patricia Bizzell and Bruce Herzberg.

their concerns this query has often loomed large and loud: Why are *you* speaking about the war, Dr. King? Why are *you* joining the voices of dissent? Peace and civil rights don't mix, they say. Aren't you hurting the cause of your people, they ask. And when I hear them, though I often understand the source of their concern, I am nevertheless greatly saddened, for such questions mean that the inquirers have not really known me, my commitment, or my calling. Indeed, their questions suggest that they do not know the world in which they live.

In the light of such tragic misunderstanding, I deem it of signal importance to try to state clearly why I believe that the path from Dexter Avenue Baptist Church — the church in Montgomery, Alabama, where I began my pastorage — leads clearly to this sanctuary tonight.

I come to this platform to make a passionate plea to my beloved nation. This speech is not addressed to Hanoi or to the National Liberation Front. It is not addressed to China or to Russia.

Nor is it an attempt to overlook the ambiguity of the total situation and the need for a collective solution to the tragedy of Vietnam. Neither is it an attempt to make North Vietnam or the National Liberation Front paragons of virtue, nor to overlook the role they can play in a successful resolution of the problem. While they both may have justifiable reasons to be suspicious of the good faith of the United States, life and history give eloquent testimony to the fact that conflicts are never resolved without trustful give and take on both sides.

Tonight, however, I wish not to speak with Hanoi and the NLF, but rather to my fellow Americans who, with me, bear the greatest responsibility in ending a conflict that has exacted a heavy price on both continents.

Since I am a preacher by trade, I suppose it is not surprising that I have seven major reasons for bringing Vietnam into the field of my moral vision. There is at the outset a very obvious and almost facile connection between the war in Vietnam and the struggle I, and others, have been waging in America. A few years ago there was a shining moment in that struggle. It seemed as if there was a real promise of hope for the poor — both black and white — through the Poverty Program. Then came the buildup in Vietnam, and I watched the program broken and eviscerated as if it were some idle political plaything of a society gone mad on war, and I knew that America would never invest the necessary funds or energies in rehabilitation of its poor so long as Vietnam continued to draw men and skills and money like some demonic, destructive suction tube. So I was increasingly compelled to see the war as an enemy of the poor and to attack it as such.

Perhaps the more tragic recognition of reality took place when it became clear to me that the war was doing far more than devastating the hopes of the poor at home. It was sending their sons and their brothers and their husbands to fight and to die in extraordinarily high proportions relative to the rest of the population. We were taking the young black men who had been crippled by our society and sending them eight thousand miles away to guarantee liberties in Southeast Asia which they had not found in Southwest Georgia and East Harlem. So we have been repeatedly faced with the cruel irony of watching Negro and white boys on TV screens as they kill and die together for a nation that has been unable to seat them together in the same schools. So we watch them in brutal solidarity burning the huts of a poor village, but we realize that they would never live on the same block in Detroit. I could not be silent in the face of such cruel manipulation of the poor.

My third reason grows out of my experience in the ghettos of the North over the last three years — especially the last three summers. As I have walked among the desperate, rejected, and angry young men, I have told them that Molotov cocktails[1] and rifles would not solve their problems. I have tried to offer them my deepest compassion while maintaining my conviction that social change comes most meaningfully through nonviolent action. But, they asked, what about Vietnam? They asked if our own nation wasn't using massive doses of violence to solve its problems, to bring about the changes it wanted. Their questions hit home, and I knew that I could never again raise my voice against the violence of the oppressed in the ghettos without having first spoken clearly to the greatest purveyor of violence in the world today — my own government.

For those who ask the question "Aren't you a Civil Rights leader?" and thereby mean to exclude me from the movement for peace, I have this further answer. In 1957 when a group of us formed the Southern Christian Leadership Conference, we chose as our motto: "To save the soul of America." We were convinced that we could not limit our vision to certain rights for black people, but instead affirmed the conviction that America would never be free or saved from itself unless the descendants of its slaves were loosed from the shackles they still wear.

Now, it should be incandescently clear that no one who has any concern for the integrity and life of America today can ignore the present war. If America's soul becomes totally poisoned, part of the autopsy must read "Vietnam." It can never be saved so long as it destroys the deepest hopes of men the world over.

As if the weight of such a commitment to the life and health of America were not enough, another burden of responsibility was placed upon me in 1964; and I cannot forget that the Nobel Prize for Peace was also a commission — a commission to work harder than I had ever worked before for the "brotherhood of man." This is a calling that takes me beyond national allegiances, but even if it were not present I would yet have to live with the meaning of my commitment to the ministry of Jesus Christ. To me the relationship of this ministry to the making of peace is so obvious that I sometimes marvel at those who ask me why I am speaking against the war. Could it be that they do not know that the good news was meant for all men — for Communist and capitalist, for their children and ours, for black and white, for revolutionary and conservative? Have they forgotten

---

[1]A Molotov cocktail is a homemade bomb commonly used in inner-city riots in the 1960s. It consists of a bottle filed with flammable liquid and stuffed with a rag that is ignited before the bomb is thrown. — EDS.

that my ministry is in obedience to the One who loved His enemies so fully that He died for them? What then can I say to the Viet Cong or to Castro or to Mao[2] as a faithful minister of this One? Can I threaten them with death, or must I not share with them my life?

And as I ponder the madness of Vietnam, my mind goes constantly to the people of that peninsula. I speak now not of the soldiers of each side, not of the junta in Saigon, but simply of the people who have been living under the curse of war for almost three continuous decades. I think of them, too, because it is clear to me that there will be no meaningful solution there until some attempt is made to know them and their broken cries.

They must see Americans as strange liberators. The Vietnamese proclaimed their own independence in 1945 after a combined French and Japanese occupation and before the Communist revolution in China. Even though they quoted the American Declaration of Independence in their own document of freedom,[3] we refused to recognize them. Instead, we decided to support France in its reconquest of her former colony.

Our government felt then that the Vietnamese people were not "ready" for independence, and we again fell victim to the deadly Western arrogance that has poisoned the international atmosphere for so long. With that tragic decision, we rejected a revolutionary government seeking self-determination, and a government that had been established not by China (for whom the Vietnamese have no great love) but by clearly indigenous forces that included some Communists. For the peasants, this new government meant real land reform, one of the most important needs in their lives.

For nine years following 1945 we denied the people of Vietnam the right of independence. For nine years we vigorously supported the French in their abortive effort to recolonize Vietnam.

Before the end of the war we were meeting 80 percent of the French war costs. Even before the French were defeated at Dien Bien Phu, they began to despair of their reckless action, but we did not. We encouraged them with our huge financial and military supplies to continue the war even after they had lost the will to do so.

After the French were defeated it looked as if independence and land reform would come again through the Geneva agreements. But instead there came the United States, determined that Ho [Chi Minh] should not unify the temporarily divided nation, and the peasants watched again as we supported one of the most vicious modern dictators — our chosen man, Premier Diem. The peasants watched and cringed as Diem ruthlessly routed out all opposition, supported their extortionist landlords and refused even to discuss reunification with the North. The peasants watched

[2]Fidel Castro (b. 1926) overthrew the corrupt Cuban government in 1959 and established a socialist state. Mao Tse-tung, or Mao Zedong (1893–1976), led the Communist revolution in China in 1949 and was a leader of the People's Republic of China until his death. — EDS.

[3]See Ho Chi Minh, "Declaration of Independence of the Democratic Republic of Vietnam," page 804. — EDS.

as all this was presided over by U.S. influence and then by increasing numbers of U.S. troops who came to help quell the insurgency that Diem's methods had aroused. When Diem was overthrown they may have been happy, but the long line of military dictatorships seemed to offer no real change — especially in terms of their need for land and peace.

The only change came from America as we increased our troop commitments in support of governments which were singularly corrupt, inept, and without popular support. All the while, the people read our leaflets and received regular promises of peace and democracy — and land reform. Now they languish under our bombs and consider us — not their fellow Vietnamese — the real enemy. They move sadly and apathetically as we herd them off the land of their fathers into concentration camps where minimal social needs are rarely met. They know they must move or be destroyed by our bombs. So they go.

They watch as we poison their water, as we kill a million acres of their crops. They must weep as the bulldozers destroy their precious trees. They wander into the hospitals, with at least twenty casualties from American firepower for each Viet Cong–inflicted injury. So far we may have killed a million of them — mostly children.

What do the peasants think as we ally ourselves with the landlords and as we refuse to put any action into our many words concerning land reform? What do they think as we test out our latest weapons on them, just as the Germans tested out new medicine and new tortures in the concentration camps of Europe? Where are the roots of the independent Vietnam we claim to be building?

Now there is little left to build on — save bitterness. Soon the only solid physical foundations remaining will be found at our military bases and in the concrete of the concentration camps we call "fortified hamlets."[4] The peasants may well wonder if we plan to build our new Vietnam on such grounds as these. Could we blame them for such thoughts? We must speak for them and raise the questions they cannot raise. These too are our brothers.

Perhaps the more difficult but no less necessary task is to speak for those who have been designated as our enemies. What of the NLF — that strangely anonymous group we call VC or Communists? What must they think of us in America when they realize that we permitted the repression and cruelty of Diem which helped to bring them into being as a resistance group in the South? How can they believe in our integrity when now we speak of "aggression from the North" as if there were nothing more essential to the war?[5] How can they trust us when now we charge *them* with violence after the murderous reign of Diem, and charge *them* with violence while we pour new weapons of death into their land?

---

[4]King is referring to strategic hamlets, villages surrounded by defensive walls to which Vietnamese peasants were moved in an attempt to insulate them from the Viet Cong. — EDS.

[5]The State Department white paper of 1965 is titled *Aggression from the North* (see p. 824). — EDS.

How do they judge us when our officials know that their membership is less than 25 percent Communist and yet insist on giving them the blanket name? What must they be thinking when they know that we are aware of their control of major sections of Vietnam and yet we appear ready to allow national elections in which this highly organized political parallel government will have no part? They ask how we can speak of free elections when the Saigon press is censored and controlled by the military junta. And they are surely right to wonder what kind of new government we plan to help form without them — the only party in real touch with the peasants. They question our political goals and they deny the reality of a peace settlement from which they will be excluded. Their questions are frighteningly relevant.

Here is the true meaning and value of compassion and nonviolence — when it helps us to see the enemy's point of view, to hear his questions, to know of his assessment of ourselves. For from his view we may indeed see the basic weaknesses of our own condition, and if we are mature, we may learn and grow and profit from the wisdom of the brothers who are called the opposition.

So, too, with Hanoi. In the North, where our bombs now pummel the land, and our mines endanger the waterways, we are met by a deep but understandable mistrust. In Hanoi are the men who led the nation to independence against the Japanese and the French, the men who sought membership in the French commonwealth and were betrayed by the weakness of Paris and the willfulness of the colonial armies. It was they who led a second struggle against French domination at tremendous costs, and then were persuaded at Geneva to give up, as a temporary measure, the land they controlled between the thirteenth and seventeenth parallels. After 1954 they watched us conspire with Diem to prevent elections which would have surely brought Ho Chi Minh to power over a united Vietnam, and they realized they had been betrayed again.

When we ask why they do not leap to negotiate, these things must be remembered. Also, it must be clear that the leaders of Hanoi considered the presence of American troops in support of the Diem regime to have been the initial military breach of the Geneva agreements concerning foreign troops, and they remind us that they did not begin to send in any large number of supplies or men until American forces had moved into the tens of thousands.

Hanoi remembers how our leaders refused to tell us the truth about the earlier North Vietnamese overtures for peace, how the president claimed that none existed when they had clearly been made. Ho Chi Minh has watched as America has spoken of peace and built up its forces, and now he has surely heard the increasing international rumors of American plans for an invasion of the North. Perhaps only his sense of humor and irony can save him when he hears the most powerful nation of the world speaking of aggression as it drops thousands of bombs on a poor, weak nation more than eight thousand miles from its shores.

At this point, I should make it clear that while I have tried here to give a voice to the voiceless of Vietnam and to understand the arguments of those who are called enemy, I am as deeply concerned about our own troops there as anything else. For it occurs to me that what we are submitting them to in Vietnam is not simply the brutalizing process that goes on in any war where armies face each other and seek to destroy. We are adding cynicism to the process of death, for our troops must know after a short period there that none of the things we claim to be fighting for are really involved. Before long they must know that their government has sent them into a struggle among Vietnamese, and the more sophisticated surely realize that we are on the side of the wealthy and the secure while we create a hell for the poor.

Somehow this madness must cease. I speak as a child of God and brother to the suffering poor of Vietnam and the poor of America who are paying the double price of smashed hopes at home and death and corruption in Vietnam. I speak as a citizen of the world, for the world as it stands aghast at the path we have taken. I speak as an American to the leaders of my own nation. The great initiative in this war is ours. The initiative to stop must be ours.

This is the message of the great Buddhist leaders of Vietnam. Recently, one of them wrote these words: "Each day the war goes on the hatred increases in the hearts of the Vietnamese and in the hearts of those of humanitarian instinct. The Americans are forcing even their friends into becoming their enemies. It is curious that the Americans, who calculate so carefully on the possibilities of military victory, do not realize that in the process they are incurring deep psychological and political defeat. The image of America will never again be the image of revolution, freedom, and democracy, but the image of violence and militarism."

If we continue, there will be no doubt in my mind and in the mind of the world that we have no honorable intentions in Vietnam. It will become clear that our minimal expectation is to occupy it as an American colony, and men will not refrain from thinking that our maximum hope is to goad China into a war so that we may bomb her nuclear installations.

The world now demands a maturity of America that we may not be able to achieve. It demands that we admit that we have been wrong from the beginning of our adventure in Vietnam, that we have been detrimental to the life of her people.

In order to atone for our sins and errors in Vietnam, we should take the initiative in bringing the war to a halt. I would like to suggest five concrete things that our government should do immediately to begin the long and difficult process of extricating ourselves from this nightmare:

1. End all bombing in North and South Vietnam.
2. Declare a unilateral cease-fire in the hope that such action will create the atmosphere for negotiation.
3. Take immediate steps to prevent other battlegrounds in Southeast Asia by curtailing our military buildup in Thailand and our interference in Laos.
4. Realistically accept the fact that the National Liberation Front

has substantial support in South Vietnam and must thereby play a role in any meaningful negotiations and in any future Vietnam government.

5. Set a date on which we will remove all foreign troops from Vietnam in accordance with the 1954 Geneva agreement.

Part of our ongoing commitment might well express itself in an offer to grant asylum to any Vietnamese who fears for his life under a new regime which included the NLF. Then we must make what reparations we can for the damage we have done. We must provide the medical aid that is badly needed, in this country if necessary.

Meanwhile, we in the churches and synagogues have a continuing task while we urge our government to disengage itself from a disgraceful commitment. We must be prepared to match actions with words by seeking out every creative means of protest possible.

As we counsel young men concerning military service we must clarify for them our nation's role in Vietnam and challenge them with the alternative of conscientious objection. I am pleased to say that this is the path now being chosen by more than seventy students at my own Alma Mater, Morehouse College, and I recommend it to all who find the American course in Vietnam a dishonorable and unjust one. Moreover, I would encourage all ministers of draft age to give up their ministerial exemptions and seek status as conscientious objectors. Every man of humane convictions must decide on the protest that best suits his convictions, but we must *all* protest.

There is something seductively tempting about stopping there and sending us all off on what in some circles has become a popular crusade against the war in Vietnam. I say we must enter that struggle, but I wish to go on now to say something even more disturbing. The war in Vietnam is but a symptom of a far deeper malady within the American spirit, and if we ignore this sobering reality we will find ourselves organizing clergy- and laymen-concerned committees for the next generation. We will be marching and attending rallies without end unless there is a significant and profound change in American life and policy.

In 1957 a sensitive American official overseas said that it seemed to him that our nation was on the wrong side of a world revolution. During the past ten years we have seen emerge a pattern of suppression which now has justified the presence of U.S. military "advisers" in Venezuela. The need to maintain social stability for our investments accounts for the counterrevolutionary action of American forces in Guatemala. It tells why American helicopters are being used against guerrillas in Colombia and why American napalm and green beret forces have already been active against rebels in Peru. With such activity in mind, the words of John F. Kennedy come back to haunt us. Five years ago he said, "Those who make peaceful revolution impossible will make violent revolution inevitable."

Increasingly, by choice or by accident, this is the role our nation has taken — by refusing to give up the privileges and the pleasures that come from the immense profits of overseas investment.

I am convinced that if we are to get on the right side of the world revolution, we as a nation must undergo a radical revolution of values. When machines and computers, profits and property rights are considered more important than people, the giant triplets of racism, materialism, and militarism are incapable of being conquered.

A true revolution of values will soon cause us to question the fairness and justice of many of our past and present policies. True compassion is more than flinging a coin to a beggar; it is not haphazard and superficial. It comes to see that an edifice which produces beggars needs restructuring. A true revolution of values will soon look easily on the glaring contrast of poverty and wealth. With righteous indignation, it will look across the seas and see individual capitalists of the West investing huge sums of money in Asia, Africa, and South America, only to take the profits out with no concern for the social betterment of the countries, and say: "This is not just." It will look at our alliance with the landed gentry of Latin America and say: "This is not just." The Western arrogance of feeling that it has everything to teach others and nothing to learn from them is not just. A true revolution of values will lay hands on the world order and say of war: "This way of settling differences is not just." This business of burning human beings with napalm, of filling our nation's homes with orphans and widows, of injecting poisonous drugs of hate into the veins of peoples normally humane, of sending men home from dark and bloody battlefields physically handicapped and psychologically deranged, cannot be reconciled with wisdom, justice, and love. A nation that continues year after year to spend more money on military defense than on programs of social uplift is approaching spiritual death.

America, the richest and most powerful nation in the world, can well lead the way in this revolution of values. There is nothing, except a tragic death wish, to prevent us from reordering our priorities, so that the pursuit of peace will take precedence over the pursuit of war. There is nothing to keep us from molding a recalcitrant status quo until we have fashioned it into a brotherhood.

This kind of positive revolution of values is our best defense against communism. War is not the answer. Communism will never be defeated by the use of atomic bombs or nuclear weapons. Let us not join those who shout war and through their misguided passions urge the United States to relinquish its participation in the United Nations. These are the days which demand wise restraint and calm reasonableness. We must not call everyone a Communist or an appeaser who advocates the seating of Red China in the United Nations and who recognizes that hate and hysteria are not the final answers to the problem of these turbulent days. We must not engage in a negative anticommunism, but rather in a positive thrust for democracy, realizing that our greatest defense against communism is to take offensive action in behalf of justice. We must with positive action seek to remove those conditions of poverty, insecurity, and injustice which are the fertile soil in which the seed of communism grows and develops.

These are revolutionary times. All over the globe men are revolting against old systems of exploitation and oppression, and out of the wombs of a frail world, new systems of justice and equality are being born. The shirtless and barefoot people of the land are rising up as never before. "The people who sat in darkness have seen a great light."[6] We in the West must support these revolutions. It is a sad fact that, because of comfort, complacency, a morbid fear of communism, and our proneness to adjust to injustice, the Western nations that initiated so much of the revolutionary spirit of the modern world have now become the arch anti-revolutionaries. This has driven many to feel that only Marxism has the revolutionary spirit. Therefore, communism is a judgment against our failure to make democracy real and follow through on the revolutions that we initiated. Our only hope today lies in our ability to recapture the revolutionary spirit and go out into a sometimes hostile world declaring eternal hostility to poverty, racism, and militarism.

We must move past indecision to action. We must find new ways to speak for peace in Vietnam and justice throughout the developing world — a world that borders on our doors. If we do not act we shall surely be dragged down the long, dark, and shameful corridors of time reserved for those who possess power without compassion, might without morality, and strength without sight.

Now let us begin. Now let us rededicate ourselves to the long and bitter — but beautiful — struggle for a new world. This is the calling of the sons of God, and our brothers wait eagerly for our response. Shall we say the odds are too great? Shall we tell them the struggle is too hard? Will our message be that the forces of American life militate against their arrival as full men, and we send our deepest regrets? Or will there be another message, of longing, of hope, of solidarity with their yearnings, of commitment to their cause, whatever the cost? The choice is ours, and though we might prefer it otherwise we *must* choose in this crucial moment of human history.

READING CRITICALLY

1. What are King's seven reasons for being concerned about the Vietnam War?

2. How does King imagine that the Vietnamese see the United States?

3. What deceptions does King accuse the U.S. government of perpetrating?

4. In the world's eyes, what are the United States' goals in Vietnam, according to King?

5. How does King explain the popularity of communism?

[6]See Isaiah 9:2. — EDS.

WRITING ANALYTICALLY

1. Senator Thomas Dodd, in his 1965 speech about the war (p. 808), opposes negotiations because the very willingness to negotiate gives encouragement to the Communists in what Dodd calls their "long war strategy" — the Communists' conviction that if they hold on long enough, their enemies will wear out. Those who seek negotiations are, Dodd implies, comforting the enemy, a treasonous act. U.S. soldiers in Vietnam similarly regarded antiwar arguments as treasonous and back-stabbing (see Kovic, for example, on p. 931). King was indeed denounced as a traitor by many — both black and white — leaders. Write an essay in which you consider the charge of treason against King. On what grounds could he be accused? How would he defend himself? What verdict would you render?

2. King predicates successful negotiation on five things that the United States should do. Write an essay analyzing the logic of his proposal. How, in other words, will the actions King suggests lead to successful negotiations? What sort of negotiations might take place if the United States followed King's recommendations? What outcome does King seem to desire?

3. King's speech was tremendously effective. The crowd at Riverside Church gave him a huge ovation, as did the demonstrators at a later rally where he gave a similar speech. In print, the speech was widely read and highly influential. King is famous for his oratory, and this speech is an excellent example of his eloquence. What makes it so powerful? Write an analysis of the speech focusing on its structure. In what order does King develop his points? How does his organization contribute to the impact that the speech makes?

LYNDON B. JOHNSON

From *"Peace in Vietnam and Southeast Asia"*

(March 31, 1968)

On the evening of March 31, 1968, looking gray and tired, President Lyndon B. Johnson (1908–73) delivered a televised address to the nation. He spoke about this plan for peace in Vietnam and ended with the surprise announcement that he would not run for reelection to the presidency. Johnson had been a congressional representative from Texas from 1937 to 1948, a senator from 1948 to 1960, and vice president under John F. Kennedy. He had become president upon Kennedy's assassination in November 1963 and

Lyndon B. Johnson, "Peace in Vietnam and Southeast Asia," *Public Papers of the Presidents of the United States, 1968—69* (Washington, D.C.: Government Printing Office, 1970), 468–76, reprinted in *Vietnam and America: A Documented History*, ed. Marvin Gettleman et al. (New York: Grove Press, 1985), 394–402.

In the notes, EDS. = Patricia Bizzell and Bruce Herzberg.

had been elected to a full term in 1964. Johnson ordered the major escalations of the Vietnam War from 1965 until 1968, when he made the speech reprinted here.

When Johnson delivered his speech, news about the war was bad, and opposition at home was growing. The Pentagon's positive reports of success in the field were being proved false by the repeated successes of the NLF (the Viet Cong) in controlling the countryside. In the United States, antiwar candidates dominated the Democratic Party primaries, and there were innumerable antiwar demonstrations in cities and on college campuses across the country. In his March 31 speech, President Johnson attempted to respond to this situation.

After he left the White House, Johnson and others in his administration spoke about how they had been deceived by the Pentagon into believing that the war was being won and into thus sustaining their commitment to the fighting. Later revelations, such as the *Pentagon Papers*, published in 1971, documented the systematic deception of both the public and the Johnson White House about the progress of the war.

GOOD EVENING, MY FELLOW AMERICANS:

Tonight I want to speak to you of peace in Vietnam and Southeast Asia.

No other question so preoccupies our people. No other dream so absorbs the 250 million human beings who live in that part of the world. No other goal motivates American policy in Southeast Asia.

For years, representatives of our government and others have traveled the world — seeking to find a basis for peace talks.

Since last September, they have carried the offer that I made public at San Antonio.

That offer was:

That the United States would stop its bombardment of North Vietnam when that would lead promptly to productive discussions — and that we would assume that North Vietnam would not take military advantage of our restraint.

Hanoi denounced this offer, both privately and publicly. Even while the search for peace was going on, North Vietnam rushed their preparations for a savage assault on the people, the government, and the allies of South Vietnam.

Their attack — during the Tet holidays[1] — failed to achieve its principal objectives.

---

[1]On the night of January 30, 1968 — during Tet, the Vietnamese lunar new year, when a truce was supposedly in force — some seventy thousand Communist troops attacked cities and villages all over South Vietnam in what became known as the Tet Offensive. The fighting was especially fierce, with Communist troops committing massacres, assassinations of minor South Vietnamese officials, and other atrocities. Although they reached even the U.S. embassy compound in Saigon, the Communists failed in their main objective — to drive out the Americans and the Saigon regime. But they shocked the United States with their ability to mount so extensive a campaign throughout the South. — EDS.

It did not collapse the elected government of South Vietnam or shatter its army — as the Communists had hoped.

It did not produce a "general uprising" among the people of the cities as they had predicted.

The Communists were unable to maintain control of any of the more than thirty cities that they attacked. And they took very heavy casualties.

But they did compel the South Vietnamese and their allies to move certain forces from the countryside into the cities.

They caused widespread disruption and suffering. Their attacks, and the battles that followed, made refugees of half a million human beings.

The Communists may renew their attack any day.

They are, it appears, trying to make 1968 the year of decision in South Vietnam — the year that brings, if not final victory or defeat, at least a turning point in the struggle.

This much is clear:

If they do mount another round of heavy attacks, they will not succeed in destroying the fighting power of South Vietnam and its allies.

But tragically, this is also clear: Many men — on both sides of the struggle — will be lost. A nation that has already suffered twenty years of warfare will suffer once again. Armies on both sides will take new casualties. And the war will go on.

There is no need for this to be so.

There is no need to delay the talks that could bring an end to this long and this bloody war.

Tonight, I renew the offer I made last August — to stop the bombardment of North Vietnam. We ask that talks begin promptly, that they be serious talks on the substance of peace. We assume that during those talks Hanoi will not take advantage of our restraint.

We are prepared to move immediately toward peace through negotiations.

So, tonight, in the hope that this action will lead to early talks, I am taking the first step to deescalate the conflict. We are reducing — substantially reducing — the present level of hostilities.

And we are doing so unilaterally, and at once.

Tonight, I have ordered our aircraft and our naval vessels to make no attacks on North Vietnam, except in the area north of the demilitarized zone where the continuing enemy buildup directly threatens allied forward positions and where the movements of their troops and supplies are clearly related to that threat.

The area in which we are stopping our attacks includes almost 90 percent of North Vietnam's population, and most of its territory. Thus there will be no attacks around the principal populated areas or in the food-producing areas of North Vietnam.

Even this very limited bombing of the North could come to an early end — if our restraint is matched by restraint in Hanoi. But I cannot in good conscience stop all bombing so long as to do so would immediately and directly endanger the lives of our men and our allies. Whether a complete bombing halt becomes possible in the future will be determined by events.

Our purpose in this action is to bring about a reduction in the level of violence that now exists.

It is to save the lives of brave men — and to save the lives of innocent women and children. It is to permit the contending forces to move closer to a political settlement.

And tonight, I call upon the United Kingdom and I call upon the Soviet Union — as cochairmen of the Geneva Conferences, and as permanent members of the United Nations Security Council — to do all they can to move from the unilateral act of deescalation that I have just announced toward genuine peace in Southeast Asia.

Now, as in the past, the United States is ready to send its representatives to any forum, at any time, to discuss the means of bringing this ugly war to an end.

I am designating one of our most distinguished Americans, Ambassador Averell Harriman, as my personal representative for such talks. In addition, I have asked Ambassador Llewellyn Thompson, who returned from Moscow for consultation, to be available to join Ambassador Harriman at Geneva or any other suitable place — just as soon as Hanoi agrees to a conference.

I call upon President Ho Chi Minh to respond positively, and favorably, to this new step toward peace.

But if peace does not come now through negotiations, it will come when Hanoi understands that our common resolve is unshakable, and our common strength is invincible.

Tonight, we and the other allied nations are contributing 600,000 fighting men to assist 700,000 South Vietnamese troops in defending their little country.

Our presence there has always rested on this basic belief: The main burden of preserving their freedom must be carried out by them — by the South Vietnamese themselves.

We and our allies can only help to provide a shield behind which the people of South Vietnam can survive and can grow and develop. On their efforts — on their determination and resourcefulness — the outcome will ultimately depend.

That small, beleaguered nation has suffered terrible punishment for more than twenty years.

I pay tribute once again tonight to the great courage and endurance of its people. South Vietnam supports armed forces tonight of almost 700,000 men — I call your attention to the fact that this is the equivalent of more than 10 million in our own population. Its people maintain their firm determination to be free of domination by the North. . . .

On many occasions I have told the American people that we would send to Vietnam those forces that are required to accomplish our mission there. So, with that as our guide, we have previously authorized a force level of approximately 525,000. . . .

Our objective in South Vietnam has never been the annihilation of the enemy. It has been to bring about a recognition in Hanoi that its objective — taking over the South by force — could not be achieved.

We think that peace can be based on the Geneva accords of 1954 — under political conditions that permit the South Vietnamese — all the South Vietnamese — to chart their course free of any outside domination or interference, from us or from anyone else.

So tonight I reaffirm the pledge that we made at Manila — that we are prepared to withdraw our forces from South Vietnam as the other side withdraws its forces to the north, stops the infiltration, and the level of violence thus subsides.

Our goal of peace and self-determination in Vietnam is directly related to the future of all Southeast Asia — where much has happened to inspire confidence during the past ten years. We have done all that we knew how to do to contribute and to help build that confidence.

A number of its nations have shown what can be accomplished under conditions of security. Since 1966, Indonesia, the fifth largest nation in all the world, with a population of more than 100 million people, has had a government that is dedicated to peace with its neighbors and improved conditions for its own people. Political and economic cooperation between nations has grown rapidly.

I think every American can take a great deal of pride in the role that we have played in bringing this about in Southeast Asia. We can rightly judge — as responsible Southeast Asians themselves do — that the progress of the past three years would have been far less likely — if not completely impossible — if America's sons and others had not made their stand in Vietnam.

At Johns Hopkins University, about three years ago, I announced that the United States would take part in the great work of developing Southeast Asia, including the Mekong Valley, for all the people of that region. Our determination to help build a better land — a better land for men on both sides of the present conflict — has not diminished in the least. Indeed, the ravages of war, I think, have made it more urgent than ever.

So, I repeat on behalf of the United States again tonight what I said at Johns Hopkins — that North Vietnam could take its place in this common effort just as soon as peace comes.

Over time, a wider framework of peace and security in Southeast Asia may become possible. The new cooperation of the nations of the area could be a foundation stone. Certainly friendship with the nations of such a Southeast Asia is what the United States seeks — and that is all that the United States seeks.

One day, my fellow citizens, there will be peace in Southeast Asia.

It will come because the people of Southeast Asia want it — those whose armies are at war tonight, and those who, though threatened, have thus far been spared.

Peace will come because Asians were willing to work for it — and to sacrifice for it — and to die by the thousands for it.

But let it never be forgotten: Peace will come also because America sent her sons to help secure it.

It has not been easy — far from it. During the past four and a half years, it has been my fate and my responsibility to be commander in chief. I have lived — daily and nightly — with the cost of this war. I know the pain that it has inflicted. I know, perhaps better than anyone, the misgivings that it has aroused.

Throughout this entire, long period, I have been sustained by a single principle: that what we are doing now, in Vietnam, is vital not only to the security of Southeast Asia, but it is vital to the security of every American.

Surely we have treaties which we must respect. Surely we have commitments that we are going to keep. Resolutions of the Congress testify to the need to resist aggression in the world and in Southeast Asia.

But the heart of our involvement in South Vietnam — under three different presidents, three separate administrations — has always been America's own security.

And the larger purpose of our involvement has always been to help the nations of Southeast Asia become independent and stand alone, self-sustaining, as members of a great world community — at peace with themselves, and at peace with all others.

With such an Asia, our country — and the world — will be far more secure than it is tonight.

I believe that a peaceful Asia is far nearer to reality because of what America has done in Vietnam. I believe that the men who endure the dangers of battle — fighting there for us tonight — are helping the entire world avoid far greater conflicts, far wider wars, far more destruction, than this one.

The peace that will bring them home someday will come. Tonight I have offered the first in what I hope will be a series of mutual moves toward peace.

I pray that it will not be rejected by the leaders of North Vietnam. I pray that they will accept it as a means by which the sacrifices of their own people may be ended. And I ask your help and your support, my fellow citizens, for this effort to reach across the battlefield toward an early peace.

Finally, my fellow Americans, let me say this:

Of those to whom much is given, much is asked. I cannot say and no man could say that no more will be asked of us.

Yet, I believe that now, no less than when the decade began, this generation of Americans is willing to "pay any price, bear any burden, meet any hardship, support any friend, oppose any foe to assure the survival and the success of liberty."

Since those words were spoken by John F. Kennedy,[2] the people of America have kept that compact with mankind's noblest cause.

And we shall continue to keep it.

---

[2]In his inaugural address, January 20, 1961. — EDS.

Yet, I believe that we must always be mindful of this one thing, whatever the trials and the tests ahead. The ultimate strength of our country and our cause will lie not in powerful weapons or infinite resources or boundless wealth, but will lie in the unity of our people.

This I believe very deeply.

Throughout my entire public career I have followed the personal philosophy that I am a free man, an American, a public servant, and a member of my party, in that order always and only.

For thirty-seven years in the service of our nation, first as a congressman, as a senator, and as vice president, and now as your president, I have put the unity of the people first. I have put it ahead of any divisive partisanship.

And in these times as in times before, it is true that a house divided against itself by the spirit of faction, of party, of region, of religion, of race, is a house that cannot stand.

There is division in the American house now. There is divisiveness among us all tonight. And holding the trust that is mine, as president of all the people, I cannot disregard the peril to the progress of the American people and the hope and the prospect of peace for all peoples.

So, I would ask all Americans, whatever their personal interests or concern, to guard against divisiveness and all its ugly consequences.

Fifty-two months and ten days ago, in a moment of tragedy and trauma, the duties of this office fell upon me. I asked then for your help and God's, that we might continue American on its course, binding up our wounds, healing our history, moving forward in new unity, to clear the American agenda and to keep the American commitment for all of our people.

United we have kept that commitment. United we have enlarged that commitment.

Through all time to come, I think America will be a stronger nation, a more just society, and a land of greater opportunity and fulfillment because of what we have all done together in these years of unparalleled achievement.

Our reward will come in the life of freedom, peace, and hope that our children will enjoy through ages ahead.

What we won when all of our people united just must not now be lost in suspicion, distrust, selfishness, and politics among any of our people.

Believing this as I do, I have concluded that I should not permit the presidency to become involved in the partisan divisions that are developing in this political year.

With America's sons in the fields far away, with America's future under challenge right here at home, with our hopes and the world's hopes for peace in the balance every day, I do not believe that I should devote an hour or a day of my time to any personal partisan causes or to any duties other than the awesome duties of this office — the presidency of your country.

Accordingly, I shall not seek, and I will not accept, the nomination of my party for another term as your president.

But let men everywhere know, however, that a strong, a confident, and a vigilant America stands ready tonight to seek an honorable peace — and stands ready tonight to defend an honored cause — whatever the price, whatever the burden, whatever the sacrifice that duty may require.

Thank you for listening.

Good night and God bless all of you.

READING CRITICALLY

1. Why does Johnson say that he is stopping most of the bombing of North Vietnam?

2. What, according to Johnson, is the goal of the war? What are the main reasons for U.S. involvement?

3. In what ways does Johnson acknowledge the antiwar movement?

4. What does Johnson seem to hope will happen in negotiations?

5. What reasons does Johnson give for declining to run for reelection?

WRITING ANALYTICALLY

1. Many commentators have noted that Johnson's speech is rather ambiguous. The policy that he is articulating seems mixed and even contradictory — promises of deescalation mixed with threats, uncertainty about the goal of negotiations, unwillingness to "widen" the war combined with a commitment to winning it if need be. One way to try to understand Johnson's position (and to get an idea of the difficulties faced by any president who makes a speech) is to consider the speech from the point of view of the different audiences that Johnson needs to address. Write an essay analyzing the way that Johnson seems to be attempting to speak to (a) supporters of the war policy, (b) the antiwar movement, (c) the South Vietnamese government, (d) the North Vietnamese government and the NLF. Option: Write the essay in the form of a series of editorials by representatives of the different audiences commenting on Johnson's ideas.

2. Senator Dodd, in his 1965 speech on the war (p. 808), opposes negotiation or even the call for negotiation as a sign of weakness that would only strengthen the Communists in their "long war" strategy. Write an essay analyzing the ways that President Johnson defends negotiation and tries to deflect or refute Dodd's argument. Do you think he succeeds? Why, or why not?

NATIONAL MOBILIZATION COMMITTEE TO END THE WAR IN VIETNAM

"A Message to GIs and to the Movement"
(November 1968)

The National Mobilization Committee to End the War in Vietnam came into existence in the spring of 1967. Leaders of a variety of civil rights and anti-war groups (including David Dellinger and A. J. Muste; see p. 840) had come together in the fall of 1966 as the Spring Mobilization Committee to organize demonstrations in New York and San Francisco for the following April. Despite some conflicts among the constituent organizations about goals and tactics, the group remained together as the National Mobilization Committee to plan further antiwar activities, becoming the chief antiwar organization in the country. Its rallies and marches succeeded both in bringing together peace groups with different constituencies and ideologies and in drawing large crowds and media attention. Its members prepared and distributed the following pamphlet in November 1968.

To GIs

YOU HAVE SEEN KIDS AGAINST THE WAR, marching around with their signs. The lifers will tell you these kids are your enemy. And the brass will issue you orders that they are your enemy. (The brass would like to issue you everything but brains.) But the truth is the kids against the war are people, most of them your own age, who want to see you come home alive.

Every kind of American is now against the war. You all know someone — a teacher, a preacher, a truck driver — who says we have no business turning over the lives of thousands of Americans to a bunch of crooks running the corrupt government of South Vietnam. You may know that even retired brass like General Shoupe and General Gavin say that American interest in Vietnam is not worth a pile of peanut shells. Probably the Americans most against this war are the men who fought it — the Vietnam veterans.

Each day, more and more Americans stand up against the senseless slaughter of GIs and Vietnamese. These Americans make up the "antiwar movement." You may only know them as the kids with long hair, the ministers of your own religion, or the guy beside you in the barracks. They get

National Mobilization Committee to End the War in Vietnam, "A Message to GIs and to the Movement," reprinted in *The New Left*, ed. Massimo Teodori (New York: Bobbs-Merrill, 1969), 314–16.

called peaceniks, Communists, and un-Americans — especially by the people who make a fortune in keeping the war going.

But as a soldier, you know better than anyone what it means to be harassed and humiliated by the lifers and the brass, especially if you open your mouth the wrong way. And everyone in the antiwar movement knows something about harassment too, for opening their mouths for American soldiers' right to return to civilian life.

Probably you resent the fact that peace demonstrations include kids who can wait out the war in college. You have every right to be mad about that. But do you know that the antiwar movement is trying to do away with the draft laws that give special privileges to some? In fact, the antiwar movement is trying to do away with all the laws that force people to fight and die in Vietnam while a few politicians haggle over how to keep the war going forever.

The lifers, the brass, and the old people who run this country will stop at nothing to keep the spirit of the antiwar movement locked out of every base. So in case your commanding officer didn't tell you, the kids against the war SUPPORT soldiers. They support the man who says he may be forced to give his body to Uncle Sam but damn if he'll turn over his brain. And they support the idea that when a war cannot be defended, even by a double-talking, money-making politician, GIs have a right to come home — now.

To the Movement

The average GI is under the thumb of the military machine; he is not the operator of it. Either he was drafted, or he volunteered under pressure from a society that won't give a noncollege man a job unless he has an honorable discharge — especially if he is black.

His first two months are spent in basic training at a huge post, far from home (by design) and far from any major city. In "basic" he is whipped into good physical shape and taught elementary skills such as rifle-firing. Most important of all, he gets broken down emotionally and intellectually by a process known as HARASSMENT. The trainee is forced to buff floors that don't need buffing, scream instead of talk, run instead of walk, memorize meaningless lists, prepare his belongings for inspections so petty that hygiene is forgotten (you have to have an UNUSED tube of tooth paste in your locker). . . .

After basic comes AIT — "advanced individual training" — or, for the vast majority, advanced infantry training. Men are given specialties: typing, machine-gunning, radio operation, and so on. Then they are assigned duty stations — Vietnam, most likely.

The GI's immediate enemy, from basic on, is the noncommissioned officer, or NCO, also known as the E-5, 6, or 7 (a reference to his pay grade) or "lifer." The lifer is a man who knows that his army standard of living beats anything he could attain in the civilian world. Most lifers are poor southerners, white and black. They have sold their souls to the military, very much like factory foremen who owe their jobs to devotion to the boss.

The officer corps has its lifers, too, but — especially in Vietnam — it is made up mostly of college graduates. Sometimes generation ties replace caste ties. That is, young second lieutenants, in the field, sometimes join their men in blowing grass while the older officers and EMs drink alcohol. In general, though, the army is like the rest of America — the well-educated give the orders, the less-educated carry them out.

From the barracks to the front-lines, the mood of the American soldier is, today, THOUGHTFUL. A basic trainee, like a college freshman of the same age, is going through a hell of a time deciding what he wants to do with his life and what he wants the world to be like. He knows that the war is costing him and his buddies more — limbs, lives — than it costs the rest of the American people. Given the huge percentage of people who oppose the war, and the fact that young people are significantly more liberal than their parents, ours is certainly one of the most reluctant armies in history.

Of course, the officers and NCOs pressure GIs constantly to stop thinking, to simply obey. But men have always overcome attempts to bully and blind them, and this is what American soldiers are doing, in rapidly increasing numbers, today.

READING CRITICALLY

1. In the message to GIs, what motives does this pamphlet attribute to the antiwar protesters?

2. What attitude does the pamphlet assume soldiers have toward the "brass" and "lifers"? Toward members of the antiwar movement?

3. What does the pamphlet assume members of the movement think about soldiers?

WRITING ANALYTICALLY

1. Both of the messages — to GIs and to the movement — appeared in the same pamphlet. Clearly, both audiences were intended to read both messages. Naturally, soldiers would wonder what was being said about them to the antiwar protesters and vice versa. Therefore, if this pamphlet was to be successful, both messages had to work for both audiences. Do you think the pamphlet manages to accomplish that goal? Write an analysis in which you explain how each message (a) seeks to find common ground between the two groups; (b) attempts to appeal to the group to whom it is addressed; and (c) attempts to appeal to the other group.

2. This pamphlet is clearly an antiwar argument, but it takes a different approach from other selections in this unit. Write an essay comparing the rhetorical strategies of the pamphlet with those of King's "Declaration of Independence from the war in Vietnam" (p. 850). What logical and emotional appeals does each use? What kinds of action does each call for? How does each see its audience or audiences?

RICHARD M. NIXON

From *"Vietnamization"* (November 3, 1969)

Richard M. Nixon (1913–94) was elected president in 1968, promising that
he had a secret plan for "peace with honor" in Vietnam. Though Nixon increased the number of U.S. troops in Vietnam at first, he instituted with-
drawals of small numbers of troops beginning in June 1969.

Nixon held officially to the bombing halt ordered in March 1968 by President Lyndon Johnson (see p. 860) but began bombing both North Vietnam
and, secretly, Cambodia in the spring of 1969. Antiwar demonstrations increased through the summer, and a set of massive protests, called Moratorium Day, was planned for October 15 and for every month thereafter. The
October 15 demonstrations drew a quarter of a million people in Washington, D.C., and large crowds in other cities; the Moratorium also engaged
people throughout the country in various other protests — such as wearing
black armbands and flying flags at half-staff. Just before the October Moratorium Day, Nixon announced that he would give a major televised address on
November 3. The timing of the announcement and the speech was intended
to deflect attention from the planned November 15 demonstrations.

Nixon's advisers made much of the fact that Nixon wrote the speech
alone, laboring over draft after draft. At last the country would learn
Nixon's plan to "Vietnamize" the war — increasing aid to South Vietnam
while slowly withdrawing U.S. forces. In terms of public reaction, the
speech could be considered a success — a Gallup poll showed 77 percent
of the American public approving. The antiwar movement, however, reacted negatively, and the November 15 demonstrations were larger than
those in October.

President Nixon was reelected in 1972; in January 1973 he announced
the agreement to end U.S. involvement in the war and withdrew all U.S.
ground troops by March. Within months, revelations of the Watergate
cover-up (see introduction to Unit Six, p. 801) began to come to light, and
in August 1974, facing probable impeachment, Nixon resigned the presidency.

GOOD EVENING, MY FELLOW AMERICANS:

Tonight I want to talk to you on a subject of deep concern to all Americans and to many people in all parts of the world — the war in Vietnam.

I believe that one of the reasons for the deep division about Vietnam is
that many Americans have lost confidence in what their government has

Richard M. Nixon, "Vietnamization," *Public Papers of the Presidents of the United States: Richard
Nixon, 1969* (Washington, D.C.: Government Printing Office, 1971), 901–9, reprinted in *Vietnam and America: A Documented History*, ed. Marvin Gettleman et al. (New York: Grove Press,
1985), 428–39.

In the notes, MG = Marvin Gettleman et al., EDS. = Patricia Bizzell and Bruce Herzberg.

told them about our policy. The American people cannot and should not be asked to support a policy which involves the overriding issues of war and peace unless they know the truth about that policy.

Tonight, therefore, I would like to answer some of the questions that I know are on the minds of many of you listening to me.

How and why did America get involved in Vietnam in the first place?

How has this administration changed the policy of the previous administration?

What has really happened in the negotiations in Paris[1] and on the battlefront in Vietnam?

What choices do we have if we are to end the war?

What are the prospects for peace?

Now, let me begin by describing the situation I found when I was inaugurated on January 20.

- The war had been going on for four years.
- thirty-one thousand Americans had been killed in action.
- The training program for the South Vietnamese was behind schedule.
- 540,000 Americans were in Vietnam with no plans to reduce the number.
- No progress had been made at the negotiations in Paris and the United States had not put forth a comprehensive peace proposal.
- The war was causing deep division at home and criticism from many of our friends as well as our enemies abroad.

In view of these circumstances there were some who urged that I end the war at once by ordering the immediate withdrawal of all American forces.

From a political standpoint this would have been a popular and easy course to follow. After all, we became involved in the war while my predecessor was in office. I could blame the defeat which would be the result of my action on him and come out as the peacemaker. Some put it to me quite bluntly: This was the only way to avoid allowing Johnson's war to become Nixon's war.

But I had a greater obligation than to think only of the years of my administration and of the next election. I had to think of the effect of my decision on the next generation and on the future of peace and freedom in America and in the world.

Let us all understand that the question before us is not whether some Americans are for peace and some Americans are against peace. The question at issue is not whether Johnson's war becomes Nixon's war.

The great question is: How can we win America's peace?

Well, let us turn now to the fundamental issue. Why and how did the United States become involved in Vietnam in the first place?

---

[1]The negotiations proposed by President Johnson in his speech of March 31, 1968 (see p. 860) began in Paris on May 13, 1968 — EDS.

Fifteen years ago North Vietnam, with the logistical support of Communist China and the Soviet Union, launched a campaign to impose a Communist government on South Vietnam by instigating and supporting a revolution.

In response to the request of the government of South Vietnam, President Eisenhower sent economic aid and military equipment to assist the people of South Vietnam in their efforts to prevent a Communist takeover. Seven years ago, President Kennedy sent sixteen thousand military personnel to Vietnam as combat advisers. Four years ago, President Johnson sent American combat forces to South Vietnam.

Now, many believe that President Johnson's decision to send American combat forces to South Vietnam was wrong. And many others — I among them — have been strongly critical of the way the war has been conducted.

But the question facing us today is: Now that we are in the war, what is the best way to end it?

In January I could only conclude that the precipitate withdrawal of American forces from Vietnam would be a disaster not only for South Vietnam but for the United States and for the cause of peace.

For the South Vietnamese, our precipitate withdrawal would inevitably allow the Communists to repeat the massacres which followed their takeover in the North fifteen years before.

- They then murdered more than fifty thousand people and hundreds of thousands more died in slave labor camps.
- We saw a prelude of what would happen in South Vietnam when the Communists entered the city of Hue last year. During their brief rule there, there was a bloody reign of terror in which three thousand civilians were clubbed, shot to death, and buried in mass graves.
- With the sudden collapse of our support, these atrocities of Hue would become the nightmare of the entire nation — and particularly for the million and a half Catholic refugees who fled to South Vietnam when the Communists took over in the North.

For the United States, this first defeat in our nation's history would result in a collapse of confidence in American leadership, not only in Asia but throughout the world.

Three American presidents have recognized the great stakes involved in Vietnam and understood what had to be done.

In 1963, President Kennedy, with his characteristic eloquence and clarity, said: ". . . we want to see a stable government there, carrying on a struggle to maintain its national independence.

"We believe strongly in that. We are not going to withdraw from that effort. In my opinion, for us to withdraw from that effort would mean a collapse not only of South Vietnam, but Southeast Asia. So we are going to stay there."

President Eisenhower and President Johnson expressed the same conclusion during their terms of office.

For the future of peace, precipitate withdrawal would thus be a disaster of immense magnitude.

- A nation cannot remain great if it betrays its allies and lets down its friends.
- Our defeat and humiliation in South Vietnam without question would promote recklessness in the councils of those great powers who have not yet abandoned their goals of world conquest.
- This would spark violence wherever our commitments help maintain the peace — in the Middle East, in Berlin, eventually even in the Western Hemisphere.

Ultimately, this would cost more lives.

It would not bring peace; it would bring more war.

For these reasons, I rejected the recommendation that I should end the war by immediately withdrawing all of our forces. I chose instead to change American policy on both the negotiating front and battlefront.

In order to end a war fought on many fronts, I initiated a pursuit for peace on many fronts.

In a television speech on May 14, in a speech before the United Nations, and on a number of other occasions I set forth our peace proposals in great detail.

- We have offered a complete withdrawal of all outside forces within one year.
- We have proposed a cease-fire under international supervision.
- We have offered free elections under international supervision with the Communists participating in the organization and conduct of the elections as an organized political force. And the Saigon government has pledged to accept the result of the elections.

We have not put forth our proposals on a take-it-or-leave-it basis. We have indicated that we are willing to discuss the proposals that have been put forth by the other side. We have declared that anything is negotiable except the right of the people of South Vietnam to determine their own future. At the Paris peace conference, Ambassador Lodge has demonstrated our flexibility and good faith in forty public meetings.

Hanoi has refused even to discuss our proposals. They demand our unconditional acceptance of their terms, which are that we withdraw all American forces immediately and unconditionally and that we overthrow the government of South Vietnam as we leave.

We have not limited our peace initiatives to public forums and public statements. I recognized, in January, that a long and bitter war like this usually cannot be settled in a public forum. That is why in addition to the public statements and negotiations I have explored every possible private avenue that might lead to a settlement. . . .

But the effect of all the public, private, and secret negotiations which have been undertaken since the bombing halt a year ago and since this administration came into office on January 20 can be summed up in one sentence: No progress whatever has been made except agreement on the shape of the bargaining table.

Well now, who is at fault?

It has become clear that the obstacle in negotiating an end to the war is not the President of the United States. It is not the South Vietnamese government.

The obstacle is the other side's absolute refusal to show the least willingness to join us in seeking a just peace. And it will not do so while it is convinced that all it has to do is to wait for our next concession, and our next concession after that one, until it gets everything it wants.

There can now be no longer any question that progress in negotiation depends only on Hanoi's deciding to negotiate, to negotiate seriously.

I realize that this report on our efforts on the diplomatic front is discouraging to the American people, but the American people are entitled to know the truth — the bad news as well as the good news — where the lives of our young men are involved.

Now let me turn, however, to a more encouraging report on another front.

At the time we launched our search for peace I recognized we might not succeed in bringing an end to the war through negotiation. I, therefore, put into effect another plan to bring peace — a plan which will bring the war to an end regardless of what happens on the negotiating front.

It is in line with a major shift in U.S. foreign policy which I described in my press conference at Guam on July 25. Let me briefly explain what has been described as the Nixon Doctrine — a policy which not only will help end the war in Vietnam, but which is an essential element of our program to prevent future Vietnams.

We Americans are a do-it-yourself people. We are an impatient people. Instead of teaching someone else to do a job, we like to do it ourselves. And this trait has been carried over into our foreign policy.

In Korea and again in Vietnam, the United States furnished most of the money, most of the arms, and most of the men to help the people of those countries defend their freedom against Communist aggression.

Before any American troops were committed to Vietnam, a leader of another Asian country expressed this opinion to me when I was traveling in Asia as a private citizen. He said: "When you are trying to assist another nation [to] defend its freedom, U.S. policy should be to help them fight the war but not to fight the war for them."

Well, in accordance with this wise counsel, I laid down in Guam three principles as guidelines for future American policy toward Asia:

- First, the United States will keep all of its treaty commitments.
- Second, we shall provide a shield if a nuclear power threatens the freedom of a nation allied with us or of a nation whose survival we consider vital to our security.
- Third, in cases involving other types of aggression, we shall furnish military and economic assistance when requested in accordance with

our treaty commitments. But we shall look to the nation directly threatened to assume the primary responsibility of providing the manpower for its defense.

After I announced this policy, I found that the leaders of the Philippines, Thailand, Vietnam, South Korea, and other nations which might be threatened by Communist aggression welcomed this new direction in American foreign policy.

The defense of freedom is everybody's business — not just America's business. And it is particularly the responsibility of the people whose freedom is threatened. In the previous administration, we Americanized the war in Vietnam. In this administration, we are Vietnamizing the search for peace.

The policy of the previous administration not only resulted in our assuming the primary responsibility for fighting the war, but even more significantly did not adequately stress the goal of strengthening the South Vietnamese so that they could defend themselves when we left.

The Vietnamization plan was launched following Secretary Laird's visit to Vietnam in March. Under the plan, I ordered first a substantial increase in the training and equipment of South Vietnamese forces.

In July, on my visit to Vietnam, I changed General Abrams' orders so that they were consistent with the objectives of our new policies. Under the new orders, the primary mission of our troops is to enable the South Vietnamese forces to assume the full responsibility for the security of South Vietnam.

Our air operations have been reduced by over 20 percent.[2]

And now we have begun to see the results of this long overdue change in American policy in Vietnam.

- After five years of Americans going into Vietnam, we are finally bringing men home. By December 15, over sixty thousand men will have been withdrawn from South Vietnam — including 20 percent of all of our combat forces.
- The South Vietnamese have continued to gain in strength. As a result they have been able to take over combat responsibilities from our American troops.

Two other significant developments have occurred since this administration took office.

- Enemy infiltration, infiltration which is essential if they are to launch a major attack, over the last three months is less than 20 percent of what it was over the same period last year.

[2]Apparently Nixon was not counting the raids in the "secret" bombing of Cambodia which had begun in March and was continuing intensively as he spoke. Nor was he probably counting the 1969 eight-month bombing campaign against the Plain of Jars in north-central Laos; some of those sorties were being reported as bombings of southern Laos while others were being reported as bombings of South Vietnam. Perhaps Nixon was counting the latter. — MG

• Most important — United States casualties have declined during the last two months to the lowest point in three years.

Let me now turn to our program for the future.

We have adopted a plan which we have worked out in cooperation with the South Vietnamese for the complete withdrawal of all U.S. combat ground forces, and their replacement by South Vietnamese forces on an orderly scheduled timetable. This withdrawal will be made from strength and not from weakness. As South Vietnamese forces become stronger, the rate of American withdrawal can become greater.

I have not and do not intend to announce the timetable for our program. And there are obvious reasons for this decision which I am sure you will understand. As I have indicated on several occasions, the rate of withdrawal will depend on developments on three fronts.

One of these is the progress which can be or might be made in the Paris talks. An announcement of a fixed timetable for our withdrawal would completely remove any incentive for the enemy to negotiate an agreement. They would simply wait until our forces had withdrawn and then move in.

The other two factors on which we will base our withdrawal decisions are the level of enemy activity and the progress of the training programs of the South Vietnamese forces. And I am glad to be able to report tonight progress on both of these fronts has been greater than we anticipated when we started the program in June for withdrawal. As a result, our timetable for withdrawal is more optimistic now than when we made our first estimates in June. Now, this clearly demonstrates why it is not wise to be frozen in on a fixed timetable.

We must retain the flexibility to base each withdrawal decision on the situation as it is at the time rather than on estimates that are no longer valid.

Along with this optimistic estimate, I must — in all candor — leave one note of caution.

If the level of enemy activity significantly increases we might have to adjust our timetable accordingly.

However, I want the record to be completely clear on one point.

At the time of the bombing halt just a year ago, there was some confusion as to whether there was an understanding on the part of the enemy that if we stopped the bombing of North Vietnam they would stop the shelling of cities in South Vietnam. I want to be sure that there is no misunderstanding on the part of the enemy with regard to our withdrawal program.

We have noted the reduced level of infiltration, the reduction of our casualties, and are basing our withdrawal decisions partially on those factors.

If the level of infiltration or our casualties increase while we are trying to scale down the fighting, it will be the result of a conscious decision by the enemy.

Hanoi could make no greater mistake than to assume that an increase in violence will be to its advantage. If I conclude that increased enemy action jeopardizes our remaining forces in Vietnam, I shall not hesitate to take strong and effective measures to deal with that situation.

This is not a threat. This is a statement of policy, which, as commander in chief of our armed forces, I am making in meeting my responsibility for the protection of American fighting men wherever they may be.

My fellow Americans, I am sure you can recognize from what I have said that we really only have two choices open to us if we want to end this war.

- I can order an immediate, precipitate withdrawal of all Americans from Vietnam without regard to the effects of that action.
- Or we can persist in our search for a just peace through a negotiated settlement if possible, or through continued implementation of our plan for Vietnamization if necessary — a plan in which we will withdraw all our forces from Vietnam on a schedule in accordance with our program, as the South Vietnamese become strong enough to defend their own freedom.

I have chosen this second course.

It is not the easy way.

It is the right way.

It is a plan which will end the war and serve the cause of peace — not just in Vietnam but in the Pacific and in the world.

In speaking of the consequences of a precipitate withdrawal, I mentioned that our allies would lose confidence in America.

Far more dangerous, we would lose confidence in ourselves. Oh, the immediate reaction would be a sense of relief that our men were coming home. But as we saw the consequences of what we had done, inevitable remorse and divisive recrimination would scar our spirit as a people.

We have faced other crises in our history and have become stronger by rejecting the easy way out and taking the right way in meeting our challenges. Our greatness as a nation has been our capacity to do what had to be done when we knew our course was right.

I recognize that some of my fellow citizens disagree with the plan for peace I have chosen. Honest and patriotic Americans have reached different conclusions as to how peace should be achieved.

In San Francisco a few weeks ago, I saw demonstrators carrying signs reading: "Lose in Vietnam, bring the boys home."

Well, one of the strengths of our free society is that any American has a right to reach that conclusion and to advocate that point of view. But as president of the United States, I would be untrue to my oath of office if I allowed the policy of this nation to be dictated by the minority who hold that point of view and who try to impose it on the nation by mounting demonstrations in the street.

For almost two hundred years, the policy of this nation has been made under our Constitution by those leaders in the Congress and the White House elected by all of the people. If a vocal minority, however fervent its cause, prevails over reason and the will of the majority, this nation has no future as a free society.

And now I would like to address a word, if I may, to the young people of this nation who are particularly concerned, and I understand why they are concerned, about this war.

I respect your idealism.

I share your concern for peace.

I want peace as much as you do.

There are powerful personal reasons I want to end this war. This week I will have to sign eighty-three letters to mothers, fathers, wives, and loved ones of men who have given their lives for America in Vietnam. It is very little satisfaction to me that this is only one-third as many letters as I signed the first week in office. There is nothing I want more than to see the day come when I do not have to write any of those letters.

— I want to end the war to save the lives of those brave young men in Vietnam.

— But I want to end it in a way which will increase the chance that their younger brothers and their sons will not have to fight in some future Vietnam someplace in the world.

— And I want to end the war for another reason. I want to end it so that the energy and dedication of you, our young people, now too often directed into bitter hatred against those responsible for the war, can be turned to the great challenges of peace, a better life for all Americans, a better life for all people on this earth.

I have chosen a plan for peace. I believe it will succeed.

If it does succeed, what the critics say now won't matter. If it does not succeed, anything I say then won't matter.

I know it may not be fashionable to speak of patriotism or national destiny these days. But I feel it is appropriate to do so on this occasion.

Two hundred years ago this nation was weak and poor. But even then, America was the hope of millions in the world. Today we have become the strongest and richest nation in the world. And the wheel of destiny has turned so that any hope the world has for the survival of peace and freedom will be determined by whether the American people have the moral stamina and the courage to meet the challenge of free world leadership.

Let historians not record that when America was the most powerful nation in the world we passed on the other side of the road and allowed the last hopes for peace and freedom of millions of people to be suffocated by the forces of totalitarianism.

And so tonight — to you, the great silent majority of my fellow Americans — I ask for your support.

I pledged in my campaign for the presidency to end the war in a way that we could win the peace. I have initiated a plan of action which will enable me to keep that pledge.

The more support I can have from the American people, the sooner that pledge can be redeemed; for the more divided we are at home, the less likely the enemy is to negotiate at Paris.

Let us be united for peace. Let us also be united against defeat. Because let us understand: North Vietnam cannot defeat or humiliate the United States. Only Americans can do that.

Fifty years ago, in this room and at this very desk, President Woodrow Wilson spoke words which caught the imagination of a war-weary world. He said: "This is the war to end war." His dream for peace after World War I was shattered on the hard realities of great power politics and Woodrow Wilson died a broken man.[3]

Tonight I do not tell you that the war in Vietnam is the war to end wars. But I do say this: I have initiated a plan which will end this war in a way that will bring us closer to that great goal to which Woodrow Wilson and every American president in our history has been dedicated — the goal of a just and lasting peace.

As president I hold the responsibility for choosing the best path to that goal and then leading the nation along it.

I pledge to you tonight that I shall meet this responsibility with all of the strength and wisdom I can command in accordance with your hopes, mindful of your concerns, sustained by your prayers.

Thank you and goodnight.

READING CRITICALLY

1. What reasons does Nixon say he might have used to justify ending the war?

2. What reasons does Nixon cite for U.S. involvement in Vietnam?

3. Why does Nixon reject "precipitate" (that is, immediate) withdrawal (p. 873)?

4. Why, according to Nixon, won't Hanoi negotiate?

5. Why won't Nixon give a timetable for withdrawal?

6. How does Nixon characterize the antiwar movement?

WRITING ANALYTICALLY

1. Nixon refers in his speech to three groups of Americans: first, the antiwar group — the "minority who hold that point of view" (p. 878), second, the "young people of this nation" (p. 879); and third, the "great silent majority of my fellow Americans" (p. 879). These three groups are his audience for this speech. In an essay, analyze how Nixon characterizes and addresses the different segments of his

[3]Wilson (1856–1924) won the Nobel Peace Prize in 1919 for his Fourteen Points, proposed in 1918 as the basis for world peace following World War I. Ironically, however, the ideals he articulated were largely ignored in the formulation of the Treaty of Versailles, which ended the war, and divisive nationalistic policies among the European powers prevented the kind of settlement Wilson envisioned. In addition, the Senate refused to ratify the treaty and thus prevented U.S. membership in the League of Nations, one of the Fourteen Points included in the treaty. — EDS.

audience. Does he try to appeal equally to all three, or does he seem to be deliberately antagonizing the antiwar segment? If so, what is his strategy?

2. Nixon devotes much of his speech to explaining why he won't follow three possible plans — immediate withdrawal, negotiation, and timed withdrawal on a fixed schedule. Write an essay analyzing Nixon's strategy for supporting "Vietnamization," focusing on the following questions about his treatment of the three possible plans. (a) One commentator, R. P. Newman, points out that though Nixon spends the most energy refuting the plan for immediate withdrawal, few critics of the war supported this plan. Why does he concentrate on it then? (b) Newman also notes that timed withdrawal on a fixed schedule was the most popular plan with members of Congress and other high-level critics. How does Nixon refute this plan? What counterarguments might you offer?

3. Write an essay comparing Nixon with Lyndon Johnson (p. 860) as presidential communicators. How do they use the authority of the office to gain credibility? What techniques of language do they use to dramatize their messages? How do they appeal to American ideals? What other methods do they use to gain acceptance?

Spiro T. Agnew

Parasites, Protesters, and the Press (1969)

Richard M. Nixon's vice president, Spiro T. Agnew (b. 1918), was a relentless critic of the antiwar movement. He became known as the spokesman for the true feelings of many in the Nixon administration — including Nixon himself — who could not be as blunt in expressing their opinions. Agnew's speeches were tremendously popular with the "silent majority," whom he courted. These were the people addressed by Nixon in his November 3, 1969 speech (see p. 871), the people who approved of the president's war policy and hated the young antiwar protesters not only for their politics but also for their appearance and lifestyle. Through Agnew, the Nixon administration thus signaled its policy in "the war at home," while the president himself maintained a somewhat more neutral tone in his own comments. Later the public would learn that Nixon ordered a massive CIA operation that collected thousands of files not only on the antiwar movement's leaders but on ordinary citizens who were suspected of antiwar sympathies.

Printed here are excerpts from three speeches Agnew delivered in 1969: one at the time of the October 15 Moratorium Day (see p. 871); one just before the president's "Vietnamization" address (see p. 871); and one at the time of the November 15 Moratorium Day demonstrations. Agnew was known for his colorful language and his lack of restraint. Nor did he hesitate

Spiro T. Agnew, _Collected Speeches of Spiro Agnew_ (New York: Audubon Books, 1971), 54–55 (October 19, 1969, speech), 70–76 (October 30, 1969, speech); _Vital Speeches of the Day_ 36 (December 15, 1969), 134–35 (November 20, 1969, speech).
    In the notes, Eds. = Patricia Bizzell and Bruce Herzberg.

to be divisive, for, as he said in a speech in the spring of 1970, "to penetrate the cacophony of seditious drivel emanating from the best-publicized clowns in our society and their fans in the fourth estate [the news media], yes, my friends, to penetrate that drivel, we need a cry of alarm, not a whisper."

In 1973, Agnew was charged with receiving payoffs for construction contracts when he was governor of Maryland (1966–68). He pleaded no contest to a charge of tax evasion associated with the kickback scheme and resigned the vice presidency in October 1973.

OCTOBER 19, 1969

New Orleans, Louisiana

SOMETIMES, IT APPEARS THAT WE ARE REACHING a time when our senses and our minds will no longer respond to moderate stimulation. We seem to be approaching an age of the gross. Persuasion through speeches and books is too often discarded for disruptive demonstrations aimed at bludgeoning the unconvinced into action.

The young — and by this I don't mean by any stretch of the imagination all the young, but I am talking about those who claim to speak for the young — at the zenith of physical power and sensitivity, overwhelm themselves with drugs and artificial stimulants. Subtlety is lost, and fine distinctions based on acute reasoning are carelessly ignored in a headlong jump to a predetermined conclusion. Life is visceral rather than intellectual, and the most visceral practitioners of life are those who characterize themselves as intellectuals.

Truth is "revealed" rather than logically proved, and the principal infatuations of today revolve around the social sciences, those subjects which can accommodate any opinion and about which the most reckless conjecture cannot be discredited.

Education is being redefined at the demand of the uneducated to suit the ideas of the uneducated. The student now goes to college to proclaim rather than to learn. The lessons of the past are ignored and obliterated in a contemporary antagonism known as the generation gap. A spirit of national masochism prevails, encouraged by an effete corps of impudent snobs who characterize themselves as intellectuals.

It is in this setting of dangerous oversimplification that the war in Vietnam achieves its greatest distortion.

The recent Vietnam Moratorium is a reflection of the confusion that exists in America today. Thousands of well-motivated young people, conditioned since childhood to respond to great emotional appeals, saw fit to demonstrate for peace. Most did not stop to consider that the leaders of the Moratorium had billed it as a massive public outpouring of sentiment against the foreign policy of the president of the United States. Most did not care to be reminded that the leaders of the Moratorium refused to disassociate themselves from the objective enunciated by the enemy in Hanoi.

If the Moratorium had any use whatever, it served as an emotional purgative for those who feel the need to cleanse themselves of their lack of ability to offer a constructive solution to the problem.

Unfortunately, we have not seen the end. The hard-core dissidents and professional anarchists within the so-called "peace movement" will continue to exacerbate the situation. November 15 is already planned — wilder, more violent, and equally barren of constructive result. . . .

OCTOBER 30, 1969

Harrisburg, Pennsylvania

A little over a week ago, I took a rather unusual step for a vice president. I said something. Particularly, I said something that was predictably unpopular with the people who would like to run the country without the inconvenience of seeking public office. I said I did not like some of the things I saw happening in this country. I criticized those who encouraged government by street carnival and suggested it was time to stop the carousel.

It appears that by slaughtering a sacred cow I triggered a holy war. I have no regrets. I do not intend to repudiate my beliefs, recant my words, or run and hide.

What I said before, I will say again. It is time for the preponderant majority, the responsible citizens of this country, to assert their rights. It is time to stop dignifying the immature actions of arrogant, reckless, inexperienced elements within our society. The reason is compelling. It is simply that their tantrums are insidiously destroying the fabric of American democracy.

By accepting unbridled protest as a way of life, we have tacitly suggested that the great issues of our times are best decided by posturing and shouting matches in the streets. America today is drifting toward Plato's classic definition of a degenerating democracy — a democracy that permits the voice of the mob to dominate the affairs of government.[1]

Last week I was lambasted for my lack of "mental and moral sensitivity." I say that any leader who does not perceive where persistent street struggles are going to lead this nation lacks mental acuity. And any leader who does not caution this nation on the danger of this direction lacks moral strength.

I believe in constitutional dissent. I believe in the people registering their views with their elected representatives, and I commend those people who care enough about their country to involve themselves in its great issues. I believe in legal protest within the constitutional limits of free

---

[1]See Book 8 of the *Republic*, where Plato describes the tendency of democracy toward mob rule. — EDS.

speech, including peaceful assembly and the right of petition. But I do not believe that demonstrations, lawful or unlawful, merit my approval or even my silence where the purpose is fundamentally unsound. In the case of the Vietnam Moratorium, the objective announced by the leaders — immediate unilateral withdrawal of all our forces from Vietnam — was not only unsound but idiotic.[2] The tragedy was that thousands who participated wanted only to show a fervent desire for peace, but were used by the political hustlers who ran the event.

It is worth remembering that our country's founding fathers wisely shaped a constitutional republic, not a pure democracy. The representative government they contemplated and skillfully constructed never intended that elected officials should decide crucial questions by counting the number of bodies cavorting in the streets. They recognized that freedom cannot endure dependent upon referendum every time part of the electorate desires it.

So great is the latitude of our liberty that only a subtle line divides use from abuse. I am convinced that our preoccupation with emotional demonstration, frequently crossing the line to civil disruption and even violence, could inexorably lead us across that line forever.

Ironically, it is neither the greedy nor the malicious, but the self-righteous who are guilty of history's worst atrocities. Society understands greed and malice and erects barriers of law to defend itself from these vices. But evil cloaked in emotional causes is well disguised and often undiscovered until it is too late.

We have just such a group of self-proclaimed saviors of the American soul at work today. Relentless in their criticism of intolerance in America, they themselves are intolerant of those who differ with their views. In the name of academic freedom, they destroy academic freedom. Denouncing violence, they seize and vandalize buildings of great universities. Fiercely expressing their respect for truth, they disavow the logic and discipline necessary to pursue truth.

They would have us believe that they alone know what is good for America; what is true and right and beautiful. They would have us believe that their reflective action is superior to our reflective action; that their revealed righteousness is more effective than our reason and experience.

Think about it. Small bands of students are allowed to shut down great universities. Small groups of dissidents are allowed to shout down political candidates. Small cadres of professional protesters are allowed to jeopardize the peace efforts of the president of the United States.

It is time to question the credentials of their leaders. And, if in questioning we disturb a few people, I say it is time for them to be disturbed. If,

---

[2]Although the original conception of the Moratorium was to hold monthly general strikes against "business as usual" until the United States withdrew from Vietnam, in fact the Vietnam Moratorium Committee, which organized the events, took a more moderate position: it sought either a negotiated peace or a U.S. commitment to withdraw. (Also see p. 871) (Also see p. 871) — EDS.

in challenging, we polarize the American people, I say it is time for a positive polarization.

It is time for a healthy in-depth examination of policies and a constructive realignment in this country. It is time to rip away the rhetoric and to divide on authentic lines. It is time to discard the fiction that in a country of 200 million people, everyone is qualified to quarterback the government. . . .

Now, we have among us, a glib, activist element who would tell us our values are lies, and I call them impudent. Because anyone who impugns a legacy of liberty and dignity that reaches back to Moses is impudent.

I call them snobs for most of them disdain to mingle with the masses who work for a living. They mock the common man's pride in his work, his family, and his country. It has also been said that I called them intellectuals. I did not. I said that they characterized themselves as intellectuals. No true intellectual, no truly knowledgeable person, would so despise democratic institutions.

America cannot afford to write off a whole generation for the decadent thinking of a few. America cannot afford to divide over their demagoguery or to be deceived by their duplicity or to let their license destroy liberty. We can, however, afford to separate them from our society — with no more regret than we should feel over discarding rotten apples from a barrel. . . .

I recognize that many of the people who participated in the past Moratorium Day were unaware that its sponsors sought immediate unilateral withdrawal. Perhaps many more had not considered the terrible consequences of immediate unilateral withdrawal.

I hope that all citizens who really want peace will take the time to read and reflect on the problem. I hope that they will take into consideration the impact of abrupt termination: that they will remember the more than three thousand innocent men, women, and children slaughtered after the Viet Cong captured Hue last year and the more than fifteen thousand doctors, nurses, teachers, and village leaders murdered by the Viet Cong during the war's early years. The only sin of these people was their desire to build their budding nation of South Vietnam.

Chanting "Peace Now" is no solution, if "Peace Now" is to permit a wholesale bloodbath. And saying that the president should understand the people's view is no solution. It is time for the people to understand the views of the president they elected to lead them.

First, foreign policy cannot be made in the streets.

Second, turning out a good crowd is not synonymous with turning out a good foreign policy.

Third, the test of a president cannot be reduced to a question of public relations. As the eighteenth-century jurist Edmund Burke wrote, "Your representative owes you not his industry only but his judgment; and he betrays instead of serving you, if he sacrifices it to your opinion."[3]

---

[3]Edmund Burke (1729–97) was a conservative British politician and author. Agnew is quoting from Burke's "Speech to the Electors of Bristol," November 3, 1774. — EDS.

Fourth, the impatience — the understandable frustration over this war — should be focused on the government that is stalling peace while continuing to threaten and invade South Vietnam — and that government's capital is not in Washington. It is in Hanoi.

This was not Richard Nixon's war — but it will be Richard Nixon's peace if we only let him make it.

Finally — and most important — regardless of the issue, it is time to stop demonstrating in the streets and start doing something constructive about our institutions. America must recognize the dangers of constant carnival. Americans must reckon with irresponsible leadership and reckless words. The mature and sensitive people of this country must realize that their freedom of protest is being exploited by avowed anarchists and Communists who detest everything about this country and want no destroy it.

This is a fact. These are the few — these are not necessarily leaders. But they prey upon the good intentions of gullible men everywhere. They pervert honest concern to something sick and rancid. They are vultures who sit in trees and watch lions battle, knowing that win, lose, or draw, they will be fed.

Abetting the merchants of hate are the parasites of passion. These are the men who value a cause purely for its political mileage. These are the politicians who temporize with the truth by playing both sides to their own advantage. They ooze sympathy for "the cause" but balance each sentence with equally reasoned reservations. Their interest is personal, not moral. They are ideological eunuchs whose most comfortable position is straddling the philosophical fence, soliciting votes from both sides. . . .

People cannot live in a state of perpetual electric shock. Tired of a convulsive society, they settle for an authoritarian society. . . .

Right now we must decide whether we will take the trouble to stave off a totalitarian state. Will we stop the wildness now before it is too late, before the witch-hunting and repression that are all too inevitable begin? . . .

NOVEMBER 20, 1969

Montgomery, Alabama

. . . Many, many strong, independent voices have been stilled in this country in recent years. And lacking the vigor of competition, some of those who have survived have — let's face it — grown fat and irresponsible.

I offer an example: When three hundred congressmen and fifty-nine senators signed a letter endorsing the president's policy in Vietnam, it was news — and it was big news. Even the *Washington Post* and the *Baltimore Sun* — scarcely house organs for the Nixon Administration — placed it prominently in their front pages.

Yet, the next morning the *New York Times*, which considers itself America's paper of record, did not carry a word. Why? Why?

If a theology student in Iowa should get up at [a] P.T.A. luncheon in Sioux City and attack the president's Vietnam policy, my guess is that you'd probably find it reported somewhere in the next morning's issue of the *New York Times*. But when three hundred congressmen endorse the president's Vietnam policy, the next morning it's apparently not considered news fit to print.

Just this Tuesday when the pope, the spiritual leader of half a billion Roman Catholics, applauded the president's effort to end the war in Vietnam and endorsed the way he was proceeding, that news was on page 11 of the *New York Times*. The same day a report about some burglars who broke into a souvenir shop at St. Peter's and stole $9,000 worth of stamps and currency — that story made page 3. How's that for news judgment?

A few weeks ago here in the South I expressed my views about street and campus demonstrations. Here's how the *New York Times* responded:

"He [that's me] lambasted the nation's youth in sweeping and ignorant generalizations, when it's clear to all perceptive observers that American youth today is far more imbued with idealism, a sense of service, and a deep humanitarianism than any generation in recent history, including particularly Mr. Agnew's generation."

That's what the *New York Times* said.

Now that seems a peculiar slur on a generation that brought America out of the Great Depression without resorting to the extremes of communism or fascism. That seems a strange thing to say about an entire generation that helped to provide greater material blessings and more personal freedom — out of that depression — for more people than any other nation in history. We have not finished the task by any means — but we are still on the job.

Just as millions of young Americans in this generation have shown valor and courage and heroism fighting the longest, and least popular, war in our history, so it was the young men of my generation who went ashore at Normandy under Eisenhower, and with MacArthur into the Philippines.

Yes, my generation, like the current generation, made its own share of great mistakes and great blunders. Among other things, we put too much confidence in Stalin and not enough in Winston Churchill.

But, whatever freedom exists today in Western Europe and Japan exists because hundreds of thousands of young men of my generation are lying in graves in North Africa and France and Korea and a score of islands in the Western Pacific.

This might not be considered enough of a sense of service or a deep humanitarianism for the perceptive critics who write editorials for the *New York Times*, but it's good enough for me. And I'm content to let history be the judge.

Now, let me talk briefly about the younger generation. I have not and I do not condemn this generation of young Americans. Like Edmund Burke,[4] I wouldn't know how to draw up an indictment against a whole

---

[4]Agnew is referring to a statement that Burke made as a member of the British Parliament in a famous speech urging conciliation with the American colonies: "I do not know the method of drawing up an indictment against an whole people" ("Second Speech on Conciliation with America: The Thirteen Resolutions," March 22, 1775). — EDS.

people. After all, they're our sons and daughters. They contain in their numbers many gifted, idealistic, and courageous young men and women.

But they also list in their numbers an arrogant few who march under the flags and portraits of dictators, who intimidate and harass university professors, who use gutter obscenities to shout down speakers with whom they disagree, who openly profess their belief in the efficacy of violence in a democratic society.

Oh, yes, the preceding generation had its own breed of losers and our generation dealt with them through our courts, our laws, and our system. The challenge is now for the new generation to put its house in order.

Today, Dr. Sydney Hook writes of "storm troopers" on the campus: that "fanaticism seems to be in the saddle." Arnold Beichman writes of "young Jacobins"[5] in our schools who "have cut down university administrators, forced curriculum changes, halted classes, closed campuses, and set a nationwide chill of fear all through the university establishment." Walter Laqueur writes in *Commentary* that "the cultural and political idiocies perpetuated with impunity in this permissive age have gone clearly beyond the borders of what is acceptable for any society, however liberally it may be constructed."

George Kennan has devoted a brief, cogent, and alarming book to the inherent dangers of what's taking place in our society and in our universities. Irving Kristol writes that our "radical students find it possible to be genuinely heartsick at the injustice and brutalities of American society, at the same time they are blandly approving of injustice and brutality committed in the name of 'the revolution.'" Or, as they like to call it, "the movement."

Now those are not names drawn at random from the letterhead of the Agnew-for-Vice-President committee. Those are men more eloquent and erudite than I, and they raise questions that I've tried to raise.

For we must remember that among this generation of Americans there are hundreds who have burned their draft cards and scores who have deserted to Canada and Sweden to sit out the war. To some Americans, a small minority, these are the true young men of conscience in the coming generation.

Voices are and will continue to be raised in the Congress and beyond asking that amnesty — a favorite word — amnesty should be provided for these young and misguided American boys. And they will be coming home one day from Sweden and from Canada and from a small minority of our citizens they will get a hero's welcome.

They are not our heroes. Many of our heroes will not be coming home; some are coming back in hospital ships, without limbs or eyes, with scars they shall carry for the rest of their lives.

Having witnessed firsthand the quiet courage of wives and parents receiving posthumously for their heroes Congressional Medals of Honor,

---

[5]The Jacobins were socialist leaders during the French Revolution of 1789. Other leftists are sometimes referred to as Jacobins. — EDS.

how am I to react when people say, "Stop speaking out, Mr. Agnew, stop raising your voice?"

Should I remain silent while what these heroes have done is vilified by some as "a dirty, immoral war" and criticized by others as no more than a war brought on by the chauvinistic anticommunism of Presidents Kennedy, Johnson, and Nixon?

These young men made heavy sacrifices so that a developing people on the rim of Asia might have a chance for freedom that they obviously will not have if the ruthless men who rule in Hanoi should ever rule over Saigon. What's dirty or immoral about that?

One magazine this week said that I'll go down as the "great polarizer" in American politics. Yet, when that large group of young Americans marched up Pennsylvania Avenue and Constitution Avenue last week, they sought to polarize the American people against the president's policy in Vietnam. And that was their right. And so it is my right, and my duty, to stand up and speak out for the values in which I believe. . . .

READING CRITICALLY

1. In the October 19 speech, what does Agnew mean by his statement that "education is being redefined at the demand of the uneducated to suit the ideas of the uneducated" (p. 882)?

2. What are Agnew's objections, in the October 19 speech, to antiwar demonstrations?

3. In the October 30 speech, Agnew explains his earlier comment about "impudent . . . snobs . . . who characterize themselves as intellectuals" (p. 883). Who is he talking about and what is his explanation?

4. What is "positive polarization" (p. 885), and how does Agnew defend it in the October 30 speech?

5. What does Agnew mean by "the dangers of constant carnival" in the October 30 speech (p. 886)?

6. Explain Agnew's statement, in the November 20 speech, that "to some Americans, a small minority," draft evaders will be considered "the true young men of conscience in the coming generation" (p. 888).

WRITING ANALYTICALLY

1. Are you familiar with any speakers or writers today who use an aggressive, attack-dog style similar to Agnew's? Talk-radio hosts such as Rush Limbaugh, for example, seem to like to take a similar approach and achieve great popularity with it. Write an essay describing this style and the reason commentators use it. How do you respond to it yourself?

2. Agnew's rhetoric is regarded as mainly emotional, appealing to those who already agree with his extreme views. Is this a fair assessment? Write an essay analyzing Agnew's arguments. What ideals does he appeal to? What logical (as opposed

to emotional) arguments does he make? Do you find them convincing? What is the effect of Agnew's elaborate and colorful language?

3. Agnew calls for "positive polarization" of the country along ideological lines (p. 885) — a very unusual position for a major political figure, even at the time of the Vietnam War. Few politicians want to be seen as divisive; indeed, they often attack their opponents as divisive. Johnson makes an impassioned plea for an end to divisiveness in his 1968 speech (p. 860), and Nixon calls for unity in his November 3 speech (p. 871). Write an essay about Agnew's dangerous move. What are the risks of calling for polarization, in general and in the particular case of Vietnam? Why does Agnew seem willing to take these risks? What does he mean by *positive* polarization. In your judgment, was Agnew's call justified or appropriate? Explain.

JOHN F. KERRY

Testimony before the U.S. Senate Foreign Relations Committee (April 22, 1971)

John F. Kerry (b. 1943) former lieutenant governor of Massachusetts (1982–84) and currently a Democratic U.S. senator from that state, fought in Vietnam, earning the Silver Star, the Bronze Star, and three Purple Hearts. A lieutenant in the navy — with fairly short hair and a fairly mild manner — Kerry became a credible and powerful representative of Vietnam Veterans Against the War (VVAW), an organization he headed for several years. In 1971 in Detroit, VVAW held hearings called the Winter Soldier Investigation to describe publicly the atrocities veterans had witnessed or participated in and to call for an end to the war. Later the same year, the group staged a week-long demonstration in Washington, performing skits, speaking to visitors, and attracting media attention. They also attracted the attention of the Senate. Toward the end of the week, John Kerry, speaking as the representative of VVAW, testified before the Senate Foreign Relations Committee in a nationally televised hearing. The following day, a group of veterans tossed their war medals on the steps of the Capitol, refusing, they said, to accept honors for committing crimes.

THANK YOU VERY MUCH, SENATOR FULBRIGHT, Senator Javits, Senator Symington, Senator Pell. I would like to say for the record, and also for the men behind me who are also wearing the uniform and their medals, that my sitting here is really symbolic. I am not here as John Kerry. I am here as

John F. Kerry, testimony before the U.S. Senate Foreign Relations Committee, *Congressional Record*, May 3, 1971, reprinted in *Vietnam and America: A Documented History*, ed. Marvin Gettleman et al. (New York: Grove Press, 1985), 453–58.
   In the notes, EDS. = Patricia Bizzell and Bruce Herzberg.

one member of the group of one thousand which is a small representation of a very much larger group of veterans in this country, and were it possible for all of them to sit at this table they would be here and have the same kind of testimony.

I would simply like to speak in very general terms. I apologize if my statement is general because I received notification yesterday you would hear me and I am afraid that because of the court injunction I was up most of the night and haven't had a great deal of time to prepare for this hearing.[1]

I would like to talk on behalf of all those veterans and say that several months ago in Detroit we had an investigation at which over 150 honorably discharged, and many very highly decorated, veterans testified to war crimes committed in Southeast Asia. These were not isolated incidents but crimes committed on a day-to-day basis with the full awareness of officers at all levels of command.

It is impossible to describe to you exactly what did happen in Detroit — the emotions in the room and the feelings of the men who were reliving their experiences in Vietnam. They relived the absolute horror of what this country, in a sense, made them do.

They told stories that at times they had personally raped, cut off ears, cut off heads, taped wires from portable telephones to human genitals and turned up the power, cut off limbs, blown up bodies, randomly shot at civilians, razed villages in fashion reminiscent of Genghis Khan,[2] shot cattle and dogs for fun, poisoned food stocks, and generally ravaged the countryside of South Vietnam in addition to the normal ravage of war and the normal and very particular ravaging which is done by the applied bombing power of this country.

We call this investigation the Winter Soldier Investigation. The term Winter Soldier is a play on words of Thomas Paine's in 1776 when he spoke of the Sunshine Patriots and summertime soldiers who deserted at Valley Forge because the going was rough.[3]

We who have come here to Washington have come here because we feel we have to be winter soldiers now. We could come back to this country, we could be quiet, we could hold our silence, we could not tell what went on in Vietnam, but we feel because of what threatens this country, not the Reds,[4] but the crimes which we are committing that threaten it, that we have to speak out.

I would like to talk to you a little bit about what the result is of the feelings these men carry with them after coming back from Vietnam. The

[1]The Supreme Court had issued an injunction against sleeping on the Mall in Washington, D.C., a move that was intended to disperse demonstrators. In protest, a group of more than eight hundred Vietnam veterans voted to stay on the Mall all night without sleeping. — EDS.

[2]The Mongol Genghis Khan (1162–1227), known for his ruthless cruelty, conquered large portions of Asia. — EDS.

[3]Thomas Paine (1737–1809), political philosopher and writer whose pamphlet *Common Sense* (1776) was a stirring argument for American independence. Kerry's reference is to an essay dated December 23, 1776, in Paine's periodical *Crisis.* — EDS.

[4]Communists. — EDS.

country doesn't know it yet but it has created a monster, a monster in the form of millions of men who have been taught to deal and to trade in violence and who are given the chance to die for the biggest nothing in history; men who have returned with a sense of anger and a sense of betrayal which no one has yet grasped.

As a veteran and one who feels this anger I would like to talk about it. We are angry because we feel we have been used in the worst fashion by the administration of this country.

In 1970 at West Point, Vice President Agnew said, "some glamorize the criminal misfits of society while our best men die in Asian rice paddies to preserve the freedom which most of those misfits abuse," and this was used as a rallying point for our effort in Vietnam.

But for us, as boys in Asia whom the country was supposed to support, his statement is a terrible distortion from which we can only draw a very deep sense of revulsion, and hence the anger of some of the men who are here in Washington today. It is a distortion because we in no way consider ourselves the best men of this country; because those he calls misfits were standing up for us in a way that nobody else in this country dared to; because so many who have died would have returned to this country to join the misfits in their efforts to ask for an immediate withdrawal from South Vietnam; because so many of those best men have returned as quadriplegics and amputees — and they lie forgotten in Veterans Administration Hospitals in this country which fly the flag which so many have chosen as their own personal symbol — and we cannot consider ourselves America's best men when we are ashamed of and hated for what we were called on to do in Southeast Asia.

In our opinion, and from our experience, there is nothing in South Vietnam which could happen that realistically threatens the United States of America. And to attempt to justify the loss of one American life in Vietnam, Cambodia, or Laos by linking such loss to the preservation of freedom, which those misfits supposedly abuse, is to us the height of criminal hypocrisy, and it is that kind of hypocrisy which we feel has torn this country apart.

We are probably much more angry than that, but I don't want to go into the foreign policy aspects because I am outclassed here. I know that all of you talk about every possible alternative for getting out of Vietnam. We understand that. We know you have considered the seriousness of the aspects to the utmost level and I am not going to try to dwell on that. But I want to relate to you the feeling that many of the men who have returned to this country express because we are probably angriest about all that we were told about Vietnam and about the mystical war against communism.

We found that not only was it a civil war, an effort by a people who had for years been seeking their liberation from any colonial influence whatsoever, but also we found that the Vietnamese whom we had enthusiastically molded after our own image were hard put to take up the fight against the threat we were supposedly saving them from.

We found most people didn't even know the difference between communism and democracy. They only wanted to work in rice paddies without helicopters strafing them and bombs with napalm burning their villages and tearing their country apart. They wanted everything to do with the war, particularly with this foreign presence of the United States of America, to leave them alone in peace, and they practiced the art of survival by siding with whichever military force was present at a particular time, be it Viet Cong, North Vietnamese, or American.

We found also that all too often American men were dying in those rice paddies for want of support from their allies. We saw firsthand how monies from American taxes were used for a corrupt dictatorial regime. We saw that many people in this country had a one-sided idea of who was kept free by our flag, and blacks provided the highest percentage of casualties. We saw Vietnam ravaged equally by American bombs and search and destroy missions, as well as by Viet Cong terrorism, and yet we listened while this country tried to blame all of the havoc on the Viet Cong.

We rationalized destroying villages in order to save them. We saw America lose her sense of morality as she accepted very coolly a My Lai[5] and refused to give up the image of American soldiers who hand out chocolate bars and chewing gum.

We learned the meaning of free fire zones, shooting anything that moves, and we watched while America placed a cheapness on the lives of Orientals.

We watched the United States falsification of body counts,[6] in fact the glorification of body counts. We listened while month after month we were told the back of the enemy was about to break. We fought using weapons against "Oriental human beings." We fought using weapons against those people which I do not believe this country would dream of using were we fighting in the European theater. We watched while men charged up hills because a general said that hill has to be taken, and after losing one platoon or two platoons they marched away to leave the hill for reoccupation by the North Vietnamese. We watched pride allow the most unimportant battles to be blown into extravaganzas, because we couldn't lose, and we couldn't retreat, and because it didn't matter how many American bodies were lost to prove that point, and so there were Hamburger Hills and Khe Sanhs and Hill 81s and Fire Base 6s, and so many others.

---

[5]On March 16, 1968, several hundred Vietnamese civilians in the village of My Lai were murdered, and many raped, by a squad of U.S. soldiers led by Lieutenant William Calley. The U.S. squad was never fired on in the raid. Official reports concealed the atrocity, but when it was leaked in 1969, twenty-five officers and enlisted men were charged with war crimes or military offenses. Of these twenty-five, only Calley was found guilty of the premeditated murder of at least twenty-two people. (The others were acquitted, or the charges against them were dismissed.) Calley was given a life sentence, which was subsequently reduced to twenty years and then to ten years. He was released on parole after serving three years. — EDS.

[6]Every week during the war the Pentagon reported the tally of "body counts"—enemy dead. Large numbers would give the impression that the U.S. forces were winning and thus bolster support for the war effort. As Kerry implies, many soldiers testified that the counts that came from the field were routinely inflated, often doubled and doubled again by the time they were officially published. — EDS.

Now we are told that the men who fought there must watch quietly while American lives are lost so that we can exercise the incredible arrogance of Vietnamizing the Vietnamese.[7]

Each day to facilitate the process by which the United States washes her hands of Vietnam someone has to give up his life so that the United States doesn't have to admit something that the entire world already knows, so that we can't say that we have made a mistake. Someone has to die so that President Nixon won't be, and these are his words, "the first president to lose a war."

We are asking Americans to think about that because how do you ask a man to be the last man to die in Vietnam? How do you ask a man to be the last man to die for a mistake? But we are trying to do that, and we are doing it with thousands of rationalizations, and if you read carefully the president's last speech to the people of this country, you can see that he says, and says clearly, "but the issue, gentlemen, is communism, and the question is whether or not we will leave that country to the Communists or whether or not we will try to give it hope to be a free people." But the point is they are not a free people now under us. They are not a free people, and we cannot fight communism all over the world. I think we should have learned that lesson by now.

But the problem of veterans goes beyond this personal problem, because you think about a poster in this country with a picture of Uncle Sam and the picture says "I want you." And a young man comes out of high school and says, "that is fine, I am going to serve my country," and he goes to Vietnam and he shoots and he kills and he does his job. Or maybe he doesn't kill. Maybe he just goes and he comes back, and when he gets back to this country he finds that he isn't really wanted, because the largest corps of unemployed in the country — it varies depending on who you get it from, the Veterans Administration says 15 percent and various other sources 22 percent — but the largest corps of unemployed in this country are veterans of this war, and of those veterans 33 percent of the unemployed are black. That means one out of every ten of the nation's unemployed is a veteran of Vietnam.

The hospitals across the country won't, or can't meet their demands. It is not a question of not trying; they haven't got the appropriations. A man recently died after he had a tracheotomy in California, not because of the operation but because there weren't enough personnel to clean the mucus out of his tube and he suffocated to death.

Another young man just died in a New York VA hospital the other day. A friend of mine was lying in a bed two beds away and tried to help him but he couldn't. He rang a bell and there was nobody there to service that man and so he died of convulsions.

[7]"Vietnamization" was President Nixon's policy of turning the responsibility for the war over to the South Vietnamese and slowly withdrawing U.S. troops. (See Nixon, "Vietnamization," p. 871). — EDS.

I understand 57 percent of all those entering the VA hospitals talk about suicide. Some 27 percent have tried, and they try because they come back to this country and they have to face what they did in Vietnam, and then they come back and find the indifference of a country that doesn't really care.

Suddenly we are faced with a very sickening situation in this country, because there is no moral indignation and, if there is, it comes from people who are almost exhausted by their past indignations, and I know that many of them are sitting in front of me. The country seems to have lain down and shrugged off something as serious as Laos,[8] just as we calmly shrugged off the loss of 700,000 lives in Pakistan, the so-called greatest disaster of all times.[9]

But we are here as veterans to say we think we are in the midst of the greatest disaster of all times now because they are still dying over there — not just Americans, but Vietnamese — and we are rationalizing leaving that country so that those people can go on killing each other for years to come.

Americans seem to have accepted the idea that the war is winding down, at least for Americans, and they have also allowed the bodies which were once used by a president for statistics to prove that we were winning that war, to be used as evidence against a man who followed orders and who interpreted those orders no differently than hundreds of other men in Vietnam.[10]

We veterans can only look with amazement on the fact that this country has been unable to see there is absolutely no difference between ground troops and a helicopter crew, and yet people have accepted a differentiation fed them by the administration.

No ground troops are in Laos so it is all right to kill Laotians by remote control. But believe me the helicopter crews fill the same body bags and they wreak the same kind of damage on the Vietnamese and Laotian countryside as anybody else, and the president is talking about allowing that to go on for many years to come. One can only ask if we will really be satisfied only when the troops march into Hanoi.

We are asking here in Washington for some action; action from the Congress of the United States of America which has the power to raise and maintain armies, and which by the Constitution also has the power to declare war.

We have come here, not to the president, because we believe that this body can be responsive to the will of the people, and we believe that the will of the people says that we should be out of Vietnam now.

[8]Beginning on February 8, 1971, South Vietnamese forces, covered by heavy U.S. bombing, invaded the politically neutral neighboring country of Laos in an attempt to cut off supply lines from North Vietnam. — EDS.

[9]On November 13, 1970, a cyclone in East Pakistan, now Bangladesh, caused this disaster. — EDS.

[10]Kerry is referring to Lieutenant William Calley. See note 5. — EDS.

We are here in Washington also to say that the problem of this war is not just a question of war and diplomacy. It is part and parcel of everything that we are trying as human beings to communicate to people in this country — the question of racism which is rampant in the military, and so many other questions such as the use of weapons; the hypocrisy in our taking umbrage at the Geneva Conventions and using that as justification for a continuation of this war when we are more guilty than any other body of violations of those Geneva Conventions; in the use of free fire zones, harassment interdiction fire,[11] search and destroy missions, the bombings, the torture of prisoners, the killing of prisoners, all accepted policy by many units in South Vietnam. That is what we are trying to say. It is part and parcel of everything.

An American Indian friend of mine who lives in the Indian Nation of Alcatraz put it to me very succinctly. He told me how as a boy on an Indian reservation he had watched television and he used to cheer the cowboys when they came in and shot the Indians, and then suddenly one day he stopped in Vietnam and he said "my God, I am doing to these people the very same thing that was done to my people," and he stopped. And that is what we are trying to say, that we think this thing has to end.

We are also here to ask, and we are here to ask vehemently, where are the leaders of our country? Where is the leadership? We are here to ask where are McNamara, Rostow, Bundy, Gilpatric[12] and so many others? Where are they now that we, the men whom they sent off to war, have returned? These are commanders who have deserted their troops, and there is no more serious crime in the laws of war. The army says they never leave their wounded. The marines say they never leave even their dead. These men have left all the casualties and retreated behind a pious shield of public rectitude. They have left the real stuff of their reputations bleaching behind them in the sun in this country.

Finally, this administration has done us the ultimate dishonor. They have attempted to disown us and the sacrifices we made for this country. In their blindness and fear they have tried to deny that we are veterans or that we served in Nam. We do not need their testimony. Our own scars and stumps of limbs are witness enough for others and for ourselves.

We wish that a merciful God could wipe away our own memories of that service as easily as this administration has wiped away their memories of us. But all that they have done and all that they can do by this denial is to make more clear than ever our own determination to undertake one last mission — to search out and destroy the last vestige of this barbaric war, to pacify our own hearts, to conquer the hate and the fear that have driven

[11]The practice of firing rounds of artillery into an area that U.S. forces thought the enemy might be interested in, so as to prevent the enemy from taking it. — EDS.

[12]Kerry is referring to Robert S. McNamara, secretary of defense from 1961 to 1968; Walt W. Rostow, national security adviser from 1966 to 1969; McGeorge Bundy, national security adviser from 1961 to 1966; and Roswell L. Gilpatric, deputy secretary of defense from 1961 to 1964. — EDS.

this country these last ten years and more, so when thirty years from now our brothers go down the street without a leg, without an arm, or a face, and small boys ask why, we will be able to say "Vietnam" and not mean a desert, not a filthy obscene memory, but mean instead the place where America finally turned and where soldiers like us helped it in the turning.

Thank you.

READING CRITICALLY

1. According to Kerry, in what ways were veterans received when they returned home?

2. What is Kerry's perception of the political situation in Vietnam and of U.S. grounds for the war?

3. What is Kerry's complaint about day-to-day military strategy?

4. What does he mean by the phrase "molded after our own image" (p. 892)?

5. What does he mean when he asks, "How do you ask a man to be the last man to die for a mistake" (p. 894)?

WRITING ANALYTICALLY

1. Underline all of Kerry's uses of the word *crime* and its various forms and synonyms. Clearly, criminality is a major issue for him, a central idea in his attempt to account for the war and the veterans' experience there. Write an essay analyzing Kerry's use of the theme of criminality. Does he conclude that the soldiers are criminals? How does the theme of criminality help him answer the question "How do you ask a man to be the last man to die for a mistake?"

2. In a rather vague paragraph on page 896, Kerry discusses the "problem of this war" that goes beyond "war and diplomacy" (and, on page 894, "beyond this personal problem"). The problem is "part and parcel of everything" (p. 896). This feeling that the war concerned larger issues was echoed by other antiwar speakers. Write an essay investigating the attempts of Kerry, Paul Potter (p. 845), and Martin Luther King Jr. (p. 850) to identify the larger social issues that they felt were reflected in the war. What do they see as the larger problems? Why do they feel that they must speak about them in their arguments against the war? Given the differences in their positions — veteran, student leader, civil rights leader — what differences do you find in their identification of problems?

VETERANS REMEMBER

TIM O'BRIEN

"On the Rainy River" (1990)

Tim O'Brien (b. 1946) was drafted into the army in 1968 upon graduating from Macalester College in St. Paul, Minnesota. He served in Vietnam from 1968 to 1970, rose to the rank of sergeant, and won a Purple Heart. O'Brien has drawn extensively on his Vietnam experiences in his numerous books and stories. His first book, *If I Die in a Combat Zone, Box Me Up and Ship Me Home* (1973), blends fiction and autobiography, and his novel *Going after Cacciato* (1978) — about a soldier who deserts and is pursued by his comrades — won the National Book Award. O'Brien's most recent novel is *In the Lake of the Woods* (1994). The story printed here is from his 1990 collection *The Things They Carried*. In "On the Rainy River," O'Brien tells the story of being drafted and his subsequent temptation to escape to Canada rather than go to Vietnam.

THIS IS ONE STORY I'VE NEVER TOLD BEFORE. Not to anyone. Not to my parents, not to my brother or sister, not even to my wife. To go into it, I've always thought, would only cause embarrassment for all of us, a sudden need to be elsewhere, which is the natural response to a confession. Even now, I'll admit, the story makes me squirm. For more than twenty years I've had to live with it, feeling the shame, trying to push it away, and so by this act of remembrance, by putting the facts down on paper, I'm hoping to relieve at least some of the pressure on my dreams. Still, it's a hard story to tell. All of us, I suppose, like to believe that in a moral emergency we will behave like the heroes of our youth, bravely and forthrightly, without thought of personal loss or discredit. Certainly that was my conviction back in the summer of 1968. Tim O'Brien: a secret hero. The Lone Ranger. If the stakes ever became high enough — if the evil were evil enough, if the good were good enough — I would simply tap a secret reservoir of courage that had been accumulating inside me over the years. Courage, I seemed to think, comes to us in finite quantities, like an inheritance, and by being frugal and stashing it away and letting it earn interest, we steadily increase our moral capital in preparation for that day when the account must be drawn down. It was a comforting theory. It dispensed with all

Tim O'Brien, "On the Rainy River," in *The Things They Carried* (Boston: Houghton Mifflin, 1990), 43–63.
In the notes, EDS. = Patricia Bizzell and Bruce Herzberg.

those bothersome little acts of daily courage; it offered hope and grace to the repetitive coward; it justified the past while amortizing the future.

In June of 1968, a month after graduating from Macalester College, I was drafted to fight a war I hated. I was twenty-one years old. Young, yes, and politically naive, but even so the American war in Vietnam seemed to me wrong. Certain blood was being shed for uncertain reasons. I saw no unity of purpose, no consensus on matters of philosophy or history or law. The very facts were shrouded in uncertainty: Was it a civil war? A war of national liberation or simple aggression? Who started it, and when, and why? What really happened to the USS *Maddox* on that dark night in the Gulf of Tonkin?[1] Was Ho Chi Minh a Communist stooge, or a nationalist savior, or both, or neither? What about the Geneva accords?[2] What about SEATO[3] and the Cold War? What about dominoes?[4] America was divided on these and a thousand other issues, and the debate had spilled out across the floor of the United States Senate and into the streets, and smart men in pinstripes could not agree on even the most fundamental matters of public policy. The only certainty that summer was moral confusion. It was my view then, and still is, that you don't make war without knowing why. Knowledge, of course, is always imperfect, but it seemed to me that when a nation goes to war it must have reasonable confidence in the justice and imperative of its cause. You can't fix your mistakes. Once people are dead, you can't make them undead.

In any case those were my convictions, and back in college I had taken a modest stand against the war. Nothing radical, no hothead stuff, just ringing a few doorbells for Gene McCarthy,[5] composing a few tedious, uninspired editorials for the campus newspaper. Oddly, though, it was almost entirely an intellectual activity. I brought some energy to it, of course, but it was the energy that accompanies almost any abstract endeavor; I felt no personal danger; I felt no sense of an impending crisis in my life. Stupidly, with a kind of smug removal that I can't begin to fathom, I assumed that the problems of killing and dying did not fall within my special province.

The draft notice arrived on June 17, 1968. It was a humid afternoon, I remember, cloudy and very quiet, and I'd just come in from a round of golf. My mother and father were having lunch out in the kitchen. I remember opening up the letter, scanning the first few lines, feeling the blood go thick behind my eyes. I remember a sound in my head. It wasn't

---

[1]A questionable confrontation between the U.S. destroyer *Maddox* and North Vietnamese gunboats led to the Tonkin Gulf Resolution in 1964. (See p. 801.) — EDS.

[2]Many of the provisions of the Geneva accords of 1954 were ignored or violated during the course of the war. (See p. 800.) — EDS.

[3]The Southeast Asia Treaty Organization (SEATO) was a Western and Asian alliance created in 1954 in part to protect Southeast Asia. It was sometimes invoked as an excuse for U.S. intervention in Vietnam. — EDS.

[4]The "domino theory" held that if Vietnam "fell" to the Communists, other Southeast Asian countries would follow. — EDS.

[5]Eugene McCarthy (b. 1916), a Democratic antiwar senator from Minnesota (1959–71), ran unsuccessfully for his party's nomination for president in 1968, with much support from young people, particularly college students. — EDS.

thinking, it was just a silent howl. A million things all at once — I was too *good* for this war. Too smart, too compassionate, too everything. It couldn't happen. I was above it. I had the world dicked — Phi Beta Kappa and summa cum laude and president of the student body and a full-ride scholarship for grad studies at Harvard. A mistake, maybe — a foul-up in the paperwork. I was no soldier. I hated Boy Scouts. I hated camping out. I hated dirt and tents and mosquitoes. The sight of blood made me queasy, and I couldn't tolerate authority, and I didn't know a rifle from a slingshot. I was a *liberal,* for Christ sake: If they needed fresh bodies, why not draft some back-to-the-stone-age hawk? Or some dumb jingo in his hard hat and Bomb Hanoi button? Or one of LBJ's pretty daughters? Or Westmoreland's[6] whole family — nephews and nieces and baby grandson? There should be a law, I thought. If you support a war, if you think it's worth the price, that's fine, but you have to put your own life on the line. You have to head for the front and hook up with an infantry unit and help spill the blood. And you have to bring along your wife, or your kids, or your lover. A *law,* I thought.

I remember the rage in my stomach. Later it burned down to a smoldering self-pity, then to numbness. At dinner that night my father asked what my plans were.

"Nothing," I said. "Wait."

I spent the summer of 1968 working in an Armour meat-packing plant in my hometown of Worthington, Minnesota. The plant specialized in pork products, and for eight hours a day I stood on a quarter-mile assembly line — more properly, a disassembly line — removing blood clots from the necks of dead pigs. My job title, I believe, was Declotter. After slaughter, the hogs were decapitated, split down the length of the belly, pried open, eviscerated, and strung up by the hind hocks on a high conveyer belt. Then gravity took over. By the time a carcass reached my spot on the line, the fluids had mostly drained out, everything except for thick clots of blood in the neck and upper chest cavity. To remove the stuff, I used a kind of water gun. The machine was heavy, maybe eighty pounds, and was suspended from the ceiling by a heavy rubber cord. There was some bounce to it, an elastic up-and-down give, and the trick was to maneuver the gun with your whole body, not lifting with the arms, just letting the rubber cord do the work for you. At one end was a trigger; at the muzzle end was a small nozzle and a steel roller brush. As a carcass passed by, you'd lean forward and swing the gun up against the clots and squeeze the trigger, all in one motion, and the brush would whirl and water would come shooting out and you'd hear a quick splattering sound as the clots dissolved into a fine red mist. It was not pleasant work. Goggles were a necessity, and a rubber apron, but even so it was like standing for eight hours a day under a lukewarm blood-shower. At night I'd go home smelling of

---

[6]General William Westmoreland (b. 1914) commanded U.S. forces in Vietnam from 1964 to 1968. — EDS.

pig. I couldn't wash it out. Even after a hot bath, scrubbing hard, the stink was always there — like old bacon, or sausage, a dense greasy pig-stink that soaked deep into my skin and hair. Among other things, I remember, it was tough getting dates that summer. I felt isolated; I spent a lot of time alone. And there was also that draft notice tucked away in my wallet.

In the evenings I'd sometimes borrow my father's car and drive aimlessly around town, feeling sorry for myself, thinking about the war and the pig factory and how my life seemed to be collapsing toward slaughter. I felt paralyzed. All around me the options seemed to be narrowing, as if I were hurtling down a huge black funnel, the whole world squeezing in tight. There was no happy way out. The government had ended most graduate school deferments; the waiting lists for the National Guard and Reserves were impossibly long; my health was solid; I didn't qualify for CO status[7] — no religious grounds, no history as a pacifist. Moreover, I could not claim to be opposed to war as a matter of general principle. There were occasions, I believed, when a nation was justified in using military force to achieve its ends, to stop a Hitler or some comparable evil, and I told myself that in such circumstances I would've willingly marched off to the battle. The problem, though, was that a draft board did not let you choose your war.

Beyond all this, or at the very center, was the raw fact of terror. I did not want to die. Not ever. But certainly not then, not there, not in a wrong war. Driving up Main Street, past the courthouse and the Ben Franklin store, I sometimes felt the fear spreading inside me like weeds. I imagined myself dead. I imagined myself doing things I could not do — charging an enemy position, taking aim at another human being.

At some point in mid-July I began thinking seriously about Canada. The border lay a few hundred miles north, an eight-hour drive. Both my conscience and my instincts were telling me to make a break for it, just take off and run like hell and never stop. In the beginning the idea seemed purely abstract, the word Canada printing itself out in my head; but after a time I could see particular shapes and images, the sorry details of my own future — a hotel room in Winnipeg, a battered old suitcase, my father's eyes as I tried to explain myself over the telephone. I could almost hear his voice, and my mother's. Run, I'd think. Then I'd think, Impossible. Then a second later I'd think, *Run*.

It was kind of schizophrenia. A moral split. I couldn't make up my mind. I feared the war, yes, but I also feared exile. I was afraid of walking away from my own life, my friends and my family, my whole history, everything that mattered to me. I feared losing the respect of my parents. I feared the law. I feared ridicule and censure. My hometown was a conservative little spot on the prairie, a place where tradition counted, and it was easy to imagine people sitting around a table down at the old Gobbler Café on Main Street, coffee cups poised, the conversation slowly zeroing in on the young O'Brien kid, how the damned sissy had taken off for Canada.

[7]Conscientious objector. — EDS.

At night, when I couldn't sleep, I'd sometimes carry on fierce arguments with those people. I'd be screaming at them, telling them how much I detested their blind, thoughtless, automatic acquiescence to it all, their simple-minded patriotism, their prideful ignorance, their love-it-or-leave-it platitudes, how they were sending me off to fight a war they didn't understand and didn't want to understand. I held them responsible. By God, yes, I *did*. All of them — I held them personally and individually responsible — the polyestered Kiwanis boys, the merchants and farmers, the pious churchgoers, the chatty housewives, the PTA and the Lions club and the Veterans of Foreign Wars and the fine upstanding gentry out at the country club. They didn't know Bao Dai[8] from the man in the moon. They didn't know history. They didn't know the first thing about Diem's[9] tyranny, or the nature of Vietnamese nationalism, or the long colonialism of the French — this was all too damned complicated, it required some reading — but no matter, it was a war to stop the Communists, plain and simple, which was how they liked things, and you were a treasonous pussy if you had second thoughts about killing or dying for plain and simple reasons.

I was bitter, sure. But it was so much more than that. The emotions went from outrage to terror to bewilderment to guilt to sorrow and then back again to outrage. I felt a sickness inside me. Real disease.

Most of this I've told before, or at least hinted at, but what I have never told is the full truth. How I cracked. How at work one morning, standing on the pig line, I felt something break open in my chest. I don't know what it was. I'll never know. But it was real, I know that much, it was a physical rupture — a cracking-leaking-popping feeling. I remember dropping my water gun. Quickly, almost without thought, I took off my apron and walked out of the plant and drove home. It was midmorning, I remember, and the house was empty. Down in my chest there was still that leaking sensation, something very warm and precious spilling out, and I was covered with blood and hog-stink, and for a long while I just concentrated on holding myself together. I remember taking a hot shower. I remember packing a suitcase and carrying it out to the kitchen, standing very still for a few minutes, looking carefully at the familiar objects all around me. The old chrome toaster, the telephone, the pink and white Formica on the kitchen counters. The room was full of bright sunshine. Everything sparkled. My house, I thought. My life. I'm not sure how long I stood there, but later I scribbled out a short note to my parents.

What it said, exactly, I don't recall now. Something vague. Taking off, will call, love Tim.

I drove north.

It's a blur now, as it was then, and all I remember is a sense of high velocity and the feel of the steering wheel in my hands. I was riding on

---

[8]Bao Dai (b.1913) was the last emperor of Vietnam. (See note 3, p. 806.) — EDS.
[9]Ngo Dinh Diem was the South Vietnamese leader from 1955 to 1963. (See pp. 799–800.) — EDS.

adrenaline. A giddy feeling, in a way, except there was the dreamy edge of impossibility to it — like running a dead-end maze — no way out — it couldn't come to a happy conclusion and yet I was doing it anyway because it was all I could think of to do. It was pure flight, fast and mindless. I had no plan. Just hit the border at high speed and crash through and keep on running. Near dusk I passed through Bemidji, then turned northeast toward International Falls. I spent the night in the car behind a closed-down gas station a half mile from the border. In the morning, after gassing up, I headed straight west along the Rainy River, which separates Minnesota from Canada, and which for me separated one life from another. The land was mostly wilderness. Here and there I passed a motel or bait shop, but otherwise the country unfolded in great sweeps of pine and birch and sumac. Though it was still August, the air already had the smell of October, football season, piles of yellow-red leaves, everything crisp and clean. I remember a huge blue sky. Off to my right was the Rainy River, wide as a lake in places, and beyond the Rainy River was Canada.

For a while I just drove, not aiming at anything, then in the late morning I began looking for a place to lie low for a day or two. I was exhausted, and scared sick, and around noon I pulled into an old fishing resort called the Tip Top Lodge. Actually it was not a lodge at all, just eight or nine tiny yellow cabins clustered on a peninsula that jutted northward into the Rainy River. The place was in sorry shape. There was a dangerous wooden dock, an old minnow tank, a flimsy tar paper boathouse along the shore. The main building, which stood in a cluster of pines on high ground, seemed to lean heavily to one side, like a cripple, the roof sagging toward Canada. Briefly, I thought about turning around, just giving up, but then I got out of the car and walked up to the front porch.

The man who opened the door that day is the hero of my life. How do I say this without sounding sappy? Blurt it out — the man saved me. He offered exactly what I needed, without questions, without any words at all. He took me in. He was there at the critical time — a silent, watchful presence. Six days later, when it ended, I was unable to find a proper way to thank him, and I never have, and so, if nothing else, this story represents a small gesture of gratitude twenty years overdue.

Even after two decades I can close my eyes and return to that porch at the Tip Top Lodge. I can see the old guy staring at me. Elroy Berdahl: eighty-one years old, skinny and shrunken and mostly bald. He wore a flannel shirt and brown work pants. In one hand, I remember, he carried a green apple, a small paring knife in the other. His eyes had the bluish gray color of a razor blade, the same polished shine, and as he peered up at me I felt a strange sharpness, almost painful, a cutting sensation, as if his gaze were somehow slicing me open. In part, no doubt, it was my own sense of guilt, but even so I'm absolutely certain that the old man took one look and went right to the heart of things — a kid in trouble. When I asked for a room, Elroy made a little clicking sound with his tongue. He nodded, led me out to one of the cabins, and dropped a key in my hand. I remember smiling at him. I also remember wishing I hadn't. The old man shook his head as if to tell me it wasn't worth the bother.

"Dinner at five-thirty," he said. "You eat fish?"

"Anything," I said.

Elroy grunted and said, "I'll bet."

We spent six days together at the Tip Top Lodge. Just the two of us. Tourist season was over, and there were no boats on the river, and the wilderness seemed to withdraw into a great permanent stillness. Over those six days Elroy Berdahl and I took most of our meals together. In the mornings we sometimes went out on long hikes into the woods, and at night we played Scrabble or listened to records or sat reading in front of his big stone fireplace. At times I felt the awkwardness of an intruder, but Elroy accepted me into his quiet routine without fuss or ceremony. He took my presence for granted, the same way he might've sheltered a stray cat — no wasted sighs or pity — and there was never any talk about it. Just the opposite. What I remember more than anything is the man's willfull, almost ferocious silence. In all that time together, all those hours, he never asked the obvious questions: Why was I there? Why alone? Why so preoccupied? If Elroy was curious about any of this, he was careful never to put it into words.

My hunch, though, is that he already knew. At least the basics. After all, it was 1968, and guys were burning draft cards, and Canada was just a boat ride away. Elroy Berdahl was no hick. His bedroom, I remember, was cluttered with books and newspapers. He killed me at the Scrabble board, barely concentrating, and on those occasions when speech was necessary he had a way of compressing large thoughts into small, cryptic packets of language. One evening, just at sunset, he pointed up at an owl circling over the violet-lighted forest to the west.

"Hey, O'Brien," he said. "There's Jesus."

The man was sharp — he didn't miss much. Those razor eyes. Now and then he'd catch me staring out at the river, at the far shore, and I could almost hear the tumblers clicking in his head. Maybe I'm wrong, but I doubt it.

One thing for certain, he knew I was in desperate trouble. And he knew I couldn't talk about it. The wrong word — or even the right word — and I would've disappeared. I was wired and jittery. My skin felt too tight. After supper one evening I vomited and went back to my cabin and lay down for a few moments and then vomited again; another time, in the middle of the afternoon, I began sweating and couldn't shut it off. I went through whole days feeling dizzy with sorrow. I couldn't sleep; I couldn't lie still. At night I'd toss around in bed, half awake, half dreaming, imagining how I'd sneak down to the beach and quietly push one of the old man's boats out into the river and start paddling my way toward Canada. There were times when I thought I'd gone off the psychic edge. I couldn't tell up from down, I was just falling, and late in the night I'd lie there watching weird pictures spin through my head. Getting chased by the Border Patrol — helicopters and searchlights and barking dogs — I'd be crashing through the woods, I'd be down on my hands and knees — people shouting out my name — the law closing in on all sides — my hometown draft board and the FBI and the Royal Canadian Mounted Police. It all seemed crazy and impossible. Twenty-one years old, an ordinary kid with all the ordinary dreams and ambitions, and all I wanted was to live the life I was born to — a mainstream life — I loved baseball and hamburgers and cherry Cokes — and now I was off on the margins of exile, leaving my country forever, and it seemed so impossible and terrible and sad.

I'm not sure how I made it through those six days. Most of it I can't remember. On two or three afternoons, to pass some time, I helped Elroy get the place ready for winter, sweeping down the cabins and hauling in the boats, little chores that kept my body moving. The days were cool and bright. The nights were very dark. One morning the old man showed me how to split and stack firewood, and for several hours we just worked in silence out behind his house. At one point, I remember, Elroy put down his maul and looked at me for a long time, his lips drawn as if framing a difficult question, but then he shook his head and went back to work. The man's self-control was amazing. He never pried. He never put me in a position that required lies or denials. To an extent, I suppose, his reticence was typical of that part of Minnesota, where privacy still held value, and even if I'd been walking around with some horrible deformity — four arms and three heads — I'm sure the old man would've talked about everything except those extra arms and heads. Simple politeness was part of it. But even more than that, I think, the man understood that words were insufficient. The problem had gone beyond discussion. During that long summer I'd been over and over the various arguments, all the pros and cons, and it was no longer a question that could be decided by an act of pure reason. Intellect had come up against emotion. My conscience told me to run, but some irrational and powerful force was resisting, like a weight pushing me toward the war. What it came down to, stupidly, was a sense of shame. Hot, stupid shame. I did not want people to think badly of me. Not my parents, not my brother and sister, not even the folks down at the Gobbler Café. I was ashamed to be there at the Tip Top Lodge. I was ashamed of my conscience, ashamed to be doing the right thing.

Some of this Elroy must've understood. Not the details, of course, but the plain fact of crisis.

Although the old man never confronted me about it, there was one occasion when he came close to forcing the whole thing out into the open. It was early evening, and we'd just finished supper, and over coffee and dessert I asked him about my bill, how much I owed so far. For a long while the old man squinted down at the tablecloth.

"Well, the basic rate," he said, "is fifty bucks a night. Not counting meals. This makes four nights, right?"

I nodded. I had three hundred and twelve dollars in my wallet.

Elroy kept his eyes on the tablecloth. "Now that's an on-season price. To be fair, I suppose we should knock it down a peg or two." He leaned back in his chair. "What's a reasonable number, you figure?"

"I don't know," I said. "Forty?"

"Forty's good. Forty a night. Then we tack on food — say another hundred? Two hundred sixty total?"

"I guess."

He raised his eyebrows. "Too much?"

"No, that's fair. It's fine. Tomorrow, though . . . I think I'd better take off tomorrow."

Elroy shrugged and began clearing the table. For a time he fussed with the dishes, whistling to himself as if the subject had been settled. After a second he slapped his hands together.

"You know what we forgot?" he said. "We forgot wages. Those odd jobs you done. What we have to do, we have to figure out what your time's worth. Your last job — how much did you pull in an hour?"

"Not enough," I said.

"A bad one?"

"Yes. Pretty bad."

Slowly then, without intending any long sermon, I told him about my days at the pig plant. It began as a straight recitation of the facts, but before I could stop myself I was talking about the blood clots and the water gun and how the smell had soaked into my skin and how I couldn't wash it away. I went on for a long time. I told him about wild hogs squealing in my dreams, the sounds of butchery, slaughterhouse sounds, and how I'd sometimes wake up with that greasy pig-stink in my throat.

When I was finished, Elroy nodded at me.

"Well, to be honest," he said, "when you first showed up here, I wondered about all that. The aroma, I mean. Smelled like you was awful damned fond of pork chops." The old man almost smiled. He made a snuffling sound, then sat down with a pencil and a piece of paper. "So what'd this crud job pay? Ten bucks an hour? Fifteen?"

"Less."

Elroy shook his head. "Let's make it fifteen. You put in twenty-five hours here, easy. That's three hundred seventy-five bucks total wages. We subtract the two hundred sixty for food and lodging, I still owe you a hundred and fifteen."

He took four fifties out of his shirt pocket and laid them on the table.

"Call it even." he said.

"No."

"Pick it up. Get yourself a haircut."

The money lay on the table for the rest of the evening. It was still there when I went back to my cabin. In the morning, though, I found an envelope tacked to my door. Inside were the four fifties and a two-word note that said EMERGENCY FUND.

The man knew.

Looking back after twenty years, I sometimes wonder if the events of that summer didn't happen in some other dimension, a place where your life exists before you've lived it, and where it goes afterward. None of it ever seemed real. During my time at the Tip Top Lodge I had the feeling that I'd slipped out of my own skin, hovering a few feet away while some poor yo-yo with my name and face tried to make his way toward a future he didn't understand and didn't want. Even now I can see myself as I was then. It's like watching an old home movie: I'm young and tan and fit. I've got hair — lots of it. I don't smoke or drink. I'm wearing faded blue jeans and a white polo shirt. I can see myself sitting on Elroy Berdahl's dock near dusk one evening, the sky a bright shimmering pink, and I'm finishing up a letter to my parents that tells what I'm about to do and why I'm doing it and how sorry I am that I'd never found the courage to talk to them about it. I ask them not to be angry. I try to explain some of my feelings, but there aren't enough words, and so I just say that it's a thing that has to be done. At the end of the letter I talk about the vacations we used to take up in this north country, at a place called Whitefish Lake, and how the scenery here reminds me of those good times. I tell them I'm fine. I tell them I'll write again from Winnipeg or Montreal or wherever I end up.

On my last full day, the sixth day, the old man took me out fishing on the Rainy River. The afternoon was sunny and cold. A stiff breeze came in from the north, and I remember how the little fourteen-foot boat made sharp rocking motions as we pushed off from the dock. The current was fast. All around us, I remember, there was a vastness to the world, an unpeopled rawness, just the trees and the sky and the water reaching out toward nowhere. The air had the brittle scent of October.

For ten or fifteen minutes Elroy held a course upstream, the river choppy and silver-gray, then he turned straight north and put the engine on full throttle. I felt the bow lift beneath me. I remember the wind in my ears, the sound of the old outboard Evinrude. For a time I didn't pay attention to anything, just feeling the cold spray against my face, but then it occurred to me that at some point we must've passed into Canadian waters, across that dotted line between two different worlds, and I remember a sudden tightness in my chest as I looked up and watched the far shore come at me. This wasn't a daydream. It was tangible and real. As we came in toward land, Elroy cut the engine, letting the boat fishtail lightly about twenty yards off shore. The old man didn't look at me or speak. Bending down, he opened up his tackle box and busied himself with a bobber and a piece of wire leader, humming to himself, his eyes down.

It struck me then that he must've planned it. I'll never be certain, of course, but I think he meant to bring me up against the realities, to guide me across the river and to take me to the edge and to stand a kind of vigil as I chose a life for myself.

I remember staring at the old man, then at my hands, then at Canada. The shoreline was dense with brush and timber. I could see tiny red berries on the bushes. I could see a squirrel up in one of the birch trees, a big crow looking at me from a boulder along the river. That close — twenty yards — and I could see the delicate latticework of the leaves, the texture of the soil, the browned needles beneath the pines, the configurations of geology and human history. Twenty yards. I could've done it. I could've jumped and started swimming for my life. Inside me, in my chest, I felt a terrible squeezing pressure. Even now, as I write this, I can still feel that tightness. And I want you to feel it — the wind coming off the river, the waves, the silence, the wooded frontier. You're at the bow of a boat on the Rainy River. You're twenty-one years old, you're scared, and there's a hard squeezing pressure in your chest.

What would you do?

Would you jump? Would you feel pity for yourself? Would you think about your family and your childhood and your dreams and all you're leaving behind? Would it hurt? Would it feel like dying? Would you cry, as I did?

I tried to swallow it back. I tried to smile, except I was crying.

Now, perhaps, you can understand why I've never told this story before. It's not just the embarrassment of tears. That's part of it, no doubt, but what embarrasses me much more, and always will, is the paralysis that took my heart. A moral freeze: I couldn't decide, I couldn't act, I couldn't comport myself with even a pretense of modest human dignity.

All I could do was cry. Quietly, not bawling, just the chest-chokes.

At the rear of the boat Elroy Berdahl pretended not to notice. He held a fishing rod in his hands, his head bowed to hide his eyes. He kept humming a soft, monotonous little tune. Everywhere, it seemed, in the trees and water and sky, a great worldwide sadness came pressing down on me, a crushing sorrow, sorrow like I had never known it before. And what was so sad, I realized, was that Canada had become a pitiful fantasy. Silly and hopeless. It was no longer a possibility. Right then, with the shore so close, I understood that I would not do what I should do. I would not swim away from my hometown and my country and my life. I would not be brave. That old image of myself as a hero, as a man of conscience and courage, all that was just a threadbare pipe dream. Bobbing there on the Rainy River, looking back at the Minnesota shore, I felt a sudden swell of helplessness come over me, a drowning sensation, as if I had toppled overboard and was being swept away by the silver waves. Chunks of my own history flashed by. I saw a seven-year-old boy in a white cowboy hat and a Lone Ranger mask and a pair of holstered six-shooters; I saw a twelve-year-old Little League shortstop pivoting to turn a double play; I saw a sixteen-year-old kid decked out for his first prom, looking spiffy in a white tux and a black bow tie, his hair cut short and flat, his shoes freshly polished. My whole life seemed to spill out into the river, swirling away from me, everything I had ever been or ever wanted to be. I couldn't get my breath; I couldn't stay afloat; I couldn't tell which way to swim. A hallucination, I suppose, but it was as real as anything I would ever feel. I saw my parents calling to me from the far shoreline. I saw my brother and sister, all the townsfolk, the mayor and the entire Chamber of Commerce and all my old teachers and girlfriends and high school buddies. Like some weird sporting event: everybody screaming from the sidelines, rooting me on — a loud stadium roar. Hotdogs and popcorn — stadium smells, stadium heat. A squad of cheerleaders did cartwheels along the banks of the Rainy River; they had megaphones and pompoms and smooth brown thighs. The crowd swayed left and right. A marching band played fight songs. All my aunts and uncles were there, and Abraham Lincoln, and Saint George, and a nine-year-old girl named Linda who had died of a brain tumor back in fifth grade, and several members of the United States Senate, and a blind poet scribbling notes, and LBJ, and Huck Finn, and Abbie Hoffman,[10] and all the dead soldiers back from the grave, and the many thousands who were later to die — villagers with terrible burns, little kids without arms or legs — yes, and the joint chiefs of staff were there, and a couple of popes, and a first lieutenant named Jimmy Cross, and the last surviving veteran of the American Civil War, and Jane Fonda dressed up as Barbarella, and an old man sprawled beside a pigpen, and my grandfather, and Gary Cooper, and a kind-faced woman carrying an umbrella and a copy of Plato's *Republic,* and a million ferocious citizens waving flags of all shapes and colors — people in hard hats, people in headbands — they were all whooping and chanting and urging me toward one shore or the other. I saw faces from my distant past and distant future. My wife was there. My unborn daughter waved at me, and my two sons hopped up and down, and a drill sergeant named Blyton sneered and shot up a finger and shook his head. There was a choir in bright purple robes. There was a cabbie from the Bronx. There was a slim young man I would one day kill with a hand grenade along a red clay trail outside the village of My Khe.

The little aluminum boat rocked softly beneath me. There was the wind and the sky.

I tried to will myself overboard.

I gripped the edge of the boat and leaned forward and thought, *Now.*

I did try. It just wasn't possible.

All those eyes on me — the town, the whole universe — and I couldn't risk the embarrassment. It was as if there were an audience to my life, that swirl of faces along the river, and in my head I could hear people screaming at me. Traitor! they yelled. Turncoat! Pussy! I felt myself blush. I couldn't tolerate it. I couldn't endure the mockery, or the disgrace, or the patriotic ridicule. Even in my imagination, the shore just twenty yards away, I couldn't make myself be brave. It had nothing to do with morality. Embarrassment, that's all it was.

And right then I submitted.

I would go to the war — I would kill and maybe die — because I was embarrassed not to.

That was the sad thing. And so I sat in the bow of the boat and cried.

It was loud now. Loud, hard crying.

---

[10]Abbie Hoffman (1936–89) was a radical and flamboyant antiwar activist, one of the Chicago Seven (see p. 840). — EDS.

Elroy Berdahl remained quiet. He kept fishing. He worked his line with the tips of his fingers, patiently, squinting out at his red and white bobber on the Rainy River. His eyes were flat and impassive. He didn't speak. He was simply there, like the river and the late-summer sun. And yet by his presence, his mute watchfulness, he made it real. He was the true audience. He was a witness, like God, or like the gods, who look on in absolute silence as we live our lives, as we make our choices or fail to make them.

"Ain't biting," he said.

Then after a time the old man pulled in his line and turned the boat back toward Minnesota.

I don't remember saying goodbye. That last night we had dinner together, and I went to bed early, and in the morning Elroy fixed breakfast for me. When I told him I'd be leaving, the old man nodded as if he already knew. He looked down at the table and smiled.

At some point later in the morning it's possible that we shook hands — I just don't remember — but I do know that by the time I'd finished packing the old man had disappeared. Around noon, when I took my suitcase out to the car, I noticed that his old black pickup truck was no longer parked in front of the house. I went inside and waited for a while, but I felt a bone certainty that he wouldn't be back. In a way, I thought, it was appropriate. I washed up the breakfast dishes, left his two hundred dollars on the kitchen counter, got into the car, and drove south toward home.

The day was cloudy. I passed through towns with familiar names, through the pine forests and down to the prairie, and then to Vietnam, where I was a soldier, and then home again. I survived, but it's not a happy ending. I was a coward. I went to the war.

READING CRITICALLY

1. At the beginning of the story, O'Brien lists a number of problems with the war, but draws no conclusions about them. What is it about these issues that makes him oppose the war?

2. What does Elroy Berdahl do that leads O'Brien to call him "the hero of my life"?

3. Why doesn't O'Brien go to Canada?

WRITING ANALYTICALLY

1. O'Brien depicts the complex set of pressures and decisions that faced draftees who opposed the war. He considers the reasons and rationalizations for the war itself but focuses on the social and emotional pressures he encountered, pressures that seem to have almost nothing to do with the politics of the situation.

At last, he says that he bases his decision on the personal questions of fear and courage.

In an essay, trace O'Brien's discussions of fear and courage. How does he define those terms? What is he afraid of? What does he hope for the courage to do? Why does he conclude that he was a coward?

2. In his November 20 speech, Spiro Agnew criticizes the men who evade the draft by going to Canada: "to some Americans, a small minority, these are the true young men of conscience" (p. 888). Agnew means this sneeringly. "They are not our heroes," he says a few sentences later. John Kerry (p. 890) criticizes Agnew for taking this view, and Ron Kovic (p. 931) would also disagree. Write an essay comparing and contrasting the positions taken by Agnew and O'Brien (include Kerry and Kovic if you wish). How do they define courage, patriotism, and heroism? Whose arguments do you find most convincing?

HAROLD "LIGHT BULB" BRYANT

Oral History (1984)

African American soldiers played a prominent role in the Vietnam War. They served in disproportionate numbers and died in disproportionate numbers. Although they made up about 11 percent of the population at the time, at the beginning of the war black soldiers accounted for 23 percent of the fatalities. Later this number dropped to 12 percent. American involvement in the war occurred during the civil rights movement at home, and African Americans on the battlefield took up the civil rights cry as well, insisting on their rights and resisting both deliberate and casual prejudice from white soldiers and officers.

Harold Bryant was one of twenty black soldiers who were interviewed by journalist Wallace Terry for a book of oral histories of the Vietnam War. Bryant, from East St. Louis, Illinois, served as a combat engineer in Vietnam from February 1966 to February 1967. Black soldiers referred to themselves as "bloods," the title Terry chose for his book.

WE WERE IN A FIRE FIGHT ONE MORNING. We had our mad minute at six o'clock. We received some fire, and so we just started shooting. I guess maybe about eight o'clock a dust-off [1] came in to take out a wounded guy.

Harold Bryant, oral history, in *Bloods: An Oral History of the Vietnam War by Black Veterans*, ed. Wallace Terry (New York: Random House, 1984), 18–32.

In the notes, EDS. = Patricia Bizzell and Bruce Herzberg.

[1]Medical evacuation by helicopter. The helicopters didn't stop their rotors during the operation and kicked up clouds of dust. — EDS.

And they came and asked for me, and they told me that I was rotating. Going home right in the middle of the fire fight. I hadn't kept up with my days. I didn't have a short-time calendar. So I was a little surprised. So they took me back to An Khe for me to clear base camp.

I went downtown and bought a few trinkets to give people. A opium pipe. Four or five of those little jackets that said on the back, "I know I'm goin' to heaven, 'cause I done spent my time in hell." I grabbed my stuff out of the connex and put it in two of those Air Vietnam suitcases and my two duffel bags. And I went to the airstrip for the Caribou that would fly me into Pleiku.

When I got to Pleiku, I guess it was about 4 P.M. They said the plane was gonna be comin' in about seven. Then Pleiku started gettin' hit, and the plane didn't come in. And they had us in a secure area with no weapons while Pleiku was being mortared. So we had to spend the night.

The plane to take us to Japan got there the next morning. And it picked up two rounds as we were leaving. And this white guy got hit. Killed. And he was rotating home, too. And his body, it stayed on the plane until we got to Japan.

From Japan, they flew us to Oakland. Then they gave us uniforms, 'cause when I left 'Nam I was still in jungle fatigues. And I took a shower, put on my Class A's, got my records. Finally they let us go, and I caught a bus over to the San Francisco airport and got home about three o'clock that morning.

My mother didn't keep up with my days left either, so she was surprised when I called from San Francisco. She met the plane. I said, "Mom, I'm happy to be home." And she said, "I'm happy to see you here with everything. It's God's blessing that you didn't get hurt." My father wasn't there 'cause he worked at night, driving eighteen-wheelers.

I went right out into the streets in my uniform and partied. Matter fact, got drunk.

I wasn't sleepy. I was still hyped up. And East St. Louis is a city that never closes. So I went to a place called Mother's, which was the latest jazz joint in town.

A lot of people knew me, so everybody was buying me drinks. Nobody was asking me how Vietnam was, what Vietnam was all about. They just was saying, "Hey, happy to see you back. Get you a drink?" They were happy I made it back, because a lot of my friends who had been over there from my city had came home dead in boxes, or disabled.

Finally, I got guys that asked me what it was really like. And when I was trying to explain it, after a while, I saw that they got disinterested. So I just didn't talk about it anymore. I was just saying, "I'm happy to be home. I hope I'll never have to go back."

I had six more months to go, so they sent me to Fort Carson in Colorado. There weren't any more airborne soldiers on post but me and maybe five or six. We either had come back from Vietnam or were getting ready to go.

Well, I ran into this officer. Second lieutenant. Just got out of OCS.[2] He asked me if I was authorized to wear a combat infantryman's badge and jump wings. I told him, "You damn right. I earned them." He didn't like that answer. So I said, "You can harass me now, sir, but you can't go over in Vietnam and do that shit." So he ended up giving me a Article 15 for disrespect. And I got busted one rank and fined $25.

That was just another nail in the coffin to keep me from re-uping.[3] I didn't want career military nohow.

I told him taking my stripe away from me wasn't shit. And he couldn't do nothing to me, 'cause they couldn't send me back to Vietnam. He didn't enjoy that, so he tried to make it hard for me until *he* got shipped out. And when I heard he had orders for 'Nam, I went and found him and laughed at him and told him that he wasn't gon' make it back.

"Somebody's gon' kill you." I said. "One of your own men is gon' kill you."

I enlisted in the army to stay out of the marines. I had went to college for a semester at Southern Illinois University at Edwardsville. But the expenses had gotten too much for my family, so I went and got me a job at McDonnell Aircraft as a sheet-metal assembler. About eight months later, two guys I went to high school with got drafted by the marines. So I joined the army so I could get a choice.

It was August of '65. I was twenty.

My father was not too hot about it. He was in World War II, in France and Germany. He was a truck driver on the Red Ball Express, gettin' gas to Patton's tanks. He resented the army because of how they treated black soldiers over there, segregated and not with the same support for white soldiers.

My left ear was pierced when I was nine just like my father's left ear was pierced when he was nine. Grandmother said all the male warriors in her mother's tribe in Africa had their ears pierced. Her mother was born in Africa. You can imagine the teasing I got in high school for wearing an earring. But I felt in this small way I carry on the African tradition. I would go in the army wearing the mark of the African warriors I descend from.

I did my basic and my AIT[4] at Fort Leonardwood, Missouri. "Lost in the Woods," yeah. Trained for combat engineer to build bridges, mountain roads. But we didn't build too many bridges. Cleared a lot of LZs.[5] Did a lot of demolition work.

I was sent to An Khe, 8th Engineers Battalion, and attached to the 1st of the 9th of the Cav. It was February, after the first battle of the Ia Drang Valley, when three hundred Cav troops got wiped out in the first real fight anybody had with the NVA.[6] I was one of those replacements.

---

[2]Officer Candidate School. — EDS.
[3]Reenlisting. — EDS.
[4]Advanced infantry training. — EDS.
[5]Landing zone for helicopters. — EDS.
[6]North Vietnamese Army. — EDS.

We probed for mines, blew up mines, disarmed and blew up booby traps. If you saw a trip wire, you could take a look at what was happening. You could see where the booby trap was, then throw a grenade at the beginning of the booby trap. Or shoot up the trail to make 'em go off. The land mines, ones you had to dig up, was the big problem, 'cause they could have another one planted somewhere next to it.

And you had to worry about crimping right and taking your time. You squeeze the blasting cap and the fuse together so they won't come apart. Crimping, right. But if you don't crimp right, like an inch from the bottom of the cap, it will blow you up. And you can't be rushed by some second lieutenant, telling you, "Hurry up, hurry up, so we can move on." If you rush, something wrong would happen. We lost three guys from rushing or crimping wrong.

One time I had to get a guy off a mine. It looked like it was impossible.

This infantry unit was on a little trail, west of Pleiku, makin' a sweep towards the Ia Drang Valley. This white dude had stepped on a mine. And knew it. He felt the plunger go down. Everybody moved away from him, about twenty meters. So they called for the engineers, and somebody asked for Light Bulb.

I have a nickname from the streets of East St. Louis. Light Bulb. Came from a friend of mine when we were growing up, 'cause he said I was always full of ideas.

When I got there on the chopper, he's been standin' there for over an hour. He really wasn't in any panic. He was very calm. He knew if he alleviated any of the pressure, both of us would have got destroyed.

I dug all around the mine with my bayonet and found out that it was a Bouncin' Betty. I told him I was gonna try to defuse it. But the three-prong primer on the Bouncin' Betty had gotten in between the cleats on his jungle boots, so there wasn't any way I could deal with it. So I said let's see if we could kind of change the pressure by him takin' his foot out of his boot and me keepin' the pressure by holding his boot down. That way he could get out uninjured. But when he started doin' that, I thought I was seein' the plunger rise, so I told him to stop.

I guess maybe I'd been working with him for maybe an hour now.

Then I got the idea. I knew when the plunger would depress, the Bouncin' Betty would bounce up about three feet and then explode. So I got the other members of his team together, and I tied a rope around his waist. And everybody, including me, moved off about twenty yards from the mine and him. And when I counted to three, everyone would pull on the rope and snatch him about fifteen feet off the mine. And it would bounce up its three feet and then explode. And it did that. And the only damage that he received was the heel of his jungle boot was blown off. No damage to him.

This was somethin' that they never taught us in school.

This guy thanked me for saving his life and the life of his squad. And whenever we were back in base camp, I would always go with them. And since a platoon would always carry three or four combat engineers with them in the bush, I would always go with them.

When I came to Vietnam, I thought we were helping another country to develop a nation. About three or four months later I found out that wasn't the case. In high school and in the papers I had been hearing about Indochina, but I couldn't find Indochina on the map. I didn't know anything about the country, about the people. Those kinds of things I had to learn on myself while I was there.

We had a Vietnamese interpreter attached to us. I would always be asking him questions. He had told me this war in Vietnam had been going on for hundreds of years. Before the Americans, they had been fighting for hundreds of years against the Chinese aggressors. I thought we had got into the beginning of a war. But I found out that we were just in another phase of their civil wars.

And we weren't gaining any ground. We would fight for a hill all day, spend two days or two nights there, and then abandon the hill. Then maybe two, three months later, we would have to come back and retake the same piece of territory. Like this Special Forces camp outside Dak To. The camp was attacked one evening. Maybe two or three platoons flew up to give them some assistance. Then somehow headquarters decided we should close down that camp. So they ended up closing down. Two or three months later, we went back to the same area to retake it. We lost twenty men the first time saving it, thirty or forty men the next time retaking it.

And they had a habit of exaggerating a body count. If we killed seven, by the time it would get back to base camp, it would have gotten to twenty-eight. Then by the time it got down to Westmoreland's[7] office in Saigon, it done went up to fifty-four. And by the time it left from Saigon going to Washington, it had went up to about 125. To prove we were really out there doing our jobs, doing, really, more than what we were doing.

I remember a place called the Ashau Valley. The 7th went in there and got cut up real bad. They had underestimated the enemy's power. So they sent in the 9th, and we cleared the Ashau Valley out. All we was doing was making contact, letting the gunships know where they were, and then we would draw back. We had twenty-five gunships circling around, and jet strikes coming in to drop napalm. We did that all day, and the next day we didn't receive any other fire.

Stars and Stripes said we had a body count of 260 something. But I don't think it was true.

By then I had killed my first VC. It was two or three o'clock in the afternoon, somewhere in the Central Highlands. I was point man. I was blazing my own trail. I was maybe forty meters in front of the rest of the squad. And I just walked up on him. He just stepped out of the bush. I didn't see

---

[7]General William Westmoreland, commander of U.S. forces in Vietnam (1964–68), who had a habit of inflating body counts. — EDS.

him until he moved. I'd say maybe fifty meters. And then he saw me. We both had a look of surprise. And I cracked him, because it just ran through my mind it would be either him or me. I just fired from the hip. And he hadn't even brought his weapon down from port arms.

But what really got to me from the beginning was not really having any information, not knowing what I was gonna be doin' next. We might be pullin' guard for some artillery one night. Then the next day some choppers would come and get us. We would never know where we were going until in the air. Then we would get word that we were going to the LZ that was really hot. Or something ignorant, like the time we went over in Cambodia to pull guard on a helicopter that had been shot down. And we got stuck there.

It was in the latter part of '66, late in the afternoon. I think it got shot down probably in 'Nam and just ended up in Cambodia. So they sent out a squad of us combat engineers to cut around the shaft so a Chinook[8] could come in, hook up, and pull it out. We didn't get there until six or seven, and it was getting dark. So the Chinook couldn't come in, so we had to stay there all night. The chopper had one door gunner and two pilots, and they were all dead. It wasn't from any rounds. They died from the impact of the chopper falling. I thought it made a lot more sense for us to get out of there and bring the bodies back with us.

When it got dark, we could see a fire maybe half a mile from us. We knew it had to be a VC camp. In the bamboo thicket right up on us we kept hearing this movement, these small noises. We thought if we fired, whoever was out there would attack us. We were so quiet that none of us moved all night. Matter of fact, one of the guy's hair turned stone gray. Because of the fear. He was just nineteen. He was a blond-headed kid when the sun went down, and when the sunlight came up, his hair was white.

We didn't find out they were monkeys until that morning.

That was about as crazy as the time we tryin' to take a shower in a monsoon rain. We had no shower for maybe ten days in the bush. We was standin' out there in the middle of a rice paddy, soapin' up. By the time all of us got soaped up, it stopped rainin'. So we had to lay down and roll around in the rice paddy to get the soap off of us. We never did call that a shower.

It seems like a lot of green guys got killed just coming in country[9] by making a mistake. I remember this white guy from Oklahoma. We got to callin' him Okie. He said that the reason he had volunteered to come over to Vietnam was because he wanted to kill gooks. He was a typical example of a John Wayne complex.

It was a week after he had just gotten there that we got into any action. He was just itching to get into some. We went out and got pinned down by machine guns. They were on our right flank. He saw where the machine-gun net was, and he tried to do the John Wayne thing. He go up, trying to

---

[8]CH-47 cargo helicopter. — EDS.
[9]Into Vietnam. — EDS.

circle around the machine-gun net. Charge the machine gun. And never made it. Whoever was firing saw him move and turned the maching gun on him. We stayed down till we could call in some gunships. Then we moved back.

There was another guy in our unit who had made it known that he was a card-carrying Ku Klux Klan member. That pissed a lot of us off, 'cause we had gotten real tight. We didn't have racial incidents like what was happening in the rear area, 'cause we had to depend on each other. We were always in the bush.

Well, we got into a fire fight, and Mr. Ku Klux Klan got his little ass trapped. We were goin' across the rice paddies, and Charlie[10] just start shootin'. And he jumped in the rice paddy while everybody else kind of backtracked.

So we laid down a base of fire to cover him. But he was just immobile. He froze. And a brother went out there and got him and dragged him back. Later on, he said that action had changed his perception of what black people were about.

But I got to find out that white people weren't as tough, weren't the number one race and all them other perceptions that they had tried to ingrain in my head. I found out they got scared like I did. I found out a lot of them were a lot more cowardly than I expected. I found out some of them were more animalistic than any black people I knew. I found out that they really didn't have their shit together.

At that time we would carry our dog tags on a chain and tie it through the buttonholes of our fatigue jacket. Wearing them around our necks would cause a rash. Also, they would make noise unless you had 'em taped around your neck.

Well, these white guys would sometimes take the dog-tag chain and fill that up with ears. For different reasons. They would take the ear off to make sure the VC was dead. And to confirm that they had a kill. And to put some notches on they guns.

If we were movin' through the jungle, they'd just put the bloody ear on the chain and stick the ear in their pocket and keep on going. Wouldn't take time to dry it off. Then when we get back, they would nail' em up on the walls to our hootch, you know, as a trophy. They was rotten and stinkin' after awhile, and finally we make 'em take 'em down.

These two guys that I can specifically think of had about twelve. I thought it was stupid. And spiritually, I was lookin' at it as damaging a dead body. After a while, I told them, "Hey man, that's sick. Don't be around me with the ears hangin' on you."

One time after a fire fight, we went for a body count. We wiped part of them out, and the rest of them took off. There were five known dead. And these two other guys be moanin'. One of them was trying to get to his weapon. One of the guys saw that and popped him. Then another guy went by and popped the other one to make sure that he was dead. Then

[10]The Viet Cong. — EDS.

this guy — one of the white guys — cut off the VC's dick and stuck it in his mouth as a reminder that the 1st Cavs had been through there. And he left the ace of spades on the body.

That happened all the time.

So did burnin' villages.

Sometimes we would get to villages, and fires would still be burnin', food still be cookin', but nobody was there. The commanding officer, this major, would say if no one is there in the village, then the village must not belong to anybody, so destroy it. But the people had probably ran off because they knew we were comin'.

If we didn't want people further down the road, like the VC, to know we were comin', we wouldn't fire the village. Or if we were movin' too fast, we wouldn't. Otherwise, you would strike your lighter. Torch it. All of 'em were thatched huts anyway. I looked at the major's orders as something he knew more about than I did.

And the villagers caught hell if they were suspect, too.

I remember at this LZ. We could sit on our bunkers and look across the road at the POW compound. The MPs had them surrounded by barbed wire. We would see MPs go in there and get them and take 'em to another bunker. Then we'd hear the Vietnamese hollerin' and shit. The MPs would take the telephone wires and wrap it around the Vietnamese fingers and crank the phone so the charge would go through the wires. Papa san, mama san, would start talkin'. And then we'd see the MPs carry 'em back into the camp.

One day at the LZ we saw a chopper maybe a mile away, high up in the air. Maybe three hundred feet. And we'd see something come out. I didn't think it was a body until I talked to the other guys. I had thought maybe the chopper had banked and then somebody had rolled out. That was a fear that we always had when we were ridin' in choppers 'cause there weren't any seat belts in the choppers at that time.

What happened was they were interrogating somebody. And the interrogation was over with.

Outside An Khe, the 1st Cav built an area for soldiers to go relieve theirselves. Bars, whorehouses. It would open at nine in the morning. We called it Sin City. And it had soul bars. A group of us would walk around to find a joint that would be playin' some soul music, some Temptations, Supremes, Sam and Dave. I would want to do my drinking somewhere where I'd hear music that I liked rather than hillbilly. But a lot of gray[11] guys who wasn't racially hung up would also be there.

The women were much more friendly there. We had heard that was because they thought of the black man as bein' more stronger, more powerful, because Buddha was black. Take a good look at a Buddha. You'll see that he has thick lips and has a very broad nose and very kinky hair. But I didn't know that until I got in country.

---

[11]White in African American slang. — EDS.

We would go to a Class 6 store and get two half-gallons of Gilby's gin for a $1.65 each. We take a bottle to papa san. Buy a girl for $5 or $10. Whatever came by, or whatever I liked. And still have a half a gallon of gin. We would have to leave the area at six o'clock.

Another good thing about the girls in Sin City was that the medical personnel in the camp would always go and check 'em once a week. And if they got disease, they'd get shots and wouldn't be able to work until they were clear. Nobody used rubbers because all the girls in Sin City were clean.

But the people got abused anyway. Like a lot of guys would have Vietnamese give them haircuts. And after papa san got through cuttin' the hair, this guy would tell him that he wouldn't like it and would walk off. He wouldn't pay papa san. And the haircut cost no more than thirty cents.

And it seemed the Vietnamese were always hung up on menthol cigarettes. Kools and things. And they knew brothers all smoked Kools. And they would always ask us for a cigarette. So a lot of guys would start givin' 'em loaded cigarettes to stop 'em from always askin' us. One of the guy's brothers had mailed him some loads from a trick shop. You take out some of the tobacco, then put in a small load of gunpowder. When the Vietnamese smokin' it, it just blow up in his face, and he wouldn't go back to that GI and ask him for a cigarette 'cause he was scared he'd get another loaded cigarette.

One night I saw a drunk GI just pull out his .45 and pop papa san. Papa san was irritatin' him or botherin' him or something. Right downtown in Sin City. After he fired, the MPs and a lot of soldiers grabbed him. They took him to the camp, and he got put up on some charges.

You could find plenty of women out in the field, too. We would set up our perimeter, and all of a sudden a little Coke girl would show up with Coca-Cola. And also some broads would show. We would set up lean-tos, or we'd put up bunkers. A guy would go outside the wire, take the broad through the wire to the bunker, knock her off, and take her back outside the wire. Normally, those kinds of deals was a C-ration deal. Or a couple of dollars. We would give the girl a a C-ration meal. Ham and lima beans, 'cause nobody in the squad would want to eat ham and lima beans. You would never give up spaghetti and meatballs.

One morning, we were sweepin' a highway near Phu Cat. Four of us in a jeep with two M-60 machine guns mounted on the back. We were coming down the road, and we looked off on to a spur and we saw three black pajama bodies start runnin' away from us. So one of the two white guys turned his gun on automatic and knocked all three down. The three of them ran over there to see what was happening and found out that two of them were women, maybe eighteen or nineteen, and one of them was a man. I stayed with the Quad 60, just pullin' guard to make sure there might have been some more VC in the area.

As I was watching, I noticed one of the white guys take his pants down and just start having sex. That kind of freaked me out, 'cause I thought the broad was dead. The brother was just standin' guard watchin'. It kind of surprised him to see this guy get off. After about twenty minutes, I ended up saying, "Hey, man. Come on. Let's go."

When they got back in the jeep, they start tellin' me what was happenin'. They had told me that they confirmed three KIA.[12] And the brother asked the dude what was wrong with him, why did he fuck a dead woman. And he said he just wanted to get his rocks off. And that was the end of it.

Today I'm constantly thinking about the war. I walk down streets different. I look at places where individuals could hide. Maybe assault me or rob me or just harass me. I hear things that other people can't hear. My wife, she had a habit at one time of buying cheap watches and leaving them on top of the dresser. I could hear it ticking, so she would put it in a drawer. I could still hear it ticking. And I dream of helicopters coming over my house, comin' to pick me up to take me to a fire fight. And when we get to the fire fight, they were dropping napalm on our own men. And I have to shoot our own soldiers to put them out of their misery. After my discharge, I lived off my unemployment until it ran out, which was about eighteen months. Then I decided to go back to school. I went two years, and then I got involved in veterans affairs. I was noticing that in my city, which is 95 percent black, that there were a lot of black combat veterans coming back not able to find any employment because of bad discharges, or killing theirselves or dopin' up. We started the Wasted Men Project at the university, and I have been counseling at veterans centers ever since.

In 1982 I transferred to the Vet Center in Tucson because I wanted to do some research on the Buffalo Soldiers.[13] In 'Nam I didn't know they were part of the original 9th Cav. These are black boys who had just received their freedom from the United States government, and they had to go to the West and suppress the freedom from another race of people who were the Indians. I think they won thirteen or fourteen Congressional Medals of Honor. But they were really policing other people, just like we were in Vietnam.

When my son, Ronnie, turned sixteen, I had him sit down and watch all thirteen hours of this film documentary about the Vietnam War so he could have an understanding of what war really was about. He had asked had I did any killing. I told him, "Yes. I had to do it. I had to do it to keep myself alive."

I wouldn't want him to go and fight an unpopular war like I did. I wouldn't want him to go down to El Salvador. And if that means that I would have to pick up me and my family baggage and move somewhere out of the country, then I would do that.

---

[12]Killed in action. — EDS.

[13]Buffalo Soldiers were African Americans recruited after the Civil War to fight Native Americans on the frontier. The Native Americans called them "buffalo soldiers" because of the texture of their hair. The most famous regiments were the 9th and 10th Cavalry. — EDS.

America should have won the war. But they wouldn't free us to fight. With all the American GIs that were in Vietnam, they could have put us all shoulder to shoulder and had us march from Saigon all the way up to the DMZ.[14] Just make a sweep. We had enough GIs, enough equipment to do that.

When I came to Washington to see the Vietnam Veterans Memorial, I looked through the book and there were about fifteen guys from my hometown who were killed. And six of them I knew.

But I looked up the memorial for James Plummer first.

Plummer was a black guy from Cincinnati. We were the same age. Twenty. We were at Camp Alpha together. That's where they assign you when you first come to 'Nam. I was in C Company, a line company. He was a truck driver, so he was in Headquarters Company, where they had all the heavy equipment.

I liked Plummer's style. He was just so easygoing. We'd sit down and just rap. Rap about music, the girls, what was happening in the world. Get high. Plummer was a John Coltrane fan. And I'm bein' a Miles Davis fan, we just automatically fell in with each other.

He was my best friend.

One day we were at the airfield at the LZ. Plummer was out of the truck, over by the ammo dump. And the ammo dump received a mortar round. It blew him up.

It freaked me out. I mean that here I saw him, and five minutes later he's instantaneously dead.

Me and two other guys ran and grabbed what we could. We pulled on the jungle fatigues, which was full of blood. It looked like maybe a dog after it crossed the street and got hit by a truck. His head was gone, both his legs from about the knee down were both gone. One arm was gone. The other was a stump left. We finally got his trunk together. The rest of it we really couldn't find, 'cause that one mortar round, it started the ammo dump to steady exploding. It constantly blew up for about an hour.

What we found was probably sent back to the States. They probably had a closed-casket funeral.

I kind of cried. I was sayin' to myself that this was such a waste because we weren't really doin' anything at the time. And him just being such a nice fella, why did he have to go this way? Go in pieces?

Everybody knew that me and him was tight, so a couple of guys took me up over to a bunker and we rapped about him all night. 'Cause we were out in the bush, I really couldn't get no booze. But when I did get back, I bought me a half gallon of gin, and I knocked it off. And that didn't make me feel any better.

When I got back, I called his mother. His mother knew me from him writing to her. I told her I was close by when he did get killed. I just told her a ammo dump blew up. I'm pretty sure she didn't have no idea what that was.

---

[14]The demilitarized zone between North and South Vietnam. — EDS.

Every year I send her a Christmas card. I just sign my name.

When I saw Plummer on the memorial, I kind of cried again.

I guess deep down in my head now I can't really believe in God like I did because I can't really see why God would let something like this happen. 'Specially like to my friend Plummer. Why He would take such a good individual away from here.

Before I went to Vietnam, I was very active in the church, because of my mother's influence. She sent me a Bible, and I carried it in my pocket everywhere I went. When I couldn't find any *Playboys* or something like that, I would read it. Matter of fact, I read it from cover to cover, starting from Genesis.

I guess I got kind of really unreligious because of my Vietnam experience. Oh, I went to church once in my uniform to please my mother. But I haven't been back since except for a funeral. I've talked to chaplains, talked to preachers about Vietnam. And no one could give me a satisfactory explanation of what happened overseas.

But each year since I've been back I have read the Bible from cover to cover. I keep looking for the explanation.

I can't find it. I can't find it.

READING CRITICALLY

1. Why does Bryant join the army?

2. What racial differences and incidents does Bryant mention?

3. What observations does Bryant make about the political situation in Vietnam? About the military mission? About the Vietnamese?

WRITING ANALYTICALLY

1. Have you ever been in the military service or considered joining? If you have been in the service, what were your motives for joining? If not, what — if anything — might motivate you to join? What is the military experience of other members of your family and how has that influenced you? Write a personal essay exploring these questions. If you have no interest in the military, explain why.

2. How does Bryant seem to feel about his experiences? Most of his descriptions are very straightforward and nonevaluative, but can you discern any reactions or opinions? Write an essay analyzing the way Bryant talks about his military experience in Vietnam. Is there any indication that he is proud, embarrassed, angry? What might you conclude from his postwar activities, his research, his feeling about his son being in the army?

LESLIE MCCLUSKY

Oral History (1987)

American women worked in Vietnam in a number of capacities — as military nurses, members of the Women's Army Corps, Red Cross volunteers, journalists, stewardesses on commercial airlines, embassy personnel, and so on. At least 7,500 women served in the military during the war, about 80 percent of them as nurses.

The stories of these women were long in coming out. There were relatively few women in Vietnam and they were ignored by the media and veterans groups. Lynda Van Devanter, an army nurse, promoted the concerns of women veterans and published her moving memoir of war and homecoming, *Home before Morning*, in 1983. Kathryn Marshall collected the oral histories of twenty women, most of them nurses, in her book *In the Combat Zone*, from which the selection here is taken. Leslie McClusky (an alias) grew up in Columbus, Ohio. She became a nurse, joined the army, and was sent to Vietnam, where she served from December 1970 to November 1971. Marshall notes that all of the women she spoke to agreed with Leslie McClusky that the war was a defining experience for them, horrible as it was, but that coming home was worse than going over.

I WAS FIRST GOING TO JOIN THE MILITARY in 1967. At that time I had a guarantee to go to Vietnam. But I made the ultimate mistake of telling my family before I was actually sworn in. Never in my life have I been bombarded by so much negative reaction.

Three years later, in early 'seventy, I decided that I really wanted to go. I was twenty-four. I still wanted to go for the same reasons, and I was very sorry that I hadn't gone before. So this time I didn't tell anybody until two weeks before I was leaving for officers' training school at Fort Sam Houston, Texas. There was the same outpouring, but now it was too late. If I'd been strong enough the first time around, I would have done it that way then.

At that time the army was taking nurses for fourteen months if they would agree to go to Vietnam. Apparently they weren't getting enough to enlist for two years; they wanted people who had been out of school for a few years and had some experience. I was assistant head nurse in a surgical intensive care unit and had had three years of real critical care

Leslie McClusky, oral history, in *In the Combat Zone: An Oral History of American Women in Vietnam, 1966–75*, ed. Kathryn Marshall (Boston: Little, Brown, 1987).

In the notes, EDS. = Patricia Bizzell and Bruce Herzberg.

experience. I'd taken care of a lot of trauma from automobile accidents, stabbings, and things. Little did I know that did not prepare me in the least for Vietnam.

I enjoyed basic training. It was the first time I'd ever really been away from home. I developed a pretty good sense of humor — you have to with the military; they take such ridiculous little things so seriously — and didn't really think of myself as being in the army. Nor did I really give much thought to Vietnam.

It wasn't until the night we were leaving that I began to realize what I had done. And I was really sorry. I remember being in the airport and feeling like a little girl.

I had my big duffel bag and a suitcase, and I was wearing my uniform and my first lieutenant's bar. There were no other women around, and nobody was really smiling. I waited with all these young men to get on this chartered plane. My remembrance is that it was a real crowded plane — they had put seats everywhere — and I was stuck in between these two guys. One of them was really big. Nobody was talking. And there wasn't any liquor because it was a military flight.

In Alaska, our first stop, everyone got off the plane, went to the bar, and had a few drinks. In Japan everybody drank again. Through this whole flight, I was never able to sleep, even though I'd had a few drinks and had brought some sleeping pills with me, because it was all very crowded and awful, and I felt awful. I didn't know what was coming up. I was scared and I felt very young, even though I was one of the oldest people on the plane. Most of the guys were eighteen or nineteen.

In Alaska I saw there was one other woman on the plane. She was sitting way in the back. I could have talked to her, but I didn't.

We landed at Bien Hoa. Bien Hoa had been rocketed the day before, so there was this mad dash to get us off and get us going. And they really meant going. This big truck came to pick us up. We were supposed to pile in the back, and here I am in my little skirt and heels — I couldn't get my feet into them after twenty-three hours of sitting, so I was carrying my heels. And I had to get my duffel bag and all my junk onto the back of this big truck that I could hardly get myself up onto. In those days I smoked two packs a day and had never dreamed about jumping up onto a truck.

There was no letup. They took us in these trucks to this room, where you were briefed. All the officers went into one room, the enlisted people into another. We got a speech about what we weren't supposed to do, and we changed our money and then they took us to get our orders. It was absolutely nonstop. Right away we were in fatigues. And then I was in this place — it was a barracks for women — way in the back with a guard out front and barbed wire all around it. I was given a blanket and two sheets and was supposed to try to sleep.

This other woman from the plane came in, but we didn't talk. We were both, I guess, so lost in our own thoughts. And she was older than me and seemed real hardened. This was her first time in Vietnam, but she was a captain, had been in the army awhile. To me she seemed sort of callous. She used a lot of language that fit in with the guys. I didn't talk that way.

This building had six or eight cots in it. The light bulbs were bare and hung down. I don't know if it was clean — in Vietnam everything seemed filthy. And it was hot and dry and there were bugs everywhere.

I had been moving around sort of like a zombie but doing everything I was supposed to do, certainly acting like I was all right. Until I went to the outhouse. It was a thing in the back with these slits you had to sit on — it wasn't exactly a flush toilet — and when I sat down a frog jumped on my leg. For some reason that was the trigger. I just burst out crying. I didn't know what I'd gotten myself into, why I was there, or what was laying in front of me. And I was just completely exhausted.

I couldn't stay in that building, so I went up to the officers' club. As soon as I walked in I knew I'd made a mistake. It was all men. This other woman was there, too, but I didn't fit in with her. So I got a drink and went outside and met some guy and sat in a bunker. We just sat there and talked. I remember I wanted my mother.

This was not exactly the best night of my life. But the worst was yet to come. Because the worst day was the day I came back home.

After three days I got orders to go to the Third Field Hospital in Saigon. The Third Field was not at all what I had in mind. It was in the city and we wore white uniforms and we were mostly taking care of Vietnamese civilians and some sort of VIPs. I didn't like it there. I didn't know anything about the Vietnamese. The army gave us absolutely no orientation to their language, their customs — the women would squat on top of the toilets — and here we had wards and wards of Vietnamese. It was very confusing. I hadn't gone there to help minister to them. In retrospect I guess I feel different. I remember there were a lot of women and children. The children, most of them, had been severely injured with mines.

Saigon itself was a very interesting city. It was dirty and real crowded, but it was so alive. There were cars, taxis, motor bikes everywhere, and on the black market you could get anything you wanted — cigarettes, decent hairspray, Breck shampoo. It's strange now to look at all the stuff on TV about Saigon, because the city looks so sterile, like it was made out of plastic models.

I was at the Third Field about a month and a half. We worked twelve hours a day, six days a week. I knew I was in a foreign city and I knew I was in the military, but mostly it just seemed like some kind of missionary camp. We weren't taking any casualties. So my experience just centered on trying to get by in this totally new environment. I thought I managed pretty well for someone who didn't think she could get by anywhere.

Our chief nurse was a pretty weird woman. When I put in for a transfer we had an argument. She started telling me that I was no longer a civilian, that I was an army officer and that I would take orders. And that I would respect her. Well, I didn't respect her. I thought she was a little crazy. She loved the Vietnamese and used to take their clothes and wash them. It seemed to me the Vietnamese were all she cared about. And she was real petty and did everything she could to keep the nurses from dating enlisted men. Anyhow, she got me transferred to Chu Lai. She thought it was punishment. But at least it was different, so it was all right with me.

Chu Lai is in the northern part of the country, right on the coast. The camp was on a cliff overlooking the ocean. It was very beautiful there. And it was all army — Chu Lai was the base camp of the Americal Division, so there were about forty thousand men stationed there.

The first guy that I saw wounded was a kid who had had his leg blown off. He had shrapnel everywhere, too. I had never seen shrapnel wounds, just like I had never seen a traumatic amputation. You know, I'd seen normal amputations under sterile conditions. But I had never seen a guy with big, black, pitted holes everywhere and a makeshift tourniquet over the amputation site. He was conscious, too. A sweet young kid. I had no idea what to say.

There were lots of others being brought in at the same time. I didn't know what to do, so I just quit functioning. That's when a corpsman sat me down and poured me some coffee. You know, the corpsmen are the people who deserve a lot of credit that I'm not sure they've gotten. They really knew what to do. They were real compassionate, too. Anyhow, after about ten minutes I said, "Shit — I'm supposed to be in charge here. I have to get some IVs, get some blood going, see who's hurt worst, who has to go in first." Only I couldn't look at anything.

But I knew that I still had eleven months to go. That I couldn't just sit there folded up in a chair not functioning. So I got up and did what I had to do. Only I didn't connect with anything. I just did it. What I didn't realize at the time is how fast a total emotional numbing sets in. I did my job well and was able to show compassion, but I worked hard at not feeling compassion. Of course I saw the kids, and of course I reacted appropriately. But it was all external. Only in the last six months have I been able to really see them, or see them again. This first kid, especially. Over the years, whenever he would flash in front of me, I'd just turn him off. I could not deal with that memory or any of the others.

There was another kid, I remember, who had had two legs and an arm blown off, probably by a mine. And the kid who was blind. You know, I've blocked so much of it that I don't remember anyone's name, even though I know I called them by their names at the time. Since I went to the Wall,[1] though, I'm remembering more and more of them. It was at the Wall that I first was able to cry.

I remember these two other guys who had malaria. They came in real dehydrated and vomiting with real high temperatures. And they acted just like little boys — little boys who were sick. I remember how I tried to make everything better, only I couldn't give them back anything they had lost. I never felt I was good enough, that what I was doing would make up for

[1] The Vietnam Veterans Memorial in Washington, D.C. — EDS.

what they were going through. So most of the time I felt real inadequate. And you can't imagine what that takes out of you.

It's true there was a lot of drinking and a lot of marijuana use. But I don't think there was that much drug abuse among medical people. Pot and alcohol, yes. No one used anything when they were working.

But when you weren't working — well, I drank. And I smoked. Because, really, there was nothing else to do. You couldn't go downtown and take in a movie. You could go to the officers' club and see war movies, and I actually think I must have seen every damn war movie that was ever made. There was this group of us, medical people and helicopter pilots and gunners, and we'd sit around and watch this stuff. That was OK. Except that, in real life, it was real helicopters and real outgoing fire and real incoming.

We got rocketed at Chu Lai. At first it was scary. But I have to tell you that, after a couple times, you just get used to it. You always had a flak jacket and a helmet on the foot of your bed. The procedure was, when there was a rocket, you put on your flak jacket and helmet and ran to the bunkers. If you were working, there was a jacket and helmet above every patient in bed. What you were supposed to do was get them on the guys who couldn't do it themselves and then roll them underneath the bed. It would usually be just at dawn when we got rocketed.

The first night I went to the bunkers. That's when I knew this was bullshit. After that I actually got under my bed once or twice, but mostly I just stuck my helmet on my head. Because they usually weren't hitting anywhere near us. And you learn to know the difference between incoming and outgoing fire.

There was a two-week period in the middle of my tour when I was sort of a basket case. I wanted out so badly I didn't think I could stand another day. And I didn't know what to do, how to deal with it. I worked every day, but I quit talking to people. After work I'd go straight to my room and sit there thinking how I could go home. First I thought I would get pregnant, but that would take too long. Or I could break a leg, only I wasn't sure that would get me out. And of course I could really go crazy, but then I would have to deal with that. Finally, after two weeks, it was over and I felt fine. So I just went back and ended the next six months.

This other stuff happened to me, too. While I was at Chu Lai, I remember, I started to really hate the Vietnamese. I had grown up real liberal — as far as I was concerned, I never had a prejudiced bone. When I first got in country[2] and everybody was talking about the "gooks," I thought they were really insensitive. Then I started hearing about things that happened. Then I started seeing the results.

Before long I started thinking of them as gooks, too. I had no love for them. Women, children, it didn't matter — I didn't want to take care of them. When helicopters would come in and there would be Vietnamese

[2]Into Vietnam. — EDS.

on them, I'd say to myself, "Shit. I do not want to go waste my energy taking care of them — " Now I'm happy I never acted on what I felt. Maybe I wasn't extremely kind, but I never did anything to hurt anybody, and I took care of them all physically, even the prisoners.

And then one day I suddenly realized what was happening to me. I was on the ward, doing something for one of the POWs, and I said to the guard — the prisoners were always guarded — "What are you sitting there with that M-16 for? Do you really think this guy is going anywhere?" I was thinking how crazy it was. Also how I never looked at them, never looked at their faces. So this time I did. I sat down and really looked at this Vietnamese as a human being. And what I saw was a fourteen-year-old kid.

I really had not cried at all, but I almost cried that day. I wanted to — wanted to cry because of what I knew had happened to me. That's when I began to see the whole thing as insane.

I started looking more at them after that. One night when I was still feeling mostly negative, there was this baby that was brought in. I said to myself, "What are we going to do with a Vietnamese baby? I don't want this baby here." I didn't want to take care of her, because I felt the same about her as about the others, even if it was a baby.

The kid wasn't really sick, but she was crying. I had to feed her, so I went and plunked this bottle in her mouth. I wasn't really looking at her. But I had to sit there and hold her — there wasn't much else to do — so after a while I started to look at her. And that time I did cry. How, I wondered, could I ever come to believe I hated a baby? I had lost all perspective, and I knew it. I also knew the numbing process was starting to wear off, but I did not know how I was going to deal with all these feelings.

Well, my year was ending. Like everyone else, I had a short-timer's calendar and short-timer's syndrome. You know, people would walk around saying, "Five days left. Four days left. I'm so short you can't see me — " And then you have your urine test to make sure you're drug-free and then you're on a plane going home. And you think it's going to be wonderful.

The flight home was certainly much louder than the flight over. I was the only woman. Everyone had thought to bring liquor. So we land in Seattle, and there's no ceremony, no one waiting to tell you what a wonderful thing you've done. I get a steak dinner, a little money, and my discharge papers. That's it. I'm out of the army. And all of a sudden I don't know why, on the plane, I was saying, "Just get me home." Because I don't have an apartment anymore. And I feel very strange. Yeah, how strange I was feeling — that was really the only thing I knew.

I didn't know anybody in Seattle, but I stayed there for a while. Then I went to Chicago, which I had never been to, and stayed a few days there. I just wandered around, kind of. Then I went to New York, where my sister lives. She didn't know I was coming or anything. I remember I woke her up.

Everything was very strange.

I remember my brother and sister wanted to go out to dinner. I mean, they were really trying, but I was sort of in shock. All I kept thinking was that I didn't care where we went to dinner — What is this about going to dinner? Except for on R and R, I haven't been in a restaurant for a year. I kept looking around thinking how incredibly superficial everything was, how nobody really understood what's going on. And I wanted to scream. I didn't want to go to a restaurant. I didn't even want to be here. All I want, I'm thinking, is to go back to 'Nam.

In New York I got a job working in a recovery room. I knew I had to have a job where I'd have minimal interaction. Because I just could not deal with any more people who were hurt. I wanted to do a mechanical job, get my money, and get out of there. And that's what I did for a long time. I went back to school and became an anesthetist so I would have less interaction with patients. I had no more to give. I didn't care. And gradually, you know, over the years, that emotional numbness took its toll.

And then, one day about seven months ago, this thing happened. I was giving anesthesia to a guy who had had some prior trauma in different areas of his body. After the surgery we were talking and I said, "I recognize you." It turned out we belonged to the same athletic club. So I asked him how he'd gotten injured before and he said he'd been a marine in Vietnam. That's when I said, "I was in Vietnam, too." And I couldn't believe it. Because for fourteen years I never told anyone.

This guy — he's a policeman — said, "Gosh, I've never met a woman who was in Vietnam." Then he said, "You women were great." And instantly I felt very close to him.

It had been a long time since I'd felt close to anybody.

One day he was on duty and driving by the club in his patrol car and I'm outside and he said, "I have something I want you to read." So he went home and got this book. It's *Home before Morning,* which I had never heard of. I took it home and started to read it. Only I couldn't read it. Because every time I read a page I'd start to see things and start to cry. I kept saying to myself, "I can't believe this. I can't believe someone else is feeling the same things I am." Because, all those years, I'd thought I was the only one.

I had never come in contact with any veterans. Meeting my policeman friend — he was the first.

So I went to the Vet Center, which, before, I never felt had anything to do with me. The guys there greeted me like a long-lost sister or something. I couldn't believe it. They were just wonderful. They had all these things organized, too.

In November — this past November — I went down to Washington for the dedication of the Monument [the Vietnam Veterans Memorial]. I had absolutely no idea what to expect. But when I saw all those guys, I felt so at home. It was, in a good sense, like being back in Vietnam. You know, you had on grungy uniforms again and everything was very recognizable and you were with people you felt truly comfortable with. Because those guys greeted me so affectionately and warmly. And you know, you just don't think of some big brute of a guy, an ex-marine, coming up to you with tears in his eyes, hugging you, thanking you, being so open about his feelings.

I was afraid because I knew the dam was trying to burst. But I went over to the Wall. I sat down and looked at all the names. And suddenly I couldn't stop crying. I was crying so hard I couldn't get up — every time I tried to get up I'd start crying again. It was as though I was never going to be able to stop. And I'd always had this thing about self-control and nobody seeing me cry.

So I was sitting there, trying to get up, when this big black guy came over and put his hand on my shoulder. "It's OK," he said. I looked up at him and couldn't talk. He backed away then — backed away but stood next to me. Finally, when I was able to stand up, I went over to him and saw tears in his eyes and he put his arms around me and I was hugging him. I couldn't believe it. And this was just the beginning.

I didn't know what to think. I was just a wreck. So I stayed with him awhile and then I went and sat on the grass. These other guys came over then. They had all been there. They just came over and they were all so gentle and we sat around and talked. It was unbelievable. It was really like being home.

READING CRITICALLY

1. Why does McClusky join the army? Do her experiences meet her expectations?

2. What is her attitude toward the Vietnamese? How does it change during her tour of duty?

3. Which of McClusky's experiences do you find most surprising or disturbing?

WRITING ANALYTICALLY

1. Many veterans have said that coming home was a terrible experience for them and McClusky asserts that coming home was worse than going over. Write an essay explaining what McClusky means by her statement. Option 1: Compare and contrast McClusky's experience of returning home with Bryant's (p. 911). Option 2: If you know a Vietnam veteran, interview him or her about the experience of returning home, and compare that person's experience to McClusky's and Bryant's.

RON KOVIC

From *Born on the Fourth of July* (1976)

Ron Kovic was born on July 4, 1946 in Levittown, Long Island, and enlisted in the army in 1964. He was severely wounded in Vietnam, received the Purple Heart and the Bronze Star, and returned to the United States in 1968, paralyzed from the waist down. After four students were killed by National Guard troops at Kent State University in 1970, he turned to antiwar activities and joined Vietnam Veterans Against the War. His boldest antiwar act was disrupting President Richard Nixon's nomination-acceptance speech, on national television, at the 1972 Republican convention in Miami. After the war, Kovic continued his work as an activist, opposing U.S. policy in Central America and advocating nuclear disarmament.

His autobiography, *Born on the Fourth of July,* was regarded as a pioneering work in the literature of Vietnam veterans. Director Oliver Stone and Kovic worked for years on a screenplay for the film version, which was released in 1989 and starred Tom Cruise as Kovic. Since that time, Kovic has been living in California and has turned down offers to run for political office.

Kovic begins his book with the story of how he is wounded in a battle in Vietnam, carried off the battlefield, and taken to a field hospital, where a priest gives him the last rites. Our excerpt begins after he returns to the United States.

I AM IN A NEW HOSPITAL NOW. Things are very different than in the last place. It is quiet in the early morning. There is no reveille here. The sun is just beginning to come in through the windows and I can hear the steady dripping of the big plastic bags that overflow with urine onto the floor. The aide comes in the room, a big black woman. She goes to Willey's bed across from me, almost stepping in the puddle of urine. She takes the cork out of the metal thing in his neck and sticks a long rubber tube in, then clicks on the machine by the bed. There is a loud sucking slurping sound. She moves the rubber tube around and around until it sucks all the stuff out of his lungs. After she is done she puts the cork back in his throat and leaves the room.

There are people talking down at the end of the hall. The night shift is getting ready to go home. They are laughing very loud and flushing the toilets, cursing and telling jokes, black men in white uniforms walking past my door. I shut my eyes. I try to get back into the dream I was having. She is so pretty, so warm and naked lying next to me. She kisses me and begins

Ron Kovic, *Born on the Fourth of July* (New York: McGraw-Hill, 1976), 32–38, 54–61, 73–74, 134–40, 170–71, 176–84.

In the notes, EDS. = Patricia Bizzell and Bruce Herzberg.

to unbutton my hospital shirt. "I love you," I hear her say. "I love you." I open my eyes. Something strange is tickling my nose.

It is Tommy the enema man and today is my day to get my enema. "Hey Kovic," Tommy is saying. "Hey Kovic, wake up, I got an enema for you."

She kisses my lips softly at first, then puts her tongue into my mouth. I am running my hands through her hair and she tells me that she loves that. She is unbuttoning my trousers now and her hand is working itself deep down into my pants. I keep driving my tongue into her more furiously than ever. We have just been dancing on the floor, I was dancing very funny like a man on stilts, but now we are making love and just above me I hear a voice trying to wake me again.

"Kovic! I have an enema for you. Come on. We gotta get you outta here."

I feel myself being lifted. Tommy and another aide, a young black woman, picked me up, carefully unhooking my tube. They put my body into the frame, tying my legs down with long white twisted sheets. They lay another big sheet over me. The frame has a long metal bar that goes above my head. My rear end sticks out of a slit that I lie on.

"Okay," shouts Tommy in his gravel voice. "This one's ready to go."

The aide pushes me into the lineup in the hallway. There are frames all over the place now, lined up in front of the blue room for their enemas. It is the Six O'Clock Special. There are maybe twenty guys waiting by now. It looks like a long train, a long assembly line of broken, twisted bodies waiting for deliverance. It is very depressing, all these bodies, half of them asleep, tied down to their frames with their rear ends sticking out. All these bodies bloated, waiting to be released. Every third day I go for my enema and wait with the long line of men shoved against the green hospital wall. I watch the dead bodies being pushed into the enema room, then finally myself.

It is a small blue room and they cram us into it like sardines. Tommy runs back and forth placing the bedpans under our rear ends, laughing and joking, a cigarette dangling from the corner of his mouth. "Okay, okay, let's go!" he shouts. There is a big can of soapy water above each man's head and a tube that comes down from it. Tommy is jumping all around and whistling like a little kid, running to each body, sticking the rubber tubes up into them. He is jangling the pans, undoing little clips on the rubber tubes and filling the bellies up with soapy water. Everyone is trying to sleep, refusing to admit that this whole thing is happening to them. A couple of the bodies in the frames have small radios close to their ears. Tommy keeps running from one frame to the other, changing the rubber gloves on his hands and squirting the tube of lubricant onto his fingers, ramming his hands up into the rear ends, checking each of the bodies out, undoing the little clips. The aide keeps grabbing the bedpans and emptying all the shit into the garbage cans, occasionally missing and splattering the stuff on the floor. She places the empty pans in a machine and closes it up. There is a steam sound and the machine opens with all the bedpans as clean as new.

Oh God, what is happening to me? What is going on here? I want to get out of this place! All these broken men are very depressing, all these bodies so emaciated and twisted in these bedsheets. This is a nightmare. This isn't like the poster down by the post office where the guy stood with the shiny shoes; this is a concentration camp. It is like the pictures of all the Jews that I have seen. This is as horrible as that. I want to scream. I want to yell and tell them that I want out of this. All of this, all these people, this place, these sounds, I want out of this forever. I am only twenty-one and there is still so much ahead of me, there is so much ahead of me.

I am wiped clean and pushed past the garbage cans. The stench is terrible. I try to breathe through my mouth but I can't. I'm trapped. I have to watch, I have to smell. I think the war has made me a little mad — the dead corporal from Georgia, the old man that was shot in the village with his brains hanging out. But it is the living deaths I am breathing and smelling now, the living deaths, the bodies broken in the same war that I have come from.

I am outside now in the narrow hallway. The young black woman is pushing my frame past all the other steel contraptions. I look at her face for a moment, at her eyes, as she pushes my frame up against another. I can hear the splashing of water next door in the shower room. The sun has come up in the Bronx and people are walking through the hallways. They can look into all the rooms and see the men through the curtains that never close. It is as if we are a bunch of cattle, as if we do not really count anymore.

They push me into the shower. The black woman takes a green plastic container and squirts it, making a long thin white line from my head to my legs. She is turning on the water, and after making sure it is not too hot she hoses me down.

It's like a car wash, I think, it's just like a big car wash, and I am being pushed and shoved through with the rest of them. I am being checked out by Tommy and hosed off by the woman. It is all such a neat, quick process. It is an incredible thing to run twenty men through a place like this, to clean out the bodies of twenty paralyzed men, twenty bloated twisted men. It is an incredible feat, a stupendous accomplishment, and Tommy is a master. Now the black woman is drying me off with a big white towel and shoving me back into the hallway.

Oh get me back into the room, get me back away from these people who are walking by me and making believe like all the rest that they don't know what's happening here, that they can't figure out that this whole thing is crazy. Oh God, oh God help me, help me understand this place. There goes the nurse and she's running down the hall, hitting the rubber mat that throws open the big green metal door with the little windows with the wire in them. Oh nurse please help me nurse, my stomach is beginning to hurt again like it does every time I come out of this place and my head is throbbing, pounding like a drum. I want to get out of this hall where all of you are walking past me. I want to get back into my bed where I can make believe this never happened. I want to go to sleep and forget I ever got up this morning.

I never tell my family when they come to visit about the enema room. I do not tell them what I do every morning with the plastic glove, or about the catheter and the tube in my penis, or the fact that I can't ever make it hard again. I hide all that from them and talk about the other, more pleasant things, the things they want to hear. I ask Mom to bring me *Sunrise at Campobello,* the play about the life of Franklin Roosevelt — the great crisis he had gone through when he had been stricken with polio and the comeback he had made, becoming governor, then president of the United States. There are things I am going through here that I know she will never understand.

I feel like a big clumsy puppet with all his strings cut. I learn to balance and twist in the chair so no one can tell how much of me does not feel or move anymore. I find it easy to hide from most of them what I am going through. All of us are like this. No one wants too many people to know how much of him has really died in the war.

At first I felt that the wound was very interesting. I saw it almost as an adventure. But now it is not an adventure any longer. I see it more and more as a terrible thing that I will have to live with for the rest of my life. Nobody wants to know that I can't fuck anymore. I will never go up to them and tell I have this big yellow rubber thing sticking in my penis, attached to the rubber bag on the side of my leg. I am afraid of letting them know how lonely and scared I have become thinking about this wound. It is like some kind of numb twilight zone to me. I am angry and want to kill everyone — all the volunteers and the priests and the pretty girls with the tight short skirts. I am twenty-one and the whole thing is shot, done forever. There is no real healing left anymore, everything that is going to heal has healed already and now I am left with the corpse, the living dead man, the man with the numb legs, the man in the wheelchair, the Easter Seal boy, the cripple, the sexlessman, the sexlessman, the man with the numb dick, the man who can't make children, the man who can't stand, the man who can't walk, the angry lonely man, the bitter man with the nightmares, the murder man, the man who cries in the shower.

In one big bang they have taken it all from me, in one clean sweep, and now I am in this place around all the others like me, and though I keep trying not to feel sorry for myself, I want to cry. There is no shortcut around this thing. It is too soon to die even for a man who has died once already. . . .

Every Saturday afternoon we'd all go down to the movies in the shopping center and watch gigantic prehistoric birds breathe fire, and war movies with John Wayne and Audie Murphy. Bobbie's mother always packed us a bagful of candy. I'll never forget Audie Murphy in *To Hell and Back.* At the end he jumps on top of a flaming tank that's just about to explode and grabs the machine gun blasting it into the German lines. He was so brave I had chills running up and down my back, wishing it were me up there. There were gasoline flames roaring around his legs, but he just kept firing that machine gun. It was the greatest movie I ever saw in my life.

Castiglia and I saw *The Sands of Iwo Jima* together. The Marine Corps hymn was playing in the background as we sat glued to our seats, humming the hymn together and watching Sergeant Stryker, played by John Wayne, charge up the hill and get killed just before he reached the top. And then they showed the men raising the flag on Iwo Jima with the marines' hymn still playing, and Castiglia and I cried in our seats. I loved the song so much, and every time I heard it I would think of John Wayne and the brave men who raised the flag on Iwo Jima that day. I would think of them and cry. Like Mickey Mantle and the fabulous New York Yankees, John Wayne in *The Sands of Iwo Jima* became one of my heroes.

We'd go home and make up movies like the ones we'd just seen or the ones that were on TV night after night. We'd use our Christmas toys — the Matty Mattel machine guns and grenades, the little green plastic soldiers with guns and flamethrowers in their hands. My favorites were the green plastic men with bazookas. They blasted holes through the enemy. They wiped them out at thirty feet just above the coffee table. They dug in on the front lawn and survived countless artillery attacks. They burned with high-propane lighter fluid and a quarter-gallon of gasoline or were thrown into the raging fires of autumn leaves blasting into a million pieces.

On Saturdays after the movies all the guys would go down to Sally's Woods — Pete and Kenny and Bobbie and me, with plastic battery-operated machine guns, cap pistols, and sticks. We turned the woods into a battlefield. We set ambushes, then led gallant attacks, storming over the top, bayonetting and shooting anyone who got in our way. Then we'd walk out of the woods like the heroes we knew we would become when we were men.

The army had a show on Channel 2 called *The Big Picture,* and after it was over Castiglia and I crawled all over the backyard playing guns and army, making commando raids all summer into Ackerman's housing project blasting away at the imaginary enemy we had created right before our eyes, throwing dirt bombs and rocks into the windows, making loud explosions like hand grenades with our voices then charging in with our Matty Mattel machine guns blazing. I bandaged up the German who was still alive and had Castiglia question him as I threw a couple more grenades, killing even more Germans. We went on countless missions and patrols together around my backyard, attacking Ackerman's housing project with everything from bazookas to flamethrowers and baseball bats. We studied the *Marine Corps Guidebook* and Richie brought over some beautiful pamphlets with very sharp-looking marines on the covers. We read them in my basement for hours and just as we dreamed of playing for the Yankees someday, we dreamed of becoming United States Marines and fighting our first war and we made a solemn promise that year that the day we turned seventeen we were both going down to the marine recruiter at the shopping center in Levittown and sign up for the United States Marine Corps.

We joined the cub scouts and marched in parades on Memorial Day. We made contingency plans for the cold war and built fallout shelters out of milk cartons. We wore spacesuits and space helmets. We made rocket ships out of cardboard boxes. And one Saturday afternoon in the basement Castiglia and I went to Mars on the couch we had turned into a rocket ship. We read books about the moon and Wernher von Braun.[1] And the whole block watched a thing called the space race begin. On a cold October night Dad and I watched the first satellite, called *Sputnik*, moving across the sky above our house like a tiny bright star. I still remember standing out there with Dad looking up in amazement at that thing moving in the sky above Massapequa. It was hard to believe that this thing, this *Sputnik*, was so high up and moving so fast around the world, again and again. Dad put his hand on my shoulder that night and without saying anything I quietly walked back inside and went to my room thinking that the Russians had beaten America into space and wondering why we couldn't even get a rocket off the pad.

It seemed that whole school year we talked about nothing but rockets and how they would break away into stages and blast their satellites into outer space. I got all the books I could on rockets and outer space and read them for hours in the library, completely fascinated by the drawings and the telescopes and the sky charts. I had an incredible rocket I got for Christmas that you had to pump compressed water into. I pulled back a plastic clip and it would send the thing blasting out across Castiglia's lawn, then out onto Hamilton Avenue in a long arc of spurting water. Castiglia and I used to tape aluminum-foil rolls from Mom's kitchen to the top of the plastic rocket then put ants and worms in the nose cone with a secret message wrapped in tissue paper. We had hundreds of rocket launchings that year. Though none of our payloads made it into orbit like the *Sputniks*, we had a lot of fun trying.

In the spring of that year I remember the whole class went down to New York City and saw the movie *Around the World in Eighty Days* on a tremendous screen that made all of us feel like we were right there in the balloon flying around the world. After the movie we went to the Museum of Natural History, where Castiglia and I walked around staring up at the huge prehistoric dinosaurs billions of years old, and studied fossils inside the big glass cases and wondered what it would have been like if we had been alive back then. After the museum they took us to the Hayden Planetarium, where the whole sixth-grade class leaned back in special sky chairs, looking up into the dome where a projector that looked like a huge mechanical praying mantis kept us glued to the sky above our heads with meteor showers and comets and galaxies that appeared like tremendous snowstorms swirling in the pitch darkness of the incredible dome. They showed the whole beginning of the earth that afternoon, as we sat back in our chairs and dreamed of walking on the moon someday or going off to Mars wondering if there really was life there and rocketing off deeper and deeper into space through all the time barriers into places and dreams we could only begin to imagine. When we got on the school bus afterward and were all seated, Mr. Serby, our sixth-grade teacher, turned around and in a soft

---

[1]Wernher von Braun (1912–77), a leading German rocket scientist, came to the United States after World War II and helped develop the American space program. — EDS.

voice told us that someday men would walk upon the moon, and probably in our lifetime, he said, we would see it happen.

We were still trying to catch up with the Russians when I heard on the radio that the United States was going to try and launch its first satellite, called *Vanguard,* into outer space. That night Mom and Dad and me and the rest of the kids watched the long pencil-like rocket on the television screen as it began to lift off after the countdown. It lifted off slowly at first. And then, almost as if in slow motion, it exploded into a tremendous fireball on the launching pad. It had barely gotten off the ground, and I cried that night in my living room. I cried watching *Vanguard* that night on the evening news with Mom and all the rest. It was a sad day for our country, I thought, it was a sad day for America. We had failed in our first attempt to put a satellite into orbit. I walked slowly back to my room. We were losing, I thought, we were losing the space race, and America wasn't first anymore.

When *Vanguard* finally made it into space, I was in junior high school, and right in the middle of the class the loudspeaker interrupted us and the principal in a very serious voice told us that something very important was about to happen. He talked about history, and how important the day was, how America was finally going to launch its first satellite and we would remember it for a long time.

There was a long countdown as we all sat on the edge of our seats, tuning our ears in to the radio. And then the rocket began to lift off the edge of the launching pad. In the background there was the tremendous roar of the rocket engines and a guy was screaming like Mel Allen that the rocket was lifting off. "It's lifting off! It's lifting off!" he kept screaming crazily. All the kids were silent for a few seconds, still straining in their chairs, waiting to see whether the rocket would make it or not, then the whole room broke into cheers and applause. America had done it! We had put our first satellite into space. "We did it! We did it!" the guy was screaming at the top of his lungs.

And now America was finally beginning to catch up with the Russians and each morning before I went to school I was watching *I Led Three Lives* on television about this guy who joins the Communists but is actually working for us. And I remember thinking how brave he was, putting his life on the line for his country, making believe he was a Communist, and all the time being on our side, getting information from them so we could keep the Russians from taking over our government. He seemed like a very serious man, and he had a wife and a kid and he went to secret meetings, calling his friends comrades in a low voice, and talking through newspapers on park benches.

The Communists were all over the place back then. And if they weren't trying to beat us into outer space, Castiglia and I were certain they were infiltrating our schools, trying to take over our classes and control our minds. We were both certain that one of our teachers was a secret Communist agent and in our next secret club meeting we promised to report anything new he said during our next history class. We watched him very carefully that year. One afternoon he told us that China was going to have a billion people someday. "One billion!" he said, tightly clenching his fist. "Do you know what that means?" he said, staring out the classroom window. "Do you know what that's going to mean?" he said in almost a whisper. He never finished what he was saying and after that Castiglia and I were convinced he was definitely a Communist. . . .

In the last month of school, the marine recruiters came and spoke to my senior class. They marched, both in perfect step, into the auditorium with their dress blue uniforms and their magnificently shined shoes. It was like all the movies and all the books and all the dreams of becoming a hero come true. I watched them and listened as they stood in front of all the young boys, looking almost like statues and not like real men at all. They spoke in loud voices and one of them was tall and the other was short and very strong looking.

"Good afternoon, men," the tall marine said. "We have come today because they told us that some of you want to become marines." He told us that the marines took nothing but the best, that if any of us did not think we were good enough, we should not even think of joining. The tall marine spoke in a very beautiful way about the exciting history of the marines and how they had never lost and America had never been defeated.

"The marines have been the first in everything, first to fight and first to uphold the honor of our country. We have served on distant shores and at home, and we have always come when our country has called. There is nothing finer, nothing prouder, than a United States Marine."

When they were finished, they efficiently picked up their papers and marched together down the steps of the stage to where a small crowd of boys began to gather. I couldn't wait to run down after them, meet with them and shake their hands. And as I shook their hands and stared up into their eyes, I couldn't help but feel I was shaking hands with John Wayne and Audie Murphy. They told us that day that the Marine Corps built men — body, mind, and spirit. And that we could serve our country like the young president had asked us to do. . . .

I was in Vietnam when I first heard about the thousands of people protesting the war in the streets of America. I didn't want to believe it at first — people protesting against *us* when we were putting our lives on the line for our country. The men in my outfit used to talk about it a lot. How could they do this to us? Many of us would not be coming back and many others would be wounded or maimed. We swore they would pay, the hippies and draft-card burners. They would pay if we ever ran into them.

But the hospital had changed all that. It was the end of whatever belief I'd still had in what I'd done in Vietnam. Now I wanted to know what I had lost my legs for, why I and the others had gone at all. But it was still very hard for me to think of speaking out against the war, to think of joining those I'd once called traitors.

I settled into my apartment again and went back to classes at the university. It was the spring of 1970. I still wore a tie and sweater every day to school and had a short haircut. I was very sensitive to people looking at me in the wheelchair. I buried myself in my books, cutting myself off from the other students. It was as if they threatened me — particularly the activists, the radicals.

I was sitting alone in my apartment listening to the radio when I first heard the news about Kent State. Four students had just been shot in a demonstration against the invasion of Cambodia. For a moment there was a shock through my body. I felt like crying. The last time I had felt that way was the day Kennedy was killed. I remember saying to myself, The whole thing is coming down now. I wheeled out to my car. I didn't know where I was going but I had to find other people who felt the way I did. I drove down the street to the university. Students were congregating in small groups all over the place. The campus looked as if it were going to explode. Banners were going up and monitors with red armbands were walking up and down handing out leaflets. There was going to be a march and demonstration. I thought carefully for a moment or two, then decided to participate, driving my car past the hundreds of students marching down to the big parking lot where the rally was to be held. I honked my horn in support but I was still feeling a little hesitant. I stayed in my car all during the rally, listening intently to each speaker and cheering and shouting with the crowd. I was still acting like an observer. The last speaker was a woman who said there would be a huge rally in Washington that Saturday and that it was hoped that everyone would make it down. I decided I would go.

That night I called my cousin Ginny's husband, Skip. He used to come and visit me at the hospital when I first came back and after I got out we became good friends. Sometimes we'd stay up all night at his house playing cards and talking about Vietnam and what had happened to me. Skip's views were very different from mine back then. He was against the war. And each time I left his house to go home, he'd give me books to read — books about the black people and poor people of the country. I laughed at him at first and didn't take the books too seriously, but it was lonely in my room and soon I began to read. And before long, every time I went to his house I asked for more books. Skip seemed surprised when I asked him to go to the rally with me but he said yes, and early Saturday morning we left for Washington.

The New Jersey Turnpike was packed with cars painted with flags and signs, and everywhere there were people hitching, holding up big cardboard peace symbols. You didn't have to ask where anyone was going. We were all going to the same place. Washington was a madhouse with buses and trucks and cars coming in from all directions.

We got a parking space and I gave up my tie and sweater for no shirt and a big red bandana around my head. Skip pushed the wheelchair for what seemed a mile or so. We could feel the tremendous tension. People were handing out leaflets reminding everyone that this was a nonviolent demonstration, and that no purpose would be served in violent confrontation. I remember feeling a little scared, the way I did before a firefight. After reading the leaflet I felt content that no one was going to get hurt.

Skip and I moved as close to the speakers' platform as we could and Skip lifted me out of my chair and laid me on my cushion. People were streaming into the Ellipse from all around us — an army of everyday people. There was a guy with a stereo tape deck blasting out music, and dogs running after Frisbees on the lawn. The Hare Krishna people started to dance and the whole thing seemed like a weird carnival. But there was a warmth to it, a feeling that we were all together in a very important place. A young girl sat down next to me and handed me a canteen of cool water. "Here," she said, "have a drink." I drank it down and passed it to Skip who passed it to someone else. That was the feeling that day. We all seemed to be sharing everything.

We listened as the speakers one after another denounced the invasion of Cambodia and the slaying of the students at Kent State. The sun was getting very hot and Skip and I decided to move around. We wanted to get to the White House where Nixon was holed up, probably watching television. We were in a great sea of people, thousands and thousands all around us. We finally made it to Lafayette Park. On the other side of the avenue the government had lined up thirty or forty buses, making a huge wall between the people and the White House. I remember wondering back then why they had to put all those buses in front of the president. Was the government so afraid of its own people that it needed such a gigantic barricade? I'll always remember those buses lined up that day and not being able to see the White House from my wheelchair.

We went back to the rally for a while, then went on down to the Reflecting Pool. Hundreds of people had taken off their clothes. They were jumping up and down to the beat of bongo drums and metal cans. A man in his fifties had stripped completely naked. Wearing only a crazy-looking hat and a pair of enormous black glasses, he was dancing on a platform in the middle of hundreds of naked people. The crowd was clapping wildly. Skip hesitated for a moment, then stripped all his clothes off, jumping into the pool and joining the rest of the people. I didn't know what all of this had to do with the invasion of Cambodia or the students slain at Kent State, but it was total freedom. As I sat there in my wheelchair at the edge of the Reflecting Pool with everyone running naked all around me and the clapping and the drums resounding in my ears, I wanted to join them. I wanted to take off my clothes like Skip and the rest of them and wade into the pool and rub my body with all those others. Everything seemed to be hitting me all at once. One part of me was upset that people were swimming naked in the national monument and the other part of me completely understood that now it was their pool, and what good is a pool if you can't swim in it.

I remember how the police came later that day, very suddenly, when we were watching the sun go down — a blue legion of police in cars and on motorcycles and others with angry faces on big horses. A tall cop walked into the crowd near the Reflecting Pool and read something into a bull-horn no one could make out. The drums stopped and a few of the naked people began to put their clothes back on. It was almost evening and with most of the invading army's forces heading back along the Jersey Turn-pike, the blue legion had decided to attack. And they did — wading their horses into the pool, flailing their clubs, smashing skulls. People were run-ning everywhere as gas canisters began to pop. I couldn't understand why this was happening, why the police would attack the people, running them into the grass with their horses and beating them with their clubs. Two or three horses charged into the crowd at full gallop, driving the invading army into retreat toward the Lincoln Memorial. A girl was crying and screaming, trying to help her bleeding friend. She was yelling something about the pigs and kept stepping backward away from the horses and the flying clubs. For the first time that day I felt anger surge up inside me. I was no longer an observer, sitting in my car at the edge of a demonstra-tion. I was right in the middle of it and it was ugly. Skip started pushing the chair as fast as he could up the path toward the Lincoln Memorial. I kept turning, looking back. I wanted to shout back at the charging police, tell them I was a veteran.

When we got to the memorial, I remember looking at Lincoln's face and reading the words carved on the walls in back of him. I felt certain that if he were alive he would be there with us.

I told Skip that I was never going to be the same. The demonstration had stirred something in my mind that would be there from now on. It was so very different from boot camp and fighting in the war. There was a to-getherness, just as there had been in Vietnam, but it was a togetherness of a different kind of people and for a much different reason. In the war we were killing and maiming people. In Washington on that Saturday after-noon in May we were trying to heal them and set them free. . . .

Every once in a while as I drive the Oldsmobile down the long, hot Texas highway, I look into the dust-covered rearview mirror and see the convoy behind me, stretching back like a gigantic snake so far I cannot even tell where it ends — cars and buses, trucks and jeeps, painted with flowers and peace signs, a strange caravan of young men wearing war rib-bons on torn utility jackets and carrying plastic guns. It is August of 1972 and we have come nearly two thousand miles with another thousand still ahead of us before we reach Miami. We have shared food and cans of Coke. We have driven like madmen across the desert and lain down in the sand in our sleeping bags. We have played and laughed around campfires. It is our last patrol together, and I know I will remember it as long as I live. It is a historic event like the Bonus March of thousands of veterans upon the Capitol in the thirties. And now it is we who are marching, the boys of the fifties. We are going to the Republican National Convention to reclaim America and a bit of ourselves. It is war and we are soldiers again, as tight as we have ever been, a whole lost generation of dope-smoking kids in worn jungle boots coming from all over the country to tell Nixon a thing or two. We know we are fighting the real enemies this time — the ones who have made profit off our very lives. We have lain all night in the rain in ambush together. We have burned anthills with kerosene and stalked through Sally's Woods with plastic machine guns, shooting people out of trees. We have been a generation of violence and madness, of dead Indians and drunken cowboys, of iron pipes full of match-heads.

There is a tremendous downpour just outside of Houston that almost tears the windshield wipers off the car. And after the rain there is one of the most beautiful rainbows ever seen, and then a second rainbow appears — a magnificent double rainbow above our heads. I am certain I want to be alive forever. I know that no matter what has happened the world is a beautiful place, and I am here with my brothers. . . .

It was the night of Nixon's acceptance speech and now I was on my own deep in his territory, all alone in my wheelchair in a sweat-soaked marine utility jacket covered with medals from the war. A TV producer I knew from the Coast had gotten me past the guards at the entrance with his press pass. My eyes were still smarting from teargas. Outside the chain metal fence around the Convention Center my friends were being clubbed and arrested, herded into wagons. The crowds were thick all around me, people dressed as if they were going to a banquet, men in expensive summer suits and women in light elegant dresses. Every once in a while someone would look at me as if I didn't belong there. But I had come almost three thousand miles for this meeting with the president and nothing was going to prevent it from taking place.

I worked my way slowly and carefully into the huge hall, moving down one of the side aisles. "Excuse me, excuse me," I said to delegates as I pushed past them farther and farther to the front of the hall toward the speakers' podium.

I had gotten only halfway toward where I wanted to be when I was stopped by one of the convention security marshals. "Where are you going?" he said. He grabbed hold of the back of my chair. I made believe I hadn't heard him and kept turning my wheels, but his grip on the chair was too tight and now two other security men had joined him.

"What's the matter?" I said. "Can't a disabled veteran who fought for his country sit up front?"

The three men looked at each other for a moment and one of them said, "I'm afraid not. You're not allowed up front with the delegates." I had gotten as far as I had on sheer bluff alone and now they were telling me I could go no farther. "You'll have to go to the back of the convention hall, son. Let's go," said the guard who was holding my chair.

In a move of desperation I swung around facing all three of them, shouting as loud as I could so Walter Cronkite and the CBS camera crew that was just above me could hear me and maybe even focus their cameras in for the six o'clock news. "I'm a Vietnam veteran and I fought in the war! Did you fight in the war?"

One of the guards looked away.

"Yeah, that's what I thought," I said. "I bet none of you fought in the war and you guys are trying to throw me out of the convention. I've got just as much right to be up front here as any of these delegates. I fought for that right and I was born on the Fourth of July."

I was really shouting now and another officer came over. I think he might have been in charge of the hall. He told me I could stay where I was if I was quiet and didn't move up any farther. I agreed with the compromise. I locked my brakes and looked for other veterans in the tremendous crowd. As far as I could tell, I was the only one who had made it in.

People had begun to sit down all around me. They all had Four More Years buttons and I was surprised to see how many of them were young. I began speaking to them, telling them about the Last Patrol and why veterans from all over the United States had taken the time and effort to travel thousands of miles to the Republican National Convention. "I'm a disabled veteran!" I shouted. "I served two tours of duty in Vietnam and while on my second tour of duty up in the DMZ I was wounded and paralyzed from the chest down." I told them I would be that way for the rest of my life. Then I began to talk about the hospitals and how they treated the returning veterans like animals, how I, many nights in the Bronx, had lain in my own shit for hours waiting for an aide. "And they never come," I said. "They never come because that man that's going to accept the nomination tonight has been lying to all of us and spending the money on war that should be spent on healing and helping the wounded. That's the biggest lie and hypocrisy of all — that we had to over there and fight and get crippled and come home to a government and leaders who could care less about the same boys they sent over."

I kept shouting and speaking, looking for some kind of reaction from the crowd. No one seemed to want to even look at me.

"Is it too real for you to look at? Is this wheelchair too much for you to take? The man who will accept the nomination tonight is a liar!" I shouted again and again, until finally one of the security men came back and told me to be quiet or they would have to take me to the back of the hall.

I told him that if they tried to move me or touch my chair there would be a fight and hell to pay right there in front of Walter Cronkite and the national television networks. I told him if he wanted to wrestle me and beat me to the floor of the convention hall in front of all those cameras he could.

By then a couple of newsmen, including Roger Mudd from CBS, had worked their way through the security barricades and begun to ask me questions.

"Why are you here tonight?" Roger Mudd asked me. "But don't start talking until I get the camera here," he shouted.

It was too good to be true. In a few seconds Roger Mudd and I would be going on live all over the country. I would be doing what I had come here for, showing the whole nation what the war was all about. The camera began to roll, and I began to explain why I and the others had come, that the war was wrong and it had to stop immediately. "I'm a Vietnam veteran," I said. "I gave America my all and the leaders of this government threw me and the others away to rot in their VA hospitals. What's happening in Vietnam is a crime against humanity, and I just want the American people to know that we have come all the way across this country, sleeping on the ground and in the rain, to let the American people see for themselves the men who fought their war and have come to oppose it. If you can't believe the veteran who fought the war and was wounded in the war, who can you believe?"

"Thank you," said Roger Mudd, visibly moved by what I had said. "This is Roger Mudd," he said, "down on the convention floor with Ron Kovic, a disabled veteran protesting President Nixon's policy in Vietnam."

The security agents were frantically trying to stop other cameras from getting through and later I was to learn that Press Secretary Ronald Ziegler had almost flipped out when he heard Mudd had interviewed me and it had gone nationwide for almost two minutes.

By this time a few other veterans had managed to get into the hall. One of them came to tell me that my old friend Bobby Muller and Bill Wieman, a double amputee, had gotten passes from Congressman McCloskey and had managed to get into the center aisle in direct line with the podium almost two hundred feet back. "Get me up there quick," I said. He turned me around and wheeled me toward the back past the smiling security officers who must have thought I was leaving. What are you smiling at? I thought to myself. I'm just warming up.

"There, up there," the vet said, pointing to the front of the aisle where Bobby and Bill were sitting in their wheelchairs.

"Where you been?" Wieman said to me, as I shook their hands.

"I've been over there," I said, pointing to the other aisle. "I wanted to get all the way to the front, but this place is great."

We lined ourselves up together, wheelchair to wheelchair, facing the platform where Nixon would speak. They had brought in a couple of Stop the War signs, and I grabbed one and held it above my head.

There was an announcement at the podium and then a tremendous roar. It was the vice president of the United States, Spiro T. Agnew. The delegates stood chanting and shaking their clasped hands over their heads, stamping their feet up and down until it seemed as though the whole convention hall was going to explode. "Four more years," the crowd shouted. "Four more years, four more years."

Agnew stood rigid at attention, accepting the tumultuous applause. Finally he raised both of his palms, signaling them all to stop so he could give his speech. Every time he spoke a few words, he was interrupted by the wild crowd, wild and enthusiastic. "Agnew in 'seventy-six!" a fat woman yelled next to me. "Agnew in 'seventy-six!"

I pulled myself up onto the siderail of my wheelchair and sat holding my sign as high as I could. I wanted everyone in the hall to be able to see it. A man came up suddenly from my blind side. Before I knew what hit me he had grabbed my sign and torn it into shreds in front of me. "You lousy commie sonofabitch!" he shouted.

Now there was only one sign left and we decided to hold on to it until it was Nixon's turn to speak. A few seconds before he was introduced, security agents began to move in all around us. We must have been an ugly sight to the National Republican Party as we sat there in perfect view of all the national networks that were perched above us.

Suddenly a roar went up in the convention hall, louder than anything I had ever heard in my life. It started off as a rumble, then gained in intensity until it sounded like a tremendous thunderbolt. "Four more years, four more years," the crowd roared over and over again. The fat woman next to me was jumping up and down and dancing in the aisle. It was the greatest ovation the president of the United States had ever received and he loved it. I held the sides of my wheelchair to keep my hands from shaking. After what seemed forever, the roar finally began to die down.

This was the moment I had come three thousand miles for, this was it, all the pain and the rage, all the trials and the death of the war and what had been done to me and a generation of Americans by all the men who had lied to us and tricked us, by the man who stood before us in the convention hall that night, while men who had fought for their country were being gassed and beaten in the street outside the hall. I thought of Bobby who sat next to me and the months we had spent in the hospital in the Bronx. It was all hitting me at once, all those years, all that destruction, all that sorrow.

President Nixon began to speak and all three of us took a deep breath and shouted at the top of our lungs, "Stop the bombing, stop the war, stop the bombing, stop the war," as loud and as hard as we could, looking directly at Nixon. The security agents immediately threw up their arms, trying to hide us from the cameras and the president. "Stop the bombing, stop the bombing," I screamed. For an instant Cronkite looked down, then turned his head away. They're not going to show it, I thought. They're going to try and hide us like they did in the hospitals. Hundreds of people around us began to clap and shout "Four more years," trying to drown out our protest. They all seemed very angry and shouted at us to stop. We continued shouting, interrupting Nixon again and again until Secret Service agents grabbed our chairs from behind and began pulling us backward as fast as they could out of the convention hall. "Take it easy," Bobby said to me. "Don't fight back."

I wanted to take a swing and fight right there in the middle of the convention hall in front of the president and the whole country. "So this is how they treat their wounded veterans!" I screamed.

A short guy with a big Four More Years button ran up to me and spat in my face. "Traitor!" he screamed, as he was yanked back by police. Pandemonium was breaking out all around us and the Secret Service men kept pulling us out backward.

"I served two tours of duty in Vietnam!" I screamed to one newsman. "I gave three-quarters of my body for America. And what do I get? Spit in the face!" I kept screaming until we hit the side entrance where the agents pushed us outside and shut the doors, locking them with chains and padlocks so reporters wouldn't be able to follow us out for interviews.

All three of us sat holding on to each other shaking. We had done it. It had been the biggest moment of our lives, we had shouted down the president of the United States and disrupted his acceptance speech. What more was there left to do but go home?

I sat in my chair still shaking and began to cry.

READING CRITICALLY

1. What effect is Kovic trying to achieve in his description of the hospital? How does he describe his own feelings about it?

2. What images of patriotism does Kovic recall from his youth?

3. What did communism seem to mean to Kovic as a child?

4. When does Kovic decide to protest the war? What was his position prior to that moment?

5. What is Kovic's goal in getting into the Republican convention?

WRITING ANALYTICALLY

1. What images of national pride do you remember from your younger days or are you aware of now? Write a personal essay in which you reflect on these images and the way you responded to them and respond to them now. How do these images of patriotism, war, international competition, personal heroism, and so on compare with those that Kovic remembers? Are the images you remember coded for gender?

2. Why is Kovic opposed to the war? Write an essay in which you trace and explain his transformation into an antiwar activist. What exactly is he upset and angry about? Certainly he is angry about being wounded and paralyzed, but a soldier might well be badly wounded without then wanting to see his country lose or run from the war. Kovic does not mention many of the issues — such as Vietnamese history, colonization, Diem, communism, or U.S. credibility — that might form his arguments about the war. What, then, makes him so opposed? How does he try to avoid the charge that his antiwar position is merely a sign of his bitterness over his injury?

3. John Kerry, another veteran, asks, "How do you ask a man to be the last man to die for a mistake?" (p. 890). Write an essay in which you imagine how Kovic might react to or try to answer Kerry's question.

ASSIGNMENT SEQUENCES

SEQUENCE 1
Why were we in Vietnam? Why did we stay?

- Ho Chi Minh, "Declaration of Independence of the Democratic Republic of Vietnam"
- Thomas J. Dodd, From a Speech to the U.S. Senate
- U.S. Department of State, From the White Paper *Aggression from the North*
- I. F. Stone, "A Reply to the 'White Paper'"
- Paul Potter, From "The Incredible War"
- Martin Luther King Jr., "Declaration of Independence from the War in Vietnam"
- Lyndon B. Johnson, From "Peace in Vietnam and Southeast Asia"
- Richard M. Nixon, From "Vietnamization"

1. Although most of the students who read *Negotiating Difference* were born at the end of the Vietnam War, many will have impressions of the war from parents and teachers who were involved in the issues raised in this unit as well as from books and the media. Write a personal essay about your knowledge of and attitudes about the war before reading the selections in this unit. What formed your attitudes — school, parents, other people you know from the Vietnam generation, reading, television and films, your own military experience? How have your ideas changed since reading the material in this unit?

2. In his argument supporting the U.S. presence in Vietnam, Thomas J. Dodd maintains that the U.S. goal is to guarantee the independence of Vietnam and to oppose communism and aggression. The "Declaration of Independence of the Democratic Republic of Vietnam" asserts that its goals are independence and opposition to French imperialism and aggression. Write an essay comparing and contrasting the two declarations. Look very closely at the kinds of arguments each offers: How does each address such issues as economics and politics? What ideals does each appeal to? What concerns does each express that are answered by the other? What concerns are not answered?

Evidently, Ho Chi Minh believed that the United States would be swayed by the ideal of political freedom and anti-imperialism, while for U.S. policymakers, anti-communism was foremost. Though this is the center of the disagreement, you need not address it directly in your essay. Your goal here should be to examine how this basic difference is expressed in the kinds of arguments each side makes to support its position.

3. The history of U.S. involvement in Vietnam is told in several different ways in the selections here. Locate the discussions of this history in the selections by Dodd, the U.S. State Department, Stone, King, and Nixon. Write an essay comparing these different versions of the history of U.S. involvement in Vietnam. You might do this by summarizing the histories, commenting on the major differences in facts or emphasis you notice, or by tracing the history chronologically, noting the differ-

ences in the versions as you go along. Whichever approach you take, you should not try to smooth over the differences, but examine them closely. What kind of story does each version tell? Who are the heroes and villains? What facts are in one version but not another? On what supposed facts is there direct disagreement?

You need not decide which version is true or closer to true than another (though you may discuss your feelings about this point if you wish). The question to ask is what we are to do when our sources of historical information differ as these do. Why do these histories differ so much? What warnings should we take from this discrepancy about how to read history?

4. The key terms in the arguments about U.S. policy in Vietnam are *communism* and *aggression*. The United States wanted to prevent the spread of communism from the Soviet Union and China to Vietnam and other countries and resented the use of force ("aggression") by one country — North Vietnam — to invade or promote revolution in another — South Vietnam. Though these principles seem quite straightforward, there were constant debates about whether they actually applied to Vietnam at all. Trace this debate in the selections by Dodd, the State Department, Stone, Potter, and King. Write an essay in which you explain the differing views on communism and aggression. You need not decide which view is correct (though you may discuss this question if you wish). Rather, try to explain what the points of disagreement are.

5. As the war progressed, did the political goals of the United States change? Write an essay tracing the use of key terms (such as *communism* and *aggression*) and the statement of U.S. goals in Vietnam focusing on the following selections: Dodd (1965), U.S. Department of State (1965), Johnson (1968), and Nixon (1969). In your essay, describe the tone of each selection.

SEQUENCE 2
What was the U.S. military mission in Vietnam?

- Thomas J. Dodd, From a Speech to the U.S. Senate
- Barbara Beidler, "Afterthoughts on a Napalm-Drop on Jungle Villages near Haiphong"
- Huy Can, "Truth Blazes Even in Little Children's Hearts"
- Paul Potter, From "The Incredible War"
- Lyndon B. Johnson, From "Peace in Vietnam and Southeast Asia"
- National Mobilization Committee, "A Message to GIs and to the Movement"
- Richard M. Nixon, From "Vietnamization"
- John F. Kerry, Testimony before the U.S. Senate Foreign Relations Committee
- Harold "Light Bulb" Bryant, Oral History
- Leslie McClusky, Oral History
- Ron Kovic, From *Born on the Fourth of July*

1. Ron Kovic describes the images of war and patriotism that influenced him to join the marines. What images have influenced your attitude toward the military?

Write a personal essay describing your attitude toward war and military service. Explain your own contacts with such service, personally or through relatives and friends. Note, in particular, any ideas you may have had about the war in Vietnam — how it was fought, how soldiers were treated, and so on — before reading the selections in this unit. How have your ideas about service in Vietnam changed as a result of your reading?

2. The military mission in Vietnam became an issue early in the war. Most internal government documents during the 1950s and 1960s (documents that are available in several collections cited in the bibliography) deal with strategies for fighting against the Communists in Vietnam, both North and South, without precipitating a war with China. There is a sense of inexorability in these documents, a constant push toward greater U.S. military involvement. The concept of the war as a fight against aggression was also very important in defining the military mission. Write an essay, based on your reading of the selections by Dodd, Johnson, and Nixon, describing the mission in Vietnam as it was presented by these government officials. Why were U.S. soldiers in Vietnam? What were they supposed to do?

3. The soldiers and nurses who served in Vietnam tell of the exceptional horrors of the war and of their own disillusionment with the ideals of the United States. Yet their experiences of the war and their reactions when they return home are not the same. Reading the pieces by Kerry, Bryant, McClusky, and Kovic — which represent only a tiny selection from the many powerful memoirs and other writings by veterans of the Vietnam War — is an emotional experience for most readers. It is worthwhile to begin by responding to these pieces through personal writing before working on a more formal question.

For a personal response, read or reread the selections by Kerry, Bryant, Mc-Clusky, and Kovic, keeping a journal of your reactions. (If this is your second reading and you kept a journal the first time, add to or react to your initial entries.) How do you feel about these people, their actions, and their experiences? In what ways do you feel connected with them? Can you imagine your own reactions in the situations they describe? What questions about the war do these selections raise for you? You can prepare your journal in several ways. You may simply turn in the pages that you have written while reading. Alternatively, recopy your journal entries so that they are legible and, as you do so, add reflective notes that explain entries that may not be clear or include further thoughts. Your instructor will indicate which method is appropriate for your course.

Alternative: Here is a more formal approach to the same selections. Write an essay examining the experiences of war and homecoming in the selections by Kerry, Bryant, McClusky, and Kovic. How do they attempt to understand, or at least describe, the conflicts they feel between the ideals or goals they initially held and the emotional effect of what they saw and did in Vietnam? How do they express and deal with disillusionment? In this essay, try to avoid your own emotions and reactions so that you can see the ways in which the writers deal with the intellectual and emotional challenges they face.

4. The conduct of the war was itself a factor in the debates about continuing the war. That is, a number of critics argued that the atrocities committed by the U.S. forces — ecological and cultural as well as personal — were reasons to stop the war. Write an essay examining this issue as it is argued in four or five of the following sources: Dodd, Beidler and Huy, Potter, King, the National Mobilization Committee, Nixon, Agnew, Kerry, and Bryant. Who was responsible for the atrocities? Is it legitimate to argue that either methods of war or the effects of war on U.S. troops in battle

should be factors in deciding whether to engage in war? How should these considerations be weighed against the ideological factors (communism, aggression, and freedom) in determining whether to engage in war? The soldiers observe that the Vietnamese themselves are not Communist ideologues. They simply want peace and to be left alone. But should this make any difference in establishing policy?

SEQUENCE 3

How was the war fought at home?

- Thomas J. Dodd, From a Speech to the U.S. Senate
- David Dellinger, A. J. Muste, et al., "Declaration of Conscience against the War in Vietnam"
- Barbara Beidler, "Afterthoughts on a Napalm-Drop on Jungle Villages near Haiphong"
- Huy Can, "Truth Blazes Even in Little Children's Hearts"
- Paul Potter, From "The Incredible War"
- Martin Luther King Jr., "Declaration of Independence from the War in Vietnam"
- Lyndon B. Johnson, From "Peace in Vietnam and Southeast Asia"
- National Mobilization Committee, "A Message to GIs and to the Movement"
- Richard M. Nixon, From "Vietnamization"
- Spiro T. Agnew, "Parasites, Protesters, and the Press"
- John F. Kerry, Testimony before the U.S. Senate Foreign Relations Committee
- Tim O'Brien, "On the Rainy River"
- Ron Kovic, From *Born on the Fourth of July*

1. Though most of the readers of *Negotiating Difference* were born at the end of the Vietnam War, the images of protest — conveyed in large part through the music of the period and the revolution in youth culture — are familiar to many. Write a personal essay describing the image you had of the country in the 1960s and early 1970s before you read the selections in this unit. What did you know of the turmoil, the demonstrations, the student protests, and what was your impression of these events? Where did your knowledge come from — your own experience, people who were present at the time, books, movies? In what ways have your ideas changed, if at all, since reading the selections here?

2. Those who opposed the war did so for a wide range of reasons, many of which are represented in the selections in this sequence. Write an essay compiling and categorizing the antiwar arguments discussed in several of the following selections: Dellinger, Muste, et al.; Beidler; Huy; Potter; King; Kerry; O'Brien; and Kovic. Though you may wish to comment on or evaluate the arguments, the goal of this assignment is to identify the arguments that were offered and sort them into groups that will help reveal, for example, who made certain kinds of arguments or when during the war certain arguments emerged or from what perspective certain arguments developed.

You may wish to work with a group or with the whole class on this project — finding all the arguments, brainstorming different categories, and then dividing up the task of categorizing the arguments.

3. Paul Potter, Martin Luther King Jr., and John Kerry link the Vietnam War to other, deeper problems in U.S. society. This connection was very powerful during the war and was evident to many groups of protesters, as we can see in these examples from a young student leader, a mature civil rights activist, and a veteran of the war. Write an essay analyzing the deeper problems connected to the war as they are described by Potter, King, and Kerry. What picture do they give of U.S. society at that time? In your judgment, have those underlying problems been addressed to any significant extent since the time of the war?

4. One of the most distressing results of the war was conflict, real and violent, within the United States. Heads were broken, students were killed, families exploded in generational conflict, individual Americans suffered crises of disillusionment and alienation, and veterans returned to find themselves outcasts. The selections here give a sense of how people with different views clashed in their arguments over the war, arguments that often led to physical clashes. To understand the strong feelings aroused by the war and the cultural issues it symbolized, analyze several sets of arguments and counterarguments. With a group or the whole class, divide the responsibility for writing essays on the following topics. In place of the topics suggested here, you may wish to work on a line of argument that you found particularly compelling when reading the selections in this sequence. Almost any combination of selections presents many possible topics. It might be valuable to share the essays that result from this assignment so that everyone can get a sense of the different issues and the perspectives that members of the class bring to them.

Topic 1: What were the arguments and counterarguments over the ideological basis for the war — communism, aggression, and freedom? Analyze the selections by Dodd, Potter, King, and Johnson. You may wish to add Nixon and Kerry.

Topic 2: What were the arguments and counterarguments over the conduct of the war? Analyze the selections by Dellinger, Muste, et al.; Beidler; Huy; Potter; Johnson; Nixon; Agnew; and Kerry.

Topic 3: What were the arguments and counterarguments over the protests themselves (including draft evasion and resistance)? Analyze the selections by Dodd; Dellinger, Muste, et al.; Potter; the National Mobilization Committee; Nixon; Agnew; Kerry; and O'Brien.

RESEARCH KIT

Negotiating Difference is an unfinished book: There are many other stories to tell in the history of "negotiating difference" in the United States. This Research Kit is intended to help you expand the readings provided in this unit. In "Ideas from the Unit Readings," we include more perspectives on the problems surrounding the war in Vietnam and its aftermath. In

"Branching Out," we point to research topics on other social issues that were significant during the war. We also suggest topics concerning the military and war resistance, both before and since the war. You can pursue these research ideas individually or as group or class projects.

To compile materials, you can start with the short bibliography included in this unit and with standard library search techniques that your teacher or a librarian can explain. Here are some other places where you can inquire for resources (not all regions will have all materials):

- Veterans groups, particularly local chapters of Vietnam Veterans Against the War, may have documents, photographs, and other unpublished materials; they may also be able to direct you to individual veterans who would be willing to be interviewed.
- Films and television documentaries are useful for learning about Vietnam and important to study to see how the media presented the war; your library and local video store may have surprising resources (see the bibliography for books and films about Vietnam).
- Since the war happened so recently, everybody who is middle-aged now should have some stories to share about the Vietnam era — faculty and staff, your parents or your parents' friends, and older students may all be resources.
- Local newspaper archives will produce a fascinating study in people's attitudes toward the war in editorials and letters to the editor.
- Your college's archives will very likely have records of protests, teach-ins, and other activities at your school.
- The Vietnam War is reflected in all the arts — photography, painting, music, and dance — so be aware of museum exhibits and shows on Vietnam-related themes.

Some of these same sources can be used for developing research papers based on writing questions that follow individual selections. Also, see other units in this book for suggestions for related topics (for example, see Unit Three for more ideas on how to research women's issues).

Keep your work focused on your research question or thesis. Remember that you cannot write an entire history of the Vietnam War.

IDEAS FROM THE UNIT READINGS

1. Investigate the U.S. role in Vietnam beginning after World War II. What was the policy of the United States toward the French efforts to regain control of Indochina? When were the first U.S. advisers sent to the area? What was the public view of the U.S. position? A particularly important time to focus on is 1954, when the Geneva accords were signed and Diem came to power. What was the United States' response to the Geneva conference, the prospect of elections in Vietnam, and Diem's rule?

2. The Gulf of Tonkin incident and the resolution passed by Congress continue to be topics of controversy. The *Pentagon Papers* reveal that the Pentagon was look-

ing for an excuse to attack North Vietnam. Did the government inflate a minor incident into a major one? Did the United States provoke the incident in the first place? Why did Congress react as it did — in effect relinquishing its own war powers?

3. Lyndon Johnson was worn out by the war, which sapped money from domestic programs to which he was committed, threatened the nation's economy in general, and caused great division in the country. Investigate Johnson's policies for conducting the war, his relationship with Secretary of Defense Robert McNamara and other advisers, and his conflict with General William Westmoreland.

4. In 1967, Secretary of Defense Robert McNamara commissioned a secret history of the Vietnam War that has come to be known as the *Pentagon Papers*. Portions of this history — which in total numbered about three thousand pages, plus another four thousand pages of documents — were photocopied and given to the *New York Times* in 1971 by Daniel Ellsberg, one of the members of McNamara's staff who had worked on the project. After a court battle, the *Times* was allowed to print the documents. Senator Mike Gravel wrote at the time, "No one who reads this study can fail to conclude that, had the true facts been made known earlier, the war would long ago have ended, and the needless deaths of hundreds of thousands of Americans and Vietnamese would have been averted." Research the story of the *Pentagon Papers*, the court fight, and the subsequent harassment of Ellsberg by the White House — a fascinating study in the systematic deception of the public by the government.

5. Investigate the experiences of Vietnam veterans as told in their memoirs. Some of the questions that need to be asked about veterans' experiences are suggested in the reading and writing questions following the selections by Kerry, Bryant, McClusky, and Kovic. Many memoirs and oral histories are available, as well as stories and novels that tell about the war, homecoming, politics, and the ongoing problems still being suffered by veterans.

6. Kerry refers to the My Lai incident, the most famous example of an atrocity committed by American soldiers. Investigate the incident and the fate of Lieutenant William Calley.

7. Look into the history of Vietnam Veterans Against the War, including the Winter Soldier hearings that led to John Kerry's testimony before the Senate and the group's other antiwar activities. As Kovic's story suggests, the veterans came to antiwar action reluctantly and, when they did, they were bitterly resisted by the government.

8. The antiwar movement offers several other research projects. (a) Early protests were led by A. J. Muste and David Dellinger. Write a biography of one of these men and investigate his antiwar philosophy. (b) The student movement was led at first by Students for a Democratic Society (SDS; see p. 845). The "Port Huron Statement" by the SDS is an impressive analysis of the underlying malaise referred to by Potter and King. Investigate the history of the SDS and analyze the "Port Huron Statement." (c) By the late 1960s, there were demonstrations on nearly every campus in the country. Check the archives at your own college (or high school) — find student newspapers and yearbooks — to see what happened there. You may well find people at your school now who were there during the antiwar activity. Write a history of antiwar and social protest in your own backyard.

9. As McClusky's story indicates, the experience of women in Vietnam was as wrenching as it was for men. Beginning with Lynda Van Devanter's memoir (see the bibliography), research women who served or worked in Vietnam.

10. Investigate the killings at Kent State University in May 1970.

11. O'Brien's story gives poignant insight into the issues draftees faced as well as the moral turmoil of a young man who ultimately decided he couldn't evade the draft. But what happened to those who made the opposite decision and left the United States for Canada or Sweden? What happened to soldiers who deserted? Research how these two groups — draft evaders and deserters — were treated both during and after the war. How was the debate over amnesty for them ultimately resolved?

12. How did Hollywood portray the war? What were the earliest movies like? How did Hollywood treat the trauma of the war and the protests at home? What are more recent films like? What attitude do they convey? For this project, you should certainly watch some of these films (see the bibliography), but also check the bibliography and your library for books that analyze the films about Vietnam.

13. How did the war end? What happened in Vietnam after 1975? What are the lasting effects of the war?

14. How did the music of the era reflect the issues surrounding the war? What purpose did the music serve — was it only an emotional rallying device or did it have a rhetorical or argumentative purpose? Did the rock music of the 1960s further alienate those who supported the war? In addition to studying the music, study its effects. Note that classical music as well as rock was influenced by the war. And toward the end of the war, popular music began to reflect the concerns of veterans.

15. Investigate the other arts that were influenced by the war: painting, photography, sculpture, dance. How do these media express concern about the war? What positions do they seem to advocate? What debates arose among critics concerning their political content? Alternative: Look into the story of the Vietnam Veterans Memorial in Washington, D.C. — the Wall. What does the design represent? Why was it chosen? What protests did its design spark? What have been people's reactions to it?

16. Look into the literature of the war. You might focus on one genre — poetry, essay, journalism, short story, novel, drama — or investigate particular themes and the way they are treated in different genres.

BRANCHING OUT

1. Though the war dominated the American consciousness, other significant issues were also on the minds of Americans at the time. The most important was the civil rights movement. There was, of course, a connection between civil rights and the war, as the selections by Martin Luther King Jr. and Harold Bryant show. Still, the main action on civil rights was elsewhere. Research the civil rights movement during the war period, paying attention to the points of contact and conflict with the antiwar movement.

2. The modern women's movement also began about this time, though neither the antiwar nor the civil rights movement was particularly supportive of women's concerns. Research the role of women in the other two movements and the beginnings of the modern women's movement.

3. Much of youth culture in the Vietnam era was connected to the antiwar movement, but not all. What were the other aspects of youth culture? Investigate

— if possible with a group that can split up the subtopics — the generation gap, the sexual revolution, hippies, drugs, Eastern religion, communes, and non-war-related music and art of the period.

4. War resistance did not begin with Vietnam. Investigate war resistance, draft resistance, conscientious objection, and so on in earlier wars. What were the grounds of resistance to the Civil War, to the world wars, to the Korea War?

5. Look into war resistance and protest since Vietnam, such as in the Gulf War in 1991. How has the Vietnam experience affected Americans' attitudes toward U.S. military action in other countries?

6. How has the military responded to the morale problem created by the Vietnam War? What images of patriotism and military service have been put forward since Vietnam by the Pentagon? What is their appeal supposed to be? How is the volunteer army's image different from the image of the army filled in large part by draftees?

UNIT SIX BIBLIOGRAPHY

Works Included or Excerpted

Agnew, Spiro T. *Collected Speeches of Spiro Agnew.* New York: Audubon Books, 1971. 54–55 (October 19, 1969, speech), 70–76 (October 30, 1969, speech).

————. *Vital Speeches of the Day* 36 (December 15, 1969), 134–35 (November 20, 1969, speech).

Beidler, Barbara. "Afterthoughts on a Napalm-Drop on Jungle Villages near Haiphong." Reprinted in Gettleman et al., *Vietnam and America.*

Bryant, Harold. Oral history. In *Bloods: An Oral History of the Vietnam War by Black Veterans,* edited by Wallace Terry. New York: Random House, 1984.

Dellinger, David, A. J. Muste, et al. "Declaration of Conscience against the War in Vietnam." In Gettleman et al., *Vietnam and America.*

Dodd, Thomas J. Speech before the U.S. Senate. Reprinted in *The Viet-Nam Reader,* edited by Marcus G. Raskin and Bernard B. Fall (New York: Random House, 1965).

Gettleman, Marvin, et al. *Vietnam and America: A Documented History.* New York: Grove Press, 1985.

Ho Chi Minh. "Declaration of Independence of the Democratic Republic of Vietnam." In *Vietnam: A History in Documents,* edited by Gareth Porter. New York: New American Library, 1981.

Huy Can. "Truth Blazes Even in Little Children's Hearts." Reprinted in Gettleman et al., *Vietnam and America.*

Johnson, Lyndon B. "Peace in Vietnam and Southeast Asia." *Public Papers of the Presidents of the United States, 1968—69.* Washington, D.C.: Government Printing Office, 1970. 468–76. Reprinted in Gettleman et al., *Vietnam and America.*

Kerry, John F. Testimony before the U.S. Senate Foreign Relations Committee. *Congressional Record,* May 3, 1971. Reprinted in Gettleman et al., *Vietnam and America.*

King, Martin Luther, Jr. "Declaration of Independence from the War in Vietnam." *Ramparts,* May 1967, 33–37. Reprinted in Gettleman et al., *Vietnam and America.*

Kovic, Ron. *Born on the Fourth of July.* New York: McGraw-Hill, 1976.

McClusky, Leslie. Oral history. In *In the Combat Zone: An Oral History of American Women in Vietnam, 1966—75,* edited by Kathryn Marshall. Boston: Little, Brown, 1987.

National Mobilization Committee to End the War in Vietnam. "A Message to GIs and to the Movement." Reprinted in *The New Left,* edited by Massimo Teodori. New York: Bobbs-Merrill, 1969.

Nixon, Richard M. "Vietnamization." *Public Papers of the Presidents of the United States: Richard Nixon, 1969.* Washington, D.C.: Government Printing Office, 1971. 901–9. Reprinted in Gettleman et al., *Vietnam and America.*

O'Brien, Tim. "On the Rainy River." In *The Things They Carried.* Boston: Houghton Mifflin, 1990.

Potter, Paul. "The Incredible War." *National Guardian,* April 29, 1965. Reprinted in *The New Left,* edited by Massimo Teodori. New York: Bobbs-Merrill, 1969.

Stone, I. F. "A Reply to the 'White Paper.'" *I. F. Stone's Weekly,* March 8, 1965. Reprinted in Gettleman et al., *Vietnam and America.*

U.S. Department of State. *Aggression from the North: The Record of North Vietnam's Campaign to Conquer South Vietnam."* Department of State Publication 7839. Far Eastern Series, no. 130. Washington, D.C., February 1965. Reprinted in Gettleman et al, *Vietnam and America.*

Other Sources

Brandon, Heather. *Casualties: Death in Vietnam, Anguish and Survival in America.* New York: St. Martin's, 1987.

Caputo, Philip. *A Rumor of War.* New York: Holt, 1977.

Edelman, Bernard, ed. *Dear America: Letters Home from Vietnam.* New York: Norton, 1985.

Ehrhart, W. D. *Marking Time.* New York: Avon, 1986.

Emerson, Gloria. *Winners and Losers: Battles, Retreats, Gains, Losses, and Ruins from a Long War.* New York: Random House, 1976.

FitzGerald, Frances. *Fire in the Lake: The Vietnamese and the Americans in Vietnam.* 1972; New York: Vintage, 1989.

Franklin, H. Bruce, ed. *The Vietnam War in American Stories, Songs, and Poems.* Boston: Bedford Books, 1995.

Greene, Bob. *Homecoming: When the Soldiers Returned from Vietnam.* New York: Putnam's, 1989.

Hayslip, Le Ly. *When Heaven and Earth Changed Places.* New York: Doubleday, 1989.

Heinemann, Larry. *Paco's Story.* New York: Farrar, Straus and Giroux, 1979.

Herr, Michael. *Dispatches.* New York: Knopf, 1978.

Karnow, Stanley. *Vietnam: A History.* Rev. ed. New York: Viking, 1991.

Lang, Daniel. *Casualties of War.* 1969; New York: Pocket Books, 1989.

MacPherson, Myra. *Vietnam and the Haunted Generation.* New York: Doubleday, 1984.

McNamara, Robert S., with Brian VanDeMark. *In Retrospect: The Tragedy and Lessons of Vietnam.* New York: Random House, Times Books, 1995.

O'Brien, Tim. *Going After Cacciato.* New York: Dell, 1978.

———. *If I Die in a Combat Zone, Box Me Up and Ship Me Home.* New York: Dell, 1973.

Pittmar, Linda, and Gene Michaud, eds. *From Hanoi to Hollywood.* New Brunswick: Rutgers University Press, 1990.

The Pentagon Papers. Senator Gravel Edition. 5 vols. Boston: Beacon Press, 1971–72. A one-volume edition, along with the articles summarizing the papers that appeared in the *New York Times,* is *The Pentagon Papers: As Published by the* New York Times. New York: Bantam, 1971.

Polner, Murray. *No Victory Parades: The Return of the Vietnam Veteran.* New York: Holt, 1971.

Porter, Gareth. *Vietnam: A History in Documents.* New York: New American Library, 1981.

Santoli, Al. *Everything We Had: An Oral History of the Vietnam War by Thirty-Three American Soldiers Who Fought It.* New York: Random House, 1981.

Sheehan, Neil. *A Bright Shining Lie: John Paul Vann and America in Vietnam.* New York: Vintage, 1989.

——— . *After the War Was Over: Hanoi and Saigon.* New York: Random House, 1991.

Small, Melvin, and William D. Hoover, eds. *Give Peace a Chance: Exploring the Vietnam Antiwar Movement.* Syracuse: Syracuse University Press, 1992.

Stone, I. F. *The Killings at Kent State: How Murder Went Unpunished.* New York: New York Review, 1971.

Sweezey, Paul, and Max Huberman. "What Every American Should Know about Indo-China." *Monthly Review,* June 1954, 49–71.

Trudeau, G. B. *The Doonesbury Chronicles.* New York: Holt, 1975.

Van Devanter, Lynda. *Home before Morning: The Story of an Army Nurse in Vietnam.* New York: Beaufort, 1983.

Vietnam Veterans Against the War. *The Winter Soldier Investigation.* Boston: Beacon Press, 1972.

Willenson, Kim. *The Bad War: An Oral History of the Vietnam War.* New York: New American Library, 1987.

Zaroulis, Nancy, and Gerald Sullivan. *Who Spoke Up? American Protest against the War in Vietnam, 1963–1975.* Garden City, N.Y.: Doubleday, 1984.

Films and Videotapes

Apocalypse Now. Dir. Francis Ford Coppola. United Artists, 1979.

Born on the Fourth of July. Dir. Oliver Stone. Universal, 1989.

Casualties of War. Dir. Brian DePalma. Columbia, 1989.

Coming Home. Dir. Hal Ashby. United Artists, 1978.

Dear America: Letters Home from Vietnam. Dir. Bill Couturie. Couturie Company, 1988.

The Deer Hunter. Dir. Michael Cimino. Columbia, 1979.

Full Metal Jacket. Dir. Stanley Kubrick. Warner, 1987.

Hamburger Hill. Dir. John Irvin. Paramount, 1987.

Hearts and Minds. Dir. Peter Davis. Touchstone, 1974.

In Country. Dir. Norman Jewison. Warner, 1988.

Know Your Enemy: The Viet Cong. U.S. Directorate for Armed Forces Information and Education, 1966.

Platoon. Dir. Oliver Stone. Orion, 1986.

Vietnam: A Television History. WGBH, 1983.

Vietnam: In the Year of the Pig. Dir. Emile de Antonio, 1968.

Vietnam: The War at Home. Catalyst Media; Glen Silver, 1978.

Why Vietnam? U.S. Directorate for Armed Forces Information and Education, 1965.

music by Sunny Clapp. © 1927 (renewed) EMI Mills Music, Inc. All rights reserved. Used by permission. Warner Bros. Publications U.S. Inc., Miami, FL 33014.

Martin Luther King, Jr. "Declaration of Independence from the War in Vietnam," the authorized version of an address published in *Ramparts,* May 1967. Reprinted by arrangement with The Heirs to the Estate of Martin Luther King, Jr., c/o Joan Daves Agency as agent for the proprietor. Copyright © 1967 by Martin Luther King, Jr.

Ron Kovic. Excerpts from *Born on the Fourth of July* by Ron Kovic. Copyright © 1976 by Ron Kovic. Reprinted by permission of McGraw-Hill, Inc.

Leslie McClusky. Oral history from *In the Combat Zone* by Kathryn Marshall. Copyright © 1981 by Kathryn Marshall. By permission of Little Brown and Company.

Mike Masaoka. Excerpt from *They Call Me Moses Masaoka* by Mike Masaoka with Bill Hosokawa. Copyright © 1987 by Mike Masaoka and Bill Hosokawa. By permission of William Morrow & Company, Inc.

Tim O'Brien. "On the Rainy River" from *The Things They Carried.* Copyright © 1990 by Tim O'Brien. Reprinted by permission of Houghton Mifflin Co./Seymour Lawrence. All rights reserved.

John Okada. Excerpt from *No-No Boy* by John Okada. Copyright © 1976 by Dorothy Okada. Reprinted by permission of the University of Washington Press.

Mary Rowlandson. Excerpt from "The Sovereignty and Goodness of God." Reprinted by permission of the publishers from *Puritans Among the Indians: Accounts of Captivity and Redemption 1676–1724* edited by Alden T. Vaughn and Edward W. Clark, Cambridge, Mass.: The Belknap Press of Harvard University Press. Copyright © 1981 by the President and Fellows of Harvard University.

Monica Sone. "Deeper into the Land." From *Nisei Daughter* by Monica Sone. Copyright © 1953, renewed copyright © 1981 by Monica Sone. By permission of Little, Brown and Company.

I. F. Stone. "A Reply to the White Paper" from *In a Time of Torment* by I. F. Stone (Random House, 1967). Copyright © 1967, 1965, by I. F. Stone. Reprinted by permission of Wylie, Aitken & Stone. Originally published in *I. F. Stone's Weekly.*

Michi Weglyn. From *Years of Infamy* by Michi Weglyn. Copyright © 1976 by Michi Nishiura Weglyn. Reprinted by permission of the University of Washington Press. Francis Biddle. Excerpts from *In Brief Authority* by Francis Biddle (Doubleday, 1962) reprinted by permission of the publisher.

Hisaye Yamamoto. "A Fire in Fontana" from *Rafu Shimpo,* December 21, 1985. Copyright © Hisaye Yamamoto DeSoto, 1985. Reprinted by permission of the author.

Minoru Yasui. Excerpts from "Minidoka" from *And Justice for All* by John Tateishi. Copyright © 1984 by John Tateishi. Reprinted by permission of Random House, Inc.

Index of Authors and Titles